SYSTEMATIC THEOLOGY

by

CHARLES HODGE

IN THREE VOLUMES

Volume III

Wm. B. Eerdmans Publishing Company
Grand Rapids, Michigan

Reprinted, November 1981

ISBN 0-8028-8135-1

PHOTOLITHOPRINTED BY EERDMANS PRINTING COMPANY
GRAND RAPIDS, MICHIGAN, UNITED STATES OF AMERICA

CONTENTS OF THE THIRD VOLUME

PART III. (*Continued.*)

CHAPTER XV.

REGENERATION.

CHAPTER XVI.

FAITH.

CHAPTER XVII.

JUSTIFICATION.

CHAPTER XVIII.

SANCTIFICATION.

CONTENTS OF THE THIRD VOLUME.

CHAPTER XIX.

THE LAW.

PART IV.
ESCHATOLOGY.
CHAPTER I.
STATE OF THE SOUL AFTER DEATH.

CHAPTER II.
RESURRECTION.

CHAPTER III.

SECOND ADVENT.

CHAPTER IV.

CONCOMITANTS OF THE SECOND ADVENT.

SYSTEMATIC THEOLOGY

PART III.—(Continued.)
SOTERIOLOGY.

SYSTEMATIC THEOLOGY

CHAPTER XV.

REGENERATION.

§ 1. *Usage of the Word.*

THE subjective change wrought in the soul by the grace of God, is variously designated in Scripture. It is called a new birth, a resurrection, a new life, a new creature, a renewing of the mind, a dying to sin and living to righteousness, a translation from darkness to light, etc. In theological language, it is called regeneration, renovation, conversion. These terms are often used interchangeably. They are also used sometimes for the whole process of spiritual renovation or restoration of the image of God, and sometimes for a particular stage of that process. Thus Calvin gives the term its widest scope : " Uno verbo pœnitentiam interpretor regenerationem, cujus non alius est scopus nisi ut imago Dei, quæ per Adæ transgressionem fœdata et tantum non obliterata fuerat, in nobis reformetur. . . . . Atque hæc quidem instauratio non uno momento, vel die, vel anno impletur, sed per continuos, imo etiam lentos interdum profectus abolet Deus in electis suis carnis corruptelas." [1]

With the theologians of the seventeenth century conversion and regeneration were synonymous terms. In the acts of the Synod of Dort, we find such expressions as " Status conversionis aut regenerationis," and "effecta ad conversionem sive regenerationem prævia." John Owen, in his work on the Holy Spirit, follows the same usage. The fifth chapter of the third book of that work is entitled " The nature of regeneration," and one of the heads under this is, " Conversion not wrought by moral suasion only.' " If the Holy Spirit," he says, " acts no otherwise on men in regeneration or conversion," then so and so follows. Turrettin, as we have seen, distinguishes between what he calls " conversio

---

[1] *Institutio,* lib. III. cap. iii. 9, edit. Berlin, 1834, vol. i. p. 389.

habitualis " and " conversio actualis." " Conversio habitualis seu passiva, fit per habituum supernaturalium infusionem a Spiritu Sancto. Actualis vero seu activa per bonorum istorum exercitium. . . . . Per illam homo renovatur et convertitur a Deo. Per istam homo a Deo renovatus et convertus convertit se ad Deum, et actus agit. Illa melius regeneratio dicitur, quia se habet ad modum novæ nativitatis, qua homo reformatur ad imaginem Creatoris sui. Ista vero conversio, quia includit hominis ipsius operationem." [1] This is clear and accurate. As these two things are distinct they should be designated by different terms. Great confusion arises from this ambiguity of terms. The questions whether man is active or passive in regeneration and whether regeneration is effected by the mediate or immediate influence of the Spirit must be answered in one way if regeneration includes conversion, and in another if it be taken in its restricted sense. In the Bible, the distinction is generally preserved ; μετάνοια, repentance, change of mind, turning to God, *i. e.*, conversion, is what man is called upon to do ; ἀναγέννησις, regeneration, is the act of God. God regenerates ; the soul is regenerated. In the Romish Church justification is making subjectively just, *i. e.*, free from sin and inwardly holy. So is regeneration. So is sanctification. These terms, therefore, in the theology of that church are constantly interchanged.

Even by the Lutherans, in the " Apology for the Augsburg Confession," regeneration is made to include justification. That is, it is made to include the whole process by which the sinner is transferred from a state of sin and condemnation into a state of salvation. In the " Form of Concord " it is said, " Vocabulum regenerationis interdum in eo sensu accipitur, ut simul et remissionem peccatorum (quæ duntaxat propter Christum contingit) et subsequentem renovationem complectatur, quam Spiritus Sanctus in illis, qui per fidem justificati sunt, operatur, quandoque etiam solam remissionem peccatorum, et adoptionem in filios Dei significat. Et in hoc posteriore usu sæpe multumque id vocabulum in Apologia Confessionis ponitur. Verbi gratia, cum dicitur : Justificatio est regeneratio. . . . . Quin etiam vivificationis vocabulum interdum ita accipitur, ut remissionem peccatorum notet. Cum enim homo per fidem (quam quidem solus Spiritus Sanctus operatur) justificatur, id ipsum revera est quædam regeneratio, quia ex filio iræ fit filius Dei, et hoc modo e morte in vitam transfertur. . . . . Deinde etiam regeneratio sæpe pro sanctificatione

[1] Locus xv. quæs. iv. 13, edit. Edinburgh, 1847, vol. ii. p. 460.

et renovatione (quæ fidei justificationem sequitur) usurpatur. In qua significatione D. Lutherus hac voce, tum in libro de ecclesia et conciliis, tum alibi etiam, multum usus est."[1]

As this lax use of terms was unavoidably attended with great confusion, the " Form of Concord " itself, and the later Lutheran theologians were more precise. They made especially a sharp distinction between justification and anything signifying a subjective change in the sinner.

In the early Church regeneration often expressed, not any inward moral change, but an external change of state or relation. Among the Jews when a heathen became a proselyte to their religion, he was said to be born again. The change of his status from without to within the theocracy, was called regeneration. This usage in a measure passed over to the Christian Church. When a man became a member of the Church he was said to be born anew ; and baptism, which was the rite of initiation, was called regeneration. This use of the word has not yet entirely passed away. A distinction is still sometimes made between regeneration and spiritual renovation. The one is external, the other internal. Some of the advocates of baptismal regeneration make this distinction, and interpret the language of the formulas of the Church of England in accordance with it. The regeneration effected in baptism, in their view, is not any spiritual change in the state of the soul, but simply a birth into the visible Church.

§ 2. *Nature of Regeneration.*

By a consent almost universal the word regeneration is now used to designate, not the whole work of sanctification, nor the first stages of that work comprehended in conversion, much less justification or any mere external change of state, but the instantaneous change from spiritual death to spiritual life. Regeneration, therefore, is a spiritual resurrection ; the beginning of a new life. Sometimes the word expresses the act of God. God regenerates. Sometimes it designates the subjective effect of his act. The sinner is regenerated. He becomes a new creature. He is born again. And this is his regeneration. These two applications of the word are so allied as not to produce confusion. The nature of regeneration is not explained in the Bible further than the account therein given of its author, God, in the exercise of the exceeding greatness of his power ; its subject, the whole soul ; and its effects, spiritual life, and all consequent holy acts

[1] III. 19, 20, 21; Hase, *Libri Symbolici,* 3d edit. p. 686.

and states. Its metaphysical nature is left a mystery. It is not the province of either philosophy or theology to solve that mystery. It is, however, the duty of the theologian to examine the various theories concerning the nature of this saving change, and to reject all such as are inconsistent with the Word of God.

Not a change in the Substance of the Soul.

Regeneration does not consist in any change in the substance of the soul. The only advocate of the opposite doctrine among Protestant theologians was Flacius Illyricus, so called from the place of his birth. He was one of the most prominent Lutheran theologians in what is called the second Reformation in Germany. He did great service in the cause of truth in resisting the synergism of Melancthon, and the concessions which that eminent but yielding reformer was disposed to make to the papists. He contributed some of the most important works of the age in which he lived to the vindication of the Protestant faith. His " Catalogus Testium Veritatis," designed to prove that the doctrines of the Reformation had had their witnesses in all ages ; his " Clavis Scripturæ Sacræ;" and especially the great historical work, " The Magdeburg Centuries " (in thirteen volumes, folio), of which he was the originator and principal author, attest his learning, talents, and untiring industry. His fervent and uncompromising spirit involved him in many difficulties and sorrows. He died worn out by suffering and labour, says his biographer ; one of those men of faith of whom the world was not worthy. Always extreme in his opinions, he held that original sin was a corruption of the substance of the soul, and regeneration such a change of that substance as to restore its normal purity. All his friends who had sided with him in his controversy with the Synergists and the supporters of the Leipzig Interim, forsook him now, and he stood alone. In the " Form of Concord," adopted to settle all the controversies of the period, these peculiar view of Flacius were condemned as a virtual revival of the Manichæa heresy. It was urged that if the substance of the soul be sinful, God, by whom each individual soul is created, must be the author of sin ; and that Christ who, in assuming our nature, became consubstantial with us, must be a partaker of sin. No Christian Church has assumed the responsibility of the doctrine of Flacius, or held that regeneration involves a change of the essence of the soul

Regeneration does not consist in an Act of the Soul.

Regeneration does not consist in any act or acts of the soul. The word here, of course, is to be understood not as including conversion, much less the whole work of sanctification, but in its restricted sense for the commencement of spiritual life. The opposite view, which makes regeneration, even in its narrowest sense, an act of the soul, has been held by very different classes of theologians. It is, of course, involved in the Pelagian doctrine which denies moral character to everything except acts of the will. If "all sin is sinning," and "all love loving," then every moral change in man must be a change from one form of voluntary activity to another. As the later Remonstrants held the principle in question they made regeneration to consist in the sinner's own act in turning unto God. The influence exerted on him was one which he could yield to or resist. If he yielded, it was a voluntary decision, and in that decision his regeneration, or the beginning of his religious life, consisted.

Dr. Emmons's View.

Dr. Emmons, holding that all sin and holiness consist in acts, which acts, whether sinful or holy, are immediately created by God, makes regeneration to consist in God's giving rise to the commencement of a series of holy acts. In his discourse on Regeneration, the first proposition which he undertakes to establish is, "that the Spirit of God, in regeneration, produces nothing but love." This is maintained in opposition to those who say that the Spirit produces a new nature, principle, disposition, or taste. "Those in the state of nature," he says, "stand in no need of having any new power, or faculty, or principle of action produced in them, in order to their becoming holy. They are just as capable of loving as of hating God. . . . . This is true of all sinners, who are as much moral agents, and the proper subjects of moral government, before as after regeneration. Whenever, therefore, the divine Spirit renews, regenerates, or sanctifies them, He has no occasion of producing anything in their minds besides love."[1] " The love which the Spirit of God produces in regeneration is the love of benevolence, and not the love of complacence."[2] "Though there is no natural or necessary connection between the first exercise of love and all future exercises of grace, yet there is a constituted connection, which renders future exer-

---

[1] Sermon 51; *Works*, edit. Boston, 1842, vol. v. p. 112.   [2] *Ibid.* p. 114.

cises of grace as certain, as if they flowed from a new nature, or holy principle, as many suppose." [1] His first inference from the doctrine of his sermon is, " If the Spirit of God produces nothing but love in regeneration, then there is no ground for the distinction which is often made between regeneration, conversion, and sanctification. They are, in nature and kind, precisely the same fruits of the Spirit. In regeneration, He produces holy exercises; in conversion, He produces holy exercises; and in sanctification, He produces holy exercises." [2] Secondly, " If the Spirit of God in regeneration produces nothing but love, then men are no more passive in regeneration than in conversion or sanctification. Those who hold that the divine Spirit in regeneration produces something prior to love as the foundation of it, that is, a new nature, or new principle of holiness, maintain that men are passive in regeneration, but active in conversion and sanctification. . . . . But if what has been said in this discourse be true, there is no new nature, or principle of action, produced in regeneration, but only love, which is activity itself." [3]

Professor Finney's Doctrine.

Professor Finney, in his " Lectures on Systematic Theology," teaches : (1.) That satisfaction, happiness, blessedness, is the only absolute good; that virtue is only relatively good, i. e., good as tending to produce happiness. (2.) That all virtue lies in the intention to promote the happiness of being, that is, of universal being. There is no virtue in emotion, feeling, or any state of the sensibility, for these are involuntary. Love to God even is not complacency in his excellence, but " willing him good." (3.) All sin is selfishness, or the choice of our own happiness in preference to the good of universal being. (4.) Every moral agent is always " as sinful or holy as with their knowledge they can be." (5.) " As the moral law is the law of nature, it is absurd to suppose that entire obedience to it should not be the unalterable condition of salvation." [4] (6.) Regeneration is an " instantaneous " change " from entire sinfulness to entire holiness." [5] It is a simple change of purpose.

The system of Professor Finney is a remarkable product of relentless logic. It is valuable as a warning. It shows to what

[1] Sermon 51; *Works*, edit. Boston, 1842, vol. v. p. 116.   [2] *Ibid.* p. 116.
[3] *Ibid.* pp. 117, 118.
[4] *Lectures on Systematic Theology*, by Charles G. Finney, edit. Oberlin, Boston, and New York, 1846, p. 364.
[5] *Ibid.* p. 500.

extremes the human mind may be carried when abandoned to its own guidance. He begins with certain axioms, or, as he calls them, truths of the reason, and from these he draws conclusions which are indeed logical deductions, but which shock the moral sense, and prove nothing but that his premises are false. His fundamental principle is that ability limits obligation. Free will is defined to be " the power of choosing, or refusing to choose, in compliance with moral obligation in every instance." [1] " Consciousness of the affirmation of ability to comply with any requisition, is a necessary condition of the affirmation of obligation to comply with that requisition." [2] " To talk of inability to obey moral law, is to talk sheer nonsense." [3]

But it is acknowledged that man's ability is confined to acts of the will, therefore moral character can be predicated only of such acts. The acts of the will are either choices or volitions. " By choice is intended the selection or choice of an end. By volition is intended the executive efforts of the will to secure the end intended." [4] We are responsible, therefore, only for our choices in the selection of an ultimate end. " It is generally agreed that moral obligation respects strictly only the ultimate intention or choice of an end for its own sake." [5] " I have said that moral obligation respects the ultimate intention only. I am now prepared to say, still further, that this is a first truth of reason." [6] " Right can be predicated only of good-will, and wrong only of selfishness. . . . . It is right for him [for a man] to intend the highest good of being as an end. If he honestly does this, he cannot, doing this, mistake his duty, for in doing this he really performs the whole of duty." [7] " Moral character belongs solely to the ultimate intention of the mind, or to choice, as distinguished from volition." [8]

The end to be chosen is " the highest good of being." " Good may be natural or moral. Natural good is synonymous with valuable. Moral good is synonymous with virtue." [9] Moral good " is only a relative good. It does meet a demand of our being, and therefore produces satisfaction. This satisfaction is the ultimate good of being." [10] " I come now to state the point upon which issue is taken, to wit : That enjoyment, blessedness, or mental satisfaction, is the only ultimate good." [11] " Of what value

---

[1] *Lectures on Systematic Theology*, by Charles G. Finney, edit. Oberlin, Boston, and New York, 1846, p. 26.

[2] *Ibid.* p. 33.   [3] *Ibid.* p. 4.   [4] *Ibid.* p. 44.
[5] *Ibid.* p. 26.   [6] *Ibid.* p. 36.   [7] *Ibid.* p. 149.
[8] *Ibid.* p. 157.   [9] *Ibid.* p. 45.   [10] *Ibid.* p. 48.   [11] *Ibid.* p. 120.

is the true, the right, the just, etc., aside from the pleasure or mental satisfaction resulting from them to sentient existences."[1]

It follows from these principles that men perform their whole duty, and are perfect, if they intend the happiness of being in general. There is no morality in emotions, sentiments, or feelings. These are involuntary states of the sensibility, and are in themselves neither good nor bad. " If any outward action or state of the feeling exists, in opposition to the intention or choice of the mind, it cannot by any possibility have moral character. Whatever is beyond the control of a moral agent, he cannot be responsible for."[2] " Love may, and often does exist, as every one knows, in the form of a mere feeling or emotion. . . . . This emotion or feeling, as we are all aware, is purely an involuntary state of mind. Because it is a phenomenon of the sensibility, and of course a passive state of mind, it has in itself no moral character."[3] Gratitude, " as a mere feeling or phenomenon of the sensibility, ... has no moral character."[4] The same is said of benevolence, compassion, mercy, conscientiousness, etc. The doctrine is, " No state of the sensibility has any moral character in itself."[5] The love which has moral excellence, and which is the fulfilling of the law, is not a feeling of complacency, but " good-will," willing the good or happiness of its object. Should a man, therefore, under the impulse of a benevolent feeling, or a sense of duty, perform a right act, he would sin as really as if, under the impulse of malice or cupidity, he should perform a bad act. The illustration is, that to pay a debt from a sense of justice, is as wicked as to steal a horse from acquisitiveness. A man " may be prevented [from committing commercial injustice] by a constitutional or phrenological conscientiousness or sense of justice. But this is only a feeling of the sensibility, and if restrained only by this, he is just as absolutely selfish as if he had stolen a horse in obedience to acquisitiveness."[6] " If the selfish man were to preach the gospel, it would be only because upon the whole it was most pleasing or gratifying to himself, and not at all for the sake of the good of being as an end. If he should become a pirate, it would be exactly for the same reason. . . . . Whichever course he takes, he takes it for precisely the same reason ; and with the same degree of light it must involve the same degree of guilt."[7] To feed the poor from a feeling of

[1] *Lectures on Systematic Theology*, by Charles G. Finney, edit. Oberlin, Boston, and New York, 1846, p. 122.
[2] *Ibid.* p. 164.   [3] *Ibid.* p. 213.   [4] *Ibid.* p. 278.
[5] *Ibid.* p. 521.   [6] *Ibid.* p. 317, 318.   [7] *Ibid.* p. 355.

benevolence, and to murder a parent from a feeling of malice, involve the same degree of guilt! Such a sacrifice to logic was never made by any man before. But still more wonderful, if possible, is the declaration that a man may " feel deeply malicious and revengeful feelings toward God. But sin does not consist in these feelings, nor necessarily imply them." [1]

Moral excellence is not an object of love. To say that we are bound to love God because He is good, is said to be " most non-sensical. What is it to love God? Why, as is agreed, it is not to exercise a mere emotion of complacency in Him. It is to will something to Him." [2] " Should it be said that God's holiness is the foundation of our obligation to love Him, I ask in what sense it can be so? What is the nature or form of that love, which his virtue lays us under an obligation to exercise? It cannot be a mere emotion of complacency, for emotions being involuntary states of mind and mere phenomena of the sensibility, are without the pale of legislation and morality." [3] " We are under infinite obligation to love God, and to will his good with all our power, because of the intrinsic value of his well-being, whether He is holy or sinful. Upon condition that He is holy, we are under obligation to will his actual blessedness, but certainly we are under obligation to will it with no more than all our heart, and soul, and mind, and strength. But this we are required to do because of the intrinsic value of his blessedness, whatever his character might be." [4] Surely such a system is a ὑπόδειγμα τῆς ἀπειθείας.

Dr. Taylor's View.

The system of Dr. Taylor of New Haven agrees with that of Professor Finney in making free agency include plenary power; in limiting responsibility and moral character to voluntary acts; in regarding happiness as the chief good; and in making regeneration to consist in a change of purpose. The two systems differ, however, essentially as to the ground of moral obligation or nature of virtue; and as to the nature of that change of purpose in which regeneration consists. Professor Finney adopts the common eudæmonistic theory which makes the happiness of being, i. e., of the universe, the chief good; and therefore makes virtue consist in the governing purpose to promote that happiness, and all sin in the purpose to seek our own happiness, instead of the hap-

[1] *Lectures on Systematic Theology*, by Charles G. Finney, Oberlin, Boston, and New York, 1846, p. 296.
[2] *Ibid.* p. 64.   [3] *Ibid.* p. 91.   [4] *Ibid.* p. 99.

piness of being ; consequently, regeneration is a change of that
purpose ; that is, it is a change from selfishness to benevolence.

Dr. Taylor, on the other hand, recognized the fact that as the
desire of happiness is a constituent element of our nature, or law
of our being, it must be innocent, and therefore is not to be confounded with selfishness. He hence inferred that this desire of
happiness is rightfully the controlling principle of action in all
sentient and rational creatures. Sin consists in seeking happiness in the creature ; holiness in seeking happiness in God ; regeneration is the purpose or decision of a sinner to seek his happiness in God and not in the world. This change of purpose, he
sometimes calls a " change of heart," sometimes " giving the
heart to God," sometimes " loving God." As regeneration is the
choice of God as our chief good, it is an intelligent, voluntary act
of the soul, and therefore must take place according to the established laws of mental action. It supposes the preliminary acts of
consideration, appreciation, and comparison. The sinner contemplates God as a source of happiness, estimates his suitableness to
the necessities of his nature, compares Him with other objects
of choice, and decides to choose God as his portion. Sometimes
the word regeneration is used in a comprehensive sense, including
the whole process of consideration and decision ; sometimes in a
restricted sense, for the decision itself.

Such being the nature of regeneration, it is of course brought
about through the influence of the truth. The Bible reveals the
nature of God, and his capacity and willingness to make his
creatures happy ; it exhibits all the motives which should determine the soul to take God for its portion. As regeneration is a
rational and voluntary act, it is inconceivable that it should take
place except in view of rational considerations. The Spirit's influence in this process is not denied. The fact is admitted that
all the considerations which ought to determine the sinner to
make choice of God, will remain without saving effect, unless the
Spirit renders them effectual.

These views are presented at length in the " Christian Spectator " (a quarterly review) for 1829. On the nature of the
change in question, Dr. Taylor says : " Regeneration, considered
as a moral change of which man is the subject — giving God the
heart — making a new heart — loving God supremely, etc., are
terms and phrases which, in popular use, denote a complex act.
. . . . These words, in all ordinary speech and writing, are used
to denote one act, and yet this one act includes a process of mental

acts, consisting of the perception and comparison of motives, the estimate of their relative worth, and the choice or willing of the external action." " When we speak of the means of regeneration, we shall use the word regeneration in a more limited import than its ordinary popular import ; and shall confine it, chiefly for the sake of convenient phraseology, to the act of the will or heart, in distinction from other mental acts connected with it ; or to that act of the will or heart which consists in a preference of God to every other object ; or to that disposition of the heart, or governing affection or purpose of the man, which consecrates him to the service and glory of God." [1]

" Self-love or desire of happiness, is the primary cause or reason of all acts of preference or choice which fix supremely on any object. In every moral being who forms a moral character, there must be a first moral act of preference or choice. This must respect some one object, God or mammon, as the chief good, or as an object of supreme affection. Now whence comes such a choice or preference ? Not from a previous choice or preference of the same object, for we speak of the first choice of the object. The answer which human consciousness gives, is, that the being constituted with a capacity for happiness desires to be happy ; and knowing that he is capable of deriving happiness from different objects, considers from which the greatest happiness may be derived, and as in this respect he judges or estimates their relative value, so he chooses or prefers the one or the other as his chief good. While this must be the process by which a moral being forms his first moral preference, substantially the same process is indispensable to a change of this preference. The change involves the preference of a new object as the chief good ; a preference which the former preference has no tendency to produce, but a direct tendency to prevent ; a preference, therefore, not resulting from, or in any way occasioned by a previous preference of any given object, but resulting from those acts of considering and comparing the sources of happiness, which are dictated by the desire of happiness or self-love." [2]

Regeneration being a change of purpose, the mode in which it is produced is thus explained. " If man without divine grace is a moral agent, then he is qualified so to consider, compare, and estimate the objects of choice as means of happiness, and capable also of such constitutional excitement in view of the good and evil set before him, as might result in his giving his heart to God, without grace. . . . . The act of giving God the heart must take place in perfect accordance with the laws of moral agency and of voluntary action.   If the interposing grace violate these laws, the effect cannot be moral action; and it must violate these laws, if it dispense with the class of mental acts now under consideration.   Whatever, therefore, be the influence which secures a change of heart in the sinner, the change itself is a moral change, and implies the exercise of all the powers and capacities of the moral agent, which in the nature of things are essential to a moral act." [1]   On a previous page it had been said, " The Scriptures authorize us to assert, generally, that the mode of divine influence is consistent with the moral nature of this change as a voluntary act of man ; and, also, that it is through the truth, and implies attention to truth on the part of man." [2] " Cannot," Dr. Taylor asks, " He who formed the mind of man, reach it with an influence of his Spirit, which shall accord with all the laws of voluntary and moral action ?   Because motives, without a divine interposition, will not secure this moral change in sinful man, and because they have no positive efficiency in its production, must God in producing it dispense with motives altogether ?   Must the appropriate connections between motives and acts of will, or between the exercise of affections and the perception of their objects, be dissolved, and have no place ?   Must God, if by his grace He brings sinners to give Him their heart in holy love, accomplish the change in such a manner that they shall have no prior perception or view of the object of their love ; and know not what or whom they love, or wherefore they love Him, rather than their former idols ?   Does a consistent theology thus limit the Holy One, and oblige Him to accomplish the veriest impossibilities, in transforming the moral character of sinful man ?" [3]   This may be a correct account of the process of conversion, with which this system confounds regeneration.   Conversion is indeed a voluntary turning of the soul from sin to God. From the nature of the case it is produced proximately by appropriate motives, or it would be neither rational nor holy.   But this proves nothing as to the nature of regeneration.   The most accurate analysis of the laws of vision can throw no light on the way in which Christ opened the eyes of the blind.

Remarks.

It is plain that these views of regeneration are mere philosophical theories.   Dr. Emmons assumes that such is the dependence

[1] *Christian Spectator*, 1829, p. 223   [2] *Ibid.* p. 17.   [3] *Ibid.* p. 489

of a creature upon the creator, that it cannot act. No creature can be a cause. There is no efficiency in second causes. Then, of course, the first cause must produce all effects. God creates everything, even volitions. In the soul there are only acts or exercises. Regeneration, therefore, is an act or volition created by God; or, it is the name given to the commencement of a new series of exercises which are holy instead of sinful.

Professor Finney assumes that plenary ability is essential to moral agency; that a man, so far as his internal life is concerned, has power only over his choices and volitions; all, therefore, for which he is responsible, all that constitutes moral character, must fall under the category of choice, the selection of an ultimate end. Assuming, moreover, that happiness is the only absolute good, all sin consists in the undue pursuit of our own happiness, and all virtue in benevolence or the purpose to seek the happiness of being. Regeneration, therefore, consists in the change of the purpose to seek our own happiness, for the purpose to seek as our ultimate end the happiness of the universe.

Dr. Taylor, agreeing with Professor Finney on the nature of free agency, and in the doctrine that happiness is the chief good, holds with him that all sin and holiness consist in voluntary action. But assuming that self-love, as distinguished from selfishness, is the motive in all rational moral action, he makes regeneration to consist in the choice of God as the source of our own happiness.

All these speculations are outside of the Bible. They have no authority or value which they do not derive from their inherent truth, and any man is at liberty to dispute them, if they do not commend themselves to his own reason and conscience. But besides the purely philosophical character of these views, it would be easy to show, not only that they have no valid ground on which to rest, but also that they are inconsistent with the teachings of Scripture and with genuine Christian experience. This will be attempted when the Scriptural account of regeneration comes to be considered.

Regeneration not a change in any one Faculty of the Soul.

Regeneration does not consist in a change in any one of the faculties of the soul, whether the sensibility, or the will, or the intellect. According to some theologians, the feelings, or heart, in the restricted sense of that word, is the exclusive seat of original sin. Hereditary corruption, in other words, is made to con-

sist in the aversion of the heart from divine things, and a preference for the things of the world. The end to be accomplished in
regeneration, therefore, is simply to correct this aversion. The
understanding, it is urged, so far as moral and religious truth is
concerned, apprehends aright and appreciates what is loved; and
in like manner, in the same sphere, we believe what we apprehend as right and good. If, therefore, the feelings are made
what they ought to be, all the other operations of the mind, or
inner man, will be right. This theory is founded in part upon
a mistaken view of the meaning of the word "heart" as used
in the Scriptures. In a multitude of cases, and in all cases
where regeneration is spoken of, it means the whole soul; that
is, it includes the intellect, will, and the conscience as well as the
affections. Hence the Bible speaks of the eyes, of the thoughts,
of the purposes, of the devices, as well as of the feelings or affections of the heart. In Scriptural language, therefore, a "new
heart" does not mean simply a new state of feeling, but a radical change in the state of the whole soul or interior man. Besides, this theory overlooks what the Bible constantly assumes:
the unity of our inward life. The Scriptures do not contemplate
the intellect, the will, and the affections, as independent, separa-
ble elements of a composite whole. These faculties are only
different forms of activity in one and the same subsistence. No
exercise of the affections can occur without an exercise of the
intellect, and, if the object be moral or religious, without including a correspondent exercise of our moral nature.

Regeneration not merely Illumination.

Another and antagonistic theory equally one-sided, is that the
intellect only is in fault, and that regeneration resolves itself into
illumination. This view is far more plausible than the preceding. The Bible makes eternal life to consist in knowledge; sinfulness is blindness, or darkness; the transition from a state of
sin to a state of holiness is a translation from darkness into
light; men are said to be renewed unto knowledge, *i. e.*,
knowledge is the effect of regeneration; conversion is said to be
effected by the revelation of Christ; the rejection of Him as the
Son of God and Saviour of men is referred to the fact that the
eyes of those who believe not are blinded by the god of this
world. These Scriptural representations prove much. They
prove that knowledge is essential to all holy exercises; that truth,
as the object of knowledge, is of vital importance, and that error

is always evil and often fatal ; and that the effects of regeneration, so far as they reveal themselves in our consciousness, consist largely in the spiritual apprehension or discernment of divine
things. These representations also prove that in the order of
nature, knowledge, or spiritual discernment, is antecedent and
causative relatively to all holy exercises of the feelings or affections. It is the spiritual apprehension of the truth that awakens
love, faith, and delight ; and not love that produces spiritual
discernment. It was the vision Paul had of the divine glory of
Christ that made him instantly and forever his worshipper and
servant. The Scriptures, however, do not teach that regeneration consists exclusively in illumination, or that the cognitive
faculties are exclusively the subject of the renewing power of the
Spirit. It is the soul as such that is spiritually dead ; and it is
to the soul that a new principle of life controlling all its exercises, whether of the intellect, the sensibility, the conscience, or
the will is imparted.

*Not a Change of the Higher, as distinguished from the Lower
Powers of the Soul.*

There is another view of the subject, which falls under this
head of what may be called partial regeneration. It is founded
on trichotomy, or the assumption of three elements in the constitution of man, namely, the body, the soul, and the spirit (the
σῶμα, ψυχή, and πνεῦμα) ; the first material, the second animal, the
third spiritual. To the second, *i. e.*, to the soul or ψυχή, are referred what man has in common with the lower animals ; life,
sensibility, will, and understanding; to the spirit what is peculiar
to us as rational, moral, and religious beings, namely, conscience
and reason. This third element, the πνεῦμα, or reason, is often
called divine ; sometimes in a literal, and sometimes in a figurative sense. In either case, according to the theory under consideration, it is not the seat of sin, and is uncorrupted by the fall.
It remains, although clouded and perverted by the disorder in
the lower departments of our nature, the point of contact and
connection between man and God. This at least is one view of
the matter. According to another view, neither the body nor the
soul (neither σῶμα nor ψυχή), has any moral character. The seat
of the moral and divine life is exclusively the πνεῦμα or spirit.
This is said to be paralyzed by the fall. It is figuratively dead ;
unsusceptible of impression from divine things. There are as
many theories of the nature of regeneration among the advocates

of this threefold division in the constitution of man, as there are systems of anthropology. The idea common to all, or to a majority of them, is that regeneration consists in restoring the πνεῦμα or spirit to its normal controlling influence over the whole man. According to some, this is a natural process in which an animal man, i. e., a man governed by the ψυχή, comes to be reasonable, or pneumatic, i. e., governed by the πνεῦμα or higher powers of his nature. According to others, it is a supernatural effect due to the action of the divine (Πνεῦμα) Spirit upon the human πνεῦμα or spirit. In either case, however, the πνευματικός, or spiritual man, is not one in whom the Holy Spirit dwells as a principle of a new, spiritual life ; but one who is governed by his own πνεῦμα or spirit. According to others again, the πνεῦμα or reason in man is God, the God-consciousness, the Logos, and regeneration is the gradually acquired ascendency of this divine element of our nature.

In reference to these views of regeneration it is sufficient to remark, (1.) That the threefold division of our nature on which they are founded is antiscriptural, as we have already attempted to prove. (2.) Admitting that there is a foundation for such a distinction, it is not of the kind assumed in these theories. The soul and spirit are not distinct substances or essences, one of which may be holy and the other unholy, or negative. This is inconsistent with the unity of our interior life which the Scriptures constantly assume. (3.) It subverts the Scriptural doctrine of regeneration and sanctification to make the governing principle in the renewed to be their own πνεῦμα or spirit, and not the Holy Spirit.

Modern Speculative Views on this Subject.

The modern speculative philosophy has introduced such a radical change in the views entertained of the nature of God, of his relation to the world, of the nature of man and of his relation to God, of the person and work of Christ, and of the application of his redemption to the salvation of men, that all the old, and, it may be safely said, Scriptural forms of these doctrines have been superseded, and others introduced which are unintelligible except in the light of that philosophy, and which to a great extent reduce the truths of the Bible to the form of philosophical dogmas. We cease to hear of the Holy Ghost as the third person of the Trinity, applying to men the redemption purchased by Christ ; of regeneration by his almighty power, or of

his dwelling in the hearts of believers. The forms of this new
theology are very diversified. They are all perhaps comprehended under three classes : first, those which are avowedly pantheistic, although claiming to be Christian; secondly, those which
are Theistic but do not admit the doctrine of the Trinity ; and
thirdly, those which endeavour to bring theology as a philosophy into the forms of Christian doctrine. In all, however, the
anthropology, christology, soteriology, and ecclesiology advocated, are so changed as to render it impossible to retain in their
exhibition the terms and formulas with which the Church from
the beginning has been familiar. Regeneration, justification, and
sanctification are almost antiquated terms ; and what remains of
the truths those terms were used to express, is merged into the
one idea of the development of a new divine life in the soul. As
to anthropology, these modern speculative, or as they often call
themselves, and are called by others, mystic, theologians teach,
(1.) That there is no dualism in man between soul and body.
There is but one life. The body is the soul projecting itself externally. Without a body there is no soul. (2.) That there is
no real dualism between God and man. The identity between
God and man is the last result of modern speculation ; and it is
the fundamental idea of Christianity.

Soul and Body one.

As to the former of these points, Schleiermacher[1] says, "There
are not a spiritual and a corporeal world, a corporeal and spiritual existence of man. Such representations lead to nothing but
the dead mechanism of a preëstablished harmony. Body and
spirit are actual only in and with each other, so that corporeal
and spiritual action can only be relatively distinguished." The
late President Rauch[2] says, " A dualism which admits of two
principles for one being, offers many difficulties, and the greatest
is, that it cannot tell how the principles can be united in a third.
A river may originate in two fountains, but a science cannot, and
much less individual life." " It would be wrong to say that man
consists of two essentially different substances, of earth and the
soul; but he is soul only, and cannot be anything else. This
soul, however, unfolds itself externally in the life of the body, and
internally in the life of the mind." So Olshausen[3] teaches that
the soul has no subsistence but in the body. Dr. J. W. Nevin[4]

. *Dialektik*, sect. 290-295 ; *Works*, Berlin, 1839, 3d div. vol. iv. part 2, pp. 245-255.
[2] *Psychology*, New York, 1840, pp. 169, 173.   [3] *Commentary*, 1 Co· xv. 20.
[4] *Mystical Presence*, edit. Philadelphia, 1846, p. 171.

says, " We have no right to think of the body in any way as a
form of existence of and by itself, into which the soul as another
form of such existence is thrust in a mechanical way. Both form
one life. The soul to be complete, to develop itself at all as a
soul, must externalize itself, throw itself out in space ; and this
externalization is the body."

God and Man one.

As to the second point, or the oneness of God and man, as the
soul externalizes itself in the body, " dividing itself only that its
unity may become thus the more free and intensely complete,"[1] so
God externalizes Himself in the world. Schleiermacher says, it is
in vain to attempt to conceive of God as existing either before or
out of the world. They may be distinguished in thought, but are
only " zwei Werthe fur dieselbe Forderung, two values of the
same postulate." According to this philosophy, it is just as true,
" No world, no God," as " No body, no soul." " The world,[2] in
its lower view, is not simply the outward theatre or stage on
which man is to act his part as a candidate for heaven. In the
midst of all its different forms of existence, it is pervaded throughout with the power of a single life, which comes ultimately to its
full sense and force only in the human person." The world,
therefore, is pervaded by " the power of a single life ;" the highest
form of that life (on earth) is man. What is that life ? What
is that pervading principle which reveals itself in such manifold
forms of existence, and culminates in man ? It is, of course,
God. Man, therefore, as Schleiermacher says, is " the existence-
form " of God on earth.[3] Ullmann[4] says that the German mystics in the Middle Ages taught " the oneness of Deity and humanity." The results reached by the mystics under the guidance
of feeling, he says, modern philosophy has reached by speculation. This doctrine of the essential oneness of God and man, the
speculative theologians adopt as the fundamental idea of Christianity. To work out that idea in a manner compatible with
Theism and the Gospel, is the problem which those theologians
have attempted to solve. These attempts have resulted, in some
cases, in avowed Christian Pantheism, as it is called; in others,

---

[1] *Mystical Presence*, edit. Philadelphia, 1846, p. 172.
[2] *Mercersburg Review*, 1850, vol. ii. p. 550.
[3] Dorner's *Christologie*, 1st edit., Stuttgart, 1839, p. 488.
[4] " Charakter des Christenthums," *Studien und Kritiken*, 1845, erstes Heft, p. 59. See
also a translation of this article at the beginning of *The Mystical Presence*, by J. W.
Nevin, D.D., Philadelphia, 1846.

in forms of doctrine so nearly pantheistic as to be hardly distinguished from Pantheism itself; and in all, in a radical modification, not only of the theology of the Church as expressed in her received standards, but also of the Scriptural form of Christian doctrines, if not of their essence. This is seen to be true in the anthropology of this system, which destroys the essential difference between the creator and his creatures, between God and man.

The christology of this modern theology has already been presented in its essential features. There is no dualism in Christ as between soul and body. The two are one life. Neither is there any dualism between divinity and humanity in Him. The divine and human in his person are one life. In being the ideal or perfect man, He is the true God. The deification which humanity reached in Christ, is not a supernatural act on the part of God; it is reached by a process of natural development in his people, *i. e.*, the Church.

Soteriology of these Philosophers.

The soteriology of this system is simple. The soul projects itself in the body. They are one life, but the body may be too much for the soul. The development of this one life in its twofold form, inward and outward, may not be symmetrical. So humanity as a generic life, a form of the life of God, as projected externally in the world from Adam onward, has not developed itself aright. If left unaided it would not reach the goal, or unfold itself as divine. A new start, therefore, must be given to it, a new commencement made. This is done by a supernatural intervention resulting in the production of the person of Christ. In Him divinity assumes the fashion of a man, — the existence-form of man, — God becomes man, and man is God. This renewed entrance, so to speak, of God into the world, this special form of divine-human life, is Christianity, which is constantly declared to be "a life," "the life of Christ," "a new theanthropic life." Men become Christians by being partakers of this life. They become partakers of this life by union with the Church and reception of the sacraments. The incarnation of God is continued in the Church; and this new principle of "divine-human life" descends from Christ to the members of his Church, as naturally and as much by a process of organic development, as humanity, derived from Adam, unfolded itself in his descendants. Christ, therefore, saves us, not so much by what He did, as by what He is.

He made no satisfaction to the divine justice ; no expiation for sin ; no fulfilling of the law. There is, therefore, really no justification, no real pardon even, in the ordinary sense of the word. There is a healing of the soul, and with that healing the removal of the evils incident to disease. Those who become partakers of this new principle of life, which is truly human and truly divine, become one with Christ. All the merit, righteousness, excellence, and power, inherent in this "divine-human life" of course belong to those who partake of that life. This righteousness, excellence, etc., are our own. They are subjective in us, and form our character, just as the nature derived from Adam was ours, with all its corruptions and infirmities.

If asked what is regeneration according to this system, the proper answer would probably be, that it is an obsolete term. There is no room for the thing usually signified by the word, and no reason for retaining the word itself. Regeneration is a work of the Holy Spirit. But this system in its integrity does not acknowledge the Holy Spirit as a distinct person or agent. And those who are constrained to make the acknowledgment of his personality, are evidently embarrassed by the admission. What the Scriptures and the Church attribute to the Spirit working with the freedom of a personal agent, when and where he sees fit, this system attributes to the "theanthropic-life" of Christ, working as a new force, according to the natural laws of development.[1]

The impression made upon the readers of the modern theologians of this school, is that made by any other form of philosophical disquisition. It has not, and from its nature it cannot have anything more than human authority. This system may be adopted as a matter of opinion, but it cannot be an object of faith. And therefore it cannot support the hopes of a soul conscious of guilt. In turning from such writings to the Word of God, the transition these theologians would have us believe, is from γνῶσις to πίστις ; but to the consciousness of the Christian, it is like the transition from the confusion of tongues at Babel, where no man understood his fellow, to the symphonious utterance of those "who spake as they were moved by the Holy Ghost."

Doctrine of Ebrard.

Of the writers who belong to the general class of "speculative" theologians, some adhere much more nearly to the Scriptures

[1] *Mystical Presence*, edit. Philadelphia, 1846, pp. 225-229.

than others. Dr. J. H. A. Ebrard, of Erlangen, has already
been repeatedly referred to as addicted to the Reformed faith ;
and where he consciously departs from it, he considers himself as
only carrying out its legitimate principles. His " Dogmatik "
has, in fact, a far more Scriptural character than most of the
modern German systems. In Ebrard, as in others, we find a
compromise attempted between the Church doctrine of regeneration, and the modern theory of the incarnation of God in the race
of man. Not only is a distinction made between repentance, conversion, and regeneration ; but also true repentance and genuine
conversion are made to precede regeneration. The two former
take place in the sphere of the consciousness. In all the states
and exercises connected with repentance and conversion, the soul
is active and coöperative · and the only influence exercised by
God or his Spirit, is mediate and moral. It is not until the sinner has obeyed the command to repent, to believe in Christ, and
to return unto God, that God gives the soul that divine something which makes it a new creature, and effects its living organic
union with Christ. In this latter process the soul is simply passive. God is the only agent. What is said to be communicated
to the soul is Christ ; the person of Christ ; the life of Christ ; his
substance, or a new substance. A distinction, however, is made
between essence and substance. Ebrard insists [1] that the most
hidden, substantial germ of our being is born again in regeneration — not merely changed, but new-born. Nevertheless, he says
that the " essentia animæ humanæ " is not changed, and assents to
the statement by Bucan, " Renovatio fit non quoad essentiam ut
deliravit Illyricus, sed quoad qualitates inhærentes." What he
asserts,[2] frequently elsewhere, is, " That Christ, real and substantial, is born in us." But he adds that the words " real and substantial " are used to guard against the assumption that regeneration consists simply in some inward exercise, or transient state of
the consciousness. It is, as he truly teaches, much more ; something lower than the consciousness ; a change in the state of the
soul, which determines the acts and exercises which reveal themselves in the consciousness, and manifest themselves in the life.
He finds his doctrine of regeneration, not in what Calvin and
some few of the Reformed theologians taught under that head,
but in what they teach of the Lord's Supper, and of the mystical
union. Calvin [3] says, " Sunt qui manducare Christi carnem, et

[1] *Dogmatik*, edit. Königsberg, 1852, vol. ii. p. 320.   [2] *Ibid.* p. 309.
[3] *Institutio*, IV. xvii. 5, edit. Berlin, 1834, vol. ii. p. 403.

sanguinem ejus bibere, uno verbo definiunt, nihil esse aliud, quam
in Christum ipsum credere. Sed mihi expressius quiddam ac
sublimius videtur voluisse docere Christus . . . . nempe vera
sui participatione nos vivificari. . . . . Quemadmodum enim non
aspectus sed esus panis corpori alimentum sufficit, ita vere ac
penitus participem Christi animam fieri convenit, ut ipsius virtute
in vitam spiritualem vegetetur." "We have here certainly,"
says Ebrard,[1] " the doctrine of a secret, mystical communication
of Christ's substance to the substantial centre in man (the
'anima'), which develops itself on the one hand in the physical,
and on the other, in the noetic life." These writers are correct
in denying that regeneration is a mere change in the purposes,
or feelings, or conscious states of any kind in man ; and also in
affirming that it involves the communication of a new and abiding principle of life to the soul. But they depart from Scripture
and from the faith of the Church universal in substituting " the
theanthropic nature of Christ," " his divine-human life," " generic humanity healed and exalted to the power of a divine life "
(i. e., deified), for the Holy Ghost. This substitution is made
avowedly in obedience to modern science, to the new philosophy which has discovered a true anthropology and revealed " the
real oneness of God and man." As already remarked, it is assumed that this communication of the " theanthropic nature of
Christ " carried with it his merits as well as his blessedness and
power. All we have of Christ, we have within us. And if we
can discover little of God, and little God-like in our souls, so
much the worse. It is all we have to expect, until our inner
life is further developed. The Christ within (as some of the
Friends also teach), is, according to this system, all the Christ
we have. Ebrard, therefore, in one view identifies regeneration
and justification. " Regeneration," he says,[2] " as the act of
Christ, is the cause ('causa efficiens') of justification ; He communicates his life to us, and awakens a new life in us." This is
justification, an inward subjective change, which involves merit
as well as holiness. This confounding the work of the Holy
Spirit in regeneration, with the judicial, objective act of justification, belongs to the system. At least it is only on the ground
of this infused life that we are pronounced righteous in the sight
of God. What we receive is " the real divine-human life of
Christ," and " whatever there may be of merit, virtue, efficacy,
or moral value in any way, in the mediatorial work of Christ, it

---

[1] *Dogmatik*, vol. ii. p. 310.   [2] *Ibid.* p. 315.

is all lodged in the life, by the power of which alone this work has been accomplished, and in the presence of which only it can have either reality or stability. The imagination that the merits of Christ's life may be sundered from his life itself, and conveyed over to his people under this abstract form, on the ground of a merely outward legal constitution, is unscriptural and contrary to all reason at the same time."[1] Regeneration consisting in the communicating the life of Christ, his substance, to the soul, and this divine-human life comprehending all the merit, virtue, or efficacy belonging to Christ and his work, — regeneration involves justification, of which it is the ground and the cause.

Doctrine of Delitzsch.

Delitzsch devotes one division of his " Biblical Psychology " to the subject of regeneration. He begins the discussion with a discourse on Christ's person. " When we wish to consider the new spiritual life of the redeemed man, we proceed from the divine human archetype, the person of the Redeemer."[2] Man was, as to his spirit and soul, originally constituted in the image of God ; the spirit was the image " of His triune nature and the latter [the soul] of His sevenfold ' doxa.' " Man was free to conform his life to the spirit, or divine principle within him, or to allow the control of his life to be assumed by the soul. Utter ruin was the consequence of the fall. This could be corrected and man redeemed only by "a new beginning of similar creative intensity."[3] This new beginning was effected in the incarnation. The Son of God became man, not by assuming our nature, in the ordinary sense of those words, but by ceasing to be almighty, omniscient, and omnipresent, and contracting Himself to the limits of humanity. It was a human life into which He thus entered ; a life including a spirit, soul, and body. There is no dualism in Christ's person, as between the corporeal and spiritual, or between the human and divine. It is the divine nature in the form of humanity, or this divine-human nature, which is purely and simply, though perfectly, human, which is communicated to the people of God in their regeneration. To this fellowship in the life of Christ, faith is indispensable, and therefore Ebrard says, infants cannot be the subjects of regeneration, while Delitzsch, a Lutheran, maintains that infants are capable of exercising faith, and

---

[1] *Mystical Presence*, by J. W. Nevin, D. D., Philadelphia, 1846, p. 191.
[2] *A System of Biblical Psychology*, by Franz Delitzsch, D. D., translated by R. E Wallis, Ph. D.; edit. Edinburgh, 1867, p. 381.
[3] *Ibid.* p. 382.

therefore are capable of being regenerated. What is received
from Christ, or that of which his people are made partakers, is
"the Spirit, the soul, the body of Christ." [1] The new man, or
second Adam, was made a "life-giving spirit," and gradually
subdues the old man, or our Adamic nature, and brings the
whole man (πνεῦμα, ψυχή, and σῶμα), spirit, soul, and body, up to
the standard of the life of Christ, in whom the divine and human are merged into one, or rather appear in their original oneness.

The communication of the theanthropic life to the soul is an
act of the divine Spirit in which we have neither agency nor consciousness. Delitzsch infers from what our Lord said to Nicodemus, John iii. that "The operation of the Spirit of regeneration
is, therefore, (1.) A free one, withdrawn from the power of human volition, of human special agency. (2.) A mysterious one,
lying beyond human consciousness, and only to be recognized by
its effects." [2] "It is peculiar to all God's creative agencies, that
the creature which is thereby brought into existence, or in which
this or that is brought into existence, has no consciousness of what
is occurring." [3]

Various as are the modifications of this doctrine as presented
by different writers of this general school, regeneration is by all
of them understood to be the communication of the life of Christ
to the soul. By the life of Christ is meant his manhood, his human nature, which was at the same time divine, and therefore is
theanthropic. It may be called human, and it may be called
divine, for although being one, one life, it is truly divine by being
perfectly human. We are all partakers of humanity as polluted
and degraded by the apostasy of Adam. Christ, or rather, the
Eternal Son of God, assumed human nature, in that He became
man, and being God, humanity in Him was filled with the treasures of wisdom and knowledge and grace and power ; of that humanity we must partake in order to have any part in the salvation of Christ. The communication of this life to us, which is our
regeneration, is through the Church, which is his body, because
animated by his human life. As we derive our deteriorated
humanity by descent from Adam, we are made partakers of this
renovated, divine humanity by union with the Church, in which
Christ as a man, and God-man, lives and dwells. And as the

---

[1] *A System of Biblical Psychology*, by Franz Delitzsch, D. D., translated by R. E.
Wallis, Ph. D.; edit. Edinburgh, 1867, p. 398.
[2] *Ibid.* p. 402.   [3] *Ibid.* p. 403.

communication of humanity as it existed in fallen Adam to his descendants is by a natural process of organic development; so the communication of the renovated humanity as it exists in Christ, to his people, and through the world, is also a natural process. It supposes no special interference or intervention on the part of God, any more than any other organic development in the vegetable or animal world. The only thing supernatural about it is the starting point in Christ.

Doctrine of the Latin Church.

In the later Latin Church the word regeneration is used as synonymous with justification, and is taken in a wide sense as including everything involved in the translation of the soul from the kingdom of darkness into the kingdom of God's dear Son. In regeneration the sinner becomes a child of God. It is made, therefore, to include, (1.) The removal of the "reatus" or guilt of sin. (2.) The cleansing away of inherent moral corruption. (3.) The "infusion of new habits of grace;" and (4.) Adoption, or recognition of the renewed as sons of God. The Council of Trent says,[1] "Justificatio . . . . non est sola peccatorum remissio, sed et sanctificatio, et renovatio interioris hominis per voluntariam susceptionem gratiæ, et donorum, unde homo ex injusto fit justus, et ex inimico amicus, ut sit heres secundum spem vitæ æternæ." The instrumental cause of justification in this sense, is declared to be "sacramentum baptismi, quod est sacramentum fidei, sine qua nulli umquam contigit justificatio." As to the effect of baptism, it is taught [2] that it takes away not only guilt, but everything of the nature of sin, and communicates a new life. "Si quis per Jesu Christi Domini gratiam; quæ in baptismate confertur, reatum originalis peccati remitti negat, aut etiam asserit, non tolli totum id, quod veram, et propriam peccati rationem habet; sed illud dicit tantum radi, aut non imputari: anathema sit. In renatis enim nihil odit Deus, quia nihil est damnationis iis qui vere consepulti sunt cum Christo per baptisma in mortem: qui non secundum carnem ambulant, sed veterem hominem exuentes, et novum, qui secundum Deum creatus est, induentes, innocentes, immaculati, puri, innoxii, ac Deo dilecti effecti sunt, heredes quidem Dei, coheredes autem Christi, ita ut nihil prorsus eos ab ingressu cœli remoretur." [3]

---

[1] Sessio vi. cap. 7.

[2] Ibid. v. 5.

[3] Streitwolf, Libri Symbolici, Göttingen, 1846, pp. 24, 25, 19.

Regeneration, therefore, as effected in baptism, is the removal of the guilt and pollution of sin, the infusion of new habits of grace, and introduction into the family of God. It is in baptism that all the benefits of the redemption of Christ are conveyed to the soul, and this is its regeneration or birth into the kingdom of God.

Doctrine of the Church of England.

1. There has always been a class of theologians in the English Church who hold the theology of the Church of Rome in its leading characteristics. They accept, therefore, the definition of regeneration, or justification, as they call it, as given by the Council of Trent, and quoted above.

2. Others make a distinction between conversion and regeneration. The latter is that grace which attends baptism, and as that sacrament without sacrilege cannot be repeated, so regeneration can be experienced only once. Conversion is "a change of heart and life from sin to holiness." "To the heathen and infidel conversion is absolutely and always necessary to salvation." To the baptized Christian conversion is not always necessary. "Some persons have confused conversion with regeneration, and have taught that all men, the baptized, and therefore in fact regenerate, must be regenerated afterwards, or they cannot be saved. Now this is in many ways false: for regeneration, which the Lord Jesus Christ himself has connected with holy baptism, cannot be repeated: moreover, not all men (though indeed most men do) fall into such sin after baptism, that conversion, or as they term it, regeneration, is necessary to their salvation ; and if a regeneration were necessary to them, it could only be obtained through repetition of baptism, which were an act of sacrilege." "They who object to the expression baptismal regeneration, by regeneration mean, for the most part, the first influx of irresistible and indefectible grace ; grace that cannot be repelled by its subject, and which must issue in its final salvation. Now, of such grace our Church knows nothing, and of course, therefore, means not by regeneration at baptism, the first influx of such grace. That the sins, original and actual, of the faithful recipient of baptism, are washed away, she doth indeed believe ; and also that grace is given to him by the immediate agency of the Holy Spirit ; yet so that the conscience thus cleansed may be again defiled, and that the baptized person may, and often does, by his own fault, fall again into sin. in which if he die he shall

without doubt perish everlastingly ; his condemnation not being avoided, but rather increased, by his baptismal privilege."[1]

3. A third form of doctrine on this subject, held by some divines of this church, is that regeneration properly expresses an external change of relation, and not an internal change of the state of the soul and of its relation to God. As a proselyte was regenerated when he professed himself a Jew, so any one initiated into the visible Church is thereby regenerated. This is held to be entirely different from spiritual renovation. Regeneration, in this outward sense, is admitted to be by baptism ; renovation is by the Spirit.

4. A large class of English theologians have ever remained faithful to the evangelical doctrine on this subject, in accordance with the views of the Reformers in their Church, who were in full sympathy both in doctrine and in ecclesiastical and Christian fellowship with other Protestant churches.

§ 3. The Evangelical Doctrine.

In the Lutheran Symbols the doctrine of Regeneration, which is made to include conversion, is thus stated : " Conversio hominis talis est immutatio, per operationem Spiritus Sancti, in hominis intellectu, voluntate et corde, qua homo (operatione videlicet Spiritus Sancti) potest oblatam gratiam apprehendere."[2]

" Hominis autem nondum renati intellectus et voluntas tantum sunt subjectum convertendum, sunt enim hominis spiritualiter mortui intellectus et voluntas, in quo homine Spiritus Sanctus conversionem et renovationem operatur, ad quod opus hominis convertendi voluntas nihil confert, sed patitur, ut Deus in ipsa operetur, donec regeneretur. Postea vero in aliis sequentibus bonis operibus Spiritui Sancto cooperatur, ea faciens, quæ Deo grata sunt."[3]

" Sicut igitur homo, qui corporaliter mortuus est, seipsum propriis viribus præparare aut accommodare non potest, ut vitam externam recipiat : ita homo spiritualiter in peccatis mortuus, seipsum propriis viribus ad consequendam spiritualem et cœlestem justitiam et vitam præparare, applicare, aut vertere non potest, nisi per Filium Dei a morte peccati liberetur et vivificetur."[4]

" Rejicimus errorem eorum qui fingunt, Deum in conversione et regeneratione hominis substantiam et essentiam veteris Adami, et

[1] A Church Dictionary, by Walter Farquhar Hook, D. D., Vicar of Leeds, article "Conversion"; 6th edition, Philadelphia, 1854.
[2] Form of Concord, II. 83.   [3] Ibid. 91.   [4] Ibid. 11.

præcipue animam rationalem penitus abolere, novamque animæ essentiam ex nihilo, in illa conversione et regeneratione creare." [1]

With these statements the doctrines taught in the Symbols and by the theologians of the Reformed churches, perfectly agree. It is sufficient to quote the standards of our own Church. The " Westminster Confession " says, " Man, by his fall into a state of sin, hath wholly lost all ability of will to any spiritual good accompanying salvation ; so as a natural man being altogether averse from that which is good, and dead in sin, is not able, by his own strength, to convert himself, or to prepare himself thereunto." " When God converts a sinner, and translates him into the state of grace, He freeth him from his natural bondage under sin, and by his grace alone enables him freely to will and to do that which is spiritually good." " All those whom God hath predestinated unto life, and those only, He is pleased, in his appointed and accepted time, effectually to call, by his Word and Spirit, out of that state of sin and death in which they are by nature, to grace and salvation by Jesus Christ; enlightening their minds, spiritually and savingly, to understand the things of God, taking away their heart of stone, and giving unto them an heart of flesh ; renewing their wills, and by his Almighty power, determining them to that which is good, and effectually drawing them to Jesus Christ; yet so as they come most freely, being made willing by his grace." " This effectual call is of God's free and special grace alone, not from anything at all foreseen in man, who is altogether passive therein, until being quickened and renewed by the Holy Ghost, he is thereby enabled to answer this call, and embrace the grace offered and conveyed in it." [2]

The Larger Catechism [3] says, " What is effectual calling? Effectual calling is the work of God's almighty power and grace, whereby (out of his free and especial love to his elect, and from nothing in them moving Him thereunto) He doth in his accepted time invite and draw them to Jesus Christ by his Word and Spirit ; savingly enlightening their minds, renewing and powerfully determining their wills, so as they (although in themselves dead in sin) are hereby made willing and able, freely to answer his call, and to accept and embrace the grace offered and conveyed therein."

Exposition of the Doctrine.

According to the common doctrine of Protestants, i. e., of Lutherans and Reformed, as appears from the above quotations,—

---

1 *Ibid.* 14 ; Hase, *Libri Symbolici*, 3d edit. Leipzig, 1836, pp. 679, 681, 658, 581.
2 ix. 3, 4; x. 1, 2   2 Question 67.

Regeneration an Act of God.

1. Regeneration is an act of God. It is not simply referred to Him as its giver, and, in that sense, its author, as He is the giver of faith and of repentance. It is not an act which, by argument and persuasion, or by moral power, He induces the sinner to perform. But it is an act of which He is the agent. It is God who regenerates. The soul is regenerated. In this sense the soul is passive in regeneration, which (subjectively considered) is a change wrought in us, and not an act performed by us.

Regeneration an Act of God's Power.

2. Regeneration is not only an act of God, but also an act of his almighty power. Agreeably to the express declarations of the Scriptures, it is so presented in the Symbols of the Protestant churches. If an act of omnipotence, it is certainly efficacious, for nothing can resist almighty power. The Lutherans indeed deny this. But the more orthodox of them mean simply that the sinner can keep himself aloof from the means through which, or, rather, in connection with which it pleases God to exercise his power. He can absent himself from the preaching of the Word, and the use of the sacraments. Or he may voluntarily place himself in such an inward posture of resistance as determines God not to exert his power in his regeneration. The assertion that regeneration is an act of God's omnipotence, is, and is intended to be, a denial that it is an act of moral suasion. It is an affirmation that it is "physical" in the old sense of that word, as opposed to moral; and that it is immediate, as opposed to mediate, or through or by the truth. When either in Scripture or in theological writings, the word regeneration is taken in a wide sense as including conversion or the voluntary turning of the soul to God, then indeed it is said to be by the Word. The restoration of sight to the blind by the command of Christ, was an act of omnipotence. It was immediate. Nothing in the way of instrumentary or secondary coöperating influence intervened between the divine volition and the effect. But all exercises of the restored faculty were through and by the light. And without light sight is impossible. Raising Lazarus from the dead was an act of omnipotence. Nothing intervened between the volition and the effect. The act of quickening was the act of God. In that matter Lazarus was passive. But in all the acts of the restored vitality, he was active and free. According to the evan-

gelical system it is in this sense that regeneration is the act of God's almighty power. Nothing intervenes between his volition that the soul, spiritually dead, should live, and the desired effect. But in all that belongs to the consciousness; all that precedes or follows the imparting of this new life, the soul is active and is influenced by the truth acting according to the laws of our mental constitution.

Regeneration in the Subjective Sense of the Word not an Act.

3. Regeneration, subjectively considered, or viewed as an effect or change wrought in the soul, is not an act. It is not a new purpose created by God (if that language be intelligible), or formed by the sinner under his influence. Nor is it any conscious exercise of any kind. It is something which lies lower than consciousness.

Not a Change of Substance.

4. It is not, however, according to the Church doctrine, any change in the substance of the soul. This is rejected universally as Manicheism, and as inconsistent with the nature of sin and holiness. It is, indeed, often assumed that there is nothing in the soul but its substance and its acts ; and, therefore, if regeneration be not a change in the acts, it must be a change of the substance of the soul. This assumption, however, is not only arbitrary, but it is also opposed to the intimate convictions of all men. That is, of all men in their normal state, when not speculating or theorizing. That such is the common judgment of men has already been proved under the heads of original righteousness and original sin. Every one recognizes, in the first place, that such constitutional principles as parental love, the social affections, a sense of justice, pity, etc., are immanent states of the soul which can be resolved neither into its essence nor acts. So also acquired habits are similar permanent and immanent states which are not acts, much less modifications or changes of the essence. The same is true of dispositions, amiable and unamiable. The refinement of taste and feeling due to education and culture, is not a change in the essence of the mind. It cannot reasonably be denied that a state of mind produced by culture, may be produced by the volition of God. What is true in every other department of our inner life, is true of our moral and religious nature. Besides those acts and states which reveal themselves in the consciousness, there are abiding states, dispositions, principles, or habits, as they are indifferently called, which con-

stitute character and give it stability, and are the proximate, determining cause why our voluntary exercises and conscious states are what they are. This is what the Bible calls the heart, which has the same relation to all our acts that the nature of a tree, as good or bad, has to the character of its fruit. A good tree is known to be good if its fruit be good. But the goodness of the fruit does not constitute or determine the goodness of the tree, but the reverse. In like manner, it is not good acts which make the man good; the goodness of the man determines the character of his acts.

It is a New Life.

5. While denying that regeneration is a change either in the essence or acts of the soul, evangelical Christians declare it to be, in the language of Scripture, " a quickening," a ζωοποιεῖν, a communication of a new principle of life. It is hard, perhaps impossible, to define what life is. Yet every man is familiar with its manifestations. He sees and knows the difference between death and life, between a dead and living plant or animal. And, therefore, when the Bible tells us that in regeneration God imparts a new form of life to the soul, the language is as intelligible as human language can be in relation to such a subject. We know that when a man is dead as to the body he neither sees, feels, nor acts. The objects adapted to impress the senses of the living make no impression upon him. They awaken no corresponding feeling, and they call forth no activity. The dead are insensible and powerless. When the Scriptures declare that men are spiritually dead they do not deny to them physical, intellectual, social, or moral life. They admit that the objects of sense, the truths of reason, our social relations and moral obligations, are more or less adequately apprehended; these do not fail to awaken feeling and to excite to action. But there is a higher class of objects than these, what the Bible calls " The things of God," " The things of the Spirit," " The things pertaining to salvation." These things, although intellectually apprehended as presented to our cognitive faculties, are not spiritually discerned by the unrenewed man. A beautiful object in nature or art may be duly apprehended as an object of vision by an uncultivated man, who has no perception of its æsthetic excellence, and no corresponding feeling of delight in its contemplation. So it is with the unrenewed man. He may have an intellectual knowledge of the facts and doctrines of the Bible, but no spiritual discernment of their excellence, and no delight in them. The same

Christ, as portrayed in the Scriptures, is to one man without form or comeliness that we should desire Him; to another He is the chief among ten thousand and the one altogether lovely; "God manifest in the flesh," whom it is impossible not to adore, love, and obey.

This new life, therefore, manifests itself in new views of God, of Christ, of sin, of holiness, of the world, of the gospel, and of the life to come; in short, of all those truths which God has revealed as necessary to salvation. This spiritual illumination is so important and so necessary and such an immediate effect of regeneration, that spiritual knowledge is not only represented in the Bible as the end of regeneration (Col. iii. 10; 1 Tim. ii. 4), but the whole of conversion (which is the effect of regeneration) is summed up in knowledge. Paul describes his conversion as consisting in Christ's being revealed to Him (Gal. i. 16); and the Scriptures make all religion, and even eternal life, to be a form of knowledge. Paul renounced everything for the excellency of the knowledge of Christ (Phil. iii. 8), and our Lord says that the knowledge of Himself and of the Father is eternal life. (John xvii. 3). The whole process of salvation is described as a translation from the kingdom of darkness into the kingdom of light. There is no wonder, therefore, that the ancients called regeneration a φωτισμός, an illumination. If a man born blind were suddenly restored to sight, such a flood of knowledge and delight would flow in upon him, through the organ of vision, that he might well think that all living consisted in seeing. So the New Testament writers represent the change consequent on regeneration, the opening the eyes on the certainty, glory, and excellence of divine things, and especially of the revelation of God in the person of his Son, as comprehending almost everything which pertains to spiritual life. Inseparably connected with this knowledge and included in it, is faith, in all the forms and exercises in which spiritual truths are its objects. Delight in the things thus revealed is the necessary consequence of spiritual illumination; and with delight come satisfaction and peace, elevation above the world, or spiritual mindedness, and such a sense of the importance of the things not seen and eternal, that all the energies of the renewed soul are (or, it is acknowledged, they should be) devoted to securing them for ourselves and others.

This is one of the forms in which the Bible sets forth the doctrine of regeneration. It is raising the soul dead in sin to spiritual life. And this spiritual life unfolds or manifests itself just as any other form of life, in all the exercises appropriate to its nature.

It is a New Birth.

The same doctrine on this subject is taught in other words when regeneration is declared to be a new birth. At birth the child enters upon a new state of existence. Birth is not its own act. It is born. It comes from a state of darkness, in which the objects adapted to its nature cannot act on it or awaken its activities. As soon as it comes into the world all its faculties are awakened ; it sees, feels, and hears, and gradually unfolds all its faculties as a rational and moral, as well as physical being. The Scriptures teach that it is thus in regeneration. The soul enters upon a new state. It is introduced into a new world. A whole class of objects before unknown or unappreciated are revealed to it, and exercise upon it their appropriate influence. The " things of the Spirit " become the chief objects of desire and pursuit, and all the energies of the new-born soul are directed towards the spiritual, as distinguished from the seen and temporal. This representation is in accordance with the evangelical doctrine on this subject. It is not consistent with any of the false theories of regeneration, which regard regeneration as the sinner's own act ; as a mere change of purpose ; or as a gradual process of moral culture.

A New Heart.

Another mode in which this doctrine is set forth is found in those passages in which God is represented as giving his people a new heart. The heart in Scripture is that which thinks, feels, wills, and acts. It is the soul ; the self. A new heart is, therefore, a new self, a new man. It implies a change of the whole character. It is a new nature. Out of the heart proceed all conscious, voluntary, moral exercises. A change of heart, therefore, is a change which precedes these exercises and determines ⁺heir character. A new heart is to a man what goodness is to .e tree in the parable of our Lord.

In regeneration, therefore, there is a new life communicated to the soul ; the man is the subject of a new birth ; he receives a new nature or new heart, and becomes a new creature. As the change is neither in the substance nor in the mere exercises of the soul, it is in those immanent dispositions, principles, tastes, or habits which underlie all conscious exercises, and determine the character of the man and of all his acts.

The whole Soul the Subject of this change.

6. According to the evangelical doctrine the whole soul is the subject of regeneration. It is neither the intellect to the exclusion of the feelings, nor the feelings to the exclusion of the intellect ; nor is it the will alone, either in its wider or in its more limited sense, that is the subject of the change in question. This is evident, —

(1.) Because the soul is a unit, and is so recognized in Scripture. Its faculties are not so dissociated that one can be good and another bad, one saved and another lost, one active in the sphere of morals and religion and the others inactive. In every such exercise the intelligence, the feelings, the will, and the conscience, or moral consciousness, are of necessity involved.

(2.) In the description of this work all the faculties of the soul are represented as affected. The mind is illuminated, the eyes of the understanding are opened ; the heart is renewed ; the will is conquered, or, the man is made willing.

(3.) When Lazarus was restored to life, it was not one member of the body, or one faculty that received the vivifying influence. It was not the heart that was set in motion, the brain and lungs being restored by its action. It was the whole man that was made alive. And it is the whole soul that is regenerated.

(4.) This is further evident from the effects ascribed to regeneration. These effects are not confined to any one department of our nature. Regeneration secures right knowledge as well as right feeling ; and right feeling is not the effect of right knowledge, nor is right knowledge the effect of right feeling. The two are the inseparable effects of a work which affects the whole soul.

(5.) When our Lord teaches that the tree must be made good in order that the fruit should be good, it was not any one part of the tree which must be changed, but the whole tree. In like manner it is the soul, in the centre and unity of its life, that is the subject of that life-giving power of the Holy Ghost, by which it becomes a new creature. The doctrine that regeneration is a change affecting only one of the faculties of the soul has its foundation entirely outside of the Scriptures. It is simply an inference from a particular psychological theory, and has no authority in theology.

§ 4. *Objections.*

The same objections which are urged against other doctrines of grace are pressed against the Augustinian view of the nature of regeneration. These objections are of three classes.

Denial of Supernaturalism.

1. The first class of objections are founded on the denial of Theism ; or at least on the denial of the Scriptural doctrine of the relation of God to the world. It is an assumption common to most of the forms of modern philosophy that the only agency of the Supreme Being (whether personal or impersonal) is according to law. It is ordered, uniform, and in, with, and through second causes, if such causes are admitted. Everything is natural, and nothing supernatural, either in the outward world or in the sphere of things spiritual. There can be no creation " ex nihilo," no miracles, no immediate revelation, no inspiration in the church sense of that term ; no supernatural work upon the heart, and therefore no regeneration in the sense of an immediate operation of almighty power on the soul. Those who depart from their principles so far as to admit the person of Christ to be supernatural in its origin contend that the supernatural in Him becomes natural, and that from Him onward the diffusion of spiritual life is by a regular process of development, as simply natural as the development of humanity from Adam through all his posterity.

This is purely a philosophical theory. It has no authority for Christians. As it is contrary to the express teaching of the Scriptures it cannot be adopted by those who recognize them as the infallible rule of faith and practice. As it contradicts the moral and religious convictions arising from the constitution of our nature, it must be hurtful in all its tendencies, and can be adopted by those only who sacrifice to speculation their interior life.

Resting on False Psychological Theories.

2. A second class of objections are founded on certain psychological theories on free agency, on the nature of the soul, and on the conditions of moral obligation. No theories on these, or any other subjects, have any authority, except those which underlie and are necessarily assumed in the facts and doctrines of the Scripture. If any theory teaches that plenary ability is essential to free agency ; that God cannot control with certainty the acts

of free agents without destroying their liberty ; or that free acts
cannot be foreseen, predicted, or foreordained, then such theory
must be false if the Scriptures assert facts which imply the contrary. If a theory teaches that men are responsible only for
acts of the will, under their own control, that theory must be
rejected if the Bible teaches that we are responsible for states
of mind over which the will has no direct power. The facts involved in the evangelical doctrine of regeneration, as stated
above, contradict the theories on which the arguments of the
Remonstrants, Pelagians, and others against that doctrine rest,
and therefore those theories must share the fate of every doctrine
which contradicts established facts. This has been demonstrated
over and over in different ages of the Church. The principles
involved in these objections have been discussed in the preceding
pages, and need not be again considered.

Objections founded on the Divine Perfection.

3. A third class of objections are drawn from the supposed
inconsistency of this doctrine with the moral perfections of God.
If all men are dead in sin, destitute of the power to restore themselves to life, then not only is it unjust that they should be condemned, but it is also incompatible with the divine rectitude that
God should exert his almighty power in the regeneration of some,
while He leaves others to perish. Justice, it is said, demands that
all should have an equal opportunity ; that all should have, by
nature or from grace, power to secure their own salvation. It
is obvious that such objections do not bear peculiarly against the
Augustinian system. They are urged by atheists against Theism.
If there be a personal God of infinite power, why does He permit
sin and misery to hold joint supremacy on earth ; why are good
and evil so unequally distributed, and why is the distribution so
arbitrary ?

Deists make the same objections against the divine authority
of the Bible. They cannot receive it as the Word of God because
it represents the Creator and Governor of the world as placing
men under circumstances which secure in some way the universality of sin, and then punishing them with inexorable severity
even for their idle words.

It is also plain that the different anti-Augustinian systems
afford no real relief from these difficulties. Admitting that regeneration is the sinner's own act; admitting that every man
has all the knowledge and all the ability necessary to secure his

salvation, it remains true that few are saved, and that God does not interpose to prevent the great majority of adult men in the present state of the world perishing in their sins.

Augustinians do not deny these difficulties. They only maintain that they are not peculiar to their system; and they rest content with the solution of them given in the Scriptures. That solution agrees with all the facts of consciousness and experience, so far as consciousness and experience extend. The Bible teaches that man was created holy; that by his voluntary transgression of the divine law he apostatized from God; that in consequence of this apostasy all men come into the world in a state of spiritual death, both guilty and polluted; that God exercises no influence to lead them into sin, but on the contrary, by his truth, his providence, and by his Spirit exerts all that influence over them which should induce rational beings to repent and seek his pardoning mercy and sanctifying gràce; that all those who sincerely and faithfully seek reconciliation with God in the way of his appointment He actually saves; that of his sovereign grace He, in the exercise of his mighty power, renews and sanctifies a multitude which no man can number, who would otherwise have continued in their sins. With these representations of the Scriptures everything within the sphere of our knowledge agrees. Consciousness and experience testify that we are an apostate race; that all men are sinners, and, being sinners, have forfeited all claims on the favour of God; that in continuing in sin and in rejecting the overtures of mercy men act voluntarily, following the desires of their own hearts. Every man's conscience, moreover, teaches him that he has never sought the salvation of his soul with the sincerity and perseverance with which men seek the things of the world, and yet failed in his efforts. Every man who comes short of eternal life knows that the responsibility rests upon himself. On the other hand, the experience of every believer is a witness to him that it is of God and not of himself that he is in Christ (1 Corinthians i. 30); every believer knows that if God had left him to himself he would have continued in unbelief and sin. Why God intervenes to save one and not another, when all are equally undeserving; why the things of God are revealed unto babes while hidden from the wise and prudent, can only be answered in the language of our Lord, "Even so, Father, for so it seemed good in thy sight." (Matthew xi. 26.)

The more popular and common objections that the Augustinian doctrine of regeneration leads to the neglect of the means of grace, " to waiting for God's time," to indifference or despair ; that it is inconsistent with exhortations and commands addressed to sinners to repent and believe, and incompatible with moral responsibility, have already been repeatedly considered. It is enough to say once more that these objections are founded on the assumption that inability, even when it arises out of our own sinfulness, is incompatible with obligation. Besides, it is the natural and actual tendency of a sense of helplessness under a burden of evil, to lead to earnest and importunate application for relief to Him who is able to afford it, and by whom it is offered.

CHAPTER XVI.

FAITH.

§ 1. *Preliminary Remarks.*

THE first conscious exercise of the renewed soul is faith; as the first conscious act of a man born blind whose eyes have been opened, is seeing. The exercise of vision in such a man is indeed attended by so many new sensations and emotions that he cannot determine how much of this new experience comes through the eye, and how much from other sources. It is so with the believer. As soon as his eyes are opened by the renewing of the Holy Ghost he is in a new world. Old things have passed away, all things are become new. The apprehension of "the things of God" as true lies at the foundation of all the exercises of the renewed soul. The discussions on the question, Whether faith precedes repentance, or repentance faith, can have no place if the meaning of of the words be agreed upon. Unless faith be limited to some of its special exercises there can be no question that in the order of nature it must precede repentance. Repentance is the turning of the soul from sin unto God, and unless this be produced by the believing apprehension of the truth it is not even a rational act. As so much prominence is assigned to faith in the Scriptures, as all the promises of God are addressed to believers, and as all the conscious exercises of spiritual life involve the exercise of faith, without which they are impossible, the importance of this grace cannot be overestimated. To the theologian and to the practical Christian it is indispensable that clear and correct ideas should be entertained on the subject. It is one of special difficulty. This difficulty arises partly from the nature of the subject; partly from the fact that usage has assigned the word faith so many different meanings; partly from the arbitrary definitions given of it by philosophers and theologians; and partly from the great diversity of aspects under which it is presented in the Word of God.

The question, What is Faith? is a very comprehensive one. In one view it is a metaphysical question. What is the psycho-

logical nature of the act or state of the mind which we designate
faith, or belief ?   In this aspect the discussion concerns the philosopher as much as the theologian.   Secondly, faith may be
viewed as to its exercise in the whole sphere of religion and
morality.   Thirdly, it may be considered as a Christian grace,
the fruit of the Spirit; that is, those exercises of faith which are
peculiar to the regenerated people of God.   This is what is
meant by saving faith.   Fourthly, it may be viewed in its relation to justification, sanctification, and holy living, or, as to those
special exercises of faith which are required as the necessary
conditions of the sinner's acceptance with God, or as essential to
holiness of heart and life.

§ 2. *The Psychological Nature of Faith.*

Faith in the widest sense of the word, is assent to the truth,
or the persuasion of the mind that a thing is true.   In ordinary
popular language we are said to believe whatever we regard as
true.   The primary element of faith is trust.   The Hebrew word
אָמַן means to sustain, to uphold.   In the Niphil, to be firm, and,
in a moral sense, to be trustworthy.   In the Hiphil, to regard as
firm, or trustworthy, to place trust or confidence in.   In like
manner the Greek πιστεύω (from πίστις, and that from πείθω, to
persuade), means to trust, *i. e.*, to be persuaded that a person or
thing is trustworthy.   Hence the epithet πιστός is applied to any
one who is, and who shows himself to be, worthy of trust.   In
Latin *credere* (whence our word credit) has the same meaning.
In mercantile matters it means to lend, to trust to ; and then in
general, to exercise trust in.   " Crede mihi," trust me, rely on
my word.   *Fides* (from *fido*, and that from πείθω), is also trust,
confidence exercised in regard to any person or thing ; then the
disposition, or virtue which excites confidence ; then the promise,
declaration, or pledge which is the outward ground of confidence.
In the cognate words, *fidens, fidelis, fiducia*, the same idea is
prominent.   The German word " Glaube " has the same general
meaning.   It is defined by Heinsius (Wörterbuch) : " der Zustand
des Gemüthes, da man eine Sache für wahr hält und sich darauf
verlässt," *i. e.*, " that state of mind in which a man receives and
relies upon a thing as true."   The English word "faith" is said to
be from the Anglo-Saxon "fægan " to covenant.   It is that state
of mind which a covenant requires or supposes ; that is, it is confidence in a person or thing as trustworthy.   " To believe," is
defined by the Latin " credere, fidem dare sive habere."   " The

etymologists," says Richardson, " do not attempt to account for this important word: it is undoubtedly formed on the Dut. *Leven ;* Ger. *Leben;* A.-S. *Lif-ian, Be-lif-ian ;* Goth. *Liban,* vivere, to live, or be-live, to dwell.   *Live* or *leve, be-* or *bi-live* or *leve,* are used indifferently by old writers, whether to denote *vivere* or *credere.* . . . . To *believe,* then, is to live by or according to, to abide by ; to guide, conduct, regulate, govern, or direct the *life* by ; to take, accept, assume or adopt as a *rule of life ;* and, consequently, to think, deem, or judge right; to be firmly persuaded of, to give credit to ; to trust, or think trustworthy ; to have or give faith or confidence ; to confide, to think or deem faithful."

The Primary Idea of Faith is Trust.

From all this it appears that the primary idea of faith is trust. The primary idea of truth is that which is trustworthy ; that which sustains our expectations, which does not disappoint, because it really is what it is assumed or declared to be.   It is opposed to the deceitful, the false, the unreal, the empty, and the worthless.   To regard a thing as true, is to regard it as worthy of trust, as being what it purports to be.   Faith, in the comprehensive and legitimate meaning of the word, therefore, is trust.

In accordance with this general idea of faith, Augustine [1] says, " Credere, nihil aliud est, quam cum assensione cogitare."   Thus, also, Reid [2] says, " Belief admits of all degrees, from the slightest suspicion to the fullest assurance. . . . . There are many operations of the mind in which . . . . we find belief to be an essential ingredient. . . . . Belief is an ingredient in consciousness, in perception, and in remembrance. . . . . We give the name of evidence to whatever is a ground of belief. . . . . What this evidence is, is more easily felt than described. . . . . The common occasions of life lead us to distinguish evidence into different kinds, ... such as the evidence of sense, the evidence of memory, the evidence of consciousness, the evidence of testimony, the evidence of axioms, the evidence of reasoning. . . . . They seem to me to agree only in this, that they are all fitted by nature to produce belief in the human mind."

[1] *De Prædestinatione Sanctorum* [II.], 5; *Works,* edit. Benedictines, Paris, 1838, vol. x. p. 1349 b.
[2] *On the Intellectual Powers,* Essay II. ch xx.; *Works,* Edinburgh, 1849, pp. 327 b, 328 a, b.

The more limited Sense of the Word.

There is, however, in most cases a great difference between the general signification of a word and its special and characteristic meaning.   Although, therefore, there is an element of belief in all our cognitions, there is an important difference between what is strictly and properly called faith, and those states or acts of the mind which we designate as sight or perception, intuition, opinions, conclusions, or apodictic judgments.   What that characteristic difference is, is the point to be determined.   There are modes of statement on this subject current among a certain class of philosophers and theologians, which can hardly be regarded as definitions of faith.   They take the word out of its ordinary and established meaning, or arbitrarily limit it to a special sphere of our mental operations.   Thus Morell[1] says, " Faith is the intuition of eternal verities."   But eternal verities are not the only objects of faith ; nor is intuition the only mode of apprehending truth which is of the nature of belief.   The same objections bear against the assertion that " Faith is the organ for the supernatural and divine ; " or, as Eschenmayer expresses it,[2] "Ein vom Denken, Fühlen und Wollen verschiedenes, eigenthümliches Organ für das Ewige und Heilige ; a special organ for the eternal and the holy."   The supernatural and divine, however, are not the exclusive objects even of religious faith.   It is by faith we know that the worlds were made by the word of God ; it was by faith Noah prepared the ark, and Abraham, being called of God, went out not knowing whither he went.   The objects of faith in these cases are not what is meant by " eternal verities."   It is, moreover, an arbitrary assumption that faith is " a special organ," even when things supernatural and divine are its object.   Our nature is adapted to the reception of all kinds of truth of which we can have any idea.   But it is not necessary to assume a special organ for historical truths, a special organ for scientific truths, and another for the general truths of revelation, and still another for " the eternal and the holy."   God has constituted us capable of belief, and the complex state of mind involved in the act of faith is of course different according to the nature of the truth believed, and the nature of the evidence on which our faith is founded.   But this does not necessitate the assumption of a distinct organ for each kind of truth.

[1] *Philosophy of Religion.*
[2] *Die einfachste Dogmatik,* § 338; Tübingen, 1826, p. 376.

Faith not to be regarded as simply a Christian Grace.

No less unsatisfactory are those descriptions of faith which regard it only in its character as a Christian and saving grace. Delitzsch, for example,[1] describes faith as the most central act of our being ; the return to God, the going out of our inner life to Him. " This longing after God's free, merciful love, as his own Word declares it, — a longing, reaching forth, and grasping it ; this naked, unselfish craving, feeling itself satisfied with nothing else than God's promised grace ; this eagerness, absorbing every ray of light that proceeds from God's reconciled love ; this convinced and safety-craving appropriation and clinging to the word of grace ; — this is faith.   According to its nature, it is the pure receptive correlative of the word of promise ; a means of approaching again to God, which, as the word itself, is appointed through the distance of God in consequence of sin ; for faith has to confide in the word, in spite of all want of comprehension, want of sight, want of experience.   No experimental *actus reflexi* belong to the nature of faith.   It is, according to its nature, *actio directa*, to wit, *fiducia supplex*."   All this is doubtless true of the believer. He does thus long after God, and appropriate the assurance of his love, and cling to his promises of grace ; but faith has a wider range than this.   There are exercises of faith not included in this description, recorded in Scripture, and especially in the eleventh chapter of the Epistle to the Hebrews.

Erdmann[2] says that religious faith, the faith on which the Scriptures lay so much stress, is, " Bewusstseyn der Versöhnung mit Gott, consciousness of reconciliation with God."   He insists that faith cannot be separated from its contents. It is not the man who holds this or that to be true, who is a believer ; but the man who is convinced of a specific truth, namely, that he is reconciled with God.   Calling faith a consciousness is not a definition of its nature.   And limiting it to a consciousness of reconciliation with God is contrary to the usage of Scripture and of theology

Definitions of Faith founded on its Subjective Nature.

The more common and generally received definitions of faith, may perhaps be reduced to three classes, all of which include the general idea of persuasion of the truth.   But some seek the dis-

---

[1] *Biblical Psychology,* p. 174.

[2] *Vorlesungen über Glauben und Wissen,* von Johann Eduard Erdmann, Berlin, 1837, p. 30.

tinguishing character of faith in its subjective nature; others, in the nature of its object; others, in the nature of the evidence, or ground on which it rests.

Faith as distinguished from Opinion and Knowledge.

To the first of these classes belong the following definitions: Faith or belief is said to be a persuasion of the truth stronger than opinion, and weaker than knowledge. Metaphysicians divide the objects of our cognitions into the possible, the real, and the necessary. With regard to the merely possible we can form only conjectures, or opinions, more or less plausible or probable. With regard to things which the mind with greater or less confidence views as certain, although it cannot justify that confidence to itself or others, i. e., cannot demonstrate the certainty of the object, it is said to believe. What it is perfectly assured of, and can demonstrate to be true so as to coerce conviction, it is said to know. Thus Locke defines faith to be the assent of the mind to propositions which are probably, but not certainly true. Bailey[1] says, " I propose to confine it [belief or faith] first, to the effect on the mind of the premises in what is termed probable reasoning, or what I have named contingent reasoning — in a word the premises in all reasoning, but that which is demonstrative ; and secondly, to the state of holding true when that state, far from being the effect of any premises discerned by the mind, is dissociated from all evidence." To believe is to admit a thing as true, according to Kant, on grounds sufficient subjectively, insufficient objectively. Or, as more fully stated, " Holding for true, or the subjective validity of a judgment in relation to conviction (which is, at the same time, objectively valid) has the three following degrees : opinion, belief, and knowledge. Opinion is a consciously insufficient judgment, subjectively as well as objectively. Belief is subjectively sufficient, but is recognized as being objectively insufficient. Knowledge is both subjectively and objectively sufficient. Subjective sufficiency is termed conviction (for myself) ; objective sufficiency is termed certainty (for all)."[2] Erdmann[3] says, " Man versteht unter Glauben eine jede Gewissheit, die geringer ist als das Wissen, und etwa stärker ist als ein blosses Meinen oder Fürmöglichhalten (z. B. ich glaube, dass es

[1] *Letters on the Philosophy of the Human Mind*, London, 1855, pp. 75, 76.
[2] Meiklejohn's *Translation of Critic of Pure Reason*, London, 1855, p. 498.
[3] *Glauben und Wissen*, Berlin, 1837, p. 29.

heute regnen wird)." "By faith is understood any persuasion which is weaker than knowledge, but somewhat stronger than a mere deeming possible or probable, as, *e. g.*, I believe it will rain to-day." This he gives as the commonly accepted meaning of the word, although he utterly repudiates it as a definition of religious faith.

It is urged in support of this definition of faith that with regard to everything of which we are not absolutely sure, and yet are persuaded or convinced of its truth, we say we believe. Thus with respect to things remembered; if the recollection is indistinct and uncertain, we say we think, *e. g.*, we think we saw a certain person at a given time and place; we are not sure, but such is our impression. If our persuasion of the fact be stronger, we say we believe it. If we have, and can have, no doubt about it, we say we know it. In like manner the testimony of our senses may be so weak as to produce only a probability that the thing is as it appears; if clearer, it produces a belief more or less decided; if so clear as to preclude all doubt, the effect is knowledge. If we see a person at a distance, and we are entirely uncertain who it is, we can only say we think it is some one whom we know. If that persuasion becomes stronger, we say, we believe it is he. If perfectly sure, we say, we know it. In all these cases the only difference between opinion, belief, and knowledge, is their relative strength. The objects are the same, their relation to the mind is the same, and the ground or evidence on which they severally rest is of the same kind. It is said that it would be incorrect to say, "We believe that we slept in our house last night;" if perfectly sure of the fact. If a witness in a court of justice simply says, "I believe I was at a certain place at a given time," his testimony would be of no value. He must be able to say that he is sure of the fact — that he knows it.

Objections to this Definition.

Of this definition of faith, it may be remarked, —

1. That the meaning which it assigns to the word is certainly legitimate, sustained by established usage. The states of mind expressed by the words, I think a thing to be true; I believe it; I know it, are distinguished from each other simply by the different degrees of certainty which enter into them respectively. The probable ground of this use of the word to believe, is, that there is more of the element of trust (or a voluntarily giving to evidence a greater influence on the mind than of necessity belongs

to it), manifest in our consciousness, than is expressed by saying, we think, or, we know. However this may be, it cannot be denied that the word belief often expresses a degree of conviction greater than opinion and less than knowledge.

2. But this is not the distinguishing characteristic of faith, or its *differentia*. There are exercises of faith into which this uncertainty does not enter. Some of the strongest convictions of which the mind is capable are beliefs. Even our assurance of the veracity of consciousness, the foundation of all other convictions, is of the nature of faith. So the primary truths which are, and must be assumed in all our researches and arguments, are beliefs. They are taken on trust. They cannot be proved. If any man denies them, there is nothing more to be said. He cannot be convinced. Sir William Hamilton[1] says, "St. Austin accurately says, ' We know what rests upon reason; we believe what rests upon authority.' But reason itself must at last rest upon authority; for the original data of reason do not rest on reason, but are necessarily accepted by reason on the authority of what is beyond itself. These data are, therefore, in rigid propriety, beliefs or trusts. Thus it is that, in the last resort, we must, perforce, philosophically admit, that belief is the primary condition of reason, and not reason the ultimate ground of belief. We are compelled to surrender the proud *Intellige ut credas* of Abelard, to content ourselves with the humble *Crede ut intelligas* of Anselm."

The same is true in other spheres. The effect on the mind produced by human testimony is universally recognized as faith. If that testimony is inadequate it does not preclude doubt; but it may be so strong as to make all doubt impossible. No sane man can doubt the existence of such cities as London and Paris. But to most men that existence is not a matter of knowledge either intuitive or discursive. It is something taken on trust, on the authority of others; which taking on trust is admitted by philosophers, theologians, and the mass of men, to be a form of faith. Again, in some moral states of mind a man's conviction of the reality of a future state of reward and punishment is as strong as his belief in his own existence, and much stronger than his confidence in the testimony of his senses. And yet a future state of existence is not a matter of knowledge. It is an object of faith, or a thing believed. We accordingly find that the Scriptures teach that there is a full assurance of faith; a faith which pre-

---

[1] Reid's *Works;* edit. Edinburgh, 1849, note A, § 5, p. 760 b.

cludes the possibility of doubt. Paul says, "I know whom I have believed, and am persuaded that he is able to keep that which I have committed unto him against that day." (2 Tim. i. 12.) As Job had said ages before, "I know that my Redeemer liveth." The Apostle declares, Hebrews xi. 1, faith to be an ὑπόστασις and ἔλεγχος, than which no stronger terms could be selected to express assured conviction. The power, also, which the Bible attributes to faith as the controlling principle of life, as overcoming the world, subduing kingdoms, stopping the mouths of lions, quenching the violence of fire, turning to flight the armies of the aliens, is proof enough that it is no weak persuasion of the truth. That definition, therefore, which makes the characteristic of faith to be a measure of confidence greater than opinion, but less than knowledge, cannot be deemed satisfactory.

Faith not a Voluntary Conviction.

A second definition of faith, founded on its nature, is that which makes it "a voluntary conviction or persuasion of the truth." This is a very old view of the matter. According to Theodoret,[1] πίστις ἐστὶν ἑκούσιος τῆς ψυχῆς συγκατάθεσις, *i. e.*, "a voluntary assent of the mind." And Thomas Aquinas says,[2] "Credere est actus intellectus assentientis veritati divinæ ex imperio voluntatis a Deo motæ per gratiam."[3] He distinguishes between knowledge and faith by representing the former as the conviction produced by the object itself seen intuitively or discursively ("sicut patet in principiis primis, ... vel . . . . sicut patet de conclusionibus") to be true; whereas in the latter the mind is not sufficiently moved to assent "ab objecto proprio, sed per quandam electionem, voluntarie declinans in unam partem magis quam in alteram. Et siquidem hæc sit cum dubitatione et formidine alterius partis, erit opinio. Si autem sit cum certitudine absque tali formidine, erit fides."

This definition admits of different explanations. The word "voluntary," if its meaning be determined by the wide sense of the word 'will," includes every operation of the mind not purely intellectual. And therefore to say that faith is a voluntary assent is to say that faith is not merely a speculative assent, an act of the judgment pronouncing a thing to be true, but includes feeling. Nitsch, therefore, defines faith to be a "gefühlsmässiges Erken-

---

[1] *Græcarum Affectionum Curatio*, sermo i. edit. Commelinus, Heidelberg(?), 1592, p. 16, lines 11, 12.

[2] *Summa*, ii. ii. quæst. ii. art. 9, edit. Cologne, 1640, p. 8 b, of third set.

[3] *Ibid.* quæst. i. art. 4, pp. 3 b, 4 a, of third set.

nen." " Die Einheit des Gefühls und der Erkenntniss ; [1] a knowledge or persuasion of truth combined with feeling, — the unity of
feeling and knowledge." But if the word " will " be taken in the
sense of the power of self-determination, then nothing is voluntary which does not involve the exercise of that power. If in
this sense faith be voluntary, then we must have the power to
believe or disbelieve at pleasure. If we believe the truth, it is
because we choose or determine ourselves to receive it; if we
reject it, it is because we will to disbelieve it. The decision is
determined neither by the nature of the object nor by the nature
or degree of the evidence. Sometimes both of these meanings of
the word voluntary seem to be combined by those who define faith
to be a voluntary assent of the mind, or an assent of the intellect
determined by the will. This appears from what Aquinas, for
example, says when he discusses the question whether faith is a
virtue. He argues that if faith be a virtue, which he admits it to
be, it must include love, because love is the form or principle of
all the virtues ; and it must be self-determined because there could
be no virtue in faith if it were the inevitable effect of the evidence or testimony. If a virtue, it must include an act of self-determination ; we must decide to do what we have the power not to
do.

Remarks on this Definition of Faith.

This definition of faith contains many elements of truth. In
the first place, it is true that faith and feeling are often inseparable. They together constitute that state of mind to which the
name faith is given. The perception of beauty is of necessity
connected with the feeling of delight. Assent to moral truth
involves the feeling of moral approbation. In like manner spiritual discernment (faith when the fruit of the Spirit) includes
delight in the things of the Spirit, not only as true, but as beautiful and good. This is the difference between a living and dead
faith. This is the portion of truth involved in the Romish doctrine of a formed and unformed faith. Faith (assent to the
truth) connected with love is the *fides formata;* faith without
love is *fides informis.* While, however, it is true that faith is
often necessarily connected with feeling, and, therefore, in one
sense of the term, is a voluntary assent, yet this is not always the
case. Whether feeling attends and enters into the exercise of
faith, depends upon its object (or the thing believed) and the
evidence on which it is founded. When the object of faith is a

[1] *System der Christlichen Lehre*, Einl. ii. A. § 8. 3, 5th edit. Bonn, 1844, p. 18.

speculative truth, or some historical event past or future ; or
when the evidence or testimony on which faith is founded is addressed only to the understanding and not to the conscience or
to our emotional or religious nature, then faith does not involve
feeling. We believe the great mass of historical facts to which
we assent as true, simply on historical testimony, and without
any feeling entering into, or necessarily connected with it. The
same is true with regard to a large part of the contents of the
Bible. They, to a great extent, are historical, or the predictions
of historical events. When we believe what the Scriptures
record concerning the creation, the deluge, the calling of Abraham, the overthrow of the cities of the plain, the history of
Joseph, and the like, our faith does not include feeling. It is
not an exercise of the will in either sense of that word. It is
simply a rational conviction founded on sufficient evidence. It
may be said, as Aquinas does say, that it is love or reverence
towards God which inclines the will to believe such facts on the
authority of his Word. But wicked men believe them, and cannot help believing them. A man can hardly be found who does
not believe that the Israelites dwelt in Egypt, escaped from
bondage, and took possession of the land of Canaan.

In the second place, it is true not only that faith is in many
cases inseparable from feeling, but also that feeling has much
influence in determining our faith. This is especially true when
moral and religious truths are the objects of faith. Want of congeniality with the truth produces insensibility to the evidence by
which it is supported. Our Lord said to the Jews, " Ye believe
not, because ye are not of my sheep." (John x. 26.) And in
another place, " If any man will do his will, he shall know of
the doctrine, whether it be of God." (vii. 17.) And the Apostle says of those that are lost, " The god of this world hath
blinded the minds of them which believe not, lest the light of the
glorious gospel of Christ, who is the image of God, should shine
unto them." (2 Cor. iv. 4.) The truth was present, attended
by appropriate and abundant evidence, but there was no susceptibility. The defect was in the organ of vision, not in the want
of light. The Scriptures uniformly refer the unbelief of those
who reject the gospel to the state of their hearts. There can
be no doubt that all the true children of God received Christ as
their God and Saviour on the evidence which He gave of his
divine character and mission, and that He was rejected only by
the unrenewed and the wicked, and because of their wickedness.

Hence unbelief is so great a sin. Men are condemned because
they believe not on the only begotten Son of God. (John iii. 18.)
All this is true. It is true of saving faith. But it is not true of
all kinds of even religious faith ; that is, of faith which has religious truth for its object. And, therefore, it cannot furnish the
differentia or criterion to distinguish faith from other forms of
assent to truth. There are states of mind not only popularly,
but correctly called belief, of which it is not true that love, or
congeniality, is an element. There is such a thing as dead faith,
or orthodoxy. There is such a thing as speculative faith. Simon
Magus believed. Even the devils believe. And if we turn to
other than religious truths it is still more apparent that faith is
not necessarily a voluntary assent of the mind. A man may hear
of something most repugnant to his feelings, as, for example, of
the triumph of a rival. He may at first refuse to believe it; but
the testimony may become so strong as to force conviction. This
conviction is, by common consent, faith or belief. It is not sight ;
it is not intuition; it is not a deduction ; it is belief; a conviction
founded on testimony. This subject, *i. e.*, the connection between
faith and feeling, will come up again in considering other definitions.

In the third place, if we take the word voluntary in the sense
which implies volition or self-determination, it is still more evident that faith cannot be defined as voluntary assent. It is,
indeed, a proverb that a man convinced against his will remains
unconvinced. But this is only a popular way of expressing the
truth just conceded, namely, that the feelings have, in many cases,
great influence in determining our faith. But, as just remarked,
a man may be constrained to believe against his will. He may
struggle against conviction ; he may determine he will not believe, and yet conviction may be forced upon him. Napoleon, at
the battle of Waterloo, hears that Grouchy is approaching. He
gladly believes it. Soon the report reaches him that the advan-
cing columns are Prussians. This he will not believe. Soon,
however, as courier after courier confirms the unwelcome fact, he
is forced to believe it. It is not true, therefore, that in faith as
faith there is always, as Aquinas says, an election " voluntarie
declinans in unam partem magis quam in alteram." There is
another frequent experience. We often hear men say they would
give the world if they could believe. The dying Grotius said he
would give all his learning for the simple faith of his unlettered
servant. To tell a man he can believe if he will is to contradict

his consciousness. He tries to believe. He earnestly prays for
faith ; but he cannot exercise it. It is true, as concerns the sinner in relation to the gospel, that this inability to believe arises
from the state of his mind. But this state of the mind lies below
the will. It cannot be determined or changed by the exercise of
any voluntary power. On these grounds the definition of faith,
whether as generic or religious, as a voluntary assent to truth,
must be considered unsatisfactory.

Definitions founded on the Object of Faith.

The preceding definitions are all founded on the assumed subjective nature of faith. The next definition is of a different kind.
It is founded on the nature of its object. Faith is said to be the
persuasion of the truth of things not seen. This is a very old and
familiar definition. " Quid est fides," asks Augustine,[1] " nisi credere quod non vides." And Lombard[2] says, " Fides est virtus
qua creduntur quæ non videntur." Hence faith is said to be
swallowed up in vision; and the one is contrasted with the other;
as when the Apostle says, " We walk by faith, not by sight."
And in Hebrews, eleventh chapter, all the objects of faith under
the aspect in which it is considered in that chapter, are included
under the categories of τὰ ἐλπιζόμενα and τὰ οὐ βλεπόμενα, " things
hoped for, and things not seen." The latter includes the former.
" We hope," says the Apostle, " for that we see not." (Romans
viii. 25.) The word sight, in this connection, may be taken in
three senses. First, in its literal sense. We are not said to believe what we see with our eyes. What we see we know to be
true. We believe that the planet Saturn is surrounded by a belt,
and that Jupiter has four satellites, on the unanimous testimony
of astronomers. But if we look through a telescope and see the
belt of the one and the satellites of the other, our faith passes
into knowledge. We believe there is such a city as Rome, and
that it contains the Colosseum, Trajan's Arch, and other monu-
ments of antiquity. If we visit that city and see these things for
ourselves, our faith becomes knowledge. The conviction is no
stronger in the one case than in the other. We are just as sure
there is such a city before having seen it, as though we had been
there a hundred times. But the conviction is of a different kind.
Secondly, the mind is said to see when it perceives an object of

---

[1] In Joannis Evangelium Tractatus, XL. 9; Works, edit. Benedictines, Paris, 1837, vol.
iii. p. 2088 b.
[2] Liber Sententiarum, III. xxiii. B., edit. 1472(?).

thought to be true in its own light, or by its own radiance. This mental vision may be either immediate or mediate—either intuitive or through a process of proof. A child may believe that the angles of a triangle are together equal to two right angles, on the authority of his teacher. When he understands the demonstration of that proposition, his faith becomes knowledge. He sees it to be true. The objects of sense-perception, the objects of intuition, and what we recognize as true on a process of proof, are not, according to this definition of the term, objects of faith. We know what we see to be true; we believe when we recognize as true what we do not see. It is true that the same thing may be an object of faith and an object of knowledge, but not at the same time. We may recognize as true the being of God, or the immortality of the soul, because the propositions, "God is," "the soul is immortal," are susceptible of proof. The arguments in support of those propositions may completely satisfy our minds. But they are truths of revelation to be believed on the authority of God. These states of mind which we call knowledge and faith, are not identical, neither are they strictly coexisting. The effect produced by the demonstration is one thing. The effect produced by the testimony of God's word, is another thing. Both include a persuasion of the truth. But that persuasion is in its nature different in the one case from what it is in the other, as it rests on different grounds. When the arguments are before the mind, the conviction which they produce is knowledge. When the testimony of God is before the mind, the conviction which it produces is faith. On this subject Thomas Aquinas says,[1] "Necessarium est homini accipere per modum fidei non solum ea, quæ sunt supra rationem : sed etiam ea, quæ per rationem cognosci possunt. Et hoc propter tria, Primo quidem, ut citius homo ad veritatis divinæ cognitionem perveniat. . . . . Secundo, ut cognitio Dei sit communior. Multi enim in studio scientiæ proficere non possunt. . . . . Tertio modo propter certitudinem. Ratio enim humana in rebus divinis est multum deficiens."

Thirdly, under the " things not seen," some would include all things not present to the mind. A distinction is made between presentative and representative knowledge. In the former the object is present at the time ; we perceive it, we are conscious of it. In representative knowledge there is an object now present, representing an absent object. Thus we have the conception of a person or thing. That conception is present, but the thing

[1] *Summa*, II. ii. quæst. ii. art. 4, edit. Cologne, 1630, pp. 6 b, 7 a, of third set.

represented is absent. It is not before the mind. It belongs to the category of things not seen. The conception which is present is the object of knowledge ; the thing represented is an object of faith. That is, we know we have the conception; we believe that the thing which it represents, does or did exist. If we visit a particular place while present to our senses we know that it exists ; when we come away and form an idea or conception of it, that is, when we recall it by an effort of memory, then we believe in its existence. " Whenever we have passed beyond presentative knowledge, and are assured of the reality of an absent object, there faith . . . . has entered as an element."[1]

Sir William Hamilton[2] says, " Properly speaking, we know only the actual and the present, and all real knowledge is an immediate knowledge. What is said to be mediately known, is, in truth, not known to be, but only believed to be." This, it may be remarked in passing, would apply to all the propositions of Euclid. For they are " mediately known," i. e., seen to be true by means of a process of proof. Speaking of memory, Hamilton says, " It is not a knowledge of the past at all; but a knowledge of the present and a belief of the past." " We are said," according to Dr. McCosh, "to know ourselves, and the objects presented to the senses and the representations (always however as presentations) in the mind ; but to believe in objects which we have seen in time past, but which are not now present, and in objects which we have never seen, and very specially in objects which we can never fully know, such as an Infinite God."[3]

Objections to this Definition.

According to this view, we know what is present to the mind, and believe what is absent. The first objection to this representation is the ambiguity of the words present and absent as thus used. When is an object present? and when is it absent? It is easy to answer this question when the object is something material or an external event. Such objects are present (" præ sensibus ") when they affect the senses ; and absent when they do not. A city or building is present when we actually see it ; absent, when we leave the place where it is, and recall the image of it. But how is it with propositions ? The Bible says all men are sinners. The truth thus announced is present to the mind.

[1] McCosh, *Intuitions of the Mind*, part II. book ii. ch. 1, edit. New York, 1860, p. 197.
[2] *Lectures on Metaphysics and Logic*, vol. i. " Metaphysics," lect. xii. sub fin., edit. Boston, 1859, pp. 152, 153.
[3] *Intuitions of the Mind*, p. 198.

We do not know it. We cannot prove it. But we believe it
upon the authority of God. The Scriptures teach that Christ
died as a ransom for many. Here, not only the historical fact
that He died is announced, but the purpose for which He died.
Here again, we have a truth present to the mind, which is an object of faith.

The second objection is involved in the first. The terms present and absent are not only ambiguous in this connection, but it
is not true, as just stated, that an object must be absent in order
to be an object of faith. The *differentia*, in other words, between knowledge and faith, is not found in the presence or absence of their objects. We can know what is absent, and we can
believe what is present.

The third objection is, that the conviction we have of the reality or truth of what we distinctly remember is knowledge, and
not distinctively faith, unless we choose to establish a new and
arbitrary definition of the word knowledge. We know what is
perceived by the senses; we know what the mind sees, either intuitively or discursively, is and must be true; and we know what
we distinctly remember. The conviction is in all these cases of
the same nature. In all it resolves itself into confidence in the
veracity of consciousness. We are conscious that we perceive
sensible objects. We are conscious that we cognize certain
truths. We are conscious that we remember certain events.
In all these cases this consciousness involves the conviction of
the reality or truth of what is seen, mentally apprehended or
remembered. This conviction is, or may be, as strong in any
one of these cases as in either of the others; and it rests in all
ultimately on the same ground. There is, therefore, no reason
for calling one knowledge and the other belief. Memory is as
much a knowledge of the past, as other forms of consciousness
are a knowledge of the present.

The fourth objection is that to deny that memory gives us the
knowledge of the past, is contrary to established usage. It is
true we are said to believe that we remember such and such
events, when we are uncertain about it. But this is because in
one of the established meanings of the word, belief expresses a
less degree of certainty than knowledge. But men never speak
of believing past events in their experience concerning which they
are absolutely certain. We know that we were alive yesterday.
No man says he believes he has seen his father or mother or any
intimate friend, whom he had known for years. Things distinctly remembered are known, and not merely believed.

The definition which makes faith to be the persuasion of the truth of things not seen, is, however, correct, if by " things not seen " are meant things which are neither objects of the senses, nor of intuition, nor of demonstrative proof. But it does not seem to be correct to include among the "things not seen," which are the special objects of faith, things remembered and not now present to mind. This definition of faith, while correct in limiting it as to its objects to things not seen, in the sense above stated, is nevertheless defective in not assigning the ground of our conviction of their truth. Why do we believe things to be true, which we have never seen and which we cannot prove ? Different answers are given to that question ; and, therefore, the definition which gives no answer to it, must be considered defective.

Definitions founded on the Nature of the Evidence on which Faith rests.

Some of the definitions of faith, as we have seen, are founded on its subjective nature ; others on its objects. Besides these there are others which seek its distinguishing characteristic in the ground on which the conviction which it includes, rests. The first of these is that which makes faith to be a conviction or persuasion of truth founded on feeling. This is by many regarded as the one most generally received. Hase[1] says, " Every cultivated language has a word for that form of conviction which, in opposition to the self-evident and demonstrable, rests on moral and emotional grounds." That word in Greek is πίστις; in English " faith." In his " Hutterus Redivivus,"[2] he says, " The common idea of faith is : unmittelbar Fürwahrhalten, ohne Vermittelung eines Schlussbeweises, durch Neigung und Bedürfniss," *i. e.*, " A persuasion of the truth, without the intervention of argument, determined by inclination and inward necessity." He quotes the definition of faith by Twesten, as " a persuasion or conviction of truth produced by feeling ; " and that of Nitzsch, given above, " the unity of knowledge and feeling." Strauss[3] says, " The way in which a man appropriates the contents of a revelation, the inward assent which he yields to the contents of the Scriptures and the doctrine of the Church, not because of critical or philosophical research, but often in opposition to them,

[1] *Dogmatik*, 3d edit. Leipzig, 1842, p. 307.
[2] Sixth edit. Leipzig, 1845, p. 4.
[3] *Dogmatik*, § 20, edit. Tübingen and Stuttgart, 1840, vol. i. p. 282.

overpowered by a feeling which the Evangelical Church calls
the testimony of the Spirit, but which in fact is only the perception of the identity of his own religious life with that portrayed
in the Scripture and prevailing in the Church, — this assent determined by feeling — in ecclesiastical language, is called Faith."
Again,[1] he says, " The pious man receives religious truth because
he feels its reality, and because it satisfies his religious wants,"
and, therefore, he adds, " No religion was ever propagated by
means of arguments addressed to the understanding, or of historical or philosophical proofs, and this is undeniably true of Christianity." Every preacher of a new religion assumes in those to
whom he presents it, an unsatisfied religious necessity, and all he
has to do is to make them feel that such necessity is met by the
religion which he proposes. Celsus, he tells us, made it a ground
of reproach against the Christians that they believed blindly ;
that they could not justify the doctrines which they held at the
bar of reason. To this Origen answered, that this was true only
of the people ; that with the educated, faith was elevated into
knowledge, and Christianity transformed into a philosophy. The
Church was divided between believers and knowers. The relation between faith and knowledge, between religion and philosophy, has been the subject of controversy from that day to this.
Some took the ground of Origen and of the Alexandrian school
generally, that it is incumbent on educated Christians to justify
their doctrines at the bar of reason, and prove them to be true on
philosophical grounds. Others held that the truths of revelation
were, at least in many cases, of a kind which did not admit of
philosophical demonstration, although they were not on that
account to be regarded as contrary to reason, but only as beyond
its sphere. Others, again, taught that there is a direct conflict
between faith and knowledge ; that what the believing Christian
holds to be true, can be shown by the philosopher to be false.
This is Strauss's own doctrine, and, therefore, he concludes his
long discussion of this point by saying, " The believer should let
the knower go his own way in peace, just as the knower does the
believer. We leave them their faith, let them leave us our philosophy. . . . . There have been enough of false irenical attempts. Henceforth only separation of opposing principles can
lead to any good."[2] On the same page he admits the great
truth, " That human nature has one excellent characteristic :
what any man feels is for him a spiritual necessity, he allows no
man to take from him."

---

[1] *Dogmatik*, edit. Tübingen ard Stuttgart, 1840, vol. i. p. 298.   [2] *Ibid.* p. 356

Remarks on this Definition.

With regard to the definition of faith which makes it a conviction founded on feeling, it may be remarked, —

First, That there are forms of faith of which this is not true. As remarked above, when treating of the cognate definition of faith as a voluntary assent of the mind, it is not true of faith in general. We often believe unwillingly, and what is utterly repugnant to our feelings.

Secondly, It is not true even of religious faith, or faith which has religious truth for its object. For there may be faith without love, i. e., a speculative, or dead faith.

Thirdly, It is not true of many of the exercises of faith in good men. Isaac believed that Jacob would be preferred to Esau, sorely against his will. Jacob believed that his descendants would be slaves in Egypt. The prophets believed in the seventy years captivity of their countrymen. The Apostles believed that a great apostasy in the Church was to occur between their age and the second coming of the Lord. The answer of Thomas Aquinas to this, is, that a man is constrained by his will (i. e., his feelings) to believe in the Scriptures, and then he believes all the Scriptures contain. So that his faith, even in the class of truths just referred to, rests ultimately on feeling. But this answer is unsatisfactory. For if the question is asked, Why did the prophets believe in the captivity, and the Apostles in the apostasy? the answer would be, not from the effect of these truths upon their feelings, but on the authority of God. And if it be further asked, Why did they believe the testimony of God? the answer may be because God's testimony carries conviction. He can make his voice heard even by the deaf or the dead. Or, the answer may be, because they were good men. But in either case, the question carries us beyond the ground of their faith. They believe because God had revealed the facts referred to. Their goodness may have rendered them susceptible to the evidence afforded, but it did not constitute that evidence.

Fourthly, It is admitted that the exercise of saving faith, i. e., of that faith which is the fruit of the Spirit and product of regeneration, is attended by feeling appropriate to its object. But this is to be referred to the nature of the object. If we believe a good report, the effect is joy; if an evil report, the effect is sorrow. The perception of beauty produces delight; of moral excellence, a glow of approbation; of spiritual things, in many cases, a joy that is unspeakable and full of glory.

Fifthly, It is also true that all these truths, if not all truth, have a self-evidencing light, which cannot be apprehended without a conviction that it really is what it is apprehended as being. It may also be admitted, that so far as the consciousness of true believers is concerned, the evidence of truth is the truth itself ; in other words, that the ground of their faith is, in one sense, subjective. They see the glory of God in the face of Jesus Christ, and therefore believe that He is God manifested in the flesh. They see that the representations made by the Scriptures of the sinfulness, guilt, and helplessness of fallen man, correspond with their own inward experience, and they are therefore constrained to receive these representations as true. They see that the plan of salvation proposed in the Bible suits their necessities, their moral judgments and religious aspirations, they therefore embrace it. All this is true, but it does not prove faith to be a conviction founded on feeling ; for there are many forms of faith which confessedly are not founded on feeling ; and even in the case of true believers, their feelings are not the ultimate ground of faith. They always fall back on the authority of God, who is regarded as the author of these feelings, through which the testimony of the Spirit is revealed to the consciousness. " We may be moved and induced," says the " Westminster Confession,"[1] " by the testimony of the Church to an high and reverend esteem of the Holy Scripture ; and the heavenliness of the matter, the efficacy of the doctrine, the majesty of the style, the consent of all the parts, the scope of the whole (which is to give all glory to God), the full discovery it makes of the only way of man's salvation, the many other incomparable excellences, and the entire perfection thereof, are arguments whereby it doth abundantly evidence itself to be the word of God ; yet, notwithstanding, our full persuasion and assurance of the infallible truth and divine authority thereof is from the inward work of the Holy Spirit, bearing witness by and with the word in our hearts." The ultimate ground of faith, therefore, is the witness of the Spirit.

Faith a Conviction of the Truth founded on Testimony.

The only other definition of faith to be considered, is that which makes it, a conviction of truth founded on testimony. We have already seen that Augustine says, " We know what rests upon reason ; we believe what rests upon authority." A definition to which Sir William Hamilton gives his adhesion.[2] In the

---

[1] Chapter i. § 5.   [2] See page 46.

Alexandrian School also, the Christian πίστις, was Auctoritäts-Glaube, a faith founded on authority, opposed, on the one hand, to the heathen ἐπιστήμη, and on the other to the Christian γνῶσις, or philosophical explanation and proof of the truths believed. Among the school-men also, this was the prevalent idea. When they defined faith to be the persuasion of things not seen, they meant things which we receive as true on authority, and not because we either know or can prove them. Hence it was constantly said, faith is human when it rests on the testimony of men; divine when it rests on the testimony of God. Thomas Aquinas[1] says, " Non fides, de qua loquimur, assentit alicui, nisi quia est a Deo revelatum." " Faith, of which we speak, assents to nothing except because it is revealed by God." We believe on the authority of God, and not because we see, know, or feel a thing to be true. This is the purport of the teaching of the great body of the scholastic divines. Such also was the doctrine of the Reformers, and of the theologians of the subsequent age, both Lutheran and Reformed. Speaking of assent, which he regards as the second act or element of faith, Aquinas says, " Hic actus fidei non rerum evidentia aut causarum et proprietatum notitia, sed Dei dicentis infallibili auctoritate." Turrettin[2] says, " Non quæritur, An fides sit scientia, quæ habeat evidentiam: Sic enim distinguitur a scientia, quæ habet assensum certum et evidentem, qui nititur ratione clara et certa, et ab opinione, quæ nititur ratione tantum probabili; ubi fides notat assensum certum quidem, sed inevidentem, qui non ratione, sed testimonio divino nititur." De Moor[3] says, " Fides subjectiva est persuasio de veritate rei, alterius testimonio nixa, quomodo fides illa generatim descripta, scientiæ et conjecturæ opponitur. . . . . Dividitur . . . . in fidem divinam, quæ nititur testimonio divino, et humanam, quæ fundata est in testimonio humano fide accepto." Owen,[4] " All faith is an assent upon testimony; and divine faith is an assent upon a divine testimony." John Howe[5] asks, " Why do I believe Jesus to be the Christ? Because the eternal God hath given his testimony concerning Him that so He is." " A man's believing comes all to nothing without this, that there is a divine testimony." Again,[6] " I believe such a thing, as God reveals it, be-

---

[1] *Summa*, II. ii. quæst. i. art. 1, edit. Cologne, 1640, p. 2, a, of third set.
[2] *Institutio*, xv. ix. 3, edit. Edinburgh, 1847, vol. ii. p. 497.
[3] *Commentarius in Johannis Marckii Compendium*, cap. xxii. § 4, Leyden, 1766, vol. iv. p. 299.
[4] *Doctrine of Justification*, ch. i. edit. Philadelphia, 1841, p. 84.
[5] *Works*, vol. ii. p. 885, Carter's edition, New York, 1869.   [6] *Ibid.* p. 1170.

cause it is reported to me upon the authority of God." Bishop Pearson [1] says, " When anything propounded to us is neither apparent to our sense, nor evident to our understanding, in and of itself, neither certainly to be collected from any clear and necessary connection with the cause from which it proceedeth, or the effects which it naturally produceth, nor is taken up upon any real arguments or reference to other acknowledged truths, and yet notwithstanding appeareth to us true, not by a manifestation, but attestation of the truth, and so moveth us to assent not of itself, but by virtue of the testimony given to it; this is said properly to be credible ; and an assent unto this, upon such credibility, is in the proper notion faith or belief."

This View almost universally Held.

This view of the nature of faith is all but universally received, not by theologians only, but by philosophers, and the mass of Christian people. The great question has ever been, whether we are to receive truth on authority, or only upon rational evidence. Leibnitz begins his " Discours de la Conformité de la Foi avec la Raison," by saying, " Je suppose, que deux vérités ne sauroient se contredire ; que l'objet de la foi est la vérité que Dieu a révélée d'une manière extraordinaire, et que la raison est l'enchainment des vérités, mais particulièrement (lorsqu'elle est comparés avec la foi) de celles où l'esprit humain peut atteindre naturellement, sans être aidé des lumières de la foi." [2]

It has already been admitted that the essential element of faith is trust ; and, therefore, in the general sense of the word to believe, is to trust. Faith is the reliance of the mind on anything as true and worthy of confidence. In this wide sense of the word, it matters not what may be the objects, or what the grounds of this trust. The word, however, is commonly used in reference to truths which we receive on trust without being able to prove them. Thus we are said to believe in our own existence, the reality of the external world, and all the primary truths of the reason. These by common consent are called beliefs. Reason begins with believing, i. e., with taking on trust what it neither comprehends nor proves. Again, it has been admitted that the word belief is often and legitimately used to express a degree of certainty less than knowledge and stronger than probability ; as when we say, we are not sure, but we believe that a certain thing happened.

[1] *An Exposition of the Creed*, 7th edit. London, 1701, p. 3.
[2] *Théodicée, Works*, edit. Berlin, 1840, 1839, part ii. p. 479.

The Strict Sense of the Word " Faith."

But in the strict and special sense of the word, as discriminated from knowledge or opinion, faith means the belief of things not seen, on the ground of testimony. By testimony, however, is not meant merely the affirmation of an intelligent witness. There are other methods by which testimony may be given than affirmation. A seal is a form of testimony; so is a sign. So is everything which pledges the authority of the attester to the truth to be established. When Elijah declared that Jehovah was God, and Baal a lie, he said, "The God that answereth by fire, let him be God." The descent of the fire was the testimony of God to the truth of the prophet's declaration. So in the New Testament God is said to have borne witness to the truth of the Gospel by signs, and wonders, and divers miracles, and gifts of the Holy Ghost (Heb. ii. 4); and the Spirit of God is said to witness with our spirits that we are the children of God (Rom. viii. 16). The word in these cases is $\mu\alpha\rho\tau\upsilon\rho\acute{\epsilon}\omega$, to testify. This is not a lax or improper use of the word testimony; for an affirmation is testimony only because it pledges the authority of him who makes it to the truth. And therefore whatever pledges that authority, is as truly of the nature of testimony, as an affirmation. When, therefore, it is said that faith is founded on testimony, it is meant that it is not founded on sense, reason, or feeling, but on the authority of him by whom it is authenticated.

Proof from the General Use of the Word.

That such is the foundation and the distinctive characteristic of faith, may be argued, — 1. From the general use of the word. We are said to know what we see or can prove; and to believe what we regard as true on the authority of others. This is admitted to be true of what is called historical faith. This includes a great deal; all that is recorded of the past; all that is true of present actualities, which does not fall within the sphere of our personal observation; all the facts of science as received by the masses; and almost all the contents of the Bible, whether of the Old or of the New Testament. The Scriptures are a record of the history of the creation, of the fall, and of redemption. The Old Testament is the history of the preparatory steps of this redemption. The New Testament is a history of the fulfilment of the promises and types of the Old in the incarnation, life, suf-

ferings, death, and resurrection of the Son of God. Whoever
believes this record has set to his seal that God is true, and is a
child of God.

Proof from Consciousness.

2. In the second place, consciousness teaches us that such is
the nature of faith not only when historical facts are its objects,
but when propositions are the things believed. The two indeed
are often inseparable. That God is the creator of the world, is
both a fact and a doctrine. It is as the Apostle says, a matter of
faith. We believe on the authority of the Scriptures, which declare that "In the beginning God created the heaven and the
earth." That God set forth his Son to be a propitiation for our
sins, is a doctrine. It rests solely on the authority of God. We
receive it upon his testimony. So with all the great doctrines of
grace ; of regeneration, of justification, of sanctification, and of a
future life. How do we know that God will accept all who believe in Christ ? Who can know the things of God, save the
Spirit of God, and he to whom the Spirit shall reveal them (1
Cor. ii. 10, 11) ? From the nature of the case, " the things of
the Spirit," the thoughts and purposes of God, can be known
only by revelation, and they can be received only on the authority of God. They are objects neither of sense nor of reason.

Proof from Scripture.

3. It is the uniform teaching of the Bible that faith is founded
on the testimony or authority of God.

The first proof of this is the fact that the Scriptures come
to us under the form of a revelation of things we could not
otherwise know. The prophets of the Old Testament were
messengers, the mouth of God, to declare what the people were
to believe and what they were to do. The New Testament is
called " The testimony of Jesus." Christ came, not as a philosopher, but as a witness. He said to Nicodemus, " We speak
that we do know, and testify that we have seen ; and ye receive
not our witness." (John iii. 11). " He that cometh from above
is above all. . . . . And what he hath seen and heard, that he
testifieth ; and no man receiveth his testimony. He that hath
received his testimony hath set to his seal that God is true "
(verses 31–33). In like manner the Apostles were witnesses.
As such they were ordained (Luke xxiv. 48). After his resurrection, and immediately before his ascension, our Lord said to
them. " Ye shall receive power, after that the Holy Ghost is

come upon you : and ye shall be witnesses unto me, both in
Jerusalem, and in all Judea, and in Samaria, and unto the
uttermost part of the earth." (Acts i. 8). When they declared the death and resurrection of Christ, as facts to be believed, they said, " Whereof we are witnesses" (Acts ii. 32,
iii. 15, v. 32). In this last passage the Apostles say they were
witnesses not only of the fact of Christ's resurrection but that
God had " exalted " Him " with his right hand to be a prince
and a saviour, for to give repentance to Israel, and forgiveness
of sins." See Acts x. 39–43, where it is said, " He commanded
us to preach unto the people, and to testify that it is he which
was ordained of God to be the judge of quick and dead. To him
give all the prophets witness, that through his name whosoever
believeth in him shall receive remission of sins."

The great complaint against the Apostles, especially in the
Grecian cities, was that they did not present their doctrines as
propositions to be proved ; they did not even state the philosophical grounds on which they rested, or attempt to sustain them at
the bar of reason. The answer given to this objection by St.
Paul is twofold : First. that philosophy, the wisdom of men,
had proved itself utterly incompetent to solve the great problems
of God and the universe, of sin and redemption. It was in fact
neither more nor less than foolishness, so far as all its speculations as to the things of God were concerned. Secondly, that the
doctrines which He taught were not the truths of reason, but
matters of revelation ; to be received not on rational or philosophical grounds, but upon the authority of God ; that they, the
Apostles, were not philosophers, but witnesses ; that they did not
argue using the words of man's wisdom, but that they simply
declared the counsels of God, and that faith in their doctrines
was to rest not on the wisdom of men, but on the powerful testimony of God.

The second proof, that the Scriptures teach that faith is the
reception of truth on the ground of testimony or on the authority of God, is, that the thing which we are commanded to do, is
to receive the record which God has given of his Son. This is
faith ; receiving as true what God has testified, and because He
has testified it. " He that believeth not God hath made him a
liar ; because he believeth not the record that God gave of his
Son." The Greek here is, οὐ πεπίστευκεν εἰς τὴν μαρτυρίαν ἣν μεμαρ-
τύρηκεν ὁ Θεὸς περὶ τοῦ υἱοῦ αὐτοῦ, " believeth not the testimony which
God testified concerning his Son." " And this is the testimony,

($\dot{\eta}$ $\mu\alpha\rho\tau\nu\rho\acute{\iota}\alpha$) that God hath given to us eternal life, and this life is in his Son" (1 John v. 10, 11).   There could hardly be a more distinct statement of the Scriptural doctrine as to the nature of faith.   Its object is what God has revealed.   Its ground is the testimony of God.   To receive that testimony, is to set to our seal that God is true.   To reject it, is to make God a liar.   " If we receive the witness of men, the witness of God is greater : for this is the witness of God which he hath testified of his son."

Such is the constant teaching of Scripture.   The ground on which we are authorized and commanded to believe is, not the conformity of the truth revealed to our reason, nor its effect upon our feelings, nor its meeting the necessities of our nature and condition, but simply, " Thus saith the Lord."   The truths of revelation do commend themselves to the reason ; they do powerfully and rightfully affect our feelings ; they do meet all the necessities of our nature as creatures and as sinners ; and these considerations may incline us to believe, may strengthen our faith, lead us to cherish it, and render it joyful and effective ; but they are not its ground.   We believe on the testimony or authority of God.

It is objected to this view that we believe the Bible to be the Word of God on other ground than testimony.   The fulfilment of prophecies, the miracles of its authors, its contents, and the effects which it produces, are rational grounds for believing it to be from God.   To this objection two answers may be made : First, that supernatural occurrences, such as prophecies and miracles, are some of the forms in which the divine testimony is given.   Paul says that God bears " witness both with signs and wonders " (Hebrews ii. 4).   And, secondly, that the proximate end of these manifestations of supernatural foresight and power was to authenticate the divine mission of the messengers of God.   This being established, the people were called upon to receive their message and to believe on the authority of God, by whom they were sent.

The third proof, that the Scriptures teach that faith is a reception of truth on the ground of testimony, is found in the examples and illustrations of faith given in the Scriptures.   Immediately after the fall the promise was made to our first parents that the seed of the woman should bruise the serpent's head.   On what possible ground could faith in this promise rest except on the authority of God.   When Noah was warned of God of the coming deluge, and commanded to prepare the ark, he believed, not because he saw the signs of the approaching flood, not because his moral judgment assured him that a just God would in that way avenge his violated law ; but simply on the testimony of God.   Thus when God promised to Abraham the possession of the land of Canaan, that he, a childless old man, should become the father of many nations, that through his seed all the nations of the earth should be blessed, his faith could have no other foundation than the authority of God.   So of every illustration of faith given by the Apostle in the eleventh chapter of his epistle to the Hebrews.   The same is true of the whole Bible.   We have no foundation for our faith in a spiritual world, in the heaven and hell described in Scripture, in the doctrines of redemption, in the security and ultimate triumph of the Church other than the testimony of God.   If faith does not rest on testimony it has nothing on which to rest.   Paul tells us that the whole Gospel rests on the fact of Christ's resurrection from the dead.   If Christ be not risen our faith is vain, and we are yet in our sins.   But our assurance that Christ rose on the third day rests solely upon the testimony which God in various ways has given to that fact.

This is a point of great practical importance.   If faith, or our persuasion of the truths of the Bible, rests on philosophical grounds, then the door is opened for rationalism ; if it rests on feeling, then it is open to mysticism.   The only sure, and the only satisfying foundation is the testimony of God, who cannot err, and who will not deceive.

Faith may, therefore, be defined to be the persuasion of the truth founded on testimony.   The faith of the Christian is the persuasion of the truth of the facts and doctrines recorded in the Scriptures on the testimony of God.

§ 3. *Different Kinds of Faith.*

Though the definition above given be accepted, it is to be admitted that there are different kinds of faith.   In other words, the state of mind which the word designates is very different in one case from what it is in others.   This difference arises partly from the nature of its objects, and partly from the nature or form of the testimony on which it is founded.   Faith in a historical fact or speculative truth is one thing; faith in æsthetic truth another thing ; faith in moral truth another thing ; faith in spiritual truth, and especially faith in the promise of salvation made to ourselves another thing.   That is, the state of mind denominated faith is very different in any one of these cases from what it is in the others.   Again, the testimony which God bears to the truth is of different kinds.   In one form it is directed especially to the understanding; in another to the conscience; in another to our regenerated nature. This is the cause of the difference between speculative, temporary, and saving faith.

Speculative or Dead Faith.

There are many men who believe the Bible to be the Word of God; who receive all that it teaches; and who are perfectly orthodox in their doctrinal belief. If asked why they believe, they may be at a loss for an answer. Reflection might enable them to say they believe because others believe. They receive their faith by inheritance. They were taught from their earliest years thus to believe. The Church to which they belong inculcates this faith, and it is enjoined upon them as true and necessary. Others of greater culture may say that the evidence of the divine origin of the Bible, both external and internal, satisfies their minds, and produces a rational conviction that the Scriptures are a revelation from God, and they receive its contents on his authority. Such a faith as this, experience teaches, is perfectly compatible with a worldly or wicked life. This is what the Bible calls a dead faith.

Temporary Faith.

Again, nothing is more common than for the Gospel to produce a temporary impression, more or less deep and lasting. Those thus impressed believe. But, having no root in themselves, sooner or later they fall away. It is also a common experience that men utterly indifferent or even skeptical, in times of danger, or on the near approach of death, are deeply convinced of the certainty of those religious truths previously known, but hitherto disregarded or rejected. This temporary faith is due to common grace; that is, to those influences of the Spirit common in a measure greater or less to all men, which operate on the soul without renewing it, and which reveal the truth to the conscience and cause it to produce conviction.

Saving Faith.

That faith which secures eternal life; which unites us to Christ as living members of his body; which makes us the sons of God; which interests us in all the benefits of redemption; which works by love, and is fruitful in good works; is founded, not on the external or the moral evidence of the truth, but on the testimony of the Spirit with and by the truth to the renewed soul.

What is meant by the Testimony of the Spirit.

It is necessary, before going further, to determine what is meant by the testimony of the Spirit, which is said to be the ground of saving faith.

God, or the Spirit of God, testifies to the truth of the Scriptures and of the doctrines which they contain. This testimony, as has been seen, is partly external, consisting in prophecies and miracles, partly in the nature of the truths themselves as related to the intellectual and moral elements of the soul, and partly special and supernatural. Unrenewed men may feel the power of the two former kinds of testimony, and believe with a faith either merely intellectual and speculative, or with what may be called from its ground, a moral faith, which is only temporary. The spiritual form of testimony is confined to the regenerated. It is, of course, inscrutable. The operations of the Spirit do not reveal themselves in the consciousness otherwise than by their effects. We know that men are born of the Spirit, that the Spirit dwells in the people of God and continually influences their thoughts, feelings, and actions. But we know this only from the teaching of the Bible, not because we are conscious of his operations. " The wind bloweth where it listeth, and thou hearest the sound thereof, but canst not tell whence it cometh, and whither it goeth: so is every one that is born of the Spirit." (John iii. 8.)

This witness of the Spirit is not an affirmation that the Bible is the Word of God. Neither is it the production of a blind, unintelligent conviction of that fact. It is not, as is the case with human testimony, addressed from without to the mind, but it is within the mind itself. It is an influence designed to produce faith. It is called a witness or testimony because it is so called in Scripture ; and because it has the essential nature of testimony, inasmuch as it is the pledge of the authority of God in support of the truth.

The effects of this inward testimony are, (1.) What the Scriptures call " spiritual discernment." This means two things: A discernment due to the influence of the Spirit ; and a discernment not only of the truth, but also of the holiness, excellence, and glory of the things discerned. The word spiritual, in this sense, means conformed to the nature of the Spirit. Hence the law is said to be spiritual, i. e., holy, just, and good. (2.) A second effect flowing necessarily from the one just mentioned is delight and complacency, or love. (3.) The apprehension of the suitableness of the truths revealed, to our nature and necessities. (4.) The firm conviction that these things are not only true, but divine. (5.) The fruits of this conviction, *i. e.*, of the faith thus produced, good works, — holiness of heart and life.

When, therefore, a Christian is asked, Why he believes the Scriptures and the doctrines therein contained, his simple answer is, On the testimony or authority of God. How else could he know that the worlds were created by God, that our race apostatized from God, that He sent his Son for our redemption, that faith in Him will secure salvation. Faith in such truths can have no other foundation than the testimony of God. If asked, How God testifies to the truth of the Bible ? If an educated man whose attention has been called to the subject, he will answer, In every conceivable way : by signs, wonders, and miracles ; by the exhibition which the Bible makes of divine knowledge, excellence, authority, and power. If an uneducated man, he may simply say, " Whereas I was blind, now I see." Such a man, and indeed every true Christian, passes from a state of unbelief to one of saving faith, not by any process of research or argument, but of inward experience. The change may, and often does, take place in a moment. The faith of a Christian in the Bible is, as before remarked, analogous to that which all men have in the moral law, which they recognize not only as truth, but as having the authority of God. What the natural man perceives with regard to the moral law the renewed man is enabled to perceive in regard to "the things of the Spirit," by the testimony of that Spirit with and by the truth to his heart.

Proof from Express Declarations of Scripture.

1. That this is the Scriptural doctrine on the subject is plain from the express declarations of the Scriptures. Our Lord promised to send the Spirit for this very purpose. " He will reprove the world of sin," especially of the sin of not believing in Christ ; " and of righteousness," that is, of his righteousness, — the rightfulness of his claims to be regarded and received as the Son of God, God manifest in the flesh, and the Saviour of the world ; "and of judgment," that is, of the final overthrow of the kingdom of darkness and triumph of the kingdom of light. (John xvi. 8.) Faith, therefore, is always represented in Scripture as one of the fruits of the Spirit, as the gift of God, as the product of his energy (πίστις τῆς ἐνεργείας τοῦ Θεοῦ) (Colossians ii. 12). Men are

said to believe in virtue of the same power which wrought in
Christ, when God raised Him from the dead. (Eph i. 19, 20.)
The Apostle Paul elaborately sets forth the ground of faith in
the second chapter of First Corinthians. He declares that he
relied for success not on the enticing words of man's wisdom, but
on the demonstration of the Spirit, in order that the faith of the
people might rest not on the wisdom of men, but on the power of
God. Faith was not to rest on argument, on historical or philosophical proof, but on the testimony of the Spirit. The Spirit
demonstrates the truth to the mind, *i. e.*, produces the conviction
that it is truth, and leads the soul to embrace it with assurance
and delight. Passages have already been quoted which teach
that faith rests on the testimony of God, and that unbelief consists in rejecting that testimony. The testimony of God is given
through the Spirit, whose office it is to take of the things of
Christ and show them unto us. The Apostle John tells his readers, " Ye have an unction from the Holy One, and ye know all
things. . . . . The anointing which ye have received of him
abideth in you : and ye need not that any man teach you : but
as the same anointing teacheth you of all things, and is truth,
and is no lie, and even as it hath taught you, ye shall abide in
him." (1 John ii. 20, 27.) This passage teaches, (1.) That
true believers receive from Christ (the Holy One) an unction.
(2.) That this unction is the Holy Ghost. (3.) That it secures
the knowledge and conviction of the truth. (4.) That this inward teaching which makes them believers is abiding, and secures
them from apostasy.

1 *Corinthians* ii. 14.

Equally explicit is the passage in 1 Corinthians ii. 14, " The
natural man receiveth not the things of the Spirit of God ; for
they are foolishness unto him : neither can he know them, because
they are spiritually discerned. But he that is spiritual judgeth
all things, yet he himself is judged of no man." The things of the
Spirit, are the things which the Spirit has revealed. Concerning
these things, it is taught : (1.) that the natural or unrenewed man
does not receive them. (2.) That the spiritual man, *i. e.*, the
man in whom the Spirit dwells, does receive them. (3.) That
the reason of this difference is that the former has not, and that
the latter has, spiritual discernment. (4.) This spiritual discernment is the apprehension of the truth and excellence of the
things discerned. (5.) It is spiritual, as just stated, both because

due to the operation of the Spirit, and because the conformity of
the truths discerned to the nature of the Spirit, is apprehended.

When Peter confessed that Jesus was the Christ the Son of
the living God, our Lord said, " Blessed art thou, Simon Bar-
jona : for flesh and blood hath not revealed it unto thee, but my
Father which is in heaven." (Matt. xvi. 17.)   Other men had
the same external evidence of the divinity of Christ that Peter
had.   His faith was due not to that evidence alone, but to the
inward testimony of God.   Our Lord rendered thanks that God
had hidden the mysteries of his kingdom from the wise and prudent and revealed them unto babes.   (Matt. xi. 25.)   The external revelation was made to both classes.   Besides this external
revelation, those called babes received an inward testimony which
made them believers.   Hence our Lord said, No man can come
unto me except he be drawn or taught of God. (John vi. 44, 45.)
The Apostle tells us that the same Gospel, the same objective
truths, with the same external and rational evidence, which was
an offence to the Jew and foolishness to the Greek, was to the
called the wisdom and the power of God.   Why this difference ?
Not the superior knowledge or greater excellence of the called,
but the inward divine influence, the κλῆσις, of which they were
the subjects. Paul's instantaneous conversion is not to be referred
to any rational process of argument ; nor to his moral suceptibility
to the truth ; nor to the visible manifestation of Christ, for no
miracle, no outward light or splendour could change the heart and
transform the whole character in a moment.   It was, as the
Apostle himself tells us (Gal. i. 15, 16), the inward revelation of
Christ to him by the special grace of God.   It was the testimony
of the Spirit, which being inward and supernatural, enabled
him to see the glory of God in the face of Jesus Christ.   The
Psalmist prayed that God would open his eyes that he might see
wondrous things out of his law.   The Apostle prayed for the
Ephesians that God would give them the Holy Spirit, that the
eyes of their souls might be opened, that they might know the
things freely given to them of God.   (Eph. i. 17, 18.)   Everywhere in the Bible the fact that any one believes is referred not
to his subjective state, but to the work of the Spirit on his heart.

Proof from the Way the Apostles acted.

2. As the Scriptures thus expressly teach that the ground of
true or saving faith is the inward witness of the Spirit, the Apostles always acted on that principle.   They announced the truth,

and demanded its instant reception, under the pain of eternal death. Our Lord did the same. " He that believeth not is condemned already, because he hath not believed in the name of the only begotten Son of God." (John iii. 18.) Immediate faith was demanded. Being demanded by Christ, and at his command by the Apostles, that demand must be just and reasonable. It could, however, be neither unless the evidence of the truth attended it. That evidence could not be the external proofs of the divinity of Christ and his Gospel, for those proofs were present to the minds of comparatively few of the hearers of the Gospel ; nor could it be rational proof or philosophical arguments, for still fewer could appreciate such evidence, and if they could it would avail nothing to the production of saving faith. The evidence of truth, to which assent is demanded by God the moment it is announced, must be in the truth itself. And if this assent be obligatory, and dissent or unbelief a sin, then the evidence must be of a nature, to which a corrupt state of the soul renders a man insensible. " If our gospel be hid," says the Apostle, " it is hid to them that are lost: in whom the God of this world hath blinded the minds of them which believe not, lest the light of the glorious gospel of Christ, who is the image of God, should shine unto them. . . . . [But] God, who commanded the light to shine out of darkness, hath shined in our hearts, to give the light of the knowledge of the glory of God in the face of Jesus Christ." (2 Cor. iv. 3–6.) It is here taught, (1.) That wherever and whenever Christ is preached, the evidence of his divinity is presented. The glory of God shines in his face. (2.) That if any man fails to see it, it is because the God of this world hath blinded his eyes. (3.) That if any do perceive it and believe, it is because of an inward illumination produced by Him who first commanded the light to shine out of darkness.

Proof from the Practice in the Church.

3. As Christ and the Apostles acted on this principle, so have all faithful ministers and missionaries from that day to this They do not expect to convince and convert men by historical evidence or by philosophical arguments. They depend on the demonstration of the Spirit.

Proof from Analogy.

4. This doctrine, that the true and immediate ground of faith in the things of the Spirit is the testimony of the Spirit, produ-

cing spiritual discernment, is sustained by analogy. If a man cannot see the splendour of the sun, it is because he is blind. If he cannot perceive the beauties of nature and of art, it is because he has no taste. If he cannot apprehend " the concord of sweet sounds," it is because he has not a musical ear. If he cannot see the beauty of virtue, or the divine authority of the moral law, it is because his moral sense is blunted. If he cannot see the glory of God in his works and in his Word, it is because his religious nature is perverted. And in like manner, if he cannot see the glory of God in the face of Jesus Christ, it is because the god of this world has blinded his eyes.

No one excuses the man who can see no excellence in virtue, and who repudiates the authority of the moral law. The Bible and the instinctive judgment of men, condemn the atheist. In like manner the Scriptures pronounce accursed all who do not believe that Jesus is the Christ the Son of the living God. This is the denial of supreme excellence; the rejection of the clearest manifestation of God ever made to man. The solemn judgment of God is, " If any man love not the Lord Jesus Christ, let him be anathema maranatha." (1 Cor. xvi. 22.) In this judgment the whole intelligent universe will ultimately acquiesce.

Faith in the Scriptures, therefore, is founded on the testimony of God. By testimony, as before stated, is meant attestation, anything which pledges the authority of the attester in support of the truth to be established. As this testimony is of different kinds, so the faith which it produces, is also different. So far as the testimony is merely external, the faith it produces is simply historical or speculative. So far as the testimony is moral, consisting in the power which the Spirit gives to the truth over the natural conscience, the faith is temporary, depending on the state of mind which is its proximate cause. Besides these, there is the inward testimony of the Spirit, which is of such a nature and of such power as to produce a perfect revolution in the soul, compared in Scripture to that effected by opening the eyes of the blind to the reality, the wonders, and glories of creation. There is, therefore, all the difference between a faith resting on this inward testimony of the Spirit, and mere speculative faith, that there is between the conviction a blind man has of the beauties of nature, before and after the opening of his eyes. As this testimony is informing, enabling the soul to see the truth and excellence of the " things of the Spirit," so far as the consciousness of the believer is concerned, his faith is a form of knowledge. He sees to be true, what the Spirit reveals and authenticates.

§ 4. *Faith and Knowledge.*

The relation of faith to knowledge is a wide field. The discussions on the subject have been varied and endless. There is little probability that the points at issue will ever be settled to the satisfaction of all parties. The ground of faith is authority. The ground of knowledge is sense or reason. We are concerned here only with Christian faith, *i. e.*, the faith which receives the Scriptures as the Word of God and all they teach as true on his authority.

Is a Supernatural Revelation needed?

The first question is, Whether there is any need of a supernatural revelation, whether human reason be not competent to discover and to authenticate all needful truth. This question has already been considered under the head of Rationalism, where it was shown, (1.) That every man's consciousness tells him that there are questions concerning God and his own origin and destiny, which his reason cannot answer. (2.) That he knows *à priori*, that the reason of no other man can satisfactorily answer them. (3.) That he knows from experience that they never have been answered by the wisdom of men, and (4.) That the Scriptures declare that the world by wisdom knows not God; that the wisdom of the world is foolishness in his estimation, and that God has therefore himself made known truths undiscoverable by reason, for the salvation of man.

Must the Truths of Revelation be Demonstrable by Reason?

A second question is, Whether truths, supernaturally revealed, must be able to authenticate themselves at the bar of reason before they can be rationally received; so that they are received, not on the ground of authority, but of rational proof. This also has been previously discussed. It has been shown that the assumption that God can reveal nothing which human reason cannot, when known, demonstrate to be true, assumes that human reason is the measure of all truth; that there is no intelligence in the universe higher than that of man; and that God cannot have purposes and plans, the grounds or reasons of which we are not competent to discover and appreciate. It emancipates the soul from the authority of God, refusing to believe anything except on the authority of reason. Why may we not believe on the testimony of God that there is a spiritual world, as well as be-

lieve that there is such a nation as the Chinese on the testimony
of men? No man acts on the principle of believing only what
he can understand and prove, in any other department. There
are multitudes of truths which every sane man receives on trust,
without being able either to prove or comprehend them. If we
can believe only what we can prove at the bar of reason to be
true, then the kingdom of heaven would be shut against all but
the wise. There could be no Christian who was not also a philosopher. In point of fact no man acts on this principle. It is
assumed in the pride of reason, or as an apology for rejecting
unpalatable truths, but men believe in God, in sin, in freedom
of the will, in responsibility, without the ability of comprehending or reconciling these truths with each other or with other
facts of consciousness or experience.

May not Revealed Truths be Philosophically vindicated?

A third question is, Whether, admitting a supernatural revelation, and moreover admitting the obligation to receive on the
authority of God the doctrines which revelation makes known,
the revealed doctrines may not be philosophically vindicated, so
as to commend them to the acceptance of those who deny revelation. May not the Scriptural doctrines concerning God, creation, providence, the trinity, the incarnation, sin, redemption,
and the future state, be so stated and sustained philosophically,
as to constrain acquiescence in them as truths of the reason.
This was the ground taken in the early Church by the theologians of the Alexandrian School, who undertook to elevate the
πίστις of the people into a γνῶσις for the philosophers. Thus the
sacred writers were made Platonists, and Christianity was transmuted into Platonism. A large part of the mental activity of the
School-men, during the Middle Ages, was expended in the same
way. They received the Bible as a supernatural revelation from
God. They received the Church interpretation of its teachings.
They admitted their obligation to believe its doctrines on the
authority of God and of the Church. Nevertheless they held
that all these doctrines could be philosophically proved. In later
times Wolf undertook to demonstrate all the doctrines of Christianity on the principles of the Leibnitzian philosophy. In our
own day this principle and these attempts have been carried further than ever. Systems of theology, constructed on the philosophy of Hegel, of Schelling, and of Schleiermacher, have almost
superseded the old Biblical systems. If any man of ordinary

culture and intelligence should take up a volume of what is called " Speculative Theology," (that is, theology presented in the forms of the speculative philosophy,) he would not understand a page and would hardly understand a sentence. He could not tell whether the theology which it proposed to present was Christianity or Buddhism. Or, at best, he would find a few drops of Biblical truth so diluted by floods of human speculation that the most delicate of chemical tests would fail to detect the divine element.

Attempts to do this Futile.

All such attempts are futile. The empirical proof of this is, that no such attempt has ever succeeded. The experiment has been made hundreds of times, and always with the same result. Where are now the philosophical expositions and vindications of Scripture doctrines by the Platonizing fathers; by the Schoolmen; by the Cartesians; by the Leibnitzians? What power over the reason, the conscience, or the life, has any of the specu lative systems of our day? Who, beyond the devotees of the systems which they represent, understand or adopt the theology of Daub, of Marheinecke, of Lange, and others? Strauss, therefore, is right when he repudiates all these vain attempts to reconcile Christianity with philosophy, or to give a form to Christian doctrine which satisfies the philosophical thinker.[1]

But apart from this argument from experience, the assumption is preposterous that the feeble intellect of man can explain, and from its own resources, vindicate and prove the deep things of God. An infant might as well undertake to expound Newton's " Principia." If there are mysteries in nature, in every blade of grass, in the insect, in the body and in the soul of man, there must be mysteries in religion. The Bible and our consciousness teach us that God is incomprehensible, and his ways past finding out; that we cannot explain either his nature or his acts ; we know not how he creates, upholds, and governs without interfering with the nature of his creatures ; how there can be three persons in the Godhead ; how in the one person of Christ there can be two intelligences and two wills ; how the Spirit inspires, renews, sanctifies, or comforts. It belongs to the " self-deifying " class of philosophers to presume to know all that God knows, and to banish the incomprehensible from the religion which he has revealed. " To the school of Hegel," says Bret-

[1] See above, p. 58.

schneider, "there are mysteries in religion only for those who
have not raised themselves to the Hegelian grade of knowledge.
For the latter all is clear; all is knowledge; and Christianity
is the solution, and therefore the revelation of all mysteries."[1]
This may be consistent in those who hold that man is God in the
highest form of his existence, and the philosopher the highest
style of man. Such an assertion, however, by whomsoever it
may be made, is the insanity of presumption.

May what is True in Religion be False in Philosophy?

A fourth question included in this general subject is, Whether
there is or may be a real conflict between the truths of reason
and those of revelation? Whether that which is true in religion
may be false in philosophy? To this question different answers
have been given.

The Fathers on this Question.

First, while the Greek fathers were disposed to bring religion
and philosophy into harmony, by giving a philosophical form to
Christian doctrines, the Latins were inclined to represent the
two as irreconcilable. "What," asks Tertullian, "has Athens
to do with Jerusalem? The academy with the Church? What
have heretics to do with Christians? Our instruction is from the
porch of Solomon, who himself taught that the Lord was to be
sought in the simplicity of the heart. . . . . We need no seeking
for truth after Christ; no research after the Gospel. When we
believe, we desire nothing beyond faith, because we believe that
there is nothing else we should do. . . . . To know nothing
beyond is to know all things."[2] He went so far as to say,
"Prorsus credibile est, quia ineptum est; . . . . certum est,
quia impossibile est."[3] Without going to this extreme, the theologians of the Latin Church, those of them at least most zealous

Systematische Entwickelung, § 29, 4th edit. Leipzig, 1841, p. 163.
[2] De Præscriptionibus adversus Hæreticos, cap. 7, 8, 14, Works, Paris, 1608 (t. iii.),
p. 331: "Quid ergo Athenis et Hierosolymis? quid Academiæ et Ecclesiæ? quid hæreticis et Christianis? Nostra institutio de porticu Solomonis est, qui et ipse tradiderat:
Dominum in simplicitate cordis esse quærendum. Viderint qui Stoicum, et Platonicum, et
Dialecticum, Christianissimum protulerunt. Nobis curiositate opus non est post Christum
Jesum, nec inquisitione post Evangelium. Cum credimus, nihil desideramus ultra credere.
Hoc enim prius credimus, non esse quod ultra credere debeamus. . . . . Cedat curiositas
fidei, cedat gloria saluti. Certe aut non obstrepant, aut quiescant adversus regulam.
Nihil ultra scire, omnia scire est."
[3] De Carne Christi, cap. 5, Works (t. iii.), p. 555: "Natus est Dei filius: non pudet,
quia pudendum est. Et mortuus est Dei filius: prorsus credibile est, quia ineptum est.
Et sepultus, resurrexit: certum est, quia impossibile est."

for Church doctrines, were inclined to deny to reason even the prerogative of a *judicium contradictionis*. They were constrained to take this ground because they were called upon to defend doctrines which contradicted not only reason but the senses. When it was objected to the doctrine that the consecrated wafer is the real body of Christ, that our senses pronounce it to be bread, and that it is impossible that a human body should be in heaven and in all parts of the earth at the same time, what could they say but that the senses and reason are not to be trusted in the sphere of faith ? That what is false to the reason and the senses may be true in religion ?

Lutheran Teaching on this Point.

The Lutherans were under the same necessity. Their doctrine of the person of Christ involves the denial of the primary truth, that attributes cannot be separated from the substance of which they are the manifestation. Their doctrine concerning the Lord's Supper involves the assumption of the ubiquity of Christ's body, which seems to be a contradiction in terms.

Luther's utterances on this subject are not very consistent. When arguing against the continued obligation of monastic vows, he did not hesitate to say that what was contrary to reason was contrary to God. " Was nun der Vernunft entgegen ist, ist gewiss dass es Gott vielmehr entgegen ist. Denn wie sollte es nicht wider die göttliche Wahrheit seyn, das wider Vernunft und menschliche Wahrheit ist."[1] But in the sacramentarian controversy he will not allow reason to be heard. " In the things of God," he says, reason or nature is stock-star-and-stone blind. " It is, indeed," he adds, " audacious enough to plunge in and stumble as a blind horse ; but all that it explains or concludes is as certainly false and wrong as that God lives." [2] In another place he says that reason, when she attempts to speculate about divine things, becomes a fool ; which, indeed, is very much what Paul says. (Rom. i. 22 ; 1 Cor. i. 18–31.)

The Lutheran theologians made a distinction between reason in the abstract, or reason as it was in man before the fall, and reason as it now is. They admit that no truth of revelation can contradict reason as such ; but it may contradict the reason of men all of whose faculties are clouded and deteriorated by sin. By this was not meant simply that the unrenewed man is opposed to the truth of God ; that " the things of the Spirit " are fool-

---

[1] *Works*, edit. Walch, vol. xix. p. 1940.   [2] *Ibid.* vol. xii. pp. 399, 400.

ishness to him ; that it seems to him absurd that God should be found in fashion as a man ; that He should demand a satisfaction for sin ; or save one man and not another, according to his own good pleasure. This the Bible clearly teaches and all Christians believe. In all this there is no contradiction between reason and religion. The being of God is foolishness to the atheist; and personal immortality is foolishness to the pantheist. Yet who would admit that these doctrines are contrary to reason ? The Lutheran theologians intended to teach, not only that the mysteries of the Bible are above reason, that they can neither be understood nor demonstrated ; and not only that "the things of the Spirit" are foolishness to the natural man, but that they are really in conflict with the human understanding; that by a correct process of reasoning they can be demonstrated to be false ; so that in the strict sense of the terms what is true in religion is false in philosophy. "The Sorbonne," says Luther, "has pronounced a most abominable decision in saying that what is true in religion is also true in philosophy ; and moreover condemning as heretics all who assert the contrary. By this horrible doctrine it has given it to be clearly understood that the doctrines of faith are to be subjected to the yoke of human reason."[1]

Sir William Hamilton.

Secondly, the ground taken by Sir William Hamilton on this subject is not precisely the same with that taken by the Lutherans. They agree, indeed, in this, that we are bound to believe what (at the bar of reason) we can prove to be false, but they differ entirely as to the cause and nature of this conflict between reason and faith. According to the Lutherans, it arises from the corruption and deterioration of our nature by the fall. It is removed in part in this world by regeneration, and entirely hereafter by the perfection of our sanctification. According to Hamilton, this conflict arises from the necessary limitation of human thought. God has so made us that reason, acting according to its own laws, of necessity arrives at conclusions directly opposed to the doctrines of religion both natural and revealed. We can prove demonstrably that the Absolute being cannot know, cannot be a cause, cannot be conscious. It may be proved with equal clearness that the Infinite cannot be a person, or possess moral attributes. Here, then, what is true in religion, what we are bound to believe, and what in point of fact all men, in virtue of

[1] *Works,* edit. Walch, vol. x. p. 1399.

the constitution of their nature do believe, can be proved to be false. There is thus an irreconcilable conflict between our intellectual and moral nature. But as, according to the idealist, reason forces us to the conclusion that the external world does not exist, while, nevertheless, it is safe and proper to act on the assumption that it is, and is what it appears to be; so, according to Hamilton, it is not only safe, but obligatory on us to act on the assumption that God is a person, although infinite, while our reason demonstrates that an infinite person is a contradiction. The conflict between reason and faith is avowed, while the obligation of faith on the testimony of our moral and religious nature and of the Word of God is affirmed. This point has been already discussed.

The View of Speculative Philosophers.

Thirdly, we note the view taken by the speculative philosophers. They, too, maintain that reason demonstrates the doctrines of revelation and even of natural religion to be false. But they do not recognize their obligation to receive them as objects of faith. Being contrary to reason, those doctrines are false, and being false, they are, by enlightened men, to be rejected. If any cling to them as a matter of feeling, they are to be allowed to do so, but they must renounce all claim to philosophic insight.

May the Objects of Faith be above, and yet not against Reason?

A fifth question is, Whether the objects of faith may be above, and yet not contrary to reason? The answer to this question is to be in the affirmative, for the distinction implied is sound and almost universally admitted. What is above reason is simply incomprehensible. What is against reason is impossible. It is contrary to reason that contradictions should be true; that a part should be greater than the whole; that a thing should be and not be at the same time; that right should be wrong and wrong right. It is incomprehensible how matter attracts matter; how the mind acts on the body, and the body on the mind. The distinction between the incomprehensible and the impossible, is therefore plain and admitted. And the distinction between what is above reason, and what is against reason, is equally obvious and just. The great body of Christian theologians have ever taken the ground that the doctrines of the Bible are not contrary to reason, although above it. That is, they are matters of faith to be received on the authority of God, and not because they can be either understood or proved. As it is incomprehensible how a soul and body can be united in one conscious life ; so it is incomprehensible how a divine and human nature can be united in one person in Christ.   Neither is impossible, and therefore neither is contrary to reason.   We know the one fact from consciousness ; we believe the other on the testimony of God.   It is impossible, and therefore contrary to reason, that three should be one.   But it is not impossible that the same numerical essence should subsist in three distinct persons.   Realists tell us that humanity, as one numerical essence, subsists in all the millions of human individuals. Thomas Aquinas takes the true ground when he says : " Ea quæ sunt supra naturam, sola fide tenemus.   Quod autem credimus, auctoritati debemus.   Unde in omnibus asserendis sequi debemus naturam rerum, præter ea, quæ auctoritate divina traduntur, quæ sunt supra naturam." [1] " Quæ igitur fidei sunt, non sunt tentanda probare nisi per auctoritates his, qui auctoritates suscipiunt. Apud alios vero sufficit defendere non esse impossibile quod prædicat fides." [2] " Quidquid in aliis scientiis invenitur veritati hujus scientiæ [sacræ doctrinæ] repugnans, totum condemnatur ut falsum." [3]

The Objects of Faith are consistent with Reason.

While, therefore, the objects of faith as revealed in the Bible, are not truths of the reason, i. e., which the human reason can discover, or comprehend, or demonstrate, they are, nevertheless, perfectly consistent with reason.   They involve no contradictions or absurdities ; nothing impossible, nothing inconsistent with the intuitions either of the intellect or of the conscience ; nothing inconsistent with any well established truth, whether of the external world or of the world of mind.   On the contrary, the contents of the Bible, so far as they relate to things within the legitimate domain of human knowledge, are found to be consistent, and must be consistent, with all we certainly know from other sources than a divine revelation.   All that the Scriptures teach concerning the external world accords with the facts of experience.   They do not teach that the earth is a plain ; that it is stationary in space ; that the sun revolves around it.   On the other hand, they do teach that God made all plants and animals, each after its own kind ; and, accordingly, all experience shows that species are immutable.   All the anthropological doctrines of the Bible agree with what we know of man from consciousness and observation. The Bible teaches that God made of one blood all nations which dwell on the face of the earth.   We accordingly find that all the

---

[1] *Summa*, I. quæst. xcix. art. 1, edit. Cologne, 1640, p. 185, a.
[2] *Ibid*. quæst. xxxii. art. 1, p. 64, a.   [3] *Ibid*. quæst. i. art. 6, p. 2, b.

varieties of our race have the same anatomical structure; the same physical nature; the same rational and moral faculties. The Bible teaches that man is a free, accountable agent; that all men are sinners; that all need redemption, and that no man can redeem himself or find a ransom for his brother. With these teachings the consciousness of all men agrees. All that the Scriptures reveal concerning the nature and attributes of God, corresponds with our religious nature, satisfying, elevating, and sanctifying all our powers and meeting all our necessities. If the contents of the Bible did not correspond with the truths which God has revealed in his external works and the constitution of our nature, it could not be received as coming from Him, for God cannot contradict himself. Nothing, therefore, can be more derogatory to the Bible than the assertion that its doctrines are contrary to reason.

Faith in the Irrational impossible.

The assumption that reason and faith are incompatible; that we must become irrational in order to become believers is, however it may be intended, the language of infidelity; for faith in the irrational is of necessity itself irrational. It is impossible to believe that to be true which the mind sees to be false. This would be to believe and disbelieve the same thing at the same time. If, therefore, as modern philosophers assert, it is impossible that an infinite being can be a person, then faith in the personality of God is impossible. Then there can be no religion, no sin, no accountability, no immortality. Faith is not a blind, irrational conviction. In order to believe, we must know what we believe, and the grounds on which our faith rests. And, therefore, the refuge which some would take in faith, from the universal scepticism to which they say reason necessarily leads, is insecure and worthless.

While admitting that the truths of revelation are to be received upon the authority of God; that human reason can neither comprehend nor prove them; that a man must be converted and become as a little child before he can truly receive the doctrines of the Bible; and admitting, moreover, that these doctrines are irreconcilable with every system of philosophy, ever framed by those who refuse to be taught of God, or who were ignorant of his Word, yet it is ever to be maintained that those doctrines are unassailable; that no created intellect can prove them to be impossible or irrational. Paul, while spurning the wisdom of the world, still claimed that he taught the highest wisdom, even the wisdom of God. (1 Cor. ii. 6, 7.) And who will venture to say that the wisdom of God is irrational?

Knowledge essential to Faith.

A sixth question, included under the head of the relation of faith to knowledge is, Whether knowledge is essential to faith? That is, whether a truth must be known in order to be believed? This Protestants affirm and Romanists deny.

Protestants of course admit that mysteries, or truths which we are unable to comprehend, may be, and are, proper objects of faith. They repudiate the rationalistic doctrine that we can believe only what we understand and what we can prove, or, at least, elucidate so that it appears to be true in its own light. What Protestants maintain is that knowledge, i. e., the cognition of the import of the proposition to be believed, is essential to faith; and, consequently, that faith is limited by knowledge. We can believe only what we know, i. e., what we intelligently apprehend. If a proposition be announced to us in an unknown language, we can affirm nothing about it. We can neither believe nor disbelieve it. Should the man who makes the declaration, assert that it is true, if we have confidence in his competency and integrity, we may believe that he is right, but the proposition itself is no part of our faith. The Apostle recognizes this obvious truth when he says, " Except ye utter by the tongue words easy to be understood (εὔσημον λόγον), how shall it be known what is spoken? for ye shall speak into the air. . . . . If I know not the meaning of the voice, I shall be unto him that speaketh a barbarian, and he that speaketh shall be a barbarian unto me. . . . . When thou shalt bless with the Spirit, how shall he that occupieth the room of the unlearned, say Amen at thy giving of thanks? seeing he understandeth not what thou sayest?" (1 Cor. xiv. 9–16.) To say Amen, is to assent to, to make one's own. According to the Apostle, therefore, knowledge, or the intelligent apprehension of the meaning of what is proposed, is essential to faith. If the proposition " God is a Spirit," be announced to the unlearned in Hebrew or Greek, it is impossible that they should assent to its truth. If they understand the language; if they know what the word " God " means, and what the word " Spirit " means, then they may receive or reject the truth which that proposition affirms. The declaration " Jesus is the Son of God," admits of different interpretations.

Some say the term Son is an official title, and therefore the proposition " Jesus is the Son of God," means that Jesus is a ruler. Others say it is a term of affection, then the proposition means that Jesus was the special object of the love of God.   Others say that it means that Jesus is of the same nature with God ; that He is a divine person. If this be the meaning of the Spirit in declaring Jesus to be the Son of God, then those who do not attach that sense to the words, do not believe the truth intended to be taught. When it is said God set forth Christ to be a propitiation for our sins, if we do not understand what the word propitiation means, the proposition to us means nothing, and nothing cannot be an object of faith.

Knowledge the Measure of Faith.

It follows from what has been said, or rather is included in it, that knowledge being essential to faith, it must be the measure of it. What lies beyond the sphere of knowledge, lies beyond the sphere of faith. Of the unseen and eternal we can believe only what God has revealed ; and of what God has revealed, we can believe only what we know. It has been said that he who believes the Bible to be the Word of God, may properly be said to believe all it teaches, although much of its instructions may be to him unknown. But this is not a correct representation. The man who believes the Bible, is prepared to believe on its authority whatever it declares to be true. But he cannot properly be said to believe any more of its contents than he knows. If asked if he believed that men bitten by poisonous serpents were ever healed by merely looking at a brazen serpent, he might, if ignorant of the Pentateuch, honestly answer, No. But should he come to read and understand the record of the healing of the dying Israelites, as found in the Bible, he would rationally and sincerely, answer, Yes. This disposition to believe whatever the Bible teaches, as soon as we know what is taught, may be called an implicit faith, but it is no real faith. It has none of its characteristics and none of its power.

Proof that Knowledge is Essential to Faith.

That knowledge, in the sense above stated, is essential to faith is obvious, —

1. From the very nature of faith. It includes the conviction of the truth of its object. It is an affirmation of the mind that a thing is true or trustworthy, but the mind can affirm nothing of that of which it knows nothing.

2. The Bible everywhere teaches that without knowledge there can be no faith. This, as just stated, is the doctrine of the Apostle Paul. He condemned the speaking in an unknown tongue in a promiscuous assembly, because the hearers could not understand what was said; and if they did not know the meaning of the words uttered, they could neither assent to them, nor be profited by them. In another place (Rom. x. 14) he asks, "How shall they believe in him of whom they have not heard?" "Faith," he says, "cometh by hearing." The command of Christ was to preach the Gospel to every creature; to teach all nations. Those who received the instructions thus given, should, He assured his disciples, be saved; those who rejected them, should be damned. This takes for granted that without the knowledge of the Gospel, there can be no faith. On this principle the Apostles acted everywhere. They went abroad preaching Christ, proving from the Scriptures that He was the Son of God and Saviour of the world. The communication of knowledge always preceded the demand for faith.

3. Such is the intimate connection between faith and knowledge, that in the Scriptures the one term is often used for the other. To know Christ, is to believe upon Him. To know the truth, is intelligently and believingly to apprehend and appropriate it. Conversion is effected by knowledge. Paul says he was made a believer by the revelation of Christ within him. The Spirit is said to open the eyes of the understanding. Men are said to be renewed so as to know. We are translated from the kingdom of darkness into the kingdom of light. Believers are children of the light. Men are said to perish for the lack of knowledge. Nothing is more characteristic of the Bible than the importance which it attaches to the knowledge of the truth. We are said to be begotten by the truth; to be sanctified by the truth; and the whole duty of ministers and teachers is said to be to hold forth the word of life. It is because Protestants believe that knowledge is essential to faith, that they insist so strenuously on the circulation of the Scriptures and the instruction of the people.

Romish Doctrine on this Subject.

Romanists make a distinction between explicit and implicit faith. By the former is meant, faith in a known truth; by the latter faith in truths not known. They teach that only a few primary truths of religion need be known, and that faith without knowledge, as to all other truths, is genuine and sufficient. On this subject Thomas Aquinas says, " Quantum ad prima credibilia, quæ sunt articuli fidei, tenetur homo explicite credere. Quantum autem ad alia credibilia non tenetur homo explicite credere, sed solum implicite, vel in præparatione animi, in quantum paratus est credere quidquid divina Scriptura continet." [1] Implicit faith is defined as, " Assensus, qui omnia, quamvis ignota, quæ ab ecclesia probantur, amplectitur." [2] Bellarmin [3] says, " In eo qui credit, duo sunt, apprehensio et judicium, sive assensus: sed apprehensio non est fides, sed aliud fidem præcedens. Possunt enim infideles apprehendere mysteria fidei. Præterea, apprehensio non dicitur proprie notitia. . . . . Mysteria fidei, quæ rationem superant, credimus, non intelligimus, ac per hoc fides distinguitur contra scientiam, et melius per ignorantiam, quam per notitiam definitur." The faith required of the people is simply, " A general intention to believe whatever the Church believes." [4] The Church teaches that there are seven sacraments. A man who has no idea what the word sacrament means, or what rites are regarded by the Church as having a sacramental character, is held to believe that orders, penance, matrimony, and extreme unction, are sacraments. So, of all other doctrines of the Church. True faith is said to be consistent with absolute ignorance. According to this doctrine, a man may be a true Christian, if he submits to the Church, although in his internal convictions and modes of thought, he be a pantheist or pagan.

It is to this grave error as to the nature of faith, that much in the character and practice of the Romish Church is to be referred, —

1. This is the reason why the Scriptures are withheld from the people. If knowledge is not necessary to faith, there is no need that the people should know what the Bible teaches.

2. For the same reason the services of public worship are conducted in an unknown language.

3. Hence, too, the symbolism which characterizes their worship. The end to be accomplished is a blind reverence and awe. For this end there is no need that these symbols should be understood. It is enough that they affect the imagination.

4. To the same principle is to be referred the practice of reserve in preaching. The truth may be kept back or concealed.

---

[1] *Summa*, II. ii. quæst. ii. art. 5, edit. Cologne, 1640, p. 7, a, of third set.
[2] *Hutterus Redivivus*, § 108, 6th edit. Leipzig, 1845, p. 271.
[3] *De Justificatione*, lib. i. cap. 7, *Disputationes*, edit. Paris, 1608, vol. iv. p. 714, a, c.
[4] Strauss, *Dogmatik*, *Die Christliche Glaubenslehre*, Tübingen and Stuttgart, 1840, vol. i. p. 284.

The cross is held up before the people, but it is not necessary that the doctrine of the sacrifice for sin made thereon should be taught. It is enough if the people are impressed; it matters not whether they believe that the sign, or the material, or the doctrine symbolized, secures salvation. Nay, the darker the mind, the more vague and mysterious the feeling excited, and the more blind the submission rendered, the more genuine is the exercise of faith. "Religious light," says Mr. Newman, "is intellectual darkness."[1]

5. It is on the same principle the Roman Catholic missions have always been conducted. The people are converted not by the truth, not by a course of instruction, but by baptism. They are made Christians by thousands, not by the intelligent adoption of Christianity as a system of doctrine, of that they may be profoundly ignorant, but by simple submission to the Church and its prescribed rites. The consequence has been that the Catholic missions, although continued in some instances for more than a hundred years, take no hold on the people, but almost uniformly die out, as soon as the supply of foreign ministers is cut off.

§ 5. *Faith and Feeling.*

It has already been seen, —

1. That faith, the act of believing, cannot properly be defined as the assent of the understanding determined by the will. There are, unquestionably, many cases in which a man believes against his will.

2. It has also been argued that it is not correct to say that faith is assent founded on feeling. On this point it was admitted that a man's feelings have great influence upon his faith; that it is comparatively easy to believe what is agreeable, and difficult to believe what is disagreeable. It was also admitted that in saving faith, the gift of God, resting on the inward illuminating testimony of the Holy Spirit, there is a discernment not only of the truth but of the divine excellence of the things of the Spirit, which is inseparably connected with appropriate feeling. It was moreover conceded that, so far as the consciousness of the believer is concerned, he seems to receive the truth on its own evidence, on its excellence and power over his heart and conscience. This, however, is analogous to other facts in his experience. When a man repents and believes, he is conscious only of his own exercises and not of the supernatural in-

---

[1] *Sermons*, vol. i. p. 124.

fluences of the Spirit, to which those exercises owe their origin and nature. Thus also in the exercise of faith, consciousness does not reach the inward testimony of the Spirit on which that faith is founded. Nevertheless, notwithstanding these admissions, it is still incorrect to say that faith is founded on feeling, because it is only of certain forms or exercises of faith that this can even be plausibly said ; and because there are many exercises of even saving faith (that is, of faith in a true believer,) which are not attended by feeling. This is the case when the object of faith is some historical fact. Besides, the Scriptures clearly teach that the ground of faith is the testimony of God, or demonstration of the Spirit. He has revealed certain truths, and attends them with such an amount and kind of evidence, as produces conviction, and we receive them on his authority.

3. Faith is not necessarily connected with feeling. Sometimes it is, and sometimes it is not. Whether it is or not, depends, — (a.) On the nature of the object. Belief in glad tidings is of necessity attended by joy ; of evil tidings with grief. Belief in moral excellence involves a feeling of approbation. Belief that a certain act is criminal, involves disapprobation. (b.) On the proximate ground of faith. If a man believes that a picture is beautiful on the testimony of competent judges, there is no æsthetic feeling connected with his faith. But if he personally perceives the beauty of the object, then delight is inseparable from the conviction that it is beautiful. In like manner if a man believes that Jesus is God manifest in the flesh, on the mere external testimony of the Bible, he experiences no due impression from that truth. But if his faith is founded on the inward testimony of the Spirit, by which the glory of God in the face of Jesus Christ is revealed to him, then he is filled with adoring admiration and love.

Religious Faith more than Simple Assent.

4. Another question agitated on this subject is, Whether faith is a purely intellectual exercise ; or Whether it is also an exercise of the affections. This is nearly allied to the preceding question, and must receive substantially the same answer. Bellarmin,[1] says, " Tribus in rebus ab hæreticis Catholici dissentiunt ; Primum, in objecto fidei justificantis, quod hæretici restringunt ad solam promissionem misericordiæ specialis, Catholici tam late patere volunt, quam late patet verbum Dei. . . . Deinde

---

[1] *De Justificatione*, lib. i. cap. 4, *Disputationes*, edit. Paris, 1608, vol. iv. p. 706, d, e.

in facultate et potentia animi quæ sedes est fidei. Siquidem
illi fidem collocant in voluntate [seu in corde] cum fiduciam
esse definiunt; ac per hoc eam cum spe confundunt. Fiducia
enim nihil est aliud, nisi spes roborata. . . . Catholici fidem
in intellectu sedem habere docent. Denique, in ipso actu intellectus. Ipsi enim per notitiam fidem definiunt, nos per assensum.
Assentimur enim Deo, quamvis ea nobis credenda proponat,
quæ non intelligimus." Regarding faith as a mere intellectual
or speculative act, they consistently deny that it is necessarily
connected with salvation. According to their doctrine, a man
may have true faith, *i. e.*, the faith which the Scriptures demand, and yet perish. On this point the Council of Trent says :
" Si quis dixerit, amissa per peccatum gratia, simul et fidem semper amitti, aut fidem, quæ remanet, non esse veram fidem, licet
non sit viva ; aut eum, qui fidem sine caritate habet, non esse
Christianum ; anathema sit." [1]

Protestant Doctrine.

On the other hand Protestants with one voice maintain that
the faith which is connected with salvation, is not a mere intellectual exercise. Calvin says : [2] " Verum observemus, fidei
sedem non in cerebro esse, sed in corde : neque vero de eo con-
tenderim, qua in parte corporis sita sit fides : sed quoniam cordis nomen pro serio et sincero affectu fere capitur, dico firmam
esse et efficacem fiduciam, non nudam tantum notionem." He
also says : [3] Quodsi expenderent illud Pauli, Corde creditur ad
justitiam (Rom. x. 10) : fingere desinerent frigidam illam qual-
itatem. Si una hæc nobis suppeteret ratio, valere deberet ad
litem finiendam : assensionem scilicet ipsam sicuti ex parte at-
tigi, et fusius iterum repetam, cordis esse magis quam cerebri, et
affectus magis quam intelligentiæ."

The answer in the Heidelberg Catechism, to the question,
What is Faith ? is, " It is not merely a certain knowledge,
whereby I receive as true all that God has revealed to us in his
Word, but also a cordial trust, which the Holy Ghost works in
me by the Gospel, that not only to others, but to me also, the
forgiveness of sin, and everlasting righteousness and life are
given by God, out of pure grace, and only for the sake of
Christ's merit." [4]

<hr>

[1] Session vi., Canon 28 ; Streitwolf, *Libri Symbolici*, Göttingen, 1846, vol. i. p. 37.
[2] *On Romans* x. 10 ; *Commentaries*, edit. Berlin, 1831, vol. v. p. 139.
[3] *Institutio*, III. ii. 8 ; edit. Berlin, 1834, vol. i. p. 358.
[4] Question 21.

That saving faith is not a mere speculative assent of the understanding, is the uniform doctrine of the Protestant symbols. On this point, however, it may be remarked, in the first place, that, as has often been stated before, the Scriptures do not make the sharp distinction between the understanding, the feelings, and the will, which is common in our day. A large class of our inward acts and states are so complex as to be acts of the whole soul, and not exclusively of any one of its faculties. In repentance there is of necessity an intellectual apprehension of ourselves as sinners, of the holiness of God, of his law to which we have failed to be conformed and of his mercy in Christ ; there is a moral disapprobation of our character and conduct ; a feeling of sorrow, shame, and remorse ; and a purpose to forsake sin and lead a holy life. Scarcely less complex is the state of mind expressed by the word faith as it exists in a true believer. In the second place, there is a distinction to be made between faith in general and saving faith. If we take that element of faith which is common to every act of believing ; if we understand by it the apprehension of a thing as true and worthy of confidence, whether a fact of history or of science, then it may be said that faith in its essential nature is intellectual, or intelligent assent. But if the question be, What is that act or state of mind which is required in the Gospel, when we are commanded to believe ; the answer is very different. To believe that Christ is " God manifest in the flesh," is not the mere intellectual conviction that no one, not truly divine, could be and do what Christ was and did ; for this conviction demoniacs avowed ; but it is to receive Him as our God. This includes the apprehension and conviction of his divine glory, and the adoring reverence, love, confidence, and submission, which are due to God alone. When we are commanded to believe in Christ as the Saviour of men, we are not required merely to assent to the proposition that He does save sinners, but also to receive and rest upon Him alone for our own salvation. What, therefore, the Scriptures mean by faith, in this connection, the faith which is required for salvation, is an act of the whole soul, of the understanding, of the heart, and of the will.

Proof of the Protestant Doctrine.

The Protestant doctrine that saving faith includes knowledge, assent, and trust, and is not, as Romanists teach, mere assent, is sustained by abundant proofs.

1. In the first place, it is proved from the nature of the object

of saving faith.   That object is not merely the general truth of
Scripture, not the fact that the Gospel reveals God's plan of saving sinners ; but it is Christ himself ; his person and work, and
the offer of salvation to us personally and individually.   From
the nature of the case we cannot, as just remarked, believe in
Christ on the inward testimony of the Spirit which reveals his
glory and his love, without the feelings of reverence, love, and
trust mingling with the act and constituting its character.   Nor
is it possible that a soul oppressed with a sense of sin should receive the promise of deliverance from its guilt and power, without any feeling of gratitude and confidence.   The act of faith in
such a promise is in its nature an act of appropriation and confidence.

2. We accordingly find that in many cases in the Bible the
word trust is used instead of faith.   The same act or state of
mind which in one place is expressed by the one word, is in
others expressed by the other.   The same promises are made to
trust as are made to faith.   The same effects are attributed to
the one, that are attributed to the other.

3. The use of other words and forms of expression as explanatory of the act of faith, and substituted for that word, shows that
it includes trust as an essential element of its nature.   We are
commanded to look to Christ, as the dying Israelites looked up
to the brazen serpent.   This looking involved trusting ; and
looking is declared to be believing.   Sinners are exhorted to flee
to Christ as a refuge.   The man-slayer fled to the city of refuge
because he relied upon it as a place of safety.   We are said to
receive Christ, to rest upon Him, to lay hold of Him.   All these,
and other modes of expression which teach us what we are to do
when we are commanded to believe, show that trust is an essential element in the act of saving faith.

4. The command to believe is expressed by the word πιστεύω
not only when followed by the accusative, but also when followed
by the dative and by the prepositions ἐπί, εἰς, ἐν.   But the literal
meaning of πιστεύειν εἰς, or ἐπί, or ἐν, is not simply *to believe*, but
to believe upon, to confide in, to trust.   Faith in a promise made
to ourselves, from the nature of the case, is an act of confidence
in him who makes the promise.

5. Unbelief is, therefore, expressed by doubt, fear, distrust,
and despair.

6. The believer knows from his own experience that when he
believes he receives and rests on Jesus Christ for salvation, as He
is freely offered to us in the Gospel.

The controversy between Romanists and Protestants on this subject turns on the view taken of the plan of salvation. If, as Protestants hold, every man in order to be saved, must receive the record which God has given of his Son ; must believe that He is God manifest in the flesh, the propitiation for our sins, the prophet, priest, and king of his people, then it must be admitted that faith involves trust in Christ as to us the source of wisdom, righteousness, sanctification, and redemption. But if, as Romanists teach, the benefits of redemption are conveyed only through the sacraments, effective *ex opere operato*, then faith is the opposite of infidelity in its popular sense. If a man is not a believer, he is an infidel, *i. e.*, a rejecter of Christianity. The object of faith is divine revelation as contained in the Bible. It is a simple assent to the fact that the Scriptures are from God, and that the Church is a divinely constituted and supernaturally endowed institute for the salvation of men. Believing this, the sinner comes to the Church and receives through her ministrations, in his measure, all the benefits of redemption. According to this system the nature and office of faith are entirely different from what they are according to the Protestant theory of the Gospel.

§ 6. *Faith and Love.*

As to the relation between faith and love there are three different views : —

1. That love is the ground of faith ; that men believe the truth because they love it. Faith is founded on feeling. This view has already been sufficiently discussed.

2. That love is the invariable and necessary attendant and consequent of saving faith. As no man can see and believe a thing to be morally good without the feeling of approbation ; so no one can see and believe the glory of God as revealed in the Scriptures without adoring reverence being awakened in his soul ; no one can believe unto salvation that Christ is the Son of God and the Son of Man ; that He loved us and gave Himself for us, and makes us kings and priests unto God, without love and devotion, in proportion to the clearness and strength of this faith, filling the heart and controlling the life. Hence faith is said to work by love and to purify the heart. Romanists, indeed, render πίστις δι' ἀγάπης ἐνεργουμένη in this passage (Gal. v. 6), " faith perfected or completed by love." But this is contrary to the constant usage of the word ἐνεργεῖσθαι in the New Testament, which is always used in a middle sense, " vim suam exserere."

According to the Apostle's teaching in Rom. vii. 4–6, love without faith, or anterior to it, is impossible. Until we believe, we
are under the condemnation of the law. While under condemnation, we are at enmity with God. While at enmity with God,
we bring forth fruit unto death. It is only when reconciled to
God and united to Christ, that we bring forth fruit unto God.
Believing that God loves us we love Him. Believing that Christ
gave Himself for us, we devote our lives to Him. Believing that
the fashion of this world passes away, that the things unseen are
eternal, those who have that faith which is the substance of things
hoped for, and the evidence of things not seen, set their affections
on things above where Christ sitteth at the right hand of God.
This necessary connection between faith and love, has already
been sufficiently insisted upon.

Romanists make Love the Essence of Faith.

3. The third doctrinal view on this subject is that of the Romanists, who make love the essence of faith. In other words, love
with them is the form (in the scholastic sense of the word) of
faith ; it is that which gives it being or character as a Christian
virtue or grace. While on the one hand they teach, as we
have seen with the Council of Trent, that faith is in itself mere
intellectual assent, without any moral virtue, and which may be
exercised by the unrenewed or by those in a state of mortal sin ;
on the other hand, they hold that there is such a Christian grace
as faith ; but in that case, faith is only another name for love.
This is not the distinction between a living and dead faith which
the Scriptures and all Evangelical Christians recognize. With
Romanists the *fides informis* is true faith, and the *fides formata*
is love. On this point, Peter Lombard [1] says : " Fides qua dicitur [creditur ?], si cum caritate sit, virtus est, quia caritas ut ait
Ambrosius mater est omnium virtutum, quæ omnes informat, sine
qua nulla vera virtus est." Thomas Aquinas [2] says : " Actus fidei
ordinatur ad objectum voluntatis, quod est bonum, sicut ad finem.
Hoc autem bonum quod est finis fidei, scilicet bonum divinum, est
proprium objectum charitatis : et ideo charitas dicitur forma fidei,
in quantum per charitatem actus fidei perficitur et formatur."
Bellarmin [3] says : " Quod si charitas est forma fidei, et fides non
justificat formaliter, nisi ab ipsa caritate formata certe multo

---

[1] *Liber Sententiarum*, iii. xxiii. C. edit. 1472(?).

[2] *Summa*, ii. ii. quæst. iv. art. 3, edit. Cologne, 1640, p. 11, a, of third set.

[3] *De Justificatione*, lib. ii. cap. 4; *Disputationes*, edit. Paris, 1608, vol. iv. pp. 789, a, b,
790, c.

magis charitas ipsa justificat. . . . . Fides quæ agitur, ac movetur, formatur, et quasi animatur per dilectionem. . . . . Apostolus
Paulus . . . . explicat dilectionem formam esse extrinsecam fidei
non intrinsecam, quæ det illi, non ut sit, sed ut moveatur." All
this is intelligible and reasonable, provided we admit subjective
justification, and the merit of good works. If justification is
sanctification, then it may be admitted that love has more to do
with making men holy, than faith considered as mere intellectual
assent. And if it be conceded that we are accepted by God on
the ground of our own virtue, then it may be granted that love is
more valuable than any mere exercise of the intellect. Romanists argue, " Maxima virtus maxime justificat. Dilectio est maxima virtus. Ergo maxime justificat." It was because this distinction between a " formed and unformed faith " was made in the
interest of justification on the ground of our own character and
merit, that Luther, with his usual vehement power, says : " Ipsi
duplicem faciunt fidem, informem et formatam, hanc pestilentissi-
mam et satanicam glossam non possum non vehementer detestari."
It is only as connected with false views of justification that this
question has any real importance. For it is admitted by all Protestants that saving faith and love are inseparably connected ;
that faith without love, *i. e.*, that a faith which does not produce
love and good works, is dead. But Protestants are strenuous in
denying that we are justified on account of love, which is the
real meaning of the Romanists when they say " fides non justificat formaliter, nisi ab ipsa caritate formata."

§ 7. *The Object of Saving Faith.*
Fides Generalis.

It is conceded that all Christians are bound to believe, and that
all do believe everything taught in the Word of God, so far as the
contents of the Scriptures are known to them. It is correct, therefore, to say that the object of faith is the whole revelation of God
as contained in his Word. As the Bible is with Protestants the
only infallible rule of faith and practice, nothing not expressly
taught in Scripture, or deduced therefrom by necessary inference,
can be imposed on the people of God as an article of faith. This
is " the liberty wherewith Christ has made us free," and in which
we are bound to stand fast. This is our protection on the one
hand, against the usurpations of the Church. Romanists claim
for the Church the prerogative of infallible and authoritative

teaching.   The people are bound to believe whatever the Church,
i. e., its organs the bishops, declare to be a part of the revelation
of God.   They do not, indeed, assume the right " to make " new
articles of faith.   But they claim the authority to decide, in such
a way as to bind the conscience of the people, what the Bible
teaches ; and what by tradition the Church knows to be included
in the teaching of Christ and his Apostles.   This gives them latitude enough to teach for doctrines the commandments of men.
Bellarmin[1] says : " Omnium dogmatum firmitas pendet ab auctoritate præsentis ecclesiæ."   On the other hand, however, it is not
only against the usurpations of the Church, that the principle
above mentioned is our security, but also against the tyranny
of public opinion.   Men are as impatient of contradiction now as
they ever were.   They manifest the same desire to have their
own opinions enacted into laws, and enforced by divine authority.
And they are as fierce in their denunciations of all who venture
to oppose them.   Hence they meet in conventions or other assemblies, ecclesiastical or voluntary, and decide what is true and what
is false in doctrine, and what is right and what is wrong in morals.   Against all undue assumptions of authority, true Protestants
hold fast to the two great principles, — the right of private judgment, and that the Scriptures are the only infallible rule of faith
and practice.   The object of faith, therefore, is all the truths revealed in the Word of God.   All that God in the Bible declares
to be true, we are bound to believe.   This is what theologians
call *fides generalis.*

Fides Specialis.

But, besides this, there is a *fides specialis* necessary to salvation.
In the general contents of the Scriptures there are certain doctrines concerning Christ and his work, and certain promises of
salvation made through Him to sinful men, which we are bound to
receive and on which we are required to trust.   The special object
of faith, therefore, is Christ, and the promise of salvation through
Him.   And the special definite act of faith which secures our salvation is the act of receiving and resting on Him as He is offered
to us in the Gospel.   This is so clearly and so variously taught in
the Scriptures as hardly to admit of being questioned.

Christ's Testimony.

In the first place, our Lord repeatedly declares that what men
are required to do, and what they are condemned because they

---

[1] *De Sacram.* lib. ii. c. 2. (?)

do not do, is to believe on Him.   He was lifted up, " That whosoever believeth in him should not perish, but have eternal life."
(John iii. 15.)   " He that believeth on him is not condemned:
but he that believeth not is condemned already, because he hath
not believed in the name of the only begotten Son of God."
(v. 18.)   " He that believeth on the Son hath everlasting life:
but he that believeth not the Son shall not see life ; but the
wrath of God abideth on him."   (v. 36.)   " This is the will of
him that sent me, that every one which seeth the Son, and believeth on him, may have everlasting life : and I will raise him
up at the last day."   (John vi. 40.)   " Verily, verily, I say unto
you, He that believeth on me hath everlasting life.   I am that
bread of life. . . . . This is the bread which cometh down from
heaven, ... if any man eat of this bread, he shall live forever."   (vers. 47–51.)   In another place our Lord says, " This
is the work of God, that ye believe on him whom he hath sent."
(John vi. 29.)   The passages, however, in which faith in Christ
is expressly demanded as the condition of salvation, are too numerous to be cited.

We are said to be saved by receiving Christ.

That Christ is the immediate object of saving faith is also
taught in all those passages in which we are said to receive
Christ, or the testimony of God concerning Christ, and in which
this act of receiving is said to secure our salvation.   For example,
in John i. 12, " As many as received him, to them gave he power
to become the sons of God."   " I am come in my Father's name,
and ye receive me not."   (John v. 43.)   " If we receive the
witness of men, the witness of God is greater : for this is the witness of God which he hath testified of his Son. He that believeth
on the Son of God hath the witness in himself : he that believeth
not God has made him a liar ; because he believeth not the record
that God gave of his Son."   (1 John v. 9, 10.)   " He that hath
the Son hath life ; he that hath not the Son of God hath not
life."   (v. 12.)   " Whosoever believeth that Jesus is the Christ
is born of God."   (v. 1.)   It is, therefore, receiving Christ ; receiving the record which God has given of his Son ; believing that
He is the Christ the Son of the living God, which is the specific
act required of us in order to salvation.   Christ, therefore, is the
immediate object of those exercises of faith which secure salvation.   And, therefore, faith is expressed by looking to Christ ;
coming to Christ ; committing the soul to Him, etc.

Teaching of the Apostles.

Accordingly the Apostle teaches we are justified " by the faith of Christ." It is not faith as a pious disposition of the mind; not faith as general confidence in God; not faith in the truth of divine revelation; much less faith " in eternal verities," or the general principles of truth and duty, but that faith of which Christ is the object. Romans iii. 22: " The righteousness of God which is by faith of Jesus Christ unto all and upon all them that believe." Galatians ii. 16: " Knowing that a man is not justified by the works of the law, but by the faith of Jesus Christ, even we have believed in Jesus Christ, that we might be justified by the faith of Christ, and not by the works of the law." iii. 24: " The law was our schoolmaster to bring us unto Christ, that we might be justified by faith." v. 26: " For ye are all the children of God by faith in Christ Jesus." Galatians ii. 20: " I live by the faith of the Son of God," etc., etc.

Christ our Ransom.

Christ declares that He gave Himself as a ransom for many; He was set forth as a propitiation for sins; He offered Himself as a sacrifice unto God. It is through the merit of his righteousness and death that men are saved. All these representations which pervade the Scriptures necessarily assume that the faith which secures salvation must have special reference to Him. If He is our Redeemer, we must receive and trust Him as such. If He is a propitiation for sins, it is through faith in his blood that we are reconciled to God. The whole plan of salvation, as set forth in the Gospel, supposes that Christ in his person and work is the object of faith and the ground of confidence.

We live in Christ by Faith.

The same thing follows from the representations given of the relation of the believer to Christ. We are in Him by faith. He dwells in us. He is the head from whom we, as members of his body, derive our life. He is the vine, we are the branches. It is not we that live, but Christ, who liveth in us. These and other representations are utterly inconsistent with the doctrine that it is a vague general faith in God or in the Scriptures which secures our salvation. It is a faith which terminates directly on Christ, which takes Him to be our God and Saviour. God sent his Son into the world, clothed in our nature, to reveal his will, to die for

our sins and to rise again for our justification. In Him dwells
the fulness of the Godhead, from his fulness we are filled. He to
us is wisdom, righteousness, sanctification, and redemption. Those
who receive this Saviour as being all He claimed to be, and commit their souls into his hands to be used in his service and saved
to his glory, are, in the Scriptural sense of the term, believers.
Christ is not only the object of their faith, but their whole inward, spiritual life terminates on Him. Nothing, therefore, can
be more foreign to the Gospel than the Romish doctrine, substantially revived by the modern philosophy which turns the mind
away from the historical, really existing, objective Christ, to the
work within us ; leaving us nothing to love and trust, but what
is in our own miserable hearts.

Christ is not received in a Special Office alone.

Admitting that Christ is the immediate and special object of
those acts of faith which secure salvation, it is asked, Whether it
is Christ in all his offices, or Christ in his priestly office, especially,
that is the object of justifying faith ? This seems an unnecessary
question. It is not raised in the Bible ; nor does it suggest itself
to the believer. He receives Christ. He does not ask himself for
what special function of his saving work he thus accepts Him. He
takes Him as a Saviour, as a deliverer from the guilt and power
of sin, from the dominion of Satan, and from all the evils of his
apostasy from God. He takes Him as his wisdom, righteousness,
sanctification, and redemption. He takes Him as his God and
Saviour; as the full, complete, satisfying, life-giving portion of
the soul. If this complex act of apprehension and surrender were
analyzed it doubtless would be found to include submission to all
his teaching, reliance on his righteousness and intercession, subjection to his will, confidence in his protection, and devotion to
his service. As He is offered to us as a prophet, priest, and king,
as such He is accepted. And as He is offered to us as a source
of life, and glory, and blessedness, as the supreme object of adoration and love, as such He is joyfully accepted.

Is the Sinner required to believe that God loves him?

Again, it is questioned, Whether the object of saving faith is
that God is reconciled to us ; that our sins are forgiven ; that we
are the objects of the saving love of God ? This is not the question above considered, namely, Whether, as Romanists say, the
object of faith is the whole revelation of God, or, as Protestants

contend, Christ and the promise of redemption through Him, although many of the arguments of the Romanists are directed against the special form of the doctrine just stated. They argue that it is contradictory to say that we are pardoned because we believe; and, in the same breath, to say that the thing to be believed is that our sins are already pardoned. Again, they argue that the only proper object of faith is some revelation of God, but it is nowhere revealed that we individually are reconciled to God, or that our sins are pardoned, or that we are the objects of that special love which God has to his own people.

In answer to the first of these objections, the Reformed theologians were accustomed to say, that a distinction is to be made between the remission of sin *de jure* already obtained through the death of Christ, and remission *de facto* through the efficacious application of it to us. In the former sense, " remissio peccatorum jam impetrata " is the object of faith. In the latter sense, it is "remissio impetranda," because faith is the instrumental cause of justification, and must precede it. " Unde," says Turrettin,[1] " ad obtinendam remissionem peccatorum, non debeo credere peccata mihi jam remissa, ut perperam nobis impingunt; sed debeo credere peccata mihi credenti et pœnitenti, juxta promissionem factam credentibus et pœnitentibus, remissum iri certissime, quæ postea actu secundari et reflexo ex sensu fidei credo mihi esse remissa."

The second objection was answered by distinguishing between the direct and the reflex act of faith. By the direct act of faith, we embrace Christ as our Saviour; by the reflex act, arising out of the consciousness of believing, we believe that He loved us and died for us, and that nothing can ever separate us from his love. These two acts are inseparable, not only as cause and effect, antecedent and consequent; but they are not separated in time, or in the consciousness of the believer. They are only different elements of the complex act of accepting Christ as He is offered in the Gospel. We cannot separate the joy and gratitude with which a great favour is accepted. Although a psychological analysis might resolve these emotions into the effects of the act of acceptance, they belong, as revealed in consciousness, to the very nature of the act. It is a cordial and grateful acceptance of a promise made to all who embrace it. If a general promise of pardon be made to criminals on the condition of the confession of guilt, every one of their number who makes the confession knows

---

[1] *Institutio,* xv. xii. 6; *Works,* edit. Edinburgh, 1847, vol. ii. p. 508.

or believes that the promise is made to him. On this point the early Reformed and Lutheran theologians were agreed in teaching that when the sinner exercises saving faith He believes that for Christ's sake he is pardoned and accepted of God. In other words, that Christ loved him and gave Himself for him. We have already seen that the " Heidelberg Catechism,"[1] the symbolical book of so large a portion of the Reformed Church, declares saving faith to be " Certa fiducia, a Spiritu Sancto per evangelium in corde meo accensa, qua in Deo acquiesco, certo statuens, non solum aliis, sed mihi quoque remissionem peccatorum æternam, justitiam et vitam donatam esse, idque gratis, ex Dei misericordia, propter unius Christi meritum." In the " Apology of the Augsburg Confession of the Lutheran Church " it is said,[2] " Nos præter illam fidem [fidem generalem] requirimus, ut credat sibi quisque remitti peccata." Calvin says,[3] " Gratiæ promissione opus est, qua nobis testificetur se propitium esse Patrem : quando nec aliter ad eum appropinquare possumus, et in eam solam reclinare cor hominis potest. . . . . Nunc justa fidei definitio nobis constabit, si dicamus esse divinæ erga nos benevolentiæ firmam certamque cognitionem, quæ gratuitæ in Christo promissionis veritate fundata, per Spiritum Sanctum et revelatur mentibus nostris et cordibus obsignatur." " Hic præcipuus fidei cardo vertitur, ne quas Dominus offert misericordiæ promissiones, extra nos tantum veras esse arbitremur, in nobis minime : sed ut potius eas intus complectendo nostras faciamus. . . . . In summa, vere fidelis non est nisi qui solida persuasione Deum sibi propitium benevolumque patrem esse persuasus, de ejus benignitate omnia sibi pollicetur : nisi qui divinæ erga se benevolentiæ promissionibus fretus, indubitatam salutis expectationem præsumit."

This is strong language. The doctrine, however, is not that faith implies assurance. The question concerns the nature of the object seen, not the clearness of the vision ; what it is that the soul believes, not the strength of its faith. This Calvin himself elsewhere beautifully expresses, saying, " When the least drop ot faith is instilled into our minds, we begin to see the serene and placid face of our reconciled Father ; far off and on high, it may be, but still it is seen." A man in a dungeon may see only a ray of light streaming through a crevice. This is very different from broad daylight. Nevertheless, what he sees is light. So what

[1] xxi.; Niemeyer, *Collectio Confessionum*, Leipzig, 1840, p. 434.
[2] v. 60; Hase, *Libri Symbolici*, Leipzig, 1846, p. 172.
[3] *Institutio*, lib. iii. ii. 7, 16; edit. Berlin, 1834, vol. i. pp. 357, 364.

the penitent sinner believes is, that God for Christ's sake is reconciled to him. It may be with a very dim and doubtful vision, he apprehends that truth ; but that is the truth on which his trust is stayed.

Proof of this Doctrine.

This is involved in the appropriation of the general promise of the Gospel. The Scriptures declare that God is love ; that He set forth his Son to be a propitiation for sin ; that in Him He is reconciled ; that He will receive all who come to Him through Christ. To appropriate these general declarations, is to believe that they are true, not only in relation to others, but to ourselves ; that God is reconciled to us. We have no right to exclude ourselves. This self-exclusion is unbelief. It is refusing to take of the waters of life, freely offered to all.

Galatians ii. 20.

Accordingly the Apostle in Galatians ii. 20, says, "The life which I now live in the flesh, I live by the faith of the Son of God, who loved me, and gave Himself for me." The object of the Apostle's faith, therefore, the truths which he believed, and faith in which gave life to his soul, were, (1.) That Christ is the Son of God ; (2.) That He loved him ; (3.) That He gave Himself for him. The faith by which a believer lives, is not specifically different in its nature or object from the faith required of every man in order to his salvation. The life of faith is only the continued repetition, it may be with ever increasing strength and clearness, of those exercises by which we first receive Christ, in all his fulness and in all his offices, as our God and Saviour. " Qui fit ut vivamus Christi fide ? quia nos dilexit, et se ipsum tradidit pro nobis. Amor, inquam, quo nos complexus est Christus, fecit ut se nobis coadunaret. Id implevit morte sua : nam se ipsum tradendo pro nobis, non secus atque in persona nostra passus est. . . . . Neque parum energiæ habet pro me : quia non satis fuerit Christum pro mundi salute mortuum reputare, nisi sibi quisque effectum ac possessionem hujus gratiæ privatim vindicet." [1]

It is objected to this view of the case that by the " love of God," or " of Christ," in the above statement, is not meant the general benevolence or philanthropy of God, but his special, electing, and saving love. When Paul said he lived by the faith of Christ who loved him, and gave Himself for him, he meant some-

[1] Calvin in loco.

thing more than that Christ loved all men and therefore him
among the rest. He evidently believed himself to be a special
object of the Saviour's love. It was this conviction which gave
power to his faith. And a like conviction enters into the faith of
every true believer. But to this it is objected that faith must
have a divine revelation for its object. But there is no revelation of God's special love to individuals, and, therefore, no individual has any Scriptural ground to believe that Christ loved
him, and gave Himself for him. Whatever force there may be in
this objection, it bears against Paul's declaration and experience.
He certainly did believe that Christ loved him and died for him.
It will not do to say that this was a conclusion drawn from his
own experience ; or to assume that the Apostle argued himself
into the conviction that Christ loved him. Christ specially loves
all who believe upon Him. I believe upon Him. Therefore
Christ specially loves me. But a conclusion reached by argument is not an object of faith. Faith must rest on the testimony
of God. It must be, therefore, that God in some way testifies
to the soul that it is the object of his love. This he does in two
ways. First, by the general invitations and promises of the Gospel. The act of appropriating, or of accepting these promises, is
to believe that they belong to us as well as to others. Secondly,
by the inward witness of the Spirit. Paul says (Rom. v. 5),
" The love of God is shed abroad in our hearts by the Holy
Ghost which is given unto us." That is, the Holy Ghost convinces us that we are the objects of God's love. This is done, not
only by the various manifestations of his love in providence and
redemption, but by his inward dealings with the soul. " He
that loveth me shall be loved of my Father, and I will love him,
and will manifest myself to him." (John xiv. 21). This manifestation is not outward through the word. It is inward. God has
fellowship or intercourse with the souls of his people. The
Spirit calls forth our love to God, and reveals his love to us.
Again, in Romans viii. 16, the Apostle says, " The Spirit itself
beareth witness with our spirit, that we are the children of God."
This does not mean that the Spirit excites in us filial feelings
toward God, from whence we infer that we are his children.
The Apostle refers to two distinct sources of evidence of our adoption. The one is that we can call God Father ; the other, the
testimony of the Spirit. The latter is joined with the former.
The word is συμμαρτυρεῖ, unites in testifying. Hence we are said
to be sealed, not only marked and secured, but assured by the

Spirit , and the Spirit is a pledge, an assurance, that we are, and ever shall be, the objects of God's saving love. (Eph. i. 13, 14 ; iv. 30.   2 Cor. i. 22.)

This is not saying that a man must believe that he is one of the elect.   Election is a secret purpose of God.   The election of any particular person is not revealed, and, therefore, is not an object of faith.   It is a thing to be proved, or made sure, as the Apostle Peter says, by the fruits of the Spirit.   All that the doctrine of the Reformers on this subject includes is, that the soul in committing itself to Christ does so as to one who loved it and died for its salvation.   The woman healed by touching our Saviour's garment, believed that she was an object of his compassionate love, because all who touched Him with faith were included in that number.   Her faith included that conviction.

§ 8. *Effects of Faith.*

Union with Christ.

The first effect of faith, according to the Scriptures, is union with Christ.   We are in Him by faith.   There is indeed a federal union between Christ and his people, founded on the covenant of redemption between the Father and the Son in the counsels of eternity.   We are, therefore, said to be in Him before the foundation of the world.   It is one of the promises of that covenant, that all whom the Father had given the Son should come to Him ; that his people should be made willing in the day of his power.   Christ has, therefore, been exalted to the right hand of God, to give repentance and the remission of sins.   But it was also, as we learn from the Scriptures, included in the stipulations of that covenant, that his people, so far as adults are concerned, should not receive the saving benefits of that covenant until they were united to Him by a voluntary act of faith.   They are " by nature the children of wrath, even as others."   (Eph. ii. 3.) They remain in this state of condemnation until they believe. Their union is consummated by faith.   To be in Christ, and to believe in Christ, are, therefore, in the Scriptures convertible forms of expression.   They mean substantially the same thing, and, therefore, the same effects are attributed to faith as are attributed to union with Christ.

Justification an Effect of Faith.

The proximate effect of this union, and, consequently, the second effect of faith, is justification. We are " justified by the faith of Christ." (Gal. ii. 16.) " There is therefore now no condemnation to them which are in Christ Jesus." (Rom. viii. 1.) "He that believeth on him is not condemned." (John iii. 18.) Faith is the condition on which God promises in the covenant of redemption, to impute unto men the righteousness of Christ. As soon, therefore, as they believe, they cannot be condemned. They are clothed with a righteousness which answers all the demands of justice. "Who shall lay anything to the charge of God's elect? It is God that justifieth. Who is he that condemneth? It is Christ that died, yea rather, that is risen again, who is even at the right hand of God, who also maketh intercession for us." (Rom. viii. 33, 34.)

Participation of Christ's Life an Effect of Faith.

The third effect of faith, or of union with Christ, is a participation of his life. Those united with Christ, the Apostle teaches (Rom. vi. 4–10), so as to be partakers of his death, are partakers also of his life. " Because I live, ye shall live also." (John xiv. 19.) Christ dwells in our hearts by faith. (Eph. iii. 17.) Christ is in us. (Rom. viii. 10.) It is not we that live, but Christ liveth in us. (Gal. ii. 20.) Our Lord's illustration of this vital union is derived from a vine and its branches. (John xv. 1–6.) As the life of the vine is diffused through the branches, and as they live only as connected with the vine, so the life of Christ is diffused through his people, and they are partakers of spiritual and eternal life, only in virtue of their union with Him. Another familiar illustration of this subject is derived from the human body. The members derive their life from the head, and perish if separated from it. (Eph. i. 22; 1 Cor. xii. 12–27, and often). In Ephesians iv. 15, 16, the Apostle carries out this illustration in detail. " The head, even Christ: from whom the whole body fitly joined together and compacted by that which every joint supplieth, according to the effectual working in the measure of every part, maketh increase of the body unto the edifying of itself in love." As the principle of animal life located in the head, through the complicated yet ordered system of nerves extending to every member, diffuses life and energy through the whole body ; so the Holy

Spirit, given without measure to Christ the head of the Church, which is his body, diffuses life and strength to every member. Hence, according to Scripture, Christ's dwelling in us is explained as the Spirit's dwelling in us. The indwelling of the Spirit is the indwelling of Christ. If God be in you; if Christ be in you; if the Spirit be in you, — all mean the same thing. See Romans viii. 9–11.

To explain this vital and mystical union between Christ and his people as a mere union of thought and feeling, is utterly inadmissible. (1.) In the first place, it is contrary to the plain meaning of his words. No one ever speaks of Plato's dwelling in men; of his being their life, so that without him they can do nothing ; and much less, so that holiness, happiness, and eternal life depend upon that union. (2.) Such interpretation supposes that our relation to Christ is analogous to the relation of one man to another. Whereas it is a relation between men and a divine person, who has life in Himself, and gives life to as many as He wills. (3.) It ignores all that the Scriptures teach of the work of the Holy Spirit and of his dwelling in the hearts of men. (4.) It overlooks the supernatural character of Christianity, and would reduce it to a mere philosophical and ethical system.

Peace as the Fruit of Faith.

The fourth effect of faith is peace. " Being justified by faith, we have peace with God, through our Lord Jesus Christ." (Rom. v. 1.) Peace arises from a sense of reconciliation. God promises to pardon, to receive into his favour, and finally to save all who believe the record which He has given of his Son. To believe, is therefore to believe this promise ; and to appropriate this promise to ourselves is to believe that God is reconciled to us. This faith may be weak or strong. And the peace which flows from it may be tremulous and intermitting, or it may be constant and assured.

Assurance.

To make assurance of personal salvation essential to faith, is contrary to Scripture and to the experience of God's people. The Bible speaks of a weak faith. It abounds with consolations intended for the doubting and the desponding. God accepts those who can only say, " Lord, I believe ; help thou mine unbelief." Those who make assurance the essence of faith, generally reduce faith to a mere intellectual assent. They are often censorious, refusing to recognize as brethren those who do not agree with them; and sometimes they are antinomian.

At the same time, Scripture and experience teach that assurance is not only attainable, but a privilege and a duty. There may indeed be assurance, where there is no true faith at all; but where there is true faith, the want of assurance is to be referred either to the weakness of faith, or to erroneous views of the plan of salvation. Many sincere believers are too introspective. They look too exclusively within, so that their hope is graduated by the degree of evidence of regeneration which they find in their own experience. This, except in rare cases, can never lead to the assurance of hope. We may examine our hearts with all the microscopic care prescribed by President Edwards in his work on "The Religious Affections," and never be satisfied that we have eliminated every ground of misgiving and doubt. The grounds of assurance are not so much within, as without us. They are, according to Scripture, (1.) The universal and unconditional promise of God that those who come to Him in Christ, He will in no wise cast out; that whosoever will, may take of the water of life without money and without price. We are bound to be assured that God is faithful and will certainly save those who believe. (2.) The infinite, immutable, and gratuitous love of God. In the first ten verses of the fifth chapter of the Epistle to the Romans, and in the eighth chapter of that epistle from the thirty-first verse to the end, the Apostle dwells on these characteristics of the love of God, as affording an immovable foundation of the believer's hope. (3.) The infinite merit of the satisfaction of Christ, and the prevalence of his continued intercession. Paul, in Romans viii. 34, especially emphasizes these points. (4.) The covenant of redemption in which it is promised that all given by the Father to the Son, shall come to Him, and that none of them shall be lost. (5.) From the witness of the Spirit, Paul says, " We . . . . rejoice in hope of the glory of God," because the love of God is shed abroad in our hearts, by the Holy Ghost given unto us. That is, the Holy Ghost assures us that we are the objects of that love which he goes on to describe as infinite, immutable, and gratuitous. (Rom. v. 3–5.) And again, "The Spirit itself beareth witness with our spirit that we are the children of God." If, therefore, any true believer lacks the assurance of faith, the fault is in himself and not in the plan of salvation, or in the promises of God.

Sanctification a Fruit of Faith.

The fifth effect of faith is sanctification. "Which are sanctified," says our Lord "by faith that is in me." Although in this verse (Acts xxvi. 18), the words "by faith" do not qualify the preceding clause, "are sanctified," alone, but are to be referred to all the preceding particulars,—illumination, deliverance from Satan, forgiveness of sins, and the eternal inheritance,—yet the immediate antecedent is not to be omitted. We are sanctified by faith as is elsewhere clearly taught. "Faith which worketh by love and purifies the heart." (Gal. v. 6, and Acts xv. 9.)

The relation of faith to sanctification is thus set forth in the Scriptures,—

1. We are justified by faith. So long as we are under the law, we are under the curse, and bring forth fruit unto death. There is, and can be no love to God, and no holy living until we are delivered from his wrath due to us for sin. We are freed from the law, delivered from its condemnation, by the body or death of Christ. It is by faith in Him as the end of the law for righteousness, that we personally are freed from condemnation and restored to the favour of God. See all this clearly taught in Romans vi., and in the first six verses of the seventh chapter. It is thus by faith we pass from judicial death to judicial life, or justification. This is the first and indispensable step of sanctification so far as it reveals itself in the consciousness of the believer.

2. It is by faith that we receive the indwelling of the Spirit. Christ (or the Spirit of Christ) dwells in our hearts by faith. Faith is the indispensable condition (so far as adults are concerned) of this indwelling of the Spirit. And the indwelling of the Spirit is the source of all spiritual life. Faith is indeed the fruit of the Spirit, and therefore the gift of the Spirit must precede the exercise of faith. It is nevertheless true that faith is the condition of the indwelling of the Spirit, and consequently of spiritual life. Life must precede breathing, and yet breathing is the necessary condition of living.

3. Faith is not only the condition of the Spirit's dwelling in us as the source of spiritual life, but we live by faith. That is, the continuance and exercise of spiritual life involve and suppose the constant exercise of faith. We live by exercising faith in God, in his attributes, in his providence, in his promises, and in all the truths which He has revealed. Especially is this life sustained by those exercises of faith of which Christ is the object; his divine

and mysteriously constituted person, as God manifest in the flesh ; his finished work for our redemption ; his constant intercession ; his intimate relation to us not only as our prophet, priest, and king, but as our living head in whom our life is hid in God, and from whom it flows into our souls. We are thus sanctified by faith, because it is through faith that all the religious affections and all the activities of spiritual life are called into exercise.

4. We are sanctified by faith, as it is the substance of things hoped for, and the evidence of things not seen. " The things of God," the truths which He has revealed concerning the spiritual and eternal world exist for us while in this world, only as the objects of faith. But faith is to the soul what the eye is to the body. It enables us to see the things unseen and eternal. It gives them substance, reality, and therefore power, — power in some little measure in proportion to their value. Thus the things seen and temporal lose their dominant power over the soul. They are not worthy to be compared with the things which God has prepared for them that love Him. The believer, — the ideal, and at times the actual believer, as we learn from Scripture and from history, is raised above the things of time and sense, overcomes the world, and becomes heavenly minded. He lives in heaven, breathes its atmosphere, is pervaded by its spirit, and has a prelibation of its joys. This renders him pure, spiritual, humble, self-denying, laborious, meek, gentle, forgiving, as well as firm and courageous. The whole of the eleventh chapter of the Epistle to the Hebrews is devoted to the illustration of the power of faith especially in this aspect. The Apostle shows that in times past, even under the dim light of the former dispensation, it enabled Noah to stand alone against the world, Abraham to offer up his only son, Moses to prefer the reproach of Christ to the treasures of Egypt ; that others through faith subdued kingdoms, wrought righteousness, stopped the mouths of lions, quenched the violence of fire ; that others were by faith made strong out of weakness, waxed valiant in fight ; that others submitted to the trial of cruel mockings and scourgings ; that others by faith endured to be stoned, sawn asunder, or slain with the sword ; and that yet others through faith consented to wander about in sheepskins and goatskins, destitute, afflicted, and tormented. All these, we are told, through faith obtained a good report.

5. Faith sanctifies because it is the necessary condition of the efficacy of the means of grace. It is through the Word, sacraments, and prayer, that God communicates constant supplies of

grace. They are the means of calling the activities of spiritual life into exercise. But these means of grace are inoperative unless they are received and used by faith. Faith does not, indeed, give them their power, but it is the condition on which the Spirit of God renders them efficacious.

That good works are the certain effects of faith is included in the doctrine that we are sanctified by faith. For it is impossible that there should be inward holiness, love, spirituality, brotherly kindness, and zeal, without an external manifestation of these graces in the whole outward life. Faith, therefore, without works, is dead. We are saved by faith. But salvation includes deliverance from sin. If, therefore, our faith does not deliver us from sin, it does not save us. Antinomianism involves a contradiction in terms.

Certainty of Salvation.

A sixth effect attributed to faith in the Scriptures is security, or, certainty of salvation. " God so loved the world, that he gave his only begotten Son, that whosoever believeth in him should not perish, but have everlasting life." (John iii. 16.) " He that heareth my word, and believeth on him that sent me, hath everlasting life, and shall not come into condemnation ; but is passed from death unto life." (John v. 24.) " I am the living bread which came down from heaven: if any man eat of this bread, he shall live forever." (John vi. 51.) " All that the Father giveth me shall come to me ; and him that cometh to me I will in no wise cast out. . . . . And this is the will of him that sent me, that every one which seeth the Son, and believeth on him, may have everlasting life: and I will raise him up at the last day." (John vi. 37, 40.) " My sheep hear my voice, and I know them, and they follow me : and I give unto them eternal life ; and they shall never perish, neither shall any man pluck them out of my hand." (John x. 27, 28.)

The Eighth Chapter of Romans.

The whole of the eighth chapter of the Epistle to the Romans is designed to prove the certain salvation of all who believe. The proposition to be established is, that there is " no condemnation to them which are in Christ Jesus." That is, they can never perish ; they can never be so separated from Christ as to come into condemnation. The Apostle's first argument to establish that proposition, is, that believers are delivered from the law by the sacrifice of Christ. The believer, therefore, is not under the law which condemns, as Paul had before said (Rom. vi. 14), " Ye are not under the law, but under grace." But if not under the law he cannot be condemned. The law has had its course, and found full satisfaction in the work of Christ, who is the end of the law for righteousness to every one that believeth. He renders every one righteous, in the sight of the law, who believes on Him. This is the first reason which the Apostle gives why those who are in Christ shall never be condemned.

His second argument is that they have already within them the principle of eternal life. That principle is the Spirit of God ; " the life-giving " as He was designated by the ancient Church. To be carnally minded is death. To be spiritually minded is life and peace. Sin is death ; holiness is life. It is a contradiction to say that those in whom the Spirit of life dwells, should die. And, therefore, the Apostle says, Although the body dies, the soul lives. And if the Spirit of Him who raised up Jesus from the dead dwell in you, He that raised up Christ from the dead shall also quicken even your mortal bodies by his Spirit that dwelleth in you. The indwelling of the Spirit, therefore, secures not only the life of the soul, but also the ultimate and glorious life of the body.

The third argument for the security of believers, is, that they are the sons of God. As many as are led by the Spirit of God, they are the sons of God. That is, they are partakers of his nature, the special objects of his love, and entitled to the inheritance which He gives. If sons then heirs, heirs of God and joint heirs with Christ. According to the Apostle's mode of thinking, that any of the sons of God should perish, is impossible. If sons they shall certainly be saved.

The fourth argument is from the purpose of God. Those whom He has predestinated to be conformed to the image of his Son, them He calls to the exercise of faith and repentance ; and whom He thus calls He justifies, He provides for them and imputes to them a righteousness which satisfies the demands of the law, and which entitles them in Christ and for his sake to eternal life ; and those whom He justifies He glorifies. There is no flaw in this chain. If men were predestinated to eternal life on the ground of their repenting and believing through their own strength, or through a coöperation with the grace of God which others fail to exercise, then their continuance in a state of grace might be dependent on themselves. But if faith and repentance are the gifts of God, the results of his effectual vocation, then be-

stowing those gifts is a revelation of the purpose of God to save
those to whom they are given.   It is an evidence that God has
predestinated them to be conformed to the image of his Son, *i. e.*,
to be like Him in character, destiny, and glory, and that He will
infallibly carry out his purpose.   No one can pluck them out of
his hands.

Paul's fifth argument is from the love of God.   As stated
above,[1] the Apostle argues from the greatness, the freeness, and
the immutability of that love that its objects never can be lost.
" He that spared not his own Son, but delivered him up for us
all, how shall he not with him also freely give us all things."   If
He has done the greater, will He not do the less?   If he gave
even his own Son, will He not give us faith to receive and constancy to persevere even unto the end?   A love so great as the
love of God to his people cannot fail of its object.   This love is
also gratuitous.   It is not founded on the attractiveness of its objects.   He loved us " while we were yet sinners ; " " when we
were enemies."   " Much more, then, being now justified by his
blood, we shall be saved from wrath through Him.   For if, when
we were enemies, we were reconciled to God by the death of his
Son, much more, being reconciled, we shall be saved by his life."
God's love in this aspect is compared to parental love.   A mother
does not love her child because it is lovely.   Her love leads her to
do all she can to render it attractive and to keep it so.   So the
love of God, being in like manner mysterious, unaccountable by
anything in its objects, secures his adorning his children with the
graces of his Spirit, and arraying them in all the beauty of holiness.   It is only the lamentable mistake that God loves us for our
goodness, that can lead any one to suppose that his love is dependent on our self-sustained attractiveness, when we should look
to his fatherly love as the source of all goodness, and the ground
of the assurance that He will not allow Satan or our own evil
hearts to destroy the lineaments of his likeness which He has impressed upon our souls.   Having loved his own, He loves them to
the end.   And Christ prays for them that their faith may not
fail.

It must be remembered that what the Apostle argues to prove
is not merely the certainty of the salvation of those that believe ;
but their certain perseverance in holiness.   Salvation in sin, according to Paul's system, is a contradiction in terms.   This perseverance in holiness is secured partly by the inward secret influ-

[1] Page 107.

ence of the Spirit, and partly by all the means adapted to secure that end — instructions, admonitions, exhortations, warnings, the means of grace, and the dispensations of his providence. Having, through love, determined on the end, He has determined on the means for its accomplishment.

The sixth argument of the Apostle is that, as the love of God is infinitely great and altogether gratuitous, it is also immutable, and, therefore, believers shall certainly be saved. Hence the conclusion, " I am persuaded that neither death, nor life, nor angels, nor principalities, nor powers, nor things present, nor things to come, nor height, nor depth, nor any other creature, shall be able to separate us from the love of God, which is in Christ Jesus our Lord."

It will be seen that the Apostle does not rest the perseverance of the saints on the indestructible nature of faith, or on the imperishable nature of the principle of grace in the heart, or on the constancy of the believer's will, but solely on what is out of ourselves. Perseverance, he teaches us, is due to the purpose of God, to the work of Christ, to the indwelling of the Holy Spirit, and to the primal source of all, the infinite, mysterious, and immutable love of God. We do not keep ourselves ; we are kept by the power of God, through faith unto salvation. (1 Peter i. 5.)

CHAPTER XVII.

JUSTIFICATION.

§ 1. *Symbolical Statement of the Doctrine.*

JUSTIFICATION is defined in the Westminster Catechism, "An act of God's free grace, wherein He pardoneth all our sins, and accepteth us as righteous in his sight, only for the righteousness of Christ imputed to us, and received by faith alone."

The Heidelberg Catechism in answer to the question, "How dost thou become righteous before God?" answers, "Sola fide in Jesum Christum, adeo ut licet mea me conscientia accuset, quod adversus omnia mandata Dei graviter peccaverim, nec ullum eorum servaverim, adhæc etiamnum ad omne malum propensus sim, nihilominus tamen (modo hæc beneficia vera animi fiducia amplectar), sine ullo meo merito, ex mera Dei misericordia, mihi perfecta satisfactio, justitia, et sanctitas Christi, imputetur ac donetur; perinde ac si nec ullum ipse peccatum admisissem, nec ulla mihi labes inhæreret; imo vero quasi eam obedientiam, quam pro me Christus præstitit, ipse perfecte præstitissem." And in answer to the question, Why faith alone justifies? it says. "Non quod dignitate meæ fidei Deo placeam, sed quod sola satisfactio, justitia ac sanctitas Christi, mea justitia sit coram Deo. Ego vero eam non alia ratione, quam fide amplecti, et mihi applicare queam."

The Second Helvetic Confession,[1] says "Justificare significat Apostolo in disputatione de justificatione, peccata remittere, a culpa et pœna absolvere, in gratiam recipere, et justum pronunciare. Etenim ad Romanos dicit apostolus, 'Deus est, qui justificat, quis ille, qui condemnet?' opponuntur justificare et condemnare. . . . . Etenim Christus peccata mundi in se recepit et sustulit, divinæque justitiæ satisfecit. Deus ergo propter solum Christum passum et resuscitatum, propitius est peccatis nostris, nec illa nobis imputat, imputat autem justitiam Christi pro nostra: ita ut jam simus non solum mundati a peccatis et purgati, vel sancti, sed etiam donati justitia Christi, adeoque absoluti a

[1] Chapter xv.

peccatis, morte vel condemnatione, justi denique ac hæredes vitæ æternæ. Proprie ergo loquendo, Deus solus nos justificat, et dun-taxat propter Christum justificat, non imputans nobis peccata, sed imputans ejus nobis justitiam."[1]

These are the most generally received and authoritative stand-ards of the Reformed Churches, with which all other Reformed symbols agree. The Lutheran confessions teach precisely the same doctrine on this subject.[2] " Unanimi consensu, docemus et confitemur. . . . . quod homo peccator coram Deo justificetur, hoc est, absolvatur ab omnibus suis peccatis et a judicio justissimæ condemnationis, et adoptetur in numerum filiorum Dei atque hæres æternæ vitæ scribatur, sine ullis nostris meritis, aut dignitate, et absque ullis præcedentibus, præsentibus, aut sequentibus nostris operibus. ex mera gratia, tantummodo propter unicum meritum, perfectissimam obedientiam, passionem acerbissimam, mortem et resurrectionem Domini nostri, Jesu Christi, cujus obedientia nobis ad justitiam imputatur."[3]

Again, " Credimus, docemus, et confitemur, hoc ipsum nostram esse coram Deo justitiam, quod Dominus nobis peccata remittit, ex mera gratia, absque ullo respectu præcedentium, præsentium, aut consequentium nostrorum operum, dignitatis, aut meriti. Ille enim donat atque imputat nobis justitiam obedientiæ Christi ; propter eam justitiam a Deo in gratiam recipimur et justi reputamur."[4] " Justificari significat hic non ex impio justum effici, sed usu forensi justum pronuntiari." And " Justi-ficare hoc loco (Rom. v. 1.) forensi consuetudine significat reum absolvere et pronuntiare justum, sed propter alienam justi-tiam, videlicet Christi, quæ aliena justitia communicatur nobis per fidem."[5] So also " Vocabulum justificationis in hoc negotio significat justum pronuntiare, a peccatis et æternis peccatorum suppliciis absolvere, propter justitiam Christi, quæ a Deo fidei imputatur."[6]

Hase,[7] concisely states the Lutheran doctrine on this subject in these words : " Justificatio est actus forensis, quo Deus, sola gra-tia ductus, peccatori, propter Christi meritum fide apprehensum, justitiam Christi imputat, peccata remittit, eumque sibi reconcil-iat."

---

[1] See Niemeyer, *Collectio Confessionum*, Leipzig, 1840.
[2] The main passages are *Augsburg Confession*, part i., article iv. ; the *Apology* for that Confession, article iii. ; and the *Form of Concord*, article iii.
[3] *Form of Concord*, III. 9.
[4] Ibid. *Epitome*, III. 4.
[5] *Apology for the Augsburg Confession*, Art. III. 131, 184.
[6] *Form of Concord* III. 17.   See Hase, *Libri Symbolici*, 3d edit., Leipzig, 1836.
[7] *Hutterus Redivivus*, § 109, 6th edit. Leipzig, 1845 p. 274.

The " Form of Concord " says, " Hic articulus, de justitia fidei, præcipuus est (ut Apologia loquitur) in tota doctrina Christiana, sine quo conscientiæ perturbatæ nullam veram et firmam consolationem habere, aut divitias gratiæ Christi recte agnoscere possunt. Id D. Lutherus suo etiam testimonio confirmavit, cum inquit: Si unicus his articulus sincerus permanserit, etiam Christiana Ecclesia sincera, concors et sine omnibus sectis permanet: sin vero corrumpitur, impossibile est, ut uni errori aut fanatico spiritui recte obviam iri possit." [1] The Lutheran theologians, therefore, speak of it as the " ἀκρόπολις totius Christianæ religionis, ac nexus, quo omnia corporis doctrinæ Christianæ membra continentur, quoque rupto solvuntur." [2]

President Edwards.

This statement of the doctrine of justification has retained symbolical authority in the Lutheran and Reformed churches, to the present day. President Edwards, who is regarded as having initiated certain departures from some points of the Reformed faith, was firm in his adherence to this view of justification, which he held to be of vital importance. In his discourse on " Justification by Faith alone," he thus defines justification: " A person is said to be justified when he is approved of God as free from the guilt of sin and its deserved punishment ; and as having that righteousness belonging to him that entitles to the reward of life. That we should take the word in such a sense and understand it as the judge's accepting a person as having both a negative and positive righteousness belonging to him, and looking on him therefore as not only quit or free from any obligation to punishment, but also as just and righteous, and so entitled to a positive reward, is not only most agreeable to the etymology and natural import of the word, which signifies to make righteous, or to pass one for righteous in judgment, but also manifestly agreeable to the force of the word as used in Scripture." He then shows how it is, or why faith alone justifies. It is not on account of any virtue or goodness in faith, but as it unites us to Christ, and involves the acceptance of Him as our righteousness. Thus it is we are justified " by faith alone, without any manner of virtue or goodness of our own."

The ground of justification is the righteousness of Christ imputed to the believer. " By that righteousness being imputed to us," says Edwards, " is meant no other than this, that that right-

---

[1] III. 6.   [2] Quenstedt.

eousness of Christ is accepted for us, and admitted instead of that perfect inherent righteousness that ought to be in ourselves : Christ's perfect obedience shall be reckoned to our account, so that we shall have the benefit of it, as though we had performed it ourselves : and so we suppose that a title to eternal life is given us as the reward of this righteousness. . . . . The opposers of this doctrine suppose that there is an absurdity in it : they say that to suppose that God imputes Christ's obedience to us, is to suppose that God is mistaken, and thinks that we performed that obedience that Christ performed.   But why cannot that righteousness be reckoned to our account, and be accepted for us, without any such absurdity ?   Why is there any more absurdity in it, than in a merchant's transferring debt or credit from one man's account to another, when one man pays a price for another, so that it shall be accepted, as if that other had paid it ?   Why is there any more absurdity in supposing that Christ's obedience is imputed to us, than that his satisfaction is imputed ?   If Christ has suffered the penalty of the law for us, and in our stead, then it will follow, that his suffering that penalty is imputed to us, *i. e.*, that it is accepted for us, and in our stead, and is reckoned to our account, as though we had suffered it.   But why may not his obeying the law of God be as rationally reckoned to our account, as his suffering the penalty of the law ? " [1]

Points included in the above Statement of the Doctrine.

According to the above statements, justification is, —

1. An act, and not, as sanctification, a continued and progressive work.

2. It is an act of grace to the sinner.   In himself he deserves condemnation when God justifies him.

3. As to the nature of the act, it is, in the first place, not an efficient act, or an act of power.   It does not produce any subjective change in the person justified.   It does not effect a change of character, making those good who were bad, those holy who were unholy.   That is done in regeneration and sanctification. In the second place, it is not a mere executive act, as when a sovereign pardons a criminal, and thereby restores him to his civil rights, or to his former status in the commonwealth.   In the third place, it is a forensic, or judicial act, the act of a judge, not of a sovereign.   That is, in the case of the sinner, or, *in foro Dei*, it is an act of God not in his character of sovereign, but in his

[1] *Works* of President Edwards, New York, 1868, vol. iv. pp. 66, 91, 92.

character of judge. It is a declarative act in which God pronounces the sinner just or righteous, that is, declares that the claims of justice, so far as he is concerned, are satisfied, so that he cannot be justly condemned, but is in justice entitled to the reward promised or due to perfect righteousness.

4. The meritorious ground of justification is not faith ; we are not justified on account of our faith, considered as a virtuous or holy act or state of mind. Nor are our works of any kind the ground of justification. Nothing done by us or wrought in us satisfies the demands of justice, or can be the ground or reason of the declaration that justice as far as it concerns us is satisfied. The ground of justification is the righteousness of Christ, active and passive, *i. e.*, including his perfect obedience to the law as a covenant, and his enduring the penalty of the law in our stead and on our behalf.

5. The righteousness of Christ is in justification imputed to the believer. That is, is set to his account, so that he is entitled to plead it at the bar of God, as though it were personally and inherently his own.

6. Faith is the condition of justification. That is, so far as adults are concerned, God does not impute the righteousness of Christ to the sinner, until and unless, he (through grace), receives and rests on Christ alone for his salvation.

That such is the doctrine of the Reformed and Lutheran churches on this important doctrine, cannot be disputed. The statements of the standards of those churches are so numerous, explicit, and discriminating as to preclude all reasonable doubt on this subject. That such is the doctrine of the Word of God appears from the following considerations.

It will not be necessary to discuss all the points above specified separately, as some of them are necessarily included in others. The following propositions include all the essential points of the doctrine.

§ 2. *Justification is a Forensic Act.*

By this the Reformers intended, in the first place, to deny the Romish doctrine of subjective justification. That is, that justification consists in an act or agency of God making the sinner subjectively holy. Romanists confound or unite justification and sanctification. They define justification as " the remission of sin and infusion of new habits of grace." By remission of sin they mean not simply pardon, but the removal of everything of the nature of sin from the soul. Justification, therefore, with them, is purely subjective, consisting in the destruction of sin and the infusion of holiness. In opposition to this doctrine, the Reformers maintained that by justification the Scriptures mean something different from sanctification. That the two gifts, although inseparable, are distinct, and that justification, instead of being an efficient act changing the inward character of the sinner, is a declarative act, announcing and determining his relation to the law and justice of God.

In the second place, the Symbols of the Reformation no less explicitly teach that justification is not simply pardon and restoration. It includes pardon, but it also includes a declaration that the believer is just or righteous in the sight of the law. He has a right to plead a righteousness which completely satisfies its demands.

And, therefore, in the third place, affirmatively, those Symbols teach that justification is a judicial or forensic act, *i. e.*, an act of God as judge proceeding according to law, declaring that the sinner is just, *i. e.*, that the law no longer condemns him, but acquits and pronounces him to be entitled to eternal life.

Here, as so often in other cases, the ambiguity of words is apt to create embarrassment. The Greek word δίκαιος, and the English word *righteous,* have two distinct senses. They sometimes express moral character. When we say that God is righteous, we mean that He is right. He is free from any moral imperfection. So when we say that a man is righteous, we generally mean that he is upright and honest ; that he is and does what he ought to be and do. In this sense the word expresses the relation which a man sustains to the rule of moral conduct. At other times, however, these words express, not moral character, but the relation which a man sustains to justice. In this sense a man is just with regard to whom justice is satisfied ; or, against whom justice has no demands. The lexicons, therefore, tell us that δίκαιος sometimes means, *leges observans ;* at others *insons, culpa vacans* (free from guilt or obligation to punishment) — *judicio Dei insons.* Pilate (Matt. xxvii. 24) said, " I am innocent of the blood of this just person ; " *i. e.*, of this person who is free from guilt ; free from anything which justifies his condemnation to death. " Christ, also," says the Apostle, " hath once suffered for sins, the just for the unjust ; " the innocent for the guilty. See Romans ii. 13 ; v. 19. " As by one man's disobedience many were made sinners, so by the obedience of one shall many be made righteous." " As the predicate of *judicandus* in his relation to the judge, 'righteousness' expresses, not a positive virtue, but a judicial negative freedom from *reatus*. In the presence of his judge, he is צַדִּיק who stands free from guilt and desert of punishment (straflos), either because he has contracted no guilt (as, *e. g.*, Christ), or, because in the way demanded by the Judge (under the Old Testament by expiatory sacrifice) he has expiated the guilt contracted."[1] If, therefore, we take the word righteous in the former of the two senses above mentioned, when it expresses moral character, it would be a contradiction to say that God pronounces the sinner righteous. This would be equivalent to saying that God pronounces the sinner to be not a sinner, the wicked to be good, the unholy to be holy. But if we take the word in the sense in which the Scriptures so often use it, as expressing relation to justice, then when God pronounces the sinner righteous or just, He simply declares that his guilt is expiated, that justice is satisfied, that He has the righteousness which justice demands. This is precisely what Paul says, when he says that God "justifieth the ungodly." (Rom. iv. 5.) God does not pronounce the ungodly to be godly ; He declares that notwithstanding his personal sinfulness and unworthiness, he is accepted as righteous on the ground of what Christ has done for him.

Proof of the Doctrine just stated.

That to justify means neither simply to pardon, nor to make inherently righteous or good is proved, —

From the Usage of Scripture.

1. By the uniform usage of the word to *justify* in Scripture. It is never used in either of those senses, but always to declare or pronounce just. It is unnecessary to cite passages in proof of a usage which is uniform. The few following examples are enough. Deuteronomy xxv. 1, "If there be a controversy between men, and they come unto judgment, that the judges may judge them ; then they shall justify the righteous, and condemn the wicked." Exodus xxiii. 7, "I will not justify the wicked." Isaiah v. 23, "Which justify the wicked for reward." Proverbs xvii. 15, "He that justifieth the wicked" is "abomination to the Lord." Luke x. 29, "He willing to justify himself." Luke xvi. 15, "Ye are they which justify yourselves before men." Matthew xi. 19, "Wisdom is justi-

---

[1] *Christliche Dogmatik*, von Johannes Heinrich August Ebrard, § 402, edit. Königsberg, 1852, vol. ii. p. 163.

fied of her children." Galatians ii. 16, "A man is not justified by the works of the law." v. 6, "Whosoever of you are
justified by the law ; ye are fallen from grace." Thus men are
said to justify God. Job xxxii. 2, "Because he justified
himself, rather than God." Psalms li. 4, "That thou mightest be justified when thou speakest." Luke vii. 29, "All the
people that heard him, and the publicans, justified God." The
only passage in the New Testament where the word δικαιόω is
used in a different sense is Revelation xxii. 11, ὁ δίκαιος, δικαιωθήτω ἔτι, "He that is righteous, let him be righteous still." Here
the first aorist passive appears to be used in a middle sense.
' Let him show himself righteous, or continue righteous.' Even
if the reading in this passage were undoubted, this single case
would have no force against the established usage of the word.
The reading, however, is not merely doubtful, but it is, in the
judgment of the majority of the critical editors, Tischendorf among
the rest, incorrect.   They give, as the true text, δικαιοσύνην ποιησάτω
ἔτι. Even if this latter reading be, as De Wette thinks, a gloss,
it shows that ὁ δίκαιος δικαιωθήτω ἔτι was as intolerable to a Greek
ear as the expression, ' He that is righteous, let him justify himself still,' would be to us.

The usage of common life as to this word is just as uniform as
that of the Bible.   It would be a perfect solecism to say of a
criminal whom the executive had pardoned, that he was justified ;
or that a reformed drunkard or thief was justified.   The word
always expresses a judgment, whether of the mind, as when one
man justifies another for his conduct, or officially of a judge.   If
such be the established meaning of the word, it ought to settle all
controversy as to the nature of justification.   We are bound to
take the words of Scripture in their true established sense.   And,
therefore, when the Bible says, "God justifies the believer," we
are not at liberty to say that it means that He pardons, or that
He sanctifies him.   It means, and can mean only that He pronounces him just.

Justification the Opposite of Condemnation.

2. This is still further evident from the antithesis between
condemnation and justification.   Condemnation is not the opposite either of pardon or of reformation.   To condemn is to pronounce guilty ; or worthy of punishment.   To justify is to
declare not guilty ; or that justice does not demand punishment ; or that the person concerned cannot justly be condemned.

When, therefore, the Apostle says (Rom. viii. 1), "There is, therefore, now no condemnation to them which are in Christ Jesus," he declares that they are absolved from guilt; that the penalty of the law cannot justly be inflicted upon them. "Who," he asks, "shall lay anything to the charge of God's elect? God who justifieth? Who is he that condemneth? Christ who died?" (vers. 33, 34.) Against the elect in Christ no ground of condemnation can be presented. God pronounces them just, and therefore no one can pronounce them guilty.

This passage is certainly decisive against the doctrine of subjective justification in any form. This opposition between condemnation and justification is familiar both in Scripture and in common life. Job ix. 20, "If I justify myself, mine own mouth shall condemn me." xxxiv. 17, "And wilt thou condemn him that is most just." If to condemn does not mean to make wicked, to justify does not mean to make good. And if condemnation is a judicial, as opposed to an executive act, so is justification. In condemnation it is a judge who pronounces sentence on the guilty. In justification it is a judge who pronounces or who declares the person arraigned free from guilt and entitled to be treated as righteous.

Argument from Equivalent Forms of Expression.

3. The forms of expression which are used as equivalents of the word "justify" clearly determine the nature of the act. Thus Paul speaks of "the blessedness of the man unto whom God imputeth righteousness without works." (Rom. iv. 6.) To impute righteousness is not to pardon; neither is it to sanctify. It means to justify, i. e., to attribute righteousness. The negative form in which justification is described is equally significant. "Blessed are they whose iniquities are forgiven, and whose sins are covered. Blessed is the man to whom the Lord will not impute sin." (Rom. iv. 7, 8.) As "to impute sin" never means and cannot mean to make wicked; so the negative statement "not to impute sin" cannot mean to sanctify. And as "to impute sin" does mean to lay sin to one's account and to treat him accordingly; so to justify means to lay righteousness to one's account and treat him accordingly. "God sent not his Son into the world to condemn the world. . . . . He that believeth on him is not condemned: but he that believeth not is condemned already." (John iii. 17, 18.)

For "as by the offence of one judgment came upon all men to

condemnation; even so by the righteousness of one the free gift came upon all men unto justification of life." (Rom. v. 18.) It was κρῖμα, a judicial sentence, which came on men for the offence of Adam, and it is a judicial sentence (justification, a δικαίωσις) which comes for the righteousness of Christ, or, as is said in ver. 16 of the same chapter, it was a κρῖμα εἰς κατάκριμα, a condemnatory sentence that came for one offence; and a χάρισμα εἰς δικαίωμα, a sentence of gratuitous justification from many offences. Language cannot be plainer. If a sentence of condemnation is a judicial act, then justification is a judicial act.

Argument from the Statement of the Doctrine.

4. The judicial character of justification is involved in the mode in which the doctrine is presented in the Bible. The Scriptures speak of law, of its demands, of its penalty, of sinners as arraigned at the bar of God, of the day of judgment. The question is, How shall man be just with God? The answer to this question determines the whole method of salvation. The question is not, How a man can become holy? but, How can he become just? How can he satisfy the claims which justice has against him? It is obvious that if there is no such attribute as justice in God; if what we call justice is only benevolence, then there is no pertinency in this question. Man is not required to be just in order to be saved. There are no claims of justice to be satisfied. Repentance is all that need be rendered as the condition of restoration to the favour of God. Or, any didactic declaration or exhibition of God's disapprobation of sin, would open the way for the safe pardon of sinners. Or, if the demands of justice were easily satisfied; if partial, imperfect obedience and fatherly chastisements, or self-inflicted penances, would suffice to satisfy its claims, then the sinner need not be just with God in order to be saved. But the human soul knows intuitively that these are refuges of lies. It knows that there is such an attribute as justice. It knows that the demands thereof are inexorable because they are righteous. It knows that it cannot be saved unless it be justified, and it knows that it cannot be declared just unless the demands of justice are fully satisfied. Low views of the evil of sin and of the justice of God lie at the foundation of all false views of this great doctrine.

The Apostle's Argument in the Epistle to the Romans.

The Apostle begins the discussion of this subject by assuming

that the justice of God, his purpose to punish all sin, to demand
perfect conformity to his law, is revealed from heaven, *i. e.*, so
revealed that no man, whether Jew or Gentile, can deny it.
(Rom. i. 18.)   Men, even the most degraded pagans, know the
righteous judgment of God that those who sin are worthy of death.
(ver. 32.)   He next proves that all men are sinners, and, being
sinners are under condemnation.   The whole world is "guilty
before God." (iii. 19.)   From this he infers, as intuitively certain
(because plainly included in the premises), that no flesh living
can be justified before God "by the deeds of the law," *i. e.*, on
the ground of his own character and conduct.   If guilty he cannot be pronounced not guilty, or just.   In Paul's argument, to
justify is to pronounce just.   Δίκαιος is the opposite of ὑπόδικος
(*i. e.*, "reus, satisfactionem alteri debens").   That is, righteous
is the opposite of guilty.   To pronounce guilty is to condemn.
To pronounce righteous, *i. e.*, not guilty, is to justify.   If a man
denies the authority of Scripture ; or if he feels at liberty, while
holding what he considers the substance of Scripture doctrines,
to reject the form, it is conceivable that he may deny that justification is a judicial act ; but it seems impossible that any one
should deny that it is so represented in the Bible.   Some men
professing to believe the Bible, deny that there is anything supernatural in the work of regeneration and sanctification.   ' Being
born of the Spirit ; ' ' quickened by the mighty power of God ; '
' created anew in Christ Jesus,' are only, they say, strong oriental expressions for a self-wrought reformation.   By a similar process it is easy to get rid, not only of the doctine of justification as
a judicial act, but of all other distinguishing doctrines of the
Scriptures.   This, however, is not to interpret, but to pervert.

The Apostle, having taught that God is just, *i. e.*, that He
demands the satisfaction of justice, and that men are sinners
and can render no such satisfaction themselves, announces that
such a righteousness has been provided, and is revealed in the
Gospel.   It is not our own righteousness, which is of the law,
but the righteousness of Christ, and, therefore, the righteousness
of God, in virtue of which, and on the ground of which, God can
be just and yet justify the sinner who believes in Christ.   As long
as the Bible stands this must stand as a simple statement of what
Paul teaches as to the method of salvation.   Men may dispute
as to what he means, but this is surely what he says.

Argument from the Ground of Justification.

5. The nature of justification is determined by its ground. This indeed is an anticipation of another part of the subject, but it is in point here. If the Bible teaches that the ground of justification, the reason why God remits to us the penalty of the law and accepts us as righteous in his sight, is something out of ourselves, something done for us, and not what we do or experience, then it of necessity follows that justification is not subjective. It does not consist in the infusion of righteousness, or in making the person justified personally holy. If the " formal cause " of our justification be our goodness ; then we are justified for what we are. The Bible, however, teaches that no man living can be justified for what he is. He is condemned for what he is and for what he does. He is justified for what Christ has done for him.

Justification not mere Pardon.

For the same reason justification cannot be mere pardon. Pardon does not proceed on the ground of a satisfaction. A prisoner delivered by a ransom is not pardoned. A debtor whose obligations have been cancelled by a friend, becomes entitled to freedom from the claims of his creditor. When a sovereign pardons a criminal, it is not an act of justice. It is not on the ground of satisfaction to the law. The Bible, therefore, in teaching that justification is on the ground of an atonement or satisfaction; that the sinner's guilt is expiated ; that he is redeemed by the precious blood of Christ ; and that judgment is pronounced upon him as righteous, does thereby teach that justification is neither pardon nor infusion of righteousness.

Argument from the Immutability of the Law.

6. The doctrine that justification consists simply in pardon, and consequent restoration, assumes that the divine law is imperfect and mutable. In human governments it is often expedient and right that men justly condemned to suffer the penalty of the law should be pardoned. Human laws must be general. They cannot take in all the circumstances of each particular case. Their execution would often work hardship or injustice. Human judgments may therefore often be set aside. It is not so with the divine law. The law of the Lord is perfect. And being perfect it cannot be disregarded. It demands nothing which ought not to be demanded. It threatens nothing which ought not to be inflicted.

It is in fact its own executioner. Sin is death. (Rom. viii. 6.)
The justice of God makes punishment as inseparable from sin, as
life is from holiness. The penalty of the law is immutable, and
as little capable of being set aside as the precept. Accordingly
the Scriptures everywhere teach that in the justification of the
sinner there is no relaxation of the penalty. There is no setting
aside, or disregarding the demands of the law. We are delivered
from the law, not by its abrogation, but by its execution. (Gal.
ii. 19.) We are freed from the law by the body of Christ.
(Rom. vii. 4.) Christ having taken our place, bore our sins in
his own body on the tree. (1 Pet. ii. 24.) The handwriting
which was against us, he took out of the way, nailing it to his
cross. (Col. ii. 14.) We are therefore not under the law, but
under grace. (Rom. vi. 14.) Such representations are inconsistent with the theory which supposes that the law may be dispensed with ; that the restoration of sinners to the favour and
fellowship of God, requires no satisfaction to its demands ; that
the believer is pardoned and restored to fellowship with God, just
as a thief or forger is pardoned and restored to his civil rights by
the executive in human governments. This is against the Scriptures. God is just in justifying the sinner. He acts according
to justice.

It will be seen that everything in this discussion turns on the
question, Whether there is such an attribute in God as justice ?
If justice be only " benevolence guided by wisdom, " then there
is no justification. What evangelical Christians so regard, is
only pardon or sanctification. But if God, as the Scriptures
and conscience teach, be a just God, as immutable in his justice
as in his goodness and truth, then there can be no remission of
the penalty of sin except on the ground of expiation, and no
justification except on the ground of the satisfaction of justice ;
and therefore justification must be a judicial act, and neither simply pardon nor the infusion of righteousness. These doctrines
sustain each other. What the Bible teaches of the justice of
God, proves that justification is a judicial declaration that justice
is satisfied. And what the Bible teaches of the nature of justification, proves that justice in God is something more than benevolence. It is thus that all the great doctrines of the Bible
are concatenated.

Argument from the Nature of our Union with Christ.

7. The theory which reduces justification to pardon and its consequences, is inconsistent with what is revealed concerning our union with Christ. That union is mystical, supernatural, representative, and vital. We were in Him before the foundation of the world (Eph. i. 4) ; we are in Him as we were in Adam (Rom. v. 12, 21 ; 1 Cor. xv. 22) ; we are in Him as the members of the body are in the head (Eph. i. 23, iv. 16 ; 1 Cor. xii. 12, 27, and often) ; we are in Him as the branches are in the vine (John xv. 1–12). We are in Him in such a sense that his death is our death, we were crucified with Him (Gal. ii. 20 ; Rom. vi. 1–8) ; we are so united with Him that we rose with Him, and sit with Him in heavenly places. (Eph. ii. 1–6.) In virtue of this union we are (in our measure) what He is. We are the sons of God in Him. And what He did, we did. His righteousness is our righteousness. His life is our life. His exaltation is our exaltation. Such is the pervading representation of the Scriptures. All this is overlooked by the advocates of the opposite theory. According to that view, Christ is no more united to his people, except in sentiment, than to other men. He has simply done what renders it consistent with the character of God and the interests of his kingdom, to pardon any and every man who repents and believes. His relation is purely external. He is not so united to his people that his merit becomes their merit and his life their life. Christ is not in them the hope of glory. (Col. i. 27.) He is not of God made unto them wisdom, righteousness, sanctification, and redemption. (1 Cor. i. 30.) They are not so in Him that, in virtue of that union, they are filled with all the fulness of God. (Col. ii. 10 ; and Eph. iii. 19.) On the other hand, the Protestant doctrine of justification harmonizes with all these representations. If we are so united to Christ as to be made partakers of his life, we are also partakers of his righteousness. What He did in obeying and suffering He did for his people. One essential element of his redeeming work was to satisfy the demands of justice in their behalf, so that in Him and for his sake they are entitled to pardon and eternal life.

Arguments from the Effects ascribed to Justification.

8. The consequences attributed to justification are inconsistent with the assumption that it consists either in pardon or in the infusion of righteousness. Those consequences are peace, reconcil-

iation, and a title to eternal life. " Being justified by faith," says the Apostle, " we have peace with God." (Rom. v. 1.) But pardon does not produce peace. It leaves the conscience unsatisfied. A pardoned criminal is not only just as much a criminal as he was before, but his sense of guilt and remorse of conscience are in no degree lessened. Pardon can remove only the outward and arbitrary penalty. The sting of sin remains. There can be no satisfaction to the mind until there is satisfaction of justice. Justification secures peace, not merely because it includes pardon, but because that pardon is dispensed on the ground of a full satisfaction of justice. What satisfies the justice of God, satisfies the conscience of the sinner. The blood of Jesus Christ cleanseth from all sin (1 John i. 7) by removing guilt, and thus producing a peace which passes all understanding. When the soul sees that Christ bore his sins upon the cross, and endured the penalty which he had incurred ; that all the demands of the law are fully satisfied ; that God is more honoured in his pardon than in his condemnation ; that all the ends of punishment are accomplished by the work of Christ, in a far higher degree than they could be by the death of the sinner ; and that he has a right to plead the infinite merit of the Son of God at the bar of divine justice, then he is satisfied. Then he has peace. He is humble ; he does not lose his sense of personal demerit, but the conscience ceases to demand satisfaction. Criminals have often been known to give themselves up to justice. They could not rest until they were punished. The infliction of the penalty incurred gave them peace. This is an element in Christian experience. The convinced sinner never finds peace until he lays his burden of sin on the Lamb of God ; until he apprehends that his sins have been punished, as the Apostle says (Rom. viii. 3), in Christ.

Again, we are said to be reconciled to God by the death of his Son. (Rom. v. 10.) But pardon does not produce reconciliation. A pardoned criminal may be restored to his civil rights, so far as the penalty remitted involved their forfeiture, but he is not reconciled to society. He is not restored to its favour. Justification, however, does secure a restoration to the favour and fellowship of God. We become the sons of God by faith in Jesus Christ. (Gal. iii. 26.) No one can read the eighth chapter of the Epistle to the Romans without being convinced that in Paul's apprehension a justified believer is something more than a pardoned criminal. He is a man whose salvation is secure because he is free from the law and all its demands : because the righteousness of the law (*i. e.*, all its righteous requirements) has been fulfilled in him; because thereby he is so united to Christ as to become a partaker of his life; because no one can lay anything to the charge of those for whom Christ died and whom God has justified; and because such believers being justified are revealed as the objects of the mysterious, immutable, and infinite love of God.

Again, justification includes or conveys a title to eternal life. Pardon is purely negative. It simply removes a penalty. It confers no title to benefits not previously enjoyed. Eternal life, however, is suspended on the positive condition of perfect obedience. The merely pardoned sinner has no such obedience. He is destitute of what, by the immutable principles of the divine government, is the indispensable condition of eternal life. He has no title to the inheritance promised to the righteous. This is not the condition of the believer. The merit of Christ is entitled to the reward. And the believer, being partaker of that merit, shares in that title. This is constantly recognized in the Scriptures. By faith in Christ we become the sons of God. But sonship involves heirship, and heirship involves a title to the inheritance. "If children, then heirs; heirs of God, and joint heirs with Christ." (Rom. viii. 17.) This is the doctrine taught in Romans v. 12–21. For the offence of one, judgment passed on all men to condemnation. For the righteousness of one, the sentence of justification of life has passed on all; that is, of a justification which entitles to life. As the sin of Adam was the judicial ground of our condemnation (*i. e.*, was the ground on which justice demanded condemnation), so the righteousness of Christ is the judicial ground of justification. That is, it is the ground on which the life promised to the righteous should in justice be granted to the believer. The Church in all ages has recognized this truth. Believers have always felt that they had a title to eternal life. For this they have praised God in the loftiest strains. They have ever regarded it as intuitively true that heaven must be merited. The only question was, Whether that merit was in them or in Christ. Being in Christ, it was a free gift to them; and thus righteousness and peace kissed each other. Grace and justice unite in placing the crown of righteousness on the believer's head.

It is no less certain that the consequences attributed to justification do not flow from the infusion of righteousness. The amount of holiness possessed by the believer does not give him peace. Even perfect holiness would not remove guilt. Repentance does not atone for the crime of murder. It does not still the murderer's conscience ; nor does it satisfy the sense of justice in the public mind. It is the πρῶτον ψεῦδος of Romanism, and of every theory of subjective justification, that they make nothing of guilt, or reduce it to a minimum. If there were no guilt, then infusion of righteousness would be all that is necessary for salvation. But if there be justice in God then no amount of holiness can atone for sin, and justification cannot consist in making the sinner holy. Besides this, even admitting that the past could be ignored, that the guilt which burdens the soul could be overlooked or so easily removed, subjective righteousness, or holiness, is so imperfect that it could never give the believer peace. Let the holiest of men look within himself and say whether what he sees there satisfies his own conscience. If not, how can it satisfy God. He is greater than our hearts, and knoweth all things. No man, therefore, can have peace with God founded on what he is or on what he does. Romanists admit that nothing short of perfect holiness justifies or gives peace to the soul. In answer to the Protestant argument founded on that admission, Bellarmin says : [1] " Hoc argumentum, si quid probat, probat justitiam actualem non esse perfectam : non autem probat, justitiam habitualem, qua formaliter justi sumus, ... non esse ita perfectam, ut absolute, simpliciter, et proprie justi nominemur, et simus. Non enim formaliter justi sumus opere nostro, sed opere Dei, qui simul maculas peccatorum tergit, et habitum fidei, spei, et caritatis infundit. Dei autem perfecta sunt opera. . . . . Unde parvuli baptizati, vere justi sunt, quamvis nihil operis fecerint." Again, " Justitia enim actualis, quamvis aliquo modo sit imperfecta, propter admixtionem venalium delictorum, et egeat quotidiana remissione peccati, tamen non propterea desinit esse vera justitia, et suo etiam quodam modo perfecta." No provision is made in this system for guilt. If the soul is made holy by the infusion of habits, or principles, of grace, it is just in the sight of God. No guilt or desert of punishment remains. " Reatus," says Bellarmin,[2] . . . . " est relatio," but if the thing of which it is a relation be taken away, where is the relation. It is impossible that such a view of justification can give peace. It makes no provision for the satisfaction of justice, and places all our hopes upon what is within, which our conscience testifies cannot meet the just requirements of God.

Neither can the theory of subjective justification account for reconciliation with God, and for the same reasons. What is in-

---

[1] De Justificatione, ii. 14 ; Disputationes, edit. Paris, 1608, vol. iv. p. 819, a, b.
[2] De Amissione Gratiæ et Statu Peccati, v. 7 ; Ibid. p. 287.

fused, the degree of holiness imparted, does not render us the objects of divine complacency and love. His love to us is of the nature of grace ; love for the unlovely. We are reconciled to God by the death of his Son. That removes the obstacle arising from justice to the outflow toward us of the mysterious, unmerited love of God. We are accepted in the beloved. We are not in ourselves fit for fellowship with God. And if driven to depend on what is within, on our subjective righteousness, instead of peace we should have despair.

Again, justification according to the Scriptures gives a title to eternal life. For this our own righteousness is utterly inadequate. So far from anything in us being meritorious, or entitled to reward, the inward state and the exercises of the holiest of men, come so far short of perfection as to merit condemnation. In us there is no good thing. When we would do good, evil is present with us. There is ever a law in our members warring against the law of the mind. Indwelling sin remains. It forced even Paul to cry out, " O wretched man that I am ! who shall deliver me from the body of this death." (Rom. vii. 24.) " Nullum unquam exstitisse pii hominis opus, quod, si severo Dei judicio examinaretur, non esset damnabile." [1] Ignoring this plain truth of Scripture and of Christian experience expressing itself in daily and hourly confession, humiliation, and prayers for forgiveness, the doctrine of subjective justification assumes that there is no sin in the believer, or no sin which merits the condemnation of God, but on the contrary that there is in him what merits eternal life. The Romanists make a distinction between a first and second justification. The first they admit to be gratuitous, and to be founded on the merit of Christ, or rather, to be gratuitously bestowed for Christ's sake. This consists in the infusion of habitual grace (i. e., regeneration). This justifies in rendering the soul subjectively just or holy. The second justification is not a matter of grace. It is founded on the merit of good works, the fruits of regeneration. But if these fruits are, as our consciousness testifies, defiled by sin, how can they merit eternal life ? How can they cancel the handwriting which is against us ? How can they be the ground of Paul's confident challenge, " Who shall lay anything to the charge of God's elect ? " It is not what is within us, but what is without us ; not what we are or do, but what Christ is and has done, that is the ground of confidence and of our title to eternal life. This is the admitted doctrine of the

---

[1] Calvin, *Institutio*, III. xiv. 11; edit. Berlin, 1834, part ii. p. 38.

Protestant Reformation. " Apud theologos Augustanæ confessionis extra controversiam positum est," says the " Form of Concord," " totam justitiam nostram extra nos, et extra omnium hominum merita, opera, virtutes atque dignitatem quærendam, eamque in solo Domino nostro, Jesu Christo consistere." As high as the heavens are above the earth, so high is a hope founded on the work of Christ for us, above a hope founded on the merit of anything wrought in us. Calvin teaches the same doctrine as Luther.[2] He quotes Lombard as saying that our justification in Christ may be interpreted in two ways : " Primum, mors Christi nos justificat, dum per eam excitatur caritas in cordibus nostris, qua justi efficimur : deinde quod per eandem exstinctum est peccatum ; quo nos captivos distinebat diabolus, ut jam non habeat unde nos damnet." To which Calvin replies, " Scriptura autem, quem de fidei justitia loquitur, longe alio nos ducit : nempe ut ab intuitu operum nostrorum aversi, in Dei misericordiam ac Christi perfectionem, tantum respiciamus. . . . . Hic est fidei sensus, per quem peccator in possessionem venit suæ salutis, dum ex Evangelii doctrina agnoscit Deo se reconciliatum : quod intercedente Christi justitia, impetrata peccatorum remissione, justificatus sit : et quanquam Spiritu Dei regeneratus, non in bonis operibus, quibus incumbit, sed sola Christi justitia repositam sibi perpetuam justitiam cogitat."

That justification is not merely pardon, and that it is not the infusion of righteousness whereby the sinner is made inherently just or holy, but a judgment on the part of God that the demands of the law in regard to the believer are satisfied, and that he has a right to a righteousness which entitles him to eternal life, has been argued, (1.) From the uniform usage of Scripture both in the Old and New Testament. (2.) From the constant opposition between justification and condemnation. (3.) From equivalent forms of expression. (4.) From the whole design and drift of the Apostle's argument in his Epistles to the Romans and to the Galatians. (5.) From the ground of justification, namely, the righteousness of Christ. (6.) From the immutability of the law and the justice of God. (7.) From the nature of our union with Christ. (8.) From the fact that peace, reconciliation with God, and a title to eternal life which according to Scripture, are the consequences of justification, do not flow either from mere pardon or from subjective righteousness, or from sanctification. That

[1] *Solida Declaratio*, III. 55; Hase, *Libri Symbolici*, 3d edit. Leipzig, 1846, p. 695.
[2] *Institutio*, III. xi. 15, 16; *ut supra*, p. 17.

this is the doctrine of Protestants, both Lutheran and Reformed, cannot with any show of reason be disputed.

Calvin's Doctrine.

It is true, indeed, that by the earlier Reformers, and especially by Calvin, justification is often said to consist in the pardon of sin. But that that was not intended as a denial of the judicial character of justification, or as excluding the imputation of the righteousness of Christ by which the believer is counted just in the sight of the law, is obvious,—

1. From the nature of the controversy in which those Reformers were engaged. The question between them and the Romanists was, Does justification consist in the act of God making the sinner inherently just or holy? or, Does it express the judgment of God by which the believer is pronounced just? What Calvin denied was that justification is a making holy. What he affirmed was that it was delivering the believer from the condemnation of the law and introducing him into a state of favour with God. The Romanists expressed their doctrine by saying that justification consists in the remission of sin and the infusion of charity or righteousness. But by the remission of sin they meant the removal of sin; the putting off the old man. In other words, justification with them consisted (to use the scholastic language then in vogue) in the removal of the habits of sin and the infusion of habits of grace. In those justified, therefore, there was no sin, and, therefore, nothing to punish. Pardon, therefore, followed as a necessary consequence. It was a mere accessary. This view of the matter makes nothing of guilt; nothing of the demands of justice. Calvin therefore, insisted that besides the subjective renovation connected with the sinner's conversion, his justification concerned the removal of guilt, the satisfaction of justice, which in the order of nature, although not of time, must precede the communication of the life of God to the soul. That Calvin did not differ from the other Reformers and the whole body of the Reformed Church on this subject appears from his own explicit declarations, and from the perfectly unambiguous statements of the Confessions to which he gave his assent. Thus he says,[1] " Porro ne impingamus in ipso limine (quod fieret si de re incognita disputationem ingrediremur) primum explicemus quid sibi velint istæ loquutiones, Hominem coram Deo justificari, Fide justificari, vel operibus. Justificari coram Deo dicitur qui judicio

---

[1] *Institutio*, III. xi. 2; *ut supra*, p. 6.

Dei et censetur justus, et acceptus est ob suam justitiam : siqui
dem ut Deo abominabilis est iniquitas, ita nec peccator in ejus oculis potest invenire gratiam, quatenus est peccator, et quamdiu
talis censetur. Proinde ubicunque peccatum est, illic etiam se
profert ira et ultio Dei. Justificatur autem qui non loco peccatoris, sed justi habetur, eoque nomine consistit coram Dei tribunali,
ubi peccatores omnes corruunt. Quemadmodum si reus innocens
ad tribunal æqui judicis adducatur, ubi secundum innocentiam
ejus judicatum fuerit, justificatus apud judicem dicitur : sic apud
Deum justificatur, qui numero peccatorum exemptus, Deum habet suæ justitiæ testem et assertorem. Justificari, ergo, operibus
ea ratione dicetur, in cujus vita reperietur ea puritas ac sanctitas
quæ testimonium justitiæ apud Dei thronum mereatur : seu qui
operum suorum integritate respondere et satisfacere illius judicio
queat. Contra, justificabitur ille fide, qui operum justitia ex-
clusus, Christi justitiam per fidem apprehendit, qua vestitus in
Dei conspectu non ut peccator, sed tanquam justus apparet. Ita
nos justificationem simpliciter interpretamur acceptionem, qua
nos Deus in gratiam receptos pro justos habet. Eamque in peccatorum remissione ac justitiæ Christi imputatione positam esse
dicimus."

This passage is decisive as to the views of Calvin ; for it is pro-
fessedly a formal statement of the " Status Quæstionis " given
with the utmost clearness and precision. Justification consists
" in the remission of sins and the imputation of the righteousness
of Christ." " He is justified in the sight of God, who is taken
from the class of sinners, and has God for the witness and as-
sertor of his righteousness."

§ 3. *Works not the Ground of Justification.*

In reference to men since the fall the assertion is so explicit and
so often repeated, that justification is not of works, that that proposition has never been called in question by any one professing to
receive the Scriptures as the word of God. It being expressly
asserted that the whole world is guilty before God, that by the
works of the law no flesh living can be justified, the only question open for discussion is, What is meant by works of the law?

To this question the following answers have been given, First,
that by works of the law are meant works prescribed in the Jewish law. It is assumed that as Paul's controversy was with those
who taught that unless men were circumcised and kept the law
of Moses, they could not be saved (Acts xv. 1, 24), all he intended

to teach was the reverse of that proposition. He is to be understood as saying that the observance of Jewish rites and ceremonies is not essential to salvation ; that men are not made righteous or good by external ceremonial works, but by works morally
good. This is the ground taken by Pelagians and by most of the
modern Rationalists. It is only a modification of this view that
men are not justified, that is, that their character before God is
not determined so much by their particular acts or works, as by
their general disposition and controlling principles. To be justified by faith, therefore, is to be justified on the ground of our
trust, or pious confidence in God and truth. Thus Wegscheider [1]
says, " Homines non singulis quibusdam recte factis operibusque
operatis, nec propter meritum quoddam iis attribuendum, sed sola
vera fide, *i. e.*, animo ad Christi exemplum ejusdemque præcepta
composito et ad Deum et sanctissimum et benignissimum converso, ita, ut omnia cogitata et facta ad Deum ejusque voluntatem
sanctissimam pie referant, Deo vere probantur et benevolentiæ
Dei confisi spe beatitatis futuræ pro dignitate ipsorum morali
iis concedendæ certissima imbuuntur. " Steudlin,[2] expresses the
same view. " All true reformation, every good act," he says,
" must spring from faith, provided we understand by faith the
conviction that something is right, a conviction of general moral
and religious principles." Kant says that Christ in a religious
aspect is the ideal of humanity. When a man so regards him
and endeavours to conform his heart and life to that ideal, he is
justified by faith.[3] According to all these views, mere ceremonial works are excluded, and the ground of justification is made
to be our own natural moral character and conduct.

Romish Doctrine.

Secondly. The doctrine of Romanists on this subject is much
higher. Romanism retains the supernatural element of Christianity throughout. Indeed it is a matter of devout thankfulness
to God that underneath the numerous grievous and destructive
errors of the Romish Church, the great truths of the Gospel are
preserved. The Trinity, the true divinity of Christ, the true
doctrine concerning his person as God and man in two distinct
natures and one person forever ; salvation through his blood, regeneration and sanctification through the almighty power of the

---

[1] *Institutiones Theologiæ*, III. iii. § 155, 5th edit. Halle, 1826, p. 476.
[2] *Dogmatik*, 2ter Theil, § 134, B, g, h; Gottingen, 1800, pp. 783, 784.
[3] See Strauss, *Dogmatik*, Tübingen and Stuttgart, 1841, vol. ii. pp. 493, 494.

Spirit, the resurrection of the body, and eternal life, are doctrines
on which the people of God in that communion live, and which
have produced such saintly men as St. Bernard, Fénélon, and
doubtless thousands of others who are of the number of God's
elect.   Every true worshipper of Christ must in his heart recognize as a Christian brother, wherever he may be found, any one
who loves, worships, and trusts the Lord Jesus Christ as God
manifest in the flesh and the only Saviour of men.   On the matter of justification the Romish theologians have marred and de-
faced the truth as they have almost all other doctrines pertaining
to the mode in which the merits of Christ are made available
to our salvation.   They admit, indeed, that there is no good in
fallen man ; that he can merit nothing and claim nothing on the
ground of anything he is or can do of himself.   He is by nature
dead in sin ; and until made partaker of a new life by the supernatural power of the Holy Ghost, he can do nothing but sin.   For
Christ's sake, and only through his merits, as a matter of grace,
this new life is imparted to the soul in regeneration (*i. e.*, as Romanists teach, in baptism).   As life expels death ; as light banishes darkness, so the entrance of this new divine life into the soul
expels sin (*i. e.*, sinful habits), and brings forth the fruits of righteousness.   Works done after regeneration have real merit, " meritum condigni," and are the ground of the second justification ;
the first justification consisting in making the soul inherently just
by the infusion of righteousness.   According to this view, we are
not justified by works done before regeneration, but we are justified for gracious works, *i. e.*, for works which spring from the principle of divine life infused into the heart.   The whole ground of
our acceptance with God is thus made to be what we are and what
we do.

Remonstrant Doctrine.

Thirdly.   According to the Remonstrants or Arminians the
works which are excluded from our justification are works of the
law as distinguished from works of the Gospel.   In the covenant
made with Adam God demanded perfect obedience as the condition of life.   For Christ's sake, God in the Gospel has entered into
a new covenant with men, promising them salvation on the condition of evangelical obedience.   This is expressed in different forms.
Sometimes it is said that we are justified on account of faith.
Faith is accepted in place of that perfect righteousness demanded
by the Adamic law.   But by faith is not meant the act of receiving and resting upon Christ alone for salvation.   It is regarded

as a permanent and controlling state of mind. And therefore it is often said that we are justified by a "fides obsequiosa," an obedient faith ; a faith which includes obedience. At other times, it is said that we are justified by evangelical obedience, *i.e.*, that kind and measure of obedience which the Gospel requires, and which men since the fall, in the proper use of " sufficient grace " granted to all men, are able to render. Limborch says, "Sciendum, quando dicimus, nos fide justificari, nos non excludere opera, quæ fides exigit et tanquam fœcunda mater producit ; sed ea includere." And again, " Est itaque [fides] talis actus, qui, licet in se spectatus perfectus nequaquam sit, sed in multis deficiens, tamen a Deo, gratiosa et liberrima voluntate, pro pleno et perfecto acceptatur, et propter quem Deus homini gratiose remissionem peccatorum et vitæ æternæ premium conferre vult." Again,[1] God, he says, demands, " obedientiam fidei, hoc est, non rigidam et ab omnibus æqualem, prout exigebat lex ; sed tantam, quantam fides, id est, certa de divinis promissionibus persuasio, in unoquoque efficere potest." Therefore justification, he says,[2] " Est gratiosa æstimatio, seu potius acceptatio justitiæ nostræ imperfectæ pro perfecta, propter Jesum Christum."

Protestant Doctrine.

Fourthly. According to the doctrine of the Lutherans and Reformed, the works excluded from the ground of our justification are not only ritual or ceremonial works, nor merely works done before regeneration, nor the perfect obedience required by the law given to Adam, but works of all kinds, everything done by us or wrought in us. That this is the doctrine of the Bible is plain, —

1. Because the language of Scripture is unlimited. The declaration is, that we are not justified " by works." No specific kind of works is designated to the exclusion of all others. But it is " works ; " what we do ; anything and everything we do. It is, therefore, without authority that any man limits these general declarations to any particular class of works.

2. The word law is used in a comprehensive sense. It includes all revelations of the will of God as the rule of man's obedience ; and, therefore, by " works of the law " must be intended all kinds of works. As νόμος means that which binds, it is used for the law of nature, or the law written on the heart (Rom. ii. 14),

---

[1] *Theologia Christiana*, VI. iv. 32, 31, 37 ; edit. Amsterdam, 1725, pp. 705, b, a, 706, a.
[2] Limborch, VI. iv. 18 ; *ut supra*, p. 703, a.

for the Decalogue, for the law of Moses, for the whole of the Old Testament Scriptures. (Rom. iii. 19.) Sometimes one, and sometimes another of these aspects of the law is specially referred to. Paul assures the Jews that they could not be justified by the works of the law, which was especially binding on them. He assures the Gentiles that they could not be justified by the law written on their hearts. He assures believers under the Gospel that they cannot be justified by works of the law binding on them. The reason given includes all possible works. That reason is, that all human obedience is imperfect; all men are sinners : and the law demands perfect obedience. (Gal. iii. 10.) Therefore, it is that " by the deeds of the law there shall no flesh be justified." (Rom. iii. 20.)

3. The law of which Paul speaks is the law which says, " Thou shalt not covet " (Rom. vii. 7) ; the law which is spiritual (ver. 14) ; which is " holy, and just, and good " (ver. 12) ; the law of which the great command is, Thou shalt love the Lord thy God with all thy heart, and thy neighbour as thyself. Besides, what are called works of the law are in Titus iii. 5 called " works of righteousness." Higher works than these there cannot be. The Apostle repudiates any ground of confidence in his " own righteousness " (Phil. iii. 9), *i. e.*, own excellence, whether habitual or actual. He censures the Jews because they went about to establish their own righteousness, and would not submit to the righteousness of God. (Rom. x. 3.) From these and many similar passages it is clear that it is not any one or more specific kinds of work which are excluded from the ground of justification, but all works, all personal excellence of every kind.

4. This is still further evident from the contrast constantly presented between faith and works. We are not justified by works, but by faith in Jesus Christ. (Gal. ii. 16, and often elsewhere.) It is not one kind of works as opposed to another ; legal as opposed to evangelical ; natural as opposed to gracious ; moral as opposed to ritual ; but works of every kind as opposed to faith.

5. The same is evident from what is taught of the gratuitous nature of our justification. Grace and works are antithetical. " To him that worketh is the reward not reckoned of grace, but of debt." (Rom. iv. 4.) " If by grace, then is it no more of works : otherwise grace is no more grace." (Rom. xi. 6.) Grace of necessity excludes works of every kind, and more especially those of the highest kind, which might have some show of merit.

But merit of any degree is of necessity excluded, if our salvation be by grace.

6. When the positive ground of justification is stated, it is always declared to be not anything done by us or wrought in us, but what was done for us. It is ever represented as something external to ourselves. We are justified by the blood of Christ (Rom. v. 9); by his obedience (Rom. v. 19); by his righteousness (ver. 18). This is involved in the whole method of salvation. Christ saves us as a priest; but a priest does not save by making those who come to him good. He does not work in them, but for them. Christ saves us by a sacrifice; but a sacrifice is effectual, not because of its subjective effect upon the offerer, but as an expiation, or satisfaction to justice. Christ is our Redeemer; he gave himself as a ransom for many. But a ransom does not infuse righteousness. It is the payment of a price. It is the satisfaction of the claims of the captor upon the captive. The whole plan of salvation, therefore, as presented in the Bible and as it is the life of the Church, is changed, if the ground of our acceptance with God be transferred from what Christ has done for us, to what is wrought in us or done by us. The Romish theologians do not agree exactly as to whether habitual or actual righteousness is the ground of justification. Bellarmin says it is the former.[1] He says, " Solam esse habitualem justitiam, per quam formaliter justi nominamur, et sumus: justitiam vero actualem, id est, opera vere justa justificare quidem, ut sanctus Jacobus loquitur, cum ait cap. 2 ex operibus hominem justificari, sed meritorie, non formaliter." This he says is clearly the doctrine of the Council of Trent, which teaches,[2] " Causam formalem justificationis esse justitiam, sive caritatem, quam Deus unicuique propriam infundit, secundum mensuram dispositionum, et quæ in cordibus justificatorum inhæret." This follows also, he argues, from the fact that the sacraments justify,[3] " per modum instrumenti ad infusionem justitiæ habitualis." This, however, only amounts to the distinction, already referred to, between the first and second justification. The infusion of righteousness renders the soul inherently righteous; then good works merit salvation. The one is the formal, the other the meritorious cause of the sinner's justification. But according to the Scriptures, both habitual and actual righteousness, both inherent grace and its fruits are excluded from any share in the ground of our justification.

[1] De Justificatione, II. 15; Disputationes, edit. Paris, 1608, vol. iv. p. 820, a.
[2] See Session vi. cap. 7. [3] Bellarmin, ut supra, p. 820, b.

7. This still further and most decisively appears from the grand objection to his doctrine which Paul was constantly called upon to answer. That objection was, that if our personal goodness or moral excellence is not the ground of our acceptance with God, then all necessity of being good is denied, and all motive to good works is removed. We may continue in sin that grace may abound. This objection has been reiterated a thousand times since it was urged against the Apostles. It seems so unreasonable and so demoralizing to say as Paul says, Romans iii. 22, that so far as justification is concerned there is no difference between Jew and Gentile; between a worshipper of the true God and a worshipper of demons; between the greatest sinner and the most moral man in the world, that men have ever felt that they were doing God service in denouncing this doctrine as a soul-destroying heresy. Had Paul taught that men are justified for their good moral works as the Pelagians and Rationalists say; or for their evangelical obedience as the Remonstrants say; or for their inherent righteousness and subsequent good works as the Romanists say, there would have been no room for this formidable objection. Or, if through any misapprehension of his teaching, the objection had been urged, how easy had it been for the Apostle to set it aside. How obvious would have been the answer, ' I do not deny that really good works are the ground of our acceptance with God. I only say that ritual works have no worth in his sight, that He looks on the heart; or, that works done before regeneration have no real excellence or merit; or, that God is more lenient now than in his dealing with Adam; that He does not demand perfect obedience, but accepts our imperfect, well-meant endeavours to keep his holy commandments.' How reasonable and satisfactory would such an answer have been. Paul, however, does not make it. He adheres to his doctrine, that our own personal moral excellence has nothing to do with our justification; that God justifies the ungodly, that He receives the chief of sinners. He answers the objection indeed, and answers it effectually; but his answer supposes him to teach just what Protestants teach, that we are justified without works, not for our own righteousness, but gratuitously, without money and without price, solely on the ground of what Christ has done for us. His answer is, that so far from its being true that we must be good before we can be justified, we must be justified before we can be good; that so long as we are under the curse of the law we bring forth fruit unto death; that it is

not until reconciled unto God by the death of his Son, that we bring forth fruit unto righteousness ; that when justified by the righteousness of Christ, we are made partakers of his Spirit; being justified we are sanctified ; that union with Christ by faith secures not only the imputation of his righteousness to our justification, but the participation of his life unto our sanctification ; so that as surely as He lives and lives unto God, so they that believe on Him shall live unto God ; and that none are partakers of the merit of his death who do not become partakers of the power of his life. We do not, therefore, he says, make void the law of God. Yea, we establish the law. We teach the only true way to become holy ; although that way appears foolishness unto the wise of this world, whose wisdom is folly in the sight of God.

§ 4. *The Righteousness of Christ the Ground of Justification.*

The imperative question remains, How shall a man be just with God ? If our moral excellence be not the ground on which God pronounces us just, what is that ground ? The grand reason why such different answers are given to this question is, that it is understood in different senses. The Scriptural and Protestant answer is absurd, if the question means what Romanists and others understand it to mean. If " just " means good, *i. e.*, if the word be taken in its moral, and not in its judicial sense, then it is absurd to say that a man can be good with the goodness of another ; or to say that God can pronounce a man to be good who is not good. Bellarmin says an Ethiopian clothed in a white garment is not white. Curcellæus, the Remonstrant, says, " A man can no more be just with the justice of another, than he can be white with the whiteness of another." Moehler [1] says, it is impossible that anything should appear to God other than it really is ; that an unjust man should appear to him, or be pronounced by him just. All this is true in the sense intended by these writers, " The judgment of God is according to truth." (Rom. ii. 2.) Every man is truly just whom He justifies or declares to be just. It is in vain to dispute until the " status quæstionis " be clearly determined. The word δίκαιος, " righteous," or " just," has two distinct senses, as above stated. It has a moral, and also a legal, forensic, or judicial sense. It sometimes expresses moral character, sometimes simply a relation to law and justice. In one sense to pronounce a man just, is to declare that he is morally good. In another sense, it is to declare that the

---

[1] *Symbolik*, § 14, 6th ed. Mainz, 1843, p. 139.

claims of justice against him are satisfied, and that he is entitled to the reward promised to the righteous. When God justifies the ungodly, he does not declare that he is godly, but that his sins are expiated, and that he has a title founded in justice to eternal life. In this there is no contradiction and no absurdity. If a man under attainder appear before the proper tribunal, and show cause why the attainder should in justice be reversed, and he be declared entitled to his rank, titles, and estates, a decision in his favour would be a justification. It would declare him just in the eye of the law, but it would declare nothing and effect nothing as to his moral character. In the like manner, when the sinner stands at the bar of God, he can show good reason why he cannot be justly condemned, and why he should be declared entitled to eternal life. Now the question is, " On what ground can God pronounce a sinner just in this legal or forensic sense ? " It has been shown that to justify, according to uniform Scriptural usage, is to pronounce just in the sense stated, that it is not merely to pardon, and that it is not to render inherently righteous or holy. It has also been shown to be the doctrine of Scripture, what indeed is intuitively true to the conscience, that our moral excellence, habitual or actual, is not and cannot be the ground of any such judicial declaration. What then is the ground ? The Bible and the people of God, with one voice answer, " The righteousness of Christ." The ambiguity of words, the speculations of theologians, and misapprehensions, may cause many of the people of God to deny in words that such is the proper answer, but it is nevertheless the answer rendered by every believer's heart. He relies for his acceptance with God, not on himself but on Christ, not on what he is or has done, but on what Christ is and has done for him.

Meaning of the Terms.

By the righteousness of Christ is meant all he became, did, and suffered to satisfy the demands of divine justice, and merit for his people the forgiveness of sin and the gift of eternal life. The righteousness of Christ is commonly represented as including his active and passive obedience. This distinction is, as to the idea, Scriptural. The Bible does teach that Christ obeyed the law in all its precepts, and that he endured its penalty, and that this was done in such sense for his people that they are said to have done it. They died in Him. They were crucified with Him. They were delivered from the curse of the law by his being made a curse for them. He was made under the law that he

might redeem those who were under the law. We are freed
from the law by the body of Christ. He was made sin that we
might be made the righteousness of God in Him. He is the end
of the law for righteousness to all them that believe. It is by
his obedience that many are made righteous. (Rom. v. 19.)
We obeyed in Him, according to the teaching of the Apostle, in
Romans v. 12–21, in the same sense in which we sinned in Adam.
The active and passive obedience of Christ, however, are only different phases or aspects of the same thing. He obeyed in suffering. His highest acts of obedience were rendered in the garden,
and upon the cross. Hence this distinction is not so presented in
Scripture as though the obedience of Christ answered one purpose, and his sufferings another and a distinct purpose. We are
justified by his blood. We are reconciled unto God by his death.
We are freed from all the demands of the law by his body (Rom.
vii. 4), and we are freed from the law by his being made under
it and obeying it in our stead. (Gal. iv. 4, 5.) Thus the same
effect is ascribed to the death or sufferings of Christ, and to his
obedience, because both are forms or parts of his obedience or
righteousness by which we are justified. In other words the obedience of Christ includes all He did in satisfying the demands of
the law.

The Righteousness of Christ is the Righteousness of God.

The righteousness of Christ on the ground of which the believer
is justified is the righteousness of God. It is so designated in
Scripture not only because it was provided and is accepted by
Him; it is not only the righteousness which avails before God,
but it is the righteousness of a divine person; of God manifest
in the flesh. God purchased the Church with his own blood.
(Acts xx. 28.) It was the Lord of glory who was crucified.
(1 Cor. ii. 8.) He who was in the form of God and thought it
not robbery to be equal with God, became obedient unto death,
even the death of the cross. (Phil. ii. 6–8.) He who is the
brightness of the Father's glory, and the express image of his
person, who upholds all things by the word of his power; whom
angels worship; who is called God; who in the beginning laid
the foundations of the earth, and of whose hands the heavens are
the workmanship; who is eternal and immutable, has, the Apostle
teaches, by death destroyed him who has the power of death and
delivered those who through fear of death (*i. e.*, of the wrath of
God) were all their lifetime subject to bondage. (Heb. i., ii.)

He whom Thomas recognized and avowed to be his Lord and
God was the person into whose wounded side he thrust his hand.
He whom John says he saw, looked upon, and handled, he declares to be the true God and eternal life.   The soul, in which
personality resides, does not die when the man dies, yet it is the
soul that gives dignity to the man, and which renders his life of
unspeakably greater value in the sight of God and man, than the
life of any irrational creature.   So it was not the divine nature
in Christ in which his personality resides, the eternal Logos, that
died when Christ died.   Nevertheless the hypostatic union between the Logos and the human nature of Christ, makes it true
that the righteousness of Christ (his obedience and sufferings)
was the righteousness of God.   This is the reason why it can
avail before God for the salvation of the whole world.   This is
the reason why the believer, when arrayed in this righteousness,
need fear neither death nor hell.   This is the reason why Paul
challenges the universe to lay anything to the charge of God's
elect.

§ 5. *Imputation of Righteousness.*

The righteousness of Christ is imputed to the believer for his
justification.   The word impute is familiar and unambiguous.
To impute is to ascribe to, to reckon to, to lay to one's charge.
When we say we impute a good or bad motive to a man, or that
a good or evil action is imputed to him, no one misunderstands
our meaning.   Philemon had no doubt what Paul meant when he
told him to impute to him the debt of Onesimus.   " Let not the
king impute anything unto his servant."   (1 Sam. xxii. 15.)
" Let not my lord impute iniquity unto me."   (2 Sam. xix. 19.)
"Neither shall it be imputed unto him that offereth it."   (Lev.
vii. 18.)   " Blood shall be imputed unto that man; he hath shed
blood."   (Lev. xvii. 4.)   " Blessed is the man unto whom the
Lord imputeth not iniquity."   (Ps. xxxii. 2.)   " Unto whom
God imputeth righteousness without works."   (Rom. iv. 6.)
God is " in Christ not imputing their trespasses unto them."
(2 Cor. v. 19.)

The meaning of these and similar passages of Scripture has
never been disputed.   Every one understands them.   We use
the word impute in its simple admitted sense, when we say that
the righteousness of Christ is imputed to the believer for his justification.

It seems unnecessary to remark that this does not, and cannot
mean that the righteousness of Christ is infused into the believer,

or in any way so imparted to him as to change, or constitute his moral character. Imputation never changes the inward, subjective state of the person to whom the imputation is made. When sin is imputed to a man he is not made sinful ; when the zeal of Phinehas was imputed to him, he was not made zealous. When you impute theft to a man, you do not make him a thief. When you impute goodness to a man, you do not make him good. So when righteousness is imputed to the believer, he does not thereby become subjectively righteous. If the righteousness be adequate, and if the imputation be made on adequate grounds and by competent authority, the person to whom the imputation is made has the right to be treated as righteous. And, therefore, in the forensic, although not in the moral or subjective sense, the imputation of the righteousness of Christ does make the sinner righteous. That is, it gives him a right to the full pardon of all his sins and a claim in justice to eternal life.

That this is the simple and universally accepted view of the doctrine as held by all Protestants at the Reformation, and by them regarded as the corner-stone of the Gospel, has already been sufficiently proved by extracts from the Lutheran and Reformed Symbols, and has never been disputed by any candid or competent authority. This has continued to be the doctrine of both the great branches of the Protestant Church, so far as they pretend to adhere to their standards. Schmid[1] proves this by a whole catena of quotations so far as the Lutheran Church is concerned. Schweizer[2] does the same for the Reformed Church. A few citations, therefore, from authors of a recognized representative character will suffice as to this point. Turrettin with his characteristic precision says : " Cum dicimus Christi justitiam ad justificationem nobis imputari, et nos per justitiam illam imputatam justos esse coram Deo, et non per justitiam ullam quæ nobis inhæreat ; Nihil aliud volumus, quam obedientiam Christi Deo Patri nomine nostro præstitam, ita nobis a Deo donari, ut vere nostra censeatur, eamque esse unicam et solam illam justitiam propter quam, et cujus merito, absolvamur a reatu peccatorum nostrum. et jus ad vitam obtinemus ; nec ullam in nobis esse justitiam, aut ulla bona opera, quibus beneficia tanta promereamur, quæ ferre possint severum judicii divini examen, si Deus juxta legis suæ rigorem nobiscum agere vellet ; nihil nos illi posse opponere,

---

[1] *Die Dogmatik der evangelisch-lutherischen Kirche, dargestellt und aus den Quellen belegt,* 3d edit. Frankfort and Erlangen, 1853.

[2] *Die Glaubenslehre der evangelisch-reformirten Kirche dargestellt und aus den Quellen belegt,* Zürich, 1844, 1847.

nisi Christi meritum et satisfactionem, in qua sola, peccatorum
conscientia territi, tutum adversus iram divinam perfugium, et
animarum nostrarum pacem invenire possumus." [1]

On the following page he refers to Bellarmin,[2] who says, " Si
[Protestantes hoc] solum vellent, nobis imputari Christi merita,
quia [a Deo] nobis donata sunt, et possumus ea [Deo] Patri
offere pro peccatis nostris, quoniam Christus suscepit super se onus
satisfaciendi pro nobis, nosque Deo Patri reconciliandi, recta esset
eorum sententia." On this Turrettin remarks, " Atqui nihil aliud
volumus; Nam quod addit, nos velle ' ita imputari nobis Christi
justitiam, ut per eam formaliter justi nominemur et simus,' hoc
gratis et falso supponit, ex perversa et præpostera sua hypothesi
de justificatione morali. Sed quæritur, Ad quid imputatio ista
fiat ? An ad justificationem et vitam, ut nos pertendimus, An
vero tantum ad gratiæ internæ et justitiæ inhærentis infusionem,
ut illi volunt ; Id est, an ita imputentur et communicentur nobis
merita Christi, ut sint causa meritoria sola nostræ justificationis,
nec ulla alia detur justitia propter quam absolvamur in conspectu
Dei ; quod volumus ; An vero ita imputentur, ut sint conditiones
causæ formalis, id. justitiæ inhærentis, ut ea homo donari possit,
vel causæ extrinsecæ, quæ mereantur infusionem justitiæ, per
quam justificatur homo ; ut ita non meritum Christi proprie, sed
justitia inhærens per meritum Christi acquisita, sic causa propria
et vera, propter quam homo justificatur ; quod illi statuunt." It
may be remarked in passing that according to the Protestant doctrine there is properly no " formal cause " of justification. The
righteousness of Christ is the meritorious, but not the formal cause
of the sinner's being pronounced righteous. A formal cause is
that which constitutes the inherent, subjective nature of a person
or thing. The formal cause of a man's being good, is goodness ;
of his being holy, holiness ; of his being wicked, wickedness. The
formal cause of a rose's being red, is redness ; and of a wall's being
white, is whiteness. As we are not rendered inherently righteous
by the righteousness of Christ, it is hardly correct to say that his
righteousness is the formal cause of our being righteous. Owen,
and other eminent writers do indeed often use the expression referred to, but they take the word " formal " out of its ordinary
scholastic sense.

Campegius Vitringa [3] says : " Tenendum est certissimum hoc
fundamentum, quod justificare sit vocabulum forense, notetque in

----

[1] *Institutio*, loc. xvi. iii. 9, edit. Edinburgh, 1847, vol. ii. p. 570.

[2] *De Justificatione*, ii. 7; *Disputationes*, Paris, 1608, p. 801, b.

[3] *Doctrina Christianæ Religionis*, iii. xvi. 2; Leyden, 1764. vol. iii. p 254, ff.

Scriptura actum judicis, quo causam alicujus in judicio justam esse declarat ; sive eum a crimine, cujus postulatus est, absolvat (quæ est genuina, et maxime propria vocis significatio), sive etiam jus ad hanc, vel illam rem ei sententia addicat, et adjudicet."

"17. Per justificationem peccatoris intelligimus actum Dei Patris, ut judicis, quo peccatorem credentem, natura filium iræ, neque ullum jus ex se habentem bona cœlestia petendi, declarat immunem esse ab omni reatu, et condemnatione, adoptat in filium, et in eum ex gratia confert jus ad suam communionem, cum salute æterna, bonisque omnibus cum ea conjunctis, postulandi."

" 27. Teneamus nullam carnem in se posse reperire et ex se producere causam, et fundamentum justificationis. 29. Quærendum igitur id, propter quod peccator justificatur, extra peccatorem in obedientia Filii Dei, quam præstitit Patri in humana natura ad mortem, imo ad mortem crucis, et ad quam præstandam se obstrinxerat in sponsione. (Rom. v. 19.)" "32. Hæc [obedientia] imputatur peccatori a Deo judice ex gratia juxta jus sponsionis, de quo ante dictum."

Owen in his elaborate work on justification,[1] proves that the word to justify, "whether the act of God towards men, or of men towards God, or of men among themselves, or of one towards another, be expressed thereby, is always used in a 'forensic' sense, and does not denote a physical operation, transfusion, or transmutation." He thus winds up the discussion : " Wherefore as condemnation is not the infusing of a habit of wickedness into him that is condemned, nor the making of him to be inherently wicked, who was before righteous, but the passing a sentence upon a man with respect to his wickedness ; no more is justification the change of a person from inherent unrighteousness to righteousness, by the infusion of a principle of grace, but a sentential declaration of him to be righteous." [2]

The ground of this justification in the case of the believing sinner is the imputation of the righteousness of Christ. This is set forth at length.[3] " The judgment of the Reformed Churches herein," he says, " is known to all and must be confessed, unless we intend by vain cavils to increase and perpetuate contentions. Especially the Church of England is in her doctrine express as to the imputation of the righteousness of Christ, both active and passive, as it is usually distinguished. This has been of late so fully manifested out of her authentic writings, that is, the ' Ar-

---

[1] *Justification*, chap. 4, edit. Philadelphia, 1841, p. 144.
[2] *Ibid*. p. 154.   [3] *Ibid*. chap. 7, p. 187.

ticles of Religion ' and ' Books of Homilies,' and other writings publicly authorized, that it is altogether needless to give any further demonstration of it."

President Edwards in his sermon on justification [1] sets forth the Protestant doctrine in all its fulness. " To suppose," he says, " that a man is justified by his own virtue or obedience, derogates from the honour of the Mediator, and ascribes that to man's virtue that belongs only to the righteousness of Christ. It puts man in Christ's stead, and makes him his own saviour, in a respect in which Christ only is the Saviour : and so it is a doctrine contrary to the nature and design of the Gospel, which is to abase man, and to ascribe all the glory of our salvation to Christ the Redeemer. It is inconsistent with the doctrine of the imputation of Christ's righteousness, which is a gospel doctrine. Here I would (1.) Explain what we mean by the imputation of Christ's righteousness. (2.) Prove the thing intended by it to be true. (3.) Show that this doctrine is utterly inconsistent with the doctrine of our being justified by our own virtue or sincere obedience.

" First. I would explain what we mean by the imputation of Christ's righteousness. Sometimes the expression is taken by our divines in a larger sense, for the imputation of all that Christ did and suffered for our redemption, whereby we are free from guilt, and stand righteous in the sight of God ; and so implies the imputation both of Christ's satisfaction and obedience. But here I intend it in a stricter sense, for the imputation of that righteousness or moral goodness that consists in the obedience of Christ. And by that righteousness being imputed to us, is meant no other than this, that that righteousness of Christ is accepted for us, and admitted instead of that perfect inherent righteousness that ought to be in ourselves : Christ's perfect obedience shall be reckoned to our account so that we shall have the benefit of it, as though we had performed it ourselves : and so we suppose that a title to eternal life is given us as the reward of this righteousness." In the same connection, he asks, " Why is there any more absurdity in supposing that Christ's obedience is imputed to us, than that his satisfaction is imputed ? If Christ has suffered the penalty of the law for us, and in our stead, then it will follow that his suffering that penalty is imputed to us, *i. e.*, that it is accepted for us, and in our stead, and is reckoned to our account, as though we had suffered it. But why may not his obeying the law of God be as rationally reckoned to our account,

[1] Serm IV. *Works*, edit. N. Y. 1868, vol. iv. pp. 91, 92.

as his suffering the penalty of the law." He then goes on to argue that there is the same necessity for the one as for the other.

Dr. Shedd says, " A second difference between the Anselmic and the Protestant soteriology is seen in the formal distinction of Christ's work into his active and his passive righteousness. By his passive righteousness is meant his expiatory sufferings, by which He satisfied the claims of justice, and by his active righteousness is meant his obedience to the law as a rule of life and conduct. It was contended by those who made this distinction, that the purpose of Christ as the vicarious substitute was to meet the entire demands of the law for the sinner. But the law requires present and perfect obedience, as well as satisfaction for past disobedience. The law is not completely fulfilled by the endurance of penalty only. It must also be obeyed. Christ both endured the penalty due to man for disobedience, and perfectly obeyed the law for him; so that He was a vicarious substitute in reference to both the precept and the penalty of the law. By his active obedience He obeyed the law, and by his passive obedience He endured the penalty. In this way his vicarious work is complete." [1]

The earlier Symbols of the Reformation do not make this distinction. So far as the Lutheran Church is concerned, it first appears in the "Form of Concord" (A. D. 1576). Its statement is as follows: " That righteousness which is imputed to faith, or to believers, of mere grace, is the obedience, suffering, and resurrection of Christ, by which He satisfied the law for us, and expiated our sins. For since Christ was not only man, but truly God and man in one undivided person, He was no more subject to the law than He was to suffering and death (if his person, merely, be taken into account), because He was the Lord of the law. Hence, not only that obedience to God his Father which He exhibited in his passion and death, but also that obedience which He exhibited in voluntarily subjecting Himself to the law and fulfilling it for our sakes, is imputed to us for righteousness, so that God on account of the total obedience which Christ accomplished (præstitit) for our sake before his heavenly Father, both in acting and in suffering, in life and in death, may remit our sins to us, regard us as good and righteous, and give us eternal salvation." [2] In this point the Reformed or Calvinistic standards agree.

It has already been remarked that the distinction between the

---

[1] *History of Christian Doctrine*, New York, 1863, vol. ii. p. 341.
[2] Hase, *Libri Symbolici*, 3d. edit., Leipz g, 1846, pp. 684, 685.

active and passive obedience of Christ is, in one view, unimportant. As Christ obeyed in suffering, his sufferings were as much a part of his obedience as his observance of the precepts of the law. The Scriptures do not expressly make this distinction, as they include everything that Christ did for our redemption under the term righteousness or obedience. The distinction becomes important only when it is denied that his moral obedience is any part of the righteousness for which the believer is justified, or that his whole work in making satisfaction consisted in expiation or bearing the penalty of the law. This is contrary to Scripture, and vitiates the doctrine of justification as presented in the Bible.

§ 6. *Proof of the Doctrine.*

That the Protestant doctrine as above stated is the doctrine of the word of God appears from the following considerations : —

1. The word δικαιόω, as has been shown, means to declare δίκαιος. No one can be truthfully pronounced δίκαιος to whom δικαιοσύνη cannot rightfully be ascribed. The sinner (ex vi verbi) has no righteousness of his own. God, therefore, imputes to him a righteousness which is not his own. The righteousness thus imputed is declared to be the righteousness of God, of Christ, the righteousness which is by faith. This is almost in so many words the declaration of the Bible on the subject. As the question, What is the method of justification ? is a Biblical question, it must be decided exegetically, and not by arguments drawn from assumed principles of reason. We are not at liberty to say that the righteousness of one man cannot be imputed to another ; that this would involve a mistake or absurdity ; that God's justice does not demand a righteousness such as the law prescribes, as the condition of justification ; that He may pardon and save as a father without any consideration, unless it be that of repentance ; that it is inconsistent with his grace that the demands of justice should be met before justification is granted ; that this view of justification makes it a sham, a calling a man just, when he is not just, etc. All this amounts to nothing. It all pertains to that wisdom which is foolishness with God. All we have to do is to determine, (1.) What is the meaning of the word to justify as used in Scripture ? (2.) On what ground does the Bible affirm that God pronounces the ungodly to be just ? If the answer to these questions be what the Church in all ages, and especially the Church of the Reformation has given, then we should rest satisfied. The Apostle in express terms says that God imputes righteousness to

the sinner. (Rom. iv. 6, 24.) By righteousness every one admits is meant that which makes a man righteous, that which the law demands. It does not consist in the sinner's own obedience, or moral excellence, for it is said to be "without works;" and it is declared that no man can be justified on the ground of his own character or conduct. Neither does this righteousness consist in faith; for it is "of faith," "through faith," "by faith." We are never said to be justified on account of faith. Neither is it a righteousness, or form of moral excellence springing from faith, or of which faith is the source or proximate cause; because it is declared to be the righteousness of God; a righteousness which is revealed; which is offered; which must be accepted as a gift. (Rom. v. 17.) It is declared to be the righteousness of Christ; his obedience. (Rom. v. 19.) It is, therefore, the righteousness of Christ, his perfect obedience in doing and suffering the will of God, which is imputed to the believer, and on the ground of which the believer, although in himself ungodly, is pronounced righteous, and therefore free from the curse of the law and entitled to eternal life.

The Apostle's Argument.

2. All the points above stated are not only clearly affirmed by the Apostle but they are also set forth in logical order, and elaborately sustained and vindicated in the Epistle to the Romans. The Apostle begins with the declaration that the Gospel "is the power of God unto salvation." It is not thus divinely efficacious because of the purity of its moral precepts; nor because it brings immortality to light; nor because it sets before us the perfect example of our Lord Jesus Christ; nor because it assures us of the love of God; nor because of the elevating, sanctifying, life-giving influence by which it is attended. There is something preliminary to all this. The first and indispensable requisite to salvation is that men should be righteous before God. They are under his wrath and curse. Until justice is satisfied, until God is reconciled, there is no possibility of any moral influence being of any avail. Therefore the Apostle says that the power of the Gospel is due to the fact that "therein is the righteousness of God revealed." This cannot mean the goodness of God, for such is not the meaning of the word. It cannot in this connection mean his justice, because it is a righteousness which is "of faith;" because the justice of God is revealed from heaven and to all men; because the revelation of justice terrifies and drives away from God; because what is here called the righteousness of God, is

elsewhere contrasted with our "own righteousness" (Rom. x. 3, Phil. iii. 9); and because it is declared to be the righteousness of Christ (Rom. v. 18), which is (Rom. v. 19) explained by his "obedience," and in Romans v. 9 and elsewhere declared to be "his blood." This righteousness of Christ is the righteousness of God, because Christ is God; because God has provided, revealed, and offers it; and because it avails before God as a sufficient ground on which He can declare the believing sinner righteous. Herein lies the saving power of the Gospel. The question, How shall man be just with God? had been sounding in the ears of men from the beginning. It never had been answered. Yet it must be answered or there can be no hope of salvation. It is answered in the Gospel, and therefore the Gospel is the power of God unto salvation to every one that believeth; *i. e.*, to every one, whether Jew or Gentile, bond or free, good or bad, who, instead of going about to establish his own righteousness, submits himself in joyful confidence to the righteousness which his God and Saviour Jesus Christ has wrought out for sinners, and which is freely offered to them in the Gospel without money and without price.

This is Paul's theme, which he proceeds to unfold and establish, as has been already stated under a previous head. He begins by asserting, as indisputably true from the revelation of God in the constitution of our nature, that God is just, that He will punish sin; that He cannot pronounce him righteous who is not righteous. He then shows from experience and from Scripture, first as regards the Gentiles, then as regards the Jews, that there is none righteous, no not one; that the whole world is guilty before God. There is therefore no difference, since all have sinned.

Since the righteousness which the law requires cannot be found in the sinner nor be rendered by him, God has revealed another righteousness (Rom. iii. 21); "the righteousness of God," granted to every one who believes. Men are not justified for what they are or for what they do, but for what Christ has done for them. God has set Him forth as a propitiation for sin, in order that He might be just and yet the justifier of them that believe.

The Apostle teaches that such has been the method of justification from the beginning. It was witnessed by the law and the prophets. There had never, since the fall, been any other way of justification possible for men. As God justified Abraham because he believed in the promise of redemption through the Messiah; so He justifies those now who believe in the fulfilment of that promise. (Rom. iv. 3, 9, 24.) It was not Abraham's believing state of mind that was taken for righteousness. It is not faith in the believer now ; not faith as a virtue, or as a source of a new life, which renders us righteous. It is faith in a specific promise. Righteousness, says the Apostle, is imputed to us, " if we believe on Him that raised up Jesus our Lord from the dead." (Rom. iv. 24.) Or, as he expresses it in Romans x. 9, "If thou shalt confess with thy mouth the Lord Jesus, and shalt believe in thine heart that God hath raised him from the dead, thou shalt be saved." The promise which Abraham believed, is the promise which we believe (Gal. iii. 14) ; and the relation of faith to justification, in his case, is precisely what it is in ours. He and we are justified simply because we trust in the Messiah for our salvation. Hence, as the Apostle says, the Scriptures are full of thanksgiving to God for gratuitous pardon, for free justification, for the imputation of righteousness to those who have no righteousness of their own. This method of justification, he goes on to show, is adapted to all mankind. God is not the God of the Jews only but also of the Gentiles. It secures peace and reconciliation with God. (Rom. v. 1–3.) It renders salvation certain, for if we are saved not by what we are in ourselves, but for what Christ has done for us, we may be sure that if we are " justified by his blood, we shall be saved from wrath through him." (Rom. v. 9.) This method of justification, he further shows, and this only, secures sanctification, namely, holiness of heart and life. It is only those who are reconciled to God by the death of his Son, that are " saved by his life." (v. 10.) This idea he expands and vindicates in the sixth and seventh chapters of this Epistle.

The Parallel between Adam and Christ.

3. Not content with this clear and formal statement of the truth that sinners can be justified only through the imputation of a righteousness not their own ; and that the righteousness thus imputed is the righteousness (active and passive if that distinction be insisted upon) of the Lord Jesus Christ; he proceeds to illustrate this doctrine by drawing a parallel between Adam and Christ. The former, he says, was a type of the latter. There is an analogy between our relation to Adam and our relation to Christ. We are so united to Adam that his first transgression was the ground of the sentence of condemnation being passed on all mankind, and on account of that condemnation we derive from him a corrupt nature so that all mankind descending from him

by ordinary generation, come into the world in a state of spiritual death. In like manner we are so united to Christ, when we
believe, that his obedience is the ground on which a sentence of
justification passes upon all thus in Him, and in consequence of
that sentence they derive from Him a new, holy, divine, and imperishable principle of spiritual life. These truths are expressed
in explicit terms. " The judgment was by one (offence) to condemnation, but the free gift is of many offences unto justification."
(Rom. v. 16.) " Therefore as by the offence of one judgment
came upon all men to condemnation ; even so by the righteousness of one the free gift came upon all men unto justification of
life. For as by one man's disobedience many were made sinners,
so by the obedience of one shall many be made righteous." (v. 18,
19.) These two great truths, namely, the imputation of Adam's
sin and the imputation of Christ's righteousness, have graven
themselves on the consciousness of the Church universal. They
have been reviled, misrepresented, and denounced by theologians,
but they have stood their ground in the faith of God's people,
just as the primary truths of reason have ever retained control
over the mass of men, in spite of all the speculations of philosophers. It is not meant that the truths just mentioned have always been expressed in the terms just given ; but the truths
themselves have been, and still are held by the people of God,
wherever found, among the Greeks, Latins, or Protestants. The
fact that the race fell in Adam ; that the evils which come upon
us on account of his transgression are penal ; and that men are
born in a state of sin and condemnation, are outstanding facts of
Scripture and experience, and are avowed every time the sacrament of baptism is administered to an infant. No less universal is the conviction of the other great truth. It is implied in
every act of saving faith which includes trust in what Christ has
done for us as the ground of our acceptance with God, as opposed
to anything done by us or wrought in us. As a single proof of
the hold which this conviction has on the Christian consciousness,
reference may be made to the ancient direction for the visitation
of the sick, attributed to Anselm, but of doubtful authorship :
" Dost thou believe that thou canst not be saved, but by the
death of Christ ? The sick man answereth, Yes. Then let it be
said unto him, Go to, then, and whilst thy soul abideth in thee,
put all thy confidence in this death alone, place thy trust in no
other thing, commit thyself wholly to this death, cover thyself
wholly with this alone, cast thyself wholly on this death, wrap

thyself wholly in this death. And if God would judge thee, say, Lord, I place the death of our Lord Jesus Christ between me and thy judgment; and otherwise I will not contend, or enter into judgment with thee. And if He shall say unto thee, that thou art a sinner, say, I place the death of our Lord Jesus Christ between me and my sins. If He shall say unto thee, that thou hast deserved damnation, say, Lord, I put the death of our Lord Jesus Christ between thee and all my sins; and I offer his merits for my own, which I should have, and have not. If He say that He is angry with thee: say, Lord, I place the death of our Lord Jesus Christ between me and thy anger." [1]

Such being the real and only foundation of a sinner's hope towards God, it is of the last importance that it should not only be practically held by the people, but that it should also be clearly presented and maintained by the clergy. It is not what we do or are, but solely what Christ is and has done that can avail for our justification before the bar of God.

Other Passages teaching the same Doctrine.

4. This doctrine of the imputation of the righteousness of Christ; or, in other words, that his righteousness is the judicial ground of the believer's justification, is not only formally and argumentatively presented as in the passages cited, but it is constantly asserted or implied in the word of God. The Apostle argues, in the fourth chapter of his Epistle to the Romans, that every assertion or promise of gratuitous forgiveness of sin to be found in the Scriptures involves this doctrine. He proceeds on the assumption that God is just; that He demands a righteousness of those whom He justifies. If they have no righteousness of their own, one on just grounds must be imputed to them. If, therefore, He forgives sin, it must be that sin is covered, that justice has been satisfied. "David, also," he says, "describeth the blessedness of the man, unto whom God imputeth righteousness without works; saying, Blessed are they whose iniquities are forgiven, and whose sins are covered. Blessed is the man to whom the Lord will not impute sin." (Rom. iv. 6–8.) Not to impute sin implies the imputation of righteousness.

In Romans v. 9, we are said to be "justified by his blood." In Romans iii. 25, God is said to have set Him forth as a propitiation for sin, that He might be just in justifying the ungodly. As to justify does not mean to pardon, but judicially to pro-

[1] See "The General Considerations," prefixed by Owen to his work on Justification.

nounce righteous, this passage distinctly asserts that the work
of Christ is the ground on which the sentence of justification is
passed.   In Romans x. 3, 4, he says of the Jews, " They being
ignorant of God's righteousness, and going about to establish
their own righteousness, have not submitted themselves unto the
righteousness of God.   For Christ is the end of the law for righteousness to every one that believeth."   It can hardly be questioned that the word (δικαιοσύνη) righteousness must have the
same meaning in both members of the first of these verses.   If
a man's " own righteousness " is that which would render him
righteous, then " the righteousness of God," in this connection,
must be a justifying righteousness.   It is called the righteousness of God, because, as said before, He is its author.   It is the
righteousness of Christ.   It is provided, offered, and accepted
of God.   Here then are two righteousnesses ; the one human,
the other divine ; the one valueless, the other infinitely meritorious.   The folly of the Jews, and of thousands since their day,
consists in refusing the latter and trusting to the former.   This
folly the Apostle makes apparent in the fourth verse.   The Jews
acted under the assumption that the law as a covenant, that is,
as prescribing the conditions of salvation, was still in force, that
men were still bound to satisfy its demands by their personal
obedience in order to be saved, whereas Christ had made an end
of the law.   He had abolished it as a covenant, in order that
men might be justified by faith.   Christ, however, has thus made
an end of the law, not by merely setting it aside, but by satisfying its demands.   He delivers us from its curse, not by mere
pardon, but by being made a curse for us.   (Gal. iii. 13.)   He
redeems us from the law by being made under it (Gal. iv. 4, 5),
and fulfilling all righteousness.

In Philippians iii. 8, 9, the Apostle says, he " suffered the
loss of all things," that he might be found in Christ, not having
his " own righteousness, which is of the law, but that which is
through the faith of Christ, the righteousness which is of God
by faith."   Here again one's own righteousness is contrasted
with that which is of God.   The word must have the same sense
in both members.   What Paul trusted to, was not his own righteousness, not his own subjective goodness, but a righteousness
provided for him and received by faith.   De Wette (no Augustinian) on this passage says, the righteousness of God here
means, " a righteousness received from God (graciously imputed)
on condition of faith " (" die von Gott empfangene (aus Gnaden
zugerechnete) Gerechtigkeit um des Glaubenswillen.")

The Apostle says (1 Cor. i. 30), Christ " of God is made unto us wisdom, and righteousness, and sanctification, and redemption." In this enumeration sanctification and righteousness are distinguished. The one renders us holy ; the other renders us just, *i. e.*, satisfies the demands of justice. As Christ is to us the source of inward spiritual life, so He is the giver of that righteousness which secures our justification. Justification is not referred to sanctification as its proximate cause and ground. On the contrary, the gift of righteousness precedes that of sanctification. We are justified in order that we may be sanctified. The point here, however, is that righteousness is distinguished from anything and everything in us which can recommend us to the favour of God. We are accepted, justified, and saved, not for what we are, but for what He has done in our behalf. God " made him to be sin for us, who knew no sin ; that we might be made the righteousness of God in him." (2 Cor. v. 21.) As Christ was not made sin in a moral sense ; so we are not (in justification) made righteousness in a moral sense. As He was made sin in that He " bare our sins ; " so we are made righteousness in that we bear his righteousness. Our sins were the judicial ground of his humiliation under the law and of all his sufferings ; so his righteousness is the judicial ground of our justification. In other words, as our sins were imputed to Him ; so his righteousness is imputed to us. If imputation of sin did not render Him morally corrupt ; the imputation of righteousness does not make us holy or morally good.

Argument from the General Teachings of the Bible.

5. It is unnecessary to dwell upon particular passages in support of a doctrine which pervades the whole Scriptures. The question is, What is the ground of the pardon of sin and of the acceptance of the believer as righteous (in the forensic or judicial sense of the word), in the sight of God ? Is it anything we do, anything experienced by us, or wrought in us ; or, is it what Christ has done for us ? The whole revelation of God concerning the method of salvation shows that it is the latter and not the former. In the first place, this is plain from what the Scriptures teach of the covenant of redemption between the Father and the Son. That there was such covenant cannot be denied if the meaning of the words be once agreed upon. It is plain from Scripture that Christ came into the world to do a certain work, on a certain condition. The promise made to Him

was that a multitude whom no man can number, of the fallen race of man, should be saved. This included the promise that they should be justified, sanctified, and made partakers of eternal life. The very nature of this transaction involves the idea of vicarious substitution. It assumes that what He was to do was to be the ground of the justification, sanctification, and salvation of his people.

In the second place this is involved in the nature of the work which He came to perform. He was to assume our nature, to be born of a woman, to take part of flesh and blood with all their infirmities, yet without sin. He was to take his place among sinners; be made subject to the law which they are bound to obey, and to endure the curse which they had incurred. If this be so, then what He did is the ground of our salvation from first to last; of our pardon, of our reconciliation with God, of the acceptance of our persons, of the indwelling of the Spirit, of our being transformed into His image, and of our admission into heaven. " Not unto us, O LORD, not unto us, but unto Thy name give glory," has, therefore, been the spontaneous language of every believer from the beginning until now.

In the third place, the manner in which Christ was to execute the work assigned as described in the prophets, and the way in which it was actually accomplished as described by Himself and by his Apostles, prove that what He did and suffered is the ground of our salvation. He says that He came " to give his life a ransom for many." (Matt. xx. 28.) " There is one God," says the Apostle, " and one mediator between God and men, the man Christ Jesus ; who gave Himself a ransom for all." (1 Tim. ii. 5, 6.) The deliverance effected by a ransom has no reference to the character or conduct of the redeemed. Its effects are due exclusively to the ransom paid. It is, therefore, to deny that Christ was a ransom, that we are redeemed by his blood, to affirm that the proximate ground of our deliverance from the curse of the law and of our introduction into the liberty of the sons of God, is anything wrought in us or done by us. Again, from the beginning to the end of the Bible, Christ is represented as a sacrifice. From the first institution of sacrifices in the family of Adam ; during the patriarchal period ; in all the varied and costly ritual of the Mosaic law ; in the predictions of the prophets ; in the clear didactic statements of the New Testament, it is taught with a constancy, a solemnity, and an amplitude, which proves it to be a fundamental and vital element of the divine plan of redemption, that the Redeemer was to save his people by offering himself as a sacrifice unto God in their behalf. There is no one characteristic of the plan of salvation more deeply engraven on the hearts of Christians, which more effectually determines their inward spiritual life, which so much pervades their prayers and praises, or which is so directly the foundation of their hopes, as the sacrificial nature of the death of Christ. Strike from the Bible the doctrine of redemption by the blood of Christ, and what have we left? But if Christ saves us as a sacrifice, then it is what He does for us, his objective work, and nothing subjective, nothing in us, which is the ground of our salvation, and of all that salvation includes. For even our sanctification is due to his death. His blood cleanses from all sin. (1 John i. 7.) It cleanses from the guilt of sin by expiation ; and secures inward sanctification by securing the gift of the Holy Spirit.

Again, the whole Bible is full of the idea of substitution. Christ took our place. He undertook to do for us what we could not do for ourselves. This is taught in every possible way. He bore our sins. He died for us and in our place. He was made under the law for us. He was made a curse for us. He was made sin for us that we might be made the righteousness of God in Him. The chastisement of our peace was laid on Him. Everything, therefore, which the Bible teaches of the method of salvation, is irreconcilable with the doctrine of subjective justification in all its forms. We are always and everywhere referred to something out of ourselves as the ground of our confidence toward God.

In the fourth place, the effects ascribed to the work of Christ, as before remarked, are such as do not flow from anything in the believer himself, but must be referred to what has been done for him. These effects are expiation of sin, propitiation, the gift and indwelling of the life-giving Spirit of God ; redemption, or deliverance from all forms of evil ; and a title to eternal life and actual participation in the exaltation, glory, and blessedness of the Son of God. It is out of all question that these wonderful effects should be referred to what we personally are ; to our merit, to our holiness, to our participation of the life of Christ. In whatever sense these last words may be understood, they refer to what we personally are or become. His life in us is after all a form of our life. It constitutes our character. And it is self-evident to the conscience that our character is not, and cannot be the ground of our pardon, of God's peculiar love, or of our eternal glory and blessedness in heaven.

In the fifth place, the condition on which our participation of the benefits of redemption is suspended, is inconsistent with any form of the doctrine of subjective justification. We are never said to be justified on account of faith, considered either as an act or as a principle, as an exercise or as a permanent state of the mind. Faith is never said to be the ground of justification. Nor are we saved by faith as the source of holiness or of spiritual life in the soul, or as the organ of receiving the infused life of God. We are saved simply " by " faith, by receiving and resting upon Christ alone for salvation. The thing received is something out of ourselves. It is Christ, his righteousness, his obedience, the merit of his blood or death. We look to Him. We flee to Him. We lay hold on Him. We hide ourselves in Him. We are clothed in his righteousness. The Romanist indeed says, that an Ethiopian in a white robe does not become white. True, but a suit of armor gives security from the sword or spear, and that is what we need before attending to the state of our complexion. We need protection from the wrath of God in the first instance. The inward transformation of the soul into his likeness is provided for by other means.

In the sixth place and finally, the fact that we are saved by grace proves that the ground of salvation is not in ourselves. The grace of God, his love for the unlovely, for the guilty and polluted, is represented in the Bible as the most mysterious of the divine perfections. It was hidden in God. It could not be discovered by reason, neither was it revealed prior to the redemption of man. The specific object of the plan of salvation is the manifestation of this most wonderful, most attractive, and most glorious attribute of the divine nature. Everything connected with our salvation, says the Apostle, is intended for the " praise of the glory of his grace " (Eph. i. 6.) God hath quickened us, he says, and raised us up, and made us sit together in heavenly places in Christ Jesus, in order " that in the ages to come, he might show the exceeding riches of his grace, in his kindness toward us, through Christ Jesus."

From their nature, grace and works are antithetical. The one excludes the other. What is of grace, is not of works. And by works in Scripture, in relation to this subject, is meant not individual acts only, but states of mind, anything and everything internal of which moral character can be predicated. When, therefore, it is said that salvation is of grace and not of works, it is thereby said that it is not founded upon anything in the believer himself. It was not any moral excellence in man, that determined God to interpose for his redemption, while He left the apostate angels to their fate. This was a matter of grace. To deny this, and to make the provision of a plan of salvation for man a matter of justice, is in such direct contradiction to every-thing in the Bible, that it hardly ever has been openly asserted. The gift of his Son for the redemption of man is ever represented as the most wonderful display of unmerited love. That some and not all men are actually saved, is expressly declared to be not of works, not on account of anything distinguishing favourably the one class from the other, but a matter of pure grace. When a sinner is pardoned and restored to the favour of God, this again is declared to be of grace. If of grace it is not founded upon any-thing in the sinner himself. Now as the Scriptures not only teach that the plan of salvation is thus gratuitous in its incep-tion, execution, and application, but also insist upon this charac-teristic of the plan as of vital importance, and even go so far as to teach that unless we consent to be saved by grace, we cannot be saved at all, it of necessity follows that the doctrine of sub-jective justification is contrary to the whole spirit of the Bible. That doctrine in all its forms teaches that that which secures our acceptance with God, is something in ourselves, something which constitutes character. If so, then salvation is not of grace ; and if not of grace, it is unattainable by sinners.

§ 7. *The Consequences of the Imputation of Righteousness.*

It is frequently said that justification consists in the pardon of sin and in the imputation of righteousness. This mode of state-ment is commonly adopted by Lutheran theologians. This exhi-bition of the doctrine is founded upon the sharp distinction made in the " Form of Concord " between the passive and active obe-dience of Christ. To the former is referred the remission of the penalty due to us for sin ; to the latter our title to eternal life. The Scriptures, however, do not make this distinction so promi-nent. Our justification as a whole is sometimes referred to the blood of Christ, and sometimes to his obedience. This is intel-ligible because the crowning act of his obedience, and that with-out which all else had been unavailing, was his laying down his life for us. It is, perhaps, more correct to say that the righteous-ness of Christ, including all He did and suffered in our stead, is imputed to the believer as the ground of his justification, and that the consequences of this imputation are, first, the remission of sin, and secondly, the acceptance of the believer as righteous. And if righteous, then he is entitled to be so regarded and treated.

By the remission of sin Romanists understand the removal of the pollution of sin. So that their definition of justification as consisting in the remission of sin and infusion of righteousness, is only a statement of the negative and positive aspects of sanctification, i. e., putting off the old man and putting on the new man. The effect of remission is constantly declared to be that nothing of the nature of sin remains in the soul. The Council of Trent says, " Justificatio . . . . non est sola peccatorum remissio, sed et sanctificatio, et renovatio interioris hominis per voluntariam susceptionem gratiæ et donorum. . . . . Quanquam nemo possit esse justus, nisi cui merita passionis Domini nostri Jesu Christi communicantur: id tamen in hac impii justificatione fit, dum ejusdem sanctissimæ passionis merito per Spiritum Sanctum caritas Dei diffunditur in cordibus eorum, qui justificantur, atque ipsis inhæret." " Quibus verbis justificationis impii descriptio insinuatur, ut sit translatio ab eo statu, in quo homo nascitur filius primi Adæ, in statum gratiæ et adoptionis filiorum Dei, per secundum Adam Jesum Christum, salvatorem nostrum: quæ quidem translatio post evangelium promulgatum sine lavacro regenerationis, aut ejus voto fieri non potest." [1] By " status gratiæ " in this definition is not meant a state of favour, but a state of subjective grace or holiness ; because in other places and most commonly justification is said to consist in the infusion of grace. In this definition, therefore, the pardon of sin in the proper sense of the words is not included. Bellarmin [2] says this translation into a state of adoption as sons of God, " non potest . . . . fieri, nisi homo per remissionem peccati desinat esse impius ; et per infusionem justitiæ incipiat esse pius. Sed sicut aër cum illustratur a sole per idem lumen, quod recipit, desinit esse tenebrosus et incipit esse lucidus: sic etiam homo per eandem justitiam sibi a sole justitiæ donatam atque infusam desinit esse injustus, delente videlicet lumine gratiæ tenebras peccatorum." The remission of sin is therefore defined to be the removal of sin. Bellarmin argues in support of this view that guilt is removed by holiness, that guilt is a relation ; the relation of sin to justice. When the thing itself is taken away, the relation itself of course ceases.[3] Hence remission of sin, even in the sense of pardon, is effected by the

[1] Sess. vi. cap. 7, 4; Streitwolf, *Libri Symbolici*, Göttingen, 1846, pp. 24, 25, 22.
[2] *De Justificatione*, ii. ii. ; *Disputationes*, edit. Paris, 1608, vol. iv. pp. 780, e, 781, a.
[3] *De Amissione Gratiæ et Statu Peccati*, v. vii., *Ibid.* p. 287, a, b.

infusion of righteousness, as darkness is banished by the introduction of light.   It is thus, as remarked above, that guilt is
either ignored, or reduced to a minimum by the Romish theory
of justification.   There is really no satisfaction of justice in the
case.   The merits of Christ avail to secure for man the gift of
the Holy Ghost, by whose power as exercised in the sacrament
of baptism, the soul is made holy, and by the introduction of holiness everything of the nature of sin is banished, and all ground
for the infliction of punishment is removed.   A scheme so opposed
to Scripture, and so inconsistent with even the natural conscience,
cannot be practically adopted by the mass of the people.   The
conviction is too intimate that the desert of punishment is not
removed by the reformation, or even by the regeneration of the
sinner, to allow the conscience to be satisfied with any scheme of
salvation which does not provide for the expiation of the guilt of
sin by what really satisfies the justice of God.

In the Bible, therefore, as well as in common life, pardon is not
a mere consequence of sanctification.   It is exemption from the
infliction of the deserved penalty of the law.   Whether this exemption is a mere matter of caprice, or unworthy partiality for
the offender, or for considerations of expediency, or at the
promptings of compassion, or upon the ground of an adequate
satisfaction to the demands of justice, makes no difference so far
as the nature of pardon is concerned.   It is in all cases the remission of a penalty adjudged to be deserved.   It is in this sense,
therefore, that justification is declared to include the pardon of
sins, founded on the imputation to the believing sinner of the
perfect righteousness of Christ.   It is this that gives the believer
peace.   He sees that he is delivered from " the wrath and curse
of God " due to him, not by any arbitrary exercise of executive
authority, but because God, as a righteous judge, can, in virtue
of the propitiation of Christ, be just and yet justify the ungodly.

The sins which are pardoned in justification include all sins,
past, present, and future.   It does indeed seem to be a solecism
that sins should be forgiven before they are committed.   Forgiveness involves remission of penalty.   But how can a penalty
be remitted before it is incurred ?   This is only an apparent difficulty arising out of the inadequacy of human language.   The
righteousness of Christ is a perpetual donation.   It is a robe
which hides, or as the Bible expresses it, covers from the eye of
justice the sins of the believer.   They are sins ; they deserve the
wrath and curse of God, but the necessity for the infliction of

that curse no longer exists. The believer feels the constant necessity for confession and prayer for pardon, but the ground of pardon is ever present for him to offer and plead. So that it would perhaps be a more correct statement to say that in justification the believer receives the promise that God will not deal with him according to his transgressions, rather than to say that sins are forgiven before they are committed.

This subject is thus presented by the Apostle : believers " are not under the law but under grace." (Rom. vi. 14.) They are not under a legal system administered according to the principles of retributive justice, a system which requires perfect obedience as the condition of acceptance with God, and which says, " Cursed is every one that continueth not in all things which are written in the book of the law to do them." They are under grace, that is, under a system in which believers are not dealt with on the principles of justice, but on the principles of undeserved mercy, in which God does not impute " their trespasses unto them." (2 Cor. v. 19.) There is therefore to them no condemnation. They are not condemned for their sins, not because they are not sins and do not deserve condemnation, but because Christ has already made expiation for their guilt and makes continual intercession for them.

The second consequence attributed to the imputation of Christ's righteousness, is a title to eternal life. This in the older writers is often expressed by the words " adoption and heirship." Being made the children of God by faith in Christ Jesus (Gal. iii. 26), they are heirs of God and joint heirs with Jesus Christ of a heavenly inheritance. (Rom. viii. 17.) The mere expiation of guilt confers no title to eternal life. The condition of the covenant under which man was placed was perfect obedience. This, from all that appears in Scripture, the perfection of God requires. As He never pardons sins unless the demands of justice be satisfied, so He never grants eternal life unless perfect obedience be rendered. Heaven is always represented as a purchased possession. In the covenant between the Father and the Son the salvation of his people was promised as the reward of his humiliation, obedience, and death. Having performed the stipulated conditions, He has a claim to the promised recompense. And this claim inures to the benefit of his people. But besides this, as the work of Christ consisted in his doing all that the law of God, or covenant of works requires for the salvation of men, and as that righteousness is freely offered to every one that believes.

every such believer has as valid a claim to eternal life as he would have had, had he personally done all that the law demands. Thus broad and firm is the foundation which God has laid for the hopes of his people. It is the rock of ages; Jehovah our righteousness.

§ 8. *Relation of Faith to Justification.*

All who profess to be Christians admit the doctrine of justification by faith. There are different views, however, as to the relation between faith and justification, as has been already intimated.

1. Pelagians and rationalists teach that faith in God's being and perfection, or in the great principles of moral and religious truth, is the source of that moral excellence on account of which we are accepted of God. It is perhaps only a different way of expressing the same idea, to say that God, in the case of Abraham, and, therefore, of other men, accepts the pious state of mind involved in the exercise of faith or confidence in God, in lieu of perfect righteousness.

2. Romanists make faith mere assent. It does not justify as a virtue, or as apprehending the offered righteousness of Christ. It is neither the formal nor the instrumental cause of justification, it is merely the predisposing or occasional cause. A man assents to the truth of Christianity, and to the more special truth that the Church is a divine institution for saving men. He therefore comes to the Church and receives the sacrament of baptism, by which, " ex opere operato," a habit of grace, or spiritual life is infused into the soul, which is the formal cause of justification ; *i. e.*, it renders the soul inherently just or holy. In this sense the sinner may be said to be justified by faith. This is the first justification. After the man is thus rendered holy or regenerated, then the exercises of faith have real merit, and enter into the ground of his second justification, by which he becomes entitled to eternal life. But here faith stands on a level with other Christian graces. It is not the only, nor the most important ground of justification. It is in this view inferior to love, from which faith indeed derives all its virtue as a Christian grace. It is then " fides formata," *i. e.*, faith of which love is the essence, the principle which gives it character.

The Romish Doctrine.

According to the Romish scheme (1.) God is the efficient cause of justification, as it is by his power or supernatural grace that the soul is made just. (2.) Christ is the meritorious cause, as it is for his sake God grants this saving grace, or influence of the Spirit to the children of men. (3.) Inherent righteousness is the formal cause, since thereby the soul is made really just or holy. (4.) Faith is the occasional and predisposing cause, as it leads the sinner to seek justification (regeneration), and disposes God to grant the blessing. In this aspect it has the merit of congruity only, not that of condignity. (5.) Baptism is the essential instrumental cause, as it is only through or by baptism that inherent righteousness is infused or justification is effected. So much for the first justification. After this justification, which makes the sinner holy, then, (6.) Good works, all the fruits and exercises of the new life, have real merit and constitute the ground of the Christian's title to eternal life.

The language of the Council of Trent on this subject is as follows : " Hujus justificationis causæ sunt, finalis quidem, gloria Dei et Christi, ac vita æterna : efficiens vero, misericors Deus, qui gratuito abluit et sanctificat, signans et ungens Spiritu promissionis sancto, ... meritoria autem dilectissimus unigenitus suus, Dominus noster, Jesus Christus, qui, cum essemus inimici, propter nimiam caritatem, qua dilexit nos, sua sanctissima passione in ligno crucis nobis justificationem [*i. e.*, regeneration] meruit et pro nobis Deo Patri satisfecit : instrumentalis item, sacramentum baptismi, quod est sacramentum fidei, sine qua nulli unquam contigit justificatio : demum unica formalis causa est justitia Dei, non qua ipse justus est, sed qua nos justos facit : qua videlicet ab eo donati, renovamur spiritu mentis nostræ, et non modo reputamur, sed vere justi nominamur, et sumus, justitiam in nobis recipientes, unusquisque suam secundum mensuram, quam Spiritus Sanctus partitur singulis prout vult, et secundum propriam cujusque dispositionem et cooperationem." Again, it is said : " Quæ enim justitia nostra dicitur, quia per eam nobis inhærentem justificamur ; illa eadem Dei est, quia a Deo nobis infunditur per Christi meritum." [1] All this relates to the first justification, or regeneration, in which the soul passes from spiritual death to spiritual life. Of the second justification, which gives a title to eternal life, Bellarmin says, [2] " Habet communis catholicorum

---

[1] Sess. vi. cap. 7, 16; Streitwolf, *Libri Symbolici*, Göttingen, 1846, vol. i. pp. 24, 25, 32.
[2] *De Justificatione*, v. 1; *Disputationes*, Paris, 1608, p. 949, a.

omnium sententia, opera bona justorum vere, ac proprie esse merita, et merita non cujuscunque præmii, sed ipsius vitæ æternæ." The thirty-second canon of the Tridentine Council at this sixth session anathematizes any one who teaches a different doctrine. "Si quis dixerit, hominis justificati bona opera ita esse dona Dei, ut non sint etiam bona ipsius justificati merita; aut ipsum justificatum bonis operibus, quæ ab eo per Dei gratiam et Jesu Christi meritum, cujus vivum membrum est, fiunt, non vere mereri augmentum gratiæ, vitam æternam, et ipsius vitæ æternæ, si tamen in gratia decesserit, consecutionem, atque etiam gloriæ augmentum ; anathema sit." It appears from all this that, according to the doctrine of the Church of Rome, faith has no special or direct connection with justification, and that "justification by faith" in that Church means something entirely different from what is intended by those words in the lips of evangelical Christians.

Remonstrant View.

3. According to the Remonstrants or Arminians, faith is the ground of justification. Under the Gospel God accepts our imperfect obedience including faith and springing from it, in place of the perfect obedience demanded by the law originally given to Adam. There is one passage in the Bible, or rather one form of expression, which occurs in several places, which seems to favour this view of the subject. In Romans iv. 3, it is said, "Abraham believed God, and it was counted unto him for righteousness;" and again in ver. 22 of that chapter, and in Galatians iii. 6. If this phrase be interpreted according to the analogy of such passages as Romans ii. 26, "Shall not his uncircumcision be counted for circumcision?" it does mean that faith is taken or accepted for righteousness. The Bible, however, is the word of God and therefore self-consistent. Consequently if a passage admits of one interpretation inconsistent with the teaching of the Bible in other places, and of another interpretation consistent with that teaching, we are bound to accept the latter. This rule, simple and obvious as it is, is frequently violated, not only by those who deny the inspiration of the Scriptures, but even by men professing to recognize their infallible authority. They seem to regard it as a proof of independence to make each passage mean simply what its grammatical structure and logical connection indicate, without the least regard to the analogy of Scripture. This is unreasonable. In Genesis xv. we are told that Abraham lamented before the Lord that he was childless, and that one born in his house was

to be his heir.   And God said unto him, " This shall not be thine heir ; but he that shall come forth out of thine own bowels, shall be thine heir.   And he brought him forth abroad, and said, Look now toward heaven, and tell the stars, if thou be able to number them.   And he said unto him, So shall thy seed be. And he believed in the LORD ; and He counted it to him for righteousness."   Taking this passage by itself, it is inferred that the object of Abraham's faith was the promise of a numerous posterity.   Supposing this to be true, which it certainly is not, what right has any one to assume that Abraham's faith's being imputed to him for righteousness, means anything more than when it is said that the zeal of Phinehas was imputed for righteousness (Ps. cvi. 31) ; or when in Deuteronomy xxiv. 13, it is said that to return a poor man's pledge " shall be righteousness unto thee before the LORD thy God."   No one supposes that one manifestation of zeal, or one act of benevolence, is taken for complete obedience to the law.   All that the phrase " to impute for righteousness " by itself means, according to Old Testament usage, is, to esteem as right, to approve.   The zeal of Phinehas was right. Returning a poor man's pledge was right.   These were acts which God approved.   And so He approved of Abraham's faith. He gained the favour of God by believing.   Now while this is true, far more, as the Apostle teaches, is true.   He teaches, first, that the great promise made to Abraham, and faith in which secured his justification, was not that his natural descendants should be as numerous as the stars of heaven, but that in his seed all the nations of the earth should be blessed ; secondly, that the seed intended was not a multitude, but one person, and that that one person was Christ (Gal. iii. 16) ; and, thirdly, that the blessing which the seed of Abraham was to secure for the world was redemption.   " Christ hath redeemed us from the curse of the law, being made a curse for us : . . . . that the blessing of Abraham (i. e., the promise made to Abraham) might come on " us.   The promise made to Abraham, therefore, was redemption through Christ.   Hence those who are Christ's, the Apostle teaches, are Abraham's seed and heirs of his promise.   What, therefore, Abraham believed, was that the seed of the woman, the Shiloh, the promised Redeemer of the world, was to be born of him.   He believed in Christ, as his Saviour, as his righteousness, and deliverer, and therefore it was that he was accepted as righteous, not for the merit of his faith, and not on the ground of faith, or by taking faith in lieu of righteousness, but because he received and rested on Christ alone for his salvation.

Unless such be the meaning of the Apostle, it is hard to see how there is any coherence or force in his arguments. His object is to prove that men are justified, not by works, but gratuitously ; not for what they are or do, but for what is done for them. They are saved by a ransom ; by a sacrifice. But it is absurd to say that trust in a ransom redeems, or is taken in place of the ransom ; or that faith in a sacrifice, and not the sacrifice itself, is the ground of acceptance. To prove that such is the Scriptural method of justification, Paul appeals to the case of Abraham. He was not justified for his works, but by faith in a Redeemer. He expected to be justified as ungodly. (Rom. iv. 5.) This, he tells us, is what we must do. We have no righteousness of our own. We must take Christ for our wisdom, righteousness, sanctification, and redemption. In the immediately preceding chapter the Apostle had said we are justified by faith in the blood of Christ, as a propitiation for sin ; and for him to prove this from the fact that Abraham was justified on account of his confiding, trusting state of mind, which led him to believe that, although a hundred years old, he should be the father of a numerous posterity, would be a contradiction.

Besides, it is to be remembered, not only that the Scriptures never say that we are justified " on account " of faith (διὰ πίστιν), but always " by," or " through " faith (διὰ or ἐκ πίστεως, or πίστει) ; but also that it is not by faith as such ; not by faith in God, nor in the Scriptures ; and not by faith in a specific divine promise such as that made to Abraham of a numerous posterity, or of the possession of the land of Canaan ; but only by faith in one particular promise, namely, that of salvation through Christ. It is, therefore, not on account of the state of mind, of which faith is the evidence, nor of the good works which are its fruits, but only by faith as an act of trust in Christ, that we are justified. This of necessity supposes that He, and not our faith, is the ground of our justification. He, and not our faith, is the ground of our confidence. How can any Christian wish it to be otherwise ? What comparison is there between the absolutely perfect and the infinitely meritorious righteousness of Christ, and our own imperfect evangelical obedience as a ground of confidence and peace !

This doctrine is moreover dishonouring to the Gospel. It supposes the Gospel to be less holy than the law. The law required perfect obedience ; the Gospel is satisfied with imperfect obedience. And how imperfect and insufficient our best obedience is, the conscience of every believer certifies. If it does not satisfy us, how can it satisfy God?

The grand objection, however, to this Remonstrant doctrine as to the relation between faith and justification, is that it is in direct contradiction to the plain and pervading teachings of the Word of God. The Bible teaches that we are not justified by works. This doctrine affirms that we are justified by works. The Bible teaches that we are justified by the blood of Christ ; that it is for his obedience that the sentence of justification is passed on men. This doctrine affirms that God pronounces us righteous because of our own righteousness. The Bible from first to last teaches that the whole ground of our salvation or of our justification is objective, what Christ as our Redeemer, our ransom, our sacrifice, our surety, has done for us. This doctrine teaches us to look within, to what we are and to what we do, as the ground of our acceptance with God. It may safely be said that this is altogether unsatisfactory to the awakened conscience. The sinner cannot rely on anything in himself. He instinctively looks to Christ, to his work done for us as the ground of confidence and peace. This in the last resort is the hope of all believers, whatever their theory of justification may be. Whether Papist, Remonstrant, or Augustinian, they all cast their dying eyes on Christ. " As Moses lifted up the serpent in the wilderness, even so must the Son of man be lifted up ; that whosoever believeth in him should not perish, but have eternal life."

Protestant Doctrine.

4. The common doctrine of Protestants on this subject is that faith is merely the instrumental cause of justification. It is the act of receiving and resting upon Christ, and has no other relation to the end than any other act by which a proffered good is accepted. This is clearly the doctrine of Scripture, (1.) Because we are constantly said to be justified by, or through faith. (2.) Because the faith which justifies is described as a looking, as a receiving, as a coming, as a fleeing for refuge, as a laying hold of, and as a calling upon. (3.) Because the ground to which our justification is referred, and that on which the sinner's trust is placed, is declared to be the blood, the death, the righteousness, the obedience of Christ. (4.) Because the fact that Christ is a ransom, a sacrifice, and as such effects our salvation, of necessity supposes that the faith which interests us in the merit of his work is a simple act of trust. (5.) Because any

other view of the case is inconsistent with the gratuitous nature of justification, with the honour of Christ, and with the comfort and confidence of the believer.

§ 9. *Objections to the Protestant Doctrine of Justification.* *It is said to lead to Licentiousness.*

1. The first, most obvious, and most persistently urged objection against the doctrine of gratuitous justification through the imputation of the righteousness of Christ, has already been incidentally considered. That objection is that the doctrine leads to license ; that if good works are not necessary to justification, they are not necessary at all; that if God accepts the chief of sinners as readily as the most moral of men, on the simple condition of faith in Christ, then what profit is there in circumcision ? in Judaism? in being in the Church ? in being good in any form ? Why not live in sin that grace may abound ? This objection having been urged against the Apostle, it needs no other answer than that which he himself gave it. That answer is found in the sixth and seventh chapters of his Epistle to the Romans, and is substantially as follows :

First, the objection involves a contradiction. To speak of salvation in sin is as great an absurdity as to speak of life in death. Salvation is deliverance from sin. How then can men be delivered from sin in order that they may live in it. Or, as Paul expresses it, " How shall we, that are dead to sin, live any longer therein ? "

Secondly, the very act of faith which secures our justification, secures also our sanctification. It cannot secure the one without securing also the other. This is not only the intention and the desire of the believer, but it is the ordinance of God ; a necessary feature of the plan of salvation, and secured by its nature. We take Christ as our Redeemer from sin, from its power as well as from its guilt. And the imputation of his righteousness consequent on faith secures the indwelling of the Holy Spirit as certainly, and for the very same reasons (the covenant stipulations), that it secures the pardon of our sins. And, therefore, if we are partakers of his death, we are partakers of his life. If we die with Him, we rise with Him. If we are justified, we are sanctified. He, therefore, who lives in sin, proclaims himself an unbeliever. He has neither part nor lot in the redemption of Him who came to save his people from their sins.

Thirdly, our condition, the Apostle says, is analogous to that of a slave, belonging first to one master, then to another. So long as he belonged to one man, he was not under the authority of another. But if freed from the one and made the slave of the other, then he comes under an influence which constrains obedience to the latter. So we were the slaves of sin, but now, freed from that hard master, we have become the servants of righteousness. For a believer, therefore, to live in sin, is just as impossible as for the slave of one man to be at the same time the slave of another. We are indeed free ; but not free to sin. We are only free from the bondage of the devil and introduced into the pure, exalted, and glorious liberty of the sons of God.

Fourthly, the objection as made against the Apostle and as constantly repeated since, is urged in the interests of morality and of common sense. Reason itself, it is said, teaches that a man must be good before he can be restored to the favour of God ; and if we teach that the number and heinousness of a man's sins are no barrier to his justification, and his good works are no reason why he should be justified rather than the chief of sinners, we upset the very foundations of morality. This is the wisdom of men. The wisdom of God, as revealed in the Scriptures, is very different. According to the Bible the favour of God is the life of the soul. The light of his countenance is to rational creatures what the light of the sun is to the earth, the source of all that is beautiful and good. So long, therefore, as a soul is under his curse, there is no life-giving or life-sustaining intercourse between it and God. In this state it can only, as the Apostle expresses it, "bring forth fruit unto death." As soon, however, as it exercises faith, it receives the imputation of the righteousness of Christ, God's justice is thereby satisfied, and the Spirit comes and takes up his dwelling in the believer as the source of all holy living. There can therefore be no holiness until there is reconciliation with God, and no reconciliation with God except through the righteousness imputed to us and received by faith alone. Then follow the indwelling of the Spirit, progressive sanctification, and all the fruits of holy living.

It may be said that this scheme involves an inconsistency. There can be no holiness until there is reconciliation, and no reconciliation (so far as adults are concerned) until there is faith. But faith is a fruit of the Spirit, and an act of the renewed soul. Then there is and must be, after all, holy action before there is reconciliation. It might be enough to say in answer to this objection, that logical order and chronological succession are different things ; or that the order of nature and order of time are not to be confounded. Many things are contemporaneous or co-instan-taneous which nevertheless stand in a certain logical, and even causal relation to each other. Christ commanded the man with a withered arm to stretch forth his hand. He immediately obeyed, but not before he received strength. He called to Lazarus to come forth from the grave ; and he came forth. But this pre-supposes a restoration of life. So God commands the sinner to believe in Christ ; and he thereupon receives Him as his Saviour ; though this supposes supernatural power or grace.

Our Lord, however, gives another answer to this objection. He says, as recorded in John xvii. 9, " I pray not for the world, but for them which thou hast given me ; for they are thine." The intercession of Christ secures for those given to Him by the Father the renewing of the Holy Ghost. The first act of the renewed heart is faith ; as the first act of a restored eye is to see. Whether this satisfies the understanding or not, it remains clear as the doctrine of the Bible that good works are the fruits and consequences of reconciliation with God, through faith in our Lord Jesus Christ.

Inconsistent with the Grace of the Gospel.

2. It is objected that the Protestant doctrine destroys the gratuitous nature of justification. If justice be satisfied ; if all the demands of the law are met, there can, it is said, be no grace in the salvation of the sinner. If a man owes a debt, and some one pays it for him, the creditor shows no grace in giving an ac-quittal. This objection is familiar, and so also is the answer. The work of Christ is not of the nature of a commercial transac-tion. It is not analogous to a pecuniary satisfaction except in one point. It secures the deliverance of those for whom it is offered and by whom it is accepted. In the case of guilt the demand of justice is upon the person of the offender. He, and he alone is bound to answer at the bar of justice. No one can take his place, unless with the consent of the representative of justice and of the substitute, as well as of the sinner himself. Among men, substitution in the case of crime and its penalty is rarely, if ever admissible, because no man has the right over his own life or lib-erty ; he cannot give them up at pleasure ; and because no human magistrate has the right to relieve the offender or to inflict the legal penalty on another. But Christ had power, *i. e.*, the right

(ἐξουσία) to lay down his life and "power to take it again." And God, as absolute judge and sovereign, the Lord of the conscience, and the proprietor of all his creatures, was at full liberty to accept a substitute for sinners. This is proved beyond contradiction by what God has actually done. Under the old dispensation every sacrifice appointed by the law was a substitute for him in whose behalf it was offered. In the clearest terms it was predicted that the Messiah was to be the substitute of his people ; that the chastisement of their sins was to be laid on Him, and that He was to make his soul an offering for sin. He was hailed as He entered on his ministry as the Lamb of God who was to bear the sins of the world. He died the just for the unjust. He redeemed us from the curse of the law by being made a curse for us. This is what is meant by being a substitute. To deny this is to deny the central idea of the Scriptural doctrine of redemption. To explain it away, is to absorb as with a sponge the life-blood of the Gospel.

It is the glory, the power, and the preciousness of the Protestant doctrine that it makes the salvation of sinners a matter of grace from the beginning to the end. On the part of the eternal Father it was of grace, *i. e.*, of unmerited, mysterious, and immeasurable love that He provided a substitute for sinners, and that He spared not his own Son, but freely gave Him up for us all. It was a matter of grace, *i. e.*, of love to sinners, to the ungodly, to his enemies, that the eternal Son of God became man, assumed the burden of our sins, fulfilled all righteousness, obeying and suffering even unto death, that we might not perish but have eternal life. It is of grace that the Spirit applies to men the redemption purchased by Christ; that He renews the heart; that He overcomes the opposition of sinners, making them willing in the day of his power; that He bears with all their ingratitude, disobedience, and resistance, and never leaves them until his work is consummated in glory. In all this the sinner is not treated according to his character and conduct. He has no claim to any one in this long catalogue of mercies. Everything to him is a matter of unmerited grace. Merited grace, indeed, is a solecism. And so is merited salvation in the case of sinners.

Grace does not cease to be grace because it is not exercised in violation of order, propriety, and justice. It is not the weak fondness of a doting parent. It is the love of a holy God, who in order to reveal that love and manifest the exceeding glory of that attribute when exercised towards the unworthy, did what was

necessary to render its exercise consistent with the other perfections of the divine nature. It was indispensable that God should
be just in justifying the ungodly, but He does not thereby cease
to be gracious, inasmuch as it was He who provided the ransom by which the objects of his love are redeemed from the curse
of the law and the power of sin.

God cannot declare the Unjust to be Just.

3. Another standing objection to the Protestant doctrine has
been so often met, that nothing but its constant repetition justifies
a repetition of the answer. It is said to be absurd that one man
should be righteous with the righteousness of another ; that for
God to pronounce the unjust just is a contradiction. This is a
mere play on words. It is, however, very serious play ; for it is
caricaturing truth. It is indeed certain that the subjective, inherent quality of one person or thing cannot by imputation become
the inherent characteristic of any other person or thing. Wax
cannot become hard by the imputation of the hardness of a stone ;
nor can a brute become rational by the imputation of the intelligence of a man ; nor the wicked become good by the imputation
of the goodness of other men. But what has this to do with one
man's assuming the responsibility of another man ? If among
men the bankrupt can become solvent by a rich man's assuming
his responsibilities, why in the court of God may not the guilty
become righteous by the Son of God's assuming their responsibilities ? If He was made sin for us, why may we not be made
the righteousness of God in Him ? The objection assumes that
the word "just" or "righteous" in this connection, expresses
moral character ; whereas in the Bible, when used in relation
to this subject, it is always used in a judicial sense, *i. e.*, it expresses the relation of the person spoken of to justice. Δίκαιος
is antithetical to ὑπόδικος. The man with regard to whom justice
is unsatisfied, is ὑπόδικος, "guilty." He with regard to whom
justice is satisfied, is δίκαιος, "righteous." To declare righteous,
therefore, is not to declare holy ; and to impute righteousness is
not to impute goodness ; but simply to regard and pronounce
those who receive the gift of Christ's righteousness, free from condemnation and entitled to eternal life for his sake. Some philosophical theologians seem to think that there is real antagonism
between love and justice in the divine nature, or that these attributes are incompatible or inharmonious. This is not so in man ;
why then should it be so in God ? The highest form of moral

excellence includes these attributes as essential elements of its perfection. And the Scriptures represent them as mysteriously blended in the salvation of man. The gospel is a revelation to principalities and powers in heaven of the πολυποίκιλος σοφία τοῦ Θεοῦ, because therein He shows that He can be just and yet justify, love, sanctify, and glorify the chief of sinners. For which all sinners should render Him everlasting thanksgiving and praise.

Christ's Righteousness due for Himself.

4. It was natural that Socinus, who regarded Christ as a mere man, should object to the doctrine of the imputation of his righteousness to the believer, that Christ was under the same obligation to obey the law and to take his share of human suffering as other men, and therefore that his righteousness being due for Himself, could not be imputed to others. This objection is substantially urged by some who admit the divinity of Christ. In doing so, however, they virtually assume the Nestorian, or dualistic view of Christ's person. They argue on the assumption that He was a human person, and that he stood, in virtue of his assumption of our nature, in the same relation to the law as other men. It is admitted, however, that the Son, who became incarnate, was from eternity the second person in the Godhead. If, therefore, humanity as assumed by him was a person, then we have two persons, — two Christs, — the one human, the other divine. But if Christ be only one person, and if that person be the eternal Son of God, the same in substance, and equal in power and glory with the Father, then the whole foundation of the objection is gone. Christ sustained no other relation to the law, except so far as voluntarily assumed, than that which God himself sustains. But God is not under the law. He is Himself the primal, immutable, and infinitely perfect law to all rational creatures. Christ's subjection to the law therefore, was as voluntary as his submitting to the death of the cross. As He did not die for Himself, so neither did He obey for Himself. In both forms of his obedience He acted for us, as our representative and substitute, that through his righteousness many might be made righteous.

As to the other form of this objection, it has the same foundation and admits of the same answer. It is said that the obedience and sufferings of Christ, being the obedience and sufferings of a mere man, or at best of only the human element in the constitution of his person, could have only a human, and, therefore, only a finite value, and consequently could be no adequate satisfaction

for the sins of the whole world. Our Lord told his disciples, " Ye
are of more value than many sparrows." If, then, in the sight of
God a man is of far greater value than irrational creatures, why
should it be thought incredible that the blood of the eternal Son
of God should cleanse from all sin ? What a man does with his
hands, the man does ; and what Christ through his human nature
did, in the execution of his mediatorial work, the Son of God did
Therefore, men who spake as they were moved by the Holy
Spirit did not hesitate to say, that the Lord of glory was crucified
(1 Cor. ii. 8), and that God purchased the Church " with his own
blood." (Acts xx. 28.)[1] If, then, the obedience rendered, and the
sufferings endured, were those of a divine person, we can only shut
our mouths and bow down before God in adoring wonder, with
the full assurance that the merit of that obedience and of those
sufferings, must be abundantly sufficient for the justification of
every sinner upon earth, in the past, the present, or the future.

Believers continue Guilty, and liable to Punishment.

5. It is sometimes objected to the Protestant doctrine on this
subject, that believers not only recognize themselves as justly exposed to condemnation for their present shortcomings and transgressions, but that the Scriptures so represent them, and constantly speak of God as punishing his people for their sins. How
is this to be reconciled with the doctrine that they are not under

---

[1] The text in this passage is indeed disputed. The common text has θεοῦ, " the Church of
God; " which is retained by Mill, Bengel, Knapp, Hahn, and others in their editions of the
New Testament. Many MSS. have κυριου και θεοῦ; and others, simply κυριου. The fact that
the phrase " the Church of God " occurs eleven times in the New Testament, while " Church
of the Lord " never occurs, is urged as a reason in favour of the latter reading, as it is assumed that transcribers would be apt to adopt a familiar, rather than an unexampled expression. There may be some force in this. On the other hand, the presumption is that
the sacred writers adhere to their own " usus loquendi." The words in Acts xx. 28 are
Paul's words, and as he, at least in ten other cases, speaks of the " Church of God," and
never once uses the expression " Church of the Lord," it is in the highest degree improbable that he uses that phrase here. Besides, it is evident that transcribers, critics, and heretics would have a strong disposition to get rid of such a phrase as " the blood of God."
Modern critics do not hesitate to assign, as one of their reasons for rejecting the common
text, that the expression is " too strong." The passage, however, though sacred, is not essential. The usage pervades the New Testament of predicating of the person of Christ
what is true of either element, the human or the divine, of his mysteriously constituted
personality. In Hebrews i. 3 the person who upholds the universe by the word of his power, is said to have purged our sins by Himself, i. e., by the sacrifice of Himself. And in
ii. 14, the person whom the sacred writer had set forth as higher than the angels, as God, as
creator of heaven and earth, as eternal and immutable, is said to have become partaker
of flesh and blood, in order that by death He might destroy him that had the power of death.
And in Philippians ii. 6, 9, he who was in the form of God and thought it not robbery to be
equal with God, became obedient unto death, even the death of the cross. Nevertheless, although Acts xx. 28 be not essential to prove any doctrine, those who believe it as it reads
in the common text, to be part of the word of God, are bound to stand by it.

condemnation; that, as regards them, justice has been fully satisfied, and that no one can justly lay anything to the charge of God's elect.

It must be admitted, or rather it is fully acknowledged that every believer feels himself unworthy of the least of God's mercies. He knows that if God were to deal with him according to his character and conduct, he must inevitably be condemned. This sense of ill-desert or demerit, is indelible. It is a righteous judgment which the sinner passes, and cannot but pass upon himself. But the ground of his justification is not in himself. The believer acknowledges that in himself he deserves nothing but indignation and wrath, not only for what he has been, but for what he now is. This is what he feels when he looks at himself. Nevertheless, he knows that there is no condemnation to them that are in Christ Jesus; that Christ has assumed the responsibility of answering for him at the bar of God; that He constantly pleads his own perfect righteousness, as a reason why the deserved penalty should not be inflicted. If punishment were not deserved, pardon would not be gratuitous; and if not felt to be deserved, deliverance could not be received as a favour. The continued sense of ill-desert, on the part of the believer, is in no wise inconsistent with the Scriptural doctrine that the claims of justice in regard to him have been satisfied by his substitute and advocate. There is a great difference, as often remarked, between demerit and guilt. The latter is the liability in justice to the penalty of the law. The former is personal ill-desert. A criminal who has suffered the legal punishment of his crime, is no longer justly exposed to punishment for that offence. He however thinks of himself no better than he did before. He knows he cannot be subjected to further punishment; but his sense of demerit is not thereby lessened. And so it is with the believer; he knows that, because of what Christ has done for him, he cannot be justly condemned, but he feels and admits that in himself he is as hell-deserving as he was from the beginning. The heart of the believer solves many difficulties which the speculative understanding finds it hard to unravel. And it need not inordinately trouble him, if the latter be dissatisfied with the solution, provided he is sure that he is under the guidance of the Spirit by the word.

This Theory concerns only the Outward.

6. Modern theologians in many instances object to the Protestant doctrine of justification, that it is outward; concerns only

legal relations ; disregards the true nature of the mystical union ; and represents Christ and his righteousness as purely objective, instead of looking upon Christ as giving Himself, his life to become the life of the believer, and with his life conveying its merits and its power.   We are not concerned at present with the theory on which this objection is founded, but simply with the objection itself.   What is urged as an objection to the doctrine is true. It does concern what is outward and objective ; what is done for the sinner rather than what is done within him.   But then it is to be considered, first, that this is what the sinner needs.   He requires not only that his nature should be renewed and that a new principle of spiritual or divine life should be communicated to him ; but also that his guilt should be removed, his sins expiated, and justice satisfied, as the preliminary condition of his enjoying this new life, and being restored to the favour of God.   And secondly, that such is the constant representation of Scripture, our only trustworthy guide in matters of religious doctrine.   The Bible makes quite as prominent what Christ does for us, as what He does in us.   It says as much of his objective, expiatory work, as of the communication of a higher spiritual life to believers.   It is only by ignoring this objective work of Christ, or by merging justification into inward renovation, that this objection has force or even plausibility.   Protestants do not depreciate the value and necessity of the new life derived from Christ, because, in obedience to the Scriptures, they insist so strenuously upon the satisfaction which He has rendered by his perfect righteousness to the justice of God.   Without the latter, the former is impossible.

§ 10. *Departures from the Protestant Doctrine.*
Osiander.

During the lifetime of the Reformers, a very earnest controversy began in the Lutheran Church on the nature of justification. This arose from the views of Andreas Osiander, a man of distinguished learning and of a speculative turn of mind ; eminent first as a preacher, and afterwards as a professor in the university of Königsberg.   His principal work is entitled " De Unico Mediatore Jesu Christo et Justificatione Fidei.   Confessio Andreæ Osiandri."   His difference of opinion from the other Reformers is clearly indicated in the following words, in which he denounces the errors which he means to oppose: " Omnes horribiliter errant. Primo, quia verbum justificare tantum pro justum reputare et pronunciare intelligunt, atque interpretantur, et non pro eo, quod est, reipsa et in veritate justum efficere. Deinde etiam in hoc, quod nullam differentiam tenent inter redemptionem et justificationem, quum tamen magna differentia sit, sicut vel inde intelligi sit, quod homines furem a suspendio redimere possunt, bonum et justum efficere non possunt. Porro etiam in hoc, quod nihil certe statuere possunt, quid tandem justitia Christi sit, quam per fidem in nobis esse, nobisque imputari oporteat. Ac postremo errant omnium rudissime etiam in hoc, quod divinam naturam Christi a justificatione separant, et Christum dividunt atque solvunt, id quod haud dubie execrandi Satanæ opus est." [1]

Osiander taught, (1.) That Christ has redeemed us by the satisfaction which He rendered to divine justice. (2.) But he denied that this was any part of our justification. (3.) He maintained that to justify does not mean to declare just, or to render righteous in a judicial or forensic sense, but to render inherently or subjectively just and holy. (4.) That the righteousness of Christ by which the believer is justified, and which he receives by faith, and which is imputed to him in the judgment of God, is not, as the Protestants taught, the work of Christ, consisting in what He did and suffered as the substitute of sinners, nor is it, as Romanists teach, the work of the Holy Spirit consisting in the infusion of a holy nature or of new habits of grace, but it is the " essential righteousness of God," "the divine essence," " God Himself." (5.) That consequently the proximate and real ground of our acceptance with God, and of our reception into heaven, is what we are, or what we become, in virtue of this indwelling of God in the soul.

The speculations of Osiander as to the nature of God and his relation to man, might have led him under any circumstances to adopt the peculiar views above stated, but the proximate cause was no doubt the reaction from the too exclusive prominence given at that time to the objective work of Christ. This is not to be wondered at, and perhaps was not to be blamed. The Romanists, with whom the Protestants had to contend, did not deny the necessity of an inward change in the nature of fallen man. But they made this almost all of Christ's redeeming work. What He did for the expiation of sin and for meeting the demands of justice, was only to open the way for God's giving renewing and sanctifying grace to sinners. Men were themselves to merit eternal life. It was unavoidable therefore, that the Reformers should strenuously insist upon what Christ did for us.

---

[1] *Confessio*, Königsberg, 1551; by count, pp. 42, 43, of the text.

and that they should protest against confounding justification
with sanctification. Osiander's cast of mind made him revolt at
this, and carried him completely over to the Romish side, so far
as the nature of justification is concerned. He said that the
Protestant doctrine of justification is " colder than ice." It is as
though a man should pay the ransom of a Turkish slave, and
leave him and his children in bondage. Still more violent is his
denunciation of the doctrine that Christ's righteousness, of which
we partake through faith, consists of his obedience and sufferings.
What good can they do us? Christ obeyed and suffered centuries
ago ; we cannot appropriate what He then did and make it our
own. Imputing it to us does not alter the case. It does not make
us better. Speculative as well as Biblical reasons, however, prevented Osiander from accepting the Romish solution of the difficulty. What we are said to receive is " the righteousness of
Christ," " the righteousness of God; " but sanctifying grace is
never called the righteousness of God. If, therefore, that righteousness by which the believer is constituted righteous, be neither
the obedience of Christ, nor infused grace, what can it be other
than the essential righteousness of God, the divine essence itself ?
Calvin, who in his " Institutes " earnestly combats the theory of
Osiander, says that he invented " monstrum nescio quod essentialis
justitiæ." " Dilucide exprimit, se non ea justitia contentum, quæ
nobis obedientia et sacrificio mortis Christi parta est, fingere nos
substantialiter in Deo justos esse tam essentia quam qualitate infusa. . . . . Substantialem mixtionem ingerit, qua Deus se in
nos transfundens, quasi partem sui faciat. Nam virtute Spiritus
sancti fieri, ut coalescamus cum Christo, nobisque sit caput et
nos ejus membra, fere pro nihilo ducit, nisi ejus essentia nobis
misceatur." [1]

But what theory of the nature of God and of his relation to
man did Osiander hold, which admitted of this doctrine of the
infusion of the divine essence into the soul? His views on this
point were not clearly brought out, but the primary idea which
underlies his speculation is the old doctrine of the oneness of God
and man. Man is God in at least one form of his existence.
He held that Christ is the image, the representative, the realized
ideal of the Godhead, not as Logos or Son, but as Godman, the
Theanthropos. As from its nature or from the nature of God
this idea must be realized, this manifestation of God in his true
idea must occur, and therefore the incarnation would have taken

[1] *Institutio*, III. xi. 5, edit. Berlin, 1834, part ii. p. 8.

place had man never sinned.   The fall of Adam only modified
the circumstances attending the incarnation, determining that it
should involve suffering and death.   But the incarnation itself,
the appearance of God in fashion as a man arose from a law of
the divine nature.   Adam was created not after the image of
God as such, but after the image of Christ; in some sort, a God-
man.   The affinity of this theory with the modern pantheistic
speculations is apparent.   Baur, therefore, is doubtless right
when he says, at the close of his apologetic notice of Osiander's
doctrine, that his idea of the relation between the divine and human "is that which at last found its adequate scientific expression
by Schleiermacher and Hegel, that Christ as Redeemer is the perfected creation of human nature; or, that the divine nature is the
truth of humanity, and human nature the reality, or existence-
form (die Wirklichkeit) of the divine nature." [1]

Stancarus.

Stancarus, a contemporary and opponent of Osiander, went to
the extreme of asserting that the righteousness of Christ was the
work of his human nature exclusively.   This doctrine was however repudiated by the Romanists as well as by Protestants.   If
it was Christ's human nature as such (and not the divine person)
who obeyed, then the human nature in Christ was a distinct subsistence, and thus the unity of his person is destroyed.   Besides,
if it was not a divine person in his human nature who obeyed
and suffered, then we have but a human Saviour, and a righteousness of no higher than a human value.   We know from Scripture that it was the Lord of glory who was crucified, the Son of
God who, being born of a woman, was made under the law.

Piscator.

The first conspicuous departure from the Protestant doctrine
of justification among the Reformed, was on the part of Piscator,
whose denial of the imputation of the active obedience of Christ
to the believer, excited for some years a good deal of discussion,
but it passed away without leaving any distinct trace in the
theology of the Reformation.   Baur, indeed, assigns to it more
importance, as he regards it as the first step in the downfall of
the whole doctrine of the satisfaction of Christ, over which he
rejoices.   Piscator was a native of Strasburg, and a member of

---

[1] Baur, *Die Christliche Lehre von der Versöhnung*, ii. i. 1, Tübingen, 1838, p. 330,
note.

the Lutheran Church, to whose service his first ministerial and professional labors were devoted.   It coming to the knowledge of the ecclesiastical authorities that in his exposition of the Epistle to the Philippians he denied the ubiquity of the human nature of Christ, and taught the doctrine of predestination, he was deprived of his position in the Lutheran Church and passed over to the Reformed.   He was soon appointed one of the professors of the new Institution of Hebron founded by the Duke of Nassau.   He remained in connection with that institution from 1584 until his death in 1625, in the seventy-ninth year of his age.   He was a prolific writer.   Besides a new translation of the Bible, he wrote numerous commentaries on books of the Old and New Testaments, and conducted many controversies with Lutherans and Romanists, before he embroiled himself with the theologians of his own church.[1]   He took the ground that the " imputatio justitiæ " and " remissio peccatorum " are identical ; the former means nothing more than the latter ; and consequently that Christ's work consists simply in the expiation of sin.   His active obedience to the divine law constitutes no part of the righteousness by which the believer is justified before God. He admits that Christ rendered a twofold obedience, — the one to the law of God as a rule of duty ; the other to the special command given to Him as Mediator.   He came to accomplish a certain work ; to do the will of the Father, which was to make satisfaction for sin.   In this we are interested ; but his obedience to the moral law was for Himself, and was the necessary condition of his satisfaction.   He could not have made atonement for others had He not been Himself holy.   " Tribuitur morti," he says,[2] " quod ei tribuendum, nimirum, quod sit plenissima satisfactio pro peccatis nostris ; sic etiam vitæ obedientiæ tribuitur, quod scriptura ei tribuendum perhibet, nimirum, quod sit causa, sine qua non potuerat Christus idoneus esse mediator inter Deum et hominem."   Although Piscator made some effort to prove exegetically that pardon and justification, the remission of sin and imputation of righteousness, are identical, yet his arguments against the received doctrine, that the obedience of Christ is part of our justifying righteousness, are not Biblical.   The question before his mind was not simply, What do the Scriptures teach ? but, What is true, logical, and symmetrical ?   He saw objections

---

[1] *Theses Theolog.*, vol. iii. locus 39 : "De causa meritoria justificationis hominis coram Deo, sive de ea re, quæ a Deo ad justitiam imputatur."

[2] Loc. xxvi, p. 331.

to the imputation of the active obedience of Christ, which seemed
to him fatal, and on the ground of those objections he rejected
the doctrine.   Thus, for example, he argues that Christ's obedience to the law was due from Himself as a man, and therefore
not imputable to others.   He argues thus,[1] " Qui Christum dicunt ubique ut hominem, Christum dicunt non hominem, dum
enim dico ubique, dico Deum, qui solus est in cœlo et in terra.
Similiter cum dico subjectum legi, dico hominem. Qui ergo
Christum subjectum legi negant, negant ipsum esse hominem."
Every man as such in virtue of being a man is individually
bound to obey the moral law.   Christ was a man; therefore He
was bound to obey the law for Himself.   He did not perceive, or
was not willing to admit, that the word "man" is taken in different senses in the different members of this syllogism, and therefore, the conclusion is vitiated.   In the first clause, "man" means
a human person; in the second clause, it means human nature.
Christ was not a human person, although He assumed human
nature.   He was a man in the sense in which we are dust and
ashes.   But because we are dust, it does not follow that all that
may be predicated of dust, may be predicated of us; *e. g.*, that
we have no life, no reason, no immortality.   In like manner,
although the eternal Son of God took upon Himself a true body
and a reasonable soul, yet as He was a divine person, it does not
follow that everything that is true of human persons must be
true of Him.   Piscator also argues that the law binds either to
punishment or to obedience, but not to both at once.   Therefore,
if Christ's obedience is imputed to us, there was no necessity
that He should die for us.   On the other hand, if He died for us,
there was no necessity that He should obey for us.   The principle
here assumed may be true with regard to unfallen man.   But
where sin has been committed there is need of expiation as well
as of obedience, and of obedience as well as expiation, if the reward of perfect obedience is to be conferred.   Again, he says,
if Christ has fulfilled the law for us, we are not bound to keep it.
This is the old objection of the Jews; if justified by grace we
may live in sin.   But Christ has fulfilled the law for us only as
a covenant of works.   In that sense, says the Apostle, we are
not under the law, but it does not thence follow that we are free
from all moral obligation arising from our relation to God, as
rational creatures.   It may be true as Baur, himself a thorough
skeptic in the English and American sense of that word, thinks,

[1] Loc. xxvi. p. 334.

that this innovation of Piscator prepared the way for the rejection of the whole Scriptural doctrine of satisfaction. Certain it is that both Lutherans and Reformed united, with scarcely a dissenting voice, in the condemnation of Piscator's doctrine. It was judicially repudiated by the national Synod of France on several different occasions; first in 1603, again at La Rochelle in 1607, and afterwards in 1612 and 1613. The Swiss churches in the "Formula Consensus Helvetica," which received symbolical authority in Switzerland, pronounced clearly in favour of the old doctrine. This matter was soon lost sight of in consequence of the rise of Arminianism of far more historical importance.

The Arminian Doctrine.

Jacobus Arminius, a man of learning, talents, attractive accomplishments, and exemplary character, was born in Holland 1560, and died professor in the University of Leyden, in 1609, having filled the chair of theology since 1603. His departures from the Reformed doctrines in which he had been educated were far less serious than those of his successors, although involving them, apparently, by a logical necessity. His great difficulty was with the doctrine of predestination or the sovereignty of God in election. He could not, however, get rid of that doctrine without denying the entire inability of man to do what is spiritually good. He, therefore, taught that although mankind fell in Adam and are born in a state of sin and condemnation, and are of themselves entirely unable to turn from sin to holiness, yet that they are able to coöperate with the grace of the Holy Spirit given to all men, especially to all who hear the Gospel, in sufficient measure to enable them to repent and believe, and to persevere in holy living unto the end. But whether any man does thus repent and believe, or, having believed, perseveres in a holy life, depends on himself and not on God. The purpose of election, therefore, is not a purpose to save, and to that end to give faith and repentance to a definite number of individuals, but a purpose to save those who repent, believe, and persevere in faith until the end. The work of Christ has, therefore, an equal reference to all men. He made full satisfaction to God for the sins of all and every man, so that God can now consistently offer salvation to all men on the conditions laid down in the Gospel.

This is a self-consistent scheme. One part implies, or necessitates the admission of the others. The above statement includes all the doctrines presented by the followers of Arminius, after his death, to the authorities in the form of a Remonstrance, as a justification of their views.   Hence the Arminians were called Remonstrants.   The document just mentioned contains the five points on which its authors and their associates differed from the Reformed faith.   The first relates to predestination, which is explained as the purpose " illos in Christo, propter Christum et per Christum servare, qui Spiritus Sancti gratia, in eundem ejus filium credunt, et in ea, fideique obedientia, per eandem gratiam in finem perseverant: contra vero eos, qui non convertentur et infideles, in peccato et iræ subjectos relinquere, et condemnare, secundum illud Evang. Joann. iii. 36."

The second relates to the work of Christ, as to which it is said, " Proinde Jesum Christum mundi servatorem pro omnibus et singulis mortuum esse, atque ita quidem, ut omnibus per mortem Christi reconciliationem et peccatorum remissionem impetravit: ea tamen conditione, ut nemo illa remissione peccatorum re ipsa fruatur, præter hominem fidelem, et hoc quoque secundum Evang. Joann. iii. 16, et 1 Joann. ii. 2."

The third, concerning the sinner's ability, declares, " Hominem vero salutarem fidem a se ipso non habere, nec vi liberi sui arbitrii, quandoquidem in statu defectionis et peccati nihil boni, quandoquidem vere bonum est, quale quid est fides salutaris, ex se possit cogitare, vel facere: sed necessarium esse eum a Deo in Christo per Spiritum Sanctum regigni et renovari mente, affectibus, seu voluntate et omnibus facultatibus, ut aliquid boni possit intelligere, cogitare, velle et perficere.   Ev. Joann. xv. 5." No Augustinian, whether Lutheran or Calvinist, can say more than that, or desire more to be said by others.

The fourth article, concerning grace, however, shows the point of departure: " Hanc Dei gratiam esse initium, progressum ac perfectionem omnis boni, atque id eo quidem usque ut ipse homo regenitus absque hac præcedentia, seu adventitia excitante, consequente et cooperante gratia, neque boni quid cogitare, velle, aut facere possit, neque etiam ulli malæ tentatione resistere; adeo quidem ut omnia bona opera, quæ excogitare possumus, Dei gratiæ in Christo tribuenda sint; quod vero modum operationis illius gratiæ, illa non irresistibilis; de multis enim dicitur eos Spiritui Sancto resistere, Act. vii. 51 et alibi multis locis."   It was not to be expected, in a brief exposition of principles designed for the justification of those who hold them, as members of a Reformed or Calvinistic church, that doubtful terms should be explained.   It is beyond controversy, however, and, it is believed, is not controverted, that irresistible is here used in the sense of certainly efficacious. The Holy Spirit operates on the hearts of all men. Some are thereby renewed and brought to faith and repentance ; others are not. This difference, according to the Remonstrants, is not to be referred to the nature of the influence exerted, but to the fact that some yield to this grace and coöperate with it; while others reject and resist it.

The fifth article refers to the perseverance of the saints, and is indefinite. It admits that the Spirit furnishes grace abundantly sufficient to enable the believer to persevere in holiness : " Sed an illi ipsi negligentia sua initium sui esse in Christo deserere non possint, et præsentem mundum iterum amplecti, a sancta doctrina ipsis semel tradita deficere, conscientiæ naufragium facere, a gratia excidere; penitus ex sacra Scriptura esset expendum, antequam illud cum plena animi tranquillitate et πληροφορία docere possent." Of course no man who believed the doctrine could write thus, and this doubtful mode of expression was soon laid aside, and " falling from grace," in the common sense of the phrase, was admitted to be an Arminian doctrine.

It will be observed that the doctrine of justification is not embraced in the five points in the Remonstrance as presented to the authorities in Holland, and as made the basis of the decisions of the Synod of Dort. The aberration of the Arminians, however, from the faith of the Reformed churches, extended to all the doctrines connected with the plan of salvation. Arminius himself, at least, held far higher and more Scriptural views on original sin, inability, and the necessity of supernatural grace, than those which have since become so prevalent even among the Reformed or Calvinistic churches themselves. In matters concerning the method of salvation, especially as to the nature of Christ's work and its application to the believer, they at first adhered closely to the language of the Reformed confessions. Thus they did not hesitate to say that Christ made full satisfaction for the sins of men ; that He was a ransom, a sacrifice, a propitiation ; that He made expiation for sin ; that his righteousness or obedience is the ground of our acceptance with God; that the faith which saves is not mere assent to truth, or pious confidence in God, but specifically faith in Christ as the Saviour of men ; and that justification is an act of God pronouncing the sinner just, or in which He pardons sin and accepts the sinner as righteous. All this is satisfactory to the ear. Language, however, admits of different interpretations; and it soon became apparent and avowed that the Remonstrants intended something very different from what the Reformed Church meant to express by the same terms.

1. They said that Christ's work was a satisfaction to divine justice. But they did not mean by satisfaction, either a " solutio," a real value rendered for what was due ; nor even an " acceptio," taking one thing for another as an equivalent ; but an " acceptilatio," a gracious acceptance as a satisfaction of that which in its own nature was no equivalent; as though God should accept the life of a brute for that of a man ; or faith for perfect obedience. Neither did the Remonstrants mean by justice the attribute which requires the righteous distribution of rewards and punishments, and which renders it necessary that the penalty of the law should be executed in case of transgression.

With regard to this latter point (the nature of justice) the language of Grotius, and of the great body of the Remonstrant or Arminian theologians, is perfectly explicit. Grotius says : " Pœnas infligere, aut a pœnis aliquem liberare, quem punire possis, quod justificare vocat Scriptura, non est nisi rectoris, qua talis primo et per se : ut, puta, in familia patris ; in republica regis, in universo Dei. . . . . Unde sequitur, omnino hic Deum considerandum, ut rectorem."[1] Again,[2] " Ratio [cur ' rectori relaxare legem talem non liceat, nisi causa aliqua accedat, si non necessaria, certe sufficiens '] . . . . est, quod actus ferendi aut relaxandi legem non sit actus absoluti dominii, sed actus imperii, qui tendere debeat ad boni ordinis conservationem."[3] " Pœna enim omnis propositum habet bonum commune." " Prudentia quoque hoc nomine rectorem ad pœnam incit it. Augetur præterea causa puniendi, ubi lex aliqua publicata est, quæ pœnam minatur. Nam tunc omissio pœnæ ferme aliquid detrahit de legis authoritate apud subditos."[4]

Here everything is purely governmental. It is not justice, in the proper and ordinary sense of the word, that is satisfied, but God's wise and benevolent regard to the interests of his moral government. This changes everything. If God's justice be not satisfied guilt is not removed, and sin is not expiated. And therefore conscience is not appeased ; nor can the real authority and honour of the law be upheld.

As to the other point, the nature of the satisfaction rendered ;

---

[1] *De Satisfactione Christi*, cap. 2; *Works*, edit. London, 1679, vol. iii. p. 306, b (19–24).
[2] *Ibid.* cap. 5; p. 317, b (35–41).   [3] *Ibid.* cap. 2; p. 308, b (62, 63).
[4] *Ibid.* cap. 5; p. 316, b (9–13).

it was not a real equivalent, which by its intrinsic value met
the obligations of the sinner, but it was something graciously accepted as such. Although Grotius rejects the use of the word
" acceptilatio," and endeavours to show that it does not express his
meaning, nevertheless, though he repudiates the word, he retains
the idea. He says,[1] " Ea est pretii natura, ut sui valore aut æstimatione alterum moveat ad concedendam rem, aut jus aliquod,
puta impunitatem." This amounts to the principle of Duns
Scotus that a thing avails (is worth) for what God pleases to
take it. Although Grotius does not carry out the principle to
the length to which the Schoolmen carried it, and say that God
might have accepted the death of one man as a satisfaction for the
sins of the world, or the blood of bulls or of goats as a real expi
ation, nevertheless, he teaches that God graciously accepted " aliquid pro aliquo," the death of Christ for the death for all the
world, not because of its being a real equivalent in itself, but because as ruler, having the right to remit sin without any satisfaction, He saw that the interests of his government could thereby
be promoted. Still more clearly is this idea expressed by Lim
borch :[2] " In eo errant quam maxime, quod velint redemtionis
pretium per omnia equivalens esse debere miseriæ illi, e qua re-
demtio fit : redemtionis pretium enim constitui solet pro libera
æstimatione illius, qui captivum detinet, non autem solvi pro cap-
tivi merito. . . . . Ita pretium, quod Christus persolvit, juxta
Dei Patris æstimationem persolutum est."

According to Grotius, Christ died as an example, " exemplum
pœnæ." The whole efficacy of his work was its moral impression on the universe. It was not an expiation or satisfaction for
past sins, but a means of deterring from the commission of sin in
the future. This, as Baur[3] and Strauss[4] remark, is the point in
which the theory of Grotius and that of Socinus coincide. They
both refer the efficacy of Christ's work to the moral impression
which it makes on the minds of intelligent creatures. They refer
that moral influence, indeed, to different causes, but moral impression is all the efficacy it has. Although the word satisfaction is
retained by Grotius, the idea attached to it by the Church is rejected. The leading Remonstrant or Arminian theologians, as
Episcopius, Curcellæus, and Limborch, differ from Grotius in their
mode of presenting this subject. Instead of regarding the work
of Christ as an example of punishment, designed to deter from

---

[1] *De Satisfactione*, cap. 8; *Works*, edit London, 1679, vol. iii. p. 328, b (12–14).
[2] *Theologia Christiana*, III. xxi. 8, edit. Amsterdam, 1715, p. 262, a.
[3] *Die christliche Lehre von der Versöhnung*, II. i. 4, Tübingen, 1838, p. 429.
[4] *Dogmatik*, Tübingen and Stuttgart, 1841, vol. ii. p. 315.

the commission of sin, they adhere to the Scriptural mode of regarding Him as a ransom and sacrifice. The difference however
is more in form than in reality. They admit that Christ redeems
us by giving Himself as a ransom for many. But a ransom, as
Curcellæus says, is not an equivalent ; it is anything the holder of
the captive sees fit to accept. It is admitted, also, that Christ
gave Himself as a sacrifice for our salvation ; but a sacrifice is
said not to be a satisfaction to justice, but simply the condition
on which pardon is granted. Under the Old Testament God
pardoned sin on the occasion of the sacrifice of irrational animals ;
under the New Testament, on the occasion of the sacrifice of
Christ. " Sacrificia," says Limborch,[1] " non sunt solutiones debi-
torum, neque plenariæ pro peccatis satisfactiones ; sed illis perac-
tis conceditur gratuita peccati remissio." " Redemtionis pretium
constitui solet pro libera æstimatione illius, qui captivum detinet."
We know, however, from Scripture that a sacrifice was not merely
an arbitrarily appointed antecedent of gratuitous forgiveness ; it
was not simply an acknowledgment of guilt. We know also that
the blood of bulls and of goats under the Old Testament could
not take away sin ; it availed only to the purifying of the flesh,
or the remission of ceremonial penalties. The only efficacy of
the Old Testament sacrifices, so far as sin committed against
God is concerned, was sacramental ; that is, they signified, sealed,
and applied the benefits of the only real and effectual expiation
for sin, to those who believed. As the victim symbolically bore
the penalty due to the offender, so the eternal Son of God really
bore our sins, really became a curse for us, and thus made a true
and perfect satisfaction to God for our offences.

2. As the Remonstrants denied that Christ's work was a real
satisfaction for sin, they of necessity denied any real justification
of the sinner. Justification with them is merely pardon. This
is asserted by Grotius in the passage above cited ; and even the
Rev. Richard Watson, whose excellent system of theology, or
" Theological Institutes," is deservedly in high repute among the
Wesleyan Methodists, not only over and over defines justification as pardon, but elaborately argues the question. "The first
point," he says, "which we find established by the language of
the New Testament is, that justification, the pardon and remission of sins, the non-imputation of sin, and the imputation of
righteousness, are terms and phrases of the same import."[2] He
then goes on to establish that position.

---

[1] *Theologia Christiana,* III. xxi. 6, 8, *ut supra,* pp. 261, a, 262
[2] II. xxiii. ; edit. New York, 1832, p. 426.

If therefore, pardon and justification are distinct things, the one the executive act of a ruler, the other a judicial act ; the one setting aside the demands of justice, the other a declaration that justice is satisfied ; then those who reduce justification to mere pardon, deny the doctrine of justification as understood and professed by the Lutheran and Reformed churches.   It of course is not intended that these Remonstrant or Arminian theologians do not hold what they call justification ; nor is it denied that they at times, at least, express their doctrine in the very language of the Symbols of the Protestant churches.   Thus the Remonstrants [1] say, " Justificatio est actio Dei, quam Deus pure pute in sua ipsius mente efficit, quia nihil aliud est, quam volitio aut decretum, quo peccata remittere, et justitiam imputare aliquando vult iis, qui credunt, id est, quo vult pœnas, peccatis eorum promeritas, iis non infligere, eosque tanquam justos tractare et premio afficere."   Nevertheless they tell us that they mean by this only pardon.   Protestants, when they say justification includes pardon " and " the imputation of righteousness, mean two distinct things by pardon and imputation of righteousness.   The Remonstrants regard them as identical, and, therefore, can use the very language of Protestants, while rejecting their doctrine.   As every one feels and knows that when a criminal is pardoned by the executive, and allowed to resume his rights of property and right of voting, he is not thereby justified ; so every candid mind must admit that there is an immense difference between the Remonstrant or Arminian doctrine of justification and that held as the cardinal principle of the Reformation by both Lutherans and Reformed.

3. This difference becomes still more apparent when we consider what the Remonstrants make the ground of justification. As they deny that Christ made any real satisfaction to divine justice (as distinguished from benevolence), so they deny that the righteousness of Christ is imputed to the believer as the ground of his justification.   On this point, Limborch [2] says, " Hæc autem, quæ nobis imputatur, non est Christi justitia ; nusquam enim Scriptura docet, Christi justitiam nobis imputari ; sed tantum fidem nobis imputari in justitiam, et quidem propter Christum."   And Curcellæus [3] says, " Nullibi docet Scriptura justitiam Christi nobis imputari.   Et id absurdum est.   Nemo enim in se injustus aliena justitia potest esse formaliter justus, non magis, quam aliena albedine Æthiops esse albus."

---

[1] *Apologia pro Confessione Remonstrantium,* cap. 11, 12; Episcopii *Opera,* edit. Rotterdam, 1665, vol. ii. p. 166, a, of second set.

[2] *Theologia Christiana.* vi. iv. 18, *ut supra,* p. 703, a.   [3] *Relig. Christ. Inst.* 7, 9, 6

As the righteousness of Christ is not imputed to the believer, the ground of his justification, that which is accepted as righteousness, is faith and its fruits, or faith and evangelical obedience. On this subject Limborch says,[1] that under the new covenant God demands " obedientiam fidei, hoc est, non rigidam et omnibus æqualem, prout exigebat lex ; sed tantam, quantam fides, id est, certa de divinis promissionibus persuasio, in unoquoque efficere potest ; in qua etiam Deus multas imperfectiones et lapsus condonat, modo animo sincero præceptorum ipsius observationi incumbamus, et continuo in eadem proficere studeamus."

And again,[2] " Deus non judicat hominum justitiam esse perfectam, imo eam judicat esse imperfectam ; sed justitiam, quam imperfectam judicat, gratiose accipit ac si perfecta esset." He, therefore,[3] thus defines justification, " Est gratiosa æstimatio, seu potius acceptatio justitiæ nostræ imperfectæ (quæ, si Deus rigide nobiscum agere vellet, in judicio Dei nequaquam consistere posset) pro perfecta, propter Jesum Christum."

The same view is presented when he speaks of faith in its relation to justification. Faith is said to be imputed for righteousness ; but Limborch says,[4] " Sciendum, quando dicimus, nos fide justificari, nos non excludere opera, quæ fides exigit et tanquam fœcunda mater producit ; sed ea includere." Again,[5] " Fides est conditio in nobis et a nobis requisita, ut justificationem consequamur. Est itaque talis actus, qui, licet in se spectatus perfectus nequaquam sit, sed in multis deficiens, tamen a Deo gratiosa et liberrima voluntate pro pleno et perfecto acceptatur et propter quem Deus homini gratiose remissionem peccatorum et vitæ æternæ præmium conferre vult."

Fletcher [6] says, " With respect to the Christless law of paradisaical obedience, we entirely disclaim sinless perfection." " We shall not be judged by that law ; but by a law adapted to our present state and circumstances, a milder law, called the law of Christ." " Our Heavenly Father never expects of us, in our debilitated state, the obedience of immortal Adam in paradise."

Dr. Peck[7] says, " The standard of character set up in the Gospel must be such as is practicable by man, fallen as he is. Coming up to this standard is what we call Christian perfection."

---

1 *Theologia Christiana*, vi. iv. 37, *ut supra*, p. 706, a.
2 *Ibid.* vi. iv. 41 ; p. 706, b, 707, a.
3 *Ibid.* vi. iv. 18 ; p. 703, a.   4 *Ibid.* vi. iv. 32 ; p. 705, b
5 *Ibid.* vi. iv. 31 ; p. 705, a.
6 *Last Check to Antinomianism*, sect. i ; *Works*, N. Y. 1833, vol. ii. pp. 493, 494.
7 *Christian Perfection*, New York, 1843, p. 294.

Under the covenant of works as made with Adam, perfect obedience was the condition of acceptance with God and of eternal life ; under the Gospel, for Christ's sake, imperfect, or evangelical obedience, is the ground of justification, *i. e.*, it is that (*propter quam*) on account of which God graciously grants us the remission of sin and the reward of eternal life.

We have then the three great systems. First, that of the Romanists, which teaches that on account of the work of Christ God grants, through Christian baptism, an infusion of divine grace, by which all sin is purged from the soul and all ground for the infliction of the penalty is removed and the sinner rendered inherently just or holy. This is the first justification. Then in virtue of the new principle of spiritual life thus imparted, the baptized or regenerated are enabled to perform good works, which are really meritorious and on account of which they are admitted to heaven.

Secondly, the Arminian theory, that on account of what Christ has done, God is pleased to grant sufficient grace to all men, and to accept the imperfect obedience which the believer is thus enabled to render in lieu of the perfect obedience required under the covenant made with Adam, and on account of that imperfect obedience, eternal life is graciously bestowed.

Thirdly, the Protestant doctrine that Christ, as the representative and substitute of sinners or of his people, takes their place under the law, and in their name and in their behalf fulfils all righteousness, thereby making a real, perfect, and infinitely meritorious satisfaction to the law and justice of God, which righteousness is imputed, or set to the account of the believer, who is thereupon and on that account freely pardoned and pronounced righteous in the sight of God, and entitled not only to the remission of sin but also to eternal life. Being united to Christ by faith, the believer becomes partaker of his life, so that it is not he that lives but Christ that liveth in him, and the life which the believer now lives in the flesh is by faith of the Son of God, who loved him, and gave Himself for him.

Comparison of the Different Doctrines.

The first remark which suggests itself on the comparison of these several schemes is, that the relation between the believer and Christ is far more close, peculiar, and constant on the Protestant scheme than on any other. He is dependent on Him every hour ; for the imputation of his righteousness ; for the supplies of the Spirit of life ; and for his care, guidance, and intercession. He must look to Him continually ; and continually exercise faith in Him as an ever present Saviour in order to live. According to the other schemes, Christ has merely made the salvation of all men possible. There his work ended. According to Romanists, He has made it possible that God should give sanctifying grace in baptism ; according to the Remonstrants, He has rendered it possible for Him to give sufficient grace to all men whereby to sanctify and save themselves. We are well aware that this is theory ; that the true people of God, whether Romanists or Remonstrants, do not look on Christ thus as a Saviour afar off. They doubtless have the same exercises towards Him that their fellow believers have ; nevertheless, such is the theory. The theory places a great gulf between the soul and Christ.

Secondly, it hardly admits of question that the Protestant view conforms to the Scriptural mode of presenting the plan of salvation. Christ in the Bible is declared to be the head of his people, their representative ; they were in Him in such a sense that they died in Him ; they are raised with Him, and sit with Him in heavenly places. They were in Him as the race was in Adam, and as branches are in the vine. They individually receive the sprinkling of that blood which cleanses from all sin. They are constituted righteous by his obedience. As He was made sin for them, so are they made the righteousness of God in Him. He is not only an example of punishment as Grotius represents, a mere governmental device, but a sacrifice substituted for us, on whose head every believer must lay his hand and to whom he must transfer the burden of his sins.

Thirdly, what is included indeed in the above, but is so important and decisive as to require distinct and repeated mention ; all schemes, other than the Protestant, refer the proximate ground of our acceptance with God to our own subjective character. It is because of our own goodness that we are regarded and treated as righteous. Whereas conscience demands, the Scriptures reveal, and the believer instinctively seeks something better than that. His own goodness is badness. It cannot satisfy his own bleared vision ; how then can it appear before the eyes of God ? It matters not how the Romanist may exalt his " inward habits of grace ; " or how the Arminian may sublimate his evangelical obedience to perfection ; neither can satisfy either the conscience or God.

Fourthly, the Protestant doctrine is the only one on which the

soul can live. This has been urged before when speaking of the
work of Christ. It is fair to appeal from theology to hymnology;
from the head to the heart; from what man thinks to what God
makes men feel. It is enough to say on this point, that Lutheran
and Reformed Christians can find nowhere, out of the Bible,
more clear, definite, soul-satisfying expression of their doctrinal
views upon this subject, than are to be found in many of the
hymns of the Latin and Arminian churches. As a single example may be cited the following stanzas from John Wesley's
' Hymns and Spiritual Songs " : —

> " Join, earth and heaven to bless
> The Lord our Righteousness.
> The mystery of redemption this,
> This the Saviour's strange design —
> Man's offence was counted his.
> Ours his righteousness divine.

> " In Him complete we shine;
> His death, his life, is mine;
> Fully am I justified,
> Free from sin, and more than free,
> Guiltless, since for me He died;
> Righteous, since He lived for me."

§ 11. *Modern Views on Justification.*
Rationalistic Theories.

These cannot be given in detail. Certain classes of opinions
can be referred to only in the briefest manner. The Rationalists
were divided into two classes; first, those who regarded the
Scriptures as a supernatural revelation of natural religion, or of
the truths of reason; and secondly, those who denied the supernatural origin of the Scriptures altogether, assigning to them no
higher authority than belongs to the writings of good and wise
men.

The former class came to agree very nearly with the latter as
to what the Bible actually teaches, or, at least, as to what is by
us to be regarded and received as true. Those who admitted the
divine origin of the Scriptures got rid of its distinctive doctrines
by the adoption of a low theory of inspiration, and by the application of arbitrary principles of interpretation. Inspiration was,
in the first instance, confined to the religious teachings of the
Bible, then to the ideas or truths, but not to the form in which
they were presented, nor to the arguments by which they were
supported. The fact that Christ saves men in some way was admitted, but not as a sacrifice nor as a ransom, nor by being a

substitute for sinners. The miracles of Christ were acknowledged as historical facts, but they were explained as mere natural events distorted by the imaginations of spectators and historians. It was granted by some that Christ and the Apostles did teach the Church doctrines, but this, it was said, was done only by way of accommodation to the prejudices, superstitions, or modes of thought of the men of that generation. The first step in this process was the denial of all distinction between the prophetic, priestly, and kingly offices of Christ. In this way a wet sponge was passed over all the doctrines of redemption, and their outlines obliterated. This unnatural process could not be long continued, and, therefore, the majority of Rationalists soon threw off all regard to the normal authority of the Bible, and avowed their faith in nothing which did not commend itself to their own understanding as true, and for that reason alone.

As to the doctrine of justification, the whole tendency of the efforts during this period was, as Baur correctly says,[1] to make the reconciliation of man to God the work of the man himself. " A man was entitled to regard himself as reconciled with God as soon as he determined to repent and to reform." God was regarded as a father. A father is displeased with a son only so long as he is disobedient. The only end of any chastisement he may inflict, is the reformation of his child. If that be accomplished, all necessity and all propriety of punishment cease. Wegscheider, a representative of this class of theologians, says,[2] "Quicunque e vita turpi, qua pœnas sibi contraxit, ad virtutem emerserit, is eadem proportione, qua jam in virtutis studio progressus fuerit, in gratiam cum Deo reversus, ab eodem præmiis dignus judicabitur."

Philosophical Theories.

The philosophical theories on this subject were as different as the systems on which they were founded. Some of these systems were theistic, others pantheistic, and others monistic, *i. e.*, founded on the oneness of God and man, without denying the distinct personality of either.

The influence of Kant's philosophy upon theology, for a time at least, was very great, and in some aspects salutary. As he exalted the power of the pure reason, making it give law to the outward, subordinating, as his disciples say, the objective to the

---

[1] *Die Christliche Lehre von der Versöhnung*, iii. i. Tübingen, 1830, p. 565.
[2] *Institutiones Theologiæ*, iii. ii. § 140, 5th edit. Halle, 1826, p. 438.

subjective, so in the sphere of religion and morality he exalted the power and authority of the practical reason. Everything was subordinate to moral excellence. Happiness was not the end. It was only a means of promoting and rewarding what is morally good. The attainment of the highest amount of moral excellence requires perfect harmony between happiness and goodness, that is, that rational creatures should be happy in exact proportion to their goodness, and miserable in proportion as they are wicked. The punishment of sin is therefore inevitable. It is determined by the immutable moral order of the universe, which can no more be changed or set aside than any physical law on which the existence or order of the external world depends.

From these principles some of the Kantian theologians inferred that the pardon of sin is impossible. Misery is as inseparable from sin as pain is from the laceration of the body. If the only punishment of sin, however, be its natural consequences, then the removal of sin effects the removal of punishment. This determines the view which many of the disciples of Kant take of the nature of redemption. It is purely subjective. Men are delivered from sin and thereby from its punishment.

To others, however, this view was unsatisfactory, (1.) Because the punishment of sin is not purely or exclusively natural. It is not so even in this world, as is proved by the deluge, by the destruction of the cities of the plain, and by a thousand other instances. Much less is it true with regard to the future world. Conscience is not the only worm that never dies, or remorse the only fire which is never quenched. (2.) Because this theory reverses the natural order of events. It makes reformation precede pardon, whereas pardon must precede reformation. On this point Bretschneider [1] quotes even Ewald [2] as saying, " It is as unpsychological as it is unchristian so to present Christian reformation, that a man must become better before he is forgiven. It is precisely through the love of God anticipating our reformation, by which the man morally dead is quickened, that the elements of all religion, gratitude, trust, and love are called into exercise." This is certainly Paul's doctrine. (3.) The theory in question overlooks guilt, responsibility to justice for sins already committed. (4.) The ends of punishment (according to the Kantians) are, first, the satisfaction of the moral excellence of God, who by necessity of his moral perfection must punish sin ; secondly,

[1] *Dogmatik*, § 159, 3d edit. Leipzig, 1828, vol. ii. p. 320, note.
[2] *Die Religionslehren der Bibel*, ii. v. zu nro. 27; Stuttgart and Tübingen, 1812, vol. ii. p. 149.

the improvement of the offender ; and thirdly, the upholding the
moral order of the universe. The two former of these ends,
Bretschneider says, may be answered by the reformation of the
sinner. When a man ceases to sin, he ceases to be opposed to
God, and God ceases to be opposed to him. But the third end of
punishment, namely, preserving the moral order of the universe,
is not answered by the sinner's reformation. He is not the only
person to be considered. The interests of morality would suffer,
if he were rendered happy notwithstanding his past transgression.
The question then is, is there any way in which the authority of
the moral law can be sustained, and yet the sinner be forgiven and
rendered blessed ? The Church answer to this question, the disciples of Kant reject as contrary to reason ; but reason, says Bretschneider, has nothing to object to the doctrine stated generally
that God can consistently pardon sin for Christ's sake. He sums
up under the following heads, what reason may accept in regard
to this whole subject. (1.) That the divine nature of Christ
rendered his sufferings more important for the spiritual world
and more available for man than they otherwise would have
been. (2.) We cannot properly say that He suffered the penalty
of the law, or the punishment of our sins, but that He endured
his unmerited sufferings for the good of the world. (3.) That
He did not make satisfaction for sin, but rendered secure the
moral order of the universe. (4.) Although He did not make
satisfaction, He procured or mediated our pardon. He is not our
sponsor, but our " mediator salutis." (5.) The expression " the
merit of Christ " does not mean any good imputed to us, or any
title belonging to us, but simply the claim of Christ that his sufferings shall avail to the good of men. (6.) The word " reconciliation " is anthropopathic. It does not express any change in
God ; but either objectively the possibility of pardon, or subjectively the hope of pardon. (7.) " To impute the merit of Christ "
does not mean that God regards Christ's obedience as our obedience, or his sufferings as our punishment, but simply that,
through love, God has determined to render his sufferings available for the good of men. (8.) That Christ's death was vicarious in so far that in consequence thereof sin may be pardoned in
the renewed. (9.) Justification is the application to individuals
of the general declaration of God that He will save all who strive
to reform. This is the highest form in which theologians regarded
as rationalistic are willing to receive the doctrines of atonement
and justification.

Speculative Theologians.

The views of the speculative theologians on these points have already been presented in the chapters on the person of Christ and on his work, as fully as is proper in such a work as this.

However much this class of theologians may differ as to their philosophical principles, or as to the length to which they carry those principles in their explanation of Christian doctrine, they agree, first, in rejecting the Church view of the plan of salvation ; they deny that Christ obeyed the law and bore its penalty vicariously, or as the substitute of sinners ; they deny that his righteousness is imputed to the believer as the ground of his justification ; they deny that saving faith consists in receiving and resting on the righteousness of Christ as something objective ; they deny that justification is a forensic or judicial act in which God pronounces the sinner just, not on the ground of his subjective state or character, but on the ground of what Christ has done for him. All this they pronounce mechanical, external, magical, unreal, and unsatisfactory.   On the other hand, they agree in representing justification as an act by which the sinner is made inherently or subjectively just ; and consequently that his acceptance with God, and his title to eternal life, are founded on what he is ; they agree in regarding faith as that state of mind which renders the sinner receptive of the infusion of whatever it is that renders him thus subjectively righteous in the sight of God.   What that is, is the main point on which their representations differ. Those who regard man as only a form of the manifestation of God, say that one man's being justified and not another, means that God is more fully developed in the one than in the other ; or that the one realizes more truly the idea of man than the other; and this, after all, consists in one's coming to the consciousness of his oneness with God, which others have not attained. " The most universal and essential idea of redemption and reconciliation is man's becoming one with God. The necessary objective assump tion, on which alone the individual can be one with God, or redeemed and reconciled, is the truth, that man as such is one with God (dass der Mensch an sich mit Gott Eins ist)." [1] This, according to one view, is an eternal process; God is ever becoming man, and man is ever returning into God. According to Schleiermacher, as already repeatedly stated, this manifestation of God in man was hindered and could never become perfect by a process

[1] Baur, *Die Christliche Lehre von der Versöhnung*, Tübingen, 1838, p. 698.

of natural development; and, therefore, by a new creative act
Christ was produced, in whom the idea of man was fully realized, or in whom the oneness of God and man was clearly exhibited, and from Him a new process of development commenced as
perfectly natural as the process before his advent, and the redemption of man consists in the communication of the sinlessness
and blessedness of Christ to the individual. This is expressed
commonly by saying that the life of Christ, — not the Holy
Spirit as derived from Him; not his divine nature; not his
humanity; but his divine-human life, — is communicated to the
Church and to all its members. In other words, as Christ is God
in human form, so is every believer. The incarnation goes forward in the Church. In the language of the older mystics, what
is communicated is " the essential righteousness of God," or
" the essence of God," the life of God, or God Himself.

According to this view the objective work of Christ, what He
did and suffered is of no avail for us; it is not that which makes
us righteous, or by which we are redeemed. Redemption and
reconciliation are a purely subjective process; something which
takes place in the sinner's own soul, and not something which
was done for him. It matters little whether there was a historical Christ or not; or, at least, whether the facts recorded of
Him be true or untrue; whether the Gospels are historical or
mythical.

According to another view, the work of Christ was in no sense
a satisfaction to divine justice; neither his obedience nor his suffering was designed to be set over to his people with its merit,
as the ground of their justification. The Word became flesh.
He assumed our fallen humanity into personal union with Him
self. This necessitated conflict and suffering as the only way in
which the new life could triumph over the law of sin and death
which belonged to our fallen humanity. This was the atonement of Christ, the triumph of health over disease. This was
the victory of Christ over sin and hell. Thus He becomes the
author of salvation to men. Humanity in Christ suffered and
died, and rose again. That humanity is our nature. It is that
which constitutes us what we are. By union with the Church,
which is the body of Christ animated by his theanthropic nature
or life, we become one with Him. What is communicated to
us is not his merit, nor his Spirit, but his essence, his substance,
his life. There is no dualism between the soul and body. They
are one life. The soul externalizes itself in the body, they are

one. So there is no dualism in Christ ; not a divine and human substance ; not a divine and human life ; but one life which is simply and purely human and yet divine ; for God and man are one ; and humanity reaches its completion only when thus identified with the divine. This divine-human life passes over from Christ to the Church ; and this takes place in the way of history, growth, and development. Partaking thus of the life of Christ, we partake of its righteousness, its holiness, and its glory. Thus redemption is purely subjective. It is wrought in us, although the source is without us. As we partake of Adam's sin and condemnation, because we partake of his nature ; so we partake of Christ's righteousness and holiness because we partake of his divine-human life, or of humanity as healed and exalted in Him.[1]

Ebrard of Erlangen.

There is an important class of modern theological writers, of whom Dr. J. H. A. Ebrard of Erlangen may be taken as a representative, who consider themselves faithful to the doctrines of the Reformation, while developing them into new forms. As Ebrard represents this class of writers among the Reformed, so Delitzsch does the same for the Lutheran theologians. These writers are abundantly orthodox in their exposition of the nature of Christ's work. This is especially true of Delitzsch in his admirable treatise on " The Vicarious Satisfaction of Christ." [2] As these writers identify regeneration and justification, their views may be found briefly stated in the chapter on regeneration.

Christ, it is admitted, made expiation for sin and satisfied the justice of God as our substitute by his vicarious obedience and sufferings. This righteousness, however, becomes ours not by being received by faith and imputed to us by the just judgment of God, but by regeneration, whereby we become partakers of the life, substance, or essence, however it may be designated, of Christ. On this subject Ebrard says : " Regeneration is the substantial objective ground both of the transient act of justification, and of the progressive work of sanctification ; whereas conversion (repentance and faith) is the subjective condition of both. And justification as the act of the Father, is a forensic judicial act ; as the act of Christ, it is identical with regenera-

---

[1] See *Mystical Presence*, by John W. Nevin, D. D. ; Morell's *Philosophy of Religion*, and *Princeton Review*, April, 1848.

[2] *Ueber den festen Schriftgrund der Kirchenlehre von der stellvertretenden Genugthnung*, printed as a second Appendix to his elaborate commentary on the Epistle to the Hebrews.

tion, *i. e.*, with the real implantation of Christ in us and of us
in Christ." Both propositions, therefore, he says, are equally
true, namely, "Christ justifies us; and faith justifies us." In
explaining this, he says: " Δίκαιος before God is one who does not
merit punishment; who is free from guilt in the sight of God's
eternal law, either because he is absolutely sinless, or holy,
never having contracted guilt, as in the case of Christ; or because his guilt has been expiated, and his lack of the righteousness demanded by the law is covered. Δικαοῦν means either to
acknowledge as δίκαιος one who is δίκαιος; or to make δίκαιος one
who is not δίκαιος." The latter is its sense when used in reference to sinners. In their case, " The act of δικαίωσις consists,
(1.) In the gift of the expiation (Sühne) made by Christ without the sinner's coöperation; and (2.) In the gift of the absolute
righteousness of Christ, in such sense that God does not regard
the sinner as he is by nature, and by self-development, but as he
is as implanted in Christ." There is, therefore, a clear distinction
to be made between the appropriation of righteousness, and the
procuring of righteousness. " Christ has procured and merited
(erworben hat) righteousness by his historical life and sufferings; it is applied by Christ's being born in us." " The Scriptures," he says, "do not speak of Christ's righteousness being
imputed to us. They teach that it comes upon us (Rom. v. 18),
and becomes our own. It is our own, however, because the person of Christ becomes ours in the strictest possible (allerrealsten,
the most literal) sense of the terms." What Ebrard contends
for is (die substantielle Lebenseinheit mit der Person Christi),
the substantial oneness of life with Christ;[1] or, as he often elsewhere expresses it, " the mysterious, mystical communication of
the substance of Christ to the central substance of man."[2] Dr.
Alexander Schweizer of Zürich,[3] although differing much in
other points from Ebrard, agrees with him in this. The essential element in the work of Christ, he says, " is the founding and
upholding a community animated or pervaded by his theanthropic life (gottmenschlichen Lebenspotenz). Dr. Nevin[4] says,
" Our nature reaches after a true and real union with the nature
of God, as the necessary complement and consummation of its
own life. The idea which it embodies can never be fully actualized, under any other form. The incarnation is the proper com-

---

[1] *Christliche Dogmatik,* ii. i. 2, § 443; Königsberg, 1852, vol. ii. pp. 311, 312, 314.
[2] *Ibid.* p. 310.
[3] *Glaubenslehre,* Zürich, 1847, vol. ii. p. 385.
[4] *Mystical Presence,* Philadelphia, 1846, pp. 200, 201.

pletion of humanity. Christ is the true ideal man." " The incarnation was no mere theophany ; no transient wonder ; no illusion exhibited to the senses. . . . . The Word became flesh ; not a single man only, as one among many ; but 'flesh,' or humanity in its universal conception. How else could He be the principle of a general life, the origin of a new order of existence for the human world as such ? How else could the value of his mediatorial work be made over to us in a real way, by a true imputation, and not a legal fiction only ? " [1] " Christianity is a life, not only as revealed at first in Christ, but as continued also in the Church. It flows over from Christ to his people, always in this form. They do not simply bear his name and acknowledge his doctrine. They are so united to Him as to have part in the substance of his life itself." [2] He had before said,[3] that " by the hypostatical union of the two natures in the person of Jesus Christ, our humanity as fallen in Adam was exalted again to a new and imperishable divine life." " The object of the incarnation was to couple the human nature in real union with the Logos, as a permanent source of life." Again,[4] " the new life of which Christ is the source and organic principle, is in all respects a true human life ; . . . . not a new humanity, wholly dissevered from that of Adam ; but the humanity of Adam itself, only raised to a higher character, and filled with new meaning and power, by its union with the divine nature. . . . . Christ's life, as now described, rests not in his separate person, but passes over to his people ; thus constituting the Church, which is his body, the fulness of Him that filleth all in all." " Christ communicates his own life substantially to the soul on which He acts, causing it to grow into his very nature. This is the mystical union ; the basis of our whole salvation ; the only medium by which it is possible for us to have an interest in the grace of Christ under any other view." [5] With his substance, his life, his divine-human nature thus communicated to the soul come his merit, his holiness, his power, his glory. These are predicates of the nature which becomes ours, constituting our personal life and character. Even the resurrection is to be effected, not by the power of Christ operating " ab extra," as when He raised Lazarus from the dead, but by " a new divine element, introduced into our nature by the incarnation." [6]

---

[1] *Mystical Presence*, Philadelphia, 1846, pp. 210, 211.　　　　[2] *Ibid*. p. 218.
[3] *Ibid*. p. 165.　　　[4] *Ibid*. p. 167.　　　[5] *Ibid*. p. 168.　　　[6] *Ibid*. p. 226.

Objections to these Theories.

In opposition to these views it may be said very briefly in the way of recapitulation of what has been more fully said in the chapters above referred to, —

1. That this is a philosophy. The scheme has its entire basis in a philosophical theory as to the nature of man and his relation to God. This is undeniable, and is hardly denied. Dr. Nevin states three "scientific principles," ignorance of which led the Reformers to a misapprehension and imperfect representation of Christianity, and the recognition of which and of their application to theology, enables the modern theologian to set forth the nature and plan of salvation in a much more satisfactory light. Those principles are, (1.) The true import of organic law. The Reformers did not make a clear distinction, he says, "between the idea of the organic law which constitutes the proper identity of a human body, and the material volume it is found to embrace as exhibited to the senses." There may be, therefore, a real communication of Christ and even of his body to his people without a communication of his flesh. (2.) The absolute unity involved in personality. In the case of Christ, body, soul, and divinity are united in "a single indivisible life," so that where the one is, all are. To communicate Christ to the soul is therefore to communicate that indivisible life, including in it as an organizing, organic principle, body, soul, and divinity. (3.) The distinction between individual and generic life. "In every sphere of life," it is said, "the individual and the general are found closely united in the same subject." The acorn, in one view, is only a single existence ; but it includes the force of a life capable of reaching far beyond itself. The life of a forest of oaks is only the expansion of the life of the original acorn, "and the whole general existence thus produced is bound together, inwardly and organically, by as true and close a unity as that which holds in any of the single existences embraced in it, separately considered." Thus also Adam, in one view, was a man ; in another, he was the man. A whole world of separate personalities lay involved in his life, as a generic principle or root. "Adam lives in his posterity as truly as he has ever lived in his own person." In like manner, although in a higher form, the life of Christ is to be viewed under the same twofold aspect. In one view the Saviour was a man ; but in another, He was the man, "the Son of man, in whose person stood revealed the true

idea of humanity, under its ultimate and most comprehensive form. Without any loss or change of character in the first view, his life is carried over in this last view continually into the persons of his people. He lives in Himself, and yet lives in them really and truly at the same time." As we participate in Adam's whole nature, soul and body, so the people of Christ participate in his whole nature, body, soul, and divinity. These are one indivisible life ; and that one theanthropic life is communicated to believers and constitutes them Christians. In this is included all their participation in the righteousness, merit, and glory of their Redeemer.[1]

Behind and under these three scientific principles there is another without which the three mentioned amount to nothing ; namely, the unity of God and man. Man in his highest form ; the ideal or perfect man ; He in whom the idea of humanity is fully realized, is God. What does it amount to, if we admit that " organic law " constitutes identity, as in the case of man ; or that personality includes the idea of " one indivisible life ; " that in man there is not one life of the body and another of the soul, that these are only different manifestations of one and the same life ; that the soul can no more be without the body than the body without the soul ; and that in Christ there is not one life of the divinity and another of his humanity ? Suppose we deny what the Church in all ages has affirmed, that there are two ἐνέργειαι in Christ, what does this amount to ? Or what does it avail to admit the realistic doctrine of a generic life ; if that life (one and indivisible) be merely human, Adamic ? How can it redeem us ? It is only on the assumption that the human and the divine are one, that this unity, fully realized in Christ, constitutes the " one indivisible life " which passes over to us ; that it has any redeeming power ; and that it exalts man from his degradation, and brings him back to conscious as well as real unity with God.

This theory as presented by Schleiermacher, its author in modern times, was undeniably pantheistic ; as held by many of his disciples, it is, in their apprehension, theistic. In either form the leading idea of the identity of God and man is retained.[2] Christ is the ideal man. In Him the idea of humanity is fully realized ; and therefore He is God. The manifestation of God in the form of man, belongs to the divine nature. The incarnation is entirely

---

[1] See *Mystical Presence*, section first of the Scientific Statement.

[2] See this clearly presented in Dr. Ullmann's paper on " The Distinctive Character of Christianity," in the *Studien und Kritiken* for January, 1845, translated by Dr. Nevin and prefixed as a Preliminary Essay to his work on *The Mystical Presence*.

independent of the fall of man ; or, admitting that the failure of the race to reach its true ideal in the first instance was the occasion of a new, special, and supernatural intervention, yet the whole end of that intervention was to realize the original idea of humanity as God made flesh.

The watchword of this whole system is, in the language of Dr. Ullmann, " The life of Christ is Christianity ; " *i. e.*, the one indivisible life of Christ ; the life of God in the form of humanity. And that life as communicated to men brings them to this real, substantial life union with God. " What," asks Dr. Ullmann, " is that in the personality of Christ by which He is constituted a perfect Saviour in the way of atonement and redemption ? We reply generally, his own substantial nature, at once human and divine ; his life filled with all the attributes of God, and representing at the same time the highest conception of nature and man ; complete and self-sufficient in its own fulness, and yet by this fulness itself the free principle of a new corresponding life-process, in the way of self-communication, for the human world. This life itself, however, has again its central heart, to which especially we must look for the peculiar being of Christ. Here the whole theology of the present time, in all its different tendencies, may be said to have but one voice. That which constitutes the special being of Christ, makes Him to be what He is and gives Him thus his highest significance for the world, is the absolute unity of the divine and human in his nature. Deity and manhood in Him come fully together and are made one. This is the last ground of Christianity. Here above all we are to look for its distinctive character." He goes on to show that on this point all are agreed. God and man are one. The difference is between the pantheistic and the Christian view which acknowledges a personal God and a positive revelation. " For the whole apprehension of Christianity, we may say, not only that much, but that all depends on the question, which of these views shall be adopted ; whether this central fact shall be regarded as a general ' unity of the divine and human ' realizing itself in the consciousness of the race as such, or be conceived of as a concrete ' union of God and man,' that actualizes itself from a definite point and only under certain moral conditions." [1] That is, whether God is incarnate in the race or in the Church. According to the latter view, the life of Christ, his human life, " filled with all the attributes of God," passes over to his people, by a process of natural

---

[1] See Nevin's *Mystical Presence*, pp. 27, 28, 29.

development. As we are fallen men by partaking of the nature
or generic life of Adam, we are God-men, and therefore redeemed
by partaking of the divine human nature or generic life of Christ.

That the oneness of God and man is the ultimate principle on
which this ἕτερον εὐαγγέλιον rests, is obvious not only from the general character of the philosophy from which it is derived, but also
from the fact that everything is made to depend upon the life of
Christ becoming the life of his people, not by his controlling their
life by his Spirit dwelling in them, but by a substantial union
and identification of their life with his, of them with Him. We
can measurably understand what is meant by life, by organic life,
by a life principle or force which develops itself, and communicates and transmits itself in a given form. We know what is
meant when it is said that the life of the acorn is developed into
an oak, and communicated to other acorns, and thus to other oaks
in endless succession and boundless multiplication. But here the
essential idea is the unity and sameness of the life transmitted.
You cannot combine the " organic law," or life, of the apple
with that of the acorn, so that the life transmitted should be " an
acorn-apple-life." Much less can you combine the organic life
principle of an animal with that of the acorn, so as to produce an
" acorn-bovine," or, " an acorn-equine life." Least of all can you
combine the intellectual life of man with that of the oak, so as to
have a " human-oak-life." Therefore if the life of God and the life
of man be so combined as to constitute one life and that a divine-
human life, then God and man must be one ; i. e., one substance,
one life differently manifested. Those who press the modern doctrine of the correlation of forces to the extreme of making thought
and gravity identical, may accept these conclusions. With them
the universe and all it contains, all its physical, mental, æsthetic,
moral, and religious phenomena are to be referred to one and the
same force variously modified. The same force modified by the
brain produces all the phenomena of mind ; as modified by animal
tissues, all the phenomena of animal life ; and as modified by vegetable organisms all the phenomena of vegetable life, — a theory
which has been annihilated as by a bolt from heaven by the single question : Where is the brain which elaborated the mind,
which framed the universe ?

It may indeed be said, and is said by modern theologians,
that God became man, and therefore man may become God.
God and man, they say, were so united as to become one nature
or life in the person of Christ. But this is contrary to Scripture

and to the faith of the Church universal. There is not a historical Church on earth, and never has been, whose creed does not teach that in the person of Christ two distinct natures or substances are united ; that He was born, not merely " per," but " ex matre sua Maria," of her substance; that He is as man consubstantial with men, as God consubstantial with the Father ; or as the Apostle expresses it, κατὰ σαρκά He is the son of David, κατὰ πνεῦμα the Son of God. Humanity and divinity in Him are no more identified or reduced to one life, than soul and body in man are identified or reduced to one life.

This whole modern theory of the Gospel rests, therefore, ultimately on the idea of the identity of God and man ; that man is a " modus existendi " of God.

The grand objection to this scheme is that it is a philosophy. It is a product of the human mind. It is the wisdom of the world. It is the recent philosophy of the speculative school of Germany, clothed in Biblical forms and phrases. The reason why the Reformers did not present the plan of salvation in this form, is declared to be that they were ignorant of modern philosophy. It is because Hegel thought that the Gospel admitted of being cast into the mould of his philosophy that he pronounced Christianity to be the absolute religion. All, therefore, that the Bible says of the " wisdom of the wise," " of the wisdom of men," of " the wisdom of the world," of " philosophy as a vain deceit," applies, and was intended to apply to this scheme and to all of like nature. " To the poor the gospel is preached." The Gospel is designed for babes and sucklings. He that runs may read and understand it. This system not one man in ten thousand can understand.

These Theories Unscriptural.

2. The second great objection to this scheme is that it is unscriptural. The Bible tells us that Christ saves us as a priest. This a child can understand. He knows that a priest takes the place of those for whom he acts ; that he approaches God in their behalf ; that he makes expiation for sin ; that he does what satisfies the demands of God's justice against the sinner, so that He can be just and yet justify the ungodly. He knows that a priest saves, not by what he does in us, not by imparting his life to us, but by what he does for us ; by an objective, and not by a subjective work. What there is of an inward work, and that is much and absolutely necessary, is not the work of a priest, under

which aspect the work of Christ is so prominently presented in the Scriptures. Again, Christ saves us as a sacrifice ; but a sacrifice is a substitute ; it bears the sins of the offender ; dies in his stead, and by its vicarious death delivers the offerer from the penalty which he had incurred. A sacrifice is not a symbol of an inward conflict between good and evil ; its proximate design is not to effect a subjective change in the sinner ; it does not produce or communicate a new principle of life, much less its own generic life to the offerer by which his real redemption is effected.

In like manner the Bible teaches that Christ gave Himself as a ransom for many. But a ransom is a price paid. Those delivered by it are bought. They are delivered by purchase. A ransom meets and satisfies the claims of a third party. This is its essential idea, and cannot be omitted without rejecting the very truth, which the Scriptures, in the use of the term, design to teach. This again is an objective work. It is something which the person redeemed neither does, nor inwardly experiences ; but which is done for him and without him and not in him.

Moreover, the whole idea of redemption, the primary truth taught in setting forth Christ as a Redeemer, is that He delivers his people not by power, not by instruction, not by moral influence, not by any subjective change wrought in them, and not by any new form of life imparted to them, but by purchase. This is the signification and the meaning of the word. The words ἀπολύτρωσις, λυτροῦν, ἀγοράζειν, ἐξαγοράζειν, are never used in Scripture in reference to the work of Christ in any other sense than that of deliverance by purchase or payment of a ransom ; and to substitute any other mode of deliverance, is to put man's thoughts in the place of God's truth ; it is to substitute the human for the divine ; the worthless for the priceless.

Moreover, Christ is constantly represented as a rock, a refuge, a hiding place. The duty required of sinners is trust ; relying on Him and his work, as something out of themselves on which to place their hope toward God.

These Theories lead Men to trust to themselves.

3. This introduces the third great objection to this scheme. It makes redemption subjective. It is what we are ; what we become ; it is the Christ within us ; the new heart, the new nature, the new life, the divine-human life of Christ, or whatever else it may be called, which is at once the ground of our justification and the source of sanctification. This is utterly inconsistent with

the Bible, and with the experience of the people of God in all ages and under all dispensations. In no instance are believers represented as trusting to what is within them, but to what is without them. The Protestant doctrine, as we have seen, makes full provision for an inward work of deliverance from the power of sin, as well as for redemption from the curse of the law; for sanctification as well as for justification. But it does not confound the two, neither does it refer either or both to the new principle of life, the new seed or leaven implanted or inserted which works as " an organic law," and by a regular process of development, as natural as the operation of any other law. The whole work of the Spirit is ignored in this new theory of redemption. What in the Bible is referred to the Spirit of God is, by the theologians of this class, referred to the " divine-human " nature of Christ. The latter, and not the former, is the proximate and efficient source of holiness of heart and life. " Christ," says Dr. Nevin, " does dwell in us, by his Spirit; but only as his Spirit constitutes the very form and power of his own presence as the incarnate and everlasting Word."[1] That is, the Spirit is the power of the incarnate Word, i. e., of the divine-human life of Christ. " The life," he adds, " thus wrought in our souls by his agency, is not a production out of nothing, but the very life of Jesus Himself organically continued in this way over into our persons." " It is with the mediatorial life of Christ that the Christian salvation, in the form now contemplated, is concerned. In this is comprehended the entire new creation revealed by the Gospel; the righteousness of Christ, and all the benefits He has procured for his people. But the mediatorial life, by the communication of which only all this grace is made to pass over to men, is one and undivided ; " and this life, as he goes on to show, includes his body, soul, and divinity. To the same effect,[2] it is said, " That the whole spiritual life of the Christian, including the resurrection of his body, is thus organically connected with the mediatorial life of the Lord Jesus, might seem to be too plainly taught in the New Testament to admit of any question , and yet we find many slow to allow the mystery, notwithstanding. A very common view appears to be, that the whole salvation of the Gospel is accomplished in a more or less outward and mechanical way, by supernatural might and power, rather than by the Spirit of the Lord as a revelation of a new historical life in the person of the believer Himself. So we have an outward

---

[1] *Mystical Presence*, pp. 197, 198.   [1] *Ibid.* p. 228, note.

imputation of righteousness to begin with ; a process of sanctification carried forward by the help of proper spiritual machinery
brought to bear on the soul, including perhaps, as its basis, the
notion of an abrupt creation ' de novo,' by the fiat of the Holy
Ghost ; and finally, to crown all, a sudden unprepared refabrica-
tion of the body, to be superadded to the life of the spirit already
complete in its state of glory." The doctrines of justification by
the imputation of the righteousness of Christ; of the regeneration and sanctification of the soul by the supernatural power of
the Spirit, and the resurrection of the body by the power of God
at the last day, are rejected and despised ; and the doctrine substituted for them is, that the divine-human life of Christ, as a new
organic law, develops itself in the Church, just as the life of the
acorn develops itself in the oak and in the forest, by a natural,
historical process, so that the members of the Church, in virtue of
their participation of this life, are justified and sanctified, and
their bodies (since the life of Christ is a human life actualizing
itself outwardly in a body as well as inwardly in a soul), ultimately raised from the dead, are fashioned after the glorious
body of Christ. The resurrection of the body is as much a
natural process as the development of a seed into a flower, or of
a grub into a butterfly. This is Dr. Nevin's own illustration :
" The birth of the butterfly, as it mounts in the air on wings of
light, is comparatively sudden, too ; but this is the revelation only
of a life which had been gradually formed for this efflorescence
before, under cover of the vile, unsightly larve." " The new
creation," he says, " is indeed supernatural ; but as such it is
strictly conformable to the general order and constitution of life.
It is a new creation in Christ Jesus, not by Him in the way of
mere outward power. The subjects of it are saved, only by being
brought within the sphere of his life, as a regular, historical,
divine-human process, in the Church. The new nature implanted
in them at their regeneration, is not a higher order of existence
framed for them at the moment out of nothing by the fiat of
God, but truly and strictly a continuation of Christ's life over in
their persons." [1]

This is the modern view of Christianity introduced by Schleiermacher, modified more or less by his disciples, and which has
passed over into England and into this country. Humanity as
revealed in Adam as a generic life was too feeble. Its development failed and would have ever failed to reach the ideal.

[1] *Mystical Presence*, pp. 228, 229.

Therefore God interposed and interrupted the process of natural development by the production of a new ideal man containing in himself a generic life, a seed, a principle, an organic law, which develops itself in the Church by a historical process, just as the life of Adam developed itself in his posterity.   We, therefore, are justified, not by what Christ did, but by his life in us, which is as truly and properly our life, as the life we derived from Adam is our own life.   We must stand before God to be justified or condemned, accepted or rejected, on the ground of what we are. We have nothing to offer but our own subjective, inherent character such as it is.   The man is to be pitied who dares to do this. It is surely better to agree with Paul, who renounced his own righteousness, his own goodness, everything pertaining to himself, everything subjective, and trusted only and confidently to the righteousness of Christ received by faith.

CHAPTER XVIII.

SANCTIFICATION.

§ 1. *Its Nature.*

SANCTIFICATION in the Westminster Catechism is said to be
" the work of God's free grace, whereby we are renewed in the
whole man after the image of God, and are enabled more and
more to die unto sin and live unto righteousness."

Agreeably to this definition, justification differs from sanctification, (1.) In that the former is a transient act, the latter a
progressive work. (2.) Justification is a forensic act, God acting as judge, declaring justice satisfied so far as the believing sinner is concerned, whereas sanctification is an effect due to the
divine efficiency. (3.) Justification changes, or declares to be
changed, the relation of the sinner to the justice of God ; sanctification involves a change of character. (4.) The former,
therefore, is objective, the latter subjective. (5.) The former is
founded on what Christ has done for us ; the latter is the effect
of what He does in us. (6.) Justification is complete and the
same in all, while sanctification is progressive, and is more complete in some than in others.

Sanctification is declared to be a work of God's free grace.
Two things are included in this. First, that the power or influence by which it is carried on is supernatural. Secondly, that
granting this influence to any sinner, to one sinner rather than
another, and to one more than to another, is a matter of favour.
No one has personally, or in himself, on the ground of anything
he has done, the right to claim this divine influence as a just recompense, or as a matter of justice.

It is a Supernatural Work.

In representing, in accordance with Scripture, sanctification as
a supernatural work, or as a work of grace, the Church intends to
deny the Pelagian or Rationalistic doctrine which confounds it
with mere moral reformation. It not unfrequently happens that
men who have been immoral in their lives, change their whole

course of living. They become outwardly correct in their deportment, temperate, pure, honest, and benevolent. This is a great and praiseworthy change. It is in a high degree beneficial to the subject of it, and to all with whom he is connected. It may be produced by different causes, by the force of conscience and by a regard for the authority of God and a dread of his disapprobation, or by a regard to the good opinion of men, or by the mere force of an enlightened regard to one's own interest. But whatever may be the proximate cause of such reformation, it falls very far short of sanctification. The two things differ in nature as much as a clean heart from clean clothes. Such external reformation may leave a man's inward character in the sight of God unchanged. He may remain destitute of love to God, of faith in Christ, and of all holy exercises or affections.

Nor is sanctification to be confounded with the effects of moral culture or discipline. It is very possible, as experience proves, by careful moral training, by keeping the young from all contaminating influences, and by bringing them under the forming influences of right principles and good associates, to preserve them from much of the evil of the world, and to render them like the young man in the Gospel whom Jesus loved. Such training is not to be undervalued. It is enjoined in the Word of God. It cannot, however, change the nature. It cannot impart life. A faultless statue fashioned out of pure marble in all its beauty, is far below a living man.

The word supernatural, as before said, is used in two senses. First, for that which is above nature, and by nature is meant everything out of God. An effect, therefore, is said to be supernatural, in the production of which nature exercises no efficiency. But secondly, the word is often used to mark the distinction between the providential efficiency of God operating according to fixed laws, and the voluntary agency of the Holy Spirit. The Bible makes a wide distinction between the providence of God and the operations of his grace. The difference between the two is, in some repects, analogous to that between the efficiency of a law, or of a uniformly acting force, and the agency of a person. The one is ordered, the other is exercised from time to time, the Spirit distributing his gifts to every one severally as He wills. In the providential agency of God, the effects produced never transcend the power of second causes as upheld and guided by Him ; whereas the effects produced by the Spirit do transcend the power of second causes. The effect is due neither to the power of the truth, nor to that of the rational subject in whom the effect is produced. It is due to the power of God over and above the power of the second causes concerned. The effects of grace, or fruits of the Spirit, are above the sphere of the natural they belong to the supernatural. The mere power of truth, argument, motive, persuasion, or eloquence cannot produce repentance, faith, or holiness of heart and life. Nor can these effects be produced by the power of the will, or by all the resources of man, however protracted or skilful in their application. They are the gifts of God, the fruits of the Spirit. Paul may plant and Apollos water, but it is God who gives the increase.

In this latter sense of the word supernatural, the coöperation of second causes is not excluded. When Christ opened the eyes of the blind no second cause interposed between his volition and the effect. But men work out their own salvation, while it is God who worketh in them to will and to do, according to his own good pleasure. In the work of regeneration, the soul is passive. It cannot coöperate in the communication of spiritual life. But in conversion, repentance, faith, and growth in grace, all its powers are called into exercise. As, however, the effects produced transcend the efficiency of our fallen nature, and are due to the agency of the Spirit, sanctification does not cease to be supernatural, or a work of grace, because the soul is active and coöperating in the process.

Proof of its Supernatural Character.

That sanctification is a supernatural work in the sense above stated is proved, —

1. From the fact that it is constantly referred to God as its author. It is referred to God absolutely, or to the Father, as in 1 Thessalonians v. 23, " The very God of peace sanctify you wholly." Hebrews xiii. 20, 21, " The God of peace that brought again from the dead our Lord Jesus . . . . make you perfect in every good work to do his will, working in you that which is well pleasing in his sight." It is also referred to the Son, as in Titus ii. 14, He " gave himself for us, that he might . . . . purify unto himself a peculiar people zealous of good works." Ephesians v. 25, He " loved the church and gave himself for it, that he might sanctify and cleanse it with the washing of water by the word, that he might present it to himself a glorious church, not having spot, or wrinkle, or any such thing ; but that it should be holy and without blemish." Predominantly sanctifica-

tion is referred to the Holy Spirit, as his peculiar work in the economy of redemption. Hence He is called the Spirit of all grace; the Spirit of joy, of peace, of love, of faith, and of adoption. All Christian graces are set forth as fruits of the Spirit. We are said to be born of the Spirit, and by Him to be enlightened, taught, led, and cleansed. We are said to be in the Spirit, to live, to walk, and to rejoice in the Spirit. The Spirit dwells in the people of God, and is the abiding source of all the actings of that spiritual life which He implants in the soul. The Bible teaches that the Son and Spirit are in the Holy Trinity subordinate to the Father, as to their mode of subsistence and operation, although the same in substance, and equal in power and glory. Hence it is that the same work is often attributed to the Father, to the Son, and to the Spirit; and as the Father and Son operate through the Spirit, the effects due to the agency of God are referred specially to the Holy Ghost.

This reference of sanctification to God proves it to be a supernatural work, because the insufficiency of second causes to produce the effect is declared to be the ground of this reference. It is because men cannot cleanse or heal themselves, that they are declared to be cleansed and healed by God. It is because rites, ceremonies, sacraments, truth, and moral suasion, cannot bring the soul back to God, that it is said to be transformed, by the renewing of the mind, through the power of the Spirit, into the image of God. We are, therefore, declared to be God's workmanship, created unto good works. And it is not we that live, but Christ that liveth in us.

All Holy Exercises referred to the Spirit as their Author.

2. This reference of sanctification to God as its author, the more decisively proves the supernatural character of the work, because the reference is not merely general, as when the wind and rain, and the production of vegetable and animal life, are referred to his universal providential agency. The reference is special. The effect is one which the Scriptures recognize as not within the sphere of second causes, and therefore ascribe to God. They recognize the free agency of man; they acknowledge and treat him as a moral and rational being; they admit the adaptation of of truth to convince the understanding, and of the motives presented to determine the will and to control the affections, and nevertheless they teach that these secondary causes and influences are utterly ineffectual to the conversion and sanctification of the

soul, without the demonstration of the Spirit. The sacred writers, therefore, constantly pray for this divine influence, " extrinsecus accidens," to attend the means of grace and to render them effectual, as well for sanctification as for regeneration and conversion. Every such prayer, every thanksgiving for grace imparted, every recognition of the Christian virtues as fruits of the Spirit, and gifts of God, are so many recognitions of the great truth that the restoration of man to the image of God is not a work of nature, either originated or carried on by the efficiency of second causes, but is truly and properly supernatural, as due to the immediate power of the Spirit producing effects for which second causes are inadequate.

We are taught to pray for Repentance, Faith, and other Graces.

3. We accordingly find the Apostle and the sacred writers generally, referring not only regeneration, the communication of spiritual life to those spiritually dead, but the continuance of that life in its activity and growth, not merely to the power of God, but to his almighty power. Paul prays in Ephesians i. 19, that his readers might know " what is the exceeding greatness of his power to us-ward who believe according to the working of his mighty power, which he wrought in Christ when he raised him from the dead." The same almighty power which was exhibited in the resurrection of Christ, is exercised in the spiritual resurrection of the believer. And as the power which raised Christ from the dead was exercised in his ascension and glorification ; so also the same power, according to the Apostle, which is exerted in the spiritual resurrection of the believer, is exercised in carrying on his sanctification, which is inward and real glorification. Accordingly, in the same Epistle (iii. 7), he ascribes all the grace whereby he was fitted for the apostleship, " to the effectual working of his power." And further on (ver. 20), to encourage the people of God to pray for spiritual blessings, he reminds them of his omnipotence whereby He was " able to do exceeding abundantly above all that we ask or think, according to the power that worketh in us." It is almighty power, therefore, and not the impotence of secondary influences, which works in the believer and carries on the work of his salvation.

They who are in Christ, therefore, are new creatures. They are created anew in Christ Jesus. This does not refer exclusively to their regeneration, but to the process by which the sinner is transformed into the image of Christ.

Argument from the Believer's Union with Christ.

4. All that the Scriptures teach concerning the union between the believer and Christ, and of the indwelling of the Holy Spirit, proves the supernatural character of our sanctification. Men do not make themselves holy; their holiness, and their growth in grace, are not due to their own fidelity, or firmness of purpose, or watchfulness and diligence, although all these are required, but to the divine influence by which they are rendered thus faithful, watchful, and diligent, and which produces in them the fruits of righteousness. Without me, saith our Lord, ye can do nothing. As the branch cannot bear fruit of itself, except it abide in the vine, no more can ye, except ye abide in me. The hand is not more dependent on the head for the continuance of its vitality, than is the believer on Christ for the continuance of spiritual life in the soul.

Argument from related Doctrines.

5. This, however, is one of those doctrines which pervade the whole Scriptures. It follows of necessity from what the Bible teaches of the natural state of man since the fall; it is assumed, asserted, and implied in all that is revealed of the plan of salvation. By their apostasy, men lost the image of God; they are born in a state of alienation and condemnation. They are by nature destitute of spiritual life. From this state it is as impossible that they should deliver themselves, as that those in the grave should restore life to their wasted bodies, and when restored, continue and invigorate it by their own power. Our whole salvation is of Christ. Those who are in the grave hear his voice. They are raised by his power. And when they live it is He who lives in them. This is the doctrine which our Lord Himself so clearly and so frequently teaches, and upon which his Apostles so strenuously insist. St. Paul in the sixth and seventh chapters of his Epistle to the Romans, where he treats of this subject " in extenso," has for his main object to prove that as we are not justified for our own righteousness, so we are not sanctified by our own power, or by the mere objective power of the truth. The law, the revelation of the will of God, including everything which He has made known to man either as a rule of obedience or as exhibiting his own attributes and purposes, was equally inadequate to secure justification and sanctification. As it demanded perfect obedience and pronounced accursed those who continue not in all things

written in the book of the law to do them, it can only condemn.
It can never pronounce the sinner just. And as it was a mere
outward presentation of the truth, it could no more change the
heart than light could give sight to the blind. He winds up his
discussions of the subject with the exclamation, " O wretched
man that I am! who shall deliver me from the body of this
death ? I thank God, through Jesus Christ our Lord." His deliverance was to be effected by God through Jesus Christ. We
learn from the eighth chapter that he was fully confident of this
deliverance, and we learn also the ground on which that confidence rested. It was not that he had in regeneration received
strength to sanctify himself, or that by the force of his own will,
or by the diligent use of natural or appointed means, the end was
to be accomplished without further aid from God. On the contrary, his confidence was founded, (1.) On the fact that he had
been delivered from the law, from its curse, and from its inexorable demand of perfect obedience. (2.) On the fact that he had
received the Spirit as the source of a new, divine, and imperishable
life. (3.) This life was not a mere state of mind, but the life of
God, or the Spirit of God dwelling in the heart ; which indwelling
secured not only the continuance of " spiritual mindedness," but
even the resurrection from the dead. " For if," says he, " the
spirit of him that raised up Jesus from the dead dwell in you, he
that raised up Christ from the dead shall also quicken ($\zeta\omega o\pi o\iota\acute{\eta}\sigma\epsilon\iota$,
make alive with the life of Christ) your mortal bodies by his Spirit
that dwelleth in you." (4.) Being led by the Spirit of God as
the controlling principle of their inward and outward life, believers
are the sons of God. The Spirit of God which is in them being
the Spirit of the Son, is in them the Spirit of sonship, i. e., it produces in them the feelings of sons toward God, and assures them
of their title to all the privileges of his children. (5.) The sanctification and ultimate salvation of believers are secured by the
immutable decree of God. For those " whom he did foreknow he
also did predestinate to be conformed to the image of his Son ;
. . . . moreover, whom he did predestinate, them he also called :
and whom he called, them he also justified : and whom he justified,
them he also glorified." This last includes sanctification ; the inward glory of the soul ; the divine image as retraced by the Spirit
of God, which to and in the believer is the Spirit of glory. (1
Pet. iv. 14.) The indwelling of the Spirit renders the believer
glorious. (6.) The infinite and immutable love which induced
God to give his own Son for our salvation, renders it certain that

all other things shall be given necessary to keep them in the love and fellowship of God. Salvation, therefore, from beginning to end is of grace ; not only as being gratuitous to the exclusion of all merit on the part of the saved, but also as being carried on by the continued operation of grace, or the supernatural power of the Spirit. Christ is our all. He is of God made unto us wisdom, and righteousness, sanctification, and redemption.

§ 2. *Wherein it consists.*

Admitting sanctification to be a supernatural work, the question still remains, What does it consist in ? What is the nature of the effect produced ? The truth which lies at the foundation of all the Scriptural representations of this subject is, that regeneration, the quickening, of which believers are the subject, while it involves the implanting, or communication of a new principle or form of life, does not effect the immediate and entire deliverance of the soul from all sin. A man raised from the dead may be and long continue to be, in a very feeble, diseased, and suffering state. So the soul by nature dead in sin, may be quickened together with Christ, and not be rendered thereby perfect. The principle of life may be very feeble, it may have much in the soul uncongenial with its nature, and the conflict between the old and the new life may be protracted and painful. Such not only may be, but such in fact is the case in all the ordinary experience of the people of God. Here we find one of the characteristic and far-reaching differences between the Romish and Protestant systems of doctrine and religion. According to the Romish system, nothing of the nature of sin remains in the soul after regeneration as effected in baptism. From this the theology of the Church of Rome deduces its doctrine of the merit of good works ; of perfection ; of works of supererogation ; and, indirectly, those of absolution and indulgences. But according to the Scriptures, the universal experience of Christians, and the undeniable evidence of history, regeneration does not remove all sin. The Bible is filled with the record of the inward conflicts of the most eminent of the servants of God, with their falls, their backslidings, their repentings, and their lamentations over their continued shortcomings. And not only this, but the nature of the conflict between good and evil in the heart of the renewed is fully described, the contending principles are distinguished and designated, and the necessity, difficulties, and perils of the struggle, as well as the method of properly sustaining it, are set forth repeatedly and in detail.   In the seventh chapter of the Epistle to the Romans we have an account of this conflict elaborately described by the Apostle as drawn from his own experience.   And the same thing occurs in Galatians v. 16, 17.   This I say then, " Walk in the Spirit, and ye shall not fulfil the lust of the flesh. For the flesh lusteth against the Spirit, and the Spirit against the flesh : and these are contrary the one to the other : so that ye cannot do the things that ye would."   Again, in Ephesians vi. 10 –18, in view of the conflict which the believer has to sustain with the evils of his own heart and with the powers of darkness, the Apostle exhorts his brethren to be strong in the Lord, and in the power of his might. . . . . " Wherefore take unto you the whole armour of God, that ye may be able to withstand in the evil day, and having done all, to stand."

With the teachings of the Scriptures the experience of Christians in all ages and in all parts of the Church agrees.   Their writings are filled with the account of their struggles with the remains of sin in their own hearts ; with confessions ; with prayers for divine aid ; and with longings after the final victory over all evil, which is to be experienced only in heaven.   The great lights of the Latin Church, the Augustines and Bernards and Fénélons, were humble, penitent, struggling believers, even to the last, and with Paul did not regard themselves as having already attained, or as being already perfect.   And what the Bible and Christian experience prove to be true, history puts beyond dispute.   Either there is no such thing as regeneration in the world, or regeneration does not remove all sin from those who are its subjects.

Putting off the Old, and putting on the New Man.

Such being the foundation of the Scriptural representations concerning sanctification, its nature is thereby determined.   As all men since the fall are in a state of sin, not only sinners because guilty of specific acts of transgression, but also as depraved, their nature perverted and corrupted, regeneration is the infusion of a new principle of life in this corrupt nature.   It is leaven introduced to diffuse its influence gradually through the whole mass.   Sanctification, therefore, consists in two things : first, the removing more and more the principles of evil still infecting our nature, and destroying their power ; and secondly, the growth of the principle of spiritual life until it controls the thoughts, feelings, and acts, and brings the soul into conformity to the image of Christ.

Paul details his own Experience in Romans vii. 7–25.

The classical passages of the New Testament on the nature of this work are the following, — Romans vii. 7–25. This is not the place to enter upon the discussion whether the Apostle in this passage is detailing his own experience or not. This is the interpretation given to it by Augustinians in all ages. It is enough to say here that the " onus probandi " rests on those who take the opposite view of the passage. It must require very strong proof that the Apostle is not speaking of himself and giving his own experience as a Christian, when, —

1. His object in the whole discussion throughout the sixth and seventh chapters, is to prove that the law, as it cannot justify, neither can it sanctify ; as it cannot deliver from the guilt, so neither can it free us from the power of sin. This is not the fault of the law, for it is spiritual, holy, just, and good. It commends itself to the reason and the conscience as being just what it ought to be ; requiring neither more nor less than what it is right should be demanded, and threatening no penalty which want of conformity to its requirements does not justly merit. What is the effect of the objective presentation of the ideal standard of moral perfection to which we are bound to be conformed on the penalty of death ? The Apostle tells us that the effects are, (*a.*) A great increase of knowledge. He had not known lust, had not the law said, Thou shalt not covet. (*b.*) A sense of moral pollution, and consequently of shame and self-loathing. (*c.*) A sense of guilt, or of just exposure to the penalty of the law of which our whole lives are a continued transgression. (*d.*) A sense of utter helplessness. The standard, although holy, just, and good, is too high. We know we never can of ourselves conform to it ; neither can we make satisfaction for past transgression. (*e.*) The result of the whole is despair. The law kills. It destroys not only all self-complacency, but all hope of ever being able to effect our own salvation. (*f.*) And thus it leads the sinner to look out of himself for salvation; *i. e.*, for deliverance from the power, as well as the guilt of sin. The law is a schoolmaster to lead us to Christ. Why could not the Apostle say all this of himself ? There is nothing here inconsistent with the character or experience of a true believer. It is as true of the Christian that he is not sanctified by moral suasion, by the objective presentation of truth, as it is of the unrenewed sinner, that he is not regenerated by any such outward influences. It is,

therefore, perfectly pertinent to the Apostle's object that he should detail his own experience that sanctification could not be effected by the law.

2. But in the second place, he uses the first person singular throughout. He says, " I had not known sin," " I died," " The commandment which was ordained to life, I found to be unto death," " I consent unto the law that it is good," " I delight in the law of God after the inward man, but I see another law in my members," etc., etc. We are bound to understand the Apostle to speak of himself in the use of such language, unless there be something in the context, or in the nature of what is said, to render the reference to him impossible. It has been shown, however, that the context favours, if it does not absolutely demand the reference of what is said to the Apostle himself. And that there is nothing in the experience here detailed inconsistent with the experience of the true children of God, is evident from the fact that the same humility, the same sense of guilt, the same consciousness of indwelling sin, the same conviction of helplessness, here expressed, are found in all the penitential portions of Scripture. Job, David, Isaiah, and Nehemiah, make the same confessions and lamentations that the Apostle here makes. The same is true of believers since the coming of Christ. There is no one of them, not even the holiest, who is not constrained to speak of himself as Paul here speaks, unless indeed he chooses to give the language of the Apostle a meaning which it was never intended to express.

3. While the passage contains nothing inconsistent with the experience of true believers, it is inconsistent with the experience of unrenewed men. They are not the subjects of the inward conflict here depicted. There is in them indeed often a struggle protracted and painful, between reason and conscience on the one side, and evil passion on the other. But there is not in the unrenewed that utter renunciation of self, that looking for help to God in Christ alone, and that delight in the law of God, of which the Apostle here speaks.

What Romans vii. 7–25 teaches.

Assuming, then, that we have in this chapter an account of the experience of a true and even of an advanced Christian, we learn that in every Christian there is a mixture of good and evil; that the original corruption of nature is not entirely removed by regeneration ; that although the believer is made a new creature.

is translated from the kingdom of darkness into the kingdom of God's dear Son, he is but partially sanctified; that his selfishness, pride, discontent, worldliness, still cleave to, and torment him; that they effectually prevent his " doing what he would," they prevent his living without sin, they prevent his intercourse with God being as intimate and uninterrupted as he could and does desire. He finds not only that he is often, even daily, overcome so as to sin in thought, word, and deed, but also that his faith, love, zeal, and devotion are never such as to satisfy his own conscience; much less can they satisfy God. He therefore is daily called upon to confess, repent, and pray for forgiveness. The Apostle designates these conflicting principles which he found within himself, the one, indwelling sin; " sin that dwelleth in me; " or the " law in my members; " " the law of sin; " the other, " the mind," " the law of my mind," " the inward man." His internal self, the Ego, was sometimes controlled by the one, and sometimes by the other.

We learn, further, that the control of the evil principle is resisted, that subjection to it is regarded as a hateful bondage, that the good principle is in the main victorious, and that through Christ it will ultimately be completely triumphant. Sanctification therefore, according to this representation, consists in the gradual triumph of the new nature implanted in regeneration over the evil that still remains after the heart is renewed. In other words, as elsewhere expressed, it is a dying unto sin and living unto righteousness. (1 Pet. ii. 24.)

Galatians v. 16–26.

Another passage of like import is Galatians v. 16–26, " Walk in the Spirit, and ye shall not fulfil the lust of the flesh. For the flesh lusteth against the Spirit, and the Spirit against the flesh; and these are contrary the one to the other : so that ye cannot do the things that ye would," etc., etc. The Scriptures teach that the Spirit of God dwells in his people, not only collectively as the Church, but individually in every believer, so that of every Christian it may be said, he is a temple of the Holy Ghost. God is said to dwell wherever He permanently manifests his presence, whether as of old in the temple, or in the hearts of his people, in the Church, or in heaven. And as the Spirit dwells in believers, He there manifests his life-giving. controlling power, and is in them the principle, or source, or controlling influence which determines their inward and outward life.

By the flesh, in the doctrinal portions of Scripture, is never, unless the word be limited by the context, meant merely our sensuous nature, but our fallen nature, *i. e.*, our nature as it is in itself, apart from the Spirit of God. As our Lord says (John iii. 6), "That which is born of the flesh is flesh; and that which is born of the Spirit is spirit." These then are the principles which "are contrary the one to the other." No man can act independently of both. He must obey one or the other. He may sometimes obey the one, and sometimes the other; but one or the other must prevail. The Apostle says of believers that they have crucified the flesh with its affections and lusts. They have renounced the authority of the evil principle; they do not willingly, or of set purpose, or habitually yield to it. They struggle against it, and not only endeavour, but actually do crucify it, although it may die a long and painful death.

Ephesians iv. 22–24.

In Ephesians iv. 22–24, we are told: "Put off concerning the former conversation the old man, which is corrupt according to the deceitful lusts; and be renewed in the spirit of your mind; and" put ye "on the new man, which after God is created in righteousness and true holiness." By the old man is to be understood the former self with all the evils belonging to its natural state. This was to be laid aside as a worn and soiled garment, and a new, pure self, the new man, was to take its place. This change, although expressed in a figure borrowed from a change of raiment, was a profound inward change produced by a creating process, by which the soul is new fashioned after the image of God in righteousness and holiness. It is a renewing as to the Spirit, *i. e.*, the interior life of the mind; or as Meyer and Ellicott, the best of modern commentators, both interpret the phrase, "By the Spirit" (the Holy Spirit) dwelling in the mind. This is a transformation in which believers are exhorted to coöperate; for which they are to labour, and which is therefore a protracted work. Sanctification, therefore, according to this representation, consists in the removal of the evils which belong to us in our natural condition, and in being made more and more conformed to the image of God through the gracious influence of the Spirit of God dwelling in us.

It is not, however, merely in such passages as those above cited that the nature of sanctification is set forth. The Bible is full of exhortations and commands addressed to the people of God, to those recognized and assumed to be regenerate, requiring them, on the one hand, to resist their evil passions and propensities, to lay aside all malice, and wrath, and pride, and jealousy; and on the other, to cultivate all the graces of the Spirit, faith, love, hope, long-suffering, meekness, lowliness of mind, and brotherly kindness. At the same time they are reminded that it is God who worketh in them both to will and to do, and that therefore they are constantly to seek his aid and to depend upon his assistance.

It follows from this view of the subject that sanctification is not only, as before proved, a supernatural work, but also that it does not consist exclusively in a series of a new kind of acts. It is the making the tree good, in order that the fruit may be good. It involves an essential change of character. As regeneration is not an act of the subject of the work, but in the language of the Bible a new birth, a new creation, a quickening or communicating a new life, and in the language of the old Latin Church, the infusion of new habits of grace; so sanctification in its essential nature is not holy acts, but such a change in the state of the soul, that sinful acts become more infrequent, and holy acts more and more habitual and controlling. This view alone is consistent with the Scriptural representations, and with the account given in the Bible of the way in which this radical change of character is carried on and consummated.

§ 3. *The Method of Sanctification.*

It has already been shown that although sanctification does not exclude all coöperation on the part of its subjects, but, on the contrary, calls for their unremitting and strenuous exertion, it is nevertheless the work of God. It is not carried on as a mere process of moral culture by moral means; it is as truly supernatural in its method as in its nature. What the Bible teaches in answer to the question, How a soul by nature spiritually dead, being quickened by the mighty power of God, is gradually transformed into the image of Christ, is substantially as follows, —

The Soul is led to exercise Faith.

1. It is led to exercise faith in the Lord Jesus Christ, to receive Him as its Saviour, committing itself to Him to be by his merit and grace delivered from the guilt and power of sin. This is the first step, and secures all the rest, not because of its inherent virtue or efficacy, but because, according to the covenant of grace, or plan of salvation, which God has revealed and which He

has pledged Himself to carry out, He becomes bound by his promise to accomplish the full salvation from sin of every one who believes.

The Effect of Union with Christ.

2. The soul by this act of faith becomes united to Christ. We are in Him by faith. The consequences of this union are, (*a.*) Participation in his merits. His perfect righteousness, agreeably to the stipulations of the covenant of redemption, is imputed to the believer. He is thereby justified. He is introduced into a state of favour or grace, and rejoices in hope of the glory of God. (Rom. v. 1–3.) This is, as the Bible teaches, the essential preliminary condition of sanctification. While under the law we are under the curse. While under the curse we are the enemies of God and bring forth fruit unto death. It is only when delivered from the law by the body or death of Christ, and united to Him, that we bring forth fruit unto God. (Rom. vi. 8 ; vii. 4–6.) Sin, therefore, says the Apostle, shall not reign over us, because we are not under the law. (Rom. vi. 14.) Deliverance from the law is the necessary condition of deliverance from sin. All the relations of the believer are thus changed. He is translated from the kingdom of darkness and introduced into the glorious liberty of the sons of God. Instead of an outcast, a slave under condemnation, he becomes a child of God, assured of his love, of his tenderness, and of his care. He may come to Him with confidence. He is brought under all the influences which in their full effect constitute heaven. He therefore becomes a new creature. He has passed from death to life ; from darkness to light, from hell (the kingdom of Satan) to heaven. He sits with Christ in heavenly places. (Eph. ii. 6.)

(*b.*) Another consequence of the union with Christ effected by faith, is the indwelling of the Spirit. Christ has redeemed us from the curse of the law by being made a curse for us, in order that we might receive the promise of the Holy Ghost. (Gal. iii. 13, 14.) It was not consistent with the perfections or purposes of God that the Spirit should be given to dwell with his saving influences in the apostate children of men, until Christ had made a full satisfaction for the sins of the world. But as with God there are no distinctions of time, Christ was slain from the foundation of the world, and his death availed as fully for the salvation of those who lived before, as for that of those who have lived since his coming in the flesh. (Rom. iii. 25, 26 ; Heb. ix. 15.) The

Spirit was given to the people of God from the beginning. But as our Lord says (John x. 10) that He came into the world not only that men might have life, but that they might have it more abundantly, the effusion, or copious communication of the Spirit is always represented as the great characteristic of the Messiah's advent. (Joel ii. 28, 29; Acts ii. 16–21; John vii. 38, 39.) Our Lord, therefore, in his last discourse to his disciples, said it was expedient for them that He went away, for " if I go not away, the Comforter (the Παράκλητος, the helper) will not come unto you; but if I depart, I will send Him unto you." (John xvi. 7.) He was to supply the place of Christ as to his visible presence, carry on his work, gather in his people, transform them into the likeness of Christ, and communicate to them all the benefits of his redemption. Where the Spirit is, there Christ is ; so that, the Spirit being with us, Christ is with us; and if the Spirit dwells in us, Christ dwells in us. (Rom. viii. 9–11.) In partaking, therefore, of the Holy Ghost, believers are partakers of the life of Christ. The Spirit was given to Him without measure, and from Him flows down to all his members. This participation of the believer in the life of Christ, so that every believer may say with the Apostle, " I live; yet not I, but Christ liveth in me " (Gal. ii. 20), is prominently presented in the Word of God. (Rom. vi. 5; vii. 4; John xiv. 19; Col. iii. 3, 4.) The two great standing illustrations of this truth are the vine and the human body. The former is presented at length in John xv. 1–8; the latter in 1 Corinthians xii. 11–27; Romans xii. 5; Ephesians i. 22, 23; iv. 15, 16; v. 30; Colossians i. 18; ii. 19; and frequently elsewhere. As the life of the vine is diffused through all the branches, sustaining and rendering them fruitful; and as the life of the head is diffused through all the members of the body making it one, and imparting life to all, so the life of Christ is diffused through all the members of his mystical body making them one body in Him; having a common life with their common head. This idea is urged specially in Ephesians iv. 15, 16, where it is said that it is from Christ that the whole body fitly joined together, through the spiritual influence granted to every part according to its measure, makes increase in love. It is true that this is spoken of the Church as a whole. But what is said of Christ's mystical body as a whole is true of all its members severally. He is the prophet, priest, and king of the Church; but He is also the prophet, priest, and king of every believer. Our relation to Him is individual and personal. The Church as a whole is the temple of God; but so is every believer. (1 Cor. iii. 16 ; vi. 19.) The Church is the bride of Christ, but every believer is the object of that tender, peculiar love expressed in the use of that metaphor. The last verse of Paul Gerhardt's hymn, " Ein Lämmlein geht und trägt die Schuld," every true Christian may adopt as the expression of his own hopes :—

> " Wann endlich ich soll treten ein
> In deines Reiches Freuden,
> So soll diess Blut mein Purpur seyn,
> Ich will mich darein kleiden ;
> Es soll seyn meines Hauptes Kron'
> In welcher ich will vor den Thron
> Des höchsten Vaters gehen,
> Und dir, dem er mich anvertraut,
> Als eine wohlgeschmückte Braut,
> An deiner Seiten stehen."

The Inward Work of the Spirit.

3. The indwelling of the Holy Spirit thus secured by union with Christ becomes the source of a new spiritual life, which constantly increases in power until everything uncongenial with it is expelled, and the soul is perfectly transformed into the image of Christ. It is the office of the Spirit to enlighten the mind: or, as Paul expresses it, " to enlighten the eyes of the understanding" (Eph. i. 18), that we may know the things freely given to us of God (1 Cor. ii. 12) ; i. e., the things which God has revealed; or, as they are called in v. 14, " The things of the Spirit of God." These things, which the natural man cannot know, the Spirit enables the believer " to discern," i. e., to apprehend in their truth and excellence ; and thus to experience their power. The Spirit, we are taught, especially opens the eyes to see the glory of Christ, to see that He is God manifest in the flesh : to discern not only his divine perfections, but his love to us, and his suitableness in all respects as our Saviour, so that those who have not seen Him, yet believing on Him, rejoice in Him with joy unspeakable and full of glory. This apprehension of Christ is transforming; the soul is thereby changed into his image, from glory to glory by the Spirit of the Lord. It was this inward revelation of Christ by which Paul on his way to Damascus was instantly converted from a blasphemer into a worshipper and self-sacrificing servant of the Lord Jesus.

It is not, however, only one object which the opened eye of the believer is able to discern. The Spirit enables him to see the glory of God as revealed in his works and in his word ; the holiness and spirituality of the law ; the exceeding sinfulness of sin ; his own guilt, pollution, and helplessness ; the length and breadth, the height and depth of the economy of redemption ; and the reality, glory, and infinite importance of the things unseen and eternal. The soul is thus raised above the world. It lives in a higher sphere. It becomes more and more heavenly in its character and desires. All the great doctrines of the Bible concerning God, Christ, and things spiritual and eternal, are so revealed by this inward teaching of the Spirit, as to be not only rightly discerned, but to exert, in a measure, their proper influence on the heart and life. Thus the prayer of Christ (John xvii. 17), " Sanctify them through thy truth," is answered in the experience of his people.

God calls the Graces of his People into Exercise.

4. The work of sanctification is carried on by God's giving constant occasion for the exercise of all the graces of the Spirit. Submission, confidence, self-denial, patience, and meekness, as well as faith, hope, and love, are called forth, or put to the test, more or less effectually every day the believer passes on earth. And by this constant exercise he grows in grace and in the knowledge of our Lord and Saviour Jesus Christ. It is, however, principally by calling his people to labour and suffer for the advancement of the Redeemer's kingdom, and for the good of their fellow-men, that this salutary discipline is carried on. The best Christians are in general those who not merely from restless activity of natural disposition, but from love to Christ and zeal for his glory, labour most and suffer most in his service.

The Church and Sacraments as means of Grace.

5. One great end of the establishment of the Church on earth, as the communion of saints, is the edification of the people of God. The intellectual and social life of man is not developed in isolation and solitude. It is only in contact and collision with his fellow-men that his powers are called into exercise and his social virtues are cultivated. Thus also it is by the Church-life of believers, by their communion in the worship and service of God, and by their mutual good offices and fellowship, that the spiritual life of the soul is developed. Therefore the Apostle says, " Let us consider one another, to provoke unto love and to good works : not forsaking the assembling of ourselves together, as the manner of some is ; but exhorting one another ; and so

much the more as ye see the day approaching." (Heb. x. 24, 25.)

6. The Spirit renders the ordinances of God, the word, sacraments, and prayer, effectual means of promoting the sanctification of his people, and of securing their ultimate salvation. These, however, must be more fully considered in the sequel.

The Kingly Office of Christ.

7. In this connection, we are not to overlook or undervalue the constant exercise of the kingly office of Christ. He not only reigns over his people, but He subdues them to Himself, rules and defends them, and restrains and conquers all his and their enemies. These enemies are both inward and outward, both seen and unseen; they are the world, the flesh, and the devil. The strength of the believer in contending with these enemies, is not his own. He is strong only in the Lord, and in the power of his might. (Eph. vi. 10.) The weapons, both offensive and defensive, are supplied by Him, and the disposition and the skill to use them are his gifts to be sought by praying without ceasing. He is an ever present helper. Whenever the Christian feels his weakness either in resisting temptation or in the discharge of duty, he looks to Christ, and seeks aid from Him. And all who seek find. When we fail, it is either from self-confidence, or from neglecting to call upon our ever present and almighty King, who is always ready to protect and deliver those who put their trust in Him. But there are dangers which we do not apprehend, enemies whom we do not see, and to which we would become an easy prey, were it not for the watchful care of Him who came into the world to destroy the works of the devil, and to bruise Satan under our feet. The Christian runs his race " looking unto Jesus; " the life he lives, he lives by faith in the Son of God; it is by the constant worship of Christ; by the constant exercise of love toward Him; by constant endeavours to do his will; and by constantly looking to Him for the supply of grace and for protection and aid, that he overcomes sin and finally attains the prize of the high-calling of God.

§ 4. The Fruits of Sanctification, or Good Works.
Their Nature.

The fruits of sanctification are good works. Our Lord says, " A good tree bringeth not forth corrupt fruit ; neither doth a

corrupt tree bring forth good fruit, For every tree is known by
his own fruit: for of thorns men do not gather figs, nor of a bram-
ble bush gather they grapes." (Luke vi. 43, 44.) By good works,
in this connection, are meant not only the inward exercises of
the religious life, but also outward acts, such as can be seen and
appreciated by others.

There are three senses in which works may be called good, —

1. When as to the matter of them they are what the law prescribes. In this sense even the heathen perform good works ; as
the Apostle says, Romans ii. 14, " The Gentiles . . . do by nature the things contained in the law." That is, they perform acts
of justice and mercy. No man on earth is so wicked as never,
in this sense of the term, to be the author of some good works.
This is what the theologians call civil goodness, whose sphere is
the social relations of men.

2. In the second place, by good works are meant works which
both in the matter of them, and in the design and motives of the
agent, are what the law requires. In other words, a work is good,
when there is nothing either in the agent or in the act which the
law condemns. In this sense not even the works of the holiest of
God's people are good. No man is ever, since the fall, in this
life, in such an inward state that he can stand before God and
be accepted on the ground of what he is or of what he does.
All our righteousnesses are as filthy rags. (Is. lxiv. 6.) Paul
found to the last a law of sin in his members. He groaned under
a body of death. In one of his latest epistles he says he had not
attained, or was not already perfect, and all Christians are required to pray daily for the forgiveness of sin. What the Scriptures teach of the imperfection of the best works of the believer,
is confirmed by the irrepressible testimony of consciousness. It
matters not what the lips may say, every man's conscience tells
him that he is always a sinner, that he never is free from moral
defilement in the sight of an infinitely holy God. On this subject the Form of Concord[1] says, " Lex Dei credentibus bona opera
ad eum modum præscribit, ut simul, tanquam in speculo, nobis
commonstret, ea omnia in nobis in hac vita adhuc imperfecta et
impùra esse ; " and [2] " Credentes in hac vita non perfecte, com-
pletive vel consummative (ut veteres locuti sunt) renovantur. Et
quamvis ipsorum peccata Christi obedientia absolutissima con-
tecta sint, ut credentibus non ad damnationem imputentur, et

[1] vi. 21 ; Hase, *Libri Symbolici*, 3d edtt. Leipzig, 1846, p. 723.
[2] vi. 7 ; *Ibid.* p. 719.

peɪ Spiritum Sanctum veteris Adami mortificatio et renovatio in spiritu mentis eorum inchoata sit : tamen vetus Adam in ipsa natura, omnibusque illius interioribus et exterioribus viribus adhuc semper inhæret." Calvin [1] says, " Seligat ex tota sua vita sanctus Dei servus, quod in ejus cursu maxime eximium se putabit edidisse, bene revolvat singulas partes : deprehendet procul dubio alicubi quod carnis putredinem sapiat, quando numquam ea est nostra alacritas ad bene agendum quæ esse debet, sed in cursu retardando multa debilitas. Quanquam non obscuras esse maculas videmus, quibus respersa sint opera sanctorum, fac tamen minutissimos esse nævos duntaxat : sed an oculos Dei nihil offendent, coram quibus ne stellæ quidem puræ sunt ? Habemus, nec unum a sanctis exire opus, quod, si in se censeatur, non mereatur justam opprobrii mercedem."

Romish Doctrine on Good Works.

Against the doctrine that the best works of the believer are imperfect, the Romanists are especially denunciatory. And with good reason. It subverts their whole system, which is founded on the assumed merit of good works. If the best works of the saints merit " justam opprobrii mercedem " (*i. e.*, condemnation), they cannot merit reward. Their argument on this subject is, that if the Protestant doctrine be true which declares the best works of the believer to be imperfect ; then the fulfilment of the law is impossible ; but if this be so, then the law is not binding ; for God does not command impossibilities. To this it may be answered, first, that the objection is inconsistent with the doctrine of Romanists themselves. They teach that man in his natural state since the fall is unable to do anything good in the sight of God, until he receives the grace of God communicated in baptism. According to the principle on which the objection is founded, the law does not bind the unbaptized. And secondly, the objection assumes the fundamental principle of Pelagianism, namely that ability limits obligation ; a principle which, in the sphere of morals, is contrary to Scripture, consciousness, and the common judgment of mankind. We cannot be required to do what is impossible because of the limitation of our nature as creatures, as to create a world, or raise the dead ; but to love God perfectly does not exceed the power of man as he came from the hands of his maker. It is not absolutely, but only relatively impossible, that is, in relation of the thing commanded, to us not

[1] *Institutio*, III. xiv. 9 ; edit. Berlin, 1834, part ii. p. 37.

as men, but as sinners. Although it is essential to the Romish
doctrine of merit, of indulgences, of works of supererogation, and
of purgatory, that the renewed should be able perfectly to fulfil
the demands of the law, nevertheless, Romanists themselves are
compelled to admit the contrary. Thus Bellarmin says,[1] " Defectus charitatis, quod videlicet non faciamus opera nostra tanto fervore dilectionis, quanto faciemus in patria, defectus quidem est,
sed culpa et peccatum non est. . . . . Unde etiam charitas nostra, quamvis comparata ad charitatem beatorum sit imperfecta,
tamen absolute perfecta dici potest." That is, although our love
is in fact imperfect, it may be called perfect. But calling it perfect, does not alter its nature. To the same effect another of the
leading theologians of the Roman Church, Andradius, says, " Peccata venalia per se tam esse minuta et levia, ut non adversentur
perfectioni caritatis, nec impedire possint perfectam et absolutam
legis obedientiam : utpote quæ non sint ira Dei et condemnatione,
sed venia digna, etiamsi Deus cum illis in judicium intret."[2]
That is, sins are not sins, because men choose to regard them as
trivial.

Works of Supererogation.

But if no work of man since the fall in this life is perfectly
good, then it not only follows that the doctrine of merit must be
given up, but still more obviously, all works of supererogation
are impossible. Romanists teach that the renewed may not
only completely satisfy all the demands of the law of God, which
requires that we should love Him with all the heart, and all the
mind, and all the strength, and our neighbour as ourselves ; but
that they can do more than the law demands, and thus acquire
more merit than they need for their own salvation, which may
be made available for those who lack.

It is impossible that any man can hold such a doctrine, unless
he first degrades the law of God by restricting its demands to
very narrow limits. The Romanists represent our relation to God
as analogous to a citizen's relation to the state. Civil laws are
limited to a narrow sphere. They concern only our social and political obligations. It is easy for a man to be a good citizen ; to
fulfil perfectly all that the law of the land requires. Such a man,
through love to his country, may do far more than the law can
demand. He may not only pay tribute to whom tribute is due,
custom to whom custom, and honour to whom honour ; but he may

---

[1] *De Justificatione*, IV. xvii ; *Disputationes*, edit. Paris, 1608, vol. iv. p. 933, b.
[2] Se Chemnitz, *Examen, De Bonis Operibus*, III. edit. Frankfort, 1574, part i. p. 209, a.

also devote his time, his talents, his whole fortune to the service of his country. Thus also, according to Romanists, men may not only do all that the law of God requires of men as men, but they may also through love, far exceed its demands. This Möhler represents as a great superiority of Romish ethics over the Protestant system. The latter, according to him, limits man's obligations to his legal liabilities, to what in justice may be exacted from him on pain of punishment. Whereas the former rises to the higher sphere of love, and represents the believer cordially and freely rendering unto God what in strict justice could not be demanded of him. " It is the nature of love, which stands far, even immeasurably higher than the demands of the law, never to be satisfied with its manifestation, and to become more and more sensitive, so that believers, who are animated with this love, often appear to men who stand on a lower level as fanatics or lunatics."[1] But what if the law itself is love? What if the law demands all that love can render? What if the love which the law requires of every rational creature calls for the devotion of the whole soul, with all its powers to God as a living sacrifice? It is only by making sin to be no sin; by teaching men that they are perfect when even their own hearts condemn them; it is only by lowering the demands of the law which, being founded on the nature of God, of necessity requires perfect conformity to the divine image, that any man in this life can pretend to be perfect, or be so insane as to imagine that he can go beyond the demands of the law and perform works of supererogation.

Precepts and Counsels.

The distinction which Romanists make between precepts and counsels, rests upon the same low view of the divine law. By precepts are meant the specific commands of the law which bind all men, the observance of which secures a reward, and non-observance a penalty. Whereas counsels are not commands; they do not bind the conscience of any man, but are recommendations of things peculiarly acceptable to God, compliance with which merits a much higher reward than the mere observance of precepts. There are many such counsels in the Bible, the most important of which are said to be celibacy, monastic obedience, and poverty.[2] No man is bound to remain unmarried, but if he voluntarily determines to do so for the glory of God, that is a great virtue. No

---

[1] Möhler, *Symbolik*, 6th edit. Mainz, 1843, p. 216.

[2] Bellarmin, *De Membris Ecclesiæ Militantis*, lib. II. *de Monachis*, cap. 7, 8; *Disputationes*, edit. Paris, 1608, vol. ii. pp. 363–365.

one is bound to renounce the acquisition of property, but if he voluntarily embraces a life of absolute poverty, it is a great merit. Our Lord, however, demands everything. He saith, " He that loveth father or mother more than me, is not worthy of me : and he that loveth son or daughter more than me, is not worthy of me." "He that findeth his life, shall lose it : and he that loseth his life for my sake, shall find it." (Matt. x. 37, 39.) " If any man come to me, and hate not his father, and mother, and wife, and children, and brethren, and sisters, yea, and his own life also, he cannot be my disciple." (Luke xiv. 26.) The law of Christ demands entire devotion to Him. If his service requires that a man should remain unmarried, he is bound to live a life of celibacy ; if it requires that he should give up all his property and take up his cross, and follow Christ, he is bound to do so ; if it requires him to lay down his life for Christ's sake, he is bound to lay it down. Greater love hath no man than this, that a man lay down his life for his friends. Nothing can go beyond this. There can be no sacrifice and no service which a man can make or render, which duty, or the law of Christ, does not demand when such sacrifice or service becomes necessary as the proof or fruit of love to Christ. There is no room, therefore, for this distinction between counsels and precepts, between what the law demands and what love is willing to render. And therefore the doctrine of works of supererogation is thoroughly anti-Christian.

The Sense in which the Fruits of the Spirit in Believers are called Good.

3. Although no work even of the true people of God, while they continue in this world, is absolutely perfect, nevertheless those inward exercises and outward acts which are the fruits of the Spirit are properly designated good, and are so called in Scripture. Acts ix. 36, it was said of Dorcas that she " was full of good works." Ephesians ii. 10, believers are said to be " created in Christ Jesus unto good works." 2 Timothy iii. 17, teaches that the man of God should be " thoroughly furnished unto all good works." Titus ii. 14, Christ gave Himself for us that He might " purify unto himself a peculiar people, zealous of good works." There is no contradiction in pronouncing the same work good and bad, because these terms are relative, and the relations intended may be different. Feeding the poor, viewed in relation to the nature of the act, is a good work. Viewed in re-

lation to the motive which prompts it, it may be good or bad. If
done to be seen of men, it is offensive in the sight of God. If
done from natural benevolence, it is an act of ordinary morality.
If done to a disciple in the name of a disciple, it is an act of
Christian virtue. The works of the children of God, therefore,
although stained by sin, are truly and properly good, because,
(1.) They are, as to their nature or the thing done, commanded
by God. (2.) Because, as to the motive, they are the fruits, not
merely of right moral feeling, but of religious feeling, i. e., of love
to God; and (3.) Because they are performed with the purpose
of complying with his will, of honouring Christ and of promoting
the interests of his kingdom.

It follows from the fundamental principle of Protestantism,
that the Scriptures are the only rule of faith and practice, that
no work can be regarded as good or obligatory on the conscience
which the Scriptures do not enjoin. Of course it is not meant that
the Bible commands in detail everything which the people of God
are bound to do, but it prescribes the principles by which their
conduct is to be regulated, and specifies the kind of acts which
those principles require or forbid. It is enough that the Scriptures require children to obey their parents, citizens the magistrate, and believers to hear the Church, without enjoining every
act which these injunctions render obligatory. In giving these
general commands, the Bible gives all necessary limitations, so
that neither parents, magistrates, nor Church can claim any authority not granted to them by God, nor impose anything on the
conscience which He does not command. As some churches have
enjoined a multitude of doctrines as articles of faith, which are
not taught in Scripture, so they have enjoined a multitude of acts,
which the Bible neither directly, nor by just or necessary inference requires. They have thus imposed upon those who recognize
their authority as infallible in teaching, a yoke of bondage which
no one is able to bear. After the example of the ancient Pharisees, they teach for doctrines the commandments of men, and
claim divine authority for human institutions. From this bondage it was one great design of the Reformation to free the people of God. This deliverance was effected by proclaiming the
principle that nothing is sin but what the Bible forbids, and nothing is morally obligatory but what the Bible enjoins.

Such, however, is the disposition, on the one hand, to usurp
authority, and, on the other, to yield to it, that it is only by the
constant assertion and vindication of this principle, that the liberty wherewith Christ has made us free can be preserved.

§ 5. *Necessity of Good Works.*

On this subject there has never been any real difference of
opinion among Protestants, although there was in the early
Lutheran Church some misunderstanding. First. It was universally admitted that good works are not necessary to our justification ; that they are consequences and indirectly the fruits of
justification, and, therefore, cannot be its ground. Secondly, it
was also agreed that faith, by which the sinner is justified, is not
as a work, the reason why God pronounces the sinner just. It
is the act by which the sinner receives and rests upon the righteousness of Christ, the imputation of which renders him righteous
in the sight of God. Thirdly, faith does not justify because it
includes, or is the root or principle of good works ; not as " fides
obsequiosa." Fourthly, it was agreed that it is only a living
faith, *i. e.*, a faith which works by love and purifies the heart,
that unites the soul to Christ and secures our reconciliation with
God. Fifthly, it was universally admitted that an immoral life is
inconsistent with a state of grace ; that those who wilfully continue in the practice of sin shall not inherit the kingdom of God.
The Protestants while rejecting the Romish doctrine of subjective justification, strenuously insisted that no man is delivered
from the guilt of sin who is not delivered from its reigning
power ; that sanctification is inseparable from justification, and
that the one is just as essential as the other.

The controversy on this subject was due mainly to a misunderstanding, but in a measure also to a real difference of opinion
as to the office of the law under the Gospel. Melancthon taught
that repentance was the effect of the law and anterior to faith,
and used forms of expression which were thought to imply that
good works, or sanctification, although not the ground of justification, were nevertheless a " causa sine qua non " of our acceptance with God. To this Luther objected, as true sanctification
is the consequence, and in no sense the condition of the sinner's
justification. We are not justified because we are holy ; but
being justified, we are rendered holy. Agricola (born in Eisle-
ben, 1492, died 1566), a pupil of Luther, and greatly influential
as a preacher, took extreme ground against Melancthon. He
not only held that repentance was not due to the operation of the
law, and was the fruit of faith, but also that the law should not
be taught under the Gospel, and that good works are not necessary to salvation. The believer is entirely free from the law ;

is not under the law but under grace; and being accepted for what Christ did, it is of little consequence what he does. Luther denounced this perversion of the Gospel, which overlooked entirely the distinction between the law as a covenant of works demanding perfect obedience as the condition of justification, and the law as the revelation of the immutable will of God as to what rational creatures should be and do in character and conduct. He insisted that faith was the receiving of Christ, not only for the pardon of sin, but also as a saviour from its power; that its object was not merely the death, but also the obedience of Christ.[1]

The controversy was renewed not long after in another form, in consequence of the position taken by George Major, also a pupil of Luther and Melancthon, and for some years professor of theology and preacher at Wittenberg. He was accused of objecting to the proposition " we are saved by faith alone " and of teaching that good works were also necessary to salvation. This was understood as tantamount to saying that good works are necessary to justification. Major, indeed, denied the justice of this charge. He said he did not teach that good works were necessary as being meritorious, but simply as the necessary fruits of faith and part of our obedience to Christ; nevertheless, he maintained that no one could be saved without good works. How then can infants be saved? And how can this unconditional necessity of good works be consistent with Paul's doctrine that we are justified by faith without works? Whom God justifies He glorifies. Justification secures salvation; and, therefore, if faith alone, or faith without works, secures justification, it secures salvation. It is very evident that this was a dispute about words. Major admitted that the sinner was in a state of salvation the moment he believed, but held that if his faith did not produce good works it was not a saving faith. In his sermon " On the Conversion of Paul," he said: " As thou art now justified by faith alone, and hast become a child of God, and since Christ and the Holy Ghost through that faith dwell in thy heart, so are good works necessary, not to obtain salvation (which thou already hast as a matter of grace, without works, through faith alone on the Lord Jesus Christ), but to hold fast your salvation, that it be not lost, and also because if thou dost not produce good works, it is an evidence that thy faith is false and dead, a mere pretence or opinion." Amsdorf, the chief representative

[1] See Dorner, *Geschichte der protestantischen Theologie*, Munich, 1867, pp. 336-344.

of the extremists in this controversy, laid down his doctrine in
the following propositions: (1.) Etsi hæc oratio: bona opera
sunt necessaria ad salutem in doctrina legis abstractive et de idea
tolerari potest, tamen multæ sunt graves causæ, propter quas
vitanda, et fugienda est non minus, quam hæc oratio: Christus
est creatura. (2.) In foro justificationis hæc propositio nullo
modo ferenda est. (3.) In foro novæ obedientiæ post reconciliationem nequaquam bona opera ad salutem, sed propter alias
causas necessaria sunt. (4.) Sola fides justificat in principio,
medio, et fine. (5.) Bona opera non sunt necessaria ad retinen-
dam salutem. (6.) Synonyma sunt et æquipollentia, seu ter-
mini convertibiles, justificatio et salvatio, nec ulla ratione distrahi
aut possunt aut debent. (7.) Explodatur ergo ex ecclesia co-
thurnus papisticus propter scandala multiplicia, dissensiones innu-
merabiles et alias causas, de quibus Apostoli Act. xv. loquuntur."

The "Form of Concord," in which this and other controversies
in the Lutheran Church were finally adjusted, took the true
ground on this subject, midway between the two extreme views.
It rejects the unqualified proposition that good works are necessary
to salvation, as men may be saved who have no opportunity to
testify to their faith by their works. On the other hand, it utterly
condemns the unwarrantable declaration that good works are hurtful to salvation; which it pronounces to be pernicious and full of
scandal. It teaches that "Fides vera nunquam sola est, quin caritatem et spem semper secum habeat." [1]

The same doctrine was clearly taught in the Lutheran Symbols
from the beginning, so that the charge made by Romanists, that
Protestants divorced morality from religion, was without foundation, either in their doctrine or practice. In the "Apology for the
Augsburg Confession" it is said: "Quia fides affert Spiritum
Sanctum, et parit novam vitam in cordibus, necesse est, quod pa-
riat spirituales motus in cordibus. Et qui sint illi motus, ostendit
propheta, cum ait: 'Dabo legem meam in corda eorum.' Postquam igitur fide justificati et renati sumus, incipimus Deum
timere, diligere, petere, et expectare ab eo auxilium. . . . . Incipimus et diligere proximos, quia corda habent spirituales et
sanctos motus. Hæc non possunt fieri, nisi postquam fide justificati sumus et renati accipimus Spiritum Sanctum. . . . . Pro-
fitemur igitur, quod necesse est, inchoari in nobis et subinde
magis magisque fieri legem. Et complectimur simul utrumque,
videlicet spirituales motus et externa bona opera. Falso igitur

1 *Epitome*, III. xi.; Hase, *Libri Symbolici*, 3d edit. 1846, p. 586.

calumniantur nos adversarii, quod nostri non doceant bona opera, cum ea non solum requirant, sed etiam ostendant, quomodo fieri possint." [1]

Antinomianism.

Antinomianism has never had any hold in the churches of the Reformation. There is no logical connection between the neglect of moral duties, and the system which teaches that Christ is a Saviour as well from the power as from the penalty of sin; that faith is the act by which the soul receives and rests on Him for sanctification as well as for justification ; and that such is the nature of the union with Christ by faith and indwelling of the Spirit, that no one is, or can be partaker of the benefit of his death, who is not also partaker of the power of his life ; which holds to the divine authority of the Scripture which declares that without holiness no man shall see the Lord (Heb. xii. 14) ; and which, in the language of the great advocate of salvation by grace, warns all who call themselves Christians : " Be not deceived : neither fornicators, nor idolaters, nor adulterers, nor effeminate, nor abusers of themselves with mankind, nor thieves, nor covetous, nor drunkards, nor revilers, nor extortioners shall inherit the kingdom of God." (1 Cor. vi. 9, 10.) It is not the system which regards sin as so great an evil that it requires the blood of the Son of God for its expiation, and the law as so immutable that it requires the perfect righteousness of Christ for the sinner's justification, which leads to loose views of moral obligation ; these are reached by the system which teaches that the demands of the law have been lowered, that they can be more than met by the imperfect obedience of fallen men, and that sin can be pardoned by priestly intervention. This is what logic and history alike teach.

§ 6. *Relation of Good Works to Reward.*

Romish Doctrine.

On this subject the Romanists make a distinction between works done before, and those done after regeneration. Works as to the matter of them good, when performed from mere natural conscience, have no other merit than that of congruity. They are necessarily imperfect, and constitute no claim on the justice of God. But works performed under the control of gracious principles infused in baptism, are perfect ; they have therefore real merit, *i. e.*, the merit of condignity. They give a claim for re-

---

[1] III. iv., v., xv.; Hase, pp. 83, 85.

ward, not merely on the ground of the divine promise, but also of the divine justice. To him that worketh is the reward not reckoned of grace, but of debt. (Rom. iv. 4.) On this subject the Council of Trent,[1] says : " Si quis dixerit, hominis justificati bona opera ita esse dona Dei, ut non sint etiam bona ipsius justificati merita ; aut ipsum justificatum bonis operibus, quæ ab eo per Dei gratiam, et Jesu Christi meritum cujus vivum membrum est, fiunt, non vere mereri augmentum gratiæ, vitam æternam, et ipsius vitæ æternæ, si tamen in gratia decesserit, consecutionem, atque etiam gloriæ augmentum ; anathema sit." Bellarmin [2] says : " Habet communis catholicorum omnium sententia, opera bona justorum vere, ac proprie esse merita, et merita non cujuscunque premii, sed ipsius vitæ æternæ."

The conditions of such meritorious works, according to Bellarmin, are: (1.) That they be good in their nature. (2.) Done in obedience to God. (3.) By a man in this life. (4.) That they be voluntary. (5.) That the agent be in a state of justification and favour with God. (6.) That they be prompted by love. (7.) That some divine promise be attached to them.

Refutation of this Romish Doctrine.

1. This whole doctrine of merit is founded on the assumption that justification, their term for regeneration, removes everything of the nature of sin from the soul ; that works performed by the renewed being free from sin are perfect ; that a renewed man can not only fulfil all the demands of the law, but also do more than the law requires. As these assumptions are contrary to Scripture, and to the experience of all Christians, the doctrine founded on them must be false.

2. The doctrine is inconsistent, not only with the express declarations of the word of God, but also with the whole nature and design of the Gospel. The immediate or proximate design of the plan of salvation, as the Scriptures abundantly teach, is the manifestation of the grace of God, and therefore it must be gratuitous in all its parts and provisions, to the entire exclusion of all merit. Unless salvation be of grace it is not a revelation of grace, and if of grace it is not of works.

3. The doctrine is so repugnant to the inward teachings of the Spirit, as well as to the teachings of his word, that it cannot be practically believed even by those who profess it. The children

---

[1] Sess. vi. canon 32; Streitwolf, *Libri Symbolici*, Göttingen, 1846, vol. i. p. 37.
[2] *De Justificatione*, v. i.; *Disputationes*, edit. Paris, 1608, vol. iv. p. 949, a.

of God, in spite of their theories and their creeds, do not trust for their salvation, either in whole or in part, to what they are or to what they do; but simply and exclusively to what Christ is and has done for them.   In proof of this, appeal may be made to the written or recorded experience of all the great lights of the Latin Church.   If every Christian is intimately convinced that he is unholy in the sight of God; that all his best acts are polluted; and that in no one thing and at no time does he come up to the standard of perfection; it is impossible that he can believe that he merits eternal life on the ground of his own works.

4. As the doctrine of merit is opposed to the nature and design of the Gospel, and to the express declarations of Scripture that we are not justified or saved by works, but gratuitously for Christ's sake, so it is derogatory to the honour of Christ as our Saviour.   He gave Himself as a ransom; he offered Himself as a sacrifice; it is by his obedience we are constituted righteous; it is, therefore, only on the assumption that his ransom, sacrifice, and obedience are inadequate that the merit of our works can be needed or admitted.   The Romanists attempt to evade the force of this objection by saying that we owe to Christ the grace or spiritual life by which we perform good works.   Had He not died for our sins, God would not in baptism wash away our guilt and pollution and impart those "habits of grace" by which we are enabled to merit eternal life.   This does not help the matter; for salvation remains a debt as a matter of justice on the ground of our good works.   It is this which is so contrary to Scripture, to the intimate conviction of every Christian, and to the glory of Christ, to whom the whole honour of our salvation is due.

Doctrine of the older Protestant Divines.

The older theologians, in order the more effectually to refute the doctrine of merit, assumed that a work, to be meritorious, must be (1.) "Indebitum," i. e., not due.   Something which we are not bound to do.   (2.) Our own.   (3.) Absolutely perfect.   (4.) Equal, or bearing a due proportion to the recompense. (5.) And, therefore, that the recompense should be due on the ground of justice, and not merely of promise or agreement.   On these conditions, all merit on the part of creatures is impossible It is, however, clearly recognized in Scripture that a labourer is worthy of his hire.   To him that worketh, says the Apostle, the reward is not reckoned of grace, but of debt.   It is something due in justice.   This principle also is universally recognized among men. Even on the theory of slavery, where the labourer himself, his time, and strength, and all he has, are assumed to belong to his master, the servant has a claim to a proper recompense, which it would be unjust to withhold from him. And in every department of life it is recognized as a simple matter of justice, that the man who performs a stipulated work, earns his wages. The payment is not a matter of favour; it is not due simply because promised; but because it has been earned. It is a debt. So in the case of Adam, had he remained perfect, there would have been no ground in justice why he should die, or forfeit the favour of God; which favour is life.

The passage in Luke xvii. 10, is relied upon as proving that a creature can in no case perform a meritorious act, i. e., an act which lays a claim in justice for a reward. Our Lord there says, " When ye shall have done all those things which are commanded you, say, ' We are unprofitable servants: we have done that which was our duty to do.' " This does not teach that the labourer is not worthy of his hire. The passage is part of a parable in which our Lord says, that a master does not thank his servant for merely doing his duty. It does not call for gratitude. But it does not follow that it would be just to withhold the servant's wages, or to refuse to allow him to eat and drink. God is just, and being just, He rewards every man according to his works, so long as men are under the law. If not under the law, they are dealt with, not on the principles of law, but of grace.

But although Protestants deny the merit of good works, and teach that salvation is entirely gratuitous, that the remission of sins, adoption into the family of God, and the gift of the Holy Spirit are granted to the believer, as well as admission into heaven, solely on the ground of the merits of the Lord Jesus Christ; they nevertheless teach that God does reward his people for their works. Having graciously promised for Christ's sake to overlook the imperfection of their best services, they have the assurance founded on that promise that he who gives to a disciple even a cup of cold water in the name of a disciple, shall in no wise lose his reward. The Scriptures also teach that the happiness or blessedness of believers in a future life, will be greater or less in proportion to their devotion to the service of Christ in this life. Those who love little, do little; and those who do little, enjoy less. What a man sows that shall he also reap. As the rewards of heaven are given on the ground of the merits of Christ, and as He has a right to do what He will with his own, there would be no injustice were the thief saved on the cross as highly exalted as the Apostle Paul. But the general drift of Scripture is in favour of the doctrine that a man shall reap what he sows; that God will reward every one according to, although not on account of his works.

§ 7. *Perfectionism.*

Protestant Doctrine.

The doctrine of Lutherans and Reformed, the two great branches of the Protestant Church, is, that sanctification is never perfected in this life; that sin is not in any case entirely subdued; so that the most advanced believer has need as long as he continues in the flesh, daily to pray for the forgiveness of sins.

The question is not as to the duty of believers. All admit that we are bound to be perfect as our Father in heaven is perfect. Nor is it a question as to the command of God; for the first, original, and universally obligatory commandment is that we should love God with all our heart and our neighbour as ourselves. Nor does the question concern the provisions of the Gospel. It is admitted that the Gospel provides all that is needed for the complete sanctification and salvation of believers. What can we need more than we have in Christ, his Spirit, his word and his ordinances? Nor does it concern the promises of God; for all rejoice in the hope, founded on the divine promise, that we shall be ultimately delivered from all sin. God has in Christ made provision for the complete salvation of his people: that is, for their entire deliverance from the penalty of the law, from the power of sin, from all sorrow, pain, and death; and not only for mere negative deliverance, but for their being transformed into the image of Christ, filled with his Spirit, and glorified by the beauty of the Lord. It is, however, too plain that, unless sanctification be an exception, no one of these promises besides that which concerns justification, is perfectly fulfilled in this life. Justification does not admit of degrees. A man either is under condemnation, or he is not. And, therefore, from the nature of the case, justification is instantaneous and complete, as soon as the sinner believes. But the question is, whether, when God promises to make his people perfectly holy, perfectly happy, and perfectly glorious, He thereby promises to make them perfect in holiness in this life? If the promises of happiness and glory are not perfectly fulfilled in this life, why should the promise of sanctification be thus fulfilled? It is, however, a mere question of fact. All admit that God can render his people perfect before death as well as after it. The only question is, Has He promised, with regard to sanctification alone, that it shall be perfected on this side of the grave? and, Do we see cases in which the promise has been actually fulfilled? The answer given to these questions by the Church universal is in the negative. So long as the believer is in this world, he will need to pray for pardon.

The grounds of this doctrine are, —

1. The spirituality of the divine law and the immutability of its demands. It condemns as sinful any want of conformity to the standard of absolute perfection as exhibited in the Bible. Anything less than loving God constantly with all the heart, all the soul, all the mind, and all the strength, and our neighbour as ourselves, is sin.

2. The express declaration of Scripture that all men are sinners. This does not mean simply that all men have sinned, that all are guilty, but that all have sin cleaving to them. " If," declares the Apostle, " we say that we have no sin, we deceive ourselves, and the truth is not in us." (1 John i. 8.) As the wise man had said before him, " There is not a just man upon earth, that doeth good, and sinneth not." (Eccles. vii. 20.) And in 1 Kings viii. 46, it is said, " There is no man that sinneth not." And the Apostle James, iii. 2, says : " In many things we offend all." It is a manifest perversion of the simple grammatical meaning of the words to make ἁμαρτίαν οὐκ ἔχομεν to refer to the past. The verb is in the present tense. The truth is not in us, says the Apostle, if we say we have no sin, i. e., that we are not now polluted by sin. In the context he sets forth Christ as the " Word of Life," as having life in Himself, and as being the source of life to us. Having fellowship with Him, we have fellowship with God. But God is light, i. e., is pure, holy, and blessed; if, therefore, we walk in darkness, i. e., in ignorance and sin, we can have no fellowship with Him. But if we walk in the light, as He is in the light, the blood of Jesus Christ cleanseth us from all sin. If we say we have no sin, and do not need now and at all times the cleansing power of Christ's blood, we deceive ourselves, and the truth is not in us.

Argument from the General Representations of Scripture.

The declarations of Scripture, which are so abundant, that there is none righteous, no not one ; that all have sinned and come short of the glory of God; that no flesh living is just in the sight of God; and that every one must lay his hand upon his mouth, and his mouth in the dust in the sight of the infinitely holy God, who accuses his angels of folly, refer to all men without exception; to Jews and Gentiles; to the renewed and unrenewed; to babes in Christ and to mature Christians. All feel, and all are bound to acknowledge that they are sinners whenever they present themselves before God; all know that they need constantly the intervention of Christ, and the application of his blood, to secure fellowship with the Holy One. As portrayed in Scripture, the inward life of the people of God to the end of their course in this world, is a repetition of conversion. It is a continued turning unto God; a constant renewal of confession, repentance, and faith; a dying unto sin, and living unto righteousness. This is true of all the saints, patriarchs, prophets, and apostles of whose inward experience the Bible gives us any account.

Passages which describe the Conflict between the Flesh and the Spirit.

3. More definitely is this truth taught in those passages which describe the conflict in the believer between the flesh and the Spirit. To this reference has already been made. That the seventh chapter of Paul's Epistle to the Romans is an account of his own inward life at the time of writing that Epistle, has already, as it is believed, been sufficiently proved; and such has been the belief of the great body of evangelical Christians in all ages of the Church. If this be the correct interpretation of that passage, then it proves that Paul, at least, was not free from sin; that he had to contend with a law in his members, warring against the law of his mind; that he groaned constantly under the burden of indwelling sin. At a still later period of his life, when he was just ready to be offered up, he says to the Philippians, iii. 12–14, "Not as though I had already attained, either were already perfect: but I follow after, if that I may apprehend that for which also I am apprehended of Christ Jesus. Brethren, I count not myself to have apprehended: but this one thing I do, forgetting those things which are behind and reaching forth unto those things which are before, I press toward the mark for the prize of the high calling of God in Christ Jesus." This is an unmistakable declaration on the part of the Apostle that even at this late period of his life he was not yet perfect; he had

not attained the end of perfect conformity to Christ, but was pressing forward, as one in a race, with all earnestness that he might
reach the end of his calling. To answer this, as has been done
by some distinguished advocates of perfectionism, by saying that
Paul's not being perfect, is no proof that other men may not be ;
is not very satisfactory.

The parallel passage in Galatians, v. 16–26, is addressed to
Christians generally. It recognizes the fact that they are imperfectly sanctified ; that in them the renewed principle, the Spirit
as the source of spiritual life, is in conflict with the flesh, the remains of their corrupt nature. It exhorts them to mortify the
flesh (not the body, but their corrupt nature), and to strive constantly to walk under the controlling influence of the Spirit.
The characteristic difference between the unrenewed and the renewed is not that the former are entirely sinful, and the latter
perfectly holy ; but that the former are wholly under the control
of their fallen nature, while the latter have the Spirit of God
dwelling in them, which leads them to crucify the flesh, and to
strive after complete conformity to the image of God. There was
nothing in the character of the Galatian Christians to render this
exhortation applicable to them alone. What the Scriptures
teach concerning faith, repentance, and justification, is intended
for all Christians ; and so what is taught of sanctification suits
the case of all believers. Indeed, if a man thinks himself perfect,
and apprehends that he has already attained what his fellow believers are only striving for, a great part of the Bible must for
him lose its value. What use can he make of the Psalms, the
vehicle through which the people of God for millenniums have
poured out their hearts ? How can such a man sympathize with
Ezra, Nehemiah, or any of the prophets ? How strange to him
must be the language of Isaiah, " Woe is me ! for I am undone ;
because I am a man of unclean lips, and I dwell in the midst of
a people of unclean lips : for mine eyes have seen the King, the
LORD of hosts."

Argument from the Lord's Prayer.

4. Not only do the holy men of God throughout the Scriptures
in coming into his presence, come with the confession of sin and
imperfection, praying for mercy, not only for what they were but
also for what they are, but our Lord has taught all his disciples
whenever they address their Father in heaven to say, " Forgive
us our trespasses." This injunction has ever been a stumbling

block in the way of the advocates of perfection from Pelagius to the present day. It was urged by Augustine in his argument against the doctrine of his great opponent that men could be entirely free from sin in the present life. The answer given to the argument from this source has been substantially the same as that given by Pelagius. It is presented in its best form by the Rev. Richard Watson.[1] That writer says, " (1.) That it would be absurd to suppose that any person is placed under the necessity of ' trespassing,' in order that a general prayer designed for men in a mixed condition might retain its aptness to every particular case. (2.) That trespassing of every kind and degree is not supposed by this prayer to be continued, in order that it might be used always in the same import, or otherwise it might be pleaded against the renunciation of any trespass or transgression whatever. (3.) That this petition is still relevant to the case of the entirely sanctified and the evangelically perfect, since neither the perfection of the first man nor that of angels is in question ; that is, a perfection measured by the perfect law, which in its obligations, contemplates all creatures as having sustained no injury by moral lapse, and admits, therefore, of no excuse from infirmities and mistakes of judgment ; nor of any degree of obedience below that which beings created naturally perfect, were capable of rendering. There may, however, be an entire sanctification of a being rendered naturally weak and imperfect, and so liable to mistake and infirmity, as well as to defect as to the degree of that absolute obedience and service which the law of God, never bent to human weakness, demands from all. These defects, and mistakes, and infirmities, may be quite consistent with the entire sanctification of the soul and the moral maturity of a being still naturally infirm and imperfect."

The first and second of these answers do not touch the point. No one pretends that men are placed under the necessity of sinning, " in order that " they may be able to repeat the Lord's prayer. This would indeed be absurd. The argument is this. If a man prays to be forgiven, he confesses that he is a sinner, and if a sinner, he is not free from sin or perfect. And therefore, the use of the Lord's prayer by all Christians, is an acknowledgment that no Christian in this life is perfect. The third answer, which is the one principally relied upon and constantly repeated, involves a contradiction. It assumes that what is not sin requires to be forgiven. Mr. Watson says the petition, " Forgive us our

---

[1] *Theological Institutes,* ii. xxix.; edit. New York, 1832, p. 545.

trespasses," may be properly used by those who are free from sin. This is saying that sin is not sin. The argument by which this position is sustained also involves a contradiction. Our "infirmities" are sins if judged by "the perfect law"; but not if judged by "the evangelical law." As we are not to be judged by the former, but by the latter, want of conformity to the law is not sin. The only inability under which men, since the fall, labour, arises from their sinfulness, and therefore is no excuse for want of conformity to that law which it is said, and said rightly, is "never bent to human weakness."

Argument from the Experience of Christians.

5. Appeal may be made on this subject to the testimony of the Church universal. There are no forms of worship, no formulas for private devotion, in any age or part of the Church, which do not contain confession of sin and prayer for forgiveness. The whole Christian Church with all its members prostrates itself before God, saying, "Have mercy upon us miserable sinners." If here and there one and another among this prostrate multitude refuse to bow and join in this confession, they are to be wondered at and pitied. They are, however, not to be found. Consciousness is too strong for theory, and therefore,

6. We may appeal to the conscience of every believer. He knows that he is a sinner. He never is in a state which satisfies his own conviction as to what he ought to be. He may call his deficiencies infirmities, weaknesses, and errors, and may refuse to call them sins. But this does not alter the case. Whatever they are called, it is admitted that they need God's pardoning mercy.

§ 8. *Theories of Perfectionism.*

Pelagian Theory.

The two radical principles of Pelagianism are, first, that the nature of man is uninjured by the fall, so that men are free from sin until by voluntary transgression they incur guilt. Secondly, that our natural powers, since, as well as before the fall, are fully competent to render complete obedience to the law.

From these principles Pelagius inferred, (1.) That a man (even among the heathen) might live from birth to death free from all sin, although he did not assert that any man ever had so lived. (2.) That when converted, men might, and numbers of men did, live without sin; perfectly obeying the law. (3.) That this obedience was rendered in the exercise of their ability, assisted by the grace of God.

By grace, Pelagius says that we are to understand, (1.) The goodness of God in so constituting our nature that we can completely obey the law in virtue of our free agency. (2.) The revelation, precepts, and example of Christ. (3.) The pardon of sins committed before conversion. (4.) The moral influences of the truth and of the circumstances in which we are placed. The effect of grace thus understood, is simply to render obedience more easy.

In the Council of Carthage, A. D. 418, the Pelagians were condemned, among other things, for teaching, (1.) That the effect of grace was merely to render obedience more easy. (2.) That the declaration of the Apostle John, "If we say that we have no sin, we deceive ourselves, and the truth is not in us," is, as to some, a mere expression of humility. (3.) That the petition in the Lord's prayer, "Forgive us our trespasses," is not suited to the saints. They use it only as expressing the desire and necessity of others.

According to the Pelagian theory, therefore, (1.) The sin from which the believer may be perfectly free is the voluntary transgression of known law. Nothing else is of the nature of sin. (2.) The law to which perfect conformity in this life is possible, and in many cases actual, is the moral law in all its strictness. (3.) This obedience may be rendered without any supernatural influence of the Holy Spirit.

Romish Theory.

Romanists teach, (1.) That by the infusion of grace in justification as effected by or in baptism, everything of the nature of sin is removed from the soul. (2.) That good works performed in a state of grace are free from the taint of sin, and are perfect. "Si quis in quolibet bono opere justum saltem venaliter peccare dixerit . . . . anathema sit."[1] (3.) That the law may be and often is, perfectly obeyed by the children of God in this life. (4.) That men may not only do all that the law requires, but may even go beyond its demands. (5.) Nevertheless, as there is a higher law than that by which men are to be judged, no man is entirely free from venial sins, *i. e.*, sins which do not bring the soul under condemnation, and therefore all men in this life have need to say, "Forgive us our trespasses."

[1] *Council of Trent*, Sess. vi. Canon 25; Streitwolf, vol. i. p. 36

From this statement it appears, —

1. That by sin from which advanced believers are said to be free, is meant only what merits condemnation, and in itself deserves the forfeiture of grace or divine favour. It is admitted that " concupiscence," or the remains of original sin, is not removed by baptism, but it is not of the nature of sin, in the sense just stated. Neither are venial sins, *i. e.*, sins which do not forfeit grace, properly sins, if judged by the law under which believers are now placed. So far, therefore, as the negative part of perfection, or freedom from sin is concerned, the Romanists do not mean freedom from moral faults, but simply freedom from what incurs the sentence of the law. It is perfection as judged by a lower standard of judgment.

2. The law to which we are now subject, and the demands of which Romanists say are satisfied by the obedience of the saints, is not the moral law in its original strictness, but the sum of that which is due from man in his present circumstances; in other words, the demands of the law are accommodated to the condition of men in this life. This is evident, because they say that the saints obey the law so far as it is now binding, and because they admit that saints commit venial sins, which can only mean sins which, under a stricter rule of judgment, would merit condemnation.

3. As stated above, they distinguish between the law and love. The former is that which all men, and especially Christians, are bound to observe, but love is a higher principle which prompts to doing more than the law or justice demands. Consequently, the positive part of perfection, or conformity to the law, does not imply the highest degree of moral excellence of which our nature is susceptible, but only such as answers to the lower demands of the law to which we are now subject. In a passage already quoted, Bellarmin says, " Defectus charitatis, quod videlicet non faciamus opera nostra tanto fervore dilectionis, quanto faciemus in patria, defectus quidem est, sed culpa, et peccatum non est. Unde etiam charitas nostra, quamvis comparata ad charitatem beatorum sit imperfecta, tamen absolute perfecta dici potest." [1] In like manner Moehler says,[2] " In modern times the attempt has been made to sustain the old orthodox doctrine by assuming that the moral law makes ideal demands, which, as every other ideal, must remain unattainable. If this be true, then the man who

---

[1] *De Justificatione*, IV. xvii.; *Disputationes*, edit. Paris, 1608, vol. iv. p. 933, b.
[2] *Symbolik*, 6th edit. Mainz, 1843, p. 216.

falls short of this ideal is as little responsible, and as little deserving of punishment, as an epic poet who should fall short of the Iliad of Homer."

The Romish theory is consistent. In baptism all sin is washed away. By the infusion of grace full ability is given to do all that is required of us. Nothing can be required beyond what we are able to perform, and, therefore, the demands of the law are suited to our present state. By obedience to this modified law, we merit increased supplies of grace and eternal life.

The perfection, therefore, which Romanists insist upon is merely relative ; not an entire freedom from sin, but only from such sins as merit condemnation ; not holiness which is absolutely perfect, but perfect only relatively to the law under which we are now placed. It is clear that there is a radical difference between Romanists and Protestants as to the nature of sin and the limits of moral obligation. If they were to adopt our definition of sin, they would not pretend to any perfection in the present life.

The Arminian Theory.

The perfection which the Arminians teach is attainable, and which, in many cases, they say is actually attained in this life, is declared to be complete conformity to the law ; including freedom from sin, and the proper exercise of all right affections and the discharge of all duties.

Episcopius defines it to be, keeping the commandments of God with a perfect fulfilment ; or loving God as much as we ought to love Him, according to the requirements of the Gospel ; or according to the covenant of grace. " By a perfection of degrees is meant that highest perfection which consists in the highest exertion of human strength assisted by grace." " This perfection includes two things, (1.) A perfection proportioned to the powers of each individual ; (2.) A desire of making continual progress, and of increasing one's strength more and more."

Limborch defines it as " keeping the precepts of the Gospel after such manner, and in such degree of perfection as God requires of us under the denunciation of eternal damnation." This obedience is " perfect as being correspondent to the stipulations contained in the divine covenant." " It is not a sinless or absolutely perfect obedience, but such as consists in a sincere love and habit of piety, which excludes all habit of sin, with all enormous and deliberate actions." [1] This perfection has three degrees

---

[1] *Theologia Christiana*, v. lxxix. 2, 8, 14; edit. Amsterdam, 1715, pp. 658, a, 659, b, 661, a.

(1.) That of beginners. (2.) That of proficients. (3.) That of the truly perfect, who have subdued the habit of sin, and take delight in the practice of virtue.

Wesley [1] says ; " Perfection is the loving God with all the heart, mind, soul, and strength. This implies that no wrong temper, none contrary to love, remains in the soul ; and that all the thoughts, words, and actions, are governed by love." Dr. Peck [2] says that it is "a state of holiness which fully meets the requirements of the Gospel."

Although these definitions differ in some respects, they agree in the general idea that perfection consists in entire conformity to the law to which we are now subject, and by which we are to be judged.

The Law to which Believers are subject.

What, according to the Arminian theory, is that law ? The answer to that question is given in a negative, and in a positive form. Negatively, it is said by Dr. Peck not to be the Adamic law, or the law originally given to Adam. Fletcher [3] says : " With respect to the Christless law of paradisiacal obedience, we utterly disclaim sinless perfection." " We shall not be judged by that law ; but by a law adapted to our present state and circumstances, called the law of Christ." " Our Heavenly Father never expects of us, in our debilitated state, the obedience of immortal Adam in paradise." The positive statements are, " It is the law of Christ." " The Gospel." " The standard of character set up in the Gospel must be such as is practicable by man, fallen as he is. Coming up to this standard is what we call Christian perfection." [4]

From this it appears that the law according to which men are pronounced perfect, is not the original moral law, but the mitigated law suited to the debilitated state of man since the fall. The sin from which the believer may be entirely free, is not all moral imperfection which in itself deserves punishment, but only such delinquencies as are inconsistent with the mitigated law of the Gospel.

On this point the language of Limborch above quoted, is explicit. It is not " an absolutely sinless perfection " that is asserted. And Fletcher says, We utterly disclaim " sinless perfection " according to the paradisiacal law. Wesley says, By sin is meant

---

[1] *Plain Account of Christian Perfection*, p. 48.
[2] *Christian Perfection*, New York, 1843, p. 292.
[3] See above, page 192.
[4] Peck, *Christian Perfection*, p. 294.

(1.) Voluntary transgression of known law. In this sense all who are born of God are free from sin. (2.) It means all unholy tempers, self-will, pride, anger, sinful thoughts. From these the perfect are free. (3.) But mistakes and infirmities are not sins. " These are," indeed, " deviations from the perfect law, and consequently need atonement. Yet they are not properly sins." " A person filled with the love of God is still liable to these involuntary transgressions. Such transgressions you may call sins, if you please, I do not." [1] The question, however, is not what Wesley or any other man chooses to call sin ; but what does the law of God condemn. Nothing which the law does not condemn can need expiation. If these transgressions, therefore, need atonement, they are sins in the sight of God. Our refusing to recognize them as such does not alter their nature, or remove their guilt.

According to the Arminian system, especially as held by the Wesleyans, this perfection is not due to the native ability, or free will of man, but to the grace of God, or supernatural influence of the Spirit. Perfection is a matter of grace, (1.) Because it is solely on account of the work of Christ that God lowers the demands of the law, and accepts as perfect the obedience which the milder law of the Gospel demands. (2.) Because the ability to render this obedience is due to the gracious influence of the Holy Spirit. (3.) Because believers constantly need the intercession of Christ as our High Priest, to secure them from condemnation for involuntary transgressions, which, judged by the law, would incur its penalty.

Oberlin Theory.

This theory is so called because its prominent advocates are the officers of the Oberlin University in Ohio. President Mahan [2] says, perfection in holiness implies a full and perfect discharge of our entire duty ; of all existing obligations in respect of God and all other beings. It is loving God with all the heart, soul, mind, and strength. It implies the entire absence of selfishness and the perpetual presence and all pervading influence of pure and perfect love.

Professor Finney says : " By entire sanctification, I understand the consecration of the whole being to God. In other words, it is the state of devotedness to God and his service required by the moral law. The law is perfect. It requires just what is right ; all that is right, and nothing more. Nothing more nor less can

---

[1] *Plain Account*, pp. 62-67.   [2] *Christian Perfection*, p. 7.

possibly be perfection or entire sanctification than obedience to the law. Obedience to the law of God in an infant, a man, an angel, and in God himself, is perfection in each of them. And nothing can possibly be perfection in any being short of this ; nor can there possibly be anything above it." [1]

The law which now binds men and to which they are bound to be perfectly conformed, is the original moral law given to Adam. But that law demands nothing more and nothing less than what every man in his inward state and outward circumstances is able to render. The law meets man at every step of his ascending or descending progress. The more grace, knowledge, or strength he has, the more does the law demand. On the other hand, the less of knowledge, culture, moral susceptibility, or strength he possesses, the less does the law require of him.

President Mahan says, Perfection does not imply that we love God as the saints do in heaven, but merely that we love Him as far as practicable with our present powers.

Professor Finney says, The law does not require that we should love God as we might do, had we always improved our time, or had we never sinned. It does not suppose that our powers are in a perfect state. The service required is regulated by our ability.

The principle of this perfect obedience is our own natural ability. A free moral agent must be able to be and to do all that the law can justly demand. Moral ability, natural ability, gracious ability, are distinctions which Professor Finney pronounces perfectly nonsensical. " It is," he says, " a first truth of reason that moral obligation implies the possession of every kind of ability which is required to render the required act possible." [2]

The Oberlin theory of perfection is founded on the following principles : —

1. Holiness consists in disinterested benevolence, *i. e.*, a perfect willingness that God should do whatever the highest good of the universe demands. A man either has, or has not, this willingness. If he has, he has all that is required of him. He is perfect. If he has not this willingness he is in rebellion against God. Therefore it is said, " Perfection, as implied in the action of our voluntary powers in full harmony with our present convictions of duty, is an irreversible condition of eternal life." [3]

2. There is no sin but in the voluntary transgression of known law.

---

[1] *Oberlin Evangelist*, vol. ii. p. 1.
[2] *Sermons*, vol. iv. No. 18.
[3] *Oberlin Quarterly Review*, May 1846, p. 468.

3. There is no moral character in anything but generic volitions, or those purposes which terminate on an ultimate end.   There is no moral character in feeling, and much less in states of mind not determined by the will.   When a man's purpose is to promote the happiness of the universe he is perfectly holy ; when it is anything else, he is perfectly sinful.

4. Every man, in virtue of being a free agent, has plenary ability to fulfil all his obligations.   This principle, though mentioned last, is the root of the whole system.

The Relation between these Theories of Perfection.

The Pelagian and the Oberlin theories agree as to their views of the nature of sin ; the ability of man ; and the extent of the obligation of the law.

They differ as to their views of the nature of virtue or holiness.   The Pelagian system does not assume that disinterested benevolence, or the purpose to promote the highest good of the universe, is the sum of all virtue ; i. e., it does not put the universe in the place of God, as that to which our allegiance is due.   They differ also in that, while the Oberlin divines maintain the plenary ability of man, they give more importance to the work of the Holy Spirit ; and in that, it is generally admitted that although men have the ability to do their whole duty, yet that they will not exert it aright unless influenced by the grace of God.

The Romish and Arminian theories agree, (1.) In that both teach that the law to which we are bound to be conformed is not " ideal excellence ; " not the Adamic law ; not the moral law in its original strictness ; but a milder law suited to our condition since the fall.   (2.) That by freedom from sin is not meant freedom from what the law in its strictness condemns, and what in its nature needs expiation and pardon, but from everything which the milder law, " the law of Christ," condemns.   (3.) They agree in denying to men since the fall ability perfectly to keep the commandments of God, but attribute the ability and disposition to obey to the grace of God ; or the supernatural influence of the Holy Spirit.

They differ as to the mode in which this grace is communicated, in that the Romanists say that it is only through the sacraments ; whereas Arminians say that sufficient grace is given to all men, which, if duly improved, secures such larger measures of grace as will enable the believer to become perfect.   They differ also as to the nature of good works in so far as Romanists include under that category many things not commanded in the Scriptures ; and as they teach the possibility of performing works of supererogatio, which the Arminians deny. The Romanists also teach that good works merit eternal life, which evangelical Arminians do not.

These theories, however, all agree in teaching that the law of God has been lowered in so far that its demands are satisfied by a less degree of obedience than was required of Adam, or of man in his normal state; and therefore in calling that perfection which in fact is not perfection, either in the sight of God or of an enlightened conscience. It is a contradiction to say that a man is perfect whose acts and shortcomings need expiation and the pardoning mercy of God.

It may be safely assumed that no man living has ever seen a fellow-man whom, even in the imperfect light in which a man reveals himself to his fellows, he deems perfect. And no sound-minded man can regard himself as perfect, unless he lowers the standard of judgment to suit his case. And here lies one of the special dangers of the whole system. If the law of God can be relaxed in its demands to suit the state of its subjects, then there is no limit to be assigned to its condescension. Thus perfectionism has sometimes, although not among the Methodists, lapsed into antinomianism.

CHAPTER XIX.

THE LAW.

§ 1. *Preliminary Principles.*

The Personality of God involved in the Idea of Law ; and, there-fore, all Morality is founded on Religion.

THE principal meanings of the word law are, (1.) An estab-lished order in the sequence of events. A law, in this sense, is a mere fact. That the planets are distant from the sun accord-ing to a determined proportion; that the leaves of a plant are arranged in a regular spiral around the stem; and that one idea by association suggests another, are simple facts. Yet they are properly called laws, in the sense of established orders of sequence or relation. So also what are called the laws of light, of sound, and of chemical affinity, are, for the most part, mere facts. (2.) A uniformly acting force which determines the regular sequence of events. In this sense the physical forces which we see in operation around us, are called the laws of nature. Gravitation, light, heat, electricity, and magnetism, are such forces. The fact that they act uniformly gives them the character of laws. Thus the Apos-tle speaks also of a law of sin in his members which wars against the law of the mind. (3.) Law is that which binds the conscience. It imposes the obligation of conformity to its demands upon all rational creatures. This is true of the moral law in its widest sense. It is also true of human laws within the sphere of their legitimate operation.

In all these senses of the word, law implies a law-giver; that is, an intelligence acting voluntarily for the attainment of an end. The irregular, or unregulated action of physical forces produces chaos; their ordered action produces the cosmos. But ordered action is action preëstablished, sustained, and directed for the accomplishment of a purpose.

This is still more obviously true with regard to moral laws. The slightest analysis of our feelings is sufficient to show that moral obligation is the obligation to conform our character and conduct to the will of an infinitely perfect Being, who has the authority to make his will imperative, and who has the power and the right to punish disobedience. The sense of guilt especially resolves itself into a consciousness of being amenable to a moral governor. The moral law, therefore, is in its nature the revelation of the will of God so far as that will concerns the conduct of his creatures. It has no other authority and no other sanction than that which it derives from Him.

The same is true with regard to the laws of men. They have no power or authority unless they have a moral foundation. And if they have a moral basis, so that they bind the conscience, that basis must be the divine will. The authority of civil rulers, the rights of property, of marriage, and all other civil rights, do not rest on abstractions, nor on general principles of expediency. They might be disregarded without guilt, were they not sustained by the authority of God. All moral obligation, therefore, resolves itself into the obligation of conformity to the will of God. And all human rights are founded on the ordinance of God. So that theism is the basis of jurisprudence as well as of morality. This doctrine is taught by Stahl, perhaps the greatest living authority on the philosophy of law. " Every philosophical science," he says, " must begin with the first principle of all things, that is, with the Absolute. It must, therefore, decide between Theism and Pantheism, between the doctrine that the first cause or principle is the personal, extramundane, self-revealing God, and the doctrine that the first principle is an impersonal power immanent in the world." [1] It is not pantheism, but fetichism to make all things God. The real question is, Whether the Absolute has personality and self-consciousness or not ? Stahl had previously said to the same effect, that every philosophy, and every religion, and especially the Christian, must proceed on a theory of the universe (a Weltanschauung). It is the Christian doctrine of God and of his relation to the world, that he makes the foundation of legal and political science (of Rechts- und Staatslehre).[2] He therefore calls his system " theological " in so far as it makes the nature and will of God the foundation of all duties and the source of all rights.

He recognizes, however, the distinction between morality and religion. " Morality," he says, " is the perfection (Vollendung) of man in himself (so far as the will is concerned) ; or the revelation

[1] *Die Philosophie des Rechts*, von Friedrich Julius Stahl; *Rechts- und Staatslehre*, I. i. 1, § 1; 4th edit. Heidelberg, 1870, vol. ii. part 1, p. 7.
[2] *Einleitung*, § 5, *ut supra*, p. 4.

of the divine being in man. Man is the image of God, and therefore in his nature is like God, perfect or complete in himself ; and
conformity to the divine image is for him the goal and command.
(Matt. v. 45.) Religion, on the other hand, is the bond between
man and God, or what binds men to God, so that we should know
and will only in Him, refer everything to Him, — entire consecration, the personal union with God. Thus, love of our neighbour,
courage, spirituality (the opposite of sensuality), may be simply
moral virtues ; whereas faith and the love of God are purely
religious. The courage of Napoleon's guard was a moral virtue
(a state of the will) ; the courage of Luther was religious (a
power derived from his relation to God)." [1]

Religion and morality, although thus different, are not independent. They are but different phases of our relation to God. Stahl,
therefore, controverts the doctrine of Grotius, that there would be
a *jus naturale* if there were no God ; which is really equivalent
to saying that there would be an obligation to goodness if there
were no such thing as goodness. Moral excellence is of the very
essence of God. He is concrete goodness ; infinite reason, excellence, knowledge, and power in a personal form ; so that there can
be no obligation to virtue which does not involve obligation to
God. Wolf carried out the doctrine of Grotius to the length of
saying that an Atheist, if consistent, would act just as the Christian acts. This principle of Grotius, says Stahl, contained the
germ of separation from religion, which unfolded itself with Kant
into an ignoring, and, with those who followed him, into the denial
of God.[2]

" The primary idea of goodness, is the essential, not the creative, will of God. The divine will in its essence is infinite love,
mercy, patience, truth, faithfulness, rectitude, spirituality, and all
that is included in holiness, which constitutes the inmost nature of
God. The holiness of God, therefore, neither precedes his will
(' sanctitas antecedens voluntatem ' of the Schoolmen), nor follows it, but is his will itself. The good is not a law for the divine
will (so that God wills it because it is good) ; neither is it a creation of his will (so that it becomes good because He wills it);
but it is the nature (das Urwollen) of God from everlasting to
everlasting." [3]   Again it is said, " Hence it follows that moral
goodness is concrete, specific, ... absolute, original, as little
determined by logical laws as by a relation to external ends. . . . .

[1] Stahl., *ut supra* I. ii. 1, § 24; *Ibid.* p. 71.   [2] *Ibid.* pp. 73,74.
[3] *Ibid.* I. ii. 2, § 29; *Ibid.* pp. 84, 85.

This is not the doctrine of modern ethics. According to the eu-
daimonistic view adopted by the English philosophers, by Thom-
asius, and others, the good is good because it tends to produce happiness. According to the rationalists, the good is conformity
with the laws of thought (Denkrichtigkeit). . . . . This was
the real doctrine of Wolf, who made morality to consist in order
(Regelmässigkeit); still more decidedly was it the doctrine of
Kant, with whom the moral law is a consequence of the laws of
thought. He says, expressly, that the idea of moral good must
be derived from preceding law, that is, the law of reason."[1]

These two principles, then, are to be taken for granted; first,
that moral good is good in its own nature, and not because of its
tendencies, or because of its conformity to the laws of reason; and,
second, that all law has its foundation in the nature and will of
God. These principles are very comprehensive. They are of
special importance in the exposition of the law in its aspect as the
revealed will of God designed to regulate human character and
conduct.

Protestant Principles limiting Obedience to Human Laws.

There is another principle regarded as fundamental by all Protestants, and that is, that the Bible contains the whole rule of
duty for men in their present state of existence. Nothing can
legitimately bind the conscience that is not commanded or forbidden by the Word of God. This principle is the safeguard of that
liberty wherewith Christ has made his people free. If it be renounced, we are at the mercy of the external Church, of the
State, or of public opinion. This is simply the principle that it
is right to obey God rather than man. Our obligation to render
obedience to human enactments in any form, rests upon our obligation to obey God; and, therefore, whenever human laws are
in conflict with the law of God we are bound to disobey them.
When heathen emperors commanded Christians to worship idols,
the martyrs refused. When popes and councils commanded
Protestants to worship the Virgin Mary, and to acknowledge the
supremacy of the bishop of Rome, the Protestant martyrs refused.
When the Presbyterians of Scotland were required by their rulers in Church and State to submit themselves to the authority of prelatical bishops, they refused. When the Puritans of
England were called upon to recognize the doctrine of "passive
obedience," they again refused. And it is to the stand thus taken

---

[1] Stahl, *ut supra*, p. 87.

by those martyrs and confessors that the world is indebted for all of the religious and civil liberty it now enjoys.

Whether any enactment of the Church or State conflicts with the truth or law of God, is a question which every man must decide for himself. On him individually rests the responsibility, and therefore to him, as an individual, belongs the right of judgment.

Although these principles, when stated *in thesi*, are universally recognized among Protestants, they are nevertheless very frequently disregarded. This is true not only of the past when the Church and State both openly claimed the right to make laws to bind the conscience. It is true at the present time. Men still insist on the right of making that sin which God does not forbid; and that obligatory which God has not commanded. They prescribe rules of conduct and terms of church fellowship, which have no sanction in the Word of God. It is just as much a duty for the people of God to resist such usurpations, as it was for the early Christians to resist the authority of the Roman Emperors in matters of religion, or for the early Protestants to refuse to recognize the right of the Pope to determine for them what they were to believe, and what they were to do. The essence of infidelity consists in a man's putting his own convictions on matters of truth and duty above the Bible. This may be done by fanatics in the cause of benevolence, as well as by fanatics in any other cause. It is infidelity in either case. And as such it should be denounced and resisted unless we are willing to renounce our allegiance to God, and make ourselves the servants of men.

Christian Liberty in Matters of Indifference.

It is perfectly consistent with the principle above stated, that a thing may be right or wrong according to circumstances, and, therefore, it may often be wrong for a man to do what the Bible does not condemn. Paul himself circumcised Timothy; yet he told the Galatians that if they allowed themselves to be circumcised, Christ would profit them nothing. Eating meat offered in sacrifice to idols was a matter of indifference. Yet the Apostle said, " If meat make my brother to offend, I will eat no flesh while the world standeth, lest I make my brother to offend."

There are two important principles involved in these Scriptural facts. The first is, that a thing indifferent in itself may become even fatally wrong if done with a wrong intention. Circumcision was nothing, and uncircumcision was nothing. It mattered little

whether a man was circumcised or not. But if any one submitted to circumcision as an act of legal obedience, and as the
necessary condition of his justification before God, he thereby rejected the Gospel, or, as the Apostle expressed it, he fell from
grace. He renounced the gratuitous method of justification, and
Christ became of no effect to him. In like manner, eating meat
which had been offered in sacrifice to an idol, was a matter of indifference. " Meat," says Paul, "commendeth us not to God: for
neither, if we eat, are we the better ; neither, if we eat not, are
we the worse." Yet if a man ate such meat as an act of reverence
to the idol, or under circumstances which implied that it was an
act of worship, he was guilty of idolatry. And, therefore, the
Apostle taught that participation in feasts held within the pre-
cincts of an idol's temple, was idolatry.

The other principle is that, no matter what our intention may
be, we sin against Christ when we make such use of our liberty,
in matters of indifference, as causes others to offend. In the first
of these cases the sin was not in being circumcised, but in making
circumcision a condition of our justification. In the second case,
the idolatry consisted not in eating meat offered in sacrifice to
idols, but in eating it as an act of worship to the idol. And in
the third case, the sin was not in asserting our liberty in matters
of indifference, but in causing others to offend.

The rules which the Scriptures clearly lay down on this subject
are : (1.) That no man or body of men has the right to pronounce
that to be sinful which God does not forbid. There was no sin
in being circumcised, or in eating meat, or in keeping the sacred
days of the Hebrews. (2.) That it is a violation of the law of
love, and therefore a sin against Christ, to make such use of our
liberty as to cause others to sin. " Take heed," says the Apostle,
" lest by any means this liberty of yours become a stumbling
block to them that are weak." " When ye sin so against the
brethren, and wound their weak conscience, ye sin against Christ."
(1 Cor. viii. 9, 12.) " It is good (i. e., morally obligatory) neither
to eat flesh, nor to drink wine, nor any thing whereby thy brother
stumbleth, or is offended, or is made weak." " All things indeed
are pure, but it is evil for that man who eateth with offence."
(Rom. xiv. 21, 20.) (3). Nothing in itself indifferent can be made
the ground of permanent and universal obligation. Because it was
wrong in Galatia to submit to circumcision, it does not follow that
it was wrong in Paul to circumcise Timothy. Because it was
wrong in Corinth to eat meat, it does not follow that it is wrong

always and everywhere. An obligation arising out of circumstances must vary with circumstances. (4.) When it is obligatory to abstain from the use of things indifferent, is a matter
of private judgment. No man has the right to decide that question for other men. No bishop, priest, or church court has the
right to decide it. Otherwise it would not be a matter of liberty.
Paul constantly recognized the right (ἐξουσία) of Christians to
judge in such cases for themselves. He does this not by implication only, but he also expressly asserts it, and condemns those
who would call it in question. " Let not him that eateth despise
him that eateth not; and let not him which eateth not judge him
that eateth: for God hath received him. Who art thou that
judgest another man's servant? to his own master he standeth or
falleth." " One man esteemeth one day above another: another
esteemeth every day alike. Let every man be fully persuaded in
his own mind." (Rom. xiv. 3, 4, 5.) It is a common saying
that every man has a pope in his own bosom. That is, the disposition to lord it over God's heritage is almost universal. Men
wish to have their opinions on moral questions made into laws to
bind the consciences of their brethren. This is just as much a
usurpation of a divine prerogative when done by a private Christian or by a church court, as when done by the Bishop of Rome.
We are as much bound to resist it in the one case as in the other.
(5.) It is involved in what has been said that the use which a man
makes of his Christian liberty can never be legitimately made the
ground of church censure, or a term of Christian communion.

Scriptural Usage of the Word Law.

The Scriptures uniformly understand by law a manifestation of
the will of God. All the operations of nature are ordered by
laws of his appointment. And his will is represented as the ultimate foundation of moral obligation. In Hebrew it is called
תּוֹרָה, instruction, because it is, as the Apostle says, " the form of
knowledge and of the truth." It is the standard of right and
wrong. In Greek it is called νόμος, custom, and then, as custom
or usage regulates the conduct of men, whatever has that authority, or does in fact control action, is called νόμος. In the New
Testament it is constantly used in this wide sense. It is sometimes applied to a rule of conduct however revealed; sometimes
to the Scriptures as the supernaturally revealed will of God, as
the rule of faith and practice; sometimes to the Pentateuch or
Law of Moses; and sometimes specifically to the moral law. It

is here to be taken to mean that revelation of the will of God which is designed to bind the conscience and to regulate the conduct of men.

How the Law is revealed.

This law is revealed in the constitution of our nature, and more fully and clearly in the written Word of God. That there is a binding revelation of the law, independently of any supernatural external revelation, is expressly taught in the Bible. Paul says of the heathen that they are a law unto themselves. They have the law written on their hearts. This is proved, he tells us, because they do, φύσει, by nature, *i. e.*, in virtue of the constitution of their nature, the things of the law. The same moral acts which the written law prescribes, the conduct of the heathen shows that they know to be obligatory. Hence their conscience approves or disapproves, as they obey or disobey this inwardly revealed law. What is thus taught in Scripture is confirmed by consciousness and experience. Every man is conscious of a knowledge of right and wrong, and of a sense of obligation, which are independent of all external revelation. He may be unable to determine whence that knowledge comes. He knows, however, that it has been in him coeval with the dawn of reason, and has enlarged and strengthened just as his reason unfolded. His consciousness tells him that the rule is within, and would be there though no positive or external revelation of duty existed. In other words, we do not refer the sense of moral obligation to an externally revealed law, as its source, but to the constitution of our nature. This is not the experience of any class of men exclusively, but the common experience of the race. Wherever there are men, there is the sense of moral obligation, and a knowledge of right and wrong.

It is frequently objected to this doctrine that men differ widely in their moral judgments. What men of one age or country regard as virtues, men of other ages or countries denounce as crimes. But this very diversity proves the existence of the moral sense. Men could not differ in judgments about beauty, if the æsthetic element did not belong to their nature. Neither could they differ on questions of morality unless the sense of right and wrong were innate and universal. The diversity in question is not greater than in regard to rational truths. That men differ in their judgments as to what is true, is no proof that reason is not a natural and essential element of their constitution. As there are certain truths of the reason which are intuitive and perceived by all men, so there are moral truths so simple that they are universally recognized. As beyond these narrow limits there is diversity of knowledge, so there must be diversity of judgment. But this is not inconsistent with the Scriptural doctrine that even the most degraded heathen are a law unto themselves, and show the work of the law written on their hearts. As the revelation which God has made of his eternal power and Godhead in his works is true and trustworthy, and sufficient to render ignorance or denial of his existence inexcusable, while it does not supersede the necessity of a clearer revelation in his word; so there is an imperfect revelation of the law made in the very constitution of our nature, by which those who have no other revelation are to be judged, but which does not render unnecessary the clearer teachings of the Scriptures.

Different Kinds of Laws.

In looking into the Bible as containing a revelation of the will of God, the first thing which arrests attention is the great diversity of precepts therein contained. This difference concerns the nature of the precepts, and the ground on which they rest, or the reason why they are obligatory.

1. There are laws which are founded on the nature of God. To this class belong the command to love God supremely, to be just, merciful, and kind. Love must everywhere and always be obligatory. Pride, envy, and malice must everywhere and always be evil. Such laws bind all rational creatures, angels as well as men. The criterion of these laws is that they are absolutely immutable and indispensable. Any change in them would imply, not merely a change in the relations of men, but in the very nature of God.

2. A second class of laws includes those which are founded on the permanent relations of men in their present state of existence. Such are the moral, as opposed to mere statute laws, concerning property, marriage, and the duties of parents and children, or superiors and inferiors. Such laws concern men only in their present state of being. They are, however, permanent so long as the relations which they contemplate continue. Some of these laws bind men as men; others husbands as husbands, wives as wives, and parents and children as such, and consequently they bind all men who sustain these several relations. They are founded on the nature of things, as it is called; that is, upon the constitution which God has seen fit to ordain. This constitution

might have been different, and then these laws would have had no place. The right of property need not have existed. God might have made all things as common as sun-light or air. Men might have been as angels, neither marrying nor giving in marriage. Under such a constitution there would be no room for a multitude of laws which are now of universal and necessary obligation.

3. A third class of laws have their foundation in certain temporary relations of men, or conditions of society, and are enforced by the authority of God. To this class belong many of the judicial or civil laws of the ancient theocracy ; laws regulating the distribution of property, the duties of husbands and wives, the punishment of crimes, etc. These laws were the application of general principles of justice and right to the peculiar circumstances of the Hebrew people. Such enactments bind only those who are in the circumstances contemplated, and cease to be obligatory when those circumstances change. It is always and everywhere right that crime should be punished, but the kind or degree of punishment may vary with the varying condition of society. It is always right that the poor should be supported, but one mode of discharging that duty may be proper in one age and country, and another preferable in other times and places. All those laws, therefore, in the Old Testament, which had their foundation in the peculiar circumstances of the Hebrews, ceased to be binding when the old dispensation passed away.

It is often difficult to determine to which of the last two classes certain laws of the Old Testament belong; and therefore, to decide whether they are still obligatory or not. Deplorable evils have flowed from mistakes as to this point. The theories of the union of Church and State, of the right of the magistrate to interfere authoritatively in matters of religion, and of the duty of persecution, so far as Scriptural authority is concerned, rest on the transfer of laws founded on the temporary relations of the Hebrews to the altered relations of Christians. Because the Hebrew kings were the guardians of both tables of the Law, and were required to suppress idolatry and all false religion, it was inferred that such is still the duty of the Christian magistrate. Because Samuel hewed Agag to pieces, it was inferred to be right to deal in like manner with heretics. No one can read the history of the Church without being impressed with the dreadful evils which have flowed from this mistake. On the other hand, there are some of the judicial laws of the Old Testament which were really founded on the permanent relations of men, and therefore, were intended to be of perpetual obligation, which many have repudiated as peculiar to the old dispensation.   Such are some of the laws relating to marriage, and to the infliction of capital punishment for the crime of murder.   If it be asked, How are we to determine whether any judicial law of the Old Testament is still in force ? the answer is first, When the continued authority of such law is recognized in the New Testament.   That for Christians is decisive.   And secondly, If the reason or ground for a given law is permanent, the law itself is permanent.

4. The fourth class of laws are those called positive, which derive all their authority from the explicit command of God. Such are external rites and ceremonies, as circumcision, sacrifices, and the distinction between clean and unclean meats, and between months, days, and years.   The criterion of such laws is that they would not be binding unless positively enacted ; and that they bind those only to whom they are given, and only so long as they continue in force by the appointment of God.   Such laws may have answered important ends, and valid reasons doubtless existed why they were imposed ; still they are specifically different from those commands which are in their own nature morally obligatory. The obligation to obey such laws does not arise from their fitness for the end for which they have been given, but solely from the divine command.

How far may the Laws contained in the Bible be dispensed with?

This is a question much discussed between Protestants and Romanists.   Protestants contended that the Church had not the power claimed by Romanists, to relieve men from the obligation of an oath, and to render marriages lawful which without the sanction of the Church would be invalid. The Church has neither the authority to set aside any law of God, nor to decide the circumstances under which a divine law ceases to be obligatory, so that it continues in force until the Church declares the parties free from its obligation.   On this subject it is plain, (1.) That none but God can free men from the obligation of any divine law, which He has imposed upon them. (2.) That with regard to the positive laws of the Old Testament, and such judicial enactments as were designed exclusively for the Hebrews living under the theocracy, they were all abolished by the introduction of the new dispensation.   We are no longer under obligation to circumcise our children, to keep the Passover, or feast of tabernacles, or to go up three times in the year to Jerusalem, or to exact an eye for an eye, or a tooth for a tooth. (3.) With regard to those laws which are founded on the permanent relations of men, such as the laws of property, of marriage, and of obedience to parents, they can be set aside by the authority of God. It was not wrong for the Hebrews to spoil the Egyptians or to dispossess the Canaanites, because He whose is the earth and the fulness thereof, authorized those acts. He had a right to take the property of one people and give it to another. The extermination of the idolatrous inhabitants of the promised land at the command of Joshua, was as much an act of God as though it had been effected by pestilence or famine. It was a judicial execution by the Supreme Ruler. In like manner, although marriage as instituted by God was and is an indissoluble covenant between one man and one woman, yet He saw fit to allow, under the Mosaic Law, within certain limitations, both polygamy and divorce. While that permission continued, those things were lawful ; when it was withdrawn, they ceased to be allowable.

When one Divine Law is superseded by another.

The above classification of the divine laws, which is the one usually adopted, shows that they differ in their relative dignity and importance. Hence when they come into conflict the lower must yield to the higher. This we are taught when God says, " I will have mercy, and not sacrifice." And our Lord also says, " The Sabbath was made for man, and not man for the Sabbath," and, therefore, the Sabbath might be violated when the duties of mercy rendered it necessary. Throughout the Scriptures we find positive laws subordinated to those of moral obligation. Christ approved of the lawyer who said that to love God with all the heart, and our neighbour as ourselves, " is more than all whole burnt-offerings and sacrifices."

Perfection of the Law.

The perfection of the moral law as revealed in the Scriptures, includes the points already considered, — (1.) That everything that the Bible pronounces to be wrong, is wrong ; that everything which it declares to be right, is right. (2.) That nothing is sinful which the Bible does not condemn ; and nothing is obligatory on the conscience which it does not enjoin. (3.) That the Scriptures are a complete rule of duty, not only in the sense just stated, but also in the sense that there is and can be no higher standard of moral excellence.   Romanists, on the contrary, teach that a man can do more than the law requires.   There are certain things which are commanded, and therefore absolutely obligatory ; and others which are recommended, but not enjoined, such as voluntary poverty, celibacy, and monastic obedience.   These are held to be virtues of a higher grade than obedience to explicit commands.   This doctrine is founded on the erroneous views of the Church of Rome on the nature of sin, and the grounds of moral obligation.   If nothing is sinful but voluntary, *i. e.*, deliberate transgression of known law ; and if the law is satisfied by voluntary action in this sense of the terms, then it is conceivable that a man may in this life render perfect obedience to the law, and even go beyond its demands.   This is also connected with the distinction which Romanists make between mortal and venial sins.   The former are those which forfeit baptismal grace, and reduce the soul to its original state of spiritual death and condemnation. The latter are sins which have not this deadly effect, but can be fully atoned for by confession and penance.   But if the law of God be spiritual, extending to the thoughts and feelings whether impulsive or cherished ; and if it demands all kinds and degrees of moral excellence, or complete congeniality with God, and conformity to his image, then there is no room for these distinctions, and no higher rule of moral conduct.   The law of the Lord, therefore, is perfect in every sense of the word.

The Decalogue.

The question whether the decalogue is a perfect rule of duty is, in one sense, to be answered in the affirmative.   (1.) Because it enjoins love to God and man, which, our Saviour teaches, includes every other duty.   (2.) Because our Lord held it up as a perfect code, when he said to the young man in the Gospel, " This do and thou shalt live."   (3.) Every specific command elsewhere recorded may be referred to some one of its several commands. So that perfect obedience to the decalogue in its spirit, would be perfect obedience to the law.   Nevertheless, there are many things obligatory on us, which without a further revelation of the will of God than is contained in the decalogue, we never should have known to be obligatory.   The great duty of men under the Gospel, is faith in Christ.   This our Lord teaches when He says, " This is the work of God, that ye believe on him whom he hath sent."   This comprehends or produces all that is required of us either as to faith or practice.   Hence he that believeth shall be saved.

Rules of Interpretation.

Theologians are accustomed to lay down numerous rules for the proper interpretation of the divine law, such as that negative precepts are to be understood as including positive, and positive, negative ; that, in forbidding an act, everything which naturally leads to it is comprehended ; that, in condemning one offence, all others of a like kind are forbidden, and the like. All such rules resolve themselves into one. The decalogue is not to be interpreted as the laws of men, which take cognizance only of external acts, but as the law of God, which extends to the thoughts and intents of the heart. In all cases it will be found that the several commandments contain some comprehensive principle of duty, under which a multitude of subordinate specific duties are included.

§ 2. *Division of the Contents of the Decalogue.*

As the law given on Sinai and written on two tables of stone, is repeatedly called in the Scriptures "The Ten Words," or, as it is in the English version of Exodus xxxiv. 28, "The Ten Commandments," there is no doubt that the contents of that law are to be divided into ten distinct precepts. (See Deut. iv. 13, and x. 4.) This summary of moral duties is also called in Scripture "The Covenant," as containing the fundamental principles of the solemn contract between God and his chosen people. Still more frequently it is called "The Testimony," as the attestation of the will of God concerning human character and conduct.

The decalogue appears in two forms which differ slightly from each other. The original form is found in Exodus the twentieth chapter ; the other in Deuteronomy v. 6–21. The principal differences between them are, first, that the command respecting the Sabbath is in Exodus enforced by a reference to God's resting on the seventh day, after the work of creation ; whereas in Deuteronomy it is enforced by a reference to God's delivering his people out of Egypt. Secondly, in the command respecting coveting, in Exodus, it is said, " Thou shalt not covet thy neighbour's house, thou shalt not covet thy neighbour's wife," etc. In both clauses the word is חָמַד. In Deuteronomy it is, "Neither shalt thou desire (חָמַד) thy neighbour's wife ; neither shalt thou covet (אָוָה) thy neighbour's house," etc. This latter difference has been magnified into a matter of importance.

The Scriptures themselves determine the number of the commandments, but not in all cases what they are. They are not numbered off as first, second, third, etc.　The consequence is that different modes of division have been adopted.　The Jews from an early period adopted the arrangement which is still recognized by them.　They regard the words in Exodus xx. 2, as constituting the first commandment, " I am the Lord thy God, which have brought thee out of the land of Egypt, out of the house of bondage."　The command is that the people should recognize Jehovah as their God; and the special ground of this recognition is made to be, that He delivered them from the tyranny of the Egyptians.　These words, however, are not in the form of a command. They constitute the preface or introduction to the solemn injunctions which follow.　In making the preface one of the commandments it became necessary to preserve the number ten, by uniting the first and second, as they are commonly arranged.　The command, " Thou shalt have no other gods before me," and " Thou shalt not make unto thee any graven image," being regarded as substantially the same; the latter being merely an amplification of the former.　An idol was a false god; worshipping idols was therefore having other gods than Jehovah.

Augustine, and after him the Latin and Lutheran churches, agreed with the Jews in uniting the first and second commandments ; but differed from them in dividing the tenth.　There is, however, a difference as to the mode of division.　Augustine followed the text as given in Deuteronomy, and made the words, Thou shalt not covet thy neighbour's wife ; " the ninth, and the words, " Thou shalt not covet thy neighbour's house," etc., the tenth commandment.　This division was necessitated by the union of the first and second, and justified by Augustine on the ground that the " cupido impuræ voluptatis " is a distinct offence from the " cupido impuri lucri."　The Romish Church, however, adheres to the text as given in Exodus, and makes the clause, " Thou shalt not covet thy neighbour's house," the ninth, and what follows, " Thou shalt not covet thy neighbour's wife, nor his man servant, nor his maid servant," etc., the tenth commandment.

The third method of arrangement is that adopted by Josephus, Philo, and Origen, and accepted by the Greek Church, and also by the Latin until the time of Augustine.　At the Reformation it was adopted by the Reformed, and has the sanction of almost all modern theologians.　According to this arrangement, the first commandment forbids the worship of false gods ; the second, the use of idols in divine worship. The command, " Thou shalt not covet," is taken as one commandment.

It is universally admitted that there are two tables of the decalogue ; the one containing the precepts concerning our duties to God, and the other those which concern our duties to our fellowmen. Philo referred five commands to each table, as he regarded reverence to parents, enjoined in the fifth, as a religious rather than a moral duty. Those who unite the first and second, and divide the tenth, refer three commandments to the first table and seven to the second. According to the third arrangement mentioned above, there are four in the first, and six in the second. The only objection urged against this is founded on the symbolism of numbers. Three and seven among the Jews are sacred and significant; four and six are not.

Arguments for the Arrangement adopted by the Reformed.

There are two questions to be determined. First, should the commandments concerning idolatry be united or separated? In favour of considering them two distinct commandments, it may be urged, (1.) That all the way through the decalogue, a new command is introduced by a positive injunction or prohibition : " Thou shalt not take the name of the Lord thy God in vain ; " " Thou shalt not steal ; " " Thou shalt not kill," etc. This is the way in which new commands are introduced. The fact, therefore, that the command, " Thou shalt have no other gods," is distinguished by the repetition of the injunction, " Thou shalt not make unto thee any graven image," is an indication that they were intended as different commands. The tenth commandment is indeed an exception to this rule, but the principle holds good in every other case. (2.) The things forbidden are in their nature distinct. Worshipping false gods is one thing ; using images in divine worship is another. They therefore called for separate prohibitions. (3.) These offences are not only different in their own nature, but they differed also in the apprehension of the Jews. The Jews regarded worshipping false gods, and using images in the worship of the true God, as very different things. They were severely punished for both offences. Both external and internal considerations, therefore, are in favour of retaining the division which has been so long and so extensively adopted in the Church.

The second question concerns the division of the tenth commandment. It is admitted that there are ten commandments.

If, therefore, the two commands, "Thou shalt have no other gods," and "Thou shalt not make any graven image," are distinct, there is no room for the question whether the command against coveting should be divided. There is, moreover, no pretext for such division, unless we follow the order given in Deuteronomy, which puts the words, "Neither shalt thou desire thy neighbour's wife," before the words, "Neither shalt thou covet thy neighbour's house, his field," etc., etc. As coveting a man's wife is a different offence, or at least a different form of a general offence, from coveting his house or land, if the order given in Deuteronomy be considered authoritative, there might be some reason for the separation. But if the order given in Exodus be adhered to, no such reason exists. The thing forbidden is cupidity, whatever be its object. That the order given in Exodus is authoritative may be argued, (1.) Because the law as there given was not only the first chronologically, but also was solemnly announced from Mount Sinai. (2.) The recension given in Deuteronomy differs from the other in many unimportant particulars. If the order in which the objects of cupidity are mentioned be a matter of indifference, then the diversity is a matter of no consequence. But if it be made a matter of importance, controlling the order and interpretation of the commandments, then it is hard to account for it. There is, therefore, every reason for regarding it as one of those diversities which were not intended to be significant. (3.) The distinction is nowhere else recognized in Scripture. On the contrary, the command, "Thou shalt not covet," is elsewhere given as one command. Paul, in Romans vii. 7, says: "I had not known sin but by the law: for I had not known lust, except the law had said, Thou shalt not covet." And in Romans xiii. 9, in enumerating the laws forbidding sins against our neighbour, Paul gives as one command, "Thou shalt not covet." (4.) Our Lord refers the sin of "coveting a man's wife" to the seventh commandment. If included under that, it would be incongruous and out of harmony with the context, to make it a distinct commandment by itself.

§ 3. *Preface to the Ten Commandments.*

"I am Jehovah thy God, which have brought thee out of the land of Egypt, out of the house of bondage. Thou shalt have no other gods before me." Theism and Monotheism, the foundation of all religion, are taught in these words. The first clause is the preface or introduction to the decalogue. It presents the ground of obligation and the special motive by which obedience is enforced.   It is because the commandments which follow are the words of God that they bind the conscience of all those to whom they are addressed.   It is because they are the words of the covenant God and Redeemer of his people that we are specially bound to render them obedience.

History seems to prove that the question whether the Infinite is a person cannot be satisfactorily answered by the unassisted reason of man.   The historical fact is, that the great majority of those who have sought the solution of that question on philosophical principles have answered it in the negative.   It is impossible, therefore, duly to estimate the importance of the truth involved in the use of the pronoun " I " in these words.   It is a person who is here presented.   Of that person it is affirmed, first, that He is Jehovah ; and secondly, that He is the covenant God of his people.

In the first place, in calling himself Jehovah, God reveals that He is the person known to his people by that name, and that He is in his nature all that that name imports.   The etymology and signification of the name Jehovah seem to be given by God Himself in Exodus iii. 13, 14, where it is written, " Moses said unto God, Behold, when I come unto the children of Israel, and shall say unto them, The God of your fathers hath sent me unto you ; and they shall say to me, What is his name ? what shall I say unto them, and God said unto Moses, I am that I am : and he said, Thus shalt thou say unto the children of Israel, I am hath sent me unto you."

Jehovah, therefore, is the I am ; a person always existing and always the same.   Self-existence, eternity, and immutability are included in the signification of the word.   This being the case, the name Jehovah is presented as the ground of confidence to the people of God; as in Deuteronomy xxxii. 40, and Isaiah xl. 28, " Hast thou not known ? hast thou not heard, that the everlasting God, Jehovah, the Creator of the ends of the earth, fainteth not, neither is weary ? there is no searching of his understanding." These natural attributes, however, would be no ground of confidence if not associated with moral excellence.   He who as Jehovah is declared to be infinite, eternal, and immutable in his being, is no less infinite, eternal, and immutable in his knowledge, wisdom, holiness, goodness, and truth.   Such is the Person whose commands are recorded in the decalogue.

In the second place, it is not only the nature of the Being who speaks, but the relation in which He stands to his people that is here revealed.   " I am Jehovah thy God."   The word God has a

definite meaning from which we are not at liberty to depart.
We may not substitute for the idea which the word in Scripture
and in ordinary language is intended to express, any arbitrary
philosophical notion of our own. God is the Being, who, because
He is all that the word Jehovah implies, is the proper object of
worship, that is, of all the religious affections, and of their appropriate expression. He is, therefore, the only appropriate object
of supreme love, adoration, gratitude, confidence, and submission.
Him we are bound to trust and to obey.

Jehovah is not only God, but He says to his people collectively
and individually, " I am thy God." That is, not only the God
whom his people are to acknowledge and worship, but who has
entered into covenant with them ; promising to be their God, to
be all that God can be to his creatures and children, on condition
that they consent to be his people. The special covenant which
God formed with Abraham, and which was solemnly renewed at
Mount Sinai, was that He would give to the children of Abraham
the land of Palestine as their possession and bless them in that
inheritance on condition that they kept the laws delivered to them
by his servant Moses. And the covenant which He has made
with the spiritual children of Abraham, is that He will be their
God for time and eternity on condition that they acknowledge,
receive, and trust his only begotten Son, the promised seed of
Abraham, in whom all the nations of the earth are to be blessed
And as in this passage the redemption of the Hebrews from their
bondage in Egypt is referred to as the pledge of God's fidelity to
his promise to Abraham, and the special ground of the obligation
of the Hebrews to acknowledge Jehovah as their God ; so the
mission of the Eternal Son for the redemption of the world is at
once the pledge of God's fidelity to the promise made to our first
parents after their fall, and the special ground of our allegiance to
our covenant God and Father.

§ 4. *The First Commandment.*

The first commandment is, " Thou shalt have no other gods
before me." I, that is, the person whose name, and nature, and
whose relation to his people are given in the preceding words,
and I only, shall be recognized by you as God.

This command, therefore, includes, first, the injunction to recognize Jehovah as the true God. As this recognition must be
intelligent and sincere, it includes, —

1. Knowledge. We must know who, or what Jehovah is. This

implies a knowledge of his attributes, of his relation to the world
as its creator, preserver, and governor, and especially his relation
to his rational creatures and to his own chosen people. This of
course involves a knowledge of our relation to Him as dependent
and responsible creatures and as the objects of his redeeming love.

2. Faith. We must believe that God is, and that He is what
He declares Himself to be; and that we are his creatures and his
children.

3. Confession. It is not enough that we secretly in our hearts
recognize Jehovah as the true God; we must openly and under
all circumstances and despite of all opposition, whether from magistrates or from philosophers, avow our faith in Him as the only
living and true God. This confession must be made, not only by
the avowal of the lips as when we repeat the Creed, but by
all appropriate acts of worship in public and private, by praise,
prayer, and thanksgiving.

4. As the law is spiritual, not only as bearing the impress of
the Spirit, and, therefore, holy, just, and good, but also as taking
cognizance of the inward as well as of the outward life, of the
thoughts and feelings as well as of external acts, this recognition
of Jehovah as our God includes the exercise towards Him of all
the religious affections; of love, fear, reverence, gratitude, submission, and devotion. And as this is not an occasional duty to
be performed at certain times and places, but one of perpetual
obligation, a habitual state of mind is the thing required. The
recognition of Jehovah as our God involves a constant sense of
his presence, of his majesty, of his goodness, and of his providence,
and of our dependence, responsibility, and obligation. We are to
have God always before our eyes; to walk and live with Him,
having a constant reference to his will in the conduct of our inward
and outward life; recognizing continually his hand in everything
that befalls us, submitting to all his chastisements and grateful
for all his mercies.

The second or negative aspect of the command is the condemnation of the failure to recognize Jehovah as the true God; failing to believe in his existence and attributes, in his government
and authority; failing to confess him before men; and failing to
render him the inward reverence and the outward homage which
are his due, that is, the first commandment forbids Atheism
whether theoretical or practical. It moreover forbids the recognition of any other than Jehovah as God. This includes the
prohibition of ascribing to any other being divine attributes;

rendering to any creature the homage or obedience due to God
alone; or exercising towards any other person or object those
feelings of love, confidence, and submission which belong of right
only to God.

It is, therefore, a violation of this commandment either to fail
in the full and sincere recognition of God as God, or to give to
any creature the place in our confidence and love due to God
alone.

This the Chief of all the Commandments.

The duty enjoined in this commandment is the highest duty of
man. It is proved to be so in the estimation of God by the express declaration of Christ. When asked, "Which is the great
commandment in the law," He answered, "Thou shalt love the
LORD thy God with all thy heart, and with all thy soul, and with
all thy mind. This is the first and great commandment." (Matt.
xxii. 37, 38.) It is so also in the sight of reason. That infinite
excellence should be reverenced; that He who is the author of
our being and giver of all our mercies; on whom we are absolutely dependent; to whom we are responsible; who is the rightful
possessor of our souls and bodies; and whose will is the highest
rule of duty, should be duly recognized by his creatures, from the
nature of the case must be the highest duty of all rational beings.
It is, moreover, the first and greatest of the commandments if
measured by the influence which obedience to its injunction has
upon the soul itself. It places the creature in its proper relation
to its Creator on which its own excellence and well-being depend.
It purifies, ennobles, and exalts the soul. It calls into exercise
all the higher and nobler attributes of our nature; and assimilates
man to the angels who surround the throne of God in heaven.
The preëminence of this commandment is further evident from
the fact that religion, or the duty we owe to God, is the foundation of morality. Without the former, the latter cannot exist.
This is plain, (1.) From the nature of the case. Morality is
the conformity of an agent's character and conduct to the moral
law. But the moral law is the revealed will of God. If there
be no God, there is no moral law; and if a man does not acknowledge or recognize God, there is no higher law than his own
reason to which he can feel any obligation to be conformed.
(2.) It is a principle of our nature that if a man disregard a higher
obligation, he will not be controlled by a lower. This principle
was recognized by our Lord when He said, "He that is faithful
in that which is least, is faithful also in much; and he that is

unjust in the least, is unjust also in much." (Luke xvi. 10.) This involves the converse : He that is unfaithful in much, is unfaithful in that which is least. (3.) It is the testimony of experience that where religion has lost its hold on the minds of the people, there the moral law is trampled under foot. The criminal and dangerous class in every community consists of those who have no fear of God before their eyes. (4.) It is the secret conviction of every man that his duty to God is his highest duty, as is evinced by the fact that the charge of atheism is one from which the human soul instinctively recoils. It is felt to be a charge of the utter degradation, or of the deadness of all that is highest and noblest in the nature of man. (5.) The most decisive and solemn evidence of this truth, however, is to be found in the revealed purpose of God to forsake those who forsake Him ; to give up to the unconstrained control of their evil passions, those who cast off their allegiance to Him. The Apostle says of the heathen world that it was " Because that when they knew God, they glorified him not as God, neither were thankful, ... God gave them up unto vile affections." (Rom. i. 21, 26.) And again in ver. 28, " As they did not like to retain God in their knowledge, God gave them over to a reprobate mind, to do those things which are not convenient ; being filled with all unrighteousness, fornication, wickedness, covetousness, maliciousness ; full of envy, murder, debate, deceit, malignity ; whisperers, backbiters, haters of God, despiteful, proud, boasters, inventors of evil things, disobedient to parents, without understanding, covenant breakers, without natural affection, implacable, unmerciful." Such are the natural, the actual, the inevitable, and the judicially ordained effects of men's refusing to retain God in their knowledge.

Notwithstanding all this we see multitudes of men of whom it may be said that God is not in all their thoughts. They never think of Him. They do not recognize his providence. They do not refer to his will as a rule of conduct. They do not feel their responsibility to Him for what they think or do. They do not worship Him ; nor thank Him for their mercies. They are without God in the world. Yet they think well of themselves. They are not aware of the dreadful guilt involved in thus forgetting God, in habitually failing to discharge the first and highest duty that rests on rational creatures. Self-respect or regard to public opinion often renders such men decorous in their lives. But they are really dead while they live ; and they have no security against the powers of darkness. It is painful also to see that scientific men and philosophers so often endeavour to invalidate the arguments for the existence of God, and advance opinions inconsistent with Theism; arguing, as they in many cases do, to prove either that there is no evidence of the existence of any power in the universe other than of physical force, or that no knowledge, consciousness, or voluntary action can be predicated of an infinite Being. This is done in apparent unconsciousness that they are undermining the foundations of all religion and morality; or that they are exhibiting a state of mind which the Scriptures pronounce worthy of reprobation.

§ 5. *The Invocation of Saints and Angels.*

Saints and angels, and especially the Virgin Mary, are confessedly objects of worship in the Romish Church. The word "worship," however, means properly to respect or honour. It is used to express both the inward sentiment and its outward manifestation. This old sense of the word is still retained in courts of law in which the judge is addressed as " Your Worship," or as " worshipful." The Hebrew word הִשְׁתַּחֲוָה and the Greek προσκυνέω, often translated in the English version by the word " worship," mean simply to bow down, or prostrate one's self. They are used whether the person to whom the homage is rendered be an equal, an earthly superior, or God Himself. It is not, therefore, from the use of any of these words that the nature of the homage rendered can be determined. Romanists are accustomed to distinguish between the *cultus civilis* due to earthly superiors; δουλεία due to saints and angels; ὑπερδουλεία due to the Virgin Mary; and λατρεία due to God alone. These distinctions, however, are of little use. They afford no criterion by which to distinguish between δουλεία and ὑπερδουλεία and between ὑπερδουλεία and λατρεία. The important principle is this: Any homage, internal or external, which involves the ascription of divine attributes to its object, if that object be a creature, is idolatrous. Whether the homage paid by Romanists to saints and angels be idolatrous is a question of fact rather than of theory; that is, it is to be determined by the homage actually rendered, and not by that which is prescribed. It is easy to say that the saints are not to be honoured as God is honoured; that He is to be regarded as the original source and giver of all good, and they as mere intercessors, and as channels of divine communications; but this does not alter the case if the homage rendered them assumes that they possess the attributes of God; and if they are to the people the objects of religious affection and confidence.

What the Church of Rome teaches on this subject may be learned from the following passages, from the decisions of the Council of Trent, from the Roman Catechism, and from the writings of the leading theologians of that Church : [1] " Mandat sancta synodus omnibus episcopis . . . . ut . . . . fideles diligenter instruant, docentes eos, sanctos, una cum Christo regnantes, orationes suas pro hominibus Deo offerre ; bonum, atque utile esse suppliciter eos invocare ; et ob beneficia impetranda a Deo per filium ejus Jesus Christum, Dominum nostrum, qui solus noster redemptor et salvator est, ad eorum orationes, opem auxiliumque confugere : illos vero, qui negant sanctos, æterna felicitate in cœlo fruentes, invocandos esse ; aut qui asserunt, vel illos pro hominibus non orare ; vel eorum, ut pro nobis etiam singulis orent, invocationem esse idolatriam ; vel pugnare cum verbo Dei ; adversarique honori unius mediatoris Dei et hominum Jesu Christi ; vel stultum esse in cœlo regnantibus voce, vel mente supplicare ; impie sentire."   " Et quamvis in honorem et memoriam sanctorum nonnullas interdum missas ecclesia celebrare consueverit ; non tamen illis sacrificium offerri docet, sed Deo soli, qui illos coronavit ; unde nec sacerdos dicere solet, offero tibi sacrificium Petre, vel Paule ; sed Deo de illorum victoriis gratias agens, eorum patrocinia implorat, ut ipsi pro nobis intercedere dignentur in cœlis, quorum memoriam facimus in terris." [2]

The Roman Catechism [3] teaches the same doctrine.

" Invocandi sunt [angeli eorum]; quod et perpetuo Deum intuentur et patrocinium salutis nostræ, sibi delatum, libentissime suscipiunt."   This invocation, it says, does not conflict with the law " de uno Deo colendo."

Thomas Aquinas says : " Quanquam solus Deus sit orandus, ut vel gratiam vel gloriam nobis donet ; sanctos nihilominus viros orare expedit, ut illorum precibus et meritis, nostræ orationes sortiantur effectum." [4]

On this subject Bellarmin lays down the following propositions, (1.) " Non licet a sanctis petere, ut nobis tanquam auctores divinorum beneficiorum, gloriam, vel gratiam aliaque ad beatitudinem media concedunt."   This, however, he virtually nullifies, when he adds, " Est tamen notandum, cum dicimus, non debere peti à sanctis, nisi ut orent pro nobis, nos non agere de verbis, sed de

---

[1] Concilii Tridentini, sess. xxv.

[2] *Ibid.* sess. xxii. caput iii.

[3] iii. ii. qu. 4 [xix. 10]. See Streitwolf, *Libri Symbolici*, Göttingen, 1846, pp. 93, 78, 79, 479.

[4] *Summa*, ii. ii. quæst. 83, art. 4, edit Cologne, 1640, p. 153, a, of third set.

sensu verborum ; nam quantum ad verba, licet dicere, S. Petre miserere mihi, salva me, aperi mihi aditum cœli : item, da mihi sanitatem corporis, da patientiam, da mihi fortitudinem." (2.) " Sancti non sunt immediati intercessores nostri apud Deum, sed quidquid a Deo nobis impetrant, per Christum impetrant." (3.) " Sancti orant pro nobis saltem in genere, secundum Scripturas." (4.) " Sancti qui regnant cum Christo, pro nobis orant, non solum in genere, sed etiam in particulari." [1] As to the question, How the saints in heaven can know what men on earth desire of them, he says four answers are given.   First, some say that the angels, who are constantly ascending to heaven and thence descending to us, communicate to the saints the prayers of the people.   Secondly, others say, " Sanctorum animas, sicut etiam angelos, mira quadam celeritate naturæ, quodammodo esse ubique ; et per se audire preces supplicantium."   Thirdly, others again say, " Sanctos videre in Deo omnia a principio suæ beatitudinis, quæ ad ipsos aliquo modo pertinent, et proinde etiam orationes nostras ad se directas."   Fourthly, others say that God reveals to them the prayers of the people.   As on earth God revealed the future to the prophets and gives to men at times the power to read the thoughts of others, so He can reveal to the saints in heaven the wants and prayers of those who call upon them.   This last solution of the difficulty Bellarmin himself prefers.[2]

The objections which Protestants are accustomed to urge against this invocation of saints are, —

1. That it is, to say the least, superstitious.   It requires faith without evidence.   It assumes not only that the dead are in a conscious state of existence in another world ; and that departed believers belong to the same living mystical body of Christ, of which their brethren still on earth are members, both of which Protestants, on the authority of God's word, cheerfully admit ; but it assumes, without any evidence from Scripture or experience, that the spirits of the dead are accessible to those who are still in the flesh ; that they are near us, capable of hearing our prayers, knowing our thoughts, and answering our requests.   The Church or the soul is launched on an ocean of fantasies and follies, without a compass, if either suffers itself to believe without evidence; then there is nothing in astrology, alchemy, or demonology which may not be received as true, to perplex, to pervert, or to torment.

---

[1] *De Ecclesia Triumphante*, lib. i., *De Sanctorum Beatitudine*, cap. xvii. xviii.; *Disputationes*, edit. Paris, 1608, vol. ii. pp. 718–721.
[2] *Ut supra*, cap. xx. p. 735.

2. The whole thing is a deceit and illusion. If in fact departed saints are not authorized and not enabled to hear and answer the prayers of suppliants on earth, then the people are in the condition of those who trust in gods who cannot save, who have eyes that see not, and ears that cannot hear. That the saints have no such office as the theory and practice of invocation suppose is plain, because the fact if true cannot be known except by divine revelation. But no such revelation exists. It is a purely superstitious belief, without the support of either Scripture or reason. The conjectural methods suggested by Bellarmin of explaining how the saints may be cognizant of the wants and wishes of men, is a confession that nothing is known or can be known on the subject ; and, therefore, that the invocation of the saints has no Scriptural or rational foundation. If this be so, then how dreadfully are the people deluded! How fearful the consequences of turning their eyes and hearts from the one divine mediator between God and man, who ever lives to make intercession for us, and whom the Father heareth always, and causing them to direct their prayers to ears which never hear, and to place their hopes in arms which never save. It is turning from the fountain of living waters, to cisterns which can hold no water.

3. The invocation of saints as practised in the Church of Rome is idolatrous. Even if it be conceded that the theory as expounded by theologians is free from this charge, it remains true that the practice involves all the elements of idolatry. Blessings are sought from the saints which God only can bestow ; and attributes are assumed to belong to them which belong to God alone. Every kind of blessing, temporal and spiritual, is sought at their hands, and sought directly from them as the givers. This Bellarmin admits so far as the words employed are concerned. He says it is right to say : " Holy Peter, save me ; open to me the gates of heaven ; give me repentance, courage," etc. God alone can grant these blessings ; the people are told to seek them at the hands of creatures. This is idolatry. Practically it is taken for granted that the saints are everywhere present, that they can hear prayers addressed to them from all parts of the earth at the same time ; that they know our thoughts and unexpressed desires. This is to assume that they possess divine attributes. In fact, therefore, the saints are the gods whom the people worship, whom they trust, and who are the objects of the religious affections.

The polytheism of the Church of Rome is in many respects analogous to that of heathen Rome. In both cases we find gods many and lords many. In both cases either imaginary beings are the objects of worship, or imaginary powers and attributes are ascribed to them. In both cases, also, the homage rendered, the blessings sought, the prerogatives attributed to the objects of worship and the affections exercised toward them, involve the assumption that they are truly divine. In both cases the hearts of the people, their confidence and hopes, are turned from the Creator to the creature. There is indeed, however, this great difference between the two cases. The objects of heathen worship were unholy; the objects of worship in the Church of Rome are regarded as ideals of holiness. This, in one view, makes an immense difference. But the idolatry is in either case the same. For idolatry consists in paying creatures the homage due to God.

Mariolatry.

The mother of our Lord is regarded by all Christians as " blessed," as " the most highly favoured of women." No member of the fallen family of man has had such an honour as she received in being the mother of the Saviour of the world. The reverence due to her as one thus highly favoured of God, and as one whose heart was pierced through with many sorrows, led the way to her being regarded as the ideal of all female grace and excellence, and gradually to her being made the object of divine honours, as the Church lost more and more of its spirituality.

The deification of the Virgin Mary in the Church of Rome was a slow process. The first step was the assertion of her perpetual virginity. This was early taken and generally conceded. The second step was the assertion that the birth, as well as the conception of our Lord, was supernatural. The third was the solemn, authoritative decision by the ecumenical council of Ephesus, A. D. 431, that the Virgin Mary was the " Mother of God." On this decision it may be remarked, (a.) That it was rendered rather as a vindication of the divinity of Christ, than as an exaltation of the glory of the Blessed Virgin. It had its origin in the Nestorian controversy. Nestorius was accused of teaching that the Logos only inhabited the man Jesus, whence it was inferred that he held that the person born of the Virgin was simply human. It was to emphasize the assertion that the " person " thus born was truly divine that the orthodox insisted that the Virgin should be called the Mother of God. (b.) There is a sense in which the designation is proper and according to the analogy of Scripture. The Virgin was the Mother of Christ;

Christ is God manifest in the flesh : therefore she was the Mother
of God.   The infant Saviour was a divine person.   Christians do
not hesitate to say that God purchased his Church with his own
blood.   According to the usage of Scripture, the person of Christ
may be designated from one nature, when the predicate belongs
to the other.   He may be called the Son of man when we speak
of his filling immensity ; and He may be called God when we
speak of his being born.   (c.) Nevertheless, although the designation be in itself justifiable, in the state of feeling which then pervaded the Church, the decision of the Council tended to increase
the superstitious reverence for the Virgin.   It was considered by
the common people as tantamount to a declaration of divinity.
The members of the Council were escorted from their place of
meeting by a multitude bearing torches, preceded by women
bearing censers filled with burning incense.   In combating the
assumed Nestorian doctrine of two persons in Christ, there was a
strong tendency to the opposite, to the doctrine of Eutyches, who
held that there was in our Lord but one nature.   According to
this view the Virgin might be regarded as the Mother of God in
the same sense that any ordinary mother is the parent of her
child.   However it may be accounted for, the fact is that the decision of the Council of Ephesus marks a distinct epoch in the
progress of the deification of the Virgin.

The fourth step soon followed in the dedication to her honour of
numerous churches, shrines, and festivals ; and in the introduction
of solemn offices designed for public and private worship in which
she was solemnly invoked.   No limit was placed to the titles of
honour by which she was addressed or to the prerogatives and
powers which were attributed to her.   She was declared to be
deificata.   She was called the Queen of heaven, Queen of queens ;
said to be exalted above all principalities and powers ; to be
seated at the right hand of Christ, to share with Him in the
universal and absolute power committed to his hands.   All the
blessings of salvation were sought at her hands, as well as protection from all enemies, and deliverance from all evils.   Prayers,
hymns, and doxologies were allowed and prescribed to be addressed to her.   The whole Psalter has been transformed into a
book of praise and confession to the Mother of Christ.   What in
the Bible is said to God and of God, is in this book addressed to
the Virgin.   In the First Psalm, for example, it is said, " Blessed
is the man who walketh not in the counsel of the ungodly," etc.
In the Psalter of the Virgin it reads, " Blessed is the man who

loveth thy name, O Virgin Mary; thy grace shall comfort his soul. As a tree irrigated by fountains of water, he shall bring forth the richest fruits of righteousness." In the second Psalm the prayer is directed to the Virgin : " Protect us with thy right hand, O Mother of God," etc. Ps. ix., "I will confess to Thee, O Lady (Domina); I will declare among the people thy praise and glory. To thee belong glory, thanksgiving, and the voice of praise." Ps. xv., " Preserve me, O Lady, for I have hoped in thee." Ps. xvii., "I will love thee O Queen of heaven and earth, and will glorify thy name among the Gentiles." Ps. xviii., " The heavens declare thy glory, O Virgin Mary; the fragrance of thy ointments is dispersed among all nations." Ps. xli., " As the hart panteth after the water brooks, so panteth my soul for thy love, O Holy Virgin." And so on to the end. The Virgin is throughout addressed as the Psalmist addressed God; and the blessings which he sought from God, the Romanist is taught to seek from her.[1]

In like manner the most holy offices of the Church are parodied. The Te Deum, for example, is turned into an address to the Virgin. " We praise thee, Mother of God; we acknowledge thee to be a virgin. All the earth doth worship thee, the spouse of the eternal Father. All the angels and archangels, all thrones and powers, do faithfully serve thee. To thee all angels cry aloud, with a never-ceasing voice, Holy, Holy, Holy, Mary, Mother of God. . . . . The whole court of heaven doth honour thee as queen. The holy Church throughout all the world doth invoke and praise thee, the mother of divine majesty. . . . . Thou sittest with thy Son on the right hand of the Father. . . . . In thee, sweet Mary, is our hope; defend us for evermore. Praise becometh thee; empire becometh thee; virtue and glory be unto thee for ever and ever." [2]

It is hardly necessary to refer to the Litanies of the Virgin Mary in further proof of the idolatrous worship of which she is the object. Those litanies are prepared in the form usually adopted in the worship of the Holy Trinity; containing invocations, deprecations, intercessions, and supplications. They contain such

---

[1] This Psalter is published under the title *Psalterium Virginis Mariæ*, a *Devoto Doctore Sancto Bonaventura compilatum*. It is given at length by Chemnitz in his *Examen Concilii Tridentini*, edit. Frankfort, 1574, part iii. pp. 166–179. Chemnitz does not refer its authorship to Bonaventura; but gives it as a document sanctioned and used in the Church of Rome.

[2] See *A Church Dictionary*. By Walter Farquhar Hook, D. D., Vicar of Leeds. Sixth edition. Philadelphia, 1854, article Mariolatry. Dr. Hook quotes the so-called " Psalter of Bonaventura;" and refers to Sancti Bonaventuræ *Opera*, tom. vi. part ii. from p. 466 to 473. Fol. Moguntiæ, 1609.

prayers as the following : " Peccatores, te rogamus audi nos ; Ut sanctam Ecclesiam piissima conservare digneris, Ut justis gloriam, peccatoribus gratiam impetrare digneris, Ut navigantibus portum, infirmantibus sanitatem, tribulatis consolationem, captivis libe- rationem, impetrare digneris, Ut famulos et famulas tuas tibi devote servientes, consolare digneris, Ut cunctum populum Chris- tianum filii tui pretioso sanguine redemptum, conservare digneris, Ut cunctis fidelibus defunctis, eternam requiem impetrare digneris, Ut nos exaudire digneris, Mater Dei, Filia Dei, Sponsa Dei, Mater carissima, Domina nostra, miserere, et dona nobis perpetuam pacem." More than this cannot be sought at the hands of God or Christ. The Virgin Mary is to her worshippers what Christ is to us. She is the object of all religious affections ; the ground of confidence ; and the source whence all the blessings of salvation are expected and sought.

There was, however, always an undercurrent of opposition to this deification of the mother of our Lord. This became more apparent in the controversy on the question of her immaculate conception. This idea was never broached in the early Church. The first form in which the doctrine appeared was, that from the fact that God says of Jeremiah, " Before thou camest forth out of the womb I sanctified thee" (Jer. i. 5), it was maintained that the same might be said of the Virgin Mary. Jeremiah indeed was sanctified before birth, in the sense that he was consecrated or set apart in the purpose of God to the prophetic office ; whereas Mary, it was held, was thus sanctified in the sense of being made holy. All the great lights of the Latin Church, Augustine, Anselm, Bernard of Clairvaux, and Thomas Aquinas, held that if the Virgin Mary were not a partaker of the sin and apostasy of man, she could not be a partaker of redemption. As Thomas Aquinas, and after him the Dominicans, took the one side in this controversy, Duns Scotus and the Franciscans took the other. The public feeling was in favour of the Franciscan doctrine of the immaculate conception. Even John Gerson, chancellor of the University of Paris, distinguished not only for his learning but also for his zeal in reforming abuses, in 1401 came out publicly in support of that view. He was, however, candid enough to admit that it had not hitherto been the doctrine of the Church. But he held that God communicated the truth gradually to the Church ; hence Moses knew more than Abraham, the prophets more than Moses, the Apostles more than the prophets ; in like manner, the Church has received from the Spirit of God many truths not

known to the Apostles. This of course implies the rejection of
the doctrine of tradition. That doctrine is, that a plenary revelation of all Christian doctrine was made by Christ to the Apostles
and by them communicated to the Church, partly in their writings
and partly by oral instructions. To prove that any doctrine is of
divine authority, it must be proved that it was taught by the
Apostles, and to prove that they taught it, it must be proved that
it has been always and everywhere held by the Church. But according to Gerson the Church of to-day may hold what the Apostles never held, and even the very reverse of what was held by
them and by the Church for ages to be true. He teaches that
the Church before his time taught that the Virgin Mary, in
common with all other members of the human race, was born with
the infection of original sin ; but that the Church of his day,
under the inspiration of the Spirit, believed in her immaculate
conception. This resolves tradition into, or rather substitutes for
it, the *sensus communis ecclesiæ* of any given time. It has already been shown [1] that Moehler in his " Symbolik " teaches substantially the same doctrine.

This question was undecided at the time of the meeting of the
Council of Trent, and gave the fathers there assembled a great
deal of trouble. The Dominicans and Franciscans, of nearly equal
influence in the Council, each urged that their peculiar views
should be sanctioned. The legates in their perplexity referred
to Rome for instructions, and were directed for fear of schism to
prevent any further controversy on the subject, and so to frame
the decision as to satisfy both parties. This could only be done
by leaving the question undecided. This was substantially the
course which the Council adopted. After affirming that all mankind sinned in Adam and derive from him a corrupt nature, it
adds : " Declarat tamen hæc ipsa Sancta Synodus, non esse suæ
intentionis comprehendere in hoc decreto, ubi de peccato originali
agitur, beatam, et immaculatam Viriginem Mariam, Dei gene-
tricem ; sed observandas esse constitutiones felicis recordationis
Xysti papæ IV., sub pœnis in eis constitutionibus contentis, quas
innovat.[2] This last clause refers to the Bull of Sixtus IV., issued
in 1483, threatening both parties in this controversy with the pains
of excommunication if either pronounced the other guilty of heresy
or mortal sin.

---

[1] Vol. i. p. 114.
[2] This is from Streitwolf, *Libri Symbolici*, Göttingen, 1846, p. 20. A foot-note says,
" Totum hanc periodum, ' Declarat-innovat,' omnes fere editiones ante Romanas omittunt."

The controversy went on, therefore, after the Council of Trent very much as it had done before, until the present Pope, himself a devoted worshipper of the Virgin, announced his purpose to have the immaculate conception of the Mother of our Lord declared. This purpose he carried into effect, and on the eighth of December, 1854, he went in great pomp to St. Peter's in Rome, and pronounced the decree that the "Virgin Mary, from the first moment of conception by the special grace of almighty God in view of the merits of Christ, was preserved from all stain of original sin." She was thus placed, as to complete sinlessness, on an equality with her adorable Son, Jesus Christ, whose place she occupies in the confidence and love of so large a part of the Roman Catholic world.

§ 6. *The Second Commandment.*

The two fundamental principles of the religion of the Bible are first, that there is one only the living and true God, the maker of heaven and earth, who has revealed Himself under the name Jehovah; secondly, that this God is a Spirit, and, therefore, incapable of being conceived of or represented under a visible form. The first commandment, therefore, forbids the worship of any other being than Jehovah; and the second, the worship of any visible object whatever. This includes the prohibition, not only of inward homage, but of all external acts which are the natural or conventional expression of such inward reverence.

That the second commandment does not forbid pictorial or sculptured representations of ideal or visible objects, is plain because the whole command has reference to religious worship, and because Moses, at the command of God himself, made many such images and representations. The curtains of the tabernacle and especially the veil separating between the Holy and Most Holy places, were adorned with embroidered figures representing cherubim; cherubim overshadowed the Ark of the Covenant with their wings; the Golden Candlestick was in the form of a tree "with branches, knops, and flowers;" the hem of the high priest's robe was adorned with alternate bells and pomegranates. When Solomon built the temple, "he carved all the walls of the house round about with carved figures of cherubim, and palm-trees, and open flowers, within and without." (1 Kings vi. 29.) The "molten sea" stood upon twelve oxen. Of this house thus adorned God said, "I have hallowed this house, which thou hast built, to put my name there forever; and mine eyes and mine heart shall be there perpetually." (1 Kings ix. 3.) There can therefore be no doubt that the second commandment was intended only to forbid the making or using the likeness of anything in heaven or earth as objects of worship.[1]

The Worship of Images forbidden.

It is equally clear that the second commandment does forbid the use of images in divine worship. In other words, idolatry consists not only in the worship of false gods, but also in the worship of the true God by images. This is clear, —

1. From the literal meaning of the words. The precise thing forbidden is, bowing down to them, or serving them, i. e., rendering them any kind of external homage. This, however, is exactly what is done by all those who employ images as the objects, or aids of religious worship.

2. This is still further plain because the Hebrews were solemnly enjoined not to make any visible representation of the unseen God, or to adopt anything external as the symbol of the invisible and make such symbol the object of worship; i. e., they were not to bow down before these images or symbols or serve them. The Hebrew word עָבַד rendered "to serve," includes all kinds of external homage, burning incense, making oblations, and kissing in token of subjection. The Hebrews were surrounded by idolaters. The nations, having forgotten God, or refusing to acknowledge Him, had given themselves up to false gods. It was nature's invisible force, of which they saw constant, and often fearful manifestations around them, that was the great object of their reverence and fear. But nature, force, the invisible, could no more satisfy them, than the invisible Jehovah. They symbolized not the unknown, but the real, first in one way and then in another. Light and darkness were the two most obvious symbols of good and evil; light, therefore, the sun, moon, and stars, the host of heaven, were among the earlier objects of religious reverence. But anything external and visible, living or dead, might be made to the people, by association or arbitrary appointment, the representative of the great unknown power by which all things

---

[1] The later Jews interpreted this commandment more strictly than either Moses or Solomon. Josephus, *Ant.* 8, 7, 5, pronounced making the figures of oxen to support the brazen laver to be contrary to the law. One of the most distinguished ministers of our Church objected to the American Sunday School Union, that they published books with pictures. When asked, What he thought of maps? he answered that so far as maps were designed simply to show the relative position of places on the face of the earth, they were allowed; but if they had any shading on them to represent mountains, they were forbidden by the second commandment.

were controlled. Most naturally, men distinguished by force of character and by their exploits would be regarded as manifestations of the unknown. Thus nature-worship and hero-worship, the two great forms of heathenism, are seen to be radically the same. It was in view of this state of the Gentile world, all nations being given to the worship of the visible as the symbol of the invisible, that Moses delivered the solemn address to the chosen people recorded in the fourth chapter of Deuteronomy. " Only take heed to thyself," said the prophet, " and keep thy soul diligently, lest thou forget the things which thine eyes have seen, and lest they depart from thy heart all the days of thy life ; but teach them thy sons, and thy sons' sons." What is it that he thus earnestly called on them to remember ? It was that in all the wonderful display of the divine presence and majesty upon Sinai, they had seen " no similitude," but only heard a voice, " Take ye therefore good heed unto yourselves ; (for ye saw no manner of similitude on the day that the LORD spake unto you in Horeb out of the midst of the fire,) lest ye corrupt yourselves, and make you a graven image, the similitude of any figure, the likeness of male or female, the likeness of any beast that is on the earth, the likeness of any winged fowl that flieth in the air, the likeness of anything that creepeth on the ground, the likeness of any fish that is in the waters beneath the earth : and lest thou lift up thine eyes unto heaven, and when thou seest the sun, and the moon, and the stars, even all the host of heaven, shouldest be driven to worship them [literally, " to prostrate thyself before them "], and serve them, which the LORD thy God hath divided unto all nations under the whole heaven. . . . . Take heed unto yourselves, lest ye forget the covenant of the LORD your God, which he made with you, and make you a graven image, the likeness of anything which the LORD thy God hath forbidden thee. For the LORD thy God is a consuming fire, even a jealous God." The thing thus repeatedly and solemnly forbidden as a violation of the covenant between God and the people, was the bowing down to, or using anything visible, whether a natural object as the sun or moon, or a work of art and man's device, as an object or mode of divine worship. And in this sense the command has been understood by the people to whom it was given, from the time of Moses until now. The worship of the true God by images, in the eyes of the Hebrews, has ever been considered as much an act of idolatry as the worship of false gods.

3. A third argument on this subject is, that the worship of

Jehovah by the use of images is denounced and punished as an act of apostasy from God.   When the Hebrews in the wilderness said to Aaron, " Make us gods which shall go before us," neither they nor Aaron intended to renounce Jehovah as their God ; but they desired a visible symbol of God, as the heathen had of their gods.   This is plain, because Aaron, when he fashioned the golden calf and built an altar before it, made proclamation, and said, " To-morrow is a feast to Jehovah." " Their sin then lay, not in their adopting another god, but in their pretending to worship a visible symbol of Him whom no symbol could represent."[1]

In like manner, when the ten tribes separated from Judah and were erected into a separate kingdom under Jeroboam, the worship of God by idols was regarded as an apostasy from the true God.   It is evident from the whole narrative that Jeroboam did not intend to introduce the worship of any other god than Jehovah.   It was the place and mode of worship which he sought to change.   He feared that if the people continued to go up to Jerusalem and worship in the temple there established, they would soon return to their allegiance to the house of David.   To prevent this, he made two golden calves, as Aaron had done, symbols of the God who had brought his people out of Egypt, and placed one in Dan and the other in Bethel, and commanded the people to resort to those places for worship.   Thus also Jehu, who boasted of his " zeal for Jehovah," and exterminated the priests and worshippers of Baal, retained the service of the golden calves, because, as Winer expresses it, " that had become the established form of the Jehovah-worship in Israel." " Er [Jehu] behielt den Kälberdienst in Dan und Bethel, als in Israel einheimisch gewordenen Jehovah-dienst."[2]   In Leviticus xxvi. 1, it is said : " Ye shall make you no idols nor graven image, neither rear you up a standing image, neither shall ye set up any image of stone in your land, to bow down unto it : for I am the LORD your God."   And Moses commanded that when the people had gained possession of the promised land, six of the tribes should be gathered on Mount Gerizim to bless, and six upon Mount Ebal to curse : " And the Levites shall speak and say unto all the men of Israel with a loud voice, cursed be the man that maketh any graven or molten image, an abomination unto the LORD, the work of the hands of the craftsman, and putteth it in a secret place.   And all the people shall answer and say, Amen."   (Deut. xxvii. 15.)

---

[1] *The Holy Bible, with an Explanatory and Critical Commentary.* By Bishops and other Clergy of the Anglican Church. New York: Charles Scribner & Co., 1871, vol. i. p. 405.

[2] *Biblisches Realwörterbuch*, von Dr. Georg Benedict Winer, 3d edit. Leipzig, 1847, art. " Jehu."

The specific thing thus frequently and solemnly forbidden is the bowing down to images, or rendering them any religious service. In this sense these commands were understood by the ancient people of God to whom they were originally given, and by the whole Christian Church until the sudden influx of nominally converted heathen into the Church after the time of Constantine, who brought with them heathenish ideas and insisted on heathen modes of worship.

The simple obvious facts with regard to the religion of the gentile world are, (1.) That the gods of the nations were imaginary beings ; that is, they either had no existence except in the imaginations of their worshippers, or they did not possess the attributes which were ascribed to them. Therefore they are called in Scripture vanity, lies, nonentities. (2.) Of these imaginary beings symbols were selected or images formed, to which all the homage supposed to be due to the gods themselves was paid. This was not done on the assumption that the symbols or images were really gods. The Greeks did not think that Jupiter was a block of marble. Neither did the heathen mentioned in the Bible believe that the sun was Baal. Nevertheless some connection was supposed to exist between the image and the divinity which it was intended to represent. With some this connection was simply that between the sign and the thing signified ; with others it was more mystical, or what in these days we should call sacramental. In either case it was such that the homage due to the divinity was paid to his image ; and any indignity offered to the latter was resented as offered to the former.

As, therefore, the heathen gods were no gods, and as the homage due to God was paid to the idols, the sacred writers denounced the heathen as the worshippers of stocks and stones, and condemned them for the folly of making gods out of wood or metal " graven by art and man's device." They made little or no difference between the worshipping of images and the worshipping false gods. The two things were, in their view, identical. Hence in the Bible the worship of images is denounced as idolatry, without regard to the divinity, whether true or false, to whom the image was dedicated.

The Reasons annexed to this Commandment.

The relation between the soul and God is far more intimate than that between the soul and any creature. Our life, spiritual and eternal, depends on our relation to our Maker. Hence our highest duty is to Him. The greatest sin a man can commit is to refuse to render to God the admiration and obedience which are his due, or to transfer to the creature the allegiance and service which belong to Him. Hence no sin is so frequently or so severely denounced in the Scriptures.

The most intimate relation which can subsist among men is that of marriage. No injury which can be rendered by one man against another is greater than the violation of that relation ; and no sin which a wife can commit is more heinous and degrading than infidelity to her marriage vows.

This being the case, it is natural that the relation between God and his people should be, as it is, in the Bible so often illustrated by a reference to the marriage relation. A people who refuse to recognize, or an individual man who refuses to recognize Jehovah as his God, who transfers the allegiance and obedience due to God alone to any other object, is compared to an unfaithful wife. And as jealousy is the strongest of human passions, the relation of God to those who thus forsake Him is illustrated by a reference to the feelings of an injured and forsaken husband. It is in this way that the Scriptures teach that the severest displeasure of God, and the most dreadful manifestations of his wrath, are the certain consequences of the sin of idolatry ; that is, of the sin of having any other God than Jehovah, or of giving to images, to stocks and stones, the external homage due to Him who is a spirit, and who must be worshipped in spirit and in truth.

The Lord, therefore, in this commandment, declares Himself to be " a jealous God, visiting the iniquities of the fathers upon the children unto the third and fourth generation ; and showing mercy unto thousands (unto the thousandth generation) of them that love me, and keep my commandments." The evil consequences of apostasy from God are not confined to the original apostates. They are continued from generation to generation. They seem indeed, and, humanly speaking, in fact are remediless. The degradation and untold miseries of the whole heathen world are the natural and inevitable consequence of their forefathers' having turned the truth of God into a lie, and worshipped and served the creature more than the Creator. These natural consequences, however, are designed, ordained, and judicial. They are not mere calamities. They are judgments, and therefore are not to be counteracted or evaded. Consequently those who teach atheism, or who undermine religion, or who corrupt and degrade the worship of God. by associating with it the worship of creat-

ures; or who teach that we may make graven images and bow
down to them and serve them, are bringing down upon themselves and upon coming generations the most direful calamities
that can degrade and afflict the children of men. Such must be
the issue unless they not only can counteract the operation of natural causes, but also can thwart the purpose of Jehovah.

It is a great cause for thankfulness, and adapted to fill the
hearts of God's faithful people with joy and confidence, to know
that He will bless their children to the thousandth generation.

The Doctrine and Usage of the Romish Church as to Images.

Salvation, our Lord said, is of the Jews. The founders of the
Christian Church were Jews. The religion of the Old Testament
in which they had been educated forbade the use of images in
divine worship. All the heathen were worshippers of idols.
Idol-worship, therefore, was an abomination to the Jews. With
the Old Testament authority against the use of images and
with this strong national prejudice against their use, it is absolutely incredible that they should be admitted in the more spiritual worship of the Christian Church. It was not until three
centuries after the introduction of Christianity, that the influence
of the heathen element introduced into the Church was strong
enough to overcome the natural opposition to their use in the
service of the sanctuary. Three parties soon developed themselves
in connection with this subject. The first adhered to the teachings of the Old Testament and the usage of the Apostolic Churches,
and repudiated the religious use of images in any form. The
second allowed the use of images and pictures for the purpose of
instruction, but not for worship. The common people could not
read, and therefore it was argued that visible representations of
Scriptural persons and incidents were allowable for their benefit.
The third contended for their use not only as a means of instruction, but also for worship.

As early as A. D. 305, the Council of Elvira in Spain condemned the use of pictures in the Church.[1] In the thirty-sixth
Canon the Council says,[2] " Placuit picturas in ecclesia esse non
debere; ne quod colitur et adoratur in parietibus depingatur."
Augustine complained of the superstitious use of images; Eusebius of Cæsarea, and Epiphanius of Salamis, protested against

---

[1] The year 305 is usually assigned as the date of this Council, although the precise time
of its session is matter of dispute.

[2] Binius, *Concilia Generalia et Provincalia*, Cologne, 1618, t. i. vol. i. p. 195, B. C.

their being made objects of worship; and Gregory the Great allowed their use only as means of instruction.[1]

In A. D. 726 the Emperor Leo III. issued an ordinance forbidding the use of images in churches as heathenish and heretical. To support his action a council was called, which met in Constantinople A. D. 754, and which gave ecclesiastical sanction to this condemnation. In A. D. 787, however, the Empress Irene, under Roman influence, called a council, which Romanists of the Italian school consider ecumenical, at Nice, by which image-worship was fully sanctioned. This Council first met in Constantinople, but there the opposition to the use of images was so strong that it was disbanded and called to meet the following year at Nice. Here the face of things had changed; enemies had been converted; opponents became advocates; even Gregory of Neo-Cæsarea, who had been a zealous supporter of the policy of Leo III. and of his son Constantine Copronymus, was brought to say, " Si omnes consentiunt, ego non dissentio." Few could withstand the promises and threats of those in power, and the cogency of the argument for image worship drawn from the numerous miracles adduced in favour of their worship. This Council, therefore, declared the previous Council, called by Leo III., heretical, and ordained the worship of pictures in the churches; not indeed with λατρεία, or the reverence due to God, but with ἀσπασμὸς καὶ τιμητικὴ προσκύνησις (with salutations and reverent prostrations). The Council announced the principle on which image-worship, whether among the heathen or Christians, has generally been defended, i. e., that the worship paid the image terminates on the object which it represents. Ἡ τῆς εἰκόνος τιμὴ ἐπὶ τὸ προτότυπον διαβαίνει καὶ ὁ προσκυνῶν τὴν εἰκόνα προσκυνεῖ ἐν αὐτῇ τοῦ ἐγγραφομένου τὴν ὑπόστασιν.

The decisions of this Council, although sanctioned by the Pope, gave offence to the Western Churches. The Emperor Charlemagne not only caused a book to be written (entitled " Libri Carolini ") to refute the doctrines inculcated, but also summoned a council to meet at Frankfort on the Main A. D. 794, at which delegates from Britain, France, Germany, Italy, and even two legates from the Bishop of Rome, were present; where the decrees of the so-called General Council of Nice were " rejected," " despised," and " condemned." All worshipping of pictures and images was forbidden, but their presence in the churches for instruction and ornament was allowed.

The friends of image-worship, however, rapidly gained the as

[1] See Guericke, *Kirchengeschichte*, II. iii. 2, § 77, 6th edit. Leipzig, 1846, vol. i. p. 350

cendancy, so that Thomas Aquinas, one of the best as well as the greatest of the Romish theologians in the thirteenth century, held the extreme doctrine on this subject. He taught that images were to be used in the churches for three purposes, first, for the instruction of the masses who could not read; secondly, that the mystery of the incarnation and the examples of the saints may be the better remembered; and thirdly, that pious feelings may be excited, as men are more easily moved by what they see than by what they hear. He taught that to the image in itself and for itself no reverence is due, but that if it represents Christ, the reverence due to Christ is due to the image. " Sic ergo dicendum est, quod imagini Christi in quantum est res quædam (puta lignum vel pictum) nulla reverentia exhibetur; quia reverentia nonnisi rationali naturæ debetur. Relinquitur ergo quod exhibeatur ei reverentia solum, in quantum est imago: et sic sequitur, quod eadem reverentia exhibeatur imagini Christi et ipsi Christo. Cum ergo Christus adoretur adoratione latriæ, consequens est, quod ejus imago sit adoratione latriæ adoranda." [1]

Tridentine Doctrine.

The Council of Trent acted with reference to the worship of images with its usual caution. It decreed that to the images of Christ and the saints " due reverence " should be paid, without defining what that reverence is. The council decided: " Imagines porro Christi, Deiparæ Virginis, et aliorum sanctorum, in templis præsertim habendas, et retinendas; eisque debitum honorem, et venerationem impertiendam; non quod credatur inesse aliqua in eis divinitas, vel virtus, propter quam sint colendæ; vel quod ab eis sit aliquid petendum; vel quod fiducia in imaginibus sit figenda; veluti olim fiebat a gentibus, quæ in idolis spem suam collocabant; sed quoniam honos, qui eis exhibetur refertur ad prototypa, quæ illæ representant: ita ut per imagines, quas osculamur, et coram quibus caput aperimus, et procumbimus, Christum adoremus; et sanctos, quorum illæ similitudinem gerunt, veneremur."

In the same session it was decreed concerning relics: " Sanctorum quoque martyrum, et aliorum cum Christo viventium sancta corpora, quæ viva membra fuerunt Christi, et templum Spiritus Sancti, ab ipso ad æternam vitam suscitanda, et glorificanda, a fidelibus veneranda esse; per quæ multa beneficia a Deo hominibus præstantur: ita ut affirmantes, sanctorum reliquiis venerationem, atque honorem non deberi; vel eas, aliaque sacra monumenta a

---

[1] *Summa*, III. quæst. xxv. art 3, edit. Cologne, 1640, p. 53 of fourth set.

fidelibus inutiliter honorari ; atque eorum opis impetrandæ causa
sanctorum memorias frustra frequentari ; omnino damnandos esse ;
prout jampridem eos damnavit, et nunc etiam damnat ecclesia." [1]
On relic-worship the Roman Catechism, says, " Cui fidem non
faciant et honoris, qui sanctis debetur, et patrocinii, quod nostri
suscipiunt, mirabiles effectæ res ad eorum sepulcra, et oculis, et
manibus membrisque omnibus captis, in pristinum statum restitu-
tis, mortuis ad vitam revocatis, ex corporibus hominum ejectis
demoniis? quæ non audisse, ut multi, non legisse, ut plurimi
gravissimi viri, sed vidisse, testes locupletissimi sancti Ambrosius
et Augustinus litteris prodiderunt. Quid multa? si vestes, su-
daria, si umbra sanctorum, priusquam e vita migrarent, depulit
morbos, viresque restituit, quis tandem negare audeat, Deum per
sacros cineres, ossa, ceterasque sanctorum reliquias eadem mirabiliter efficere? Declaravit id cadaver illud, quod forte illatum in
sepulcrum Elisei, ejus tacto corpore, subito revixit." [2]

Bellarmin.

The whole of the Liber Secundus of Bellarmin's Disputation
" De Ecclesia Triumphante " in the second volume of his works,
is devoted to the discussion of the question of the worship of the
relics and images of the saints. As to the worship of images he
says there are three opinions among Romanists themselves :
" Prima, quod imago non sit ullo modo in se colenda, sed solum
coram imagine colendum exemplar." " Secunda opinio est, quod
idem honor debeatur imagini ut exemplari, et proinde Christi
imago sit adoranda cultu latriæ, Beatæ Mariæ cultu hyperduliæ,
sanctorum aliorum, cultu duliæ." " Tertia opinio versatur in
medio, estque eorum, qui dicunt, ipsas imagines in se, et proprie
honorari debere, sed honore minori, quam ipsum exemplar, et
proinde nullam imaginem adorandam esse cultu latriæ." [3] His
own opinion is given in the following propositions : " Prima sententia, sive propositio. Imagines Christi, et sanctorum venerandæ
sunt, non solum per accidens, vel improprie, sed etiam per se proprie, ita ut ipsæ terminent venerationem ut in se considerantur,
et non solum ut vicem gerunt exemplaris." " Secunda propositio.
Quantum ad modum loquendi præsertim in concione ad populum,
non est dicendum imagines ullas adorari debere latria, sed e con-
trario non debere sic adorari." " Tertia propositio. Si de re

[1] Sess. xxv.; Streitwolf, Libri Symbolici, Göttingen, 1846, vol. i. pp. 93, 94.
[2] III. ii. 8 (15, xxx., xxxi.); Streitwolf, vol. i. p. 482.
[3] De Ecclesia Triumphante, lib. II., De Imaginibus Sanctorum, cap. xx.; Disputationes, Par s, 1608, vol. ii. pp. 801, 802.

ipsa agatur, admitti potest, imagines posse coli improprie, vel per
accidens, eodem genere cultus, quo exemplar ipsum colitur."
" Quarta propositio. Imago per se, et proprie non est adoranda
eodem cultu, quo ipsum exemplar, et proinde nulla imago est
adoranda cultu latriæ per se, et proprie." " Quinta conclusio,
Cultus, qui per se, proprie debetur imaginibus, est cultus quidam
imperfectus, qui analogice et reductive pertinet ad speciem ejus
cultus, qui debetur exemplari." [1]

Relics.

Bellarmin in his defence of the " cultus reliquiarum " begins
with an attempted refutation of Calvin's five arguments against
such worship. He then presents his own in favour of it.[2] They
are such as these : First, from Scriptural examples : (*a.*) Moses
carried the bones " sancti Josephi " with him when he left Egypt ;
(*b.*) God honoured the remains of Moses by burying them with
his own hands; (*c.*) A dead man was restored to life by contact
with the bones of Elisha (2 Kings xiii. 21) ; (*d.*) Isaiah predicted
that the sepulchre of the Messiah should be glorious. The Vulgate renders Isaiah xi. 10, " Et erit sepulcrum ejus gloriosum ; "
which Bellarmin understands as foretelling " ut sepulcrum Domini,
ab omnibus honoraretur." And adds, " Ex quo refellitur Lutheri
blasphemia, qui in libro de abolenda Missa dicit, Deo non majo-
rem curam esse de sepulcro Domini, quam de bobus. " (*e.*) The
woman mentioned in the Gospel was healed by touching Christ's
garment ; the sick, according to Acts v. 15, were placed in the
streets " that at least the shadow of Peter passing by might over-
shadow some of them " ; again, in Acts xix. 11, 12, it is said : " God
wrought special miracles by the hands of Paul : so that from his
body were brought unto the sick handkerchiefs or aprons, and
the diseases departed from them, and the evil spirits went out of
them." If, says Bellarmin, Christ were now on earth, and we
should kiss his garment, the Protestants would call us idolaters.

His second argument is from the decisions of councils ; the
third from the testimony of the fathers ; the fourth and fifth
from the miracles wrought by and in the relics of the saints, of
which he cites numerous examples ; the sixth from the miraculous
discovery of the remains of the saints, " Si enim Deo cultus reliquiarum non placeret, cur ipse servis suis corpora sanctorum,
quæ latebant, ostenderet ? " the seventh, from the translation
of relics from one place to another. He also argues from the

---

[1] *Ut supra*, cap. xxi.-xxv. pp. 802–809.   [2] *Ut supra*, cap. iii. pp. 746–753.

custom of depositing the remains of the saints under altars, and burning incense and lamps before their tombs.[1]

Remarks.

1. From all this it appears that the Romanists worship im-ages in the same way that the heathen of old did, and pagans of our own day still do. They " bow down to them and serve them." They pay them all the external homage which they render to the persons they are intended to represent.

2. The explanations and defence of such worship are the same in both cases. The heathen recognized the fact that the images made of gold, silver, wood, or marble were lifeless and insensible in themselves ; they admitted that they could not see, or hear, or save. They attributed no inherent virtue or supernatural power to them. They claimed that the homage paid to them terminated on the gods which they represented ; that they only worshipped before the images, or at most through them. So far as the Greeks and Romans are concerned, they were less reverential to the mere image, and claimed far less of the supernatural in con-nection with their use.

3. Both among the heathen and the Romanists, for the unedu-cated people the images themselves were the objects of worship. It would be hard to find in any heathen author such justification of image-worship as the Romish theologians put forth. What heathen ever said that the same homage was due to the image of Jupiter as to Jupiter himself? This Thomas Aquinas says of the images of Christ and of the saints. Or what heathen ever has said, as Bellarmin says, that although the homage to be paid

---

[1] In the *Decreta et Articuli fidei jurandi per Episcopos et alios Prælatos in susceptione muneris consecrationis, publicati Romæ in Consistorio ap. S. Marcum d. IV. Septbr. a. MDLX.*, are the following articles: " Virgo Dei genitrix, Angeli, et Sancti, religiose coli debent, et invocari, ut eorum meritis, et precibus juvemur.

" Crux Christi, et imagines, ac quæcunque attigerunt, adoranda sunt, juxta Ecclesiæ catholicæ doctrinam, et fidem.

" Deiparæ Virginis Mariæ, angelorum, et sanctorum sunt imagines adorandæ (id est in honore habendæ, as it reads in the margin) tum corpora, et reliquiæ quævis." See Streit-wolf, *Libri Symbolici Ecclesiæ Catholicæ*, Göttingen, 1846, vol. ii. p. 328.

Notwithstanding such authoritative declarations, Bellarmin enumerates it as among the " mendacia " of the Centuriators and of Calvin that they say that the Catholics " Non solum sanctos Christi loco adorant, sed etiam eorum ossa, vestes, calceos, et simulacra;" and asks: " At quis unquam Catholicorum reliquias invocavit? Quis unquam auditus est in precibus, aut litaniis dixisse: 'Sanctæ reliquiæ, orate pro me?' Et quis easdem un-quam divino honore affecit, vel Christi loco adoravit: nos enim reliquias quidem hono-ramus, et osculamur ut sacra pignora patronorum nostrorum: sed nec adoramus ut Deum nec invocamus ut sanctos, sed minore cultu veneramur, quam sanctorum spiritus, nedum quam Deum ipsum." *De Ecclesia Triumphante*, lib. ii., *De Reliquiis Sanctorum*, cap. ii.; *Disputationes*, edit. Paris, 1608, vol. ii. pp. 745, e, 746, a.

to the image is not strictly and properly the same as that due to
its prototype, it is nevertheless improperly and analogically the
same ; the same in kind although not in degree ?   What can the
common people know of the difference between *proprie* and *improprie ?*   They are told to worship the image, and they worship
it just as the heathen worshipped the images of their gods.   As
the Bible pronounces and denounces as idolatry not only the worship of false gods, but also the worship of images, ' the bowing
down to them and serving them,' it is clear that the Roman Church
is as wholly given to idolatry as was Athens when visited by Paul.

4. The moral and religious effects of image worship are altogether evil.   It is enough to prove that it is evil in its consequences that God has forbidden it, and threatened to visit the
worshippers of idols with his severe judgments.   It degrades the
worship of God.   It turns off the minds of the people from the
proper object of reverence and confidence, and leads the uneducated masses to put their trust in gods who cannot save.

5. As to the worship of relics, it is enough to say, (*a.*) That
it has no support from Scripture.   The outline of Bellarmin's
arguments given above, is sufficient to show that the Bible furnishes no apology for this superstitious custom.   (*b.*) What pass
for relics, in the great majority of cases, are spurious.   There is
no end to the deceptions practised on the people in this regard.
There are, it is said, enough fragments of the cross exhibited in
different sanctuaries, to build a large ship ; and there are innumer
able nails which are reverenced as the instruments of our Lord's
torture.   Bones not only of ordinary men, but even of brutes,
are set before the people as relics of the saints.[1]   In one of the
cathedrals of Spain there is a magnificent ostrich feather preserved
in a gorgeous casket, which the priests affirm fell from the wing
of the angel Gabriel.   Romanists themselves are obliged to resort
to the doctrine of " economics " or pious fraud, to justify these
palpable impositions on the credulity of the people.   Of such
impositions the most flagrant example is the blood of St. Januarius, which is annually liquefied in Naples.   (*c.*) Ascribing mirac-

---

[1] Luther in the Smalcald Articles, says: " Reliquiæ sanctorum refertæ multis mendaciis,
ineptis et fatuitatibus.   Canum et equorum ossa ibi sæpe reperta sunt."   In German it
reads thus: " Das Heiligthum (reliquiæ sanctorum), darinne so manche öffentliche Lügen
und Narrenwerk erfunden, von Hunds- und Rossknochen, das auch um solcher Büberei
willen, das der Teufel gelacht hat, längst sollte verdammt worden seyn, wenn gleich etwas
Gutes daran wäre, dazu auch ohne Gottes Wort, weder geboten noch gerathen, gänz un-
nöthig und unnütz Ding ist."   Pars ii. art. ii. 22.

In the church at Wittenberg there hangs an original portrait of Luther under which is
written, " All his words were thunderbolts."

ulous powers to these pretended relics as Romanists do, is to the last degree superstitious and degrading. It is true that a little more than a century ago belief in necromancy and witchcraft was almost universal even among Protestants. But there is the greatest possible difference between superstitious beliefs prevailing for a time among the people, and those beliefs being adopted by the Church and enacted into articles of faith to bind the conscience of the people in all time. The Church of Rome is chained down by the decisions of her popes and councils pronouncing the grossest superstitions to be matters of divine revelation sanctioned and approved by God. She has rendered it impossible for men entitled to be called rational to believe what she teaches. The great lesson taught by the history of image-worship and the reverencing of relics, is the importance of adhering to the word of God as the only rule of our faith and practice; receiving nothing as true in religion but what the Bible teaches, and admitting nothing into divine worship which the Scriptures do not either sanction or enjoin.

Protestant Doctrine on the Subject.

As the worship of images is expressly forbidden in the Scriptures, Protestants, as well Lutheran as Reformed, condemned their being made the objects of any religious homage. As, however, their use for the purposes of instruction or ornament is not thus expressly forbidden, Luther contended that such use was allowable and even desirable. He, therefore, favoured their being retained in the Churches. The Reformed, however, on account of the great abuse which had attended their introduction, insisted that they should be excluded from all places of worship.

The Lutheran standards do not dilate on this subject. In the Apology for the Augsburg Confession it is said : " Primum quia cum alii mediatores præter Christum quæruntur, collocatur fiducia in alios, obruitur tota notitia Christi, idque res ostendit. Videtur initio mentio sanctorum, qualis est in veteribus orationibus, tolerabili consilio recepta esse. Postea secuta est invocatio, invocationem prodigiosi et plus quam ethnici abusus secuti sunt. Ab invocatione ad imagines ventum est, hæ quoque colebantur, et putabatur eis inesse quædam vis, sicut Magi vim inesse fingunt imaginibus signorum cœlestium certo tempore sculptis." [1]

Luther was tolerant of the use of images in the churches. On this subject he says: " If the worship of images be avoided, we

---

[1] IX. 34; Hase, *Libri Symbolici*, 3d edit. Leipzig, 1846, p. 229.

may use them as we do the words of Scripture, which bring things
before the mind and cause us to remember them." [1]   " Who is so
stone blind," he asks, " as not to see that if sacred events may
be described in words without sin and to the profit of the hearers,
they may with the same propriety, for the benefit of the uneducated, be portrayed or sculptured, not only at home and in
our houses, but in the churches." [2] In another place he says that
when one reads of the passion of Christ, whether he will or not,
an image of a man suspended on a cross is formed in his mind,
just as certainly as his face is reflected when he looks into the
water.   There is no sin in having such an image in the mind ;
why then should it be sinful to have it before the eyes ? [3]

The Reformed went further than this.   They condemned not
only the worship of images, but also their introduction into
places of worship, because they were unnecessary, and because
they were so liable to abuse.   The Second Helvetic Confession
says, " Rejicimus non modo gentium idola, sed et Christianorum
simulachra.   Tametsi enim Christus humanam assumpserit naturam, non ideo tamen assumpsit, ut typum præferret statuariis
atque pictoribus. . . . . Et quando beati spiritus et divi cœlites,
dum hic viverent, omnem cultum sui averterunt, et statuas op-
pugnarunt, cui verisimile videatur divis cœlestibus et angelis suas
placere imagines, ad quas genua flectunt homines, detegunt capita,
aliisque prosequuntur honoribus ? "   In another paragraph of the
same chapter it is said : "Idcirco approbamus Lactantii veteris,
scriptoris sententiam, dicentis, Non est dubium, quin religio nulla
est, ubicunque simulachrum est." [4]

The Heidelberg Catechism, says,[5] " Is it forbidden to make any
images or statues ? God cannot and ought not in any way to be
depicted ; and although it is lawful to make representations of
creatures, yet God forbids that they should be worshipped, or He
through them.   But may not images be tolerated in the churches
for the instruction of the uneducated ? By no means ; for it does
not become us to be wiser than God, who has willed that his
Church be instructed, not by dumb images, but by the preaching
of his word."

No one who has ever seen any of the masterpieces of Christian
art, whether of the pencil or of the chisel, and felt how hard it

---

[1] On Micah i. 7; *Works*, edit. Walch, vol. vi. p. 2747.   [2] *Ibid*. p. 2740.
[3] *Wider die himmlischen Propheten*, von den Bildern und Sacrament, 65; *Ibid*. vol. xx.
p. 213.
[4] *Confessio Helvetica Posterior*, cap. iv.; Niemeyer, *Collectio Confessionum*, Leipzig,
1840, p. 472.
[5] Quest. 97, 98: Niemeyer, pp. 453. 454.

is to resist the impulse to " bow down to them and serve them," can doubt the wisdom of their exclusion from places of public worship.

§ 7. *The Third Commandment.*

" Thou shalt not take the name of the Lord thy God in vain ; for the Lord will not hold him guiltless that taketh his name in vain."

The literal meaning of this command is doubtful. It may mean, "Thou shalt not utter the name of God in a vain or irreverent manner ;" or, " Thou shalt not utter the name of God to a lie," *i. e.*, " Thou shalt not swear falsely." The Septuagint renders the passage thus ; Οὐ λήψῃ τὸ ὄνομα κυρίου τοῦ θεοῦ σου ἐπὶ ματαίῳ. The Vulgate has, " Non assumes nomen Domini Dei tui in vanum." Luther, as usual, freely *ad sensum* : " Du sollst den Namen des Herrn, deines Gottes, nicht missbrauchen." Our translators have adopted the same rendering.

The ancient Syriac Version, the Targum of Onkelos, Philo, and many modern commentators and exegetes understand the command as directed against false swearing : " Thou shalt not utter the name of God to a lie." So the elder Michaelis in his annotated Hebrew Bible, explains " *ad vanum* confirmandum : non frustra, nedum, falso." Gesenius in his Hebrew Lexicon renders the passage,[1] " Du sollst den Namen Jehova's nicht zur Lüge aussprechen ; nicht falsch schwören." Rosenmüller[2] renders it : " Nolli enunciare nomen Jova Dei tui ad falsum sc. comprobandum." Knobel[3] reads : " Nicht sollst du erheben den Namen Jehova's zur Nichtigkeit ; " and adds, " The prohibition is directed specially against false swearing."

This interpretation is consistent with the meaning of the words, as שָׁוְא, here rendered " vanity," or with the preposition, " in vain," elsewhere means " falsehood." (See Ps. xii. 3 (2) ; xli. 7 (6) ; Isaiah lix. 4 ; Hos. x. 4.) To lift up, or pronounce the name of God for a lie, naturally means, to call upon God to confirm a falsehood. The preposition לְ also has its natural force. Compare Leviticus xix. 12, " Ye shall not swear by my name [לַשֶּׁקֶר ' to a lie '] falsely." The general import of the command remains the same, whichever interpretation be adopted. The command not to misuse the name of God, includes false swearing, which is the

---

[1] Edit. Leipzig, 1857, *sub voce*, שָׁוְא.

[2] *Scholia in Vetus Testamentum in Compendium redacta*, Leipzig, 1828, vol. i. p. 404.

[3] *Kurzgefasstes exegetische Handbuch zum Alten Testament : Exodus und Leviticus er klärt* von August Knobel, Leipzig, 1857, p. 205.

greatest indignity which can be offered to God. And as the command, " Thou shalt do no murder," includes all indulgence of malicious feelings · so the command, " Thou shalt not forswear thyself," includes all lesser forms of irreverence in the use of the name of God.

It is urged, as an objection to the second interpretation given above, that perjury is an offence against our neighbour, and therefore belongs to the second table of the Law; and that it is in fact included in the ninth commandment, " Thou shalt not bear false witness against thy neighbour." Bearing false testimony and false swearing are, however, different offences. The first and second commandment forbid the worship of any other being than Jehovah, and worshipping Him in any way not appointed in his word; and the third, supposing it to forbid false swearing, is here in place, as false swearing is a practical denial of the being or perfections of God.

Import of the Command.

The word " name " is used in reference to God in a very comprehensive sense. It often means a personal or individual designation; as when God says, " This is my name, " i. e., Jehovah. Frequently the " name of God " is equivalent to God himself. To call on the name of the Lord, and to call on God, are synonymous forms of expression. As names are intended to distinguish one person or thing from another, anything distinguishing or characteristic may be included under the term. The name of God, therefore, includes everything by which He makes Himself known. This commandment, therefore, forbids all irreverence towards God ; not only the highest act of irreverence in calling on Him to bear witness to a falsehood, but also all irreverent use of his name; all careless, unnecessary reference to Him, or his attributes ; all indecorous conduct in his worship ; and in short, every indication of the want of that fear, reverence, and awe due to a Being infinite in all his perfections, on whom we are absolutely dependent, and to whom we are accountable for our character and conduct.

The third commandment, therefore, specially forbids not only perjury, but also all profane, or unnecessary oaths, all careless appeals to God, and all irreverent use of his name. All literature, whether profane or Christian, shows how strong is the tendency in human nature to introduce the name of God even on the most trivial occasions. Not only are those formulas, such as

Adieu, Good-bye or God be with you, and God forbid, which may
have had a pious origin, constantly used without any recognition
of their true import, but even persons professing to fear God
often allow themselves to use his name as a mere expression of
surprise. God is everywhere present. He hears all we say. He
is worthy of the highest reverence ; and He will not hold him
guiltless who on any occasion uses his name irreverently.

Oaths.

The command not to call upon God to confirm a lie, cannot be
considered as forbidding us to call upon Him to confirm the truth.
And such is the general nature of an oath. Oaths are of two
kinds, assertatory, when we affirm a thing to be true ; and promissory, when we bring ourselves under an obligation to do, or to
forbear doing certain acts. To this class belong official oaths
and oaths of allegiance. In both cases there is an appeal to God
as a witness. An oath, therefore, is in its nature an act of worship. It implies, (1.) An acknowledgment of the existence of God.
(2.) Of his attributes of omnipresence, omniscience, justice, and
power. (3.) Of his moral government over the world ; and (4.) Of
our accountability to Him as our Sovereign and Judge. Hence
" to swear by the name of Jehovah," and to acknowledge Him as
God, are the same thing. The former involves the latter.

Such being the case, it is evident that a man who denies the
truths above mentioned cannot take an oath. For him the words
he utters have no meaning. If he does not believe that there is a
God ; or suppose that he admits that there is some being or force
which may be called God, if he does not believe that that Being
knows what the juror says, or that He will punish the false
swearer, the whole service is a mockery. It is a great injustice,
tending to loosen all the bonds of society, to allow atheists to give
testimony in courts of justice.[1]

The imprecation usually introduced in the formula of an oath, is
not essential to its nature. It is indeed involved in the appeal to
God to bear witness to the truth of what we say, but its direct
assertion is not necessary. Indeed, it is not found in any of the
oaths recorded in the Bible. Some strenuously object to its intro-

[1] In a recent murder trial in one of the courts of New York, a young scientific physician
was called to give testimony on what constitutes insanity. He distinctly asserted that
thought was a function of the brain; that where there is no brain there can be no thought;
and that a disordered brain necessitates disordered mental action. Of course, God having
no brain cannot be intelligent; in other words, there can be no God. Such a man may
be a good chemist or a good surgeon; but he is no more competent to be a witness in a
court of justice, than he is fit to be a preacher.

duction, as involving a renunciation of all hope of the mercy and grace of God, and as an equivalent to an imprecation on one's self of everlasting perdition.

The Lawfulness of Oaths.

The lawfulness of oaths may be inferred, —

1. From their nature. Being acts of worship involving the acknowledgment of the being and attributes of God, and of our responsibility to Him, they are in their nature good. They are not superstitious, founded on wrong ideas of God or of his relation to the world; nor are they irreverent; nor are they useless. They have a real power over the consciences of men; and that power is the greater according as the faith of the juror and of society in the truths of religion, is the more intelligent and the stronger.

2. In the Scriptures, oaths, on proper occasions, are not only permitted, but commanded. "Thou shalt fear the LORD thy God, and shalt swear by his name. (Deut. vi. 13.) "He who blesseth himself in the earth, shall bless himself in the God of truth; and he that sweareth in the earth, shall swear by the God of truth." (Is. lxv. 16.) "It shall come to pass, if they will diligently learn the ways of my people, to swear by my name, Jehovah liveth; (as they taught my people to swear by Baal;) then shall they be built in the midst of my people." (Jer. xii. 16; iv. 2.) God Himself is represented as swearing. (Psalms cx. 4; Hebrews vii. 21.) "When God made promise to Abraham, because he could swear by no greater, he sware by himself." (Heb. vi. 13.) Our blessed Lord also, when put upon his oath by the high priest, did not hesitate to answer. (Matt. xxvi. 63.) The words are, Ἐξορκίζω σε κατὰ τοῦ Θεοῦ τοῦ ζῶντος, which are correctly rendered by our version, "I adjure thee (call on thee to swear) by the living God." Meyer in his comment on this passage says: "An affirmative answer to this formula was an oath in the full meaning of the word." And our Lord's reply, "Thou sayest," is the usual Rabbinical form of direct affirmation.[1] The Hebrew word הִשְׁבִּיעַ is rendered in the Septuagint by ὁρκίζω and ἐξορκίζω, and in the Vulgate by adjuro. See Genesis l. 5, "My father made me swear, ὥρκισέ με." Num. v. 19, "The priest shall charge her by an oath, ὁρκιεῖ αὐτήν." It appears from this passage as well as from others in the Old Testament, that oaths were on certain occasions enjoined by God himself. (Ex. xxii. 10.) They cannot, therefore, be unlawful.

---

[1] See Schoettgen's *Hor. Hebr. et Talm.*, Matt. v. 34; Dresden and Leipzig, 1733, p. 40.

Seeing, then, that an oath is an act of worship ; that it is enjoined on suitable occasions ; that our Lord himself submitted to be put upon his oath ; and that the Apostles did not hesitate to call God to witness to the truth of what they said ; we cannot admit that Christ intended to pronounce all oaths unlawful, when he said, as recorded in Matthew v. 34, " Swear not at all." This would be to suppose that Scripture can contradict Scripture, and that Christ's conduct did not conform to his precepts. Nevertheless, his words are very explicit. They mean in Greek just what our version makes them mean. Our Lord did say, " Swear not at all." But in the sixth commandment it is said, " Thou shalt not kill." That, however, does not mean that we may not kill animals for food ; for that is permitted and commanded. It does not forbid homicide in self-defence, for that also is permitted. Neither does it forbid capital punishment ; for that is not only permitted but even commanded. The meaning of this command has never been doubted or disputed, because it is sufficiently explained by the context and occasion, and by the light shed upon it by other parts of Scripture. As, therefore, the command, " Thou shalt not kill," forbids only unlawful killing ; so also the command, " Swear not at all," forbids only unlawful swearing.

This conclusion is confirmed by the context. A great part of our Lord's Sermon on the Mount is devoted to the correction of perversions of the law, introduced by the Scribes and Pharisees. They made the sixth commandment to forbid only murder ; our Lord said that it forbade all malicious passions. They limited the seventh commandment to the outward act ; He extended it to the inward desire. They made the precept to love our neighbour consistent with hating our enemies ; Christ says, " Love your enemies, bless them that curse you." In like manner, the Scribes taught that the law allowed all kinds of swearing, and swearing on all occasions, provided a man did not forswear himself ; but our Lord said, I say unto you, in your communications swear not at all ; this is plain from ver. 37, " Let your communications (λόγος, word, talk) be Yea, yea ; Nay, nay : for whatsoever is more than these, cometh of evil." It is unnecessary, colloquial, irreverent swearing our Lord condemns. This has nothing to do with those solemn acts of worship, permitted and commanded in the word of God. The Jews of that age were especially addicted to colloquial swearing, holding that the law forbade only false swearing, or swearing by the name of false gods ; [1]

---

[1] See Meyer on this passage, who refers to Philo. *De Spec. Leg.*; A. Lightfoot, *Horæ* ;

hence our Lord had the more occasion to rebuke this sin, and show the evil of any such adjurations.

When are Oaths lawful.

1. As an oath involves an act of worship, it is plain that it should not be taken on any trivial occasion, or in an irreverent manner.

2. An oath is lawful when prescribed and administered by duly authorized officers of the State, or of the Church; they are the " ministers of God," acting in his name and by his authority. There are many who do not regard it as proper that an oath should ever be taken, except when thus imposed by those in authority. The Church of England in the thirty-ninth article, says: " As we confess that vain and rash swearing is forbidden Christian men by our Lord Jesus Christ, and James his Apostle; so we judge that Christian religion doth not prohibit, but that a man may swear when the magistrate requireth, in a cause of faith and charity, so it be done according to the prophet's teaching, in justice, judgment, and truth." The same ground has been taken by many moral philosophers and theologians.

There does not, however, seem to be any sufficient reason for this restriction, either in the nature or design of an oath, or in the teachings of Scripture. The oath being an appeal to God to bear witness to the truth of our declarations, or the sincerity of our promises, there is no reason why this appeal should not be made whenever any important end is to be accomplished by it. There should be a necessity for it; that is, no man should swear lightly or profanely, but only when all the conditions which justify this appeal to God are present. According to the old law those conditions are, " judicium in jurante, justitia in objecto, veracitas in mente." That is, the juror must be competent. He must have a just judgment of the nature and obligation of an oath, so as to understand what he is about to do. Therefore an idiot, a child, or an unbeliever cannot properly be put upon his oath. By " justitia in objecto," is meant that the object concerning which the oath is taken, should be a proper object. If it be a promissory oath, the thing we engage to do must be possible and lawful; if an assertatory oath, the object must have due importance; it must be within the knowledge of the juror; and there must be an adequate reason why this appeal to God

and Meuschen, *N. T. ex Talm. illustr.* See, also, Winer's *Realwörterbuch*, and Tholuck's *Auslegung der Bergpredigt Christi*, 3d edit. Hamburg, 1845.

should be made.   The " veracitas in mente," includes the sincere purpose of doing what we promise, or of telling the whole truth, and nothing but the truth, to the best of our knowledge in the case in which we testify.   This excludes all intention to deceive, all mental reservation, and all designed ambiguity of language. All these conditions may be present in private, as well as in judicial or official oaths.

Then again, as the design of an oath is to produce conviction of the truth, to satisfy others of our sincerity and fidelity, and to make an end of controversy, it is evident that circumstances may arise in private life, or in the intercourse of a man with his fellow-men, when an oath may be of the greatest importance. If we risk a great deal on the fidelity or veracity of a man, we have a right to bind him by the solemnity of an oath ; or if it is of great importance that others should confide in our veracity or fidelity, it may be right to give them the assurance which an oath is suited and intended to afford.

As to the Scriptural examples, by far the greater number of the oaths recorded in the Bible, and that with the implied approbation of God, are of a non-judicial character.   Abraham swore to Abimelech. (Gen. xxi. 23.)   Abraham made his servant swear to him.   (Gen. xxiv. 3.)   Isaac and Abimelech interchanged oaths. (Gen. xxvi. 31.)   Jacob caused Joseph to swear not to bury him in Egypt. (xlvii. 31.)   Joseph exacted a similar oath from his brethren.   So we read of David's swearing to Saul, and to Jonathan, of Jonathan's to David, and of David's to Shimei.   Such private oaths seem at times to have been prescribed in the Mosaic law. In Exodus xxii. 19, it is said, if a man deliver any animal to his neighbour for safe-keeping, and it die on his hands, " then shall an oath of the LORD be between them both, that he hath not put his hand unto his neighbour's goods."   In the New Testament we find the Apostle frequently appealing to God to witness to the truth of what he said (Rom. i. 9 ; Phil. i. 8 ; 1 Thess. ii. 5, 10) ; doing this also in the most formal manner, as in 2 Corinthians i. 23, " I call God for a record upon my soul."

Augustine's rule on this subject is good : " Quantum ad me pertinet, juro ; sed quantum mihi videtur, magna necessitate compulsus." [1]   The multiplicity of oaths is a great evil.   The rapid and irreverent administration of them is profane.

---

[1] Sermo CLXXX. 10 [ix.]; *Works*, edit. Benedictines, Paris, 1837, vol. v. p. 1250, a.

The Form of an Oath.

Under the Old Testament, in voluntary oaths the usual form was, " The LORD do so to me, and more also." (Ruth i. 17; 2 Sam. iii. 9, 35; 1 Kings ii. 23; 2 Kings vi. 31.) Or simply, "As the LORD liveth." (Ruth iii. 13; Judges viii. 19; 2 Sam. ii. 27. Jer. xxxviii. 16); or as it is in Jeremiah xlii. 5, " The LORD be a true and faithful witness." In judicial proceedings the oath consisted in a simple assent to the adjuration, which assent was expressed in Hebrew by אָמֵן, and in Greek by σὺ εἶπας. The form is a matter of indifference; any form of words which implies an appeal to God as a witness is an oath. In swearing, the right hand was usually elevated towards heaven. Genesis xiv. 22, " Abram said to the king of Sodom, I have lift up mine hand unto the LORD, the most high God, the possessor of heaven and earth." Hence "to lift up the hand " was to swear. (See Deut. xxxii. 40; Ex. vi. 8 (in the Hebrew); Ezek. xx. 5.) Lifting up the hand was evidently intended to intimate that the juror appealed to the God of heaven. Among Christians it is usual to put the hand upon the Bible, to indicate that the oath is taken in the name of the God of the Bible, and that the judgment invoked in case of perjury is that which the Bible denounces against false swearing. Kissing the Bible, another usual part of the ceremonial of an oath, is an expression of faith in the Bible as the word of God. There is nothing unseemly or superstitious in this. On the contrary, instead of appealing to the God of nature, it is most appropriate that the Christian should appeal to the God of the Bible, who, through Jesus Christ, is our reconciled God and Father.

Rules which determine the Interpretation and Obligation of an Oath.

An oath must be interpreted according to the plain natural meaning of the words, or the sense in which they are understood by the party to whom the oath is given or by whom it is imposed. This is a plain dictate of honesty. If the juror understands the oath in a sense different from that attached to it by the party to whom it is given, the whole service is a deceit and mockery. The commander of whom Paley speaks, who swore to the garrison of a besieged town that if they surrendered, a drop of their blood should not be shed, and buried them all alive, was guilty, not only of perjury, but also of dastardly and cruel mockery. The *animus imponentis*, as is universally admitted, must therefore determine the interpretation of an oath. It was the fact that the Jesuits inculcated the lawfulness of mental reservation, which more than anything else made them an abomination in the eyes of all Christendom. It was this which furnished the sharpest thong to the scourge with which Pascal drove them out of Europe.

This is a matter about which men who mean to be honest are not always sufficiently careful. Their conscience is satisfied if what they say will bear an interpretation consistent with the truth, although the obvious sense is not true.[1]

No oath is obligatory which binds a man to do what is unlawful or impossible. The sin lies in taking such an oath, not in breaking it. The reason of this rule is, that no man can bring himself under an obligation to commit a sin. Herod was not bound to keep his oath to the daughter of Herodias when she demanded the head of John the Baptist. Neither were the forty men, who had bound themselves with "an oath of execration" to kill Paul. But an oath voluntarily taken to do what is lawful and within the power of the juror binds the conscience, (*a.*) Even when fulfilling it involves injury to the temporal interests of the juror. The Bible pronounces the man blessed who "sweareth to his own hurt and changeth not." (Ps. xv. 4.) (*b.*) When the oath is obtained by deceit or violence. In the latter case the juror makes a choice of evils. He swears to make a sacrifice to save himself from what he dreads more than the loss of what he promises to relinquish. This may often be a hard case. But such is the solemnity of an oath, and such the importance of its inviolable sanctity being preserved, that it is better to suffer injustice than that an oath should be broken. The case where an oath is obtained by deceit is more difficult, for when such deceit is practised the juror did not intend to assume the obligation which the oath imposes. He might, therefore, plausibly argue that if he did not intend to assume an obligation, it was not assumed. But, on the other hand, the principle involved in the commercial maxim, *caveat emptor*, applies to oaths. A man is bound to guard against deception; and if deceived he must take the consequences. Besides, those to whom the oath is given trust to it, and act upon it, and, in a certain sense at least, acquire rights under it. The Scriptures, however, in this as in all other cases, are our safest guide. When

---

[1] A gentleman was charged with having written a certain article in a newspaper. He declared that he did not write it. That was true. But he had dictated it.

the Israelites conquered Canaan, the Gibeonites who dwelt in the land, sent delegates to Joshua pretending that they were from a distant country, and " Joshua made peace with them, and made a league with them, to let them live : and the princes of the congregation sware unto them." When the deception was discovered, the people clamoured for their extermination. " But all the princes said unto all the congregation, We have sworn unto them by the LORD God of Israel : now, therefore, we may not touch them." (Joshua ix. 15, 19.) This oath, as appears from 2 Samuel xxi. 1, was sanctioned by God and the people were punished for violating it.

Romish Doctrine.

The principle on which the authorities of the Roman Church assume the right to free men from the obligation of their oaths, is that no man can bind himself to do what is sinful. It is the prerogative of the Church to decide what is sinful. If therefore the Church decide that an oath to obey a sovereign disobedient to the Pope, to preserve inviolate a safe conduct, or to keep faith with heretics or infidels is sinful, the obligation of every such oath ceases as soon as the judgment of the Church is rendered.

In answer to the question, " Cui competit potestas dispensandi super juramento ? " the Romish theologians answer : " Principaliter competit summo Pontifici ; non tamen nisi ex rationabili causa, quia dispensat in jure alieno : competit etiam jure ordinario Episcopis, non Parochis. Requirit autem hæc dispensatio potestatem jurisdictionis majoris."[1] The casuists, on this as on all other practical subjects, go into the most minute details and subtle distinctions. Dens, for example, in the section above quoted, gives no less than ten conditions under which the obligation of an oath ceases. To the question : " Quibus modis potest cessare obligatio juramenti promissorii ? " he answers : " 1. Irritatione. 2. Dispensatione et relaxatione. 3. Commutatione. 4. Materiæ mutatione vel subtractione. 5. Cessante fine totali complete. 6. Ratione conditionis non adimpletæ. 7. Cessante principali obligatione cessat juramentum pure accessorium. 8. Non acceptatione, et condonatione, seu remissione. 9. Si juramentum incipiat vergere in deteriorem exitum, vel in præjudicium boni communis, vel etiam alicujus particularis, v. g. quis juravit occultare furtum alterius, sed inde alter liberius prolabitur ad alia furta : item cessat juramentum, quando directe est majoris boni impeditivum. 10. Deni-

---

[1] *Theologia Moralis Dogmatica Reverendi et Eruditissimi Domini Petri Dens ; de Juramento*, N. 177. edit. Dublin, 1832, vol. iv. pp. 214–216.

que cessat obligatio juramenti, licet improprie, per adimpletionem sive totalem solutionem rei juratæ : et e contra dicitur cessare ab initio, quia juramentum fuit nullum, sive quia nullam ab initio obligationem produxit." Number nine opens a very wide door the last clause especially seems to teach that a promissory oath ceases to bind whenever it is expedient to break it.[1]

The whole Romish system is the masterpiece of the " wisdom of the world." As many promissory oaths are not obligatory, it would seem to be wise, instead of leaving the question of their continued obligation to be decided by the individual juror, who is so liable to be unduly biased, to refer the matter to some competent authority. This would tend to prevent false judgments, to satisfy the conscience of the juror and the public mind. And as the question is a matter of morals and religion, it would seem to be proper that the decision should be referred to the organs of the Church. Rome makes all these seemingly wise arrangements. But as God has exalted no human authority over the individual conscience, as no man can delegate his responsibility to another, but every man must answer to God for himself, it is clear that no such arrangement can be consistent with the divine will. Again, if it were true that the Church were divinely guided so as to be infallible in its judgment, this tremendous power over the consciences of men might be safely intrusted to it ; but as in fact the representatives of the Church are men of like passions as other men, and no more infallible than their fellows, Romanism is nothing more than a device to put the prerogatives and power of God into the hands of sinful men. History teaches how this usurped power has been used.

Vows.

Vows are essentially different from oaths, in that they do not involve any appeal to God as a witness, or any imprecation of his displeasure. A vow is simply a promise made to God. The conditions of a lawful vow are, first, as to the object, or matter of the vow, (1.) That it be something in itself lawful. (2.) That it be acceptable to God. (3.) That it be within our own power. (4.) That it be for our spiritual edification. Secondly, as to the person making the vow, (1.) That he be competent ; that is, that he have sufficient intelligence, and that he be *sui*

---

[1] In conversation with a very intelligent Romish priest who had been educated at Maynooth, the question was asked, What was the effect of a course of " Moral Theology " designed to train priests for the confessional ? The prompt answer was, Utterly to destroy the moral sense.

iuris. A child is not competent to make a vow; neither is one under authority so that he has not liberty of action as to the matter vowed. (2.) That he act with due deliberation and solemnity; for a vow is an act of worship. (3.) That it be made voluntarily, and observed cheerfully.

All these principles are recognized in the Bible. " When thou shalt vow a vow unto the LORD thy God, thou shalt not slack to pay it: for the LORD thy God will surely require it of thee ; and it would be sin in thee. But if thou shalt forbear to vow, it shall be no sin in thee. That which is gone out of thy lips thou shalt keep and perform: even a freewill offering, according as thou hast vowed unto the LORD thy God, which thou hast promised with thy mouth." (Deut. xxiii. 21–23.) In Numbers xxx. 3–5, it is enacted that if a woman in her father's house make a vow, and her father disallow it, it shall not stand, " and the LORD shall forgive her, because her father disallowed her." The same rule is applied to wives and to children, on the obvious principle, that where the rights of others are concerned, we are not at liberty to disregard them.

All the conditions requisite to the lawfulness of a vow, may be included under the old formula, " judicium in vovente, justitia in objecto, veritas in mente." There are two conditions insisted upon by Romanists to which Protestants do not consent. The one is that a vow must be " de meliore bono," *i. e.*, for a greater good. If a man vows to devote himself to the priesthood, to make a pilgrimage, to found a church, or to become a monk, the thing vowed is not only good in itself, but it is better than its opposite. The other condition is, that the thing vowed must be in itself not obligatory, so that the sphere of duty is enlarged by the vow. These conditions are included in those laid down by Dens. [1] He says: " Quinque ex causis provenire, quod aliquid non sit apta materia voti; 1°. quia est impossibile ; 2°. quia est necessarium ; 3°. quia est illicitum ; 4°. quia est indifferens vel inutile ; 5°. quia non est bonum melius." The two conditions just specified no doubt concur in many vows acceptable to God, but they are not essential. A man may vow to do what he is bound to do, as is the case with every man who consecrates himself to God in baptism. Nor is it necessary that the thing vowed should be in its own nature a greater good. A man may bind himself to a work out of gratitude to God, which in its own nature is indifferent. This was the case with many

[1] *Tractatus de Voto; Theologia,* edit. Dublin, 1832, vol. iv. N. 91, p. 111.

of the particulars included in the vows of the Nazarite. There was no special virtue in abstaining from wine, vinegar, grapes moist or dry, or in letting " the locks of the hair of his head grow." (Num. vi. 3–5.) The Romish doctrine on this subject is connected with the distinction which Papists make between precepts and counsels. The former bind the conscience, the others do not. There is special merit, according to their theory, in doing more than is commanded. No man is commanded to devote himself to a life of obedience, celibacy, and poverty, but if he does, so much the better ; he has the greater merit.

As usual, the Romanists connect so many subordinate rules with the general principles laid down that they are explained away, or rendered of little use. Thus the rule that the matter of a vow must be " bonum melius," is explained to mean better in itself considered, and not better in relation to the person making the vow. Thus it may be very injurious to a man's spiritual interests to be bound by monastic vows ; nevertheless, as the monastic life is in itself a " bonum melius," the vows once taken are obligatory. Then as to the condition of possibility ; if possible as to the substance, but impossible as to the accidents, the vow is binding. Thus if a man vows to make a pilgrimage to Jerusalem on his knees, although going on his knees be impossible, he is bound to go in some way.

Lawfulness of Vows.

On this subject there is little or no diversity of opinion. That they are lawful appears, —

1. From their nature. A vow is simply a promise made to God. It may be an expression of gratitude for some signal favour already given, or a pledge to manifest such gratitude for some blessing desired should God see fit to grant it. Thus Jacob vowed that if God would bring him back in peace to his father's house, he would consecrate to Him the tenth of all that he possessed. The Bible, and especially the Psalms, abound with examples of such vows of thank-offerings to God. Even Calvin, notwithstanding his deep sense of the evils entailed on the Church by the abuse of vows by the Romanists, says, " Ejusmodi vota hodie quoque nobis in usu esse possunt, quoties nos Dominus vel a clade aliqua, vel a morbo difficili, vel ab alio quovis discrimine eripuit. Neque enim a pii hominis officio tunc abhorret, votivam oblationem, velut sollenne recognitionis symbolum, Deo consecrare : ne ingratus erga ejus benignitatem videatur." [1] He

---

[1] *Institutio,* IV. xiii. 4, edit. Berlin, 1834, par. ii. p. 338.

also recognizes the propriety of vows of abstinence from indulgences which we have found to be injurious ; and also of vows
the end of which is to render us more mindful of duties which
we may be inclined to neglect. In all such vows there is a devout recognition of God, and of our obligations to Him. They,
therefore, as well as oaths, are acts of worship. They are
regarded as such in the Symbols of the Reformed Churches.
Thus, for example, the "Declaratio Thoruniensis"[1] includes,
under acts of worship, "jusjurandum legitimum, quo Deum cor-
dium inspectorem, ut veritatis testem, et falsitatis vindicem appellamus. Denique votum sacrum, quo vel nos ipsos, vel res
aut actiones nostras Deo, velut sacrificium quoddam spirituale,
consecramus et devovemus."

2. The fact that the Scriptures contain so many examples of
vows, and so many injunctions to their faithful observance, is a
sufficient proof that in their place, and on proper occasions, they
are acceptable in the sight of God.

3. This is further evident from the fact that the baptismal
covenant is of the nature of a vow. In that ordinance we solemnly promise to take God the Father to be our Father, Jesus
Christ his Son to be our Saviour, the Holy Ghost to be our
Sanctifier, and his word to be the rule of our faith and practice.
The same is true of the sacrament of the Lord's Supper ; in that
ordinance we consecrate ourselves to Christ as the purchase of
his blood, and vow to be faithful to Him to the end. The same
thing is true also of the marriage covenant, because the promises
therein made are not merely between the parties, but by both
parties to the contract, to God.

But while the lawfulness of vows is to be admitted, they
should not be unduly multiplied, or made on slight occasions, or
allowed to interfere with our Christian liberty. Not only have
the violation of these rules been productive of the greatest evils
in the Church of Rome, but Protestant Christians also have
often reduced themselves to a miserable state of bondage by the
multiplication of vows. When such cases occur, it is healthful
and right for the Christian to assert his liberty. As a believer
cannot rightfully be brought into bondage to men, so neither
can he rightfully make a slave of himself. He should remember
that God prefers mercy to sacrifice ; that no service is acceptable to Him which is injurious to us ; that He does not require
us to observe promises which we ought never to have made

[1] *De Cultu Dei*, 5; Niemeyer, *Collectio Confessionum*, Leipzig, 1840, p. 678.

and that vows about trifles are irreverent, and should neither be
made nor regarded, but should be repented of as sins.   Even
Thomas Aquinas says, " Vota quæ sunt de rebus vanis et inu-
tilibus, sunt magis deridenda, quam servanda." [1]

Monastic Vows.

At the time of the Reformation the doors of all the monasteries in lands in which Protestants had the power, were thrown
open, and their inmates declared free in the sight of God and
man, from the vows by which they had hitherto been bound.
Protestants did not maintain that there was anything intrinsic-
ally wrong in a man, or a company of men renouncing the ordinary avocations of life, and devoting himself or themselves to a
religious life.   Nor did they object to such men living together
and conforming to a prescribed rule of discipline; nor did they
deny that such institutions under proper regulations, might be,
and in fact had been of great and manifold utility.   They had
been places of security for those who had no taste for the conflicts
by which all Christendom was so long agitated.   In many cases
they were places of education and seats of learning.   Their objections to them were, —

1. That they had been perverted from their original design,
and had become the sources of evil and not of good, in every part
of the Church.   Instead of its being free to every one to enter
and to leave these institutions at discretion, those once initiated
were bound for life by the vows which they had made, and instead of the obligations assumed being rational and Scriptural,
they were unreasonable and unscriptural.   Instead of the inmates
of these institutions supporting themselves by their own labour,
they were allowed to live in idleness, supported by alms or by the
revenues of the convents, which had in many cases become enormous.   This objection was directed to the very principle on which
the monastic institutions of the Romish Church were founded.
On this point Calvin says, " Proinde meminerint lectores, fuisse
me de monachismo potius quam de monachis loquutum, et ea
vitia notasse, non quæ in paucorum vita hærent, sed quæ ab ipso
vivendi instituto separari nequeunt." [2]

2. To this, however, was added the argument from experience.
Monastic institutions had become the sources of untold evils to
the Church.   Being in a great measure independent of the ordi-

---

[1] *Summa*, II. ii. quæst. lxxxviii. 2; edit. Cologne, 1640, p. 164, b, of third set.
[2] *Institutio*, IV. xiii. 15 ; edit. Berlin, 1834, vol. ii. p. 345.

nary ecclesiastical authorities, they were the cause of conflict and
agitation. Each order was an "imperium in imperio," and one
order was arrayed against another, as one feudal baron against
his fellows. Besides, the corruption of manners within the convents as portrayed by Romanists themselves, rendered them such
a scandal and offence as to justify their summary suppression.
Much is implied in the answer of Erasmus to Frederick the Wise,
" Lutherus peccavit in duobus, nempe quod tetigit coronam pon
tificis et ventres monachorum." [1]

3. Practical evils might be reformed, but Protestants objected
that the whole system of monkery was founded on the false principle of the merit of good works. It was only on the assumption that men could work out a righteousness of their own, that
they submitted to the self-denial and restraints of the monastic
life. If, however, as Protestants believe, there is no merit in the
sight of God in anything fallen men can do, and the righteousness of Christ is the sole ground of our acceptance with God, the
whole ground on which these institutions were defended is undermined. To enter a monastery, on the theory of the Romish
Church, was to renounce the doctrine of salvation by grace. Besides, it was also taught that celibacy, obedience, and voluntary
poverty, being uncommanded, the monastic vow to observe these
rules of life, involved special merit. This was a twofold error.
First, it is an error to suppose that there can be any work of supererogation. The law of God demanding absolute perfection of
heart and life, there can be no such thing as going beyond its requirements. And, secondly, it is an error to assume that there is
any virtue at all in celibacy, monastic obedience, or voluntary
poverty. These are not " meliora bona " in the Romish sense of
the words. In this view, also, monastic vows are antichristian.

4. A fourth reason urged by Protestants for pronouncing monastic vows invalid, was that they were unlawful, not only for the
reason just assigned, but also because they were contrary to the
law of Christ. No man has the right to swear away his liberty ;
to reduce himself to a state of absolute subjection to a fellow-
mortal. To his own master he must stand or fall. The vow of
obedience made by every monk or nun was a violation of the
apostolic injunction, " Be not ye the servants of men." The
same remark is applicable to the vow of celibacy. No one has a
right to take that vow ; because celibacy is right or wrong according to circumstances. It may be a sin, and therefore no such
vow can bind the conscience.

[1] Guericke's *Kirchengeschichte*, VII. I. ii. § 174, 6th edit. Leipzig, 1846, vol. iii. p. 69.

5. Monastic life, instead of being subservient to holiness of heart, was in the vast majority of cases injurious to the monks themselves. The fearful language of Jerome is full of instruction: " O quoties ego ipso in eremo constitutus in illa vasta solitudine, quæ exusta solis ardoribus, horridum monachis præstat habitaculum, putavi me Romanis interesse deliciis. . . . . Ille igitur ego, qui ob Gehennæ metum tali me carcere ipse damnaveram, scorpiorum tantum socius et ferarum, sæpe choris intereram puellarum. Pallebant ora jejuniis, et mens desideriis æstuabat in frigido corpore, et ante hominem sua jam in carne præmortuum, sola libidinum incendia bulliebant." [1] In the day when that which is hidden shall be made manifest, there will probably be no such fearful revelation of self-torture as that made by unveiling the secret life of the inmates of monastic institutions. They are in necessary conflict with the laws of nature and with the law of God.

The Protestants adopted the rule announced by Calvin: [2] " Omnia non legitima nec rite concepta, ut apud Deum nihili sunt, sic nobis irrita esse debere." For, he immediately adds, as in human contracts only that continues binding, which he to whom the promise is made wishes us to observe, so it is to be supposed that we are not bound to do what God does not wish us to do, simply because we have promised Him to do it. On these grounds the Reformers with one accord pronounced all monastic vows to be null and void. Thus the Gospel became a proclamation of liberty to the captive, and the opening of the prison to those who were bound.

§ 8. *The Fourth Commandment.*
Its Design.

The design of the fourth commandment was, (1.) To commemorate the work of creation. The people were commanded to remember the Sabbath-day and to keep it holy, because in six days God had made the heavens and the earth. (2.) To pre-

---

[1] *Epistola xxii; Ad Eustochium, Paulæ Filiam, De Custodia Virginitatis, Opera*, ed. Migne, Paris, 1845, vol. i. p. 398. This long epistle is addressed to a young Roman lady of rank and wealth ; and is designed to confirm her in her resolution not to marry. It is founded on the assumption that virginity was not only a great virtue, but also that a special reward, a glory not otherwise attainable, was attached to it. He says to her : " Cave, quæso, ne quando de te dicat Deus : ' Virgo Israel cecidit, et non est qui suscitet eam ' (Amos v. 2). Audenter loquar : Cum omnia possit Deus, suscitare virginem non potest post ruinam. Valet quidem liberare de pœna, sed non vult coronare corruptam." *Ibid.* p. 394. He enjoins upon her all kinds of ascetic observances even while confessing their inefficacy in his own case.

[2] *Institutio*, iv. xiii. 20; edit. Berlin, 1834, vol. ii. p. 349.

serve alive the knowledge of the only living and true God.   If heaven and earth, that is, the universe, were created, they must have had a creator; and that creator must be extramundane, existing before, out of, and independently of the world.   He must be almighty, and infinite in knowledge, wisdom, and goodness; for all these attributes are necessary to account for the wonders of the heavens and the earth.   So long, therefore, as men believe in creation, they must believe in God.   This accounts for the fact that so much stress is laid upon the right observance of the Sabbath.   Far more importance is attributed to that observance than to any merely ceremonial institution.   (3.) This command was designed to arrest the current of the outward life of the people and to turn their thoughts to the unseen and spiritual.   Men are so prone to be engrossed by the things of this world that it was, and is, of the highest importance that there should be one day of frequent recurrence on which they were forbidden to think of the things of the world, and forced to think of the things unseen and eternal.   (4.) It was intended to afford time for the instruction of the people, and for the public and special worship of God.   (5.) By the prohibition of all servile labour, whether of man or beast, it was designed to secure recuperative rest for those on whom the primeval curse had fallen: " In the sweat of thy face shalt thou eat bread."   (6.) As a day of rest and as set apart for intercourse with God, it was designed to be a type of that rest which remains for the people of God, as we learn from Psalms xcv. 11, as expounded by the Apostle in Hebrews iv. 1– 10.   (7.) As the observance of the Sabbath had died out among the nations, it was solemnly reënacted under the Mosaic dispensation to be a sign of the covenant between God and the children of Israel.   They were to be distinguished as the Sabbath-keeping people among all the nations of the earth, and as such were to be the recipients of God's special blessings.   Exodus xxxi. 13, " Verily my Sabbaths ye shall keep: for it is a sign between me and you throughout your generations; that ye may know that I am the Lord that doth sanctify you."   And in verses 16, 17, " Wherefore the children of Israel shall keep the Sabbath, to observe the Sabbath throughout their generations, for a perpetual covenant. It is a sign between me and the children of Israel forever."   And in Ezekiel xx. 12, it is said, " Moreover, also, I gave them my Sabbaths, to be a sign between me and them, that they might know that I am the Lord that sanctify them."

The Sabbath was instituted from the Beginning, and is of Perpetual Obligation.

1. This may be inferred from the nature and design of the institution. It is a generally recognized principle, that those commands of the Old Testament which were addressed to the Jews as Jews and were founded on their peculiar circumstances and relations, passed away when the Mosaic economy was abolished; but those founded on the immutable nature of God, or upon the permanent relations of men, are of permanent obligation. There are many such commands which bind men as men; fathers as fathers; children as children; and neighbours as neighbours. It is perfectly apparent that the fourth commandment belongs to this latter class. It is important for all men to know that God created the world, and therefore is an extramundane personal being, infinite in all his perfections. All men need to be arrested in their worldly career, and called upon to pause and to turn their thoughts Godward. It is of incalculable importance that men should have time and opportunity for religious instruction and worship. It is necessary for all men and servile animals to have time to rest and recuperate their strength. The daily nocturnal rest is not sufficient for that purpose, as physiologists assure us, and as experience has demonstrated. Such is obviously the judgment of God.

It appears, therefore, from the nature of this commandment as moral, and not positive or ceremonial, that it is original and universal in its obligation. No man assumes that the commands, " Thou shalt not kill," and " Thou shalt not steal," were first announced by Moses, and ceased to be obligatory when the old economy passed away. A moral law is one that binds from its own nature. It expresses an obligation arising either out of our relations to God or out of our permanent relations to our fellow-men. It binds whether formally enacted or not. There are no doubt positive elements in the fourth commandment as it stands in the Bible. It is positive that a seventh, and not a sixth or eighth part of our time should be consecrated to the public service of God. It is positive that the seventh rather than any other day of the week should be thus set apart. But it is moral that there should be a day of rest and cessation from worldly avocations. It is of moral obligation that God and his great works should be statedly remembered. It is a moral duty that the people should assemble for religious instruction and for the

united worship of God.   All this was obligatory before the time
of Moses, and would have been binding had he never existed.
All that the fourth commandment did was to put this natural
and universal obligation into a definite form.

2. The original and universal obligation of the law of the
Sabbath may be inferred from its having found a place in the
decalogue.   As all the other commandments in that fundamental
revelation of the duties of men to God and to their neighbour, are
moral and permanent in their obligation, it would be incongruous
and unnatural if the fourth should be a solitary exception.   This
argument is surely not met by the answer given to it by the advocates of the opposite doctrine.   The argument they say is valid
only on the assumption " that the Mosaic law, because of its divine origin, is of universal and permanent authority." [1]   May it
not be as well said, If the command, " Thou shalt not steal," be
still in force, the whole code of the Mosaic law must be binding ?
The fourth commandment is read in all Christian churches, whenever the decalogue is read, and the people are taught to say,
" Lord, have mercy upon us, and incline our hearts to keep this
law."

3. Another argument is derived from the penalty attached to
the violation of this commandment.   " Ye shall keep the Sabbath, therefore, for it is holy unto you : every one that defileth it
shall surely be put to death."   (Ex. xxxi. 14.)   The violation
of no merely ceremonial or positive law was visited with this
penalty.   Even the neglect of circumcision, although it involved
the rejection of both the Abrahamic and the Mosaic covenant, and
necessarily worked the forfeiture of all the benefits of the theocracy, was not made a capital offence.   The law of the Sabbath
by being thus distinguished was raised far above the level of
mere positive enactments.   A character was given to it, not only
of primary importance, but also of special sanctity.

4. We accordingly find that in the prophets as well as in the
Pentateuch, and the historical books of the Old Testament, the
Sabbath is not only spoken of as " a delight," but also its faithful observance is predicted as one of the characteristics of the
Messianic period.   Thus Isaiah says, " If thou turn away thy
foot from the Sabbath, from doing thy pleasure on my holy day ;
and call the Sabbath a Delight, the Holy of the LORD, Honourable ; and shalt honour him, not doing thine own ways, nor
finding thine own pleasure, nor speaking thine own words : then

---

[1] Palmer, in Herzog's *Real-Encyklopädie*, art. " Sonntagsfeier."

shalt thou delight thyself in the LORD ; and I will cause thee to ride upon the high places of the earth, and feed thee with the heritage of Jacob thy father ; for the mouth of the LORD hath spoken it." (Is. lviii. 13, 14.) Gesenius is very much puzzled at this. The prophets predicted that under the Messiah the true religion was to be extended to the ends of the earth. But the public worship of God was by the Jewish law tied to Jerusalem. That law was neither designed nor adapted for a universal religion. To those, therefore, who believe that the Sabbath was a temporary Mosaic institution to pass away when the old economy was abolished, it is altogether incongruous that a prophet should represent the faithful observance of the Sabbath as one of the chief blessings and glories of the Messiah's reign.

These considerations, apart from historical evidence or the direct assertion of the Scriptures, are enough to create a strong, if not an invincible presumption, that the Sabbath was instituted from the beginning, and was designed to be of universal and permanent obligation. Whatever law had a temporary ground or reason for its enactment, was temporary in its obligation. Where the reason of the law is permanent the law itself is permanent.

The greater number of Christian theologians who deny all this, still admit the Sabbath to be a most wise and beneficent institution. Nay, many of them go so far as to represent its violation, as a day of religious rest, as a sin. This, however, is a conces sion that the reason for the command is permanent, and that iↄ God has not required its observance, the Church or State is bound to do so.

Direct Evidence of the ante-Mosaic institution of the Sabbath.

Presumptive evidence may be strong enough to coerce assent. The advocates of the early institution of the Sabbath, however, are not limited to that kind of evidence. There is direct proof of the fact for which they contend, —

1. In Genesis ii. 3, it is said, " God blessed the seventh day, and sanctified it ; because that in it he had rested from all his work which God created and made." It is indeed easy to say that this is a prolepsis ; that the passage assigns the reason why in the times of Moses, God selected the seventh, rather than any other day of the week to be the Sabbath. This is indeed possible, but it is not probable. It is an unnatural interpretation which no one would adopt except to suit a purpose. The narrative purports to be an account of what God did at the time of the crea-

tion. When the earth was prepared for his reception, God created man on the sixth day, and rested from the work of creation
on the seventh, and set apart that day as a holy day to be a perpetual memorial of the great work which He had accomplished.[1]
This is the natural sense of the passage, from which only the
strongest reasons would authorize us to depart. All collateral
reasons, however, are on its side.

In support of this interpretation the authority of the most
impartial, as well as the most competent interpreters might be
quoted. Grotius did not believe in the perpetuity of the Sabbath,
yet he admits that in Genesis ii. 3, it is said that the seventh day
was set apart as holy from the creation. He assumes, on the authority, as he says, of many learned Hebrews, that there were
two precepts concerning the Sabbath. The one given at the
beginning enjoined that every seventh day should be remembered
as a memorial of the creation. And in this sense, he says, the
Sabbath was doubtless observed by the patriarchs, Enoch, Noah,
Abraham, etc. The second precept was given from Mount Sinai
when the Sabbath was made a memorial of the deliverance of the
Israelites from Egyptian bondage. This latter law enjoined rest
from labour on the Sabbath. The Scriptural argument which he
urges in support of this theory, is, that in all the accounts of the
journeyings of the patriarchs, we never read of their resting on
the seventh day ; whereas after the law given from Mount Sinai,
this reference to the resting of the people on the Sabbath is of
constant occurrence.[2]

Delitzsch says " Hengstenberg understands Genesis ii. 3, as
though it were written from the stand-point of the Mosaic law, as
if it were said, God for this reason in after times blessed the seventh
day ; which scarcely needs a refutation. God himself, the Creator,
celebrated a Sabbath immediately after the six days' work, and
because his σαββατισμός could become the σαββατισμός of his creatures, He made for that purpose the seventh day, by his blessing,
to be a perennial fountain of refreshment, and clothed that day
by hallowing it with special glory for all time to come." [3]

Baumgarten in his comment on this verse says the separa-

---

[1] The force of this argument does not depend on the supposition that the days of creation
were periods of twenty-four hours. Admitting that they were geologic periods, at the end
of the sixth of which man appeared, and that then followed a period of permanent rest,
that would be reason enough why every seventh day should be selected as a memorial of
the creation, to teach Adam and his descendants that the earth did not owe its existence to
a olind process of development, but to the fiat of Jehovah.

[2] *De Veritate Religionis Christianæ*, v. 10; *Works*, London, 1679, vol. iii. p. 79.

[3] *Die Genesis Ausgelegt*, von Franz Delitzsch, Leipzig, 1852, pp. 84, 85.

tion of this day from all others was made so that "the return of this blessed and holy day should be to him a memorial, and participation of the divine rest."[1] And Knobel, one of the most pronounced of the rationalistic commentators, says, "That the author of Genesis makes the distinction of the seventh day coeval with the creation, although the carrying out of the purpose thus intimated was deferred to the time of Moses. Nothing is known of any ante-Mosaic celebration of the Sabbath."[2]

2. Apart from the fact that the reason for the Sabbath existed from the beginning, there is direct historical evidence that the hebdomadal division of time prevailed before the deluge. Noah in Genesis viii. 10, 12, is said twice to have rested seven days. And again in the time of Jacob, as appears from Genesis xxix. 27, 28, the division of time into weeks was recognized as an established usage. As seven is not an equal part either of a solar year or of a lunar month, the only satisfactory account of this fact, is to be found in the institution of the Sabbath. This fact moreover proves not only the original institution, but also the continued observance of the seventh day. There must have been something to distinguish that day as the close of one period or the commencement of another. It is altogether unnatural to account for this hebdomadal division by a reference to the worship of the seven planets. There is no evidence that the planets were objects of worship at that early period of the world, or for a long time afterwards, especially among the Shemitic races. Besides, this explanation is inconsistent with the account of the creation. The divine authority of the book of Genesis is here taken for granted. What it asserts, Christians are bound to believe. It is undeniably taught in this book that God created the heavens and the earth in six days and rested on the seventh. It matters not how the word "days" may be explained, we have in the history of the creation this hebdomadal division of time. No earlier cause for the prevalence of that division can be given, and no other is needed, or can reasonably be assumed.

This division of time into weeks, was not confined to the Hebrew race. It was almost universal. This fact proves that it must have had its origin in the very earliest period in the history of the world.[3]

[1] *Theologische Commentar zum Pentateuch*, Kiel, 1843, vol. i. p. 29.
[2] *Die Genesis Erklärt*, von August Knobel, Leipzig, 1852.
[3] Of this general prevalence in the ancient world, of a special reverence for the seventh day and of the division of time into weeks, Grotius gives abundant evidence in his work, *De Veritate Religionis Christianæ*, i. 16; *Works*, vol. iii. p. 16. On this subject, see Winer's

3. That the law of the Sabbath was not first given on Mount Sinai, may also be inferred from the fact that it was referred to as a known and familiar institution, before that law was promulgated. Thus in the sixteenth chapter of Exodus the people were directed to gather on the sixth day of the week manna sufficient for the seventh, as on that day none would be provided. And more particularly in the twenty-third verse, it is said, " To-morrow is the rest of the holy Sabbath unto the LORD : bake that which ye will bake to-day, and seethe that ye will seethe ; and that which remaineth over lay up for you, to be kept until morning." And in the twenty-sixth verse we read, " Six days ye shall gather it; but on the seventh day, which is the Sabbath, in it there shall be none." There was therefore a Sabbath before the Mosaic law was given. Again, the language used in the fourth commandment, " Remember the Sabbath day to keep it holy," naturally implies that the Sabbath was not a new institution. It was a law given in the beginning, that had doubtless in a good measure, especially during their bondage in Egypt, become obsolete, which the people were henceforth to remember and faithfully observe.

The objection to the pre-Mosaic institution of the Sabbath founded on the silence of Genesis on the subject in the history of the patriarchs, is of little weight. It is to be remembered that the book of Genesis, comprised in some sixty octavo pages, gives us the history of nearly two thousand years. All details not bearing immediately on the design of the author were of necessity left out. If nothing was done but what is there recorded, the antediluvians and patriarchs lived almost entirely without religious observances.

The Sabbath does not stand alone. It is well known that Moses adopted and incorporated with his extended code many of the ancient usages of the chosen people. This was the case with sacrifices and circumcision, as well as with all the principles of the decalogue. That a particular law, therefore, is found in the Mosaic economy is not sufficient evidence that it had its origin with the Hebrew Lawgiver, or that it ceased to be binding when the old dispensation was abrogated. If the reason for the law remains, the law itself remains ; and if given to mankind before the birth of Moses, it binds mankind. On this point even Dr.

Realwörterbuch, word " Sabbath." Winer refers, among other authorities discussing this question of the antiquity of the Sabbath, to Selden, *Jus Nat. et Gent.;* Spencer, *Legg. ritual.;* Eichhorn, *Urgesch.;* Hebenstreit, *De Sabb. ante legg. Mos. existente ;* Michaelis, *Mos. Recht.*

Paley says: "If the divine command was actually delivered at the creation, it was addressed, no doubt, to the whole human species alike, and continues, unless repealed by some subsequent revelation, binding upon all who come to the knowledge of it."[1] That the law of the Sabbath was thus given is, as has been shown, the common opinion even of those who deny its perpetual obligation, and therefore its permanence cannot reasonably be questioned by those who admit the principle that what was given to mankind was meant for mankind.

4. It is a strong argument in favour of this conclusion, that the law of the Sabbath was taken up and incorporated in the new dispensation by the Apostles, the infallible founders of the Christian Church. All the Mosaic laws founded on the permanent relations of men either to God or to their fellows, are in like manner adopted in the Christian Code. They are adopted, however, only as to their essential elements. Every law, ceremonial or typical, or designed only for the Jews, is discarded. Men are still bound to worship God, but this is not now to be done especially at Jerusalem, or by sacrifices, or through the ministration of priests. Marriage is as sacred now as it ever was, but all the special laws regulating its duties, and the penalty for its violation, are abrogated. Homicide is as great a crime now as under the Mosaic economy, but the old laws about the avenger of blood and cities of refuge are no longer in force. The rights of property remain unimpaired under the gospel dispensation, but the Jewish laws regarding its distribution and protection, are no longer binding. The same is true with regard to the Sabbath. We are as much bound to keep one day in seven holy unto the Lord, as were the patriarchs or Israelites. This law binds all men as men, because given to all mankind, and because it is founded upon the nature common to all men, and the relation which all men bear to God. The two essential elements of the command are that the Sabbath should be a day of rest, that is, of cessation from worldly avocations and amusements; and that it should be devoted to the worship of God and the services of religion. All else is circumstantial and variable. It is not necessary that it should be observed with special reference to the deliverance of the Israelites out of Egypt; nor are the details as to the things to be done or avoided, or as to the penalty for transgression obligatory on us. We are not bound to offer the sacrifices required of the Jews, nor are we bound to abstain from lighting a fire on that day. In

[1] *Principles of Moral and Political Philosophy*, v. 7; edit. Boston, 1848, vol. ii. p. 48.

like manner the day of the week is not essential. The change
from the seventh to the first was circumstantial. If made for
sufficient reason and by competent authority, the change is obligatory. The reason for the change is patent. If the deliverance
of the Hebrew from the bondage in Egypt should be commemo-
rated, how much more the redemption of the world by the Son
of God. If the creation of the material universe should be kept
in perpetual remembrance, how much more the new creation secured by the resurrection of Jesus Christ from the dead. If men
wish the knowledge of that event to die out, let them neglect to
keep holy the first day of the week ; if they desire that event to
be everywhere known and remembered, let them consecrate that
day to the worship of the risen Saviour. This is God's method
for keeping the resurrection of Christ, on which our salvation
depends, in perpetual remembrance.

This change of the Sabbath from the seventh to the first day
of the week was made not only for a sufficient reason, but also by
competent authority. It is a simple historical fact that the
Christians of the apostolic age ceased to observe the seventh, and
did observe the first day of the week as the day for religious worship. Thus from the creation, in unbroken succession, the people
of God have, in obedience to the original command, devoted one
day in seven to the worship of the only living and true God. It
is hard to conceive of a stronger argument than this for the perpetual obligation of the Sabbath as a divine institution. It is not
worth while to stop to answer the objection, that the record of
this uninterrupted observance of the Sabbath is incomplete.
History does not record everything. We find the fountain of
this river of mercy in paradise ; we trace its course from age to
age ; we see its broad and beneficent flow before our eyes. If
here and there, in its course through millenniums, it be lost from
view in a morass or cavern, its reappearance proves its identity
and the divinity of its origin. The Sabbath is to the nations
what the Nile is to Egypt, and you might as well call the one a
human device as the other. Nothing but divine authority and
divine power can account for the continued observance of this
sacred institution from the beginning until now.

5. It is fair to argue the divine origin of the Sabbath from its
supreme importance. As to the fact of its importance all Christians are agreed. They may differ as to the ground on which
the obligation to observe it rests, and as to the strictness with
which the day should be observed, but that men are bound to

observe it, and that its due observance is of essential importance, there is no difference of opinion among the churches of Christendom. But if so essential to the interests of religion, is it conceivable that God has not enjoined it? He has given the world the Church, the Bible, the ministry, the sacraments; these are not human devices. And can it be supposed that the Sabbath, without which all these divine institutions would be measurably inefficient, should be left to the will or wisdom of men? This is not to be supposed. That these divinely appointed means for the illumination and sanctification of men, are in a great measure without effect, where the Sabbath is neglected or profaned, is a matter of experience. It is undeniable that the mass of the people are indebted to the services of the sanctuary on the Lord's Day, for their religious knowledge. Any community or class of men who ignore the Sabbath and absent themselves from the sanctuary, as a general thing, become heathen. They have little more true religious knowledge than pagans. But without such knowledge morality is impossible. Religion is not only the lifeblood of morality, so that without the former the latter cannot be; but God has revealed his purpose that it shall not be. If men refuse to retain Him in their knowledge, He declares that He will give them up to a reprobate mind. (Rom. i. 28.) Men do not know what they are doing, when by their teaching or example they encourage the neglect or profanation of the Lord's Day. We have in the French Communists an illustration and a warning of what a community without a Sabbath, i. e., without religion, must ultimately and inevitably become. Irreligious men of course sneer at religion and deny its importance, but the Bible and experience are against them.

Objections.

The general objections against the doctrine that the law of the Sabbath is of universal and perpetual obligation, have already been incidentally considered. Those derived from the New Testament are principally the following: —

1. An objection is drawn from the absence of any express command. No such command was needed. The New Testament has no decalogue. That code having been once announced, and never repealed, remains in force. Its injunctions are not so much categorically repeated, as assumed as still obligatory. We find no such words as, "Thou shalt have no other gods before me," or "Thou shalt not make unto thee any graven image." Paul says,

" I had not known lust, except the law had said, Thou shalt not covet." (Rom. vii. 7.) The law which said " Thou shalt not covet," is in the decalogue. Paul does not reënact the command, he simply takes for granted that the decalogue is now as ever the law of God.

2. It is urged not only that there is no positive command on the subject, but also that there is a total silence in the New Testament respecting any obligation to keep holy one day in seven. Our Lord in his Sermon on the Mount, it is said, while correcting the false interpretations of the Mosaic law given by the Pharisees, and expounding its precepts in their true sense, says nothing of the fourth commandment. The same is true of the council in Jerusalem. That council says nothing about the necessity of the heathen converts observing a Sabbath. But all this may be said of other precepts the obligation of which no man questions. Neither our Lord nor the council say anything about the worshipping of graven images. Besides, our Lord elsewhere does do, with regard to the fourth commandment, precisely what He did in the Sermon on the Mount with regard to other precepts of the decalogue. He reproved the Pharisees for their false interpretation of that commandment, without the slightest intimation that the law itself was not to remain in force.

3. Appeal is made to such passages as Colossians ii. 16, " Let no man therefore judge you in meat, or in drink, or in respect of an holy day, or of the new moon, or of the Sabbath days ; " and Romans xiv. 5, " One man esteemeth one day above another ; another esteemeth every day alike. Let every man be fully persuaded in his own mind." Every one knows, however, that the apostolic churches were greatly troubled by Judaizers, who insisted that the Mosaic law continued in force, and that Christians were bound to conform to its prescriptions with regard to the distinction between clean and unclean meats, and its numerous feast days, on which all labour was to be intermitted. These were the false teachers and this was the false doctrine against which so much of St. Paul's epistles was directed. It is in obvious reference to these men and their doctrines that such passages as those cited above were written. They have no reference to the weekly Sabbath, which had been observed from the creation, and which the Apostles themselves introduced and perpetuated in the Christian Church.

4. It also frequently said that a weekly Sabbath is out of keeping with the spirit of the Gospel, which requires the consecration

of the whole life and of all our time to God. With the Christian, it is said, every day is holy, and one day is not more holy than another. It is not true, however, that the New Testament requires greater consecration to God than the Old. The Gospel has many advantages over the Mosaic dispensation, but that is not one of them. It was of old, even from the beginning, required of all men that they should love God with all the heart, with all the mind, and with all the strength; and their neighbour as themselves. More than this the Gospel demands of no man. If it consists with the spirituality of the Church that believers should not neglect the assembling themselves together; and that they should have a stated ministry, sacramental rites, and the power of excommunication, and all this by Divine appointment; then it is hard to see why the consecration of one day in seven to the service of God, should be inconsistent with its spiritual character. So long as we are in the body, religion cannot be exclusively a matter of the heart. It must have its institutions and ordinances; and any attempt to dispense with these would be as unreasonable and as futile as for the soul, in this our present state of existence, to attempt to do without the body.

5. Another ground is often taken on this subject. The importance of the Sabbath is not denied. The obligation to keep it holy is admitted. It is declared to be sinful to engage in worldly avocations or amusements on that day; but it is denied that this obligation to consecrate the day to God rests upon any divine command. It is denied that the original sanctification of the seventh day at the creation binds all men to keep one day in seven holy to the Lord. It is maintained that the fourth commandment, both as to its essence and as to its accidents is abrogated; and, therefore, that there is no express command of God now in force requiring us to keep holy the Sabbath. The obligation is either self-imposed, or it is imposed by the Church. The Church requires its members to observe the Lord's Day, as it requires them to observe Christmas or Good Friday; and Christians, it is said, are bound to obey the Church, as citizens are bound to obey the state. But Protestants deny that the Church has power to make laws to bind the conscience. That is the prerogative of God. If the Church may do it in one case it may in another; and we should be made the servants of men. It is by this simple principle, that men are bound to obey the Church, that Rome has effectually despoiled all who acknowledge her authority of the liberty wherewith Christ has made his people free.

Most of the modern evangelical theologians in Germany say
that the obligation to observe the Sabbath is self-imposed. That
is, that every man, and especially every Christian, is bound to
do all he can to promote the interests of religion and the good of
society. The consecration of the Lord's Day to the worship of
God is eminently conducive to these ends; therefore men are
bound to keep it holy. But an obligation self-imposed is limited
to self. One man thinks it best to devote Sunday to religion;
another that it should be kept as a day of relaxation and amusement. One man's liberty cannot be judged by another man's
conscience. Expediency can never be the ground of a universal
and permanent obligation. The history of the Church proves
that no such views of duty are adequate to coerce the conscience
and govern the lives of men. The Sabbath is not in fact consecrated to religion, where its divine authority is denied. The
churches may be more or less frequented, but the day is principally devoted to amusement. A German theologian[1] says that
the doctrine that the religious observance of the Sabbath rests
on an express divine command, "prevails throughout the whole
English-speaking part of Christendom," and that in the Evangelical Church in Germany, some either from a too legal view of
Christianity, or from servile subjection to the letter of the Bible,
or impressed by the solemn stillness of an English Sunday as
contrasted with its profanation elsewhere, have ever been inclined
to the same views. Although this writer, the representative of
a large class, asserts his Christian liberty to observe one day
above another, or all days alike, he admits that the religious observance of the Lord's Day is not a matter of indifference; on
the contrary, he says that "its profanation (Verleztung) is a sin."
To make a thing sinful, however, he says it is not necessary that
it should be against an express divine command. A Christian's
conscience, "guided by the word, and enlightened by the Spirit
of God," is his rule of conduct. Conscience thus guided and
enlightened, may enjoin or forbid much for which no explicit
directions can be found in the Scriptures. No man denies all
this; but a man's conscience is a guide for himself, and not for
other people. If we hold fast the fundamental principle of our
Protestant faith and freedom, "that the Scriptures are the only
infallible rule of faith and practice," we must be able to plead
express divine authority for the religious observance of the Lord's
Day, or allow every man so to keep it or not as he sees fit. To

[1] Palmer in Herzog's *Real-Encyklopädic.*

his own master he stands or falls; to Him alone is he accountable for the use which he makes of his Christian liberty. But as no man is at liberty to steal or not to steal as he sees fit, so all " English speaking" Christians with one voice say, he is not at liberty to sanctify or profane the Sabbath, as he sees fit. He is bound by the primal and immutable law given at the creation, to keep one day in seven holy to the Lord.

If it be true that it is peculiar to the Anglo-Saxon race to hold this view of the obligation of the Christian Sabbath, then they have special reason for profound gratitude to God. God of old said to the Israelites, " Hallow my Sabbaths; and they shall be a sign between me and you, that ye may know that I am the LORD your God." That is, it shall be for a sign that you are my people. So long as you keep the Sabbath holy I will bless you; when you neglect and profane it, your blessings shall depart from you. (Jer. xvii. 20–27.) If it be then the distinction of Anglo-Saxon Christians, that they are a sabbath-keeping people, it is one to be highly prized and sedulously guarded; and in this country especially, we should be watchful lest the influx of immigrants of other nationalities deprive us of this great distinction and its blessings.

It is a popular objection against the religious observance of the Lord's Day, that the labouring classes need it as a day of recreation. On this it is obvious to remark, (1.) That there are many grievous evils in our modern civilization, but these are not to be healed by trampling on the laws of God. If men crowd labourers into narrow premises, and overwork them in heated factories six days in the week, they cannot atone for that sin by making the Lord's Day a day for amusement. (2.) So far from Sunday, as generally spent by the labouring class, being a day of refreshment, it is just the reverse. Monday is commonly with them the worst day in the week for labour; it is needed as a day for recovery from the effects of a misspent Sunday. (3.) If the labouring classes are provided with healthful places of abode and are not overworked, then the best restorative is entire rest from ordinary occupations, and directing their thoughts and feelings into new channels, by the purifying and elevating offices of religion. This is the divinely appointed method of preserving the bodies and souls of men in a healthful state, a method which no human device is likely to improve.

How is the Sabbath to be Sanctified?

It may be said in general terms to be the opinion of the whole Jewish and Christian Church, that the sanctification required by God, consists not merely in cessation from worldly avocations, but also in the consecration of the day to the offices of religion. That this is the correct view is proved, (1.) Not only by the general consent of the people of God under both dispensations, but also by the constant use of the words to " hallow," to " make " or, " keep holy," and to " sanctify." The uniform use of such expressions, shows that the day was set apart from a common to a sacred use. (2.) From the command to increase the number of sacrifices in the temple service, which proves that the day was to be religiously observed. (3.) From the design of the institution, which from the beginning was religious ; the commemoration of the work of creation, and after the advent, of the resurrection of Christ. (4.) In Leviticus xxiii., a list is given of those days on which there was to be " a holy convocation " of the people ; i. e., on which the people were to be called together for public worship, and the Sabbath is the first given. (5.) The command is constantly repeated that the people should be faithfully instructed out of the law, which was to be read to them on all suitable occasions. To give opportunity for such instruction was evidently one of the principal objects of these " holy convocations." (Deut. vi. 6, 7, 17–19 ; Josh. i. 8.) This instruction of the people was made the special duty of the Levites (Deut. xxxiii. 10) ; and of the priests. (Lev. x. 11, comp. Mal. ii. 7.) The reading of the law was doubtless a regular part of the service on all the days on which the people were solemnly called together for religious worship. Thus in Deuteronomy xxxi. 11, 12, we read, " When all Israel is come to appear before the LORD thy God in the place which he shall choose, thou shalt read this law before all Israel in their hearing. Gather the people together, men, and women, and children, and thy stranger that is within thy gates, that they may hear, and that they may learn, and fear the LORD your God, and observe to do all the words of this law." Such was the design of the convocation of the people. We know from the New Testament that the Scriptures were read every Sabbath in the synagogues ; and the syn agogues were among the earliest institutions of the chosen people. 2 Kings iv. 23, at least proves that at that period it was customary for the people to resort on the Sabbath to holy men for instruction. In Psalm lxxiv. 8, it is said of the heathen, " They have burned up all the synagogues of God in the land." The word here rendered " synagogues," means " assemblies," but burning up " assemblies " can only mean places of assembly; as burning up churches, in our mode of expression, can only mean the edifices where churches or congregations are accustomed to assemble. What other places of assembling the Psalmist could refer to, if synagogues did not then exist, it is hard to understand. But admitting that synagogues were not common among the Jews until after the exile, which is a very improbable supposition, the fact that reading the Scriptures on the Sabbath was an established part of the synagogue service, goes far to prove that it was a sabbatical service long before the exile. (6.) The place of the fourth command in the decalogue; the stress laid upon it in the Old Testament; the way in which it is spoken of in the prophets; and the Psalms appointed to be used on that day, as for example the ninety-second, all show that the day was set apart for religious duties from the beginning. (7.) This may also be argued from the whole character of the old dispensation. All its institutions were religious; they were all intended to keep alive the knowledge of the true God, and to prepare the way for the coming of Christ. It would be entirely out of keeping with the spirit of the Mosaic economy to assume that its most important and solemn holy day was purely secular in its design.[1]

It is admitted that the precepts of the decalogue bind the Church in all ages; while the specific details contained in the books of Moses, designed to point out the way in which the duty they enjoined was then to be performed, are no longer in force. The fifth commandment still binds children to obey their parents; but the Jewish law giving fathers the power of life and death over their children, is no longer in force. The seventh commandment forbids adultery, but the ordeal enjoined for the trial of a woman suspected of that crime, is a thing of the past. The same principle applies to the interpretation of the fourth commandment. The command itself is still in force; the Mosaic

---

[1] The doctrine that the Jewish sabbath was simply a day of relaxation from labour, was advanced among Protestants towards the close of the seventeenth century, by Selden, in his work *De Legibus Hebræorum*. This opinion was adopted by Vitringa in the first book of his *Observationes Sacræ*. It is also advocated by Bähr in his *Symb. des Mos. Cultus*. The contrary doctrine was adopted by all the Reformers, and by the great body of Christian theologians; and is ably sustained by Hengstenberg in his treatise *Ueber den Tag des Herrn*, pp. 29–41. This subject is discussed in the January number of the *Princeton Review* for 1831, pp. 86–134.

laws respecting the mode of its observance have passed away with the economy to which they belonged. It is unjust therefore to represent the advocates of the continued obligation of the fourth commandment, as Judaizers. They are no more Judaizers than those who hold that the· other precepts of the decalogue are still in force.

There are two rules by which we are to be guided in determining how the Sabbath is to be observed, or in deciding what is, and what is not lawful on that holy day. The first is, the design of the commandment. What is consistent with that design is lawful ; what is inconsistent with it, is unlawful. The second rule is to be found in the precepts and example of our Lord and of his Apostles. The design of the command is to be learned from the words in which it is conveyed and from other parts of the word of God. From these sources it is plain that the design of the institution, as already remarked, was in the main twofold. First, to secure rest from all worldly cares and avocations ; to arrest for a time the current of the worldly life of men, not only lest their minds and bodies should be overworked, but also that opportunity should be afforded for other and higher interests to occupy their thoughts. And secondly, that God should be properly worshipped, his word duly studied and taught, and the soul brought under the influence of the things unseen and eternal. Any man who makes the design of the Sabbath as thus revealed in Scripture his rule of conduct on that day, can hardly fail in its due observance. The day is to be kept holy unto the Lord. In Scriptural usage to hallow or make holy is to set apart to the service of God. Thus the tabernacle, the temple, and all its utensils were made holy. In this sense the Sabbath is holy. It is to be devoted to the duties of religion, and what is inconsistent with such devotion, is contrary to the design of the institution.

It is however to be remembered that the specific object of the Christian Sabbath is the commemoration of the resurrection of Jesus Christ from the dead. All the exercises of the day, therefore, should have a special reference to Him and to his redeeming work. It is the day in which He is to be worshipped, thanked, and praised ; in which men are to be called upon to accept his offers of grace, and to rejoice in the hope of his salvation. It is therefore a day of joy. It is utterly incongruous to make it a day of gloom or fasting. In the early Church men were forbidden to pray on their knees on that day. They were to stand erect, exulting in the accomplishment of the work of God's redeeming love.

The second rule for our guidance is to be found in the precepts and example of our Lord. In the first place, He lays down the principle, " The Sabbath was made for man, and not man for the Sabbath." It is to be remarked that Christ says, "the Sabbath was made for man," not for the Jews, not for the people of any one age or nation, but for man ; for man as man, and therefore for all men. Moral duties, however, often conflict, and then the lower must yield to the higher. The life, the health, and the well-being of a man are higher ends in a given case, than the punctilious observance of any external service. This is the rule laid down by the prophet (Hosea vi. 6) : " I desired mercy, and not sacrifice ; and the knowledge of God more than burnt offering." This passage our Lord quotes twice in application to the law of the Sabbath, and thus establishes the general principle for our guidance, that it is right to do on the Sabbath whatever mercy or a due regard to the comfort or welfare of ourselves or others requires to be done. Christ, therefore, says expressly, " It is lawful to do well (καλῶς ποιεῖν, that is, as the context shows, to confer benefits) on the Sabbath days." (Matt. xii. 12. See also Mark iii. 4.)

Again, we are told by the same authority, that " the priests in the temple profane the Sabbath and are blameless." (Matt. xii. 5.) The services of the temple were complicated and laborious, and yet were lawful on the Sabbath. On another occasion He said to his accusers, " If a man on the Sabbath day receive circumcision, that the law of Moses should not be broken ; are ye angry at me, because I have made a man every whit whole on the Sabbath day ? Judge not according to the appearance, but judge righteous judgment." (John vii. 23, 24.) From this we learn that whatever is necessary for the due celebration of religious worship, or for attendance thereon, is lawful on the Sabbath.

Again in Luke xiv. 1–14, we read, " And it came to pass, as he went into the house of one of the chief Pharisees, to eat bread on the Sabbath day, that they watched him. And, behold, there was a certain man before him, which had the dropsy. And Jesus answering, spake unto the lawyers and Pharisees, saying, Is it lawful to heal on the Sabbath day ? And they held their peace. And he took him, and healed him, and let him go. . . . . And he put forth a parable to those which were bidden, when he marked how they chose out the chief rooms ; saying unto them," etc., etc. This was evidently a large entertainment to which guests were " bidden." Christ, therefore, thought right, in the prosecution of his work, to attend on such entertainments on the Sabbath.

The frequency with which our Lord was accused of Sabbath-breaking by the Pharisees, proves that his mode of observing that day was very different from theirs, and the way in which He vindicated himself proves that He regarded the Sabbath as a divine institution of perpetual obligation. It had been easy for Him to say that the law of the Sabbath was no longer in force; that He, as Lord of the Sabbath, erased it from the decalogue. It may indeed be said that as the whole of the Mosaic law was in force until the resurrection of Christ, or until the day of Pentecost, the observance of the Sabbath was as a matter of course then obligatory, and therefore that Christ so regarded it. In answer to this, however, it is obvious to remark, that Christ did not hesitate to abrogate those of the laws of Moses which were in conflict with the spirit of the Gospel. This He did with the laws relating to polygamy and divorce. Under the old dispensation it was lawful for a man to have more than one wife; and also to put away a wife by giving her a bill of divorcement. Both of these things Christ declared should not be allowed under the Gospel. The fact that He dealt with the Sabbath just as He did with the fifth, sixth, and seventh precepts of the decalogue, which the Pharisees had misinterpreted, shows that He regarded the fourth commandment as belonging to the same category as the others. His example affords us a safe guide as to the way in which the day is to be observed.

The Sunday Laws.

It is very common, especially for foreign-born citizens, to object to all laws made by the civil governments in this country to prevent the public violation of the Lord's Day. It is urged that as there is in the United States an entire separation of the Church and State, it is contrary to the genius of our institutions, that the observance of any religious institution should be enforced by civil laws. It is further objected that as all citizens have equal rights irrespective of their religious opinions, it is an infringement of those rights if one class of the people are required to conform their conduct to the religious opinions of another class. Why should Jews, Mohammedans, or infidels be required to respect the Christian Sabbath? Why should any man, who has no faith in the Sabbath as a divine institution, be prevented from doing on that day whatever is lawful on other days? If the State may require the people to respect Sunday as a day of rest, why may it not require the people to obey any or all other precepts of the Bible ?

State of the Question.

It is conceded, (1.) That in every free country every man has equal rights with his fellow-citizens, and stands on the same ground in the eye of the law. (2.) That in the United States no form of religion can be established ; that no religious test for the exercise of the elective franchise or for holding of office can be imposed ; and that no preference can be given to the members of one religious denomination above those of another. (3.) That no man can be forced to contribute to the support of any church, or of any religious institution. (4.) That every man is at liberty to regulate his conduct and life according to his convictions or conscience, provided he does not violate the law of the land.

On the other hand it is no less true, —

1. That a nation is not a mere conglomeration of individuals. It is an organized body. It has of necessity its national life, its national organs, national principles of action, national character, and national responsibility.

2. In every free country the government must, in its organization and mode of action, be an expression of the mind and will of the people.

3. As men are rational creatures, the government cannot banish all sense and reason from their action, because there may be idiots among the people.

4. As men are moral beings, it is impossible that the government should act as though there were no distinction between right and wrong. It cannot legalize theft and murder. No matter how much it might enrich itself by rapine or by the extermination of other nations, it would deserve and receive universal condemnation and execration, should it thus set at nought the bonds of moral obligation. This necessity of obedience to the moral law on the part of civil governments, does not arise from the fact that they are instituted for the protection of the lives, rights, and property of the people. Why have our own and other Christian nations pronounced the slave-trade piracy and punishable with death ? Not because it interferes with the rights or liberty of their citizens but because it is wicked. Cruelty to animals is visited with civil penalties, not on the principle of profit and loss, but because it is a violation of the moral law. As it is

impossible for the individual man to disregard all moral obligations, it is no less impossible on the part of civil governments.

5. Men moreover are religious beings. They can no more
ignore that element of their nature than their reason or their
conscience. It is no matter what they may say, or may pretend
to think, the law which binds them to allegiance to God, is just
as inexorable as the law of gravitation. They can no more
emancipate themselves from the one than they can from the other.
Morality concerns their duty to their fellow-men; religion concerns their duty to God. The latter binds the conscience as
much as the former. It attends the man everywhere. It must
influence his conduct as an individual, as the head of a family, as
a man of business, as a legislator, and as an executive officer.
It is absurd to say that civil governments have nothing to do
with religion. That is not true even of a fire company, or of a
manufactory, or of a banking-house. The religion embraced by
the individuals composing these associations must influence their
corporate action, as well as their individual conduct. If a man
may not blaspheme, a publishing firm may not print and dis-
seminate a blasphemous book. A civil government cannot ignore
religion any more than physiology. It was not constituted to
teach either the one or the other, but it must, by a like necessity,
conform its action to the laws of both. Indeed it would be far
safer for a government to pass an act violating the laws of health,
than one violating the religious convictions of its citizens. The
one would be unwise, the other would be tyrannical. Men put
up with folly, with more patience than they do with injustice.
It is vain for the potsherds of the earth to contend with their
Maker. They must submit to the laws of their nature not only
as sentient, but also as moral and religious beings. And it is
time that blatant atheists, whether communists, scientists, or philosophers, should know that they are as much and as justly the
objects of pity and contempt, as of indignation to all right-minded
men. By right-minded men, is meant men who think, feel, and
act according to the laws of their nature. Those laws are ordained, administered, and enforced by God, and there is no escape
from their obligation, or from the penalties attached to their
violation.

6. The people of this country being rational, moral, and religious beings, the government must be administered on the principles of reason, morality, and religion. By a like necessity of right,
the people being Christians and Protestants, the government

must be administered according to the principles of Protestant Christianity. By this is not meant that the government should teach Christianity, or make the profession of it a condition of citizenship, or a test for office. Nor does it mean that the government is called upon to punish every violation of Christian principle or precept. It is not called upon to punish every violation of the moral law. But as it cannot violate the moral law in its own action, or require the people to violate it, so neither can it ignore Christianity in its official action. It cannot require the people or any of its own officers to do what Christianity forbids, nor forbid their doing anything which Christianity enjoins. It has no more right to forbid that the Bible should be taught in the public schools, than it has to enjoin that the Koran should be taught in them. If Christianity requires that one day in seven should be a day of rest from all worldly avocations, the government of a Christian people cannot require any class of the community or its own officers to labour on that day, except in cases of necessity or mercy. Should it, on the ground that it had nothing to do with religion, disregard that day, and direct that the custom-houses, the courts of law, and the legislative halls should be open on the Lord's Day, and public business be transacted as on other days, it would be an act of tyranny, which would justify rebellion. It would be tantamount to enacting that no Christian should hold any office under the government, or have any share in making or administering the laws of the country. The nation would be in complete subjection to a handful of imported atheists and infidels.

Proof that this is a Christian and Protestant Nation.

The proposition that the United States of America are a Christian and Protestant nation, is not so much the assertion of a principle as the statement of a fact. That fact is not simply that the great majority of the people are Christians and Protestants, but that the organic life, the institutions, laws, and official action o. the government, whether that action be legislative, judicial, or ex ecutive, is, and of right should be, and in fact must be, in accord ance with the principles of Protestant Christianity.

1. This is a Christian and Protestant nation in the sense statec in virtue of a universal and necessary law. If you plant an acorn, you get an oak. If you plant a cedar, you get a cedar. Il a country be settled by Pagans or Mohammedans, it develops intc a Pagan or Mohammedan community. By the same law if a

country be taken possession of and settled by Protestant Christians, the nation which they come to constitute must be Protestant and Christian.   This country was settled by Protestants. For the first hundred years of our history they constituted almost the only element of our population.   As a matter of course they were governed by their religion as individuals, in their families, and in all their associations for business, and for municipal, state, and national government.   This was just as much a matter of necessity as that they should act morally in all these different relations.

2. It is a historical fact that Protestant Christianity is the law of the land, and has been from the beginning.   As the great majority of the early settlers of the country were from Great Britain, they declared that the common law of England should be the law here.   But Christianity is the basis of the common law of England, and is therefore of the law of this country; and so our courts have repeatedly decided.   It is so not merely because of such decisions.   Courts cannot reverse facts.   Protestant Christianity has been, is, and must be the law of the land,   Whatever Protestant Christianity forbids, the law of the land (within its sphere, *i. e.*, within the sphere in which civil authority may appropriately act) forbids.   Christianity forbids polygamy and arbitrary divorce, so does the civil law.   Romanism forbids divorce even on the ground of adultery ; Protestantism admits it on that ground.   The laws of all the states conform in this matter to the Protestant rule. Christianity forbids all unnecessary labour, or the transaction of worldly business, on the Lord's Day ; that day accordingly is a *dies non*, throughout the land.   No contract is binding, made on that day.   No debt can be collected on the Christian Sabbath.   If a man hires himself for any service by the month or year, he cannot be required to labour on that day.   All public offices are closed, and all official business is suspended.   From Maine to Georgia, from ocean to ocean, one day in the week, by the law of God and by the law of the land, the people rest.

This controlling Influence of Christianity is Reasonable and Right.

It is in accordance with analogy.   If a man goes to China, he expects to find the government administered according to the religion of the country   If he goes to Turkey, he expects to find the Koran supreme and regulating all public action.   If he goes to a Protestant country, he has no right to complain, should he find the Bible in the ascendancy and exerting its benign influence not only on the people, but also on the government.

The principle that the religion of a people rightfully controls the action of the government, has of course its limitation. If the religion itself be evil and require what is morally wrong, then as men cannot have the right to act wickedly, it is plain that it would be wrong for the government to conform to its requirements. If a religion should enjoin infanticide, or the murder of the aged or infirm, neither the people nor the government should conform their conduct to its laws. But where the religion of a people requires nothing unjust or cruel or in any way immoral, then those who come to live where it prevails are bound to submit quietly to its controlling the laws and institutions of the country.

The principle contended for is recognized in all other departments of life. If a number of Christian men associate themselves as a manufacturing or banking company, it would be competent for them to admit unbelievers in Christianity into their association, and to allow them their full share in its management and control. But it would be utterly unreasonable for such unbelievers to set up a cry of religious persecution, or of infringement of their rights and liberty, because all the business of the company was suspended upon the Lord's Day. These new members knew the character and principles of those with whom they sought to be associated. They knew that Christians would assert their right to act as Christians. To require them to renounce their religion would be simply preposterous.

When Protestant Christians came to this country they possessed and subdued the land. They worshipped God, and his Son Jesus Christ as the Saviour of the world, and acknowledged the Scriptures to be the rule of their faith and practice. They introduced their religion into their families, their schools, and their colleges. They abstained from all ordinary business on the Lord's Day, and devoted it to religion. They built churches, erected school-houses, and taught their children to read the Bible and to receive and obey it as the word of God. They formed themselves as Christians into municipal and state organizations. They acknowledged God in their legislative assemblies. They prescribed oaths to be taken in his name. They closed their courts, their places of business, their legislatures, and all places under the public control, on the Lord's Day. They declared Christianity to be part of the common law of the land. In the process of time thousands have come among us, who are neither Protestants nor Christians. Some are papists, some Jews, some infidels, and some atheists. All are welcomed; all are admitted to equal rights and privileges. All are

allowed to acquire property, and to vote in every election, made
eligible to all offices, and invested with equal influence in all public affairs.   All are allowed to worship as they please, or not to
worship at all, if they see fit.   No man is molested for his religion
or for his want of religion.   No man is required to profess any
form of faith, or to join any religious association.   More than this
cannot reasonably be demanded.   More, however, is demanded.
The infidel demands that the government should be conducted on
the principle that Christianity is false.   The atheist demands that
it should be conducted on the assumption that there is no God,
and the positivist on the principle that men are not free agents.
The sufficient answer to all this is, that it cannot possibly be
done.

The Demands of Infidels are Unjust.

The demands of those who require that religion, and especially
Christianity, should be ignored in our national, state, and municipal laws, are not only unreasonable, but they are in the highest degree unjust and tyrannical.   It is a condition of service in
connection with any railroad which is operated on Sundays, that
the employee be not a Christian.   If Christianity is not to control the action of our municipal, state, and general governments,
then if elections be ordered to be held on the Lord's Day, Christians cannot vote.   If all the business of the country is to go on,
on that as on other days, no Christian can hold office.   We
should thus have not a religious, but an anti-religious test-act.
Such is the free-thinker's idea of liberty.[1]   But still further, if
Christianity is not to control the laws of the country, then as
monogamy is a purely Christian institution, we can have no
laws against polygamy, arbitrary divorce, or " free love."   All
this must be yielded to the anti-Christian party ; and consistency
will demand that we yield to the atheists, the oath and the
decalogue ; and all the rights of citizenship must be confined to
blasphemers.   Since the fall of Lucifer, no such tyrant has been
made known to men as August Comte, the atheist.   If, therefore, any man wishes to antedate perdition, he has nothing to do
but to become a free-thinker and join in the shout, " Civil government has nothing to do with religion ; and religion has
nothing to do with civil government."

[1] A free-thinker is a man whose understanding is emancipated from his conscience.   It
is therefore natural for him to wish to see civil government emancipated from religion.

Conclusion.

We are bound, therefore, to insist upon the maintenance and faithful execution of the laws enacted for the protection of the Christian Sabbath. Christianity does not teach that men can be made religious by law; nor does it demand that men should be required by the civil authority to profess any particular form of religious doctrine, or to attend upon religious services; but it does enjoin that men should abstain from all unnecessary worldly avocations on the Lord's Day. This civil Sabbath, this cessation from worldly business, is what the civil government in Christian countries is called upon to enforce. (1.) Because it is the right of Christians to be allowed to rest on that day, which they cannot do, without forfeiting their citizenship, unless all public business be arrested on that day. (2.) Because such rest is the command of God; and this command binds the conscience as much as any other command in the decalogue. So far as the point in hand is concerned, it matters not whether such be the command of God or not; so long as the people believe it, it binds their conscience; and this conscientious belief the government is bound to respect, and must act accordingly. (3.) Because the civil Sabbath is necessary for the preservation of our free institutions, and of the good order of society. The indispensable condition of social order is either despotic power in the magistrate, or good morals among the people. Morality without religion is impossible; religion cannot exist without knowledge; knowledge cannot be disseminated among the people, unless there be a class of teachers, and time allotted for their instruction. Christ has made all his ministers, teachers; He has commanded them to teach all nations; He has appointed one day in seven to be set apart for such instruction. It is a historical fact that since the introduction of Christianity, nine tenths of the people have derived the greater part of their religious knowledge from the services of the sanctuary. If the Sabbath, therefore, be abolished, the fountain of life for the people will be sealed.[1]

Hengstenberg, after referring to the authority of the Church and other grounds, for the observance of the Lord's Day, closes

[1] *The Sabbath and Free Institutions.* A paper read before the National Sabbath Convention, Saratoga, August 13, 1863, by the Rev. Mark Hopkins, D. D., President of Williams College, Mass. See also an able article from the pen of the Rev. Joshua H. McIlvaine, D. D., entitled, " A Nation's Right to Worship God," in the *Princeton Review* for October, 1859; also the article on " Sunday Laws," in the same number of that journal.

his discussion of the subject with these words: " Thank God
these are only the outworks; the real fortress is the command
that sounded out from Sinai, with the other divine commands
therewith connected, as preparatory, confirmatory, or explanatory. The institution was far too important, and the temptations too powerful, that the solid ground of Scriptural command
could be dispensed with. . . . It is as plain as day that the
obligation of the Old Testament command instead of being lessened is increased. This follows of course from the fact that the
redemption through Christ is infinitely more glorious than the
deliverance of the Israelites out of Egypt, which in the preface
to the Ten Commandments is referred to as a special motive to
obedience. No ingratitude is blacker than refusing to obey Him
who for our sakes gave up his only begotten Son."[1] He had said
before that the Sabbath " rests on the unalterable necessities of
our nature, inasmuch as men inevitably become godless if the
cares and labours of their earthly life be not regularly interrupted."[2]

§ 9.   The Fifth Commandment.
Its Design.

The general principle of duty enjoined in this commandment,
is that we should feel and act in a becoming manner towards
our superiors. It matters not in what their superiority consists,
whether in age, office, power, knowledge, or excellence. There
are certain feelings, and a certain line of conduct due to those
who are over us, for that very reason, determined and modified
in each case by the degree and nature of that superiority. To
superiors are due, to each according to the relation in which he
stands to us, reverence, obedience, and gratitude. The ground
of this obligation is to be found, (1.) In the will of God, who has
enjoined this duty upon all rational creatures. (2.) In the
nature of the relation itself. Superiority supposes, in some form
or degree, on the part of the inferior, dependence and indebted-
ness, and therefore calls for reverence, gratitude, and obedience;
and, (3.) In expediency, as the moral order of the divine government and of human society depend upon this due submission to authority.

In the case of God, as his superiority is infinite the submission
of his creatures must be absolute. To Him we owe adoration
or the profoundest reverence, the most fervent gratitude, and

[1] *Ueber den Tag des Herrn,* Berlin, 1852, pp. 92–94.   [2] *Ibid.* p. 40.

implicit obedience. The fifth commandment, however, concerns our duty to our fellow-creatures. First in order and in impor tance is the duty of children to their parents, hence the general duty is embodied in the specific command, " Honour thy father and thy mother."

The Filial Relation.

When a child is born into the world it is entirely helpless and dependent. As it derives its existence from its parents, so it would immediately perish without their assiduous and constant care. The parents are not only its superiors in knowledge, in power, and in every other attribute of humanity ; but they are also the proximate source of all good to the child. They protect, cherish, feed, clothe, educate, and endow it. All the good bestowed, is bestowed disinterestedly. Self is constantly sacrificed. The love of parents to their children is mysterious and immutable, as well as self-sacrificing. It is a form of love which none but a parent can know. A mother's love is a mystery and a wonder. It is the most perfect analogue of the love of God.

As the relation in which parents stand to their children has this close analogy to the relation in which God stands to his rational creatures, and especially to his own people, so the duties resulting from that relation are analogous. They are expressed by the same word. Filial piety is as correct an expression as it is common. Parents stand to their dependent children, so to speak, in the place of God. They are the natural objects of the child's love, reverence, gratitude, confidence, and devotion. These are the sentiments which naturally flow out of the relation; and which in all ordinary cases do flow from it ; so that Calvin is justified in saying that children destitute of these feelings, " monstra sunt non homines." This endearing and intimate relation between parents and children (which cannot exist where monogamy is not the law), binding all in the closest union which can exist among men, makes the family the corner-stone of the well-being of society on earth, and the type of the blessedness of heaven. The Church is the family of God. He is the Father, its members are brethren.

While the relative duties of parents and children must be everywhere and always essentially the same, yet they are more or less modified by varying conditions of society. There are laws on this subject in the Bible, which being intended for the state of things existing before the coming of Christ, are no longer binding

upon us. It was unavoidable in the patriarchal state of society,
and especially in its nomadic state, that the father of a family
should be at once father, magistrate, and priest. And it was
natural and right that many of the parental prerogatives necessary in such a state of society, should be retained in the temporary and transition state organized under the Mosaic institutions.
We find accordingly that the laws of Moses invested parents
with powers which can no longer properly belong to them; and
sustained parental authority by penal enactments which are no
longer necessary. Thus it was ordered, "He that curseth (or
revileth, Septuagint ὁ κακολογῶν, Vulgate 'qui maledixerit') his
father or his mother shall surely be put to death." (Exod. xxi.
17.) In the fifteenth verse of the same chapter it is said, "He
that smiteth his father or his mother, shall be surely put to
death." (Compare Deut. xxvii. 16; Prov. xx. 20; Matt. xv. 4.)
It may be remarked here, in passing, that our Lord's comment on
this commandment given in Matthew xv. 4–6, shows that the
honouring of their parents required of children, does not mean
simply the cherishing right feelings towards them, but as well
the ministering to their support when necessary. Christ said to
the Pharisees, "God commanded, saying, Honour thy father and
mother; . . . . but ye say, Whosoever shall say to his father
or his mother, It is a gift (consecrated to God), by whatsoever
thou mightest be profited by me, and honour not his father or
his mother, he shall be free." That is, the Pharisees taught that
a son might evade the obligation to honour, i. e., to support his
father or mother, by saying that his property was consecrated to
God.

The Mosaic law also enacted that "If a man have a stubborn
and rebellious son, which will not obey the voice of his father, or
the voice of his mother, and that, when they have chastened him,
will not hearken unto them; then shall his father and his mother
lay hold on him, and bring him out unto the elders of his city,
and unto the gates of his place: and they shall say unto the elders
of his city, This our son is stubborn and rebellious; he will not
obey our voice; he is a glutton, and a drunkard. And all the
men of the city shall stone him with stones, that he die." (Deut.
xxi. 18–21.)

Fathers under the old economy had the right to choose wives
for their sons and to give their daughters in marriage. (Gen.
xxiv.; Ex. xxi. 9; Judges xiv. 2; Gen. xxix. 18; xxxiv. 12.)
Children also were liable to be sold to satisfy the debts of their

fathers. (Levit. xxv. 39–41 ; 2 Kings iv. 1 ; Is. l. 1 ; Matt.
xviii. 25.) These judicial enactments have passed away. They
serve to prove, however, how intimate in the sight of God is the
relation between parents and children. A father's benediction
was coveted as the greatest blessing ; and his curse deprecated
as a fearful evil. (Gen. xxvii. 4, 12, 34–38 ; xlix. 2 ff.)

In the New Testament the duty enjoined in the fifth commandment is frequently recognized and enforced. Our blessed
Lord himself was subject to his parents. (Luke ii. 51.) The
Apostle commands children to obey their parents in the Lord
(Eph. vi. 1), and to obey them in all things, for this is well pleasing unto the Lord. (Col. iii. 20.) This obedience is to be not
only religious, but specifically Christian, as the word Lord, in
Ephesians vi. 1, refers to Christ. This is plain because in ch. v. 21,
the Apostle says that these specific duties are to be performed
" in the fear of Christ ; " [1] because the Lord is always in the New
Testament to be understood of Christ, unless the context forbids ;
and because especially throughout these chapters Lord and Christ
are interchanged, so that it is evident that both words refer to
the same person. Children are required to obey their parents in
the Lord, *i. e.*, as a religious duty, as part of the obedience due
to the Lord. They are to obey them " in all things ; " *i. e.*, in
all things falling within the sphere of parental authority. God
has never committed unlimited power to the hands of men. The
limitations of parental authority are determined partly by the
nature of the relation, partly by the Scriptures, and partly by
the state of society or the law of the land. The nature of the
relation supposes that parents are to be obeyed as parents, out of
gratitude and love ; and that their will is to be consulted and respected even where their decisions are not final. They are not
to be obeyed as magistrates, as though they were invested with
the power to make or to administer civil laws ; nor yet as prophets or priests. They are not lords of the conscience. They cannot control our faith or determine for us questions of duty so as
to exonerate us from personal obligation. Being a service of love,
it does not admit of strictly defined boundaries. Children are to
conform to the wishes and to be controlled by the judgments of
their parents, in all cases where such submission does not conflict
with higher obligations.

---

[1] The common text indeed in Ephesians v. 21, has Θεοῦ, but the authority of the MSS.
is so decidedly in favour of Χριστοῦ that that reading is almost universally adopted by
editors and commentators.

The Scriptural rule is simple and comprehensive. It does not go into unnecessary details. It prescribes the general rule of obedience. The exceptions to that rule must be such as justify themselves to a divinely enlightened conscience, *i. e.*, a conscience enlightened by the Word and Spirit of God. The general principle given in the Bible in all such cases is, " It is right to obey God rather than man."

The Promise.

This commandment has a special promise attached to it. This promise has a theocratical form as it stands in the decalogue, " That thy days may be long upon the land which the LORD thy God giveth thee." The Apostle, in Ephesians vi. 3, by leaving out the last clause generalizes it, so that it applies to no one land or people, but to obedient children everywhere. The promise announces the general purpose of God and a general principle of his providential government. " The hand of the diligent maketh rich," that is the general rule, which is not invalidated if here and there a diligent man remains poor. It is well with obedient children ; they prosper in the world. Such is the fact, and such is the divine promise. The family being the corner-stone of social order and prosperity, it follows that those families are blessed in which God's plan and purpose are most fully carried out and realized.

Parental Duties.

As children are bound to honour and obey their parents, so parents have duties no less important in reference to their children. These duties are summarily expressed by the Apostle in Ephesians vi. 4, first in a negative, and then in a positive form. " Ye fathers provoke not your children to wrath." This is what they are not to do. They are not to excite the bad passions of their children by anger, severity, injustice, partiality, or any undue exercise of authority. This is a great evil. It is sowing tares instead of wheat in a fruitful soil. The positive part of parental duty is expressed by the comprehensive direction, " but bring them up in the nurture ($\pi a\iota\delta\epsilon i a$) and admonition ($\nu o\nu\theta\epsilon\sigma i a$) of the Lord." The former of these words is comprehensive, the latter specific. The one expresses the whole process of education or training ; the other the special duty of warning and correction. The " nurture and admonition " is to be Christian; that is, not only such as Christ approves and enjoins, but which is truly his.

i. e., that which He exercises by his word and Spirit through the
parent as his organ. "Christ is represented as exercising this
nurture and admonition, in so far as He by his Spirit influences
and controls the parent."[1] According to the Apostle, this religious or Christian element is essential in the education of the
young. Man has a religious as well as an intellectual nature.
To neglect the former would be as unreasonable as to neglect the
latter and make all education a matter of mere physical training.
We must act in accordance with facts. It is a fact that men
have a moral and religious nature. It is a fact that if their moral
and religious feelings are enlightened and properly developed, they
become upright, useful, and happy ; on the other hand, if these
elements of their nature are uncultivated or perverted, they become degraded, miserable, and wicked. It is a fact that this department of our nature as much needs right culture as the intellectual or the physical. It is a fact that this culture can be
effected only by the truth instilled into the mind and impressed
upon the conscience. It is a fact that this truth, as all Christians
believe, is contained in the Holy Scriptures. It is a fact, according to the Scriptures, that the eternal Son of God is the only
Saviour of men, and that it is by faith in Him and by obedience
to Him, men are delivered from the dominion of sin ; and therefore it is a fact that unless children are brought up in the nurture
and admonition of the Lord, they, and the society which they constitute or control, will go to destruction. Consequently, when
a state resolves that religious instruction shall be banished from
the schools and other literary institutions, it virtually resolves on
self-destruction. It may indeed be said that such a resolution
does not imply that religious education is to be neglected. It
simply declares that it is not a function of the state, that it is a
duty which belongs to the family and to the Church. This is
plausible, but it is fallacious.

1. All the education received by a large portion of the people
of any country, is received in its primary schools. If that be irreligious (in the negative sense, if in this case there be such a
sense), their whole training is irreligious.

2. It is to be remembered that the Christian people of a country are the Church of that country. The Christians of Antioch
were the Church of Antioch, and the Christians of Rome were the
Church of Rome. In like manner the Christians in the United
States are the Church in the United States. As therefore the

---

[1] Meyer, Commentary *in loco.*

schools belong to the people, as they are their organs for the
education of their children ; if the people be Christians, the schools
of right must be Christian.   Any law which declares that they
shall not be so, is tyrannical.   It may be said that the law does
not forbid Christians having religious schools, it only says that
such schools shall not be supported by the public money.   But
the people are the public ; and if the people be Christians, Christians are the public.   The meaning of such a law, therefore,
really is, that Christians shall not use their own money for the
support of their own schools.

3. If Christian men therefore constitute a nation, a state, a
county, a town, or a village, they have the right, with which no
civil power can justly interfere, of having Christian schools.   If
any who are not Christians choose to frequent such schools, they
should not be required to attend upon the religious instruction.
They can derive all the benefit they seek, although they omit
attendance on what is designed for the children of Christian
parents.

4. It is true that Church and State are not united in this country as they ever have been in Europe.   It is conceded that this
separation is wise.   But it is not to be inferred from that concession that the state has nothing to do with religion ; that it must
act as though there were no Christ and no God.   It has already
been remarked that this is as impossible as it would be for the
state to ignore the moral law.   It may be admitted that Church
and State are, in this country, as distinct as the Church and a
banking company.   But a banking company, if composed of
Christians, must conduct its business according to Christian principles, so far as those principles apply to banking operations.   So
a nation, or a state, composed of Christians, must be governed by
Christianity, so far as its spirit and precepts apply to matters of
civil government.   If therefore the state assumes that the education of the people is one of its functions, it is bound in a
Christian country, — a country in which ninety hundredths of the
population consist of Christians,— to conduct the schools on Christian principles, otherwise it tramples on the most sacred rights of
the people.   This the people never will submit to, until they lose
all interest in their religion.   No one doubts that the Bible does
require that education should be religiously conducted.   " These
words which I command thee this day, shall be in thine heart:
and thou shalt teach them diligently unto thy children, and shalt
talk of them when thou sittest in thine house, and when thou walk-

est by the way, and when thou liest down, and when thou risest up." (Deut. vi. 6, 7. and xi. 19.) "He established a testimony in Jacob, and appointed a law in Israel, which he commanded our fathers, that they should make them known to their children; that the generation to come might know them, even the children which should be born, who should arise and declare them to their children; that they might set their hope in God, and not forget the works of God, but keep his commandments." (Ps. lxxviii. 5, 6, 7.) "Train up a child in the way he should go; and when he is old he will not depart from it." (Prov. xxii. 6.) Fathers bring up your children "in the nurture and admonition of the Lord." (Eph. vi. 4.) These are not ceremonial or obsolete laws. They bind the consciences of men just as much as the command, "Thou shalt not steal." If parents themselves conduct the education of their children, these are the principles upon which it must be conducted. If they commit that work to teachers, they are bound, by the law of God, to see that the teachers regard these divine prescriptions; if they commit the work to the state, they are under equally sacred obligation to see that the state does not violate them. This is an obligation which they cannot escape.

5. When the Sunday laws were under discussion, on a previous page, it was urged that it would be unreasonable and unjust for a man who joined a business association of moral men, to insist that the affairs of the association should be conducted on immoral principles; if he joined a company of Christian manufacturers, it would be unjust for him to require that they should violate the laws of Christianity. So if a Christian should go to Turkey, it would be preposterous for him to insist that the Koran should be banished from the public schools. No less preposterous is it for any man to demand that Christians in this country should renounce their religion. Christianity requires that education in all its departments should be conducted religiously. If any set of men should found a school or a university from which all religious instruction should be banished, the law of the land would doubtless permit them to do so. But for the law to forbid that the religion of the people should be taught in schools sustained by the money of the people, ought not to be submitted to.

6. The banishment of religious influence from our schools is impossible. If a man is not religious, he is irreligious; if he is not a believer, he is an unbeliever. This is as true of organizations and institutions, as it is of individuals. Byron uttered a

profound truth when he put into the mouth of Satan the words "He that does not bow to God, has bowed to me." If you banish light, you are in darkness. If you banish Christianity from the schools, you thereby render them infidel. If a child is brought up in ignorance of God, he becomes an atheist. If never taught the moral law, his moral nature is as undeveloped as that of a pagan. This controversy, therefore, is a controversy between Christianity and infidelity; between light and darkness; between Christ and Belial.[1]

It is admitted that this subject is encumbered with practical difficulties where the people of a country differ widely in their religious convictions. In such cases it would be far better to refer the matter to the people of each school district, than by a general law to prohibit all religious instruction from the public schools. This would, in fact, be to make them infidel, in deference to a numerically insignificant minority of the people. It is constantly said that the state, if it provides for anything more than secular education, is travelling out of its sphere ; that civil government is no more organized to teach religion than a fire company is. This latter assertion may be admitted so far as this, — that the same rule applies to both cases. That is, all individual men, and all associations of men, are bound to act according to the principles of morality and religion, so far as those principles are applicable to the work which they have to do. Men cannot lawfully cheat in banking, nor can they rightfully conduct their business on the Lord's Day. In like manner if God requires that education should be conducted religiously, the state has no more right to banish religion from its schools, than it has to violate the moral law. The whole thing comes to this : Christians are bound by the express command of God, as well as by a regard to the salvation of their children and to the best interests of society, to see to it that their children are brought up " in the nurture and admonition of the Lord ; " this they are bound to do ; through the state if they can ; without it, if they must.

Obedience due to Civil Magistrates.

If the fifth commandment enjoins as a general principle, respect and obedience to our superiors, it includes our obligations

---

[1] So little is this matter understood, that one of the most respectable and influential journals in the land, recently announced the fact that one of the cantons of Switzerland had prohibited all religious instruction in the schools, as a proof that "the world was getting tired of sacerdotalism." Thus religion is reduced to sacerdotalism or priestcraft.

to civil rulers; we are commanded to " Submit ourselves to
every ordinance of man for the Lord's sake: whether it be to
the king as supreme; or unto governors, as unto them that are
sent by him for the punishment of evil doers, and for the praise
of them that do well. For so is the will of God." (1 Peter ii.
13–15.) The whole theory of civil government and the duty of
citizens to their rulers, are comprehensively stated by the Apostle in Romans xiii. 1–5. It is there taught, (1.) That all
authority is of God. (2.) That civil magistrates are ordained of
God. (3.) That resistance to them, is resistance to Him; they
are ministers exercising his authority among men. (4.) That
obedience to them must be rendered as a matter of conscience,
as a part of our obedience to God.

From this it appears, — First, that civil government is a divine
ordinance. It is not merely an optional human institution;
something which men are free to have or not to have, as they
see fit. It is not founded on any social compact; it is something
which God commands. The Bible, however, does not teach that
there is any one form of civil government which is always and
everywhere obligatory. The form of government is determined
by the providence of God and the will of the people. It changes
as the state of society changes. Much less is it implied in the
proposition that government is a divine institution, that God
designates the persons who are to exercise the various functions
of the government; or the mode of their appointment; or the
extent of their powers.

Secondly, it is included in the Apostle's doctrine, that magistrates derive their authority from God; they are his ministers;
they represent Him. In a certain sense they represent the people, as they may be chosen by them to be the depositaries of
this divinely delegated authority; but the powers that be are
ordained by God; it is his will that they should be, and that
they should be clothed with authority.

Thirdly, from this it follows that obedience to magistrates and
to the laws of the land, is a religious duty. We are to submit
to " every ordinance of man," for the Lord's sake, out of our
regard to Him, as St. Peter expresses it; or for " conscience
sake," as the same idea is expressed by St. Paul. We are
bound to obey magistrates not merely because we have promised
to do so; or because we have appointed them; or because they
are wise or good; but because such is the will of God. In like
manner the laws of the land are to be observed, not because we

approve of them, but because God has enjoined such obedience. This is a matter of great importance; it is the only stable foundation of civil government and of social order. There is a great difference between obedience to men and obedience to God; between lying to men and lying to God, and between resistance to men and resistance to God. This principle runs through the Bible, which teaches that all authority is of God, and therefore all obedience to those in authority is part of our obedience to God. This applies not only to the case of citizens and rulers, but also to parents and children, husbands and wives, and even masters and slaves. In all these relations we are to act not as the servants of men, but as the servants of God. This gives to authority by whomsoever exercised a divine sanction; it gives it power over the conscience; and it elevates even menial service into an element of the glorious liberty of the sons of God. No man can have a servile spirit who serves God in rendering obedience to men. None but a law-abiding people can be free or prosperous; and no people can be permanently law-abiding who do not truly believe that " the powers that be are ordained of God. " Whosoever, therefore, resisteth the power (those in authority), resisteth the ordinance of God: and they that resist shall receive to themselves damnation ($\kappa\rho\hat{\iota}\mu\alpha$)." That is, God will punish them.

Fourthly, another principle included in the Apostle's doctrine is, that obedience is due to every *de facto* government, whatever its origin or character. His directions were written under the reign of Nero, and enjoined obedience to him. The early Christians were not called to examine the credentials of their actual rulers, every time the prætorian guard chose to depose one emperor and install another. The people of England were not free from their obligation to William and Mary when once established on the throne, because they might think that James II. was entitled to the crown. We are to obey " the powers that be." They are in authority by the will of God, which is revealed by facts, as clearly as by words. It is by Him that " kings reign and princes decree justice." " He raiseth up one, and putteth down another."

Fifthly, the Scriptures clearly teach that no human authority is intended to be unlimited. Such limitation may not be expressed, but it is always implied. The command " Thou shalt not kill," is unlimited in form, yet the Scriptures recognize that homicide may in some cases be not only justifiable but obligatory. The principles which limit the authority of civil government and of its agents are simple and obvious. The first is that governments and magistrates have authority only within their legitimate spheres. As civil government is instituted for the protection of life and property, for the preservation of order, for the punishment of evil doers, and for the praise of those who do well, it has to do only with the conduct, or external acts of men. It cannot concern itself with their opinions, whether scientific, philosophical, or religious. An act of Parliament or of Congress, that Englishmen or Americans should be materialists or idealists, would be an absurdity and a nullity. The magistrate cannot enter our families and assume parental authority, or our churches and teach as a minister. A justice of the peace cannot assume the prerogatives of a governor of a state or of a president of the United States. Out of his legitimate sphere a magistrate ceases to be a magistrate. A second limitation is no less plain. No human authority can make it obligatory on a man to disobey God. If all power is from God, it cannot be legitimate when used against God. This is self-evident. The Apostles when forbidden to preach the Gospel, refused to obey. When Daniel refused to bow down to the image which Nebuchadnezzar had made ; when the early Christians refused to worship idols ; and when the Protestant martyrs refused to profess the errors of the Romish Church, they all commended themselves to God, and secured the reverence of all good men. On this point there can be no dispute. It is important that this principle should be not only recognized, but also publicly avowed. The sanctity of law, and the stability of human governments, depend on the sanction of God. Unless they repose on Him, they rest on nothing. They have his sanction only when they act according to his will; that is in accordance with the design of their appointment and in harmony with the moral law.

Sixthly, another general principle is that the question, When the civil government may be, and ought to be disobeyed, is one which every man must decide for himself. It is a matter of private judgment. Every man must answer for himself to God, and therefore, every man must judge for himself, whether a given act is sinful or not. Daniel judged for himself. So did Shadrach, Meshech, and Abednego. So did the Apostles, and so did the martyrs.

An unconstitutional law or commandment is a nullity ; no man sins in disregarding it. He disobeys, however, at his peril. If his judgment is right, he is free. If it be wrong, in the view of the proper tribunal, he must suffer the penalty. There is an obvious distinction to be made between disobedience and resistance.

A man is bound to disobey a law, or a command, which requires him to sin, but it does not follow that he is at liberty to resist its execution. The Apostles refused to obey the Jewish authorities; but they submitted to the penalty inflicted. So the Christian martyrs disobeyed the laws requiring them to worship idols, but they made no resistance to the execution of the law. The Quakers disobey the law requiring military service, but quietly submit to the penalty. This is obviously right. The right of resistance is in the community. It is the right of revolution, which God sanctions, and which good men in past ages have exercised to the salvation of civil and religious liberty. When a government fails to answer the purpose for which God ordained it, the people have a right to change it. A father, if he shamefully abuses his power, may rightfully be deprived of authority over his children.[1]

Obedience to the Church.

The Apostle commands Christians "Obey them that have the rule over you, and submit yourselves : for they watch for your souls." "Remember them which have the rule over you, who have spoken unto you the word of God." (Heb. xiii. 17, 7.) Our Lord said to his disciples, that if an offending brother resisted other means to bring him to repentance, his offence must be told to the Church ; and that if he neglected to hear the Church, he was to be regarded as a heathen man and a publican. (Matt. xviii. 17.)

The principles which regulate our obedience to the Church, are very much the same as those which concern our relation to the State, —

1. The visible Church is a divine institution. In one sense indeed it is a voluntary society, in so far as that no man can be coerced to join it. If he joins it at all, it must be of his own free will. Nevertheless it is the will of God that the visible Church as an organized body should exist ; and every man who hears the Gospel, is bound to enroll himself among its members and to submit to its authority.

2. All Church power is of God, and all legitimate Church officers are his ministers. They act in his name and by his authority. Resistance to them, therefore, is resistance to the ordinance of God.

---

[1] All these subjects are fully expounded in the great works on Jurisprudence and Civil Polity. For a popular discussion of them, reference may be made to, *Discussions of Church Principles.* By William Cunningham, D. D., Principal of New College, Edinburgh. Edinburgh: T. and T. Clark, 1863, particularly chapters vi. and vii. See also the *Princeton Review* for January, 1851, article "Civil Government."

3. All the prerogatives of the Church and all the powers of its officers are laid down in the word of God.

4. The prerogatives of the Church are, first, to teach. Its great commission is to teach all nations. It is to teach what God has revealed in his word as to what men are to believe and what they are to do. Beyond the limits of the revelation contained in the Scriptures the Church has no more authority to teach than any other association among men. Secondly, the Church has the right and duty to order and conduct public worship, to administer the sacraments, to select and ordain its own officers, and to do whatever else is necessary for its own perpetuity and extension. Thirdly, it is the prerogative of the Church to exercise discipline over its own members, and to receive or to reject them as the case may be.

5. As to the external organization of the Church all Christians agree that there are certain rules laid down in the word of God which are of universal and perpetual obligation. All Christian churches, however, have acted on the assumption, that beyond these prescribed rules, the Church has a certain discretion to modify its organization and its organs to suit varying emergencies.

6. The visible Church being organized for a definite purpose, its power being derived from God, and its prerogatives being all laid down in the Scriptures, it follows not only that its powers are limited within the bounds thus prescribed, but also that the question, whether its decisions and injunctions are to be obeyed, is to be determined by every one concerned, on his own responsibility. If the decision is within the limits to which God has confined the action of the Church, and in accordance with the Scriptures, it is to be obeyed. If it transcends those limits, or is contrary to the word of God, it is to be disregarded. If therefore the Church through any of its organs should assume to decide questions of pure science, or of political economy, or of civil law, such decisions would amount to nothing. Or, if it should declare that to be true which the Scriptures pronounce to be false; or that to be false which the Scriptures declare to be true, such judgment would bind no man's conscience. And in like manner, should the Church declare any thing to be sinful which the word of God teaches to be right or indifferent; or that to be right and obligatory which that word pronounces to be evil, then again its teaching is void of all authority. All this is included in the principle that we must obey God rather than man; and that as to when obedience to man conflicts with our allegiance to God, every man

from the nature of the case must judge for himself. No man can estimate the importance of these simple principles. It was by disregarding them that the Church came gradually to deny the right of private judgment; to subordinate the Scriptures to its decisions; and to put itself in the place of God. In this way it has imposed unscriptural doctrines upon the faith of men; made multitudes of things to be obligatory which God never enjoined; and declared the greatest sins, such as treason, persecution, and massacre to be Christian duties.

While, therefore, the duty of obedience to our superiors, and submission to law, as enjoined in the fifth commandment, is the source of all order in the family, the Church, and the State; the limitation of this duty by our higher obligation to God, is the foundation of all civil and religious liberty.

§ 10. *The Sixth Commandment.*
Its Design.

This commandment, as expounded by our Lord (Matt. v. 21, 22), forbids malice in all its degrees and in all its manifestations. The Bible recognizes the distinction between anger and malice. The former is on due occasion allowable; the other is in its nature, and therefore always, evil. The one is a natural or constitutional emotion arising out of the experience or perception of wrong, and includes not only disapprobation but also indignation, and a desire in some way to redress or punish the wrong inflicted. The other includes hatred and the desire to inflict evil to gratify that evil passion. Our Lord is said to have been angry; but in Him there was no malice or resentment. He was the Lamb of God; when He was reviled, He reviled not again; when He suffered, He threatened not; He prayed for his enemies even on the cross.

In the several commandments of the decalogue, the highest manifestation of any evil is selected for prohibition, with the intention of including all lesser forms of the same evil. In forbidding murder, all degrees and manifestations of malicious feeling are forbidden. The Bible assigns special value to the life of man, first, because he was created in the image of God. He is not only like God in the essential elements of his nature, but he is also God's representative on earth. An indignity or injury inflicted on him, is an act of irreverence toward God. And secondly, all men are brethren. They are of one blood; children of a common father. On these grounds we are bound to love and respect all men as men; and to do all we can not only to protect

their lives but also to promote their well-being. Murder, therefore, is the highest crime which a man can commit against a fellow-man.

Capital Punishment.

As the sixth commandment forbids malicious homicide, it is
plain that the infliction of capital punishment is not included in
the prohibition. Such punishment is not inflicted to gratify revenge, but to satisfy justice and for the preservation of society.
As these are legitimate and most important ends, it follows that
the capital punishment of murder is also legitimate. Such punishment, in the case of murder, is not only lawful, but also obligatory.

1. Because it is expressly declared in the Bible, " Whoso
sheddeth man's blood, by man shall his blood be shed : for in
the image of God made he man." (Gen. ix. 6.) That this is of
perpetual obligation is clear, because it was given to Noah, the
second head of the human race. It was, therefore, not intended
for any particular age or nation. It is the announcement of
a general principle of justice ; a revelation of the will of God.
Moreover the reason assigned for the law is a permanent reason.
Man was created in the image of God ; and, therefore, whoso
sheds his blood, by man shall his blood be shed. This reason has
as much force at one time or place as at any other. Rosenmüller's
comment on this clause is, " Cum homo ad Dei imaginem sit factus,
æquum est, ut, qui Dei imaginem violavit et destruxit, occidatur,
cum Dei imagini injuriam faciens, ipsum Deum, illius auctorem,
petierit." [1] This is a very solemn consideration, and one of wide
application. It applies not only to murder and other injuries inflicted on the persons of men, but also to anything which tends to
degrade or to defile them. The Apostle applies it even to evil
words, or the suggestion of corrupt thoughts. If it is an outrage
to defile the statue or portrait of a great and good man, or of a
father or mother, how much greater is the outrage when we defile
the imperishable image of God impressed on the immortal soul
of man. We find the injunction, that the murderer should surely be put to death, repeated over and over in the Mosaic law.
(Ex. xxi. 12, 14; Lev. xxiv. 17 ; Num. xxxv. 21 ; Deut. xix.
11, 13.)

There are clear recognitions in the New Testament of the continued obligation of the divine law that murder should be punished with death. In Romans xiii. 4, the Apostle says that the

[1] *Scholia in Vetus Testamentum*, Leipzig, 1795.

magistrate "beareth not the sword in vain." The sword was worn as the symbol of the power of capital punishment. Even by profane writers, says Meyer, " bearing the sword " by a magistrate was the emblem of the power over life and death. The same Apostle said (Acts xxv. 11): " If I be an offender, or have committed anything worthy of death, I refuse not to die; " which clearly implies that, in his judgment, there were offences, for which the appropriate penalty is death.

2. Besides these arguments from Scripture, there are others drawn from natural justice. It is a dictate of our moral nature that crime should be punished ; that there should be a just proportion between the offence and the penalty ; and that death, the highest penalty, was the proper punishment for the greatest of all crimes. That such is the instinctive judgment of men is proved by the difficulty often experienced in restraining the people from taking summary vengeance in cases of atrocious murder. So strong is this sentiment that a species of wild justice is sure to step in to supply the place of judicial remissness. Such justice, from being lawless and impulsive, is too often misguided and erroneous, and, in a settled state of society, is always criminal. It being the nature of men, that if the regular, lawful infliction of death as a judicial penalty be abolished, it will be inflicted by the avenger of blood, or by tumultuous assemblies of the people, society has to choose between securing to the homicide a fair trial by the constituted authorities, and giving him up to the blind spirit of revenge.

3. Experience teaches that where human life is undervalued, it is insecure ; that where the murderer escapes with impunity or is inadequately punished, homicides are fearfully multiplied. The practical question, therefore, is, Who is to die ? the innocent man or the murderer ?

Homicide in Self-Defence.

That homicide in self-defence is not forbidden by the sixth commandment, is plain, (1.) Because such homicide is not malicious, and, therefore, does not come within the scope of the prohibition. (2.) Because self-preservation is an instinct of our nature, and therefore, a revelation of the will of God. (3.) Because it is a dictate of reason and of natural justice that if of two persons one must die, it should be the aggressor and not the aggrieved. (4.) Because the universal judgment of men, and the Word of God, pronounce the man innocent who kills another in defence of his own life or that of his neighbor.

War.

It is conceded that war is one of the most dreadful evils that can be inflicted on a people ; that it involves the destruction of property and life ; that it demoralizes both the victors and the vanquished ; that it visits thousands of non-combatants with all the miseries of poverty, widowhood, and orphanage ; and that it tends to arrest the progress of society in everything that is good and desirable. God overrules wars in many cases, as He does the tornado and the earthquake, to the accomplishment of his benevolent purposes, but this does not prove that war in itself is not a great evil. He makes the wrath of man to praise Him. It is conceded that wars undertaken to gratify the ambition, cupidity, or resentment of rulers or people, are unchristian and wicked. It is also conceded that the vast majority of the wars which have desolated the world have been unjustifiable in the sight of God and man. Nevertheless it does not follow from this that war in all cases is to be condemned.

1. This is proved because the right of self-defence belongs to nations as well as to individuals. Nations are bound to protect the lives and property of their citizens. If these are assailed by force, force may be rightfully used in their protection. Nations also have the right to defend their own existence. If that be endangered by the conduct of other nations, they have the natural right of self-protection. A war may be defensive and yet in one sense aggressive. In other words, self-defence may dictate and render necessary the first assault. A man is not bound to wait until a murderer actually strikes his blow. It is enough that he sees undeniable manifestations of a hostile purpose. So a nation is not bound to wait until its territories are actually invaded and its citizens murdered, before it appeals to arms. It is enough that there is clear evidence on the part of another nation of an intention to commence hostilities. While it is easy to lay down the principle that war is justifiable only as a means of self-defence, the practical application of this principle is beset with difficulties. The least aggression on national property, or the slightest infringement of national rights, may be regarded as the first step toward national extinction, and therefore justify the most extreme measures of redress. A nation may think that a certain enlargement of territory is necessary to its security, and, therefore, that it has the right to go to war to secure it. So a man may say that a portion of his neighbour's farm is necessary to the full en-

joyment of his own property, and therefore that he has the right
to appropriate it to himself. It is to be remembered that nations
are as much bound by the moral law as individual men ; and
therefore that what a man may not do in the protection of his
own rights, and on the plea of self-defence, a nation may not do.
A nation therefore is bound to exercise great forbearance, and to
adopt every other available means of redressing wrongs, before it
plunges itself and others into all the demoralizing miseries of war.

2. The lawfulness of defensive war, however, does not rest exclusively on these general principles of justice ; it is distinctly
recognized in Scripture. In numerous cases, under the Old Testament, such wars were commanded. God endowed men with
special qualifications as warriors. He answered when consulted
through the Urim and Thummim, or by the prophets, as to the
propriety of military enterprises (Judges xx. 27 f., 1 Sam.
xiv. 37, xxiii. 2, 4 ; 1 Kings xxii. 6 ff.) ; and He often interfered
miraculously in behalf of his people when they were engaged in
battle. Many of the Psalms of David, dictated by the Spirit,
are either prayers for divine assistance in war or thanksgivings
for victory. It is very plain, therefore, that the God whom the
patriarchs and prophets worshipped did not condemn war, when
the choice was between war and annihilation. It is a very clear
case that if the Israelites had not been allowed to defend themselves against their heathen neighbours they would have soon been
extirpated, and their religion would have perished with them.

As the essential principles of morals do not change, what was
permitted or commanded under one dispensation, cannot be
unlawful under another, unless forbidden by a new revelation.
The New Testament, however, contains no such revelation. It
does not say, as in the case of divorce, that war was permitted
to the Hebrews because of the hardness of their hearts, but that
under the Gospel a new law was to prevail. This very silence
of the New Testament leaves the Old Testament rule of duty
on this subject still in force. Accordingly, although there is
no express declaration on the subject, as none was needed, we
find the lawfulness of war quietly assumed. When the soldiers
inquired of John the Baptist what they should do to prepare for
the kingdom of God, he did not tell them that they must forsake
the profession of arms. The centurion, whose faith our Lord so
highly commended (Matt. viii. 5–13), was not censured for
being a soldier. So also the centurion, a devout man, whom
God in a vision commanded to send for Peter, and on whom,

and his associates, according to the record in the tenth chapter of Acts, the Holy Ghost came with miraculous gifts, was allowed to remain in the army of even a heathen emperor. If magistrates, as we learn from the thirteenth chapter of Romans, are armed with a right or power of life and death over their own citizens, they certainly have the right to declare war in self-defence.

In the early ages of the Church there was a great disinclination to engage in military service, and the fathers at times justified this reluctance by calling the lawfulness of all wars into question. But the real sources of this opposition of Christians to entering the army, were that they thereby gave themselves up to the service of a power which persecuted their religion ; and that idolatrous usages were inseparably connected with military duties. When the Roman empire became Christian, and the cross was substituted for the eagle on the standards of the army, this opposition died away, till at length we hear of fighting prelates, and of military orders of monks.

No historical Christian Church has pronounced all war to be unlawful. The Augsburg Confession [1] expressly says that it is proper for Christians to act as magistrates, and among other things "jure bellare, militare," etc. And Presbyterians especially have shown that it is not against their consciences to contend to the death for their rights and liberties.

Suicide.

It is conceivable that men who do not believe in God or in a future state of existence, should think it allowable to take refuge in annihilation from the miseries of this life. But it is unaccountable, except on the assumption of temporary or permanent insanity, that any man should rush uncalled into the retributions of eternity. Suicide, therefore, is most frequent among those who have lost all faith in religion.[2] It is a very complicated crime ; our life is not our own ; we have no more right to destroy our life than we have to destroy the life of a fellow-man. Suicide is, therefore, self murder. It is the desertion of the post which God has assigned us ; it is a deliberate refusal to submit to his will ; it is a crime which admits of no repentance, and consequently involves the loss of the soul.

---

[1] I. xvi. 2; Hase, *Libri Symbolici*, 3d edit. p. 14.

[2] It is estimated that one death out of 175 in London is suicide; in New York, one in 172; in Vienna, one in 160; in Paris, one in 72.

Duelling.

Duelling is another violation of the sixth commandment. Its advocates defend it on the same principle on which international war is defended. As independent nations have no common tribunal to which they can resort for the redress of injuries, they are justifiable, on the principle of self-defence, in appealing to arms for the protection of their rights. In like manner, it is said, there are offences for which the law of the land affords no redress, and therefore, the individual must be allowed to seek redress for himself. But (1.) There is no evil for which the law does not, or should not, afford redress. (2.) The redress sought in the duel is unjustifiable. No one has the right to kill a man for a slight or an insult. Taking a man's life for a hasty word, or even for a serious injury, is murder in the sight of God, who has ordained the penalty of death as the punishment for only the most atrocious crimes. (3.) The remedy is preposterous; for most frequently it is the aggrieved party who loses his life. (4.) Duelling is the cause of the greatest suffering to innocent parties, which no man has a right to inflict to gratify his pride or resentment. (5.) The survivor in a fatal duel entails on himself, unless his heart and conscience be seared, a life of misery.

§ 11. *The Seventh Commandment.*

This commandment, as we learn from our Lord's exposition of it, given in his sermon on the mount, forbids all impurity in thought, speech, and behaviour. As the social organization of society is founded on the distinction of the sexes, and as the well-being of the state and the purity and prosperity of the Church rest on the sanctity of the family relation, it is of the last importance that the normal, or divinely constituted relation of the sexes be preserved in its integrity.

Celibacy.

Among the important questions to be considered under the head of this commandment, the first is, Whether the Bible teaches that there is any special virtue in a life of celibacy? This is really a question, whether there was an error in the creation of man.

1. The very fact that God created man, male and female, declaring that it was not good for either to be alone, and constituted marriage in paradise, should be decisive on this subject. The

doctrine which degrades marriage by making it a less holy state, has its foundation in Manicheeism or Gnosticism. It assumes that evil is essentially connected with matter; that sin has its seat and source in the body; that holiness is attainable only through asceticism and "neglecting of the body;" that because the "vita angelica" is a higher form of life than that of men here on earth, therefore marriage is a degradation. The doctrine of the Romish Church on this subject, therefore, is thoroughly anti-Christian. It rests on principles derived from the philosophy of the heathen. It presupposes that God is not the author of matter; and that He did not make man pure, when He invested him with a body.

2. Throughout the Old Testament Scriptures marriage is represented as the normal state of man. The command to our first parents before the fall was, " Be fruitful, and multiply, and replenish the earth." Without marriage the purpose of God in regard to our world could not be carried out; it is, therefore, contradictory to the Scriptures to assume that marriage is less holy, or less acceptable to God than celibacy. To be unmarried, was regarded under the old dispensation as a calamity and a disgrace. (Judges xi. 37 ; Ps. lxxviii. 63; Is. iv. 1; xiii. 12.) The highest earthly destiny of a woman, according to the Old Testament Scriptures, which are the word of God, was not to be a nun, but to be the mistress of a family, and a mother of children. (Gen. xxx. 1 ; Ps. cxiii. 9 ; cxxvii. 3 ; cxxviii. 3, 4 ; Prov. xviii. 22 ; xxxi. 10, 28.)

3. The same high estimate of marriage, characterizes the teachings of the New Testament. Marriage is declared to be "honourable in all." (Heb. xiii. 4.) Paul says, " Let every man have his own wife, and let every woman have her own husband." (1 Cor. vii. 2.) In 1 Timothy v. 14, he says : "I will, that the younger women marry." In 1 Timothy iv. 3, "forbidding to marry " is included among the doctrines of devils. As the truth comes from the Holy Spirit, so false doctrines, according to the Apostle's mode of thinking, come from Satan, and his agents, the demons ; they are " the seducing spirits " spoken of in the same verse.[1] Our Lord more than once (Matt. xix. 5 ; Mark x. 7)

---

[1] Calvin in his comment on this verse says: " Non multo post Apostoli mortem exorti sunt Encratitæ (qui nomen sibi a continentia indiderunt) Taciani; Cathari; Montanus cum sua secta, et tandem Manichæi, qui ab esu carnium et conjugio abhorrerent, et tanquam res profanas damnarent. . . . . Excipiunt [Papistæ] se Encratitis et Manichæis esse dissimiles, quia non simpliciter usum conjugii et carnium interdicunt, sed certis tantum diebus cogunt ad carnis abstinentiam, solos autem monachos et sacerdotes cum monialibus ad votum cœlibatus cogunt. Verum hæc . . . . nimis frivola est excusatio. Nam sanctimoniam nihilo-

quotes and enforces the original law given in Genesis ii. 24, that a
man shall "leave his father and his mother, and shall cleave unto
his wife, and they shall be one flesh." The same passage is
quoted by the Apostle as containing a great and symbolical truth.
(Eph. v. 31.) It is thus taught that the marriage relation is the
most intimate and sacred that can exist on earth, to which all
other human relations must be sacrificed. We accordingly find
that from the beginning, with rare exceptions, patriarchs, prophets, apostles, confessors, and martyrs, have been married men. If
marriage was not a degradation to them, surely it cannot be to
monks and priests.

The strongest proof of the sanctity of the marriage relation in
the sight of God, is to be found in the fact that both in the Old
and in the New Testaments, it is made the symbol of the relation
between God and his people. "Thy Maker is thy husband," are
the words of God, and contain a world of truth, of grace, and of
love. The departure of the people from God, is illustrated by a
reference to a wife forsaking her husband; while God's forbearance, tenderness, and love, are compared to those of a faithful
husband to his wife. "As the bridegroom rejoiceth over the
bride, so shall thy God rejoice over thee." (Is. lxii. 5.) In the
New Testament, this reference to the marriage relation, to illustrate the union between Christ and the Church, is frequent and
instructive. The Church is called "the Bride, the Lamb's wife."
(Rev. xxi. 9.) And the consummation of the work of salvation is
set forth as the marriage, or the marriage-supper of the Lamb.
(Rev. xix. 7, 9.) In Ephesians v. 22–33, the union between husbands and wives, and the duties thence resulting, are set forth as
so analogous to the union between Christ and his Church, that in
some cases it is hard to determine to which union the language of
the Apostle is to be applied. It is a matter of astonishment, in
view of all these facts, that marriage has so extensively and persistently been regarded as something degrading, and celibacy or perpetual virginity as a special and peculiar virtue. No more striking evidence of the influence of a false philosophy in perverting
the minds of even good men, is afforded in the whole history of
the Church. Even the Reformers did not escape altogether from
its influence. They often speak of marriage as the less of two
evils; not as in itself a good; and not as the normal and appropriate state in which men and women should live, as designed

minus in his rebus locant; deinde falsum et adulterinum Dei cultum instituunt: postremi
conscientias alligant necessitati, a qua debebant esse liberæ." Edit. Berlin, 1831.

by God in the very constitution of their nature, and as the best adapted to the exercise and development of all social and Christian virtues.   Thus Calvin says : " Unde constat et aliam quamlibet, extra conjugium, societatem coram ipso [Deo] maledictam esse; et illam ipsam conjugalem in necessitatis remedium esse ordinatam, ne in effrenem libidinem proruamus. . . . . Jam quum per naturæ conditionem et accensa post lapsum libidine, mulieris consortio bis obnoxii simus, nisi quos singulari gratia Deus inde exemit; videant singuli quid sibi datum sit. Virginitas, fateor, virtus est non contemnenda : sed quoniam aliis negata est, aliis nonnisi ad tempus concessa, qui ab incontinentia vexantur, et superiores in certamine esse nequeunt ad matrimonii subsidium se conferant, ut ita in suæ vocationis gradu castitatem colant." [1] That is, virginity is a virtue. Celibacy is a higher state than marriage. Those who cannot live in that state, should descend to the lower platform of married life. With such dregs of Manichean philosophy was the pure truth of the Bible contaminated even as held by the most illustrious Reformers.

4. The teaching of Scripture as to the sanctity of marriage is confirmed by the experience of the world. It is only in the marriage state that some of the purest, most disinterested, and most elevated principles of our nature are called into exercise. All that concerns filial piety, and parental and especially maternal affection, depends on marriage for its very existence. Yet on the purifying and restraining influence of these affections the well-being of human society is in a large measure dependent. It is in the bosom of the family that there is a constant call for acts of kindness, of self-denial, of forbearance, and of love. The family, therefore, is the sphere the best adapted for the development of all the social virtues; and it may be safely said that there is far more of moral excellence and of true religion to be found in Christian households, than in the desolate homes of priests, or in the gloomy cells of monks and nuns. A man with his children or grandchildren on his knees, is an object of higher reverence than any emaciated anchorite in his cave.

5. Our Lord teaches that a tree is known by its fruits. There has been no more prolific source of evil to the Church than the unscriptural notion of the special virtue of virginity and the enforced celibacy of the clergy and monastic vows, to which that notion has given rise. This is the teaching of history. On this point the testimony of Romanists as well as of Protestants is de-

[1] *Institutio*, II. viii. 41, 42; edit. Berlin, 1834, vol. i. pp. 264, 265.

cisive and overwhelming.   It may be admitted that the Catholic
clergy in this and in some other countries are as decorous in their
lives, as the clergy of other denominations, without invalidating
the testimony of history as to the evils of vows of celibacy.

Protestants, while asserting the sanctity of marriage and denying the superior virtue of a life of celibacy, do not deny that there
are times and circumstances in which celibacy is a virtue : *i. e.*,
that a man may perform a virtuous act in resolving never to
marry.   The Church often has work to do, for which single men
are the only proper agents.   The cares of a family, in other words,
would unfit a man for the execution of the task assigned.   This,
however, does not suppose that celibacy is in itself a virtue.   It
may also happen that a rich man may be called upon to undertake a work which would necessitate his disencumbering himself
of the care of his estate, and subjecting himself to a life of poverty.   The same is true of the state.   In fact military service,
for the great majority of the rank and file of an army, is an estate of forced celibacy so long as the service continues.   And even
with regard to the officers, the liberty to marry is very much restricted in the standing armies of Europe.   There are times when
marriage is inexpedient.   Our Lord in foretelling the destruction
of Jerusalem said, " Woe unto them that are with child, and to
them that give suck in those days."   It is the part of wisdom to
escape such woes.   When Christians had no security for life or
home ; when they were liable to be torn away from their families,
or to have all means of providing for their wants taken out of
their hands, it was better for them not to marry.   It is in reference to such times and circumstances that the words of Christ, in
the nineteenth chapter of Matthew, were uttered, and the advice
of the Apostle, in the seventh chapter of First Corinthians was
given.   The Pharisees asked our Lord whether a man could put
away his wife at pleasure.   He referred them to the original institution of marriage, as showing that it was intended to be an
indissoluble connection.   His disciples said, In that case it is better that a man should not marry.   Our Lord replied : Whether
it is better for a man to marry or not, is not a question for every
man to decide for himself.   " That the unmarried state is better,
is a saying not for every one, and indeed only for such as it is
divinely intended for." [1]   That is, those to whom the requisite

[1] *Commentary, Critical and Explanatory, on The Old and New Testament.*   Matthew
xix. 11. By Rev. Robert Jamieson, St. Paul's, Glasgow, Scotland; Rev. A. R. Fausset, A.
M., St. Cuthbert, York, England; and the Rev. David Brown D. D., Aberdeen, Scotland.
Hartford, Conn. 1871.

grace is given, " Omnes hujus dicti capaces esse negans, significat electionem non esse positam in manu nostra, acsi de re nobis subjecta esset consultatio. Si quis utile sibi esse putat uxore carere, atque ita nullo examine habito, cœlibatus legem sibi edicit, longe fallitur. Deus enim, qui pronuntiavit bonum esse, ut viro adjutrix sit mulier, contempti sui ordinis pœnam exiget : quia nimium sibi arrogant mortales, dum se a cœlesti vocatione eximere tentant. Porro non esse omnibus liberum, eligere utrum libuerit, inde probat Christus, quia speciale sit continentiæ donum : nam quum dicit, non omnes esse capaces, sed quibus datum est, clare demonstrat non omnibus esse datum." [1] Those to whom it is given to lead an unmarried life, as our Lord teaches (Matt. xix. 10), are not only those who by their natural constitution are unfit for the marriage state, but those whom God calls to special service in his Church and whom He fits for that work.

The doctrine which Paul teaches on this subject is perfectly coincident with the teachings of our Lord. He recognizes marriage as a divine institution ; as in itself good ; as the normal and proper state in which men and women should live ; but as it is necessarily attended by many cares and distractions, it was expedient in times of trouble, to remain unmarried. This is the purport of Paul's teachings in First Corinthians vii. No one of the sacred writers, whether in the Old or in the New Testament, so exalts and glorifies marriage as does this Apostle in his Epistle to the Ephesians. He, therefore, is not the man, guided as he was in all his teachings by the Spirit of God, to depreciate or undervalue it, as only the less of two evils. It is a positive good : the union of two human persons to supplement and complement the one the other in a way which is necessary to the perfection or full development of both. The wife is to her husband what the Church is to Christ. Nothing higher than this can possibly be said.

[1] Calvin on Matthew xix. 10, 11, in *N. T. Comment.* Berlin, 1838, vol. ii. p. 159. Although Calvin sometimes speaks disparagingly of marriage, at other times, especially when writing against the Papists, he vindicates its sanctity. Thus in connection with the passage quoted above, he says: "Si conjugium instituit Deus in communem humani generis salutem, licet quædam minus grata secum trahat, non ideo protinus spernendum est. Discamus ergo, si quid in Dei beneficiis nobis non arridet, non tam lauti esse ac morosi, quin reverenter illis utamur. Præsertim nobis in sancto conjugio cavenda est hæc pravitas: nam quia multis molestiis implicitum est, semper conatus est Satan odio et infamia gravare, ut homines ab eo subduceret. Et Hieronymus nimis luculentum maligni perversique ingenii specimen in eo edidit, quod non tantum calumniis exagitat sacrum illum et divinum vitæ ordinem, sed quascunque potest ex profanis auctoribus λοιδορίας accumulat, quæ ejus honestatem deforment." — *Ibid.* p. 158.

History.

No one can read the Epistles of Paul, especially those to the Ephesians and Colossians, without seeing clear indications of the prevalence, even in the apostolic churches, of the principles of that philosophy which held that matter was contaminating; and which inculcated asceticism as the most efficacious means of the purification of the soul.   This doctrine had already been adopted and reduced to practice by the Essenes among the Jews.   Farther East, under a somewhat different form, it had prevailed for ages before the Christian era, and still maintains its ground.   According to the Brahminical philosophy the individuality of man depends on the body.   Complete emancipation from the body, therefore, secures the merging of the finite into the infinite.   The drop is lost in the ocean, and this is the highest and ultimate destiny of man.   It is not therefore to be wondered at, that the early fathers came more or less under the influence of these principles, or that asceticism gained so rapidly and maintained so long its ascendancy in the Church.   The depreciation of the divine institution of marriage, and the exaltation of virginity into the first place among Christian virtues, was the natural and necessary consequence of this spirit.   Ignatius called voluntary virgins " the jewels of Christ."   Justin Martyr desired celibacy to prevail to the "greatest possible extent."   Tatian regarded marriage as inconsistent with spiritual worship.   Origen " disabled himself in his youth " and regarded marriage as a pollution.   Hieracas made " virginity a condition of salvation."   Tertullian denounced second marriage as criminal, and represented celibacy as the ideal of Christian life, not only for the clergy, but also for the laity.   Second marriage was early prohibited so far as the clergy were concerned, and soon came in their case the prohibition of marriage altogether.   The Apostolical Constitutions prohibited priests from contracting marriage after consecration. 'The Council of Ancyra, A. D. 314, allowed deacons to marry, provided they stipulated for the privilege before ordination.   The Council of Elvira, A. D. 305, forbade the continuance of the marriage relation (according to the common interpretation of its canons) to bishops, presbyters, and deacons on pain of deposition.[1]   Jerome was fanatical in his denunciation of marriage ; and even Augustine was carried away by the spirit of the age.   In answer to the objection that if men acted on his principles the world would be depopulated, he answered :

[1] See Schaff, *History of The Christian Church*, New York, 1867, vol. i. §§ 91, 96.

So much the better, for in that case Christ would come the sooner. [1] Siricius, Bishop of Rome A. D. 385, decided that marriage was inconsistent with the clerical office; and was followed in this view by his successors. Great opposition, however, was experienced in enforcing celibacy, and it required all the energy of Gregory VII. to have the decisions of councils carried into effect. Ultimately, however, the rule, so far as the clergy are concerned, was acquiesced in, and received the authoritative sanction of the Council of Trent. That Council decided,[2] " Si quis dixerit, statum conjugalem anteponendum esse statui virginitatis, vel cœlibatus, et non esse melius, et beatius manere in virginitate aut cœlibatu, quam jungi matrimonio : anathema sit." On this assumed higher virtue of celibacy, in the preceding canon it was ordered : " Si quis dixerit, clericos in sacris ordinibus constitutos, vel regulares, castitatem solemniter professos, posse matrimonium contrahere, contractumque validum esse, non obstante lege ecclesiastica, vel voto : et oppositum nil aliud esse, quam damnare matrimonium ; posseque omnes contrahere matrimonium, qui non sentiunt se castitatis, etiam si eam voterint, habere donum ; anathema sit; cum Deus id recte petentibus non deneget, nec patiatur nos supra id, quod possumus, tentari."

Although the doctrine that virginity, as the Roman Catechism expresses it, " summopere commendatur," as being better, and more perfect and holy than a state of marriage, is made the ostensible ground of the enforced celibacy of the clergy, it is manifest that hierarchical reasons had much to do in making the Romish Church so strenuous in insisting that its clergy should be unmarried. This Gregory VII. avows when he says,[3] " Non liberari potest ecclesia a servitute laicorum, nisi liberentur clerici ab uxoribus." And Melancthon felt authorized to say in reference to the celibacy of the clergy in the Church of Rome, " Una est vera et sola causa tuendi cœlibatus, ut opes commodius administrentur et splendor ordinis retineatur." [4]

As the Reformation was a return to the Scriptures as the only infallible rule of faith and practice ; and as in the Scriptures marriage is exalted as a holy state, and no preëminence in excellence is assigned to celibacy or virginity ; and as the Reformers denied the authority of the Church to make laws to bind the conscience or to curtail the liberty with which Christ had made his people

[1] Augustine, *De Bono Conjugali*, 10; *Works*, edit. Benedictines, Paris, 1837, vol. vi. p. 551, c.
[2] Sess. xxiv., canon 10; Streitwolf, *Libri Symbolici*, Göttingen, 1846, p. 91.
[3] *Epist.* lib. iii. p. 7.   [4] See Herzog's *Real-Encyklopädie*, Art. " Cölibat."

free, Protestants pronounced with one voice against the obligation of monastic vows and of the celibacy of the clergy.

The Greek Church petrified at an early date. It assumed the
form which it still retains, before the doctrine of the special sanctity of celibacy had gained ascendancy. It abides therefore by
the decisions of the Council of Chalcedon, A. D. 451, and of
Trullo, A. D. 692, which permitted marriage to priests and deacons. Those Greeks who are in communion with the Church of
Rome enjoy the same liberty. Benedict XIV. declared in reference to them, " Etsi expetendum quam maxime esset, ut Græci,
qui sunt in sacris ordinibus constituti, castitatem non secus ac
Latini servarent. Nihilominus, ut eorum clerici, subdiaconi,
diaconi et presbyteri uxores in eorum ministerio retineant, dum-
modo ante sacros ordines, virgines, non viduas, neque corruptas
duxerint, Romana non prohibet Ecclesia. Eos autem, qui viduam
vel corruptam duxerunt, vel ad secunda vota, prima uxore mortua,
convolarunt, ad subdiaconatum, diaconatum et presbyteratum pro-
moveri omnino prohibemus." [1] In the Russian Church the priests
are required to be married men; but second marriages are for
them prohibited. The bishops are chosen from the monks and
must be unmarried.

Marriage a Divine Institution.

Marriage is a divine institution. (1.) Because founded on the
nature of man as constituted by God. He made man male and
female, and ordained marriage as the indispensable condition of
the continuance of the race. (2.) Marriage was instituted before
the existence of civil society, and therefore cannot in its essential
nature be a civil institution. As Adam and Eve were married
not in virtue of any civil law, or by the intervention of a civil
magistrate, so any man and woman cast together on a desert
island, could lawfully take each other as husband and wife. It
is a degradation of the institution to make it a mere civil contract. (3.) God commanded men to marry, when He commanded them to increase, and multiply and replenish the earth.
(4.) God in his word has prescribed the duties belonging to the
marriage relation; He has made known his will as to the parties

---

[1] Bulla lvii. § 7–26; *Magn. Bull. Rom., Luxemburg*, 1752, vol. xvi. The controversies
in the Church on this subject are detailed by the leading modern ecclesiastical historians,
as Neander, Gieseler, and Schaff. The merits of the question are discussed in numerous
separate treatises, as well as in such books as Burnet's *Exposition of the Thirty-nine
Articles*, Jeremy Taylor's *Ductor Dubitantium* (iii. iv. *Works*, London, 1828, vol. xiii.,
pp. 549-616), Elliott's *Delineation of Romanism*, Thiersch's *Vorlesungen über Katholicis-
mus und Protestantismus*, 2nd edit. Erlangen, 1848.

who may lawfully be united in marriage ; He has determined the
continuance of the relation ; and the causes which alone justify
its dissolution. These matters are not subject to the will of the
parties, or to the authority of the State. (5.) The vow of mutual
fidelity made by husband and wife, is not made exclusively by
each one to the other, but by each to God. When a man connects himself with a Christian Church he enters into covenant
with his brethren in the Lord ; mutual obligations are assumed ;
but nevertheless the covenant is made with God. He joins the
Church in obedience to the will of God ; he promises to regulate
his faith and practice by the divine word ; and the vow of fidelity
is made to God. It is the same in marriage. It is a voluntary,
mutual compact between husband and wife. They promise to be
faithful to each other ; but nevertheless they act in obedience to
God, and promise to Him that they will live together as man and
wife, according to his word. Any violation of the compact is,
therefore, a violation of a vow made to God.

Marriage is not a sacrament in the sense which in baptism
and the Lord's Supper are sacraments, nor in the sense of
the Romish Church ; but it is none the less a sacred institution.
Its solemnization is an office of religion. It should, therefore, be
entered upon with due solemnity and in the fear of God ; and
should be celebrated, i. e., the ceremony should be performed by
a minister of Christ. He alone is authorized to see to it that the
law of God is adhered to ; and he alone can receive and register
the marriage vows as made to God. The civil magistrate can
only witness it as a civil contract, and it is consequently to ignore
its religious character and sanction to have it celebrated by a
civil officer. As the essence of the marriage contract is the
mutual compact of the parties in the sight of God and in the presence of witnesses, it is not absolutely necessary that it should be
celebrated by a minister of religion or even by a civil magistrate.
It may be lawfully solemnized, as among the Quakers, without
the intervention of either. Nevertheless as it is of the greatest
importance that the religious nature of the institution should be
kept in view, it is incumbent on Christians, so far as they themselves are concerned, to insist that it should be solemnized as a
religious service.

Marriage as a Civil Institution.

As a man's being a servant of God and bound to make his word
the rule of his faith and practice, is not inconsistent with his

being a servant of the state, and bound to render obedience to its laws ; so it is not inconsistent with the fact that marriage is an ordinance of God, that it should be, in another aspect, a civil institution.   It is so implicated in the social and civil relations of men that it of necessity comes under the cognizance of the state. It is therefore a civil institution.   (1.) In so far as it is, and must be, recognized and enforced by the state.   (2.) It imposes civil obligations which the state has the right to enforce.   The husband is bound to sustain his wife, for example, and he is constrained by the civil law to the performance of this duty. (3.) Marriage also involves, on both sides, rights to property ; and the claims of children born in wedlock to the property of their parents.   All these questions concerning property fall legitimately under the control of the civil law.   In many countries not only property, but rank, title, and political prerogatives are implicated with the question of marriage.   (4.) It belongs to the state, therefore, as the guardian of these rights, to determine what marriages are lawful and what unlawful ; how the contract is to be solemnized and authenticated ; and what shall be its legal consequences.   All these laws Christians are bound to obey, so far as obedience to them is consistent with a good conscience.

The legitimate power of the state in all these matters is limited by the revealed will of God.   It can make nothing an impediment to marriage which the Scriptures do not declare to be a bar to that union.   It can make nothing a ground of dissolving the marriage contract which the Bible does not make a valid ground of divorce.   And the state can attach none other than civil pains and penalty to the violation of its laws concerning marriage. This is only saying that a Christian government is bound to respect the conscientious convictions of the people.   It is a violation of the principles of civil and religious liberty for the state to make its will paramount to the will of God.   Plain as this principle seems to be, it is nevertheless constantly disregarded in almost all Christian nations, whether Catholic or Protestant.   In England, for example, it is still the law, that no member of the royal family can marry without the consent of the reigning sovereign.   If this meant nothing more than that any member of the royal family thus marrying, should forfeit for himself and his children all right of succession to the crown, it might be all right. But the real meaning is that such a marriage is null and void ; that parties otherwise lawfully married and whom God has joined together as man and wife, are not man and wife.   This is to bring the law of man and the law of God into direct collision, and make the human supersede the divine. In Prussia a subordinate officer of the army cannot marry without the consent of his commander. If he should marry without that consent, it might be right to make him throw up his commission; but to say that his wife is not a wife, is not only untrue, but it is a monstrous injustice and cruelty. In England, until of late years, no marriage was valid unless solemnized in church, within canonical hours, and by a man in priest's orders. This law was designed specially for the protection of heiresses from the wiles of fortune-hunters. It might be just to determine that no marriage not thus solemnized should convey any right to property; but to say that parties married five minutes after twelve o'clock, noon, are not married at all, whereas had the ceremony been performed ten minutes sooner, they would be truly man and wife, shocks the conscience and common sense of men. So in this country before the abolition of slavery, according to the laws of our Southern States, no slave could marry. A young white man married a young woman, whom no one in the community supposed had a drop of African blood in her veins. It was proved, however, that she was a slave. Her husband purchased her, manumitted her, repudiated her, married another woman, and was received into the communion of a Presbyterian Church. The law of God was thus regarded as a mere nullity.[1]

Because marriage is in some of its aspects a civil institution, to be regulated within certain limits, by the civil law, men have treated it as though it were a mere business engagement. They ignore its character as a divine institution, regulated and controlled by divine laws. Civil legislatures should remember that they can no more annul the laws of God than the laws of nature. If they pronounce those not to be married who, by the divine law, are married; or if they separate those whom God hath joined together, their laws are absolute nullities at the bar of conscience and in the sight of God.

[1] This however was in accordance with the canonical law, which made error as to the condition of one of the parties, as bond or free, a ground of annulling the marriage contract. Stahl, *De Matrimonio Rescindendo.* Berlin, 1841. Canon Leg. cap. 2, 4, x., de conjugio servorum, 4, 9. See Göschen in Herzog's *Encyklopädie,* art. "Ehe." This is still the doctrine of the Romish Church. See Dens, *Tractatus de Matrimonio; Theologia,* edit. Dublin, 1832, vol. vii., N. 72, p. 109. See also *Commentaries on the Law of Marriage and Divorce,* by Joel Prentiss Bishop. 4th edition. Boston. 1864, vol. i. chap. x. §§ 154–163.

Monogamy.

Marriage is a compact between one man and one woman to live together, as man and wife, until separated by death. According to this definition, first, the marriage relation can subsist only between one man and one woman; secondly, the union is permanent, *i. e.*, it can be dissolved only by the death of one or both of the parties, except for reasons specified in the word of God; and thirdly, the death of one of the parties dissolves the union, so that it is lawful for the survivor to marry again.

As to the first of these points, or that the Scriptural doctrine of marriage is opposed to and condemns polygamy, it is be remarked, —

1. That such has been the doctrine of the Christian Church in all ages and in every part of the world. There has never been a church calling itself Christian which tolerated a plurality of wives among its members. There could hardly be a stronger proof than this fact that such is the law of Christ. It is morally certain that the whole Church cannot have mistaken, on such a subject as this, the mind and will of its divine Head and Master.

2. Marriage as originally constituted and ordained by God was between one man and one woman. And the language of Adam when he received Eve from the hands of her Maker, proves that such was the essential nature of the relation: " And Adam said, This is now bone of my bones, and flesh of my flesh. . . . . Therefore shall a man leave his father and his mother, and shall cleave unto his wife and they shall be one flesh." (Gen. ii. 23, 24.) Or, as our Lord quotes and expounds the passage, " They twain shall be one flesh: so then they are no more twain, but one flesh." (Mark x. 8.) " The two," and no more than two, become one. This was not only the language of unfallen Adam in Paradise, but the language of God uttered through the lips of Adam, as appears not only from the circumstances of the case, but also from our Lord's attributing to them divine authority, as He evidently does in the passage just quoted. Thus the law of marriage as originally instituted by God, required that the union should be between one man and one woman. This law could be changed only by the authority by which it was originally enacted. Delitzsch remarks on this passage: [1] " In these words not only the deepest spiritual union, but a union comprehending the whole nature of man, an all comprehending personal communion, is rep-

[1] *Die Genesis*, Leipzig, 1852, p. 114.

resented as the essence of marriage; and monogamy is set forth as its natural and divinely appointed form."

3. Although this original law was partially disregarded in later times, it was never abrogated. Polygamy and divorce were in a measure tolerated under the Mosaic law, yet in all ages among the Hebrews, monogamy was the rule, and polygamy the exception, as it was among other civilized nations of antiquity. Polygamy first appears among the descendants of Cain. (Gen. iv. 19.) Noah and his sons had each but one wife. Abraham had but one wife, until the impatience of Sarah for children led him to take Hagar as a concubine. The same rule of marriage was observed by the prophets as a class. Polygamy was confined in a great measure to kings and princes. There was also an honour-able distinction made between the wife and the concubine. The former retained her preëminence as the head of the family. Numerous passages of the Old Testament go to prove that monogamy was considered as the law of marriage, from which plurality of wives was a departure. Throughout the Proverbs, for example, it is the blessing of a good wife, not of wives, that is continually set forth. (Prov. xii. 4; xix. 14; xxxi. 10 ff.) The apocryphal books contain clear evidence that after the exile monogamy was almost universal among the Jews; and it may be inferred from such passages as Luke i. 5; Acts v. 1, and many others, that the same was true at the time of the advent of Christ.

With regard to the toleration of polygamy under the Mosaic law, it is to be remembered that the seventh commandment belongs to the same category as the sixth and eighth. These laws are not founded on the essential nature of God, and therefore are not immutable. They are founded on the permanent relations of men in their present state of existence. From this it follows, (1.) That they bind men only in their present state. The laws of property and marriage can have no application, so far as we know, to the future world, where men shall be as angels, neither marrying nor giving in marriage. (2.) These laws being founded on the permanent and natural relations of men, cannot be set aside by human authority, because those relations are not subject to the will or ordinance of men. (3.) They may however be dispensed with by God. He commanded the Israelites to despoil the Egyptians and to dispossess the Canaanites, but this does not prove that one nation may, of its own motion, seize on the inheritance of another people. If God, therefore, at any time and to any people granted permission to practise polygamy, then so long as that permission lasted and for those to whom it was given, polygamy was lawful, and at all other times and for all other persons it was unlawful. This principle is clearly recognized in what our Saviour teaches concerning divorce. It was permitted the Jews under the Mosaic law to put away their wives; as soon as that law was abolished, the right of divorce ceased.

4. Monogamy, however, does not rest exclusively on the original institution of marriage, or upon the general drift of the Old Testament teaching, but mainly on the clearly revealed will of Christ. His will is the supreme law for all Christians, and rightfully for all men. When the Pharisees came to Him and asked Him whether a man could lawfully put away his wife, He answered, that marriage as instituted by God was an indissoluble union between one man and one woman; and, therefore, that those whom God had joined together no man could put asunder. This is the doctrine clearly taught in Matthew xix. 4–9; Mark x. 4–9; Luke xvi. 18; Matthew v. 32. In these passages our Lord expressly declares that if a man marries while his first wife is living he commits adultery. The exception which Christ himself makes to this rule, will be considered under the head of divorce.

The Apostle teaches the same doctrine in Romans vii. 2, 3: " The woman which hath an husband is bound by the law to her husband, so long as he liveth; but if the husband be dead, she is loosed from the law of her husband. So then, if while her husband liveth, she be married to another man, she shall be called an adulteress: but if her husband be dead, she is free from that law; so that she is no adulteress, though she be married to another man." The doctrine of this passage is that marriage is a compact between one man and one woman, which can be dissolved only by the death of one of the parties. So in 1 Corinthians vii. 2: " Let every man have his own wife, and let every woman have her own husband," it is taken for granted that, in the Christian Church, a plurality of wives is as much out of the question as a plurality of husbands. This assumption runs through the whole New Testament. We not only never read of a Christian's having two or more wives; but whenever the duty of the marriage relation is spoken of, it is always of the husband to his wife, and of the wife to her husband. In the judgment, therefore, of the whole Christian Church, marriage is a covenant between one man and one woman to live together as husband and wife, until separated by death.

5. This Scriptural law is confirmed by the providential law which secures the numerical equality of the sexes. Had polygamy been according to the divine purpose, we should naturally expect that more women would be born than men. But the reverse is the fact. There are more men than women born into the world. The excess, however, is only sufficient to provide for the greater peril to life to which men are exposed. The law of providence is the numerical equality of the sexes ; and this is a clear intimation of the will of God that every man should have his own wife, and every woman her own husband. Such being the will of God, as revealed both in his word and in his providence, everything which tends to counteract it must be evil in its nature and consequences. The doctrine which depreciated marriage, and made celibacy a virtue, flooded the Church with corruption. And everything in our modern civilization and modes of living which renders marriage difficult, and consequently infrequent, is to be deprecated, and if possible removed. That every man should have his own wife and every woman her own husband, is the divinely appointed preventive of the " Social Evil" with all its unutterable horrors.[1] Every other preventive is human and worthless. Rather than that the present state of things should continue, it would be better to return to the old patriarchal usage, and let parents give their sons and daughters in marriage as soon as they attained the proper age, on the best terms they can.

6. As all the permanently obligatory laws of God are founded on the nature of his creatures, it follows that if He has ordained that marriage must be the union of one man and one woman, there must be a reason for this in the very constitution of man and in the nature of the marriage relation. That relation must be such that it cannot subsist between one and many ; between one man and more than one woman. This is plain, first, from the nature of the love which it involves ; and secondly, from the nature of the union which it constitutes. First, conjugal love is peculiar and exclusive. It can have but one object. As the love of a mother for a child is peculiar, and can have no other object than her own child, so the love of a husband can have no other object than his wife, and the love of a wife no other object than her husband. It is a love not only of complacency and delight, but also of possession, of property, and of rightful ownership. This is the reason why jealousy in man or woman is the fiercest of all

---

[1] The fact that men and women, who make the murder of infants a profession, are rolling in wealth, is enough to rouse any community from its false security.

human passions. It involves a sense of injury; of the violation of the most sacred rights; more sacred even than the rights of property or life. Conjugal love, therefore, cannot by possibility exist except between one man and one woman. Monogamy has its foundation in the very constitution of our nature. Polygamy is unnatural, and necessarily destructive of the normal, or divinely constituted relation between husband and wife.

Secondly, in another aspect, the union involved in marriage cannot exist except between one man and one woman. It is not merely a union of feeling and of interests. It is such a union as to produce, in some sense, identity. The two become one. Such is the declaration of our Lord. Husband and wife are one, in a sense which justified the Apostle in saying as he does, in Ephesians v. 30, that the wife is bone of her husband's bone, and flesh of his flesh. She is his body. She is himself (v. 28). Such is this union that " Qui uxorem repudiat, quasi dimidiam sui partem a seipso avellit. Hoc autem minime patitur natura, ut corpus suum quisque discerpat." What all this means it may be hard for us to understand. It is certain, — (1.) That it does not refer to anything material, or to any identification of substance. When Adam said of Eve, " This is bone of my bones, and flesh of my flesh," he doubtless referred to her being formed out of his body. But as these words are used by the Apostle to express the relation of all wives to their husbands, they must be understood of something else than identity of substance. (2.) The oneness of man and wife, of which the Scriptures speak, cannot be understood in any sense inconsistent with their distinct subsistence or personality. They may be very different in character and destiny. The one may be saved, the other lost. (3.) It is evident, however, that the meaning of the strong language of Scripture on this subject is not exhausted, by representing the marriage union as being merely one of affection; or by saying that the husband is the complement of the wife and the wife of the husband; that is, that the marriage relation is necessary to the completeness of our nature and to its full development in the present state of existence; that there are capacities, feelings, and virtues which are not otherwise or elsewhere called into exercise. All this may be true, but it is not the whole truth. (4.) There is, in a certain sense, a community of life between husband and wife. We are accustomed to say, and to say truly, that the life of parents is communicated to their children. Each nation and every historical family has a form of life by which it is distinguished. As, therefore, the life of a father and the life of his son are the same, in that the blood (*i. e.*, the life) of the parent flows in the veins of his children; so in an analogous sense the life of the husband and wife is one. They have a common life, and that common or joint life is transmitted to their offspring. This is the doctrine of the early Church. The Apostolical Constitutions say : [1] ἡ γυνὴ κοινωνός ἐστι βίου, ἐνουμένη εἰς ἓν σῶμα ἐκ δύο παρὰ θεοῦ.

The analogy which the Apostle traces out in Ephesians v. 22–33, between the conjugal relation and the union between Christ and his Church, brings out the Scriptural doctrine of marriage more clearly than perhaps any other passage in the Bible. No analogy is expected to answer in all respects, and no illustration borrowed from earthly relations can bring out all the fulness of the things of God. The relation, therefore, between a husband and his wife, is only an adumbration of the relation of Christ to his Church. Still there is an analogy between the two, (1.) As the Apostle teaches, the love of Christ to his Church is peculiar and exclusive. It is such as He has for no other class or body of rational creatures in the universe. So the love of the husband for his wife is peculiar and exclusive. It is such as he has for no other object; a love in which no one can participate. (2.) Christ's love for his Church is self-sacrificing. He gave himself for it. He purchased the Church with his blood. So the husband should, and when true, does, in all things sacrifice himself for his wife. (3.) Christ and his Church are one; one in the sense that the Church is his body. So the husband and wife are in such a sense one, that a man in loving his wife loves himself. (4.) Christ's life is communicated to the Church. As the life of the head is communicated to the members of the human body; and the life of the vine to the branches, so there is, in a mysterious sense, a community of life between Christ and his Church. In like manner, in a sense no less truly mysterious, there is a community of life between husband and wife.

From all this it follows that as it would be utterly incongruous and impossible that Christ should have two bodies, two brides, two churches, so it is no less incongruous and impossible that a man should have two wives. That is, the conjugal relation, as it is set forth in Scripture, cannot by possibility subsist, except between one man and one woman.

[1] Lib. vi. cap. xiv.; *Works* of Clement of Rome, edit. Migne, Paris, 1857, vol. i. p 945, c.

Conclusions.

1. If such be the true doctrine of marriage, it follows, as just stated, that polygamy destroys its very nature. It is founded on a wrong view of the nature of woman; places her in a false and degrading position; dethrones and despoils her; and is productive of innumerable evils.

2. It follows that the marriage relation is permanent and indissoluble. A limb may be violently severed from the body, and lose all vital connection with it; and husband and wife may be thus violently separated, and their conjugal relation annulled; but in both cases the normal connection is permanent.

3. It follows that the state can neither constitute nor dissolve the marriage relation. It can no more free a husband or wife " a vinculo matrimonii," than it can free a father " a vinculo paternitatis." It may protect a child from the injustice or cruelty of its father, or even, for due cause, remove him from all parental control, and it may legislate about its property, but the natural bond between parents and children is beyond its control. So the state may legislate about marriage, and determine its accidents and legal consequences , it may decide who, in the sight of the law, shall be regarded as husband and wife, and when, or under what circumstances, the legal or civil rights and privileges arising out of the relation shall cease to be enforced; and it may protect the person and rights of the wife, and, if necessary, remove her from the control of her husband, but the conjugal bond it cannot dissolve. All decrees of divorce " a vinculo matrimonii," issued by civil or ecclesiastical authorities, so far as the conscience is concerned, are perfectly inoperative, unless antecedently to such decree and by the law of God, the conjugal relation has ceased to exist.

4. It follows from the Scriptural doctrine of marriage that all laws are evil which tend to make those two whom God pronounces to be one; such laws, for example, as give to the wife the right to conduct business, contract debts, and sue and be sued, in her own name. This is attempting to correct one class of evils at the cost of incurring others a hundred-fold greater. The Word of God is the only sure guide of legislative action as well as of individual conduct.

5. It need hardly be remarked that it rollows from the nature of marriage, that next to murder, adultery is the greatest of all social crimes. Under the Old Dispensation it was punishable

with death. And even now it is practically impossible to convict a husband of murder who kills the man who has committed
adultery with his wife. This comes from human laws being in
conflict with the laws of nature and of God. The law of God regards marriage as identifying a man and his wife; the laws of the
state too often regard it as merely a civil contract, and give an
injured husband no redress but a suit for damages for the pecuniary loss he has sustained by being deprived of the services of his
wife. The penalty for adultery, to be in any due proportion to
the magnitude of the crime, should be severe and degrading.

6. The relative duties of husband and wife arising out of their
relation, may be expressed in a few comprehensive words. The
husband is to love, protect, and cherish his wife as himself, *i. e.*,
as being to him another self. The duties of the wife are set
forth in the time-honoured Christian formula, "love, honour, and
obey."

Converted Polygamists.

The question has been mooted, Whether a polygamist, when
converted to Christianity, should be required to repudiate all his
wives but one, as a condition of his admission into the Christian
Church? The answer to this question has been sought from
three sources: First, the Scriptural doctrine of marriage; secondly, the example of the Apostles when dealing with such cases;
and thirdly, from a consideration of the effects which would follow
from making monogamy an indispensable condition of admission
to the Church.

As to the first point, it is admitted by all Christians, that it is
the law of God, the law of Christ, and consequently the law of
the Christian Church that polygamy is sinful, being a violation
of the original and permanently obligatory law of marriage. As
every man who enters the Church professes to be a Christian,
and as every Christian is bound to obey the law of Christ, it
seems plain that no man should be received into the communion
of the Church who does not conform to the law of Christ concerning marriage. The only question is, Whether Christ has made
a special exception in favour of those who in the times of their
ignorance, contracted the obligations of marriage with more than
one woman? It is of course possible that such an exception
might have been made. It would be analogous to the temporary
suspension of the original law of marriage in favour of the hard-
hearted Jews. Has then such an exception been made? This is
the second point to be considered. It concerns a matter of fact.

Those who assume that such an exception has been made, are bound to produce the clearest evidence of the fact. This is necessary not only to satisfy the consciences of the parties concerned, but also to justify a departure from a plainly revealed law of God. It would be a very serious matter to set up in a heathen country, a church not conformed in this matter to the usual law of Christendom. Missionaries are sent forth to teach not only Christian doctrines but Christian morals. And the churches which they found, profess to be witnesses for Christ as to what He would have men to believe, and as to what He would have them to do. They ought not to be allowed to bear false testimony. It is certain that there is no clear and definite expression of the will of Christ, recorded in the New Testament, that the case contemplated should be an exception to the Scriptural law of marriage. There is no instance recorded in the New Testament, of the admission of a polygamist to the Christian Church. It has, indeed, been inferred from 1 Timothy iii. 2, where the Apostle says, a bishop must be " the husband of one wife," that a private member of the Church might have more wives than one. But this is in itself a very precarious inference ; and being inconsistent with Christ's express prohibition, it is altogether inadmissible. The meaning of the passage has been much disputed. What the Apostle requires is that a bishop should be in all respects an exemplary man : not given to wine, no striker, not greedy of filthy lucre ; the husband of one wife, i. e., not a polygamist. This no more implies that other men may be polygamists, than his saying that a bishop must not be greedy of filthy lucre and not a brawler, implies that other men may be covetous or contentious. According to another and widely accepted interpretation of the passage in 1 Timothy iii. 2, and the corresponding passage in Titus i. 6, the injunction of the Apostle is that a man who has been married more than once, must not be appointed a bishop or presbyter. If this be the true meaning of the Apostle, his language affords still less ground for the argument drawn from it in favour of the lawfulness of polygamy in church members. If even second marriage was forbidden to presbyters, *a fortiori* must polygamy be regarded as inconsistent with the law of Christ.

This interpretation was very generally adopted in the early Church, during the Middle Ages, and by Romanists, and is sustained by many of the recent commentators. Bishop Ellicott decides in favour of this interpretation. His reasons are, — (1.) The opinion of the early writers and of some councils. (2.) The special respect paid among pagans to a woman who was "univira." (3.) The propriety, in the case of ἐπίσκοποι and διάκονοι, of a greater temperance. (4.) And the manifestation of a greater sanctity (σεμνότης) of a single marriage, which he thinks is indicated even in Scripture (Luke ii. 36, 37). The objections to it are, —

In the first place, that it rests on an unscriptural view of marriage. According to the Bible, marriage is a better, higher, and holier, because the normal state, than celibacy. It was only in the interest of the doctrine of the peculiar sanctity of celibacy, that this interpretation was adopted by the fathers.

In the second place, it rests on the no less unscriptural assumption of the superior holiness of the clergy. No higher degree of moral purity is required of them than of other men, for the simple reason that every man is required to be perfectly holy in heart and life. The interpretation in question gained the stronger hold of the Church as the doctrine of "the grace of orders," and of the priesthood of the clergy gained ascendancy. When the Reformation came and swept away these two doctrines, it removed the two principal supports of the interpretation in question. It is not to be admitted that there can be anything unholy in second marriages, which an infinitely holy God declares to be lawful (Rom. vii. 3), nor can it be conceded that the clergy are holier than other believers, seeing that the only priesthood in the Church on earth is the priesthood common to all believers.

In the third place, the interpretation which makes the Apostle interdict second marriages to bishops and deacons, is contrary to the natural meaning of the words. The parallel passage in Titus i. 5, 6, reads thus : " That thou shouldest, ... ordain elders in every city, as I had appointed thee : if any be blameless, the husband of one wife, etc ; " εἴ τις ἐστὶν . . . μιᾶς γυναικὸς, ἀνήρ, ' if any one is at this present time the husband of one wife.' It is the present state and character of the man that are to be taken into the account. He might before have been unmarried, or even a polygamist, but when ordained, he must, if married at all, be the husband of but one woman. " Qui sit : non autem, Qui fuerit," says Calvin in his comment on 1 Timothy iii. 2. And on Titus i. 6 he says, " Qui defuncta uxore alteram jam cœlebs inducit, nihilominus unius uxoris maritus censeri debet. Non enim eligendum docet qui fuerit maritus unius uxoris, sed qui sit." Whichever of these interpretations of 1 Timothy iii. 2, be adopted, whether we understand the Apostle to forbid that a

polygamist, or that a man twice married, should be admitted to
the ministry, in neither case does the passage give authority to
receive a polygamist into the fellowship of the Church. Consid
ering, then, that monogamy is the undoubted law of Christ
considering that we have no evidence that He made an exception
in favour of heathen converts ; and considering the great importance that churches, founded in heathen lands, should bear true
witness of the doctrines and precepts of Christianity, it would
seem clear that no man having more than one wife should be
admitted to Christian fellowship.

The third aspect of this question concerns the effects of enforcing the Christian law of marriage in heathen lands. It is urged
that this would result in great cruelty and injustice. For a man
to cast off women whom he had engaged to protect and cherish,
to abandon not only them but their children, it is said, cannot be
reconciled with any right principle. To this it may be replied, —
(1.) That in many heathen countries it is not the husband who
supports the wives, but the wives who support the husband. They
are his slaves, and sustain him by their labour. There would be
no great hardship in his setting them free. (2.) But when this is
not the case, it does not follow that because a man ceases to regard several women as his wives, he should cease to provide for
them, and for the welfare of his children. This in any event, as a
Christian, he is bound to do.

It is also suggested, as a difficulty in this matter, that it is hard
to determine which of his several wives a converted polygamist
should retain. Some say, that it is the one first married ;
others say, that he should be allowed to make his own selection.
If marriage among the heathen were what it is in Christian
countries, there would be no room for doubt on this subject.
Then the first contract would be the only binding one, and all
the rest null and void. But in the Christian sense of the word
there has been no marriage in any case. There has been no
promise and vow of mutual fidelity. The relation of a heathen polygamist to the women of his harem, is more analogous
to concubinage than to Christian marriage. The relation of a
heathen polygamist to his numerous wives, is so different from
the conjugal relation as contemplated in Scripture, as to render
it at least doubtful whether the husband's obligation is exclusively, or preëminently, to the woman first chosen. This is a
point of casuistry to which those who expect to labour in heathen
countries should direct their attention. The Romish Church de-

cides in favour of the first wife. The Roman Catechism[1] says :
" Atque ob eam rem fieri intelligimus, ut, si infidelis quispiam,
gentis suæ more et consuetudine, plures uxores duxisset, cum ad
veram religionem conversus fuerit, jubeat eum Ecclesia ceteras
omnes relinquere, ac priorem tantum justæ et legitimæ uxoris
loco habere."

Divorce.

The questions which call for, at least a brief consideration.
under this head are, (1.) What is divorce, and what are its legitimate effects? (2.) What are the Scriptural grounds of divorce?
(3.) What are the Romish doctrine, and practice on this subject ?
(4.) What are the doctrine and practice of Protestant Churches
and countries ? (5.) What is the duty of the Church and of its
officers in cases where the laws of the state on this subject are in
conflict with the law of God ? Works on civil and canon law,
when treating of divorce, take a much wider range than this, but
the points above indicated seem to include those of most interest
and importance to the theologian.

Divorce ; its Nature and Effects.

Divorce is not a mere separation, whether temporary or permanent, " a mensa et thoro." It is not such a separation as leaves
the parties in the relation of husband and wife, and simply re-
lieves them from the obligation of their relative duties. Divorce
annuls the " vinculum matrimonii," so that the parties are no
longer man and wife. They stand henceforth to each other in
the same relation as they were before marriage. That this is the
true idea of divorce is plain from the fact that under the old
dispensation if a man put away his wife, she was at liberty to
marry again. (Deut. xxiv. 1, 2.) This of course supposes that
the marriage relation to her former husband was effectually dissolved. Our Lord teaches the same doctrine. The passages in
the Gospels, referring to this subject, are Matthew v. 31, 32 ; xix.
3–9 ; Mark x. 2–12 ; and Luke xvi. 18. The simple meaning
of these passages seems to be, that marriage is a permanent compact, which cannot be dissolved at the will of either of the parties. If, therefore, a man arbitrarily puts away his wife and
marries another, he commits adultery. If he repudiates her on
just grounds and marries another, he commits no offence. Our
Lord makes the guilt of marrying after separation to depend
on the ground of the separation. Saying, ' that if a man puts

[1] II. viii. 17 (19, xxvi.); Streitwolf, *Libri Symbolici*, Göttingen, 1846, vol. i. p. 458.

away his wife for any cause save fornication, and marries another, he commits adultery'; is saying that 'the offence is not committed if the specified ground of divorce exists.' And this is saying that divorce, when justifiable, dissolves the marriage tie.

Although this seems so plainly to be the doctrine of the Scriptures, the opposite doctrine prevailed early in the Church, and soon gained the ascendancy. Augustine himself taught in his work " De Conjugiis Adulterinis,"[1] and elsewhere, that neither of the parties after divorce could contract a new marriage. In his " Retractions," however, he expresses doubt on the subject. It passed, however, into the canon law, and received the authoritative sanction of the Council of Trent, which says,[2] " Si quis dixerit, ecclesiam errare, cum docuit et docet, juxta evangelicam et apostolicam doctrinam, propter adulterium alterius conjugum matrimonii vinculum non posse dissolvi ; et utrumque, vel etiam innocentem, qui causam adulterio non dedit, non posse, altero conjuge vivente, aliud matrimonium contrahere ; mœcharique eum, qui, dimissa adultera, aliam duxerit, et eam, quæ, dimisso adultero, alii nupserit ; anathema sit." This is the necessary consequence of the doctrine, that the marriage relation can be dissolved only by death. The indisposition of the mediæval and Romish Church to admit of remarriages after divorce, is no doubt to be attributed in part to the low idea of the marriage state prevailing in the Latin Church. It had its ground, however, in the interpretation given to certain passages of Scripture. In Mark x. 11, 12, and in Luke xvi. 18, our Lord says without any qualification : " Whosoever putteth away his wife, and marrieth another, committeth adultery ; and whosoever marrieth her that is put away from her husband, committeth adultery." This was taken as the law on the subject, without regard to what is said in Matthew v. 31, 32, and xix. 3–9. As, however, there is no doubt of the genuineness of the passages in Matthew, they cannot be overlooked. One expression of the will of Christ is as authoritative and as satisfactory as a thousand repetitions could make it. The exception stated in Matthew, therefore, must stand. The reason for the omission in Mark and Luke may be accounted for in different ways. It is said by some that the exception was of necessity understood from its very nature, whether mentioned or not. Or having been stated twice, its repetition was unnecessary. Or what perhaps is most probable, as our Lord was speak-

---

[1] *Works*, edit. Benedictines, Paris, 1837, vol. vi. p. 658.
[2] Sess. xxiv. Canon 7; Streitwolf, *Libri Symbolici*, Göttingen, 1846, vol. i. pp. 90, 91.

ing to Pharisees, who held that a man might put away his wife
when he pleased, it was enough to say that such divorces as they
were accustomed to, did not dissolve the bonds of marriage, and
that the parties remained as much man and wife as they were
before. Under the Old Testament, divorce on the ground of
adultery, was out of the question, because adultery was punished by death. And, therefore, it was only when Christ was
laying down the law of his own kingdom, under which the death
penalty for adultery was to be abolished, that it was necessary
to make any reference to that crime.

It has been earnestly objected to the doctrine that adultery
dissolves the marriage bond, that both parties, the guilty as
well the innocent become free, and either may contract a new
marriage. If this be so, it is said, that all that a man, who
wishes to get rid of his wife, has to do, is to commit that offence.
He will then be at liberty to marry whom he chooses. To this
it might be a sufficient answer to say that the objection bears
rather against the wisdom of the law, than against the fact that
it is the law ; or in other words, the objection is against the
plain meaning of the words of Christ. But it is to be remembered, that adultery is a crime in the sight of man as well as in
the sight of God, and as such it ought to be punished. Under
the old dispensation it was punished by death ; under the new,
it may be punished by imprisonment, or by prohibition of any
future marriage. Christ leaves the punishment of this, as of other
crimes, to be determined by his disciples in their civil capacity.
All He does is to teach what its effects are, " in foro conscientiæ," as to the marriage bond.

Grounds of Divorce.

As already stated, marriage is an indissoluble compact between
one man and one woman. It cannot be dissolved by any voluntary act of repudiation on the part of the contracting parties ;
nor by any act of the Church or State. " Those whom God
has joined together, no man can put asunder." The compact
may, however, be dissolved, although by no legitimate act of
man. It is dissolved by death. It is dissolved by adultery ;
and as Protestants teach, by wilful desertion. In other words,
there are certain things which from their nature work a dissolution of the marriage bond. All the legitimate authority the
state has in the premises is to take cognizance of the fact that the

marriage is dissolved ; officially to announce it, and to make suitable provision for the altered relation of the parties.

Under the preceding head it has already been shown that according to the plain teaching of our Saviour the marriage bond is annulled by the crime of adultery. The reason of this is, that the parties are no longer one, in the mysterious sense in which the Bible declares a man and his wife to be one.[1] The Apostle teaches on this subject the same doctrine that Christ had taught. The seventh chapter of his First Epistle to the Corinthians is devoted to the subject of marriage, in reference to which several questions had been proposed to him.

He first lays down the general principle, founded on the Word of God and the nature of man, that it is best that every man should have his own wife and every wife her own husband ; but in view of the "present (or imminent) distress," he advises his readers not to marry. He writes to the Corinthians as a man would write to an army about to enter on a most unequal conflict in an enemy's country, and for a protracted period. He tells them : ' This is no time for you to think of marriage. You have a right to marry. And in general it is best that all men should marry. But in your circumstances marriage can only lead to embarrassment and increase of suffering.' This limitation of his advice not to marry, to men in the circumstances of those to whom the advice is given, is not only stated in so many words in verse 26, but it is the only way in which Paul can be reconciled with himself or with the general teaching of the Bible. It has already been remarked, that no one of the sacred writers speaks in more exalted terms of marriage than this Apostle. He represents it as a most ennobling spiritual union, which raises a man out of himself and makes him live for another ; a union so elevated and refining as to render it a fit symbol of the union between Christ and his Church. Marriage, according to this Apostle, does for man in the sphere of nature, what union with Christ does for him in the sphere of grace.

Having thus given it as a matter of advice that it was best, under existing circumstances, for Christians not to marry, he

---

[1] That the word πορνεία, as used in Matthew v. 32, and xix. 9, means adultery, there can be no reasonable doubt. Πορνεία is a general term including all unlawful sexual cohabitation, as Theodoret on Romans i. 29 (edit. Halle, 1771), says, καλεῖ πορνείαν τὴν οὐ κατὰ γάμον γινομένην συνουσίαν; whereas μοιχεία is the same offence when committed by a married person. For the definite use of the word πορνεία, see 1 Corinthians v. 1. Tholuck discusses the meaning of this word as used by Matthew, at great length in his *Bergpredigt*, 3d edit. Hamburg, 1845, pp. 225-230.

proceeds to give directions to those who were already married. Of these there were two classes : first, those where both husband and wife were Christians ; and secondly, those where one of the parties was a believer and the other an unbeliever, *i. e.*, a Jew or a heathen. With regard to the former he says, that as according to the law of Christ the marriage is indissoluble, neither party had the right to repudiate the other. But if, in violation of the law of Christ, a wife had deserted her husband, she was bound either to remain unmarried, or to be reconciled to her husband. The Apostle thus impliedly recognizes the principle that there may be causes which justify a woman's leaving her husband, which do not justify a dissolution of the marriage bond.

With regard to those cases in which one of the parties was a Christian and the other an unbeliever, he teaches, first, that such marriages are lawful, and, therefore, ought not to be dissolved. But, secondly, that if the unbelieving partner depart, *i. e.*, repudiates the marriage, the believing partner is not bound ; *i. e.*, is no longer bound by the marriage compact. This seems to be the plain meaning. If the unbelieving partner is willing to continue in the marriage relation, the believing party is bound ; bound, that is, to be faithful to the marriage compact. If the unbeliever is not willing to remain, the believer in that case is not bound ; *i. e.*, bound by the marriage compact. In other words, the marriage is thereby dissolved. This passage is parallel to Romans vii. 2. The Apostle there says, a wife " is bound by the law to her husband, so long as he liveth ; but if the husband be dead, she is loosed from the law of her husband." So here he says, ' A wife is bound to her husband if he is willing to remain with her ; but if he deserts her, she is free from him.' That is, wilful desertion annuls the marriage bond. This desertion, however, must be deliberate and final. This is implied in the whole context. The case contemplated is where the unbelieving husband refuses any longer to regard his believing partner as his wife.

This interpretation of the passage is given not only by the older Protestant interpreters, but also by the leading modern commentators, as De Wette, Meyer, Alford, and Wordsworth, and in the Confessions of the Lutheran and Reformed Churches. Even the Romanists take the same view. They hold, indeed, that among Christians marriage is absolutely indissoluble except by the death of one of the parties. But if one of the partners be an unbeliever, then they hold that desertion annuls the marriage contract. On this point Cornelius à Lapide, of Louvain and Rome, says, "Nota, Apostolum permittere hoc casu non tantum thori divortium sed etiam matrimonii ; ita ut possit conjux fidelis aliud matrimonium inire." Lapide refers to Augustine, Thomas Aquinas, and Ambrose in support of this opinion.[1] The Canon Law, under the title "Divortiis" teaches the same doctrine. Wordsworth's comment on the passage is, "Although a Christian may not put away his wife, being an unbeliever, yet if the wife desert her husband (χωρίζεται) he may contract a second marriage."

The Romanists indeed rest their sanction to remarriage in the case supposed, on the ground that there is an essential difference between marriage where one or both the parties are heathen, and marriage where both parties are Christians. This, however, makes no difference. Paul had just said that such unequal marriages were lawful and valid. Neither party could legitimately repudiate or leave the other. The ground of divorce indicated is not difference of religion, but desertion.

There is a middle ground taken by many, both ancients and moderns, in the interpretation of this passage. They admit that desertion justifies divorce, but not the remarriage of the party deserted. To this it may be objected, —

1. That this is inconsistent with the nature of divorce. We have already seen that divorce among the Jews, as explained by Christ, and as understood in the apostolic Church, was such a separation of man and wife as dissolved the marriage bond. This idea was expressed in the use of the words ἀπολύειν, ἀφιέναι, χωρίζειν, and these are the words here used.

2. This interpretation is inconsistent with the context and with the design of the Apostle. Among the questions submitted to his decision, was this, 'Is it lawful for a Christian to remain in the marriage relation with an unbeliever?' Paul answers, 'Yes ; such marriages are lawful and valid. Therefore if the unbeliever is willing to continue the marriage relation, the believer remains bound ; but if the unbeliever refuses to continue the marriage, the believer is no longer bound by it.' To say that the believer is no longer bound to give up his or her religion, which seems to be Neander's idea, or is not bound to force himself or herself upon an unwilling partner, would be nothing to the point. No Christian could think himself bound to give up his religion, and no one could think it possible that married life could be continued without the consent of the parties. The question, in this sense, was not worth either asking or answering.

[1] *Comment.* 1 Cor. vii. 15 : edit. Venice, 1717

3. Desertion, from the nature of the offence, is a dissolution of the marriage bond. Why does death dissolve a marriage? It is because it is a final separation. So is desertion. Incompatibility of temper, cruelty, disease, crime, insanity, etc., which human laws often make grounds of divorce, are not inconsistent with the marriage relation. A woman may have a disagreeable, a cruel, or a wicked husband, but a man in his grave, or one who refuses to recognize her as his wife, cannot be her husband.

It is said, indeed, that this doctrine makes marriage depend on the option of the parties. Either may desert the other; and then the marriage is dissolved. The same objection was made to our Lord's doctrine that adultery destroys the marriage bond. It was said that if this be so, either party might dissolve the marriage, by committing that crime. As the objections are the same, the answer is the same. As adultery is a crime, so is desertion; and both should be punished. The question is not what these crimes deserve, but what are their legitimate effects, according to the Scriptures, on the marriage relation.

That desertion is a legitimate ground of divorce, was therefore, as before mentioned, the doctrine held by the Reformers, Luther, Calvin, and Zwingle, and almost without exception by all the Protestant churches.[1]

Doctrine of the Church of Rome.

Marriage is thus defined in the Roman Catechism: " Matrimonium est viri, et mulieris maritalis conjunctio inter legitimas personas, individuam vitæ consuetudinem retinens." The clause "inter legitimas personas," is explained by saying, " Qui a nuptiarum conjunctione legibus omnino exclusi sunt, ii matrimonium inire non possunt; neque, si ineant, ratum est, exempli enim gratia: qui intra quartum gradum propinquitate conjuncti sunt, puerque ante decimum quartum annum, aut puella ante duodecimum, quæ ætas legibus constituta est, ad matrimonii justa fœdera ineunda apti esse non possunt." The clause, " Individuam vitæ consuetudinem retinens," it is said, " indissolubilis vinculi naturam declarat quo vir, et uxor colligantur." [2]

Marriage is to be contemplated under two aspects. It is an institution founded in nature, and therefore exists wherever men

---

[1] See the elaborate article on " Ehe " in Herzog's *Encyklopädie*, and President Woolsey's recent *Essay on Divorce*, New York, 1869, chap. IV. President Woolsey does not, for himself, understand 1 Corinthians vii. 15, to teach that desertion justifies divorce.

[2] *Catechismus, ex Decreto Concilii Tridentini, ad Parochos, Pii V. Pont. Max. Jussu editus*, II. viii. quæst. 3; Streitwolf, vol. i. p. 448.

exist. It is a lawful institution among the heathen as well as among Christians. But as it is an ordinance of God it has a character among those who know the true God and thus regard it, far higher than it has for those who are the worshippers of false gods. And, therefore, marriage, under the old dispensation, had a much higher character than it had among the heathen. Nevertheless, among Christians marriage is something far more sacred than it was under the Mosaic economy. Christ had raised it to the dignity of a sacrament.[1]

Marriage a Sacrament.

The word sacrament is one of vague and various meaning. Sometimes it means that which is sacred or consecrated; sometimes that which has, or is intended to have a sacred meaning; i. e., an external sign of some religious truth or grace; sometimes a divinely appointed external rite instituted to be a means of grace; and sometimes a divinely appointed external sign that contains and conveys the grace which it signifies. It is in this last sense that the word is used by Romanists; and it is in this sense they teach that marriage is a sacrament. The principal Scriptural authority for this doctrine they find in Ephesians v. 32, where, as they understand the passage, the words τὸ μυστήριον τοῦτο μέγα ἐστίν, rendered in the Vulgate, "Sacramentum hoc magnum est," are spoken of marriage. According to this version and interpretation, the Apostle does indeed directly assert that marriage is a mystery. But (1.) The words do not refer to marriage, but to the mystical union between Christ and his people as appears from the Apostle's own explanation in the following clause: "I speak concerning Christ and the Church." The two subjects, the union of husband and wife and the union between Christ and his people, had been so combined and interwoven in the preceding verses, that it would have been difficult to determine to which the words, "This is a great mystery," were intended to refer, had not the Apostle himself told us. But (2.) Even if the Apostle does say that the marriage union is a great mystery, which in one sense it clearly is, that would not prove that it is a sacrament. The word "mystery," as used in the Bible, means something hidden or unknown; something which can be known only by divine revelation. Thus the Gospel itself is repeatedly said to be a mystery (Eph. iii. 3–9); the future conversion of the Jews is said to be a mystery (Rom. xi. 25); the incarnation is

---

[1] *Catechismus Romanus*, II. viii. quæst. 14, 16; Streitwolf, vol. i. pp. 454–457.

said to be the great mystery of godliness (1 Tim. iii. 16); and anything obscure or enigmatical is called a mystery (Rev. xvii. 5); thus the mystery of the seven candlesticks is their secret meaning. If, therefore, Paul says that marriage is a great mystery in the sense that no one can fully understand what is meant when God says that husband and wife are one, or even in the sense that marriage has a sacred import, that it is a symbol of a great religious truth, this is what all Protestants admit and what is clearly taught in Scripture. Paul had himself just set forth marriage as the great analogue of the mystical union of Christ and the Church. (3.) Admitting still further that marriage was properly called "sacramentum," that would prove nothing to the purpose. That Latin word had not the sense attached to it by Romanists until long after the apostolic age. It has not that sense even in the Vulgate. In 1 Timothy iii. 16, the manifestation of God in the flesh is declared to be the "great mystery of godliness," which the Vulgate translates " magnum pietatis sacramentum;" but Romanists do not hold that the incarnation is a sacrament in the ecclesiastical sense of that term. The Latin Church, however, having gradually come to attach to the word the idea of a divinely appointed rite or ceremony, which signifies, contains, and conveys grace, and finding, as the words were understood, marriage declared in Ephesians v. 32 to be a " sacramentum," it came to teach that it was a sacrament in the same sense as baptism and the Lord's Supper.

Romanists then teach that marriage is a sacrament not merely because it is the sign or symbol of the union of Christ and his Church. The Roman Catechism says,[1] (1). That no one should doubt " quod scilicet viri, et mulieris conjunctio, cujus Deus auctor est, sanctissimi illius vinculi, quo Christus dominus cum Ecclesia conjungitur, sacramentum, id est, sacrum signum sit." If this were all, no Protestant could object. (2). But Romanists teach that marriage is a sacrament because it not only signifies but also confers grace. The ceremony, including the consent of the parties, the benediction, and the intention of the priest, renders the bride and groom holy. It sanctifies them. " Ex opere operato," it transforms mere natural human love into that holy spiritual affection which renders their union a fit emblem of the union of Christ and the Church. On this point the Council of Trent says:[2] " Gratiam, vero, quæ naturalem illum amorem perficeret

---

[1] II. viii. quæst. 15; Streitwolf, vol. i. pp. 455, 456.
[2] Sess. XXIV.: *Ibid.* vol. i. p. 89.

et indissolubilem unitatem confirmaret, conjugesque sanctificaret, ipse Christus, venerabilium sacramentorum institutor, atque perfector, sua nobis passione promeruit." It would be a great blessing if this were so. Facts, however, prove that the sacramental efficacy of matrimony no more so sanctifies husbands and wives as to make their mutual love like the holy love of Christ for his Church, than baptism confers (to those not opposing an obstacle) all the benefits, subjective and objective, of the redemption of Christ. If the sacramentarian theory were true, all Christians would be perfect and Christendom would be paradisiacal.

Marriage between Christians, according to Romanists, is indissoluble. Neither adultery nor desertion justifies divorce. Death alone can sever the bond. It is not to be inferred from this, however, that marriage is a more sacred institution among Romanists than among Protestants. Any departure from Scriptural rules is sure to work evil. The denial that adultery destroys the marriage bond, leads naturally, and in fact has led, not only to render that crime more frequent, but also to unscriptural devices to remedy the injustice of forcing a husband or wife to maintain the conjugal relation with a guilty partner. One of these devices is the multiplication of the causes of separation " a mensa et thoro " ; and another still more unscriptural, is the multiplying the reasons which render marriage null and void " ab initio." No less than sixteen causes which render marriages null are enumerated by Romish theologians.[1]

The causes which justify separation without divorce, are vows, adultery, apostasy, and crimes. Under the last head they include cruelty and prodigality. If the parties had not been baptized, divorce " a vinculo " was allowed when one of the partners became a Romanist and the other refused to, and also for any serious crime. The whole matter is in the hands of the Church, which claims the right of making and unmaking impediments to marriage at pleasure. " Si quis dixerit Ecclesiam non potuisse constituere impedimenta, matrimonium dirimentia, vel in iis constituendis errasse; anathema sit." [2] At one period the

---

[1] These sixteen causes are expressed in the following lines: —
"Error, conditio, votum, cognatio, crimen,
Cultus disparitas, vis, ordo, ligamen, honestas,
Amens, affinis, si clandestinus et impos,
Si mulier sit rapta, loco nec reddita tuto;
Si impubes, ni forte potentia suppleat annos:
Hæc socianda vetant connubia, facta retractant."
—Dens, *Theologia Moralis et Dogmatica, De Matrimonio,* N. 70, edit. Dublin, 1832, vol. vii. p, 194.
[2] Council of Trent, Sess. xxiv. canon 4: Streitwolf, vol. i. p. 90.

Church of Rome made consanguinity within the seventh degree an impediment to marriage; at present it forbids marriage within the fourth degree inclusive. "The old Catholic theory of marriage," says President Woolsey, "was practically a failure in all its parts, in its ascetic frown on marriage, in its demand from the clergy of an abstinence not required from the Christian laity, in teaching that nothing but death could release the married pair from their obligations. When it sought for impracticable virtue, and forbade to some what God had allowed to all, it opened a fountain of vice with the smallest incitement to virtue." [1]

Laws of Protestant Countries concerning Divorce.

It has already been shown that Protestants, making the Scriptures their guide, taught that the dissolution of the bond of marriage was allowable only for the two offences of adultery and wilful desertion. So far as the churches and their confessions are concerned, this is still the doctrine of almost all Protestant denominations. When, however, marriage came to be regarded as essentially a civil contract, it gradually fell under the jurisdiction of the state, and laws were passed varying in different countries, as legislators were influenced by mere views of justice or expediency. The legislation of all European nations was greatly influenced by the old Roman law; and, therefore, when marriage was removed from the exclusive jurisdiction of the Church, the laws concerning it were more or less adopted from that ancient code. The Roman laws concerning divorce were very lax. Mutual consent was, even after the Roman emperors became Christian, regarded as a sufficient reason for dissolving the bond of marriage. When the Church gained the ascendancy over the State, and the pope became the virtual legislator of Christendom, divorce for any reason was forbidden; and when and where the pope in his turn was dethroned, there was a general tendency to return to the laxity of the Roman legislation.

England.

England was an exception to this rule. It discarded less of popish usages than any other Protestant nation. For a long time after the Reformation no special law concerning divorce was passed. The ecclesiastical courts could decree separation "a mensa et thoro," but a full divorce "a vinculo" could be

---

1 *Essay on Divorce*, by Theodore D. Woolsey, D. D., LL. D., New York, 1869, p. 127.

obtained only by a special act of Parliament. Under the reign
of the present sovereign all such questions were removed from
the ecclesiastical courts and remitted to a civil tribunal. That
tribunal is authorized to grant judicial separation "a mensa et
thoro" on the ground of adultery, or cruelty, or desertion without just cause for two years and upward; and dissolution of
marriage on account of simple adultery on the part of the wife,
or aggravated adultery on the part of the husband. Such divorce
gives both parties liberty to contract a new marriage. "On the
whole, with serious defects," says President Woolsey, "it seems
to us to be an excellent law. It does honour to the Christian
country where it is in force, and it is certainly a great improvement on the former mode of regulating divorce in England."[1]
It may be a good law in comparison with the lawlessness that
preceded it, and in comparison with the lax legislation of other
Protestant nations, but it is not good so far as it is not conformed to the Scriptures. The New Testament makes no such
distinction as is made in this law, between adultery on the part
of the wife and the same offence on the part of the husband.
And it is not good in not allowing wilful desertion to be a legitimate ground of divorce, if, as Protestants almost universally
believe, the Bible teaches the contrary.

France.

In France the laws of the Romish Church were in force until
the Revolution. That event threw everything into confusion,
and the sanctity of marriage was in a great degree disregarded.
Under the empire of the first Napoleon, the civil code allowed
divorce, (1.) for simple adultery on the part of the wife; (2.) for
aggravated adultery on the part of the husband; (3.) for outrages
and cruelty; (4.) for the condemnation of either party to an infamous punishment; and (5.) for mutual persistent consent. The
restoration of the Bourbons put an end to these laws and led to
the entire probibition of divorce.

Germany.

Among the Protestants of Germany, the views of the Reformers,
as a general thing, controlled the action of the several states on
this subject until about the middle of the eighteenth century,
when the laws of marriage were greatly relaxed. Göschen attributes this change in a great measure to the influence of Tho-

[1] *Essay on Divorce*, p. 178.

masius († 1728), who regarded marriage as merely a civil institution designed for the purposes of the state, and which, therefore, might be set aside whenever it failed to answer the desired end.[1] The present law of Prussia, although an improvement on the previous legislation, is far below the Scriptural standard. Besides adultery and wilful desertion, it makes many other offences grounds of divorce, for example, plots endangering the life or health of the other party; gross injuries; dangerous incompatibility of temper; crimes entailing an infamous punishment; habitual drunkenness and extravagance; and deliberate mutual consent, if there be no children fruit of the marriage to be dissolved.

The United States.

The laws of the several states of this Union on the subject of divorce vary from the extreme of strictness to the extreme of laxness. In South Carolina no divorce has ever been given. The effect of refusing to regard adultery as a dissolution of the marriage bond is, as proved by the experience of Catholic countries, to lead the people to regard that crime as a pardonable offence. It was indictable. In New York adultery is the only ground of divorce; but separation from bed and board is granted for cruelty, desertion, and refusal on the part of the husband to make provision for the support of the wife. In several of the other states, besides adultery and desertion, many other grounds are made sufficient to justify divorce; of these grounds the following are the principal: imprisonment, neglect to provide for the maintenance of the wife, habitual drunkenness, and cruelty. In some states the whole matter is left to the discretion of the courts. In the laws of Maine it is said that divorce " a vinculo " may be granted by any justice of the Supreme Court, " when in the exercise of a sound discretion, he deems it reasonable and proper, conducive to domestic harmony, and consistent with the peace and morality of society." The law of Indiana says divorce may be granted for any cause for which the court deems it proper.[2] In Rhode Island to the enumeration of specific causes is added, " and for any other gross misbehaviour and wickêdness in either of the parties, repugnant to and in violation of the marriage covenant." In Connecticut the statute passed in 1849 allows divorce for " any such

---

[1] See his elaborate article on " Ehe " in Herzog's *Real-Encyklopädie*, Stuttgart and Hamburg, 1855, vol. iii. p. 703.

[2] Bishop, *Marriage and Divorce*, book VII. chap. xl. §§ 827 [542], 830 [544], 4th edit. Boston, 1864, vol. i.

misconduct as permanently destroys the happiness of the petitioner and defeats the purpose of the conjugal relation." [1]

Duty of the Church and of its Officers.

There are certain principles bearing on this subject which will be generally conceded, (1.) Every legislative body is bound to conform its enactments to the moral law. This may be assumed as a self-evident proposition. (2.) Every Christian legislature is bound to conform its action to the laws of Christianity. By a Christian legislature is meant one which makes laws for a Christian people. It is not necessary that it should represent them as Christians, to be their agents in teaching, propagating, or enforcing the principles of the Christian religion. It is enough to constitute it a Christian legislature that the great body of its constituents who are bound to obey its laws are Christians. No one hesitates to say that Italy, Spain, and France are Catholic countries ; or that England, Sweden, and Prussia are Protestant. As all the powers of legislatures are derived from the people, it is irrational to suppose that the people would delegate to their representatives authority to violate their religion. No legislature of a Christian state, therefore, can have the right to make laws inconsistent with the Christian religion. This principle, so reasonable and obvious, is conceded in the abstract. No state in this Union would dare to legalize adultery or bigamy. Before the Reformation all questions concerning marriage were under the jurisdiction of the Church ; after that event they were, in Protestant countries, referred to the authorities of the state. "It never, however," says Stahl, "entered the minds of the Reformers, to assert that marriage was purely a civil institution, to be determined by civil, and not religious laws, or that the testimony of the Church as to the divine laws of marriage was not a binding rule for the legislation of the state." [2] And in still more general terms he declares that "What the Church as such [the body of Christians] testifies to be an unchangeable divine law, 'jus divinum,' and upholds within its sphere, is the impassable rule and limit for the legislation of a Christian state." [3]

3. No act of any human legislature contrary to the moral law can bind any man, and no such act contrary to the law of Christ can bind any Christian. If, therefore, a human tribunal annuls

---

[1] See Woolsey, *Essay on Divorce*, New York, 1869, p. 205.

[2] *Die Philosophie des Rechts, Rechts- und Staatslehre*, I. iii. 3. 1. § 69, 4th edit. Heidelberg, 1870, vol. ii. part 1, p. 441.

[3] *Ibid.* § 68; p. 435.

a marriage for any reason other than those assigned in the Bible, the marriage is not thereby dissolved. In the judgment of Christians it remains in full force; and they are bound so to regard it. And on the other hand, if the state pronounces a marriage valid, which the Bible declares to be invalid, in the view of Christians it is invalid. There is no help for this. Christians cannot give up their convictions; nor can they renounce their allegiance to Christ. This state of conflict between the laws and the conscience of the people, is the necessary consequence, if a body making laws for a Christian people disregards an authority which the people recognize as divine.

4. The laws of many of the states of this Union, on the matter of divorce, are unscriptural and immoral. If the former, they are the latter in the view of all who believe in the divine authority of the Bible. If the Scriptures be the only infallible rule of faith and practice, they contain the only standard of right and wrong. The moral law is not something self-imposed. It is not what any man or body of men may think right or expedient. It is the revealed will of God as to human conduct; and whatever is contrary to that will is morally wrong. If this be so, then there can be no doubt that the divorce laws of many of our states are immoral. They contravene the law of God. They annul marriages for other reasons than those allowed in Scripture, and even, in some cases, at the discretion of the courts. They pronounce persons not to be man and wife, who by the law of God are man and wife. They pronounce those to be legally married, whose union Christ declares to be adulterous. That is, they legalize adultery. This is a conclusion which cannot be avoided, except by denying either the authority of the Bible, or that it legislates on the subject of marriage. If marriage were a mere civil compact, with regard to which the Scriptures gave no special directions, it might be regulated by the state according to its views of wisdom or expediency. But if it be an ordinance of God; if He has revealed his will as to who may, and who may not intermarry, and who, when married, may or may not be released from the marriage bond, then the state has no more right to alter these laws than it has to alter the decalogue, and to legalize idolatry or blasphemy. There is no use in covering this matter over. It is wrong to regard anti-Christian laws as matters of small importance.

The action of the state in this matter is not merely negative. It does not simply overlook or refuse to punish the violation of the Scriptural law of divorce, but it intervenes by its positive action, and declares that certain parties are not man and wife, between whom, according to the law of God, the bond of marriage still subsists. It condemns bigamy, but it sanctions what the Bible pronounces bigamy. The law of the state and the law of God, in this regard, are so opposed to each other, that he who obeys the one violates the other.

5. As the Church and its officers are under the highest obligations to obey the law of Christ, it follows that where the action of the state conflicts with that law, such action must be disregarded. If a person be divorced on other than Scriptural grounds and marries again, such person cannot consistently be received to the fellowship of the Church. If a minister be called upon to solemnize the marriage of a person improperly divorced, he cannot, in consistency with his allegiance to Christ, perform the service. This conflict between the civil and divine law is a great evil, and has often, especially in Prussia, given rise to great difficulty.

As all denominations of Christians, Romanists and Protestants, are of one mind on this subject, it is matter of astonishment that these objectionable divorce laws are allowed to stand on the statute-books of so many of our states. This fact proves either that public attention has not to a sufficient degree been called to the subject, or that the public conscience is lamentably blinded or seared. The remedy is with the Church, which is the witness of God on earth, bound to testify to his truth and to uphold his law. If Christians, in their individual capacity and in their Church courts, would unite in their efforts to arouse and guide public sentiment on this subject, there is little doubt that these objectionable laws would be repealed.

The Social Evil.

This is not a subject to be discussed in these pages; a few remarks, however, in reference to it may not be out of place.

1. It is obviously Utopian to expect that all violations of the seventh commandment can be prevented, any more than that the laws against theft or falsehood should never be disregarded.

2. The history of the world shows that the instinct which leads to the evil in question can never be kept within proper limits, except by moral principle, or by marriage.

3. To these two means of correction, therefore, the efforts of the friends of virtue should be principally directed. There can

be no efficient moral culture without religious training. If we would reform our fellow-men, we must bring and keep them from the beginning to the end of their lives under the influence of the truth and ordinances of God ; to accomplish this work is the duty assigned to the Church. Besides this general moral culture, there is needed special effort to produce a proper public sentiment with regard to this special evil. So long as the seventh commandment can be violated without any serious loss of self-respect or of public confidence, one of the strongest barriers against vice is broken down. If loss of character as certainly followed a breach of the seventh commandment, as it follows theft or perjury, the evil would be to a good degree abated. This is already the fact with regard to certain classes. It is so with regard to women ; and it is so in the case of the clergy. If a minister of the gospel be guilty of this offence, he is as certainly and effectually ruined as he would be by the commission of any other crime short of murder. The same moral law, however, binds all men. Theft in the case of one man is, in its essential character, just what it is in the case of any other man.

4. The divinely appointed preventive of the social evil is laid down in 1 Corinthians vii. 2: " Let every man have his own wife, and let every woman have her own husband." That there are serious difficulties, in the present state of society, in the way of frequent and early marriages, cannot be denied. The principal of these is no doubt the expensive style of living generally adopted. Young people find it impossible to commence life with the conveniences and luxuries to which they have been accustomed in their fathers' houses, and therefore marriage is neglected or postponed. With regard to the poorer classes, provision might be made to endow young women of good character, so as to enable them to begin their married life in comfort. Arrangements may also be made in various ways to lessen the expense of family living. The end to be accomplished is to facilitate marriage. Those who are so happy as to find in a dictum of Scripture the ultimate reason and the highest motive, may see the end to be attained, although, as in the present case, they are obliged to leave the means of its accomplishment to experts in social science.

Prohibited Marriages.

That certain marriages are prohibited is almost the universal judgment of mankind. Among the ancient Persians and Egyptians, indeed, the nearest relations were allowed to intermarry, and in the corrupt period of the Roman Empire, equal laxness more or less prevailed. These isolated facts do not invalidate the argument from the general judgment of mankind. What all men think to be wrong, must be wrong. This unanimity cannot be accounted for, except by assuming that the judgment in which men thus agree is founded on the constitution of their nature, and that constitution is the work of God. There are cases, therefore, in which the " vox populi " is the " vox Dei."

The Ground or Reason of such Prohibitions.

The reason why mankind so generally condemn the intermarriage of near relations cannot be physical. Physiology is not taught by instinct. It is, therefore, not only an unworthy, but is an altogether unsatisfactory assumption, that such marriages are forbidden because they tend to the deterioration of the race. The fact assumed may, or may not be true ; but if admitted, it is utterly insufficient to account for the condemnatory judgment in question.

The two most natural and obvious reasons why the intermarriage of near relations is forbidden are, first, that the natural affection which relatives have for each other is incompatible with conjugal love. They cannot coexist. The latter is a violation and destruction of the former. This reason need only be stated. It requires no illustration. These natural affections are not only healthful, but in the higher grades of relationship, even sacred. The second ground for such prohibitions is a regard to domestic purity. When persons are so nearly related to each other as to justify their living together as one family, they should be sacred one to the other. If this were not the case, evil could hardly fail to occur, when young people grow up in the familiarity of domestic life. The slightest inspection of the details of the law as laid down in the eighteenth chapter of Leviticus, shows that this principle underlies many of its specifications.

J. D. Michaelis, in his work on the law of Moses, makes this the only reason for the Levitical prohibitions. He goes to the extreme of denying that " nearness of kin " is in itself any bar to marriage. His views had great influence, not only on public opinion, but even on legislation in Germany. That influence, however, passed away when a deeper moral and religious feeling gained ascendancy.[1]

---

[1] *Commentaries on the Laws of Moses.* By Sir John David Michaelis, Professor of Philosophy in the University of Göttingen. Translated by Alexander Smith, D. D., London 1814, vol. ii. arts. 104–108, pp. 54–76.

Augustine's Theory.

Augustine advanced a theory on this subject, which still has its earnest advocates. He held that the design of all these prohibitory laws was to widen the circle of the social affections. Brothers and sisters are bound together by mutual love. Should they intermarry the circle is not extended. If they choose husbands and wives from among strangers, a larger number of persons are included in the bonds of mutual love. " Habita est ratio rectissima charitatis, ut homines quibus esset utilis atque honesta concordia, diversarum necessitudinum vinculis necterentur ; nec unus in uno multas haberet, sed singulæ spargerentur in singulos ; ac sic ad socialem vitam diligentius colligandam plurimæ plurimos obtinerent." Thus it would come to pass, " Ut unus homo haberet alteram sororem, alteram uxorem, alteram consobrinam, alterum patrem, alterum avunculum, alterum socerum, alteram matrem, alteram amitam, alteram socrum : atque ita se non in paucitate coarctatum, sed latius atque numerosius propinquitatibus crebris vinculum sociale diffunderet." [1]

A writer in Hengstenberg's " Evangelische Kirchen-Zeitung," adopts and elaborately vindicates this theory. He endeavours to show that it answers all the criteria by which any theory on the subject should be tested. These marriages are called " abominations ; " and he asks, Is it not shameful that the benevolent ordinance of God for extending the circle of the social affections should be counteracted ? They are called " confusion," because they unite those whom God commands to remain separate. It also accounts for the propriety of the intermarriage of brothers and sisters in the family of Adam ; for in the beginning the circle of affection did not admit of being enlarged. It even meets the case of the Levirate law which bound a man to marry the childless widow of his brother. The law which forbids the marriage of relations, holds only where the relationship is close. There must, therefore, be cases just on the line beyond which relationship is no bar to marriage. And with regard to those just within the line, there must be considerations which sometimes outweigh the objections to a given marriage. That God dispensed with the law forbidding the marriage of a man with his brother's widow, when the brother died without children, this German writer regards as impossible. " Evil," he says, " may be tolerated,

---

[1] *De Civitate Dei*, xv. xvi. 1; *Works*, edit. Benedictines, Paris, 1838, vol. vii. pp. 633, 634.

but not commanded." He adds that it provokes a smile (man muss es naiv nennen) that Gerhard finds an analogy between the case in question and the permission given to the Israelites to despoil the Egyptians.[1] It is probable that the venerable Gerhard would smile at the writer's criticisms. In the first place, God can no more allow evil than He can command it. An act otherwise evil, ceases to be so when He either allows (*i. e.*, sanctions) it, or commands it. If He commands a man to be put to death, it ceases to be murder to put him to death. There are two principles of morality generally accepted and clearly Scriptural; one of which is, that any of those moral laws which are founded, not on the immutable nature of God, but upon the relations of men in the present state of existence, may be set aside by the divine law-giver whenever it seems good in his sight; just as God under the old dispensation set aside the original monogamic law of marriage. Polygamy was not sinful as long as God permitted it. The same principle is involved in the words of Christ, God loves mercy and not sacrifice. When two laws conflict, the weaker yields to the stronger. It is wrong to labour on the Sabbath, but any amount of labour on that day becomes a duty, if necessary to save life. In the case of the Levirate law, the prohibition to marry a brother's widow, yielded to what under the Mosaic economy was regarded as a higher obligation, that is, to perpetuate the family. To die childless was considered one of the greatest calamities.

The question, however, concerning the rationale of these laws is one of minor importance. We may not be able to see exactly in all cases why certain things are forbidden. The fact that they are forbidden should satisfy the reason and the conscience. The two important questions in connection with this subject, to be considered, are, first, is the Levitical law respecting prohibited marriages still in force? and, second, how is that law to be interpreted, and what marriages does it forbid?

Is the Levitical Law of Marriage still in force?

1. It is a strong *à priori* argument in favour of an affirmative answer to that question, that it always has been regarded as obligatory by the whole Christian Church.

2. The reason assigned for the prohibition contained in that law, has no special reference to the Jews. It is not found in their peculiar circumstances, nor in the design of God in select-

---

[1] *Evangelische Kirchen-Zeitung*, June 1840, pp. 369–416; see p. 378.

ing them to be depositaries of his truth to prepare the world for the coming of the Messiah. The reason assigned "is nearness of kin." This reason has as much force at one time as at another, for all nations as for any one nation. There was nothing peculiar in the relation in which Hebrew parents and children, Hebrew brothers and sisters, and Hebrew uncles and nieces, stood, which was the ground of these prohibitions. That ground was the nearness of the relationship itself as it exists in every and in all ages. There is, therefore, in the sight of God, a permanent reason why near relations ought not to intermarry.

3. If the Levitical law be not still in force, we have no divine law on the subject. Then there is no such sin as incest. It is an offence only against the civil law, and a sin against God only in so far as it is sinful to violate the law of the state. But this is contrary to the universal judgment of men, at least of Christian men. For parents and children, brothers and sisters, to intermarry is universally considered as sin against God, irrespective of any human prohibition. But if a sin against God, it must be forbidden in his Word, or we must give up the fundamental principle of Protestantism, that the Scriptures are the only infallible rule of our faith and practice. As such marriages are nowhere in the Bible forbidden except in the Levitical law, if that law does not forbid them, the Bible does not forbid them.

4. The judgments of God are denounced against the heathen nations for permitting the marriages which the Levitical law forbids. In Leviticus xviii. 3, it is said, "After the doings of the land of Egypt, wherein ye dwelt shall ye not do: and after the doings of the land of Canaan, whither I bring you, shall ye not do ; neither shall ye walk in their ordinances." This is the introduction to the law of prohibited marriages, containing the specification of the " ordinances " of the Egyptians and Canaanites, which the people of God were forbidden to follow. And in the twenty-seventh verse of the same chapter, at the close of these specifications, it is said, " All these abominations have the men of the land done, which were before you, and the land is defiled." Again, in ch. xx. 23, still in reference to these marriages, it is said, " Ye shall not walk in the manners of the nations which I cast out before you: for they committed all these things, and therefore I abhorred them." This is a clear proof that these laws were binding, not on the Jews alone, but upon all people and at all times.

5. The continued obligation of the Levitical law on this subject

is also recognized in the New Testament. This recognition is involved in the constant reference to the law of Moses as the law of God. If in any of its parts or specifications it is no longer obligatory, that is to be proved. It contains much which we learn from the New Testament was designed simply to keep the Hebrews a distinct people; much which was typical; much which was a shadow of things to come, and which passed away when the substance was revealed. It contained, however, much which was moral and of permanent obligation. If God gives a law to men, those who deny its perpetual obligation are bound to prove it. The presumption is that it continues in force until the contrary is proved. It must be hard to prove that laws founded on the permanent social relations of men were intended to be temporary.

Besides this general consideration, we find specific recognitions of the continued obligation of the Levitical law in the New Testament. John the Baptist, as recorded in Mark vi. 18 and Matthew xiv. 4, said to Herod that it was not lawful for him to have his brother Philip's wife. It matters not, as to the argument, whether Philip was living or not. The offence charged was not that he had taken another man's wife, but that he had taken his brother's wife. It may be objected to this argument that during the ministry of John the Baptist the law of Moses was still in force. This Gerhard denies, who argues from Matthew xi. 13, "All the prophets and the law prophesied until John," that the Baptist's ministry belongs to the new dispensation.[1] This may be doubted. Nevertheless John expressed the moral sentiment of his age; and the record of the fact referred to by the Evangelists whose Gospels were written after the Christian Church was fully organized, is given in a form which involves a sanction of the judgment which the Baptist had expressed against the marriage of Herod with his brother's wife. It is also to be remembered that the Herodian family was Idumean, and therefore, that a merely Jewish law would have no natural authority over them.

The Apostle Paul, moreover, in 1 Corinthians v. 1, speaks of a man's marrying his step-mother as an unheard of offence. That this was a case of marriage and not of adultery is plain because the the phrase γυναῖκα ἔχειν is never used in the New Testament except of marriage. This, therefore, is a clear recognition of the

---

[1] *Loci Theologici,* xxvi. v. ii. 2. 1. 1. § 129, edit. Tübingen, 1776, vol. xv. p. 285. Gerhard subjects the whole subject of prohibited marriages to a protracted discussion.

continued obligation of the law forbidding marriage between
near relations, whether the relationship was by consanguinity or
affinity.

6. The Bible everywhere enforces those laws which have their
foundation in the natural constitution of men. That this Levitical law is a divine authentication of a law of nature, may be inferred from the fact that with rare exceptions the intermarriage
of near relations is forbidden among all nations. Paul says that
the marriage of a man with his step-mother was unheard of
among the heathen; *i. e.*, it was forbidden and abhorred. Cicero
exclaims, " Nubit genero socrus. . . . . O mulieris incredibile et
præter hanc unam in omni vita inauditum ! " [1] Beza says, It
must not be overlooked that the civil laws of the Romans agree
completely in reference to this subject with the divine law.
They seemed to have copied from it.[2]

No Christian Church doubts the continued obligation of any of
the laws of the Pentateuch, of which it can be said that the reason assigned for their enactment is the permanent relations of
men ; that the heathen are condemned for their violation ; and
that the New Testament refers to them as still in force: and
which heathen nations under the guidance of natural conscience
have enacted.

How is the Levitical Law to be interpreted?

Admitting the Levitical law of marriage to be still in force, the
next question is, How is it to be interpreted ? Is it to be understood as specifying the degrees of relation, whether of consanguinity or of affinity, within which intermarriage is forbidden ? or,
is it to be viewed as an enumeration of particular cases, so that
no case not specifically mentioned is to be included in the prohibition ?

The former of these rules of interpretation is the one generally
adopted; for the following reasons : —

1. The language of the law itself. It begins with a general
prohibition of marriage between those who are near of kin.
Nearness of kindred is made the ground of the prohibition. The
specifications which follow are intended to show what degree of
nearness of kindred works a prohibition. This reason applies to
many cases not particularly mentioned in Leviticus xviii. or else-

[1] *Pro A. Cluentio*, v. vi. (14, 15); *Works* edit. Leipzig, 1850, p. 374, b.
[2] Beza, *De Repudiis et Divortiis, Tractationes Theologicæ*, edit. Eustathius Vignon, 1582.
vol. ii. p. 52.

where. The law would seem to be applicable to all cases in which the divinely assigned reason for its enactment is found to exist.

2. The design of the law, as we have seen, is twofold: first, to keep sacred those relationships which naturally give rise to feelings and affections which are inconsistent with the marriage relation; and secondly, the preservation of domestic purity. As the natural affections are due partly to the very constitution of our nature, and partly to the familiarity and constancy of intercourse, and the interchange of kindly offices, it is natural that in the enumeration of the prohibited cases regard should be had, in the selection, to those in which this familiarity of intercourse, at the time the law was enacted, actually prevailed. In the East the family is organized on different principles from those on which it is organized in the West. Among the early Oriental nations especially, the males of a family with their wives remained together; while the daughters, being given in marriage, went away and were amalgamated with the families of their husbands. Hence it would happen that relatives by the father's side would be intimate associates, while those of the same degree on the mother's side might be perfect strangers. A law, therefore, constructed on the principle of prohibiting marriage between parties so related as to be already in the bonds of natural affection and who were domesticated in the same family circle, would deal principally in specifications of relationships on the father's side. It would not follow, however, from this fact, that relations of the same grade of kindred might freely intermarry, simply because they were not specified in the enumeration. The law in its principle applies to all cases, whether enumerated or not, in which the nearness of kin is the source of natural affection, and in which it leads to and justifies intimate association.

3. Another consideration in favour of the principle of interpretation usually adopted, is, that the opposite rule would introduce the greatest inconsistencies into the law. The law forbids marriage between those near of kin; and, according to this rule, it goes on alternately permitting and forbidding marriages where the relationship is precisely the same. Thus, a man cannot marry the daughter of his son; but a woman may marry the son of her daughter; a man cannot marry the widow of his father's brother, but he may marry the widow of his mother's brother; a woman cannot marry two brothers, but a man may marry two sisters. These inconsistencies might be intelligible if the law were a temporary and local enactment, designed for a transient

state of society; but they are utterly unaccountable if the law
be one of permanent and universal obligation. A rule of interpretation which brings uniformity and consistency into these
enactments of Scripture, is certainly to be preferred to one which
renders them confused and inconsistent.

Prohibited Degrees.

The cases specifically mentioned are : 1. Mother. 2. Step-
mother. 3. Grand-daughter. 4. Sister and half-sister, " born
at home or born abroad," *i. e.*, legitimate or illegitimate. 5. Aunt
on the father's side. 6. Maternal aunt. 7. The wife of a father's
brother. 8. Daughter-in-law. 9. Brother's wife. 10. A woman
and her daughter. 11. A wife's grand-daughter. 12. Two
sisters at the same time.

The meaning of Leviticus xviii. 18, has been much disputed.
The question is, Whether the words אִשָּׁה אֶל־אֲחֹתָהּ, " a woman to
her sister," are to be understood in their idiomatic sense, "one to
another," so that the law forbids bigamy, the taking of one wife
to another during her lifetime; or, Whether they are to be taken
literally, so that this law forbids a man's marrying the sister of his
wife while the latter is living. It is certain that the words in question have in several places the idiomatic sense ascribed to them.
In Exodus xxvi. 3, " Five curtains shall be coupled together one
to another," literally, " a woman to her sister ; " so in verse 5, the
loops take hold, " a woman and her sister ; " ver. 6, the taches of
gold unite the curtains, " a woman and her sister." Also in ver.
17. Thus also in Ezekiel i. 9, it is said, " their wings were joined
one to another," " a woman to her sister ; " and again in ch. iii. 13.
The words therefore admit of the rendering given in the margin
of the English version. But it is objected to this interpretation
in this case : (1.) That the words in question never mean " one
to another," except when preceded by a plural noun ; which is not
the case in Leviticus xviii. 18. (2.) If this explanation be adopted,
the passage contains an explicit prohibition of polygamy, which
the law of Moses permitted. (3.) It is unnatural to take the words
" wife " and " sister " in a sense different from that in which they
are used throughout the chapter. (4.) The ancient versions agree
with the rendering given in the text of the English Bible. The
Septuagint has γυναῖκα ἐπ᾽ ἀδελφῇ αὐτῆς ; the Vulgate, " sororem
uxoris tuæ."

In this interpretation the modern commentators almost without
exception agree. Thus Maurer renders the passage : " ' Uxorem

ad (*i. e.*, præter) sororem ejus ne ducito,' *i. e.*, Nolli præter tuam
conjugem aliam insuper uxorem ducere, quæ illius soror est." [1]
Baumgarten's comment is: " From the fact that the prohibition
of the marriage of a wife's sister is expressly conditioned on the
life of the former, we must infer with the Rabbins, that after the
death of the wife this marriage is permitted. True, the degree
of affinity is here the same as in ver. 16, but there the relationship
is on the male, here on the female side ; this makes a difference, because under the Old Testament the woman had not attained to the same degree of personality and independence as the
man." [2] Rosenmüller says : " Uxorem ad sororem ejus ne ducas,
duas sorores ne ducas in matrimonium, scil. בְּחַיֶּיהָ in vita ejus, *i. e.*,
uxore tua vivente. Non igitur prohibet Moses matrimonium cum
sorore uxoris mortuæ." [3] Knobel says : " Finally, a man shall
not marry . . . . the sister of his wife, so long as the latter lives.
. . . . To marry one after the other, after the death of the
other, is not forbidden." [4] Keil understands v. 18 in the same
way. It forbids, according to his view, a man's having two sisters, at the same time, as his wives. " After the death of the
first wife," he adds, " marriage with her sister was allowed." [5]

The inference which these writers draw from the fact that in
this passage the marriage of a wife's sister is forbidden during
the life of the wife, that the marriage of the sister, after the death
of the wife, is allowed, is very precarious. All that the passage
teaches is, that if a man chooses to have two wives, at the same
time, which the law allowed, they must not be sisters ; and the
reason assigned is, that it would bring the sisters into a false relation to each other. This leaves the question of the propriety
of marrying the sister of a deceased wife just where it was. This
verse has no direct bearing on that subject.

The cases not expressly mentioned in Leviticus xviii., although
involving the same degree of kindred as those included in the
enumeration, are : 1. A man's own daughter. This is a clear
proof that the enumeration was not intended to be exhaustive.
2. A brother's daughter. 3. A sister's daughter. 4. A maternal

---

[1] *Commentarius Grammaticus Criticus in Vetus Testamentum*, Leipzig, 1835, vol. i.
p. 51.

[2] *Theologischer Commentar zum Pentateuch*, Kiel, 1844, vol. i. part 2, p. 204.

[3] *Scholia in Vetus Testamentum in Compendium redacta*, Leipzig, 1828, vol. i. p.
539.

[4] *Kurzgefasstes exegetisches Handbuch zum Alten Testament. Exodus und Leviticus
erklärt*, von August Knobel, Leipzig, 1857, pp. 505, 506.

[5] *Biblischer Commentar über das Alte Testament*, Heraüsgegeben von Carl Friedr. Keil
und Frank Delitzsch ; *Die Bücher Moses*, von C. F. Keil, Leipzig, 1862, vol. ii. p. 117.

uncle's widow. 5. A brother's son's widow. 6. A sister's son's widow. 7. The sister of a deceased wife.

As nearness of kindred is made the ground of prohibition, and as these cases are included within " the degrees " specified, the Church has considered them as belonging to the class of prohibited marriages. It is, however, to be considered that the word " prohibited," as here used, is very comprehensive. Some of the marriages specified in the Levitical law are prohibited in very different senses. Some are pronounced abominable, and those who contract them are made punishable with death. Others are pronounced unseemly, or evil, and punished by exclusion from the privileges of the theocracy. Others again incur the penalty of dying childless; probably meaning that the children of such marriages should not be enrolled in the family registers which the Jews were so careful to preserve.

As this distinction is recognized in the law itself, so it is founded in the nature of the case. As nearness of kin varies from the most intimate relationship to the most distant, so these marriages vary in their impropriety from the highest to the lowest degree. Some of them may, in certain cases, be wrong, not in themselves, but simply from the obligation to uphold a salutary law. That is, there may be cases to which the law, but not the reason of the law applies. For example ; a man may go thousands of miles from home and marry : his wife would stand in a very different relation to her husband's brothers, than had she lived in the same house with them. The law forbidding a woman to marry the brother of her deceased husband, would apply to her; but the reason of that law would affect her in a very slight degree ; nevertheless, even in her case, the law should be observed.

There is another obvious remark that ought to be made. Strong repugnance is often felt and expressed against the Levitical law, not only because it is regarded as placing all the marriages specified on the same level, representing all as equally offensive in the sight of God, but also from the assumption that all the marriages forbidden are, if contracted, invalid. This is a wrong view of the subject. It is inconsistent with the law itself, and contrary to the analogy of Scripture. The law recognizes a great disparity in the impropriety of these marriages. Some, as just remarked, are utterly abominable and insufferable. Others are specified because inexpedient or dangerous, as conflicting with some ethical or prudential principle.

It is in this as in many other cases. The Mosaic law discountenanced and discouraged intermarriage between the chosen people and their heathen neighbours. With regard to the Canaanites, such intermarriages were absolutely forbidden; with other heathen nations, although discountenanced, they were tolerated. Joseph married an Egyptian; Moses, a Midianite; Solomon married Pharaoh's daughter. Such marriages, in the settled state of the Jewish nation, may have been wrong, but they were valid. Even now under the Christian dispensation, believers are forbidden to be unequally yoked together with unbelievers. It does not follow from this that every marriage between a believer and an unbeliever is invalid. These remarks are not out of place. The truth suffers from being misapprehended. If the Bible is made to teach what is contrary to the common sense, or the intuitive judgments of men, it suffers great injustice. No man can force himself to believe that a man's marrying the sister of a deceased wife is the same kind of offence as a father's marrying his own daughter. The Bible teaches no such doctrine; and it is a slander so to represent it.

Concluding Remarks.

The laws of God are sacred. They are founded, not only on his infinite wisdom, but also on the nature of his creatures, and, therefore, should be sedulously observed. There may, in some cases, be honest difference of opinion as to what the law or will of God is, but when ascertained, it is our wisdom and duty to make it the rule of our conduct. This is so obvious that the statement of it may seem entirely superfluous. It is so common, however, for men professing to be Christians to make their own feelings, opinions, and views of expediency, the rule of action for themselves and others, that it is by no means a work of supererogation, to reiterate on all proper occasions the truism that there is no wisdom like God's wisdom, and that men are never wise except when they follow the wisdom of God as revealed in his Word, even when they have to do it blindly.

There are certain principles which underlie the marriage laws of the Bible, which all men in their private capacity and when acting as legislators, would do well to respect, —

1. The first is, that marriage is not a mere external union; it is not simply a mutual compact; it is not merely a civil contract. It is a real, physical, vital, and spiritual union, in virtue of which man and wife become, not merely in a figurative sense, but really, although in a mysterious sense, one flesh. This is not only expressly

declared by Christ himself to be the nature of marriage, but it is
the doctrine which underlies the whole Levitical law on this subject. Nearness of kin is expressed constantly by saying that one
is "flesh of the flesh" of the other, שְׁאֵר בְּשָׂרוֹ, "Carnem carnis
suæ s. corporis sui esse cognatam propinquam, quæ est ut caro
ejusdem corporis." [1] According to the Scriptures, therefore, husband and wife are the nearest of all relations to each other. According to the spirit, and most of the legislation of the present
age, they are no relations at all. They are simply partners. If
one member of a business firm die, his property does not go to
his partner, but to his own family ; so if a wife die, without children, her property does not go to her husband, but to her third
or fourth cousins. They, in the eye of the law, are more nearly
related to her than her husband. This is not the light in which
God looks upon marriage.

2. The second principle which underlies these marriage-laws is,
that affinity is as real a bond of relationship as consanguinity.
Fully one half of the marriages specified in Leviticus are prohibited on the ground of affinity. The same form of expression
is used to designate both kinds of relationship. Those related to
each other by affinity are said to be "flesh of the flesh," one of
the other, just as blood relations ; because all the specifications
contained in the eighteenth chapter of Leviticus are included under the general prohibition contained in the sixth verse, "None
of you shall approach to any that is near of kin to him ; " under this head are included step-mothers ; mothers-in-law ; step-
daughters ; sisters-in-law (as when a man is forbidden to marry
the widow of his brother) ; uncle's wife, etc. These relationships are traced out in the line of affinity, just as far as they are
in that of consanguinity. The declaration, therefore, contained
in the Westminster Confession,[1] "The man may not marry any
of his wife's kindred nearer in blood than he may of his own, nor
the woman of her husband's kindred nearer in blood than of her
own," is a simple and comprehensive statement of the law as laid
down in Leviticus. In saying that affinity is as real a bond of
relationship as consanguinity, it is not meant that it is as strong.
A daughter is a nearer relation than a step-daughter, or daughter-in-law ; a mother than a step-mother ; a sister than a sister-
in-law. This, as we have seen, is recognized in the law itself.

---

[1] Rosenmüller, *Scholia in Vetus Testamentum in Compendium redacta,* Leipzig. 1838.
vol. i. pp. 536, 537.

[2] Chap. xxiv. 4.

The Bible asserts nothing inconsistent with fact or nature. In making affinity a real bond of kindred, it is meant that it is not merely nominal, or conventional, or arbitrary. It has its foundation in nature and fact.

Mr. Bishop, in his elaborate work on " Marriage and Divorce," says, " A truly enlightened view will doubtless discard altogether affinity as an impediment, while it will extend somewhat the degrees of consanguinity within which marriages will be forbidden." [1] He also teaches [2] that " the relationship by affinity " ceases " with the dissolution which death brings to the marriage. . . . . If, when a man's wife dies, she is still his wife, then, of course, her sister is still his sister. . . . . If, on the other hand, the wife is no more the wife after her death, then is her sister no more the sister of the husband. And though men who have no other idea of religion than to regard it as a bundle of absurd and loathed forms, may not be able to see how the termination of the relationship by the death of the wife is of any consequence in the case, yet men who discern differently and more wisely, will discover nothing unseemly in practically acting upon a fact which everybody knows to exist."

It is very evident that Mr. Bishop never asked himself what, in the present connection, the word " relationship " means. Had he had any clear idea of the meaning of the word, he never could have written the above sentences. By relationship is here meant the relation in which parties stand to each other ; and that, in the case supposed, is a matter of feeling, affection, and intimacy. This relationship is not dissolved by the death of the person through whom it arose. A wife's sister continues to cherish to her widowed brother-in-law the same sisterly affection after, as before her sister's death. She can live with him, guide his house, and take charge of his children, without the slightest violation of her self-respect, and without fear of incurring the disrespect of others.

Besides, if relationship by affinity is dissolved by death, then a son may, on the death of his father, marry his step-mother, which Paul says (1 Cor. v. 1) was not tolerated among the heathen. We have not come to that yet. On the principle of Mr. Bishop, a man may marry his mother-in-law, his daughter-in-law, and, on the death of the mother, his step-daughter. All this the Bible forbids ; and whatever religion in some of its manifestations may

---

[1] *Commentaries on the Law of Marriage and Divorce*, by Joel Prentiss Bishop, Boston, 1864, vol. i. § 320.

[2] *Ibid.* § 314, note 2.

be, the Bible, surely, is not "a bundle of absurd and loathed forms." It is the wisdom of God, in the presence of which the wisdom of man is foolishness.

3. The great truth contained in these laws is, that it is the will of God, the dictate of his infinite and benevolent wisdom that the affections which belong to the relation in which kindred (whether by consanguinity or affinity) stand to each other, should not be disturbed, perverted, or corrupted by that essentially different kind of love which is appropriate and holy in the conjugal relation ; and that a protecting halo should be shed around the family circle.

§ 12. *The Eighth Commandment.*

This commandment forbids all violations of the rights of property. The right of property in an object is the right to its exclusive possession and use.

The foundation of the right of property is the will of God. By this is meant, (1.) That God has so constituted man that he desires and needs this right of the exclusive possession and use of certain things. (2.) Having made man a social being, He has made the right of property essential to the healthful development of human society. (3.) He has implanted a sense of justice in the nature of man, which condemns as morally wrong everything inconsistent with the right in question. (4.) He has declared in his Word that any and every violation of this right is sinful.

This doctrine of the divine right of property is the only security for the individual or for society. If it be made to rest on any other foundation, it is insecure and unstable. It is only by making property sacred, guarded by the fiery sword of divine justice, that it can be safe from the dangers to which it is everywhere and always exposed.

Numerous theories have been advanced on this subject. These theories have had a twofold object : the one to explain the nature and ground of the right ; the other to explain how the right was originally acquired. These objects are distinct and should not be confounded.

1. The modern philosophical theory that might is right, that the strongest is always the best, includes indeed both these objects. If being is the only good, and if it is true the more of being the more of good, then he who has the most of being, he in whom the infinite is most fully revealed, has the right to have and to hold whatever he chooses to possess.

2. If a regard to our individual well-being be the only ground of moral obligation, then a man has the right to whatever will make him happy. He may, and he certainly would, make a great mistake, if he supposed that taking what does not belong to him would promote his happiness; but he is restrained from such injustice only by a sense of prudence. He is entitled to have whatever in fact would make him happy, and for that reason.

3. If regard to the general good, the greatest happiness of the greatest number, or expediency, as Paley makes it, be the rule and ground of duty, then it will always be a matter of opinion, a matter on which men will ever differ, what is, and what is not expedient. One might think that a community of goods would promote the greatest good, and then he would, at least in his own conscience, be entitled to act on that principle. Others might think that agrarianism, or the periodic distribution of all the land of the country in equal portions among the people, would promote the general good, and then that would be to them the rule of action. There would be no end to the devices to promote the greatest good, if the rights of men rested on no other foundation than that of expediency.

Some of the most distinguished legal and philosophical writers of the present age teach that "property is founded on utility." With some, however, utility is not the ground, but rather the test of human rights and duties. The fact that an institution or a course of conduct is conducive to the public good, is not so much the reason why it is right, as a proof that it is right and in accordance with the will of God. " God designs the happiness of all his sentient creatures. Some human actions forward that benevolent purpose, or their tendencies are beneficent and useful. Other human actions are adverse to that purpose, or their tendencies are mischievous or pernicious. The former, as promoting his purpose, God has enjoined. The latter, as opposed to his purpose, God has forbidden. He has given us the faculty of observing; of remembering; and of reasoning; and by duly applying those faculties, we may collect the tendencies of our actions. Knowing the tendencies of our actions, and knowing his benevolent purpose, we know his tacit commands." [1] It is no doubt true that it is a fair and conclusive argument that a thing is right or wrong in itself and conformed or opposed to the will of God, that its tendency is of necessity and always to produce, on the one

---

[1] *Lectures on Jurisprudence, or the Philosophy of Positive Law*, by the late John Austin. ed edit. revised and edited by Robert Campbell, London, 1869, vol. i. p. 109.

hand, good, or, on the other, evil. But this is a roundabout way
of getting at the truth. Whether an institution or a course of
action be useful or not, must be a matter of opinion. And if a
matter of opinion, men will differ about it; and the opinion of
one man, or even of the majority of men, will have no authority
over others. God has revealed his will in his Word, and in the
constitution of our nature. Paul says that even the heathen " do
by nature the things contained in the law," that the law is " written in their hearts." (Rom. ii. 14, 15.) Property is sacred, not
because in our opinion it is a useful institution, and hence infer-
entially approved by God, but He has said in the Bible, and says
in every man's conscience, " Thou shalt not steal." Mr. Austin's
theory does not prevent his teaching that " property *jus in rem*,"
depends on " principles of utility." [1]

4. Paley says also that " the real foundation of our right [to
property] is the law of the land." He admits, however, that the
law may authorize the most flagitious injustice. He therefore
makes a distinction between the words and the intention of the
law ; and adds : " With the law, we acknowledge, resides the disposal of property ; so long, therefore, as we keep within the design
and intention of a law, that law will justify us, as well in *foro conscientiæ*, as in *foro humano*, whatever be the equity or expediency
of the law itself." [2] The law of the land has indeed legitimately
much to do with questions of property ; but the right itself does
not rest upon that law, and is, in the sight of God, independent of
it. The right exists prior to all law of the state. The law cannot
ignore that right. It cannot rightfully deprive a man of his property, except in punishment of crime, or on the ground of stringent
necessity, and, in the latter case, with due compensation. Property,
however, is not the creature of the law. No unjust law gives a title
to property, valid in the sight of God ; that is, a title which should
satisfy a conscientious man in entering upon its possession and
use. Even when the law is not unjust, it may work, not legal,
but moral injustice. A will, for example, may clearly express
the wishes and intention of a testator, but for some clerical or
technical error be set aside and the property go to a person for
whom it was not intended. Such person would have a legal, but
not a morally valid title to the property. Good men are sometimes heard to say : " We will take all the law gives us ; " in

[1] *Jurisprudence*, vol. i. pp. 132, 382; vol. ii. pp. 1161.
[2] *The Principles of Moral and Political Philosophy*, book iii. part i. ch. iv. ; edit. Boston.
1848 vol. i. pp. 87–89.

saying this, they do not apprehend the full meaning of their
words ; it amounts to saying that in matters of property they
will make the law of the land, and not the law of God, the rule
of their conduct.

5. It is a very common doctrine that the right of property
is founded on common consent, or on the social compact.
Men agree that each man may appropriate to himself a portion of what originally is common to all.   But this consent
only recognizes a right ; it does not create it.   If a man takes a
glass of water from a stream common to all, it is of right his ;
and he has no need to appeal to any compact or consent to justify
his appropriating it to himself.   The question how a man ac-
quires a right to property, and the nature of the right itself, as
before remarked, are different questions, although intimately related.

6. Both are included in the common theory on the subject.   If
a man puts under culture a portion of unappropriated land, it is
for the time being his, on the principle that a man owns himself,
and therefore the fruits of his labour.   Exclusive possession and
use of the land in question are necessary to secure the man those
fruits ; he has, therefore, the right to the land as long as he uses
it.   If he abandons it, his right ceases.   On the other hand, if
his use is continued, so as to involve occupancy, his right of possession becomes permanent.   It is on this principle men act in
mining districts in unoccupied lands.   Each man, the first comer,
stakes out for himself a claim ; this he works, or is entitled to
keep to himself.   If he abandons it and goes elsewhere, it ceases
to be his.   If he permanently occupies it, it is permanently his.
The right of property is thus made to rest on occupancy and use ;
in other words, on labour.   But even this, according to Blackstone,
is not a natural right.   "All property," he says, "must cease
upon death, considering men as absolute individuals, and uncon-
nected with civil society : for then, by the principles before established, the next immediate occupant would acquire a right in
all that the deceased possessed.   But as, under civilized governments which are calculated for the peace of mankind, such a
constitution would be productive of endless disturbances, universal law of almost every nation (which is a kind of secondary law of nature) has either given the dying person a power of
continuing his property, by disposing of his possessions by will ;
or, in case he neglects to dispose of it, or is not permitted to make
any disposition at all, the municipal law of the country then steps

in, and declares who shall be the successor, representative, or heir of the deceased ; that is, who alone shall have a right to enter upon this vacant possession, in order to avoid that confusion which its becoming again common would occasion." On the same page, speaking of the right of inheritance, he says : " We are apt to conceive at first view that it has nature on its side ; yet we often mistake for nature what we find established by long and inveterate custom. It is a wise and effectual, but clearly a political establishment ; since the permanent right of property, vested in the ancestor himself, was no natural, but merely a civil right." [1] He had said before,[2] " Necessity begat property ; and in order to insure that property, recourse was had to civil society, which brought along with it a long train of inseparable concomitants ; states, government, laws, punishments, and the public exercise of religious duties." This seems to be inverting the natural order of things. Disregard of the moral law would result in endless evil, and there is an absolute necessity that its commands should be observed and enforced ; but the obligation of the law does not rest on that necessity ; it is altogether anterior and independent of it. So the right of property is anterior and independent of the necessity of its being held sacred, in order to secure the well-being of mankind. The fact is, that the right of property is analogous to the right of life, liberty, or pursuit of happiness. It does not come from men ; it is not given by man ; and it cannot be ignored, or arbitrarily interfered with by man. It rests on the will of God as revealed in the constitution of our nature and in our relation to persons and things around us.

7. Stahl, the distinguished German jurist, gives substantially the following account of the matter. Man was formed out of the earth ; but a divine spirit was breathed into him. He is, therefore, on the one hand, dependent on the material world ; on the other, exalted above it. He is placed here as its lord and owner. The things of the outer world are given to him for the satisfaction of his physical wants, and of his spiritual necessities. He, therefore, has power and right over things external, and they must be permanently and securely under his control. This is the foundation of the right of property. Property is the means for the development of the individuality of the man. The manner in which it is acquired and used, reveals what the man is ; his

---

[1] *Commentaries on the Laws of England*, II. i. by Sir William Blackstone, Knt. 16th edit. London, 1825, vol. ii. p. 10.

[2] *Ibid.* p. 7.

food, clothing, and habitation ; his expenditures for sensual enjoyment, for objects of taste, of art, and of science, and for hospi-
tality, benevolence, and the good of society ; and the consecration
of his acquisitions to the interests of a higher life, — these in their
totality as they rest on the right of property, make out a man's
portrait. Property, however, is specially designed to enable a
man to discharge his moral duties. Every man has duties of his
own to perform ; duties which belong to him alone, not to others,
not to society ; duties which arise out of his personal vocation
and standing, especially such as belong to his own family. Therefore he must have what is exclusively his own. Property, therefore, is not intended for mere self-gratification or support ; nor is
it a mere objectless mastery over things external ; it is the necessary means to enable a man to fulfil his divinely-appointed destiny. Herein lies the divine right of property ! [1]

The right of property, therefore, is not founded on the law of
the land, or on any explicit or implied contract among men ; but
upon the law of nature. It is true that natural, as distinguished
from positive laws, have been differently explained. "As the
science of ethics," says Lord Mackenzie, "embraces the whole
range of moral duties, its province is evidently much wider than
that of jurisprudence, which treats only of those duties that can
be enforced by external law." [2] The duties, however, which can
be thus enforced are of two kinds ; those which arise from the
natural, and those which arise from common or statute law. "By
the law of nature," says Chancellor Kent,[3] "I understand those
fit and just rules of conduct which the Creator has prescribed to
man as a dependent and social being, and which are to be ascertained from the deduction of right reason, though they may be
more precisely known and more explicitly declared by divine revelation." Cicero, teaches that God is the author of natural law,
and that its duties are of unchangeable obligation. He says, "Nec
erit alia lex Romæ, alia Athenis, alia nunc, alia posthac ; sed et
omnes gentes et omni tempore una lex et sempiterna et immu-
tabilis continebit, unusque erit communis quasi magister et im-
perator omnium deus." [4]

[1] *Die Philosophie des Rechts, Rechts- und Staatslehre*, I. iii. 2, 1, § 22, 4th edit.
Heidelberg, 1870, vol. ii. part 1, p. 350 f. The paragraph in the text is not a translation, but a condensation.

[2] *Studies in Roman Law, with Comparative Views of the Laws of France, England, and
Scotland*, by Lord Mackenzie, one of the Judges of the Court of Session in Scotland, 2d
edit. Edinburgh and London, 1865, p. 45.

[3] Chancellor Kent, quoted by Lord Mackenzie.

[4] *De Republica*, III. xxii. 33. 16, edit. Leipzig, 1850, p. 1193, a.

Lord Mackenzie gives the doctrine of Cicero the sanction of his own judgment : " Where," he says, " the law of nature absolutely commands or forbids, it is immutable and of universal obligation, so that, although it may be confirmed, it cannot be controlled by human laws without a manifest violation of the divine will." [1]

In these days, when so many are disposed to throw off the authority of God, and regard marriage and property as mere creatures of the law, which may be regulated or ignored at the caprice or will of the people, it is well to remind them that there is a law higher than any law of man, enforced by the authority of God, which no man and no community can violate with impunity.

Although the right of property involves the right of absolute control, so that a man can do what he will with his own, it does not follow that this right is unlimited, or that the civil law has no legitimate control over the use or distribution of his property. A man has no right to use his knowledge or strength to the injury of his fellow-men ; neither can he use his property so as to make it a public nuisance ; nor can he devote it to any immoral or hurtful object ; nor can he dispose of it by will so as to militate against the public policy. Of course, as different nations are organized on different principles, the laws regulating the use and distribution of property must also differ. Among the Hebrews the land of Canaan was originally distributed equitably among the several families. The head of the family had not the unrestricted control of what was thus given him. He could not finally alienate it. His sons, not his daughters, unless there were no sons, were his heirs. The first-born had a double portion. (Deut. xxi. 15 ff.) These limitations of the right of property were ordained by God, in order that the ends of the theocracy might be accomplished. God saw fit to render it impossible that any large portion of the land should be engrossed by one or by a few families. In England public policy has assumed that it is important to maintain a powerful order of nobility. To secure that end the laws of primogeniture and entail have been long in force, with the result that the greater part of the land in Great Britain is in the hands of comparatively few families. This unequal distribution of property has gone on rapidly increasing, so that Hugh Miller, when editor of the " Edinburgh Witness," said that England was now like a pyramid poised on its apex. In France the right of a testator to dispose of his property is very much limited. " If any one die without issue or ascendants, he may leave his whole property to

[1] *Studies in Roman Law*, etc., p. 49.

strangers; but if a man at his death has one lawful child, he can only so dispose of the half of his estate; if he leave two children, the third; and if he leave three or more children, the fourth." In Scotland " if a man die without either wife or issue, his whole property is at his own disposal; if he leave a wife and issue, his goods or personal property are divided into three equal parts, one of which goes to his wife as *jus relictæ*, another to his children as *legitim* (i. e., *legitima portio*), and the third is at his own disposal; if he leave no wife, he may dispose of one half, and the other half goes to his children, and so *e converso*, if he leave no children, the wife is entitled to one half, and he may bequeath the other." [1] These facts are referred to simply as illustrations of the way in which the law, both divine and human, may limit the exercise of the right of property while the sacredness of that right, as higher than any human law, is fully recognized.

Community of Goods.

Community of goods does not necessarily involve the denial of the right of private property. When Ananias, having sold a possession, kept back part of the price, Peter said to him: " While it remained was it not thine own? and after it was sold, was it not in thine own power?" (Acts v. 4.) Any number of men may agree to live in common, putting all their possessions and all the fruits of their labour into a common fund, from which each member is supplied according to his wants. This experiment was tried on a small scale and for a short time, by the early Christians in Jerusalem. " The multitude of them that believed were of one heart and of one soul: neither said any of them that ought of the things which he possessed was his own; but they had all things common. . . . . Neither was there any among them that lacked: for as many as were possessors of lands or houses, sold them, and brought the prices of the things that were sold, and laid them down at the Apostles' feet: and distribution was made unto every man as he had need." (Acts iv. 32–35.) Some indeed say that these passages do not imply any actual community of goods. Having " all things common " is understood to mean, " No one regarded his possessions as belonging absolutely to himself, but as a trust for the benefit of others also." This interpretation seems inconsistent with the whole narrative. Those who had possessions sold them. They renounced all control over what was once their own. The price was handed over to the Apostles and distributed by them or under their direction.

1 Lord Mackenzie, *ut supra*, p. 270.

On the narrative as given in the Acts it may be remarked, —

1. That the conduct of these early Christians was purely spontaneous. They were not commanded by the Apostles to sell their possessions and to have all things in common. There is not the slightest intimation that the Apostles gave any encouragement to this movement. They seem simply to have permitted it. They allowed the people to act under the impulse of their own feelings, each one doing what he pleased with his own.

2. It can hardly be deemed unnatural that the early Christians were led into this experiment. To us the wonders of redemption are " the old, old story," inexpressibly precious indeed, but it has lost the power of novelty. In those to whom it was new it may well have produced an ecstatic bewilderment, which led their judgment astray. There are two great truths involved in the Gospel, the clear perception of which may account for the determination of those early converts to have all things in common. The one is that all believers are one body in Christ Jesus ; all united to Him by the indwelling of the Holy Spirit ; all equally partakers of his righteousness ; all the objects of his love ; and all destined to the same inheritance of glory. The other great truth is contained in the words of Christ, " Inasmuch as ye have done it unto one of the least of these my brethren, ye have done it unto me." It was no wonder, then, that men whose minds were filled with these truths, were oblivious of mere prudential considerations.

3. This experiment, for all that appears, was confined to the Christians in Jerusalem, and was soon abandoned. We never hear of it elsewhere or afterwards. It has, therefore, no preceptive force.

4. The conditions of the success of this plan, on any large scale, cannot be found on earth. It supposes something near perfection in all embraced within the compass of its operation. It supposes that men will labour as assiduously without the stimulus of the desire to improve their condition and to secure the welfare of their families as with it. It supposes absolute disinterestedness on the part of the more wealthy, the stronger, or the more able members of the community. They must be willing to forego all personal advantages from their superior endowments. It supposes perfect integrity on the part of the distributors of the common fund, and a spirit of moderation and contentment in each member of the community, to be satisfied with what others, and not he, may think to be his equitable share. We shall have to

wait till the millennium before these conditions can be fulfilled. The attempt to introduce a general community of goods in the present state of the world, instead of elevating the poor, would reduce the whole mass of society to a common level of barbarism and poverty. The only secure basis of society is in those immutable principles of right and duty which God has revealed in his Word, and written upon the hearts of men. And these truths, even if acknowledged as matters of opinion, lose their authority and power if they cease to be regarded as revelations of the mind and will of God, to which human reason and human conduct must conform.

Communism and Socialism.

Heaven is not higher than "the lower parts of the earth," than the principles and aims of the early Christians were exalted above those of the modern advocates of the community of goods. This idea is not of modern origin. It appears in different forms in all ages of the world. It entered into the scheme of Plato's Republic, for in his view private property was the chief source of all social evils. It was included in the monasticism of the Middle Ages. Renunciation of the world included the renunciation of all property. Voluntary poverty was one of the vows of all monastic institutions. It was adopted by many of the mystical and fanatical sects which appeared before the Reformation, as the Beghards, and "Brethren of the Free Spirit," who taught that the world should be restored to its paradisiacal state, and that all the distinctions created by law, whether of social organization, property, or marriage, should be done away. At the time of the Reformation the followers of Münzer adopted the same principles, and their efforts to carry them into practice led to the miseries of the "peasant-war." All these movements were connected with fanatical religious doctrines. The leaders of these sects claimed to be inspired, and represented themselves as the organs and messengers of God.

Modern communism, on the contrary, so far as its general character is concerned, is materialistic and atheistic, and in some of its forms pantheistic.[1] This is consistent with the admission that

[1] Enfantin, a disciple of St. Simon, began one of his public discourses, delivered in Paris in 1831, with the words, "Dieu est tout ce qui est; Tout est en lui, tout est par lui, Nul de nous n'est hors de lui;" and Henri Heine called himself a Hegelian. On the other hand, one of St. Simon's books is entitled Le nouveau Christianisme. See Guerike's Kirchen-Geschichte, vii. D. § 220, 6th edit. Leipzig, 1846, vol. iii. p. 679, foot-notes. We are tempted to quote a single characteristic sentence from Guerike, ut supra, pp. 678-682:

some of its advocates, as St. Simon, Fourier, and others, were sincere and benevolent men. Some of them, indeed, said that they only desired to carry out the principle of brotherly love so often inculcated by Christ. Communism and socialism are not properly convertible terms, although often used to designate the same system. The one has reference more especially to the principle of community in property; the latter to the mode of social organization. With Fourier, the former was subordinate to the latter. He did not entirely deny the right of property, but insisted that society was badly organized. Instead of living in distinct families, each struggling for support and advancement, men should be gathered in large associations having common property, and all labouring for a common fund. That fund was to be distributed according to the capital contributed by each member, and according to the time and skill employed in the common service. Proudhon, immortalized by the book in which the question "What is property?" is answered by saying, "Property is theft," makes the rule for the distribution of the common fund to be the time devoted to labour. Louis Blanc puts capital, labour, and skill out of consideration, and makes the wants of the individual the only rule of distribution. It is common to all these schemes that the right to property in land or its productions is denied. The two latter deny to a man all property in his own skill or talents; and the last, even in his labour, so that the idlest and least efficient member of society

"Die originellste und selbständigste religiös-politische Secte der neuesten Zeit aber, von einem Manne gegründet, dem erst durch verunglückten, Selbstmord 'der göttliche Mensch sich kund that' (dem französischen Grafen Claude Henri St. Simon, geb. zu Paris 1760, gest. am 19. Mai 1825), und sodann durch die Juli-Revolution 1830 erst in rechten Schwung gebracht, welche, als die Quintessenz des tief verderbten antichristlichen Zeitgeistes, als die einzig ganz consequente unter allen widergöttlichen Richtungen der Zeit, Welt und Gott, Staat und Kirche, Fleisch und Geist, Diesseits und Jenseits, Böse und Gut, (auch Weib und Mann) sowohl wissenschaftlisch als praktisch unirte und identificirte, unbeschränkte vollständig organisirte Herrschaft des widergöttlichen Fleisches, ungebundenes systematisches Leben nur für diesseitige (die einzige) Welt, unbedingte Geltung eines consequenten politisch-religiösen Materialismus in glühender Beredtsamkeit predigte, und auf den Thron des heiligen Gottes den 'reizenden' Fürsten dieser Welt setzte, wollte nicht etwa eine christliche Parthei oder Secte, sondern die neue Welt-religion sein; und diese seligen 'Menschen der Zukunft,' so verschollen auch mit all ihrer abenteuerlich glänzenden Aeusserlichkeit sie wieder für den Moment sind, — aber in einem 'Jüngen-Deutschland,' (zuerst 1834 und besonders 1835) sowie im vollkommen organisirten englischen Socialisten- und in den continentalischen Communisten-Vereinen, und nun nach modischerem Schnitt, verjüngt auch bereits wider erstanden, und in allerlei neuen Formen stets neu erstehend, — bahnten so einer fürchterlichen Weltepoche den grässlich anmuthigen Weg." Unless the reader is somewhat accustomed to find his way through the mazes of Dr. Guericke's sentences, he may experience some difficulty in threading the above labyrinth. It is, however, interesting, as characteristic of the man and of his book. One of his countrymen called his history a Strafpredigt.

should, according to it, receive as much as the most industrious and useful.

The denial of the right of property is, to a great extent, connected with the rejection of religion and of marriage. Marriage, next to religion and property, was declared to be the greatest means of social misery. Children were not to belong to their parents, but to the state; inclination and enjoyment were to be the motive and the end and the rule of life.[1]

International Society.

France has been the birthplace and the principal seat of Communism in its modern form. The principles involved in the system have made wide progress in other countries, and leavened to a fearful extent the minds of the labouring classes both in Europe and in America. Organization and combination among the scattered millions said to be included in the membership of this society have given it an importance which has forced itself on the attention of almost all Christian states. What the principles and aims of this formidable body are, it is not easy satisfactorily to state. There has been no authoritative annunciation of principles recognized by all the affiliated societies. They differ, within certain limits, doubtless, among themselves. Some find their fit representatives in the Communists of Paris as they revealed themselves during the current year (1871). Others would shrink from the excesses which rendered the name of Communists an object of execration and abhorrence in all parts of the civilized world. Enough, however, is known of the designs of the society in question, to render it certain that its success would involve the overthrow of all existing governments; in placing all power in the hands, not of the people, but of a particular class, the operatives, the *proletariat* (the men without land); in the dissolution of society as at present organized; the abolition of private property; the extinction of the family; the abrogation of all marriage laws; and the proscription of religion, and especially of Christianity, as a public evil. Such are the avowed objects of some of the leaders of the movement, and such are the logical consequences of the principles advocated by the more reticent of their number.

---

[1] See Herzog's *Real-Encyklopädie*, art. "Communismus und Socialismus." Stahl's *Philosophie des Rechts, Rechts- und Staatslehre*, I. iii. 2. 2. §§ 31-34; 4th edit. Heidel-berg, 1870, vol. ii. part 1. pp. 367-376. *Cyclopædia of Biblical, Theological, and Ecclesiastical Literature*, prepared by the Rev. John McClintock, D. D., and James Strong, S. T. D., New York, 1869, art. "Communism." The Cyclopædias above referred to give copious references to the literature of this subject.

It is a historical fact that Communism had its origin in its modern form in materialistic atheism ; in the denial of God, who has the right to give laws to men, and the power and the purpose to enforce those laws by the retributions of justice ; in the belief that the present life is the whole period of existence allotted to men ; and that the enjoyments of this life are, therefore, all that men have to desire or expect. These principles had long been inculcated by such men as Rousseau, Voltaire, d'Holbach, Diderot, and others. To produce a conflagration, however, there must be not only fire, but combustible materials. These materialistic principles would have floated about as mere speculations, had there not been such a mass of suffering and degradation among the people. It was minds burdened with the consciousness of misery and the sense of injustice which were inflamed by the new doctrines, and which burst forth in a fire that for a time set all Europe in a blaze. We must not attribute all the evil either to the infidels or to the people. Had it not been for the preceding centuries of cruelty and oppression, France had not furnished such a bloody page to the history of modern Europe.

" L'Internationale " for March 27th, 1870, expressed succinctly the object of the International Society : " The rights of the working-men, that is our principle ; the organization of the working-men, that is our means of action ; social revolution, that is our end." It is " working-men," artisans, not the mass of the people, educated or uneducated ; but a single class whose interests are to be regarded. It is not a political revolution, the change of one form of government for another, that is the end aimed at ; but a social revolution, a complete upturning of the existing order of society.

As this institution is looming up with such portentous aspect in every direction, the question is, How is it to be met, and its influence counteracted ? Open outbreaks may be suppressed by force, but the evil cannot be healed by any such means. Artillery is inefficient against opinions. If Communism, as organized in this society, owes its origin to the causes above specified, the rational method of procedure is, to correct or remove those causes. If Communism is the product of materialistic Atheism, its cure is to be found in Theism ; in bringing the people to know and believe that there is a God on whom they are dependent and to whom they are responsible ; in teaching them that this is not the only life, that the soul is immortal, and that men will be rewarded or punished in the world to come according to their character and

conduct in the present life ; that consequently well-being here is
not the highest end of existence; that the poor here may hereafter be far more blessed than their rich neighbours ; and that it
is better to be Lazarus than Dives.   It will be necessary to bring
them to believe that there is a divine providence over the affairs
of the world; that events are not determined by the blind operation of physical causes ; but that God reigns ; that He distributes
to every one severally as He pleases ; " that the Lord maketh
poor and maketh rich ; " that it is not the rich and the noble,
but the poor and the lowly, that are his special favourites; and
that the right of property, the right of marriage, the rights of
parents and magistrates, are all ordained by God, and cannot be
violated without incurring his displeasure and the certain infliction of divine punishment.   To imbue the minds of the mass of
the people, especially in great cities, will be a slow and difficult
work ; but it is absolutely necessary.   If Materialism and Atheism are practically embraced by the mass of any community, it
will inevitably perish.   The religious training of the people, however, is only one half of the task which society has to accomplish,
to secure its own existence and prosperity.   The great body of
the people must be rendered comfortable, or at least have the
means of becoming so ; and they must be treated with justice.
Misery and a sense of wrong are the two great disturbing elements in the minds of the people.   They are the slumbering fires
which are ever ready to break out into destructive conflagration.

Violations of the Eighth Commandment.

It may well be doubted whether society is more in danger from
the destructive principles of Communism, than from the secret or
tolerated frauds which, to so great an extent, pervade almost all
the departments of social life.   If this commandment forbids all
unfair or unjust appropriation of the property of others to our
own use or advantage, if every such appropriation is stealing in
the sight of God, then theft is the most common of all the outward transgressions of the decalogue.   It includes not merely
vulgar theft such as the law can detect and punish, but,—

1. All false pretences in matters of business ; representing an
article proposed for purchase or exchange to be other and better
than it is.   This includes a multitude of sins.   Articles produced
at home are sold as foreign productions, and the price asked and
given is determined by this fraudulent representation.   Shawls of
Paris are sold as Indian ; wines manufactured in this country are

sold as the productions of France, Portugal, or Madeira. It is said that more Champagne wine is drunk in Russia than is made in France. More cigars are consumed in this country, under the name of Havanas, than Cuba produces. A great part of the paper made in the United States bears the stamp of London or Bristol. This kind of fraud has scarcely any limit. It does not seem to disturb any man's conscience. Worse than this is the selling things as sound and genuine, which in fact are spurious and often worthless. So wide-spread is fraud in matters of trade that it has become a legal maxim, " Let the buyer take care of himself." He should expect to be cheated, and therefore is required to be always on his guard. It is not uncommon to hear men say to a clergyman, " If I were dealing with a man of business, I would of course try to cheat him ; for I know he would try to cheat me. But as you are not a man of business, I make an exception in your case, and will deal honestly."

Under this head of false pretences comes the adulteration of articles of food, of medicine, and of the materials for clothing. The extent to which this is carried is fearful. The English Parliament not long since appointed a commission to examine into the adulterations of articles of food sold by the green grocers in London. The result of the examination was that only six out of every hundred of the specimens collected were pure, *i. e.*, were what they were represented or declared to be. There is no reason to suppose that London is peculiar or preëminent in this kind of fraud. The same complaint is made of the adulteration of drugs. This evil was so great that some governments have taken the preparation of medicine for their navies and armies into their own hands. If we are to believe the public papers, the greater part of the wines and other liquors, spirituous and malt, sold to the public, are not only adulterated but mixed with poisonous drugs. The clothing furnished soldiers in active service, exposed to all the severities, and changes of weather, was and often is, made of worthless materials. There would be no end to the enumeration of frauds of this kind. A prominent English journal recently said that the great part of the revenue of the British government was taken up in endeavouring to prevent and detect frauds against the public.

2. Another large class of violations of the eighth commandment comprises attempts to take undue advantage of the ignorance or of the necessities of our fellow-men. It is of the nature of theft if a man sells an article knowing it to be of less value

than he to whom he offers it for sale takes it to be. If a man is aware that the credit of a bank is impaired, or that the affairs of a railroad, or of any other corporation, are embarrassed, and takes advantage of that knowledge, to dispose of the stock or notes of such corporations to those ignorant on the subject, demanding more for them than their actual worth, he is guilty of theft, if the command, "Thou shalt not steal," forbids all unfair acquisition of the property of our neighbour. In like manner all unfair attempts to enhance or depress the value of articles of commerce, are violations of the law of God. Unfounded reports are often designedly circulated to have this enhancing or depressing effect on values, so that advantage may be taken of the unwary or uninformed. It is an offence of the same kind to engross commodities to enhance their price. " He that withholdeth corn, the people shall curse him : but blessing shall be upon the head of him that selleth it." (Prov. xi. 26.) Again it is a violation of the law to take advantage of the necessities of our fellow-men and to demand an exorbitant price for what they may need. In the recent dreadful conflagration in Chicago a thousand dollars were demanded for the use of a horse and wagon for a single hour. It may be said that there is no fixed standard of value ; that a thing may be worth what it costs the man who owns it ; or what it is worth to the man who demands it ; or what it will bring in open market. If an hour's use of the horse and wagon was worth more to the man in Chicago than a thousand dollars, it may be said that it was not unfair to demand that sum. If this be so, then if a man perishing of thirst is willing to give his whole estate for a glass of water, it would be right to exact that price ; or if a man in danger of drowning should offer a thousand dollars for a rope, we might refuse to throw it to him for a less reward. Such conduct every man feels would be worthy of execration. The fact is that things have an intrinsic value, however determined, which cannot be enhanced because our suffering fellow-men may be in pressing need of them.

3. This commandment forbids also depriving men of property, on the ground of any mere technical flaw, or legal defect in their title. Such defect may be the effect of unavoidable ignorance ; or loss by shipwreck, fire, theft, or other so called accident, of the evidence of their right. The law may in such cases be inexorable : it may be on the whole right that it should be so, but nevertheless the man who avails himself of such defect to get possession of his neighbour's property, breaks the command which says,

" Thou shalt not steal ; " *i. e.*, thou shalt not take what in the sight of God does not belong to you. Gambling falls under the same category where advantage is taken of the unwary or unskilful, to deprive them of their property without compensation. It is, however, impossible to enumerate or to classify the various methods of fraud. The code of morals held by many business and professional men is very far below the moral law as revealed in the Bible. This is especially true in reference to the eighth commandment in the decalogue. Many who have stood well in society, and even in the Church, will be astonished at the last day to find the word " Thieves " written after their names in the great book of judgment.

§ 13. *The Ninth Commandment.*

This commandment forbids all violations of the obligations of veracity. The most aggravated of this class of offences is bearing false witness against our neighbour. But this includes every offence of the same general character ; as the command thou shalt not kill, forbids all indulgence or manifestation of malice.

The command to keep truth inviolate belongs to a different class from those relating to the Sabbath, to marriage, or to property. These are founded on the permanent relations of men in the present state of existence. They are not in their own nature immutable. God may at any time suspend or modify them. But truth is at all times sacred, because it is one of the essential attributes of God, so that whatever militates against, or is hostile to truth is in opposition to the very nature of God. Truth is, so to speak, the very substratum of Deity. It is in such a sense the foundation of all the moral perfections of God, that without it they cannot be conceived of as existing. Unless God really is what He declares Himself to be ; unless He means what He declares Himself to mean ; unless He will do what He promises, the whole idea of God is lost. As there is no God but the true God, so without truth there is and can be no God. As this attribute is the foundation, so to speak, of the divine, so it is the foundation of the physical and moral order of the universe. What is the immutability of the laws of nature, but a revelation of the truth of God ? They are manifestations of his purposes. They are promises on which his creatures rely, and by which they must regulate their conduct. If those laws were capricious, if the same effects did not uniformly follow from the same causes, the very existence of living beings would be impossible. The food of one day might be poison the next. If a man did not reap what he sowed, there could be no security for anything. The truth of God, therefore, is written on the heavens. It is the daily proclamation made by the sun, moon, and stars in their solemn procession through space, and it is echoed back by the earth and all that it contains.

The truth of God, too, is the foundation of all knowledge. How do we know that our senses do not deceive us ; that consciousness is not mendacious ? that the laws of belief which by the constitution of our nature we are forced to obey, are not false guides ? Unless God be true there can be no certainty in anything ; much less can there be any security ; we can have no confidence in the future : no assurance that evil will not ultimately triumph over good, darkness over light, and confusion and misery over order and happiness. There is, therefore, something awfully sacred in the obligations of truth. A man who violates the truth, sins against the very foundation of his moral being. As a false god is no god, so a false man is no man ; he can never be what man was designed to be ; he can never answer the end of his being. There can be in him nothing that is stable, trustworthy, or good.

There are two classes of sins which the ninth commandment forbids. The first is, all forms of detraction ; everything which is unjustly or unnecessarily injurious to our neighbour's good name ; and the second, all violations of the laws of truth. This latter, indeed, includes the former. Bearing false witness, however, being the definite thing forbidden, should be separately considered.

Detraction.

The highest form of this offence is bearing false testimony in a court of justice. This includes the guilt of malice, falsehood, and mockery of God ; and its commission justly renders a man infamous, and places him outside of the pale of society. As it strikes at the security of character, property, and even of life, it is an offence which cannot be passed by with impunity. The false swearer is, therefore, a criminal in the sight of the civil law, and subject to public disgrace and punishment.

Slander is an offence of the same character. It differs from the sin of bearing false witness, only in not being committed in a judicial process, and in not being attended by the same effects. The slanderer, however, does bear false witness against his neighbour. He does it in the ears of the public, and not in those of a jury. The offence includes the elements of malice and falsehood against which this command is specially directed. The circulation of false reports, " tale-bearing," as it is called in Scripture, is indicative of the same state of mind, and comes under the same condemnation. As the law of God takes cognizance of the thoughts and intents of the heart, in condemning an external act it condemns the disposition which tends to produce it. In condemning all speaking ill of our neighbour, the Scriptures condemn a suspicious temper, a disposition to impute bad motives, and an unwillingness to believe that men are sincere and honest in the avowal of their principles and aims. This is the opposite of that charity which "thinketh no evil," " believeth all things, hopeth all things." It is still more opposed to the spirit of this law, that we should cherish or express satisfaction in the disgrace of others, even if they be our competitors or enemies. We are commanded to " rejoice with them that do rejoice and weep with them that weep." (Rom. xii. 15.)

The usages of life, or the principles of professional men, allow of many things which are clearly inconsistent with the requirements of the ninth commandment. Lord Brougham is reported to have said in the House of Lords, that an advocate knows no one but his client. He is bound *per fas et nefas*, if possible, to clear him. If necessary for the accomplishment of that object, he is at liberty to accuse and defame the innocent, and even (as the report stated) to ruin his country.[1] It is not unusual, especially in trials for murder, for the advocates of the accused to charge the crime on innocent parties and to exert all their ingenuity to convince the jury of their guilt. This is a cruel and wicked injustice, a clear violation of the command which says, " Thou shalt not bear false witness against thy neighbour."

Falsehood.

1. The simplest and most comprehensive definition of falsehood is, *enunciatio falsi*. This enunciation need not be verbal. A sign or gesture may be as significant as a word. If, to borrow Paley's illustration, a man is asked which of two roads is the right one to a given place, and he intentionally points to the wrong one, he is as guilty of falsehood as if he had given the wrong directions in words. This is true; nevertheless there is a power peculiar to words. A thought, a feeling, or a conviction

---

[1] Lord Brougham, according to the public papers, uttered these sentiments in vindication of the conduct of the famous Irish advocate Phillips, who on the trial of Courvoisier for the murder of Lord Russell, endeavored to fasten the guilt on the butler and housemaid, whom he knew to be innocent, as his client had confessed to him that he had committed the crime.

is not only more clearly revealed in the consciousness when clothed in words, but it is thereby strengthened. Every man feels this when he says, " I believe ; " or, " I know that my Redeemer liveth."

2. The above definition of falsehood, although resting on high authority, is too comprehensive. It is not every *enunciatio falsi* which is a falsehood. This enunciation may be made through ignorance or mistake, and therefore be perfectly innocent. It may even be deliberate and intentional. This we see in the case of fables and parables, and in works of fiction. No one regards the Iliad or the Paradise Lost as a repertorium of falsehoods. It is not necessary to assume that the parables of our Lord, are veritable histories. They were not designed to give a narrative of actual occurrences. Intention to deceive, therefore, is an element in the idea of falsehood. But even this is not always culpable. When Pharaoh commanded the Hebrew midwives to slay the male children of their countrywomen, they disobeyed him. And when called to account for their disobedience, they said, " The Hebrew women are not as the Egyptian women; for they are lively, and are delivered ere the midwives come in unto them. Therefore God dealt well with the midwives : and the people multiplied, and waxed very mighty." (Ex. i. 19, 20.) In 1 Samuel xvi. 1, 2, we read that God said to Samuel, " I will send thee to Jesse the Bethlehemite : for I have provided me a king among his sons. And Samuel said, How can I go? if Saul hear it, he will kill me. And the Lord said, Take an heifer with thee, and say, I am come to sacrifice to the Lord." Here, it is said, is a case of intentional deception actually commanded. Saul was to be deceived as to the object of Samuel's journey to Bethlehem. Still more marked is the conduct of Elisha as recorded in 2 Kings vi. 14–20. The king of Syria sent soldiers to seize the prophet at Dothan. " And when they came down to him, Elisha prayed unto the Lord, and said, Smite this people I pray thee with blindness. And He smote them with blindness, according to the word of Elisha. And Elisha said unto them, This is not the way neither is this the city : follow me and I will bring you to the man whom ye seek. But he led them to Samaria. And it came to pass, when they were come into Samaria, that Elisha said, Lord, open the eyes of these men, that they may see. And the Lord opened their eyes, and they saw ; and behold, they were in the midst of Samaria ; " that is, in the hands of their enemies. The prophet, however, would not allow them to be injured ; but com-

manded that they should be fed and sent back to their master.
Examples of this kind of deception are numerous in the Old
Testament. Some of them are simply recorded facts, without
anything to indicate how they were regarded in the sight of God;
but others, as in the cases above cited, received either directly or
by implication the divine sanction. Of our blessed Lord himself
it is said in Luke xxiv. 28, " He made as though (προσεποιεῖτο, he
made a show of) he would have gone further." He so acted as
to make the impression on the two disciples that it was his purpose to continue his journey. (Comp. Mark vi. 48.) Many theologians do not admit that the fact recorded in Luke xxiv. 28,
involved any intentional deception; because the "simulatio non
fuerit in verbis veritati contradicentibus, sed in gestibus veritati
consentientibus. Christus . . . . agebat, ut qui iturus esset
longius, et revera iturus fuerat, nisi rogatus fuisset a discipulis,
alia fortasse ratione se iis manifesturus. . . . . Alii dicunt, simu-
lationem fuisse tentatoriam, æque ac illam, quæ in Abrahami
historia a scriptore sacro commemoratur Gen. xxii. 2. In eandem
sententiam descendunt Beausobre et L'Enfant, qui in notis gal-
licis ad Luc. xxiv. 28, ita scribunt: C'est un feinte innocente et
pleine d'amour, par laquelle Jésus-Christ veut éprouver la foi de
ses disciples. Ainsi en usent les medicins à l'égard des malades,
et les pères à l'égard de leurs enfans." [1]

It is the general sentiment among moralists that stratagems
in war are allowable; that it is lawful not only to conceal intended
movements from an enemy, but also to mislead him as to your
intentions. A great part of the skill of a military commander is
evinced in detecting the intentions of his adversary, and in con-
cealing his own. Few men would be so scrupulous as to refuse to
keep a light in a room, when robbery was apprehended, with the
purpose of producing the impression that the members of the
household were on the alert.

On these grounds it is generally admitted that in criminal falsehoods there must be not only the enunciation or signification of
what is false, and an intention to deceive, but also a violation of
some obligation. If there may ·be any combination of circumstances under which a man is not bound to speak the truth, those
to whom the declaration or signification is made have no right to
expect him to do so. A general is under no obligation to reveal
his intended movements to his adversary; and his adversary has
no right to suppose that his apparent intention is his real purpose.

[1] Gerhard, *Loci Theologici*, xiii. 177; edit. Tübingen, 1766, vol. v. p. 346, Cotta's note.

Elisha was under no obligation to aid the Syrians in securing his
person and taking his life; and they had no right to assume that
he would thus assist them. And, therefore, he did no wrong in
misleading them. There will always be cases in which the rule
of duty is a matter of doubt. It is often said that the rule above
stated applies when a robber demands your purse. It is said to
be right to deny that you have anything of value about you. You
are not bound to aid him in committing a crime; and he has no
right to assume that you will facilitate the accomplishment of his
object. This is not so clear. The obligation to speak the truth
is a very solemn one; and when the choice is left a man to tell a
lie or lose his money, he had better let his money go. On the
other hand, if a mother sees a murderer in pursuit of her child,
she has a perfect right to mislead him by any means in her power;
because the general obligation to speak the truth is merged or
lost, for the time being, in the higher obligation. This principle
is not invalidated by its possible or actual abuse. It has been
greatly abused. Jesuits taught that the obligations to promote the
good of the Church absorbed or superseded every other obligation. And, therefore, in their system not only falsehood and
mental reservation, but perjury, robbery, and assassination became lawful if committed with the design of promoting the interests of the Church. Notwithstanding this liability to abuse,
the principle that a higher obligation absolves from a lower stands
firm. It is a dictate even of the natural conscience. It is evidently right to inflict pain in order to save life. It is right to subject travellers to quarantine, although it may grievously interfere
with their wishes or interests, to save a city from pestilence. The
principle itself is clearly inculcated by our Lord when He said, " I
will have mercy and not sacrifice ; " and when He taught that it
was right to violate the Sabbath in order to save the life of an ox,
or even to prevent its suffering. The Jesuits erred in assuming
that the promotion of the interests of the Church (in their sense
especially of the word Church) was a higher duty than obedience
to the moral law. They erred also in assuming that the interests
of the Church could be promoted by the commission of crime;
and their principle was in direct violation of the Scriptural rule
that it is wrong to do evil that good may come.

The question now under consideration is not whether it is ever
right to do wrong, which is a solecism ; nor is the question whether
it is ever right to lie ; but rather what constitutes a lie. It is not
simply an " *enunciatio falsi,*" nor, as it is commonly defined by

the moralists of the Church of Rome, a " locutio contra mentem loquentis ; " [1] but there must be an intention to deceive when we are expected and bound to speak the truth.   That is, there are circumstances in which a man is not bound to speak the truth, and therefore there are cases in which speaking or intimating what is not true is not a lie.   The Roman moralists just referred to, answer the question, Whether it is ever lawful to lie ? in the negative.   Dens, for example goes so far as to say : " Non licet mentiri (*i. e.*, to utter what is not true, as he defines the word ' mendacium ') ad avertendum mortem aut interitum Reipublicæ, vel quæcunque alia mala : in hujusmodi perplexitatibus debent homines confugere ad auxilium Dei, angeli custodis," etc.[2]   This is a sound rule, provided the obligation to speak the truth exists.   It is far better that a man should die or permit a murder to be committed, than that he should sin against God.   Nothing could tempt the Christian martyrs to save their own lives or the lives of their brethren by denying Christ, or by professing to believe in false gods ; in these cases the obligation to speak the truth was in full force.   But in the case of a commanding general in time of war, the obligation does not exist to intimate his true intentions to his adversary.   Intentional deception in his case is not morally a falsehood.   Although the Romanist theologians lay down the rule that a *mendacium* is never lawful, and although they define *mendacium* as stated above, yet they teach that if a confessor is asked whether he knows a fact confided to him in the confessional, he is at liberty to answer, No ; meaning that he does not know it *scientia communicabili*.   That is, he is authorized, according to their own definition of the word, to tell a downright falsehood. He may be right to reply to the question, Whether he knows a fact communicated to him in his character of confessor, by saying, " I am not at liberty to answer ; " but it is hard to see how he could be justified in a direct falsehood.[3]

In order to include the third element entering into the nature of criminal falsehood, Paley defines a lie to be a violation of a promise.   Every violation of a promise is not a lie, for it may not

---

[1] This definition is given by Dens, *Theologia, De Mendacio*, N. 242, edit. Dublin, 1832, vol. iv. p. 306.

[2] *Ibid.* N. 243, p. 308.

[3] " Confessarius interrogatus a tyranno an Titius confessus sit homicidium, respondere potest et debet: ' nescio;' quia confessarius id nescit scientia communicabili. Imo, etiamsi instaret tyrannus, et diceret, ' An hoc nescis scientia sacramentali ? ' Respondere adhuc posset: ' nescio.' Ratio est, quia tyrannus bene scit se de hoc jus interrogandi non habere, nec confessarius ut homo scit se scire, sed uti vicarius Dei et scientia incommunicabili." John Peter Gury, *Compendium Theologiæ Moralis*, new edit. Tornaci, vol. i. p. 201.

include the other elements of a falsehood; but every lie is a violation of a promise. It arises out of the very nature of human society, and from the relation in which men of necessity stand to each other, that every man is expected to speak the truth, and is under a tacit but binding promise not to deceive his neighbours by word or act. If in any case he is guilty of intentional deception, he must be able to show that in that particular case the obligation does not exist; that is, that the party deceived has no right to expect the truth, and that no virtual promise is violated in deceiving him. This is certainly the fact in military manœuvres, and in some other cases of rare occurrence.

This, however, is not always admitted. Augustine, for example, makes every intentional deception, no matter what the object or what the circumstances, to be sinful. "Ille mentitur," he says, "qui aliud habet in animo, et aliud verbis vel quibuslibet significationibus enuntiat." [1] Again he says,[2] "Nemo autem dubitat mentiri eum qui volens falsum enuntiat causa fallendi : quapropter enuntiationem falsam cum voluntate ad fallendum prolatam, manifestum est esse mendacium." He reviews the cases recorded in the Bible which seem to teach the opposite doctrine. This would be the simplest ground for the moralist to take. But, as shown above, and as generally admitted, there are cases of intentional deception which are not criminal.

Kinds of Falsehood.

Augustine divides falsehood into no less than eight classes. But these differ for the most part simply as to their subject matter, or their effects. The division as given by Thomas Aquinas and very generally adopted since,[3] is into three classes ; the pernicious, the benevolent, and the jocose. Under the first head come all falsehoods which are instigated by any evil motive and are designed to promote some evil end. It includes not only the direct enunciation of what is false, but also all quibbling or prevarication.

[1] *De Mendacio*, 3; *Works*, edit. Benedictines, Paris, 1837, vol. vi. p. 712, a.
[2] *Ibid.* 5, (iv.), p. 715, a.
[3] Aquinas, *Summa*, II. ii. 110, 2; edit. Cologne, 1640, p. 203, a, of third set. "Potest dividi mendacium, in quantum habet rationem culpæ, secundum ea quæ aggravant, vel diminuunt culpam mendacii ex parte finis intenti. Aggravat autem culpam mendacii, si aliquis per mendacium intendat alterius nocumentum: quod vocatur mendacium perniciosum. Diminuitur autem culpa mendacii, si ordinetur ad aliquod bonum, vel delectabile, et sic est mendacium jocosum: vel utile, et sic est mendacium officiosum, quo intenditur juvamentum alterius, vel remotio nocumenti. Et secundum hoc dividitur mendacium in tria prædicta." The first, according to Romanists, is a mortal sin, the two latter are regarded as venial.

Mental Reservation.

This class includes also all cases of mental reservation. It should be said in justice to the teachers of Moral Theology in the Romish Church, that, although the Jesuits made themselves so obnoxious by asserting the propriety of mental reservation, they at least in general terms condemn it. " Restrictio mentalis," says Gury, " est actus mentis verba alicujus propositionis ad alium sensum quam naturalem et obvium detorquentis vel restringentis." This he says is unlawful, because it is " simpliciter mendacium." It is true these theologians make serious modifications of this rule. It is only of reservation " proprie mentalis," that is, when the true meaning of the speaker cannot be detected, that this condemnation is pronounced. If it be possible, from the circumstances or the mode of expression, to know what he means, the rule does not always apply. There are cases in which it is allowable to permit a man to deceive himself. Under this head is brought in the case above referred to. It is said that a confessor may properly say that he does not know a thing, when he means that he does not know it as a man, or with a knowledge that is communicable. So it is said that if a man be asked by one who has no right to interrogate him, whether he has committed a crime, he may say, No ; meaning none that he was bound to confess. So also it is taught that public persons, ambassadors, magistrates, advocates, etc., may use mental reservation in its wider sense. In like manner a servant may say his master is not at home, whom he knows to be in the house, because such denial so often means that the person inquired for does not wish to be seen.[1] This opens a very wide door of which not only Jesuits, but men professing to be Protestants and Christians freely avail themselves. To an unsophistical mind all the instances above specified are cases of unmitigated falsehood.

The extent to which the Jesuits carried the principle of mental reservation is a matter of notoriety. The three rules by which they perverted the whole system of morals, and which threatened to overturn the very foundations of society, and which led at one time to the suppression of the order, were, —

1. The doctrine that the character of an act depended solely on the intention. If the intention be good, the act is good ; whether it be falsehood, perjury, murder, or any other conceivable crime. Pascal quotes the Jesuit moralist Escobar as laying down the gen-

[1] Gury, *ut supra*, vol. i. pp. 200, 201.

eral principle, " that promises are not binding unless there was
an intention of keeping them, at the time they were made." [1]
On the same principle, that the intention determines the character
of the act, the murder of Henry III. in 1589; of the Prince of
Orange in 1584 ; of Henry IV. of France in 1610; and especially
the massacres on the feast of St. Bartholomew, were all justified.
This principle is not confined to the Jesuits. When in 1819 young
Sand murdered Kotzebue, the poet, from political motives, he not
only justified the act to the last, but perhaps the general sentiment among his younger countrymen was that of approbation.
Even De Wette, the distinguished theologian and commentator,
in a letter of consolation to the mother of Sand, spoke of the assassination as " a favourable sign of the times." [2] It was regarded
very much as the killing of Marat by Charlotte Corday is regarded by the public to this day. When the doctrine comes to be
formalized as a moral principle that the intention determines the
character of the act, so that murder committed for the good of
the Church or the State is commendable, then the law of God is
set at nought and the bonds of society are unloosed.

2. The doctrine of probability. If it was probable that an act
was right there was no sin in committing it, although in the conviction of the agent the act was wrong ; and an act was probably
right, if among the moralists there was a difference of opinion
on the subject.

3. The above-mentioned doctrine of mental reservation. It
was taught that a man might innocently swear he did not do a
certain thing, provided he said to himself, not audibly to others,
" I mean I did not do it ten years ago." All these different
kinds of lying, though referred to different heads by the Jesuit
teachers, belong properly to the class of pernicious falsehoods,
such as the law of God utterly condemns.

The second class, called " mendacia officiosa," includes all
falsehoods uttered for a good object. Such as those told the sick
by their attendants, to comfort or encourage them ; those told by

---

[1] Blaise Pascal, *Lettres écrites a un Provincial*, edit. Paris, 1829, p. 180; Escobar, III.
ex. iii. n. 48.

[2] De Wette did not approve of the assassination of Kotzebue in a moral point of view.
His language was: " So wie die That geschehen ist, mit diesem Glauben, mit dieser Zuver-
sicht, ist sie ein schönes Zeichen der Zeit. — Die That ist — allgemein betrachtet — unsitt-
lich und der sittlichen Gesetzgebung zuwiderlaufend. Das Böse soll nicht durch das Böse
überwunden werden, sondern allein durch das Gute. Durch Unrecht, List und Gewalt
kann kein Recht gestiftet werden, und der gute Zweck heiligt nicht das ungerechte Mittel."
Quoted in the *Conversations-Lexicon*, 7th edit. Leipzig, 1827, art. Wette (de). The letter, although thus guarded, led to the loss of his professorship in Berlin and his virtual banishment from the city.

detectives for the discovery of crimes; or those which are designed to prevent evil or secure good for ourselves or others.
All such falsehoods are pronounced by Romanists to be venial
sins, mere peccadilloes.[1] The example given by Dens, in the
place referred to, of this class of sins, is the case of a man having
money, denying that he has it to avoid being robbed. This is
very different from the doctrine of Augustine, who teaches that it
is unlawful to lie to save life, or even to save a soul.[2] Augustine's position is consistent with what was said above, that there
are occasions on which a higher obligation absolves from a lower,
as our Lord himself teaches. But that principle applies to the
case of falsehood only when the enunciation of what is untrue
ceases to be falsehood in the criminal sense of the word. It has
been seen that three elements enter into the nature of falsehood properly so called, (1.) The enunciation of what is false.
(2.) The intention to deceive. (3.) The violation of a promise;
that is, the violation of the obligation to speak the truth, the
obligation which rests upon every man to keep faith with his
neighbour. In military manœuvres, as above remarked, there is
no expectation, and no right for expectation, that a general will
reveal his true intentions to his adversary, and therefore in that
case deception is not falsehood, because there is no violation of
an obligation. But when a confessor was called upon by a
heathen magistrate to say whether he was a Christian, he was
expected, and bound to speak the truth, although he knew the
consequence would be a cruel death. So when a man is asked if
he has money about him, he is expected to speak the truth, and
has no right to lie any more than a Christian had a right to lie
to save his life. The doctrine that "mendacia officiosa" are only
venial sins, rests on the principle that the intention determines
the character of the act. The simple Scriptural rule is, that he
who does "evil that good may come," his "damnation is just."

It is a fact of experience, that, so far as our inner life at least
is concerned, exorbitant attention to how to do a thing destroys
the ability to do it. An adept in logic may be a very poor rea-
soner; and a man who spends his life in studying the rules of
elocution may be a very indifferent orator. So a man versed in

<hr/>

[1] Dens, *ut supra*, vol. iv. N. 242, p. 307. "Mendacium officiosum dicitur, quod com-
mittitur solum causa utilitatis propriæ vel alienae: v. g. quis dicit, se non habere pecunias,
ne iis spolietur a militibus." And on the same page he says, "Officiosum autem et jocosum sunt ex genere suo peccatum veniale." So also Gury, vol. i. p. 199. "Mendacium
officiosum peccatum venale est, per se, quia in eo gravis deordinatio non apprehenditur."
[2] *De Mendacio*, 9, (vi.); *Works, ut supra*, vol. vi. p. 719 ff.

all the subtleties of casuistry is apt to lose the clear and simple
apprehension of right and wrong.   Professor Gury has for the
motto of his book on moral theology, the words of St. Gregory :
" Ars artium regimen animarum."   Very true, but it is a bad
way to lead a man to a given point to put him into a labyrinth.
These books of casuistry only serve to mystify the plainest subjects.   Indulging in such subtleties can hardly fail to lead to the
adoption of false principles.   It is very plain that the man who
was at once a prince and a bishop, could not well be drunk as
prince and sober as bishop; yet, as we have seen, these books
teach that a priest may lie as a man, and yet speak truth as a
vicar of God.   The plain directions of the Word of God and a
conscience enlightened by his Spirit, are safer guides in matters
of duty than all the books on moral theology the Jesuits ever
wrote.   This is not saying that morals are not a proper subject
of study, or that there is not a call in that field for the exercise
of discrimination and distinction.   The objection is not to the
study of morals, but to inordinate devotion to that department,
and to the perplexing and perverting subtleties of casuistry.

Pious Frauds.

Pious fraud was reduced by Romanists to a science and an
art.   It was called economics, from οἰκονομία, " dispensatio rei
familiaris," the discretionary use of things in a family according
to circumstances.   The theory is founded on the principle that if
the intention be lawful, the act is lawful.   Any act, therefore,
designed to promote any " pious " end is justifiable "in foro
conscientiæ."   This principle was introduced at an early period
into the Christian Church.   Mosheim attributes to it a heathen
origin.[1]   He says that the Platonists and Pythagoreans taught
that it was commendable to lie to promote a good end.   The
evil, however, had probably an independent origin wherever it
appeared.   It is plausible enough to rise spontaneously in any
mind not under the control of the Word and Spirit of God.

Augustine had to contend against this error in his day.   There
were certain orthodox Christians who thought it right falsely to
assert that they were Priscillianists in order to gain their confidence and thus be able to convict them of heresy.   This brought
up the question whether it was allowable to commit a fraud for a
good end ; in other words, whether the intention determined the
character of the act.   Augustine took the negative of the ques-

---

[1] *Ecclesiastical History*, I. ii. 2. 3. § 15; edit. New York, 1859, vol. i. p. 130.

tion, and argued that a lie was always a lie, and always wicked; that it was not lawful to tell a falsehood for any purpose whatever. "Interest quidem plurimum," he says, "qua causa, quo fine, qua intentione quid fiat: sed ea quæ constat esse peccata, nullo bonæ causæ obtentu, nullo quasi bono fine, nulla velut bona intentione facienda sunt. . . . . Cum vero jam opera ipsa peccata sunt; sicut furta, stupra, blasphemiæ, vel cætera talia; quis est qui dicat causis bonis esse facienda, ut vel peccata non sint, vel quod est absurdius, justa peccata sint? Quis est qui dicat: ut habeamus quod demus pauperibus, faciamus furta divitibus; aut, testimonia falsa vendamus, maxime si non inde innocentes læduntur, sed nocentes potius damnaturis judicibus eruuntur?"[1] He specially condemns all "pious frauds," i. e., frauds committed in pretended service of religion.

Notwithstanding the authority of Augustine, the doctrine that it was right to use fraud in efforts to promote the interests of the Church, was openly avowed by some of his contemporaries and many of his immediate successors, and during the Middle Ages was the practical rule of the Romish Church, as it is at the present day. Among the early advocates of this lax principle of morals is found the name even of Jerome. In his epistle to Pammachius, he says, that in teaching, a man is bound to be honest, but in dealing with an adversary, he may do what he pleases; it is right "nunc hæc nunc illa proponere. Argumentari ut libet, aliud loqui, aliud agere, panem, ut dicitur, ostendere, lapidem tenere."[2] The principle that the intention sanctifies the deed, is clearly asserted by John Cassian, a disciple of Chrysostom. Falsehood, he says, is like poison: taken moderately and in illness, it may be salutary; but if taken inopportunely, it is fatal. "Non enim Deus verborum tantum actuumque nostrorum discussor et judex, sed etiam propositi ac destinationis inspector est. . . . . Ille tamen intimam cordis inspiciens pietatem, non verborum sonum, sed votum dijudicat voluntatis, quia finis, operis et affectus considerandus est perpetrantis."[3]

---

[1] Contra Mendacium ad Consentium, 18; Works, edit. Benedictines, Paris, 1837, vol. vi. pp. 767, d, 768, a, b.

[2] Epistola, xlviii. [30 seu 50] 13, seu Liber Apologeticus ad Pammachium; Works, edit. Migne, Paris, 1845, vol. i. p. 502.

[3] Collationes, xvii. 17; Magna Bibliotheca Veterum Patrum, t. v. par. ii. Cologne, 1618, p. 189, f, g.

Forgeries.

The principle having been once admitted that it is right to deceive in order to accomplish a good object, there was no limit set in practice to its application. Hence, --

1. Even from the earliest times genuine works of the apostolic fathers were corrupted by interpolations; and works were issued bearing the names of authors who were dead long before the works were written. Besides the apocryphal books which are now admitted to be spurious, the Letters of Ignatius, a portion of which are generally received as authentic, were so corrupted as to be the source of an extended and permanent evil influence. Of these letters there are, as is well known, three recensions, the larger containing fifteen epistles, the shorter, and the Syrian, founded on a Syriac translation. The larger collection is given up by scholars as spurious; as to the others, many who admit their authenticity, insist that they are more or less corrupted by interpolation.[1]

The so-called "Apostolical Constitutions" are a collection of rules or canons derived partly from the New Testament, partly from the decisions of early provincial councils, and partly from tradition; all, however, imposed on the Church as of apostolical authority. As the number of councils increased there was a necessity for renewed collections of their decisions. These collections included "decretals" issued by the Bishop of Rome; both classes being included under the name of "canons," these collections were gradually consolidated into the Canon Law. It was a natural and easy method of imposing on the Church to insert spurious decretals in the collections from time to time, and to found on these forgeries exorbitant pretensions to priestly dignity and power. The most notorious of these impositions is what is known as the Decretals of Isidore, Bishop of Seville, the most distinguished writer of the seventh century. He died A. D. 636. The collection which went under his name did not make its appearance until the ninth century. It contains many genuine decretals and canons, but also many that are manifest forgeries. The author of the collection and of the spurious documents it

---

[1] A brief account of this much debated question is given by Uhlhorn in Herzog's *Real-Encyklopädie*, art. "Ignatius."

Neander says of these assumed letters of Ignatius, "Even the briefer revision, which is the one most entitled to confidence, has been very much interpolated. . . . . A hierarchical purpose is not to be mistaken." *General History of the Christian Religion and Church*, by Dr. Augustus Neander. Translated by Joseph Torrey, Professor in the University of Vermont, 2d edit. Boston, 1849, vol. i. p. 661.

contains is unknown. Its date is fixed by Gieseler between 829
and 845. These decretals " were soon circulated," says that historian, " in various collections, appealed to without suspicion in
public transactions, and used by the popes, from Nicolaus I., immediately after he had become acquainted with them (864),
without any opposition being made to their authenticity, and
continued in undiminished reputation, till the Reformation led
to the detection of the cheat. On these false decretals were
founded the pretensions of the popes to universal sway in the
Church; while the pretended ' donatio Constantini M.,' a fiction of an earlier time, but soon adopted into them, was the
first step from which the papacy endeavoured to elevate itself
even above the state." [1] The authenticity of these documents
was first seriously attacked by the Magdeburgh Centuriators,
who were answered by the Jesuit Turrianus. " The question
was decided by Dav. Blondelli Pseudoisidorus et Turrianus vapu-
lantes, Genev. 1628. The Ultramontanists, though they admit
the deception, deny the revolution of ecclesiastical principles
caused by it." [2] These decretals attribute to the pope absolute
supremacy over the Church, over patriarchs, bishops, and priests.
To him an appeal lies in all questions of doctrine, and his decisions are final. The gift of Constantine conferred on the pontiff
more than imperial dignity and power. It conveyed the sovereignty of the city of Rome, of Italy, and of the western provinces. Among other things it says, " Et sicut nostram terrenam
imperialem potentiam, sic ejus (Petri) sacrosanctam Romanam
Ecclesiam decrevimus veneranter honorari, et amplius quam nostrum imperium terrenumque thronum, sedem sacratissimam b.
Petri gloriose exaltari: tribuentes ei potestatem et gloriæ dignitatem, atque vigorem et honorificentiam imperialem. Unde ut
pontificalis apex non vilescat, sed magis quam imperii dignitas,
gloria et potentia decoretur, ecce tam palatium nostrum, ut
prædictum est, quam Romanam urbem, et omnes Italiæ, seu
occidentalium regionum provincias, loca et civitates præfato
beatissimo Pontifici nostro Sylvestro, universali papæ, contradi-
mus atque relinquimus: et ab eo et a successoribus ejus per
hanc divalem nostram, et pragmaticum constitutum decernimus
disponenda, atque juri sanctæ Romanæ Ecclesiæ concedimus per-
mansura." [3]

[1] Gieseler, *Ecclesiastical History*, Per. iii. ii. 1. 1. § 20; edit. Edinburgh, 1848, vol. ii.
pp. 331–336.
[2] *Ibid.* p. 335, foot-notes.
[3] Quoted by Gieseler, *ut supra*, vol. ii. p. 337, from the *Decreta Gratiani*.

False Miracles.

The second great class of pious frauds by which the Church of
Rome has for ages endeavoured to sustain its errors and confirm
its power, is that of pretended miracles. On this subject it may
be remarked, —

1. That there is nothing in the New Testament inconsistent
with the occurrence of miracles in the post-apostolic age of the
Church. The Apostles were indeed chosen to be the witnesses
of Christ, to bear testimony to the facts of his history and to the
doctrines which He taught. And among the signs of an Apostle, or necessary credentials of his commission, was the power
to work miracles. (Rom. xv. 18, 19 ; 2 Cor. xii. 12.) When
the Apostles had finished their work, the necessity of miracles, so
far as the great end they were intended to accomplish was concerned, ceased. This, however, does not preclude the possibility
of their occurrence, on suitable occasions, in after ages. It is a
mere question of fact to be decided on historical evidence. In
some few cases the nature of the event, its consequences, and the
testimony in its support, have constrained many Protestants to
admit the probability, if not the certainty of these miraculous
interventions.[1] Among the controversial writings which the great
questions in debate in the late Vatican Council have called forth,
there are two of special interest which have already been translated and circulated in this country. The one is entitled " The
Pope and The Council," [2] a series of papers written by German
Catholic scholars of distinction. It is a historical argument
against Ultramontanism. Among other things it demonstrates
that the claims of the Ultramontanists have been sustained by a
regular system of forgeries in all ages of the Church.[3]

The other work is by the late Abbe Gratry,[4] one of the most

---

[1] Grotius in his annotations on Mark xvi. 17, says: "Cum vero multo etiam seriora
secula plena sint testimoniis ejus rei, nescio qua ratione moti quidam id donum ad prima
tantum tempora restringant; quibus ut uberiorem fuisse miraculorum copiam, ad jacienda
tanti ædificii fundamenta contra vim mundi, facile concedo, ita cum illis expirasse hanc
Christi promissionem cur credamus non video. Quare si quis nunc etiam gentibus Christi
ignaris (illis enim proprie miracula inserviunt 1 Cor. xiv. 22). Christum, ita ut ipse annun-
tiari voluit, annuntiet, promissionis vim duraturam arbitror. Sunt enim ἀμεταμέλητα τοῦ
Θεοῦ δῶρα (sine pœnitentia dona Dei). Sed nos cujus rei culpa est in nostra ignavia aut
indifferentia id solemus in Deum rejicere." *Works*, edit. London, 1679, tome II. vol. i. p.
328, b, 18–32.

[2] *The Pope and the Council*, by Janus. Authorized Translation from the German.
Boston, 1870.

[3] See especially chap. III. § 7, pp. 76–122.

[4] *Papal Infallibility Untenable*. Three Letters by A. Gratry, Priest of the Oratory, and
member of the French Academy. Hartford, 1870.

distinguished Romish ecclesiastics of France, whose death has
just been announced. In these masterly letters the writer establishes two points, as he says truly beyond the possibility of
rational denial. The first is, that the popes have erred when
speaking " ex cathedra," and therefore are not infallible; and
the second, that the claims of Papal infallibility have been sustained by the most bare-faced and persistent forgeries and frauds.
Both of these points are proved specially in the case of Pope
Honorius. Yet, sad to say, this eminent man, not long before
his death, submitted to the decree of the Vatican Council by
which the infallibility of the Pope was made an article of faith.
He said he " erased " all he had written against that doctrine.[1]

2. During the first hundred years after the death of the Apostles we hear little or nothing of the working of miracles by
the early Christians. On this point Bishop Douglass says, " If
we except the testimonies of Papias and Irenæus, who speak of
raising the dead, ... I can find no instances of miracles mentioned by the fathers before the fourth century, as what were
performed by Christians in their times, but the cures of diseases,
particularly the cures of demoniacs, by exorcising them; which
last, indeed, seems to be their favourite standing miracle, and the
only one which I find (after having turned over their writings
carefully and with a view to this point): they challenged their
adversaries to come and see them perform."[2] The fathers of
the fourth century freely speak of the age of miracles as past;
that such interpositions, being no longer necessary, were no longer
to be expected. Thus Chrysostom says: " Ne itaque ex eo, quod
nunc signa non fiunt, argumentum ducas tunc etiam non fuisse.
Etenim tunc utiliter fiebant, et nunc utiliter non fiunt."[3] And
Augustine says: " Cur, inquiunt, nunc illa miracula, quæ præ-
dicatis facta esse, non fiunt? Possem quidem dicere, necessaria
fuisse priusquam crederet mundus, ad hoc ut crederet mundus."[4]

---

[1] It is perfectly intelligible that a man who admits the infallibility of general councils,
may be able to subject his strongest personal convictions to the judgment of the Church.
But no less than three œcumenical councils and twenty Popes had pronounced Honorius
a heretic. How could the council of the Vatican reverse those decisions? Besides, Gratry
and his Gallican and German coadjutors denied that the late council was either œcumenical
or free. Father Hyacinth wrote to Gratry on his recantation, and said to him, "You speak
of erasing what you have written, but how can you erase the facts which you have demonstrated, or the convictions you have produced in the minds of the faithful?"

[2] *Criterion, or, the Rules by which the True Miracles recorded in the New Testament are
distinguished from the Spurious Miracles of Pagans and Papists.* 4th edit. Oxford, 1832,
pp. 228–232. The author was Dean of Windsor, Bishop of Carlisle, and afterwards of
Salisbury.

[3] *In Epistolam* ɪ. *ad Corinthios, Homilia,* vi. 2; *Works,* edit. Montfaucon, Paris, 1837,
vol. x. p. 53, a.

[4] *De Civitate Dei,* XXII. viii. 1; *Works,* edit. Benedictines, Paris, 1838, vol. vii. p. 1057, d.

However these declarations may be reconciled with the fact that these fathers, themselves, give accounts of what passed for miracles in their day, they at least show that in their view there was such a difference between the Scriptural and ecclesiastical miracles that they did not belong to the same category. Although these miracles were unfrequent in the early ages of the Church, yet they rapidly increased in number until they became matters of every day's occurrence.

3. They admit of being classified on different principles. As to their nature, some are grave and important; others are trifling, childish, and even babyish; others are indecorous; and others are irreverent and even blasphemous. Professor Newman, one of the richest prizes gained by the Romanists from the Church of England in this generation, is candid enough to admit the contrast between the Scriptural and what he calls ecclesiastical miracles. Of the former, he says,[1] " The miracles of Scripture are, as a whole, grave, simple, and majestic: those of ecclesiastical history often partake of what may not unfitly be called a romantic character, and of that wildness and inequality which enters into the notion of romance." He says,[2] " It is obvious to apply what has been said to the case of the miracles of the Church, as compared with those in Scripture. Scripture is to us a garden of Eden, and its creations are beautiful as well as ' very good,' but when we pass from the Apostolic to the following ages, it is as if we left the choicest valleys of the earth, the quietest and most harmonious scenery, and the most cultivated soil, for the luxuriant wildernesses of Africa or Asia, the natural home or kingdom of

---

[1] *Two Essays on Scripture Miracles and on Ecclesiastical.* By John Henry Newman, formerly Fellow of Oriel College, Oxford, 2d edit. London, 1870, p. 116. These Essays, it should be stated, were first published before Dr. Newman entered the Church of Rome. The former was written in 1825–26, and the latter in 1842–43. He was reconciled to Rome in 1845. In the second edition of the united essays published in 1870, he endorses them anew with slight qualification. His words are (p. viii.), " These distinct views of miraculous agency, thus contrasted, involve no inconsistency with each other; but it must be owned that, in the essay upon the Scripture miracles, the author goes beyond both the needs and the claims of his argument, when, in order to show their special dignity and beauty, he depreciates the purpose and value of the miracles of Church history. To meet this undue disparagement in his first essay, of facts which have their definite place in the divine dispensation, he points out in his second the essential resemblance which exists between many of the miracles of Scripture and those of the later times; and it is with the same drift that, in this edition, a few remarks at the foot of the page have been added in brackets." This qualification was hardly necessary, as the fourth chapter of the second essay contains the most ingenious defence of ecclesiastical miracles anywhere to be found. It is generally understood that Prof. Newman was in heart a Romanist some years before his secession from the Church of England. Of this his famous Tract Number 90 of the Oxford series, is a sufficient proof.

[2] *Ibid* p. 150.

brute nature, uninfluenced by man." A more felicitous illustration can hardly be imagined. The contrast between the Gospels and the legends of the saints, is that between the divine and the human and even the animal; between Christ (with reverence be it spoken) and St. Anthony. Another principle on which these ecclesiastical miracles may be classified, is the design for which they were wrought or adduced. Some are brought forth as proofs of the sanctity of particular persons, or places, or things; some to sustain particular doctrines, such as purgatory, transubstantiation, the worshipping of the saints and of the Virgin Mary, etc., some for the identification of relics. It is no injustice to the authorities of the Church of Rome, to say, that whatever good ends these miracles may in any case be intended to serve, they have in the aggregate been made subservient to the accumulation of money and to the increase of power. The amount of money drawn from the single doctrine of purgatory and the assumed power of the keys over that imaginary place of torture, is beyond all computation. And the whole fabric of priestly power, the most absolute and the most dreaded ever exercised over men, would fall to the ground if it were not the belief of the people, founded mainly on " lying wonders," that the priests have power to forgive sin, to save or to destroy souls at will, or at discretion. If this doctrine be false, the whole Romish system is false. Romanists, therefore, have everything at stake on this question. Bishop Jeremy Taylor, writing to a lady " seduced to the Church of Rome," said long ago, " All the points of difference between us and your Church are such as do evidently serve the ends of covetousness and ambition, of power and riches." [1]

4. A fourth general remark on this subject is, that it is no just matter of reproach to the authorities and people of the Romish Church that they believed in these false miracles. Faith in the frequently recurring interference of supernatural influences in the affairs of men, was for ages universal. Even so late as the seventeenth century Protestants as well as Catholics, of all ranks, believed in ghosts, witches, necromancy, and demonocracy. Cotton Mather's " Magnalia " is a match for the Legends of the Saints.

5. It is not that Romanists believed in the frequent occurrence of miracles, but that they propagated reports of miracles, knowing them to be false; that this was done for the purposes of deceit; that this is persisted in to the present day; and that the

[1] *First Letter to One Seduced to the Church of Rome; Works,* edit. London, 1828, vol. xi. p. 189.

honour, truth, integrity, and infallibility of the Church are pledged in support of their actual occurrence. The truth of Christianity depends on the historical truth of the account of the miracles recorded in the New Testament. The truth of Romanism depends on the truth of the miracles to which it appeals. What would become of Protestantism if it depended on the demonology of Luther, or the witch stories of our English forefathers. The Romish Church, in assuming the responsibility for the ecclesiastical miracles, has taken upon itself a burden which would crush the shoulders of Atlas. These "lying wonders" are endorsed, not only by the negative action of the authorities of the Church, by allowing them to be believed and cited in proof of its doctrines and divine mission ; not only by the recognized expounders of its faith referring to them and asserting their truth ; but also by solemn official action of the highest ecclesiastical dignitaries, including a long succession of popes. As no one could be canonized unless his saintship was sustained by at least four miracles, when any one was proposed for canonization a commission was appointed to ascertain the facts of his life, and especially of the miracles which he wrought. This commission reported to the Pope, who, if satisfied, decreed the enrolment of the candidate in the list of saints. These official documents contain the record of the most trivial, and, on other grounds, most objectionable miracles.[1] And to such miracles the Church of Rome has given her sanction, and on the truth of these it must stand or fall.

[1] Accounts of these miracles may be found, not only in the original documents, but also in numerous works, as those of Bishop Stillingfleet and others, written to expose the impostures of the Romish Church. The Rev. John Cumming of London, in his *Lectures on Romanism* (Boston, 1854), has cited from these official records examples sufficiently numerous to satisfy any ordinary man. For example, it is said of Santa Rosa Maria of Lima, among many other things, that the Virgin often appeared to her and talked with her; that the Saviour came to her in the form of a child leaning on his mother's arm, to collect roses scattered on the ground, and then the Divine infant took one of them and said "Thou art this rose." (Cumming, p. 629.) When her tomb was opened fifteen years after death, her remains "exhaled the odor of roses." Of St. Philip Neri it is said that he was so agitated by the love of God, that the Lord broke two of his ribs to give freer action to his heart. (p. 634.) Of Sister Maria Francisca, it is certified that when placing a holy Bambino (*i. e.*, image of the infant Jesus) into the manger, such a light emanated from the Bambino as to blind her for three days. On another occasion, when dressing the image, she said, "My little child, if you do not stretch out your feet I cannot put on your shoes and stockings," and the wooden image immediately stretched out its feet. It is also asserted that she obtained from Christ permission to suffer vicariously for a limited time, in the place of some of her friends, the pains of purgatory, and accordingly endured for a month the most intense agonies. It is further said, that she had imparted to her the sufferings of Christ, his bloody sweat, the anguish of the crown of thorns, his scourging and agonies on the cross, and had his wounds visibly impressed upon her. (Cumming, pp. 649-653.) Cardinal Wiseman edited a book including the lives of several saints, and among them that of St. Veronica Giuliani, who was canonized so recently as 1839. Of this saint, he says, among many similar things, that God recompensed her readiness to drink of the chalice of

There are, however, two special and standing miracles to which Romanists are fully committed, and which in the judgment probably of nine tenths of the educated men in Christendom are barefaced impostures. The Church of Rome by its highest dignitaries and representatives asserted and still continues to assert that the house in which the Virgin Mary dwelt in Nazareth was, when that city fell into the hands of the infidels, transported by angels and deposited at Loretto, a village a few miles from Ancona in Italy. The first step in this transportation occurred in 1291 from Nazareth to Dalmatia; the second in 1294 to the neighbourhood of Recanati; and the third in 1295 to its present location. The house is thirty feet long, fifteen wide, and eighteen high, and is built of wood and brick. It is now greatly adorned, having a silver door and a silver grating, and stands in the midst of a large church erected over and around it. Its shrine was enriched with offerings of priceless value, and is regarded as the Mecca of Italy; the number of pilgrims amounting sometimes to two hundred thousand in a single year. The annual income of the house, apart from presents, is stated to be thirty thousand dollars.[1] The original house is said to be a *fac-simile* of hundreds of others in the neighborhood of Ancona. It is obvious that such a frail building could not, without a miracle, have been preserved thirteen hundred years; another miracle would be required to identify it after so long a period; another stupendous miracle to account for its transportation to Dalmatia; and two more nearly as great to explain its reaching its present location. The only conceivable design of all these miracles, must be to sustain the doctrines and authority of the Romish Church, and to pour money into its treasury. Both these objects they have accomplished to a wonderful degree. No man who is not prepared to accept all these miracles without a particle of evidence, can rationally believe in the Church of Rome.

The other standing miracle for which the Romish Church is responsible before the whole world, is the annual liquefaction of the blood of St. Januarius at Naples. The tradition concerning him is, that he was thrown by his heathen persecutors into a heated oven, where he remained three days uninjured. He was afterwards exposed to wild beasts, who became as lambs in his

suffering, by making her a partaker of the torments of Christ's passion. Christ accordingly appeared to her and took the crown of thorns and placed it on her head. (Cumming, pp. 665–675.) Such are some of the miracles on which Rome rests her claims to be the only true Church and the infallible teacher of man.

[1] *Conversations-Lexicon*, 7th edit. Leipzig, 1827, art. "Loretto."

presence. He was finally beheaded, A. D. 305. A woman is said to have caught and preserved a portion of his blood. This with other of his remains was carried to Naples, being identified as usual by a miracle, as it is said, " Neapolitani beatum Januarium revelatione commoti sustulerunt." The blood, preserved with great care in the cathedral, is contained in two crystal vials, a larger and smaller one. In its ordinary state it is a hard substance, sometimes represented as filling the vial, and sometimes as appearing in a hard round lump. The blood of other saints is said to liquefy on the anniversaries of their martyrdom, but the blood of Januarius becomes liquid whenever the vial containing it is brought near to the skull of the saint, which is still preserved. It turns readily when good is impending, and refuses to change when evil is at hand. It thus serves the purpose of an oracle. It is annually produced and exhibited to crowds of devotees gathered in the cathedral on the first Sunday of May, and also on the nineteenth day of September and twentieth of December, and at other times on extraordinary emergencies. To this miracle the Church of Rome is fully committed as it is exhibited every year under the eyes of the pope and the highest dignitaries of the Church. There is not a particle of evidence for the facts above stated concerning this saint, which may not be pleaded for any one of the thousands of stories of fairies and witches with which the histories of all nations abound, except the liquefaction of the blood. As to that, however, it is to be said that there is no evidence that the substance contained in the vial is blood; or if blood, that it is human blood ; or if human, that it is the blood of Januarius ; or if his, that the cause of the liquefaction is bringing the vial into proximity to the saint's cranium. All that the people are allowed to see, the change of a dark-red solid substance into a fluid, any chemist could effect at five minutes' notice. It is true, as Dr. Newman admits, that these miracles do not so much prove the truth of the Church, as the Church proves the truth of the miracles. Then what are they worth.

Relics.

Relics are the remains of sacred persons and things, which are not only to be cherished as memorials, but to which "cultus " or a certain degree of religious worship is due, and which are imbued with supernatural power. They heal the sick, restore sight to the blind, hearing to the deaf, soundness to the maimed, and even, at times, life to the dead. Of these the Catholic world is

full.[1] Dr. Newman in his " Lectures on the Present Position of
Catholics in England," delivered after his reconciliation with the
Church of Rome, says, " At Rome there is the True Cross, the
Crib of Bethlehem, and the Chair of St. Peter ; portions of the
Crown of Thorns are kept at Paris ; the Holy Coat is shown at
Tréves ; the Winding-sheet at Turin : at Monza the iron Crown
is formed out of a nail of the Cross ; and another nail is claimed
for the Duomo of Milan ; and pieces of Our Lady's habit are to
be seen in the Escurial. The Agnus Dei, blest medals, the
Scapula, the cord of St. Francis, all are the medium of divine
manifestations and graces." [2]

There is here opened an illimitable field for pious fraud. First,
in palming upon the credulous people spurious relics, and, secondly in falsely attributing to them supernatural power. It has
been proved in many cases that remains passed off as relics of the
saints were bones of animals. In other cases it is impossible that
all should be genuine, as bodies, or the same parts of bodies, of one
and the same man are exhibited in different places. There is,
as has often been asserted, enough wood of the true cross, held
sacred in different localities, out of which to construct a large
building. Writing not long after the alleged discovery of the
cross on which the Saviour died, Cyril of Jerusalem says, " Sanctum crucis lignum testatur, quod ad hodiernum usque diem apud
nos conspicitur, ac per eos qui fide impellente ex eo frusta decerp-
unt orbem fere totum hinc jam opplevit." And again, he speaks
of " crucis lignum, quod per particulas ex hoc loco per totum
orbem distributum est." [3] St. Paulinas, who is one of the long
list of witnesses quoted in defence of the veneration of relics, says
" that a portion of the cross kept at Jerusalem gave off fragments
of itself without diminishing." This is the only way in which

---

[1] The language of the Council of Trent in reference to the honour due to the relics of the
saints has already been quoted when treating of the second commandment. Perrone in his
Prælectiones Theologicæ, De Cultu Sanctorum, iv. 71, edit. Paris, 1861, vol. ii. p. 112, b,
adduces as one of his arguments in favour of the worship of relics the declaration of the
Epistle of the Church of Smyrna, that the heathen feared " ne Christiani, relicto Christo,
Polycarpum adorare inciperent; omni idcirco qua poterant ratione martyrum corpora,
ne a Christianis colerentur, ethnici gladiatorum corporibus commiscebant; in amphitheatris
feris, in aquis piscibus ut vorarentur exponebant; aut saltem igne illa cremabant, cinere
dispergentes, uti ex martyrum actis constat." It was " adoration," " worship," that was
to be rendered to these relics. The distinctions between the different kinds of worship, had
little effect on the popular mind. Perrone himself teaches that the " material heart of
Christ " was to be adored *latriæ cultu*. *De Incarnatione*, ii. iv. 454; *Ibid*. p. 81, a.

[2] Quoted by Dr. Cumming in his *Lectures on Romanism*, p. 595.

[3] *Catechesis Illuminandorum.* x. 19. and viii 4; *Opera*, Venice, 1763, pp. 146, c. and
184, c.

the fact in question can be accounted for. If this solution be not admitted, then it must be acknowledged that, at least, the great majority of the portions of the cross now on exhibition must be spurious. There is no historical evidence of any value that any portion of the true cross has been preserved. Nothing was heard of it until A. D. 327. About that time, according to the legend, the Empress Helena, in searching for the Holy Sepulchre, found at the depth of thirty feet from the surface of the earth, three crosses, assumed to be those mentioned in the Gospels. The true cross was identified, some say, by its inscription ; others, by a sick woman being touched by the one and the other without effect, but restored to perfect health the moment the true cross came in contact with her body. Others say that a corpse was restored to life by the touch of the true cross. In reference to this account it may be remarked, (1.) That there is a strong antecedent improbability that the crosses used on Calvary were ever buried. The assumption that it was the custom of the Jews to bury those implements of torture, rests on a very precarious foundation. (2.) The cross was a very slight structure, as it could be borne by one man ; and, therefore, if buried superficially, as it must have been at first, it could hardly have continued undecayed three hundred years, especially considering the ploughings and over-turnings to which the Holy City was subjected. (3.) The historical evidence in support of this legend is of little account. Cyril of Jerusalem, twenty years after the date assigned to the discovery, does indeed say that the true cross was then in Jerusalem, as Jerome does some sixty years later, but neither of them makes any mention of Helena in connection with the cross or the sepulchre. It may, therefore, be admitted that what passed for the true cross was then in Jerusalem, but the account of its recovery and identification remains without support. (4.) The historian Eusebius, a contemporary and eye-witness, makes no mention of the finding of the cross, an event the belief in which agitated all Christendom, and led to the immense aggrandizement of the bishopric of Jerusalem. It is inconceivable that such an event, if within his knowledge, should have been passed over in silence by such a historian, who had so much at heart to enchance the glory of his patron the Emperor. (5.) Calvary and the sepulchre we know were without the city. The place where the cross is said to have been found is in the centre of the modern city. Whether the city has so changed its limits as to bring the place of the crucifixion and burial of Christ within its boundaries, is a much debated question. Dr.

Robinson, one of the most reliable of explorers, says, " The hypothesis which makes the second wall so run as to exclude the alleged site of the Holy Sepulchre, is on topographical grounds untenable and impossible." [1]   That is, assuming the truth of the statement of the Evangelists that Christ was crucified without the walls, it is topographically impossible that the alleged site of the Holy Sepulchre should be the true one.   And thus the whole foundation of the legend of finding the cross on that spot falls to the ground.   Dr. Robinson winds up his long discussion of this question in the following words : " Thus in every view which I have been able to take of the question, both topographical and historical, whether on the spot or in the closet, and in spite of all my previous prepossessions, I am led irresistibly to the conclusion, that the Golgotha and the tomb now shown in the Church of the Holy Sepulchre, are not upon the real places of the crucifixion and resurrection of our Lord.   The alleged discovery of them by the aged and credulous Helena, like her discovery of the cross, may not improbably have been the work of pious fraud.   It would perhaps not be doing injustice to the Bishop Macarius and his clergy, if we regard the whole as a well laid and successful plan for restoring to Jerusalem its former consideration, and elevating his see to a higher degree of influence and dignity." [2]

Dr. Newman says we must either admit the discovery of the cross, or believe the Church of Jerusalem guilty of imposture.[3] It is hard to decide how much is due in this matter to fraud, and how much to superstitious credulity.   That both prevailed for ages in the Church is an undoubted historical fact.   Are we to believe all that Gregory of Nyssa said of Gregory of Neo-Cæsarea, or what the fathers relate of St. Anthony ; are we to admit all the legends of the saints, to avoid charging credulity or fraud against good men ?   It is lamentable that good men advocated the principle that it is right to deceive for a good end.   It is undeniable that the doctrine of pious frauds has been avowed and acted upon in the Church of Rome ever since it began to aspire to ecclesiastical supremacy.   Was not the pretended donation of Italy by Constantine to the pope a fraud ?   Are not the Isidorian Decretals a fraud ?   Are not the miracles wrought in proof of the delivery of souls from purgatory, frauds ?   Is not the alleged house of the

---

[1] *Biblical Researches in Palestine, Mount Sinai, and Arabia Petræa. A Journal of Travels in the year* 1838, *by E. Robinson and E. Smith. Drawn up from the Original Diaries, etc.* By Edward Robinson, Professor of Biblical Literature in the Union Theological Seminary, New York. Boston, 1841, vol. ii. p. 69.

[2] *Ibid.* p. 80.   [3] *Essays on Miracles,* p. 297.

Virgin Mary at Loretto a fraud? Is not the foot-print (ex pede Hercules) on a marble slab in the Cathedral of Rouen, a fraud? Is not the feather from the wing of the Archangel Gabriel preserved in one of the Cathedrals of Spain, a fraud? The whole Catholic world is full of frauds of this kind; and the only possible ground for Romanists to take is, that it is right to deceive the people for their good. " Populus vult decipi," is the excuse a Romish priest once made to Coleridge in reference to this matter.

Secondly, pious frauds are practised, not only in the exhibition of false relics, but also in falsely attributing to them supernatural power. Dr. Newman says: " The store of relics is inexhaustible; they are multiplied through all lands, and each particle of each has in it at least a dormant, perhaps an energetic virtue of supernatural operation." [1] Bellarmin of course teaches the same [2] doctrine. Cyril of Jerusalem says, " Et Elisæum qui semel et iterum suscitavit, dum viveret, et post mortem : vivus resurrectionem per suam ipsius animam operatus est, ut autem non animæ solum justorum honorarentur, sed crederetur etiam in justorum corporibus jacere vim, projectus in monumentum Elisæi mortuus prophǝtæ corpus attingens, vitam concepit, 4 Kin. iv. 13, ut ostenderetur, absente etiam anima inesse vim corpori sanctorum propter animam justam, quæ in eo habitaverat." [3] Dr. Newman says that miracles wrought by relics are of daily occurrence in all parts of the world. It is not that people are favourably affected by them through the imagination or feelings, but that the relics themselves are imbued with supernatural power. Thus Dr. Newman, one of the most cultivated men of the nineteenth century, has come round to the pure, simple, undiluted fetichism of Africa.

Our Lord warned his disciples against being deceived by lying wonders. The Bible (Deut. xiii. 1–3) teaches that any sign or wonder given or wrought in support of any doctrine contrary to the Word of God, is, without further examination, to be pronounced false. If, therefore, such doctrines as the supremacy of the pope; the power of priests to forgive sins; the absolute necessity of the sacraments as the only channels of communicating the merits and grace of Christ; the necessity of auricular confession; purgatory; the adoration of the Virgin and of the consecrated wafer; and the worship of saints and angels, are contrary to the

[1] *Lectures on the Position of Catholics in England*, p. 284.
[2] See above, pp. 300, 301.
[3] *Catechesis Illuminandorum*, xviii. 16; *Opera*, Venice, 1763, p. 293, a, b.

Holy Scriptures, then to a certainty all the pretended miracles wrought in their support are " lying wonders ; " and those who promulgate and sustain them are guilty of pious fraud. If, therefore, as Newman says, The Catholic Church, from east to west, from north to south, is, according to our conceptions, hung with miracles ; so much the worse. It is hung all over with the symbols or ensigns of apostasy.

§ 14. *The Tenth Commandment*

Is a general prohibition of covetousness. " Thou shalt not covet," is a comprehensive command. Thou shalt not inordinately desire what thou hast not; and especially what belongs to thy neighbour. It includes the positive command to be contented with the allotments of Providence ; and the negative injunction not to repine, or complain on account of the dealings of God with us, or to envy the lot or possessions of others. The command to be contented does not imply indifference, and it does not enjoin slothfulness. A cheerful and contented disposition is perfectly compatible with a due appreciation of the good things of this world, and diligence in the use of all proper means to improve our condition in life.

Contentment can have no other rational foundation than religion. Submission to the inevitable is only stoicism, or apathy, or despair. The religions of the East, and of the ancient world generally, so far as they were the subject of thought, being essentially pantheistic, could produce nothing but a passive consent to be borne along for a definite period on the irresistible current of events, and then lost in the abyss of unconscious being. The poor and the miserable could with such a faith have little ground for contentment, and they would be under the strongest temptation to envy the rich and the fortunate. But if a man believes that there is a personal God infinite in power, wisdom, and love ; if he believes that God's providence extends over all creatures and over all events ; and if he believes that God orders everything, not only for the best on the whole, but also for the best for each individual who puts his trust in Him and acquiesces in his will, then not to be contented with the allotments of infinite wisdom and love must be folly. Faith in the truths referred to cannot fail to produce contentment, wherever that faith is real. When we further take into view the peculiar Christian aspects of the case ; when we remember that this universal government is administered by Jesus Christ, into whose hands, as He himself tells us, all power in heaven and earth has been committed, then we know that our lot is determined by Him who loved us and gave Himself for us, and who watches over his people as a shepherd watches over his flock, so that a hair of our heads cannot perish without his permission. And when we think of the eternal future which He has prepared for us, then we see that the sorrows of this life are not worthy to be compared with the glory that shall be revealed in us, and that our light afflictions, which are but for a moment, shall work out for us a far more exceeding and an eternal weight of glory; then mere contentment is elevated to a peace which passes all understanding, and even to a joy which is full of glory. All this is exemplified in the history of the people of God as recorded in the Bible. Paul could not only say, "I have learned, in whatsoever state I am, therewith to be content" (Phil. iv. 11); but he could also say: "I take pleasure in infirmities, in reproaches, in necessities, in persecutions, in distresses for Christ's sake." (2 Cor. xii. 10.) This has measurably been the experience of thousands of believers in all ages. Of all people in the world Christians are bound in whatsoever state they are therewith to be content. It is easy to utter these words, and easy for those in comfort to imagine that they are exercising the grace of contentment; but when a man is crushed down by poverty and sickness, surrounded by those whose wants he cannot supply; seeing those whom he loves, suffering and wearing away under their privations, then contentment and submission are among the highest and rarest of Christian graces. Nevertheless, it is better to be Lazarus than Dives.

The second form of evil condemned by this commandment is envy. This is something more than an inordinate desire of unpossessed good. It includes regret that others should have what we do not enjoy; a feeling of hatred and malignity towards those more favoured than ourselves; and a desire to deprive them of their advantages. This a real cancer of the soul; producing torture and eating out all right feelings. There are, of course, all degrees of this sin, from the secret satisfaction experienced at the misfortunes of others, or the unexpressed desire that evil may assail them or that they may be reduced to the same level with ourselves, to the Satanic hatred of the happy because of their happiness, and the determination, if possible, to render them miserable. There is more of this dreadful spirit in the human heart, than we are willing to acknowledge. Montesquieu says that every man has a secret satisfaction in the misfortunes even of his dearest friends. As envy is the antithesis of love, it is of all sins the most opposed to the nature of God, and more effectually than any other excludes us from his fellowship.

Thirdly, the Scriptures, however, make mention most frequently of covetousness under the form of an inordinate desire of wealth. The man of whom covetousness is the characteristic has the acquisition of wealth as the main object of his life. This fills his mind, engrosses his affections, and absorbs his energy. Of covetousness in this form the Apostle says it is the root of all evil. That is, there is no evil — from meanness, deceit, and fraud, up to murder — to the commission of which covetousness has not prompted men, or to which it does not always threaten to impel them. Of the covetous man in this sense of the word the Bible says, (1.) That he cannot enter heaven. (1 Cor. vi. 10.) (2.) That he is an idolater. (Eph. v. 5.) Wealth is his God, *i. e.*, that to which he gives his heart and consecrates his life. (3.) That God abhors him. (Ps. x. 3.)

This commandment has a special interest, as it was the means, as St. Paul tells us, of leading him to the knowledge of sin. " I had not known lust, except the law had said, Thou shalt not covet." (Rom. vii. 7.) Most of the other commandments forbid external acts, but this forbids a state of the heart. It shows that no external obedience can fulfil the demands of the law ; that God looks upon the heart, that He approves or disapproves of the secret affections and purposes of the soul ; that a man may be a pharisee, pure outwardly as a whited sepulchre, but inwardly full of dead men's bones and of all uncleanness.

CHAPTER XX.

By means of grace are not meant every instrumentality which God may please to make the means of spiritual edification to his children. The phrase is intended to indicate those institutions which God has ordained to be the ordinary channels of grace, i, e., of the supernatural influences of the Holy Spirit, to the souls of men. The means of grace, according to the standards of our Church, are the word, sacraments, and prayer.

§ 1. *The Word.*

1. The word of God, as here understood, is the Bible. And the Bible is the collection of the canonical books of the Old and New Testaments.

2. These books are the word of God because they were written by men who were prophets, his organs, or spokesmen, in such a sense that whatever they declare to be true or obligatory, God declares to be true and binding. These topics have already been considered in the first volume of this work, so far as they fall within the limits of systematic theology.

3. The word of God, so far as adults are concerned, is an indispensable means of salvation. True religion never has existed, and never can exist, where the truths revealed in the Bible are unknown. This point also has already been discussed when speaking of the insufficiency of natural religion.

4. The word of God is not only necessary to salvation, but it is also divinely efficacious to the accomplishment of that end. This appears, (*a.*) From the commission given to the Church. After his resurrection our Lord said to his disciples: " Go ye therefore, and teach all nations, baptizing them in the name of the Father, and of the Son, and of the Holy Ghost; teaching them to observe all things, whatsoever I have commanded you: and, lo, I am with you alway, even unto the end of the world. Amen." (Matt. xxviii. 19, 20). The words as recorded in Mark xvi. 15, 16, are, " Go ye into all the world, and preach the gos-

pel to every creature. He that believeth and is baptized shall be saved; but he that believeth not shall be damned." The end to be accomplished, was the salvation of men. The means of its accomplishment was teaching. The disciples were to teach what Christ had taught them. That is, they were to teach the Gospel to every creature under heaven. All means derive their efficiency from the ordinance of God; as He has ordained the Gospel to be the means of salvation, it must be efficacious to that end. (*b.*) This appears further from the manner in which the Apostles executed the commission which they had received. They went everywhere, preaching Christ. They were sent to teach; and teaching was their whole work. " I determined," said Paul, " not to know anything among you, save Jesus Christ and him crucified." (1 Cor. ii. 2.) (*c.*) The power of the Word is proved from many direct assertions in the Bible. Paul tells the Romans that he was not ashamed of the Gospel of Christ, because " it is the power of God unto salvation." (Rom. i. 16.) To the Corinthians he says, in view of the utter impotence of the wisdom of the world, that " it pleased God by the foolishness of preaching to save them that believe." (1 Cor. i. 21.) The preaching of Christ crucified was " unto the Jews a stumbling-block, and unto the Greeks foolishness; but unto them which are called, both Jews and Greeks, Christ the power of God, and the wisdom of God." (Vers. 23, 24.) In the Epistle to the Hebrews it is said: " The word of God is quick, and powerful, and sharper than any two-edged sword, piercing even to the dividing asunder of soul and spirit, and of the joints and marrow, and is a discerner of the thoughts and intents of the heart." (Heb. iv. 12.)

The sacred writers, under the guidance of the Holy Spirit, are exuberant in their praise of the Word of God, as its power was revealed in their own experience. " The law of the LORD," says the Psalmist, " is perfect, converting the soul." (Ps. xix. 7.) By the law of the Lord is meant the whole revelation which God has made in his Word to determine the faith, form the character, and control the conduct of men. It is this revelation which the Psalmist pronounces perfect, that is, perfectly adapted to accomplish the end of man's sanctification and salvation. " Thy word," he says, " is a lamp unto my feet, and a light unto my path." (Ps. cxix. 105.) " The testimony of the LORD is sure, making wise the simple : the statutes of the LORD are right, rejoicing the heart : the commandment of the LORD is pure, enlightening the eyes: the fear of the LORD is clean, enduring forever: the judgments of the LORD are true and righteous altogether.   More to be desired are they than gold, yea, than much fine gold; sweeter also than honey and the honeycomb." (Ps. xix. 7-10.) Almost every one of the hundred and seventy-six verses of the one hundred and nineteenth Psalm contains some recognition of the excellence or power of the Word of God. " Is not my word like as a fire? saith the Lord; and like a hammer that breaketh the rock in pieces?" (Jer. xxiii. 29.)

In the New Testament the same divine efficacy is attributed to the Word of God. It is the gospel of our salvation, i. e., that by which we are saved. Paul said that Christ commissioned him to preach the Gospel to the Gentiles, saying, for this purpose I appeared unto thee to make thee minister and a witness, delivering thee from the Gentiles, "unto whom now I send thee, to open their eyes, and to turn them from darkness to light, and from the power of Satan unto God, that they may receive forgiveness of sins, and inheritance among them which are sanctified by faith that is in me." (Acts xxvi. 17, 18.)   All this was to be effected by the Gospel. The same Apostle writing to Timothy says: " From a child thou hast known the Holy Scriptures, which are able to make thee wise unto salvation, through faith which is in Christ Jesus. All Scripture is given by inspiration of God, and is profitable for doctrine, for reproof, for correction, for instruction in righteousness." (2 Tim. iii. 15, 16.) The Apostle Peter says that men are "born again, not of corruptible seed, but of incorruptible, by the word of God which liveth and abideth forever." (1 Pet. i. 23.) Our Lord prayed, "Sanctify them through thy truth: thy word is truth." (John xvii. 17.)

Testimony of History.

There can, therefore, be no doubt that the Scriptures teach that the Word of God is the specially appointed means for the sanctification and the salvation of men. This doctrine of the Bible is fully confirmed by the experience of the Church and of the world. That experience teaches, — First, that no evidences of sanctification, no indications of the saving influences of the Spirit are found where the Word of God is unknown. This is not saying that none such occur. We know from the Bible itself, " That God is no respecter of persons; but in every nation he that feareth him, and worketh righteousness, is accepted with him." (Acts x. 34, 35.) No one doubts that it is in the power of God to call whom He pleases from among the heathen and to reveal to them enough truth to secure their salvation.[1] Nevertheless it remains a fact patent to all eyes that the nations where the Bible is unknown sit in darkness. The absence of the Bible is just as distinctly discernible as the absence of the sun. The declaration of the Scriptures is that " the whole world lieth in wickedness " (1 John v. 19) ; and that declaration is confirmed by all history.

A second fact on which the testimony of experience is equally clear is, that true Christianity flourishes just in proportion to the degree in which the Bible is known, and its truths are diffused among the people. During the apostolic age the messengers of Christ went everywhere preaching his Gospel, in season and out of season ; proving from the Scriptures that Jesus is the Christ, the Son of the living God ; requiring those to whom they preached to search the Scriptures ; exhorting younger ministers to preach the Word ; to hold forth the Word of life ; to give attendance to reading, exhortation, and doctrine ; to meditate upon these things and to give themselves wholly to them. During this period the Gospel made more rapid progress, and perhaps brought forth more abundant fruits than during any equally long period of its history. When, however, the truth began to be more and more corrupted by the speculations of philosophy, and by the introduction of the Jewish doctrines concerning ceremonies and the priesthood ; when " reserve " in preaching came into vogue, and it was held to be both lawful and wise to conceal the truth, and awaken reverence and secure obedience by other means ; and when Christian worship was encumbered by heathen rites, and the trust of the people turned away from God and Christ, to the virgin and saints, then the shades of night overspread the Church, and the darkness became more and more intense, until the truth or light was almost entirely obscured. At the Reformation, when the chained Bible was brought from the cloisters, given to the press, and scattered over Europe, it was like the bright rising of the sun : the darkness was dissipated; the Church arose from the dust, and put on her beautiful garments, for the glory of God had arisen upon her. Wherever the reading and preaching of the Word was unrestricted, there light, liberty, and true religion prevailed, in a proportionate

---

[1] In the Second Helvetic Confession, chapter i., it is said: " Cum hodie hoc Dei verbum per prædicatores legitime vocatos annunciatur in ecclesia, credimus ipsum Dei verbum annunciari, et a fidelibus recipi, neque aliud Dei verbum vel fingendum vel cœlitus esse expectandum. . . . . Agnoscimus interim, Deum illuminare posse homines etiam sine externo ministerio, quos et quando velit: id quod ejus potentiæ est. Nos autem loquimur de usitata ratione instituendi homines, et præcepto et exemplo tradita nobis a Deo." — Niemeyer, *Collectio Confessionum*, Leipzig, 1840, pp. 467, 468.

degree.   Wherever the Bible was suppressed and the preaching of its truths was forbidden, there the darkness continued and still abides.

A third important fact equally well established is, that true religion prevails in any community, in proportion to the degree in which the young are instructed in the facts and indoctrinated in the truths of the Bible.   This, in one view, is included under the previous head, but it deserves separate notice.   The question does not concern the reason why the religious education of the young is so important; or the way in which that education can most advantageously be secured; but simply the fact that where the young are from the beginning imbued with the knowledge of the Bible, there pure Christianity abides ; and where they are allowed to grow up in ignorance of divine truth, there true religion languishes and loses more and more its power.   Such is the testimony of experience.

It is, therefore, the united testimony of Scripture and of history that the Bible, the Word of God, is the great means of promoting the sanctification and salvation of men, that is, of securing their temporal and eternal well being.   Those consequently who are opposed to religion ; who desire the reign of indifferentism, or the return of heathen doctrines and heathen morality, are consistent and wise in their generation, in endeavouring to undermine the authority of the Bible ; to discourage its circulation ; to discountenance attendance on its preaching ; and especially to oppose its being effectually taught to the young.   Those on the other hand who believe that without holiness no man can see God, and that without the light of divine truth, holiness is impossible, are bound as pastors, as parents, and as citizens to insist that the Bible shall have free course, and that it shall be faithfully taught to all under their influence or for whose training they are responsible.

To what is the Power of the Word to be attributed?

It being admitted as a fact that the Bible has the power attributed to it, the question arises, To what is that due?   To this question different answers are given.   Some say that its whole power lies in the nature of the truths which it contains. This is the doctrine held by Pelagians and Rationalists.   On this subject it may be remarked, (1.) That all truth has an adaptation to the human mind and tends to produce an impression in accordance with its nature.   If a mind could be conceived of destitute of all truth, it would be in a state of idiocy.   The mind is roused to action and expanded, and its power is increased by the truth, and, other things being equal, in proportion to the amount of truth communicated to it. (2.) It is the tendency of all moral truth in itself considered, to excite right moral feelings and to lead to right moral action. (3.) It is further conceded that the truths of the Bible and the sources of moral power therein contained are of the highest possible order. The doctrine, for example, therein taught concerning God, that He is a Spirit, infinite, eternal, and unchangeable in being, wisdom, power, holiness, justice, goodness, and truth, is immeasurably above all that human reason ever discovered or human philosophy ever taught. There is more moral power in that single truth, than in all the systems of moral philosophy. The same may be said of what the Bible teaches of God's relation to the world. He is not merely its creator and architect, but also its constant preserver and governor; everywhere present, working with and by his creatures, using each according to its nature, and overruling all things to the accomplishment of the highest and most beneficent designs. To his rational creatures, especially to men, He reveals Himself as a father, loving, guiding, and providing for them; never afflicting them willingly, but only when it would be morally wrong to do otherwise. The Bible doctrine concerning man is not only true, conformed to all that man reveals himself to be, but it is eminently adapted to make him what he was designed to be: to exalt without inflating; to humble without degrading him. The Bible teaches that God made man out of the dust of the earth and breathed into him the breath of life, and he became a living soul conformed to the image of God in knowledge, righteousness, and holiness. Thus man is apparently the lowest of God's rational creatures, but made capable of indefinite progress in capacity, excellence, and blessedness. The actual state of man however exhibits a sad contrast with this account of his original condition. The Bible accordingly informs us that man fell from the state in which he was created by sinning against God. Thus sin was introduced into the world: all men are sinners, that is, guilty, polluted, and helpless. These are facts of consciousness, as well as doctrines of the Bible. The Scriptures however inform us that God so loved the world that He gave his only begotten Son, that whoso believeth on Him might not perish but have everlasting life. We are told that this Son is the image of God, equal with God. By Him were all things created that are in

heaven, and that are in earth, visible and invisible, whether they
be thrones, or dominions, or principalities or powers: all things
were created by Him and for Him; and He is before all things,
and by Him all things consist.   This divine Person, for us and
for our salvation, took upon Him our nature, fulfilled all righteousness, bore our sins in his own body on the tree; and having
died for our offences, rose again for our justification; and is now
seated at the right hand of the majesty on high; all power in
heaven and earth having been committed to his hands.   There is
more of power to sanctify, to elevate, to strengthen and to cheer
in the single word JESUS, which means " Jehovah-saviour," than
in all the utterances of men since the world began.   This divine
and exalted Saviour has sent forth his disciples to preach his
Gospel to every creature, promising pardon, sanctification, and
eternal life, including a participation in his glory, to every one,
on the sole condition that he receive Him as his God and Saviour, and, trusting in Him alone for salvation, honestly endeavour to do his will; that is, to love God with all his heart and
his neighbour as himself, and to do to others as he would have
others do to him.   In view of all these truths, God asks, " What
could have been done more to my vineyard, that I have not done
in it?"   All the resources of moral power are exhausted in the
Bible.   Every consideration that can affect the intellect, the con
science, the feelings, and the hopes of man is therein presented :
yet all in vain.

There are two conditions necessary for the production of a
given effect.   The one is that the cause should have the requisite
efficiency; and the other, that the object on which it acts should
have the requisite susceptibility.   The sun and rain shed their
genial influences on a desert, and it remains a desert; when
those influences fall on a fertile plain, it is clothed with all the
wonders of vegetable fertility and beauty.   The mid-day brightness of the sun has no more effect on the eyes of the blind than a
taper; and if the eye be bleared the clearest light only enables it
to see men as trees walking.   It is so with moral truth: no matter what may be its inherent power, it fails of any salutary effect
unless the mind to which it is presented be in a fit state to
receive it.

The minds of men since the fall are not in a condition to receive
the transforming and saving power of the truths of the Bible;
and therefore it is necessary, in order to render the Word of God
an effectual means of salvation, that it should be attended by the

supernatural power of the Holy Spirit. The Apostle says expressly, " The natural man receiveth not the things of the Spirit of God : for they are foolishness unto him : neither can he know them, because they are spiritually discerned." (1 Cor. ii. 14.) In the preceding chapter he had said, that the same gospel which to the called was the power and wisdom of God, was to the Jews a stumbling-block, and to the Greeks foolishness. Our Lord said to the Jews : " Why do ye not understand my speech ? even because ye cannot hear my Word. He that is of God heareth God's words : ye therefore hear them not because ye are not of God." (John viii. 43, 47.) Everything that the Scriptures teach of the state of men since the fall proves that until enlightened by the Holy Ghost they are spiritually blind, unable to discern the true nature of the things of the Spirit, and therefore incapable of receiving a due impression from them.

Experience confirms this teaching of the Bible. It shows that no mere moral power of truth as presented objectively to the mind is of any avail to change the hearts of men. There once appeared on earth a divine person clothed in our nature ; exhibiting the perfection of moral excellence in the form of a human life : holy, harmless, undefiled, and separate from sinners ; humble, disinterested, beneficent, tender, patient, enduring, and dispensing blessings on all who approached him. Yet this person was to the men of his generation without form or comeliness. He came to his own and his own received him not. They rejected him and preferred a murderer. And in what respect are we better than they ? How is Christ regarded by the mass of the men of this generation. Multitudes blaspheme Him. The majority scarcely think of Him. He is to them no more than Socrates or Plato. And yet there is in Him such a revelation of the glory of God, as would constrain every human heart to love and adore Him, had not the god of this world blinded the eyes of those who believe not. It is vain therefore to talk of the moral power of truth converting men.

There are some who throw a vail over this rationalistic doctrine, and delude themselves and others into the belief that they stand on more Scriptural ground than Rationalists, because they admit that the Spirit is operative in the truth. Every theist believes that God is everywhere present in the world and always sustaining and coöperating with physical causes in the production of their various effects. So the Spirit is in the world, everywhere present and everywhere active, coöperating with moral causes in producing their legitimate effects. There is nothing in the operation of physical causes transcending their legitimate effects; and there is nothing in the regeneration, conversion, and sanctification of men which transcends the legitimate effects of moral truth. The one series of effects is just as natural, and just as little supernatural, as the other. It has already been shown on a previous page,[1] that this is all that the most advanced rationalists require. It excludes the supernatural, which is all they demand. In the effects produced by physical causes guided by the providential efficiency of God, there is nothing which exceeds the power of those causes; and in the effects produced by the moral power of the truth under the coöperation of the Spirit, there is nothing which exceeds the power of the truth. The salvation of the soul is as much a natural process as the growth of a plant. The Scriptures clearly teach that there is an operation of the Spirit on the soul anterior to the sanctifying influence of the truth, and necessary to render that influence effective. A dead man must be restored to life, before the objects of sense can produce upon him their normal effect. Those spiritually dead must be quickened by the almighty power of God, before the things of the Spirit can produce their appropriate effect. Those spiritually blind must have their eyes opened before they can discern the things freely given, or revealed, to them of God. This influence being anterior to, cannot be through, the truth. Hence we find numerous prayers in every part of the Scriptures for this antecedent work of the Spirit; prayers that God would change the hearts, open the eyes, and unstop the ears of men; or that He would give them ears to hear, and eyes to see. The Spirit is everywhere represented as a personal agent, distributing his gifts to every one severally as He will. He arouses their attention, controls their judgments, and awakens their affections. He convinces them of sin, righteousness, and judgment. He works in the people of God both to will and to do. He teaches, guides, comforts, and strengthens. His influence is not confined to one activity producing an initial change, and then leaving the renewed soul to the influences of the truth and of the ordinances. It is abiding. It is not however the influence of a uniformly acting force coöperating with the truth; but that of a person, acting when and where He pleases; more at one time than at another, sometimes in one way and sometimes in another. He is a " Helper " who can be invoked, or who can be grieved and resisted. All these

---

[1] See vol. ii. p. 657, ff.

representations of the Scriptures, which are utterly inconsistent
with the purely rationalistic doctrine, as well as with the doctrine
which either confounds the operations of the Spirit with the
providential efficiency of God, or regards them as analogous, have
impressed themselves on the general consciousness of the Church.
Every believer feels that he stands to the Holy Spirit in the relation which one person sustains to another : a person on whom he
is dependent for all good ; whose assistance must be sought, and
whose assistance may be granted or withheld at pleasure ; and
who may come or withdraw either for a season or forever. Such
has been the faith of the Church in all ages, as is manifest from
its creeds, its hymns, and its prayers. While all Christians admit
that God's providential efficiency extends over all his works, and
that all good in fallen man is due to the presence and power of his
Holy Spirit, yet they have ever felt and believed, under the guidance of the Scriptures, that the divine activity in these different
spheres is entirely different. The spheres themselves are different ; the ends to be accomplished are different ; and the mode
of operation is different. In nature (especially in the external
world) God acts by law ; his providential efficiency is a " potentia ordinata ; " in grace it is more a " potentia absoluta," untram-
melled by law. It is personal and sovereign. He does not ˉact
continuously or in any one way ; but just as He sees fit. He
works in us " both to will and to do of his good pleasure." (Phil.
ii. 13.) As just remarked, therefore, every Christian feels his dependence not upon law, but on the good-will of a person. Hence
the prayers so frequent in Scripture, and so constantly on the
lips of believers, that the Spirit would not cast us off ; would
not give us up ; would not be grieved by our ingratitude or resistance : but that He would come to us, enlighten us, purify,
elevate, strengthen, guide, and comfort us ; that He would come
to our households, renew our children, visit our churches, and
multiply his converts as the drops of the morning dew ; and that
He would everywhere give the Word of God effect.

This sovereignty in the operations of the Spirit is felt and recognized by every parent, by every pastor, and by every missionary. It is the revealed purpose of God that it must be acknowledged. " See your calling brethren," says the Apostle ; not the
wise, the great, the good, but the foolish, those who are of no account, hath God chosen in order " that no flesh should glory in
his presence." (1 Cor. i. 26-29.) No man is to be allowed to
attribute his conversion or salvation to himself, to law, or to the

efficiency of means. It is in the hands of God. It is of Him
that any man is in Christ Jesus. (1 Cor. i. 30.) In like manner
He so gives or withholds the influences of the Spirit that every
minister of the Gospel, as the Apostles themselves did, should
feel and acknowledge that his success does not depend on his official dignity, or his fidelity, or his skill in argument, or his power
of persuasion, but simply and solely on the demonstration of the
Spirit, given or withheld as He sees fit. Why was it that so few
were converted under the ministry of Christ, and so many thousands under that of the Apostles ? Why is it that a like experience has marked the whole history of the Church ? The only
Scriptural or rational answer that can be given to that question
is, " Even so, Father : for so it seemed good in thy sight." We
know indeed that the Spirit's sovereignty is determined in its
action by infinitely wise and good reasons ; and we know that
his withholding his coöperation is often judicial and punitive ;
that He abandons individuals, churches, communities, and nations
who have sinned away their day of grace. It is important that
we should remember, that, in living under the dispensation of the
Spirit, we are absolutely dependent on a divine Person, who
gives or withholds his influence as He will; that He can be
grieved and offended ; that He must be acknowledged, feared,
and obeyed ; that his presence and gifts must be humbly and
earnestly sought, and assiduously cherished, and that to Him all
right thoughts and right purposes, all grace and goodness, all
strength and comfort, and all success in winning souls to Christ,
are to be ascribed.

The Office of the Word as a Means of Grace.

Christians then do not refer the saving and the sanctifying
power of the Scriptures to the moral power of the truths which
they contain ; or to the mere coöperation of the Spirit in a manner analogous to the way in which God coöperates with all second
causes, but to the power of the Spirit as a divine Person acting
with and by the truth, or without it, as in his sovereign pleasure
He sees fit. Although light cannot restore sight to the blind, or
heal the diseases of the organs of sight, it is nevertheless essential
to every exercise of the power of vision. So the Word is essential to all holy exercises in the human soul.

In every act of vision there are three essential conditions:
1. An object. 2. Light. 3. An eye in a healthful or normal
state. In all ordinary cases this is all that is necessary. But

when the object to be seen has the attribute of beauty, a fourth condition is essential to its proper apprehension, namely, that the observer have æsthetic discernment or taste natural or acquired. Two men may view the same work of art. Both have the same object before them and the same light around them. Both see alike all that affects the organ of vision ; but the one may see a beauty which the other fails to perceive ; the same object therefore produces on them very different effects. The one it delights, elevates, and refines ; the other it leaves unmoved if it does not disgust him. So when our blessed Lord was upon earth, the same person went about among the people ; the same Word sounded in their ears ; and the same acts of power and love were performed in their presence. The majority hated, derided, and finally crucified Him. Others saw in Him the glory of the only begotten Son of God full of grace and truth. These loved, adored, worshipped, and died for Him. Without the objective revelation of the person, doctrines, work, and character of Christ, this inward experience of his disciples had been impossible. But this outward revelation would have been, and in fact was to most of those concerned, utterly in vain, without the power of spiritual discernment. It is clear, therefore, what the office of the Word is, and what that of the Holy Spirit is in the work of sanctification. The Word presents the objects to be seen and the light by which we see ; that is, it contains the truths by which the soul is sanctified, and it conveys to the mind the intellectual knowledge of those truths. Both these are essential. The work of the Spirit is with the soul. That by nature is spiritually dead ; it must be quickened. It is blind ; its eyes must be opened. It is hard ; it must be softened. The gracious work of the Spirit is to impart life, to open the eyes, and to soften the heart. When this is done, and in proportion to the measure in which it is done, the Word exerts its sanctifying influence on the soul.

It is a clear doctrine of the Bible and fact of experience that the truth when spiritually discerned has this transforming power. Pau was full of pride, malignity, and contempt for Christ and his Gospel. When the Spirit opened his eyes to behold the glory of Christ, he instantly became a new man. The effect of that vision — not the miraculous vision of the person of the Son of God, but the spiritual apprehension of his divine majesty and love — lasted during the Apostle's life, and will last to all eternity. The same Apostle, therefore, teaches us that it is by beholding the glory of Christ that we are transformed into his image, from

glory to glory, by the Spirit of the Lord. (2 Cor. iii. 18.)
Hence the Scriptures so constantly represent the heavenly state,
as seeing God. It is the beatific vision of the divine glory, in
all its brightness, in the person of the Son of God, that purifies,
ennobles, and enraptures the soul; filling all its capacities of
knowledge and happiness. It is thus that we are sanctified
by the truth; it is by the spiritual discernment of the things
of the Spirit, when He opens, or as Paul says, enlightens
the eyes of our understanding. We thus learn how we must
use the Scriptures in order to experience their sanctifying
power. We must diligently search them that we may know the
truths therein revealed; we must have those truths as much as
possible ever before the mind; and we must pray earnestly and
constantly that the Spirit may open our eyes that we may see
wondrous things out of his law. It matters little to us how
excellent or how powerful the truths of Scripture may be, if we
do not know them. It matters little how well we may know
them, if we do not think of them. And it matters little how
much we think of them, if we cannot see them; and we cannot
see them unless the Spirit opens the eyes of our heart.

We see too from this subject why the Bible represents it as
the great duty of the ministry to hold forth the Word of life; by
the manifestation of the truth to commend themselves to every
man's conscience in the sight of God. This is all they need do.
They must preach the Word in season and out of season, whether
men will hear, or whether they will forbear. They know that
the Gospel which they preach is the power of God unto salvation,
and that if it be hid, it is hid to them that are lost: in whom
the God of this world hath blinded the minds of them which
believe not, lest the light of the glorious Gospel of Christ, who
is the image of God, should shine unto them. (2 Cor. iv. 4.)
Paul may plant and Apollos water, but God only can give the
increase.

Besides this general sanctifying power of the Word of God,
when spiritually discerned, it is to be further remarked that it is
the means of calling forth all holy thoughts, feelings, purposes,
and acts. Even a regenerated soul without any truth before it,
would be in blank darkness. It would be in the state of a
regenerated infant; or in the state of an unborn infant in relation to the external world; having eyes and ears, but nothing to
call its faculties of sight and hearing into exercise. It is obvious
that we can have no rational feelings of gratitude, love, adora-

tion and fear toward God, except in view of the truths revealed concerning Him in his Word. We can have no love or devotion to Christ, except so far as the manifestation of his character and work is accepted by us as true. We can have no faith except as founded on some revealed promise of God; no resignation or submission except in view of the wisdom and love of God and of his universal providence as revealed in the Scriptures; no joyful anticipation of future blessedness which is not founded on what the Gospel makes known of a future state of existence. The Bible, therefore, is essential to the conscious existence of the divine life in the soul and to all its rational exercises. The Christian can no more live without the Bible, than his body can live without food. The Word of God is milk and strong meat, it is as water to the thirsty, it is honey and the honeycomb.

The Lutheran Doctrine.

This doctrine has already been briefly, and, perhaps, sufficiently discussed on a preceding page;[1] it cannot, however, be properly overlooked in this connection. The Lutherans agree in words with Rationalists and Remonstrants, in referring the efficiency of the Word of God in the work of sanctification to the inherent power of the truth. But Rationalists attribute to it no more power than that which belongs to all moral truth; such truth is from its nature adapted to form the character and influence the conduct of rational creatures, and as the truths of the Bible are of the highest order and importance, they are willing to concede to them a proportionate degree of power. The Lutherans, on the other hand, teach, — First, that the power of the Word which is inherent and constant, and which belongs to it from its very nature as the Word of God, is supernatural and divine. Secondly, that its efficiency is not due to any influence of the Spirit, accompanying it at some times and not at others, but solely to its own inherent virtue. Thirdly, that its diversified effects are due not to the Word's having more power at one time than at another; or to its being attended with a greater or less degree of the Spirit's influence, but to the different ways in which it is received. Christ, it is said, healed those who had faith to be healed. He frequently said: "According to your faith be it unto you," or "Thy faith hath saved thee." It was not because there was more power in the person of Christ when the woman touched his garment, than at other times, that she

was healed, but because of her faith.   Fourthly, that the Spirit
never operates savingly on the minds of men, except through and
in the Word.   Luther in the Smalcald Articles says : " Constanter
tenendum est, Deum nemini Spiritum vel gratiam suam largiri
nisi per verbum et cum verbo externo et præcedente, ut ita
præmuniamus nos adversum enthusiastas, *i. e.*, spiritus, qui jac-
titant se ante verbum et sine verbo Spiritum habere." [1]   And
in the Larger Catechism,[2] he says : " In summa, quicquid Deus
in nobis facit et operatur, tantum externis istius modi rebus et
constitutionibus operari dignatur."   Luther went so far as to
refer even the inspiration of the prophets to the " verbum vocale,"
or external word.[3]

  This divine power of the Word, however, is not, as before
remarked, to be referred to the mere moral power of the truth.
On this point the Lutheran theologians are perfectly explicit.
Thus Quenstedt [4] says : " Verbum Dei non agit solum persua-
siones morales, proponendo nobis objectum amabile; sed vero,
reali, divino et ineffabili influxu potentiæ suæ gratiosæ."   This
influx of divine power, however, is not something occasional,
giving the word a power at one time which it has not at another.
It is something inherent and permanent.   Quenstedt says : [5]
' Verbo Dei virtus divina non extrinsecus in ipso usu demum
accedit, sed . . . . in se et per se, intrinsice ex divina ordinatione et communicatione, efficacia et vi conversiva et regeneratrice
præditum est, etiam ante et extra omnem usum."   And Hollaz [6]
says it has this power " propter mysticam verbi cum Spiritu Sancto
unionem intimam et individuam."

  Professor Schmid, of Erlangen, in his " Dogmatik der evangelisch-lutherischen Kirche," quotes from the leading Lutheran theologians their views on this subject.   Hollaz, for example, says
that this " vis divina " is inseparably conjoined with the Word ;
that the Word of God cannot be conceived of without the Spirit ;
that if the Holy Spirit could be separated from the Word, it would

---

[1] II. viii. 3; Hase, *Libri Symbolici*, 1846, p. 331.

[2] IV. 30; Hase, p. 540.

[3] See Smalcald Articles, II. viii. 10, 11: "Quare in hoc nobis est, constanter perseve-
randum, quod Deus non velit nobiscum aliter agere, nisi per vocale verbum et sacramenta,
et quod, quidquid sine verbo et sacramentis jactatur, ut spiritus, sit ipse diabolus.   Nam
Deus etiam Mosi voluit apparere per rubum ardentem et vocale verbum.   Et nullus
propheta, sive Elias, sive Elisæus, Spiritum sine decalogo sive verbo vocali accepit."
Hase, p. 333.

[4] *Theologia Didactico-Polemica*, I. IV. ii. quæst. xvi. ἐχθεσις, 4; edit. Leipzig, 1715,
p. 248.

[5] *Ibid.* I. IV. ii. quæst. xvi. *fontes solutionum*, 7; p. 268.

[6] *Examen Theologicum Acroamaticum*. III. ii. 1, quæst. 4; edit. Leipzig, 1763, p. 992.

not be the Word of God, but the word of man.[1] Quenstedt says
that the action of the Word and of the Spirit is one and indivisible. Baier says :[2] " Nempe eadem illa infinita virtus, quæ es-
sentialiter, per se et independenter in Deo est, et per quam Deus
homines illuminat et convertit, verbo communicata est: et tanquam verbo communicata, divina tamen, hic spectari debet." A distinction, says Quenstedt, is to be made between the natural instruments, such as the staff of Moses, or rod of Aaron, which God uses
to produce supernatural effects, and those, as the Word and sacraments, which are " sua essentia supernaturalia. . . . . Illa indigent
novo motu et elevatione nova ad effectum novum ultra propriam
suam et naturalem virtutem producendum ; hæc vero a prima institutione et productione sufficienti, hoc est, divina et summa vi ac
efficacia prædita sunt, nec indigent nova et peculiari aliqua elevatione ultra efficaciam ordinariam, jamdum ipsis inditam ad producendum spiritualem effectum."[3] That the Word is not always
efficacious is not because it is attended by greater power in one
case than another, but because of the difference in the moral state
of those to whom it is presented. On this point Quenstedt says,
" Quanquam itaque effectus Verbi divini prædicati nonnunquam
impediatur, efficacia tamen ipsa, seu virtus intrinseca a verbo tolli
et separari non potest. Et ita per accidens fit inefficax, non potentiæ defectu, sed malitiæ motu, quo ejus operatio impeditur, quo
minus effectum suum assequatur."[4] A piece of iron glowing
with heat, if placed in contact with anything easily combustible,
produces an immediate conflagration. If brought in contact with
a rock, it produces little sensible effect. So the Word of God
fraught with divine power, when presented to one mind regenerates, converts, and sanctifies, and when presented to another
leaves it as it was, or only exasperates the evil of its nature. It
is true these theologians say that the operation of the Word is not
physical, as in the case of opium, poison, or fire ; but moral, " illus-
trando mentem, commovendo voluntatem," etc. Nevertheless the
illustration holds as to the main point. The Word has an inherent,
divine, and constant power. It produces different effects according to the subjective state of those on whom it acts. The Spirit
acts neither on them nor on it more at one time than at another.

[1] Hollaz, *Examen*, III. ii. 1, 4; edit. Holmiæ et Lipsiæ, 1741, p. 987.
[2] *Compendium Theologiæ Positivæ*, Prolegg. II. xxxix. d; edit. Frankfort and Leipzig, 1739, p. 106.
[3] Quenstedt, *Theologia*, I. IV. ii. quæst. xvi. ἐχθεσις, 7, *ut supra*, p. 249.
[4] *Ibid.* quæst. xvi. 9.

Remarks.

1. It is obvious that this peculiar theory has no support from Scripture. The Bible does indeed say that the Word of God is quick and powerful; that it is the wisdom of God and the power of God; and that it convinces, converts, and sanctifies. But so does the Bible say that Christ gave his Apostles power to work miracles; and that they went about communicating the Holy Ghost by the laying on of hands, healing the sick, and raising the dead. But the power was not in them. Peter was indignant at such an imputation. " Why look ye so earnestly on us," he said to the people, " as though by our own power or holiness we had made this man to walk?" If the Apostles' working miracles did not prove that the power was in them, the effects produced by the Word do not prove that the power is in it.

2. This doctrine is inconsistent with the constant representations of the Scriptures, which set forth the Spirit as attending the Word and giving it effect, sometimes more and sometimes less; working with and by the truth as He sees fit. It is inconsistent with the command to pray for the Spirit. Men are not accustomed to pray that God would give fire the power to burn or ice to cool. If the Spirit were always in mystical, indissoluble union with the Word, giving it inherent divine power, there would be no propriety in praying for his influence as the Apostles did, and as the Church in all ages has ever done, and continues to do.

3. This theory cuts us off from all intercourse with the Spirit and all dependence upon Him as a personal voluntary agent. He never comes; He never goes; He does not act at one time more than at another. He has imbued the Word with divine power, and sent it forth into the world. There his agency ends. God has given opium its narcotic power, and arsenic its power to corrode the stomach, and left them to men to use or to abuse as they see fit. Beyond giving them their properties, He has nothing to do with the effects which they produce. So the Spirit has nothing to do with the conviction, conversion, or sanctification of the people of God, or with illuminating, consoling, or guiding them, beyond once for all giving his Word divine power. There it is: men may use or neglect it as they please. The Spirit does not incline them to use it. He does not open their hearts, as He opened the heart of Lydia, to receive the Word. He does not enlighten their eyes to see wondrous things out of the law.

4. Lutherans do not attribute divine power to the visible words,

or to the audible sounds uttered, but to the truth which these
conventional signs are the means of communicating to the mind.
They admit that this truth, although it has inherent in it divine
power, never produces any supernatural or spiritual effect unless
it is properly used. They admit also that this proper use includes
the intellectual apprehension of its meaning, attention, and the
purpose to believe and obey. Yet they believe in infant regeneration. But if infants are incapable of using the Word ; and if the
Spirit never operates except in the Word and by its use, how is it
possible that infants can be regenerated. If, therefore, the Bible
teaches that infants are regenerated and saved, it teaches that the
Spirit operates not only with and by the Word, but also without
it, when, how, and where He sees fit. If Christ healed only those
who had faith to be healed, how did He heal infants, or raise the
dead ?

5. The theory in question is contrary to Scripture, in that it
assumes that the reason why one man is saved and another not,
is simply that one resists the supernatural power of the Word and
another does not. Why the one resists, is referred to his own free
will. Why the other does not resist, is referred not to any special influence, but to his own unbiased will. Our Lord, however,
teaches that those only come to Him who are given to Him by
the Father; that those come who besides the outward teaching of
the Word, are inwardly taught and drawn of God. The Apostle
teaches that salvation is not of him that willeth or of him that
runneth, but of God who showeth mercy. The Lutheran doctrine
banishes, and is intended to banish, all sovereignty in the distribution of saving grace, from the dispensations of God. To those
who believe that that sovereignty is indelibly impressed on the
doctrines of the Bible and on the history of the Church and of
the world, this objection is of itself sufficient. The common
practical belief of Christians, whatever their theories may be, is
that they are Christians not because they are better than other
men ; not because they coöperate with the common and sufficient
grace given to all men ; not because they yield to, while others
resist the operation of the divine Word ; but because God in his
sovereign mercy made them willing in the day of his power ; so
that they are all disposed to say from the heart, " Not unto us, O
LORD, not unto us, but unto thy name give glory."

6. This Lutheran doctrine is inconsistent with the experience
of believers individually and collectively. On the day of Pentecost, what fell upon the Apostles and the brethren assembled with

them ?   It was no " verbum vocale; " no sound of words; and no
new external revelation.   The Spirit of God Himself, enlightened
their minds and enabled them to remember and to understand all
that Christ had taught, and they spoke every man, as the Spirit
(not the Word) gave them utterance.   Here was a clear manifestation of the Spirit's acting directly on the minds of the Apostles.
To say that the effects then exhibited were due to the divine
power inherent in the words of Christ; and that they had resisted
that power up to the day of Pentecost, and then yielded to its
influence, is an incredible hypothesis.   It will not account for the
facts of the case.   Besides, our Lord promised to send the Spirit
after his ascension.   He commanded the disciples to remain in
Jerusalem until they were imbued with power from on high.
When the Spirit came they were instantly enlightened, endowed
with plenary knowledge of the Gospel, and with miraculous gifts.
How could the " verbum vocale" impart the gift of tongues, or
the gift of healing.   What according to the Lutheran theory is
meant by being full of the Holy Ghost ? or, by the indwelling of
the Spirit ? or, by the testimony of the Spirit ? or, by the demonstration of the Spirit ? or, by the unction of the Holy One which
teaches all things ? or, by the outpouring of the Spirit ?   In
short, the whole Bible, and especially the evangelical history and
the epistles of the New Testament, represents the Holy Spirit not
as a power imprisoned in the truth, but as a personal, voluntary
agent acting with the truth or without it, as He pleases.   As such
He has ever been regarded by the Church, and has ever exhibited
himself in his dealings with the children of God.

7. Luther, glorious and lovely as he was — and he is certainly
one of the grandest and most attractive figures in ecclesiastical
history — was impulsive and apt to be driven to extremes.[1]   The
enthusiasts of his age undervalued the Scriptures, pretending to
private revelations, and direct spiritual impulses, communicating
to them the knowledge of truths unrevealed in the Bible, and a
rule of action higher than that of the written Word.   This doctrine
was a floodgate through which all manner of errors and extrava-
gances poured forth among the people and threatened the overthrow of the Church and of society.   Against these enthusiasts all
the Reformers raised their voices, and Luther denounced them
with characteristic vehemence.   In opposition to their pretensions

---

[1] No one knows Luther who has not read pretty faithfully the five octavo volumes of his
letters, collected and edited by De Wette.   These exhibit not only his power, fidelity, and
courage, but also his gentleness, disinterestedness, and his childlike simplicity, as well as
his joyousness and humour.

he took the ground that the Spirit never operated on the minds of men except through the Word and sacraments; and, as he held the conversion of sinners to be the greatest of all miracles, he was constrained to attribute divine power to the Word. He was not content to take the ground which the Church in general has taken, that while the Word and sacraments are the ordinary channels of the Spirit's influence, He has left himself free to act with or without these or any other means, and when He makes new revelations to individuals they are authenticated to others by signs, and miracles, and divers gifts; and that in all cases, however authenticated, they are to be judged by the written Word as the only infallible rule of faith or practice; so that if an Apostle or an angel from heaven should preach any other gospel than that which we have received, he is to be pronounced accursed. (Gal. i. 8.) " We are of God:" said the Apostle John, " he that knoweth God heareth us; he that is not of God heareth not us. Hereby we know the spirit of truth and the spirit of error." (1 John iv. 6.) The Scriptures teach that not only the Holy Spirit, but also other spirits good and evil have access to the minds of men, and more or less effectually control their operations. Directions, therefore, are given in the Bible to guide us in discriminating between the true and false.

The power of individual men, who appear in special junctures, over the faith and character of coming generations, is something portentous. Of such " world controllers," at least in modern times, there are none to compare with Martin Luther, Ignatius Loyola, and John Wesley. Though so different from each other, each has left his impress upon millions of men. Our only security from the fallible or perverting influence of man, is in entire, unquestioning submission to the infallible Word of God.

§ 2. *The Sacraments. Their Nature.*
Usage of the Word Sacrament.

1. In classical usage the word " sacramentum " means, in general, something sacred. In legal proceedings the money deposited by contending parties was called " sacramentum," because when forfeited it was applied to sacred purposes. " Ea pecunia, quæ in judicium venit in litibus, sacramentum a sacro." " Sacramentum æs significat, quod pœnæ nomine penditur, sive eo quis interrogatur sive contenditur." Then in a secondary sense it meant a judicial process. In military usage it expressed the ob-

ligation of the soldier to his leader or country; then the oath by
which he was bound; and generally an oath; so that in ordinary
language "sacramentum dicere" meant to swear.[1]

2. The ecclesiastical usage of the word was influenced by various circumstances. From its etymology and signification it was
applied to anything sacred or consecrated. Then to anything
which had a sacred or hidden meaning. In this sense it was
applied to all religious rites and ceremonies. This brought it into
connection with the Greek word μυστήριον, which properly means a
secret; something into the knowledge of which a man must be
initiated. Hence in the Vulgate "sacramentum" is used as
the translation of μυστήριον in Ephesians i. 9, iii. 9, v. 32; Colossians i. 27; 1 Timothy iii. 16; Revelation i. 20, xvii. 7. It was
therefore used in the wide sense for any sign which had a secret
import. Thus Augustine says,[2] "Nimis autem longum est, con-
venienter disputare de varietate signorum, quæ cum ad res divinas
pertinent, sacramenta appellantur." And again he says,[3] "Ista
fratres dicuntur sacramenta, quia in eis aliud videtur, aliud intelligitur. Quod videtur speciem habet corporalem, quod intelligitur,
fructum habet spiritualem." All religious rites and ceremonies,
the sign of the cross, anointing with oil, etc., were therefore called
sacraments. Augustine frequently calls the mystical or allegor-
ical exposition of Scripture, a sacrament. Jerome[4] says, "Sacramenta Dei sunt prædicare, benedicere ac confirmare, communionem
reddere, visitare infirmos, orare.[5] Lombard says, "Sacramentum
est sacræ rei signum."[6]

The Theological Usage and Definition of the Word.

3. It is evident that the signification of the word "sacrament"
is so comprehensive and its usage so lax, that little aid can be derived from either of those sources in fixing definitely its meaning
in Christian theology. Hence theologians soon began to frame
definitions of the word more or less exact, derived from the teachings of the New Testament on the subject. The two simplest
and most generally accepted of such definitions are the one by
Augustine and the other by Peter Lombard. The former says,[7]

---

[1] Freund's *Lateinische Wörterbuch.*
[2] *Epistola* cxxxviii. (5); *Works,* edit. Benedictines, Paris, 1836, vol. vii. p. 615, c.
[3] *Sermo* cclxxii. (16); *Ibid.* vol. v. p. 1614, b, c.   [4] *Works,* tom. ix. p. 59. (?)
[5] See Gerhard, *Loci Theologici,* xix. i. §§ 6, 9; edit. Tübingen, 1768, vol. viii. pp. 204,
205.
[6] Lombard, *Magister Sententiarum,* lib. iv. dist. i. B. edit. (?) 1472.
[7] *In Joannis Evangelium Tractatus,* lxxx. 3; *Works,* edit. Benedictines, Paris, 1837, vol.
iii. 2290, a.

" Accedit verbum ad elementum, et fit sacramentum;" the latter,[1]
" Sacramentum est invisibilis gratiæ visibilis forma." These definitions however are too vague.

It is obvious that the only safe and satisfactory method of ar-
riving at the idea of a sacrament, in the Christian sense of the
word, is to take those ordinances which by common consent are
admitted to be sacraments, and by analyzing them determine
what are their essential elements or characteristics. We should
then exclude from the category all other ordinances, human or
divine, in which those characteristics are not found. Baptism
and the Lord's Supper are admitted to be sacraments. They are
(1.) Ordinances instituted by Christ. (2.) They are in their
nature significant, baptism of cleansing ; the Lord's Supper of
spiritual nourishment. (3.) They were designed to be perpetual.
(4.) They were appointed to signify, and to instruct; to seal,
and thus to confirm and strengthen ; and to convey or apply, and
thus to sanctify, those who by faith receive them. On this principle the definition of a sacrament given in the standards of our
Church is founded. " A sacrament," it is said, " is an holy ordinance instituted by Christ; wherein, by sensible signs, Christ
and the benefits of the New Covenant are represented, sealed,
and applied to believers." [2]

To the same effect the other Reformed Symbols speak. For
example, the Second Helvetic Confession says : " Sunt sacramenta
symbola mystica, vel ritus sancti, aut sacræ actiones, a Deo ipso
institutæ, constantes verbo suo, signis, et rebus significatis, quibus in ecclesia summa sua beneficia, homini exhibita, retinet in
memoria, et subinde renovat, quibus item promissiones suas obsignat, et quæ ipse nobis interius præstat, exterius repræsentat, ac
veluti oculis contemplanda subiicit, adeoque fidem nostram, Spiritu Dei in cordibus nostris operante, roborat et auget : quibus
denique nos ab omnibus aliis populis et religionibus separat,
sibique soli consecrat et obligat, et quid a nobis requirat, significat." [3]

The definition given in the Geneva Catechism is that a sacrament is " externa divinæ erga nos benevolentiæ testificatio, quæ
visibili signo spirituales gratias figurat, ad obsignandas cordibus
nostris Dei promissiones, quo earum veritas melius confirmetur." [4]

The Heidelberg Catechism says, that sacraments are " sacra et

---

[1] Lombard, *ut supra.*
[2] *Westminster Shorter Catechism,* quest. 92.
[3] xix.; Niemeyer, *Collectio Confessionum,* Leipzig, 1840, p. 512.
[4] v. *de Sacramentis; Ibid.* p. 160.

in oculos incurrentia signa, ac sigilla, ob eam causam a Deo instituta, ut per ea nobis promissionem Evangelii magis declarat et
obsignet: quod scilicet non universis tantum, verum etiam singulis
credentibus, propter unicum illud Christi sacrificium in cruce
peractum, gratis donet remissionem peccatorum, et vitam æternam." [1]

The Thirty-nine Articles of the Church of England teach [2]
that "Sacraments ordained of Christ be not only badges or tokens
of Christian men's profession; but rather they be certain sure
witnesses and effectual signs of grace, and God's will toward us,
by the which He doth work invisibly in us, and doth not only
quicken, but also strengthen and confirm our faith in Him."

Lutheran Doctrine.

The Lutheran definition of the sacraments agrees in all essential
points with that of the Reformed churches. In the Augsburg
Confession, its authors say: "De usu sacramentorum docent,
quod sacramenta instituta sint, non modo ut sint notæ professionis
inter homines, sed magis ut sint signa et testimonia voluntatis
Dei erga nos, ad excitandam et confirmandam fidem in his, qui
utuntur, proposita.   Itaque utendum est sacramentis ita, ut fides
accedat, quæ credat promissionibus, quæ per sacramenta exhibentur et ostenduntur." [3]

In the Apology for that Confession it is said: "Si sacramenta
vocamus ritus, qui habent mandatum Dei, et quibus addita est
promissio gratiæ, facile est judicare, quæ sint proprie sacramenta.
Nam ritus ab hominibus instituti non erunt hoc modo proprie dicta
sacramenta.   Non est enim auctoritatis humanæ, promittere gratiam.   Quare signa sine mandato Dei instituta, non sunt certa
signa gratiæ, etiamsi fortasse rudes docent, aut admonent aliquid." [4]

"Dicimus igitur ad sacramenta proprie sic dicta duo potissi-
mum requiri, videlicet verbum et elementum, juxta vulgatum illud
Augustini: 'Accedit verbum ad elementum, et fit sacramentum.'
Fundamentum hujus adsertionis ex ipsa natura et fine sacramentorum pendet, cum enim sacramenta id, quid in verbo evangelii
prædicatur, externo elemento vestitum sensibus ingerere debeant,
ex eo sponte sequitur, quod nec verbum sine elemento, nec elementum sine verbo constituat sacramentum.   Per verbum intelligitur
primo mandatum atque institutio divina, per quam elementum

---

[1] lxvi.; Niemeyer, p. 444.   [2] Art. xxv.
[3] I. xiii. 1, 2; Hase, Leipzig, 1846, p. 13.   [4] vii. 3; Hase, p. 200.

. . . . separatur ab usu communi, et destinatur usui sacramentali; deinde promissio atque ea quidem evangelio propria, per
sacramentum adplicanda et obsignanda. Per elementum non
quodvis, sed certum et verbo institutionis expressum accipitur."[1]
In all this the Reformed and Lutherans are agreed. The
differences between them in relation to the sacraments do not
concern their nature.

Romish Doctrine.

The distinctive doctrine of the Romish Church on this subject is
that the sacraments contain the grace which they signify, and that
such grace is conveyed " ex opere operato." That is, they have
a real inherent and objective virtue, which renders them effectual
in communicating saving benefits to those who receive them. In
a certain sense these words may be used to express the Lutheran
doctrine; but that doctrine differs from the Romanist doctrine, as
will appear when the efficacy of the sacraments comes to be considered. The language of the Council of Trent on this subject
is: " Si quis dixerit sacramenta novæ legis non continere gratiam,
quam significant; aut gratiam ipsam non ponentibus obicem non
conferre; quasi signa tantum externa sint acceptæ per fidem
gratiæ, vel justitiæ, et notæ quædam Christianæ professionis, quibus apud homines discernuntur fideles ab infidelibus; anathema
sit."[2]

The Roman Catechism defines a sacrament " Rem esse sensibus subjectam, quæ ex Dei institutione sanctitatis et justitiæ tum
significandæ, tum efficiendæ vim habet."[3] As the task devolved
on the Council of Trent was to present and harmonize the doctrines elaborated by the Schoolmen in opposition to the doctrines
of the Reformers, the definitions and explanations given by the
writers of the Middle Ages throw as much light on the decrees
of the Council as the expositions of the later theologians of the
Latin Church. On this point Thomas Aquinas says : " Oportet,
quod virtus salutifera a divinitate Christi per ejus humanitatem
in ipsa sacramenta derivetur. . . . . Sacramenta ecclesiæ speciali-
ter habent virtutem ex passione Christi, cujus virtus quodammodo
nobis copulatur per susceptionem sacramentorum."[4] Again :
" Ponendo quod sacramentum est instrumentalis causa gratiæ,
necesse est simul ponere, quod in sacramento sit quædam virtus

[1] Gerhard, *Loci Theologici*, xix. 2. § 11; edit. Tübingen, 1768, vol. viii. p. 207.
[2] Sess. VII. *De Sacramentis in genere*, canon 6; Streitwolf, vol. i. p. 39.
[3] II. i. quæst. 6 (x. 11); Streitwolf, vol. i. p. 241.
[4] *Summa*, III. lxii. 5; edit. Cologne, 1640, p. 129, b, of fourth set.

instrumentalis ad inducendum sacramentalem effectum. . . . . Sicut virtus instrumentalis acquiritur instrumento, ex hoc ipso quod
movetur ab agente principali, ita et sacramentum consequitur
spiritualem virtutem ex benedictione Christi et applicatione ministri ad usum sacramenti." Thus Thomas's own opinion was adopted
by the Council as opposed to that of the Scotists to which Thomas
refers, in the same connection : " Illi qui ponunt quod sacramenta
non causant gratiam, nisi per quandam concomitantiam ponunt
quod in sacramento non sit aliqua virtus, quæ operetur ad sacramenti effectum, est tamen virtus divina sacramento assistens, quæ
sacramentalem effectum operatur." [1] This is very nearly the
doctrine of the Reformed Church upon the subject. Bellarmin's
illustration of the point in hand is that as fire is the cause of
combustion when brought into contact with proper materials, so
the sacraments produce their effect by their own inherent virtue.
" Exemplum," he says, " esse potest in re naturali. Si ad ligna
comburenda, primum exsiccarentur ligna, deinde excuteretur ex
silice, tum applicaretur ignis ligno, et sic tandem fieret combustio ;
nemo diceret, causam immediatam combustionis esse siccitatem
aut excussionem ignis ex silice aut applicationem ignis ad ligna,
sed solum ignem, ut causam primariam, et solum calorem seu
calefactionem, ut causam instrumentalem." [2]

" Jam vero sacramenta gratiam, quam significant, continere,
eamque conferre virtute sibi insita, seu ex opere operato, Scripturæ, patres, constansque Ecclesiæ sensus traditionalis luculentis-
sime docent." [3]   According to Romanists, therefore, a sacrament
is a divine ordinance which has the inherent or intrinsic power of
conferring the grace which it signifies.

Remonstrant Doctrine.

It has already been shown that it was the tendency of the
Remonstrants to eliminate, as far as possible, the supernatural
element from Christianity. They therefore regarded the sacraments not properly as means of grace, but as significant rites
intended to bring the truth vividly before the mind, which truth
exerted its moral influence on the heart. " Sacramenta cum dicimus, externas ecclesiæ ceremonias seu ritus illos sacros ac solennes
intelligimus, quibus veluti fœderalibus signis ac sigillis visibili-
bus, Deus gratiosa beneficia sua, in fœdere præsertim evangelico

---

[1] Aquinas, *ut supra*, lxii. 4; p. 129, a.

[2] Bellarmin, *De Sacramentis*, II. i.; *Disputationes*, Paris, 1608, vol. iii. p. 109, a.

[3] Joannes Perrone, *Prælectiones Theologicæ, De Sacramentis in genere*, II. i. 39: edit.
Paris, 1861, vol. ii. p. 221, a.

promissa, non modo nobis repræsentat et adumbrat, sed et certo
modo exhibet atque obsignat: nosque vicissim palam publiceque
declaramus ac testamur, nos promissiones omnes divinas vera,
firma atque obsequiosa fide amplecti, et beneficia ipsius jugi et
grata semper memoria celebrare velle." [1]

" Restat, ut dicamus, Deum gratiam suam per sacramenta nobis
exhibere, non eam actu per illa conferendo ; sed per illa tanquam
signa clara ac evidentia eam repræsentando et ob oculos ponendo
non eminus aut sub figuris quibusdam tanquam multo post fu-
turam, sed tanquam præsentem : ut ita in signis istis tanquam in
speculo quodam, exhibitionem illam gratiæ, quam Deus nobis con-
cessit, quasi conspiciamus.   Estque hæc efficacia nulla alia quam
objectiva, quæ requirit facultatem cognitivam rite dispositam,
ut apprehendere possit illud, quod signum objective menti offert.
Hinc videmus, quomodo sacramenta in nobis operentur, nimirum
tanquam signa repræsentantia menti nostræ rem cujus signa sunt.
Neque alia in illis quæri debet efficacia." [2]

Zwingle alone of the Reformers seems inclined to this view of
the sacraments : " Sunt . . . . sacramenta," he says, " signa vel
ceremoniæ, pace tamen omnium dicam, sive neotericorum sive
veterum, quibus se homo Ecclesiæ probat aut candidatum aut
militem esse Christi, redduntque Ecclesiam totam potius certi-
orem de tua fide quam te.   Si enim fides tua non aliter fuerit absoluta, quam ut signo ceremoniali egeat, fides non est: fides enim
est, qua nitimur misericordiæ Dei inconcusse, firmiter et indis-
tracte, ut multis locis Paulus habet." [3]   Elsewhere he says : " Credo,
imo scio omnia sacramenta, tam abesse ut gratiam conferant, ut
ne adferant quidem aut dispensent. . . . . Dux autem vel vehiculum Spiritui non est necessarium, ipse enim est virtus et latio qua
cuncta feruntur, non qui ferri opus habeat: neque id unquam leg-
imus in scripturis sacris, quod sensibilia, qualia sacramenta sunt,
certo secum ferrent Spiritum, sed si sensibilia unquam lata sunt
cum Spiritu, jam Spiritus fuit qui tulit, non sensibilia.   Sic cum
ventus vehemens ferretur, simul adferebantur linguæ venti virtute, non ferebatur ventus virtute linguarum." [4]   It is obvious
that all that Zwingle here says of the sacraments, might be said
of the Word of God ; and, therefore, if he proves anything he

[1] *Confessio Remonstrantium*, xxiii. 1; *Episcopii Opera*, edit. Rotterdam, 1665, vol. ii. p.
92, a, of second set.
[2] Limborch, *Theologia Christiana*, v. lxvi. 31, 32; edit. Amsterdam, 1715, p. 606, b.
[3] *De Vera et Falsa Religione*, *Works*, edit. Schuler and Schultess, Turici, 1832, vol. iii.
p. 231.
[4] *Ad Carolum Rom. Imperatorem, Fidei Huldrychi Zwinglii Ratio*, § 7; Niemeyer's
Collectio Confessionum, p. 24.

proves that the sacraments are not means of grace; he proves the same concerning the Word, to which the Scriptures attribute such an important agency in the sanctification and salvation of men.

§ 3. *Number of the Sacraments.*

If the word sacrament be taken in the wide sense in which it was used in the early Church for any significant religious rite, it is obvious that no definite limit can be set to their number. If the word be confined to such divine ordinances as answer the conditions which characterize baptism and the Lord's Supper, then it is evident that they are the only sacraments under the Christian dispensation; and such is the view taken by all Protestants. It is true that in the Apology for the Augsburg Confession it is said: " Vere sunt sacramenta, baptismus, Cœna Domini, absolutio, quæ est sacramentum pœnitentiæ. Nam hi ritus habent mandatum Dei et promissionem gratiæ, quæ,est propria Novi Testamenti." The last was soon dropped out of the list of sacraments, although the Lutherans retained confession as a distinct Church institution. The confession however was to be general, an enumeration of sins not being required, and the absolution which followed was simply declarative, and not judicial, as among the Romanists. The Reformed symbols required private confession to be made to God, and general confession in the congregation of the people; and recommended in extraordinary cases, where the conscience is burdened or the mind perplexed, private confession to the pastor or spiritual adviser.

The Romanists have seven sacraments, adding to baptism and the Lord's Supper, matrimony, orders, penance, confirmation, and extreme unction. Matrimony, however, although a divine institution, was not ordained for signifying, sealing, and applying to believers the benefits of redemption, and therefore, is not a sacrament. The same may be said of orders. And as to confirmation, penance, and extreme unction, in the sense in which Romanists use those terms, they are not divine institutions at all.

Confirmation.

Confirmation indeed, or a service attending the introduction of those baptized in infancy, into full communion in the Church, was early instituted and long continued among Protestants as well as among Romanists. Those who had been baptized in infancy, had their standing in the Church on the ground of the profession of faith and the engagements made in their name, by their parents or sponsors. When they came to years of discretion, they were examined as to their knowledge and conduct, and if found competently instructed and free from scandal, they assumed the obligation of their baptismal vows upon themselves, and their church membership was confirmed. In all this, however, there was nothing of a sacramental character.

This simple service the Romanists have exalted into a sacrament. The " material," they say, is the anointing with oil, or the imposition of hands; or as Thomas Aquinas and Bellarmin say, the two united. Perrone makes the anointing the essential thing. The gift or grace conveyed, " ex opere operato," is that supernatural influence of the Holy Ghost, which enables the recipient to be faithful to his baptismal vows. The administrator must be a prelate, as prelates only are the official successors of the Apostles, and, therefore, they only have the power of conveying the Holy Spirit by the imposition of hands, which was one of the prerogatives of the apostleship.

Penance.

Romanists distinguish between " pœnitentia," repentance or penitence, as a virtue and as a sacrament. As a virtue it consists in sorrow for sin, a determination to forsake it, and a purpose " ad sui vindictam in compensationem injuriæ Deo per peccatum illatæ; " *i. e.*, a purpose to make satisfaction to God. As a sacrament it is an ordinance instituted by Christ for the remission of sins committed after baptism, through the absolution of a priest having jurisdiction. The matter of the sacrament is the act of the penitent including contrition, confession, and satisfaction. The form is the act of absolution on the part of the priest. By contrition is meant sorrow, or remorse. It is not necessary that this contrition should be anything more than a natural, as distinguished from a gracious, exercise or state of mind; or as the Romanists express it, it is not necessary that contrition should be " caritate perfecta." The confession included in this assumed sacrament, must be auricular; it must include all mortal sins; a sin not confessed is not forgiven. This confession is declared by the Council of Trent to be necessary to salvation. " Si quis negaverit, confessionem sacramentalem vel institutam, vel ad salutem necessariam esse jure divino; aut dixerit, modum secreti confitendi soli sacerdoti, quem Ecclesia catholica ab initio semper observavit, et observat, alienum esse ab institutione et mandato Christi, et inventum esse humanum; anathema sit."[1] In sin there is both a "reatus culpæ" and a "reatus pœnæ." The former, together with the penalty of eternal death, is removed by absolution; but "reatus pœnæ" as to temporal punishment, to be endured either in this life or in purgatory, remains or may remain. Hence the necessity of satisfaction for sin in the sense above stated. The absolution granted by the priest, is not merely declaratory, but judicial and effective. On this point the Romish Church teaches "1° Christum delere peccata sacerdotum ministerio; 2° sacerdotes sedere judices in tribunali pœnitentiæ; 3° illorum sententiam ratam in cœlis esse; 4° sacerdotes hac potestate præstare angelis et archangelis ipsis."[2] This doctrine that no real sin, committed after baptism, can be forgiven unless confessed to a priest; that the priest has the power to remit or retain; that he carries at his girdle the keys not only of the visible Church on earth, but also of heaven and hell; and that he opens and no man shuts, and shuts and no man opens, is one of the strongest links of the chain by which the Church of Rome leads captive the souls of men. No wonder that she says that the power of a priest is above that even of angels and archangels.

Orders.

Orders or ordination is made a sacrament, because instituted or commanded by Christ, and because therein the supernatural power of consecrating the body and blood of Christ and of forgiving sin is conferred. It is thus defined: " Ordo sacer et sacramentum divinitus institutum, quo tribuitur potestas consecrandi corpus et sanguinem Domini, nec non remittendi et retinendi peccata." On this subject the Council of Trent says: " Si quis dixerit, per sacram ordinationem non dari Spiritum Sanctum, ac proinde frustra episcopos dicere: Accipe Spiritum Sanctum; aut per eam non imprimi characterem; vel eum, qui sacerdos semel fuit, laicum rursus fieri posse; anathema sit."[3] The right and power to ordain belong exclusively to prelates, for they alone possess the apostolical prerogative of communicating the Holy Spirit by the imposition of hands. The Apostles, however, had only the power of communicating miraculous gifts. They nei-

---

[1] Sess. xiv. canon 6; Streitwolf, vol. i. p. 68.
[2] Perrone, *Prælectiones Theologicæ, De Pœnitentia,* v. i. 155; edit. Paris, 1861, vol. ii. p. 351, a.
[3] Sess. xxiii. canon 4; Streitwolf, vol. i. p. 88.

ther claimed nor pretended to exercise the power of conferring the sanctifying or saving influences of the Spirit. As the
Church of Rome claims for its clergy a power far above that of
angels or archangels, so it claims for its bishops powers far transcending those of the Apostles.

Matrimony.

Matrimony is declared to be a sacrament because, although
not instituted by Christ, it was made by Him the symbol of the
mystical union between the Church and its divine head ; and because by its due celebration divine grace is conferred upon the
contracting parties. It is thus defined : " Sacramentum novæ
legis, quo significatur conjunctio Christi cum Ecclesia, et gratia
confertur ad sanctificandam viri et mulieris legitimam conjunc-
tionem, ad uniendos arctius conjugum animos, atque ad prolem
pie sancteque in virtutis officiis et fide christiana instituendam."[1]

Extreme Unction.

This is defined to be a sacrament wherein by the anointing
with oil (per unctionem olei benedicti) and prayer in the prescribed form, by the ministration of a priest, grace is conferred to
the baptized dangerously ill, whereby sins are remitted and the
strength of the soul is increased. " Si quis dixerit, sacram in-
firmorum unctionem non conferre gratiam, nec remittere peccata,
nec alleviare infirmos ; sed jam cessasse, quasi olim tantum
fuerit gratia curationum ; anathema sit." " Si quis dixerit,
presbyteros Ecclesiæ, quos B. Jacobus adducendos esse infirmum
inunguendum hortatur, non esse sacerdotes ab Episcopo ordinatos,
sed ætate seniores, in quavis communitate ; ob idque proprium
extremæ unctionis ministrum non esse solum sacerdotem ; anathema sit."[2]

Reasons for fixing the Number of the Sacraments at Seven.

It is a work of supererogation for Romanists to assign any
reason for making the number of the sacraments seven, and
neither more nor less, other than the decision of the Church. If
the Church be infallible her judgment on the question is decisive ; if it be not infallible no other reason is of any avail. They
admit that there is no authority from Scripture on this point,

---

[1] Perrone, *ut supra*, *De Matrimonio*, 1. vol. ii. p. 407.
[2] Conc. Trident. sess. xiv. " De sacramento extremæ unctionis," can. 2, 4; Streitwolf,
vol. i. pp. 70, 71.

and on no subject in dispute between them and Protestants, can appeal be made with less show of reason to the testimony of tradition. Romish theologians, therefore, while they claim common consent in support of their doctrine on this subject, avail themselves of all the collateral aid they can command. Thomas Aquinas says that there is an analogy between the natural and spiritual life of man. He is born; he is strengthened; he is nourished; he needs means of recovery from illness; he needs to propagate his race; to live under the guidance of legitimate authority; and to be prepared for his departure from this world. The sacraments provide for all these necessities of his spiritual life. He is born in baptism; strengthened by confirmation; nourished by the Lord's Supper; recovered from spiritual illness by penance; the Church is continued by holy matrimony; the sacrament of orders provides for the Christian a supernaturally endowed guide; and extreme unction prepares him for death. Thus through the seven sacraments all his spiritual wants are supplied.

Then again as there are seven cardinal virtues, there should be seven sacraments. Besides seven is a sacred number: there are seven days in the week; every seventh year was Sabbatical; and there were seven golden candlesticks, and seven stars in the right hand of Christ. It is not wonderful therefore that there should be seven sacraments. It is obvious that all this amounts to nothing. The two sacraments instituted by Christ for the definite purpose of " signifying, sealing, and applying to believers," the benefits of redemption, stand alone in the New Testament. No other ordinance has the same characteristics or the same design. Admitting, therefore, that the Fathers and the Church were unanimous in calling any number of other sacred institutions sacraments, that would not prove that they belong to the same category as baptism, and the Lord's Supper.

It is, however, notorious that no such general consent can be pleaded in support of the seven sacraments of the Romanists. The simple facts on this subject are, — (1.) As already remarked, in the early Church every sacred rite was called a sacrament. Then their number was indefinite. (2.) The preëminence of baptism and the Lord's Supper over all other sacred rites being recognized, they were called, as by Augustine, the chief sacraments. (3.) When attention was directed to the fact that something is true of baptism and the Lord's Supper, which is true of no other sacred ordinances or rites, that they, and they only, of external ceremonies were appointed to be " means of grace," then they were declared in this light to be the only Christian sacraments.   Justin Martyr,[1] Cyril of Jerusalem,[2] and Augustine,[3] so speak of them.[4]   (4.) As a ritualistic spirit increased in the Church, first one and then another rite was assumed to be a " means of grace," not always, however, the same rites, and thus the number of sacraments was increased.   (5.) For centuries, however, no definite number was admitted by anything like general consent.   Some made the number three; the Pseudo Dionysius in the sixth century made six.   Peter Damiani, the friend of Gregory VII., made twelve.   " Ratherius, Bishop of Verona († 974), Fulbert, Bishop of Chartres († 1028), Bruno, Bishop of Wurzburg († 1045), Rupert, Abbot of Deutz († 1135), admitted only baptism and the Lord's Supper; others, as Theodulf, Bishop of Orleans († 821), Agobard, Bishop of Lyons († 840), Lanfranc, Bishop of Canterbury († 1089), Hildebert, Bishop of Tours († 1134), Hugo, of St. Victor († 1141), call them ' duo sanctæ ecclesiæ sacramenta.' "[5]   (6.) It is certain, says the writer just quoted, that Peter Lombard († 1164) is the first who enumerated the seven sacraments as held by the Romanists.   He gives no reason for fixing on the number seven; but that which was already on hand in the traditional sanctity, attributed to that number.   It was regarded as the symbol of universality and perfection.   This was sufficient for deciding on an arbitrary number.   What has been said is enough to show that Romanists have not even any plausible ground for their appeal to common consent in support of their doctrine on this subject.   Such appeal on their theory is unnecessary.   If the Church be infallible, and if the Church testifies that Christ ordained matrimony, extreme unction, etc., to be sacraments; that testimony is decisive.   If, however, the Church, in the papal sense of the word, be the very reverse of infallible, then its testimony, so far as the faith of Christians is concerned, amounts to nothing.

[1] *Apologia* I [II.] *AdAntoninum Pium*, 65, 66; *Works*, edit. Commelinus, Heidelberg, 1593, p. 76.

[2] *Catechesis Mystagogicæ Quinque*, Schram, *Analysis Patrum*, Augsburg, 1789, vol. x. pp. 250–268.

[3] *Enarratio in Psalmum* ciii. 14; *Works*, edit. Benedictines, Paris, 1836, vol. iv. p. 1626, d.

[4] Perrone in his *Prælectiones Theologicæ, De Sacramentis in genere*, i. 14; edit. Paris, 1861, vol. ii. p. 217; refers to these and tries to explain the facts away.

[5] Herzog's *Real-Encyklopädie*, Art. " Sacramente," vol. xiii., p. 241.   The writer of the elaborate article in Herzog refers to the thorough investigation of this question in the Dissertation by G. L. Hahn, entitled, *Doctrinæ Rom. de numero Sacramentorum septenario ationes historicæ,*Vratisl. 1859.

§ 4. *The Efficacy of the Sacraments.*

Zwinglian and Remonstrant Doctrine.

According to the doctrine of Zwingle afterwards adopted by the Remonstrants, the sacraments are not properly " means of grace." They were not ordained to signify, seal, and apply to believers the benefits of Christ's redemption.   They were indeed intended to be significant emblems of the great truths of the Gospel. Baptism was intended to teach the necessity of the soul's being cleansed from guilt by the blood of Christ and purified from the pollution of sin by the renewing of the Holy Ghost.   They were urther designed to be perpetual memorials of the work of re- lemption, and especially to be the means by which men should, n the sight of the Church and of the world, profess themselves :o be Christians.   As a heathen, when he desired to be admitted into the commonwealth of Israel, received circumcision, which was the divinely appointed seal of the Abrahamic covenant, so par- ticipation in the Christian sacraments was the appointed means for the public profession of faith in Christ.   Paul presents the matter in this light in 1 Corinthians x. 15–22, where he argues that participation in the sacred rites of a religion involves a pro- fession of that religion, whether it be Christian, Jewish, or hea- then.   The sacraments, therefore, are " badges of Christian men's profession."   This doctrine, however, attributes to them no other than what Zwingle calls in the passage above quoted, " an objec- tive power;" that is, the objective presentation of the truth which they signify to the mind.

" Ex quibus hoc colligitur sacramenta dari in testimonium publicum ejus gratiæ, quæ cuique privato prius adest. . . . . Ob hanc causam sacramenta, quæ sacræ sunt cerimoniæ (accedit enim verbum ad elementum et fit sacramentum), religiose colenda, hoc est in precio habenda, et honorifice tractanda sunt, ut enim gra- tiam facere non possunt, Ecclesiæ tamen nos visibiliter sociant, qui prius invisibiliter sumus in illam recepti, quod cum simul cum promissionis divinæ verbis in ipsorum actione pronunciatur ac promulgatur, summa religione suscipiendum est." [1]   In his treatise on true and false religion, Zwingle says : " Impossibile est, ut res aliqua externa fidem hominis internam confirmet et stabiliat." [2] And again he says [3] that the sacraments as other memorials can

1 *Zwinglii Fidei Ratio,* Niemeyer, vol. i. pp. 25, 26.
2 *Works,* edit. Schuler und Schultess.(?) See Strauss, *Dogmatik,* vol. ii. p. 519.
3 *Expositio Christianæ Fidei,* 70; Niemeyer, vol. i. p. 49.

only produce historical, but not religious faith. Zwingle in the use of such language, had doubtless more a negative, than an affirmative object before his mind. He was more intent on denying the Romish doctrine of the inherent power of the sacraments, than of asserting anything of their real efficacy. Nevertheless it is true that Zwingle has ever been regarded as holding the lowest doctrine concerning the sacraments of any of the Reformers. They were to him no more means of grace than the rainbow or the heaps of stone on the banks of the Jordan. By their significancy and by association they might suggest truth and awaken feeling, but they were not channels of divine communication.

Doctrine of the Reformed Church.

The first point clearly taught on this subject in the Symbols of the Reformed Church is that the sacraments are real means of grace, that is, means appointed and employed by Christ for conveying the benefits of his redemption to his people. They are not, as Romanists teach, the exclusive channels; but they are channels. A promise is made to those who rightly receive the sacraments that they shall thereby and therein be made partakers of the blessings of which the sacraments are the divinely appointed signs and seals. The word grace, when we speak of the means of grace, includes three things. 1st. An unmerited gift, such as the remission of sin. 2d. The supernatural influence of the Holy Spirit. 3d. The subjective effects of that influence on the soul. Faith, hope, and charity, for example, are graces.

The second point in the Reformed doctrine on the sacraments concerns the source of their power. On this subject it is taught negatively that the virtue is not in them. The word virtue is of course here used in its Latin sense for power or efficiency. What is denied is that the sacraments are the efficient cause of the gracious effects which they produce. The efficiency does not reside in the elements, in the water used in baptism, or in the bread and wine used in the Lord's Supper. It is not in the sacramental actions; either in giving, or in receiving the consecrated elements. Neither does the virtue or efficiency due to sacraments reside in, or flow from the person by whom they are administered. It does not reside in his office. There is no supernatural power in the man, in virtue of his office, to render the sacraments effectual. Nor does their efficiency depend on the character of the administrator in the sight of God; nor upon his intention; that is, his purpose to render them effectual. The man who administers the sacraments is not a worker of miracles. The Apostles and others at that time in the Church, were endued with supernatural power ; and they had to will to exercise it in order to its producing its legitimate effect. It is not so with the officers of the Church in the administration of the sacraments. The affirmative statement on this subject is, that the efficacy of the sacraments is due solely to the blessing of Christ and the working of his Spirit. The Spirit, it is to be ever remembered, is a personal agent who works when and how He will. God has promised that his Spirit shall attend his Word ; and He thus renders it an effectual means for the sanctification of his people. So He has promised, through the attending operation of his Spirit, to render the sacraments effectual to the same end.

The third point included in the Reformed doctrine is, that the sacraments are effectual as means of grace only, so far as adults are concerned, to those who by faith receive them. They may have a natural power on other than believers by presenting truth and exciting feeling, but their saving or sanctifying influence is experienced only by believers.

All these points are clearly presented in the standards of our own Church. The sacraments are declared to be means of grace, that is, means for signifying, sealing, and applying the benefits of redemption. It is denied that this virtue is in them, or in him by whom they are administered. It is affirmed that their efficiency in conveying grace, is due solely to the blessing of Christ and the coöperation of his Spirit ; and that such efficiency is experienced only by believers. Thus in the Shorter Catechism, the sacraments are said to be holy ordinances "instituted by Christ ; wherein, by sensible signs, Christ and the benefits of the new covenant are represented, sealed, and applied to believers."[1] In the Larger Catechism the sacraments are said to be instituted "to signify, seal, and exhibit unto those that are within the covenant of grace, the benefits of his [Christ's] mediation."[2] The word "exhibit," as here used, means to confer, or impart, as the Latin word "exhibere" also sometimes means. That such is the sense of the word in our standards, is plain because the exhibition here spoken of is confined to those within the covenant ; and because this word is interchanged and explained by the word "confer." Thus in the Confession of Faith[3] it is said, "The grace which is exhibited in, or by the sacraments, rightly used, is not conferred by any virtue in them." And again,[4] that by the right

---

[1] Ques. 9.   [2] Ques. 162.   [3] Chap. xxvii. 3.   [4] Chap. xxviii. 6.

use of baptism "the grace promised is not only offered, but really exhibited and conferred by the Holy Ghost, to such (whether of age or infants) as that grace belongeth unto, according to the counsel of God's own will, in his appointed time." With this view of the sacraments as means of grace all the other leading symbols of the Reformed Churches agree. Thus the First Helvetic Confession [1] says, "Asserimus, sacramenta non solum tesseras quasdam societatis Christianæ, sed et gratiæ divinæ symbola esse, quibus ministri, Domino, ad eum finem, quem ipse promittit, offert et efficit, cooperentur." The Gallican Confession says : "Fatemur talia esse signa hæc exteriora, ut Deus per illa Sancti sui Spiritus virtute, operetur, ne quicquam ibi frustra nobis significetur." [2] In the Geneva Catechism [3] it is said : "Quid est sacramentum? Externa divinæ erga nos benevolentiæ testificatio, quæ visibili signo spirituales gratias figurat, ad obsignandos cordibus nostris Dei promissiones, quo earum veritas melius confirmetur. . . . . Vim efficaciamque sacramenti non in externo elemento inclusam esse existimas, sed totam a Spiritu Dei manare? Sic sentio : nempe, ut virtutem suam exerere Domino placuerit per sua organa, quem in finem ea destinavit." The language of the Belgic Confession [4] is to the same effect : "Sunt enim sacramenta signa, ac symbola visibilia rerum internarum et invisibilium, per quæ, ceu per media, Deus ipse virtute Spiritus Sancti in nobis operatur. Itaque signa illa minime vana sunt, aut vacua : nec ad nos decipiendos aut frustrandos instituta."

These symbols of the Reformed Churches on the continent of Europe agree with those of our own Church, not only in representing the sacraments as real means of grace, but also in denying that their efficacy is due to their inherent virtue, or to him who administers them, and in affirming that it is due to the attending operation of the Spirit, and is conditioned on the presence of faith in the recipient. This is plain from the quotations already made, which might be multiplied indefinitely. On this point Calvin says : "Neque sacramenta hilum proficere sine Spiritu Sancti virtute." And again : "Spiritus Sanctus (quem non omnibus promiscue sacramenta advehunt, sed quem Dominus peculiariter suis confert) is est qui Dei gratias secum affert, qui dat sacramentis in nobis locum, qui efficit ut fructificent." [5] Guerike [6] gives as one

---

[1] Art. XXI.; Niemeyer, *Collectio Confessionum*, Leipzig, 1840, p. 120.

[2] Art. XXXIV.; *Ibid.* p. 337.

[3] v. *De Sacramentis*, 2 and 5; *Ibid.* pp. 160, 161.   [4] Art. XXXIII.; *Ibid.* p. 383.

[5] *Institutio*, IV. xiv. 9, 17; edit. Berlin, 1834, part ii. pp. 355, 360.

[6] *Allgemeine Christliche Symbolik*, von H. E. Ferdinand Guerike, D. D., Leipzig, 1839, p. 378.

of the main points of difference between the Lutherans and Reformed on this subject, that the latter deny the inherent power of the sacraments, and insist that the "virtus Spiritus Sancti extrinsecus accidens" is the source of all their sanctifying influence.

There is, therefore, a strict analogy, according to the Reformed doctrine, between the Word and the sacraments as means of grace. (1.) Both have in them a certain moral power due to the truth which they bring before the mind. (2.) Neither has in itself any supernatural power to save or to sanctify. (3.) All their supernatural efficiency is due to the coöperation or attending influence of the Holy Spirit. (4.) Both are ordained by God to be the channels or means of the Spirit's influence, to those who by faith receive them. Nothing is said in the Bible to place the sacraments above the Word as a means of communicating to men the benefits of Christ's redemption. On the contrary, tenfold more is said in Scripture of the necessity and efficiency of the Word in the salvation of men, than is therein said or implied of the power of the sacraments.

Besides the points already referred to as characteristic of the Reformed doctrine on the sacraments, there is a fourth, which is, that the grace or spiritual benefits received by believers in the use of the sacraments, may be attained without their use. This, however, may perhaps be more properly considered, when the necessity of the sacraments comes under consideration.

The Lutheran Doctrine.

There are two points specially insisted upon by Lutherans in reference to the efficacy of the sacraments. The first is, the absolute necessity of faith in order to any real sanctifying or saving benefit being derived from the use of those ordinances. On this point they are in perfect accord with the Reformed. Hase is right when he says that the idea, "That a sacrament can confer saving benefit without faith is utterly destructive of Protestantism."[1]   Augustine had long ago taught the doctrine, "Unde ista tanta virtus aquæ, ut corpus tangat, et cor abluat, nisi faciente verbo: non quia dicitur, sed quia creditur."[2]   And Bernard of Clairvaux says: "Sacramentum enim sine re sacramenti sumenti

[1] *Evangelische Dogmatik*, II. ii. 1, § 213; 3d edit. Leipzig, 1842, p. 442.
[2] *In Joannis Evangelium Tractatus*, LXXX. 3; *Works*, edit. Benedictines, Paris, 1837, vol. iii. p 2290, a.

mors est : res vero sacramenti, etiam, præter sacramentum, sumenti vita æterna est." [1]

The Lutheran symbols on this point are perfectly explicit. In
the " Augsburg Confession " [2] it is said: " Itaque utendum est
sacramentum ita, ut fides accedat, quæ credat promissionibus,
quæ per sacramenta exhibentur et ostenduntur. Damnant igitur
illos, qui docent, quod sacramenta, ex opere operato justificent,
nec docent fidem requiri in usu sacramentorum, quæ credat remitti peccata."

In the " Apology for the Augsburg Confession " [3] it is said :
" Damnamus totum populum scholasticorum doctorum, qui docent, quod sacramenta non ponenti obicem conferant gratiam ex
opere operato, sine bono motu utentis. Hæc simpliciter Judaica
opinio est, sentire, quod per ceremoniam justificemur, sine bono
motu cordis, hoc est, sine fide. . . . . At sacramenta sunt signa
promissionum. Igitur in usu debet accedere fides. . . . . Loquimur hic de fide speciali, quæ præsenti promissioni credit, non tantum quæ in genere credit Deum esse, sed quæ credit offerri remissionem peccatorum."

The second point in the doctrine of Lutherans in regard to the
efficacy of the sacraments is one in which they differ from the
Reformed, and as Guerike, himself a strenuous Lutheran, correctly says, approximate to the Romanists. They hold that the
efficacy of the sacraments is due to their own inherent virtue or
power ; a power independent, on the one hand, of the attendant
influences of the Spirit (extrinsecus accidens), and, on the other
hand, of the faith of the recipient. Faith, indeed, is necessary to
any saving or sanctifying effect, but that is only a subjective condition on which the beneficial operation of the power, inherent in
the sacraments, is suspended. Bellarmin's illustration is applicable to the Lutheran doctrine as well as to his own. Fire will not
cause wood to burn unless the wood be dry ; but its dryness does
not give fire its power. Luther's own favourite illustration was
drawn from the case of the woman who touched the Saviour's
garment. There was inherent healing virtue in Christ. Those
who touched him without faith received no benefit. The woman
having faith was healed the moment she touched the hem of his
garment. Her faith, however, was in no sense the source of the
power which resided in Christ. Guerike complains that the Re-

[1] Guigo (attributed to St. Bernard); *Works* of St. Bernard, edit. Migne, Paris, 1859, vol.
ii. p. 327, b, c (ii. 214).
[2] I. xiii.; Hase, *Libri Symbolici*, Leipzig, 1846, p. 13.   [3] VII. 18–21; *Ibid.* p. 203.

formed teach that " the visible signs do not as such convey any
invisible divine grace ; that without the sacraments the Christian
may enjoy through faith the same divine gifts which the sacraments are intended to convey, and hence do not admit their absolute necessity, much less that they are the central point of the
Christian method of salvation (der christlichen Heilsanstalt)." [1]

Luther did not at first hold this inherent power of the sacraments, but seemed disposed to adopt even the low views of Zwingle.   In his work on the Babylonish Captivity he says, " Baptismus neminem justificat, nec ulli prodest, sed fides in verbum
promissionis, cui additur baptismus. . . . . Nec verum esse potest, sacramentis inesse vim efficacem justificationis seu esse signa
efficacia gratiæ." [2]   Melancthon uses much the same language :
" Non justificant signa, ut Apostolus ait, Circumcisio nihil est :
ita baptismus nihil est.   Participatio mensæ Domini nihil est :
sed testes sunt καὶ σφραγῖδες divinæ voluntatis erga te, quibus conscientia tua certa reddatur, si de gratia, de benevolentia Dei erga
se dubitet. . . . . Quæ alii sacramenta, nos signa appellamus,
aut si ita libet, signa sacramentalia.   Nam sacramentum ipsum
Christum Paulus vocat." [3]   " Hinc apparet, quam nihil signa sint,
nisi fidei exercendæ μνημόσυνα." [4]

As, however, Luther understood our Lord's words in John iii.
5, as teaching the necessity of baptism, he inferred that if the
sacrament is necessary to salvation it must have saving power.
But as the Bible teaches that no one can be saved without faith,
he held that the sacraments could have no saving effect unless
the recipient was a believer.   We have thus the two essential
elements of the Lutheran doctrine of the sacraments ; they have
inherent, saving, sanctifying power ; but that power takes effect
for good only upon believers.

The necessity of faith is clearly stated in the passages already
quoted from the " Augsburg Confession " and the " Apology ; "
the inherent power of the sacraments in opposition to the Reformed
doctrine is as clearly taught in the Lutheran standards.   Both
points are included in some of the proof passages which follow.
Guerike says : " It is undoubtedly the Lutheran, in opposition
to the Reformed doctrine of ' virtus Spiritus sancti extrinsecus

---

[1] *Allgemeine Christliche Symbolik*, § 54, Leipzig, 1839, pp. 375, 376.

[2] Luther, *Captivitas Babylonica, de Sacramento Baptismi ; Works*, edit. Wittenberg
(Latin), 1546, vol. ii. leaf 79, page 2.

[3] *Loci Communes ; De Signis;* edit. Strasburg, 1523, in *Dodecas Scriptorum Theolog-
icorum*, Nuremberg, 1646, pp. 774, 775.

[4] *Ibid.,* De Baptismo, p. 778.

accedens,' that the grace is in, and not merely with or by (mit oder neben), the sacraments." [1] He refers to the language of Luther in his Larger Catechism in reference to baptism. Luther says : " Interrogatus, quid baptismus sit ? ita responde : non esse prorsus aquam simplicem, sed ejusmodi, quæ verbo et præcepto Dei comprehensa, et illi inclusa sit, et per hoc sanctificata ita ut nihil aliud sit, quam Dei seu divina aqua." He adds, however, " non quod aqua hæc per sese quavis alia sit præstantior, sed quod ei verbum ac præceptum Dei accesserit. Quocirca mera sycophantia est et diaboli illusio, quod hodie nostri novi spiritus, ut blasphement et contumelia afficiant baptismum, verbum et institutionem Dei ab eo divellunt, nec aliter intuentur eum, quam aquam e putreo haustam ac deinceps ita blasphemo ore blaterant : Quid vero utilitatis manus aquæ plena præstaret animæ ? Quis vero adeo vecors et inops animi est, qui hoc ignoret, divulsis baptismi partibus, aquam esse aquam ? Qua vero fronte tu tibi tantum sumis, ut non verearis ab ordinatione Dei pretiosissimum κειμήλιον avellere, quo Deus illam constrinxit et inclusit, neque inde divelli vult aut sejungi ? Quippe verbum Dei, aut præceptum, item nomen Dei, in aqua ipse solet esse nucleus, qui thesaurus ipso cœlo et terra omnibus modis nobilior est et præstantior." [2]

Lutherans are wont to refer to the analogy between the Word and sacraments. The difference between them and the Reformed as to the sacraments, is analogous to the difference between the two churches as to the Word. The Reformed refer the supernatural power of the Word, not to the literal Word as written or spoken ; not to the mere moral truth therein revealed, but to the coöperation, or as Paul calls it, the demonstration, of the Spirit. The Lutherans, on the other hand, teach that there is inherent in the divine Word (not in the letters or the sound but in the truth), a supernatural, divine virtue, inseparable from it, and independent of its use; and which is the same to believers and unbelievers ; sanctifying and saving the former, because of their faith, and not benefiting the latter, because of their voluntary resistance. So the sacraments have an inherent, divine power, certain of producing saving effects, if they meet with faith in those who receive them. " The Lutheran Church," says Guerike, " regards the sacraments as actions, wherein God, through external signs by Him appointed, offers and confers his invisible and heavenly

[1] *Symbolik*, Leipzig, 1839, p. 393, note.
[2] *Catechismus Major*, par. iv., *De Baptismo;* Hase, *Libri Symbolici*, edit. Leipzig, 1846, p. 537

gifts ; they see in the sacraments visible signs, which in virtue of the divine word of promise pronounced over them, in such sense contain the invisible divine gifts they signify, that they communicate them (mittheilen) to all who partake of them, although only to believers to their good." [1]

This inherent divine virtue of the sacraments does not reside in the elements ; nor does it flow from him who administers them ; nor is it due to the concurrent operation of the Holy Spirit ; but to the Word. The elements employed are in themselves mere elements ; with the Word, they are divinely efficacious, because the divine Word, wherever it is, is fraught with this divine, supernatural, saving, and sanctifying power which always takes effect on those who have faith to receive it.

Dr. Schmid of Erlangen, however, admits that there is a difference of view on this subject, between the earlier and later theologians of his Church. The former made the sacrament consist of the element and the Word, and referred its supernatural effect to the inherent divine power of the latter, agreeably to Luther's representation in his Larger Catechism, where, when speaking of baptism, he says, in words already quoted : " non tantum naturalis aqua sed etiam divina, cœlestis, sancta et salutifera aqua (est) . . . . hocque nonnisi verbi gratia, quod cœleste ac sanctum verbum est." The later theologians, however, from the time of Gerhard, did not make the sacrament consist of the element and the Word ; but of something terrestrial and something celestial. The former is the element or external symbol, " quod est res corporea visibilis . . . . ordinata ad hoc ; ut sit rei cœlestis vehiculum et medium exhibitivum." The latter, or " res cœlestis," is " res invisibilis et intelligibilis, re terrena visibili, tanquam medio divinitus ordinato exhibita, a qua fructus sacramenti principaliter dependet." According to this view the efficacy of the sacrament does not depend upon the Word, but upon this " res cœlestis," of which the " res terrena " is the vehicle and medium. The office of the Word is to unite the two. It is called the " αἴτιον ποιητικόν, hoc est, efficere, ut duæ illæ partes essentiales unum sacramentum constituant in usu sacramentorum." [2] This doctrine of the later Lutherans is attended with serious difficulties. It brings them into conflict with Luther and Lutherans of the older school who are strenuous

---

[1] Guerike's *Symbolik*, p. 372.

[2] Schmid, *Die Dogmatik der evangelisch-lutherischen Kirche.* Frankfort and Erlangen, 1853, pp. 415–417.

in referring the efficacy of the sacraments to the Word. The elements without the Word, are mere elements. It is the Word in which the supernatural power resides which produces the effect the sacrament is intended to accomplish. But according to this later view there are in the sacraments two things, the sign and the thing signified; a " res terrena " and a " res cœlestis." They are so united that where the one is given and received by faith, the other is received. This " res cœlestis," however, is not the Word. In the case of the eucharist, for example, it is the real body and blood of Christ, and these being inseparably united with his soul and divinity, it is this marvellous gift, and not the Word, which makes the Lord's Supper the life-sustaining food of the soul.

So far as the efficacy of the sacraments is concerned, the main point of difference between the Lutherans and the Reformed is, that the latter attribute their sanctifying power to the attending influences of the Spirit; the former to the inherent, supernatural power of the Word which is an essential part of these divine ordinances. Even on this point Chemnitz expresses himself in a way to which any Reformed theologian may assent. " Recte Apologia Augustanæ confessionis dicit, eundem esse effectum, eandem virtutem, seu efficaciam, et verbi et sacramentorum, quæ sunt sigilla promissionum. . . . . Sicut igitur Evangelium est potentia Dei ad salutem omni credenti : non quod magica quædam vis characteribus, syllabis, aut sono verborum inhæreat, sed quia est medium, organon seu instrumentum, per quod Spiritus Sanctus efficax est, proponens, offerens, exhibens, distribuens et applicans meritum Christi, et gratiam Dei, ad salutem omni credenti : ita etiam sacramentis tribuitur vis et efficacia : non quod in sacramentis extra seu præter meritum Christi, misericordiam Patris, et efficaciam Spiritus Sancti, quærenda sit gratia ad salutem ; sed sacramenta sunt causæ instrumentales ita, quod per illa media seu organa, Pater vult gratiam suam exhibere, donare, applicare : Filius meritum suum communicare credentibus : Spiritus Sanctus efficaciam suam exercere, ad salutem omni credenti." [1]

The Lutheran doctrine as generally presented and as stated above, stands opposed, (1.) To the doctrine of the Romanists which denies the necessity of a living faith in the recipient in order to his experiencing the efficacy of the sacraments ; and which not only represents them as imbued with an inherent power, but also

---

[1] *Examen Concilii Tridentini, de Efficacia et Usu Sacramentorum*, edit. Frankfort-on-the-Main, 1573, 1574, part ii. p. 22, b.

teaches that they confer grace " ex opere operato." (2.) To the doctrine which makes the sacraments merely badges of a Christian profession. (3.) To the doctrine which represents them as mere allegories or significant exhibitions of truth. (4.) To the doctrine which regards them as merely commemorative, as a portrait or monument may be. (5.) To the doctrine which denies to them inherent efficacy and refers their sanctifying influence to the accompanying power of the Holy Spirit; and (6.) To the doctrine which assumes that they confer nothing which may not be obtained by faith without them. In all these points, with the exception of the last two, Lutherans and Reformed are agreed.

Doctrine of the Church of Rome on the Efficacy of the Sacraments.

It has already been stated that the Romanists teach, (1.) That the sacraments contain the grace which they signify. (2.) That they convey that grace " ex opere operato." (3.) That there is a certain efficacy common to all the sacraments. They all convey grace, i. e., " gratia gratum faciens, sanctificans ; " and besides this common influence, in baptism, confirmation, and orders, there is conveyed an indelible character (quoddam indelebile) in virtue of which they can never be repeated. (4.) That the conditions of the efficacy of the sacraments on the part of the administrator are, first, that he have authority (this is limited in its application to baptism) ; and second, that he have the intention of doing what the Church designs to be done ; and in regard to the recipient, that he does not oppose an obstacle. The sacraments are declared to be effectual " non ponentibus obicem."

In what Sense do the Sacraments contain Grace ?

By this is meant that they possess in them inherent virtue of rendering holy those to whom they are administered. Their power in the sphere of religion is analogous to that of articles of the " materia medica " in the sphere of physics. Some have a narcotic power ; some act on one organ and some on another ; some are stimulants, and some are sedatives. Or to refer to the illustration so familiar with Bellarmin ; the inherent virtue of the sacraments to confer grace, is analogous to that of fire to burn. Fire produces combustion because it is ordained by God and imbued with power to that end. The sacraments confer grace because they are endowed with grace-imparting efficacy, and are ordained by God for that purpose. " Containing grace "

and " conferring grace " " virtute sibi insita," are explanatory
forms of expression. The sacraments are said to contain grace
because they confer it by their inherent virtue. This is intended
as a denial that their efficacy is due to the moral, or to the supernatural power of the truth ; or to the attending influences of the
Spirit, or to the subjective state of those who receive them.

As to the peculiar effect ascribed to baptism, confirmation, and
orders, little is said. These sacraments are never repeated. For
this some reason was to be assigned, and, therefore, it was assumed that they left an indelible impression on the soul. What
that is, cannot be stated further than by saying that it is a " Signum quoddam spirituale et indelebile in anima impressum. Qui
eo insigniti sunt, deputantur ad recipienda vel tradenda aliis ea,
quæ pertinent ad cultum Dei." [1] The language of the Council
of Trent sheds no light on the subject. It simply says : [2] " Si
quis dixerit, in tribus sacramentis, baptismo scilicet confirmatione,
et ordine, non imprimi characterem in anima, hoc est signum
quoddam spirituale et indelebile, unde ea iterari non possunt;
anathema sit." The only passages of Scripture referred to by
Perrone in support of this assumption, are 2 Corinthians i. 22,
and Ephesians i. 13, in which the Apostle speaks of all believers
being sealed by the Holy Spirit. In those passages there is not
the slightest reference to any sacramental impression. In the
second part of the Roman Catechism in answer to the question,
What " character " in this connection signifies, it is said that it
is something which cannot be removed, and which renders the
soul fit to receive or to perform certain spiritual benefits or functions. Thus in baptism a certain something is impressed upon
the soul by which it is prepared to receive the benefit of other
sacraments, and by which it is distinguished from the souls of
the unbaptized. In confirmation the soul is marked as a soldier
of Christ and prepared to contend against all spiritual enemies.
In orders something is received which fits the recipient to administer the sacraments, and which distinguishes him from all other
Christians.

Ex Opere Operato.

The Council of Trent anathematizes, as we have seen, not only
those who deny that the sacraments convey grace, but also those
who deny that they convey it " ex opere operato." The meaning

---

[1] Perrone, *Prælectiones Theologicæ, De Sacramentis in genere*, cap. ii. 1, 2; edit. Paris,
861, vol. ii. pp. 220, a, 224.

[2] Sess. vii. *de Sacramentis in genere*, canon 9; Streitwolf, vol. i. p. 39.

of this phrase is intelligible enough if left unexplained. It has been obscured by the explanations given by Romanists themselves, as well as by the conflicting views of Protestants on the subject. To say that the sacraments contain grace; that they convey it "virtute sibi insita," that they convey it "ex opere operato," all amount to the same thing. The simple meaning is that such is the nature of the sacraments that, when duly administered, they produce a given effect. There is no necessity and no propriety in looking beyond them to account for the effect produced. If you place a coal of fire on a man's hand, it produces a certain effect. That effect follows without fail. It follows from the very nature of the thing done and from the act of doing it. It makes no difference, whether we say that the coal contains heat; or, that it burns in virtue of its inherent nature; or that the effect is produced "ex opere operato."

Of course there are certain conditions necessary in order to the production of the effect. The hand must be alive, otherwise it is not the hand of a man; it is simply a lump of clay. There must be no obstacle. If you interpose a porcelain plate between the coal and the hand, the hand will not be burnt. The coal must be ignited, not simply a piece of carbon. So the thing done must be a real sacrament. It must have everything essential to the integrity of the ordinance. The coal, in the case supposed, must be brought into contact with the hand; but whether it be placed there by the use of a silver spoon, or of a pair of iron tongs, makes no difference. So it makes no difference whether the priest who administers the sacrament be a good man or a bad man, whether he be orthodox or heretical. He must, however, do the thing; and he cannot do it without intending to do it. If the man's hand is to be burnt, in a given time and place, the coal must be intentionally placed upon it.

Although the doctrine of the Church of Rome as to the way in which the sacraments convey grace, seems to be thus simple, there is no little apparent diversity among the theologians of that Church in their views on the subject. This diversity, however, is really more in the mode of stating the doctrine, than in the doctrine itself. Lutherans agree with Romanists in denying that the efficacy of the sacraments is due to the attending influences of the Holy Spirit; and they agree with them in attributing to them an inherent supernatural power. The main point of difference between them is that the Lutherans insist on the presence and exercise of faith in the recipient. According to them the sacra-

ments convey grace only to believers. Whereas Romanists, as
understood by Lutherans and indeed by all Protestants, deny
this necessity of faith or of good dispositions in order to the
due efficacy of the sacraments. This, however, Bellarmin pronounces a deliberate falsehood on the part of the Protestants;
and he uses language on this subject which Luther himself
might have employed, " Est merum mendacium," he says, " quod
Catholici dicant, sacramenta prodesse peccatoribus : omnes enim
Catholici requirunt pœnitentiam, tanquam dispositionem ad gratiam recipiendam."   "Falsum est Catholicos non habere pro
obice incredulitatem : omnes enim Catholici requirunt necessario
in adultis actualem fidem, et sine ea dicunt neminem justificari."[1]
" Voluntas, fides, et pœnitentia in suscipiento adulto necessario
requiruntur, ut dispositiones ex parte subjecti, non ut causæ
activæ : non enim fides et pœnitentia efficiunt gratiam sacramentalem, neque dant efficaciam sacramento ; sed solum tollunt
obstacula quæ impedirent, ne sacramenta suam efficaciam exercere possent ; unde in pueris, ubi non requiritur dispositio, sine
his rebus fit justificatio."[2]   Luther would not agree with this
last clause about infants ; but to the rest of the paragraph he
could hardly object.   Then follows in Bellarmin the illustration
quoted above.[3] Fire does not owe its efficacy to the dryness of
the wood ; nevertheless the dryness is a necessary condition of
combustion.

In another passage Bellarmin is still more explicit : " Igitur
ut intelligamus, quid sit opus operatum, notandum est, in justificatione, quam recipit aliquis, dum percipit sacramenta, multa
concurrere ; nimirum ex parte Dei, voluntatem utendi illa re sensi-
bili ; ex parte Christi, passionem ejus ; ex parte ministri potestatem, voluntatem, probitatem ; ex parte suscipientis voluntatem,
fidem, et pœnitentiam ; denique ex parte sacramenti ipsam ac-
tionem externam, quæ consurgit, ex debita applicatione formæ
et materiæ. Cæterum ex his omnibus id, quod active, et proxime
atque instrumentaliter efficit gratiam justificationis, est sola actio
illa externa, quæ sacramentum dicitur, et hæc vocatur opus
operatum, accipiendo passive (operatum) ita ut idem sit sacramentum conferre gratiam ex opere operato, quod conferre gratiam
ex [vi] ipsius actionis sacramentalis a Deo ad hoc institutæ, non
ex merito agentis vel suscipientis."[4]

[1] Bellarmin, *De Sacramentis*, I. 2; *Disputationes*, Paris, 1608, vol. iii. p. 6, b, c.
[2] *Ibid.* II. i.; pp. 108, d, 109, a.   [3] See p. 496.
[4] *De Sacramentis in genere*, II. i.; *ut supra*, p. 108, c.

Notwithstanding all this the Romanists do teach the very doctrine which the Reformers charged upon them, and which the Protestant Symbols so strenuously condemn. This is clear, —

1. Because the same words do not always mean the same thing. Bellarmin says that Romanists teach that faith on the part of the recipient is necessary in order to the efficacy of the sacraments, at least in the case of adults. Protestants say the same thing ; and yet their meaning is entirely different. By faith, Protestants mean saving faith ; that faith which is one of the fruits of the Spirit, which, if a man has, his salvation is certain. Romanists, however, mean by faith mere assent, which a man may have, and be in a state of condemnation, and perish forever. This is their formal definition of faith, as given by Bellarmin himself; and the Council of Trent pronounces accursed those who say that the assent given by unrenewed men to the truth, is not true faith. Romanists do not hold that sacraments convey grace to avowed atheists or professed infidels; but that they exert saving power on those having the kind of faith in the Church which the bandits of Italy profess and cherish. So also the repentance required is not the godly sorrow of which the Apostle speaks, but that remorse which wicked men often experience. These points have been abundantly proved in the preceding pages.[1] A coal of fire will burn a man's hand ; it is true the man must be alive, but whether he is a good or bad man makes no difference. The sacraments confer grace by their inherent efficacy. It is true the recipient must be a believer ; but whether he has what St. Peter calls " the precious faith of God's elect," or the same kind of faith that Simon Magus had, makes no difference.

2. That this is the true doctrine of the Church of Rome is evident from the manner in which it is presented by its leading theologians. This appears from the great distinction which they make between the sacraments of the Old, and those of the New Testament. The former only signified, the latter confer grace. The latter are effectual " ex opere operato;" the former, as Thomas Aquinas says, were effectual only " ex fide et devotione suscipientis." Again, the necessity of anything good in the recipient is expressly denied. Thus Gabriel Biel (†1495) says : " Sacramentum dicitur conferre gratiam ex opere operato, ita quod ex eo ipso, quod opus illud, puta sacramentum, exhibitur, nisi impediat obex peccati mortalis, gratia confertur utentibus ; sic quod præter exhibitionem signi foris exhibiti non requiritur bonus motus

1 See above, the chapter on Faith.

seu devotio interior in suscipiente."[1] In like manner also Duns Scotus declares,[2] "præter istam (primam causam meritoriam sc. Christum) non oportet dare aliam intrinsecam in recipiente, qua conjungatur Deo, antequam recipiat gratiam;" and Petrus de Palude,[3] " In sacramentis novæ legis non per se requiritur, quod homo se disponat: ergo per ipsum sacramentum disponitur." The later Romish theologians teach the same doctrine. Thus Klee[4] says that the sacraments, when rightly dispensed, are of necessity effectual. And Moehler says: " The Catholic Church teaches that the sacrament works in us, in virtue of its character as an ordinance of Christ, appointed for our salvation (' ex opere operato, scl. a Christo,' instead of ' quod operatus est Christus '), i. e., the sacraments bring from the Saviour a divine power, which can be caused by no human frame of mind (Stimmung), nor by any spiritual state or effort, but which is given by God for Christ's sake directly in the sacrament."[5] It is true, he immediately adds, " Man must receive them, and must be susceptible of their impression, and this susceptibility expresses itself in repentance, in sorrow for sin, in longing for divine help, and in trusting faith ; nevertheless he can only receive them, and hence only have the requisite susceptibility." All this, however, according to the Romish system, the unrenewed man has, or may have. In the case of infants there is nothing but passivity: simple non-resistance ; and this is all that is required in the case of adults.

3. One of the points of controversy between the Jansenists and Jesuits related to this very subject. The Jansenists maintained that the efficacy of the sacraments depended on the inward state of the recipient. If he were not in a state of grace, and in the exercise of faith when they were received, they availed nothing. This doctrine the Jesuits controverted, and their influence prevailed in the Church. Jansenism was condemned and suppressed.

4. Another argument is derived from the constant practice of the Romish Church. There is no pretence of her recognized ministers demanding the profession, or evidence of what Protestants understand by saving faith in order to the reception of the

---

[1] *Collectorium in Quatuor Libros Sententiarum,* lib. iv. dis. 1, qu. 3; Basle, 1508, by count, p. 14, b, of the text of book iv.

[2] *In Lib. iv. Sentent.,* lib. iv. dis. 4, qu. 2; Venice, 1506, by count, p. 34, b, of book iv.

[3] In his commentary on the Sentences, lib. iv. dis. 1, qu. 1 ; Paris, 1514, by count, p. 4, a, b, of book iv.

[4] *Dogmatik, Specielle Dogmatik,* iii. ii. 1, § 7; Mainz, 1835, vol. iii. p. 95.

[5] *Symbolik oder Darstellung der dogmatischen Gegensätze der Katholiken und Protestanten;* von Dr. J. A. Möhler, iv. § 28; 6th edit. Mainz. 1843, p. 255.

sacraments, or as the condition of their sanctifying influence. On the contrary, they act on the principle, that the sacraments confer grace in the first instance. They baptize crowds of uninstructed heathen, without the slightest pretence that they are penitents or believers. If faith be a fruit of regeneration, and if, as Romanists all teach, regeneration is effected in baptism, how can the presence of faith in the recipient be a condition of the efficacy of baptism.[1]

The Administrator.

Lutherans and Reformed agree in teaching, first, that the efficacy of the sacraments does not depend on anything in him who administers them ; and second, that as the ministry of the Word and sacraments are united in the Scriptures, it is a matter of order and propriety that the sacraments should be administered by those only who have been duly called and appointed to that service. In the Second Helvetic Confession,[2] therefore, it is said, " Baptismus pertinet ad officia ecclesiastica." According to the Westminster Confession,[3] " There be only two sacraments ordained by Christ our Lord in the Gospel. That is to say, baptism and the supper of the Lord : neither of which may be dispensed by any, but by a minister of the Word, lawfully ordained."

The doctrine of the Lutheran Church is thus stated by Hollaz : " Jus dispensandi sacramenta Deus concredidit ecclesiæ, quæ exsecutionem aut exercitium hujus juris, observandi ordinis et εὐσχημοσύνης causa commendavit ministris verbi divini vocatis et ordinatis. In casu autem extremæ necessitatis, ubi sacramentum est necessarium nec nisi periculo salutis omitti potest, quilibet homo Christianus (laicus aut femina) sacramentum initiationis valide celebrare potest." [4] This is considered as not inconsistent with the Augsburg Confession, which says : [5] " De ordine ecclesiastico docent, quod nemo debeat in ecclesia publice docere, aut sacramenta administrare, nisi rite vocatus."

The doctrine of the Church of Rome on this subject is briefly stated in the canons enacted during the seventh session of the

---

[1] See *Historischer Anhang über die Wirksamkeit der Sacramente* " *ex opere operato.*" vol. ii. § 107, p. 363, of Köllner's *Symbolik.* Köllner comes to the conclusion that there is no great difference between the Lutheran and Romish doctrines on the efficacy of the sacraments; a conclusion in conflict with the conviction of Luther and his associates.

[2] xx.; Niemeyer, *Collectio Confessionum,* Leipzig, 1840, p. 518.

[3] Chap. xxvii. 4.

[4] *Examen,* iii. ii. 3, quæst. 6; edit. Leipzig, 1840, p. 518.

[5] i. 14; Hase, *Libri Symbolici,* 3d edit. Leipzig, 1846, p. 13.

Council of Trent.[1]   We read thus : " Si quis dixerit, Christianos omnes in verbo, et omnibus sacramentis administrandis habere potestatem ; anathema sit." The Council say in "all" the sacraments ; for the Church of Rome, although denying the power of any but canonically ordained priests to render the administration of the sacraments efficacious, admits of the efficacy of lay baptism. Again, " Si quis dixerit, in ministris, dum sacramentis conficiunt, et conferunt, non requiri intentionem saltem faciendi, quod facit ecclesia ; anathema sit." Intention is defined to be the purpose of doing what Christ ordained and what the Church is accustomed to do.   On this subject Bellarmin says, (1.) It is not necessary (in baptism at least) that the administrator should have an intelligent intention of doing what the Church does; for he may be ignorant of the doctrine of the Church ; all that is required is that he intend to administer a Church ordinance.   (2.) It is not necessary that he intend to do what the Church of Rome does ; but what the true Church, whatever that may be, is accustomed to do.   Hence, he says, the Catholic Church does not rebaptize those who have been baptized by the Geneva churches. ·" Non tollit efficaciam sacramenti error ministri circa ecclesiam, sed defectus intentionis."   (3.) That not actual intention, but only virtual, is required.   " Virtualis dicitur, cum actualis intentio in præsenti non adest ob aliquam evagationem mentis, tamen paulo ante adfuit et in virtute illius sit operatio." [2]   On this account the Roman Catechism says, that baptism administered by a heretic, a Jew, or a heathen, is efficacious: " Si id efficere propositum eis fuerit, quod ecclesia Catholica in eo administrationis genere efficit." [3]   This agrees with the popular view of the doctrine of intention.   The administrator must intend to produce the effect which the sacrament was designed to accomplish.   If he baptizes, he must intend to regenerate ; if he absolves, he must intend to absolve ; if he consecrates the bread and wine, he must intend their transmutation ; if he offers the host, he must intend it as a sacrifice ; and if offered for a particular person, he must intend it to take effect for his benefit.   According to this view everything depends on the will of the officiating priest.

[1] Sess. vii.; *Canones de Sacramentis in genere*, 10, 11; Streitwolf, vol. i. p. 40.

[2] Bellarmin, *De Sacramentis in genere*, i. xxvii.; *Disputationes*, edit. Paris, 1608, vol. iii. pp. 94, d, 95.

[3] *Catechismus Romanus*, ii. ii. 18 (xxii. 24); Streitwolf. *Libri Symbolici*, vol. i. p. 270.

§ 5. *The Necessity of the Sacraments.*

The distinction between the necessity of precept and the necessity of means, is obvious and important. No one would be willing to say, without qualification, that it is unnecessary to obey an explicit command of Christ. And as He has commanded his disciples to baptize all who are received as members of his Church, in the name of the Father, of the Son, and of the Holy Ghost, and required his disciples statedly to commemorate his death by the celebration of the Lord's Supper, the strongest moral obligation rests upon his people to obey these commands. But the obligation to obey any command, such as to observe the Sabbath, to visit the sick, and to relieve the poor, depends on circumstances. No opportunity may be offered; or the discharge of the duty may be hindered by external circumstances; or we may lack the ability to render the service required. So with regard to the command to be baptized and to commemorate the Lord's death at his table, it is evident that many circumstances may occur to prevent obedience even on the part of those who have the disposition and purpose to do whatever their Lord requires at their hands. And even where obedience is not prevented by external circumstances, it may be prevented by ignorance, or by unfounded scruples of conscience.

By the necessity of means is usually understood an absolute necessity, a " sine qua non."   In this sense food is a necessity of life; light is necessary to the exercise of vision; the Word is necessary to the exercise of faith, for it is its object, the thing which is to be believed; and faith is, on the part of adults, necessary to salvation, for it is the act of receiving the grace of God offered in the Bible.   And therefore times almost without number, it is said in Scripture, that we are saved by faith, that he that believeth shall be saved, and that he that believeth not shall not see life.

The question between the Reformed on the one hand, and Lutherans and Romanists on the other, is in which of these senses are the sacraments necessary.   According to the Reformed they have the necessity of precept.   The use of them is enjoined as a duty; but they are not necessary means of salvation.   Men may be saved without them.   The benefits which they signify and which they are the means of signifying, sealing, and applying to believers, are not so tied to their use that those benefits cannot be secured without them.   Sins may be forgiven, and the soul regenerated and saved, though neither sacrament has ever been received. The Lutherans and Romanists, on the other hand, hold that the sacraments are necessary means of grace, in the sense that the grace which they signify is not received otherwise than in their use. There is no remission of sin or regeneration without baptism ; no reception of the body and blood of Christ to our spiritual nourishment and growth in grace, without the Lord's Supper ; and, according to Romanists, no forgiveness of post-baptismal sins without priestly absolution ; no grace of orders without canonical ordination ; and no special preparation for death without extreme unction. This question is of importance chiefly in reference to baptism, and will therefore come up when that sacrament is under consideration. At present it is only the general teachings of these several churches that need be referred to. The " Consensus Tigurinus " is the most carefully considered and cautiously worded exposition of the doctrine of the Reformed in relation to the sacraments, belonging to the period of the Reformation. It was drawn up to settle the differences on this subject between the churches of Geneva and those of Zurich. It contains the statements in reference to the sacraments to which both parties agreed. It teaches[1] (1.) That the sacraments are " notæ ac tesseræ " of Christian fellowship and brotherhood ; incitements to gratitude, faith, and a holy life, and " syngraphæ " binding us thereto. They were ordained especially that therein God might testify, represent, and seal to us his grace. (2.) The things signified are not to be separated from the signs. Those who by faith receive the latter receive also the former. (3.) That respect is to be had rather to the promise to which our faith is directed ; for the elements without Christ " nihil sint quam inanes larvæ." (4.) The sacraments confer nothing " propria eorum virtute ; " God alone works in us by his Spirit. They are organs or means by which God efficaciously operates. (5.) They are sometimes called seals, but the Spirit alone is properly the seal as well as the beginner and finisher of our faith. (6.) God does not operate in all who receive the sacraments, but only in his own chosen people. (7.) Hence the doctrine is to be rejected that the sacraments convey grace to all who do not oppose the obstacle of mortal sin. The grace of God is not so bound to the signs, that all who have the latter have the former. (8.) Believers receive without the sacraments the blessings which they receive in their use. " Extra eorum usum fidelibus constat, quæ

[1] Niemeyer, *Collectio Confessionum*, Leipzig, 1840, pp. 193–195.

illic figuratur veritas." Paul received baptism for the remission
of sins ; but his sins were remitted before he was baptized. Baptism was to Cornelius the laver of regeneration, but he had received the Spirit before he was thus externally washed. In the
Lord's Supper we receive Christ, but Christ dwells in every believer, and we must have faith before we can acceptably approach
the table of the Lord. (9.) The benefit of the sacraments is
not confined to the time in which they are administered or received. God often regenerates long after baptism those baptized
in infancy ; some in early youth, some in old age. The benefit
of baptism, therefore, continues through the whole life, because
the promise signified therein continues always in force.

As to the Lutheran doctrine on this subject, Guerike says that
the three churches, the Greek, Roman, and Lutheran, "are agreed
in holding that in the sacraments the visible signs as such really
convey the invisible divine things, and therefore, that a participation of the sacraments is necessary in order to a participation of
the heavenly gifts (göttliche Sache) therein contained. While on
the contrary the Reformed Church teaches that the visible signs
as such do not convey the invisible grace, and that the Christian
can by faith receive the same divine benefits without the use of
the sacraments, and consequently that the sacraments are not absolutely necessary, much less the middle point of the Christian
plan of salvation." [1] The language of the Lutheran Symbols
justifies this strong language of Guerike. Thus the signers of
the Augsburg Confession,[2] "Damnant Anabaptistas qui improbant baptismum puerorum et affirmant pueros sine baptismo salvos
fieri." And in the comment on that article in the "Apology for
the Confession," it is said,[3] "Nonus articulus approbatus est, in
quo confitemur, quod baptismus sit necessarius ad salutem, et
quod pueri sint baptizandi, et quod baptismus puerorum non sit
irritus, sed necessarius et efficax ad salutem." The Lutheran
theologians, however, in treating of the necessity of baptism,
make a distinction between adults and infants. With regard to
the former, regeneration should precede baptism. In reference to
them, the design of baptism is to seal and confirm the grace
already received. In regard to infants it is the organ or means
of regeneration. Thus Baier says : [4] "Hic autem, quod ad
finem proximum attinet, diversitas occurrit, respectu subjectorum

---

[1] *Symbolik*, p. 374.
[2] Par. I. ix. 3 ; Hase, *Libri Symbolici*, 3d edit. Leipzig, 1846, p. 12.
[3] *Apologia*, iv. 51 ; *Ibid.* p. 156.
[4] *Compendium Theologiæ Positivæ*, III. x. 10 ; edit. Frankfort and Leipzig, 1739, p. 643.

diversorum. Nam infantibus quidem æque omnibus per baptismum primum confertur et obsignatur fides, per quam meritum
Christi illis applicetur : Adultis vero illis tantum, qui fidem ex
verbo conceperunt ante baptismi susceptionem, baptismus eam
obsignat et confirmat." So also Gerhard says : " Infantibus
baptismus principaliter est medium ordinarium regenerationis et
mundationis a peccatis, etc. Secundario autem sigillum justitiæ
et fidei confirmatio ; adultis credentibus baptismus principaliter
præstat usum obsignationis ac testificationis de gratia Dei, υιοθεσία
et vita æterna ; sed minus principaliter renovationem et dona
Spiritus Sancti auget. Infantes, per baptismum primitias Spiritus et fidei accipiunt: adulti qui per verbum primitias fidei et
Spiritus Sancti acceperunt, per baptismum incrementa ejusdem
consequuntur." [1]

The doctrine of the Church of Rome on this subject is, not
that all the seven sacraments are necessary to salvation, but that
each is necessary to the reception of the gift or grace which it is
intended to convey. There can be no "grace of orders " without
canonical ordination, but it is not necessary that every man should
be ordained. The sacrament of penance is necessary only in
the case of post-baptismal sin, and even the eucharist, which
they regard as far the greatest of their sacraments " in dignity
and mystery," is not necessary to infants. Baptism, however,
being the only channel through which remission of sins and regeneration are conveyed, is absolutely necessary to salvation.
And priestly absolution is absolutely necessary for the remission
of sins committed after baptism. Such revolting consequences
would flow from carrying this principle rigorously out, that Romanists shrink from its assertion. It would exclude many confessors and martyrs from the kingdom of heaven. It is, therefore, taught that when circumstances render it impossible that
these sacraments can be received, the purpose and desire to
receive them secure their benefits. These cases are, however,
exceptions, and are generally overlooked in the statement of the
doctrine. This exception does not apply to infants, and, therefore, they cannot enjoy its benefits. It is the doctrine of the
Church of Rome that all unbaptized persons fail of eternal life.
This is included in their idea of the Church. None are saved
who are not within the pale of the true Church. None are
within the pale of the Church who have not been baptized, and
who are not subject to canonical bishops, and especially to the

[1] *Loci Theologici*, XXI. vii. § 124; edit. Tübingen, 1769, vol. ix. p. 169.

bishop of Rome. The unbaptized, therefore, not being in the
Church, as defined by Romanists, are of necessity excluded from
the kingdom of heaven.

The language of the Roman standards is perfectly explicit.
The Council of Trent says :[1] " Si quis dixerit, non dari gratiam
per hujusmodi sacramenta semper, et omnibus, quantum est ex
parte Dei, etiam si rite ea suscipiant, sed aliquando, et aliquibus ;
anathema sit."   And again :[2] " Si quis dixerit baptismum liberum esse, hoc est non necessarium ad salutem ; anathema sit."
In the Roman Catechism[3] we find the following : " Estne Baptismus ad salutem omnibus necessarius ? " the answer is : " Sed cum
ceterarum rerum cognitio; quæ hactenus expositæ sunt, fidelibus
utillissima habenda sit, tum vero nihil magis necessarium videri
potest, quam ut doceantur, omnibus hominibus baptismi legem
a Domino præscriptam esse, ita ut, nisi per baptismi gratiam Deo
renascantur, in sempiternam miseriam, et interitum a parentibus,
sive illi fideles, sive infideles sint, procreentur."   According to
the Church of Rome, therefore, all the unbaptized, whether their
parents be believers or infidels, are doomed to eternal misery and
perdition.   With regard to penance, the Council of Trent says :[4]
" Est hoc sacramentum pœnitentiæ lapsis post baptismum ad salutem necessarium, ut nondum regeneratis ipse baptismus."   It
also teaches that full confession of all sins committed after baptism is " jure divino " necessary, because our Lord Jesus Christ,
about to ascend into heaven, left his priests as his vicars, as
" præsides et judices," to whom all mortal sins, into which Christians may fall, are to be communicated, and who are authorized
to pronounce the sentence of remission or retention.   It is said,
moreover, that our Lord teaches that priests, who themselves are
in a state of mortal sin, in virtue of the power of the Holy Spirit
given them in ordination, exercise, as ministers of Christ, this
function of remitting sins, and those err who contend that wicked
priests have not this power.   All this is reiterated in the canons
and amplified and enforced in the Catechism.[5]

In this connection it is sufficient to remark, —

1. That the doctrine that the sacraments are necessary to salvation, on the ground that they are the only channels for conveying to men the benefits of Christ's redemption, is clearly contrary
to the express teachings of the Bible.   The Scriptures everywhere

---

[1] Sess. vii., *De Sacramentis in genere,* canon 7; Streitwolf, vol. i. p. 39.

[2] *Ibid., De Baptismo,* canon 5; *Ibid.* p. 41.

[3] Par. ii. cap. ii. quæs. 25 (31, xxx.); *Ibid.* p. 274.

[4] Sess. xiv. cap. 2; *Ibid.* p. 55.   [5] Sess. xiv. cap. 5, 6; *Ibid.*

teach that God looks upon the heart; that He requires of fallen men simply faith in our Lord Jesus Christ and repentance toward God as the only indispensable conditions of salvation; that all men have free access to God, through the mediation of Christ, to obtain at his hands the remission of sins and all the benefits of redemption; that they need no intervention of priests to secure for them this access or the communication of those benefits; and that no external rites have power in themselves to confer grace. God so loved the world, that He gave his only begotten Son, that whosoever believeth on Him should not perish but have everlasting life. He that believeth on Him is not condemned; but he that believeth not is condemned already. Believe on the Lord Jesus Christ and thou shalt be saved. Whosoever calleth on the name of the Lord, shall be saved. Whoso believeth that Jesus is the Christ, is born of God. The Scripture cannot be broken. It cannot be that he who truly believes the record which God has given of his Son should fail of eternal life. We become the sons of God by faith in Jesus Christ. It is true we are commanded to be baptized, as we are commanded to confess Christ before men or to love the brethren. But these are duties to which faith secures obedience; they are not the means of salvation.

2. This ritual system is utterly inconsistent with the whole genius of Christianity. God is a Spirit, and He requires those who worship Him, to worship Him in spirit and in truth. External rites are declared to be nothing. Circumcision is nothing, and uncircumcision is nothing. "He is not a Jew, which is one outwardly; neither is that circumcision, which is outward in the flesh: but he is a Jew, which is one inwardly; and circumcision is that of the heart, in the spirit, and not in the letter; whose praise is not of men, but of God." (Rom. ii. 28, 29.) This is not merely a fact, but a principle. What St. Paul here says of circumcision and of Jews, may be said, and is substantially said by St. Peter in reference to baptism and Christianity. A man who is a Christian outwardly only, is not a Christian; and the baptism which saves, is not the washing of the body with water, but the conversion of the soul. (1 Peter iii. 21.) The idea that a man's state before God depends on anything external, on birth, on membership in any visible organization, or on any outward rite or ceremony, is utterly abhorrent to the religion of the Bible. It did not belong to Judaism except in the corrupt form of Pharisaism. It is true, that under the old dispensation a man could not be saved unless he belonged to the commonwealth of Israel,

and was one of the children of Abraham.   But according to St.
Paul (Rom. ix. 8 ; Gal. iii. 7 and 29), this only meant that they
must believe in Abraham's God and the promise of redemption
through his seed.   If a man of heathen birth and culture came to
the knowledge of the truth, believed the doctrines which God
had revealed to his chosen people, relied on the promise of salvation through Christ, and purposed to obey the law of God, then
he was a Jew inwardly and one of Abraham's seed.   His circumcision was only " a seal of the righteousness of the faith which he
had, yet being uncircumcised." (Rom. iv. 11.)   The doctrine that
such a man, notwithstanding this thorough change in his inward
state in knowledge, conviction, and character, is under the wrath
and curse of God, until a little piece of flesh is cut from his body,
never was a part of the religion of God.   It is part and parcel of
the religion of his great adversary.   Any one, therefore, who
teaches that no man can be saved without the rite of baptism,
and that by receiving that rite he is made a child of God and heir
of heaven, is antichrist, and " even now are there many antichrists."   (1 John ii. 18.)

3. This ritualistic system, which makes the sacraments the only
channels of grace, and consequently absolutely necessary to salvation, naturally leads to the divorce of religion and morality.   A
man, according to this system, may be in the true Church a child
of God, and assured of heaven, and yet utterly frivolous, worldly,
and even immoral in his inward and outward life.   This is illustrated on a large scale in every Roman Catholic country.   In such
countries some of the greatest devotees are openly wicked men.
And wherever this system prevails we find its most zealous advocates among people of the world, who live at ease in full security
of salvation, because they are in the Church and faithful in observing " days, and months, and times, and years ; " and are
punctiliously " subject to ordinances, touch not, taste not, handle
not." [1]   The great question at issue in the controversy with ritualism is, Whether a man's salvation depends on his inward state,
or upon outward rites ; or, as some would give it, Whether his
state is determined by outward rites, or whether the rites depend
for their value and efficacy on his inward state.   In either form
the question is, Are we saved by faith or by sacraments ?   The
Apostle teaches us that " in Christ Jesus neither circumcision
availeth anything nor uncircumcision, but a new creature." (Gal.
vi. 15.)

[1] A gentleman of discrimination and candour, not long since said to a friend, " You are
very pious, but you have no religion.   I am religious, but I have no piety."

4. The above remarks are not intended to apply, and in fact are not applicable to the Lutheran system. Lutherans do, indeed, teach the necessity of the sacraments, but as they also teach that true, living, saving faith is the indispensable condition of their efficacy ; and, as they further teach that in the case of adults such faith produced by the Word precedes baptism, they do not make baptism the ordinary and indispensable channel for the communication of the saving influences of the Holy Spirit. They hold that all who, through the reading or hearing of the Word, are led to embrace the Lord Jesus Christ as their God and Saviour, are thereby made children of God and heirs of eternal life. They believe with the Apostle (Gal. iii. 26), that we " are all the children of God by faith in Christ Jesus." It is this doctrine of salvation by faith, or as Luther has it, " by faith alone," that has saved the Lutheran system from the *virus* of ritualism.

§ 6. *Validity of the Sacraments.*

That is valid which avails for the end intended. The question, therefore, as to the validity of the sacraments is a question as to what is necessary to their being that which they purport to be. The answer to this question is that they must conform to the prescriptions given in the Bible concerning them. The elements employed must be those which Christ ordained. The form, or the manner in which those elements are given and received, must be in accordance with his directions ; and the ordinance must be administered with the intention of doing what He has commanded. Thus if baptism be a washing with water, then it is necessary that water should be the element employed in its administration. If it be a washing with water in the name of the Father, of the Son, and of the Holy Ghost, then those words, or that form, must be used ; and the ordinance must be administered and received in the faith of the Trinity. The general faith of the Church has been in favour of the validity of heretical baptism ; but heresy was made to include other departures from the standard of faith, than the denial of the essential doctrines of the Gospel. Baptism is a Christian ordinance. It involves on the part of both the administrator and the recipient the profession of the Christian religion. It is perfectly evident that the same service, as to matter and form, performed by a heathen to a heathen, who attached an entirely different meaning to what was done, could not be regarded as a Christian ordinance.

The other condition necessary to the validity of the sacraments concerns the intention of those engaged in the service. They must intend to do what Christ commanded. If a man receives the ordinance of baptism, he must intend to profess his faith in the Gospel and to accept the terms of salvation therein presented. And the administrator must have the purpose to initiate the recipient into the number of the professed disciples of Christ. A sacrament, therefore, administered by an idiot, or a maniac, or in sport, or in mockery, is utterly null and void. It has no meaning and is entirely worthless.

The only question on which there is much diversity of opinion on this subject, is, Whether the validity of the sacraments depends on the official standing of the person by whom they are administered? We have seen that Romanists make canonical ordination or consecration absolutely essential. If any man but a bishop (in their sense of the word) should confirm or ordain, nothing is done. The service in either case is an empty one, conveying neither grace nor authority. If any other than a priest should absolve a penitent, no absolution takes place ; and so of the Lord's Supper, the words of consecration pronounced by any lips but those of a canonically ordained priest, produce no change in the elements. The reason of this is, not merely that the officiator acts in such cases disorderly and improperly, but that he has neither the prerogative nor the power to render the sacraments effectual. They are invalid, because they do not avail to accomplish the end for which they were appointed. Romanists are guilty of a benevolent inconsistency in making baptism an exception to this rule. There is the same logical or theoretical reason that baptism should be invalid when administered by an unordained person, as that confirmation, ordination, or absolution, when thus administered, should be null and void. But as baptism is held to be essential to salvation, souls must often perish, when a priest is inaccessible, unless lay baptism be allowed. In cases of such emergency the Church of Rome, therefore, pronounces baptism to be valid (*i. e.*, efficacious) when administered by a layman, a woman, or even by a pagan, provided the administrator really intends to baptize, *i. e.*, to do what the Church contemplates in the administration of that ordinance.

The standards of the Lutheran and Reformed Churches place preaching the Word and the administration of the sacraments on the same ground. They teach (1.) That Christ has appointed certain officers in his Church. (2.) That by his Spirit he calls and qualifies certain men for the discharge of the duties of those offices. (3.) That those who aspire to them are to be examined as to their call and qualifications. (4.) That if found competent they are to be set apart or ordained in an orderly manner to the office to which they deem themselves called. (5.) That the special functions of one class of these officers, are preaching and the administration of the sacraments. (6.) It follows from all this that for any one not thus called and ordained to undertake the exercise of either of these functions of the ministry, in a settled state of the Church, is wrong; it is a violation of the divinely constituted order of Christ's Church. According to this view, lay preaching and lay administration of the ordinances (in ordinary circumstances) are equally wrong. But are they invalid? That is a very different question. We know that Romanists, when they pronounce a sacrament invalid, mean that it is powerless. We know that when the old English law pronounced any marriage invalid if not solemnized by a man in holy orders, the meaning was, that the ceremony was null and void; that the parties were not married. But what can be meant by lay preaching being invalid? Is the Gospel invalid? Does it lose its truth, authority, or power? This cannot be. Neither its authority nor its power depend upon the clay lips by which it is proclaimed. Again, if a number of pious Christians assemble, where no minister can be had, to celebrate the Lord's Supper, in what sense is such a service invalid? Do they not commemorate the death of Christ? Are not the bread and wine to them the symbols of his body and blood? If faith be in exercise, may they not receive those symbols to their spiritual nourishment and growth in grace? Again, if baptism be a washing with water in the name of the Holy Trinity, to signify and seal our engrafting into Christ, does it cease to be, or to signify this if not administered by an ordained minister? Does not the man thus baptized make a profession of his faith in Christ? and does he not thereby become a member of that great body which confesses Him before men? Can it, therefore, be any more invalid than the Gospel, when preached by a layman?

What the Bible, therefore, seems to teach on this subject is, that Christ having appointed certain officers in his Church to preach his Word and to administer his ordinances, for any man, under ordinary circumstances not duly appointed, to assume the functions of the ministry, is irregular and wrong, because contrary to the order of Christ's Church. Further than this the Reformed and Lutheran standards do not appear to have gone.

§ 7. *Baptism.*

" Baptism is a sacrament, wherein the washing with water, in the name of the Father, and of the Son, and of the Holy Ghost, doth signify and seal our engrafting into Christ and partaking of the benefits of the covenant of grace, and our engagement to be the Lord's." [1]

The Mode of Baptism.

According to the definition given above, baptism is a washing with water. By washing is meant any such application of water to the body as effects its purification. This may be done by immersion, affusion, or sprinkling. The command, therefore, to baptize is simply a command to wash with water. It is not specifically a command to immerse, to affuse, or to sprinkle. The mode of applying water as the purifying medium is unessential. The only necessary thing is to make such an application of water to the person, as shall render the act significant of the purification of the soul.

The first argument in favour of this view of the ordinance is an *à priori* one. As by common consent the design of the institution is either to symbolize or to effect the cleansing of the soul from the guilt and pollution of sin, by the blood and spirit of Christ, it would seem to follow that washing with water, however done, is all that is necessary to the integrity of the ordinance. The idea of purification is as clearly and as frequently signified by affusion as by immersion. Besides, to make anything so purely circumstantial as the manner in which water is used in the act of cleansing, essential to a Christian sacrament, which, according to some, is absolutely necessary to salvation; and, according to others, is essential to membership in the visible Church of Christ, is opposed to the whole nature of the Gospel. It is to render Christianity more Judaic than Judaism, even as understood by the Pharisees; for they purified themselves, their offerings, and holy places and utensils, by immersion, affusion, or sprinkling as was most appropriate or convenient.

Use of the Word in the Classics.

The second argument on this subject, is drawn from the usage of the word. In the Classics; in the Septuagint and the Apocryphal writings of the Old Testament; in the New Testament; and in the writings of the Greek fathers, the words βάπτω,

---

[1] *Westminster Shorter Catechism*, Ques. 94.

βαπτίζω, and their cognates, are used with such latitude of meaning, as to prove the assertion that the command to baptize is a
command to immerse, to be utterly unauthorized and unreasonable.

Ever since the Reformation and the rise of the Baptists as a
distinct denomination, who hold that " baptizing is dipping, and
dipping is baptizing," the meaning of the Greek words in question has been a matter of dispute, on which hundreds of volumes
have been written. It is evidently impossible to enter on that
discussion in these pages. All that can be attempted is a brief
statement of the conclusions believed to be established, while the
proofs on which those conclusions rest must be sought in works
devoted to the subject. As to the classic use of the words in
question, it is clear that βάπτω means (1.) To dip. (2.) To dye
by dipping. (3.) To dye without regard to the mode in which
it is done ; as a lake is said to be baptized (*i. e.*, dyed) by the
blood shed in it ; a garment is spoken of as baptized by colour-
ing matter dropping on it. (4.) It also means to gild; also to
glaze, as when earthenware is covered with any vitreous matter.
(5.) To wet, moisten, or wash. (6.) To temper, as hot iron is
tempered; this may be done by plunging or pouring. " Tempered, ὑπὸ ἐλαίου," does not mean plunged into oil. (7.) To imbue. The mind is said to be baptized with fantasies; not
plunged into them, for it is ὑπὸ τῶν φαντασίων.[1]

A man is said to be " imbued with righteousness." This cannot mean " dipped." It is obvious, therefore, that a command to
baptize, made in the use of the word βάπτω, cannot be limited to a
command to dip, plunge, or immerse.

As to the classic use of βαπτίζω, it means, (1.) To immerse, or
submerge. It is very frequently used when ships are spoken of
as sunk or buried in the sea. They are then said to be baptized.
(2.) To overflow or to cover with water. The sea-shore is said
to be baptized by the rising tide. (3.) To wet thoroughly, to
moisten. (4.) To pour upon or drench. (5.) In any way to be
overwhelmed or overpowered. Hence men are said to be baptized
with wine (οἱ βεβαπτισμένοι are the intoxicated), with opium,
with debts, with puzzling questions. Wine is said to be baptized
by having water poured into it.[2]

---

[1] There are two recent American writers whose works contain all that most students
would be disposed to read on this subject. The one is the Rev. Dr. Conant, in his book,
Meaning and Use of the Word Baptizein, New York, 1868; and the other the Rev. James
W. Dale, in his *Classic Baptism; Judaic Baptism;* and *Johannic Baptism;* to be followed
by *Christian Baptism*.

[2] Illustrations of some of these uses of the word may be found in Stephen's *Thesaurus*

The word βαπτίζω, as Dr. Dale so strenuously argues, belongs
to that class of words which indicate an effect to be produced
without expressing the kind of action by which that effect is to
be brought about. In this respect it is analogous to the word "to
bury." A man may be buried by being covered up in the ground;
by being placed in an empty cave; by being put into a sarcoph-
agus; or even, as among our Indians, by being placed upon a
platform elevated above the ground. The command to bury, may
be executed in any of these ways. So with regard to the word
βαπτίζω, there is a given effect to be produced, without any specific
injunction as to the manner; whether by immersion, pouring, or
sprinkling.

Use of the Words in the Septuagint and Apocrypha.

These words are of rare occurrence in the Greek version of
the Old Testament. In the fifth chapter of Second Kings we
have the history of Naaman the Syrian, who came to the prophet
to be healed of his leprosy. And "Elisha sent a messenger unto
him, saying, Go and wash in Jordan seven times" (ver. 10).
"Then went he down and dipped himself (ἐβαπτίσατο) seven
times in Jordan" (ver. 14). The only special interest in this
passage is the proof it affords that baptism and washing are
identical. The command to wash was obeyed by baptizing himself. The Vulgate does not change the words in the two passages,
"Vade et lavare septies in Jordane" (ver. 10). "Descendit et
lavit in Jordane septies" (ver. 14). The Septuagint has λοῦσαι
in verse 10, and ἐβαπτίσατο in verse 14.

In Daniel iv. 33, it is said that the body of Nebuchadnezzar
"was wet (baptized, ἐβάφη, [LXX. ver. 30]) with the dew of
heaven." Here the idea of dipping is absolutely precluded.

The word βάπτω, when meaning to dip, does not necessarily
include the idea of entire immersion. A mere touch or partial
immersion is often all the word is intended to express; as in Leviticus iv. 17: "The priest shall dip (βάψει) his finger in some
of the blood." Leviticus xiv. 6: "As for the living bird, he shall
take it, and the cedar wood, and the hyssop, and shall dip (βάψει)
them and the living bird in the blood of the bird that was killed
over the running water." All these things could not be immersed
in the blood of a bird. Boaz said to Ruth, at meal-time "dip
(βάψεις) thy morsel in the vinegar." (Ruth ii. 14.) Joshua iii. 15:

and Scapula's *Lexicon*, and of all in the works of Dr. Conant and Dr. Dale, who discuss
the bearing of each on the matter in debate from their respective stand-points.

" The feet of the priests that bare the ark were dipped (ἐβά-
φησαν) in the brim of the water." 1 Samuel xiv. 27 : Jonathan
" dipped " (ἐβαψεν) the end of the rod which was in his hand " in
an honey-comb." Psalm lxviii. 23 (24), " That thy foot may
be dipped (βαφῇ) in the blood of thine enemies." These examples prove that even βάπτω, as used in the Septuagint, does not,
when it means to dip, include the idea of complete immersion.

βαπτίζω (according to Trommius), besides the passage already
quoted from 2 Kings v. 14, occurs in the Septuagint only in Isaiah
xxi. 4, where the Greek is ἡ ἀνομία με βαπτίζει, " iniquity baptizes
(or overwhelms) me." The English version, adhering to the
Hebrew, reads, " Fearfulness affrighted me." The Vulgate has
" Tenebræ stupefecerunt me." The word occurs twice in the
Apocrypha, Judith xii. 7, and Sirach xxxiv. 27 [xxxi. 25].
Wahl,[1] referring to these two passages, defines " βάπτομαι, me lavo
= νίπτομαι," " I wash myself." In Sirach the expression is, βαπ-
τιζόμενος ἀπὸ νεκροῦ, " baptized from a dead body," i. e., purified
from the uncleanness contracted by touching a dead body. Or,
as Fritzsche translates it, " Der sich wäscht von einem Todten,
einer Leiche, sich reinigt von der Befleckung, die ihm die Berü-
hrung des Leichn aus zugezogen, vrgl. 4 Moses xix. 11."[2] That
is, " He that washes from a corpse purifies himself from the
defilement occasioned by touching it." We learn from the passage referred to for illustration (Numbers xix. 11–13), that this
purification was effected by sprinkling the ashes of a heifer. (See
ver. 9, and compare Heb. ix. 13.) In Numbers xix. 13, it is said,
" Whosoever toucheth the dead body of any one that is dead, and
purifieth not himself, defileth the tabernacle of the LORD ; and
that soul shall be cut off from Israel, because the water of separation was not sprinkled upon him, he shall be unclean ; his uncleanness is yet upon him." The water of separation was the
water in which the ashes of a red heifer had been mingled, as
described in the preceding part of the chapter. And it was the
sprinkling of that water which effected the baptism, or purification, of the defiled person.

The passage in Judith determines nothing either way as to the
meaning of the word. It merely says, ἐβαπτίζετο ἐν τῇ παρεμβολῇ
ἐπὶ τῆς πηγῆς τοῦ ὕδατος, " she baptized herself in the camp at a
fountain of water." If it be a settled point that βαπτίζω always

---

[1] *Clavis Librorum V. T. Apocryphorum Philologica*, Auctore Christ. Abrah. Wahl, Philos.
et Theol! Doctore, Leipzig, 1853.

[2] *Kurzgefasstes exegetisches Handbuch zu den Apokryphen des Alten Testamentes*, von
Otto Fridolin Fritzsche, Leipzig, 1859, vol. v. p. 195.

means to immerse, then this passage asserts that Judith immersed
herself in the fountain. But if, as the vast majority of Christians believe, the word often means to wash, or purify, without
regard to the way in which the purification is effected, then the
passage cannot be proved to assert anything more than that
Judith washed herself at the fountain. The circumstances of
the case are all in favour of the latter interpretation. According
to the narrative, the land had been invaded by an immense host
of Assyrians under the command of Holofernes. Resistance
seemed hopeless, and utter destruction was imminent. In this
emergency Judith, a young, beautiful, and rich woman, inflamed
with zeal for her country and her religion, determined to make a
desperate effort for the salvation of her people. For this purpose,
arrayed to the best advantage, she made her way into the enemies' camp and presented herself to Holofernes and promised to
aid him in the conquest of the land. The Assyrian general, cap-
tivated by her charms, treated her with great favour. She remained undisturbed in her tent for three days, but was permitted
at night to resort to the fountain for purification. On the fourth
day she was invited to a great feast, at which Holofernes drank
to excess, so that when the guests had retired and the general
was in a state of helpless intoxication, Judith, with the assistance
of her maid, cut off his head and carried it to the camp of her
own people. This led to the overthrow of the Assyrians and the
deliverance of the land.

The circumstances in this case which favour the assumption
that Judith went to the fountain not for immersion, but for ablution, are, (1.) It was within the camp, necessarily, for such a
host, of large dimensions. But a camp filled with soldiers does
not seem to be an appropriate bathing-place for a lady of distinction even at night. (2.) Dr. Conant says : " There was evidently no lack of water for the immersion of the body, after
the Jewish manner, namely by walking into the water to the
proper depth, and then sinking down till the whole body was
immersed." [1] The probability, however, seems all the other way.
It must have been an extraordinary fountain, if it allowed of
immersion in any such way. If the word βαπτίζω can only mean
" to immerse," these considerations amount to nothing. But if
the word means to wash or to purify as well as to immerse, then
they are of sufficient weight to turn the scale in favour of the
former explanation. Of itself, however, the passage proves nothing.

[1] *Meaning and Use of Baptizein*, New York, 1868, p. 85.

The New Testament Usage.

The word βάπτειν is used four times in the New Testament, in no one of which does it express the idea of entire immersion. In Luke xvi. 24, " That he may dip (βάψῃ) the tip of his finger in water." The finger, when dipped in water, is not submerged When placed horizontally on the water and slightly depressed, it retains more of the moisture than if plunged perpendicularly into it. John xiii. 26, speaks twice of dipping the sop (βάψας and ἐμβάψας). But a morsel held in the fingers, is only partly immersed. In Revelation xix. 13, the words περιβεβλημένος ἱμάτιον βεβαμμένον αἵματι obviously means ' clothed with a vesture stained or dyed with blood.' The allusion is probably to Isaiah lxiii. 1 ff. : " Who is this that cometh from Edom, with dyed garments from Bozrah ? . . . . Wherefore art thou red in thine apparel, and thy garments like him that treadeth in the wine-fat ? I have trodden the wine-press alone ; . . . . and their blood shall be sprinkled upon my garments, and I will stain all my raiment." In this case, therefore, the baptism was by sprinkling. Βαπτίζω occurs in the New Testament about eighty times ; βάπτισμα some twenty times ; and βαπτισμός four times. As every one admits that baptism may be effected by immersion, and as the purifications under the Old Testament (called by the Apostle, Hebrews ix. 10, in Greek, " diverse baptisms ") were effected by immersion, affusion, and sprinkling, it would not be surprising if in some of these numerous passages, the baptism spoken of necessarily implied immersion. It so happens, or, it has been so ordered, however, that there is no such passage in the whole of the New Testament. The places in which these words occur may be arranged in the following classes : (1.) Those in which, taken by themselves, the presumption is in favour of immersion. (2.) Those in which the idea of immersion is necessarily excluded. (3.) Those which in themselves are not decisive, but where the presumption is altogether in favour of affusion.

To the first class belong those passages which speak of the persons baptized going into (εἰς) the water, and " coming up out of the water." (Matt. iii. 16 ; Acts viii. 38, 39.) Such passages, however, must be isolated in order to create a presumption in favour of immersion. According to ancient accounts, the common way of baptizing was for the person to step into water, when water was poured on his head, and then he came up out of the water, not in the least incommoded by dripping garments. And when we remember that it is said concerning John, that " Then went out to him Jerusalem, and all Judea, and all the region round about Jordan, and were baptized of him in Jordan, confessing their sins " (Matt. iii. 5, 6), it seems physically impossible that he should have immersed all this multitude.   When all the circumstances are taken into view, the presumption in favour of immersion, even in this class of passages, disappears.

2. The second class of passages, those from which the idea of immersion is excluded, includes all those which relate to the baptism of the Spirit.   The Spirit is frequently said to be poured out on men ; but men are never said to be dipped or immersed into the Holy Spirit.   Such an idea is altogether incongruous. When, therefore, it is said that men are baptized by the Holy Spirit, as is so often done, the reference must be to effusion, or affusion of the Spirit by which the soul is cleansed from sin.   As the Holy Spirit is a person, and not a mere influence or force, the preposition ἐν used in this connection (Matt. iii. 11 ; Mark i. 8 ; John i. 33 ; Acts i. 5, xi. 16 ; 1 Cor. xii. 13) must have its instrumental force.   The work performed in us by the Holy Spirit is a baptism.   As water in the hands of John was the purifying medium for the body, so the Holy Spirit, as sent or given by Jesus Christ, purifies the soul.   Some of the modern commentators are such purists that they are unwilling to allow of the slightest departure from classic usage in the Greek of the New Testament.   They speak as though the sacred writers were Greek grammarians, instead of, as was in most cases the fact, unlettered men writing in what to them was a foreign language.   Thus because the particle ἵνα in classic Greek has always a telic force, they deny that it is ever used ecbatically in the New Testament, even in such cases as Luke xxii. 30, " I appoint unto you a kingdom, ... in order that ye may eat and drink at my table." John vi. 7, " Two hundred pennyworth of bread is not sufficient for them, in order that every one of them may have a little." Romans xi. 11, " Have they stumbled with the design that they should fall ? "   1 Corinthians xiv. 13, " Let him that speaketh in an unknown tongue pray in order that he may interpret," etc., etc.   Thus, also, because the words πιστεύω, πίστις, and πιστός in the classics are rarely found in construction with the preposition ἐν, they give the most unnatural interpretation to many passages in order to avoid admitting that construction in the New Testament.   This is done in the face of such passages as Mark i. 15, πιστεύετε ἐν τῷ εὐαγγελίῳ.   Galatians iii. 26, " Ye are all the

children of God, διὰ τῆς πίστεως ἐν Χριστῷ Ἰησοῦ.   Ephesians i. 15,
" After I heard of your, πίστιν ἐν τῷ Κυρίῳ Ἰησοῦ," and many others
of like kind.   In like manner because the instrumental force of
ἐν is rare in the classics, it is avoided as much as possible in the
Scriptures.   Baptism ἐν πνεύματι, instead of being understood as
meaning a baptism by, or with the Spirit, is made to mean " in
the sphere of the Spirit," and baptism ἐν πυρί, baptism " in the
sphere of fire."   What this means, it would be difficult for most
of those for whom the Bible is intended to understand.   The baptism of John and that of Christ are contrasted.   The one baptized
with water , the other with the Holy Spirit.   In Acts i. 5, it is
said, " John truly baptized with water (ὕδατι, the simple instrumental dative); but ye shall be baptized (ἐν Πνεύματι ἁγίῳ) with
the Holy Ghost not many days hence."   As to baptize ὕδατι cannot mean to immerse in water, so neither can baptizing ἐν τῷ
Πνεύματι mean immersing in the Spirit.   The fact is βαπτίζειν does
not express any particular mode of action.   As to dye, expresses
any kind of action by which an object is coloured; to bury, any
kind of action by which an object is hidden and protected; so to
baptize, expresses any act by which a person or thing is brought
into the state of being wet, purified, or even stupefied, as by
opium or wine.

Another passage in which this word occurs where the idea of
immersion is precluded, is 1 Corinthians x. 1, 2, " All our fathers
were under the cloud, and all passed through the sea ; and were
all baptized unto Moses in the cloud and in the sea."   The people went through the sea dry shod.   As far as known not a drop
of water touched them.   The cloud referred to was doubtless the
pillar of cloud by day and the pillar of fire by night which guided
the people through the wilderness.   The simple and generally
accepted meaning of the passage is, that as a man is brought by
Christian baptism into the number of the professed and avowed
disciples of Christ, so the Hebrews were brought by the supernatural manifestations of divine power specified, into the relation
of disciples and followers to Moses.   There is no allusion to immersion, affusion, or sprinkling in the case.

Another passage belonging to this class is Mark vii. 4, " When
they come from the market, except they wash (βαπτίσωνται), they
eat not.   And many other things there be, which they have
received to hold, as the washing of cups, and pots, brazen vessels, and of tables (κλινῶν, couches)."   To maintain that beds or
couches were immersed, is a mere act of desperation.   Baptism

means here, as it does everywhere when used of a religious rite, symbolical purification by water, without the slightest reference to the mode in which that purification was effected.

3. The third class of passages includes all those in which the idea of immersion, though not absolutely precluded, is to the last degree improbable. The late Dr. Edward Robinson, than whom there is no higher authority on all that relates to the topography and physical geography of Palestine and the habits of its inhabitants, so far as they are determined by the nature of the country, says : (1.) " The idea of private baths in families in Jerusalem and Palestine generally is excluded." (2.) " In Acts ii. 41, three thousand persons are said to have been baptized at Jerusalem apparently in one day at the season of Pentecost in June ; and in Acts iv. 4, the same rite is necessarily implied in respect to five thousand more. Against the idea of full immersion in these cases there lies a difficulty, apparently insuperable, in the scarcity of water. There is in summer no running stream in the vicinity of Jerusalem, except the mere rill of Siloam a few rods in length ; and the city is and was supplied with water from its cisterns and public reservoirs.[1] From neither of these sources could a supply have been well obtained for the immersion of eight thousand persons. The same scarcity of water forbade the use of private baths as a general custom ; and thus also further precludes the idea of bathing" in such passages as Luke xi. 38 ; Mark vii. 2–8. He confirms his conclusion by further remarking, (3.) " In the earliest Latin versions of the New Testament, as, for example, the Itala, which Augustine regarded as the best of all,[2] which goes back apparently to the second century and to usage connected with the apostolic age, the Greek verb, βαπτίζω, is uniformly given in the Latin form, " baptizo," and is never translated by "immergo," or any like word, showing that there was something in the rite of baptism to which the latter did not correspond.[3] (4.) The baptismal fonts still found[4] among the ruins of the most ancient Greek churches in Palestine, as at Tekoa and Gophna, and going back apparently to very early times, are not large enough to admit of the baptism of adult persons by immersion, and were obviously never intended for that use." [5]

[1] See *Biblical Researches in Palestine*, vol. i. pp. 479–516.

[2] *De Doctrina Christiana*, ii. 22 [xv.]; *Works*, edit. Benedictines, Paris, 1836, vol. iii. p. 54, d.

[3] See Blanchini, *Evangeliorum Quadruplex*, etc., Rom. 1749.

[4] See Robinson's *Biblical Researches in Palestine*, edit. Boston, 1841, vol. ii. p. 182; vol. iii. p. 78.

[5] See Robinson's *Lexicon of the New Testament*, word βαπτίζω. New York. 1850

It is, therefore, to the last degree improbable that the thousands mentioned in the early chapters of Acts were baptized by immersion. The same improbability exists as to the case of the centurion in Cæsarea and the jailer at Philippi. With regard to the former, Peter said, " Can any man forbid water? " which naturally implies that water was to be brought to Cornelius, and not he be taken to the water. As to the jailer, it is said (Acts xvi. 33) that he and all his were baptized within the prison, as the narrative clearly implies, at midnight. There is the same improbability against the assumption that the eunuch, mentioned in Acts viii. 27–38, was baptized by immersion. He was travelling through a desert part of the country towards Gaza, when Philip joined him, " And as they went on their way they came unto a certain water (ἐπί τι ὕδωρ, to some water)." There is no known stream in that region of sufficient depth to allow of the immersion of a man. It is possible, indeed, that there might have been a reservoir or tank in that neighbourhood. But that is a fact to be assumed without evidence and against probability. It is said they " went down both into the water," and came " up out of the water." But that might be said, if the water were not deep enough to cover their ankles.

The presumption is still stronger against immersion in the case mentioned in Mark vii. 4. It is there said of "the Pharisees and all the Jews," that "when they come from the market, except they baptize themselves (ἐὰν μὴ βαπτίσωνται) they eat not." Let it be here considered, (1.) That private baths were in Jerusalem very rare, from the necessity of the case. (2.) That what is said, is not said merely of men of wealth and rank who might be supposed to have conveniences and luxuries which the common people could not command. It is said of the " Pharisees," a large class, and not only of that class, but of " all the Jews." It is wellnigh incredible, under such circumstances, that " all the Jews " should immerse themselves every time they came from the ἀγορά, i. e., " a place of public resort in towns and cities ; any open place, where the people came together either for business or to sit and converse. In oriental cities such open places were at the inside of the gates ; and here public business was transacted, and tribunals held, as also markets." [1] That all the Jews immersed themselves every time they came from such a place of public resort, is very hard to believe, considering that the facilities for such immersion were not at their command. (3.) The

---

[1] Robinson, *sub voce.*

words baptize and wash are interchanged in this whole connection in such a way as to show that, in the mind of the writer, they were synonymous expressions. The Pharisees complained that the disciples ate with unwashen (ἀνίπτοις) hands; for they eat not unless they wash (νίψωνται) their hands; and when they come from the market they do not eat unless they wash (βαπτίσωνται); and they hold to the washing (βαπτισμούς) of cups, and pots, of brazen vessels, and of tables or couches. To baptize the hands was to wash the hands, and the usual mode of ablution in the east is by pouring water on the hands (see 2 Kings iii. 11).

It is notorious that the various ablutions prescribed by the Mosaic law were effected sometimes by immersion, sometimes by affusion, and sometimes by sprinkling. And it is no less true that all these modes of purification are called by the sacred writers διάφοροι βαπτισμοί, as in Hebrews ix. 10, and Mark vii. 4.

So far, therefore, as the New Testament is concerned, there is not a single case where baptism necessarily implies immersion; there are many cases in which that meaning is entirely inadmissible, and many more in which it is in the highest degree improbable. If immersion were indispensable, why was not the word καταδύω used to express the command? If sprinkling were exclusively intended, why was not ῥαίνω or ῥαντίζω used? It is simply because the mode is nothing and the idea everything, that a word was chosen which includes all the modes in which water can be applied as the means of purification. Such a word is βαπτίζω, for which there is no legitimate substitute, and therefore that word has been retained by all the Churches of Christendom, even by the Baptists themselves.

The Patristic Usage.

This is a wide and densely wooded field, in which a man may find anything he chooses to look for, unless it be for proof that the fathers always used the word βαπτίζω in the sense of immersion. They speak of the waters of chaos as baptized by the Spirit of God brooding over them; they were thereby sanctified and a sanctifying power was imparted to the waters. The only point of interest here is, that Tertullian, for example, regarded this as "baptismi figura," a figure of baptism. The point of resemblance assuredly was not immersion.

But besides this, Suicer gives and copiously illustrates, from the writing of the fathers, no less than eight "significations of the word baptism (vocis βάπτισμα significationes)." (1.) The deluge was a baptism, not only for the world, purging away its sins, but also for Noah and his family, as a means of salvation. As they were saved by the waters buoying up the ark, so are we saved by baptism. (2.) The baptism of Moses when he passed through the Red Sea. The sea was the symbol of the water of baptism ; the cloud, of the Holy Spirit. (3.) That of the Hebrews, as among them any person or thing impure, ἐλούετο ὕδατι, was washed with water. This washing, however done, was baptism. (4.) The baptism of John, which was regarded as introductory, not spiritual, or conferring the Spirit, but simply leading to repentance. (5.) The baptism of Jesus. Βαπτίζει Ιησοῦς, ἀλλ᾽ ἐν πνεύματι. Here immersion is precluded. (6.) Of tears, διὰ δακρύων. " I know a fifth," says Gregory Nazianzen,[1] " by tears, but very laborious, when a man washes (ὁ λούων) his pillow and his bed every night with his tears." (7.) Of blood. The martyrs were baptized with blood. Christ's cross and death were called his baptism, because thereby purification was made for the sins of men. (8.) The baptism of fire. This is sometimes understood of the Holy Spirit, who purifies as fire does ; at others of the final conflagration when the earth is to be purified by fire. With the fathers, therefore, the act of purification, and not simply or only the act of immersion, was baptism.[2]

It is not denied that βαπτίζειν means to immerse, or that it is frequently so used by the fathers as by the classic authors ; it is not denied that the Christian rite was often administered, after the apostolic age, by immersion ; it is not even denied that during certain periods of the history of the Church, and in certain regions, immersion was the common method in which baptism was administered. But it is denied that immersion is essential to baptism ; that it was the common method in the apostolic Churches ; that it was at any time or in any part of the Church the exclusive method ; and more especially is it denied that immersion is now and everywhere obligatory or necessary to the integrity of Christian baptism.[3]

[1] *Oratio* xxxix.; *Opera*, Cologne, 1630, vol. i. p. 634.

[2] Joh. Caspari Suiceri, *Thesaurus Ecclesiasticus e Patribus Græcis ordine alphabetico exhibens Quæcunque Phrases, Ritus, Dogmata, Hæreses, et hujusmodi alia spectant. Opus viginti annorum indefesso labore adornatum*, 2d edit., Amsterdam, 1728.

[3] See Hermann Cremer, *Biblisch-Theologisches Wörterbuch der Neutestamentlichen Grä-cität*, Gotha, 1866. After referring to the Old Testament ablutions the author says, on p. 87: " We must, therefore, by βαπτίζειν understand a washing, the design of which, as of the theocratical washings and purifications, was the purification of the soul from sin (Entsündigung)." On p. 89 it is said, " We find the secondary meaning of βαπτίζειν in Matthew iii. 11: Βαπτ. ἐν πνεύματι ἁγίῳ καὶ πυρί, opp. ἐν ὕδατι εἰς μετάνοιαν, comp. Luke iii. 16; John i. 33. That it is not the meaning of immersion, but of ' washing with the design of

The Catholicity of the Gospel.

The third general argument on this subject is derived from the fact that the Gospel is designed for all classes of persons and for all parts of the earth. It is not intended exclusively for the strong and robust, but also for the weak, the sick, and the dying. It is not to be confined to the warm or temperate regions of the earth, but it is to be preached and its ordinances are to be administered wherever fallen men can be found. Baptism by immersion would be to many of the sick certainly fatal; to the dying impossible. To the inhabitants of Greenland, if possible, it would be torture; and to those dwelling in the deserts of Arabia or Africa, it could be administered only at long intervals or at the end of a long pilgrimage. Yet baptism is an imperative duty. The command of Christ is, "Go ye, therefore, and teach all nations, baptizing them in the name of the Father, and of the Son, and of the Holy Ghost." It is not to be believed that our blessed Lord would have enjoined an external rite as the mode of professing his religion, the observance of which, under many circumstances, would be exceedingly difficult, and sometimes impossible.

Argument from the Design of the Ordinance.

This argument was adverted to in the beginning of this section. It requires, however, a more particular consideration. (1.) It is admitted that baptism is a sign, and that the blessing which it signifies is purification from sin. (2.) It is admitted that the theocratical purifications, having the same general import, were effected by immersion, affusion, and sprinkling. (3.) It is admitted that the soul is cleansed from the guilt of sin by the blood of Christ. (4.) It is admitted that under the Old Testament the application of the blood of the sacrifices for sin was expressed by the act of sprinkling. It was sprinkled on the people (Ex. xxiv. 8) for whose benefit the sacrifices were offered; it was sprinkled upon the altar; and, by the High Priest, upon the mercy seat. In the New Testament the application of the blood of Christ is expressed by the same word. "Elect . . . . unto . . . . sprinkling of the blood of Jesus Christ." (1 Pet. i. 2.) "The blood of sprinkling, that speaketh better things than that of Abel." (Heb. xii. 24,) (5.) It is admitted, further, that the purification of the soul from the moral pollution of sin is effected by the renewing

purification,' that is transferred, is plain from the antithesis between ἐν ὕδ. and ἐν πν., whereby the two baptisms are distinguished."

of the Holy Ghost. (6.) It is admitted that the communication of the sanctifying influences of the Spirit is expressed in the use of two familiar figures, that of anointing with oil, and that of the pouring of water. Kings, priests, and prophets were anointed. The people of God are called his " anointed." The Apostle John says to believers : " Ye have an unction from the Holy One, and ye know all things. . . . . The anointing which ye have received of Him abideth in you." (1 John ii. 20 and 27.) The other figure is no less familiar. (Is. xxxii. 15; Joel ii. 28.) The Spirit's influences are compared to rain which waters the earth, and to the dew which falls on the mown grass. From all this it appears that the truth symbolized in baptism may be signified by immersion, affusion, or sprinkling; but that the ordinance is most significant and most conformed to Scripture, when administered by affusion or sprinkling.

§ 8. *The Formula of Baptism.*

This is authoritatively prescribed in Matthew xxviii. 19. Christ gave a command perpetually binding on his Church to baptize men "in the name of the Father, and of the Son, and of the Holy Ghost." In this passage the preposition εἰς (εἰς τὸ ὄνομα) means unto, or, in reference to. Paul asks the Corinthians " were ye baptized εἰς τὸ ὄνομα Παύλου;" (1 Cor. i. 13. Did your baptism make you the disciples of Paul?) He tells them (1 Cor. x. 2) that the fathers, " were baptized unto Moses " εἰς τὸν Μωσήν, they were made and professed to be the disciples of Moses. So in Romans vi. 3, it is said we " were baptized εἰς Χριστὸν Ιησοῦν unto Jesus Christ." Galatians iii. 27, " Baptized into (εἰς) Christ." According to this formula, he who receives baptism as a Christian rite, thereby professes to stand in that relation to the Father, Son, and Spirit which those who receive the religion of Christ sustain. That is, he professes to receive God the Father, as his father ; God the Son, as his Saviour, and God the Holy Ghost as his teacher and sanctifier ; and this involves the engagement to receive the Word, of which the Spirit is the author, as the rule of his faith and practice.[1]

[1] Fritzsche on Romans vi. 3, says: "Loquutio, βαπτίζω τινὰ εἰς τινα (εἰς τι) per se non minus late patet, quam vernacula Jemanden auf Jemanden (aut etwas) taufen. Non enim nisi hanc generalem notionem complectitur: aliquem aquæ ita immergere, ut ejus cogitationes in aliquem (aliquod) dirigas, Jemanden unter Beziehung, Hindeutung auf jemanden (etwas) taufen. At multis de causis ei qui lavatur res memorabilis monstrari potest, v. c., ut in aliquo fidem collocet, ut aliquem ducem sequatur, ut aliquid pie revereatur, ut aliquid effectum reddat, ut aliquid sibi evenisse sciat et sic porro. . . . . Sic dubitare non potest, quin βαπτίζω τινά εἰς Χριστόν (Gal. iii. 27), aquæ aliquem sic immergere, ut animum ad

There are several cases in which baptism is said to have been administered ἐν τῷ ὀνόματι in, or on, the name of Christ, instead of εἰς τὸ ὄνομα into, or, in reference to. And in Acts ii. 38, the preposition ἐπί is used, ἐπὶ τῷ ὀνόματι. It is doubtful whether anything materially different was intended to be expressed by this change of the prepositions and cases. To baptize, ἐπί or ἐν ὀνόματι, means to baptize "upon the name," sc., of Christ, that is, upon the authority of Christ. The rite is administered in obedience to his command, in the form in which he prescribed, and with the intent for which he ordained it.

In the Acts it is repeatedly said that the Apostles baptized their converts in "the name of Christ." It is not to be inferred from this fact that they departed from the form prescribed in Matthew xxviii. 19, and administered the ordinance in the use of the words, ' I baptize thee in the name of Christ;' or, ' I baptize thee εἰς Χριστόν unto Christ.' Such inference is unnecessary; as baptism administered in the way prescribed in Matthew xxviii. 19, is a baptism both in the name, or, by the authority of Christ, and unto or in reference to Him. As this inference is unnecessary so it is improbable. It is in the highest degree improbable that the Apostles would have departed from the form so solemnly prescribed by their Divine Master; and it is moreover improbable that any such departure took place from the fact that the form prescribed in Matthew has been used in all ages and parts of the Church.

§ 9. *The Subjects of Baptism.*

" Baptism is not to be administered to any that are out of the visible Church, till they profess their faith in Christ and obedience to Him : but the infants of such as are members of the visible Church are to be baptized." [1]

The question, Who are the proper subjects of baptism ? is determined by the design of the ordinance and the practice of the Apostles. It has been shown that, according to our standards, the sacraments (and of course baptism) were instituted, to signify, seal, and apply to believers the benefits of the redemption of Christ. The reception of baptism, so far as adults are concerned, is an intelligent, voluntary act, which from its nature in-

---

Christum applicare eum jubeas, valeat ita aliquem aqua lustrare ut Christo fidem habendam esse ei significes (Act. xix. 4), et βαπτίζω τινα εἰς τὸ ὄνομα τοῦ Πατρός, κτλ. . . . . notet lustro aliquem reverentia, quæ Patris — nomini debeatur, eum obstringens." Edit. Halle, 1836, vol. i. pp. 359, 360.

[1] *Westminster Shorter Catechism*, quest. 95.

volves, (1.) A profession of faith in Christ, and (2.) A promise of allegiance to Him.

This is clear, —

1. From the command of Christ to make disciples of all nations, baptizing them in the name of the Father, of the Son, and of the Holy Ghost. A disciple, however, is both a recipient of doctrines taught, and a follower. Every one, therefore, who is made a disciple by baptism, enrolls himself among the number of those who receive Christ as their teacher and Lord, and who profess obedience and devotion to his service.

2. This is further clear from the uniform practice of the Apostles. In every case on record of their administering the rite, it was on the condition of a profession of faith on the part of the recipient. The answer of Philip to the eunuch who asked, What doth hinder me to be baptized? "If thou believest with all thine heart thou mayest," discloses the principle on which the Apostles uniformly acted in this matter.

3. This has in all ages been the practice of the Church. No man was admitted to baptism without an intelligent profession of faith in Christ, and a solemn engagement of obedience to Him. The practice of Romanist missionaries in baptizing the heathen in crowds, can hardly be considered as invalidating this statement.

Although this has been the principle universally admitted, there has been no little diversity as to its application, according to the different views of the nature of the faith, and of the character of the obedience required by the Gospel. In some points, however, there has ever been a general agreement.

Qualifications for Adult Baptism.

1. Faith supposes knowledge of at least the fundamental doctrines of the Gospel. Some may unduly enlarge, and some unduly restrict the number of such doctrines; but no Church advocates the baptism of the absolutely ignorant. If baptism involves a profession of faith, it must involve a profession of faith in certain doctrines; and those doctrines must be known, in order to be professed. In the early Church, therefore, there was a class of catechumens or candidates for baptism who were under a regular course of instruction. This course continued, according to circumstances, from a few months, to three years. These catechumens were not only young men, but often persons in mature life, and of all degrees of mental culture. Where Christian

churches were established in the midst of large heathen cities, the Gospel could not fail to excite general attention. The interest of persons of all classes would be more or less awakened. Many would be so impressed with the excellence of the new religion, as to desire to learn its doctrines and join themselves to the company of believers. These candidates for baptism, being in many cases men of the highest culture, it was necessary that their teachers should be men thoroughly instructed and disciplined. We accordingly find such men as Pantænus, Clemens, and Origen successively at the head of the catechetical school of Alexandria.[1] These schools, although primarily designed for converts from among the Jews and heathen, on account of their high character, soon began to be frequented by other classes, and especially by those who were in training for the ministry. When Christianity became the prevalent religion, and the ranks of the Church were filled up, not by converts of mature age, but by those born within its pale and baptized in their infancy, the necessity for such schools no longer existed. Their place, however, was supplied by the systematic instruction of the young in preparation for their confirmation or their first communion.

2. All churches are agreed in demanding of adults who are candidates for baptism, a profession of their faith in Christ and the Gospel of his salvation.

3. They agree in requiring of those who are baptized the renunciation of the world, the flesh, and the devil. This involves a turning from sin, and a turning to God.

Although these principles are, as just remarked, generally admitted, there is, in practice, great diversity in their application. Where the Church was pure and its ministers faithful, these requisitions were strenuously enforced ; but where the reverse was the case, the most formal, and often evidently insincere, assent to the creed of the Church was taken for a profession of faith ; and a renunciation of the world compatible with devotion to its pleasures and its sins, was accepted in the place of genuine repentance. It is well, however, to have a clear idea of what the Church has a right to demand of adults when they apply for baptism. It is evident from the teachings of Scripture, and from the avowed principles of all Christian churches, that we are bound to require of all such candidates, (1.) A competent knowledge of the Gospel. (2.) A credible profession of faith. (3.) A conversation void of offence.

---

[1] H. E. F. Guerike, *De Schola quæ Alexandriæ floruit, catechetica,* Halle, 1824.

The question, although thus simple in its general statement, is nevertheless one of great difficulty. As it is almost universally the fact that, so far as adults are concerned, the qualifications for baptism are the same as those for admission to the Lord's table, the question, What are the qualifications for adult baptism ? resolves itself into the question, What are the qualifications for church-membership ? The answer to that question, it is evident, must be determined by the views taken of the nature and the prerogatives of the Church. We accordingly find that there are three general views of the qualifications for adult baptism, founded on the three generic views of the nature of the Church.

Romish Theory of the Church.

First, the theory derived from the ancient theocracy and from the analogy between the Church and a civil commonwealth. The theocracy, or the Church, under the old dispensation, was essentially an externally organized body. All the natural descendants of Abraham, through Isaac, were, in virtue of their birth, members of the " Commonwealth of Israel." As such, independently of their own moral character or that of their parents, they were entitled to all the privileges of the economy under which they lived. They were freely admitted to the services of the Temple, to the Passover, and to all the sacred festivals, and typical institutions of the Mosaic dispensation, even to those which were truly of a sacramental character. The Hebrews were, of course, subject to the laws of the theocracy under which they lived; for minor offences they forfeited this or that privilege, or were subjected to some specified penalty ; and for graver offences they were excommunicated or cut off from among the people. All this finds a parallel in the kingdoms of this world. All native born Englishmen are subjects of the crown, and are entitled to all the privileges of Englishmen ; they may be good or bad citizens, but their citizenship does not depend upon their character ; they may be punished for their offences, but they cannot be deprived of their rights as citizens unless they are outlawed.

This theory has, by Romanists and Romanizers, been transferred bodily to the Church. The Church, according to them, is essentially an externally organized society. All born within its pale are " ipso facto " its members, and entitled to all its privileges. They are entitled to all its sacraments and ordinances, not in virtue of their character, but in virtue of their birthright. Thus Mr. Palmer,[1] of the Oxford Anglican School, says that the

[1] Palmer, *On the Church*, New York, 1841, vol. i. p. 377.

Scriptures make no mention of regeneration, sanctity, or real piety visible or invisible, as prerequisites for admission to the sacrament of baptism.[1]   No doubt a pious Hebrew priest would exhort those who came to offer sacrifices or to celebrate the Passover, that they should attend on those services in a devout spirit and in the exercise of faith, assuring them that the mere external service was of no account.   The Romanist, with his " ex opere operato " theory of the sacraments, could hardly go as far as that, but he would doubtless exhort the candidate for baptism, and all who come to the sacraments of the Church, to perform those duties in a proper spirit.   But this has nothing to do with the right of approach.   We may exhort citizens to exercise their civil rights conscientiously, and with a due regard to the interests of the country, but the rights themselves are not to be disputed.

The same result is reached, although on a different theory, in all those countries in which Church and State are so united that the head of the State is the head of the Church ; and that membership in the Church is a condition of citizenship in the State. This was the case for centuries in England, and is so to a great extent to the present day.   The reigning sovereign is still the head of the Church, the supreme authority in administering its government.   The laws of the Church are acts of Parliament; every Englishman, unless he voluntarily makes himself an exception, has a right to all the services of the Church, including the right to be buried as a Christian " in the sure hope of a blessed resurrection."   Until of late years no man could hold any important office, especially in the army or navy, who was not in communion with the established Church.   So also in Prussia, the head of the State governs the Church.   No man, unless a Romanist or a Hebrew, can marry, become an apprentice, or enter on the practice of a profession without producing a certificate of baptism and confirmation.

Puritan Theory of the Church.

The second general theory of the nature of the Church is that, which for convenience sake, may be called the Puritan.   The word Puritan has in history a much wider sense than that assigned to it in modern usage.   In English history the designation Puritan was applied to all those, who under the reigns of Eliza-

---

[1] This is not inconsistent with what was said above of all churches requiring as the conditions of adult baptism, competent knowledge, a profession of faith, and the renunciation of the world.   What was there said concerned the reception of members into the Church, *ab extra*.   What is here said concerns those who are members of the Church by birth.

beth and Charles I. were desirous of a further reformation of the Church. Many prelates, and thousands of Episcopalians and Presbyterians, were included in that class. Modern usage has confined the term to the Independents or Congregationalists, the followers of Brown and Robinson. They were, therefore, often called Brownists. According to them the visible Church consists of the regenerate ; and it is the duty and the prerogative of the Church to sit in judgment on the question whether the applicant for admission to the sacraments is truly born of God. Hence in New England, there was a broad distinction made between the Church and the parish. The former consisted of the body of communicants ; the latter of those who, though not communicants, frequented the same place of worship and contributed to the support of the minister and to other congregational expenses. " To join the Church," thus came to mean joining the number of those who were admitted to the Lord's Supper. This of course implies, that communicants only are in the Church. This view has gained ascendancy in this country even, to a great extent, among Presbyterians.

The Common Protestant Theory.

According to our standards the visible Church consists of all those who profess the true religion together with their children. The common Protestant theory of the Church agrees with that of the Puritans in the following points. (1.) That the true or invisible Church as a whole consists of the elect. This is the Church which Christ loved, for which He gave Himself, that He might sanctify it, and present it to Himself a glorious Church without spot or wrinkle. (Eph. v. 25–27.) (2.) That the true or invisible Church on earth consists of all true believers. (3.) That the profession of faith made by those who are baptized, or come to the table of the Lord, is a profession of true faith. That is, those baptized profess to be Christians. The point of difference between the theories concerns the duty and prerogative of the Church in the matter. According to the one view the Church is bound to be satisfied in its judgment that the applicant is truly regenerate ; according to the other, no such judgment is expressed or implied in receiving any one into the fellowship of the Church. As Christ has not given his people the power to search the heart, He has not imposed upon them the duty which implies the possession of any such power. Both parties require a credible profession of faith on the part of the

applicant for membership.   But the one means by credible, that
which constrains belief ; the other, that which may be believed,
i. e., that against which no tangible evidence can be adduced.   If
such applicant be a heretie, or if his manner of life contradicts
his profession, he ought not to be received ; and if already in the
Church, he ought, as the Apostle says, to be rejected.   The common Protestant doctrine is that nothing authorizes us to refuse a
man admission to the Church, which would not justify his exclusion if already a member of it.   If guilty of any " offence " or
" scandal," he ought to be excluded ; and if chargeable with any
such " offence " or " scandal," he ought not to be admitted to
membership, no matter what his profession or detail of experience
may be.   The late Dr. John M. Mason clearly and forcibly expresses the common doctrine on this subject, when he says : " A
credible profession of Christianity, is all that she [the Church]
may require in order to communion.   She may be deceived ; her
utmost caution may be, and often has been, ineffectual to keep
bad men from her sanctuary.   And this, too, without her fault,
as she is not omniscient.   But she has no right to suspect sincerity, to refuse privilege, or inflict censure, where she can put
her finger upon nothing repugnant to the love or the laws of
God." [1]   And on the following page he says : " A profession of
faith in Christ, and of obedience to Him, not discredited by
other traits of character, entitles an adult to the privileges of his
Church."

This is not the place for the discussion of the question concerning the nature of the Church.   These theories are simply mentioned here because of their bearing on the subject of adult baptism.   According to all these theories believing adults are, by the
command of Christ, entitled to Christian baptism.   Much more
difficulty attends the question concerning

§ 10. *Infant Baptism.*

The difficulty on this subject is that baptism from its very
nature involves a profession of faith ; it is the way in which by
the ordinance of Christ, He is to be confessed before men ; but
infants are incapable of making such confession ; therefore they
are not the proper subjects of baptism.   Or, to state the matter
in another form : the sacraments belong to the members of the
Church ; but the Church is the company of believers ; infants

[1] *Essays on the Church of God*, by John M. Mason, D. D., New York, 1843, Essay III.
p. 57.

cannot exercise faith, therefore they are not members of the Church, and consequently ought not to be baptized.

In order to justify the baptism of infants, we must attain and authenticate such an idea of the Church as that it shall include the children of believing parents. The word Church is used in Scripture and in common life, in many different senses, (1.) It means the whole body of the elect, as in Ephesians v. 25, and when the Church is said to be the body, or the bride of Christ, to be filled by his Spirit, etc.   (2.) It means any number of believers collectively considered ; or the whole number of believers residing in any one place, or district, or throughout the world. In this sense we use the word when we pray God to bless his Church universal, or his Church in any particular place. (3.) It is used as a collective term for the body of professed believers in any one place ; as when we speak of the Church of Jerusalem, of Ephesus, or of Corinth.   (4.) It is used of any number of professed believers bound together by a common standard of doctrine and discipline ; as the Church of England, the Church of Scotland, the Lutheran Church, and the Reformed Church.   And (5.) It is used for all the professors of the true religion throughout the world, considered as united in the adoption of the same general creed and in common subjection to Christ.

It is evident that no one definition of the Church can include all the senses in which the word is legitimately used ; and, therefore, that we may affirm of the Church in one sense of the word, what must be denied of it in a different sense ; and the same person may be said to be, or not to be a member of the Church according to the meaning attached to the word. In the present discussion, by the Church is meant what is called the visible Church ; that is, the whole body of those who profess the true religion, or, any number of such professors united for the purpose of the public worship of Christ, and for the exercise of mutual watch and care. With regard to infant baptism the following propositions may be maintained.

First Proposition.   The Visible Church is a Divine Institution.

Concerning the Church in this sense, it is clearly taught in Scripture, that it is the will of God that such a Church should exist on earth. This no Christian denies. God has imposed duties upon his people which render it necessary for them thus to associate in a visible organized body. They are to unite in his worship ; in teaching and propagating his truth ; in testifying for

God in all ages and in all parts of the world. He has prescribed the conditions of membership in this body, and taught who are to be excluded from its communion. He has appointed officers, specified their qualifications, their prerogatives, and the mode of their appointment. He has enacted laws for its government. Its rise, progress, and consummation are traced in history and prophecy, from the beginning to the end of the Bible. This is the kingdom of God of which our Lord discourses in so many of his parables, and which it is predicted is ultimately to include all the nations of the earth.

Second Proposition.   The Visible Church does not consist exclusively of the Regenerate.

It is no less clearly revealed that it is not the purpose of God that the visible Church on earth should consist exclusively of true believers. This is plain, (1.) Because the attainment of such a result in any society or government administered by men is an impossibility. It would require that the officers of the Church or the Church itself should have the power to read the heart, and be infallible in judgments of character. (2.) The conditions which, under both dispensations, He has prescribed for admission into this visible society of his professed worshippers, are such as men not truly regenerated may possess. Those qualifications, as we have seen, are competent knowledge, and a credible profession of faith and obedience. (3.) Our Lord expressly forbids the attempt being made. He compares his external kingdom, or visible Church, to a field in which tares and wheat grow together. He charged his disciples not to undertake to separate them, because they could not, in all cases, distinguish the one from the other. Both were to be allowed to grow together until the harvest. (4.) Christ, to whom all hearts are known, admitted Judas to the number of his most favoured disciples, and even made him an Apostle. (5.) All attempts to make a Church consisting exclusively of the regenerate, have failed. So far as known, no such Church has ever existed on the face of the earth. This of itself is proof that its existence did not enter into the purpose of God.

Third Proposition.   The Commonwealth of Israel was the Church.

(1.) It is so called in Scripture. (Acts vii. 38.) (2.) The Hebrews were called out from all the nations of the earth to be the peculiar people of God. They constituted his kingdom. (3.) To them were committed the oracles of God. They were Israelites; to them pertained the adoption, and the glory, and the covenants, and the giving of the law, and the service, and the promises. (Rom. ix. 4.) Nothing more can be said of the Church under the new dispensation. They were selected for a Church purpose, namely, to be witnesses for God in the world in behalf of the true religion; to celebrate his worship; and to observe his ordinances. Their religious officers, prophets, and priests, were appointed by God and were his ministers. No man could become a member of the Commonwealth of Israel, who did not profess the true religion; promise obedience to the law of God as revealed in his Word; and submit to the rite of circumcision as the seal of the covenant. There is no authorized definition of the Church, which does not include the people of God under the Mosaic law.

Fourth Proposition. The Church under the New Dispensation is identical with that under the Old.

It is not a new Church, but one and the same. It is the same olive-tree. (Rom. xi. 16, 17.) It is founded on the same covenant, the covenant made with Abraham. It has, indeed, often been said that it is to belittle the truth to put the idea of a covenant between God and man in the place of a general law or economy. It is, however, to be remembered that God is a person, capable of speaking with other persons, of promising and threatening. These promises are not merely announcements of the results of cosmical laws, physical or moral. That Christ should be born of the seed of Abraham, of the tribe of Judah, and of the house of David, is not to be attributed to the working of any general law. Nothing pertaining to his advent, his person, his work, or to the application of his redemption, is to be accounted for in any such way. Our Lord gives us an infinitely higher idea of God's relation to the world when He tells us that He feeds the young ravens when they cry; and that the hairs of our heads are all numbered; than when He is regarded as merely the author or source of the physical and moral order of the universe. A covenant is a promise suspended upon a condition. It is beyond controversy that God did make such a promise to Adam, to Abraham, and to the Hebrew nation through Moses; and these transactions are in Scripture constantly called covenants. It does not, therefore, seem very reverent to speak of God as belittling his truth by the form in which He presents it.

God, then, did enter into covenant with Abraham. In that covenant He promised that Abraham, although nearly a hundred years old, should have a son. He promised that his descendants, through Isaac, should be as numerous as the stars in heaven; that He would give them the land of Canaan for a possession; that He would be their national God, and that the Hebrews as a nation should be His peculiar people; and above all He promised the patriarch that in his seed all the nations of the earth should be blessed. By seed was not meant his descendants collectively, but one person, that is, Christ. (Gal. iii. 16.) The blessing promised, therefore, was the blessing of redemption through Christ, his promise to Abraham was a repetition of the promise made to our first parents after the fall, this promise was the Gospel. The Gospel or εὐαγγέλιον has a definite meaning in the Scriptures. It means the announcement of the plan of salvation through Christ, and the offer of that salvation to every one that believes. This Gospel, Paul says, was preached before unto Abraham. The pious Hebrews are, therefore, described as (τοὺς προηλπικότας ἐν τῷ Χριστῷ) those who hoped in Christ before his advent. (Eph. i. 12.) This promise of redemption made to Abraham was that " unto which," Paul says, " our twelve tribes, instantly serving God day and night, hope to come." (Acts xxvi. 7.) The condition of all these Abrahamic promises was faith. This the Apostle abundantly teaches, especially in the fourth chapter of Romans and the third chapter of Galatians. Abraham believed in the promise of the birth of Isaac. (Rom. iv. 19, 20.) Those of his descendants who believed in the promises of national blessings made to the Hebrews, received those blessings, those who believed in the promise of redemption through Christ were made partakers of that redemption.

Such being the nature of the covenant made with Abraham, it is plain that so far as its main element is concerned, it is still in force. It is the covenant of grace under which we now live, and upon which the Church is now founded. This cannot be doubted by any who admit the account just given of the Abrahamic covenant. This is clear because the promise is the same. Paul says (Gal. iii. 14) that the blessing promised to Abraham has come upon us. In his speech before Agrippa, he said: " I stand, and am judged for the hope of the promise made of God unto our fathers. . . . . For which hope's sake, king Agrippa, I am accused of the Jews." (Acts xxvi. 6, 7.) As the promise is the same, so also the condition is the same. The Apostle argues that men now

must be justified by faith, because Abraham was thus justified.
Christians, therefore, are said to be the sons or heirs of Abraham,
because faith in the promise of redemption secures their redemption just as faith in the same promise secured his.   And he tells
the Galatians, " If ye be Christ's, then are ye Abraham's seed,
and heirs according to the promise." (Gal. iii. 29.)   This doctrine, that the Church now rests on the Abrahamic covenant, in
other words, that the plan of salvation revealed in the Gospel
was revealed to Abraham and to the other Old Testament saints,
and that they were saved just as men since the advent of Christ
are saved, by faith in the promised seed, is not a matter incidentally revealed.   It is wrought into the very substance of the Gospel.   It is involved in all the teachings of our Lord, who said that
He came not to destroy, but to fulfil ; and who commanded in
quirers to search the Old Testament Scriptures if they would
learn what He taught.   The Apostles did the same thing.   The
Bereans were commended, because they searched the Scriptures
daily to see whether the doctrines taught by the Apostles ac-
corded with that infallible standard. (Acts xvii. 11.)   The messengers of Christ constantly quoted the Old Testament in support
of their teachings.   Paul says that the Gospel which he preached
had been taught already in the law and the prophets. (Rom. iii.
21.)   He tells the Gentiles that they were grafted in the old
olive-tree and made partakers of its root and fatness.

The conclusion is that God has ever had but one Church in the
world.   The Jehovah of the Old Testament is our Lord ; the
God of Abraham, Isaac, and Jacob, is our covenant God and
Father ; our Saviour was the Saviour of the saints who lived
before his advent in the flesh.   The divine person who delivered
the Israelites out of Egypt ; who led them through the wilderness ; who appeared in his glory to Isaiah in the temple ; towards
whose coming the eyes of the people of God were turned in faith
and hope from the beginning, is He whom we recognize as God
manifest in the flesh, our Lord and Saviour Jesus Christ.   He,
therefore, who was the head of the theocracy is the head of the
Church.   The blood which He shed for us, was shed from the
foundation of the world, as much " for the redemption of the
transgressions which were under the first testament " (Heb. ix.
15), as for us and for our salvation.   The promise unto which
the twelve tribes, instantly serving God day and night, hoped
to come (Acts xxvi. 7), is the promise on which we rely.   The
faith which saved Abraham was, both as to its nature and

as to its object, that which is the condition of salvation under the Gospel. " The city which hath foundations, whose builder and maker is God" (Heb. xi. 10), is "Jerusalem the golden," the heaven to which we aspire.

Fifth Proposition. The terms of admission into the Church before the Advent were the same that are required for admission into the Christian Church.

Those terms were a credible profession of faith in the true religion, a promise of obedience, and submission to the appointed rite of initiation. Every sincere Israelite really received Jehovah as his God, relied upon all his promises, and especially upon the promise of redemption through the seed of Abraham. He not only bound himself to obey the law of God as then revealed, but sincerely endeavoured to keep all his commandments. Those who were Israelites only in name or form, or, as the Apostle expresses it, were "Jews outwardly," made the same professions and engagements, but did so only with the lips and not with the heart. If any from among the heathen assayed to enter the congregation of the Lord, they were received upon the terms above specified, and to a place equal to, and in some cases better than, that of sons and of daughters. If any Israelite renounced the religion of his fathers, he was cut off from among the people. All this is true in reference to the Church that now is. The Christian Church requires of those whom it receives to membership in visible communion, nothing more than a credible profession of faith, the promise of obedience to Christ, and submission to baptism as the rite of initiation. There has, therefore, been no change of the terms of admission to the Church, effected by the introduction of the Gospel.

Sixth Proposition. Infants were Members of the Church under the Old Testament Economy.

This is conclusively proved by the fact that infants, by the command of God, were circumcised on the eighth day after their birth. It is indeed said that circumcision was the sign of the national covenant between God and the Hebrews; and, therefore, that its administration to children was only a recognition of their citizenship in the commonwealth of Israel.

To this it may be answered, first, that under the old economy, the Church and State were identical. No man could be a member of the one without being a member of the other. Exclusion

from the one was exclusion from the other. In the pure theocracy the high priest was the head of the State as well as the
head of the Church. The priests and Levites were civil as well as
religious officers. The sacrifices, and the festivals, even the Passover, ever regarded as a sacrament, were national as well as religious services. If, therefore, circumcision was a sign and seal of
membership in the Hebrew nation, it was a sign and seal of membership in the Hebrew Church. All this arose from the nature
of God's covenant with Abraham. In that covenant, as we have
seen, were included both national and religious promises. God
selected the descendants of that patriarch through Isaac to be a
people peculiar to himself, He constituted them a nation to be
secluded and hedged around from other nations, He gave them
the land of Canaan for a habitation, and He enacted for them
a code of laws, embracing their civil, national, social, personal,
and religious duties. All these enactments were mingled together. The people were not regarded as bearing distinct relations
to the magistrate and to God. All their obligations were to
Him. They were a holy people ; a Church in the form of a nation. The great promise, as we have seen, was the promise of
the redemption of the world by the Messiah. To this everything else was subordinate. The main design of the constitution
of the Hebrews as a distinct nation, and of their separation from
all other people, was to keep alive the knowledge of that promise.
Almost the whole significancy and value of the priesthood, sacrifices, and temple service, were to prefigure the person, offices, and
work of the Messiah. To the Hebrews as a people were committed the " oracles of God ; " this was their grand distinction.
Those oracles had reference to the great work of redemption.
To suppose a man to be a Jew, and not at least a professed believer in those promises and predictions, is a contradiction. A
man, therefore, was a member of the Jewish commonwealth, only
in virtue of his being a member of the Jewish Church ; at least,
he could not be the former without being the latter. Consequently, every child who was circumcised in evidence that he was
one of the chosen people, was thereby sealed as a member of the
Church of God as it then existed.

Secondly, that circumcision was not the sign exclusively of the
national covenant with the Hebrews, is plain because it was enjoined upon Abraham and continued in practice hundreds of years
before the giving of the law on Mount Sinai, when the people
were inaugurated as a nation. It was instituted as the sign of

the covenant (that is the Scriptural and proper word) made with Abraham. The essential features of that covenant we learn from such passages as Genesis xii. 3, " In thee shall all families of the earth be blessed." xvii. 7, " I will establish my covenant between me and thee, and thy seed after thee, in their generations, for an everlasting covenant, to be a God unto thee, and to thy seed after thee." These passages are explained in the New Testament. They are shown to refer, not to temporal or national blessings, but to the blessings of redemption. Thus in Romans xv. 8, it is said, " Jesus Christ was a minister of the circumcision for the truth of God, to confirm the promises made unto the fathers." Christ has redeemed us from the curse of the law, that the blessing of Abraham might come on us. (Gal. iii. 14.) This covenant, the Apostle goes on to argue, " that was confirmed before of God in Christ, the law, which was four hundred and thirty years after, cannot disannul, that it should make the promise of none effect." In short, the whole New Testament is designed to show that the covenant made with Abraham, and the promises therein contained, were executed and fulfilled in Jesus Christ. Of that covenant circumcision was the sign and seal.

Thirdly, this is directly asserted by the Apostle in Romans iv. 9–12, where he proves that circumcision cannot be the ground of justification, because Abraham was justified before he was circumcised, and " received the sign of circumcision, a seal of the righteousness of the faith which he had being yet uncircumcised." This is saying that circumcision is the seal of the covenant which promises salvation on the condition of faith. That is, it is the seal of the covenant of grace, or of the plan of salvation which has been the only ground of hope for man since his apostasy. If, therefore, children were circumcised by the command of God, it was because they were included in the covenant made with their fathers.

Fourthly, that circumcision was not merely a civil or national institution, is further plain from its spiritual import. It signifies the cleansing from sin, just as baptism now does. Thus we read even in the Old Testament of the circumcision of the heart. (Deut. x. 16 ; Jer. iv. 4 ; Ezek. xliv. 7.) Therefore uncircumcised lips are impure lips, and an uncircumcised heart is an unclean heart. (Ex. vi. 12 ; Lev. xxvi. 41. See, also, Acts vii. 51.) Paul says the true circumcision is not that which is outward in the flesh ; but that which is inward, of the heart, by the Spirit. (Rom. ii. 28, 29.) Therefore the Apostle speaking of himself and of other believers says, "We are the circumcision, which worship God in the Spirit, and rejoice in Christ Jesus, and have no confidence in the flesh." (Phil. iii. 3.) Such being the spiritual import of circumcision, its reference to the national covenant was a very subordinate matter. Its main design was to signify and seal the promise of deliverance from sin through the redemption to be effected by the promised seed of Abraham.

Children, therefore, were included in the covenant of grace as revealed under the old dispensation, and consequently were members of the Church as it was then constituted. In the sight of God parents and children are one. The former are the authorized representatives of the latter; they act for them; they contract obligations in their name. In all cases, therefore, where parents enter into covenant with God, they bring their children with them. The covenant made with Adam included all his posterity; the promise made to Abraham was to him and to his seed after him; and when the Mosaic covenant was solemnly inaugurated, it was said, " Ye stand this day all of you before the LORD your God; your captains of your tribes, your elders, and your officers, with all the men of Israel, your little ones, your wives, and thy stranger that is in thy camp, from the hewer of thy wood unto the drawer of thy water : that thou shouldst enter into covenant with the LORD thy God, and into his oath, which the LORD thy God maketh with thee this day." (Deut. xxix. 10–12.) It is vain to say that children cannot make contracts or take an oath. Their parents can act for them; and not only bring them under obligation, but secure for them the benefits of the covenants into which they thus vicariously enter. If a man joined the commonwealth of Israel he secured for his children the benefits of the theocracy, unless they willingly renounced them. And so when a believer adopts the covenant of grace, he brings his children within that covenant, in the sense that God promises to give them, in his own good time, all the benefits of redemption, provided they do not willingly renounce their baptismal engagements.

This is really the turning point in the controversy concerning infant church-membership. If the Church is one under both dispensations; if infants were members of the Church under the theocracy, then they are members of the Church now, unless the contrary can be proved. The next proposition, therefore, on this subject, to be established is, the

Seventh Proposition, that there is nothing in the New Testament which justifies the Exclusion of the Children of Believers from Membership in the Church.

The " onus probandi " rests on those who take the negative on this subject. If children are to be deprived of a birthright which they have enjoyed ever since there was a Church on earth, there must be some positive command for their exclusion, or some clearly revealed change in the conditions of membership, which renders such exclusion necessary. It need hardly be said that Christ did not give any command no longer to consider the children of believers as members of the Church, neither has there been any change in the conditions of church-membership which necessarily works their exclusion. Those conditions are now what they were from the beginning. It was inevitable, there-fore, when Christ commanded his Apostles to disciple all nations, baptizing them in the name of the Father, of the Son, and of the Holy Spirit, that they should act on the principle to which they had always been accustomed. When under the Old Testa-ment, a parent joined the congregation of the Lord, he brought his minor children with him. When, therefore, the Apostles baptized a head of a family, it was a matter of course, that they should baptize his infant children. We accordingly find several cases of such household baptism recorded in the Acts of the Apostles. In Acts xvi. 15, it is said Lydia " was baptized, and her household," and of the jailer at Philippi (ver. 33), that " he and all his " were baptized ; and in 1 Corinthians i. 16, Paul says that he baptized the household of Stephanas. The Apostles, therefore, acted on the principle which had always been acted on under the old economy. It is to be remembered that the history of the Apostolic period is very brief, and also that Christ sent the Apostles, not to baptize, but to preach the Gospel, and, therefore. it is not surprising that so few instances of household baptism are recorded in the New Testament. The same remark applies sub-stantially to the age immediately succeeding that of the Apostles. The Church increased with great rapidity, but its accessions were from without ; adult converts from among the Jews and Gentiles, who in becoming Christians, brought, as a matter of course, their children with them into the fold of Christ. Little, therefore, during this period is heard of the baptism of infants. As soon, however, as children born within the Church constituted the chief source of supply, then we hear more of baptisms for the dead; the ranks of the Church, as they were thinned by the decease of believers, being filled by those who were baptized to take their places. In the time of Tertullian and Origen infant baptism is spoken of, not only as the prevailing usage of the Church, but as having been practised from the beginning. When Pelagius was sorely pressed by Augustine with the argument in support of the doctrine of original sin derived from the baptism of infants, he did not venture to evade the argument by denying either the prevalence of such baptisms or the divine warrant for them. He could only say that they were baptized, not on account of what they then needed, but of what they might need hereafter. The fact of infant baptism and its divine sanction were admitted. These facts are here referred to only as a collateral proof that the practice of the New Testament Church did not in this matter differ from that of the Church as constituted before the advent of Christ.

The conduct of our Lord in relation to children, in its bearing on this subject must not be overlooked. So far from excluding them from the Church in whose bosom they had always been cherished, He called them the lambs of his flock, took them into his arms, and blessed them, and said, of such is the kingdom of heaven. If members of his kingdom in heaven, why should they be excluded from his kingdom on earth? Whenever a father or mother seeks admission to the Christian Church, their heart prompts them to say: Here Lord am I and the children whom thou hast given me. And his gracious answer has always been: Suffer little children to come unto me and forbid them not.

Eighth Proposition. Children need, and are capable of receiving the Benefits of Redemption.

On this point all Christians are agreed. All churches — the Greek, the Latin, the Lutheran, and the Reformed — unite in the belief that infants need "the sprinkling of the blood of Jesus Christ" and the renewing of the Holy Ghost in order to their salvation. The Reformed, at least, do not believe that those blessings are tied to the ordinance of baptism, so that the reception of baptism is necessary to a participation of the spiritual benefits which it symbolizes; but all agree that infants are saved by Christ, that they are the purchase of his blood, and that they need expiation and regeneration. They are united, also, in believing that all who seek the benefits of the work of Christ, are bound to be baptized in acknowledgment of its necessity and of their faith, and that those who need, but cannot seek, are, by the ordinance of God, entitled to receive the appointed sign and seal of redemption, whenever and wherever they are presented by those who have the right to represent them.

§ 11. *Whose Children are entitled to Baptism ?*

This is a very delicate, difficult, and important question. No answer which can be given to it can be expected to give general satisfaction. The answers will be determined by the views taken of the nature of the Church and the design of the sacraments. Probably the answer which would include most of the views entertained on the subject, is, that the children of the members of the visible Church, and those for whose religious training such members are willing to become responsible, should be baptized. But this leaves many questions undecided, and allows room for great diversity of practice.

Difference between the Jewish and Christian Usage.

We have already seen under the old dispensation, (1.) That God made a nation his Church and his Church a nation. (2.) Consequently that membership in the one involved membership in the other, and exclusion from the one, exclusion from the other. (3.) That the conditions of admission to the Church were, therefore, the same as the conditions of admission into the commonwealth. (4.) That those conditions were profession of faith in the true religion, and a promise of obedience to the will of God as revealed in his word. (5.) That the State exacted this profession and enforced this obedience so far as the external conduct was concerned. All the people were required to be circumcised, to offer sacrifices, to observe the festivals, and to frequent the temple services. And, (6.) That this was God's way of preserving the knowledge of the true religion in that age of the world. And it succeeded. When Christ came, the uncorrupted Scriptures were read in the synagogues ; the sacrifices as divinely appointed were offered in the temple ; the high priest in his offices and work still stood before the people, as the type of Him who was to come. Under this system there could be no question as to whose children were to be circumcised.

When Christ came and broke down the wall of partition between the Jews and Gentiles, and announced his Gospel as designed and adapted for all men, all this was changed. It followed from the fact that the Church was to embrace all nations.

(1.) That the Church and State could no longer be united or identified as they had been under the theocracy. The Christian Church at the first was established in an enemy's country. For three centuries it was not only independent and separate from the State, but it was in every way opposed and persecuted by the civil power. It is still the fact that the Christian Church exists in Pagan and Mohammedan countries. (2.) From the necessity of the case it is a body independent of the State. It has its own organization, its own laws, its own officers, and its own conditions of membership. It has the right to administer its own discipline agreeably to the laws of Christ its king and head. (3.) As it was intended by Christ that his Church should be thus catholic or universal, existing under all forms of human government, civilized or savage, it was clearly his intention that it should be thus independent and distinct from the State. He declared that his kingdom was not of this world. It is not of the same kind with worldly kingdoms; it has different ends to accomplish, and different means for the attainment of those ends. It is spiritual, that is, concerned with the religious or spiritual, as distinguished from the secular interests of men. It moves, therefore, in a different sphere from the State, and the two need never come into collision. (4.) As the Church, since the advent is identical with the Church which existed before the advent, although so different in its organization, in its officers, and in its mode of worship, the conditions of church-membership are now what they were then. Those conditions still are credible profession of faith, and obedience to the divine law. But it is no longer the duty of the State to require such profession or to enforce such obedience, so that every citizen of the State should be "ipso facto" a member of the Church. The two bodies are now distinct. A man may be a member of the one, and not a member of the other. The Church has the right to exercise its own discretion, within the limits prescribed by Christ, as to the admission or exclusion of members.

Doctrine of the Church of Rome on the Baptism of Children.

It has already been remarked that the Romish theory of the Church is founded on that of the ancient theocracy. That theory, however, is necessarily modified by the catholicity of the Church. Being designed for all nations, it could not be identified with any one nation. National citizenship is no longer the condition of church-membership. Rome, however, teaches,—

1. That the Church is, in its essential character, an external,

organized society, so that no man can be a member of Christ's body and a partaker of his life, who is not a member of that society.

2. The Church is an institute of salvation. Its sacraments are exclusively the channels for conveying to men the benefits of the redemption of Christ.

3. As the sacraments are the only channels of grace, no gracious affections or fruits of the Spirit can be required of those who receive them. Being designed to make men good, goodness cannot be the condition of their reception or efficacy.

4. The sacraments, and especially baptism, being thus necessary to salvation, it is the duty of all men to apply that they should be administered to them and to their children.

5. With regard to those children whose parents, through ignorance or indifference, neglect to bring them to the Church for baptism, they may be presented by any one who takes an interest in their salvation, that they may be baptized on the faith of the Church, or on that of those who are willing to act as their sponsors. It is no matter, therefore, whether the parents of such children are Christians, Jews, Mohammedans, or Pagans, as they all need, so they are all entitled to the sacrament of baptism. To exclude them from baptism, is to exclude them from heaven.

The Roman Catechism[1] declares that the people must be taught that our Lord has enjoined baptism on all men, so that they will all perish eternally unless they be renewed by the grace of baptism, whether their parents be believers or unbelievers. In the answer to the next question the Scriptural authority for the baptism of infants is given ; and in answer to the following question it is taught that infants, when baptized, receive the grace signified, not because they believe by the assent of their own mind, but because of the faith of their parents if believers, and if not, then by the faith of the Church universal ; and they may be properly offered for baptism by any one who is willing to present them, by whose charity they are brought into the communion of the Holy Spirit.

6. Although not identified with the State, the Church theoretically absorbs the State, and does so in fact wherever it has the ascendancy. The Church is a body which has two arms — a spiritual and a secular. It demands that the State require all its subjects to profess its faith, to receive its sacraments, and to submit to its discipline ; and where it has not the power thus to ren-

[1] II. ii. quæs. 25 [31, xxx.]; Streitwolf, vol. i. p. 274.

der the State its tool, it openly asserts its right to do so. One of the encyclical letters of the present pope so openly denied the liberty of conscience, the liberty of the press, and the lawfulness of tolerating any other religion than that of the Church of Rome, that the late Emperor of the French forbade its publication in France; yet the Archbishop of New York read it in his cathedral to an immense and approving audience.

The Roman Church, therefore, believing that baptism is essential to salvation, baptizes all children presented for that ordinance without regard to their immediate parentage or remote descent.

Theories on which many Protestants contend for the propriety of the baptism of children other than those of believing parents.

There are two principles on which the baptism of children whose parents are not members of the visible Church, is defended. The first is, that the promise is to parents and their children, and their children's children even to the thousandth generation. Children, therefore, whose immediate parents may have no connection with the Church, have not forfeited their privileges as children of the covenant. If the promise be to them, its sign and seal belongs to them. The second principle is, that of spiritual adoption. Children who are orphans, or whose parents are unfit or unwilling to bring them up in a Christian manner, may be so far adopted by those willing and qualified to assume the responsibility of their religious education as to become proper subjects of baptism. This principle is sanctioned in the Scriptures. In Genesis xvii. 12, God said to Abraham, " He that is eight days old shall be circumcised among you, every man child in your generations; he that is born in the house, or bought with money of any stranger, which is not thy seed." Our Church on the same principle in 1787 enjoined with regard to apprentices that " Christian masters and mistresses, whose religious professions and conduct are such as to give them a right to the ordinance of baptism for their own children, may and ought to dedicate the children of their household to God, in that ordinance, when they have no scruple of conscience to the contrary." In 1816, it was decided, " (1.) It is the duty of masters who are members of the Church to present the children of parents in servitude to the ordinance of baptism, provided they are in a situation to train them up in the nurture and admonition of the Lord, thus securing to them the rich advantages which the Gospel provides.   (2.) It is the duty of Christ's ministers to inculcate this doctrine, and to baptize all children of this description when presented by their masters." On the baptism of heathen children the Church in 1843 decided that such children are to be baptized, " who are so committed to the missions, or other Christian tuition, as to secure effectually their entire religious education." [1]

It was on the authority of the two principles above mentioned that many of the most distinguished theologians of Holland contend that foundlings, whose parents were unknown, illegitimate children, and the children of excommunicated persons, should be admitted to baptism. The question whether heathen children, committed to the care of Christian missionaries, should be baptized was submitted to the Synod of Dort. There was a diversity of opinion on the subject among the members, but the majority decided against it; not, as would appear, from the language employed, because of either of the above principles being denied, but because of the uncertain tenure by which such children were held. It was feared that they might return to heathenism, and thus the scandal of baptized persons practising heathen rites be afforded.[2]

A second theory advanced on this subject was that of a twofold covenant; one external, the other internal; answering to the distinction between the Church visible and invisible. God, under the old dispensation, entered into a covenant with the Hebrew nation constituting them his visible Church, which covenant was distinct from that in which eternal life was promised to those that truly believe in the Redeemer who was to come. The conditions of admission into this external, visible society, were outward profession of the true religion, and external obedience. The condition of admission into the invisible Church, was true and saving faith. The sacraments were attached to the external covenant. All who made this external profession and yielded this outward obedience to the Mosaic law, were of right entitled to circumcision, to the passover, and to all the privileges of the theocracy. So it is now, according to the theory in hand. Christ designed

---

[1] Baird's *Digest of the Acts, Deliverances, and Testimonies of the Supreme Judicatory of the Presbyterian Church*, Philadelphia, pp. 106, 107; edit. 1856, pp. 82, 83.

[2] *Doctrina Christianæ Religionis per Aphorismos summatim Descripta*. Editio sexta. Cui nunc accedit Υποτυπωσις Theologiæ Elencticæ in usum Scholarum Domesticarum Campegii Vitringæ. Curante Martino Vitringa, cap. xxiv. Lyons, 1779, vol. vii. p. 153, note I. Bernhardini de Moor, *Commentarius Perpetuus in Johannis Marckii Compendium Theologiæ Christianæ*. Pars v: cap. 30, § 19, γ.; Lyons, 1768, vol. v. pp. 500-502.

to form an external, visible Church, furnished with a constitution, laws, and proper officers for their administration.   The conditions of admission into this visible society, were the profession of speculative, or historical faith in his religion, and external conformity to its laws and the laws of his Church.   To this external body all the ordinances of his religion are attached.   Those, therefore, who apply for baptism or the Lord's Supper, do not profess to be the regenerated children of God.   They simply profess to be believers as distinguished from infidels or scorners, and to be desirous to avail themselves of Church privileges for their own benefit and for the good of their children.   From this body Christ gathers the great majority of his own people, making them members of his mystical body.

De Moor gives a long account of the controversy.   Vitringa, it appears, strenuously opposed this theory of a twofold covenant in its application to the New Testament economy.   Marck as strenuously defended it.[1]

This seems substantially the ground taken by the Rev. Mr. Stoddard, grandfather of President Edwards.   Mr. Stoddard published, in 1707, a sermon on the Lord's Supper, in which he maintained, " That sanctification is not a necessary qualification to partaking of the Lord's Supper," and " That the Lord's Supper is a converting ordinance."   This was answered in a " Dissertation" by Dr. Increase Mather.   To this Mr. Stoddard replied in " An Appeal to the Learned ; being a Vindication of the right of visible saints to the Lord's Supper, though they be destitute of a saving work of God's Spirit on their hearts ; against the exceptions of Mr. Increase Mather."   President Edwards succeeded his grandfather as pastor of the Church in Northampton, Mass., in 1727, and for twenty years continued to act on the same principle on this subject as his grandfather.   Having become convinced that that principle was unscriptural, he published, in 1749, " An humble Inquiry into the Rules of the Word of God, concerning the qualifications requisite to a complete standing and full communion in the visible Christian Church."   His design was to prove that no one should be admitted to the Lord's table who is not in the judgment of the Church truly regenerate. This doctrine was very obnoxious to the people of his charge, and opposed to the sentiment and practice of the majority of the neighbouring churches.[2]   The difficulty arising from this contro-

---

[1] De Moor, *ut supra*, cap. xxx. § xvi. vol. v. pp. 470–473.
[2] It is stated in the *Life of President Edwards*, by Sereno E. Dwight, prefixed to an

versy was one of the principal causes which led to the dismission of President Edwards from his pastoral charge at Northampton. The views of Edwards soon gained the ascendancy in the Evangelical churches of New England, and to a great extent also among Presbyterians.

The Rev. John Blair, a prominent minister of our Church, took substantially the ground of a twofold covenant. Mr. Blair, as well as his more distinguished brother, Rev. Samuel Blair, took an active part with Whitefield and the Tennents in the great revival which occurred about the middle of the last century, and belonged to what were called the New Lights in the controversy which issued in the schism of 1741. He does not, indeed, admit of a twofold covenant, but he teaches the same doctrine which that expression was intended to assert. The Church of Christ, he says, is very properly distinguished as visible and invisible. By the former is meant "the whole number of true believers wherever they are." "The visible Church consists of all those who by an external profession of the doctrines of the Gospel, and subjection to the laws and ordinances of Christ, appear as a society separated from the world, and dedicated to God and his service. In this view, in the present imperfect state, the Church comprehends branches that are withered, as well as those that bear fruit. Now the covenant of grace subsists between the blessed God and the Church, as such a visible Society,[1] and is rendered visible by a visible transaction and external administration in various ordinances; and comprehends sundry external privileges for the advantage and spiritual edification of the Church. Here are not two covenants, one for the invisible Church and another for the visible." Gomarus, a leader in the Synod of Dort, says two covenants should be distinguished. That with the visible Church he calls hypothetical, that with the invisible Church absolute. In the main point, however, they agree, for Mr. Blair goes on to say: "It is [to] the covenant of grace

edition of Edwards' *Works*, in ten vols., New York, 1829, vol. i. p. 307, that "All the churches in the county, except two, and all the clergy, except three, approved of the lax mode of admission." That is, were opposed to Edwards' doctrine on the subject.

[1] To this sentence Mr. Blair appends the following note: "In no other way can we conceive the covenant to subsist between God and believers as a Church. In the exercise of faith, believers have union to, and communion with Jesus Christ; but by this alone, they could have no fellowship with one another; for each one could only be conscious of his own exercise of faith, and could have no society with any other therein. Whatever real relation to each other is founded in their common union to Christ, yet they could not at all perceive it. They would be members of Christ, but utterly detached from each other, and so not formally a body. It is only as incorporated in the visible Church, that they are fitly placed in the body, and have any knowledge one of another, and so have fellowship."

in this view, namely, as visibly subsisting between God and his Church, considered as a visible society, a public body separated and distinguished from the world, and dedicated to God, that the sacraments are annexed as visible signs and seals thereof." [1]

A man, therefore, in coming to the Lord's table, or in presenting himself or his children for baptism, does not profess to be a member of the invisible, but only of the visible Church. God has commanded men not to steal, and not to neglect their religious duties; He commands them to pray; to hear his word; to attend the assemblies of his saints gathered for his worship; to be baptized; and to commemorate the Redeemer's death in the way of his appointment. All these duties are obligatory; and they are all to be performed in a right spirit. But a man, argues Mr. Blair, is not to wait until he thinks himself regenerate and is so regarded by the Church, before he attempts to obey them. The sacraments, he says,[2] " are not instituted to be visible signs of persons' opinion or judgment concerning the exercises of their own hearts." He no more professes to be regenerated when he comes to be baptized than when he prays. His prayer is from its nature a profession of faith in the divine existence and perfections, in the power of God to hear and answer his requests; it is a confession of his necessities and of his dependence. And this profession and confession are sincere; so sincere that it is not only his duty, but his right to pray — a right which no man may take from him. In like manner a man may be, in the same sense, sincere in his belief of the truth of the Gospel; sincere in his desire to obey the command of Christ, and secure the benefits of his salvation. " When the sons of the stranger," says Mr. Blair, " are instructed in the doctrines of the Gospel, are convinced in their judgment and conscience, they are true and exhibit the true religion; that they are bound by the authority of God to embrace it, and yield obedience to the divine laws; it is their immediate duty to embrace it, and that publicly and avowedly by joining themselves to the Lord, and his Church, in the sacrament of baptism; and thus make a public profession of the true religion, come under solemn obligations to walk in the ways of God's commandments, and under the care and discipline

---

[1] *Essays on,* I. *The Nature, Uses, and Subjects of the Sacraments of the New Testament;* II. *On Regeneration, wherein the principle of Spiritual Life thereby implanted is particularly considered;* III. *On the Nature and Use of the Means of Grace.* By John Blair, A. M., Pastor of the Church of Good-Will (alias Wallkill), in the Province of New York. New York: printed by John Holt, at the Exchange, 1771. Essay I. pp. 13–15.

[2] *Ibid.* p. 35.

of the Church." [1] Such persons "are brought under the bond of the covenant. This should be early laid before them, to let them see that by this dedication to God, they are bound to perform all duties of religion for which they have capacity, to receive instruction and appear for religion as the professors thereof. As soon as they have a competency of knowledge, and are capable of the discipline of the Church, they are bound to commemorate the death of Christ, and renew their engagements to Him at his table, unless debarred by discipline for unchristian conduct. When they shall become parents, they are bound to dedicate their children to God in baptism." [2]

Such were the views on this subject entertained by some of the most evangelical ministers of our Church during the last century and long afterwards. The same views prevailed, to some extent, also in New England.

A third theory on which the baptism of children, whose parents are not communicants, is contended for, makes a distinction between baptism and the Lord's Supper. More is required for the latter than for the former; and, therefore, adults who are entitled to baptism for themselves and for their children, may not be entitled to admission to the Lord's table. This is one of the views on this general subject referred to by Vitringa and De Moor in the works above mentioned. The advocates of this theory appeal to the fact that the Apostles, who were no more able than other men to read the heart, baptized thousands on the spot, on a simple external profession of faith. So Paul baptized the jailer at Philippi and his family "straightway," that is, as would appear, at midnight in the prison. Philip baptized the eunuch of Ethiopia as soon as he confessed that Jesus is the Son of God, although he knew nothing, so far as appears in the narrative, of his conduct either before or after. On the other hand, it is urged that these same Apostles required all who came to the Lord's Supper to examine themselves, and see whether they were in the faith, or whether Christ dwelt in them. This seems to have been the ground taken by Mr. Blair in the earlier part of his ministry; for he says in his preface [3] to his Essays: "Many of my friends will, probably, be surprised, to find I have changed my sentiments with respect to some subjects of one of the sacraments; for they know it was formerly my opinion, that the unregenerate ought not, by any means, to adventure to the Lord's table; though they ought to dedicate their children to God in baptism."

---

[1] Blair, *Essays, ut supra,* p. 28.   [2] *Ibid.* p. 43.   [3] *Ibid.* p. 4.

This is also the theory which was known in New England as the " Half-Way Covenant." Many were recognized as entitled to present their children for baptism, who were not prepared for admission to the Lord's Supper. The controversy on this subject began in Hartford, Connecticut, in 1654, 1655. Several councils were called, which failed to produce unanimity. The question was referred to a Synod of divines to meet in Boston. The Synod met and sat two or three weeks. " As to the case of such baptized persons as, without being prepared to come to the Lord's Supper, were of blameless character, and would own for themselves their baptismal obligations, it decided that they ought to be allowed to present their children for baptism. This assuming of baptismal obligations was called by opponents, taking the Half-way Covenant." [1]

The Synod decided in favour of the following propositions : —

" 1. They that, according to Scripture, are members of the visible Church, are the subjects of baptism.

" 2. The members of the visible Church, according to Scripture, are confederate visible believers, in particular churches, and their infant seed, i. e., children in minority, whose next parents, one or both, are in covenant.

" 3. The infant seed of confederate visible believers, are members of the same Church with their parents, and when grown up are personally under the watch, discipline, and government of that church.

" 4. These adult persons are not, therefore, to be admitted to full communion, merely because they are, and continue members, without such further qualifications as the Word of God requireth thereunto.

" 5. Church-members who were admitted in minority, understanding the doctrine of faith, and publicly professing their assent thereto, not scandalous in life, and solemnly owning the covenant before the Church, wherein they give up themselves and their children to the Lord, and subject themselves to the government of Christ in the Church, their children are to be baptized.

" 6. Such church-members, who either by death, or some other extraordinary providence, have been inevitably hindered from publicly acting as aforesaid, yet have given the Church cause, in judgment of charity, to look at them as so qualified, and such as, had

---

[1] *A History of New England, from the Discovery by Europeans to the Revolution of the Seventeenth Century, being an Abridgment of his " History of New England during the Stuart Dynasty."* By John Gorham Palfrey. New York, 1866, vol. ii. p. 19.

they been called thereunto, would have so acted, their children are to be baptized.

" 7. The members of orthodox churches, being sound in the faith and not scandalous in life, and presenting due testimony thereof ; these occasionally coming from one church to another may have their children baptized in the church, whither they come, by virtue of communion of churches. But if they remove their habitation they ought orderly to covenant and subject themselves to the government of Christ in the church where they settle their abode, and so their children to be baptized. It being the church's duty to receive such into communion, so far as they are regularly fit for the same." [1]

These propositions are founded on the following principles : —

1. That as under the old economy the Temple was one, it had its outer and inner courts, and those who had access to the former were not thereby entitled to enter the latter ; so under the new dispensation the visible Church is one, but it includes two classes of members ; baptized professors of the true religion, and those who, giving evidence of regeneration, are admitted to the Lord's Supper.

2. That the qualifications for baptism and for full communion are not identical. Many may properly be admitted to the former, who are not prepared for the latter.

3. That baptism being a sign and seal of the covenant of grace, all who are baptized, whether adults or infants, are properly designated " fœderati," members of the visible Church, believers, saints, Christians.

4. That those baptized in infancy remain members of the visible Church until they are " discovenanted," as the Congregationalists express it ; or, separated from it by a regular act of discipline.

5. That being members of the Church, if free from scandal and continuing their profession, they are entitled to present their children for baptism.

The decision of this Synod did not put an end to the controversy. It was, however, in accordance with the views of the majority of the New England churches. Its chief opponents were found among " the more conservative class of laymen. Its advocates among the clergy were from the first a majority, which

---

[1] *Magnalia Christi Americana*, by Rev. Cotton Mather, D. D., F. R. S., Hartford, 1853, vol. ii. pp. 276–316. The passage referred to contains a full account of the controversy. The words above are on page 279.

went on increasing from generation to generation ; and the Half-way Covenant, as it was opprobriously called, came to be approved by the general practice of the Congregational churches of New England." [1]   Such, also, it is believed, although on somewhat different principles, was the general practice of the Presbyterian Church in this country until within a comparatively recent period of its history.

The Puritan Doctrine on this Subject.

The Puritans, in the restricted sense of that word, held, (1.) That the Church consists of the regenerate.   (2.) That a particular church consists of a number of true believers united together by mutual covenant.   (3.) That no one should be admitted to church-membership who did not give credible evidence of being a true child of God.   (4.) They understood by credible evidence, not such as may be believed, but such as constrains belief.   (5.) All such persons, and no others, were admitted to the Lord's Supper.   They, therefore, constituted the Church, and to them exclusively belonged the privileges of church-membership, and consequently to them was confined the right of presenting their children for baptism.   All other professors of the true religion, however correct in their deportment, were denied that privilege.

These principles, when introduced by the Brownists in England, were opposed by the great body of Protestants in Great Britain and upon the Continent.   They were brought to this country by the disciples of Robinson, and controlled the New England churches for many years.   They were gradually relaxed when the theory above stated gained the ascendancy, which it retained until President Edwards published his "Essay," to which we have referred, which gradually changed the opinions and practice of the Congregational churches throughout the land, and to a great extent those of Presbyterians also.

President Edwards, however, lays down one proposition, and devotes his whole treatise to proving another.   The proposition which he undertakes to establish is, that none " ought to be admitted to the communion and privileges of members of the visible Church of Christ in complete standing, but such as are in profession, and in the eye of the Church's Christian judgment, godly or gracious persons." [2]   What he proposes to prove, therefore, is that those only who, in the judgment of the Church, are godly

---

[1] Palfrey, p. 103.　　　　　　　[2] *Works*, edit. New York, 1868, vol. 1. p. 89.

or gracious persons are to be admitted to the sacraments. All his arguments, however, ten in number, are directed to prove that those who come to the Christian sacraments profess to be Christians. These propositions are very different. Many who assent to the latter, reject the former. The one has reference to the qualifications for church-membership in the sight of God; the other concerns the legitimate power of the Church in receiving or rejecting those who apply for access to the ordinances which Christ has appointed as means of grace for the people. Edwards had far higher notions of Church power in this matter, than those entertained by the great body of Protestants. The reason why President Edwards confounded the propositions above mentioned, was, that those against whom he wrote did not deny the prerogative of the Church to sit in judgment on those who applied for Church privileges; that, with them, was not the matter in dispute. The question concerned the divinely appointed qualifications for membership in the Christian Church. Did Christ intend and ordain that those only whom the Church judged to be truly regenerated should be admitted; or did He design the sacraments, as Stoddard contended, for the unconverted; they, as well as preaching, being appointed as means of conversion. This being, then, the only matter of debate, to it Edwards naturally confined his attention.

Edwards is very explicit in his statement of the prerogative and duty of the Church in acting as a judge of the real character of those who profess to be Christians. He says: " By Christian judgment I intend something further than a kind of mere negative charity, implying that we forbear to censure and condemn a man, because we do not know but that he may be godly, and therefore forbear to proceed on the foot of such a censure or judgment in our treatment of him: as we would kindly entertain a stranger, not knowing but in so doing we entertain an angel or precious saint of God. But I mean a positive judgment, founded on some positive appearance, or visibility, some outward manifestations that ordinarily render the thing probable. There is a difference between suspending our judgment, or forbearing to condemn, or having some hope that possibly the thing may be so, and so hoping the best; and a positive judgment in favour of a person." [1]

Edwards is careful not to make any detail of religious experience the ground upon which the Church was to rest its judgment.

[1] *Works*, edit. New York, 1868, vol. i. pp. 91, 92.

This was one of the charges brought against his scheme which
he earnestly resists. In reply to this objection [1] he quotes the
following passage from his work on " Religious Affections : "
" In order to persons' making a proper profession of Christianity,
such as the Scripture directs to, and such as the followers of
Christ should require in order to the acceptance of the professors
with full charity, as of their society, it is not necessary they
should give an account of the particular steps and method, by
which the Holy Spirit, sensibly to them, wrought and brought
about those great essential things of Christianity in their hearts.
There is no footstep in Scripture of any such way of the Apostles, or primitive ministers and Christians requiring any such
relation in order to their receiving and treating others as their
Christian brethren, to all intents and purposes ; or of their first
examining them concerning the particular method and order of
their experiences. They required of them a profession of the
things wrought ; but no account of the manner of working was
required of them. Nor is there the least shadow in the Scripture
of any such custom in the Church of God, from Adam to the
death of the Apostle John."

According to this theory, therefore, the Church consists of
those who are " judged " to be regenerate. None but those thus
declared to be true believers are to be received as members of the
Church. They alone are entitled to the sacraments either for
themselves or for their children, and consequently only the children of communicants are to be admitted to baptism. It may be
remarked on this theory, —

1. That it is a novelty. It had never been adopted or acted
upon by any church on earth, until the rise of the Independents.

2. It has no warrant from Scripture either by precept or example. Under the old economy those who professed the true religion were admitted to the theocracy ; but no body of men sat in
judgment on the question of their regeneration. Those thus
admitted, unless excluded judicially, had a right to the sacraments of the Church for themselves and for their children. The
Apostles acted upon precisely the same principle. It is impossible that they should have examined and decided favourably as to
the regeneration of each of the five thousand persons added to the
Church in one day in Jerusalem. The whole Church, for more
than a thousand years, followed the example of the Apostles in
this matter.

[1] *Misrepresentations Corrected and Truth Vindicated, in a Reply to the Rev. Solomon
Williams' Book; Works,* edit. New York, 1868, vol. i. pp. 206, 207.

3. The attempt to make the visible Church consist exclusively of true believers must not only inevitably fail of success, but it must also be productive of evil. Dr. Cotton Mather, in defending the decision of the Synod of Boston, which allowed baptism to the children of non-communicants, quotes Paræus as saying, " In church reformation, 'tis an observable truth that those that are for too much strictness, do more hurt than profit the Church." And he, himself, says, " Baptism is a seal of the whole covenant of grace ; but it is by way of initiation. Hence it belongs to all that are within the covenant or have the first entrance there-into. And is there no danger of corruption by overstraining the subject of baptism ? Certainly, it is a corruption to take from the rule, as well as add to it. Moses found danger in not apply-ing the initiating seal, to such for whom it was appointed. Is there no danger of putting those out of the visible Church, whom our Lord would have kept in? . . . . If we do not keep in the way of a converting, grace-giving covenant, and keep persons un-der those church dispensations, wherein grace is given, the Church will die of a lingering, though not violent, death. The Lord hath not set up churches only that a few old Christians may keep one another warm while they live, and then carry away the Church into the cold grave with them when they die ; no, but that they might with all care, and with all the obligations and advantages to that care that may be, nurse up still successively another generation of subjects to our Lord, that may stand up in his kingdom when they are gone." [1]

4. Experience proves that it is a great evil to make the Church consist only of communicants and to cast out into the world, without any of that watch and care which God intended for them, all those together with their children, who do not see their way clear to come to the Lord's table. Admitting with gratitude all that can be said of the great advance made by the Church in this country within the last fifty or sixty years, there are loud and almost universal complaints made of the decay of family religion, of family training, and especially of the ecclesiastical instruction of the young. It is within the memory of many now living that in almost every Presbyterian and every Congregationalist family in the land, as a matter of course, the children were regularly taught the " Westminster Catechism." It is not so now.[2]

[1] Mather's *Magnalia*, vol. ii. p. 309.

[2] The venerable Mr. Spaulding, during his recent visit to this country, after spending thirty-five years as a missionary of the American Board in Ceylon, was so much struck with the change in these respects which had taken place during his absence, that he said

Doctrine and Usage of the Reformed Churches.

The language of the Reformed Churches as the proper subjects of infant baptism is perfectly uniform. In the " Second Helvetic Confession " it is said,[1] " Damnamus Anabaptistas, qui negant baptisandos esse infantulos recens natos a fidelibus. Nam juxta doctrinam evangelicam, horum est regnum Dei, et sunt in fœdere Dei, cur itaque non daretur eis signum fœderis Dei ? "

The " Gallic Confession " says : [2] " Quamvis baptismus sit fidei et resipiscentiæ sacramentum, tamen cum una cum parentibus posteritatem etiam illorum in ecclesia Deus recenseat, affirmamus, infantes sanctis parentibus natos, esse ex Christi authoritate baptizandos."

The " Belgic Confession " says : [3] " (Infantes e fidelibus parentibus natos) baptizandos et signo fœderis obsignandos esse credimus."

The " Westminster Confession " says : [4] " Now only those that do actually profess faith in, and obedience unto Christ, but also the infants of one or both believing parents are to be baptized."

The " Larger Catechism " says : [5] " Infants descending from parents, either both or but one of them, professing faith in Christ, and obedience to Him, are, in that respect, within the covenant, and are to be baptized."

The " Shorter Catechism " says : [6] " Baptism is not to be administered to any that are out of the visible Church, till they profess their faith in Christ and their obedience to Him ; but the children of such as are members of the visible Church, are to be baptized."

The " Directory for Worship " says : [7] " The seed of the faithful have no less right to this ordinance, under the Gospel, than the seed of Abraham to circumcision."

It is, therefore, plain that according to the standards of the Reformed Church, it is the children of the members of the visible Church who are to be baptized. Agreeably to Scriptural usage such members are called " fœderati," saints, believers, faithful, holy brethren, partakers of the heavenly calling. The Apostles in addressing professing Christians in the use of such

he thought the time would come when the Tamul people would be called upon to send missionaries to America.

[1] Cap. xx.; Niemeyer, *Collectio Confessionum*, Leipzig, 1840, p. 518.
[2] Art. xxxv. *Ibid.* p. 338.   [3] Art. xxxiv. *Ibid.* p. 384.   [4] Chap. xxviii. 4.
[5] Quest. 166.   [6] Quest. 95.   [7] Chap. vii. 4.

terms did not express any judgment of their state in the sight
of God. They designated them according to their profession.
If they professed to be believers, they were called believers, and
were treated as such ; unless they gave tangible evidence to the
contrary, and in that case they were excommunicated. The Reformed, as well as the Lutheran theologians, therefore, speak of
the members of the visible Church as believers, and of their
children as born of believing parents. All that is intended,
therefore, by the language above cited is, that the sacraments of
the Church are to be confined to members of the Church and
to their children. It never entered the minds of the authors of
those symbols that the visible Church consists exclusively of the
regenerate, or of those who gave such evidence of their regeneration as to constrain a judgment in their favour.

It has already been stated that the common doctrine of Protestants on this whole subject is, —

1. That the visible Church has always consisted of those who
professed the true religion, together with their children.

2. That the terms of church-membership under all dispensations
have been the same, namely, profession of faith and promise of
obedience.

3. The requirements for participation in the sacraments were
the same. That is, any one entitled to the rite of circumcision,
was entitled to partake of the passover ; those, under the Christian dispensation, entitled to baptism, are entitled to the Lord's
Supper. Those who, unbaptized, would be entitled to baptism
for themselves, are entitled, and they only, to present their children for baptism. This is only saying that the privileges of the
Church are confined to members of the Church.

4. The profession of faith required for admission to the Church
or its ordinances is a profession of true faith ; and the promise
of obedience is a promise of the obedience of the heart as well
as of the outward life. When a man professed to be a Jew
he professed to be truly a Jew. It is inconceivable that God
required of him only an insincere, hypocritical, or formal faith.
This point is strenuously urged by President Edwards. He
argues that those who enter the Christian Church enter into
covenant with God, because under the Mosaic economy all the
people thus pledged themselves to be the sincere worshippers of
God. He appeals to such passages as Deuteronomy vi. 13, x. 20,
" Thou shalt fear the LORD thy God ; Him shalt thou serve, and
to Him shalt thou cleave, and swear by his name." " This insti-

tution, in Deuteronomy, of swearing into the name of the LORD, or visibly and explicitly uniting themselves to Him in covenant, was not prescribed as an extraordinary duty, or a duty to be performed on a return from a general apostasy, and some other extraordinary occasions : but is evidently mentioned in the institution as a part of the public worship of God to be performed by all God's people." [1] This was an institution, he adds, belonging not only to Israel under the Old Testament, but also to Gentile converts, and to Christians under the New Testament. This explicit open covenanting with God, he argues,[2] ought to be required of persons before they are admitted to the privileges of adult members of the Church. Circumcision and the passover were not designed for the conversion of the Gentiles. Those only were admitted to these ordinances who professed to be converted. In like manner baptism and the Lord's Supper are not converting ordinances. They are to be administered only to those who profess to be Christians. It is plain, from the nature of the case, that those who partake of the Christian sacraments profess to be Christians. This is not so much asserted as assumed as self-evident by the Apostle, when he dissuades the Corinthians from frequenting the feasts given in the temples of idols. As, he says, those who partake of the bread and wine in the Lord's Supper thereby profess to be in communion with Christ ; and as those who partake of the Jewish altar, thereby profess to be the worshippers of Jehovah ; so those who partake of feasts given in honour of idols, thereby profess to be idolators. (1 Cor. x. 14–21.) In baptism the recipient of that ordinance publicly declares that he takes God the Father to be his father ; God the Son to be his Saviour ; and God the Holy Ghost to be his sanctifier. More than this no Christian can profess. That this profession should not be insincere or hypocritical, or merely a matter of form, need not be argued. When a parent presents his child for baptism, he makes precisely these professions and engagements ; and he can do no more when he comes to the Lord's Supper.

5. The prerogative of the Church is limited to the demand of a credible profession of faith and promise of obedience. And by a credible profession is to be understood, such as may be believed ; that is, one against which no decisive, tangible evidence can be adduced. If a man professes faith who is an avowed heretic, or avows a purpose of obedience while leading an ungodly life, the

---

[1] *Works*, edit. New York, 1868, vol. i. pp. 106, 107.   [2] *Ibid*. p. 109.

Church is authorized and bound to refuse to receive him.   Nothing, however, can consistently be made a ground of such refusal, which would not be regarded as a sufficient ground for the discipline of one already in the communion of the Church.   Two things are to be considered, the one concerns the applicants for Church privileges.   They are bound to obey the command of Christ to be baptized and to present their children for baptism ; and they are bound to commemorate his death in the way of his appointment.   They assume a grave responsibility who refuse to allow them to comply with those commands.   It is moreover not only a duty, but a right, a privilege, and a blessing to receive the sacraments of the Church.   They are divinely appointed means of grace.   We must have good reasons if we venture to refuse any of our fellow sinners the use of the means of salvation which Christ has appointed.   It is to be feared that many have come short of eternal life, who, had they been received into the bosom of the Church and enjoyed its guardian and fostering care, might have been saved.   (This is not inconsistent with the doctrine of election, as that doctrine is taught in Scripture.)

Besides the duties and rights of the people, the other thing to be considered in this matter, is the proper office of the Church. The Church has a solemn duty to perform.   That duty is clearly laid down in the Word of God.   It is bound to refuse to recognize as Christian brethren those who deny the faith, and those whose manner of life is inconsistent with the law of Christ.   The Bible gives a list of offences which exclude those who commit them from the kingdom of heaven, and for which the Church is commanded to exclude men from her communion.   In doing this it secures all the purity it is possible, in the present state of existence, to attain.   Beyond this the Church has neither the right nor the power to go.   It cannot legitimately assume the prerogative of sitting in judgment on the hearts of men.   It has no right to decide the question whether those who apply for the privileges of Christ's house are regenerate or unregenerate.   The responsibility as to their inward spiritual state rests upon those who seek to become members of the Church.   They should be taught what it is they profess and promise.

That the Church is not called upon to pronounce a judgment as to the real piety of applicants for membership is plain, —

1. Because no such prerogative was assumed under the Old Testament.   The terms of membership were then what they are now.   The same inward sincerity was required then as now

This Edwards insists upon, yet he does not venture to assert that all Jews admitted to circumcision and the passover, were, in the judgment of charity, truly regenerate persons.

2. The New Testament contains no command to the Church to assume the prerogative in question. There is the command often repeated to recognize as brethren all who profess their faith in Christ. There are explicit directions given as to those who, although calling themselves brethren, are to be rejected. (1 Cor. v. 9, 10; Rom. xvi. 17; 2 Thess. iii. 6; Tit. iii. 10; Matt. vii. 15–17.) But there is no command to exclude those whom the Church or its officers do not in their hearts believe to be the true children of God. The gates of the kingdom of God are not to be opened or shut at the discretion of weak, fallible men. Every man has a right and is bound to enter those gates, except those whom Christ has commanded his Church to reject.

3. The Apostles, it is plain, never acted on the principle in question. This is clear, as remarked above, from their baptizing converts immediately after the profession of their faith. It is obviously impossible that there should have been any protracted examination of the religious experience of the three thousand converted on the day of Pentecost, or of the five thousand brought in by the sermon of Peter, recorded in the third chapter of Acts. The Acts of the Apostles and the Epistles of the New Testament afford abundant evidence that the early churches did not consist exclusively of those whom the Apostles " judged " to be regenerated persons. The Church of Jerusalem was filled with men who were so " zealous of the law," that Paul feared that they would not receive him even when he came to bring alms to the people. Paul charges the churches of Galatia with having turned aside to another gospel. He reproves the Corinthians with the grossest irregularities; and the Epistles of John are no less objurgatory.

4. Experience proves that all attempts to preserve the purity of the Church by being more strict than the Bible, are utterly futile. The tares cannot be separated from the wheat.

5. Such attempts are not only futile, they are seriously injurious. They contravene the plan of God. They exclude from the watch and care of the Church multitudes whom He commands his people to look after and cherish. In confining the visible Church to communicants, it unchurches the great majority even of the seed of the faithful.

6. There is an obvious inconsistency in having one rule for

admission into the Church, and another for continued membership. If Christ requires us to reject all whom in the judgment of charity we are not constrained to believe to be regenerate, then He requires us to excommunicate all those of whom this belief is not entertained. But no Church acts, or can act on that principle. No man once admitted to Church privileges can be debarred from them, except after a trial and conviction on the charge of some "scandal" or "offence."

The sacraments as all admit are to be confined to members of the Church. But the Church does not consist exclusively of communicants. It includes also all who having been baptized have not forfeited their membership by scandalous living, or by any act of Church discipline. All members of the Church are professors of religion. They profess faith in Christ and are under a solemn vow to obey his laws. If they are insincere or heartless in this profession, the guilt is their own. The Church is, and can be responsible only for their external conduct; so long as that is not incompatible with the Christian character, and so long as the faith is held fast, the privileges of membership continue.

This seems clearly the doctrine of the standards of our own Church. Those standards teach, (1.) That the sacraments are signs and seals of the covenant of grace. (2.) That consequently all who partake of them do thereby profess to accept of that covenant for their own salvation; they profess to receive the Lord Jesus Christ as He is offered to them in the gospel. (3.) That although a man may doubt of his being in Christ he may be a worthy partaker of the sacraments, if he "unfeignedly desires to be found in Christ, and to depart from iniquity." [1] (4.) That the Church has no authority to exclude from the sacraments any except those who, although they may profess faith, are ignorant or scandalous. In answer to the question, " May any who profess the faith, and desire to come to the Lord's Supper, be kept from it ? " it is answered, " Such as are found to be ignorant or scandalous, notwithstanding their profession of the faith, and desire to come to the Lord's Supper, may and ought to be kept from that sacrament by the power which Christ hath left in his Church, until they receive instruction, and manifest their reformation." This, according to Presbyterians, is the extent of the power of the Church, in the matter of shutting the doors of the kingdom of God.

---

[1] Larger Catechism, answer to the 172d Question.

Those, therefore, who, having been themselves baptized, and still professing their faith in the true religion, having competent knowledge, and being free from scandal, should not only be permitted but urged and enjoined to present their children for baptism, that they may belong to the Church, and be brought up under its watch and care. To be unbaptized is a grievous injury and reproach ; one which no parent can innocently entail upon his children. The neglect of baptism, which implies a want of appreciation of the ordinance, is one of the crying sins of this generation.

§ 12. *Efficacy of Baptism.*

Doctrine of the Reformed Churches.

In the section which treats of the efficacy of the sacraments in general, it was shown that according to the Reformed Church the sacraments (1.) Are ordinances of divine appointment. (2.) That they are means of grace, and therefore are not to be undervalued or neglected. (3.) That their efficacy does not depend upon any virtue in them or in him by whom they are administered, but upon the attending influence of the Holy Spirit. (4.) That their efficacy is not tied to the time of their administration ; and that they are not the exclusive channels of the spiritual benefits which they signify, so that such benefits can be received only through and in the use of the sacraments. We have by faith alone, and by the free gift of God, all that the sacraments are made the means of communicating. The same may be said of reading and hearing the Word of God : neither is to be neglected, because either, or one without the other, may be made effectual. The sacraments are not to be neglected or undervalued, because men can be saved without them. (5.) That, so far as adults are concerned, true, living faith in those who receive the sacraments is the indispensable condition of their saving or sanctifying influence.

All these positions are affirmed to be true of baptism as well as of the Lord's Supper. Of the former the principal Reformed symbols use such language as the following : " Obsignantur hæc omnia baptismo. Nam intus regeneramur, purificamur, et renovamur a Deo per Spiritum Sanctum : foris autem accipimus obsignationem maximorum donorum, in aqua, qua etiam maxima illa beneficia repræsentantur, et veluti oculis nostris conspicienda proponuntur." [1]

---

[1] *Confessio Helvetica posterior*, xx ; Niemeyer, *Collectio Confessionum*, Leipzig, 1840 p. 517.

" Baptismus nobis testificandæ nostræ adoptioni datus, quoniam in eo inserimur Christi corpori, ut ejus sanguine abluti simul etiam ipsius Spiritu ad vitæ sanctimoniam renovemur." [1]

" (Baptismi significatio) duas partes habet.   Nam ibi remissio peccatorum, deinde spiritualis renovatio figuratur. . . . . Annon aliud aquæ tribuis nisi ut ablutionis tantum sit figura ?   Sic figuram esse sentio ut simul annexa sit veritas.   Neque enim sua nobis dona pollicendo nos, Deus frustratur.   Proinde et peccatorum veniam et vitæ novitatem offeri nobis in baptismo et recipi a nobis, certum est." [2]

" Baptism is not only a sign of profession, and mark of difference, whereby Christian men are discerned from others that be not christened ; but it is also a sign of regeneration or new birth, whereby as by an instrument they who receive baptism rightly are grafted into the Church.   The promises of the forgiveness of sins, of our adoption to be the sons of God by the Holy Ghost, are visibly signed and sealed ; faith is confirmed and grace increased by virtue of prayer to God." [3]

The Heidelberg Catechism says : " Is then the external baptism of water, the washing away of sins ?   It is not : For the blood of Jesus Christ alone cleanses us from all sin.   Why then does the Holy Spirit call baptism the washing of regeneration, and the washing away of sins ?   God speaks thus not without sufficient cause, not only that He may teach us, that just as pollution of the body is purged by water, so our sins are expiated by the blood and Spirit of Christ ; but much more that He may assure us by this divine symbol and pledge, that we not less truly are cleansed from our sins by inward washing, than that we are purified by external and visible water." [4]

The Consensus Tigurinus is the most carefully prepared and guarded statement of the doctrine of the Reformed Church which has come down from the age of the Reformation.   It was drawn up to adjust the difficulties arising from the diverging views on this subject between Calvin and the clergy of Geneva on the one hand, and the Zwinglian clergy of Zurich on the other.   In the ninth article it is said, " that although we distinguish, as is proper, between the sign and the things signified ; yet we do not disjoin the truth from the signs : moreover all who embrace by faith the promises therein offered, spiritually receive Christ to-

---

[1] *Confessio Gallicana*, Art. xxxv.; *Ibid.* p. 338.
[2] *Catechismus Genevensis* [v.], Niemeyer, pp. 162, 163.
[3] Thirty-nine Articles, xxvii.   [4] Ques. 72 and 73, Niemeyer, pp. 445, 446

gether with his spiritual gifts ; and so those who before had been
made partakers of Christ, continue and renew that participation."
In articles immediately following it is taught that regard is to be
had, not to the naked signs, but to the promises annexed to them ;
that the signs without Christ are " inanes larvæ ; " that if any
good be conferred by the sacraments, it is not from their proper
inherent virtue ; for it is God alone who acts through his Spirit.
Article sixteenth is in these words, " Præterea sedulo docemus,
Deum non promiscue vim suam exerere in omnibus qui sacramenta recipiunt, sed tantum in electis.   Nam quemadmodum non
alios in fidem illuminat, quam quos preordinavit ad vitam : ita
arcana Spiritus sui virtute efficit, ut percipiant electi quæ offerunt
sacramenta."   Article nineteenth teaches that the benefits signified by the sacraments may be obtained without their use. Paul's
sins were remitted before he was baptized.   Cornelius received
the Spirit before he received the external sign of regeneration.
In the twentieth article it is taught that the benefit of the sacraments is not confined to the time of their administration.   God
sometimes regenerates in their old age those who were baptized
in infancy or youth.[1]

In the Westminster Confession it is said : " Although it be a
great sin to contemn or neglect this ordinance [baptism], yet
grace and salvation are not so inseparably annexed unto it, as
that no person can be regenerated or saved without it, or that
all that are baptized, are undoubtedly regenerated.   The efficacy
of baptism is not tied to that moment of time wherein it is administered ; yet, notwithstanding, by the right use of this ordinance the grace promised is not only offered, but really exhibited
and conferred by the Holy Ghost, to such (whether of age or
infants) as that grace belongeth unto, according to the counsel
of God's own will, in his appointed time." [2]

Calvin controverts the Romish doctrine that the Sacraments of
the New Testament have greater efficacy than those of the Old.
" Nihilo splendidius de illis Apostolus quam de his loquitur, quum
docet patres eandem nobiscum spiritualem escam manducasse ; et
escam illam Christum interpretatur." (1 Cor. x. 3.) And again,
in the same paragraph, " Nec vero baptismo nostro plus tribuere
fas est, quam ipse alibi circumcisioni tribuit, quum vocat ' sigillum
justitiæ fidei.' (Rom. iv. 11.) Quicquid ergo nobis hodie in
sacramentis exhibetur, id in suis olim recipiebant Judæi, Christum
scilicet cum spiritualibus suis divitiis. Quam habent nostra vir-

<hr>

[1] Niemeyer, pp. 194, 195.   [2] Chap. xxviii. §§ 5, 6.

tutem, eam quoque in suis sentiebant: ut scilicet essent illis divinæ erga se benevolentiæ sigilla in spem salutis æternæ." [1]

The doctrine of the Reformed Church, therefore, on the efficacy of baptism includes in the first place the rejection or denial of certain false doctrines on the subject. (1.) That baptism conveys grace " ex opere operato " in the sense which Romanists attach to those words, by any objective supernatural power belonging to the ordinance itself; or in virtue of the divine efficiency inherent in the word or promise of God connected with the sacrament. (2.) That the coöperation of the Spirit, to which the efficacy of the ordinance is due, always attends its administration, so that those who are baptized, in all cases, if unresisting, experience the remission of sins and the renewing of the Holy Ghost. (3.) That baptism was appointed to be the ordinary means or channel of conveying, in the first instance, the merits of Christ's death and the saving influences of the Spirit, so that those benefits may not, except in extraordinary cases, be obtained before or without baptism.

In the second place the Reformed doctrine on this subject affirms, (1.) That baptism is a divine ordinance. (2.) That it is a means of grace to believers. (3.) That it is a sign and seal of the covenant of grace. (4.) That the ordinance was intended to be of perpetual obligation, in the sense that all, not baptized in infancy, are required to submit to baptism as the divinely appointed way of publicly professing their faith in Christ and their allegiance to Him as their God and Saviour; and that all such professors of the true religion are bound to present their children for baptism as the divinely appointed way of consecrating them to God. (5.) That God, on his part, promises to grant the benefits signified in baptism to all adults who receive that sacrament in the exercise of faith, and to all infants who, when they arrive at maturity, remain faithful to the vows made in their name when they were baptized.

Proof of the Reformed Doctrine.

As to the affirmations included in the doctrine of the Reformed churches concerning baptism, little need be said, as they are generally conceded. In all ages, since the apostolic, the tendency in the Church has been not to detract from the importance of the Christian sacraments, but unduly to exalt them. Nothing is plainer from the whole tenor of the New Testament than that the

---

[1] *Institutio*, IV. xiv. 23, edit. Berlin, 1834, part ii. p. 364.

sacraments hold a place much below that of the truth. Whereas
in all churches in a state of decay the reverse is the fact. The
Jewish Church in the time of Christ, had become completely ritualistic. Rites and ceremonies had usurped the place of truth
and holy living. A man might be proud, avaricious, unjust, and
as our Lord expresses it, in every way a " child of the devil," yet
if punctilious in the observance of church rites and church festivals, he esteemed himself and was esteemed by others, a saint so
holy as to be contaminated by fellowship or contact with those
who were the true children of God. This was the form in which
corruption entered the Christian Church soon after the age of
the Apostles. This " mystery of iniquity " even in that age had
begun to work, and when he that " did let " was taken out of
the way, the evil was fully revealed, and the Christian Church
became as thoroughly ritualistic as the Jewish Church had been
when Christ came. The Reformation was in its essential character a protest against ritualism. It proclaimed salvation by a living faith which purified the heart, in opposition to the doctrine of
salvation by rites and ceremonies. It insisted that religion was
a matter of the heart, and therefore denounced as apostasy the
Church returning to " weak and beggarly elements," to observing " days, and months, and times, and years," subjecting the
people to " ordinances, touch not ; taste not ; handle not ; which
are all to perish with the using ; after the commandments and doctrines of men." Ritualism is a broad, smooth, and easy road to
heaven, and is always crowded. It was much easier in Paul's
time to be a Jew outwardly than to be one inwardly ; and circumcision of the flesh was a slight matter when compared to the circumcision of the heart. A theory which allows a man to be religious, without being holy ; to serve both God and mammon ; to
gain heaven without renouncing the world, will never fail to find
numerous supporters. That there is such a theory ; that it has
prevailed extensively and influentially in the Church ; and that
it is prevalent over a large part of Christendom, cannot be disputed. It does not follow, however, that all who are called ritual-
ists, or who in fact attribute undue importance to external rites,
are mere formalists. Many of them are, no doubt, not only sincere, but spiritual Christian men. This is no proof that the
system is not false and evil. All Protestants cheerfully admit
that many Romanists are holy men ; but they no less strenuously
denounce Romanism as an apostasy from the pure Gospel.

As the corruption of the Church of Rome consisted largely in making Christianity to consist in the punctual attendance on church rites ; in teaching that the merits of Christ and the renewing of the Holy Ghost were conveyed in baptism even to unbelievers (*i. e.*, to those destitute of saving faith) ; that when those blessings had been forfeited by sin, they could be restored by confession and absolution; that the eucharist is a true propitiatory sacrifice for the living and the dead ; and that, in short, the religion of Christ is purely ritualistic, its benefits being conferred through external rites, and in no other way, so that those rites were indispensably necessary to salvation; it would have been natural had the Reformers gone to the opposite extreme, and unduly depreciated the importance of the sacraments which Christ himself had appointed.   From this extreme, however, they were mercifully preserved.   They taught, first, that in one sense, —

Baptism is a Condition of Salvation.

This is included in the commission which Christ gave to the Apostles, " Go ye into all the world, and preach the gospel to every creature. He that believeth and is baptized shall be saved." (Matt. xvi. 15, 16.) Baptism, therefore, has the necessity of precept, not that of a means. Our Lord does not say that he that is unbaptized shall be damned. That denunciation falls only on those who believe not. In this respect baptism is analogous to confession. Christ attributes the same necessity to the latter as to the former. In Matthew x. 32, it is written, " Whosoever shall confess me before men, him will I confess also before my Father which is in heaven. But whosoever shall deny me before men, him will I also deny before my Father which is in heaven." And St. Paul says (Rom. x. 9, 10), " If thou shalt confess with thy mouth the Lord Jesus, and shalt believe in thy heart that God hath raised Him from the dead, thou shalt be saved. For with the heart man believeth unto righteousness ; and with the mouth confession is made unto salvation." Confession does not make a man a Christian. It is the public avowal that he is a Christian ; that he is a believer in Christ, in his divinity, in his incarnation, and in his being and doing all that He claimed to be, and that the Scriptures declare He did for us and our salvation. Such confession is a duty, a privilege, and a dictate of gratitude and loyalty, which cannot be repressed. His people will glory in confessing Him. While there is this desire and purpose to acknowledge Christ before men, due occasion for this confession may not be afforded, or it may be hindered by self-diffidence or ignorance.

As our Lord intended not only to save men by the renewing of the Holy Ghost, and thus to bring them into membership in his mystical body, but also to constitute a visible church to consist of all those who confessed Him to be their God and Saviour, He appointed an outward visible sign by which they should be known and enrolled among his people. This was in accordance with the example set in the Old Testament. When God determined to organize Abraham and his descendants into a visible church, to be the depository of the truth and the treasure-house of his gifts, he appointed circumcision to be the sign of the covenant and the badge of membership in the commonwealth of Israel. This also is according to the common usage in human society. When a foreigner wishes to become a citizen of another state, he is called upon to take an oath of allegiance to his adopted country. When a man is elected or appointed to an important office, he must be duly inaugurated, and take the oath of fidelity. The oath taken by the President of the United States does not make him President; it neither confers the right to the office, nor does it confer the qualifications for the proper discharge of its duties. Circumcision did not make a man a Jew. It gave him neither the knowledge nor the grace necessary to his being one of the true children of Israel. It was the appointed means of avowing that he was a Jew; it was the sign of his being included among the worshippers of the true God; and it secured for him the privileges of the theocracy. In like manner, baptism does not make a man a Christian. It is the appointed means of avowing that he is a Christian; it is the badge of his Christian profession before men, it secures for him the privileges of membership in the visible Church, and it is a pledge on the part of God that, if sincere and faithful, he shall partake of all the benefits of the redemption of Christ. It is only in this sense that the Reformed Church teaches the necessity of baptism. It has the necessity of a divine precept. It is the condition of salvation, in the same sense in which confession is, and in which circumcision was. The uncircumcised child was cut off from among the people. He forfeited his birthright. But he did not forfeit his salvation. The Apostle teaches us that if an uncircumcised man kept the law, his uncircumcision was counted for circumcision. To this the Jews objected by asking, What profit then is there in circumcision? Paul answered, Much every way. It is not useless, because not essential. The same is true of baptism. Although not the means of salvation or necessary to its attainment, its benefits are great and manifold.

Baptism as a Duty.

The Reformed Church teaches that baptism is a duty. If a man wishes to be and to be regarded as a disciple of Christ, he is bound to be baptized. If he wishes to consecrate his children to God, he is bound to do it in the way of his appointment. This is plain, —

1. From the command of Christ. If He directed the Apostles to make disciples by baptizing them, He thereby commanded those who claimed to be disciples to submit to baptism. After such a command, the refusal to be baptized, unless that refusal arises from mistake of the nature of the command or through ignorance, is tantamount to refusing to be a disciple at all.

2. This is further plain from the conduct of the Apostles. Under the first sermon preached by the Apostle Peter after the effusion of the Spirit, multitudes were " pricked in their heart," and Peter " said unto them, Repent and be baptized." " Then they that gladly received the Word were baptized." When Philip preached the Word in Samaria, those who believed were baptized, both men and women ; and when he was sent to join the " man of Ethiopia," and " preached unto him," in that short discourse, probably less than an hour long, he must have insisted on the duty of baptism, for the man said, " Here is water ; what doth hinder me to be baptized." It is not probable that a minister of our day in his first brief discourse with an inquirer would urge upon him the duty of being baptized. As soon as Cornelius received the Spirit, Peter ordered water to be brought that he might be baptized. When Ananias came to Paul who was blind from his vision of the glory of Christ, he at once baptized him. And Paul himself, as soon as the jailer in Philippi professed his faith, baptized him and his straightway. It is obvious, therefore, that the Apostles regarded baptism as an imperative duty binding on all those who professed to be the disciples of Christ.

3. This is still further plain from the uniform practice of the Christian Church in all ages and in all parts of the world. All Christians have felt themselves bound by the authority of Christ to confess Him before men in the ordinance of baptism. It is incredible that they should be mistaken in such a matter as this ; that they should regard an external rite as universally obligatory, if it had not in fact been enjoined by their divine Master. Those, therefore, who look upon baptism as an unimportant ceremony which may be neglected with impunity, are acting in opposition to the convictions of the Apostles as manifested by their

conduct, and to the faith of the Church universal. It is not good for a man to have the people of God of all ages against him.

4. The duty of baptism may be argued from its manifold advantages. In the first place, it is a great honour and distinction. If among men it is a coveted distinction to wear the badge of the Legion of Honour, it is a far more desirable distinction to wear the badge of disciples of Christ, to be enrolled among his professed followers, and to be marked as belonging to Him and not to the world. In the second place, those who are baptized, unless they renounce their privilege, are members of the visible Church. The visible Church is an institution of God; it is his treasure-house. The Church under the new dispensation has great advantage over the ancient theocracy, and yet the Apostle speaks in glowing terms of the privileges of the Jews. " Who are Israelites; to whom pertaineth the adoption, and the glory, and the covenants, and the giving of the law, and the service of God, and the promises." (Rom. ix. 4.) Notwithstanding, when in 2 Corinthians iii. 6–11, he compares the two dispensations, he says, " If the ministration of death, written and engraven in stones, was glorious, ... how shall not the ministration of the Spirit be rather glorious? . . . . For even that which was made glorious had no glory in this respect, by reason of the glory that excelleth." This contrast between the Old and New Economies is presented in still stronger terms throughout the Epistle to the Galatians, and in that to the Hebrews. In Galatians he makes Hagar the slave the symbol of the one, and Sarah the free woman the symbol of the other. And in Hebrews the Mosaic economy, with its temples, sacrifices, priesthood, and ritual, is declared to be the unsubstantial shadow, of which the gospel dispensation is the substance. If, then, it was such a distinction to belong to the old theocracy, what, in the view of Paul, must be the honour and blessedness of membership in the Christian Church.

Membership in the visible Church is not only a great honour, it is a great advantage. To the Church are committed the oracles of God. It is the depository of that truth which is able to make men wise unto salvation. It is the divinely appointed instrumentality for preserving and communicating that truth. Every one admits that it is a blessing to be born in a Christian, instead of in a heathen land. It is no less obviously true that it is a blessing to be within the pale of the Church and not cast out into the world. It is good to have the vows of God upon us. It is good to be under the watch and care of the people of God. It is good to have a special claim upon their prayers and upon their efforts to bring us into, or keep us in the paths of salvation. And above all, it is good to be of the number of those to whom God has made a special promise of grace and salvation. For the promise is unto us and to our children. It is a great evil to be " aliens from the commonwealth of Israel, and strangers from the covenants of promise." They, therefore, sin against God and their own souls who neglect the command to be baptized in the name of the Lord ; and those parents sin grievously against the souls of their children who neglect to consecrate them to God in the ordinance of baptism. Do let the little ones have their names written in the Lamb's book of life, even if they afterwards choose to erase them. Being thus enrolled may be the means of their salvation.

Baptism as a Means of Grace.

The Reformed Church teaches that baptism is a means of grace.

1. It is a sign. It signifies the great truths that the soul is cleansed from the guilt of sin by the sprinkling of the blood of Christ, and purified from its pollution by the renewing of the Holy Ghost. The Bible teaches that God sanctifies and saves men through the truth ; that the Spirit works with and by the truth in conveying to men the benefits of redemption. It matters not whether that truth be brought before the mind by hearing or reading it, or in the use of significant divinely appointed emblems. The fact and the method of the deliverance of the children of Israel from their bondage in Egypt, were as clearly taught in the sacrament of the Passover, as in the written words of Moses. So the fundamental truths just mentioned are as clearly and impressively taught in the sacrament of baptism, as in the discourses of our blessed Lord himself. It is, therefore, just as intelligible how the Spirit makes the trnth signified in baptism the means of sanctification, as how he makes that same truth, as read or heard, an effectual means of salvation. The Spirit does not always coöperate with the truth as heard, to make it a means of grace ; neither does He always attend the administration of baptism, with his sanctifying and saving power.

2. Baptism is a seal or pledge. When God promised to Noah that He would never again drown the world in a deluge, He set the rainbow in the heavens as a pledge of the promise which He had made. When he promised to Abraham to be a God to him and to his seed after him, He appointed circumcision as the seal and pledge of that promise. So when He promised to save men

by the blood of Christ and by the renewing of the Holy Ghost, he appointed baptism to be, not only the sign, but also the seal and pledge of those exceeding great and precious promises. No believer in the Bible can look on the rainbow without having his faith strengthened in the promise that a deluge shall never again destroy the earth. No pious Jew could witness the rite of circumcision administered, or advert to that sign in his own person, without an increased confidence that Jehovah was his God. And no Christian can recall his own baptism, or witness the baptism of others, without having his faith strengthened in the great promises of redemption. Every time the ordinance of baptism is administered in our presence, we hear anew the voice from heaven proclaiming, " The blood of Jesus Christ his Son cleanseth us from all sin ; " " He saved us, by the washing of regeneration and renewing of the Holy Ghost."

3. Baptism, however, is not only a sign and seal ; it is also a means of grace, because in it the blessings which it signifies are conveyed, and the promises of which it is the seal, are assured or fulfilled to those who are baptized, provided they believe. The Word of God is declared to be the wisdom and power of God to salvation ; it is the means used by the Holy Spirit in conferring on men the benefits of redemption. Of course all who merely hear or read the Word of God are not saved ; neither do all who receive the baptism of water experience the baptism of the Holy Ghost ; but this is not inconsistent with the Word's being the means of salvation, or with baptism's being the washing of regeneration. Our Lord says we are sanctified by the truth. Paul says we put on Christ in baptism (Gal. iii. 27). When a man receives the Gospel with a true faith, he receives the blessings which the Gospel promises ; when he receives baptism in the exercise of faith, he receives the benefits of which baptism is the sign and seal. Unless the recipient of this sacrament be insincere, baptism is an act of faith, it is an act in which and by which he receives and appropriates the offered benefits of the redemption of Christ. And, therefore, to baptism may be properly attributed all that in the Scriptures is attributed to faith. Baptism washes away sin (Acts xxii. 16) ; it unites to Christ and makes us the sons of God (Gal. iii. 26, 27) ; we are therein buried with Christ (Rom. vi. 3) ; it is (according to one interpretation of Titus iii. 5) the washing of regeneration. But all this is said on the assumption that it is what it purports to be, an act of faith. The gospel of our salvation is, to those who believe not, a

savour of death unto death. Circumcision to the unbelieving Jew, was uncircumcision. Baptism, without faith, is without effect. Such being the case, it is plain that baptism is as truly a means of grace as the Word. It conveys truth to the mind; it confirms the promise of God; and it is the means in the hands of the Spirit of conveying to believers the benefits of redemption. Hence it is a grievous mistake and a great sin to neglect or undervalue it.

All this is plain so far as adults are concerned. But if the saving benefits of baptism are suspended on the condition of faith in the recipient, what benefit can there be in the baptism of infants? To this it may be answered, —

1. That it is the commandment of God. This should be enough. It might as well be asked what benefit could there be in the circumcision of infants under the law. Paul tells us that the benefit to them as well as to others was much every way. It secured their membership in the commonwealth of Israel, which was a greater honour and privilege than the highest peerage on earth. So baptism secures the membership of infants in the visible Church of God, which is a still greater distinction and blessing.

2. Infants are the objects of Christ's redemption. They are capable of receiving all its benefits. Those benefits are promised to them on the same conditions on which they are promised to their parents. It is not every one who says Lord, Lord, who shall enter into the kingdom of God. It is not every baptized adult who is saved; nor are all those who are baptized in infancy made partakers of salvation. But baptism signs, seals, and actually conveys its benefits to all its subjects, whether infants or adults, who keep the covenant of which it is the sign. As a believer who recalls some promise of the Scriptures which he has read or heard, receives the full benefit of that promise; so the infant when arrived at maturity receives the full benefit of baptism, if he believes in the promises signified and sealed to him in that ordinance. Baptism, therefore, benefits infants just as it does adults, and on the same condition.

It does not follow from this that the benefits of redemption may not be conferred on infants at the time of their baptism. That is in the hands of God. What is to hinder the imputation to them of the righteousness of Christ, or their receiving the renewing of the Holy Ghost, so that their whole nature may be developed in a state of reconciliation with God? Doubtless this often occurs; but whether it does or not, their baptism stands good; it assures them of salvation if they do not renounce their baptismal covenant.

Baptismal Regeneration.

Different meanings are attached to the words baptismal regeneration. It has been already stated, in a preceding chapter, that by regeneration is sometimes meant an external change,—translation from the world, as the kingdom of darkness, into the Church, as the kingdom of light. In this sense it implies no subjective change. Sometimes it means the life-long process by which a soul is more and more transformed into the image of God. Sometimes it means the whole process which takes place in the consciousness when a sinner turns from sin through Christ unto God. It is then synonymous with conversion. In our day, in ordinary theological language, it means that supernatural change effected by the Spirit of God by which a soul is made spiritually alive. " You hath He quickened (ἐζωοποίησε)," (see Eph. ii. 1, 5), says the Apostle to the Ephesians. In their former state they were dead in trespasses and sins. Their regeneration consisted in their being made spiritually alive ; or, in their having the principle of a new spiritual life imparted to them. Such being the diversity of meaning attached to the word in question, the phrase baptismal regeneration may be understood in very different senses. The sense in which it is to be here taken is that in which, as is believed, it is generally understood. According to the faith of the Church universal, Greek, Latin, and Protestant, all men since the fall are born in a state of sin and condemnation — spiritually dead. It is a wide-spread belief that when baptism is administered to new-born infants, they are regenerated inwardly by the Holy Spirit ; they are so born again as to become the children of God and heirs of his kingdom. The word, however, includes more than simply the renewing of the soul. Prior to baptism, according to the Catechism of the Church of England, infants are in a state of sin and the children of wrath ; by baptism they are said to be made members of Christ, children of God, and inheritors of the kingdom of heaven. In other words, in baptism the blessings signified in that ordinance are conveyed to the soul of the infant. Those blessings are the cleansing from guilt by the blood of Christ, and purification from pollution by the renewing of the Holy Ghost.

The doctrine of baptismal regeneration, in this sense of the term, has been very extensively held in the Church. The passages of Scripture relied upon for its support, are principally the following : John iii. 5, " Except a man be born of water and of the Spirit, he cannot enter into the kingdom of God." Our Lord is understood in these words to teach the necessity of baptism to salvation. But none of the fallen family of man can be saved without " the sprinkling of the blood of Jesus Christ," and " sanctification of the Spirit; " if baptism saves the soul, it must be by communicating to it those blessings; or, in other words, those blessings must attend its administration. The principal support of this interpretation is tradition. It has been handed down from age to age in the Church, until its authority seems firmly established. It may be remarked in reference to this passage, —

1. That if it be admitted that the words " born of water " are to be understood of baptism, the passage does not prove the doctrine of baptismal regeneration. It asserts the necessity of baptism to admission into the kingdom of God, just as our Lord insists on the necessity of the public confession of his name. Confession is not a means of salvation. It does not convey the benefits of Christ's redemption. It is a duty which Christ imposes on all who desire to be confessed by Him in the last day. The Reformed acknowledge that baptism has this necessity of precept.

2. The phrase " kingdom of God " sometimes means heaven, the future state of blessedness ; sometimes the external or visible Church, as consisting of those who profess to acknowledge Christ as their king ; and sometimes the invisible Church, consisting of those in and over whom Christ actually reigns. At other times the phrase is used comprehensively as including, without discriminating, these several ideas. In this last sense the conditions of admission into the kingdom of God are the conditions of discipleship, and the conditions of discipleship are baptism and inward regeneration ; precisely as under the old dispensation, for a man to become truly a Jew it was necessary that he should be circumcised and believe the true religion as then revealed. But this does not imply that circumcision of the flesh was circumcision of the heart ; or that the latter uniformly attended the former. Neither does our Lord's language in John iii. 5, even, if understood of baptism, imply that the inward grace uniformly attends the outward ordinance. John the Baptist (Matt. iii. 11, 12) made a marked distinction, not only between his baptism and Christian baptism, but between baptism with water and baptism of the Holy Ghost. He could administer the former, Christ only could impart the latter. The two were not necessarily connected. A man might receive the one and not the other. Thousands did then, and do now, receive baptism with water who did not, and do not, experience the renewing of the Holy Ghost.

3. There is no necessity for assuming that there is any reference in John iii. 5, to external baptism.   The passage may be explained after the analogy suggested by what is said in Matthew
iii. 11.   There it is said that Christ would baptize with the Holy
Ghost and with fire.   No one understands this of literal fire.
Fire was one of the familiar Scriptural emblems of purification.
(Is. iv. 4; Jer. v. 14; Mal. iii. 2; Acts ii. 3.)   To baptize with
fire, was to effect a real, and not merely an outward purification.
According to this analogy, to be born of water and of the Spirit,
is to experience a cleansing of the soul analogous to that effected
for the body by water.   This is the interpretation generally
adopted by the Reformed theologians.   It is in accordance, not
only with the passage in Matthew iii. 11, but with the general
usage of Scripture.   In that usage the sign and the thing signified are often united, often interchanged, the one being used for
the other.   Water, essential to the existence of all living creatures on the face of the earth, not only the means of cleansing and
refreshment, but also one of the elements of life, is familiarly used
for the divine blessing, and especially for the saving, sanctifying,
refreshing, and sustaining influences of the Holy Spirit.   Thus in
the gracious invitation of the prophet, " Ho, every one that thirst-
eth, come ye to the waters."   (Is. lv. 1.)   Before in chapter xii.
3, he had said, " With joy shall ye draw water out of the wells of
salvation."   Isaiah xxxv. 6, " In the wilderness shall waters break
out, and streams in the desert."   Isaiah xliv. 3, " I will pour
water upon him that is thirsty."   Ezekiel xxxvi. 25, " Then will
I sprinkle clean water upon you, and ye shall be clean."   Jeremiah ii. 13, God says, My people " have forsaken me, the fountain
of living waters."   Zechariah xiv. 8, " Living waters shall go out
from Jerusalem."   (Compare Ezekiel xlvii. 1–5.)   Our Lord said
to the woman of Samaria, " If thou knewest the gift of God, and
who it is that saith to thee, Give me to drink; thou wouldest have
asked of him, and he would have given thee living water."   (John
iv. 10.)   On another occasion, he said, " If any man thirst, let
him come unto me and drink.   He that believeth on me as the
Scripture hath said, out of his belly shall flow rivers of living
waters.   But this he spake of the Spirit."   (John vii. 37, 38.)
Revelation xxi. 6, " I will give unto him that is athirst of the
fountain of the water of life freely."   xxii. 17, " Whosoever will,
let him take the water of life freely."   It would be a sad mistake
to understand by water in all these passages, the physical element,
or even sacramental water.   When God promises to sprinkle clean

water upon us, He promises the renewing of the Holy Ghost ; and
when Christ says, we must be born of water, He explains it by
saying, we must be born of the Spirit.

That our Lord, in John iii. 5, does not make baptism essential to admission into the kingdom of God, but regeneration by
the Spirit, is the more probable, because Christian baptism was
not instituted when the words there recorded were uttered.   It is
impossible that Nicodemus, or any who heard those words, could
understand them of that sacrament.   Christ, however, intended
to be understood.   He intended that Nicodemus should understand what was necessary to his salvation.   He was accustomed
to hear the sanctifying influence of God's grace called water ; he
knew what the Scriptures meant by being washed with clean
water ; and it was easy for him to understand that being " born
of water " meant to be purified ; but he could not know that it
meant baptism.   To make the passage refer to the baptism of
John is out of the question, although sustained by the authority of
Grotius, Episcopius, Bengel, Neander, Baumgarten-Crusius, Hof-
man, and others.   The baptism of John was confined to the Jews.
It admitted no man to the kingdom of Christ.   Our Lord is laying down the conditions of salvation for all men, and therefore
cannot be understood to refer to a baptism of which the Gentiles
were not partakers, and of which, in the vast majority of cases,
they had never heard.[1]

Another argument on this subject is derived from the fact that
in the sixth and eighth verses of this chapter, where our Lord insists on the necessity of regeneration, he says nothing of being
born of water.   It is simply regeneration by the Spirit that He
declares to be necessary.   It cannot be supposed that one doctrine is taught in the fifth verse and another in the sixth and
eighth verses ; the former teaching that baptism and the renewing of the Holy Ghost are both necessary, and the latter insisting
only on a new birth by the Spirit.   If the two passages teach the
same doctrine, then the fifth verse must teach that being born of

---

[1] That the baptism of John was not Christian baptism would seem plain, (1.) Because
it belonged to the old dispensation.   The Christian Church was not yet established.   (2.) It
bound no man to faith in Jesus Christ as the Son of God and Saviour of the world.   (3.) He
baptized all Judea, but all the people in Judea, pharisees and others, were not thereby
made professing Christians.   (4.) It was a baptism simply unto repentance, as a preparation for the coming of Christ.   (5.) Those who were baptized by John were rebaptized
when they professed to become Christians.   Of the multitudes converted on the day of
Pentecost and immediately after, many no doubt had been baptized by John, and yet they
were baptized anew.   And according to the interpretation, almost universally received in
our day, of Acts xix. 1–6, Paul baptized in Ephesus " certain disciples " in the name of
the Lord Jesus, who had already been baptized by John.

water and being born of the Spirit are one and the same thing,
the one expression being figurative, and the other literal, precisely
as in Matthew iii. 11, where the baptism of the Holy Ghost and
of fire are spoken of.

Again, if " born of water" means baptism, and " born of the
Spirit," spiritual regeneration, then the two things are distinct.
Accordingly Lücke says that being " born of water " is a figurative expression for repentance, which must precede regeneration
by the Spirit.   " The spirit of wisdom flees the sinful soul," as is
said in the Book of Wisdom.   Only the pure in heart can see
God, our Lord himself teaches, and therefore Lücke argues only
those who truly repent are susceptible of regeneration.[1]   This
disjoining the two things as distinct is natural, if the one refers to
baptism and the other to inward regeneration, and therefore would
indicate that regeneration is not by baptism, contrary to the doctrine of the advocates of baptismal regeneration.   Hengstenberg
also makes the two things distinct.   Water, he says, signifies the
remission of sins ; this is effected in baptism ; the new-birth by
the Spirit follows after, which, in his view, is a slow process.[2]

All the arguments against the doctrine in question drawn from
the general teachings of the Bible are, of course, arguments against
the traditionary interpretation of this particular passage.

Another passage on which special reliance is placed as a support of the doctrine of baptismal regeneration is Titus, iii. 5.
The Apostle there says, God saves us " by the washing of regeneration, and renewing of the Holy Ghost."   By " the washing of
regeneration " is understood baptism ; and the Apostle is understood to assert two things, first, that baptism is necessary to salvation ; and second, that baptism is, or is the means of, regeneration.   It is, as the commentators say, the *causa medians* of an
inward change of heart ; or, as Bishop Ellicott says : " The genitive παλιγγενεσίας apparently marks the attribute or inseparable
accompaniments of the λουτρόν, thus falling under the general head
of the possessive genitive." [3]   On this interpretation it may be
remarked, —

1. That, taking the words λουτρὸν παλιγγενεσίας by themselves,

---

[1] *Commentar über das Evangelium des Johannes,* von Dr. Friedrich Lücke, Professor der
Theologie zu Göttingen, 3d edit. Bonn, 1840; part i. p. 522.

[2] *Das Evangelium des heiligen Johannes erläutert,* von E. W. Hengstenberg: Berlin,
1861, vol. i. pp. 186–189.

[3] *A Critical and Grammatical Commentary on the Pastoral Epistles, with a revised
Translation.* By Rt. Rev. Charles J. Ellicott, D.D., Lord Bishop of Gloucester and Bristol.
Andover, 1865, p. 213.

they may have the meaning attached to them. They may mean that baptism is the cause or means of regeneration; or, that regeneration is its inseparable accompaniment. But this is very far from proving that they either have or can have that sense in this connection.

2. Admitting that these words are to be understood of baptismal regeneration, they do not teach that regeneration is insep arably connected with baptism. When Paul speaks of the " gospel of your salvation," he does not mean to say that salvation is inseparable from the mere hearing of the Gospel. When he says, " Faith cometh by hearing," he does not mean that all who hear believe. When our Lord says, We are sanctified by the truth, He does not teach that the truth always has this sanctifying efficacy. The Bible teaches that the Word does not profit unless "mixed with faith in them that " hear it. So St. Paul teaches that baptism does not effect our union with Christ, or secure the remission of sins, or the gift of the Spirit, unless it be, and because it is an act of faith. This Bishop Ellicott admits. He says we must remember " that St. Paul speaks of baptism on the supposition that it was no mere observance, but that it was a sacrament in which all that was inward properly and completely accompanied all that was outward."

3. Still, admitting that the words refer to baptism, they may just as fairly be explained ' Baptism which is the sign and seal of regeneration,' as ' Baptism which is the means or invariable antecedent of regeneration.' The construction indicates the intimate relation between the two nouns, without determining what that relation is, whether it be that of cause and effect, or of a sign and the thing signified. Calvin's comment, " partam a Christo salutem baptismus nobis obsignat," [1] is therefore fully justified.

4. There are, however, strong reasons for denying that there is any reference to baptism as an external rite in this passage.

First, the genitive παλιγγενεσίας may be the simple genitive of apposition; ' the washing which is regeneration.' There are two kinds of washing, the outward and the inward. We are saved by that washing which is regeneration, namely, the renewing of the Holy Ghost. The latter clause being exegetical of the former. This interpretation is simple and natural. It does no violence to the meaning of the words or to the construction of the passage.

Secondly, if the latter clause be not exegetical, it must be accessary. It must express something new, something not expressed

---

[1] *In Novum Testamentum Commentarii*, edit. Berlin, 1831, vol. vi. p. 360.

by the former clause.   The Apostle would then be made to say,
We are saved by the washing of regeneration, and also by the
renewing of the Holy Ghost.   Which amounts to saying, We are
saved by regeneration and by regeneration.   This argument can
only be met by making regeneration mean the commencement, and
the renewing of the Holy Ghost, the progress and development of
the new life.   But this is contrary to the analogy between this
passage and that in John iii. 5.[1]

[1] Bishop Ellicott refers to "the able treatise on this text by Waterland, a tract which,
though extending only to thirty pages, will be found to include and to supersede much that
has been written on this subject."   The treatise thus commended furnishes an excellent
illustration of the difficulty of those understanding each other, who differ seriously in their
modes of thinking and in their use of terms.   To Waterland himself, and to those who agree
with him in his theory of religion and in his use of words, this tract doubtless appears well
ordered and consistent; by the majority of evangelical Christians of our day it can hardly
fail to be regarded as full of confusion and contradictions.   (This treatise may be found in
Waterland; *Works*, edit. Oxford, 1843, vol. iv. pp. 425–458.)   Waterland begins by saying, (1.) That Titus iii. 5, teaches that under the Christian dispensation, God saves men
" by the sacrament of Christian baptism, considered in both its parts, the outward visible
sign, which is water, and the inward things signified and exhibited, namely, a death unto
sin, and a new birth unto righteousness, therein wrought by the Holy Spirit of God." (Page
427.)   (2.) The passage distinctly speaks both of a regeneration, and of a renovation, as two
things, and both of them wrought ordinarily in one and the same baptism, here called the
laver of regeneration and of renewing.   (3.)   " Regeneration," he says, " passively considered, is but another name for the new birth of a Christian: and that new birth, in general,
means a spiritual change wrought upon any person, by the Holy Spirit in the use of baptism; whereby he is translated from his natural state in Adam, to a spiritual state in
Christ." (Page 429.)   Most persons in our day would understand this to mean that regeneration is a subjective change in the state of the soul; a change from spiritual death to
spiritual life.   This, however, is afterwards denied.   Regeneration is not a change of mind.
It is a change of state.   It is a change in the relation which the sinner bears to God.   " A
translation from the curse of Adam into the grace of Christ.   This change, translation, or
adoption, carries in it many Christian blessings and privileges, but all reducible to two,
namely, remission of sins (absolute or conditional), and a covenant claim, for the time being, to eternal happiness." (Page 433.)   " Regeneration on the part of the grantor, God Almighty, means admission or adoption into sonship or spiritual citizenship: and on the part
of the grantee, namely, man, it means his birth, or entrance into that state of sonship, or
citizenship." (Page 432.)   In this sense regeneration implies no subjective change.   The
soul remains precisely in the same inward state in which it was before.   Adoption does not
change a man's inward state.   Waterland, therefore, maintains that Simon Magus was regenerated although it did him no good, leaving him in "the gall of bitterness and in the
bond of iniquity."   Sonship was granted him, but he did not accept it.   He did not, however, need a second regeneration, but only to repent, then his regeneration or adoption in
baptism would take effect. (Pages 442–444.)   In this sense also he teaches that renovation
or "the renewing of the Holy Ghost," must precede baptism, as well as attend and follow
it.   It must precede it to produce faith and repentance, without which regeneration or
adoption does no good. (Page 434.)   In infants, "their innocence and incapacity are to
them instead of repentance, which they do not need, and of actual faith which they cannot
have." (Page 439.)   Infant baptism, however, effects no inward or subjective change.   It
leaves the soul in the same condition, not in the same state or relative position in which it
was before.   On page 433, in stating the difference between regeneration and renovation,
the renewing of the Holy Ghost, he says, "Regeneration is itself a kind of renewal; but
then it is of the spiritual state considered at large; whereas renovation is a " renewal of
heart or mind," a " renewal, namely, of the inward frame, or disposition of the man."
In proof of this difference between regeneration and renovation he says: " Regeneration

Thirdly, if the doctrine of baptismal regeneration can be shown to be thoroughly anti-scriptural, then it cannot be taught in Titus iii. 5. If any passage admit of two interpretations, one opposed to the analogy of Scripture, and the other in harmony with it, we are bound to adopt the latter.

The same remark applies to Acts xxii. 16, where it is recorded that Ananias said to Paul, " Arise, and be baptized, and wash away thy sins, calling on the name of the Lord." If it were the clear doctrine of the Bible that baptism does wash away sin, that

may be granted and received (as in infants) where that renovation has no place at all, for the time being: and therefore, most certainly, the notions are very distinct." Baptismal regeneration, therefore, involves no change "of heart or mind," no change "of the inward frame or disposition." On page 443, in justifying the assumption that Simon Magus was regenerated by his baptism, he makes the benefits of baptism merely outward. He says that "As the Holy Spirit consecrates and sanctifies the waters of baptism, giving them an outward and relative holiness: so He consecrates the persons also in an outward and relative sense, whether good or bad, by a sacred dedication of them to the worship and service of the whole Trinity: which consecration is forever binding, and has its effect; either to the salvation of the parties, if they repent and amend, or to their greater damnation if they do not."

Thus we have three, if not four different definitions of regeneration mixed up together in this treatise, and interchanged one for the other to suit emergencies. First, the word is taken in the sense which it now usually bears. It is the new birth, a change of heart, the commencement of spiritual life in the soul; a change from a state of spiritual death to that of spiritual life. The Christian is said to be the subject of three births. " Once he is born into the natural life, born of Adam; once he is born into the spiritual life, born of water and the Spirit; and once also into a life of glory, born of the resurrection at the last day." (Page 432.) In this sense regeneration and renovation differ as the commencement and the development of life differ; or, as in ordinary language, regeneration and the life-long process of sanctification differ. Secondly, regeneration is made to mean "the death unto sin." Romanists teach that in baptism there is the removal of sin both as to its guilt and power, and an infusion of new habits of grace. Waterland, on page 427, appears to confine it to the death of sin, which on page 439 he explains by the words "plenary remission." In words already quoted, God saves us "by the sacrament of Christian baptism considered in both its parts, the outward visible sign, which is water, and the inward things signified and exhibited, namely, a death unto sin, and a new birth unto righteousness." It will be observed he says "inward things," a death and a new birth, which he after distinguishes as regeneration and renovation. In baptism, therefore, we have simply "remission of sin," renovation precedes and follows it. Thirdly, he makes baptism to confer a covenant claim to the privileges or blessings all included under the heads of remission of sins and a title to eternal happiness. These are granted to adults conditionally, i. e., provided they have faith and repentance; and to infants absolutely, because in their case innocence supplies the place of faith and repentance. This implies no subjective change. It is simply adoption, such as Paul says, in Romans ix. 4, pertained to the Jews as a nation. And fourthly, he teaches that baptism confers on the recipient, whether good or bad, an outward and relative holiness, by consecrating him to the worship and service of God. (Page 443.)

It would thus appear that every theory of baptism, whether Romanist or Protestant, High Church or Low Church, Evangelical or Ritual, can find support in this treatise. If the clear-headed Bishop Ellicott has a clew through this labyrinth, he would do well to impart it to the public. The great characteristic of a large and representative class of the learned theologians of the Church of England during the seventeenth and eighteenth centuries, was that they derived their theology from the Bible through the medium of the Fathers. Whereas the theologians of the Continent drew their doctrines immediately from the Bible; and this makes the difference between biblical and patristical Christianity; the difference, to common eyes, between twilight and noon.

such ablution can be effected in no other way, then we should be forced to admit that Paul's sins had not been remitted until he was baptized. But as this would contradict the plainest teachings of Scripture ; as Paul himself says that God called him by his grace, and made him a true Christian by revealing his Son in him, by opening his eyes to see the glory of God in the face of Jesus Christ, which revelation attended the vision he had on his way to Damascus ; and as the effect of that spiritual revelation was to transform his whole nature and lead him to fall to the ground, and say, " Lord, what wilt thou have me to do ? " no one can believe that he was under the wrath and curse of God, during the three days which intervened between his conversion and his baptism. He did not receive baptism in order that his sins should be washed away ; but as the sign and pledge of their forgiveness on the part of God. He was to be assured of his forgiveness in the ordinance of baptism ; just as a Gentile proselyte to Judaism was assured of his acceptance as one of the people of God, by the rite of circumcision ; but circumcision did not make him a child of God. This passage is perfectly parallel to Acts ii. 38, where it is said, " Repent, and be baptized every one of you in the name of Jesus Christ for the remission of sins, εἰς ἄφεσιν ἁμαρτιῶν." The remission of sins was that to which baptism was related ; that of which it was the sign and seal. John's baptism was εἰς μετάνοιαν unto repentance. This does not mean that his baptism made men penitent. But it was a confession on the part of those who received it, that they needed repentance, and it bound them to turn from their sins unto God. In Luke iii. 3, it is said, John came " preaching the baptism of repentance for the remission of sins." No man understands this to mean that his baptism secured the remission, or the washing away, of sin in the experience of all the multitude who flocked to his baptism. Neither does the Bible anywhere teach that Christian baptism effects either pardon or regeneration in those still out of Christ.

Direct Arguments against the Doctrine of Baptismal Regeneration.

It has been shown in the note on the preceding page that the word regeneration in the phrase " baptismal regeneration," is used in very different senses. The sense usually attached to it, in our day, is that inward change in the state of the soul wrought by the Holy Spirit, by which it passes from death unto life ; by which it is born again so as to become a child of God and an heir of eternal life. The doctrine of baptismal regeneration is the doctrine that this inward saving change is effected in baptism; so that those who are baptized are the subjects of that new birth which Christ declares to be necessary to salvation; and those who are not baptized have not experienced that new birth and are not in a state of salvation.

1. The first, the most obvious, and the most decisive argument against this doctrine is, that, so far as any work or act of the sinner is concerned, the Bible everywhere teaches that the only indispensable condition of salvation is faith in Jesus Christ. "As Moses lifted up the serpent in the wilderness, even so must the Son of man be lifted up: that whosoever believeth in him should not perish, but have eternal life. For God so loved the world, that he gave his only begotten Son, that whosoever believeth in him should not perish, but have everlasting life." (John iii. 14–16.) "He that believeth on the Son hath everlasting life: and he that believeth not the Son shall not see life; but the wrath of God abideth on him" (ver. 36). "I am the bread of life: he that cometh to me shall never hunger; and he that believeth on me shall never thirst." (John vi. 35.) "This is the will of him that sent me, that every one which seeth the Son, and believeth on him, may have everlasting life: and I will raise him up at the last day" (ver. 40). "He that believeth in me, though he were dead, yet shall he live: and whosoever liveth and believeth in me shall never die." (John xi. 25, 26.) These are the words of Jesus. This is the gospel which the Apostles preached, going everywhere and saying to every sinner whom they met, "Believe on the Lord Jesus Christ, and thou shalt be saved." (Acts xvi. 31.) "Whosoever believeth that Jesus is the Christ is born of God." (1 John v. 1.) "Who is he that overcometh the world, but he that believeth that Jesus is the Son of God?" (ver. 5.) Heaven and earth shall pass away, but these words can never pass away. No man may add to them, or detract from them. Whosoever believes on the Son hath everlasting life. This stands firm. It matters not to what Church he may belong; it matters not whether he be Jew or Gentile, bond or free, learned or unlearned, good or bad, baptized or unbaptized, whosoever believes shall be saved.

Not every one, however, who says he believes is a true believer; not every one who believes as the devils believe; but he who has that faith which works by love and purifies the heart, the precious faith of God's elect, every such believer is sure of eternal life. It does not follow from this that faith stands alone; that obedience is not necessary. But obedience is the fruit of faith. He that does not obey, does not believe. For any one, therefore, to say that although a man truly believes the record God has given of his Son, yet that he is not a Christian, unless he belongs to some particular church organization, unless he is baptized with water, unless he comes to the Lord's table, contradicts not the general teaching of the Bible only, but the fundamental principle of the gospel method of salvation. Even Gabriel would not dare to shut the gates of paradise on the thief converted on the cross, because he had not been baptized.

2. It is plain that baptism cannot be the ordinary means of regeneration, or the channel of conveying in the first instance the benefits of redemption to the souls of men, because, in the case of adults, faith and repentance are the conditions of baptism. But faith and repentance, according to the Scriptures, are the fruits of regeneration. He who exercises repentance towards God and faith in our Lord Jesus Christ is in a state of salvation before baptism and therefore in a state of regeneration. Regeneration consequently precedes baptism, and cannot be its effect, according to the ordinance of God. That the Apostles did require the profession of faith and repentance before baptism, cannot be denied. This is plain, not only from their recorded practice but also from the nature of the ordinance. Baptism is a profession of faith in the Father, and the Son, and the Holy Spirit; not of a faith to be obtained through the ordinance, but of a faith already entertained. When the Eunuch applied to Philip for baptism, he said: " If thou believest with all thine heart thou mayest." Of those who heard Peter's sermon on the day of Pentecost it is said, " they that gladly received his word were baptized." (Acts ii. 41.) On this point, however, there can be no dispute. The only way in which Romanists and Romanizers evade this argument, is by denying that faith and repentance are the fruits of the Spirit, or of regeneration. They are in their view not gracious, but natural works, works done before regeneration; works which leave the soul in a state of perdition. But in this they contradict the express words of Christ, who says, whosoever believes shall be saved. And, in contradicting Christ, they contradict the whole Bible.

3. The doctrine of baptismal regeneration, in the sense above explained, is opposed to the whole nature of true religion as set forth in the Scriptures. The two great errors against which

the Gospel, as taught by Christ and unfolded by his Apostles, was directed ; were first the doctrine of human merit ; the merit of good works, the doctrine that men are to be saved on the ground of their own character or conduct ; and the second was ritualism, the doctrine of the necessity and inherent supernatural virtue of external rites and ceremonies. Our Lord taught that men were saved by looking to Him as the dying Hebrews in the wilderness were saved by looking to the brazen serpent. He further taught that unless a man, no matter how punctilious in observing the ceremonial law, was born of the Spirit, he could not enter into the kingdom of God. And the great burden of apostolic teaching was first, that we are saved, not by works but by faith, not for our own righteousness, but on the ground of the righteousness of Christ ; and secondly, that religion is a matter of the heart, not of ritual or ceremonial observances. The Jews of that day taught that no uncircumcised man could be saved. Romanists and Romanizers teach that no unbaptized person, whether infant or adult, is saved. The Jews taught that " no circumcised person ever entered hell," provided he remained within the pale of the theocracy. Romanists and Romanizers say that no baptized person is ever lost, provided he remains within the pale of the Roman Church. The Jews believed that circumcision secured its benefits, not only as a seal of the covenant, but from its own sanctifying power. This was only one aspect of the doctrine of salvation by works, against which the sacred writers so earnestly protested. " He is not a Jew," says St. Paul, " which is one outwardly ; neither is that circumcision, which is outward in the flesh : but he is a Jew, which is one inwardly ; and circumcision is that of the heart, in the spirit and not in the letter ; whose praise is not of men, but of God." (Rom. ii. 28, 29.) The doctrine of the Bible, therefore, is that he is not a Christian who is one outwardly, but that he is a Christian who is one inwardly ; and the baptism which saves the soul is not baptism with water, but the baptism of the heart by the Holy Ghost. This doctrine of salvation by rites was, in the view of the Apostles, a much lower form of doctrine, more thoroughly Judaic, than the doctrine of salvation by works of righteousness.

It is evident that the doctrine of baptismal regeneration, as held by Romanists and their followers, changes the whole nature of religion. It makes mere external observances the conditions of salvation, assuming that outward rites are exclusively the channels through which the benefits of redemption are conveyed to the souls of men. It excludes from the hope of heaven men who truly believe, repent, and lead a holy life; and it assures those of their title to eternal life, who are unrenewed and unsanctified.

4. A fourth argument against the doctrine under consideration, is derived from the analogy between the Word and sacraments everywhere presented in the Bible. God, it is said, saves men by preaching; the gospel is declared to be the power of God unto salvation; faith is said to come by hearing: we are begotten by the Word: we are sanctified by the truth. No Christian, whether Romanist or Protestant, believes that all who hear the Gospel are saved; that it is always the vehicle of conveying the saving and sanctifying influences of the Spirit. Why then should it be assumed, because we are said to be united to Christ by baptism, or to wash away our sins in that ordinance, either that baptism " ex opere operato " produces these effects, or that the Spirit always attends its administration with his saving influences.

5. Again, all Christians admit that multitudes of the baptized come short of eternal life, but no regenerated soul is ever lost. Our Lord in teaching that none but those who are born of the Spirit, enter into the kingdom of heaven, thereby teaches that those who are thus new-born are certainly saved. This is included also in his repeated declarations, that those who believe in Him have eternal life; being partakers of his life, if He lives they shall live also. And the Apostle, in Romans viii. 30, expressly declares that all the regenerate are saved. Whom God predestinates, he says, them He also calls (regenerates), and whom He calls, them he also justifies; and whom He justifies, them he also glorifies. If baptism, therefore, is, in all ordinary cases, attended by the regeneration of the soul, then all the baptized will be saved. If they are not made the heirs of salvation, they are not made the subjects of regeneration.

6. The doctrine of baptismal regeneration is contradicted by the facts of experience. Regeneration is no slight matter. It is a new birth; a new creation; a resurrection from spiritual death to spiritual life. It is a change, wrought by the exceeding greatness of God's power, analogous to that which was wrought in Christ, when He was raised from the dead, and exalted to the right hand of the majesty on high. It cannot therefore remain without visible effect. It controls the whole inward and outward life of its subject, so that he becomes a new man in Christ Jesus. The mass of those baptized, however, exhibit no evidence of any such change. There is no apparent difference between them and

the unbaptized. The whole population of Europe, speaking in general terms, are baptized. Are they all regenerated? Then regeneration amounts to nothing. This doctrine, therefore, utterly degrades regeneration, the precious life-giving gift of the Holy Spirit. To say that those who receive regeneration by baptism in infancy fall away; that the principle of life imparted to them, being uncherished, remains undeveloped, is no satisfactory answer to this argument. Life, especially the life of God in the soul, is not thus powerless. To say that a dead body is restored to life, when it exhibits no evidence of vitality; or, that a dead tree is made alive which puts forth no foliage and bears no fruit, is to say that it is alive and yet dead. It is true that a seed may have a principle of life in it which remains long undeveloped, but unfolds itself when placed under the normal conditions of growth. But the normal conditions of growth of the principle of spiritual life in an infant, are the development of the intelligence and the presence of the truth. If these conditions occur, the growth of the germ of spiritual life is certain. It is to be remembered that that germ is the Holy Spirit, who has life in Himself, and gives life to all in whom He dwells. The doctrine of baptismal regeneration is contradicted by facts. The baptized as a body remain unchanged in heart and life.

§ 13. *Lutheran Doctrine of Baptism.*

Its Necessity.

On this point the Lutheran standards hold the following language. In the Augsburg Confession those who adopt that symbol say: " De baptismo docent, quod sit necessarius ad salutem, quodque per baptismum offeratur gratia Dei ; et quod pueri sint baptizandi, qui per baptismum oblati Deo recipiantur in gratiam Dei. Damnant Anabaptistas, qui improbant baptismum puerorum et affirmant pueros sine baptismo salvos fieri." The Apology for that Confession repeats that declaration, and affirms "that the baptism of infants is not in vain but necessary and effectual to salvation." [1] The same doctrine is taught in the two catechisms of Luther, the larger and smaller.

This doctrine the Lutheran divines have softened down. They affirm that baptism is ordinarily necessary ; yet that the necessity is not absolute, so that if its administration be prevented by una-

[1] *Confessio* I. ix. et *Apologia* IV. 51; Hase, *Libri Symbolici*, p. 12 and p. 156. "Quod oaptismus puerorum non sit irritus, sed necessarius et efficax ad salutem."

voidable circumstances, the want of baptism is not fatal. Thus Gerhard,[1] says Docemus, " baptismum esse quidem ordinarium initiationis sacramentum et regenerationis medium omnibus omnino etiam fidelium liberis ad regenerationem et salutem necessarium; interim tamen in casu privationis sive impossibilitatis salvari liberos Christianorum per extraordinariam et peculiarem dispensationem divinam." Again [2] he says : " Infantes illos, qui vel in utero materno [3] vel repentino quodam casu ante baptismi susceptionem exstinguuntur, temere damnare nec possumus nec debemus, quin potius statuimus, preces piorum parentum, vel si parentes hac in parte negligentes fuerunt, preces Ecclesiæ ad Deum pro his infantibus fusas clementer exaudiri, eosdemque in gratiam et vitam a Deo recipi." In this view the great body of Lutheran divines concur. Dr. Krauth says : " On God's part it is not so necessary that He may not, in an extraordinary case, reach, in an extraordinary way, what baptism is his ordinary mode of accomplishing. Food is ordinarily necessary to human life ; so that the father who voluntarily withholds food from his child is at heart its murderer. Yet food is not so absolutely necessary to human life that God may not sustain life without it." [4]

Its Effects.

As Lutherans regard baptism as ordinarily the necessary means of salvation, they must hold that it communicates all that is essential to that end. It must be the ordinary means of conveying the merits of Christ for the remission of sin and the inward renovation or regeneration of the soul. Such is, therefore, the doctrine taught in the standards of the Lutheran Church. In Luther's Larger Catechism it is said, " Quare rei summam ita simplicissime complectere, hanc videlicet baptismi virtutem, opus, fructum et finem esse, ut homines salvos faciat. Nemo enim in

---

[1] Gerhard, *Loci Theologici*, XXI. viii. 238; edit. Tübingen, 1769, vol. ix. p. 282.

[2] *Ibid.* p. 284.

[3] Romanists, when a child is in imminent peril, baptize it *in utero*.

[4] *The Conservative Reformation and its Theology, as represented in the Augsburg Confession, and in the History and Literature of the Evangelical Lutheran Church.* By Charles P. Krauth, D.D., Norton Professor of Theology in the Evangelical Lutheran Seminary, and Professor of Intellectual and Moral Philosophy in the University of Pennsylvania, Philadelphia: J. B. Lippincott & Co. 1871, pp. 431. We are sorry to see that Dr. Krauth labours to prove that the Westminster Confession teaches that only a certain part, or some of those who die in infancy, are saved ; this he does by putting his own construction on the language of that Confession. We can only say that we never saw a Calvinistic theologian who held that doctrine. We are not learned enough to venture the assertion that no Calvinist ever held it; but if all Calvinists are responsible for what every Calvinist has ever said, and all Lutherans are responsible for everything Luther or Lutherans have ever said, then Dr. Krauth as well as ourselves will have a heavy burden to carry.

hoc baptizatur, ut princeps evadat, verum sicut verba sonant, ut
salvus fiat. Cæterum salvum fieri scimus nihil aliud esse, quam
a peccati, mortis et diaboli tyrannide liberari, in Christi regnum
deferri, ac cum eo immortalem vitam agere." [1] Gerhard says all
the effects of baptism may be included under the two heads
mentioned in Titus iii. 5, regeneration and renovation. The
former he says includes, (1.) The gift of faith. (2.) The remission of sins. (3.) Reception into the covenant of grace.
(4.) Putting on Christ. (5.) Adoption into the number of the
sons of God. (6.) Deliverance from the power of Satan, and,
(7.) The possession of eternal life. Under the head of renovation he includes : the gift of the Holy Spirit, who begins to renew
the intellect, the will, and all the powers of the soul; so that the
lost image of God begins to be restored ; the inward man is renewed, the old man put off, and the new man put on ; the Spirit
resists and gains dominion over the flesh, that sin may not reign
in the body. The same doctrine, in different words, is taught by
all the leading Lutheran theologians.[2]

To what is this Efficacy of Baptism to be referred ?

The effects attributed to baptism are not to be referred to any
power inherent in the water ; nor to the power of the Holy Spirit
" extrinsecus accidens ; " but to the power of the Spirit inherent
in the Word. It has been repeatedly mentioned that Lutherans
teach that there is a divine, supernatural power in the Word of
God, which always produces a saving effect upon those who hear
it, unless it is voluntarily resisted. In the case of infants there
is no such voluntary resistance ; and therefore to them baptism is
always efficacious in conveying to them all the benefits of redemption, which, however, may be forfeited by neglect, unbelief,
or bad conduct in after life. The word connected with baptism
includes the command to baptize ; the formula, the ordinance being
administered in the name of the Holy Trinity ; and especially the
promise, " He that believeth and is baptized, shall be saved."
In Luther's Shorter Catechism, in answer to the question, " Qui
potest aqua tam magnas res efficere ? it is said, " Aqua certe
tantas res non efficit, sed verbum Dei, quod in et cum aqua est,
et fides, quæ verbo Dei aquæ addito credit. Quia aqua sine verbo
Dei est simpliciter aqua, et non est baptismus : sed addito verbo

---

[1] *Catechismus Major*, iv. 24, 25; Hase, *ut supra*, p. 539.

[2] Gerhard, *ut supra*, vol. ix. pp. 148–157. For other Lutheran theologians see Schmid,
Dogmatik der evangelisch-lutherischen Kirche, Frankfort and Erlangen, 1853.

Dei est baptismus, hoc est, salutaris aqua gratiæ et vitæ, et lavacrum regenerationis in Spiritu Sancto, sicut Paulus ait ad Tit.
iii. 5." [1] These ideas are expanded in the Larger Catechism.
Among other things it is there said, " Ad hunc modum ita dis-
cerne, longe aliam rem esse baptismum, atque omnes alias aquas :
non naturalis essentiæ gratia, sed quod huic aliquid præstantioris
rei adjungitur. Ipse enim Deus baptismum suo honestat nomine,
suaque virtute confirmat. Eam ob rem non tantum naturalis
aqua, sed etiam divina, cœlestis, sancta et salutifera aqua, quo-
cunque alio laudis titulo nobilitari potest, habenda et dicenda est ;
hocque non nisi verbi gratia, quod cœleste ac sanctum verbum est,
neque a quoquam satis ampliter, digne et cumulate laudari potest,
siquidem omnem Dei virtutem et potentiam in se habet compre-
hensam. Inde quoque baptismus suam accipit essentiam, ut sacramenti appellationem mereatur, quemadmodum sanctus etiam
docet Augustinus : Accedit, inquit, verbum ad elementum, et fit
sacramentum, hoc est, res sancta et divina." [2] If the Word comprehends in itself, " all the virtue and power of God," and if that
Word is united with the water of baptism, it is easy to understand
how the ordinance has all the potency attributed to it.

The Condition on which the Efficacy of Baptism is suspended.

That condition is faith. It is the clearly pronounced doctrine
of the Lutheran Church that baptism is altogether useless or void
of any saving effect, unless the recipient be a believer. And by
faith is not meant mere speculative assent, such as Simon Magus
had, but true, living, and saving faith. On these points the
Lutheran standards are explicit. In the Larger Catechism, it is
said : " Qui crediderit et baptizatus fuerit, salvus erit. Hoc est :
sola fides personam dignam facit, ut hanc salutarem et divinam
aquam utiliter suscipiat. Cum enim hoc in verbis una cum aqua
nobis offeratur et proponatur, non alia ratione potest suscipi, quam
ut hoc ex animo credamus. Citra fidem nihil prodest baptismus,
tametsi per sese cœlestis et inæstimabilis thesaurus esse negari
non possit." And again it is said, " Absente fide, nudum et inefficax signum tantummodo permanet." [3]

From this it follows that in the case of adults, faith and therefore regeneration, must precede baptism. And consequently in
their case the design and effect of baptism cannot be to convey
the remission of sin and renovation of the heart, but simply to con-

---

[1] *Catechismus Minor,* iv. 9, 10; Hase, p. 377.
[2] *Catechismus Major,* iv. 17, 18; *Ibid.* pp. 537, 538.
[3] iv. 33, 34, and 73; Hase, pp. 541, 549.

firm and strengthen a faith already possessed. Thus Gerhard and Baier as quoted above, say : [1] " Adultis credentibus principaliter præstat usum obsignationis ac testificationis de gratia Dei," and " Infantibus quidem æque omnibus per baptismum primum confertur et obsignatur fides, per quam meritum Christi applicatur. Adultis vero illis tantum, qui fidem ex verbo conceperunt ante baptismi susceptionem, baptismus eam obsignat et confirmat."

With regard to infants Lutherans teach that they have true faith.   Gerhard says : " Nos non de modo fidei sumus solliciti, sed in illa simplicitate acquiescimus, quod infantes vere credant." [2] Chemnitz says : " Nequaquam concedendum est, infantes, qui baptizantur, vel sine fide esse, vel in aliena fide baptizari. . . . . Aliena quidem vel parentum vel offerentium fides, parvulos ad Christum in baptismo adducit Marc. x. 13, et orat, ut propria fide donentur.   Sed per lavacrum aquæ in verbo, Christum Spiritu suo infantibus qui baptizantur, operari et efficacem esse, ut regnum Dei accipiant, non est dubium : licet, quomodo illud fiat, non intelligamus."   Again, " Sicut enim circumcisio etiam parvulorum in V. T. fuit signaculum justitiæ fidei, ita, quia in N. T. infantes baptizati Deo placent, et salvi sunt, non possunt, nec debent inter infideles rejici, sed recte annumerantur fidelibus." [3]

As the word produces faith in those who hear it, provided they do not resist its influence, so baptism in which the word is embodied (so that it is *verbum visibile*), produces faith in infants who are incapable of resistance.   On this subject Dr. Krauth says : " That this grace is offered whenever baptism is administered, and is actually conferred by the Holy Spirit, whenever the individual receiving it does not present in himself a conscious voluntary barrier to its efficacy.   This barrier, in the case of an individual personally responsible, is unbelief.   In the case of an infant, there is no conscious voluntary barrier, and there is a divinely wrought receptivity of grace.   The objector says, the infant cannot voluntarily receive the grace, therefore grace is not given.   We reverse the proposition and reply, the infant cannot voluntarily reject grace, therefore the grace is given.   When we speak of a divinely wrought receptivity of grace, we imply that whatever God offers in the Word or element bears with the offer the power of being received.   When He says to the man with a withered arm, ' Reach forth thine arm ! ' that which was impossible by nature is made possible by the very word of command.

---

[1] Pages 518, 519.

[2] *Loci Theologici*, XXI. viii. § 230; edit. Tübingen, 1769, vol. ix. pp. 275, 276.

[3] *Loc. Theol.* III. *De Baptismo*, edit. Frankfort and Wittenberg, 1653, p. 147, b. of third set.

The Word and Sacraments *per se* break up the absoluteness of the natural bondage; they bring an instant possibility of salvation. Grace is in them so far prevenient that he who has them may be saved, and if he be lost, is lost by his own fault alone." [1]

§ 14. *Doctrine of the Church of Rome.*

The Canons of the Council of Trent on the subject of baptism are brief and comprehensive. The Canons anathematize those who teach that Christian baptism has no superior efficacy to that of John; that true, natural water is not essential in the administration of this sacrament, or that the language of our Lord in John iii. 5, "Except a man be born of water," etc., is to be understood metaphorically; that heretical baptism if performed in the right way and with the intention of doing what the Church does is not valid; that baptism is a matter of indifference, and not necessary to salvation; and also those who deny the propriety, necessity, or efficacy of infant baptism, etc. The Roman Catechism enters much more fully on the subject. It defines baptism as the "sacramentum regenerationis per aquam in verbo." Its material is " omne naturalis aquæ genus, sive ea maris sit, sive fluvii, sive paludis, sive putei, aut fontis, quæ sine ulla adjunctione aqua dici solet." [2] The form prescribed by Christ in Matthew xxviii. 19, is to be observed. As baptism is an ablution it may be performed by immersion, affusion, or sprinkling. There should be sponsors to assume the responsibility of the religious education of the newly baptized. Sponsorship is such an impediment to marriage that if a sponsor should marry his or her godchild, the marriage would be null and void. Baptism by laymen or by women, in cases of necessity, is allowable. Infants receive in baptism spiritual grace; " non quia mentis suæ assensione credant, sed quia ' parentum fide, si parentes fideles fuerint, sin minus, fide (ut D. Augustini verbis loquamur) universæ societatis sanctorum muniuntur.' " Those who are admitted to baptism must desire to be baptized. Hence the unwilling, the insane, the unconscious (nisi vitæ periculum immineat), are not the proper subjects of baptism. In the case of infants, the will of the Church answers for their will. Faith also is necessary; for our Lord says, " He that believeth and is baptized shall be saved." So also is repentance. " Cum baptismus ob eam rem expetendus sit, ut Christum induamus, et cum eo conjungamur, plane constat,

---

[1] *The Conservative Reformation and its Theology*, p. 439.
[2] II. ii. quæs. 4, 6 [7]; Streitwolf, *Libri Symbolici*, vol. i. pp. 259, 260

merito a sacra ablutione rejiciendum esse, cui in vitiis et peccatis perseverare propositum est; præsertim vero, quia nihil eorum, quæ ad Christum, et Ecclesiam pertinent, frustra suscipiendum est: inanemque baptismum, si justitiæ, et salutis gratiam spectemus, in eo futurum esse, satis intelligimus, qui secundum carnem ambulare, non secundum Spiritum cogitat: etsi, quod ad sacramentum pertinet, perfectam ejus rationem sine ulla dubitatione consequitur, si modo, cum rite baptizatur, in animo habeat id accipere, quod a sancta Ecclesia administratur." [1]

The first effect of baptism is the remission of sin. And by remission is meant not only pardon, but the removal of sin. The soul is so cleansed that nothing of the nature of sin remains in it. " Hoc primum tradere oportet, peccatum sive a primis parentibus origine contractum, sive a nobis commissum, quamvis etiam adeo nefarium sit, ut ne cogitari quidem posse videatur, admirabili hujus sacramenti virtute remitti, et condonari." The Catechism quotes the anathema pronounced by the Council of Trent on those who teach, " Quamvis peccata in baptismo remittantur, ea tamen prorsus non tolli, aut radicitus evelli, sed quodam modo abradi, ita ut peccatorum radices animo infixæ adhuc remaneant." [2] The language of the Council is, " In renatis nihil odit Deus, quia nihil est damnationis iis, qui vere consepulti sunt cum Christo per baptisma in mortem: qui non secundum carnem ambulant, sed veterem hominem exuentes, et novum, qui secundum Deum creatus est, induentes, innocentes, immaculati, puri, innoxii, ac Deo dilecti effecti sunt." [3] " Concupiscentia, quæ ex peccato est, nihil aliud est, nisi animi appetitio, natura sua rationi repugnans: qui tamen motus si voluntatis consensum, aut negligentiam conjunctam non habeat, a vera peccati natura longe abest." [4]

One of the propositions which Perrone lays down on this subject, is, that " Per D. N. J. C. gratiam, quæ in baptismo confertur, reatus originalis peccati remittitur, ac tollitur totum id, quod veram et propriam peccati rationem habet." [5]

Baptism, according to Romanists, avails not only for the remission and removal of all sin, but also for the inward sanctification of the soul. "Exponendum erit, hujus sacramenti virtute nos non solum a malis, quæ vere maxima dicenda sunt, liberari, verum etiam eximiis bonis augeri. Animus enim noster divina gratia

---

[1] ii. ii. 27 [xxxiii.] 30 [xxxviii.]; Streitwolf, pp. 276, 279.
[2] *Catechismus Romanus*, ii. ii. 31 [xlii.]; Streitwolf, vol. i. pp. 280, 281.
[3] Sess. v. 5; *Ibid.* vol. i. p. 19.
[4] *Catechismus Romanus*, ii. ii. 32 [xliii.]; *Ibid.* pp. 281, 282.
[5] *Prælectiones Theologicæ, De Baptismo*, cap. vi. 170, 5th edit. Turin, 1839, vol. vi. p. 59.

repletur, qua justi, et filii Dei effecti, æternæ quoque salutis heredes instituimur." [1] It thus appears, that, according to the Church of Rome, all the benefits of the redemption of Christ are conveyed to the soul by baptism; and that there is no other divinely appointed channel of their communication.

The Council of Trent declared, " Si quis dixerit, in tribus sacramentis, baptismo scilicet, confirmatione, et ordine, non imprimi characterem in anima, hoc est signum quoddam spirituale, et indelebile, unde ea iterari non possunt; anathema sit." [2] What this internal spiritual something is, does not admit of explanation. It neither reveals itself in the consciousness nor manifests itself in the life. It is assumed to be something analogous in the spiritual sphere, to the insignia of merit or decorations of nobility in the sphere of civil or social life.

§ 15. *The Lord's Supper.*

The passages of Scripture directly referring to the sacrament of the Lord's Supper are the following: Matthew xxvi. 26–28, " And as they were eating, Jesus took bread, and blessed it (εὐλογήσας), and brake it, and gave it to the disciples, and said, Take, eat; this is my body. And he took the cup and gave thanks (εὐχαριστήσας), and gave it to them, saying, Drink ye all of it: for this is my blood of the new testament, which is shed for many for the remission of sins."

Mark xiv. 22–24, " And as they did eat, Jesus took bread, and blessed, and brake it, and gave to them, and said, Take, eat; this is my body. And he took the cup; and when he had given thanks, he gave it to them: and they all drank of it. And he said unto them, This is my blood of the new testament, which is shed for many."

Luke xxii. 19, 20, " And he took bread, and gave thanks, and brake it, and gave unto them, saying, This is my body which is given for you: this do in remembrance of me. Likewise also the cup after supper, saying, This cup is the new testament in my blood, which is shed for you."

1 Corinthians x. 15–17, " I speak as to wise men; judge ye what I say. The cup of blessing which we bless, is it not the communion of the blood of Christ? The bread which we break, is it not the communion of the body of Christ? For we being many are one bread, and one body; for we are all partakers of that one bread."

---

1 *Catechismus Romanus*, II. ii. 38 [1]; Streitwolf, vol. i. p. 286.
2 Sess. vii. *De Sacramentis in genere*, canon 9; Streitwolf, pp. 39, 40.

1 Corinthians xi. 23–29, " For I have received of the Lord that which also I delivered unto you, That the Lord Jesus, the same night in which he was betrayed, took bread: and when he had given thanks, he brake it, and said, Take, eat; this is my body, which is broken for you: this do in remembrance of me. After the same manner also he took the cup, when he had supped, saying, This cup is the new testament in my blood: this do ye, as oft as ye drink it, in remembrance of me. For as often as ye eat this bread, and drink this cup, ye do shew the Lord's death till he come. Wherefore, whosoever shall eat this bread, and drink this cup of the Lord, unworthily, shall be guilty of the body and blood of the Lord. But let a man examine himself, and so let him eat of that bread, and drink of that cup. For he that eateth and drinketh unworthily, eateth and drinketh damnation to himself, not discerning the Lord's body."

Apart from matters of doubtful interpretation, these passages plainly teach, First, that the Lord's Supper is a divine institution of perpetual obligation. Second, that the material elements to be used in the celebration, are bread and wine. Third, that the important constituent parts of the service are, (1.) The consecration of the elements. (2.) The breaking of the bread and pouring out of the wine. (3.) The distribution and the reception by the communicants of the bread and wine. Fourth, that the design of the ordinance is, (1.) To commemorate the death of Christ. (2.) To represent, to effect, and to avow our participation in the body and blood of Christ. (3.) To represent, effect, and avow the union of believers with Christ and with each other. And (4.) To signify and seal our acceptance of the new covenant as ratified by the blood of Christ. Fifth, the conditions for profitable communion are, (1.) Knowledge to discern the Lord's body. (2.) Faith to feed upon Him. (3.) Love to Christ and to his people.

The main points of controversy concerning this ordinance are: (1.) The sense in which the bread and wine are the body and blood of Christ. (2.) The sense in which the communicant receives the body and blood of Christ in this ordinance. (3.) The benefits which the sacrament confers, and the manner in which those benefits are conveyed. (4.) The conditions on which the efficacy of the ordinance is suspended.

The Lord's Supper is a divine Ordinance of perpetual Obligation.

This has never been doubted in the Christian Church. That Christ intended that the ordinance should continue to be ob-

served in his Church until his second advent is plain, (1.) From
his express command given in Luke xxii. 19, and repeated by the
Apostle in 1 Corinthians xi. 24. (2.) The design of the ordinance
which is declared to be the commemoration of Christ; the constantly repeated proclamation of his expiatory death in the ears of
men; and the communication of the benefits of that death to his
people, necessarily assumes that it is to be observed so long as
Christ, in the visible manifestation of his person, is absent from his
Church. (3.) That the Apostles so understood the command of
Christ is plain from their continuing to observe this ordinance
to which such frequent reference is made in their writings, under
the designations, "breaking of bread," "the Lord's Supper," and
" The Lord's table." (4.) The uniform practice of the Church on
this subject admits of no other solution, than the appointment of
Christ and the authority of the Apostles.

The names given to this sacrament in the early Church were very
various. It was called, (1.) Εὐχαριστία, not only by the Greeks but
also by the Latins, because as Chrysostom says, πολλῶν ἐστιν εὐεργε-
τημάτων ἀνάμνησις.[1]   It is a solemn thanksgiving for the blessings of
redemption. This designation being so appropriate, all English speaking Christians are fond of calling it the eucharist.
(2.) Εὐλογία, for the same reason. The words εὐχαριστέω and εὐλογέω
are interchanged. Sometimes the one and sometimes the other is
used for the same act, and hence εὐχαριστία and εὐλογία are used in
the same sense. In 1 Corinthians x. 16, St. Paul calls the sacramental cup τὸ ποτήριον τῆς εὐλογίας, "the cup of blessing," in allusion
to the כּוֹס הַבְּרָכָה drunk at the paschal supper. (3.) Προσφορά,
" offering," because of the gifts or offerings for the poor and for
the service of the Church made when the Lord's Supper was celebrated. (4.) Θυσία, " sacrifice." Properly, the act of sacrificing; metonymically, the thing sacrificed or the victim; tropically
of anything offered to God, as obedience or praise. In Philippians ii. 17, Paul speaks of " the sacrifice and service of faith; "
and in iv. 18, he says that the contributions of the saints were " an
odour of a sweet smell, a sacrifice acceptable, well pleasing to God."
And in Hebrews xiii. 15 we read of a θυσία αἰνέσεως, " a sacrifice of
praise." The praise was the sacrifice or offering made to God.
The Lord's Supper in this sense was at first called a sacrifice,
both because it was itself a thank-offering to God and because
attended by alms which were regarded as tokens of gratitude to

---

[1] *In Mattheum Homilia* xxv. [xxvi.] 3 ; *Works,* edit. Montfaucon, Paris, 1836, vol. vii.
p. 352 [310. d].

Christ for the benefits of his redemption. Afterwards, it was so
called, because it was a commemoration of the sacrifice of Christ
upon the cross; and finally because it came to be regarded by
Romanists as itself an expiatory sacrifice. For this reason the
consecrated wafer is by them called "hostia," the host, or victim,
because it was assumed to be the true body of Christ offered to
God in expiation of the sins of the faithful. (5.) Μυστήριον,
something secret, or having a sacred or secret import. As the
Lord's Supper was a significant memorial of the greatest of all
mysteries, the death of the Son of God upon the cross, it was appropriately designated μυστήριον. This word, however, is applied
in its general sense to both sacraments and even to other sacred
rites. Another reason may be assigned for this designation. The
Lord's Supper was celebrated in secret; in so far that the promiscuous body of attendants on Christian worship was dismissed
before the sacrament was administered. (6.) Σύναξις, "the assembly," because from the nature of the service it implied the coming
together of believers. (7.) "Sacramentum," in the general sense
of μυστήριον, by way of eminence applied to the Lord's Supper
as "the" sacrament. It was also after the idea of the sacrificial
character of the eucharist became prevalent, called "sacramentum altaris," the sacrament of the altar. This designation sur-
vived the doctrine on which it was founded, as it was retained by
Luther, who earnestly repudiated the idea that the Lord's Supper
is a sacrifice. (8.) "Missa," or mass. This word has been
variously explained; but it is almost universally, at the present
time, assumed to come from the words used in dismission of the
congregation. "Ite, missa est," "Go, the congregation is dismissed." First the unconverted hearers were dismissed, and then
the catechumens, the baptized faithful only remaining for the
communion service. Hence there was in the early Church a
"missa infidelium," a "missa catechumenorum," and finally a
"missa fidelium." There seems to have been a different service
adapted to these several classes of hearers. Hence the word
"missa" came to be used in the sense of the Greek word λειτουργία
or service. As under the Old Testament the offering of sacrifices
was the main part of the temple service, so in the Christian
Church, when the Lord's Supper was regarded as an expiatory
offering, it became the middle point in public worship and was
called emphatically the service, or mass. Since the Reformation
this has become universal as the designation of the eucharist as
celebrated in the Church of Rome.

The Elements to be used in the Lord's Supper.

The word element, in this connection, is used in the same sense as the Latin word " elementum," and the Greek word στοιχεῖα, for the component parts of anything; the simple materials or rudiments. Bread and wine are the elements employed in the celebration of the Lord's Supper, because they are the simple corporeal materials employed as the symbols of the body and blood of Christ.

As the Lord's Supper was originally instituted in connection with the Passover, there is no doubt that unleavened bread was used on that occasion. It is evident, however, from the apostolic history, that the Apostles used whatever kind of bread was at hand. There is no significancy either in the kind of bread or in the form of the loaf. It is enough that it is bread. This makes it the proper emblem of Him who declared Himself to be the true bread which came down from heaven.

Although it seems so obvious that it is a matter of indifference what kind of bread is used in the Lord's Supper, a serious controversy arose on this subject in the eleventh century between the Greek and Latin churches: the former condemning the use of unleavened bread as a remnant of Judaism, and the latter insisting not only on its propriety, but on its being the only kind allowable, because used by Christ himself when He instituted the sacrament. The two churches adhere to their ancient convictions and practice to the present day. The Lutherans in this matter side, in their practice, with the Romanists. The Reformed regard it as a matter of indifference ; although they object to the " placentulæ orbiculares," or round wafers, used by Romanists in this ordinance ; because flour and water or flour and some glutinous substance is not bread in the ordinary sense of the word. It is not used for nourishment. The use, therefore, is inconsistent with the analogy between the sign and the thing signified. The eucharist is a supper ; it represents our feeding upon Christ for our spiritual nourishment and growth in grace. Besides, the use of the wafer was introduced with the rise of the doctrine of transubstantiation. The consecrated bread being regarded as the real body of Christ, it was natural that it should be made in a form which precluded the danger of any particle of it being profaned.[1]

[1] The question of the kind of bread used in the eucharist at different times and in different churches is discussed with great minuteness of detail in the recent work, *Notitia*

Some of the Reformed theologians raise the question whether in places where bread and wine cannot be obtained, it is lawful to use in their stead other articles of nourishment, the most allied to them in nature? This question they answer affirmatively; while they insist that the command of Christ and the practice of the Apostles should be strictly adhered to where such adherence is possible.

By wine as prescribed to be used in this ordinance, is to be understood " the juice of the grape ; " and " the juice of the grape " in that state which was, and is, in common use, and in the state in which it was known as wine. The wine of the Bible was a manufactured article. It was not the juice of the grape as it exists in the fruit, but that juice submitted to such a process of fermentation as secured its preservation and gave it the qualities ascribed to it in Scripture. That οἶνος in the Bible, when unqualified by such terms as *new*, or *sweet*, means the fermented juice of the grape, is hardly an open question. It has never been questioned in the Church, if we except a few Christians of the present day. And it may safely be said that there is not a scholar on the continent of Europe, who has the least doubt on the subject. Those in the early Church, whose zeal for temperance led them to exclude wine from the Lord's table, were consistent enough to substitute water. They were called Tatiani, from the name of their leader, or Encratitæ, Hydroparastatæ, or Aquarii, from their principles. They not only abstained from the use of wine and denounced as " improbos atque impios " those who drank it, but they also repudiated animal food and marriage, regarding the devil as their author.[1] They soon disappeared from history. The plain meaning of the Bible on this subject has controlled the mind of the Church, and it is to be hoped will continue to control it till the end of time.[2]

In most churches, the wine used in the Lord's Supper is mixed with water. The reasons assigned for this custom, are, (1.) That

---

Eucharistica, a Commentary. Explanatory, Doctrinal and Historical on the Order for the Administration of the Lord's Supper or Holy Communion, according to the Use of the Church of England. By W. E. Scudamore, M. A., Rector of Ditchingham and formerly Fellow of St. John's College, Cambridge; Rivingtons, London, Oxford and Cambridge, 1872, pp. 749–765.

[1] Suicer, *Thesaurus Ecclesiasticus, sub voce* Σύναξις ; edit. Amsterdam, 1728, vol. ii. p. 1123.

[2] This is not the place for the discussion of what, in this country, is called " The Wine Question." The reader will find it amply ventilated in the *Princeton Review* for April and October, 1841, in two articles from the pen of Rev. John Maclean, D. D., and more recently by the Rev. Lyman H. Atwater, D. D., in the same Review, October, 1871, and January, 1872.

the eucharist having been instituted at the table of the Paschal supper, and the wine used in the Passover being mixed with water, it is morally certain that the wine used by Christ when instituting this sacrament, was also thus mixed. Hence it was inferred that his disciples in all ages should follow his example. That the Paschal cup contained wine mixed with water rests on the authority of Jewish writers. " It was the general practice of the Jews to dilute their wine with water. ' Their wine was very strong,' says an ancient Jewish writer,[1] 'and not fit for drinking unless water was mixed with it.' " [2] It is certain, from the writings of the fathers, that this custom prevailed extensively in the primitive Church. As the Greeks and Romans were in the habit of mixing water with their wine on all ordinary occasions, it is the more natural that the same usage should prevail in the Church. It is still retained, both by Romanists and by the Oriental Church. (2.) Besides this historical reason for the usage in question, it was urged that it adds to the appropriate significance of the ordinance. As water and blood flowed from the side of our Lord on the cross, it is proper, it is said, that water should be mixed with the wine in the service intended to be commemorative of his death. This being the case, the quantity of the water used was declared to be a matter of indifference. In the First Book of Edward VI. prepared for the Church of England, the minister was ordered to put into the cup " a little pure and clean water." This order was omitted from the rubric, and has never been restored. Merati, of the Church of Rome, says: " A little water ought to be mixed by the priest with the wine on the altar, not . . . . for necessity of the sacrament or divine precept, ... but only of ecclesiastical precept obliging under mortal sin." [3]

The Sacramental Actions.

The first of these is the introductory and consecrating prayer. The object of this prayer is threefold : —

1. To give thanks to God for the gift of his Son, whose death we are about to commemorate.

2. To prepare the hearts of the communicants for the solemn service on which they are attending. To this end the prayer must be appropriate. And to be appropriate, it should be well considered. This is a matter of great importance. It often

---

[1] Gloss in Lightfoot, *Horæ Hebraicæ* in St. Matthew xxvi. 27, n. v. *Opp.* tom. ii. p. 380.

[2] Scudamore, *ut supra*, p. 350.

[3] Note by Merati in Gavanti. *Commentaria in Rubricas Missalis Romani.* pars III. tit. iv. n. vi.; *Thesaurus Sacrorum Rituum,* auctore Gavanto. Augsburg, 1763, vol. i. p. 333. b.

happens that the prayers offered on such occasions are long and rambling. Petitions are offered for all classes of men; for the young and old; for the sick and afflicted; for Sunday-schools; for missions, and all the other objects usually embraced in the long prayer before the sermon. The consequence is, that the minds of the people are distracted. Their attention is turned away from the service before them; and they are much less prepared to celebrate the Lord's death when the prayer is ended, than they were before it began. This is as inappropriate and as hurtful as it would be for a minister to spend his strength in praying for the conversion of the heathen or the Jews, when kneeling at the bedside of a dying sinner. The officiating clergyman little thinks of the pain he inflicts by such desultory prayers. He not only puts himself out of sympathy with the people, but there is a constant antagonism between him and them during the progress of the prayer, and when it is over there is a painful effort to collect their scattered thoughts, and to suppress the feelings of disapprobation, displeasure, and sense of injury awakened by the want of thought or want of tact on the part of the pastor.

3. The third object of this introductory prayer, is the consecration of the elements. Bread and wine in themselves, or as found in common use, are not the symbols of the body and blood of Christ. They become such only by being set apart for that purpose. This is an important part of the service; and therefore, is made prominent in the liturgies of all Churches, and especially enjoined not only in our Directory for Worship, but also in the Confession of Faith and in our Larger Catechism.[1]

In all these points there is an analogy between this prayer and "the grace before meat," used at an ordinary meal. In that service we recognize the goodness of God in providing food for our bodies; we prepare our minds for the thankful reception of his gifts; and we pray that the portion received may be set apart or rendered effectual for the renewal of our strength. When, therefore, it is said that our Lord gave thanks or blessed the cup and the bread, it is to be understood that He not only thanked God for his mercies, but that He also invoked his blessing, or, in other words, prayed that the bread and wine might be, what He intended them to be, the symbols of his body and blood, and the means of spiritual nourishment to his disciples. This is also taught by the Apostle in 1 Corinthians x. 16, where

---

[1] *Directory*, viii. 5; *Confession*, xxix. 3; *Larger Catechism*, Q. 169.

he speaks of " the cup of blessing," *i. e.*, the cup which has been blessed, or consecrated by prayer to a sacred use ; as is explained by the following words, " which we bless."

Breaking the Bread.

This is the second of the prescribed sacramental actions. It is an important, because it is a significant, part of the service. Christ broke the bread which He gave to his disciples. The bread is the symbol not merely of Christ's body, but of his body as broken for us. " The bread which we break," says the Apostle, thereby showing that the breaking was a constituent part of the service. So significant is this act that it was used as a designation of the sacrament itself, which was called the " breaking of bread," Acts ii. 42. The breaking of the bread enters into the significancy of the ordinance not only as referring to the broken body of Christ, but also as the participation of one bread is the symbol of the unity of believers. There is one bread, and one body. This significance is lost, when separate wafers are distributed to the communicants. Above all it is expressly commanded. It is recorded that Christ blessed, broke, and gave the bread ; and then added: " This do." The command includes the blessing, the breaking, and the giving.

This important part of the service continued to be observed in the Church until the doctrine that the bread after consecration is the real body of Christ began to prevail. Then the use of the wafer was introduced, which is placed unbroken in the mouth of the communicant. This is clearly a departure from apostolic usage, and evinces a departure from apostolic doctrine.

The Distribution and Reception of the Elements.

It is recorded that Christ after having blessed the bread and broken the bread, gave it to his disciples, saying: " Take, eat." And in like manner after having blessed the cup, he gave it to them, saying: " Drink ye all of it." All this is significant. Christ gives ; the disciples, each one for himself, receive and partake of the offered gifts.

From all this it is clear, (1.) That it is contrary to the rule prescribed in Scripture when the communicant does not for himself, receive with his own hand the elements of bread and wine. (2.) That it is utterly inconsistent with the nature of the sacrament, when, as in the private masses of the Romanists, the officiating priest alone partakes of the consecrated bread or wine.

(3.) That it is against the nature of the sacrament, when instead of the two elements being distributed separately, the bread is dipped into the wine, and both are received together. This mode of administering the Lord's Supper, was, it is said, introduced at first, only in reference to the sick; then it was practised in some of the monasteries; and was partially introduced into the parishes. It never, however, received the sanction of the Roman Church. In the Greek and the other oriental churches it became the ordinary method, so far as the laity are concerned. The bread and wine are mixed together in the cup, and, by a spoon, placed in the mouth of the recipient. Among the Syrians the usual custom was for the priest to take a morsel of bread, dip it in the wine and place it in the mouth of the communicant. From the East this passed for a time over to the West, but was soon superseded by a still greater departure from the Scriptural rule.[1] (4.) The most flagrant violation of the integrity of this sacrament is that of which the Church of Rome for the last seven hundred years has been guilty, in withholding the cup from the laity. This is inconsistent not only with the command of Christ, and the example of the Apostles, but also with the practice of the Universal Church for eleven hundred years. This is not denied by Romanists themselves. They do not pretend to claim the authority of antiquity for this custom. They fall back on the authority of the Church. They deny, indeed, that the words of Christ include a command that the wine as well as the bread should be distributed in the Lord's Supper; but they affirm that after consecration, the whole substance of the bread is transmuted into the substance of Christ's body; and that as his body and blood are inseparable, they who receive the bread do thereby receive his blood; and, therefore, that the whole benefit of the sacrament is experienced by the laity although the cup be withheld from them. This being the case, they maintain that it is wise in the Church, for prudential reasons, especially to avoid the danger of the blood of Christ being spilled and profaned, to confine the administration of the cup to the clergy. On the principle that the whole Christ is in the bread, the language of the Council of Trent is:[2] " Si quis negaverit, in venerabili sacramento eucharistiæ sub unaquaque specie, et sub singulis cujusque speciei partibus, separatione facta, totum Christum contineri;

---

[1] Suicer, *Thesaurus Ecclesiasticus, ut supra,* vol. ii. p. 1127.   Scudamore, *Notitia Eucharistica, ut supra,* pp. 614–618.

[2] Sess. xiii. canon 3; Streitwolf, *Libri Symbolici,* vol. i. p. 51.

anathema sit." The comment of Perrone on these words is as follows : " Hæc porro veritas est corollarium dogmatis de transubstantione ; panis enim et vinum per consecrationem convertuntur in illud Christi corpus et sanguinem, qui in cœlis est, et in eodem statu glorioso ; jam vero corpus illud inseparabile est a sanguine, anima et divinitate, et e converso pariter sanguis separari nequit a corpore, anima, et divinitate, ergo sub quavis specie totus Christus præsens fiat necesse est." [1] Withholding the cup from the laity is therefore founded on the doctrine of transubstantiation, and must fall with it. The custom was introduced gradually, and it was not until the Council of Constance, A. D. 1415, that it was made a law in the Latin Church. And that Council admits that its action was contrary to the primitive practice, for it says : " Although in the primitive Church this sacrament was received under both kinds, yet has this custom been introduced, that it should be taken by the celebrants under both kinds, and by the laity under the kind of bread only. Wherefore since this custom has been introduced by the Church and the holy fathers on reasonable grounds, and has been very long observed, it is to be accounted for a law, etc." [2]

The Design of the Lord's Supper.

As the death of the incarnate Son of God for us men and for our salvation is of all events the most important, it should be held in perpetual remembrance. It was to this end that our blessed Lord instituted this sacrament, and accompanied the institution with the command, " This do in remembrance of me." And the Apostle in 1 Corinthians xi. 26, tells his readers, " As often as ye eat this bread, and drink this cup, ye do shew the Lord's death till he come." This itself is of great importance. The fact that the Lord's Supper has been celebrated without interruption in the Church, from the day of the crucifixion to the present time, is an irresistible proof of the actual occurrence of the event which it is intended to commemorate. It is, therefore, just as certain that Christ died upon the cross as that Christians everywhere celebrate the Lord's Supper. It is not only, however, the fact of Christ's death, which this sacrament thus authenticates ; but also its design. Our Lord declared that He died as a substitute and sacrifice. " This is my body which is given for you ; " or, as the Apostle reports it, " broken for you." " This is my blood of the New

---

[1] *Prælectiones Theologicæ*, 5th edit. Turin, 1839, vol. vi. p. 168.
[2] *Notitia Eucharistica, ut supra*, p. 624.

Testament, which is shed for many for the remission of sins."
Redemption, therefore, is not by power, or by teaching, or by
moral influence, but by expiation. It is this truth which the
Lord's Supper exhibits and authenticates. Still further, as Christ
affirms that his body was to be broken and his blood shed for the
remission of sin, this from the nature of the case involves on his
part the promise and pledge, that the sins of those who receive
and trust Him, shall certainly be forgiven. The sacrament thus
becomes not only a sign but also a seal. It is the handwriting
and signet of the Son of God attached to the promise of redemption. As, therefore, the truth revealed in the Word has the
highest power that can belong to truth in its normal influence on
the human mind ; so even the natural effect of the truths symbolized and authenticated in the Lord's Supper, is to confirm the
faith of the believer. But as the natural or objective power of
the truth as revealed in the Word is insufficient for conversion or
sanctification without the supernatural influences of the Spirit, so
the truths set forth in the eucharist avail nothing towards our
salvation unless the Spirit of all grace gives them effect. On the
other hand, as the Word when attended by the demonstration of
the Spirit, becomes the wisdom and power of God unto salvation ;
so does the sacrament of the Lord's Supper, when thus attended,
become a real means of grace, not only signifying and sealing, but
really conveying to the believing recipient, Christ and all the
benefits of his redemption.

In the Lord's Supper, therefore, the believer receives Christ.
He receives his body and blood. The Apostle asserts that the
bread which we break is a participation (κοινωνία) of the body of
Christ, and that the cup which we bless is a participation of the
blood of Christ. (1 Cor. x. 16.) Our Lord in John vi. 53 says,
" Except yet eat the flesh of the Son of man, and drink his blood,
ye have no life in you." There must be a sense, therefore, in
which believers receive the body and blood of Christ. The effect
of this reception of Christ is two fold. First, He and his people
become one ; and secondly, all true believers in virtue of this union
with Christ become one body " and every one members one of another." Christ and his people are one in such a sense that it is
not they that live, but Christ that liveth in them. (Gal. ii. 20.)
He dwells in them ; his life is their life ; because He lives they
shall live also. (John xiv. 19.) They are one in a sense analogous to that in which the head and members of the human body
are one. The Holy Spirit given to Him without measure is com-

municated to his people so that they become one body fitly joined together. (Eph. iv. 16.) By one Spirit they are all baptized into one body. (1 Cor. xii. 13.) This union between Christ and his people is also illustrated by the union between the vine and its branches. The life of the vine and of its branches is one. (John xv.) Again, Christ and his people are one, as husband and wife are one flesh. "We are members of his body, of his flesh, and of his bones." (Eph. v. 30.)

In being thus united to Christ as their common head, believers become one body, in a mystical sense. The Holy Spirit dwelling in each and in all constitutes them one. They have one principle of life. The Spirit works in all alike "both to will and to do." They have, consequently, one faith, and one religious experience, as well as one Lord, and one God and Father. They are so bound together that if one member suffer, all the members suffer with it; or if one member be honoured, all the members rejoice with it. (1 Cor. xii. 26.) So far as this all churches seem to agree. They all admit that in the Lord's Supper believers are thus united to Christ and to one another.

Qualifications for the Lord's Supper.

It is plain from the preceding account of the nature and design of this sacrament, that it is intended for believers; and that those who come to the table of the Lord do thereby profess to be his disciples. If sincere in this profession, they receive the inestimable gifts which it is intended to convey. If insincere, they eat and drink judgment to themselves. The Apostle, therefore, argues that as those who partook of the Jewish altars did thereby profess to be Jews; and as those who participated in the heathen sacrifices, did thereby profess to be heathen; so those who partake in the Lord's Supper, do thereby profess to be Christians. But to be a Christian a man must have competent knowledge of Christ and of his gospel. He must believe the record which God has given of his Son. He must believe that Christ died for our sins; that his body was broken for us. He must accept of Christ as He is thus offered to him as a propitiation for sin. All this, or, the profession of all this is involved in the very nature of the service. The faith, however, of those who would acceptably partake of the Lord's Supper, is faith not only in Christ, but also in the sacrament itself. That is, faith in its divine appointment, and in its being what in the New Testament it is declared to be. We must not look upon it as a mere human device, as a mere ritual

observance or ceremony ; but as a means ordained by God of signifying, sealing, and conveying to believers Christ and the benefits of his redemption.   The reason why believers receive so little
by their attendance on this ordinance is, that they expect so little.
They expect to have their affections somewhat stirred, and their
faith somewhat strengthened ; but they perhaps rarely expect so
to receive Christ as to be filled with all the fulness of God.   Yet
Christ in offering Himself to us in this ordinance, offers us all of
God we are capable of receiving.   For we are complete ($\pi\epsilon\pi\lambda\eta\rho\omega$-
$\mu\acute{\epsilon}\nu\omega$) filled, $i.$ $e.$, filled with the fulness of God in Him.   (Col.
ii. 10.)

It is impossible that the faith which this sacrament demands
should exist in the heart, without producing supreme love and
gratitude to Christ, and the fixed purpose to forsake all sin and
to live devoted to his service.   Our Church, therefore, teaches
that it is required of them who would worthily partake of the
Lord's Supper, that they examine themselves, of their knowledge
to discern the Lord's body, of their faith to feed upon Him, of
their repentance, love, and new obedience.

It is, however, not to be inferred from this that a man must be
assured that he is a true believer before he can properly approach
the Lord's table.   It often happens that those who are most confident that they are Christians, have the least of Christ's Spirit.
And therefore we are taught in the Larger Catechism,[1] that
" One who doubteth of his being in Christ, or of his due preparation to the sacrament of the Lord's Supper, may have true interest in Christ, though he be not assured thereof ; and in God's
account hath it, if he be duly affected with the apprehension of
the want of it, and unfeignedly desires to be found in Christ, and
to depart from iniquity ; in which case (because promises are made,
and this sacrament is appointed, for the relief even of weak and
doubting Christians) he is to bewail his unbelief, and labour to
have his doubts resolved ; and so doing, he may and ought to come
to the Lord's Supper, that he may be further strengthened."

It is no valid objection to the doctrine that faith, love, and new
obedience are the qualifications for an acceptable approach to the
Lord's table, that under the Old Testament all the people were
allowed to partake of the Passover.   This only shows the difference between what God demands, and what fallible men are
authorized to enforce.   It cannot be doubted that it was required
of the Jews in coming to the paschal supper that they should

1 Ques. 172.

believe the fact of their miraculous deliverance out of Egypt; that they should be duly grateful to God for that great mercy; and that they should have faith in the promise of that still greater redemption through Him of whom their paschal lamb was the divinely appointed type. All this was implied in an intelligent and sincere attendance on the Jewish Passover. The priests, however, were not authorized to sit in judgment on the sincerity of the worshippers, and to exclude all whom they deemed insincere. So while faith, love, and the purpose of new obedience are clearly required of all who come to the table of the Lord, all that the Church can demand is a credible profession; that is, a profession against which no tangible evidence can be adduced. Even to acceptable prayer, faith and love and the purpose of obedience are demanded, and yet we cannot exclude from access to God all whom we do not deem true believers. Confounding the Church and the world is a great evil, but the Church cannot be kept pure by any human devices. Men must be so instructed that they will be kept back from making profession of a faith they do not possess, by their own consciences; and those who act unworthily of their Christian profession should be subjected to the discipline of the Church. Further than this the Bible does not authorize us to go, and all attempts to improve upon the Bible must be productive of evil. According to our Directory for Worship, the minister "is to warn the profane, the ignorant, and scandalous, and those that secretly indulge themselves in any known sin, not to approach the holy table." To these classes his power of exclusion is confined. "On the other hand, he shall invite to this holy table, such as, sensible of their lost and helpless state of sin, depend upon the atonement of Christ for pardon and acceptance with God; such as, being instructed in the Gospel doctrine, have a competent knowledge to discern the Lord's body, and such as desire to renounce their sins, and are determined to lead a holy and godly life." [1]

Although all churches substantially agree as to the nature and design of the Lord's Supper, so far as the general statements above given are concerned, they differ essentially in their explanations of those statements; just as all profess to receive what the Scriptures say of this ordinance, while they differ so widely as to what the Bible really teaches. So far as these differences of views concern the qualifications for participating in the Lord's Supper; the benefits the ordinance is intended to convey; and the nature

---

[1] *Westminster Directory*, chap. viii. p. 4.

of the efficacy attributed to it, they have been already sufficiently considered when teaching of the sacraments in general.   There are, however, certain points in reference to this sacrament in particular, which are so important that they have determined the course of ecclesiastical history.   Those points are all intimately related.   (1.) In what sense are the bread and wine in the eucharist the body and blood of Christ.   (2.) In what sense are his body and blood received in that ordinance by the communicant. (3.) In what sense is Christ in the Lord's Supper.   These points are so related that they cannot well be considered separately. These are the points as to which the Reformed, the Lutheran, and the Roman Churches are opposed to each other.

§ 16. *Doctrine of the Reformed Church on the Lord's Supper.*

It is a very difficult matter to give an account of the Reformed doctrine concerning the Lord's Supper satisfactory to all parties.   This difficulty arises partly from the fact that words have changed their meaning since the days of the Reformation. The Reformed as well as Lutherans asserted that there is " a real presence" of Christ in the Lord's Supper ; and that the believer receives the true body and blood, or the substance of the body and blood of Christ.   Such expressions would be understood in our day very differently from what they were then.   Another source of difficulty on this subject is that the statements of the Reformed had for one great object the prevention of a schism in the ranks of the Protestants.   They did all they could to conciliate Luther.   They adopted forms of expression which could be understood in a Lutheran sense.   So far was this irenical spirit carried that even Romanists asked nothing more than what the Reformed conceded. Still another difficulty is that the Reformed were not agreed among themselves.   There were three distinct types of doctrine among them, the Zwinglian, the Calvinistic, and an intermediate form, which ultimately became symbolical, being adopted in the authoritative standards of the Church.

Zwinglian Statements.

It was the tendency of the Zwinglian element of the Reformed Church, to make less of the supernatural aspect of the sacraments than their associates did.   There was, however, no essential difference, as afterwards appeared between the Churches of Zurich and those of Geneva.   Zwingle taught that " The Lord's Supper is nothing else than the food of the soul, and Christ instituted the ordinance as a memorial of Himself. When a man commits himself to the sufferings and redemption of Christ he is saved. Of this He has left us a certain visible sign of his flesh and blood, both of which He has commanded us to eat and drink in remembrance of Him." This is said in a document presented to the council of Zurich in 1523.

In his "Expositio Christianæ Fidei," written just before his death, and published by Bullinger in 1536, he says: "The natural substantial body of Christ in which He suffered, and in which He is now seated in heaven at the right hand of God, is not in the Lord's Supper eaten corporeally, or as to its essence, but spiritually only. . . . . Spiritually to eat Christ's body is nothing else than with the spirit and mind to rely on the goodness and mercy of God through Christ. . . . . Sacramentally to eat his body, is, the sacrament being added, with the mind and spirit to feed upon Him." [1]

The Confessions most nearly conformed to the views of Zwingle are the "Confessio Tetrapolitana," the "First Basil," and the "First Helvetic." These are all apologetic. The last mentioned protests against the representation that the Reformed regard the sacraments as mere badges of profession, and asserts that they are signs and means. The Lord's Supper is called "cœna mystica" "in which Christ truly offers his body and blood, and hence Himself, to his people; not as though the body and blood of Christ were naturally united with the bread and wine, locally included in them, or sensibly there present, but in so far as the bread and wine are symbols, through which we have communion in his body and blood, not to the nourishment of the body, but of the spiritual or eternal life." [2]

In "The Sincere Confession of the Ministers of the Church of Zurich," dated 1545, we find the following precise statement of their doctrine: "We teach that the great design and end of the

---

[1] "In cœna domini naturale ac substantiale istud corpus Christi, quo et hic passus est et nunc in cœlis ad dexteram patris sedet, non naturaliter atque per essentiam editur, sed spiritualiter tantum. . . . . Spiritualiter edere, corpus Christi, nihil est aliud quam spiritu ac mente niti misericordia et bonitate Dei per Christum. . . . . Sacramentaliter edere corpus Christi, cum proprie volumus loqui, est, adjuncto sacramento, mente ac spiritu corpus Christi edere." Niemeyer, *Collectio Confessionum*, Leipzig, 1840, pp. 44, 47.

[2] "Cœnam mysticam, in qua dominus corpus et sanguinem suum, id est, seipsum suis vere ad hoc offerat, ut magis, magisque in illis vivat, et illi in ipso. Non quod pani et vino corpus et sanguis domini vel naturaliter uniantur: vel hic localiter includantur, vel ulla huc carnali præsentia, statuantur. Sed quod panis et vinum ex institutione domini symbola sint, quibus ab ipso domino per ecclesiæ ministerium vera corporis et sanguinis ejus communicatio, non in periturum ventris cibum, sed in æternæ vitæ alimoniam exhibeatur." Art. xxii.; Niemeyer, pp. 120, 121.

Lord's Supper, that to which the whole service is directed, is the remembrance of Christ's body devoted, and of his blood shed for the remission of our sins. This remembrance, however, cannot take place without true faith. And although the things of which the service is a memorial, are not visible or present after a visible or corporal manner, nevertheless believing apprehension and the assurance of faith renders them present in one sense to the soul of the believer. He has truly eaten the bread of Christ . . . . who believes on Christ, very God and very man, crucified for us, on whom to believe is to eat, and to eat is to believe. . . . . Believers have in the Lord's Supper no other life-giving food than that which they receive elsewhere than in that ordinance. The believer, therefore, receives both in and out of the Lord's Supper, in one and the same way, and by the same means of faith, one and the same food, Christ, except that in the supper the reception is connected with the actions and signs appointed by Christ, and accompanied with a testifying, thanksgiving, and binding service. . . . . Christ's flesh has done its work on earth, having been offered for our salvation; now it no longer benefits on earth and is no longer here."

Calvin's Doctrine.

While Calvin denied the real presence of the body and blood of Christ in the eucharist, in the sense in which that presence was asserted by Romanists and Lutherans, yet he affirmed that they were dynamically present. The sun is in the heavens, but his light and heat are present on earth. So the body of Christ is in heaven, but from that glorified body there radiates an influence, other than the influence of the Spirit (although through his agency), of which believers in the Lord's Supper are the recipients. In this way they receive the body and blood of Christ, or, their substance, or life-giving power. He held, therefore, that there was something not only supernatural, but truly miraculous, in this divine ordinance.

He says :[1] " We conclude that our souls are fed by the flesh and

---

[1] *Institutio* iv. xvii. 10; edit. Berlin, 1834, part ii. p. 407. "Summa sit, non aliter animas nostras carne et sanguine Christi pasci, quam panis et vinum corporalem vitam tuentur et sustinent. Neque enim aliter quadraret analogia signi, nisi alimentum suum animæ in Christo reperirent: quod fieri non potest, nisi nobiscum Christus vere in unum coalescat nosque reficiat carnis suæ esu et sanguinis potu. Etsi autem incredibile videtur, in tanta locorum distantia penetrare ad nos Christi carnem, ut nobis sit in cibum, meminerimus, quantum supra sensus omnes nostros emineat arcana Spiritus sancti virtus et quam stultum sit, ejus immensitatem modo nostro velle metiri. Quod ergo mens nostra non comprehendit, concipiat fides, Spiritum vere unire, quæ locis disjuncta sunt. Jam sacram illam carnis et sanguinis sui communicationem, qua vitam suam in nos transfundit Christus,

blood of Christ, just as our corporal life is preserved by bread and wine. For the analogy of the signs would not hold, if our souls did not find their aliment in Christ, which, however, cannot be the case, unless Christ truly coalesce into one with us, and support us through the use of his flesh and blood. It may seem incredible indeed that the flesh of Christ should reach us from such an immense local distance, so as to become our food. But we must remember how far the power of the Holy Spirit transcends all our senses, and what folly it must be even to think of reducing his immensity to our measure. Let faith then embrace what the understanding cannot grasp, namely, that the spirit truly unites things which are totally separated. Now this sacred communication of his flesh and blood, by which Christ transfuses his life into us, just as if He penetrated our bones and marrow, He testifies and seals in the holy supper ; not by the exhibition of a vain and empty sign, but by putting forth such an energy of his Spirit as fulfils what He promises."

In 1561 Calvin wrote in answer to the Lutheran Hesshuss, and with an irenical purpose, his tract " De participatione carnis et sanguinis Christi in sacra cœna." In an appendix to that Tract, he says, " The same body then which the Son of God once offered in sacrifice to the Father, he daily offers to us in the supper, that it may be our spiritual aliment. Only that must be held which was intimated as to the mode, that it is not necessary that the essence of the flesh should descend from heaven in order that we may feed upon it ; but that the power of the Spirit is sufficient to penetrate through all impediments and to surmount all local distance. At the same time we do not deny that the mode here is incomprehensible to human thought; for flesh naturally could neither be the life of the soul, nor exert its power upon us from heaven ; and not without reason is the communication, which makes us flesh of his flesh, and bone of his bones, denominated by Paul a great mystery. In the sacred supper we acknowledge it a miracle, transcending both nature and our understanding, that Christ's life is made common to us with Himself, and his flesh given to us as aliment." [1]

Again, " These things being disposed of, a doubt still appears with respect to the word ' substance '; which is readily allayed if we put away the gross imagination of a manducation of the flesh,

non secus acsi in ossa et medullas penetraret, in cœna etiam testatur et obsignat; et quidem non objecto inani aut vacuo signo, sed efficaciam Spiritus sui illic proferens, qua impleat, quod promittit."

[1] *Works*, Amsterdam, 1667; vol. viii. p. 744, a, b.

as though it were corporal food, that, being taken into the mouth,
is received into the stomach.   For if this absurdity be removed,
there no reason why we should deny that we are fed with Christ's
flesh substantially, since we truly coalesce with Him in one body
by faith, and are made one with Him.   Whence it follows that
we are joined with Him in substantial connection, just as substantial vigour flows down from the head into the members.   The
definition there must stand that we are made to partake of
Christ's flesh substantially; not in the way of carnal mixture, or
as if the flesh of Christ drawn down from heaven entered into us,
or were swallowed by the mouth ; but because the flesh of Christ,
as to its power and efficacy, vivifies our souls, not otherwise than
the body is nourished by the substance of bread and wine." [1]

The Reformed symbols which most nearly conform to the peculiar views of Calvin are the Gallican, the Belgian, and the early
Scottish.   The first mentioned teaches [2] " Quamvis [Christus]
nunc sit in cœlis, ibidem etiam mansurus donec veniat mundum
judicaturus: credimus tamen, eum arcana et incomprehensibili
Spiritus sui virtute per fidem apprehensa, nos nutrire et vivificare
sui corporis et sanguinis substantia.   Dicimur autem hoc spiritualiter fieri, non ut efficaciæ et veritatis loco imaginationem aut
cogitationem supponamus, sed potius, quoniam hoc mysterium nostræ cum Christo coalitionis tam sublime est, ut omnes nostros sensus totumque adeo ordinem naturæ superet: denique quoniam sit
divinum ac cœleste, non nisi fide percipi ac apprehendi potest."

" Credimus, sicut antea dictum est, tam in cœna quam in baptismo, Deum nobis reipsa, id est, vere et efficaciter donare quicquid
ibi sacramentaliter figurat, ac proinde cum signis conjungimus
veram possessionem ac fruitionem ejus rei, quæ ita nobis offertur.
Itaque affirmamus eos qui ad sacram mensam Domini puram fidem
tanquam vas quoddam afferunt, vere recipere quod ibi signa testi-

---

[1] At the meeting of the national Synod of France in 1571, Beza being president, an application was made by certain deputies to have the clause in Article 37 of the Confession
altered, which asserts that we are nourished with "the substance of Christ's body and
blood."   The Synod refused to make the alteration, and explained the expression by saying they did not understand by it, " any confusion, commixture, or conjunction, ... but
this only, that by his virtue all that is in Him that is needful to our salvation, is hereby
most freely given and communicated to us.   Nor do we agree with those who say we communicate in his merits and gifts and Spirit, without his being made ours; but with the
Apostle (Eph. v. 23), admiring this supernatural, and to us, incomprehensible, mystery, we
believe we are partakers of his body delivered to death for us, and of his blood shed for us,
so that we are flesh of his flesh and bone of his bones, and that we receive Him together
with his gifts by faith, wrought in us by the incomprehensible virtue and efficacy of the
Holy Spirit."   This decision offended the Zurich ministers.

[2] Art. xxxvi. xxxvii.; Niemeyer, p. 338.

ficantur, nempe corpus et sanguinem Jesu Christi, non minus esse cibum ac potum animæ, quam panis et vinum sunt corporis cibus."

In the Scotch Confession of 1560, it is said, "We confess that believers in the right use of the Lord's Supper thus eat the body and drink the blood of Jesus Christ, and we firmly believe that He dwells in them, and they in Him, nay, that they thus become flesh of his flesh and bone of his bones. For as the eternal Deity gives life and immortality to the flesh of Christ, so also his flesh and blood, when eaten and drunk by us, confer on us the same prerogatives." [1]

In the Belgic Confession adopted in 1563, it is said, " Ut iis nobis [Christus] testificatur, quam vere accipimus et tenemus manibus nostris hoc sacramentum, illudque ore comedimus (unde et postmodum vita hæc nostra sustentatur), tam vere etiam nos fide (quæ animæ nostræ est instar et manus et oris) recipere verum corpus et verum sanguinem Christi, in animis nostris, ad vitam spiritualem in nobis fovendam. . . . . Dicimus itaque id quod comeditur esse ipsissimum Christi corpus naturale, et id quod bibitur verum ipsius sanguinem : at instrumentum seu medium quo hæc comedimus et bibimus non est os corporeum, sed spiritus ipse noster, idque per fidem." [2]

Confessions in which Zwinglians and Calvinists agree.

The most important of these, as already mentioned, is the " Consensus Tigurinus," because drawn up for the express purpose of settling the disputes between the two parties, and because it was adopted by both. It was written by Calvin and published under the title " Consensio mutua in re Sacramentaria Ministrorum Tigurinæ Ecclesiæ, et D. Joannis Calvini Ministri Genevensis Ecclesiæ, jam nunc ab ipsis authoribus edita." This " Consensus" was vehemently attacked by the Lutherans ; and Calvin, four years after its publication, felt called upon to publish an explanation and defence of it. In his letter prefixed to that defence and addressed to the ministers of Zurich and other Swiss churches, he says : The Lutherans now see that those whom they denounced as Sacramentarians agree, and then adds : " Nec vero si superstites hodie essent optimi et eximii Christi servi Zwinglius et Oecolampadius, verbulum in ea sententia mutarent." [3] No document, therefore, can have a higher claim to represent the true

---

[1] Art. xxi.; Niemeyer, p. 352.   [2] Art. xxxv.; *Ibid.* pp. 385, 386.
[3] See his *Letter to the Swiss Churches* prefixed to his *Consensionis Capitum Expositio ;* Niemeyer, *ut supra,* p. 201

doctrine of the Reformed Church than this "Consensus." This document has already been quoted on a previous page to prove that its authors, (1.) Did not regard the sacraments as mere signs, or as simply badges of a Christian profession. (2.) But as means of grace, appointed, not only to signify and seal, but also to convey the benefits of redemption. (3.) That their saving and sanctifying efficacy is not due to any virtue in them or in him that doth administer them, but solely to the blessing of God and the working of his Spirit. (4.) That the sacraments are not means of grace to all indiscriminately, or to all who are their passive recipients, but only to believers or the chosen people of God. (5.) That their efficacy is not tied to the time of their administration. (6.) That the grace or saving gifts which the sacraments, when God so wills, are made the channels of communicating, may be, and in fact are, received before and without their use.

The last seven articles of the "Consensus" concern the Lord's Supper. In the twenty-first the local presence of Christ in that sacrament is denied. "Præsertim vero tollenda est quælibet localis præsentiæ imaginatio. Nam quum signa hic in mundo sint, oculis cernuntur, palpentur manibus: Christus quatenus homo est, non alibi quam in cœlo, nec aliter quam mente et fidei intelligentia quærendus est. Quare perversa et impia superstitio est, ipsum sub elementis hujus mundi includere."

The twenty-second article teaches that the words, "This is my body," in the form of institution, are to be understood figuratively. "Proinde, qui in solennibus Cœnæ verbis, Hoc est corpus meum, Hic est sanguis meus: præcise literalem, ut loquuntur, sensum urgent, eos tanquam præposteros interpretes repudiamus. Nam extra controversiam ponimus, figurate accipienda esse, ut esse panis et vinum dicantur id quod significant. Neque vero novum hoc aut insolens videri debet, ut per metonymiam ad signum transferatur rei figuratæ nomen, quum passim in Scripturis ejusmodi locutiones occurrant: et nos sic loquendo nihil asserimus, quod non apud vetustissimos quosque et probatissimos Ecclesiæ scriptores extet."

Article twenty-third relates to spiritual manducation. "Quod autem carnis suæ esu et sanguinis potione, quæ hic figurantur, Christus animas nostras per fidem Spiritus sancti virtute pascit, id non perinde accipiendum, quasi fiat aliqua substantiæ vel commixtio vel transfusio: sed quoniam ex carne semel in sacrificium oblata et sanguine in expiatione effuso vitam hauriamus."

Article twenty-fourth is directed against transubstantiation and other errors. " Hoc modo non tantum refutatur Papistarum commentum de transubstantione, sed crassa omnia figmenta atque futiles argutiæ, quæ vel cœlesti ejus gloriæ detrahunt vel veritati humanæ naturæ minus sunt consentaneæ. Neque enim minus absurdum judicamus, Christus sub pane locare vel cum pane copulare, quam panem transubstantiare in corpus ejus."

Article twenty-fifth teaches that Christ's body is locally in heaven. "Ac ne qua ambiguitas restet, quum in cœlo quærendum Christum dicimus, hæc locutio locorum distantiam nobis sonat et exprimit. Tametsi enim philosophice loquendo supra cœlos locus non est; quia tamen corpus Christi, ut fert humani corporis natura et modus, finitum est et cœlo, ut loco, continetur, necesse est a nobis tanto locorum intervallo distare, quanto cœlum abest a terra."

Article twenty-sixth, the last of the series, is directed against the adoration of the host, or consecrated wafer.[1]

The Heidelberg Catechism was prepared at the command of Frederick III., Elector of the Palatinate, by Caspar Olevian, a disciple of Calvin, and by Ursinus, a friend of Melancthon, and adopted by a General Synod held at Heidelberg in 1563. This Catechism, having symbolical authority both in the German and in the Dutch Reformed Churches, is entitled to special respect as a witness to the faith of the Reformed Church.

The sacraments are declared to be " Sacred, visible signs, and seals, instituted by God, that through them He may more clearly present and seal the promise of the gospel, namely, that He, for the sake of the one offering of Christ accomplished on the cross, grants not to all only but even to separate believers the forgiveness of sin and eternal life."

" How art thou reminded and assured, in the Holy Supper, that thou art a partaker of the one offering of Christ on the cross, and of all his benefits?"

" Thus, that Christ has commanded me and all believers, to eat this broken bread, and to drink this cup in remembrance of Him; adding these promises: that his body was offered and broken on the cross for me, and his blood shed for me, as certainly as I see with my eyes the bread of the Lord broken for me, and the cup communicated to me: and further, that He feeds and nourishes my soul to everlasting life, with his crucified body and shed blood, as assuredly as I receive from the hands of the minister, and take with my mouth, the bread and cup, as certain signs of the body and blood of Christ."

[1] Niemeyer, *Collectio Confessionum*, Leipzig, 1840, p. 196.

" What is it then to eat the crucified body, and drink the shed blood of Christ? "

" It is not only to embrace with a believing heart all the sufferings and death of Christ, and thereby to obtain the pardon of sin and eternal life ; but also, besides that, to become more and more united to his sacred body by the Holy Ghost, who dwells at once both in Christ and in us ; so that we, though Christ is in heaven, and we on earth, are notwithstanding, flesh of his flesh and bone of his bone ; and we live and are governed forever by one Spirit, as the members of the same body are by one soul."

" Do then the bread and wine become the very body and blood of Christ? "

" Not at all : but as the water in baptism is not changed into the blood of Christ, neither is the washing away of sin itself, being only the sign and pledge of the things sealed to us in baptism ; so the bread in the Lord's Supper is not changed into the very body of Christ ; though agreeably to the nature and properties of sacraments, it is called the body of Christ Jesus." [1]

The Confession of Faith of the Reformed Dutch Church was revised by the Synod of Dort in 1618 and 1619. In the thirty-fifth article of that Confession, it is said that as man has a natural life common to all men, so believers have besides, a spiritual life given in their regeneration ; and as God has provided food for our natural life, He has in like manner provided food for our spiritual life. That food is Christ, who is the true bread which came down from heaven ; " who nourishes and strengthens the spiritual life of believers, when they eat Him, that is to say, when they apply and receive Him by faith in the Spirit." As we receive the bread and wine by the mouth " we also do as certainly receive by faith (which is the hand and mouth of our soul) the true body and blood of Christ our only Saviour in our souls for the support of our spiritual life." The manner of this reception is hidden and incomprehensible. " In the mean time we err not, when we say, that what is eaten and drunk by us is the proper and natural body, and the proper blood of Christ. But the manner of our partaking of the same, is not by the mouth, but by the Spirit through faith."

The Second Helvetic Confession is, on some accounts, to be regarded as the most authoritative symbol of the Reformed Church, as it was more generally received than any other, and was sanctioned by different parties. It was drawn up by Bullinger in

[1] Ques. lxvi. xxv. lxxvi. lxxviii.; Niemeyer, pp. 444–447.

1562. In 1565, the Elector Frederick, distressed at the contentions respecting the sacraments which agitated the Church, wrote to Bullinger to send him a confession which might if possible unite the conflicting parties, or, at least meet the objections of the Lutherans. Bullinger sent him this Confession which he had prepared some years before; with which the Elector was perfectly satisfied. To give it the greater authority it was adopted by the Helvetic churches. As it was drawn up by Bullinger the successor of Zwingle at Zurich, it cannot be supposed to contain anything to which a Zwinglian could object. The nineteenth chapter treats of the sacraments in general, and teaches, (1.) That they are mystic symbols, or holy rites, or sacred actions, including the word, signs, and thing signified. (2.) That there were sacraments under the old, as well as under the new economy. (3.) That God is their author, and operates through them. (4.) That Christ is the great object presented in them, the substance and matter of them, the lamb slain from the foundation of the world, the rock from which all the fathers drank, etc. (5.) Therefore, as far as the substance is concerned, the sacraments of the two dispensations are equal; they have the same author, the same significancy, and the same effects. (6.) The old have been abolished, and baptism and the Lord's Supper introduced in their place.   (7.) Then follows an exposition of the constituent parts of a sacrament. First, the word, by which the elements are constituted sacred signs. Water, bread, and wine, are not in themselves, apart from the divine appointment, sacred symbols; it is the word of God added to them, consecrating, or setting them apart, which gives them their sacramental character. Secondly, the signs, being thus consecrated, receive the names of the things signified. Water is called regeneration; the bread and wine are called the body and blood of Christ. They are not changed in their own nature. They are called by the names of the things signified, because the two are sacramentally united, that is, united by mystical significance and divine appointment. (8.) In the next paragraph, this Confession rejects, on the one hand the Romish doctrine of consecration, and on the other, the idea that the sacraments are mere empty signs. (9.) The benefits signified are not so included in the sacraments or bound to them, that all who receive the signs receive the things which they signify; nor does their efficacy depend on the administrator; nor their integrity upon the receiver. As the Word of God continues his Word, whether men believe or not; so is it with the sacraments.

The twenty-first chapter is devoted to the Lord's Supper. It contains the following passages : " Ut autem rectius et perspicacius intelligatur, quomodo caro et sanguis Christi sint cibus et potus fidelium, percipianturque a fidelibus ad vitam æternam, paucula hæc adjiciemus. Manducatio non est unius generis. Est enim manducatio corporalis, qua cibus in os percipitur ab homine, dentibus atteritur, et in ventrem deglutitur. . . . . Est et spiritualis manducatio corporis Christi, non ea quidem, qua existimemus cibum ipsum mutari in spiritum, sed qua, manente in sua essentia et proprietate corpore et sanguine Domini, ea nobis communicantur spiritualiter, utique non corporali modo, sed spirituali, per Spiritum Sanctum, qui videlicet ea, quæ per carnem et sanguinem Domini pro nobis in mortem tradita, parata sunt, ipsam inquam remissionem peccatorum, liberationem, et vitam æternam, applicat et confert nobis, ita ut Christus in nobis vivat, et nos in ipso vivamus, efficitque ut ipsum, quo talis sit cibus et potus spiritualis noster, id est, vita nostra, vera fide percipiamus. . . . . Et sicut oportet cibum in nosmetipsos edendo recipere, ut operetur in nobis, suamque in nobis efficaciam exerat, cum extra nos positus, nihil nobis prosit : ita necesse est nos fide Christum recipere, ut noster fiat, vivatque in nobis, et nos in ipso. . . . . Ex quibus omnibus claret nos, per spiritualem cibum, minime intelligere imaginarium, nescio quem, cibum, sed ipsum Domini corpus pro nobis traditum, quod tamen percipiatur a fidelibus, non corporaliter, sed spiritualiter per fidem. . . . . Fit autem hic esus et potus spiritualis, etiam extra Domini cœnam, quoties, aut ubicunque homo in Christum crediderit. Quo fortassis illud Augustini pertinet, Quid paras dentem et ventrem ? crede, et manducasti."

" Præter superiorem manducationem spiritualem, est et sacramentalis manducatio corporis Domini, qua fidelis non tantum spiritualiter et interne participat vero corpore et sanguine Domini, sed, foris etiam accedendo ad mensam Domini, accipit visibile corporis et sanguinis Domini sacramentum." [1]

It is a remarkable fact that the confessions of the Church of England conform more nearly to the Zwinglian than to the Calvinistic ideas and phraseology in respect to the Lord's Supper. This may be accounted for by the fact that it was less important for the English than for the German churches to conciliate the Lutherans. In the articles adopted by the Synod of London in 1552, and approved by Edward VI., the first clause of the statement of the doctrine of the Lord's Supper is in the language of

1 See Niemeyer, *Collectio Confessionum*, Leipzig, 1840, pp. 512-521.

Scripture: " To those who receive it worthily and with faith, the bread which we break is the communion of the body of Christ." The second clause rejects transubstantiation. The third is directed against the Lutheran doctrine, and asserts that as Christ is in heaven; " non debet quisquam fidelium carnis ejus et sanguinis realem et corporalem (ut loquuntur) præsentiam in eucharistia vel credere vel profiteri."

Article twenty-eight of the Thirty-nine Articles adopted in 1562, contains the first three clauses substantially as they appeared in the article of Edward VI., and then adds : " The body of Christ is given, taken, and eaten in the supper only after a heavenly and spiritual manner ; and the mean whereby the body of Christ is received and eaten in the supper, is faith. The sacrament of the Lord's Supper was not by Christ's ordinance reserved, carried about, lifted up, and worshipped." In the early edition of these articles, the clause against transubstantiation was amplified as follows: " Forasmuch as the truth of man's nature requireth, that the body of one and the selfsame man cannot be at one time in divers places, but must needs be in one certain place ; therefore the body of Christ cannot be present at one time in many and divers places : and because as Holy Scripture doth teach, Christ was taken up into heaven, and there shall continue unto the end of the world ; a faithful man ought not either to believe, or openly confess the real and bodily presence, as they term it, of Christ's flesh and blood in the sacrament of the Lord's Supper." [1] All this is implied in the form in which the article now stands. It affords clear evidence what were the sentiments of the English Reformers on this subject. It is principally interesting as it repudiates the idea of the " real presence " of the flesh and blood of Christ in the sacrament; which even Zwingle was willing to allow. He, however, used the word " real " in a very different sense from that in which it is used by either Romanists or Lutherans.

The Sense in which Christ is present in the Lord's Supper.

The extracts from the symbols of the Reformed Church enable us to answer, First, the question in what sense according to that Church, Christ is present in the Lord's Supper. The Reformed theologians are careful to explain what they mean by the word presence. Anything is said to be present when it operates duly on our perceiving faculties. A sensible object is present (præ sensi-

1 See *Exposition of Thirty-nine Articles* by Gilbert [Burnet], 6th edit. Dublin, 1790, p 403.

bus) when it affects the senses. A spiritual object is present when it is intellectually apprehended and when it acts upon the mind. It is said of the wicked, " God is not in all their thoughts." They are without God. They are " far off." On the other hand, God is present with his people when He controls their thoughts, operates on their hearts, and fills them with the sense of his nearness and love. This presence is not imaginary, it is in the highest sense real and effective. In like manner Christ is present when He thus fills the mind, sheds abroad his love in our hearts by the Holy Ghost given unto us ; and not only communicates to us the benefits of his sufferings and death, that is, the remission of our sins and reconciliation with God, but also infuses his life into us. Nothing is plainer from Scripture than that there is this communication of life from Christ to his people. It is not only directly asserted as when Paul says, " I live ; yet not I, but Christ liveth in me " (Gal. ii. 20) ; and, He " is our life " (Col. iii. 4) ; but it is also illustrated in every way. As the body derives life from the head (Col. ii. 19) and the branches from the vine, so do believers derive their life from Him : on this point there is no dispute among Christians. This, again, is a presence to us and in us which is not imaginary, but in the highest sense real and effective.

But what is meant by the word Christ when He is said to be thus present with us ? It does not mean merely that the Logos, the eternal Son of God, who fills heaven and earth, is present with us as He is with all his creatures ; or, simply that He operates in us as He operates throughout the universe. Nor does it mean merely that his Spirit dwells in believers and works in them both to will and to do of his good pleasure. Something more than all this is meant. Christ is a person ; a divine person with a human nature ; that is with a true body and a reasonable soul. It is that person who is present with us. This again does not mean, that Christ's human nature, his body and soul are ubiquitous; but it does mean that a divine person with human affections and sympathies is near us and within us. We have now a high-priest who can be touched with a sense of our infirmities. (Heb. iv. 15.) He and we are one in such a sense that He is not ashamed to call us brethren. (Heb. ii. 11.) In all things He was made like unto his brethren that He might be what He still is, a merciful and faithful high-priest. (Heb. ii. 17.) Of this every Christian is assured.[1] The

---

1 The late Dr. Cutler, of precious memory, formerly rector of St. Ann's Church, Brooklyn, a short time before his death, met the writer in Chestnut Street, Philadelphia, and, without a word of salutation, said, " Have you ever thought of the difference between com-

prayers and hymns of the Church addressed to Christ all assume that He has human sympathies and affections which make his relation to us entirely different from what it is to any other order of beings in the universe. If any one asks, How the humanity of Christ, his body and soul in heaven, can sympathize with his people on earth? the answer is, that it is in personal union with the Logos. If this answer be deemed insufficient, then the questioner may be asked, How the dust of which the human body is formed can sympathize with the immortal spirit with which it is united? Whether the mystery of this human sympathy of Christ can be explained or not, it remains a fact both of Scripture and of experience. In this sense, and not in a sense which implies any relation to space, it may be said that wherever the divinity of Christ is, there is his humanity, and as, by common consent, He is present at his table, He is there in the fulness of his human sympathy and love.

But this presence of Christ in the eucharist is predicated, not of his person only, but also of his body and blood. This presence the Reformed, as Zwingle said, " if they must have words," were willing to call real. But then they explained the word " real " as the opposite of " imaginary." The negative statements concerning this presence of the body and blood of Christ in the Lord's Supper are, —

1. That it is not local or corporeal. It is not material or of the matter.

2. It is not to the senses.

3. It is not peculiar to this sacrament. Christ and his benefits, his body and blood, and all their influences on the believer, are said to be accessible to him, and as truly received by him out of the supper as in it.

On this point the Confessions, even those signed by Calvin, are perfectly explicit. In the Zurich Confession, A. D. 1545, it is said, " Believers have in the Lord's Supper no other life-giving food than that which they receive elsewhere than in that ordinance." In the Second Helvetic Confession this is taught at length, and the doctrine vindicated from the objection that it renders the sacrament useless, that if we can receive without it what we receive in it, the importance of the sacrament is gone. The answer is, that as we continually need food for the body, so we continually need food for the soul; and that the sacra-

munion with God and communion with Christ? " and passed on without adding a word. These were the last words the writer ever heard from lips which the Spirit had often touched with a coal from the altar.

ments as well as the Word are divinely appointed means for conveying that spiritual nourishment. That the sacraments are means
of grace, does not render the Word unnecessary; neither does the
Word's being effectual and sufficient unto salvation, render the
sacraments useless.   Calvin teaches the same doctrine:[1] "The
verity which is figured in the sacraments believers receive outside
of the use of them.   Thus in baptism, Paul's sins were washed
away, which had already been blotted out.   Baptism was to Cornelius the laver of regeneration, although he had before received
the Spirit.   And so in the Lord's Supper, Christ communicates
Himself to us, although He had already imparted Himself to us
and dwells within us."   The office of the sacraments, he teaches,
is to confirm and increase our faith.   In his defence of this " Consensus," he expresses surprise that a doctrine so plainly proved by
Scripture and experience should be called into question.[2]   In the
decree of the French National Synod of 1572, it is said, " The same
Lord Jesus both as to his substance and gifts, is offered to us in
baptism and the ministry of the word, and received by believers."

The Church of England teaches the same doctrine, for in the
office for the communion of the sick, the minister is directed to
instruct a parishioner who is prevented from receiving the sacrament " that if he do truly repent him of his sins, and steadfastly
believe that Jesus Christ hath suffered death upon the cross for
him, and shed his blood for his redemption, earnestly remembering the benefits he hath thereby, and giving Him hearty thanks
therefor, he doth eat and drink the body and blood of our
Saviour Christ profitably to his soul's health, although he do not
receive the sacrament with his mouth."   On this point there was
no diversity of opinion in the Reformed Church.   There is no
communion with Christ, no participation of his body and blood
in the Lord's Supper, which is not elsewhere offered to believers
and experienced by them.

4. There is still another position maintained by the Reformed
which is especially important as determining their doctrine on
this subject.   They not only deny that believers receive the body
and blood of Christ in the Lord's Supper otherwise than these are

---

[1] " Extra eorum [sacramentorum] usum fidelibus constat, quæ illic figuratur veritas. Sic
baptismo abluta sunt Pauli peccata, quæ jam prius abluta erant. Sic idem baptismus Cor
nelio fuit lavacrum regenerationis, qui tamen jam Spiritu Sancto donatus erat. Sic in cœna
se communicat Christus, qui tamen et prius se nobis impertierat et perpetuo manet in
nobis."   *Consensus Tigurinus*, art. xix.; Niemeyer, *Collectio Confessionum*, p. 195.
[2] Niemeyer, p. 212.   " Quod deinde prosequimur, fidelibus spiritualium bonorum effectum
quæ figurant sacramenta, extra eorum usum constare, quando et quotidie verum esse ex-
perimur et probatur Scripturæ testimoniis mirum est s cui displiceat."

received through the Word, but they deny that believers receive anything in the eucharist that was not granted and communicated to the saints under the Old Testament. This of course is decisive. Under the old dispensation it was only the sacrificial efficacy of his broken body and shed blood that could be enjoyed. He died for the remission of sins "under the first testament." (Heb. ix. 15.) Therefore the fathers as well as we, and they as fully as we, are cleansed by the sprinkling of his blood ; to them, as well as to us, He was the true bread which came down from heaven ; they all drank of that Spiritual Rock which was Christ. Calvin devotes several pages to the refutation of the doctrine of the Romanists that the sacraments of the Old Testament only signified grace, while those of the New actually convey it. He maintains that, though different in form, they are the same in nature, object, and effect. " Scholasticum autem illud dogma, quo tam longum discrimen inter veteris ac novæ Legis sacramenta notatur, perinde acsi illa non aliud quam Dei gratiam adumbrarint, hæc vero præsentem conferant, penitus explodendum est. Siquidem nihilo splendidius de illis Apostolus quam de his loquitur, quum docet patres eandem nobiscum spiritualem escam manducasse : et escam illam Christum interpretatur (1 Cor. x. 3). . . . . Quicquid ergo nobis hodie in sacramentis exhibetur, id in suis olim recipiebant Judæi, Christum scilicet cum spiritualibus suis divitiis. Quam habent nostra virtutem, eam quoque in suis sentiebant ; ut scilicet essent illis divinæ erga se benevolentiæ sigilla in spem æternæ salutis." He quotes freely from Augustine to prove that that eminent father taught " Sacramenta Judæorum in signis fuere diversa : in re quæ significatur, paria, diversa specie visibili, paria virtute spirituali." [1]

With these negative statements agree all the affirmations concerning the presence of the body and blood in the Lord's Supper. What is affirmed to be present is not the body and blood of Christ absolutely, but his body as broken, and his blood as shed. It is the sacrifice which He offered that is present and of which the believer partakes. It is present to the mind, not to our bodies. It is perceived and received by faith and not otherwise. He is not present to unbelievers. By presence is meant not local nearness, but intellectual cognition and apprehension, believing appropriation, and spiritual operation. The body and blood are present to us when they fill our thoughts, are apprehended by

---

[1] See *Institutio*, iv. xiv. §§ 20–26, especially §§ 23, 26; edit. Berlin, 1834, part ii. pp. 362-367.

faith as broken and shed for our salvation, and exert upon us their proper effect.[1] " The body of Christ is in heaven at the right hand of God," says the Helvetic Confession. " Yet the Lord is not absent from his Church when celebrating his supper. The sun is absent from us in heaven, nevertheless it is efficaciously present with us ; how much more is Christ, the sun of righteousness, though absent as to the body, present with us, not corporally in deed, but spiritually, by his vivifying influence." Calvin says : " Every imagination of local presence is to be entirely removed. For while the signs are upon earth seen by the eyes and handled by the hands, Christ, so far as He is a man, is nowhere else than in heaven ; and is to be sought only by the mind and by faith. It is, therefore, an irrational and impious superstition to include Him in the earthly elements." He likewise teaches that Christ is present in the promise and not in the signs.[2] Ursinus, one of the principal authors of the Heidelberg Catechism, in his Exposition of that formulary, says : " These two, I mean the sign and the thing signified, are united in this sacrament, not by any natural copulation, or corporal and local existence one in the other ; much less by transubstantiation, or changing one into the other; but by signifying, sealing, and exhibiting the one by the other ; that is, by a sacramental union, whose bond is the promise added to the bread, requiring the faith of the receivers. Whence it is clear, that these things, in their lawful use, are always jointly exhibited and received, but not without faith of the promise, viewing and apprehending the thing promised, now present in the sacrament ; yet not present or included in the sign as in a vessel containing it ; but present in the promise, which is the better part, life, and soul of the sacrament. For they want judgment who affirm that Christ's body cannot be present in the sacrament except it be in or under the bread ; as if, forsooth, the bread alone, without the promise, were either a sacrament, or the principal part of a sacrament."

---

[1] " Corpus Christi in cœlis est ad dextram patris.   Sursum ergo elevanda sunt corda, et non defigenda in panem, nec adorandus dominus in pane. Et tamen non est absens ecclesiæ suæ celebranti cœnam dominus. Sol absens a nobis in cœlo, nihilominus efficaciter præsens est nobis: quanto magis sol justitiæ Christus, corpore in cœlis absens nobis, præsens est nobis, non corporaliter quidem, sed spiritualiter per vivificam operationem. (xxi.; Niemeyer, *Collectio Confessionum*, Leipzig, 1840, p. 522.) Calvin says (*Consensus Tigurinus*, xxi.; *Ibid.* p. 196): " Præsertim vero tollenda est quælibet localis præsentiæ imaginatio. Nam quum signa hic in mundo sint, oculis cernantur, palpentur manibus: Christus quatenus homo est, non alibi quam in cœlo, nec aliter quam mente et fidei intelligentia quærendus est.   Quare perversa et impia superstitio est, ipsum sub elementis hujus mundi includere."

[2] *Consensus Tigurinus*, x.; p. 194.

[3] *Summe of Christian Religion*, by Zacharias Ursinus, London, 1645; *Catechism of Christian Religion*, quest. 77, p. 434.

There is, therefore, a presence of Christ's body in the Lord's Supper; not local, but spiritual; not to the senses, but to the mind and to faith; and not of nearness, but of efficacy. If the presence is in the promise, then the body of Christ is present, offered to and received by the believer whenever and wherever he embraces and appropriates the promise. So far the doctrine of the Reformed Church is clear.

Manducation.

Our Lord in John vi. 53–58, expressly and solemnly declares that except a man eat of his flesh, and drink his blood, he has no life in him; and that whoso eateth his flesh and drinketh his blood, hath eternal life. It is here taught that the eating spoken of is necessary to salvation. He who does not eat of the flesh of the Son of Man, has no life in him. He who does thus eat, shall live forever. Now as no Christian Church, not even the Roman, maintains that a participation of the Lord's Supper is essential to salvation, it is plain that no such Church can consistently believe that the eating spoken of is that which is peculiar to that ordinance. Again, the Scriptures so clearly and variously teach that those who believe in Christ; who receive the record God has given of his Son; who receive Him; who flee to Him for refuge; who lay hold of Him as their God and Saviour, shall never perish but have eternal life; it is plain that what is expressed in John vi. by eating the flesh of Christ and drinking his blood, must be the same thing that is elsewhere expressed in the various ways just referred to. When we eat our food we receive and appropriate it to the nourishment of our bodies; so to eat the flesh of Christ, is to receive and appropriate Him and his sacrificial work for the life of our souls. Without this appropriation of Christ to ourselves we have no life; with it, we have life eternal, for He is our life. As this appropriation is an act of faith, it is by believing that we eat his flesh and drink his blood. We accordingly find that this is recognized in all the leading Confessions of the Reformed Church. Thus in the Zurich Confession it is said, "Eating is believing, and believing is eating." The Helvetic Confession, as quoted above,[1] says, that this eating takes place as often as and wherever a man believes in Christ. The Belgic Confession says,[2] "God sent Christ as the true bread from heaven which nourishes

---

[1] Page 636.

[2] "Deus panem vivificum misit, qui de cœlo descendit, nempe Jesum Christum: is nutrit et sustentat vitam fidelium spiritualem, si comedatur, id est, applicetur et recipiatur Spiritu per fidem." xxxv.; Niemeyer. *Collectio Confessionum*, p. 385.

and sustains the spiritual life of believers, if it be eaten, that is, if it be applied and received by the Spirit through faith." Faith, as shown above, is, in all these Confessions, declared to be the hand and the mouth by which this reception and appropriation are effected. A distinction may be, and often is, made between spiritual and sacramental manducation. But the difference between them is merely circumstantial. In the former the believer feeds on Christ to his spiritual nourishment, without the intervention and use of the elements of bread and wine ; in the latter, he does the same thing in the use of those elements as the divinely appointed sign and seal of the truth and promise of God.

Although the Confessions are thus uniform and clear in their assertion, " that eating is believing," the theologians, in some instances, make a distinction between them. Thus Calvin says : [1] " There are some who define in a word, that to eat the flesh of Christ, and to drink his blood, is no other than to believe on Christ Himself. But I conceive that in that remarkable discourse, in which He recommends us to feed upon his body, He intended to teach us something more striking and sublime ; namely, that we are quickened by a real participation of Him, which he designates by the terms eating and drinking, that no person might suppose the life which we receive from Him to consist in simple knowledge. . . . . At the same time, we confess there is no eating but by faith, and it is impossible to imagine any other ; but the difference between me and those whose opinion I now oppose is this, ... they consider eating to be faith itself, but I apprehend it to be rather a consequence of faith." Among the moderns Dean Alford makes much the same distinction. " What is this eating and drinking ? Clearly, not merely faith : for faith answers to the hand reached forth for the food, — but not the act of eating. Faith is a necessary condition of the act : so that we can hardly say, with Augustine, ' Crede, et manducasti ; ' but ' crede et manucabis.' " [2] Eating, he says, implies the act of ap-

---

[1] " Sunt enim qui manducare Christi carnem, et sanguinem ejus bibere, uno verbo definiunt, nihil esse aliud, quam in Christum ipsum credere. Sed mihi expressius quiddam ac sublimius videtur voluisse docere Christus in præclara illa concione, ubi carnis suæ manducationem nobis commendat: nempe vera sui participatione nos vivificari, quam manducandi etiam ac bibendi verbis ideo designavit, ne, quam ab ipso vitam percipimus, simplici cognitione percipi quispiam putaret. Quemadmodum enim non aspectus, sed esus panis corpori alimentum sufficit, ita vere ac penitus participem Christi animam fieri convenit, ut ipsius virtute in vitam spiritualem vegetetur. Interim vero hanc non aliam esse, quam fidei manducationem fatemur, ut nulla alia fingi potest. Verum hoc inter mea et istorum verba interest, quod illis manducare est duntaxat credere: ego credendo manducari Christi carnem, quia fide noster efficitur, eamque manducationem fructum effectumque esse fidei dico." *Institutio*, IV. xvii. 5; edit. Berlin, 1834, pp. 403, 404.

[2] *Greek Testament*, John vi. 53; edit. London, 1859, vol. i. p. 723.

propriation. This is a distinction without a difference. It concerns simply the extent given to the meaning of the word faith. If faith be merely knowledge and assent, then there is a difference between believing and eating, or appropriating. But if by faith we not merely receive as with the hand, but appropriate and apply what is thus received, the difference between believing and eating disappears. When we are commanded to eat the flesh and to drink the blood of Christ, we are commanded to act; and the act required is an act of faith; the act of receiving and appropriating Christ and the benefits of his redemption. The language of Calvin above quoted is to be taken in connection with his explicit declaration already cited, that the Christian receives and feeds on Christ whenever he truly believes; and with the fact that he admits that the believer eats Christ as fully elsewhere as in the Lord's Supper; and especially with the fact that the saints under the old dispensation ate of the same spiritual meat and drank of the same spiritual drink as fully and as really as believers now do. The Reformed understood that " eating and drinking," as used in John vi. 51–58, must be understood " figuratively of the spiritual appropriation of Christ by faith," because our Lord makes such eating and drinking essential to salvation. On this point the Lutherans are of one mind with the Reformed, in so far as their leading theologians understand all that is said in John vi. of eating his flesh and drinking his blood, of the appropriation of his sacrificial death by the act of believing.

What is received in the Lord's Supper.

The question, What is the act we perform in eating? and, What it is we eat? are distinct, though the answer to one may determine the answer to the other. If the manducation is not with the mouth but by faith, then the thing eaten must be spiritual and not material. Nevertheless our Lord says we must eat his flesh and drink his blood , and all the Reformed Confessions teach that we receive the body and blood of Christ, although not " after a corporal or carnal manner." In answer to the question, What is here meant by the body and blood of Christ? the almost uniform answer is, (1.) That it is not the matter of his body and blood. (2.) That it is not his body and blood as such. (3.) That it is not his glorified body now in heaven. His body and blood were received by the disciples before his death, and consequently before his ascension and glorification, and it is not disputed that believers since the apostolic age receive what the Apostles received when this sacrament was instituted. (4.) That we receive Christ's body as broken, or as given unto death for us, and his blood as shed for the remission of sins. (5.) That therefore to receive the body and blood as offered in the sacrament, or in the Word, is to receive and appropriate the sacrificial virtue or effects of the death of Christ on the cross. And, (6.) That as Christ and his benefits are inseparable, they who receive the one receive also the other; as by faith through the indwelling of the Holy Ghost we are united to Christ so as to be members of that body of which He is the head and the perpetual source of life. By faith, therefore, we become one with Him, so as to be flesh of his flesh, in a sense analogous to that in which husband and wife are no more two, but one flesh.

Although Calvin admitted all these propositions, he nevertheless, at times, teaches that what the believers receive is specifically an influence from the glorified body of Christ in heaven. Thus he says: " We admit without circumlocution that the flesh of Christ is life-giving, not only because in it once our salvation was obtained, but because now, we being united to Him in sacred union, it breathes life into us. Or, to use fewer words, because, being by the secret power of the Spirit engrafted into the body of Christ, we have a common life with Him ; for from the hidden fountain of divinity, life is, in a wonderful manner, infused into the flesh of Christ, and thence flows out to us." [1]   Again, " Christ is absent from us as to the body ; by his Spirit, however, dwelling in us, He so lifts us to Himself in heaven, that he transfuses the life-giving vigour of his life into us, as we grow by the vital heat of the sun." [2]   If by the word " flesh," in this connection, we understand the humanity of Christ, there is a sense in which the passages above quoted may be understood in accordance with the common doctrine not only of the Reformed, but of all Christian churches.   When Paul said " I live; yet not I, but Christ liveth in me," he no doubt meant by Christ the incarnate Son of God clothed in our nature at the right hand of God.   It is a divine-human Saviour, He who is both God and man in two distinct natures and one person forever, in whom and by whom we live, and who dwells in us by his Spirit.   Unless we are willing to accuse the illustrious Calvin of inconsistency, his meaning must be made to harmonize with what he says elsewhere.   In the " Consensus Tigurinus," he says : " Christus quatenus homo est, non alibi quam in cœlo, nec aliter quam mente et fidei intelligentia quæ-

---

[1] See his *Consensionis Capitum Expositio*, Niemeyer, pp. 213, 214.   [2] *Ibid.* p. 215.

rendus est ; " and again, " Quod autem carnis suæ esu et sanguinis potione, quæ hic figurantur, Christus animas nostras per fidem
Spiritus sancti virtute pascit, id non perinde accipiendum, quasi
fiat aliqua substantiæ vel commixtio vel transfusio : sed quoniam
ex carne semel in sacrificium oblata et sanguine in expiationem
effuso vitam hauriamus." [1] It is here expressly said that what the
believer receives in the Lord's Supper is not any supernatural influence flowing from the glorified body of Christ in heaven ; but
the benefits of his death as an expiation for sin. It is to be remarked that Calvin uses the very words of the twenty-third article of the Consensus in explanation of what he meant by saying,
" ex abscondito Deitatis fonte in Christi carnem mirabiliter infusa
est vita, ut inde ad nos flueret." [2] To preserve the consistency of
the great Reformer his language must be interpreted so as to harmonize with the two crucial facts for which he so earnestly contends ; first, that believers receive elsewhere by faith all they
receive at the Lord's table ; and secondly, that we Christians
receive nothing above or beyond that which was received by the
saints under the Old Testament, before the glorified body of Christ
had any existence. It is also to be remembered that Calvin
avowed his agreement with Zwingle and Oecolampadius on all
questions relating to the sacraments.[3]

The Efficacy of the Lord's Supper as a Sacrament.

This includes two points, first, The effect produced ; and second,
The agency or influence to which the effect is due. In the Lord's
Supper we are said to receive Christ and the benefits of his redemption to our spiritual nourishment and growth in grace. As our
natural food imparts life and strength to our bodies, so this sacrament is one of the divinely appointed means to strengthen the
principle of life in the soul of the believer, and to confirm his faith
in the promises of the gospel. The Apostle teaches that by partaking of the bread and wine, the symbols of Christ's body and
blood given for us, we are thereby united to him as our head, and
with all our fellow believers as joint members of his mystical body.
The union between the head and members of the human body
and between the vine and its branches, is a continuous union.
There is a constant flow of vital influence from the one to the
other. In like manner the union between Christ and his people is continuous. He constantly imparts his life-giving influence
to all united to Him by faith and by the indwelling of his Spirit.

[1] Art. xxi. xxiii.; Niemeyer, p. 196.   [2] Niemeyer, p. 214.   [3] See page 631.

It has often been stated already that the Bible teaches, (1.) That Christ and his people are one; that this union is not merely a union of congeniality or feeling, but such as constitutes them one in a real but mysterious sense. (2.) That the bond of union is faith and the indwelling of the Holy Spirit, who dwelling in Him without measure is communicated from Him to all his members. As God is everywhere present and everywhere operative by his Spirit, so Christ dwells in our hearts by faith through or in virtue of the indwelling of the Holy Ghost. (3.) He is thus our life. He works in us to will and to do according to his own good pleasure. As God works everywhere throughout nature continually controlling all natural causes each after its kind, to produce the effects intended; so does Christ work in us according to the laws of our nature in the production of everything that is good; so that it is from Him that " all holy desires, all good counsels, and all just works do proceed." It is not, therefore, we that live, but Christ that liveth in us.

As our Lord in addressing the Apostles and through them all his disciples, said this is my body and blood given for you, He says the same in the most impressive manner in this ordinance to every believing communicant : " This is my body broken for you." " This is my blood shed for you." These words when received by faith fill the heart with joy, confidence, gratitude, love, and devotion; so that such a believer rises from the Lord's table refreshed by the infusion of a new life.

The efficacy of this sacrament, according to the Reformed doctrine, is not to be referred to any virtue in the ordinance itself, whether in its elements or actions ; much less to any virtue in the administrator; nor to the mere power of the truths which it signifies ; nor to the inherent, divine power in the word or promise by which it is attended ; nor to the real presence of the material body and blood of Christ (*i. e.*, of the body born of the Virgin), whether by the way of transubstantiation, consubstantiation, or impanation ;[1] nor to a supernatural life-giving influence emanating

---

[1] One of the numerous theories concerning the eucharist prevalent more or less in the early church, was that which is known in the history of doctrine as impanation. As in man the soul is united to the body imparting to it life and efficiency without itself becoming material, or rendering the body spirit; and as the Eternal Logos became flesh by taking to Himself a true body and a reasonable soul, without receiving anything human into his divine nature, or imparting divinity to his humanity; so the same Logos becomes united with the consecrated bread, without any substantial change in it or in Him. His relation to the bread, however, is analogous to that of the soul to the body in man and of the Logos to humanity in the person of our Lord. As the assumption of our nature by the Son of God is expressed by the word " incarnation," so his assumption and union with the bread in the Lord's Supper is called " impanation." The only distinguished modern theologian (so

from the glorified body of Christ in heaven, nor to the communication of the theanthropic nature of Christ, but only to " the blessing of Christ, and the working of his Spirit in them that receive " the sacrament of his body and blood.

By some of the early fathers the resurrection of the body was regarded as a specific effect of the Lord's Supper, which was therefore called, as by Ignatius,[1] φάρμακον ἀθανασίας, ἀντίδοτος τοῦ ἀποθανεῖν. This idea was connected in their minds with the doctrine of impanation referred to in the foregoing foot-note. Of this there is little trace in the theology of either the Reformed or Lutheran Church. In the Scotch Confession of 1560, it is indeed said : " As the eternal deity gives life and immortality to the flesh of Christ, so also his flesh and blood, when eaten and drunk by us, confer on us the same prerogatives ; " and in the confession adopted by the Lutherans in 1592 it is said, the body of Christ is received by the mouth " in pignus et certificationem resurrectionis nostrorum corporum ex mortuis ; " on which Philippi remarks that those words do not imply any " immediate corporeal operation or any implanting in us of a germ of a resurrection body. They only teach that this sacrament is a pledge of our resurrection ; and as this idea is introduced only in one place in the acknowledged standards of the Church, and there only incidentally, it is to be considered as a subordinate matter. The main point is the pledge of the pardon of sin and of eternal life which includes an assurance of the resurrection of the body." [2]

According to the standards of the Reformed Church, therefore :

far as known to the writer), who advocated this doctrine, was the late Dr. August Hahn of the University of Leipzig. "Bread and wine," he says, "in the Lord's Supper, are what the human body formerly was when the Son of God (the divine Logos) was here on earth; that is, the means of his perceptible presence and efficiency on those who receive Him in a penitent and believing heart; they are therefore = the body and blood of Christ; since in them the Lord, who is the Light, the Life, and the Resurrection, communicates Himself actually, truly, and essentially (wirklich und wahrhaftig und wesentlich) to his people, and makes this bread, the bread of eternal life." See *Lehrbuch des Christlichen Glaubens*, von August Hahn, Leipzig, 1828, p. 602. On page 603, he says, Luther was right in rejecting the doctrine of transubstantiation, and "he would have been right had he taught that with *in*, *with*, and *under* the bread and wine in the Holy Supper, we actually and essentially or really (wirklich und wesentlich) receive the present person Jesus Christ or the Logos, and hence this bread and this wine are the body and the blood of Christ, wherein He now communicates the bread which is from heaven to believers, as formerly when He came in literal flesh and blood He gave Himself to them. But Luther erred when he asserted that with, in, and under the bread and wine, the real body which suffered for us, and the blood of Jesus Christ which was shed for us, are communicated, because according to the Scriptures (1 Cor. xv. 45-50), the spiritual, heavenly body of our glorified Lord, is not flesh and blood; and a body, whatever be its nature, cannot as body be ubiquitous."

[1] *Ad Ephesios*, xx. ; *Epistles*, edit. Oxford, 1709, p. 19.

[2] *Kirchliche Glaubenslehre*, von D. Fr. Ad. Philippi, ordentlichem Professor der Theologie zu Rostock, Gütersloh, 1871, vol. v. p. 266.

The Lord's Supper is a holy ordinance instituted by Christ ; as a memorial of his death, wherein, under the symbols of bread and wine, his body as broken and his blood as shed for the remission of sins, are signified, and, by the power of the Holy Ghost, sealed and applied to believers ; whereby their union with Christ and their mutual fellowship are set forth and confirmed, their faith strengthened, and their souls nourished unto eternal life.

Christ is really present to his people in this sacrament, not bodily, but in spirit ; not in the sense of local nearness, but of efficacious operation. They receive Him, not with the mouth but by faith ; they receive his flesh and blood, not as flesh, not as material particles, not its human life, not the supernatural influence of his glorified body in heaven ; but his body as broken and his blood as shed. The union thus signified and effected is not a corporeal union, not a mixture of substances, but a spiritual and mystical union due to the indwelling of the Holy Spirit. The efficacy of this sacrament, as a means of grace, is not in the signs, nor in the service, nor in the minister, nor in the word, but in the attending influence of the Holy Ghost.

§ 17. *Modern Views concerning the Lord's Supper.*

The modern philosophy has introduced certain principles as to the nature of God and his relation to the world, and as to the nature of man and his relation to God, which when applied to Christian doctrines have produced a revolution in theology. It has already been shown that the principles of this philosophy in their application to the origin and present state of man, to the person and work of Christ, and to the way in which men are made partakers of his salvation, have introduced a method of presenting the gospel utterly unintelligible to those unacquainted with the modern speculations. The word philosophy is to be understood in a sense wide enough to include a great diversity of systems, which although they have certain principles in common, differ widely from each other. They belong to two general classes, the pantheistic and theistic, which merge off into each other in every variety of form, and in different degrees of approximation towards identity.

According to the pantheistic theory, the world is the ever varying and unfolding existence form of God ; and man is the form in which He comes to consciousness on this earth. According to the theistic theory, the world owes its existence to the will of God, in which He is immanent and of which He is the life. Man is the form in which generic humanity is manifested in connection with a given corporeal organization. On neither view is there any real dualism between God and the world, or God and man except as occasioned by sin. The oneness of God and man is affirmed by both classes, by Cousin and Ullman for example, with equal earnestness. This is a oneness which admits of diversity ; it is a unity in plurality ; but it is a oneness of life ; and such a unity of nature that God may become man, and man God.

The individuality or personality of man depends on the body. Generic humanity is not in itself a person. It becomes personal only by its union with an organized body. It loses its personality when it has no body ; and therefore the immortality of the soul, as distinct from the body, is pronounced by Olshausen an anti-Christian or pagan idea. Whatever of conscious existence the soul has between death and the resurrection must be connection with its body, which is not the prison, or garment, or shell, or hull of the soul ; it is not in any way one form of existence and the soul another ; both form one life. The soul to be complete to develop itself, as a soul, must externalize itself, throw itself out in space ; and this externalization is the body. All is one process, one and the same organic principle, dividing itself only that its unity may become the more free and intensely complete. The soul and body are one ; one and the same organic principle.[1]

The same principles are applied to the explanation of the doctrine of the person of Christ. According to the decisions of the ecumenical councils of Chalcedon and Constantinople, which have been accepted by all Christendom, the Eternal Son of God became man by taking to Himself a true body and a reasonable soul, and so was, and continues to be, both God and man in two distinct natures and one person forever. By nature ($\phi\acute{v}\sigma\iota\varsigma$) is meant substance ($o\mathring{v}\sigma\acute{\iota}a$), as these words are used interchangeably. By the one nature He is consubstantial with us men ; and by the other He is consubstantial with the Father.

This dualism, this hypostatic union of two distinct substances in the person of Christ, involves, as taught by those councils and believed by all Christendom, two $\grave{\epsilon}v\acute{\epsilon}\rho\gamma\epsilon\iota a\iota$, two operations, two wills. There is no mixture or confusion of these two natures ; no transfer of the properties of the one to the other, but each retains its own peculiar attributes.

On the other hand, the modern German theology rejects this

---

[1] The commonly received distinction of mind and matter on this theory must be given up. They are not two distinct substances having distinct and incompatible properties or attributes.

distinction of natures in Christ.   It denies all dualism in the constitution of his person.   It teaches that Christ did not assume
" a reasonable soul " into personal union with Himself, but either
that He himself became, by a process of self-limitation, such a
soul, or that He assumed generic humanity, so that He did not
become a man, but the man.   His assumption of humanity was
something general, and not merely particular.   The Word became flesh ; not a single man only as one of many ; but flesh or
humanity in its universal conception ; otherwise He could not be
the principle of a new order of existence for the human world as
such.   By this assumption of humanity, the divine and human,
God and man, become one in such a sense as to exclude all dualism.   There are not a divine and a human, but there is a theanthropic, or divine-human nature or life.   As in man there is not
one life of the body and another of the soul, but the two are
one and the same organic principle, so in the case of Christ the
divine and human are one and the same.   The divine nature of
Christ is at the same time human in the fullest sense.   Humanity
is never complete till it reaches his person.   It includes in its very
constitution a struggle towards the form in which it is here exhibited, and can never rest until this end is attained.   Our nature
reaches after a true and real union with the nature of God, as the
necessary complement and consummation of its own life.   The
idea which it embodied can never be fully actualized under any
other form.   The incarnation, then, is the proper completion of
humanity.   Christ is the true ideal man.   Here is reached ultimately the highest summit of human life, which is of course the
crowning sense of the word, or that in which it finds its last and
full significance.

The first man, Adam, is to be viewed under a twofold character.
In one respect he was simply a man ; in another, he was the man,
in whose person was included the whole human race.   His individual personality was limited wholly to himself ; but a whole
world of like separate personalities lay involved in his life, at the
same time, as a generic principle or root.   All these in a deep
sense, form at last but one and the same life.   Adam lives in his
posterity as truly as he ever lived in his own person.   They
participate in his whole nature, soul and body, and are truly bone
of his bone and flesh of his flesh.   So the life of Christ is to be
viewed under the same twofold aspect.   He, as was Adam, is an
individual person.   But as Adam included in himself the race, he
included all other human persons in his life ; so Christ, having

assumed generic humanity into personal union with Himself, includes in a still higher sense a world of other personalities. " He
was Himself the race." He has assumed generic humanity into
personal union with Himself and thereby rendered it divine ; it is
indeed a true human life, but it is nevertheless divine. It is one
life ; not the life of the Logos separately considered, but the life
of the Word made flesh. He was man more perfectly than Adam
himself, before the fall ; humanity stood revealed in Him under its
most perfect form. The humanity which He assumed was not
new, but the humanity of Adam raised to a higher character, and
filled with new meaning and power, by its union with the divine
nature. The identity of Adam and his race is not material. Not
a particle of Adam's body has come into ours. The identity resolves itself into an invisible law ; and it is not one law for the
body and another law for the soul ; but one and the same law involves the presence of both, as the power of a common life.
Where the law works, there Adam's life is reproduced, body and
soul together. And still the individual Adam is not blended with
his posterity in any such way as to lose his own personality or to
swallow up theirs. His identity with his posterity is generic ; but
none the less real or close on that account. The case in regard
to Christ and his people is analogous. His life, generic humanity
as united in one life with the divine in his person passes over to
his people. And as the race of individual men is developed by a
regular, natural, organic process from the generic humanity in the
person of Adam, so the life of Christ rests not in his separate
person, but passes over to his people ; this takes place in the way
of history, growth, or regular living development. In regeneration we become partakers of this new principle of life, that is, of
generic humanity as united with the divine nature, which involves
a participation of the entire humanity of Christ. We are not
joined in a real life unity with the everlasting Logos, apart from
Christ's manhood, in the way of direct personal in-being. This
would make us equal with Christ. The mystical union would then
be the hypostatical union itself repeated in the person of every
believer. It is not the divine life of the Logos as such, but the
theanthropic life of Christ which passes over to his people. " The
personality of the Son," says Olshausen[1] " as comprehensive, includes in itself all the personalities of his people and pervades
them with his own life, as the living centre of an organism, from
which life flows forth and to which it returns."

[1] *John* xiv. 20; *Commentar*, 3d edit. Königsberg, 1838, vol. ii. p. 352

The life' which is thus conveyed to us is a true human life, controlling not only the soul but also the body. It is corporeal as well as incorporeal. It must put on an outward form and project itself in space. It is to be remembered that human life is not to be split into two lives, one of the body and another of the soul, thus constituting a dualism in our nature, instead of the absolute unity which belongs to it in fact. Soul and body, are, in their ground, but one life; identical in their origin; bound together by interpenetration subsequently at every point, and holding together in the presence and power of the same organic law. The life of Christ, lodged in us, works in us according to the law which it includes in its own constitution. That is, it works as a human life; and as such becomes the law of regeneration in the body as truly as in the soul. This does not suppose any actual approach of Christ's body to the persons of his people; nor any ubiquity or idealistic dissipation of that body; nor any fusion of this personality with ours. We must distinguish between the simple man and the universal man, here joined in the same person. Adam was an individual and the whole race. There is no dissipation of Christ's personality into the general consciousness of the Church involved in the affirmation that his person forms the ground, out of which and in the power of which only, the whole life of the Church continually subsists. In this view Christ is personally present always in the Church, that is, of course, in the power of his divine nature. But his divine nature is at the same time human, in the fullest sense, and wherever his presence is revealed in a real way, it includes the person necessarily under the one aspect as well as under the other; with all this, however, which is something very different from the conception of a proper ubiquity in the case of Christ's body, we do not relinquish the thought of his separate human individuality. We distinguish between his universal humanity in the Church, and his humanity as a particular man, whom the heavens have received till the time of the restitution of all things. His glorified body, we doubt not, is possessed of qualities, attributes, and powers, that transcend immeasurably all we know or can think of a human body here. Still it is a body, a particular human body, having organized parts and an outward form. As such of course it must be defined and circumscribed by local limits, and cannot be supposed to be present in different places at the same time.

The life of Christ as communicated to his people is a true human life; and all life, in the case of man, is actualized, and can be actualized, only in the way of process or gradual historical development.   All that belongs, then, to the new life of the Christian, conceived as complete at the last day, must be allowed to be involved in it as principle and process from the beginning.   In every stage of its progress it is a true human life answerable to the nature of its organic root, and to the nature also of the subject in which it is lodged.   The bodies of the saints in glory will be only the last result, in organic continuity, of the divine life of Christ implanted in their souls at their regeneration.   There is nothing abrupt in Christianity.   It is a supernatural constitution indeed; but as such it is clothed in a natural form, and involves in itself as regular a law of historical development, as the old creation itself.   The resurrection body will be simply the ultimate outburst of the life that had been ripening for immortality under cover of the old Adamic nature before.   The winged psyche has its elemental organization in the worm, and does not lose it in the tomb-like chrysalis.   The resurrection of the body is, therefore, as much a natural process as the development of the butterfly from the grub, or the flower from the seed.[1]

1 To avoid the danger of misrepresentation the exhibition of the principles of this modern aspect of theology has been given in great measure in the language of its advocates.   No reference to names is given, so that no one is made responsible for the views expressed.   Experience teaches that quoting a man's words is no security against the charge of misrepresentation.   The writer was grieved to learn that his friend of more than forty years standing, Dr. John W. Nevin, considers himself to be unjustly charged by us with holding doctrines which he earnestly repudiates.   On page 429 of the second volume of this work he is quoted as saying that Hegel's Christological ideas, "are very significant and full of instruction."   This has been construed as charging him with being a thorough Hegelian.   As to this construction, we would say, first, that nothing was further from the writer's mind than the intention of making such an imputation; and secondly, that the language used gives no fair ground for such an interpretation.   On the preceding page (428) Dorner is quoted as saying that "the foundations of the new Christology were laid by Schelling, Hegel, and Schleiermacher."   Dorner certainly did not mean to intimate that all the modern Christologists, himself included, were Hegelians.   Neither did we intend to intimate that Dr. Nevin adopted Hegel's philosophy as a system, which we know, from his own authority, he abhors.

Again, it is said that Dr. Nevin is represented as denying the divinity of Christ, because he is quoted as saying that our Lord was the ideal, or perfect man, that "his divine nature is at the same time human in the fullest sense."   (*Mystical Presence*, Philadelphia, 1846, p. 174.)   Those who understand this language as necessarily involving the denial of the divinity of Christ are forgetful of the fact that the oneness of God and man is the primary principle of the New Theology.   Even Lutherans hold that the humanity of Christ is capable of receiving the attributes of divinity, that as a man He is omniscient, omnipresent, and almighty.   Schleiermacher, as we understand him, had no other personal God, than Christ.   We doubt not, and have never intimated anything to the contrary, that Dr. Nevin, although he makes Christ the ideal or perfect man, attributes to Him in his theory and in his heart, all the perfections with which the most devout believer in his divinity invests the adorable Redeemer.   How he reconciles this with his representing Him as the Ideal man; and with the assertion that He has but one life and that life in the fullest sense human, it is not for us to say.   The same thing, however, is done by many others besides Dr. Nevin.

Applications of these Principles to the Lord's Supper.

It is obvious that as the principles above stated must modify the whole method, and, so to speak, theory of salvation, so they must also determine the view taken of the Lord's Supper. They necessarily exclude the Romish doctrine of transubstantiation; and the Lutheran doctrine that the real natural body and blood of Christ are present in, with, and under the bread and wine in this sacrament, and received after a corporal manner (" corporaliter ") by the mouth. No less obviously do they exclude the doctrine of Calvin that what is received by the believer in the Lord's Supper is a supernatural influence emanating from the glorified body of Christ in heaven. In like manner they exclude the Reformed doctrine that what is received are the sacrificial benefits of the broken body of Christ, which benefits are not only the forgiveness of sins and reconciliation with God, but the indwelling of the Holy Spirit by which we are united to Christ and made partakers of his salvation. As our redemption, according to this theory, is effected by introducing into the centre of our being a new principle of life, a new organic law, which by its operation and gradual development works out our salvation; and as this new life is generic humanity united with the divine nature of Christ so as to become truly divine while it is still truly human, and yet only one and the same life, it follows that it is not the body and blood of Christ, but his theanthropic nature that we receive in the Holy Communion.

We are therefore told that the real communication which believers have with Christ in the Holy Supper, extends to his whole person. To be real and not simply moral, it must be thus comprehensive. We may divide Christ in our thoughts, abstracting his divinity from his humanity, or his soul from his body. But no such dualism has place in his actual person — that is, no dualism between his divinity and humanity, or, between his soul and body. If therefore He be received by us at all, He must be received in a whole way. We partake not of certain rights and privileges only, which have been secured for us by the breaking of his body and the shedding of his blood, but of the veritable substantial life of the beloved Immanuel Himself, as the fountain and channel by which alone all these benefits can be conveyed into our souls. We partake not of his divinity only, nor yet of his Spirit as separate from Himself, but also of his true and proper humanity. Not of his humanity in a separate form, his flesh and blood disjoined from his Spirit; but of the one life which is the union of both — Spirit in such connections seems to stand not for the Holy Spirit, but for the divine nature of Christ, for the life of Christ is not the union of the Holy Spirit with his humanity — and in virtue of which the presence of the one must ever involve in the same form, and to the same extent, the presence of the other. What we receive is therefore his whole life, as a single undivided form of his existence, by one and the same process. The participation of Christ's life in the sacrament is in no sense corporeal, but altogether spiritual, as the necessary condition of its being real. It is the soul or spirit of the believer that is immediately fed with the grace which is conveyed to it mystically in the holy ordinance. But this is in fact a fruition which belongs to the entire man, for the life made over to him under such central form, becomes at once in virtue of its own human character, and of the human character of the believer himself, a renovating force which reaches out into his person on all sides, and fills with its presence the totality of his nature.

The same system substantially is unfolded by Ebrard in his "Christliche Dogmatik." What is taught concerning the Lord's Supper presupposes what is taught of the nature of man and of the person of Christ. In the sacrament of the supper we are united to Christ; but the nature of our union with Christ depends upon the nature of the parties to that union. Humanity as a generic life developed from Adam as its root and centre, being corrupted by sin, is healed by its union with the divine nature in the person of Christ, or according to Ebrard's mode of representation, by the Logos becoming a man by a process of self-limitation. Every man from the first moment of his existence possesses " ein substantielles Centrum seines mikrokosmischen Lebens, ... ein Centrum, welches da war, ehe der Mensch bewusste Gedanken hatte, und welches bleiben wird, wenn der Leib dem Tode verfällt, welches also an sich weder Gedanke (mens) noch materieller Stoff ist." [1] That is, every man has from the commencement of his being " a substantial centre of life, which precedes conscious mental activity, and which will remain when the body dies, and therefore in itself is neither mind (mens) nor matter." This life-centre is instinct with a force which develops itself as mind and body, physically and psychologically. It is the Ego, the personality. It is the seat of regeneration which consists in introducing into this substantial centre of our being a new organic

---

[1] *Christliche Dogmatik*, III. iii. 2, § 444; Königsberg, 1852, vol. ii. p. 316.

law which gives rise to a new development. This new law, or
principle of life is the substance of Christ. Herein consists the
mystical union. " This union is a central, that is, an organic union
between the soul-centre, (seelischen Centrum) of the exalted Incarnate one and our soul-centre, so that Christ from our centre
pervades, controls, and sanctifies, both our physical-somatic, and
our noetic life." [1] A few lines further on it is said, " This communication is real, not imaginary, ... in that before all our
thought, the substantial centre of our physical and noetic life is
organically united with Christ's centre, [so that in the Lord's Sup-
per] we receive a new communication of the substance (Substanz-
mittheilung] of the glorified Son of man." [2] What is communicated is sometimes said to be " the person of Christ," sometimes
" the whole Christ," sometimes " his life," sometimes " his whole
human life," and sometimes the " organic law of Christ's human
life." The Lord's Supper, therefore, is by Ebrard declared to be
an ordinance " wherein Christ renews the mystical union, the real
life-bond, with his people, in that He renewedly implants Himself, his person, and glorified humanity in them, objectively, really,
and centrally, and thus confirms and renews their participation
in the benefits of his death." [3]

This theory repudiates the doctrine of transubstantiation, the
Lutheran doctrine of oral manducation of the true, natural body
and blood of Christ ; the Calvinistic idea of an emanation from
the glorified body of Christ, the Reformed doctrine of the reception of the benefits of Christ's sacrificial death, and of Christ
Himself by the indwelling of his Spirit, and insists on the communication of the divine humanity of Christ to the soul of the
believer as a new organic law, somewhat in the same way as
magnetism is added to iron as a new controlling law. Philippi [4]
reviews the exhibitions of the doctrine of the eucharist given by
the leading German theologians from Schleiermacher to Lange.
The epithet of " mystic-theosophical," which he applies to the
doctrine of Lange, applies with more or less propriety to all the

---

[1] *Christliche Dogmatik*, III. iii. 2. 2. B. § 545 ; Königsberg, 1852, vol. ii. p. 651.

[2] On page 322, Ebrard, when treating of regeneration and of the mystical union with
Christ thereby effected, quotes the following passage from *The Mystical Presence*, by
Dr. J. W. Nevin, Philadelphia, 1846, p 160, as expressing his own views on the subject :
"Christ's person is one, and the person of the believer is one ; and to secure a real communication of the whole human life of the first over into the personality of the second, it is
only necessary that the communication should spring from the centre of Christ's life and
pass over to the centre of ours."

[3] *Christliche Dogmatik*, III. iii. 2. 2. B. § 545 ; Königsberg, 1852, vol. ii. p. 650.

[4] *Kirchliche Glaubenslehre*, von D. Fr. Ad. Philippi, Gütersloh, 1871, vol. v. pp. 364-380.

modern German theories.   They are unintelligible to the majority
of educated men, and as to the poor, for whom the gospel is especially designed, they are absolutely meaningless.

Remarks.

As the theory above referred to, in its main features has been
repeatedly brought under review in these pages, there is the less
need for any remarks in its application to the doctrine of the
Lord's Supper.   It may be sufficient to call attention to the following points: —

1. If there be no such thing as generic humanity, no such objective reality ; if Adam were not the human race ; if he and his
posterity are not identical in such a sense that his acts were their
acts as truly as they were his own ; in other words, if the scholastic
doctrine of realism, which until of late, has been regarded as utterly exploded, be not true, then this whole theory collapses.
Its foundation is gone.

2. If it be not true that in man the soul and body are one ;
one living substance developing itself under two aspects, so that
there can be no soul without a body ; if in the person of Christ
there are two substances or natures hypostatically united, and not
only one nature and life, so that his divine nature is in the fullest
sense human, and his human, divine, then again the whole foundation of the theory is gone ; then there can be no communication of his divine humanity or theanthropic life to his people
to be in them the germ of a new life, noetic and somatic, to be
historically developed as was the nature derived from Adam, until
it issues in the resurrection and final consummation.

3. It is to be remembered that it is said that this generic humanity which constitutes the identity between Adam and his
race which is the analogue of the mystical union between Christ
and his people, resolves itself into " an invisible law."   Now what
does that mean?   What is a law ?   In the lips of philosophers
and scientists the word law often means nothing more than a fact.
What are the laws of Kepler but facts ?   By the laws of nature is
often meant nothing more than generalizations concerning the
orderly sequence of events.   At other times a law means a uniformly acting force.   An organic law is a force uniformly acting
to produce a given organic result.   The germ of a bird and of a
fish are undistinguishable by the microscope or by chemical
agents ; yet by an organic law, a uniformly acting force, the one
develops into a bird, the other into a fish.   What then is meant by

saying that generic humanity resolves itself in a law ? Can it mean anything more than a uniformly acting force ? Then when it is said that generic humanity as united with the divine nature, so as to become itself divine while it continues human, is communicated to us, does it mean anything more than that a new uniformly acting force is implanted in our nature, as when the magnetic force is introduced into a piece of iron — an illustration, obviously imperfect indeed, used by the advocates of the theory ? Then what becomes of a personally present Christ ? All Christ does for us is to implant a new law in our nature, which by its natural, historical development works out our salvation. It is this aspect of the case that made the German opposers of Schleiermacher, say that after all he had a Christ that was, but is not now. Christ appeared in the world, and produced a certain effect, and then passed away, leaving nothing but his memory. It is not said that the advocates of the theory in question view the matter in this light ; but it is said that some of the first minds among his countrymen regarded this as the logical consequence of Schleiermacher's system. That system passed in Germany for what it was worth, an ingenious philosophical theory. In this country it is propounded as the truth of God.

4. It is a part of the theory under consideration that we become partakers of Christ's redemption only in virtue of our participation of his life. His life brings with it his merit and his power. He is our wisdom, righteousness, sanctification, and redemption only so far as, and only because, we become subjectively wise, righteous, holy, and free from the consequences of our sins. It is the Christ within us and not the Christ without us and above us, that is our confidence and glory. It is hard to see on this theory what meaning there is in praying to Christ for his intercession, his guidance, his protection, or his love. He has implanted a new law within us which works out our salvation by just as natural a process of development, as that by which a seed expands into plant and flower. It is not for other men to say how a theory lies in the minds of its advocates, or to sit in judgment on their religious experience ; but they have the right to protest against any theory which, in their apprehension of it, takes away their personal Saviour and gives them nothing but a new invisible law in their members ; which substitutes for the Incarnate Son of God " the organic law of Christ's human life."

5. This new doctrine is a philosophy ; and philosophy we know from an infallible authority, is a vain deceit. It is vain

(κενή) empty; void of truth, weightless and worthless.   It is moreover, a deceit; it disappoints and misleads.   This is not said of natural philosophy, which concerns itself with the facts and laws of nature; nor of moral philosophy, which treats of the phenomena and laws of our moral nature; nor of intellectual philosophy, which deals with the operations and laws of mind as revealed in consciousness.   But it is said of speculative philosophy; of every system which undertakes to determine on à priori speculative principles, the nature of God, the origin and constitution of the universe, the nature of man and of his relation to God, or to use common language, of the finite to the infinite.   It was the oriental philosophy which the Spirit of God by the pen of St. Paul, in his Epistle to the Colossians, pronounced " a vain deceit."   He says the same thing in the Epistle to the Corinthians of the Greek philosophy, whether Eleatic or Platonic.   This judgment of inspiration is confirmed by experience.   Who now cares a straw for the speculations of the ancients, of the schoolmen, or of their modern successors.   Who is now a Hegelian?   Forty years ago, who was not?   We were told then, as we are told now, that certain scientific principles have a right to be respected and employed in the exposition of the doctrine of the Bible.   But what is called science — in the sphere of speculation — in one age, is repudiated as nonsense in another.   No philosophy has the right to control or modify the exposition of the doctrines of the Bible, except the philosophy of the Bible itself; that is, the principles which are therein asserted or assumed.

§ 18. *The Lutheran Doctrine concerning the Lord's Supper.*

Protestants at the time of the Reformation agreed on all the great doctrines of the Gospel.   Luther was as thorough an Augustinian as Calvin.   There would have been no schism had it not been for the difference of views which gradually arose on the true nature of the sacrament of the Lord's Supper.   And even on this point, such was the desire to avoid division, and such the spirit of concession manifested by the Reformed, that a schism would have been avoided, had it not been that Luther insisted on the adoption of the very words in which he stated his doctrine on the subject. That there was a real difference between the parties must be admitted, but that difference was not such as to justify a division in the ranks of Protestants; and the Reformed were willing to adopt a mode of stating the doctrine which both parties could receive without a violation of conscience.   One attempt after another designed to effect a compromise failed, and the Lutherans and Reformed separated into two ecclesiastical denominations, and so remain at the present time. In the Evangelical Church of Prussia under the pressure of the government, the two parties have been brought into one Church which comprehends the greater part of the people. But beyond the limits of Prussia the two Churches remain distinct, though no longer in a state of mutual alienation.

Luther took his stand on the words of Christ, "This is my body," which he insisted must be understood literally. He would admit of no figure in the subject, copula, or predicate. Christ affirmed that "This," that which I hold in my hand, and which I give you to eat, is my body.[1] This position having been as-

---

[1] Lutherans lay great stress on the fact that in Matthew xxvi. 26, τοῦτο (this) is neuter, and ἄρτος (bread) is masculine, and therefore that the meaning cannot be ' This bread is my body,' but ' This that I give you to eat is my body.' It must be admitted that the neuter pronoun cannot be referred to the masculine noun grammatically, but it evidently does refer to it *ad sensum*. ' This thing which I hold in my hand and which I give you to eat is my body.' But the thing which Christ gave his disciples was the bread which he had taken and broken; and therefore it was the bread which He affirmed was, either literally or figuratively, his body. Lutherans themselves cannot avoid saying and admitting that the bread in the Lord's Supper is the body of Christ. Thus Luther (*Larger Catechism*, v. 12, 13; Hase, *Libri Symbolici*, p. 554) tells his catechumen to say, " Though infinite myriads of devils and all fanatics should impudently demand, How bread and wine can be the body and blood of Christ? I know that all spirits and all learned men put together have not as much intelligence as Almighty God has in his little finger." The bread therefore he teaches is the body of Christ. And Dr. Krauth (p. 609) says, " Just as it would be blasphemy to say, ' Man is God,' and is yet literally true of Christ, ' This man is God,' so would it be blasphemy to say, ' Bread is Christ's body,' and yet it is literally true, ' This bread is Christ's body.' " It is conceded, therefore, that after all, the pronoun " This " (τοῦτο), in the words of institution, does refer to the noun "bread," and that if the language of Christ is to be understood literally, He affirms that the bread in the Lord's Supper is his body. On this concession it may be remarked, (1.) That it seems to yield everything to the Romanists. If the bread is literally the body of Christ, it is no longer bread; for no one asserts that the same thing can be bread and flesh at the same time. If, therefore, the words of Christ are to be taken literally, they teach the doctrine of transubstantiation. (2.) It will not do to say that the bread remains bread and that the body of Christ is in, with, and under it, for that makes the language figurative, and the literal interpretation, the main, if not the only, prop of the Lutheran doctrine, is given up. When Christ says, "This cup is the New Testament," it is admitted that the cup is used metonymically for the wine in the cup. And if the language of our Lord, ' This bread is my body,' means, This bread is the vehicle of my body, then He spoke figuratively and not literally; and whether the figure used be metonymy or metaphor is a question to be determined by the nature of the proposition, the context, and the analogy of Scripture. But the advocates of the metonymical sense are not entitled to charge those who adopt the metaphorical meaning, with giving up the literal sense. That is done by the one party as well as by the other.

A great deal of discussion has been expended on the meaning of the substantive verb "is," in the proposition, "This is my body." The Reformed are wont to say that it means, "signifies," "represents," or "symbolizes" my body. The Lutherans maintain that it is the mere copula between the subject and predicate, and never has, or can have the meaning assigned to it by the Reformed ; and in this they are right. Yet it seems to be a dispute about words. There is no real difference between the parties. When the Re-sumed it necessarily led to a statement of what is meant by the body and blood of Christ; in what sense the bread is his body and the wine his blood; how they are given and received; and what are the effects of such reception. On all these points the surest sources of information on the real doctrine of the Lutheran Church is to be found in its authorized symbols.

Statement of the Doctrine in the Symbolical Books.

The tenth article of the first part of the Augsburg Confession is very short, and is couched in language which Calvin would not, and did not, hesitate to adopt. "De Cœna Domini docent, quod corpus et sanguis Christi vere adsint et distribuantur vescentibus in Cœna Domini, et improbant secus docentes." [1]

The language of the Apology is more explicit: "Decimus articulus approbatus est, in quo confitemur, nos sentire, quod in Cœna Domini vere et substantialiter adsint corpus et sanguis Christi, et vere exhibeantur cum illis rebus, quæ videntur, pane et vino, his, qui sacramentum accipiunt." "Non negamus recta nos fide caritateque sincera Christo spiritualiter conjungi; sed nullam nobis conjunctionis rationem secundum carnem cum illo esse, id profecto pernegamus, idque a divinis Scripturis omnino alienum dicimus." [2]

In the Smalcald Articles [3] it is said: "De sacramento altaris sentimus, panem et vinum in Cœna esse verum corpus et sanguinem Christi, et non tantum dari et sumi a piis, sed etiam impiis christianis."

---

formed say that "is" means or may mean "signifies," all they intend is that the one word, in the case in question, may be properly substituted for the other. The idea intended to be expressed by the words, "The seven ears are seven years," may be expressed by saying, 'The seven ears signify seven years.' This does imply that "are" means "signify." Dr. Krauth tells us that Luther in his version of the Bible employs forty-six different substitutes for the substantive verb as used in the Hebrew and Greek. It would hardly be fair to say that Luther gives forty-six different lexicographical meanings to the Hebrew word הָיָה, or the Greek εἰμι. Whether the proposition "This is my body" is to be understood literally or figuratively is an open question; but there can be no question as to the lexicographical meaning of the word "is." No one doubts that such propositions as "I am the living bread," "That rock was Christ," "The seven candlesticks . . . are the seven churches," and hundreds of others of like kind occurring in the Bible and in ordinary language, are to be understood figuratively. And it may be safely said that if the proposition, "This (bread) is my body" were submitted to a thousand intelligent men, who knew nothing of Christianity, not one of them would hesitate to say that the words, according to all the laws of interpretation, must be understood figuratively. The fact that they have been understood literally by so large a part of Christendom, is to be accounted for by other reasons than any ambiguity in the words themselves.

[1] Hase, *Libri Symbolici*, p. 12.
[2] IV. 54–56; Hase, pp. 157, 158. Cyril on John XV.
[3] VI. 1, 5; Hase, p. 330.

" De transubstantione subtilitatem sophisticam nihil curamus, qua fingunt, panem et vinum relinquere et amittere naturalem suam substantiam, et tantum speciem et colorem panis, et non verum panem remanere. Optime enim cum sacra Scriptura congruit, quod panis adsit et maneat, sicut Paulus ipse nominat: Panis quem frangimus. Et: Ita edat de pane."

In the Smaller Catechism it is asked: " Quid est sacramentum altaris ? Responsio. Sacramentum altaris est verum corpus et verus sanguis Domini nostri Jesu Christi, sub pane et vino, nobis Christianis ad manducandum ac bibendum ab ipso Christo institutum. Quid vero prodest, sic comedisse et bibisse? Responsio. Id indicant nobis hæc verba: Pro vobis datur; et: Effunditur in remissionem peccatorum. Nempe quod nobis per verba illa in sacramento remissio peccatorum, vita, justitia et salus donentur. Ubi enim remissio peccatorum est, ibi est et vita et salus. Qui potest corporalis illa manducatio tantas res efficere ? Responsio. Manducare et bibere ista certe non efficiunt, sed illa verba, quæ hic ponuntur: Pro vobis datur, et: Effunditur in remissionem peccatorum ; quæ verba sunt una cum corporali manducatione caput et summa hujus sacramenti. Et qui credit his verbis, ille habet, quod dicunt, et sicut sonant, nempe remissionem peccatorum." [1]

Luther in his Larger Catechism enlarges on all these points ; answers various objections to his doctrine ; insists upon the necessity of faith in order to the profitable reception of the ordinance; and exhorts to frequent attendance on the ordinance.

The Form of Concord gives the affirmative statement of the doctrine ; and then the negation of all the opposing views. It affirms: First, the true and substantial presence of the body and blood of Christ in this sacrament. Second, that the words of institution are to be understood literally, so that the bread does not signify the absent body, nor the wine the absent blood of Christ, but on account of the sacramental union "panis et vinum vere sint corpus et sanguis Christi." Third, that the cause of this presence is not the consecration by man, but is due solely to the omnipotent power of our Lord Jesus Christ. Fourth, the prescribed words of institution are on no account to be omitted. Fifth, the fundamental principles on which the doctrine rests are, (1.) That Jesus Christ is inseparably true, essential, natural, perfect God and man in one person. (2.) That the right hand of God is everywhere, and, therefore, Christ, " ratione human-

[1] v. 1-8; Hase, pp. 380, 381.

itatis suæ," being truly and actually at the right hand of God is, as to his humanity, everywhere present. (3.) " Quod verbum Dei non est falsum, aut mendax." (4.) That God knows, and has in his power various modes of presence, and is not bound to that particular mode which philosophers are accustomed to call local or circumscriptive. Sixth, that the body and blood of Christ are received not only spiritually by faith, but also by the mouth, yet not " capernaitice," but in a supernatural and celestial way, as sacramentally united with the bread and wine. Seventh, that not only the worthy and believing, but also the unworthy and unbelieving communicants received the body and blood of Christ in this sacrament.[1] Such are the most important affirmations concerning the Lord's Supper.

The Form of Concord, on the other hand, denies or rejects, (1.) The papal doctrine of transubstantiation. (2.) The doctrine of the sacrifice of the Mass. (3.) The withholding the cup from the laity. (4.) The figurative interpretation of the words of institution. (5.) The doctrine that the body of Christ is not received by the mouth. (6.) That the bread and wine are only symbols or signs of a Christian profession. (7.) That the bread and wine are only symbols, signs, or types of the absent body of Christ. (8.) That they are merely signs and seals by which our faith is confirmed, by being directed heavenward, and there made partaker of the body and blood of Christ. (9.) That our faith is strengthened by receiving the bread and wine and not by the true body and blood really present in the supper. (10.) That in the sacrament only the virtue, efficacy, and merit of the absent body and blood are dispensed. (11.) That the body of Christ is so shut up in heaven, that " nullo prorsus modo " can it be present at one and the same time in many or all places where the Lord's Supper is celebrated. (12.) That Christ could not have promised or offered the presence of his body in the eucharist, because such presence is inconsistent with the nature of a body. (13.) That God cannot by his omnipotence make the body of Christ to be present in more than one place at the same time. (14.) That faith and not the omnipotent word of Christ, is the cause of the presence of the body and blood of Christ in the supper. (15.) That believers are to seek the Lord's body in heaven and not in the sacrament. (16.) That the impenitent and unbelievers do not receive the body and blood of Christ, but only the bread and wine. (17.) That the dignity of the

---

[1] *Epitome*, VII. 1-16; Hase, pp. 599, 600.

communicants in this ordinance is not alone from true faith in
Christ, but from some human source.   (18.) That true believers may eat the Lord's Supper to condemnation if imperfect
in their conversation.   (19.) That the visible elements of bread
and wine in this sacrament should be adored.   (20.) Præter hæc
justo Dei judicio relinquimus omnes curiosas, sannis virulentis
tinctas, et blasphemas quæstiones, quæ honeste, pie et sine gravi
offensione recitari nequeunt, aliosque sermones, quando de supernaturali et cœlesti mysterio hujus sacramenti crasse, carnaliter,
capernaitice, et plane abominandis modis, blaspheme, et maximo
cum ecclesiæ offendiculo, Sacramentarii loquuntur.   (21.) Finally any corporal manducation of the body of Christ is denied,
as though it was masticated by the teeth or digested as ordinary
food.   A supernatural manducation is again affirmed ; a manducation which no one by his senses or reason can comprehend.[1]

Although the Lutheran doctrine on this subject may be regarded as stated with sufficient clearness in the Epitome of the
Form of Concord, it becomes still plainer by the more expanded
and controversial exposition in the second, and much more extended portion of that document, called the " Solida Declaratio."
The seventh chapter of that Declaration, in giving the " Status
Controversiæ," between the Lutherans and the Reformed, says
that although the Sacramentarians (as the Reformed were called)
laboured to come as near as possible to the language of the Lutherans and used the same forms of expression, yet when pressed,
it became apparent that their true meaning was very different.
They admitted the presence of the body and blood of Christ in
the supper, but it was a presence to faith.   The real body of
Christ is in heaven and not on earth ; therefore they denied that
his body and blood, " in terra adesse," and taught that nothing
in the sacrament is received by the mouth but the bread and
wine.   This is one point of difference between the Lutherans and
the Reformed.   The former teaching that the literal, natural body
of Christ, born of the Virgin Mary, is actually present in, with, and
under the bread, and his blood shed upon the cross and which
was the life of his body while on earth, is present in, with, and
under the consecrated wine.   The latter teach that the natural
body of Christ is in heaven, and is not on earth, and therefore
is not present in the elements of bread and in the supper of
the Lord.   What is present, according to Calvin, is not the natural body and blood of Christ, but a supernatural, life-giving

[1] *Epitome*, VII. 22–42 ; Hase, pp. 602–604.

influence emanating from his glorified body in heaven, and conveyed to the believer by the power of the Holy Ghost. According to the Reformed generally, it is not this supernatural power of the glorified body of Christ that is present and received, but the sacrificial efficacy of his body broken and his blood shed for the remission of sins.

Secondly, as the thing received, according to the two doctrines, is different, so are the mode and organ and condition of reception. According to the Lutherans the body and blood are received " corporaliter ; " the organ is the mouth ; the only condition is the actual reception of the bread and wine. The body and blood of Christ are received equally by believers and unbelievers ; although to their spiritual good only by the former. According to the Reformed, the mode of reception is not corporeal, but spiritual ; the organ is not the mouth, but faith ; and the condition of reception is the presence and exercise of faith on the part of the communicant. This point of difference is clearly recognized in the Form of Concord, when it says that the Reformed think that the body and blood of Christ, " tantum in cœlis, et præterea nullibi esse, ideoque Christum nobis cum pane et vino verum corpus et verum sanguinem manducandum et bibendum dare, spiritualiter, per fidem, sed non corporaliter ore sumendum." [1]

Manducation.

Thirdly, another point of difference, which the Form of Concord points out between the two Churches, concerns the manducation or eating which takes place in the Lord's Supper. Our Lord in the sixth chapter of St. John's Gospel, although not there treating of the Eucharist, says, that He is the true bread which came down from heaven, and that whosoever eateth of that bread shall live forever. And in the same chapter, with a change of language but not of meaning, He says, " The bread that I will give is my flesh." " Except ye eat the flesh of the Son of man, and drink his blood, ye have no life in you. Whoso eateth my flesh, and drinketh my blood, hath eternal life ; and I will raise him up at the last day." Such being the language of Christ, every Christian must admit that there is a sense in which the believer may properly be said to eat the flesh and to drink the blood of the Son of man. The only question is, What does such

---

[1] *Solida Declaratio*, VII. 6; Hase, *Libri Symbolici*, p. 727. See also Dr. Julius Müller. *Vergleichung der Lehren Luthers und Calvins vom heiligen Abendmahl*, in his *Dogmatische Abhandlungen*, Bremen, 1870, p. 425.

language mean ? According to the Reformed the meaning is that it is the indispensable condition of eternal life, that we should receive Christ as He is offered to us in the gospel ; and as He is there offered to us as a sacrifice for our sins, his body broken and his blood shed for us, we must receive and appropriate Him in that character. To receive Him as the true bread, and to eat of that bread, is to receive and appropriate Him as being to us the source of eternal life ; and to eat his flesh and drink his blood is to receive and appropriate Him as the broken and bleeding sacrifice for our sins. In other words, to eat is to believe. The Form of Concord correctly recognizes this as the doctrine of the Reformed Church. It says,[1] that the Reformed in rejecting the literal sense of the words " eat, this is my body," teach " ut edere corpus Christi nihil aliud ipsis significet, quam credere in Christum, et vocabulum corporis illis nil nisi symbolum, hoc est, signum seu figuram corporis Christi denotet, quod tamen non in terris in sacra cœna præsens, sed tantum in cœlis sit." That the Reformed are right in this matter may, in passing, be argued, (1.) From the fact that our Lord in John vi. interchanges as equivalent the words " eating " and " believing." He says, " If any man eat of this bread, he shall live forever ; " and, " He that believeth on me hath everlasting life. I am that bread of life." The same specific effect is ascribed to eating and believing, and therefore the two words express the same act. (2.) The eating spoken of is declared to be the indispensable condition of eternal life. " Except ye eat the flesh of the Son of man, and drink his blood, ye have no life in you." But it is the clear doctrine of the Bible, and the common doctrine of the Lutheran and Reformed Churches, that the only eating which is necessary to eternal life is that which consists in believing. Lutherans are as far as the Reformed from making the sacramental eating of the body and blood of Christ in the supper essential to salvation. (3.) Nothing is essential to salvation under the new dispensation that was not essential under the old. This also is a part of the common faith of both Churches. But under the Old Testament there could be no other eating of the flesh of Christ, than believing on Him as the passover, or, lamb of God that taketh away the sins of the world. (4.) Any corporal eating of the flesh of Christ's body and drinking of his blood, as He sat at table with his disciples, would seem to be inconceivable. (5.) Our Lord Himself, in opposition to the sense put upon his words by the people of Capernaum, said : " It

[1] vii. 7; Hase, *Libri Symbolici*, p. 727.

is the Spirit that quickeneth ; the flesh profiteth nothing ; the words that I speak unto you, they are spirit, and they are life." It was not his literal flesh that He was to give us to eat, for that would profit nothing. His words, on that subject, were to be understood in a spiritual sense.[1]

But although the Lutherans reject the doctrine of the Reformed who teach that the eating of the body of Christ in the sacrament is spiritual and by faith, and assert that it is corporal (corporaliter) and by the mouth, yet they strenuously resist the idea that it is after the manner of ordinary food. They maintain that the manner is supernatural and incomprehensible. The Lutherans distinguish between a spiritual manducation, of which says the Form of Concord, Christ treats especially in the sixth chapter of St. John, and which is by faith, and a sacramental manducation which is by the mouth, when in the Lord's Supper, " verum et substantiale corpus et sanguis Christi ore accipiuntur atque participantur ab omnibus, qui panem illum benedictum et vinum in cœna Dominica edunt et bibunt." The words of Christ, it is said, "non potest nisi orali, non autem de crassa, carnali, capernaitica, sed de supernaturali et incomprehensibili manducatione corporis Christi intelligi." [2] Being incomprehensible, it is of course inexplicable.

However, although the Lutherans reject the idea that the body of Christ in the Lord's Supper is eaten after the manner of ordinary food, yet the language of Luther on this subject, adopted or defended by his followers, can hardly be understood in any other sense. In his instruction to Melancthon,[3] he says, " Of our doctrine this is the sum, that the body of Christ is truly eaten in and with the bread, so that what the bread does and suffers, the body of Christ does and suffers ; it is distributed, eaten, and masticated (zerbissen) by the teeth." On this passage Philippi [4] remarks that as Luther says that this is *propter unionem sacramentalem*, it is not inconsistent with the language of the Form of Concord which denies that the body of Christ is lacerated by the teeth and digested as ordinary food. He says it is analogous to the proposition, God died, not as to his divine nature

---

[1] There are two modes of interpreting the passage John vi. 50–58. According to the one, it is to be understood as referring to a participation of the benefit of Christ's sacrificial death, according to the other, of the reception of his body and blood in the Supper. A large portion of the Lutheran theologians adopt the former.

[2] *Form of Concord*, vii. 63, 64; Hase, *Libri Symbolici*, pp. 744, 745.

[3] *Works*, edit. Walch, 1745, vol. xvi. p. 2489.

[4] *Kirchliche Glaubenslehre*, vol. v. p. 350.

but as to his assumed human nature. The language of Luther
on this subject is seldom now heard from the lips of Lutherans.

Mode of Presence.

A thing is present where it is perceived and where it acts. The
nature of that presence varies with the nature of the object of
which it is affirmed. A body is present where it is perceived by
the senses or acts upon them. The soul is present where it perceives and acts. It is somewhere, and not everywhere. God is
present everywhere, as He fills immensity. There is no portion
of space from which He is absent as to his essence, knowledge, or
power.[1] As the Lutherans affirm the presence of the substance
of Christ's natural body and blood in the Lord's Supper, of that
body which was born of the Virgin and suffered on the cross;
and as that body was and is material, it would seem to follow
that the presence affirmed is local. It is a presence in a definite
place. The Reformed, therefore, always understood the Lutherans to assert the local presence of the body of Christ in the
Lord's Supper. The Lutherans, however, deny that they teach
any such presence. This after all may be a dispute about words.[2]
The parties may take the word " local " in different senses. The
Lutherans say that the body and blood of Christ are with, in,
and under the bread and wine. They are held in the hand and
taken into the mouth. This is all the Reformed mean when they
speak of a local presence; a presence in a definite portion of space.
Magnetism is locally present in the magnet; electricity in the
Leyden jar. The soul is locally present in the body. The man
is locally present in mind and body where he perceives and acts and
where he is perceived and acted upon. Lutherans appear to take

---

[1] Luther and Lutherans speak of three modes of Christ's presence: First, that in which
He was present when here on earth; "raumerfüllende und vom Raum umschollene," space-
filling and by space circumscribed; Second, that which is in space, but does not fill any portion of it, and is not circumscribed by it. In this state Christ's body rose from the grave
and passed through closed doors. This kind of presence belongs to angels. Third, the
divine and celestial mode of presence, according to which Christ, in virtue of the union of
the two natures in his person, is present in his humanity, in his soul and body, wherever
God is present. It is specially in the second and third modes (the definitive and the re-
pletive) that Luther asserted the presence of Christ's body in the eucharist; although he
asserted that the first was possible, " Denn er wolle in keiner Weise läugnen, dass Gottes
Gewalt nicht sollte so viel vermögen, dass ein Leib zugleich an vielen Orten sein möge,
auch leiblicher, begreiflicher Weise.'ᶜ Philippi, *ut supra*, vol. v. p. 346.

[2] On this word Gerhard remarks: " Terminum localis præsentiæ esse ambiguum. Corpus
Christi præsens esse dicimus in illo loco, in quo celebratur cœna, sed modo locali et cir-
cumscriptivo præsens esse negamus. Si præsentiam localem sensu posteriori intelligunt,
habent nos sibi consentientes; si priori, repugnamus." *Loci Theologici*, xxii. xi. § 106;
edit. Tübingen, 1770, vol. x. p. 186.

the word "local" in a sense in which it characterizes the presence of a body which is present exclusively, *i. e.*, both in the sense of excluding all other bodies from the same portion of space, being bounded by it, and of being nowhere else. The Reformed say that it is contrary to the nature of such a body as that which belongs to man, that it should be in many places at the same time, much less that it should fill all space. The idea that the flesh and blood of Christ are omnipresent, seems to involve a contradiction. It is in vain to appeal to the omnipotence of God. Contradictions are not the objects of power. It is no more a limitation of the power of God to say that He cannot do the impossible, that He cannot make right wrong, or the finite infinite, than it is a limitation of his wisdom that He cannot teach the untrue or the unwise. All such assumptions destroy the idea of God as a rational Being. If the body and blood of Christ be everywhere present, then they are received in every ordinary meal as well as in the Lord's Supper. The answer which Lutherans give to this objection, namely, that it is one thing for the body of Christ to be omnipresent, and another for it to be accessible, or everywhere given, is unsatisfactory; because the virtue resides in the body and blood, and if they are everywhere present and received they are everywhere operative, at least to believers. If this omnipresence of the body of Christ was actual only after his ascension, then, as Müller[1] argues, the Apostles must, at the institution of the Lord's Supper, have partaken of his body and blood in a manner peculiar to that one occasion, and Christ, so far as other Christians are concerned, only foretold that his body would be ubiquitous and therefore present in the eucharist. Luther, therefore, says, "If Christ at the Last Supper had not uttered the words 'this is my body,' yet the words, Christ sits at the right hand of God, prove that his body and blood may be in the Lord's Supper as well as everywhere else."[2] As Christ in his human nature and therefore in his human body sits at the right hand of God; and as the right hand of God is everywhere, his body must be everywhere, and therefore in the bread as used in the sacrament. The current representations, however, of the Lutheran theologians on this point are, that the presence of the body of Christ in the Lord's Supper is peculiar, something which occurs there and nowhere else. This presence is due, not to the words of consecration as uttered by the minister, but to the almighty power which

---

[1] *Dogmatische Abhandlungen*, Bremen, 1870, p. 455, note.
[2] *Das diese Worte, etc.*, § 118; *Works*, edit. Walch's, vol. xx. p. 1011.

attended the original utterance of the words, This is my body, and continues to operate whenever and wherever this sacrament is administered.

This presence of the body and blood of Christ in, with, and under the bread and wine has been generally expressed by non-Lutherans by the word consubstantiation, as distinguished from the Romish doctrine of transubstantiation. The propriety of this word to express the doctrine of Luther is admitted by Philippi, if it be understood to mean, what in fact is meant by it when used by the Reformed, " das reale Zusammensein beider Substanzen," *i. e.*, the real coexistence of the two substances, the earthly and the heavenly. But Lutherans generally object to the word because it is often used to express the idea of the mixing two substances so as to form a third ; or the local inclusion of the one substance by the other.[1]

The Lutheran doctrine of the mode of the presence of the body and blood of Christ in the eucharist, is thus carefully stated by Gerhard :[2] " Quam vere in sacra cœna præsens est res terrena, panis et vinum : tam vere etiam præsens res cœlestis, corpus et sanguis Christi : proinde credimus, docemus et confitemur in eucharistiæ sacramento veram, realem et substantialem corporis et sanguinis Christi præsentiam, exhibitionem, manducationem et bibitionem, quæ præsentia non est essentialis conversio panis in corpus et vini in sanguinem Christi, quam transubstantionem vocant, neque est corporis ad panem, ac sanguinis ad vinum extra usum cœnæ localis aut durabilis, neque est panis et corporis Christi personalis unio, qualis est divinæ et humanæ naturæ in Christo unio, neque est localis inclusio corporis in panem, neque est impanatio, neque est incorporatio in panem, neque est consubstantio, qua panis cum corpore Christi, et vinum cum ipsius sanguine in unam massam physicam coalescat : neque est naturalis inexistentia, neque delitescentia corpusculi sub pane, neque quidquam hujusmodi carnale aut physicum ; sed est præsentia et unio sacramentalis, quæ ita comparata est, ut juxta ipsius salvatoris nostri, veracis, sapientis, et omnipotentis institutionem, pani benedicto tanquam medio divinitus ordinato corpus : et vino benedicto tanquam medio itidem divinitus ordinato, sanguis Christi modo nobis incomprehensibili uniatur, ut cum illo pane corpus Christi una manducatione sacramentali et cum illo vino sanguinem Christi una bibitione sacramentali in sublimi mysterio suma-

[1] Philippi, *ut supra*, vol. v, p. 356, and Krauth, *ut snpra*, pp. 130, 339.
[2] John Gerhard, *Loci Theologici*, XXII. X. § 69; edit. Tübingen, 1769, vol. X. pp. 116, 117.

mus, manducemus ac bibamus.   Breviter non ἀπουσίαν absentiam, non ἐνουσίαν inexistentiam, non συνουσίαν consubstantionem, non μετουσίαν transubstantionem, sed παρουσίαν corporis et sanguinis Christi in sacra cœna statuimus.''

The whole doctrine of the Lutheran Church on the Lord's Supper is briefly and authoritatively stated in the " Articuli Visitatorii " issued in 1592 for the Electorate and northern provinces of of Saxony, which all church officers and teachers were required to adopt.   The first Article is as follows : " Pura et vera doctrina nostrarum Ecclesiarum de Sacra Cœna.   (1.)   Quod verba Christi: Accipite et comedite, hoc est corpus meum : Bibite, hic est sanguis meus simpliciter, et secundum literam, sicut sonant, intelligenda sint.   (2.)   Quod in sacramento duæ res sint, quæ exhibentur et simul accipiuntur: una terrena, quæ est panis et vinum ; et una cœlestis, quæ est corpus et sanguis Christi.   (3.)   Quod hæc unio, exhibitio et sumptio fiat hic inferius in terris, non superius in cœlis.   (4.)   Quod exhibeatur et accipiatur verum et naturale corpus Christi, quod in cruce pependit, et verus ac naturalis sanguis, qui ex Christi latere fluxit.   (5.)   Quod corpus et sanguis Christi non fide tantum spiritualiter, quod etiam extra cœnam fieri potest, sed cum pane et vino oraliter, modo tamen imperscrutabili, et supernaturali, illic in cœna accipiantur, idque in pignus et certificationem resurrectionis nostrorum corporum ex mortuis.   (6.)   Quod oralis perceptio corporis et sanguinis Christi non solum fiat a dignis, verum etiam ab indignis, qui sine pœnitentia et vera fide accedunt ; eventu tamen diverso.   A dignis enim percipitur ad salutem, ab indignis autem ad judicium." [1]

The Benefit received at the Lord's Supper.

In the Augsburg Confession, in the Apology, in the Shorter and Larger Catechism, and in the Form of Concord, the benefits conferred upon believers in this sacrament are declared to be forgiveness of sin and confirmation of faith.   These are said to be its special and intended effects.   Thus in the Shorter Catechism the question is asked, " Quid vero prodest, sic comedisse et bibisse ? " The answer is " Id indicant hæc verba : Pro vobis datur ; et : effunditur in remissionem peccatorum.   Nempe nobis per verba illa in sacramento remissio peccatorum, vita, justitia et salus donentur.   Ubi enim remissio peccatorum est, ibi est et vita et salus." The next question is, " Qui potest corporalis illa manducatio tantas res efficere ?"   To which the following answer is given:

---

[1] Hase, *Libri Symbolici*, 3d edit. Leipzig, 1846, pp. 857, 858.

" Manducare et bibere ista certe non efficiunt, sed illa verba, quæ hic ponuntur : Pro vobis datur, et : Effunditur in remissionem peccatorum; quæ verba sunt una cum corporali manducatione caput et summa hujus sacramenti. Et qui credit his verbis, ille habet, quod dicunt, et sicut sonant, nempe remissionem peccatorum." [1] To the same effect in the Larger Catechism, after referring to the words of institution it is said that in coming to the Lord's Supper we receive the remission of sins. " Quare hoc? Ideo, quod verba illic extant et hæc dant nobis. Siquidem propterea a Christo jubeor edere et bibere, ut meum sit, mihique utilitatem afferat, veluti certum pignus et arrhabo, imo potius res ipsa, quam pro peccatis meis, morte et omnibus malis ille opposuit et oppignoravit. Inde jure optimo cibus animæ dicitur, novum hominem alens atque fortificans." [2]

All that is here said is in perfect accord with the Reformed doctrine both as to the benefits to be derived from this sacrament and as to the source from which those benefits are to be received. The believing communicant receives at the Lord's table the benefits of his redeeming death, and his faith is confirmed by the divinely appointed seals and pledge of the promises of God. And the sacrament has these effects, because through the grace of the Holy Spirit the worthy communicant embraces by faith the offer of pardon and acceptance made in the ordinance. This implies the ignoring or repudiation of the idea that the benefits conferred are to be attributed to any magical or supernatural influence from the actual, natural body and blood of Christ, which, according to the Lutheran doctrine, are orally received in this ordinance; or to a divine influence emanating from the glorified body of Christ in heaven; or to the theanthropic life of Christ conveyed into the believer as a new organic law. Nevertheless there is another mode of representation occurring in the writings of Luther and of Lutherans. According to this representation there is a divine, supernatural power inherent in the body and blood of Christ, which being received in the Lord's Supper conveys to the believer, as to his soul and body, a new spiritual and immortal life. Thus, in his Larger Catechism, in answer to the question how bread and wine can have the power attributed to the Lord's Supper, he says it is not bread as such which produces the effect, " but such bread and wine which are the body and blood of Christ, and which have the words [of

[1] v. 5–8; Hase, *Libri Symbolici*, pp. 381, 382.
[2] v. 22, 23; *Ibid.* pp. 555, 556.

institution] connected with them." To this he adds : " Quin etiam illud pro certo constat, Christi corpus et sanguinem nequaquam rem otiosam et infrugiferam esse posse, quæ nihil fructus aut utilitatis afferat." [1] Luther's Catechisms have symbolical authority, having been adopted by the whole Lutheran Church. The same authority does not belong to his private writings, in which the idea advanced of the life-giving power of the body and blood of Christ as received in the sacrament is (at least as often understood) more fully expanded. In his work entitled " Das diese Worte Christi, ' das ist mein Leib u. s. w.,' noch fest stehen wider die Schwarmgeister," published in 1527,[2] he says Christ gives us his own body and blood as food " in order that with such a pledge he may assure and comfort us, that our body shall live forever, because it here on earth enjoys eternal living food." [3] " The mouth, which corporeally eats Christ's flesh, knows not, it is true, what it eats, but the heart knows : by itself it would gain nothing, for it cannot comprehend the word [of promise]. But the heart knows well what the mouth eats. For it comprehends the word and eats spiritually, what the mouth eats corporeally." But since the mouth is a member of the heart, it must live forever, on account of the heart, which through the word lives forever, because the body corporeally eats the same everlasting food, which the soul with it spiritually eats. Again : [4] " The heart cannot eat corporeally, and the mouth cannot eat spiritually. God, however, has arranged it, that the mouth eats for the heart corporeally, and the heart eats for the body spiritually, so both are satisfied with the same food and are saved. For the body having no understanding, knows not that it eats such food whereby it shall live forever. Because it feels it not, but dies and moulders away, as though it had eaten other food, as an irrational brute. But the soul sees and understands, that the body must live forever, because it is a partaker of an everlasting food; which will not allow it to decay and waste away in the grave." [5] Still more strongly is this idea expressed in such passages as the following. When a man eats this food [6] " it changes

---

[1] v. 28–30; Hase, *Libri Symbolici*, p. 557.

[2] *Das diese Worte*, etc., edit. Walch, vol. xx.

[3] *Ibid*, § 186, p. 1045.

[4] *Ibid*, p. 1046.

[5] Philippi, *Kirchliche Glaubenslehre*, vol. v. p. 267. Philippi admits that these passages appear to teach that the seeds of immortality are implanted in the bodies of believers by the corporeal participation of the body of Christ, though he endeavours to explain them as teaching that the Lord's Supper is a pledge of the believer's resurrection. On p. 268, however, he admits that there are other passages which cannot be thus explained.

[6] *Das diese Worte*, §§ 207, 208, pp. 1055,1056.

(verdäut) and transmutes his flesh, so that it becomes spiritual, that is, endued with immortal life and blessed, as Paul, 1 Corinthians xv. 44, says : It is raised a spiritual body." Luther gives what he calls a gross illustration. He supposes a wolf to devour a sheep and the flesh of the sheep to have power enough to transmute the wolf into a sheep. " So we, when we eat Christ's flesh corporeally and spiritually, the food is so strong that it changes us into itself, so that out of carnal, sinful, mortal men, we are made spiritual, holy, and living men ; such we already are, but hidden in faith and hope, and not yet revealed; at the last day we shall see it." Again : [1] " God is in this flesh. It is divine and spiritual (a weak translation of ein Gottesfleisch, ein Geistfleisch), it is in God, and God is in it, therefore it is living and gives life both as to soul and body to all who eat it." Again : [2] " If we eat Him corporeally, so He is in us corporeally, and we in Him. He is not digested and assimilated, but He continually transmutes us, the soul into righteousness, the body into immortality." After quoting these and similar passages, Philippi admits that they teach that " the body of Christ is not only the pledge of our resurrection, but also that it is the life-giving, operative power through which our bodies are prepared for our final resurrection." [3]

There were two views of the benefit of the Lord's Supper in the mind of Luther. He commonly represents its special benefit to be the forgiveness of sins, which is received whenever faith in the gospel is exercised. This effect is due, not to what is in the sacrament received by the mouth, but to the Word as received by faith. According to this view, as Dorner [4] says, the Lord's supper is a sign and pledge of the forgiveness of sin. To this view, he adds, the Lutheran Church has adhered. Therefore, the

---

[1] *Das diese Worte*, p. 125. (?)   [2] *Ibid*, p. 132. (?)

[3] See Philippi, *ut supra*, p. 269. So also, Gerhard, *Loci Theologici*, xxii. xi. § 103; edit. Tübingen, 1770, vol. x. p. 175, says that the fathers teach that our bodies " suscipiant ex contactu carnis Christi vim quandam ad gloriosam resurrectionem et vitam æternam; " an opinion to which Gerhard accedes. Calvin (*Institutio*, iv. xvii. 32, edit. Berlin, 1834, part ii. p. 426) uses language of similar import: " De carnis etiam nostræ immortalitate securos nos reddat, siquidem ab immortali ejus carne jam vivificatur et quodammodo ejus immortalitate communicat." There is, however, an essential difference, as to this point between Luther and Calvin. Luther held that what is received in the Supper is the true, natural body of Christ; that it is received corporeally, by the mouth, that it is received by unbelievers as well as by the believers; and that it is to the natural body thus received, that the believer owes the glorious resurrection that awaits him. All these points Calvin denies. It is not the natural body of Christ, which hung upon the cross, that is received. It is not received corporeally by the mouth, but only by the soul through faith. It is received out of the Lord's Supper as well as in that ordinance. The resurrection of believers, therefore, according to Calvin, is due to our union with Christ, effected by faith; and not to eating his true, natural body.

[4] *Geschichte der protestantischen Theologie*, Munich, 1867, p. 152.

Apology says : " Idem effectus est verbi et ritus, sicut præclare dictum est ab Augustino, sacramentum esse verbum visibile, quia ritus oculis accipitur, et est quasi pictura verbi, idem significans, quod verbum. Quare idem est utriusque effectus." [1]

At other times, however, Luther, as appears from the passages above quoted, attributes to the Lord's Supper a peculiar effect due to the real, natural body of Christ therein received, which, in virtue of its union with his divine nature, is imbued with a supernatural, life-giving power. To this power he refers the glorious future resurrection of the believer. In this he made some approximation to the modern doctrine that the redemptive work of Christ consists in the infusion into our nature of a new force, or organic law which, by a process of natural, historical development, works out the salvation of soul and body. Julius Müller rejoices that this view did not take root in the Lutheran Church, as it is, as he says, plainly contrary to Scripture. If the resurrection of believers be due to the body of Christ as received in the Lord's Supper, what is to become of children, of confessors and martyrs, and of all the Old Testament saints, who never partook of the Lord's Supper.[2]

§ 19. *Doctrine of the Church of Rome on the Lord's Supper.*

Romanists regard the eucharist under two distinct aspects as a sacrament and as a sacrifice. The latter in their system is by far the more important. Möhler in his " Symbolik " almost entirely overlooks its sacramental character. And in the worship of the Romish Church the sacrifice of the mass is the central point. In the symbolical books, however, the two views are kept distinct. It is a sacrament inasmuch as it signifies, contains, and conveys grace. It includes an external sign and things signified. The external signs are bread and wine, which retain their form after consecration and after the change in their substance thereby affected. The things signified are, (1.) The passion of Christ. (2.) The grace of God given in the sacrament. (3.) Eternal life.[3] It has virtue to produce grace. " On voit," says Cardinal Gousset in the place referred to, " que le signe eucharistique est un signe qui a la vertu de produire la grace ; mais il n'a cette vertu que par l'institution de Jésus Christ."

The grace bestowed is not spiritual life, for that is communi-

---

[1] VII. 5; Hase, *Libri Symbolici*, p. 201.

[2] *Dogmatische Abhandlungen*, pp. 417, 418.

[3] *Théologie Dogmatique.* Par S. É. Le Cardinal Gousset, Archevêque de Reims. *De l'Eucharistie* I. i. 695, 10th edit. Paris, 1866, vol. ii. p. 452.

cated in baptism, and is presupposed in those who receive the
eucharist as a sacrament. On this point the language of the Roman Catechism and other Roman authorities is explicit, and in
tone evangelical and Protestant. Thus the Catechism says,
" Constat quemadmodum mortuis corporibus naturale alimentum
nihil prodest, ita etiam animæ, quæ spiritu non vivit, sacra mysteria non prodesse, ac propterea panis, et vini speciem habent, ut
significetur, non quidem revocandæ ad vitam animæ, sed in vita
conservandæ causa instituta esse."[1] The benefits received are
analogous to those which the body receives from its natural food.
Bread and wine strengthen and refresh the body ; so the eucharist
strengthens and refreshes the soul. And more than this, the food
of the body is transmuted into the body ; whereas the divine
food received in this sacrament transmutes the soul into its own
nature.   " Neque enim hoc sacramentum in substantiam nostram,
ut panis, et vinum, mutatur ; sed nos quodam modo in ejus naturam convertimur : ut recte illud D. Augustini ad hunc locum
transferri possit :[2] ' Cibus sum grandium ; cresce, et manducabis
me. Nec tu me in te mutabis, sicut cibum carnis tuæ ; sed tu
mutaberis in me.' "[3]

Lutherans make the forgiveness of sins, a blessing which the
believer constantly needs, the great benefit of this ordinance.
This is not its design in the view of Romanists, for they teach
that for a man to approach the altar in a state of mortal sin, is a
dreadful profanation.   They enjoin, therefore, confession and absolution in the sacrament of penance, as a necessary preparation
for this ordinance.   Only venial sins are remitted by receiving
the sacrament of the Lord's Supper.   Nevertheless, as according
to Romanists, Christ is really in both natures present in the eucharist, they say " necessario fons omnium gratiarum dicenda est,
cum fontem ipsum cœlestium charismatum, et donorum, omnium-
que sacramentorum auctorem Christum dominum admirabili modo
in se contineat."[4]   The virtue of the eucharist, both as a sacrament and as a sacrifice, rests, according to Romanists, in the doctrine of

Transubstantiation.

Christ is present in this ordinance, not spiritually as taught by
the Reformed, nor by the real presence of his body and blood in,
with, and under the bread and wine, but by the bread and wine

---

[1] *Catechismus Romanus,* II. iv. quæst. 40 [60, li.] ; Streitwolf, Göttingen, 1846, vol. i. p.
344.
[2] *Confessionum,* VII. x. 16 ; *Works,* edit. Benedictines, Paris, 1836, vol. i. p. 241, c.
[3] *Catechismus Romanus, ut supra,* quæst. 39 ; p. 343.   [4] *Ibid.* p. 342.

being by the almighty power of God changed into his body and blood. As at the feast in Cana of Galilee, the water was changed into wine, so in the eucharist, the bread and wine are changed into, and remain the body and blood of Christ. This doctrine is thus set forth in the Canons of the Council of Trent: —

" 1. Si quis negaverit, in sanctissimæ eucharistiæ sacramento contineri vere, realiter, et substantialiter corpus et sanguinem una cum anima, et divinitate Domini nostri, Jesu Christi, ac proinde totum Christum, sed dixerit tantummodo esse in eo, ut in signo, vel figura aut virtute; anathema sit.

" 2. Si quis dixerit in sacrosancto eucharistiæ sacramento remanere substantiam panis, et vini, una cum corpore et sanguine Domini nostri, Jesu Christi, negaveritque mirabilem illam et singularem conversionem totius substantiæ panis in corpus, et totius substantiæ vini in sanguinem, manentibus duntaxat speciebus panis, et vini, quam quidem conversionem catholica ecclesia aptissime transubstantionem appellat; anathema sit.

" 3. Si quis negaverit, in venerabili sacramento eucharistiæ sub unaquaque specie, et sub singulis cujusque speciei partibus, separatione facta, totum Christum contineri; anathema sit.

" 4. Si quis dixerit, peracta consecratione, in admirabili eucharistiæ sacramento non esse corpus, et sanguinem Domini nostri Jesu. Christi, sed tantum in usu dum sumitur, non autem ante, vel post; et in hostiis, seu particulis consecratis, quæ post communionem reservantur, vel supersunt, non remanere verum corpus Domini; anathema sit.

" 5. Si quis dixerit, vel præcipuum fructum sanctissimæ eucharistiæ esse remissionem peccatorum, vel ex ea non alios effectus provenire; anathema sit.

" 6. Si quis dixerit, in sancto eucharistiæ sacramento Christum, unigenitum Dei filium, non esse cultu latriæ, etiam externo, adorandum; atque ideo nec festiva peculiari celebritate venerandum; neque in processionibus, secundum laudabilem, et universalem ecclesiæ ritum, et consuetudinem, solemniter circumgestandum, vel non publice, ut adoretur, populo proponendum, et ejus adoratores esse idololatras; anathema sit.

" 7. Si quis dixerit, non licere sacram eucharistiam in sacrario reservari, sed statim post consecrationem adstantibus necessario distribuendam, aut non licere, ut illa ad infirmos honorifice deferatur; anathema sit.

" 8. Si quis dixerit, Christum, in eucharistia exhibitum, spiritualiter tantum manducari, et non etiam sacramentaliter, et realiter: anathema sit.

" 9. Si quis negaverit, omnes, et singulos Christi fideles utriusque sexus, cum ad annos discretionis pervenerint, teneri singulis
annis, saltem in paschate, ad communicandum, juxta præceptum
sanctæ matris ecclesiæ; anathema sit.

" 10. Si quis dixerit, non licere sacerdoti celebranti seipsum
communicare; anathema sit.

" 11. Si quis dixerit, solam fidem esse sufficientem præpara-
tionem ad sumendum sanctissimæ eucharistiæ sacramentum;
anathema sit.   Et ne tantum sacramentum indigne atque ideo in
mortem, condemnationem sumatur, statuit, atque declaret ipsa
sancta synodus, illis, quos conscientia peccati mortalis gravat,
quantumcunque etiam se contritos existiment, habita copia con-
fessoris, necessario præmittendam esse confessionem sacramentalem.   Si quis autem contrarium docere, prædicare, vel pertinaciter
asserere, seu etiam publice disputando defendere præsumpserit eo
ipso excommunicatus existat." [1]

From this statement it appears, first, as concerns the elements
of bread and wine, that in and by the act of consecration, their
whole substance is changed.   Nothing of the substance or essence
of either remains.   The accidents, or sensible properties, however, continue as they were.   The form, colour, taste, odour, the
specific gravity, their chemical affinities, and their nutritive qualities remain the same.   So far as the senses, chemical analysis,
and physics are concerned or are to be trusted, no change has
taken place.   As the sensible properties of the bread and wine do
not and cannot inhere in the substance of Christ's body and blood,
and as their own substance no longer exists, those properties do
not inhere in any substance.   " Cum antea demonstratum sit, corpus Domini, et sanguinem vere in sacramento esse, ita nulla amplius subsit panis, et vini substantia; quoniam ea accidentia
Christi corpori, et sanguini inhærere non possunt: relinquitur, ut
supra omnem naturæ ordinem ipsa se, nulla alia re nisa, sustentent,
hæc perpetua, et constans fuit catholicæ Ecclesiæ doctrina." [2]

Secondly, as to what is said to be present under the species of
bread and wine, it is the body and blood of Christ; the body
which hung upon the cross; the blood which flowed from his side;
with the nerves, bones, and whatever pertains to the completeness
of man.   (" Ossa, nervi, et quæcumque ad hominis perfectionem
pertinent.") [3]   As, however, the body of Christ is inseparably connected with his soul, so that where the one is, the other must be;

1 *Council of Trent*, Sess. xiii. canones; Streitwolf, vol. i. pp. 50-52.
2 *Catechismus Romanus*, II. iv. quæst. 37 [45, xliv.]; *Ibid.* p. 341.
3 *Ibid.* quæst. 27 [33. xxxi.], p. 333.

and as his soul is in like manner connected with his divinity, it follows that the whole Christ, body, soul, and divinity, is present, and is received orally, *i. e.*, by the mouth, by the communicant. "Docere autem oportet, Christum nomen esse Dei, et hominis, unius scilicet personæ, in qua divina, et humana natura conjuncta sit, quare utramque substantiam, et quæ utriusque substantiæ consequentia sunt, divinitatem, et totam humanam naturam, quæ ex-anima, et omnibus corporis partibus, et sanguine etiam constat, complectitur: quæ omnia in sacramento esse credendum est, nam cum in cœlo tota humanitas divinitati, in una persona, et hypostasi conjuncta sit, nefas est suspicari, corpus, quod in sacramento inest, ab eadem divinitate sejunctum esse."[1]

Thirdly, the whole Christ is in the bread and the whole Christ is in the wine:[2] and not only so, but in each and every particle of both species. Thus the Catechism, says "non solum in utra-que specie, sed in quavis utriusque speciei particula totum Christum contineri."

Fourthly, Lutherans teach that the presence of the body and blood of Christ in, with, and under the bread and wine, is confined to the time of the administration of the sacrament. Romanists, on the other hand, teach that as there is an entire change of the substance of the elements into the substance of the body and blood of Christ, that change is permanent. From this it is inferred, (1.) That the consecrated wafer as containing the whole Christ, may be preserved. (2.) That it may be carried to the sick. (3.) That it may be borne about in processions. (4.) That it should be adored.

It is well known that Romanists distinguish between the "cultus civilis," or worship (*i. e.*, respect) due to our superiors among men; δουλεία, due to saints and angels; ὑπερδουλεία, due to the Virgin Mary, and λατρεία, due to God alone. The ground of this worship is the real or supposed possession of divine perfections in its object. When our Lord was upon the earth He was the proper object of this divine worship, because He was God manifested in the flesh. The worship terminated on the person; and that person is and was divine. If Christians err in believing that the person known in history as Jesus of Nazareth, was, and is the Eternal Son of God clothed in our nature, then their worship of Him is idolatry. They ascribe divine perfections and render di-

---

[1] *Catechismus Romanus, ut supra*, quæst. 27 [33, xxxi.], p. 334.

[2] Romanists teach that even after consecration, it is proper to call the elements bread and wine, because, although the substance is changed, the accidents of bread and wine remain. *Catechismus Romanus, ut supra*, quæst, 30 [xxxv. 36], p. 335.

vine honours to a creature, and therein consists the essence of idolatry. In like manner Romanists teach that λατρεία, the worship
due to God alone, is to be rendered to the host, or consecrated
wafer. This worship, of course, is not rendered to the wafer
as such, any more than the worship of Christians was rendered
to the body and blood of Christ, when He was here on earth.
But Romanists worship the host on the assumption that it is the
body of Christ, with which his soul and divinity are inseparably
connected. If their doctrine of transubstantiation be false ; if
the host be no more the body of Christ than any other piece of
bread ; if his soul and divinity be no more present in it than in
other bread, then they must admit that the worship of the host
is as pure and simple idolatry as the world has ever seen. As
all Protestants believe the doctrine of transubstantiation to be
utterly unscriptural and false, they are unanimous in pronouncing
the worship of the consecrated elements to be idolatry.

Proof of the Doctrine.

The arguments urged by Romanists in support of the fearful
dogma of transubstantiation, are derived partly from Scripture
and partly from tradition. Without the latter, the former, to all
appearance, even in the estimation of Romanists themselves,
would be of little account. The Scriptural passage principally
relied upon, is John vi. 48–65. As to this discourse of our
Lord, Cardinal Gousset lays down two propositions : first, that
it is to be understood of the Lord's Supper ; and second, that the
eating of which it speaks is oral, by the mouth, and not merely
spiritual, by faith. If these points be granted, then it follows
that our Lord does speak of a literal eating of his flesh, and
therefore that his flesh must be in the literal sense of the words
eaten at the Lord's Supper. Such eating it must be conceded
necessitates the admission of the doctrine of transubstantiation.
It is enough, in this place, to say of this argument, that it proves
too much. Our Lord expressly declares that the eating of which
He speaks is essential to salvation. If, therefore, his words are
to be understood of the Lord's Supper, then a participation in
that sacrament is essential to salvation. But this the Church
of Rome explicitly denies, and must in consistency with its whole
system, insist on denying. Romanists teach that spiritual life is as
necessary to an experience of the benefits of this sacrament, as
natural life is to the body's being nourished by food.[1]

---

[1] *Catechismus Romanus*, ii. iv. 40 [li. 50], Streitwolf, vol. i. p. 344.

They further teach that baptism, which precedes the eucharist, conveys all the saving benefits of Christ's redemption ; they therefore cannot make the eucharist essential, and consequently they cannot, without contradicting Christ or themselves, interpret John vi. 48–65 as referring to the Lord's Supper.[1]

Appeal, of course, is also made to the words of institution, " This is my body." In this argument enough has already been said. There is no more necessity for understanding those words literally than the declaration of Christ, " I am the true bread," or, " I am the door." The elements are declared to be bread and wine both by Christ and by the Apostles, after as well as before consecration.

Romanists, however, teach that there are many doctrines which Christ and his Apostles taught, which are either not revealed at all, or but very imperfectly in Scripture, and which are to be received on the authority of tradition. On that authority they rely for the support of all their peculiar doctrines. As to that argument, as urged in behalf of the doctrine of transubstantiation, Protestants say, first, that the Scriptures are the only infallible rule of faith and practice, and, therefore, that no doctrine, which cannot be proved from the Bible, can be received as an article of faith. And as the doctrine of transubstantiation cannot be so proved, it is to be rejected as a mere human theory. And, secondly, that even admitting the authority of tradition, it can be demonstrated that the doctrine in question has no claim to support from the rule, " quod semper, quod ubique, quod ab omnibus." The rise and gradual development of this doctrine can be historically traced. The conflicts attending its introduction as an article of faith are matters of record, and it can no more be proved, even by tradition, than the doctrine of purgatory and extreme unction. This is the conclusion reached after years of controversy, and it is not likely ever to be shaken. It was on this point that the leading divines of the Church of England laid out their strength in their controversy with the Church of Rome.[2]

It is a valid objection to this doctrine that it involves an im-

[1] "Le sacrement de l'eucharistie n'est point nécessaire au salut, d'une nécessité de moyen; on peut être sauvé sans avoir reçu la communion. La raison, c'est que se sacrement n'a point été institué comme moyen de conférer la première grace sanctifiante ou de remettre le péché mortel, ce qui est réservé aux sacrements de baptême et de pénitence." Gousset, *Théologie*, Paris, 1866, vol. ii. p. 516.

[2] In Herzog's *Real-Encyklopädie*, vol. xvi., there is, under the head of " Transubstantiation," an elaborate article of fifty-five royal octavo pages on the history of this doctrine, n which its rise through the patristical and mediæval periods is minutely traced.

possibility. The impossible cannot be true, and, therefore, cannot, rationally, be an object of faith. It is impossible that the
accidents or sensible properties of the bread and wine should remain if the substance be changed. Such a proposition has no
more meaning in it than the assertion that an act can be without
an agent. Accidents or properties are the phenomena of substance ; and it is self-evident that there can be no manifestations
where there is not something to be manifested. In other words
nothing, a " non-ens " cannot manifest itself. Romanists cannot
turn to the theory that matter is not a substance ; for that is not
their doctrine. On the contrary, they assert that the substance
of the bread is transmuted into the substance of Christ's body.
Nor can they help themselves by resorting to the pantheistic doctrine that all accidents are phenomena of God, for that would upset their whole system.

It is moreover impossible that the well-attested testimony of
our senses should be deceptive. If it once be assumed that we
cannot trust to the laws of belief impressed on our nature, of
which faith in our sense perceptions is one of the most important,
then the foundation of all knowledge, faith, and religion is over-
turned. What has Catholicism to say for itself, if the people
cannot trust their ears when they hear the teachings of the
Church, or their eyes when they read its decrees ? It has nothing
to stand upon. It is engulfed with all things else in the abyss of
nihilism. To believe in transubstantiation we must disbelieve
our senses, and this God requires of no man. It involves disbelief
in Him who is the author of our nature and of the laws which
are impressed upon it. There is no more complete and destructive infidelity than the want of faith in the veracity of consciousness, whether it be consciousness of our sense perceptions, or of
the truths involved in our rational, moral, or religious nature.

It is another objection to this doctrine that it logically leads,
and in fact has led, to the greatest practical evils. It has led to
superstitious, in the place of rational and Scriptural reverence for
the sacrament ; to the idolatrous worship of the consecrated wafer;
to attributing to it magical, or supernatural virtue contrary to
Scripture ; to perverting a simple sacrament into a propitiatory
sacrifice, and to investing the ministers of Christ with the character of sacrificing priests, empowered to offer, for money, a propitiatory oblation securing forgiveness even for the sins of the departed. It has been made a mine of wealth to the priesthood
and the Church. It was principally the popular belief in this

great error, that secured the transfer of the greater part of the land and wealth of Europe into the hands of the clergy and gave them almost unlimited power over the people.

Withholding the Cup from the Laity.

The Romish Church admits that this is contrary to the original institution of the ordinance, and to the usage of the primitive Church. It is defended, (1.) On the ground that the cup is unnecessary to the completeness of the sacrament. The blood is in the body ; he therefore who receives the latter receives the former. And as the whole Christ, as to his body, soul, and divinity is not only in each species, but in every particle of both, he who receives the consecrated bread receives the whole Christ, and derives all the benefit from communing, the sacrament is capable of affording. (2.) That there is great danger in passing the cup from one communicant to another that a portion of its contents should be spilt ; and as the cup after consecration contains the real blood of Christ, its falling to the ground and being trodden under foot, is a profanation, by every means to be avoided. (3.) The Church did not of its own motion introduce this innovation. It was introduced and had become general, before the Church saw fit, for sufficient reasons, to interfere and change a custom into a law.

The Lord's Supper as a Sacrifice.

On this subject the Church of Rome teaches, according to the Council of Trent, —

" 1. Si quis dixerit, in missa non offerri Deo verum, et proprium sacrificium ; aut quod offerri non sit aliud, quam nobis Christum ad manducandum dari ; anathema sit.

" 2. Si quis dixerit, illis verbis, ' Hoc facite in meam commemorationem ; ' Christum non instituisse Apostolos sacerdotes ; aut non ordinasse, ut ipsi, aliique sacerdotes offerent corpus, et sanguinem suum ; anathema sit.

" 3. Si quis dixerit, missæ sacrificium tantum esse laudis, et gratiarum actionis, aut nudum commemorationem sacrificii in cruce peracti, non autem propitiatorium ; vel soli prodesse sumenti ; neque pro vivis, et defunctis, pro peccatis, pœnis, satisfactionibus, et aliis necessitatibus offerri debere ; anathema sit.

" 4. Si quis dixerit, blasphemiam irrogari sanctissimo Christi sacrificio, in cruce peracto, per missæ sacrificium ; aut illi per hoc derogari ; anathema sit.

" 5. Si quis dixerit, imposturam esse, missas celebrare in honorem sanctorum, et pro illorum intercessione, apud Deum obtinenda, sicut ecclesia intendit ; anathema sit.

" 6. Si quis dixerit, canones missæ errores continere, ideoque abrogandum ; anathema sit.

" 7. Si quis dixerit, cæremonias, vestes, et externa signa, quibus in missarum celebratione ecclesia catholica utitur, irritabula impietatis esse, magis quam officia pietatis ; anathema sit.

" 8. Si quis dixerit, missas, in quibus solus sacerdos sacramentaliter communicat, illicitas esse, ideoque abrogandas ; anathema sit.

" 9. Si quis dixerit, ecclesiæ Romanæ ritum, quo summissa voce pars canonis, et verba consecrationis proferuntur, damnandum esse ; aut lingua tantum vulgari missam celebrari debere ; aut aquam non miscendam esse vino in calice offerendo, eo quod sit contra Christi institutionem ; anathema sit." [1]

From this it appears, —

1. That, according to the Church of Rome, the eucharist is a real, propitiatory sacrifice, for the expiation of sin, for reconciliation with God, and for securing providential and gracious blessings from his hands.

2. That what is offered is Christ, his body, soul, and divinity, all which are present under the form of bread and wine. The sacrifice of the mass is the same, therefore, as the sacrifice of the cross ; the former being a constant repetition of the latter. " Unum itaque et idem sacrificium esse fatemur, et haberi debet, quod in missa peragitur, et quod in cruce oblatum est : quemadmodum una est et eadem hostia Christus, videlicet Dominus noster, qui se ipsum in ara crucis semel tantummodo cruentum immolavit. Neque enim cruenta, et incruenta hostia, duæ sunt hostiæ, sed una tantum, cujus sacrificium, postquam Dominus ita præcepit, ' Hoc facite in meam commemorationem,' in eucharistia quotidie instauratur." [2]

3. As the sacrifice is the same, so also is the priest. Christ offered Himself once on the cross, and He offers Himself daily in the mass. " Sed unus etiam atque idem sacerdos est Christus dominus, nam ministri, qui sacrificium faciunt, non suam, sed Christi personam suscipiunt, cum ejus corpus et sanguinem conficiunt, id quod et ipsius consecrationis verbis ostenditur, neque enim sacerdos inquit, Hoc est corpus Christi, sed, ' Hoc est corpus meum : ' personam videlicet Christi domini gerens, panis, et vini

---

[1] Sess. xxii. canones; Streitwolf, vol. i. pp. 81, 82.
[2] *Catechismus Romanus*, par. II. cap. iv. quæst. 60 [lxxxii. 76], *Ibid.* p. 359.

substantiam, in veram ejus corporis, et sanguinis substantiam
convertit." [1]   On this statement it may be remarked in passing,
that if the ministers are not the real offerers, they are not real
priests.   A priest is one appointed to offer sacrifices.   But according to the theory, the officiating minister in the service of the
mass, does not offer the sacrifice.   He is a supernumerary.   He
has no function.   There is no reason why without his intervention, Christ should not when his people meet to commemorate his
death, offer Himself anew to God.   The Roman theory in this,
as in many other points, is not self-consistent.   Romanists represent ministers as true priests; mediators between God and the
people, without whose intervention, no sinner can have access to
God or obtain pardon or acceptance.   They are not only invested
with priestly authority and prerogatives, but imbued with supernatural power.   The words of consecration pronounced by other
than sacerdotal lips, are inoperative.   The mass unless performed
by a priest is no sacrifice.   All this supposes that their office is a
reality, that ministers are really priests; but according to the
passage just quoted, they are not priests at all.   According to
the common mode of representation, however, the minister in
the mass as truly offers the body and blood of Christ, as the
priests under the Old Testament offered the blood of lambs or of
goats.   Cardinal Gousset, for example, says: " According to the
faith of the Catholic Church, the mass is a sacrifice of the new
law, in which the priest offers to God the body and blood of Jesus
Christ under the form of bread and wine.   The mass is a true sacrifice instituted by Jesus Christ."   " A sacrifice, from its nature,
is an act of supreme worship, due to God alone.   Hence when a
mass is celebrated in the name of a saint, it is not to be believed
that the sacrifice is offered to the saint; but simply in his memory, to implore his protection, and to secure his intercession.   It
is a sacrifice in which is offered the body and blood of Christ.
Jesus Christ, whose body and blood are present under the forms
of bread and wine, is Himself the victim.   Finally, the eucha-
ristic sacrifice is made by the hands of the priest, but Jesus Christ
is the principal minister ; He is at once priest and victim, offering himself to God the Father by the ministry of his priests." [2]

4. As under the Old Testament some of the sin offerings
availed for those who brought the victims, and for whose benefit
they were offered ; and others, as the morning and evening sacri-

[1] *Catechismus Romanus*, II. iv. quæst. 61 [lxxxiii. 77], Streitwolf, vol. i. pp. 359, 360.
[2] Gousset, *Théologie, ut supra*, vol. II. p. 522.

fices, and those offered on the feast days, and especially that on
the great day of atonement, were intended for the whole nation ;
so according to Romanists, the propitiatory sacrifice, in the ordinary public service, is offered for the sins of the faithful in general, while at other times it is offered for particular individuals.
And as it matters not whether such individuals be living or
dead, it is obvious that such masses may be indefinitely multiplied.   As according to the Church of Rome the great majority
of those dying within the pale of the Church, pass into purgatory, where they remain in a state of suffering for a period to
which there is no certainly known termination before the day
of judgment ; for their benefit, to alleviate or shorten their sufferings, masses may be, and should be offered by their surviving
friends.   It has ever been found that men at the approach of
death, or the affectionate relatives of the departed, are willing to
appropriate money at their command, to pay for masses for their
benefit.   This, as just remarked, has proved an inexhaustible
mine of wealth to the Church.   " Hujus sacrificii eam vim esse,
parochi docebunt, ut non solum immolanti, et sumenti prosit, sed
omnibus etiam fidelibus, sive illi nobiscum in terris vivant, sive
jam in Domino mortui, nondum plane expiati sint.   Neque enim
minus ex Apostolorum certissima traditione, pro his utiliter offertur, quam pro vivorum peccatis, pœnis, satisfactionibus, ac quibus-
vis calamitatibus, et angustiis." [1]

Remarks.

No doctrine of the Church of Rome is more portentous or more
fruitful of evil consequences than this doctrine of the mass ; and
no doctrine of that Church is more entirely destitute of even a
semblance of Scriptural support.   The words of Christ, " This do
in remembrance of me," are made to mean, " Offer the sacrifice
which I myself have just offered " (Offrez le sacrifice que je vien
d'offrir moi-meme).[2]   These words constituted the Apostles and all
their successors priests.   The Council of Trent even anathematizes all who do not put that preposterous interpretation on those
simple words.[3]   Romanists also appeal to the fact that Christ is
said to be a priest forever after the order of Melchizedek, from
which they infer that He continually repeats the sacrifice once
offered on the cross.   They even argue from such passages as

---

[1] *Catechismus Romanus*, par. II. cap. iv. quæst. 63 [86, lxxxvi], Streitwolf, vol. i. pp.
360, 361.
[2] Gousset, *Théologie, ut supra*, vol. ii. p. 538.
[3] See Sess. xxii. canon 2; quoted above on page 685.

Malachi i. 11, in which the universal spread of the true religion is predicted by saying that from the rising of the sun to the going down of the same, " in every place incense shall be offered unto my name, and a pure offering." [1]

Protestants reject the doctrine that the eucharist is a true propitiatory sacrifice, —

1. Because it is not only destitute of all support from the Scriptures, but is directly contrary to the whole nature of the ordinance, as exhibited in its original institution and in the practice of the apostolic church. There it is set forth as a sacred feast commemorative of the death of Christ.

2. Because it is founded on the monstrous doctrine of transubstantiation. If the whole substance of the bread be not changed into the substance of Christ's body, and the whole substance of the wine into the substance of his blood, and if the whole Christ, body, soul, and divinity be not really and truly present under the form (or species) or appearance of the bread and wine, then the priest in the mass has nothing to offer. He in fact offers nothing, and the whole service is a deceit. Just so certainly, therefore, as the impossible and the unscriptural cannot be true, just so certain is it, that the mass is not a propitiatory sacrifice.

3. The Romish doctrine is that the Apostles were priests, and were invested with authority and power to continue and perpetuate in the Church the priestly office by ordination and the imposition of hands by which the supernatural gifts of the Holy Spirit are conveyed. All this is unscriptural and false. First, because a priest is a man appointed to be a mediator between God and other men, drawing near to Him in behalf of those who have not liberty of access for themselves, and whose function it is to offer gifts and sacrifices for sin. But there is no such office under the Christian dispensation, save in the person of Jesus Christ. He is our only, and all sufficient priest; everywhere present and everywhere accessible, who has opened for us a new and living way of access to God, available to all sinners of the human race without the intervention of any of their fellow sinners. Every believer is as much a priest under the Gospel, as any other be-

---

[1] In this passage the words מְקְטָר מֻגָּשׁ, correctly rendered in the English version "incense shall be offered," in the Vulgate are translated "sacrificatur." In the Septuagint it is θυμίαμα προσάγεται. Luther's version is, "geräuchert." Even if the Vulgate version were correct, and the prophet had said that "in every place sacrifice should be made," that would prove nothing to the point. The Old Testament prophets predicted the spread of the true religion under the Gospel dispensation in the use of terms borrowed from the Old Testament ritual.

liever, for through Christ they all have equal freedom of access unto God. It subverts the whole nature of the gospel, to make the intervention of any human priest necessary to our reconciliation with God. Secondly, Christian ministers are never called priests in the New Testament. Every title of dignity, every term expressive of the nature of their office, is bestowed on them, but the title priest, so familiar to Jewish and Gentile ears, is never given to them. Nor is any priestly function ascribed to them. They are not mediators. They are not appointed to offer sacrifices for sin. Every priest is a mediator, but it is expressly declared that Christians have but one mediator, the man Christ Jesus. There is but one sacrifice for sin, the all sufficient sacrifice of Christ upon the cross, who died once for all to bring us near to God. Thirdly, Christ Himself and the Apostles after Him in all their addresses to the people, instead of directing them to go to ministers as priests to obtain the benefits of redemption, uniformly assume that the way is open for the return of every sinner to God without human intervention. " Come unto me " is the invitation of Christ to every heavily laden sinner. " Believe on the Lord Jesus Christ, and thou shalt be saved," is the gospel preached by the Apostles both to Jews and Gentiles. The emancipation of the Christian world effected by the Reformation, consisted in large measure in freeing man from the belief that Christian ministers are priests through whom alone sinners can draw near to God. It was preaching deliverance to captives, and the opening of the prison to those who were bound, to announce that believers through Christ are all made kings and priests unto God; subject to no authority but the authority of God (and of course to such as He has ordained), and all having access by one Spirit unto the Father. If then ministers are not priests, the eucharist is not a sacrifice.

4. The Romish doctrine is derogatory to the sacrifice of the cross. It supposes that the work of Christ in making satisfaction for the sins of men, needs to be constantly repeated. This is directly contrary to Scripture, which teaches that by the one offering of Himself, He has forever perfected them that believe. His one sacrifice has done all that need be done, and all that a sacrifice can do. Romanists say that the same sacrifice which was made on the cross, is made in the mass. The only difference between the two is modal. It concerns only the manner of oblation. Then why is the latter needed? Why does not the one offering of Christ suffice? Certain it is the Bible refers us to nothing else ; and the believer craves nothing else.

5. The doctrine of the sacrificial character of the eucharist, is an integral part of the great system of error, which must stand or fall as a whole. Romanism is another gospel. It proposes a different method of salvation from that presented in the word of God. It teaches that no one can be saved who is out of the pale of that visible society of which the pope of Rome is the head ; and that all are saved who die within that pale. It teaches that no one can be regenerated who is not baptized ; and that there is no forgiveness for post-baptismal sins, except by the sacrament of penance and absolution at the hands of a priest. It teaches that no one can have the benefit of the Lord's Supper, who does not receive it at the hands of a properly ordained officer of the Church of Rome. It teaches that there is no valid ministry, and that there are no valid ordinances except in the line of the apostolic succession as recognized by the pope. It follows men beyond the grave. It teaches that the souls in purgatory are still under the power of the keys ; that their stay in that place or state of torment, can be prolonged or shortened at the will of the Church. The pope assumes, and has often pretended to exercise, the power of granting indulgences for even a thousand years. This whole theory hangs together. If one assumption be false, the whole is false. And if the theory in its primary principle of a perpetual apostleship, infallible in teaching and of plenary power in government and discipline, be false, then every particular doctrine involving that principle must be false.

Moehler, whose philosophical and mitigated Romanism, has called down upon him no little censure from his stricter brethren, represents the doctrine of the eucharist as the point in which all the differences between Romanists and Protestants converge. On the view taken of this doctrine depends the question whether the Christian Church has a true living " cultus " or not. With him the Church, of course, is the body, which, professing the true religion, is united in the reception of the same sacraments, in subjection to bishops canonically consecrated, and especially to the pope of Rome. For him, and all Romanists, this Church is Christ. He dwells in it ; animates it ; operates through it exclusively in the salvation of men. The teaching of the Church is his teaching ; its commands are his commands ; He regenerates only through its sacrament of baptism ; He remits sin only through the sacrament of penance ; He strengthens in confirmation ; He nourishes his people with his body and blood in the eucharist : and in the ordination of priests. He appoints the organs through which all this is done by his ceaseless activity. " The Church," says Moehler, "is vicariously (auf eine abbildlich-lebendige Weise) Christ manifested and working through all time. The Redeemer did not merely live eighteen hundred years ago, and then disappear, to be remembered only as a historical person as any other of the departed ; on the contrary He is ever living in the Church."[1] Romanists, therefore, practically take away Christ, and give us the Church in his stead. It is to be remembered that by the Church they do not mean the body consisting of true believers, but the external, organized body of which the pope is the head. It is this body represented in history by the Hildebrands, the Borgias, and the Leos, which Romanism puts in the place of Christ, clothing it with his prerogatives, and claiming for it the obedience, the reverence, and the confidence due to God alone. It is against this theory, which practically puts man in the place of God, that the most fearful denunciations of the Scriptures are pronounced.

§ 20. *Prayer.*

Prayer is the converse of the soul with God. Therein we manifest or express to Him our reverence, and love for his divine perfection, our gratitude for all his mercies, our penitence for our sins, our hope in his forgiving love, our submission to his authority, our confidence in his care, our desires for his favour, and for the providential and spiritual blessings needed for ourselves and others. As religion, in the subjective sense of the word, is the state of mind induced by the due apprehension of the character of God and of our relation to Him as our Creator, Preserver, and Redeemer ; so prayer is the expression, uttered or unuttered, of all the feelings and desires which that state of mind produces or excites. A prayerless man is of necessity, and thoroughly irreligious. There can be no life without activity. As the body is dead when it ceases to act, so the soul that goes not forth in its actions towards God, that lives as though there were no God, is spiritually dead.

Prayer takes a great deal for granted. It assumes, in the first place, the personality of God. Only a person can say I, or be addressed as Thou ; only a person can be the subject and object of intelligent action, can apprehend and answer, can love and be loved, or hold converse with other persons. If God, therefore, be only a name for an unknown force, or for the moral order of the

<hr>

[1] *Symbolik,* von Dr. J. A. Moehler, 6th edit. Mainz, 1843, p. 300.

universe, prayer becomes irrational and impossible.[1] Secondly, God, however, although a person, may dwell far off in immensity, and have no intercourse with his creatures on earth. Prayer, therefore, assumes not only the personality of God, but also that He is near us; that He is not only able, but also willing to hold intercourse with us, to hear and answer; that He knows our thoughts afar off; and that unuttered aspirations are intelligible to Him. Thirdly, it assumes that He has the personal control of all nature, i. e., of all things out of Himself; that He governs all his creatures and all their actions. It assumes that He has not only created all things and endowed matter and mind with forces and powers, but that He is everywhere present, controlling the operation of such forces and powers, so that nothing occurs without his direction or permission. When it rains, it is because He wills it, and controls the laws of nature to produce that effect. When the earth produces fruit in abundance, or when the hopes of the husbandman are disappointed, these effects are not to be referred to the blind operation of natural laws, but to God's intelligent and personal control. There is no such reign of law as makes God a subject. It is He who reigns, and orders all the operations of nature so as to accomplish his own purposes.

This does not suppose that the laws of nature are mutable, or that they are set aside. There is scarcely any effect, either in nature or in the acts of men, due to the operation of any one natural force. We produce effects by combining such forces, so that the result is due to this intelligent and voluntary combination. In like manner, in the ordinary operations of nature, God accomplishes his purpose by a similar intelligent and voluntary combination of natural causes. When He wills that it should rain, He wills that all the secondary causes, productive of that effect, should be brought into operation. The doctrine of providence only supposes that God does, on the scale of the universe, what we do within the limited sphere of our efficiency. We, indeed, so far as effects out of ourselves are concerned, are tied to the use of

---

[1] Philosophers, says Dr. Chalmers, "look on the Supreme Principle to be in every way as inflexible and sure as they have uniformly found of the subordinate principles; and that He is as unfit to be addressed by a petition or the expression of a wish, as any fancied spirit that may reside in a volcano or a storm, in any other department of nature's vast machinery — that the cries of urgency and distress are of no more avail when sent up to Him who wields the elements of the world, as if they were only lifted to the elements themselves — that the same unchangeableness which pervades all nature, is also characteristic of nature's God: and so they deem to be an aberration from sound philosophy, both the doctrine of a special providence and the observation of prayer." Chalmers, *Works*, ed. New York, 1844, vol. ii. p. 31⁰

secondary causes. We can act neither against them, nor without them. God is not thus limited. He can operate without second causes as well as with them, or against them. There seems to be no little confusion in the minds of many writers on this subject. They insist on the immutability of the laws of nature, and sometimes speak of God as constantly controlling their operation by combining and directing their forces ; and yet they resolve all second causes into the divine efficiency ; that is, an efficiency directed by intelligence and will.   " It is but reasonable," says Sir John Herschel, " to regard the force of gravitation as the direct or indirect result of a consciousness or will existing somewhere." [1] " It may be that all natural forces are resolvable in some one force, and indeed in the modern doctrine of the correlation of forces, an idea which is a near approach to this, has already entered the domain of science. It may also be that this one force, into which all others return again, is itself but a mode of action of the Divine Will." [2]   It is a common remark that the only force of which we have any direct knowledge is mind-force, and hence that it is unphilosophical to assume any other.   From this it is inferred that all the forces operating in nature are the energy of the one Supreme Intelligence. This doctrine, as shown when treating of the doctrine of Providence, almost inevitably leads to pantheism. But it is difficult to see how those who take this view can consistently speak of the immutability of law, or of God's being free only within its limits. It is essential to the idea of mind-power, that it should be free ; that it should act when, where, and how it pleases. In the case of God, indeed, it cannot act unwisely or unjustly. But if all the forces of nature are only manifestations of the divine efficiency, what meaning can be attached to the proposition that He operates with, and through, and never independently of natural law ?

The Scriptural doctrine is that God is an extra-mundane, personal Being, independent of the world, who has created it, and endowed all things material with their several properties or powers, which He in his omnipresent, and infinitely wise omnipotence, constantly controls. This doctrine is presupposed in prayer ; for " prayer and the answer of prayer, are simply . . . . the preferring of a request upon the one side, and compliance with that request upon the other. Man applies, God complies. Man asks a favour, God bestows it. These are conceived to be the two

---

[1] *Outlines of Astronomy*, 5th ed. p. 292.
[2] *The Reign of Law*, by the Duke of Argyle, 5th ed. London, 1867, p. 129.

terms of a real interchange that takes place between the parties
— the two terms of a sequence, in fact, whereof the antecedent is
a prayer lifted up from earth, and the consequent is the fulfilment
of that prayer in virtue of a mandate from heaven." [1]

Prayer also supposes that the government of God extends over
the minds of men, over their thoughts, feelings, and volitions ;
that the heart is in his hands, and that He can turn it even as
the rivers of water are turned.

It is evident, therefore, that not only atheism, pantheism, materialism, and every other system of philosophy which involves the
denial of the existence or the personality of God, but also all
other theories, whether scientific or philosophical, which do not
admit of the control of God over the operations of nature and the
character and conduct of men, are inconsistent with prayer.   According to all these systems there is either no one to pray to, or
nothing to pray for.   If there be no personal God, there is no
one to pray to ; and if God, supposing such a Being to exist,
has no control over nature or man, then there is no rational motive for prayer; there is nothing to be accomplished by it.   The
idea that the service would still be of value for its subjective
effect is irrational, because its subjective effect is due to faith in
its objective efficiency.   If a man believes that there is no God,
he cannot make himself a better man by acting hypocritically,
and pouring forth his prayers and praises to a nonentity.   Or, if
a believer in the existence of God, if he has such a theory of his
nature or of his relation to the world, as precludes the possibility
of his hearing, or if He hears, of his answering our prayers, then
prayer becomes irrational.   Candid men, therefore, who in their
philosophy hold any of the theories referred to, do not hesitate
to pronounce prayer superstitious or fanatical.   Kant, although a
theist, regards all as unphilosophical enthusiasts who assume that
God hears or answers prayer.[2]

Professor Tyndall, one of the representative scientific men of
the age, says, " One by one natural phenomena have been associated with their proximate causes ; and the idea of direct personal volition, mixing itself in the economy of nature, is retreating
more and more."   Science, he tells us " does assert, for example,
that without a disturbance of natural law, quite as serious as the
stoppage of an eclipse, or the rolling the St. Lawrence up the

---

[1] Chalmers, *ut supra*, p. 321.
[2] Kant's *Leben*, von Borowsky, p. 199 (Büchner's *Biblische Real und Verbal-Concor-
danz*, word " Bitte "); Halle, 1840, 6th ed. p. 560.

Falls of Niagara, no act of humiliation, individual or national, could call one shower from heaven, or deflect towards us a single beam of the sun." [Man may deflect the beams of the sun at pleasure, but God cannot. Man, according to Professor Espy, can make it rain, but God cannot.] " Those, therefore, who believe that the miraculous is still active in nature, may with perfect consistency join in our periodic prayers for fair weather and for rain : while those who hold that the age of miracles is past, will refuse to join in such petitions." [1] With Professor Tyndall and the large class of scientists to which he belongs, there never has been an event in the external world due to the exercise of any other force than the undirected operation of physical causes. " Nothing has occurred to indicate that the operation of the law [of gravity] has for a moment been suspended ; nothing has ever intimated that nature has been crossed by spontaneous action, or that a state of things at any time existed which could not be rigorously deduced from the preceding state. Given the distribution of matter and the forces in operation in the time of Galileo, the competent mathematician of that day could predict what is now occurring in our own." [2] What is meant by "spontaneous action " ? Spontaneous is antithetical to necessary. Spontaneous action, therefore, is free action ; the action of intelligence and will ; such action as Professor Tyndall displays in writing or delivering his lectures. His assertion, therefore, is that there has never occurred in nature any effect which may not be referred to necessary, *i. e.*, to blind, unintelligent causes. This of course precludes the possibility of miracles. For a miracle is an event in the external world which cannot be referred to any natural cause, but which must from its nature be ascribed to the immediate efficiency, or the "spontaneous action " of God. When Christ said, " I will; be thou clean," and the leper was cleansed, the only cause, or efficient antecedent of the cure, was his will ; a volition. So when He said, " Lazarus come forth," or when He " said unto the sea, Peace, be still. And the wind ceased and there was a great calm." The scientific man has no idea how small he looks, when, in the presence of Christ, he ventures to say that nature has never been crossed by " spontaneous action ; " that Christ's will was not a cause, when he healed the sick, or opened the eyes of the blind, or raised the dead, by a word ; or

---

[1] *Fragments of Science for Unscientific People*, by John Tyndall, LL. D., F. R. S., London 1871, pp. 31, 32, and 36.
[2] *Ibid.* pp. 63, 64.

when He himself rose by his own power from the grave. To say that these facts never occurred, simply because, according to the ephemeral theory of the hour, they could not occur, is the infinite of folly. It is a thousand fold more certain that they occurred than that the best authenticated facts of history are true. For such facts we have only ordinary historical evidence; for the truth of Christ's miracles, and especially of his resurrection, we have the evidence of all the facts of history from his day to the present. The actual state of the world, and the existence of the Church, necessitate the admission of those facts, to which God himself bore witness of old in signs, and wonders, and divers miracles, as He does still in a manner absolutely irresistible, in the gift of the Holy Ghost. To hear the whole gospel, even constructively, pronounced a lie, is a sore trial to those who have even a glimmer of the faith of Paul, and who can only say with quivering lips, what he said with the fulness of assurance, " I know whom I have believed." [1]   Scientific men are prone to think that there is no other evidence of truth, than the testimony of the senses. But the reason has its intuitions, the moral nature its *à priori* judgments, the religious consciousness its immediate apprehensions, which are absolutely infallible and of paramount authority. A man might as easily emancipate himself from the operation of the laws of nature, as from the authority of the moral law, or his responsibility to God. When, therefore, men of science advance theories opposed to these fundamental convictions, they are like bats impinging against the everlasting rocks.

But apart from the case of miracles, it may be safely said, that so far from its being true that nature has never been " crossed by spontaneous action," such action in nature is familiar, constant, and almost universal. What is an organism, but the product of spontaneous action? that is, of the intelligent (and therefore voluntary) selection and application of appropriate means for the accomplishment of a foreseen and intended end? If the world is full of the evidences of spontaneous action on the part of man, nature is full of evidence of such action on the part of God. The evidence is of the same kind, and just as palpable and irresistible in the one case as in the other. It is admitted of necessity by those who deny it. Darwin's books, for example, are full of such expressions as " wonderful contrivance," " ingenious device,"

---

[1] In the volume above referred to, there is an article entitled, "Miracles and Special Providences," being a review by Professor Tyndall of the Rev. Mr. Mozley's *Bampton Lectures on Miracles*. In that review "magic, miracles, and witchcraft" are placed in the same category.

" marvellous arrangements." These expressions reveal the perception of spontaneous action. They have no meaning except on
the assumption of such action. " Contrivance," " device," imply
design, and would not be used if the perception of intention did
not suggest and necessitate them. Some twenty times already,
in the course of this work, it has been shown that, in many cases,
those who begin with denying any spontaneous action in nature,
end with asserting that there is no other kind of action anywhere;
that all force is mind-force, and therefore spontaneous as well
as intelligent.

Spontaneous action cannot be got rid of. If denied in the
present, it must be admitted in the past. If, as even Professor
Huxley teaches, " Organization is not the cause of life; but life
is the cause of organization," [1] the question is, Whence comes
life ? Not out of nothing, surely. It must have its origin in the
spontaneous, voluntary act of the ever, and the necessarily Living One.

The theory of the universe which underlies the Bible, which is
everywhere assumed or asserted in the sacred volume, which accords with our moral and religious nature, and which, therefore,
is the foundation of natural, as well as of revealed religion, is
that God created all things by the word of his power ; that He
endowed his creatures with their properties or forces ; that He is
everywhere present in the universe, coöperating with and controlling the operation of second causes on a scale commensurate
with his omnipresence and omnipotence, as we, in our measure,
coöperate with, and control them within the narrow range of our
efficiency. According to this theory, it is not irrational that we
should pray for rain or fair weather, for prosperous voyages or
healthful seasons ; or that we should feel gratitude for the innumerable blessings which we receive from this ever present,
ever operating, and ever watchful benefactor and Father. Any
theory of the universe which makes religion, or prayer, irrational,
is self-evidently false, because it contradicts the nature, the consciousness, and the irrepressible convictions of men. As this
control of God extends over the minds of men, it is no less rational that we should pray, as all men instinctively do pray, that
He would influence our own hearts, and the hearts of others, for
good, than that we should pray for health.

It is also involved in the assumptions already referred to, that
the sequence of events in the physical and moral world is not

[1] *Elements of Comparative Anatomy*, pp. 10, 11.

determined by any inexorable fate. A fatalist cannot consistently pray. It is only on the assumption that there is a God, who does his pleasure in the army of heaven and among the inhabitants of the earth, that we can rationally address Him as the hearer of prayer.

In like manner it is assumed that there is no such foreordination of events as is inconsistent with God's acting according to the good pleasure of his will. When a man enters upon any great enterprise, he lays down beforehand the plan of his operations; selects and determines his means, and assigns to each subordinate the part he is to act; he may require each to apply continually for guidance and directions; and may assure him that his requests for assistance and guidance shall be answered. Were it possible that every instance of such application or request could be foreseen and the answer predetermined, this would not be inconsistent with the duty or propriety of such requests being made, or with the liberty of action on the part of the controller. This illustration may amount to little; but it is certain that the Scriptures teach both foreordination and the efficacy of prayer. The two, therefore, cannot be inconsistent. God has not determined to accomplish his purposes without the use of means; and among those means, the prayers of his people have their appropriate place. If the objection to prayer, founded on the foreordination of events, be valid, it is valid against the use of means in any case. If it be unreasonable to say, 'If it be foreordained that I should live, it is not necessary for me to eat,' it is no less unreasonable for me to say, 'If it be foreordained that I should receive any good, it is not necessary for me to ask for it.' If God has foreordained to bless us, He has foreordained that we should seek his blessing. Prayer has the same causal relation to the good bestowed, as any other means has to the end with which it is connected.

The God of the Bible, who has revealed Himself as the hearer of prayer, is not mere intelligence and power. He is love. He feels as well as thinks. Like as a father pitieth his children, so the LORD pitieth them that fear Him. He is full of tenderness, compassion, long-suffering, and benevolence. This is not anthropomorphism. These declarations of Scripture are not mere "regulative truths." They reveal what God really is. If man was made in his image, God is like man. All the excellences of our nature as spirits belong to Him without limitation, and to an infinite degree. There is mystery here, as there is everywhere. But we are all used to mysteries, the naturalist as well as the

theologian. Both have been taught the folly of denying that a
thing is, because we cannot tell how it is. It is enough for us to
know that God loves us and cares for us ; that a sparrow does not
fall to the ground without his notice, and that we are, in his
sight, of more value than many sparrows. All this for the
believer is literal truth, having in its support the highest kind of
evidence. The " how " he is content to leave unexplained.

It is an objection often urged against the propriety of addressing prayer to God, that it is inconsistent with his dignity as an
infinite Being to suppose that He concerns Himself with the
trifling affairs of men. This objection arises from a forgetfulness that God is infinite. It assumes that his knowledge, power,
or presence, is limited ; that He would be distracted if his attention were directed to all the minute changes constantly occurring
throughout the universe. This supposes that God is a creature
like ourselves ; that bounds can be set to his intelligence or efficiency. When a man looks out on an extended landscape, the
objects to which his attention is simultaneously directed are too
numerous to be counted. What is man to God ? The absolute
intelligence must know all things ; absolute power must be able
to direct all things. In the sight of God, the distinction between
few and many, great and small, disappears. In Him all creatures
live, and move, and have their being.

The Object of Prayer.

As prayer involves the ascription of divine attributes to its object, it can be properly addressed to God alone. The heathen
prayed to imaginary beings, or to idols, who had eyes that saw
not, and hands that could not save. Equally unscriptural and
irrational are prayers addressed to any creature of whose presence
we have no knowledge, and of whose ability either to hear or
answer our petitions we have no evidence.

In the Old Testament, the prayers therein recorded are uniformly addressed to God, as such ; to the one Divine Being, because the distinction of the persons in the Godhead was then but
imperfectly revealed. In the New Testament, prayer is addressed
either to God, as the Triune God, or to the Father, to the Son,
and to the Holy Spirit, as distinct persons. In the Christian
doxology, used wherever the Bible is known, the several persons
of the Trinity are separately addressed. The examples of prayer
addressed to Christ, recorded in the New Testament, are very
numerous. As prayer, in the Scriptural sense of the term, in-

cludes all converse with God either in the form of praise, thanksgiving, confession, or petition ; all the ascriptions of glory to Him, as well as all direct supplications addressed to Him, come under this head. The Apostles prayed to Him while He was yet with them on earth, asking of Him blessings which God only could bestow, as when they said, " Lord, increase our faith." The dying thief, taught by the Spirit of God, said, " Lord, remember me, when thou comest into thy kingdom." The last words of the first martyr, Stephen, were, " Lord Jesus, receive my spirit." Paul besought the Lord thrice that the thorn in his flesh might depart from him. So in 1 Timothy i. 12, he says, " I thank Christ Jesus our Lord, who hath enabled me, for that He counted me faithful, putting me into the ministry." In Revelation i. 5, 6, it is said, " Unto him that loved us, and washed us from our sins in his own blood, and hath made us kings and priests unto God and his Father ; to Him be glory and dominion for ever and ever. Amen." Revelation v. 13, " Every creature which is in heaven, and on the earth, and under the earth, and such as are in the sea, and all that are in them, heard I saying, 'Blessing, and honour, and glory, and power, be unto Him that sitteth upon the throne, and unto the Lamb, for ever and ever.' " As the Bible so clearly teaches that Christ is God manifest in the flesh ; that all power in heaven and earth is committed to his hands ; that He is exalted to give repentance and the remission of sins ; as He gives the Holy Ghost ; and as He is said to dwell in us, and to be our life ; it does thereby teach us that He is the proper object of prayer. Accordingly, as all Christians are the worshippers of Christ, so He has ever been the object of their adoration, thanksgivings, praises, confessions, and supplications.

Requisites of Acceptable Prayer.

1. The first and most obviously necessary requisite of acceptable prayer, is sincerity. God is a Spirit. He searches the heart. He is not satisfied with words, or with external homage. He cannot be deceived and will not be mocked. It is a great offence, therefore, in his sight, when we utter words before Him in which our hearts do not join. We sin against Him when we use terms, in the utterance of which the angels veil their faces, with no corresponding feelings of reverence ; or use the formulas of thanksgiving without gratitude ; or those of humility and confession without any due sense of our unworthiness ; or those of petition without desire for the blessings we ask. Every one must ac-

knowledge that this is an evil often attending the prayers of sincere Christians; and with regard to the multitudes who, in places
of public worship, repeat the solemn forms of devotion or profess
to unite with those who utter them, without any corresponding
emotions, the service is little more than mockery.

2. Reverence. God is an infinitely exalted Being; infinite in
his holiness as well as in knowledge and power. He is to be
had in reverence by all who are round about Him. This holy
fear is declared to be the first element of all true religion. His
people are designated as those who fear his name. We are
required to serve Him with reverence and godly fear. And
whenever heaven is opened to our view, its inhabitants are seen
prostrate before the throne. We offend God, therefore, when
we address Him as we would a fellow creature, or use forms of
expression of undue familiarity. Nothing is more characteristic
of the prayers recorded in the Bible, than the spirit of reverence
by which they are pervaded. The Psalms especially may be regarded as a prayer-book. Every Psalm is a prayer, whether of
worship, of thanksgiving, of confession, or of supplication. In
many cases all these elements are intermingled. They relate to
all circumstances in the inward and outward life of those by
whom they were indited. They recognize the control of God
over all events, and over the hearts of men. They assume that
He is ever near and ever watchful, sustaining to his people the
relation of a loving Father. But with all this, there is never any
forgetfulness of his infinite majesty. There is a tendency sometimes in the best of men, to address God as though He were one
of ourselves. Luther's familiar formula was, Lieber Herr, or
Lieber Herr Gott (dear Lord, dear Lord God). As Lieber Herr
is the usual mode of address among friends (equivalent to our
Dear Sir), it sounds strangely when God is thus addressed. In
Luther it was the expression of faith and love; in many who
imitate him it is the manifestation of an irreverent spirit.

3. Humility. This includes, first, a due sense of our insignifi-
cance as creatures; and secondly, a proper apprehension of our
ill-desert and uncleanness in the sight of God as sinners. It is
the opposite of self-righteousness, of self-complacency and self-
confidence. It is the spirit manifested by Job, when he placed
his hand upon his mouth, and his mouth in the dust, and said, I
abhor myself, and repent in dust and ashes; by Isaiah when he
said, Woe is me! because I am a man of unclean lips, and I dwell
in the midst of a people of unclean lips; and by the publican, who

was afraid to lift up so much as his eyes unto heaven, but smote upon his breast, and said, God be merciful to me a sinner. Such language is often regarded as exaggerated or hypocritical. It is, however, appropriate. It expresses the state of mind which cannot fail to be produced by a proper apprehension of our character as sinners, in the sight of a just and holy God. Indeed there is no language which can give adequate expression to that rational sense of sin which the people of God often experience.

4. Importunity. This is so important that on three different occasions our Lord impressed its necessity upon his disciples. This was one evident design of the history of the Syrophenician woman, who could not be prevented from crying, " Have mercy on me, O Lord, thou son of David." (Matt. xv. 22.) Thus also in the parable of the unjust judge, who said, " Because this widow troubleth me, I will avenge her, lest by her continual coming she weary me. And the Lord said, Hear what the unjust judge saith. And shall not God avenge his own elect, which cry day and night unto Him, though He bear long with them ? I tell you that He will avenge them speedily." (Luke xviii. 5–8.) Again in Luke xi. 5–8, we read of the man who refused to give his friend bread, of whom Christ said, " Though he will not rise and give him, because he is his friend, yet because of his importunity he will rise and give him as many as he needeth." God deals with us as a wise benefactor. He requires that we should appreciate the value of the blessings for which we ask, and that we should manifest a proper earnestness of desire. If a man begs for his own life or for the life of one dear to him, there is no repressing his importunity. He will not be refused. If the life of the body is to be thus earnestly sought, can we expect that the life of the soul will be granted to those who do not seek it with importunate earnestness.

5. Submission. Every man who duly appreciates his relation to God, will, no matter what his request, be disposed to say, " Lord, not my will but thine be done." Even a child feels the propriety· of subjecting his will in all his requests to his earthly father. How much more should we submit to the will of our Father in heaven. He alone knows what is best ; granting our request might, in many cases, be our destruction. Our Lord in the garden of Gethsemane set us an example in this matter, that should never be forgotten.

6. Faith. We must believe. (*a.*) That God is. (*b.*) That He is able to hear and answer our prayers. (*c.*) That He is dis-

posed to answer them. (*d.*) That He certainly will answer
them, if consistent with his own wise purposes and with our best
good. For this faith we have the most express assurances in the
Bible. It is not only said, " Ask, and ye shall receive ; seek and
ye shall find," but our Lord says explicitly, " Whatsoever ye shall
ask in my name, that will I do." (John xiv. 13.) And again,
" If two of you shall agree on earth, as touching anything that
they shall ask, it shall be done for them of my Father which is in
heaven." (Matt. xviii. 19.) All the promises of God are conditional. The condition, if not expressed, is implied. It cannot
be supposed that God has subjected Himself in the government
of the world, or in the dispensation of his gifts, to the short-
sighted wisdom of men, by promising, without condition, to do
whatever they ask. No rational man could wish this to be the
case. He would of his own accord supply the condition, which,
from the nature of the case and from the Scriptures themselves,
must be understood. In 1 John v. 14, the condition elsewhere
implied is expressed. " This is the confidence that we have in
Him, that if we ask anything according to his will, He heareth
us." The promise, however, gives the assurance that all prayers
offered in faith, for things according to the will of God, will be
answered. The answer, indeed, may be given, as in the case of
Paul when he prayed to be delivered from the thorn in the flesh,
in a way we do not expect. But the answer will be such as we,
if duly enlightened, would ourselves desire. More than this we
need not wish. Want of confidence in these precious promises of
God ; want of faith in his disposition and readiness to hear us, is
one of the greatest and most common defects in the prayers of
Christians. Every father desires the confidence of his children,
and is grieved by any evidence of distrust; and God is our
Father; He demands from us the feelings which children ought
to have towards their earthly parents.

7. The prayers of Christians must be offered in the name of
Christ. Our Lord said to his disciples : " Hitherto have ye asked
nothing in my name : ask, and ye shall receive." (John xvi. 24.)
" I have chosen you . . . . that whatsoever ye shall ask of the
Father in my name, He may give it you." (xv. 16.) " Whatsoever ye shall ask in my name, that will I do." (xiv. 13.) By
" the name of God " is meant God himself, and God as manifested in his relation to us. Both ideas are usually united.
Thus to believe " in the name of the only begotten Son of God "
is to believe that Christ is the Son of God, and that as such He

is manifested as the only Saviour of men. To act in the name of any one is often to act by his authority, and in the exercise of his power. Thus our Lord speaks of the works which He did " in his Father's name ; " that is, by the Father's authority and in the exercise of his efficiency. And of the Apostles it is fre- quently said that they wrought miracles in the name of Christ, meaning that the miracles were wrought by his authority and power. But when one asks a favour in the name of another, the simple meaning is, for his sake. Regard for the person in whose name the favour is requested, is relied on as the ground on which it is to be granted. Therefore, when we are told to pray in the name of Christ, we are required to urge what Christ is and what He has done, as the reason why we should be heard. We are not to trust to our own merits, or our own character, nor even simply to God's mercy ; we are to plead the merits and worth of Christ. It is only in Him, in virtue of his mediation and worth, that, according to the Gospel, any blessing is conferred on the apostate children of men.

Different Kinds of Prayer.

As prayer is converse with God, it includes those spiritual ex- ercises, those goings forth of the soul towards God in thought and feeling, which reveal themselves in the forms of reverence, grati- tude, sorrow for sin, sense of dependence, and obligation. In this sense, the man who lives and walks with God, prays always. He fulfils to the letter the injunction " Pray without ceasing." It is our duty and high privilege to have this constant converse with God. The heart should be like the altar of incense, on which the fire never went out.

It is, however, a law of our nature that we should clothe our thoughts and feelings in words. And therefore, prayer is in one form speech. Even when no audible utterance is given, words as the clothing or expression of inward states are present to the mind. There is power, however, in articulate words. The thought or feeling is more distinct and vivid even to ourselves, when audibly expressed. Prayer, in this sense, is usually dis- tinguished as secret, social, and public. It would be a great mistake, if a Christian should act on the assumption that the life of God in his soul could be adequately preserved by that form of prayer, which consists in habitual communion with God. The be- liever needs, in order to maintain his spiritual health and vigour, regular and stated seasons of prayer, as the body needs its daily meals. "When thou prayest," is the direction given by our Lord, "enter into thy closet, and when thou hast shut thy door, pray to thy Father which is in secret; and thy Father, which seeth in secret, shall reward thee openly." (Matt. vi. 6.) The Bible presents to us the example of the people of God, and of our blessed Lord himself, as a rule of conduct on this subject. We read that Christ often retired for the purpose of prayer, and not unfrequently spent whole nights in that exercise. If the spotless soul of Jesus needed these seasons of converse with God, none of his followers should venture to neglect this important means of grace. Let each day, at least, begin and end with God.

Social prayer includes family prayer, and prayer in the assemblies of the people for social worship. As man's nature is social, he must have fellowship with his fellow men in all that concerns his inward and outward life. No man lives, or can live for himself, in religion any more than in any other relation. As the family is the most intimate bond of fellowship among men, it is of the utmost importance that it should be hallowed by religion. All the relations of parents, children, and domestics are purified and strengthened, when the whole household is statedly assembled, morning and evening, for the worship of God. There is no substitute for this divinely appointed means of promoting family religion. It supposes, indeed, a certain amount of culture. The head of the family should be able to read the Scriptures as well as to lead in the prayer. Those, however, who cannot do the former, may at least do the latter. All persons subject to the watch or care of the Church should be required to maintain in their households this stated worship of God. The character of the Church and of the state depends on the character of the family. If religion dies out in the family, it cannot elsewhere be maintained. A man's responsibility to his children, as well as to God, binds him to make his house a Bethel; if not a Bethel, it will be a dwelling place of evil spirits.

When and where the mass of the people were so ignorant as to be incompetent profitably to maintain religious services in their families, it was natural and proper for the Church daily to open its doors, and call the people to matins and vespers. It was far better to have this opportunity for daily worship, than that such stated service should be neglected. It is not wise, however, to continue a custom when the grounds on which it was introduced no longer exist; or to make a church ordinance the substitute for a divine institution.

Public Prayer.

The public services of the sanctuary are designed for worship and instruction. The former includes prayer and singing; the latter, the reading the word of God and preaching. These elements should be preserved in due proportion. In some churches, instruction is made entirely subordinate to worship; twice the time being devoted to the latter that is allotted to the former. This seems to be contrary to the Scriptural rule. Knowledge in the Bible is represented as the essential element of religion. There can be no true worship of God without adequate knowledge of God; there can be no repentance, faith, or holy living unless the truths on which these exercises and this living are dependent are understood, and are present to the mind. Religion is a reasonable, that is (λογική) a rational service, with which ignorance is incompatible. Christian ministers, therefore, are always in the New Testament called διδάσκαλοι, teachers. Their great commission received from Christ was " to teach all nations." The Apostles, therefore, went everywhere, preaching. Paul says Christ did not send him to baptize, or to perform mere religious services, but to preach the Gospel, which he declared to be the wisdom of God and the power of God unto salvation. No human authority could have transformed Paul from a preacher into an offerer of prayers. It was not until pagan ideas of worship began to pervade the Church, and ministers were transmuted from teachers into priests, that the teaching element was made so entirely subordinate to that of worship, as it has been for ages in the Church of Rome.

While teaching should be, as it clearly was during the apostolic age, the prominent object in the services of the Lord's day, the importance of public prayer can hardly be overestimated. This, it is often said, is the weak point in the Presbyterian Sabbath service. This is probably true. That is, it is probably true that there are more good preachers than good prayers. The main reason for this is, that the minister devotes a great part of the labour of the week to the preparation of his sermon, and not a thought to his prayers. It is no wonder, therefore, that the one should be better than the other.

In order that this part of divine service should be conducted to the edification of the people, it is necessary, (1.) That the officiating minister should have a truly devout spirit; that the feelings and desires, of which the prayers are the utterance, should be in exercise in his own heart. (2.) That his mind and memory should be well stored with the thoughts and language of Scripture. Holy men of old spake as they were moved by the Holy Ghost. Their utterances, whether in adoration, thanksgiving, confession, or supplication, were controlled by the Spirit of God. Hence they express the mind of the Spirit; they are the most appropriate vehicles for the expression of those feelings and desires which the Spirit awakens in the minds of God's people. No prayers, therefore, are more edifying, other things being equal, than those which abound in the appropriate use of Scriptural language. (3.) The prayer should be well ordered, so as to embrace all the proper parts and topics of prayer in due proportion. This will prevent its being rambling, diffuse, or repetitious. (4.) It should also be suited to the occasion, whether that be the ordinary service on the Lord's day, or the administration of the sacraments, or the special service on days of thanksgiving or of fasting and humiliation. (5.) It is hardly necessary to say that the language employed should be simple, solemn, and correct. (6.) The prayers should be short. Undue length in this service is generally owing, not more to diffuseness than to useless repetitions.

Prayer as a Means of Grace.

Means of grace, as before stated, are those means which God has ordained for the end of communicating the life-giving and sanctifying influences of the Spirit to the souls of men. Such are the word and sacraments, and such is prayer. It has not only the relation which any other cause has to the end for which it was appointed, and thus is the condition on which the blessings of God, providential or spiritual, are bestowed ; but it brings us near to God, who is the source of all good. Fellowship with Him, converse with Him, calls into exercise all gracious affections, reverence, love, gratitude, submission, faith, joy, and devotion. When the soul thus draws near to God, God draws near to it, manifests his glory, sheds abroad his love, and imparts that peace which passes all understanding. Our Lord says, " If a man love me, he will keep my words: and my Father will love him, and we will come unto him, and make our abode with him." (John xiv. 23.) In such fellowship, the soul must be holy and must be blessed.

The Power of Prayer.

The course of human events is not controlled by physical force alone. There are other powers at work in the government of the world.　There is the power of ideas, true or false; the power of truth; the power of love and human sympathy; the power of conscience; and above all, the Supreme Power, immanent in the world as well as over it, which is an intelligent, voluntary, personal power, coöperating with and controlling the operations of all creatures, without violating their nature.　This Supreme Power is roused into action by prayer, in a way analogous to that in which the energies of a man are called into action by the entreaties of his fellow-men.　This is the doctrine of the Bible; it is perfectly consistent with reason, and is confirmed by the whole history of the world, and especially of the Church.　Moses by his prayer saved the Israelites from destruction; at the prayer of Samuel the army of the Philistines was dispersed; "Elias was a man subject to like passions as we are, and he prayed earnestly that it might not rain: and it rained not on the earth by the space of three years and six months.　And he prayed again, and the heavens gave rain, and the earth brought forth her fruit." These facts are referred to by the Apostle James, for the purpose of proving that the prayer of a righteous man availeth much. Paul constantly begged his Christian brethren to pray for him, and directed that prayer should " be made for all men: for kings, and for all that are in authority; that we may lead a quiet and peaceable life in all godliness and honesty."　This of course supposes that prayer is a power.　Queen Mary of Scotland was not beside herself, when she said she feared the prayers of John Knox, more than an army.　Once admit the doctrine of theism, that is of the existence of a personal God, and of his constant control over all things out of Himself, and all ground for doubt as to the efficacy of prayer is removed, and it remains to us, as it has been to the people of God in all ages, the great source of spiritual joy and strength, of security for the present and confidence for the future.　The Forty-sixth Psalm still stands: " The LORD of Hosts is with us; the God of Jacob is our refuge."

SYSTEMATIC THEOLOGY.

PART IV.

ESCHATOLOGY.

CHAPTER I.

§ 1. *Protestant Doctrine.*

THE Protestant doctrine on the state of the soul after death includes, first of all, the continued conscious existence of the soul after the dissolution of the body. This is opposed, not only to the doctrine that the soul is merely a function of the body and perishes with it, but also to the doctrine of the sleep of the soul during the interval between death and the resurrection.

The former doctrine belongs to the theory of materialism, and stands or falls with it. If there be no substance but matter, and no force but such as is the phenomenon of matter; and if the form in which physical force manifests itself as mind, or mental action, depends on the highly organized matter of the brain, then when the brain is disorganized the mind ceases to exist. But if the soul and body are two distinct substances, then the dissolution of the latter does not necessarily involve the end of the conscious existence of the former.

There is another view on this subject adopted by many who are not materialists, but who still hold that mind cannot act or manifest itself without a material organ. Thus, for example, the late Isaac Taylor says that as extension is an attribute of matter, the soul without a body cannot be extended. But extension is a relation to space; what is not extended is consequently nowhere. "We might as well," he says, "say of a pure spirit that it is hard, heavy, or red, or that it is a cubic foot in dimensions, as say that it is here or there, or that it has come, and is gone." "When we talk of absolute immateriality, and wish to withdraw mind altogether from matter, we must no longer allow ourselves to imagine that it is, or that it can be, in any place, or that it has any kind of relationship to the visible and extended universe." In like manner, he argues that mind is dependent upon its corporeity, or union with matter, for its relationship to time. A pure spirit could not tell the difference between a moment and a century; it could have no perception of the equable flow of duration, for that is a knowledge drawn from the external world and its regular motions.   To its union with matter, mind is indebted also for its sensibility or sensations, for its power over matter, for its imaginative emotions, and for its " defined, recognizable individuality," and of course for its personality.   The soul after death, therefore, must either cease its activity, at least in reference to all out of itself, or be furnished at once with a new body.   The latter assumption is the one commonly adopted. " Have the dead ceased to exist ? " he asks, " Have those who are fallen asleep perished ?   No ; — for there is a spiritual body, and another vehicle of human nature, as well as a natural body ; and, therefore, the dissolution of this animal structure leaves the life untouched.   The animal body is not itself the life, nor is it the cause of life ; nor again is the spiritual body the life, nor the cause of it ; but the one as well as the other are the instruments of the mind, and the necessary medium of every productive exercise of its faculties." [1]

On this theory of the dependence of mind on matter, " for every productive exercise of its faculties," for its individuality, and its susceptibilities, it may be remarked, (1.) That the theory is admitted to be untrue in relation to God.   He has no body ; and He can act and be acted upon, and his activity is productive.   If such be the case with God who is a pure spirit, it is altogether arbitrary to deny that it is true with regard to the human soul.   Man as a spirit is of the same nature with God. He is like Him in all that is essential to the nature of a spirit. (2.) The theory has no support from Scripture, and, therefore, has no right to intrude itself into the explanation of Scriptural doctrines.   The Bible never attributes corporeity to angels; yet it ascribes to them a " ubi "; speaks of their coming and going ; and of their being mighty in power to produce effects in the material and spiritual worlds.   It never speaks of man's having any other body besides his earthly tabernacle, and the body which he is to have at the resurrection.   And yet it speaks of the soul as active and conscious when absent from the body and present with the Lord.   (3.) If the soul is a substance it has power, power of self-manifestation, and productive power according to its nature. Electricity may be a force in nature manifested to us, in our present state, only under certain conditions.   But that does not prove that it is active only under those conditions, or that beings consti-

---

[1] *Physical Theory of Another Life*. By Isaac Taylor. New York, 1852, p. 23, and the whole of chap. ii.

tuted differently from what we are, may not be cognizant of its
activity. It is enough, however, that the theory in question is
extra-scriptural, and therefore has no authority in matters of
faith.

It is no less evident that according to the pantheistic theory,
in all its phases, which regards man as only one of the transient
forms of God's existence, there is no room for the doctrine of the
conscious existence of the soul after death. The race is immortal, but the individual man is not. Trees and flowers cover the
earth from generation to generation ; yet the same flower blooms
but once. The mass of men whose convictions, on such subjects,
are founded on their moral and religious nature, have in all ages
believed in the continued existence of the soul after death. And
that universality of belief is valid evidence of the truth believed.
But men whose opinions are under the control of the speculative
understanding, have never arrived at any settled conviction on
this subject. To be, or not to be ? was a question speculation
could not answer. The dying Hume said he was about to take
a leap in the dark. The continued existence of the soul after
death is a matter of divine revelation. It was part of the faith
of the Church before the coming of Christ. The revelation of all
the great doctrines which concern the destiny and salvation of
men has been indeed progressive. It is not, therefore, a matter
of surprise that the doctrine of the future state is much less
clearly unfolded in the Old Testament than in the New. Still it
is there. When the Apostle Paul (2 Tim. i. 10) speaks of " Our
Saviour Jesus Christ, who hath abolished death, and hath brought
life and immortality to light through the Gospel," he is not to be
understood as saying that the future life was unknown, as Archbishop Whately argues, before the coming of Christ. This
would be inconsistent with the most explicit declarations elsewhere. It is often said that Christ came to preach the Gospel,
to make propitiation for sin, and to reveal the way of reconciliation with God. Paul says in Galatians iii. 23, " before faith
came we were kept under the law." Yet he strenuously insists
that the Gospel, or plan of salvation which he taught, was taught
by the law and prophets (Rom. iii. 21) ; and that the patriarchs
were saved by faith in the same promise on which sinners are
now called upon to rely. What was imperfectly revealed under
the old economy, is clearly revealed under the new. This is all
that those passages which speak of the Gospel bringing new
truths to light, are intended to teach. Christ shed a flood of

light on the darkness beyond the grave. Objects before dimly discerned in that gloom, now stand clearly unveiled; so that it may well be said He brought life and immortality to light. He revealed the nature of this future state, and showed how, for the people of God, that state was one of life. It may be observed in passing, that many Christian writers who speak of the doctrine of a future life being unknown, at least to the patriarchs, and to the writers of the Psalms, mean "the Christian doctrine" on that subject. They do not intend to deny that the people of God from the beginning believed in the conscious existence of the soul after death. This Hengstenberg, for example, distinctly asserts concerning himself.[1]

Doctrine of a Future Life revealed under the Old Testament.

1. The first argument on this subject is an *à priori* one. That the Hebrews, God's chosen people, the recipients and custodians of a supernatural revelation, should be the only nation on the face of the earth, in whose religion the doctrine of a future state had no place, would be a solecism. It is absolutely incredible, for it supposes human nature in the case of the Hebrews to be radically different from what it is in other men.

2. Instead of the Hebrews having lower views of man than other nations, they alone were possessed of the truth concerning his origin and nature. They had been taught from the beginning that man was created in the image of God, and, therefore, like God, of the same nature as a spirit, and capable of fellowship with his maker. They had also been taught that man was created immortal; that the death even of the body, was a punishment; that the sentence of death (in the sense of dissolution) concerned only the body. "Dust thou art, and unto dust shalt thou return." The soul is not dust, and therefore, according to the earliest theology of the Hebrews, was not to return to dust; it was to return to God who gave it.

3. We accordingly find that throughout the Old Testament Scriptures the highest views are presented of the nature and destiny of man. He is the child of God, destined to enjoy his fellowship and favour; the possessions and enjoyments of earth are always represented as temporary and insignificant, not adapted to meet the soul's necessities; they were taught not to envy the

---

[1] *Commentar über die Psalmen*, von G. W. Hengstenberg. *Abhandlung* No. 7. *Zur Glaubenslehre der Psalmen*, edit. Berlin, 1847, vol. iv. part 2. On p. 321, he says, "When we deny the doctrine of immortality to the writers of the Psalms, it is in the Christian sense" of the word.

wicked in their prosperity, but to look to God as their portion; they were led to say, " Whom have I in heaven but thee? and there is none upon earth that I desire besides thee; " and " I had rather be a door-keeper in the house of my God, than to dwell in the tents of wickedness." In the Old Testament, the righteous are always represented as strangers and pilgrims upon the earth, whose home and whose reward are not in this world; that their portion is in another world, and, therefore, that it is better to be the humblest and most afflicted of God's people than to be the most prosperous of the wicked. The judgments of God are represented as falling on the wicked in a future state, and thus effectually vindicating the justice of God in his dealings with men. The Psalmist said, he was envious at the foolish, when he saw the prosperity of the wicked, until he went into the sanctuary of God and understood their end. In contrasting his own state and prospects with theirs, he said, " I am continually with thee. . . . . Thou shalt guide me with thy counsel, and afterward receive me to glory." (Ps. lxxiii. 23, 24.) Such is the drift and spirit of the Old Testament Scriptures. Their whole tendency was to raise the thoughts of the people from the present and turn them towards the future; to make men look not at the things seen, but at the things unseen and eternal.

4. The dead in the Old Testament are always spoken of as going to their fathers, as descending into " Sheol," *i. e.*, into the invisible state, which the Greeks called Hades. Sheol is represented as the general receptacle or abode of departed spirits, who were there in a state of consciousness; some in a state of misery, others in a state of happiness. In all these points the pagan idea of Hades corresponds to the Scriptural idea of Sheol. All souls went into Hades, some dwelling in Tartarus, others in Elysium. That the Hebrews regarded the souls of the dead as retaining their consciousness and activity is obvious from the practice of necromancy, and is confirmed by the fact of the appearance of Samuel to Saul, as recorded in 1 Samuel xxviii. The representation given in Isaiah xiv. of the descent of the King of Babylon, when all the dead rose to meet and to reproach him, takes for granted and authenticates the popular belief in the continued conscious existence of departed spirits.

5. In several passages of the Old Testament, the doctrine of a future life is clearly asserted. We know upon the authority of the New Testament that the Sixteenth Psalm is to be understood of the resurrection of Christ, with which, the Apostle teaches us,

that of his people is inseparably connected. His soul was not to be left in Sheol; nor was his body to see corruption. In Psalm xvii. 15, after having described the cruelty and prosperity of the wicked, the Psalmist says, in regard to himself: " I will behold thy face in righteousness: I shall be satisfied, when I awake, with thy likeness." Isaiah xxvi. 19, says : " Thy dead men shall live, together with my dead body shall they arise. Awake and sing, ye that dwell in dust, for my dew is as the dew of herbs, and the earth shall cast out the dead." (Dan. xii. 2.) " And many of them that sleep in the dust of the earth shall awake; some to everlasting life, and some to shame and everlasting contempt. And they that be wise, shall shine as the brightness of the firmament; and they that turn many to righteousness, as the stars forever and ever." These prophetic declarations are indeed often explained as referring to the restoration of the nation from a state of depression to one of prosperity and glory. But the language employed, the context in which there is clear reference to the Messianic period, and the sanction given by Christ and his Apostles to the doctrine taught by the literal sense of the words here used, are considerations decisive in favour of the ordinary interpretation, which is adopted by Delitzsch,[1] Hengstenberg,[2] Oehler,[3] and many others of the modern interpreters. Even Mr. Alger, in his elaborate work on the doctrine of a future life, concedes the point so far as the passage in Daniel is concerned. " No one," he says, " can deny that a judgment, in which reward and punishment shall be distributed according to merit, is here clearly foretold."[4] Those German writers whose views of inspiration are so low as to enable them to interpret each book of the Bible as the production of an individual mind, and to represent the several writers as teaching different doctrines, in many cases take the ground that in the early books of the Scriptures, the simple fact of a future life is taken for granted, but not taught, and that nothing was made known as to the nature of that life. Thus Schultz says, " That all the books of

---

[1] *Commentar über den Psalter*, Leipzig, 1860, vol. ii. p. 420.

[2] *Commentar über die Psalmen, Abhandlung No. 7.* Berlin, 1847, vol. iv. part 2, p. 273 ff.

[3] *Veteris Testamenti Sententia de Rebus post Mortem Futuris.* G. F. Oehler, Stuttgart, 1846, p. 50.

[4] *A Critical History of the Doctrine of a Future Life, with a Complete Bibliography of the Subject.* By William Rounseville Alger. Philadelphia, 1846, p. 149. The Appendix, an instructive volume, being " A Catalogue of Works relating to the Nature, Origin, and Destiny of the Soul. The Titles classified and arranged chronologically, with Notes and Indexes of Authors and Subjects. By Ezra Abbot," is a marvel of ability and learning.

the Old Testament assume that men are in some way or other to
live after death. Even in the Pentateuch this is taken for
granted. It is not taught, but assumed as a self-evident truth,
immanent in the consciousness of the people." [1]

6. It is to be remembered that we have in the New Testament
an inspired, and, therefore, an infallible commentary on the Old
Testament Scriptures. From that commentary we learn that the
Old Testament contains much which otherwise we should never
have discovered. Not only is the compass of the truths revealed
to the fathers shown to be far greater than the simple words
would suggest, but truths are declared to be therein taught, which,
without divine assistance, we could not have discovered. There
is another thing concerning the faith of the Old Testament saints
to be taken into consideration. They may have understood, and
probably did understand their Scriptures far better than we are
disposed to think possible. They had the advantage of the constant presence of inspired men to lead them in their interpretation of the written word, and they enjoyed the inward teaching
of the Holy Spirit. What that spiritual illumination availed in
their case, we cannot tell; but we know that now the humble
Christian who submits himself to the teachings of the Spirit, understands the Bible far better than any mere verbal critic.

We have then in the New Testament the most explicit declarations, not only that the doctrine of a future state was revealed
in the Old Testament, but that from the beginning it was part
of the faith of the people of God. Our Lord in refuting the
Sadducees, who denied not only the resurrection of the body, but
also the conscious existence of man after death, and the existence
of any merely spiritual beings, appeals to the fact that in the
Pentateuch, the authority of which the Sadducees admitted, God
is familiarly called the God of Abraham, Isaac, and Jacob; but
as He is the God not of the dead but of the living, the designation referred to proves that Abraham, Isaac, and Jacob are now
living, and living too in the fellowship and enjoyment of God.
" Christ," says Mr. Alger, whom we quote the rather because he
belongs to the class of men who call themselves liberal Christians,[2] " Christ once reasoned with the Sadducees ' as touching

---

[1] *Die Voraussetzungen der christlichen Lehre von der Unsterblichkeit dargestellt* von
Hermann Schultz, Dr. der Philosophie, Licent. der Theologie, etc., Göttingen, 1861, p.
207.

[2] On page 438, he says: "The essence of rationalism is the affirmation that neither the
fathers, nor the Church, nor the Scriptures, nor all of them together, can rightfully establish any proposition opposed to the logic of sound philosophy, the principles of reason, and

the dead, that they rise;' in other words, that the souls of men
upon the decease of the body pass into another and an unending state of existence: — 'Neither can they die any more; for
they are equal with the angels, and are the children of God,
being children of the resurrection.' His argument was, that God
is the God of the living, not of the dead; that is, the spiritual
nature of man involves such a relationship with God as pledges
his attributes to its perpetuity. The thought which supports this
reasoning penetrates far into the soul and grasps the moral relations between man and God. It is most interesting, viewed
as the unqualified affirmation by Jesus, of the doctrine of a
future life which shall be deathless."[1] The reasoning of Christ,
however, is not only an affirmation of the truth of the doctrine
of a future deathless life, but an affirmation also that that doctrine is taught in the Old Testament. The words which He
quotes are contained in the book of Exodus; and those words,
as explained by Him, teach the doctrine of the blessed and unending life of the righteous.

That the Jews when Christ came, universally, with the exception of the sect of the Sadducees, believed in a future life, is beyond dispute. The Jews at this period were divided into three
sects: the Sadducees, who were materialistic skeptics, believing
neither in the resurrection, nor in angels, nor in spirits; the Essenes, who were a philosophical and ascetic sect, believing that
the souls of the just being freed at death from the prison of the
body, rejoice and are borne aloft where a happy life forever is
decreed to the virtuous; but the wicked are assigned to eternal
punishment in a dark cold place;[2] and the Pharisees, who, as
we know from the New Testament, believed in the resurrection
of the body in the sense in which Paul believed that doctrine
(Acts xxvi. 6), for he claimed in his controversy with the Sad-

the evident truth of nature. Around this thesis the battle has been fought and the victory
won; and it will stand with spreading favour as long as there are unenslaved and cultivated
minds in the world. This position is, in logical necessity, and as a general thing in fact,
that of the large though loosely-cohering body of believers known as ' Liberal Christians;'
and it is tacitly held by still larger and evergrowing numbers nominally connected
with sects that officially eschew it with horror." Mr. Alger doubtless considered this as
simply a declaration of independence of human authority in matters of religion. To
other, and perhaps to wiser men, it sounds like a declaration of independence of God, the
infinite Reason; as an assertion that the Infinite God can teach him nothing; or, at least,
that He cannot so authenticate his teachings as to render them authoritative. The men
are to be pitied who have no better knowledge of the mysteries of the present and the
future than is to be found in themselves.

[1] Alger, *ut supra*, p. 340.

[2] Josephus, *De Bello Judaico*, II. viii. 11; *Works*. edit. Leipzig, 1827, vol. v. pp. 215,
216, [165.]

ducees, that the Pharisees were on his side. They believed that
the soul was in its nature immortal; that the righteous only are
happy after death, and that the wicked are eternally miserable.
That the Jews derived their doctrine from their own Scriptures is
plain, (1.) Because they admitted no other source of religious
knowledge. The Scriptures were their rule of faith, as those
Scriptures had been understood and explained by their fathers.
(2.) There is no other known source from which the doctrine of
a future state as held by the Jews in the time of Christ, could
have been obtained. The doctrines, whether religious or philosophical, of their heathen neighbours were antagonistic to their
own. This is true even of the doctrines of Zoroaster, which in
some points had most affinity with those of the Jews. (3.) The
inspired writers of the New Testament teach the same doctrines,
and affirm that their knowledge was derived not from men, but
from the revelation of God as contained in the Old Testament,
and as made by Christ.

A few of the passages in which the Apostles teach that the
doctrine of a future life was known to the patriarchs before the
coming of Christ, are the following: Paul was arraigned before
the council in Jerusalem, and "when Paul perceived that the
one part were Sadducees, and the other Pharisees, he cried out
in the council, Men and brethren, I am a Pharisee, the son of a
Pharisee: of the hope and resurrection of the dead I am called in
question." (Acts xxiii. 6.) He here declares that in the dispute
between these two parties, on the question whether the doctrine
of a future life and of the resurrection of the dead was taught in
the Scriptures which both parties acknowledged, he sided with
the Pharisees. Again in his speech before Agrippa, he said:
"I stand, and am judged for the hope of the promise made of
God unto our fathers: unto which promise our twelve tribes instantly serving God day and night, hope to come. For which
hope's sake, King Agrippa, I am accused of the Jews. Why
should it be thought a thing incredible with you, that God should
raise the dead?" (Acts xxvi. 6–8.) The promise to which he
refers is the promise of redemption through the Messiah, which
redemption includes the deliverance of his people from the power
of death and other evil consequences of sin. This was the promise to which the twelve tribes hoped to come. The belief, therefore, in a future life is thus declared to have been a part of the
religion of the whole Hebrew nation.

In Galatians iii. 8, the Apostle says, God "preached before

the gospel unto Abraham." The Gospel, however, in the Apostle's sense of the term, is the glad tidings of salvation; and salvation is deliverance from the penalty of the law and restoration to the image and favour of God. This of necessity involves the idea of a future life; of a future state of misery from which the soul is delivered, and of a future state of glory and blessedness into which it is introduced. In teaching, therefore, that men before the coming of Christ needed and desired salvation, in the Christian sense of the word, the Apostle assumed that they had a knowledge of the evils which awaited unpardoned sinners in the world to come. The evidence, however, that the New Testament affords of the fact that the Hebrews believed in a future state, is not found exclusively in direct assertions of that fact, but in the whole nature of the plan of salvation therein unfolded. The New Testament takes for granted that all men, since the apostasy of Adam, are in a state of sin and condemnation; that from that state no man can be delivered except through the Messiah, the Lord Jesus Christ, who is the only Saviour of men. It is, therefore, taught that the knowledge of this Redeemer was communicated to our race from the beginning, and in express terms in the promise made to Abraham; that the condition of salvation was then, as it is now, faith in Christ; that the blessings secured for believers were enjoyed before the advent of the Son of God in the flesh, as well as since. The heaven of believers is called the bosom of Abraham. All this of course assumes that the truths made known in the New Testament are in their germs revealed in the Old; just as all the doctrines unfolded in the Epistles are contained in the words of Christ as recorded in the Gospels.

The Epistle to the Hebrews is specially devoted to the object of unfolding the relation between the Old Dispensation and the New. The former was the shadow, or image, of the latter. What in the New is taught in words, in the Old, was taught through types. That men are sinners, and as such under condemnation; that sin can only be cleansed by blood, or that the expiation of guilt by a vicarious sacrifice is necessary in order to forgiveness; that men therefore are saved by a priest appointed to draw near to God in their behalf and to offer gifts and sacrifices for sin; and that the effect of this priestly intervention is eternal salvation, are said to be the truths which underlie the religion of the Old Testament, as they constitute the life of the religion of the New. Faith was to the saints of old as it is to us,

" the substance of things hoped for, the evidence of things not seen." They walked by faith, and not by sight. They lived with their eyes fixed on the unseen and eternal. It was the future that filled their vision and elevated them above the present. They " died in faith, not having received the promises, but having seen them afar off, and were persuaded of them, and embraced them, and confessed that they were strangers and pilgrims on the earth. For they that say such things declare plainly that they seek a country. And truly, if they had been mindful of that country from whence they came out, they might have had opportunity to have returned ; but now they desire a better country, that is, an heavenly ; wherefore God is not ashamed to be called their God : for He hath prepared for them a city." (Heb. xi. 13–16.) Moses by faith chose rather " to suffer affliction with the people of God, than to enjoy the pleasures of sin for a season." It was through faith, the belief and hope of a better life hereafter, that the saints of old " subdued kingdoms, wrought righteousness, obtained promises, stopped the mouths of lions, quenched the violence of fire, escaped the edge of the sword, out of weakness were made strong, waxed valiant in fight, turned to flight the armies of the aliens. Women received their dead raised to life again : and others were tortured, not accepting deliverance ; that they might obtain a better resurrection : and others had trial of cruel mock- ings and scourgings, yea, moreover of bonds and imprisonment : they were stoned, they were sawn asunder, were tempted, were slain with the sword : they wandered about in sheep-skins and goat-skins ; being destitute, afflicted, tormented (of whom the world was not worthy) ; they wandered in deserts, and in moun- tains, and in dens and caves of the earth." Nothing more than this can be said of Christian confessors and martyrs. The faith of the Old Testament saints in the unseen and eternal was, there- fore, as strong as that of any set of men since the creation. It has been said that the opinion of the New Testament writers is of no weight in a matter of criticism, and, therefore, it is of no consequence what they thought about the teachings of the Old Testament. This is true, if those writers were ordinary men ; but if they spoke as they were moved by the Holy Ghost, then what they said, God said. We have, therefore, the sure word of inspiration that the people of God from the beginning of the world have believed in a state of conscious existence beyond the grave. That such is the doctrine of the New Testament is not disputed, and therefore need not be argued.

The Intermediate State.

As all Christians believe in the resurrection of the body and a future judgment, they all believe in an intermediate state. That is, they believe that there is a state of existence which intervenes between death and the resurrection ; and that the condition of the departed during that interval is, in some respects, different from that which it is to be subsequent to that event. It is not, therefore, as to the fact of an intermediate state, but as to its nature, that diversity of opinion exists among Christians.

The common Protestant doctrine on this subject is that " the souls of believers are at their death, made perfect in holiness, and do immediately pass into glory ; and their bodies, being still united to Christ, do rest in their graves till the resurrection." According to this view the intermediate state, so far as believers are concerned, is one of perfect freedom from sin and suffering, and of great exaltation and blessedness. This is perfectly consistent with the belief that after the second coming of Christ, and the resurrection of the dead, the state of the soul will be still more exalted and blessed.

In support of the Protestant doctrine as thus stated, it may be remarked,

1. That it is simply a question of fact. What do the Scriptures teach as to the state of the soul of a believer immediately after death ? It is not legitimate to decide this question on psychological grounds ; to argue that such is the nature of the soul that it cannot retain its individuality, or personality, when separated from the body ; or, that it is a mere function of the brain ; or, that it cannot act or be acted upon — can neither perceive nor be perceived except through and by means of the senses ; or, that as vegetable and animal life are only manifest and active in connection with some form of matter, in other words, as there must be a physical basis of life, so the soul necessarily requires a material basis for its manifestation and activity. All these speculations, or theories, are, for the Christian, of no account, if the Bible teaches the fact of the continued, personal, individual existence of the soul after the death and dissolution of the body. The Bible does not formally teach anthropology in either of the branches of physiology or psychology, as a department of human science, but it assumes a great deal that falls under these several heads. It assumes that soul and body in man are two distinct substances united in a vital union so as to constitute the man, in

the present state of existence, one individual person. It assumes that the seat of this personality is the soul. The soul is the self, the Ego, of which the body is the organ. It assumes that the soul continues its conscious existence, and its power of acting and of being acted upon after its separation from the body. This we have seen to be the doctrine of the whole Bible. The dead, according to the Scriptures, do not cease to be; they do not cease to be conscious and active.

There is, therefore, nothing in the psychology of the Scriptures, which is that of the vast majority of men, learned or unlearned, inconsistent with the doctrine that the souls of believers do, at death, immediately pass into glory.

2. According to the Scriptures and the faith of the Church, the probation of man ends at death. As the tree falls, so it lies. He that is unjust let him be unjust still, and he that is righteous let him be righteous still. When the bridegroom comes, they that are ready enter in, and the door is shut. According to the parable of the rich man and Lazarus, there is no passing after death from one state to another; there is a great gulf between the righteous and the wicked from that time for evermore. It is appointed unto all men once to die, and after that the judgment. The destiny of the soul is decided at death.

3. There is no satisfaction to be rendered in the future life for the sins done in the body. The Romish doctrine of satisfactions renders necessary the assumption of a purgatorial state after death for those who have not in this life made full expiation for their sins. But if the one offering of Christ forever perfects them that believe; if his sacrifice be a perfect satisfaction for our sins, then there is no reason why believers should be kept out of blessedness until they have expiated their sins by their own sufferings.

4. There is nothing contrary to Scripture, or to analogy, in the assumption of a sudden and immediate change from imperfect to perfect holiness. The Protestant doctrine is that the souls of believers are at death made perfect in holiness. But it is asked, what sanctifying power is there in death? Progress in moral excellence is gradual; as no one becomes thoroughly evil by one act, or in a moment, so, it is said, it is unreasonable to suppose that a sudden change from imperfect to perfect moral excellence takes place at the moment of death. This objection supposes that the salvation of men is a natural process; if it be a supernatural work, the objection has no force. Curing a man of leprosy was a slow process; but when Christ said to the leper " I will;

be thou clean," he was healed in a moment. The change which takes place in a believer at death, can hardly be much greater than that instantaneously produced in Paul on his journey to Damascus. Paul, in Galatians i. 16, attributes that change to the revelation of the Son of God to him. If the momentary vision of the divine glory of Christ produced such an effect upon the Apostle, is it strange that the Scriptures should teach that the souls of believers, when separated from the world and the flesh, and redeemed from the power of the devil, and bathed in the full brightness of the glory of the blessed Redeemer, should in a moment be purified from all sin?

If, therefore, there be nothing in the nature of the soul inconsistent with its separate existence ; if the body be not a necessary condition of its consciousness or activity ; if its probation terminates at death ; if the perfection of Christ's work precludes all necessity of future satisfaction for sin ; and if the immediate change from imperfect to perfect holiness be consistent with the analogy of faith, then there is no *à priori* objection to the doctrine that the souls of believers at death do immediately pass into glory.

5. That such is the doctrine of Scripture may be argued from the general drift of the sacred volume, so far as this subject is concerned. The Bible constantly speaks of the present life as a state of conflict, of labour, and of suffering ; and of death as the entrance into rest. There remains a rest for the people of God. That rest follows the state of labour and trial. Believers then cease from their works. The rest on which they enter is not merely a rest from conflict and sin, but a rest which arises from the attainment of the end of their being, from their restoration to their proper relation to God, and all their capacities being satisfied and filled.

6. Besides these general considerations the doctrine in question is taught in many passages of Scripture with more or less distinctness. Thus, in Revelation xiv. 13, the Apostle says, " I heard a voice from heaven saying unto me, Write, Blessed are the dead which die in the Lord from henceforth : Yea, saith the Spirit, that they may rest from their labours ; and their works do follow them." The simple meaning of this passage is that those who die in the Lord are, from that moment onward, in a state of blessednesss ; because they cease from their labours, and enter on the reward of the righteous. Death is for them emancipation from evil, and the introduction into a state of happiness.

Our Lord constantly teaches concerning those who believe in Him, (1.) That they are not condemned. They are no longer under the sentence of the law. (2.) That they have eternal life. That the effect of the union between Himself and them, consummated by faith, is that they partake of his life in a sense analogous to that in which the branch partakes of the life of the vine. As He lives always, those who partake of his life can never perish. And as He lives unto God, so the life of his people is a holy and divine life. That life, from its nature, is an unfailing source of blessedness. It purifies, exalts, and glorifies. It is impossible that the souls in which Christ thus lives should remain in a state of misery and degradation, or in that dreamy state of existence in " the under-world " which so many of the fathers imagined to be the abode of the departed spirits of believers, awaiting the second coming of Christ. (3.) Our Lord promised that He would raise his people from the dead on the last day. It would seem, therefore, to be involved in the nature of the redemption of Christ, and of the union between Him and his people, that when absent from the body they are present with the Lord. It is inconceivable that with the Spirit of God dwelling in them, which is the Spirit of holiness and of glory, they should sink at death into a lower state of existence than that which they enjoyed in this world. We accordingly find that in the parable of the rich man and Lazarus, Christ says : " The beggar died, and was carried by the angels into Abraham's bosom." (Luke xvi. 22.) The implication is undeniable that in his case the transition was immediate from earth to heaven. Still more explicit is the declaration of our Lord to the penitent thief, " To-day shalt thou be with me in paradise." (Luke xxiii. 43.) The word paradise occurs in two other places in the New Testament. In 2 Corinthians xii. 4, Paul says he was caught up into paradise, which he explains by saying that he was caught up into the third heaven. And in Revelation ii. 7, Christ says : " He that hath an ear, let him hear what the Spirit saith unto the churches : To him that overcometh will I give to eat of the tree of life, which is in the midst of the paradise of God." There can, therefore, be no doubt that paradise is heaven, and consequently when Christ promised the dying thief that he should that day be in paradise, he promised that he should be in heaven. It would, therefore, seem impossible that any who do not rest their faith on the fathers rather than on the Bible, should deny that the souls of believers do at death immediately pass into heaven. The fathers made a distinction between paradise and heaven which is not found in the Scriptures. Some of them regarded the former as one division of Hades, corresponding to the Elysium of the pagans; others located it somewhere on the earth; while others regarded it as a locality high up above the earth, but below the dwelling-place of God. These are mere fancies. The word heaven is indeed a term of wide application in the Bible as it is in common life. We speak of the fowls of heaven; of the stars of heaven; of our Father who is in heaven; and of believers being the citizens of heaven. In each of these cases the word has a different sense. Whether paradise and heaven are the same is a mere dispute about words. If the word heaven be taken in one of its legitimate senses, they are the same; if it be taken in another of its senses, they are not the same. It would not be in accordance with Scriptural usage to say that believers are now in paradise; but the Apostle does say they are now ἐν τοῖς ἐπουρανίοις (Eph. ii. 6), i. e., in heaven. Paradise, as the word is used by Christ and his Apostles, is the place where Christ now is, and where He manifests his presence and glory. Whether it is the place where He will finally establish his kingdom; and whether all the redeemed, clothed in their resurrection bodies, shall there be gathered together, is a matter of which we have no knowledge, and in which we need take no interest. All we need know is that it is where Christ is; that it is a place and state in which there is neither sin nor sorrow, and where the saints are as exalted and happy as, in the existing circumstances of their being, it is possible for them to be. Whether any, in obedience to patristic usage, choose to call this paradise a department of Hades, is a matter of no concern. All that the dying believer need know is that he goes to be with Christ. That to him is heaven.

In 2 Corinthians v. 2, the Apostle says: "We know, that if our earthly house of this tabernacle were dissolved, we have a building of God, an house not made with hands, eternal in the heavens." There are three ways in which these words, in connection with those which follow, are interpreted. (1.) According to one view, the house not made with hands into which the believer is received at death, is heaven. (2.) According to another view the meaning of the Apostle is, that when our present body is dissolved the soul will not be found naked, but will be immediately clothed with another and more spiritual body suited to the altered state of its existence. (3.) That the new house or body intended is the resurrection body. The second of these interpretations is founded on a gratuitous assumption. It assume that the soul is furnished with a body of which the Scriptures make no mention, and of the existence of which we have no evidence. The Bible knows nothing of any human body save that which we now have, and that which we are to have at the resurrection; the one natural, the other spiritual. The third interpretation assumes that the Apostles erred not only in their own convictions, but in their teaching. It assumes that what they taught could be true only on the condition that the second coming of Christ was to occur while the men of that generation were alive. The point, however, in which all these views of this passage agree, is the only one which concerns the question under consideration. They all suppose that the soul is received into a state of blessedness immediately after death. This the Apostle clearly teaches. As soon as our earthly house is destroyed, the soul, instead of being left houseless and homeless, is received in that house which is eternal in the heavens. " We are always confident," he says, "knowing that, whilst we are at home in the body, we are absent from the Lord: we are confident, I say, and willing rather to be absent from the body, and to be present with the Lord."

In Philippians i. 23, he expresses the same confidence: " For," he says, " I am in a strait betwixt two, having a desire to depart, and to be with Christ; which is far better: nevertheless, to abide in the flesh is more needful for you." Two things are here perfectly plain; first, that Paul regards the state of the soul after death as more exalted than its condition while in the flesh. This he distinctly asserts. And, secondly, that this change for the better takes place immediately after death. He was confident that as soon as he departed he would be with Christ. Both these points are conceded, even by those who deny the doctrine which they evidently involve. Some say that Paul, finding that Christ did not come as soon as he expected, changed his opinion, and held that the souls of believers were admitted at death into heaven, instead of awaiting the second advent in the underworld. The fathers said that while the great body of believers at death went into Hades, some few, especially the martyrs, were admitted at once into heaven. Mr. Alger conjectures that " we may assume . . . . that Paul believed there would be vouchsafed to the faithful Christian during his transient abode in the underworld a more intimate and blessed spiritual fellowship with his Master than he could experience while in the flesh." [1] All this is

---

[1] Alger, *ut supra*, p. 290.

floundering.   The simple fact is that the inspired Apostle confidently anticipated for himself, and evidently for his fellow-believ-
ers, immediate admission at death to the presence of Christ.   The
ancients regarded the "under-world" or Hades, as "a gloomy
prison," as Mr. Alger himself calls it.   That Paul should have
desired death in order that he should be thrust into a dungeon,
no man can believe.

The Scriptures represent Abraham, Isaac, and Jacob as being
in heaven.   The good, at death, are carried by angels to Abraham's bosom.   Moses and Elijah appeared in glory on the mount
of transfiguration, conversing with Christ.   In the Epistle to the
Hebrews, it is said, "Ye are come unto Mount Sion, and unto the
city of the living God, the heavenly Jerusalem, and to an innumerable company of angels, to the general assembly and church
of the first born, which are written in heaven, and to God the
Judge of all, and to the spirits of just men made perfect, and to
Jesus the mediator of the new covenant, and to the blood of
sprinkling, that speaketh better things than that of Abel."
Nothing can be more utterly inconsistent with the nature of the
Gospel, than the idea that the fire of divine life as it glows in the
hearts of God's elect, is, at death, to be quenched in the damp
darkness of an underground prison, until the time of the resurrection.

§ 2. *The Sleep of the Soul.*

The doctrine that the soul exists, during the interval between
death and the resurrection, in a state of unconscious repose,
properly supposes the soul to be a distinct substance from the
body.   It is therefore to be distinguished from the materialistic
theory, which assumes that as matter in certain states and combinations exhibits the phenomena of magnetism or light, so in other
combinations it exhibits the phenomena of life, and in others the
phenomena of mind, and hence that vital and mental activity are
as much the result or effect of the molecular arrangements of
matter, as any physical operations in the external world.   As in
this view it would be absurd to speak of the sleep or quietude of
magnetism or light when the conditions of their existence are
absent, so it would be equally absurd, on this theory, to speak of
the sleep of the soul after the dissolution of the body.

The doctrine of the sleep of the soul, moreover, is not identical with that which assumes that, although matter is in none of
its combinations the cause of mental activity, yet that it is the
necessary condition (so far as man is concerned) of its manifesta-

tion. The best of scientific men teach with regard to life, or vital force, that it is not the result of material combinations, but that such combination is necessary to its manifestation. "We recognize that these [vital] phenomena," says Professor Nicholson, " are never manifested except by certain forms of matter, or, it may be, by but a single form of matter. We conclude, therefore, that there must be an intimate connection between vital phenomena and the ' matter of life ; ' but we can go no further than this, and the premises do not in any way warrant the assertion that life is the result of living matter, or one of its properties." " The more philosophical view as to the nature of the connection between life and its material basis, is the one which regards vitality as something superadded and foreign to the matter by which vital phenomena are manifested. Protoplasm is essential as the physical medium through which vital action may be manifested ; just as a conductor is essential to the manifestation of electric phenomena, or just as a paint-brush and colours are essential to the artist. Because metal conducts the electric current, and renders it perceptible to our senses, no one thinks of therefore asserting that electricity is one of the inherent properties of a metal, any more than one would feel inclined to assert that the power of painting was inherent in the camel's hair or in the dead pigments. Behind the material substratum, in all cases, is the active and living force ; and we have no right to assume that the force ceases to exist when its physical basis is removed, though it is no longer perceptible to our senses. It is, on the contrary, quite conceivable theoretically that the vital forces of an organism should suffer no change by the destruction of the physical basis, just as electricity would continue to subsist in a world composed universally of non-conductors. In neither case could the force manifest its presence, or be brought into any perceptible relation with the outer world ; but in neither case should we have the smallest ground for assuming that the power was necessarily non-extant." [1]

This view when transferred to the soul, or mental phenomena, may be applied in three different forms to the doctrine of the state of man after death. First, God may be regarded as the universal mind-force which manifests itself through the human brain as electricity does through a conductor. When the brain is

1 *Introduction to the Study of Biology*, by H. Alleyne Nicholson, M. D., D. Sc., Ph. D., F. R. S. E., F. G. S., etc., Professor of Natural History and Botany in University College, Toronto, etc., etc. Edinburgh and London, 1872, pp. 8 and 11.

disintegrated, the mind-force remains, but not the individual man. Secondly, we may assume the realistic doctrine of generic humanity, manifesting itself in connection with proper corporeal organizations. Here again, it would seem to follow that when any individual human body is dissolved, the generic human life remains, but not the man. This is nearly the doctrine of Olshausen, before referred to. He held that the individuality of man depends on the body ; so that without a body there can be no soul ; that the only existence of the soul of man possible between death and the resurrection must be the scattered dust of its human frame. Thirdly, we may take the doctrine of Swedenborg, who taught that man has two bodies, an exterior and interior, a material and spiritual, and that it is the former only that dies ; the latter remains as the organ of the soul. Or, as others believe, the new, or spiritual, or resurrection body is provided at the moment of death, so that the soul passes from its earthly to its heavenly tabernacle in a moment. In none of these forms, however, is this theory of the absolute dependence of the soul for its power of self-manifestation properly applicable to the doctrine of the sleep of the soul after death. It is nevertheless probable that those who advocated this doctrine, in different periods in the history of the Church, had some such theory underlying their views.

Eusebius [1] mentions a small sect of Christians in Arabia who held that the soul remained unconscious from death to the resurrection. At the time of the Reformation there was such a revival of that doctrine that Calvin deemed it expedient to write an essay devoted to its refutation. Socinus also taught that the soul after death perceived and received nothing out of itself, although it remained self-conscious and self-contemplative. Archbishop Whately [2] says that, so far as the Scriptures are concerned, it is an open question whether the soul remains in a conscious state after death or not. In the third lecture he gives reasons which favour the view of continued consciousness ; and in the fourth, those which seem to teach the opposite doctrine. To the understanding, he says, there is no difference between the two views ; although to the imagination, the difference is great. In the consciousness of the soul of the believer, in either case, entrance into heaven would instantaneously succeed death. An in-

---

[1] *Ecclesiastica Historia*, VI. xxxvii.; edit. Cambridge, 1720, p. 299.
[2] *A View of the Scripture Revelations concerning a Future State*, by Richard Whately, D. D., Archbishop of Dublin. Philadelphia, 1856.

terval of which the soul was unconscious, would, for it, have no existence. The archbishop for himself thinks that the arguments on the one side are as strong as those on the other. The two considerations which seem to him to favour the doctrine of the sleep of the soul between death and the resurrection, are, first the fact that death is so often called a sleep. The dead are those who are asleep. (1 Thess. xiv. 4.) This expression cannot properly be understood of the body. A dead body can no more be said to sleep than a stone. The fair intimation, therefore, is, as the Archbishop thinks, that the soul sleeps when the body dies. The second consideration is that the New Testament clearly teaches that there is a solemn final judgment at the last day, when the destiny of each soul will be decided for eternity. But this appears inconsistent with the doctrine that the fate of the soul is decided immediately after it leaves the body. He admits that, according to the Scriptures, probation ends with this life, and therefore if the righteous at death pass into a state of happiness and the wicked into a state of misery, they are thereby judged; and there is no apparent necessity for a future judgment. It is obvious that these arguments have little force against the clear teachings of the Bible, and the faith of the Church universal, and indeed of all mankind. As to the first of the above mentioned arguments, it is enough to say, that as a dead body and a body asleep are so much alike in appearance, it is the most natural thing in the world to speak of death as an unending sleep. This is done continually by those who are firm believers in the continued conscious activity of the soul after death. The other argument has, if possible, still less weight. Although the fate of every man should be decided for himself and to his knowledge at the moment of death, there may be important and numerous reasons why there should be a public, solemn adjudication at the last day, when the secrets of all hearts shall be made known, and the justice of God revealed in the presence of men and angels.

§ 3. *Patristic Doctrine of the Intermediate State.*

Although the true doctrine concerning the state of the dead was, as has been shown, revealed in the Old Testament, it was more or less perverted in the minds of the people. The prevalent idea was that all souls after death descended into Sheol, and there remained in expectation of the coming of the Messiah. When He came it was expected that the Jews, or at least, the faithful, would be raised from the dead, and made partakers of all the glories and blessedness of the Messiah's reign. The views presented in the writings of the Rabbins of the condition of the souls in Sheol are not only diverse but inconsistent. The common representation was that Sheol itself was a gloomy, subterraneous abode, whose inhabitants were shades, weak and powerless, existing in a dreamy state; the best of them not in a state of suffering, and yet with no other enjoyment than the anticipation of deliverance when the Messiah should come. At other times, however, more life was attributed to the souls of the departed; and Sheol was represented as divided into two departments, Paradise and Gehenna. In the former were, according to some, all Jews, according to others only those who had faithfully observed the law; and in the other, the Gentiles. The common opinion was that all the Jews would be raised from the dead, when the Messiah came, and all the Gentiles left forever in the abode of darkness. Paradise, according to this view, was a place of positive enjoyment, and Gehenna a place of positive suffering. It is evident that there is no great difference between this Jewish doctrine in its essential features, and the true doctrine as presented by our Lord in the parable of the rich man and Lazarus. Both are represented as going into Sheol or Hades. The one was comforted, the other tormented. There was an inseparable barrier between the two. So far both doctrines agree. When the Rabbi Jochanan was dying, he said, "Two paths open before me, the one leading to bliss, the other to torments; and I know not which of them will be my doom." [1] "Paradise is separated from hell by a distance no greater than the width of a thread." [2]

According to many modern interpreters the New Testament writers adopted this Jewish doctrine not only in substance but in its details. (1.) They are represented as teaching that all the people of God who died before the advent of Christ, were confined in Sheol, or the under-world. Sheol or Hades, as stated above, is constantly spoken of "as the gloomy realm of shades, wherein are gathered and detained the souls of all the dead generations." The soul at death is said to be dismissed "naked into the silent, dark, and dreary region of the under-world." (2.) That when Christ died upon the cross, He descended "ad inferos," into Hades, or Hell, for the purpose of delivering the

---

[1] *Talmud, Tract. Barachoth;* quoted by Alger, p. 167.
[2] Eisenmenger, *Entdecktes Judenthum,* Königsberg, 1711; ii. cap. v. p. 315.

pious dead from their prison; and that they were the redeemed captives of whom the Apostle speaks in Ephesians iv. 8–10, as led by Christ into heaven. (3.) That those who die in the Lord since his advent, instead of being admitted into heaven, pass into the same place and the same state into which the patriarch passed at death before his coming. (4.) And as the Old Testament saints remained in Sheol until the first coming of the Messiah, so those who die under the New Testament, are to remain in Hades, until his second coming. Then they are not only to be delivered from Sheol, but their bodies are to be raised from the dead, and soul and body, reunited and glorified, are to be admitted into heaven.

Such is the scheme of doctrine said to be taught in the New Testament. Our Lord is regarded as giving it his sanction in the parable concerning Lazarus. Paul is made to teach it when he speaks of Christ as descending to " the lower parts of the earth," which is said to mean " the parts lower than the earth," that is, the under-world. His object in thus descending was, according to the theory, to deliver the souls confined in the gloomy prison of Sheol. Christ's triumph over principalities and powers is referred to the same event, his descent into Hades. Mr. Alger, representing a large class of writers, says that according to Paul's doctrine, " Christ was the first person clothed with humanity and experiencing death, admitted into heaven. Of all the hosts who had lived and died, every one had gone down into the dusky under-world. They were all held in durance waiting for the Great Deliverer." [1] The fate of those who die since the advent is no better, for they, as Paul is made to teach, are " all to remain in the under-world " until the second coming of Christ, " when they and the transformed living shall ascend together with the Lord." [2]

St. Peter is made to teach the same doctrine in still more explicit terms. In his discourse delivered on the day of Pentecost, he argued that Jesus is the Christ from the fact that God raised Him from the dead. That He was thus raised he argued from the sixteenth Psalm, where it is written, " Thou wilt not leave my soul in hell, neither wilt thou suffer thine Holy One to see corruption." That these words cannot refer to David, Peter argued, because he did see corruption, and his sepulchre remained until that day. The words of the Psalmist, therefore, must be understood of Christ, whose soul was not left in hell (Sheol),

---

[1] Alger, *ut supra*, p. 284.   [2] *Ibid.* p. 288.

neither did his flesh see corruption. As for David, he " is not ascended into heaven." (Acts ii. 34.) Something, therefore, happened to Christ that did not happen to David or to any other man. Christ was not left in hell; David and all other men were thus left. Christ did ascend to heaven; David did not; and if David did not, then other saints of his time did not. Thus it is that Peter is made to teach that the souls of the pious dead do not ascend to heaven, but descend to the gloomy abode of Sheol, Hades, or Hell, all these terms being equivalent. This exposition of the Apostle's teaching is plausible, and if consistent with other parts of Scripture, might be accepted. But as it contradicts what the Bible clearly teaches in many other places, it must be rejected. Peter's object was to prove the Messiahship of Christ from the fact of the resurrection of his body. The essential idea of " rising from the dead " was the restoration of the body to life. The soul does not die, and is not raised. The Apostle proved that Christ's body did not see corruption, but was restored to life; first, because it was a historical fact of which he and his brethren were witnesses; and secondly, from the prediction of the Psalmist that the Messiah was not to remain in the grave. That the sixteenth Psalm does not refer to David, he argued, because David died and was buried; his body did see corruption; his sepulchre remained among them; he, his body, he, as a man composed of soul and body, had not ascended to heaven. The whole argument concerns the body; because it is true only of the body, that it dies, is buried, sees corruption, and does not ascend to heaven. The simple meaning of Psalm xvi. 10, is that the person there spoken of was not to remain under the power of death. He was to rise from the dead before his body had time to see corruption. This is all that the passage teaches. This is true of Christ; it was not true of David or of any of the saints who died before the advent; and it is not true of those who have died since the advent. In this respect, as in so many others, Christ stands gloriously alone.

The difficult passage 1 Peter iii. 18, 19, however it may be interpreted, proves nothing against the Protestant doctrine that the souls of believers do at death immediately pass into glory. What happens to ordinary men happened to Christ when He died. His cold and lifeless body was laid in the tomb. His human soul passed into the invisible world. This is all that the creed, commonly called the Apostle's, means, when it says Christ was buried, and descended into Hell, or Hades, the unseen world. This is all that the passage in question clearly teaches. Men may doubt and differ as to what Christ did during the three days of his sojourn in the invisible world. They may differ as to who the spirits in prison were to whom he preached, or, rather, made proclamation (ἐκήρυξεν); whether they were the antediluvians; or, the souls of the people of God detained in Sheol; or, the mass of the dead of all antecedent generations and of all nations, which is the favorite hypothesis of modern interpreters. They may differ also as to what the proclamation was which Christ made to those imprisoned spirits; whether it was the gospel; or his own triumph; or deliverance from Sheol; or the coming judgment. However these subordinate questions may be decided, all that remains certain is that Christ, after his death upon the cross, entered the invisible world, and there, in some way, made proclamation of what He had done on earth. All this is very far from teaching the doctrine of a "Limbus Patrum," as taught by the Jews, the Fathers, or the Romanists.

It is a great mistake in interpretation of the New Testament, to bring down its teachings to the level of Jewish or Pagan ideas. Because the Jews expected the Messiah to establish an earthly kingdom, it is inferred that the kingdom of God, as proclaimed by Christ and his Apostles, was to be realized in this life. Because they expected that the Messiah was to deliver the souls of their fathers from Sheol, it is assumed that this was the work actually effected by Christ. Because the Jews regarded imprisonment in the under-world as the special penalty of sin, it is inferred that deliverance from that imprisonment was the redemption our Lord actually effected. This is to interpret the Scriptures by the Talmud and Cabala, and not Scripture by Scripture. This is historical interpretation "en oûtre." It is true that Christ proclaimed that the kingdom of God was at hand; but his kingdom was not of this world. It is true that He came to open the prison doors and proclaim liberty to the captives; but the prison was not Sheol, and the captives were not the souls of departed patriarchs. It is true that He came to redeem his people; but the redemption which He effected was from the curse of God's violated law, and not deliverance from the gloomy land of Shades.

We all know that the great evil with which the Apostles had to contend in the early Church, and the great source of corruption in the Church in after ages, was a Judaizing spirit. Most of the early Christians were Jews, and most of the converts from the Gentiles were proselytes imbued with Jewish doctrines. These doctrines, moreover, were congenial with what the Apostle calls "the carnal mind." It is not wonderful, therefore, that they were transferred to the Christian Church, and proved in it a permanently corrupting leaven. Modern critics are going back to the beginning, and doing in our day what the Judaizers did in the age of the Apostles. They are eliminating Christianity from the Gospel, and substituting Judaism, somewhat spiritualized, but still essentially Judaic.

It is notorious that the Jewish doctrines of the merit of works; of the necessity and saving efficacy of external rites; of a visible kingdom of Christ of splendour and worldly grandeur; of an external church out of whose pale there is no salvation; of the priestly character of the ministry; and of a church hierarchy, soon began to spread among Christians, and at last became ascendant. This being the case it would be strange if the Jewish doctrine of Sheol, or of an intermediate state, had not been adopted by many of the fathers, together with the other elements of the corrupt Judaism of the apostolic age. We accordingly find that as the Jews, contrary to the teaching of their own Scripture, held that the souls of those who died before the coming of the Messiah descended into Sheol, and there awaited the advent of the Redeemer, so the Christians began to believe, contrary to the teaching of their Scriptures, that the souls of believers at death, instead of passing into glory, are shut up in Hades, awaiting the second coming of Christ. It is true there were varying and inconsistent notions entertained of the nature of this intermediate state; and the same is true also with regard to the views on this subject which long prevailed in the Church. There are two facts which stand out so plainly in the New Testament Scriptures that they could not be always overlooked or denied. The one is that Christ, forty days after his resurrection, ascended into heaven, and is now seated at the right hand of the Majesty on high. The other is that the souls of believers when absent from the body are present with the Lord. As many of the Jews, therefore, assumed that in Sheol there were two departments, Paradise and Gehenna, the one the abode of the righteous, the other of the wicked; so the Christians, in many cases, made the same distinction with regard to the intermediate state; the souls of believers went to paradise; the souls of the wicked into hell. And they often so exalted the blessedness of the former as to make it a mere dispute about words whether they went to heaven or into an intermediate state. The real controversy, so far as any exists, is not as to whether

there is a state intermediate between death and the resurrection
in which believers are less glorious and exalted than they are to
be after the second advent of Christ, but what is the nature of
that state. Are believers after death with Christ? Do their
souls immediately pass into glory? or, are they in a dreamy,
semi-conscious state, neither happy nor miserable, awaiting the
resurrection of the body. That this latter view was for a long
time prevalent in the Church may be inferred, (1.) From the
fact that this was the view of the intermediate state commonly
adopted by the Jews. (2.) It is the view attributed to the
writers of the New Testament. (3.) It is the doctrine avowed
by many of the patristic and mediæval writers. (4.) There
would otherwise be no ground for the opposition manifested to
the doctrine of Protestants on this subject. Daillé says, "The
doctrine that heaven shall not be opened till the second coming
of Christ, — that during that time the souls of all men, with few
exceptions, are shut up in the under-world, — was held by Justin
Martyr, Irenæus, Tertullian, Augustine, Origen, Lactantius,
Victorinus, Ambrose, Chrysostom, Theodoret, Œcomenius, Are-
tas, Prudentius, Theophylact, Bernard, and many others, as is
confessed by all. . . . . This doctrine is literally held by the
whole Greek Church at the present day; nor did any of the Latins expressly deny any part of it until the Council of Florence, in
the year of our Lord 1439." [1]

Flügge [2] says in reference to the early fathers, that they
"were not in doubt as to the fate of the soul when separated
from the body until the resurrection, because they rested on the
Jewish doctrine on that subject." Justin Martyr speaks in this
way : [3] [Φημὶ :] Τὰς μὲν [ψυχὰς] τῶν εὐσεβῶν ἐν κρειττονί ποι χώρῳ μένειν, τὰς
δὲ ἀδίκους καὶ πονερὰς ἐν χείρονι, τὸν τῆς κρίσεως ἐκδεχομένας χρόνον τοτε,
that is, "I say, that the souls of the pious dwell in some better
place, and ungodly and wicked souls in a worse place, thus awaiting the time of judgment."

The fathers say but little about Hades. Hippolytus, however,
gives an account of it which is in substance as follows : [4] Hades,
in which the souls of the righteous and unrighteous are detained,
was left at the creation in a state of chaos, to which the light of

---

[1] *De Usu Patrum*, II. iv. ; edit. Geneva, 1656, pp. 290, 291.

[2] *Geschichte des Glaubens an Unsterblichkeit, Auferstehung, Gericht und Vergeltung*,
von W. Flügge, Universitätsprediger in Göttingen, III. i. 3; Leipzig, 1799, vol. iii. part 1,
p. 87.

[3] *Dialogus cum Tryphone Judæo*, 5; edit. Commelinus, Heidelberg, 1593, p. 172, 16-19.

[4] *Against Plato on the Cause of the Universe*, (fragment): *Ante-Nicene Christian Library*, Edinburgh, 1869, vol. ix. Hippolytus, vol. ii. p. 46 ff.

the sun never penetrates, but where perpetual darkness reigns. This place is the prison of souls, over which the angels keep watch. In Hades there is a furnace of unquenchable fire into which no one has yet been cast. It is reserved for the banishment of the wicked at the end of the world, when the righteous will be made citizens of an eternal kingdom. The good and the bad, although both in Hades, are not in the same part of it. They enter the under-world by the same gate. When this gate is passed, the guardian angels guide the souls of the departed different ways; the righteous are guided to the right to a region full of light; the wicked are constrained to take the left hand path, leading to a region near the unquenchable fire. The good are free from all discomfort, and rejoice in expectation of their admission into heaven. The wicked are miserable in constant anticipation of their coming doom. An impassable gulf separates the abode of the righteous from that of the wicked. Here they remain until the resurrection, which he goes on to explain and defend.

Flügge admits that there was no uniformity of representation on this subject in the early Church. The same general idea, however, is constantly reproduced; the Latins agreeing substantially with the Greeks. Tertullian represents the underworld as the general receptacle of departed spirits who retain their consciousness and activity. In this unseen world there are two divisions, both called " Inferi." " Nobis inferi non nuda cavositas, nec subdivalis aliqua mundi sentina creduntur: sed in fossa terræ et in alto vastitas, et in ipsis visceribus ejus abstrusa profunditas." [1] In this region there are two divisions; the one called " infernum," by way of eminence, or Gehenna, " quæ est ignis arcani subterraneus ad pœnam thesaurus; " the other is the bosom of Abraham or paradise, " divinæ amœnitatis recipiendis sanctorum spiritibus destinatum, materia [maceria] quadam igneæ illius zonæ a notitia orbis communis segregatum." [2] According to this mode of representation, the intermediate state was itself a state of reward and punishment; at other times, however, this was denied; all retribution being reserved to the day of judgment. In the early Greek Church, this latter view was the more prevalent; [3] but later both the Greeks and Latins agreed in regarding the state of the righteous after death as far more favourable than that of the wicked.

[1] Tertullian, De Anima, 55; Works, edit. Basle, 1562, p. 685.

[2] Tertullian, Apologeticus, 47; ut supra, p. 892.

[3] Flügge, III. i. 4; ut supra, pp. 215, 216.

The common views on this subject are perhaps fairly represented in the elaborate work of the Honourable Archibald Campbell, on "the doctrine of a middle state between death and the resurrection." [1] He thus sums up the points which he considers himself to have proved to be the doctrine of the Bible, of the Fathers, and of the Church of England.

" First. That the souls of the dead do remain in an intermediate, or middle state between death and the resurrection."

" That the proper place appointed for the abode of the righteous during the interim between death and the resurrection, called paradise, or Abram's bosom, is not the highest heavens where alone God is at present, fully to be enjoyed, but it is, however, a very happy place, one of the lower apartments or mansions of heaven, a place of purification and improvement, of rest and refreshment, and of divine contemplation. A place from whence our blessed Lord's humanity is sometimes to be seen, though clouded or veiled if compared with the glory He is to appear with, and be seen in, at and after his second coming. Into which middle state and blessed place, as they are carried by the holy angels, whose happy fellowship they there enjoy; so afterward at the resurrection, after judgment, they are led into the beatific vision by the Captain of our salvation, Jesus Christ Himself, where they shall see Him fully as He is, and there they shall enjoy God for ever and ever, or sempiternally."

The souls of the wicked at death do not go into hell, but into a middle state, "which state is dark, dismal, and uncomfortable, without light, rest, or any manner of refreshment, without any company but that of devils and such impure souls as themselves to converse with, and where these miserable souls are in dismal apprehensions of the deserved wrath of God."

" Secondly, That there is no immediate judgment after death, no trial on which sentence is pronounced, of neither the righteous nor the wicked, until Christ's second coming. And that, therefore, none of any age or class from the beginning of the world to the glorious appearing of our blessed Saviour at his second coming, are excepted from continuing in their proper middle state, from their death until their resurrection, whether they be patriarchs, prophets, Apostles, or martyrs."

" Thirdly, That the righteous in their happy middle state, do improve in holiness, and make advances in perfection, and yet

---

[1] *The Doctrines of a Middle State between Death and the Resurrection, of Prayers for the Dead, etc., etc.,* by Honourable Archibald Campbell. London, 1721, folio, p. 44.

they are not for all that carried out of that middle state into glory, or into the beatific vision, until after their resurrection."

" Fourthly, That prayers for those who are baptized according to Christ's appointment, and who die in the pale and peace of his Church, which the ancients called dying with the sign of faith, I say that prayers for such are acceptable to God as being fruits of our ardent charity, and are useful both to them and to us, and are too ancient to be popish."

" Lastly, That this doctrine for an intermediate state between death and the resurrection, as I have proved it, does effectually destroy the popish purgatory, invocation of the saints departed, popish penances, commutations of those penances, their indulgences, and treasures of merits purchased by supererogation."

As an example of the prayers for the dead he gives the following extract from the Office to be used at the Burial of the Dead in the first Liturgy of King Edward the Sixth : [1] " O Lord, with whom do live the spirits of them that be dead, and in whom the souls of them that be elected, after they be delivered from the burden of the flesh be in joy and felicity ; grant unto this thy servant that the sins which he committed in this world be not imputed unto him, but that he, escaping the gates of hell and pains of eternal darkness, may ever dwell in the region of light, with Abraham, Isaac, and Jacob, in the place where is no weeping, sorrow, nor heaviness ; and when that dreadful day of the general resurrection shall come, make him to rise also with the just and righteous, and receive this body again to glory, then made pure and incorruptible."

Jeremy Taylor, bishop of Down and Connor, says : [2] " Paradise is distinguished from the heaven of the blessed ; being itself a receptacle of holy souls, made illustrous with visitation of angels, and happy by being a repository for such spirits, who, at the day of judgment, shall go forth into eternal glory."

Again, he says : [3] " I have now made it as evident as questions of this nature will bear, that in the state of separation, the spirits of good men shall be blessed and happy souls, — they have an antepast or taste of their reward ; but their great reward itself, their crown of righteousness, shall not be yet ; that shall not be until the day of judgment. . . . . This is the doctrine of

---

[1] Published at London in the year 1549 ; folio cxlix. p. 2.
[2] *Life and Death of Jesus Christ*, iii. xvi. ad. 1 ; 3d edit. London, 1657, p. 588.
[3] *Sermon at Funeral of Sir George Dalston ; Works.* edit. London, 1828, vol. vi. pp. 553, 557.

the Greek Church unto this day, and was the opinion of the greatest part of the ancient Church both Latin and Greek; and by degrees was, in the west, eaten out by the doctrine of purgatory and invocation of saints; and rejected a little above two hundred years ago, in the Council of Florence."

It appears, therefore, that there is little difference between the advocates of an intermediate state and those who are regarded as rejecting that doctrine. Both admit, (1.) That the souls of believers do at death pass into a state of blessedness. (2.) That they remain in that state until the resurrection. (3.) That at the second coming of Christ, when the souls of the righteous are to be clothed with their glorified bodies, they will be greatly exalted and raised to a higher state of being. Bishop Hickes in his highly commendatory review of the work of the Honourable Archibald Campbell just referred to, which is appended to that volume, although he lays great stress on the doctrine in question, says that those who call the state into which the righteous enter, heaven; and that into which the wicked are introduced when they die, hell, may continue to do so, provided they mean by heaven a state which is less perfect than that which awaits them after the coming of Christ; and by hell, a condition less miserable than that which will be assigned to the wicked.

The Church of England agrees with other Protestant churches in its teachings on this subject. In the Liturgy of Edward VI. just quoted, it is said, (1.) That the spirits of all the dead live after the dissolution of the body. (2.) That the righteous are with God in a state of joy and felicity. (3.) That they have escaped the gates of hell and the pains of eternal darkness into which, as is necessarily implied, the souls of those who die unreconciled to God immediately enter. All the members of that Church are taught to say daily : " The glorious company of the Apostles praise thee. The goodly fellowship of the Prophets praise thee. The noble army of Martyrs praise thee." These, therefore, are all with God, and engaged in his service. In one of the prayers appointed to be used in the visitation of the sick, these words occur : " O Almighty God, with whom do live the souls of just men made perfect, after they are delivered from their earthly prisons." The souls of the just, therefore, are made perfect when they are delivered from the body.

§ 4. *Doctrine of the Church of Rome.*

Although Romanists reject the doctrine of an intermediate

state in the sense of the ancient Church, they nevertheless divide the world into which the souls of men enter at death, into many different departments.

The Limbus Patrum.

They hold that the souls of the righteous before the coming of Christ descended into Sheol, where they remained in a state of expectancy awaiting the coming of the Messiah. When Christ came and had accomplished his work of redemption by dying upon the cross, He descended into Hades, or the under-world, where the souls of the patriarchs were confined, delivered them from their captivity, and carried them in triumph to heaven. In other words they hold the common Jewish doctrine as to the state of the dead, so far as the saints of the Old Testament period are concerned. Their views on that subject have an intimate relation, whether causal or inferential is uncertain and unimportant, with their doctrine of the sacraments. Holding, first, that the sacraments are the only channels by which the saving blessings of redemption are conveyed to men ; and, secondly, that the sacraments of the Old Testament signified but did not communicate grace, they could not avoid the conclusion that those who died before the coming of Christ were not saved. The best that could be hoped concerning them was that they were not lost, but retained in a salvable state awaiting the coming deliverer. Whether they inferred that the Old Testament saints were not saved because they had no grace-bearing sacraments, or concluded that their sacraments were ineffectual, because those who had no others were not saved, it is not easy to determine. The latter is the more probable ; as most naturally they received the doctrine of Sheol from the Jews, as they did so many other doctrines ; and being led to believe that the patriarchs were not in heaven, they could not avoid the conclusion that circumcision and the passover were very far inferior in efficacy to the Christian sacraments.

The Limbus Infantum.

This is the name given to the place and state pertaining to the departed souls of unbaptized infants. As this class includes, perhaps, a moiety of the whole human race, their destiny in the future world is a matter of the deepest interest. The doctrine of the Church of Rome on this subject is that infants dying without baptism are not at death, or ever after it, admitted into the kingdom of heaven. They never partake of the benefits of redemption. This doctrine is explicitly stated in the symbols of that Church, and defended by its theologians. Cardinal Gousset, for example, says that original sin, of which all the children of Adam are partakers, is the death of the soul. Its consequences in this life are ignorance or obscuration of the understanding, feebleness of the will which can do nothing spiritually good without the assistance of divine grace, concupiscence or revolt of our lower nature, infirmities, sorrow, and the death of the body. Its consequences in the life to come are exclusion from the kingdom of heaven, privation of life eternal, of the beatific vision ; " no one can enter into the kingdom of God unless he be born again in Jesus Christ by baptism ; ' Except a man be born of water and of the Spirit, he cannot enter into the kingdom of God.' This is what faith teaches, but it goes no further. The Church leaves to the discussions of the schools the different opinions of theologians touching the fate of those who are excluded from the kingdom of heaven on account of original sin ; infants, for example, who die without having received the sacrament of baptism." [1]

Perrone speaking on this subject says, " We must distinguish the certain from the uncertain. What is certain, yea, a matter of faith, we have from the decisions of the Second Council of Lyons and the Council of Florence, both of which declare concerning infants and idiots : ' Credimus .... illorum animas, qui in mortali peccato vel cum solo originali decedunt, mox in infernum descendere, poenis tamen disparibus puniendas.' Ita quidem Florentinum ' in decreto Unionis,' quod descripsit verba Lugdunensis in fidei professione. De fide igitur est, (1.) parvulos ejusmodi in infernum descendere seu damnationem incurrere ; (2.) poenis puniri disparibus ab illis quibus puniuntur adulti. Quæ proinde spectant ad hunc inferni locum, ad poenarum disparitatem, seu in quo hæc disparitas constituenda sit, ad parvulorum statum post judicii diem incerta sunt omnia, nec fidem attingunt. Hinc variæ de his sunt patrum ac theologorum sententiæ." [2] Perrone goes on to show that the Latin fathers represent infants as suffering " poenam sensus ; " while most of Greek fathers say that they incur only " poenam damni," a sense of loss in being deprived of the blessedness of heaven. What that involves, however, he says is much disputed among theologians.

The Scriptural proof of this doctrine, as argued by Romanists,

---

[1] *Théologie Dogmatique*, par S. É. le Cardinal Gousset, Archevêque de Reims, 10th edit. Paris, 1866, vol. ii. pp. 95, 96.

[2] *Prælectiones Theologicæ*, edit. Paris, 1861, vol. i. p. 494.

is principally twofold ; the first is derived from the doctrine of original sin. They admit that the sin of Adam brought guilt and spiritual death upon all mankind. Baptism is the only means appointed for the deliverance of men from these dreadful evils. Hence it follows that the unbaptized remain under this guilt and pollution. The second great argument is founded upon John iii. 5, "Except a man be born of water, and of the Spirit, he cannot enter into the kingdom of God." This Romanists understand as an explicit declaration that the unbaptized cannot be saved. On this, however, as on all other subjects, their main dependence is upon the decision of Councils and the testimony of the fathers. Besides the Councils of Lyons and Florence, both regarded as ecumenical by Romanists, appeal is made to the canons of the Council of Trent, " Si quis parvulos recentes ab uteris matrum baptizandos negat, etiam si a baptizatis parentibus orti ; aut dicit in remissionem quidem peccatorum eos baptizari, sed nihil ex Adam trahere originalis peccati, quod regenerationis lavacro necesse sit expiari ad vitam æternam consequendam. . . . . anathema sit." [1] The Synod of Carthage, A. D. 416, is also quoted, which decided: [2] " Quicunque negat, parvulos per baptismum Christi a perditione liberari, et salutem percipere posse; anathema sit." Although the councils declare that the souls of unbaptized infants descend immediately into hell, Cardinal Gousset remarks, it is to be remembered that there are many departments in hell. There was one for the impenitent who died before the coming of Christ, and another for the souls of the righteous who awaited the advent of the Messiah ; so there is no reason for denying that there is still another for the souls of unbaptized infants. " We repeat," he says, [3] " that neither the Council of Florence nor that of Lyons pronounces on the nature of the punishment of those who die with only the guilt of original sin, except to show that they are forever excluded from the kingdom of heaven." We can, therefore, without going counter to the decisions of the Church, maintain the sentiment which exempts such unfortunates from the punishment of hell, and the rather because the opposite opinion is generally abandoned, and this abandonment is in accord with Pope Innocent III., who, distinguishing between the punishment of original and of actual sin, makes the latter to be the pain of

---

[1] Sess. v., canon 4; Streitwolf, vol. i. pp. 18, 19.

[2] Quoted by Perrone, *Prælectiones Theologicæ*, iii. vi. 599; edit. Paris, 1861, vol. i. pp. 496, 497.

[3] Gousset, *ut supra*, p. 96.

eternal fire; the former, the simple loss of the beatific (or intuitive) vision: " Pœna originalis peccati est carentia visionis Dei, actualis vero pœna peccati est gehennæ perpetuæ cruciatus."[1] On the following page he says, " We will go still further, and say with St. Thomas, that although unbaptized infants are deprived forever of the happiness of the saints, they suffer neither sorrow nor sadness in consequence of that privation." It is a matter of rejoicing that the doctrine of Romanists on the condition of unbaptized infants in a future life has admitted of this amelioration, although it is hard to reconcile it with the decisions of councils which declare that the souls of such infants do at death immediately descend into hell, if that word be understood according to the sense in which it was generally used when those decisions were made. The current representations of the theologians of the Latin Church are against this modified form of the doctrine. The Council of Trent anathematizes those who say that baptism is not necessary for the expiation of original sin; as that of Carthage those who affirm that it does not save infants from perdition. Romanists, however, of our day, have the right to state their doctrine in their own way, and should not be charged with holding sentiments which they repudiate.

Hell.

Hell is defined by Romanists as the place or state in which the fallen angels and men who die in a state of mortal sin, or, as it is also expressed, of final impenitence, suffer forever the punishment of their sins.

That the punishment of the wicked is unending they prove from the express declarations of Scripture, from the faith of the Church universal, and from the general belief of men. As to the nature of the sufferings of those who perish, they say they are those of loss; they are deprived of the favour, vision, and presence of God; and those " of sense," or of positive infliction. To this latter class are to be referred such sufferings as arise from wicked passions, from remorse and despair, as well as those which spring from the external circumstances in which the finally condemned are placed. Whether the unquenchable fire of which the Bible speaks, is to be understood literally or figuratively, is a question about which Romanists differ. Gousset proposes the question, and says that it is one on which the Church has given no decisions. " It is of faith," he says, "that the condemned

[1] Innocent III. *Caput " Majores " de Baptismo.*

shall be eternally deprived of the happiness of heaven, and that they shall be eternally tormented in hell ; but it is not of faith that the fire which causes their suffering is material. Many doctors, whose opinion has not been condemned, think that as 'the worm which never dies' is a figurative expression, so also is ' the fire that is never quenched;' and that the fire means a pain analogous to that by fire rather than the real pain produced by fire. Nevertheless the idea that the fire spoken of is real material fire is so general among Catholics, that we do not venture to advance a contrary opinion." [1]

Into this place and state of endless misery do pass, at death, all who die out of the pale of the Catholic Church ; all the unbaptized (at least among adults) ; all schismatics ; all heretics; all who die impenitent, or in a state of mortal sin, that is, sin the penalty of which is eternal death, which has not been remitted by priestly absolution.

Heaven.

Heaven, on the other hand, is the place and state of the blessed, where God is ; where Christ is enthroned in majesty, and where are the angels and the spirits of the just made perfect. Those who enter heaven are in possession of the supreme good. " The happiness of the saints above is complete ; they possess God, and in that possession they find perfect rest, and the enjoyment of all good." Their blessedness is perfect because it is everlasting. They see God face to face. They will eternally love Him and be loved by Him. " Beatitudo, quæ etiam summum bonum aut ultimus finis nuncupatur, a Bœtio [2] definitur : ' status bonorum omnium congregatione perfectus ;' a S. Augustino,[3] ' Bonorum omnium summa et cumulus;' a scholasticis autem : ' summum bonum appetivus rationalis satiativum.' " [4] It is, therefore, heaven in the highest sense of the term, into which the saints are said to enter.

There are, however, degrees in this blessedness. " The elect," says Cardinal Gousset, " in heaven, see God in a manner more or less perfect, according as they have more or less of merit, ' pro meritorum diversitate,' as it is expressed by the Council of Florence, which agrees with the words of our Lord, who says, ' In my Father's house are many mansions.' " [5] Into this only a

---

1 Gousset, *ut supra,* p. 160.
2 *Consolatio Philosophiæ,* Lib. iii, prosa 2; Lyons, 1671, p. 107.
3 *Enarratio in Psalmum,* ii. 11; *Works,* Paris, 1835, vol. iv. p. 8, c.
4 Perrone, *ut supra,* vol. i. p. 467.   5 Gousset, p. 132.

few, however, even of true believers, according to Romanists, enter at death. The advocates of the doctrine of an intermediate state, as has been shown, assert that none of the human family, whether patriarch, prophet, Apostle, or martyr, is admitted to the vision of God when he leaves the body; and that none of the wicked goes into the place of final retribution. Both the righteous and the wicked remain in a middle state, awaiting their final doom and location at the second coming of Christ. As to both these points, Romanists are more nearly agreed with the great body of Protestants.

On this point the Council of Florence says : " Credimus . . . . illorum animas, qui post baptismum susceptum nullam omnino peccati maculam incurrerunt, illas etiam animas quæ post contractam peccati maculam vel in suis corporibus, vel eisdem exutæ corporibus sunt purgatæ in cœlum mox recipi, et intueri clare ipsum Deum trinum et unum sicuti est." This doctrine Romanists assert not only in opposition to those who teach that the soul dies with the body and is revived at the resurrection, but also to those who say that the souls even of the perfectly purified " in aliqua requie degere, donec post corporum resurrectionem adipiscantur æternam beatitudinem, quam interim expectant." This error, Perrone says, widely disseminated among the Greeks, was adopted by Luther and Calvin.[1]

Two classes of persons, therefore, according to this view, enter heaven before the resurrection; first, those who are perfectly purified at the time of death; and second, those who, although not thus perfect when they leave this world, have become perfect in purgatory.

Purgatory.

According to Romanists, all those who die in the peace of the Church, but are not perfect, pass into purgatory; with regard to which they teach, (1.) That it is a state of suffering. The commonly received traditional, though not symbolical, doctrine on this point is, that the suffering is from material fire. The design of this suffering is both expiation and purification. (2.) That the duration and intensity of purgatorial pains are proportioned to the guilt and impurity of the sufferers. (3.) That there is no known or defined limit to the continuance of the soul in purgatory, but the day of judgment. The departed may remain in this state of suffering for a few hours or for thousands of years. (4.) That souls in purgatory may be helped; that is, their suffer-

---

[1] *Ut supra*, p. 473.

ings alleviated or the duration of them shortened by the prayers of the saints, and especially by the sacrifice of the Mass. (5.) That purgatory is under the power of the keys. That is, it is the prerogative of the authorities of the Church, at their discretion, to remit entirely or partially the penalty of sins under which the souls there detained are suffering.

This doctrine is deeply rooted in the whole Romish system. According to that system, (1.) Christ delivers us only from the " reatus culpæ," and exposure to eternal death. (2.) For all sins committed after baptism the offender must make satisfaction by penance or good works. (3.) This satisfaction must be complete and the soul purified from all sin, before it can enter heaven. (4.) This satisfaction and purification, if not effected in this life, must be accomplished after death. (5.) The eucharist is a propitiatory sacrifice intended to secure the pardon of post-baptismal sins, and takes effect according to the intention of the officiating priest. Therefore, if he intends it for the benefit of any soul in purgatory, it inures to his advantage. (6.) The pope, being the vicar of Christ on earth, has full power to forgive sin ; that is, to exempt offenders from the obligation to make satisfaction for their offences.

Moehler, and other philosophical defenders of Romanism, soften down the doctrine by representing purgatory simply as a state of gradual preparation of the imperfectly sanctified for admission into heaven, making no mention of positive suffering, much less of material fire.   Cardinal Gousset does not go so far as this, yet he says : [1] " It is of faith, (1.) That the righteous who die without having entirely satisfied divine justice, must make satisfaction after this life by temporary pains, which are called pains of purgatory ; (2.) That the souls in purgatory are relieved by the prayers of the Church. This is what the faith teaches ; but it stops there. Is purgatory a particular place rather than a state, or a state rather than a particular place ? Are the pains of purgatory due to fire, or are the pains those which arise from the consciousness of having offended God ? What are the severity and duration of those pains ? These and other questions of like kind, are not included in the domain of Catholic doctrine. These are questions about which there exists no decision or judgment of the Church. Nevertheless it should be known that in the opinion of the majority of theologians the torments of purgatory consist in part in those of fire, or, at least, in such as are analogous to

[1] Gousset, *ut supra*, vol. ii. 143.

the pain produced by fire. We will add that, according to Saint
Augustine and Saint Thomas, whose opinion is generally adopted
(dont le sentiment est assez suivi), the pains of purgatory sur-
pass those of this life: " Pœna purgatorii," says the angelic Doctor,[1] "quantum ad pœnam damni et sensus,, excedit omnem
pœnam istius vitæ."

Cardinal Wiseman,[2] in his lecture on this subject, speaks in the
mildest terms. He says nothing of the pains of purgatory except
that they are pains. The satisfaction for sin demanded by the
Church of Rome, to be rendered in this world, consists of prayers,
fastings, almsgiving, and the like ; and we are told that if this
satisfaction be not made before death, it must be made after it.
This is all that the Cardinal ventures to say. He has not courage
to lift the veil from the burning lake in which the souls in purgatory are represented as suffering, according to the common faith
of Romanists. Although it is true that the Church of Rome has
wisely abstained from any authoritative decision as to the nature
and intensity of purgatorial sufferings, it does not thereby escape
responsibility on the subject. It allows free circulation with ecclesiastical sanction, expressed or implied, of books containing the
most frightful exhibitions of the sufferings of purgatory which the
imagination of man can conceive. This doctrine, therefore, however mildly it may be presented in works designed for Protestant
readers, is nevertheless a tremendous engine of priestly power.
The feet of the tiger with the claws withdrawn are as soft as vel-
vet ; when those claws are extended, they are fearful instruments
of laceration and death.

Arguments used in favour of the Doctrine.

1. Romanists make comparatively little use of Scripture in defence of their peculiar doctrines.[3] Their main support is tradition

---

[1] See Aquinas, *Summa*, III. xlvi. 6, 3.

[2] *Lectures on the Principal Doctrines and Practices of the Catholic Church.* By Cardinal Wiseman. Two volumes in one. Sixth American from the last London edition. Revised and Corrected. Baltimore, 1870. *Lecture XI. On Satisfaction and Purgatory.*

[3] Cardinal Wiseman says: "I have more than once commented on the incorrectness of
that method of arguing which demands that we prove every one of our doctrines individually from the Scriptures. I occupied myself, during my first course of lectures, in dem-
onstrating the Catholic principle of faith that the Church of Christ was constituted by Him
the depositary of his truths, and that, although many were recorded in his holy word, still
many were committed to traditional keeping, and that Christ Himself has faithfully promised to teach in his Church, and has thus secured her from error." *Lectures, ut supra,* xi.
vol. ii. p. 45. This resolves all controversies with Romanists into two questions. First,
what is the prerogative of the Church as a teacher; and secondly, is the Church of Rome,
or any other external organized body, the body of Christ to which the prerogatives and
promises of the Church belong?

and the authority of the Church. Cardinal Wiseman cites but two passages from the New Testament in favour of the doctrine of purgatory. The first is our Lord's saying that the sin against the Holy Ghost shall never be forgiven either in this world or in the world to come. This is said to imply that there are sins which are not forgiven in this life which may be forgiven hereafter; and therefore that the dead, or at least a part of their number, are not past forgiveness when they die. This is a slender thread on which to hang so great a weight. The words of Christ contain no such implication. To say that a thing can never happen either here or hereafter, in this world or in the world to come, is a familiar way of saying that it can never happen under any circumstances. Our Lord simply said that blasphemy of the Holy Ghost can never be forgiven. The other passage is from Revelation xxi. 27, where it said that nothing that defileth shall enter heaven. But as very few, if any of the human family, are perfectly pure when they die, it follows that, if there be no place or process of purification after death, few if any of the sons of men could be saved; or, as Cardinal Wiseman puts the argument, " Suppose that a Christian dies who had committed some slight transgression; he cannot enter heaven in this state, and yet we cannot suppose that he is to be condemned forever. What alternative, then, are we to admit? Why, that there is some place in which the soul will be purged of the sin, and qualified to enter into the glory of God."[1] But does not the blood of Christ cleanse from all sin? Were not the sins of Paul all forgiven the moment he believed? Did the penitent thief enter purgatory instead of paradise? To minds trained under the influence of evangelical doctrine, such arguments as the above cannot have the slightest weight.

2. Great stress is laid upon the fact that the custom of praying for the dead prevailed early and long in the Church. Such prayers take for granted that the dead need our prayers; and this supposes that they are not in heaven. But if not in heaven where can they be except in a preparatory or purgatorial state? To this it may be answered, (1.) That praying for the dead is a superstitious practice, having no support from the Bible. It was one of the corruptions early introduced into the Church. It will not do to argue from one corruption in support of another. (2.) Those who vindicate the propriety of praying for the dead are often strenuous opposers of the doctrine of purgatory. Dr. Pusey, for example, says: " Since Rome has blended the cruel in

vention of purgatory with the primitive custom of praying for the dead, it is not in communion with her that any can seek comfort from this rite." [1] The early Christians prayed for the souls of Apostles and martyrs, whom they assuredly believed were already in heaven. It was not, therefore, for any alleviation of their sufferings, as Dr. Pusey argues, that such prayers were offered, but for the augmentation of their happiness, and the consummation of their blessedness at the last day.

3. The argument of most logical force to those who believe the premises whence it is derived, is drawn from the doctrine of satisfaction. The Romish doctrine on this subject includes the following principles : " (1.) That God, after the remission of sin, retains a lesser chastisement in his power, to be inflicted on the sinner. (2.) That penitential works, fasting, alms-deeds, contrite weeping, and fervent prayer, have the power of averting that punishment. (3.) That this scheme of God's justice was not a part of the imperfect law, but the unvarying ordinance of his dispensation, anterior to the Mosaic ritual, and amply confirmed by Christ in the gospel. (4.) That it consequently becomes a part of all true repentance to try to satisfy this divine justice by the voluntary assumption of such penitential works as his revealed truth assures have efficacy before Him." [2] In connection with this is to be taken the doctrine of indulgences. This doctrine, we are told, rests on the following grounds : (1.) " That satisfaction has to be made to God for sin remitted, under the authority and regulation of the Church. (2.) That the Church has always considered herself possessed of the authority to mitigate, by diminution or commutation, the penance which she enjoins ; and she has always reckoned such a mitigation valid before God, who sanctions and accepts it. (3.) That the sufferings of the saints, in union with, and by virtue of Christ's merits, are considered available towards the granting this mitigation. (4.) That such mitigations, when

---

[1] *An earnest Remonstrance to the author of the " Pope's Pastoral Letter to certain Members of the University of Oxford,"* London, 1836, p. 25. The Hon. Archibald Campbell, whose work is quoted above, says that all the authorities to which he refers from among the English Bishops and theologians, side with him in defending prayers for the dead and in denouncing purgatory.

[2] Wiseman, *ut supra,* vol. ii. p. 40. It will be observed that the Cardinal, in detailing the kind of satisfaction to be made, mentions fasting, alms-giving, and prayer, but says nothing of scourgings, hair shirts, spiked girdles, and all other means of self-torture so common and so applauded in the Romish Church. In this way he softens down and understates all " Catholic Doctrines and Practices," to render them less revolting to the reason and conscience of his readers. Purgatory with him is a bed of roses with here and there a thorn, instead of the lake of real fire and brimstone which glares through all Church history.

prudently and justly granted, are conducive toward the spiritual weal and profit of Christians." [1]

We have thus a broad foundation laid for the whole doctrine of purgatory. God in the forgiveness of sin remits only the penalty of eternal death. There remain temporal pains to be endured in satisfaction of divine justice. If such satisfaction be not made in this world, it must be rendered in the next. The Church has the power of regulating these satisfactions, of directing what they shall be, of mitigating or commuting them in this life, and of lessening their severity or duration in the life to come. The infinite merit of Christ, and the superfluous merits of all the saints, gained by works of supererogation, form an inexhaustible treasury, from which the Pope and his subordinates may draw at discretion for the mitigation, or plenary dispensation, of all the satisfaction due for sin in the way of penance in this life, or the pains of purgatory in the life to come. Now when it is considered that the pains of purgatory are authoritatively and almost universally represented by Romanists to be intolerably severe, it will be seen that no such engine of power, no such means of subjugating the people, or of exalting and enriching the priesthood has ever been claimed or conceded by man. Men really invested with this power, of necessity, and of right, are the absolute masters of their fellow men; and those who wrongfully claim it, who assume without possessing it, are the greatest impostors (consciously or unconsciously) and the greatest tyrants the world ever saw.

4. With Romanists themselves the greatest argument in favour of the doctrine of purgatory is tradition. They claim that it has always been held in the Church; and in support of that claim they quote from the fathers all passages which speak of purification by fire, or of praying for the dead. They usually begin with the Second Book of Maccabees xii. 43, where it is said that Judas Maccabeus sent " 2,000 drachmas of silver to Jerusalem for sacrifice, to be offered for the sins " of the dead. They cite Tertullian,[2] who advised a widow to pray for her husband, and to offer oblations for him on the anniversary of his death; Cyprian,[3] who says that if a man committed a certain offence, " no oblation should be made for him, nor sacrifice offered for his repose;" Basil, who says of Isaiah ix. 19, " The people shall be as the fuel of the fire," οὐκ ἀφανισμὸν ἀπειλεῖ, ἀλλὰ τὴν κάθαρσιν ὑποφαίνει, that is, " it does not threaten extermination, but denotes purification;"[4] Cyril of Je-

---

[1] *Ibid.* vol. ii. p. 70. [2] *De Monogamia*, 10; *Works*, edit. Basle, 1562, p. 578.
[3] Ep. xlvi. p. 114. (?)
[4] *In Esaiæ*, ix. 19; *Works*, edit. Paris, 1618, vol. i. p. 1039. d.

rusalem, who says : " Deinde et pro defunctis sanctis patribus et
episcopis, et omnibus generatim, qui inter nos vita functi sunt,
oramus, maximum hoc credentes adjumentum illis animabus fore,
pro quibus oratio defertur, dum sancta et tremenda coram jacet
victima ; " [1] that is, " Then we pray for the holy fathers and the
bishops that are dead ; and, in short, for all those who are departed this life in our communion ; believing that the souls of those
for whom the prayers are offered, receive very great relief while
this holy and tremendous victim lies upon the altar ; " Gregory of
Nyssa,[2] who says that in this life the sinner may " be renovated
by prayers and by the pursuit of wisdom ; " but when he has
quitted his body, " he cannot be admitted to approach the Divinity till the purging fire shall have expiated the stains with which
his soul was infected ; " Ambrose,[3] who thus comments upon 1
Corinthians iii. 15, " He . . . . shall be saved, yet so as by fire."
The Apostle says, " ' Yet so as by fire,' in order that his salvation
be not understood to be without pain.   He shows that he shall be
saved indeed, but he shall undergo the pain of fire, and be thus
purified ; not like the unbelieving and wicked man, who shall be
punished in everlasting fire ;" Jerome,[4] who says : " As we believe the torments of the devil, and of those wicked men, who said
in their hearts, ' There is no God,' to be eternal ; so, in regard to
those sinners, impious men and even Christians, whose works
will be proved and purged by fire, we conclude that the sentence
of the judge will be tempered by mercy ; " and Augustine,[5] who
says : " The prayers of the Church, or of good persons, are heard

1 *Catechesis Mystagogica*, v. 9 ; *Opera*, Venice, 1763, p. 328, a, b.
2 *Oratio de Mortuis ; Works*, Paris, 1615, vol. ii. pp. 1066–1068.
3 "Dixit: 'Sic tamen quasi per ignem,' ut salus hæc non sine pœna sit: . . . . ostendit
salvum illum quidem futurum; sed pœnas ignis passurum, ut per ignem purgatus fiat salvus,
et non sicut perfidi æterno igne in perpetuum torqueatur." *Works*, edit. Paris, 1661, vol.
iii. p. 351, a.
4 *Comment. in c. lxv. Isai., Opera*, Paris, 1579, tome iv. p. 502, d, e.
5 " Nam pro defunctis quibusdam, vel ipsius Ecclesiæ, vel quorumdam piorum exauditur
oratio: sed pro his quorum in Christo regeneratorum nec usque adeo vita in corpore male
gesta est ut tali misericordia judicentur digni non esse, nec usque adeo bene, ut talem misericordiam reperiantur necessariam non habere.   Sicut etiam facta resurrectione mortuorum
non deerunt quibus post pœnas, quas patiuntur spiritus mortuorum, impertiatur misericordia, ut in ignem non mittantur æternum.   Neque enim de quibusdam veraciter diceretur,
quod non eis remittatur neque in hoc sæculo, neque in futuro, nisi essent quibus, etsi non
in isto, tamen remittetur in futuro." *De Civitate Dei*, XXI. xxiv. 2; *Works*, 2d Benedic-
tine edition, Paris, 1838, vol. vii. p. 1028, c, d.   "Ædificarent autem aurum, argentum,
lapides pretiosos, et de utroque igne securi essent; non solum de illo æterno qui in æternum
cruciaturus est impios, sed etiam de illo qui emendabit eos qui per ignem salvi erunt. . . . .
Et quia dicitur, 'salvus erit,' contemnitur ille ignis. . . . . Gravior tamen erit ille ignis
quam quidquid potest homo pati in hac vita." *Enarratio in Psalmum* xxxvii. 2, 3;
Works, vol. iv. pp. 418, d, 419, a.

in favour of those Christians who departed this life not so bad as to be deemed unworthy of mercy, nor so good as to be entitled to immediate happiness. So, also, at the resurrection of the dead, there will some be found to whom mercy will be imparted, having gone through those pains to which the spirits of the dead are liable. Otherwise it would not have been said of some with truth, that their sin ' shall not be forgiven, neither in this world, nor in the world to come,' unless some sins were remitted in the next world." And again : " If they had built ' gold and silver, and precious stones,' they would be secure from both fires ; not only from that in which the wicked shall be punished forever, but likewise from that fire that purifies those who shall be saved by fire. But because it is said ' shall be saved,' that fire is thought lightly of ; though the suffering will be more grievous than anything man can undergo in this life." " These passages," says Cardinal Wiseman, " contain precisely the same doctrine as the Catholic Church teaches ;" they may be found in great abundance in all the standard works of Catholic theologians.

With regard to this argument from the fathers, it may be remarked, (1.) That if any one should quote Döllinger, Dupanloup, Wiseman, and Manning in favour of any Christian doctrine, it would have more weight with Protestants than the same number of these early writers ; not only because they are, speaking generally, men of far more ability and higher culture, but because they are in more favourable circumstances to learn the truth. The fathers looked at everything through an atmosphere filled with the forms of pagan traditions and ideas. The modern leaders of the Church of Rome are surrounded by the light of Protestant Christianity. (2.) All the ancient writers, quoted in support of the doctrine of purgatory, held doctrines which no Romanist is now willing to avow. If they discard the authority of the fathers when teaching a Jewish millennium, or sovereign predestination, once the doctrine of the universal Church, they cannot reasonably expect Protestants to bow to that authority when urged in favour of the pagan idea of a purification by fire. (3.) The witnesses cited in support of the doctrine of purgatory come very far short of proving the universal and constant belief of the doctrine in question. And, according to Romanists themselves, no doctrine can plead the support of tradition that cannot stand the crucial test, " quod semper, quod ubique, quod ab omnibus." (4.) That purgatory is, what Dr. Pusey calls it, " a modern invention," has been demonstrated by tracing historically its origin, rise, and development in the Church.

Arguments against the Doctrine.

1. The first, most obvious, and, for Protestants, the most decisive argument against the doctrine is, that it is not taught in the Bible. This is virtually admitted by its advocates. The most that is pretended is, that having adopted the doctrine on other grounds, they can find in Scripture here and there a passage which can be explained in accordance with its teachings. There is no passage which asserts it. There is no evidence that it formed a part of the instructions of Christ or his Apostles.

2. It is not only destitute of all support from Scripture, but it is opposed to its clearest and most important revelations. If there be anything plainly taught in the Bible, it is that if any man forsakes his sins, believes in the Lord Jesus Christ as the eternal Son of God, trusts simply and entirely to Him and his work, and leads a holy life, he shall certainly be saved. This the doctrine of purgatory denies. It rests avowedly on the assumption that notwithstanding the infinitely meritorious sacrifice of Christ, the sinner is bound to make satisfaction for his own sins. This the Bible declares to be impossible. No man does or can perfectly keep the commandments of God, much less can he not only abstain from incurring new guilt, but also make atonement for sins that are past.

The doctrine moreover assumes the merit of good works. Here again it is clearer than the sun that the New Testament teaches that we are saved by grace and not by works; that to him that worketh, the reward is a matter of debt; but to him who simply believes, it is a matter of grace; and that the two are incompatible. What is of grace is not of works; and what is of works is not of grace. There is nothing more absolutely incompatible with the nature of the Gospel than the idea that man can " satisfy divine justice " for his sins. Yet this idea lies at the foundation of the doctrine of purgatory. If there be no satisfaction of justice, on the part of the sinner, there is no purgatory, for, according to Romanists, purgatory is the place and state in which such satisfaction is rendered. As the renunciation of all dependence upon our own merit, of all purpose, desire, or effort to make satisfaction for ourselves, and trusting exclusively to the satisfaction rendered by Jesus Christ, is of the very essence of Christian experience, it will be seen that the doctrine of purgatory is in conflict not only with the doctrines of the Bible but also with the religious consciousness of the believer. This is not saying that no man who believes in purgatory can be a true Christian. The history of the Church proves that Christians can be very inconsistent; that they may speculatively adhere to doctrines which are inconsistent with what their hearts know to be true.

It is, however, not only the doctrine of satisfaction, but also the absolutely preposterous doctrine of supererogation which must be admitted, if we adopt the creed of the Church of Rome in this matter. The idea is that a man may be more than perfect; that he may not only do more than the law requires of him, but even render satisfaction to God's justice so meritorious as to be more than sufficient for the pardon of his own sins. This superfluous merit, is the ground on which the sins of those suffering in purgatory may be forgiven. This is a subject which does not admit of argument. It supposes an impossibility. It supposes that a rational creature can be better than he ought to be; *i. e.*, than he is bound to be. Romanists moreover strenuously deny the possibility that Christ's righteousness can be imputed to the believer as the ground of his justification; and yet they teach that the merits of the saints may be imputed to sinners in purgatory as the ground of their forgiveness.

Another antiscriptural assumption involved in the doctrine is that the pope, and his subordinates, have power over the unseen world; power to retain or to remit the sins of departed souls; to deliver them from purgatorial fire or to allow them to remain under its torments. This is a power which could not be trusted in the hands of an angel. Nothing short of infinite knowledge and infinite rectitude could secure it from fatal abuse. No such power we may be assured has ever been committed to the hands of sinful men.

There are two entirely different things involved in this priestly power to forgive sins. There are two kinds of punishment denounced against sin. The one is the sentence of eternal death; the other is the temporary punishment to which the sinner remains subject after the eternal penalty is remitted.[1] With regard

---

[1] In the passage quoted in part on a preceding page, Cardinal Wiseman says: "No fasting, no prayers, no alms-deeds, no works that we can conceive to be done by man, however protracted, however expensive or rigorous they may be, can, according to the Catholic doctrine, have the most infinitesimal weight for obtaining the remission of sin, or of the eternal punishment allotted to it. This constitutes the essence of forgiveness, of justification, and in it we hold that man has no power. Now, let us come to the remaining part of the sacrament [of penance]. We believe that upon this forgiveness of sins, that is, after the remission of that eternal debt, which God in his justice awards to transgressions against his law, He has been pleased to reserve a certain degree of inferior or temporary punishment appropriate to the guilt which had been incurred; and it is on this part of the punishment alone, that, according to the Catholic doctrine, satisfaction can be made to God." *Lectures, ut supra*, vol. ii. p. 35.

to both the priest interferes. Neither can be remitted without his intervention. The eternal penalty is remitted in the sacrament of penance. The latter is exacted, mitigated, or dispensed with at the discretion of the Church, or its organs. As to the remission of the eternal penalty the intervention of the priest is necessary because he alone can administer the sacrament of penance, which includes contrition, confession, and satisfaction. All are necessary. It is not enough that the sinner be penitent in heart and truly turn from sin unto God; he must confess his sins to the priest. The Church " maintains that the sinner is bound to manifest his offences to the pastors of his Church, or, rather, to one deputed and authorized by the Church for that purpose ; to lay open to him all the secret offences of his soul, to expose all its wounds, and in virtue of the authority vested by our Blessed Saviour in him, to receive through his hands, on earth, the sentence which is ratified in heaven, of God's forgiveness." Christ also " gave to the Church power of retaining sins, that is, of withholding forgiveness, or delaying it to more seasonable time."[1] " Here is a power, in the first place, truly to forgive sin. For this expression ' to forgive sins,' in the New Testament, always signifies to clear the sinner of guilt before God." " The Apostles, then, and their successors, received this authority ; consequently, to them was given a power to absolve, or to cleanse the soul from its sins. There is another power also : that of retaining sins. What is the meaning of this ? clearly the power of refusing to forgive them. Now, all this clearly implies — for the promise is annexed, that what sins Christ's lawful ministers retain on earth, are retained in heaven — that there is no other means of obtaining forgiveness, save through them. For the forgiveness of heaven is made to depend upon that which they forgive on earth ; and those are not to be pardoned there, whose sins they retain."[2] This is sufficiently explicit. It is to be remembered the power of forgiveness here claimed has reference, not to the temporary punishment imposed in the way of penance or satisfaction, but to the remission of " the eternal debt." Now, as to the temporary punishment, which, as we have seen, may last thousands of years and exceed in severity any sufferings on earth, Romanists teach, (1.) That " they are expiatory of past transgression."[3] (2.) That they are of the same nature with the penances imposed by the discipline of the early Church. That discipline was naturally, perhaps necessarily, very severe ; the Church was then sur-

[1] Wiseman, *Lectures*, vol. ii. p. 15   [2] *Ibid*. pp. 19 20.   [3] *Ibid*. p. 39.

rounded by heathenism, and many of its members were heathen converts. What tendencies, and what temptations to unchristian conduct, were unavoidable under such circumstances, may be learned from the state of the Church in Corinth as depicted in Paul's epistles. The great danger was that Christians should be involved, intentionally or unintentionally, in the idolatrous services to which they had been accustomed. As the worship of idols in any form, was a renunciation of the Gospel, it was against that offence the discipline of the Church was principally directed. One party contended that the " lapsed " ought never to be restored to Christian fellowship ; another, which allowed their readmission to the Church, insisted that they should be restored only after a long and severe course of penance. Some were required " to lay prostrate for a certain period of months or years before the doors of the Church, after which they were admitted to different portions of the divine service ; while others were often excluded through their whole lives from the liturgical exercises of the faithful, and were not admitted to absolution until they were at the point of death." These penances Romanists pronounce " meritorious in the sight of God," they " propitiate his wrath." This is the doctrine of satisfaction ; and such satisfaction for sin is the necessary condition of its forgiveness. (3.) As these penances or satisfactions are imposed by the Church, they can be mitigated or remitted by the Church. (4.) As the pains of purgatory are of the nature of satisfactions, " expiatory," " meritorious," and " propitiatory," they are as much under the control of the Church, as the penances to be endured in this life.

This is the true, and it may be said, the virtually admitted genesis of the doctrine of purgatory in the Church of Rome. It is a perversion of the ecclesiastical discipline of the early Christians. To be sure, the genesis, or birth, is spurious ; there is no legitimate connection between the premises and the conclusion. Admitting the fact that the early Church imposed severe penances on offenders before restoring them to fellowship ; admitting that this was right on the part of the Church ; admitting that such penances were of the nature of satisfactions, so far as they were designed to satisfy the Church that the repentance of the offender was sincere ; and admitting that these penances being matters of Church discipline were legitimately under the power of the Church, how does all this prove that they were " expiatory in the sight of God," that " they satisfied divine justice," or that they were the necessary conditions of forgiveness at his bar ?

Satisfactory to the Church as evidences of repentance, and satisfactory to God's justice, are two very different things, which Romanists have confounded. Besides, how does it follow, because the visible Church has control of the discipline of its members, in this life, that it has control of the souls of men in the life to come ? Yet Romanists reason from the one to the other.

3. Another decisive argument against the doctrine of purgatory is drawn from the abuses to which it has led, and which are its inevitable, being its natural consequences. It is *à priori* evident that a power committed to weak and sinful men which is safe in no other hands but those of God Himself, must lead to the most dreadful abuses. The doctrine, as we have seen, is, (1.) That the priest has power to remit or retain, the penalty of eternal death denounced against all sin. (2.) That he (or the appropriate organ of the Church) has power to alleviate, to shorten, or to terminate, the sufferings of souls in purgatory. That this power should fail to be abused, in the hands of the best of men, is impossible. Vested in the hands of ordinary men, as must be generally the case, or in the hands of mercenary and wicked men, imagination can set no limit to its abuse ; and imagination can hardly exceed the historical facts in the case. This is not a matter of dispute. Romanists themselves admit the fact. Cardinal Wiseman acknowledges that " flagrant and too frequent abuses, doubtless, occurred through the avarice, and rapacity, and impiety of men ; especially when indulgence was granted to the contributors towards charitable or religious foundations, in the erection of which private motives too often mingle." [1] The reader must be referred to the pages of history for details on this subject. The evils which have in fact flowed from this doctrine of purgatory and of the priestly power of retaining or remitting sin, are such as to render it certain that no such doctrine can be of God.

4. Romanists, however, confidently appeal, in support of their doctrine, to the express declaration of Christ, " Whose soever sins ye remit, they are remitted unto them ; and whose soever sins ye retain, they are retained." (John xx. 23.) To the same effect it is said, in Matthew xvi. 19, " I will give unto thee the keys of the kingdom of heaven : and whatsoever thou shalt bind on earth, shall be bound in heaven : and whatsoever thou shalt loose on earth, shall be loosed in heaven." The first remark to be made on these passages is, that whatever power is granted in them to the Apostles, is granted in Matthew xviii. 18 to all Chris-

---

[1] *Lectures, ut supra,* xii.; vol. ii. p. 75.

tians, or, at least, to every association of Christians which constitutes a Church. " If thy brother shall trespass against thee, go and tell him his fault between thee and him alone : if he shall hear thee, thou hast gained thy brother. But if he will not hear thee, then take with thee one or two more, that in the mouth of two or three witnesses every word may be established. And if he neglect to hear them, tell it unto the Church : but if he neglect to hear the Church, let him be unto thee as an heathen man and a publican. Verily, I say unto you, whatsoever ye shall bind on earth, shall be bound in heaven : and whatsoever ye shall loose on earth shall be loosed in heaven." This power, therefore, of binding and loosing, whatever it was, was not vested exclusively in the Apostles and their successors, but in the Church. But the true Church to which the promises and prerogatives of the Church belong, consists of true believers. This is not only the doctrine of the Bible and of all Protestants at the time of the Reformation, but would seem to be a matter of course. Promises made to the Apostles were made to true apostles, not to those who pretended to the office, and were false apostles. So the promises made to Christians are made not to nominal, pretended, or false Christians, but to those who truly are what they profess to be. If this be clear, then it is no less clear that the power of binding and loosing, of remitting or retaining sin, was never granted by Christ to unregenerated, wicked men, no matter by what name they may be called. This is a great point gained. The children of God in this world are not under the power of the children of the devil, to be forgiven or condemned, saved or lost, at their discretion. Therefore, when Luther was anathematized by the body calling itself the Church, as Athanasius had been before him, it did not hurt a hair of his head.

Secondly, the power granted by Christ to his Church of binding and loosing, of forgiving or retaining sin, is not absolute, but conditional. The passages above quoted are analogous to many others contained in the Scriptures, and are all to be explained in the same way. For example, our Lord said to his disciples ; They who hear you, hear me. That is, the people were as much bound to believe the gospel when preached by the disciples, as though they heard it from the lips of Christ Himself. Or, if these words are to be understood as addressed exclusively to the Apostles, and to include a promise of infallibility in teaching, the meaning is substantially the same. Men were as much bound to receive the doctrines of the Apostles, as the teachings of Christ, for what they taught He taught. St. John, therefore, says, " He that knoweth God heareth us; he that is not of God, heareth not us." (1 John iv. 6.) Nevertheless, although Christ required all men to hear his Apostles as though He himself were speaking; yet no man was bound to hear them unless they preached Christ's gospel. Therefore St. Paul said, " Though we, or an angel from heaven, preach any other gospel unto you than that which we have preached unto you, let him be accursed." (Gal. i. 8.) If the Apostles taught anything contrary to the authenticated revelation of God, they were to be rejected. If they undertook to bind or loose, to remit or retain sin on any other terms than those prescribed by Christ, their action amounted to nothing; it produced no effect. In teaching and in absolution their power was simply declarative. In the one case, they, as witnesses, declared what were the conditions of salvation and the rule of life prescribed in the gospel; and in the other case, they simply declared the conditions on which God will forgive sin, and announced the promise of God that on those conditions He would pardon the sins of men. A child, therefore, may remit sin just as effectually as the pope; for neither can do anything more than declare the conditions of forgiveness. It once required the heroism of Luther to announce that truth which emancipated Europe; now it is an every-day truth.

There is, of course, a great difference between the Apostles and other Christian teachers. Christ bore witness to the correctness of their testimony as to his doctrines, and sanctioned their declarations, by signs, and wonders, and gifts of the Holy Ghost, thus giving the seal of infallibility to their teachings as uttered by the lips and as we have them recorded in the Bible. And, there is also a difference between the official ministers of the gospel and other men, in so far as the former are specially called to the work of preaching the word. But in all cases, in that of the Apostles, in that of office-bearers in the Church, and in that of laymen, the power is simply declaratory. They declare what God has revealed. What difference does it make in the authority of the message, whether the gospel be read at the bed of a dying sinner, by a child, or by an archbishop? None in the world.

There is another class of passages analogous to those under consideration. When our Lord says, Ask and ye shall receive, Whatsoever ye ask in my name I will do it, no one understands these promises as unconditional. No one believes that any prayer of the Christian is ever heard, if it be not for something agreeable to the will of God. When then it is said, " Whose soever sins ye remit, they are remitted," why should it be inferred that no condition is implied? The language is not more explicit in the one case than in the other. As no man's prayers are heard unless he asks for things agreeable to the will of God ; so no man's sins are remitted unless he truly repents and truly believes in the Lord Jesus Christ. One man has no more power to forgive sins, than another. The forgiveness of sin is the exclusive prerogative of God.

Thirdly, there is another remark to be made about this power of binding and loosing. Christ has ordained that the terms of admission to the Church, should be the same as those of admission into heaven ; and that the grounds of exclusion from the Church, should be the same as those of exclusion from heaven. He, therefore, virtually said to his disciples, Whom ye receive into the Church, I will receive into heaven ; and whom ye exclude from the Church, I will exclude from heaven. But this, of course, implies that they should act according to his directions. He did not bind Himself to sanction all their errors in binding and loosing ; any more than He was bound by his promise to hear their prayers, to grant all the foolish or wicked petitions his people might offer ; or by his promise in reference to their teaching, to sanction all the false doctrines into which they might be seduced. If we interpret Scripture by Scripture, we escape a multitude of errors.

Fourthly, Romanists rest their doctrine of absolution and of the power of the keys over souls in purgatory, very much upon the special gifts granted to the Apostles and to their successors. In reference to this agreement it may be remarked, —

1. That the Apostles never claimed, never possessed, and never pretended to exercise, the power assumed by Romanists, in the remission of sins. They never presumed to pronounce the absolution of a sinner in the sight of God. Christ could say " Thy sins be forgiven thee ; " but we never hear such language from the lips of an Apostle. They never directed those burdened with a sense of sin to go to the priest to make confession and receive absolution. They had no authority in this respect above that which belongs to the ordinary officers of the Church. They could declare the terms on which God had promised to forgive sins ; and they could suspend or excommunicate members, for cause, from the communion of the visible Church. In the case

of the incestuous man whom the Church in Corinth allowed to remain in its fellowship, Paul determined to do what he censured the Church for not doing; that is, in virtue of his apostolic jurisdiction extending over all the churches, he excommunicated the offender, or, delivered him to Satan, that he might repent. (1 Cor. v.) When the man did repent, the Apostle exhorted the Corinthians to restore him to their fellowship, saying, " To whom ye forgive anything, I forgive also." (2 Cor. ii. 10.) He claimed for himself no power which he did not recognize as belonging to them. It was a mere matter of Church discipline from beginning to end. This power of discipline, which all Churches recognize and exercise, the Romanists have perverted into the priestly power of absolution.

2. Admitting, what, however, is not conceded, that the Apostles had special power to forgive sin, that power must have rested on their peculiar gifts and qualifications. They were infallible men ; not infallible indeed in reading men's hearts, or in judging of their character, but simply infallible as teachers ; and they had authority to organize the Church, and to lay down laws for its future government and discipline. These gifts and prerogatives, indeed, in no way qualified them to sit in judgment on the souls of men, to pardon or condemn them at discretion , but, such as they were, they were personal. Those who claim to be their official successors, and arrogate their peculiar prerogatives, do not pretend to possess their gifts ; they do not pretend to personal infallibility in teaching, nor do they claim jurisdiction beyond their own dioceses. As no man can be a prophet without the gifts of a prophet, so no man can be an Apostle without the gifts of an Apostle. The office is simply authority to exercise the gifts ; but if the gifts are not possessed what can the office amount to ?

But even if the impossible be admitted ; let it be conceded that the prelates have the power of remitting and retaining sin, as claimed by Romanists, in virtue of their apostleship, how is this power granted to priests who are not Apostles ? It will not do to say that they are the representatives and delegates of the bishop. The bishop is said to have this power because he has received the Holy Ghost. If this means anything, it means that the Holy Spirit dwells in him, and so enlightens his mind and guides his judgment, as to render his decisions in retaining or remitting sin, virtually the decisions of God ; but this divine illumination and guidance can no more be delegated than the knowledge of the lawyer or the skill of the surgeon. How can a prophet delegate his power to foresee the future to another man? It is impossible to believe that God has given men the power of forgiving or retaining sin, unless He has given them the power of infallible judgment; and that such infallibility of judgment belongs to the Romish priesthood, no man can believe.

It has already been urged as valid arguments against the Romish doctrine of purgatory, (1.) That it is destitute of all Scriptural support. (2.) That it is opposed to many of the most clearly revealed and most important doctrines of the Bible. (3.) That the abuses to which it always has led and which are its inevitable consequences, prove that the doctrine cannot be of God. (4.) That the power to forgive sin, in the sense claimed by Romanists, and which is taken for granted in their doctrine of purgatory, finds no support in the words of Christ, as recorded in John xx. 23, and Matt. xvi. 19, which are relied on for that purpose. (5.) The fifth argument against the doctrine is derived from its history, which proves it to have had a pagan origin, and to have been developed by slow degrees into the form in which it is now held by the Church of Rome.

History of the Doctrine.

The details on this subject must be sought in the common books on the history of doctrine. Here only the most meagre outline can be expected. A full exposition on this subject would require first an account of the prevalence of the idea of a purification by fire among the ancients before the coming of Christ, especially among the people of central Asia; secondly, an account of the early appearance of this idea in the first three centuries in the Christian Church, until it reached a definite form in the writings of Augustine; and thirdly, the establishment of the doctrine as an article of faith in the Latin Church, principally through the influence of Gregory the Great.

Fire is the most effectual means of purification. It is almost the only means by which the dross can be separated from the gold. In the Scriptures it is frequently referred to, in illustration of the painful process of the sanctification of the human soul. In Zechariah xiii. 9, it is said, " I will bring the third part through the fire, and will refine them as silver is refined, and will try them as gold is tried: they shall call on my name, and I will hear them : I will say, It is my people ; and they shall say, The LORD is my God." It is in allusion to the same familiar fact, that afflictions are so often compared to a furnace, and the trials of God's people are said to be by fire. " The fire," says the Apostle, "shall try every man's work, of what sort it is." With the ancient Persians fire was sacred. It became an object of worship, as the symbol of the divinity; and elemental fire was even for the soul the great means of purification. In the Zend-avesta, Ormuz is made to say to Zoroaster, " Thine eyes shall certainly see all things live anew. — For the renovated earth shall yield bones and water, blood and plants, hair, fire and life as at the beginning. — The souls will know their bodies. — Behold my father! my mother! my wife! Then will the inhabitants of the universe appear on earth with mankind. Every one will see his good or evil. Then a great separation will occur. Everything corrupt will sink into the abyss. Then too through the fierceness of the fire all mountains shall melt; and through the flowing stream of fire, all men must pass. The good will go through as easily as through flowing milk. The wicked find it real fire; but they must pass through and be purified. Afterward the whole earth shall be renewed." [1]

With the Greek Stoics also, fire was the elementary principle and soul of the world, and they also taught a renovation of the world through fire. With the Stoics, " The universe is one whole, which comprises all things; yet contains a passive principle, matter, τὸ πάσχον, and an active principle, τὸ ποιοῦν, which is reason, or God. The soul of man is part of this divine nature, and will be reabsorbed into it and lose its individual existence. The Deity in action, if we may so speak, is a certain active æther, or fire, possessed of intelligence. This first gave form to the original chaos, and, being an essential part of the universe, sustains it in order. The overruling power, which seems sometimes in idea to have been separated from the Absolute Being, was εἱμαρμένη, fate, or absolute necessity. To this the universe is subject, both in its material and divine nature. Men return to this life totally oblivious of the past, and by the decrees of fate are possessed of a renovated existence, but still in imperfection and subject to sorrow as before." [2]   This is an inchoate form of

[1] Kleuker's *Zendavesta im Kleinem*, 2 Thl. s. 128.

[2] *The Mutual Influence of Christianity and the Stoic School.* By James Henry Bryant, B. D., St. John's College, Cambridge, Incumbent of Astley, Warwickshire. The Hulsean Dissertation for the year 1865. London and Cambridge, 1866, p. 22. Sir Alexander Grant, in his *Ethics of Aristotle*, Essay vi., *The Ancient Stoics* (first an Oxford Essay, 1858), London, 1866, vol. i. p. 246, remarks: "If we cast our eyes on a list of the early Stoics and their native places, we cannot avoid noticing how many of this school appear to have come of an Eastern and often of a Semitic stock." This circumstance in connec-

the pantheism of the present day. The system as stated is not self-consistent ; as it says that the souls of men are to be absorbed into the soul of the world, and yet that they are to return to this life, although oblivious to the past; which amounts to saying that there will be a new generation of men.

The idea of a purification by fire after death became familiar to the Greek mind, and was taken up by Plato, and wrought into his philosophy; he taught that no one could become perfectly happy after death, until he had expiated his sins ; and that if they were too great for expiation, his sufferings would have no end.[1] That this doctrine passed from the Gentiles to the Jews may be inferred not only from the fact already mentioned that Judas Maccabeus sent money to Jerusalem to pay for sacrifices to be offered for the sins of the dead ; but also from the doctrine of the Rabbins, that children, by means of sin offerings, could alleviate the sufferings of their deceased parents.[2] Some of them also taught that all souls, not perfectly holy, must wash themselves in the fire-river of Gehenna; that the just would therein be soon cleansed, but the wicked retained in torment indefinitely.[3] It was in this general form of a purification by fire after death that the doctrine was adopted by some of the fathers. Nothing more than this can be proved from the writings of the first three centuries. Origen taught first that this purification was to take place after the resurrection. " Ego puto," he says, " quod et post resurrectionem ex mortuis indigeamus sacramento eluente nos atque purgante : nemo enim absque sordibus resurgere poterit : nec ullam posse animam reperiri quæ universis statim vitiis careat." [4] And secondly, that in the purifying fire at the end of the world, all souls, and all fallen angels, and Satan himself, will ultimately be purged from sin, and restored to the favour of God. In his comment on Romans viii. 12, he says : " Qui vero verbi Dei et doctrinæ Evangelicæ purificationem spreverit, tristibus et pœnalibus purificationibus semetipsum reservat, ut ignis gehennæ in cruciatibus purget, quem nec apostolica doctrina nec evangelicus sermo purgavit." [5] This doctrine was condemned in the Church ; but, as

tion with affinity in doctrine, goes to show the eastern origin of the Stoic system. It includes the pantheism of the Orientals with some of the elements peculiar to the religion of the Semitic race as we find them in the Bible.

[1] Hœpfner, *De Origine Dogmatis de Purgatorio*, Halle, 1792–98 ; quoted by Flügge, *ut supra*, p. 323.

[2] Eisenmenger, *Endecktes Judenthum*, ii. vi.; Königsberg, 1711, pp. 357, 358.

[3] *Kabbala Denudata*, edit. Frankfort, 1684, vol. ii. part 1, pp. 108, 109, 113.

[4] *Homil. xv. in Luc. Works*, edit. Delarue, Paris, 1740, vol. iii. p. 948, B, a.

[5] *Ibid.* Paris, 1759, vol. iv. p. 640, B, b, c.

Flügge [1] says : " This anathema was the less effective because the
eastern views on this subject differed so much from the western
or Church doctrine.   The former, or Origen's doctrine, contemplated the purification of the greatest sinners and of the devil
himself ; the Latin Church thought only of believers justified by
the blood of Christ.   The one supposed the sinner to purify himself from his desire of evil ; the other, asserted expiation by suffering.   According to the former, the sinner was healed and
strengthened ; according to the latter, divine justice must be satisfied."   It is not to be inferred from this, that the Greek Church
adopted Origen's views as to " the restoration of all things ; "
but it nevertheless maintained until a much later period the views
by which it was distinguished from the Latins on the doctrine of
the future state.

It was, therefore, in the western Church that the development
of the doctrine of purgatory took place.   Augustine first gave it
a definite form, although his views are not always consistently or
confidently expressed.   Thus he says : It is doubtful whether a
certain class of men are to be purified by fire after death, so as to
be prepared to enter heaven ; " utrum ita sit," he says, " quæri
potest : et aut inveniri, aut latere, nonnullos fideles per ignem
quemdam purgatorium ; quanto magis minusve bona pereuntia
dilexerunt, tanto tardius citiusque salvari." [2]   In other places,
however, he teaches the two essential points in the doctrine of
purgatory, first, that the souls of a certain class of men who are
ultimately saved, suffer after death ; and secondly, that they are
aided through the eucharist, and the alms and prayers of the
faithful.[3]

It was, however, Gregory the Great who consolidated the
vague and conflicting views circulating through the Church, and
brought the doctrine into such a shape and into such connection
with the discipline of the Church, as to render it the effective
engine for government and income, which it has ever since remained.   From this time onward through all the Middle Ages,
purgatory became one of the prominent and constantly reiterated
topics of public instruction.   It took firm hold of the popular
mind.   The clergy from the highest to the lowest, and the different orders of monks vied with each other in their zeal in its incul-
cation ; and in the marvels which they related of spiritual appa-

---

[1] *Ut supra*, p. 327.

[2] *Enchiridion de Fide, Spe et Charitate*, 69 ; *Works*, Paris, 1837, vol. vi. p. 382, b.

[3] *De Civitate Dei*, xxi. xiii.; *Ibid.* vol. vii. p. 1015, d.   *Enchiridion de Fide, Spe et Charitate*, 110 ; *Ibid.* vol. vi. p. 403, b, c.

ritions, in support of the doctrine. They contended fiercely for the honour of superior power of redeeming souls from purgatorial pains. The Franciscans claimed that the head of their order descended annually into purgatory, and delivered all the brotherhood who were there detained. The Carmelites asserted that the Virgin Mary had promised that no one who died with the Carmelite scapulary upon their shoulders, should ever be lost.[1] The chisel and pencil of the artist were employed in depicting the horrors of purgatory, as a means of impressing the public mind. No class escaped the contagion of belief; the learned as well as the ignorant; the high and the low; the soldier and the recluse; the skeptic and the believer were alike enslaved.[2] From this slavery the Bible, not the progress of science, has delivered all Protestants.

[1] Mosheim, *Historia Ecclesiæ*, Sæculum XIII. pars ii. 2, § 29; edit. Helmstadt, 1764, p. 454.

[2] All experience proves that infidelity is no protection against superstition. If men will not believe the rational and true, they will believe the absurd and the false. When the writer was returning from Europe, he had as a fellow passenger a distinguished French diplomatist. One evening when admiring the moon shining in its brightness, that gentleman adverted to the idea of creation, and pronounced it absurd, avowing himself an atheist. But he added immediately, "Don't misunderstand me. I am a good Catholic, and mean to die in the faith of the Catholic Church. You Protestants are all wrong. You tell every man to think for himself. Ho! then I'll think what I please. I want a religion which tells me I sha'n't think; only submit. Well! I mean to submit, and be buried in consecrated ground."

CHAPTER II.

THE RESURRECTION.

§ 1. *The Scriptural Doctrine.*

BY the resurrection is not meant the continued existence of the soul after death. The fact that the Sadducees in the time of Christ, against whom most of the arguments found in the New Testament in favour of the doctrine of the resurrection were directed, denied not only that doctrine, but also that of the continued existence of the soul after death, sufficiently accounts for the sacred writings combining the two subjects. Thus our Lord, in reasoning with the Sadducees, said : " As touching the dead, that they rise; have ye not read in the book of Moses, how in the bush God spake unto him, saying, I am the God of Abraham, and the God of Isaac, and the God of Jacob ? He is not the God of the dead, but the God of the living." (Mark xii. 26.) All that this passage directly proves is that the dead continue alive after the dissolution of the body. But as this is Christ's answer to a question concerning the resurrection, it has been inferred that the resurrection means nothing more than that the soul does not die with the body, but rises to a new and higher life. Thus also the Apostle in the elaborate argument contained in 1 Corinthians xv. evidently regards the denial of the resurrection as tantamount with the denial of the future life of the soul. Hence many maintain that the only resurrection of which the Bible speaks is the resurrection of the soul when the body dies. The first position, therefore, to be defended, in stating the Scriptural doctrine on this subject is, that our bodies are the subjects of the resurrection spoken of in the Scriptures.

The Bodies of Men are to rise again.

This is denied, first, by those who take the word resurrection in a figurative sense, expressing the rising of the soul from spiritual death to spiritual life. At the grave of Lazarus Martha said to our Lord, " I know that he shall rise again in the resurrection at the last day." To which our Lord, according to Mr. Alger, replies substantially, " You suppose that in the last day the Messiah will restore the dead to live again upon the earth. I am the Messiah, and the last days have therefore arrived. I am commissioned by the Father to bestow eternal life upon all who believe on me ; but not in the manner you have anticipated. The true resurrection is not calling the body from the tomb, but opening the fountains of eternal life in the soul. I am come to open the spiritual world to your faith. He that believeth in me and keepeth my commandments, has passed from death unto life — become conscious that though seemingly he passes into the grave, yet really he shall live with God forever. The true resurrection is, to come into the experience of the truth that, ' God is not the God of the dead but of the living ; for all live unto Him.' Over the soul that is filled with such an experience, death has no power. Verily, I say unto you, the hour is coming, and now is, when the dead, the ignorant and guilty, buried in trespasses and sins, shall lay hold of the life thus offered, and be blessed." [1]

Secondly, the resurrection of the body is denied by those who, with the Swedenborgians, hold that man, in this life, has two bodies, an external and internal, a material and psychical.[2] The former dies and is deposited in the grave, and there remains never to rise again. The other does not die, but in union with the soul passes into another state of existence. The only resurrection, therefore, which is ever to occur, takes place at the moment of death.

Thirdly, it is denied by those who assume that the soul as pure spirit, cannot be individualized or localized ; that it cannot have any relation to space, or act or be acted upon, without a corporeity of some kind ; and who, therefore, assume that it must be furnished with a new, more refined, ethereal body, as soon as its earthly tabernacle is laid aside. The resurrection body is according to this view also furnished at the moment of death.

That the Scriptures, however, teach a literal resurrection of the body is proved, (1.) From the meaning of the word. Resurrection signifies a rising again ; a rising of that which was buried ; or a restoration of life to that which was dead. But the soul, according to the Scriptures, does not die when the body is dissolved. It, therefore, cannot be the subject of a resurrection,

---

[1] Alger, *ut supra*, p. 324.
[2] Bonnet, *Palingénésie Philosophique. Essai Analytique sur l'Ame*, chap. xxiv., part xxii., Neufchatel, 1783, vol. xiv. p. 205 ff., especially p. 230 ff., and vol. xvi. p. 481 ff. Lange, *Beiträge zu der Lehre von den letzten Dingen*, Meurs, 1841. Lange's doctrine, however, as will appear in the sequel, is not that of Swedenborg.

except in the sense antithetical to spiritual death, which is not now in question. The same is true of the psychical body, if there be such a thing. It does not die, and, therefore, cannot rise again. The same may also be said of a new body furnished the soul when its earthly house of this tabernacle is dissolved.

(2.) Those who are in the dust of the earth ; those "that are in the graves " are said to rise. But it is only of the body that it can be said, it is in the grave ; and, therefore, it is of the body the resurrection spoken of, must be understood.

(3.) It is "our mortal bodies" which are to rise again. This form of expression is decisive of the Apostle's meaning. "He that raised Christ from the dead shall also quicken your mortal bodies, by his Spirit that dwelleth in you." (Rom. viii. 11.) It is "our vile body" which is to be fashioned like unto Christ's glorious body. (Phil. iii. 21.)

(4.) This also is clearly the doctrine taught in the fifteenth chapter of First Corinthians. There were certain errorists in Corinth who denied the fact and the desirableness of the resurrection of believers. Paul's argument is directed to both those points. As to the fact that the dead can rise, he refers to what no Christian could deny, the rising of Christ from the dead. This, as a historical fact, he supports by historical evidence. He then shows that the denial of the resurrection of Christ, is the denial of the whole Gospel, which rests on that fact. " If Christ be not risen, then is our preaching vain, and your faith is also vain." But if Christ rose from the dead, all his people must. Christ rose as the first fruits of them that sleep. There is in Paul's view, the same divinely appointed, and therefore necessary connection between the resurrection of Christ and that of his people, as between the death of Adam and that of his descendants. As surely as all in Adam die, so surely shall all in Christ be made alive. And finally, on this point, the Apostle condescends to argue from the faith and practice of the Church. What is the use, he asks, of being baptized for the dead, if the dead rise not? The whole daily life of the Christian is founded, he says, on the hope of the resurrection ; not of the continued existence of the soul merely, but of the glorious existence of the whole man, soul and body, with Christ in heaven. As to the second point, the desirableness of the resurrection of the body, he shows that all objections on this score are founded on the assumption that the future is to be like the present body. He says that the man who makes that objection is a fool. The two are no more alike than a seed and a flower, a clod of earth and a star, the earthly and the heavenly. " It [the body of course] is sown in corruption, it is raised in incorruption : it is sown in dishonour, it is raised in glory : it is sown in weakness, it is raised in power : it is sown a natural body, it is raised a spiritual body." This whole discourse, therefore, is about the body. To the objection that our present bodies are not adapted to our future state of existence, he answers, Granted ; it is true that flesh and blood cannot inherit the kingdom of God ; this corruptible must put on incorruption, and this mortal must put on immortality. It would seem that the Apostle in this chapter must have had in his eye a host of writers in our day who make themselves merry with the doctrine of the resurrection, on much the same grounds as those relied upon by the errorists of Corinth, whose fragments he scattered to the winds eighteen centuries ago.

(5.) Another argument on this subject is drawn from the analogy constantly presented, between the resurrection of Christ and that of his people. The sacred writers, as we have seen, argue the possibility and the certainty of the resurrection of our bodies, from the fact of Christ's resurrection ; and the nature of our future bodies from the nature of his body in heaven. There would be no force in this argument if the body were not the thing which is to rise again.

(6.) Finally, as Paul argued from the faith of the Church, we cannot err in following his example. The Bible is a plain book, and the whole Christian world, in all ages, has understood it to teach, not this or that, but the literal rising from the dead of the body deposited in the grave. All Christians of every denomination are taught to say, I believe in " The forgiveness of sins ; The resurrection of the body ; And the life everlasting."

The Identity of the Future with our Present Body.

There are two distinct questions to be here considered. First, Do the Scriptures teach that the resurrection body is to be the same as that deposited in the grave ? Second, Wherein does that sameness or identity consist ? The first of these questions we may be able to answer with confidence ; the second we may not be able to answer at all.

The arguments to prove that we are hereafter to have the same bodies that we have in the present life, are substantially the same as those already adduced. Indeed, identity is involved in the very idea of a resurrection ; for resurrection is a living again of that which was dead ; not of something of the same nature, but of the very thing itself. And all the passages already quoted as proving the resurrection of the body, assume or declare that it is the same body that rises. It is our present " mortal bodies ; " " our vile body ; " it is " this corruptible," " this mortal ; " it is that which is sown, of which the resurrection and transformation is predicted and promised. Our resurrection is to be analogous to that of Christ ; but in his case there can be no doubt that the very body which hung upon the cross, and which laid in the tomb, rose again from the dead. Otherwise it would have been no resurrection. This identity was the very thing Christ was anxious to prove to his doubting disciples. He showed them his pierced hands and feet, and his perforated side. On this subject, however, there is little difference of opinion. Wherever the resurrection of the body is an article of faith the identity of the present and future body has been admitted. The usual form of Christian burial, in the case of the faithful, has ever been, " We commit this body to the grave in the sure hope of a blessed resurrection."

Wherein does this Identity consist?

It is obvious that identity in different cases depends on very different conditions. First, in the case of unorganized matter, as a clod of earth or a stone, the identity depends on the continuity of substance and of form. If the stone be reduced to powder and scattered abroad, the same substance continues, but not in the same combination ; and therefore the identity is gone. In what sense is water in a goblet the same from hour to hour, or from day to day ? It is the same substance resulting from the combination of oxygen and hydrogen, and it is the same portion of that substance. If that goblet be emptied into the ocean, what becomes of the identity of the water which it contained ? If you separate the water into its constituent gases, the elementary substances continue, but they are no longer water. You may change its state without destroying its identity. If frozen into ice and again thawed, it is the same water. If evaporated into steam, and then condensed, it is the same water still. This sameness, of which continuance of the same substance is the essential element, is the lowest form of identity. In the Church it has often been assumed that sameness of substance is essential to the identity between our present and future bodies. This idea has been pressed sometimes to the utmost extreme. Augustine seems to have thought that all the matter which at any period entered into the organism of our present bodies, would in some way be restored in the resurrection body.   Every man's body, however dispersed here, shall be restored perfect in the resurrection.   Every body shall be complete in quantity and quality.   As many hairs as have been shaved off, or nails cut, shall not return in such vast quantities as to deform their original places ; but neither shall they perish ; they shall return into, the body into that substance from which they grew.[1]   Thomas Aquinas was more moderate.   He taught that only those particles which entered into the composition of the body at death, would enter into the composition of the resurrection body.   This idea seems to have entered into the theology of Romanists, as some at least of the theologians of the Church of Rome labour to remove the objection to this view of the subject derived from the fact that the particles of the human body after death are not only dispersed far and wide and mingled with the dust of the earth, but also enter into the composition of the bodies of plants, of animals, and of men.   To this Perrone answers, " Difficile Deo non est moleculas omnes ad corpus aliquod spectantes, etiam post innumeros transitus ex uno in aliud colligere.   Hæc mutatio seu transitus accidentalis est, minime vere essentialis, ut ex physiologia ac zoobiologia constat universa." [2]   It is true, as our Lord teaches us : " With God all things are possible ; " and if sameness of substance be essential to that identity between our present and future bodies, which the Bible asserts, then we should have to submit to these difficulties, satisfied that it is within the power of omniscient omnipotence to do whatever God has promised to effect.

Others assume that it is not necessary to the identity contended for that all the particles of the body at death should be included in the resurrection body.   It is enough that the new body should be formed exclusively out of particles belonging to the present body.   But as the body after the resurrection is to be refined and ethereal, a tenth, a hundredth, or a ten thousandth portion of those particles would suffice.   It would take very little of gross matter to make a body of light.   Tertullian thought that God had rendered the teeth indestructible in order to furnish material for the future body.   Many others also suppose that there is somewhere an indestructible germ in our present body, which is to be developed into the body of the future.[3]

[1] De Civitate Dei, xxii., xix., xx.; Works, Paris, 1838, vol. vii. pp. 1085–1089.
[2] Prælectiones, edit. Paris, 1861, vol. i. p. 503.
[3] See Essay on the Identity and General Resurrection of the Human Body, by Samuel Drew, chapter vi. section 7, Brooklyn, 1811, p. 315 ff.

Secondly, in works of art sameness of substance holds a very subordinate part. The Apollo Belvidere once lay dormant in a block of marble. The central portion of that block containing every particle of matter in the statue was not the Apollo of the artist. Could every particle clipped off, be restored, the substance would remain, but the statue would be gone. Here form, expression, the informing idea are the main constituents of identity. If a penitentiary should be taken down, and the materials be employed in the construction of a cathedral, the substance would be the same, but not the building. When you look into a mirror the image reflected remains the same, but not the substance; for that is changed with every new reflection. And if it were possible, or proved, that in like manner the Madonna del Sixti of Raphael had a thousand times changed its substance, it would remain the same picture still. The soul here informs the body. The character is more or less visibly impressed upon the face. We know the former by looking at the latter. If this be so, if the soul have power thus to illuminate and render intelligent the gross material of our present frames, why may it not hereafter render its ethereal vestment so expressive of itself as to be at once recognized by all to whom it was ever known. Thus we may at once recognize Isaiah, Paul, and John. It is not said that this will be so; that herein lies the identity of their heavenly and earthly bodies; but should it prove to be true, we should not stop to inquire or to care how many particles of the one enter into the composition of the other.

Thirdly, identity in living organisms is something still higher, and more inscrutable than in works of art. The acorn and the oak are the same; but in what sense? Not in substance, not in form. The infant and the man are the same, through all the stages of life; boyhood, manhood, and old age; the substance of the body, however, is in a state of perpetual change. It is said this change is complete once every seven years. Hence if a man live to be seventy years old, the substance of his body has, during that period, been entirely changed ten times. Here, then, is an identity independent of sameness of substance. Our future bodies, therefore, may be the same as those we now have, although not a particle that was in the one should be in the other.

The object of these remarks on the different kinds of identity, is not to explain anything. It is not intended to teach wherein the identity of the earthly and heavenly consists; whether it be an identity of substance; or of expression and idea, as in works of art; or of the uninterrupted continuity of the same vital force as in the plant and animal through their whole progress of growth and decay ; or whether it is a sameness which includes all these ; or something different from them all.   Nothing is affirmed. The subject is left where the Bible leaves it.   The object aimed at is twofold ; first, to show that it is perfectly rational for a man to assert the identity between our present and our future bodies, although he is forced to admit that he does not know wherein that identity is to consist.   This is no more than what all men have to admit concerning the continued sameness of our present bodies. And, secondly, to stop the mouths of gainsayers.   They ridicule the idea of a resurrection of the body ; asking if the infant is to rise as an infant ; the old man, wrinkled and decrepid ; the maimed as maimed ; the obese with their cumbrous load ; and by such questions think they have refuted a Scripture doctrine.   The Bible teaches no such absurdities ; and no Church goes beyond the Scriptures in asserting two things, namely : that the body is to rise, and that it is to be the same after the resurrection that it was before ; but neither the Bible nor the Church determines wherein that sameness is to consist.

With regard to our present bodies, the fact of their continued identity is not denied.   According to one view the principle of this identity is in the body and perishes, or, ceases, with it.   According to another, although in the body, it does not perish with it, but remains united to the soul, and under appropriate circumstances fashions for itself a new body.   According to others, this vital principle is in the soul itself.   Agassiz, as a zoölogist, teaches that with every living germ there is an immaterial principle by which one species is distinguished from another, and which determines that the germ of a fish develops into a fish ; and that of a bird, into a bird, although the two germs are exactly the same ($i.$ $e.$, alike) in substance and structure.   When the individual dies, this immaterial principle ceases to exist.   This is Agassiz's doctrine.   Dr. Julius Müller[1] thinks that this vital organizing force continues in union with the soul, but is not operative between death and the resurrection.   He says, " it is not the $\sigma \acute{a} \rho \xi$, the mass of earthly material, ... but the $\sigma \hat{\omega} \mu a$, the organic whole, to which the Scriptures promise a resurrection. . . . . The organism, as the living form which appropriates matter to itself, is the true body, which in its glorification becomes the $\sigma \hat{\omega} \mu a$ $\pi \nu \epsilon \upsilon \mu a \tau \iota \kappa \acute{o} \nu$." But he understands the Apostle in 2 Corinthians v. 4, as clearly teaching that the soul during the interval between death and the

[1] *Studien und Kritiken*, 1835, pp. 777, 785.

resurrection remains unclothed. Dr. Lange, whose imagination often dominates him, teaches that the soul was created to be incarnate; and therefore was endowed with forces and talents to that end. In virtue of its nature, it as certainly gathers from surrounding matter the materials for a body, as a seed gathers from the earth and air the matter suited to its necessities. He assumes, therefore, that there is in the soul " a law or force, which secures its forming for itself a body suited to its necessities and sphere; or more properly," he adds, " the organic identity " may be characterized as the " Schema des Leibes," which is included in the soul, or, as the " Incarnationstrieb des Geistes ; " a "nisus formativus " which belongs to the human soul.[1] The soul while on earth forms for itself a body out of earthly materials ; when it leaves the earth it fashions a habitation for itself out of the materials to be found in the higher sphere to which it is translated ; and at the end of the world, when the grand palingenesia is to occur, the souls of men, according to their nature, will fashion bodies for themselves out of the elements of the dissolving universe. " The righteous will clothe themselves with the refined elements of the renovated earth; they shall shine as the sun. The wicked shall be clothed with the refuse of the earth; they shall awake to shame and everlasting contempt."[2]

Leaving out of view what is fanciful in this representation, it may be readily admitted by those who adhere to the generally received doctrine that man consists of soul and body (and not of spirit, soul, and body), that the soul, besides its rational, voluntary, and moral faculties, has in it what may be called a principle of animal life. That is, that it has not only faculties which fit it for the higher exercises of a rational creature capable of fellowship with God, but also faculties which fit it for living in organic union with a material body. It may also be admitted that the soul, in this aspect, is the animating principle of the body, that by which all its functions are carried on. And it may further be admitted that the soul, in this aspect, is that which gives identity to the human body through all the changes of substance to which it is here subjected. And finally it may be admitted, such being the case, that the body which the soul is to have at the resurrection, is as really and truly identical with that which it had on earth, as the body of the man of mature life is the same which he had when he was an infant. All this may pass for what it is worth. What stands sure is what the Bible

[1] *Beiträge zu der Lehre von den Letzten Dingen*, Meurs, 1841, p. 235. [2] *Ibid.* p. 251.

teaches, that our heavenly bodies are in some high, true, and real sense, to be the same as those which we now have.

Nature of the Resurrection Body.

It is obvious that this is a subject of which we can know nothing, except from divine revelation. We are of necessity as profoundly ignorant of this matter, as of the nature of the inhabitants of the planets or of the sun. The speculations of men concerning the nature of the future body have been numerous; some merely fanciful, others, revolting.

There are two negative statements in the Bible on this subject, which imply a great deal. One is the declaration of Christ, That in the resurrection men neither marry nor are given in marriage, but are as the angels of God. The other is the words of Paul in 1 Corinthians xv. 50, " Flesh and blood cannot inherit the kingdom of God." There seem to be plainly three things implied or asserted in these passages. (1.) That the bodies of men must be specially suited to the state of existence in which they are to live and act. (2.) That our present bodies, that is, our bodies as now organized, consisting as they do of flesh and blood, are not adapted to our future state of being. And (3.) That everything in the organization or constitution of our bodies designed to meet our present necessities, will cease with the life that now is. Nothing of that kind will belong to the resurrection body. If blood be no longer our life, we shall have no need of organs of respiration and nutrition. So long as we are ignorant of the conditions of existence which await us after the resurrection, it is vain to speculate on the constitution of our future bodies. It is enough to know that the glorified people of God will not be cumbered with useless organs, or trammeled by the limitations which are imposed by our present state of existence.

The following particulars, however, may be inferred with more or less confidence from what the Bible has revealed on this subject, —

1. That our bodies after the resurrection will retain the human form. God, we are told, gave to all his creatures on earth each its own body adapted to its nature, and necessary to attain the end of its creation. Any essential change in the nature of the body would involve a corresponding change in its internal constitution. A bee in the form of a horse would cease to be a bee; and a man in any other than a human form, would cease to be a man. His body is an essential element in his constitution. Ev-

ery intimation given in Scripture on this subject, tends to sustain this conclusion. Every time Christ appeared to his disciples not only before, but also after his ascension, as to Stephen, Paul, and John, it was in human form. Origen conceited that, because the circle is the most perfect figure, the future body will be globular. But a creature in that form would not be recognized either in earth or heaven as a man.

2. It is probable that the future body will not only retain the human form, but that it will also be a glorified likeness of what it was on earth. We know that every man has here his individual character, — peculiarities mental and emotional which distinguish him from every other man. We know that his body by its expression, air, and carriage more or less clearly reveals his character. This revelation of the inward by the outward will probably be far more exact and informing in heaven than it can be here on earth. How should we know Peter or John in heaven, if there were not something in their appearance and bearing corresponding to the image of themselves impressed by their writings on the minds of all their readers ?

3. This leads to the further remark that we shall not only recognize our friends in heaven, but also know, without introduction, prophets, apostles, confessors, and martyrs, of whom we have read or heard while here on earth. (*a.*) This is altogether probable from the nature of the case. If the future body is to be the same with the present, why should not that sameness, whatever else it may include, include a certain sameness of appearance. (*b.*) When Moses and Elias appeared on the mount with Christ, they were at once known by the disciples. Their appearance corresponded so exactly with the conceptions formed from the Old Testament account of their character and conduct, that no doubt was entertained on the subject. (*c.*) It is said that we are to sit down with Abraham, Isaac, and Jacob in the kingdom of heaven. This implies that Abraham, Isaac, and Jacob will be known; and if they are known surely others will be known also. (*d.*) It is promised that our cup of happiness will then be full; but it could not be full, unless we met in heaven those whom we loved on earth. Man is a social being with a soul full of social affections, and as he is to be a man in heaven, is it not likely that he will retain all his social affections there ? God would hardly have put this pure yearning in the hearts of his people if it were never to be gratified. David weeping over his dead son, said, " I shall go to him, but he shall not

return to me." And this has been the language of every be-
reaved heart from that day to this. (*e.*) The Bible clearly teaches
that man is to retain all his faculties in the future life. One of
the most important of those faculties is memory. If this were
not retained there would be a chasm in our existence. The past
for us would cease to exist. We could hardly, if at all, be conscious of our identity. We should enter heaven, as creatures
newly created, who had no history. Then all the songs of heaven
would cease. There could be no thanksgiving for redemption ; no
recognition of all God's dealings with us in this world. Memory,
however, is not only to continue, but will doubtless with all our
faculties be greatly exalted, so that the records of the past may
be as legible to us as the events of the present. If this be so, if
men are to retain in heaven the knowledge of their earthly life ;
this of course involves the recollection of all social relations, of
all the ties of respect, love, and gratitude which bind men in the
family and in society. (*f.*) The doctrine that in a future life we
shall recognize those whom we knew and loved on earth, has entered into the faith of all mankind. It is taken for granted in
the Bible, both in the Old Testament and in the New. The patriarchs always spoke of going to their fathers when they died.
The Apostle exhorts believers not to mourn for the departed as
those who have no hope ; giving them the assurance that they
shall be reunited with all those who die in the Lord.

4. We know certainly that the future bodies of believers are
to be, — (*a.*) Incorruptible ; not merely destined never to decay,
but not susceptible of corruption. By the certain action of physical laws, our present body, as soon as deserted by the soul, is
reduced to a mass of corruption, so revolting that we hasten to
bury our dead out of our sight. The future body will be liable
to no such change; neither, as we learn from Scripture, will it be
subject to those diseases and accidents which so often mar the
beauty or destroy the energy of the bodies in which we now
dwell. Being unsusceptible of decay, they will be incapable of,
or at least, carefully preserved from, suffering, by Him who has
promised to wash all tears from our eyes.

(*b.*) The future body is to be immortal. This is something different from, something higher than incorruptible ; the latter is
negative, the other positive ; the one implies immunity from
decay ; the other not merely immunity from death, but perpetuity of life. There is to be no decrepitude of age ; no decay of
the faculties ; no loss of vigour ; but immortal youth.

(*c.*) The present body is sown in weakness, it will be raised in power. We know very well how weak we now are, how little we can effect; how few are our senses; how limited their range; but we do not yet know in what ways, or in what measure our power is to be increased. It is probable that however high may be our expectations on this subject, they will fall short of the reality; for it doth not yet appear, it is not revealed in experience or in hope, what we shall be. We may have new senses, new and greatly exalted capabilities of taking cognizance of external things, of apprehending their nature and of deriving knowledge and enjoyment from their wonders and their beauties. Instead of the slow and wearisome means of locomotion to which we are now confined, we may be able hereafter to pass with the velocity of light or of thought itself from one part of the universe to another. Our power of vision, instead of being confined to the range of a few hundred yards, may far exceed that of the most powerful telescope. These expectations cannot be extravagant, for we are assured that eye hath not seen, nor ear heard, neither has it entered into the heart of man to conceive the things which God hath prepared for them that love Him.

(*d.*) The body is sown in dishonour, it shall be raised in glory. Glory is that which excites wonder, admiration, and delight. The bodies of the saints are to be fashioned like unto Christ's glorious body. We shall be like Him when we see Him as He is. More than this cannot be said; what it means we know not now, but we shall know hereafter. We already know that when the body of Christ was transfigured upon the mount, the Apostles fainted and became as dead men in its presence; and we know that when He shall come again the second time unto salvation, the heavens and the earth shall flee away at the sight of his glory. Let it suffice us to know that as we have borne the image of the earthly, we shall also bear the image of the heavenly. Well might the Apostle exhort believers not to mourn for the pious dead, whom they are to see again, arrayed in a beauty and glory of which we can now have no conception.

(*e.*) It is sown a natural body, it is raised a spiritual body. When words are used thus antithetically, the meaning of the one enables us to determine the meaning of the other. We can, therefore, in this case learn what the word " spiritual " means, from what we know of the meaning of the word "natural." The word ψυχικόν, translated "natural," as every one knows, is derived from ψυχή, which means sometimes the life; sometimes the

principle of animal ·life which men have in common with the
brutes; and sometimes the soul in the ordinary and comprehensive sense of the term; the rational and immortal principle of our
nature; that in which our personality resides; so that to say
" My soul rejoices," or, " My soul is exceeding sorrowful," is
equivalent to saying, " I rejoice," or, " I am sorrowful." Such
being the signification of the ψυχή, it is plain that σῶμα ψυχικόν,
the psychical, or natural, body, cannot by possibility mean a body
made out of the ψυχή. In like manner it is no less plain that
σῶμα πνευματικόν cannot by possibility mean a body made of spirit.
That indeed would be as much a contradiction in terms, as to
speak of a spirit made out of matter. Again, we know that man
has an animal as well as a rational nature; that is, his soul is endowed not only with reason and conscience, but also with sensi-
bilities, or faculties which enable it to take cognizance of the appetites of the body, as hunger and thirst, and of its sensations of
pleasure and pain. These appetites and sensations are states of
consciousness of the soul. The σῶμα ψυχικόν, or natural body,
therefore, is a body adapted to the soul in this aspect of its nature; and the σῶμα πνευματικόν, or spiritual body, is a body adapted
to the higher attributes of the soul. We know from experience
what the former is; it is an earthly body, made of the dust of
the earth. The chemist can analyze it, and reduce it to its constituents of ammonia, hydrogen, carbon, etc.; and in the grave
it soon becomes undistinguishable from other portions of the
earth's surface. It is a body which, while living, has constant
need of being repaired; it must be sustained by the oxygen of
the air, and by the chemical elements of its food. It soon grows
weary, and must be refreshed by rest and sleep. In a little more
than seventy years, it is worn out, and drops into the grave. The
reverse of this is true of the spiritual body; it has no such necessities, and is not subject to such weariness and decay. It is no
doubt involved in the fact, that while our present bodies are
adapted to the lower faculties of our nature, and the spiritual
body to our higher faculties, that the latter must be more refined,
ætherial, and, as Paul says, heavenly, than the other. Even now
the soul, in one sense, pervades the body. It is in every part of
it; it is sensible of all its changes of state; it gives to it a look
and carriage which reveal man as the lord of this world. To a
far greater degree may the soul permeate the refined and glorified
body which it is to receive at the resurrection of the just; and
thus render it to a degree now incomprehensible, in its very na-

ture spiritual.   If the face of man formed out of the dust of the
earth often beams with intelligence and glows with elevated emotions, what may be expected of a countenance made like unto
that of the Son of God.

If then our future bodies are to retain the human form ; to be
easily distinguished by those who knew and loved us on earth ; if
they are to be endued with an unknown power ; if they are to
be incorruptible, immortal, and spiritual ; if we are to bear the
image of the heavenly, we may well bow down with humble and
joyful hearts and receive the exhortation of the Apostle : " Therefore, my beloved brethren, be ye steadfast, unmovable, always
abounding in the work of the Lord, forasmuch as ye know that
your labour is not in vain in the Lord."

§ 2. *History of the Doctrine.*

The doctrine of the resurrection of the body is not exclusively
a doctrine of the Bible.   It is found, in different forms, in many of
the ancient religions of the world.   This is the more remarkable
as it is in itself so improbable, and so much out of the analogy
of nature.   One generation of plants and animals succeeds another in uninterrupted succession ; but the same individuals never
reappear.   The case is the more remarkable when we consider
the difficulties with which the doctrine is beset ; difficulties so
great that it is rejected and even ridiculed by all in this generation who do not recognize the sacred Scriptures as an authority
from which they dare not dissent.   When such doctrines are
found not only in the Bible but also in the religions of heathen
nations it may be assumed that the Hebrews borrowed them
from their heathen neighbours.   This is the hypothesis adopted
generally by rationalists.   They urge in its support that the doctrine of Satan, of the resurrection of the body, and of the destruction and renovation of the earth, do not appear in those
portions of the Scriptures which were written before the Babylonish captivity.   To carry out this argument they refer Job, Daniel, and a large portion of Isaiah to a period subsequent to the
exile, contrary to evidence both external and internal in favour of
the greater antiquity of those books.   Even if it be conceded
that the doctrines do not appear distinctly in any but the later
writings of the Old Testament, that would not justify the assumption of their heathen origin, provided that their genesis can
be traced in the earlier books of Scripture.   Nothing is more obvious, or more generally admitted than the progressive character

of the divine revelations.   Doctrines at first obscurely intimated, are gradually developed.   This is the case with the doctrines of the Trinity, of the personality of the Holy Spirit, of the divinity of Christ, of the nature of his redemption, of the future state ; and, as might be expected, of the resurrection of the dead.   It is just as unreasonable and as unhistorical to say that the Church received the doctrine of the resurrection of the body from the heathen, as that it received from Plato the doctrine of the Trinity. There is another consideration on this subject, which for the Christian is decisive.   The doctrines which in the New Testa- ment are declared to be part of the revelation of God, are thereby declared not to be of heathen origin.   The heathen may have held them, as they hold the doctrine of the existence of God and of the immortality of man ; that does not prove that such doc- trines have only a human origin and human authority.

These things being premised, it is admitted as a remarkable fact that belief in the resurrection of the body did prevail among the ancients prior to the advent of Christ.   Reference is some- times made to the Brahminic doctrine of the constant succession of cycles of countless ages in the history of the universe, one cycle being a reproduction or renewal of another, as having an analogy to the Christian doctrine of the resurrection.   " The first appear- ance of this notion of a bodily restoration," says Mr. Alger,[1] " which occurs in the history of opinions, is among the ancient Hindus.   With them it appears as a part of a vast conception, embracing the whole universe in an endless series of total growths, decays, and exact restorations.   In the beginning the Supreme Being is one and alone.   He thinks to himself ' I will become many ' [This is a figure of speech ; for according to the Hindu sys- tem the Supreme Being, the Absolute, cannot think].   Straight- way the multiform creation germinates forth, and all beings live. Then for an inconceivable period — a length of time commensu- rate with the existence of Brahma, the Demiurgus [This again is a mixture of ideas, for Brahma of the Hindus does not corre- spond with the Demiurgus of the Greeks] — the successive gen- erations flourish and sink.   At the end of this period all forms of matter, all creatures, sages, and gods, fall back into the Uni- versal Source whence they arose.   Again the Supreme Being is one and alone.   After an interval the same causes produce the same effects, and all things recur exactly as they were before." [2]

[1] Alger, *ut supra,* p. 488.
[2] Wilson, *Lectures on the Religion of the Hindus,* London, 1862, vol. ii. pp. 91, 95, 100- 103.

According to the Hindu system men have not to wait for the conclusion of one of these great cycles to be absorbed in the Supreme Being. By a life strictly conformed to prescribed rules, and by a process of complete self-abnegation, they attain a state in which they are lost in the Infinite as drops of rain in the ocean. As individuals they can never be reproduced, any more than the drops of rain can be recovered from the ocean. The ocean, by evaporation may produce other clouds which shall fall in other drops of rain; but this is not a reproduction of those which fell a thousand years ago. There is therefore no analogy between this theory and the Christian doctrine of the resurrection.

"The same general conception," continues Mr. Alger,[1] "in a modified form was held by the Stoics of later Greece, who doubtless borrowed it from the East, and who carried it out in greater detail. 'God is an artistic fire, out of which the cosmopœia issues.' This fire proceeds in a certain fixed course, in obedience to a fixed law, passing through certain intermediate gradations, and established periods, until it returns into itself and closes with a universal conflagration. . . . . The Stoics supposed each succeeding formation to be perfectly like the preceding. Every particular that happens now, has happened exactly so a thousand times before, and will happen a thousand times again. This view they connected with astronomical calculations making the burning and recreating of the world coincide with the same position of the stars as that at which it previously occurred. This they called the restoration of all things. The idea of these enormous revolving identical periods — Day of Brahm, Cycle of the Stoics, or Great Year of Plato — is a physical fatalism, effecting a universal resurrection of the past, by reproducing it over and over forever." [2]

In the first volume of this work the attempt was made to show that the Brahminical and several Grecian systems of philosophy, were only different modifications of the pantheistic theory of the Infinite by fixed and necessary laws manifesting itself in the finite in all its endless diversities of forms. This endless succession of individuals, however, has no affinity with the Bible doctrine of the resurrection of the dead. The flora and fauna of this are not a resurrection of the plants and animals of the geologic periods.

In the religion of Zoroaster there is a far nearer approach to the doctrines of the Bible.[3] As the Scriptures teach that God at

[1] Alger, *ut supra*, p. 489.

[2] Ritter's *Geschichte d. Philosophie d. alt. Zeit.*, 3ter Th. xi. 4; Hamburg, 1831, p. 582.

[3] See *Ten Great Religions: an Essay in Comparative Theology.* By James Freeman Clarke. Boston, 1872, ch. v., specially p. 200.

first created all things good, and made man after his own image, and placed him upon probation in Eden ; so Zoroaster taught that Ormuzd created all things good, and that all were sinless and happy, and fitted for immortality. And as the Bible teaches that through the seduction of Satan man fell from his original state, and became the subject of sin, misery, and death ; so in the religion of the ancient Persians it is taught, that Ahriman, the personal principle of evil, co-eternal with Ormuzd the principle of good, effected the ruin of man for this world and the next. Such was the origin of evil ; such was the beginning of the conflict between good and evil, of which our earth has been the theatre. Both systems teach the ultimate triumph of the good, and the redemption of man ; both teach a future state, the resurrection of the body, and the renewal of the earth, or, that there are to be a new heaven and a new earth. It is certain from the teachings of the New Testament that the Hebrews did not derive these doctrines from the Persians; it is, therefore, in the highest degree probable that the Persians derived them from their neighbours of the family of Shem, who were the depositaries of the revelations of God.

It has already been seen that the doctrine of the resurrection of the body was clearly taught in the Old Testament, and in the apocryphal books of the Jews ; that it was a cardinal article of faith among the Jews when Christ came into the world ; and that it was emphatically asserted by Christ and his Apostles. We have also seen that the Bible teaches nothing on this subject beyond (1.) That the body is to rise again. (2.) That its identity will be preserved. And (3.) That it is to be so changed and refined as to adapt it to the high state of existence to which it is destined. In this simple form the doctrine has ever been held by the Church, which is not responsible for the fanciful theories adopted by many of its members.

The philosophical theologians of the Alexandrian school, in the early Church, were disposed to spiritualize all the Bible says of the resurrection of the body, and of its future state. The Latins, on the other hand, adhered to a literal interpretation of Scriptural language, often to the grossest extremes. Augustine, as we have seen, thought the resurrection body was to be composed of all the matter that ever belonged to it in this world, and Jerome asks : " If men are not raised with flesh and bones, how can the damned gnash their teeth in hell ? " [1]

---

[1] See Jerome. *Cŏntra Joannnem Hierosolumitanum*, **33**, *Works*, edit. Migne, vol. ii. pp. 384, 385 [441].

During the Middle Ages, the faith of the Church, on this subject, remained unchanged. The speculations of individual writers
were diverse, inconsistent, and of little interest, because of no
authority.

At the time of the Reformation the simple doctrine of the
Bible was reaffirmed ; and theologians beyond those limits were
left to their own guidance. The form in which the doctrine was
usually presented by the theologians of the seventeenth century,
was : (1.) That the resurrection body is to be numerically, and
in substance, one with the present body. (2.) That it is to have
the same organs of sight, hearing, etc., as in this life. (3.) Many
held that all the peculiarities of the present body as to size or
stature, appearance, etc., are to be restored. (4.) As the bodies
of the righteous are to be refined and glorified, those of the
wicked, it was assumed, would be proportionately repulsive. The
later Protestant theologians, as well Lutheran as Reformed, confine themselves more strictly within the limits of Scripture.

Rationalism, as far as it prevailed, swept the whole doctrine
away. Reason does not teach the doctrine, and cannot explain
it ; therefore, it has no title to recognition. Deistical rationalists
admitted that the doctrine was taught in the Scriptures, but this
was to them only an additional reason for denying their divine
origin. The more moderate rationalists, who admitted the Bible
to be a revelation of the truths of reason, or of natural religion,
explained away all that it teaches concerning the resurrection,
making it refer to the rising of the soul from a state of sin to a
state of holiness ; or, as relating not to the resurrection of the
body, but to the continued life of the soul in a future state.

Of course the modern speculative, or pantheistic theology, ignores the doctrine of a resurrection. It does not even admit of
the existence of the soul after the dissolution of the body. The
race is immortal, but the individuals of which it is composed are
not. Scientific materialism admits of no other resurrection than
the reappearance of the same chemical elements which now form
our bodies, in the bodies of future plants, animals, or men. The
lime in our bones may help to form the bones of those who come
after us. Thus philosophy and science, when divorced from the
Bible, lead us only to negations, darkness, and despair.

CHAPTER III.

§ 1. *Preliminary Remarks.*

THIS is a very comprehensive and very difficult subject. It is intimately allied with all the other great doctrines which fall under the head of eschatology. It has excited so much interest in all ages of the Church, that the books written upon it would of themselves make a library. The subject cannot be adequately discussed without taking a survey of all the prophetic teachings of the Scriptures both of the Old Testament and of the New. This task cannot be satisfactorily accomplished by any one who has not made the study of the prophecies a specialty. The author, knowing that he has no such qualifications for the work, purposes to confine himself in a great measure to a historical survey of the different schemes of interpreting the Scriptural prophecies relating to this subject.

The first point to be considered is the true design of prophecy, and how that design is to be ascertained. Prophecy is very different from history. It is not intended to give us a knowledge of the future, analogous to that which history gives us of the past. This truth is often overlooked. We see interpreters undertaking to give detailed expositions of the prophecies of Isaiah, of Ezekiel, of Daniel, and of the Apocalypse, relating to the future, with the same confidence with which they would record the history of the recent past. Such interpretations have always been falsified by the event. But this does not discourage a certain class of minds, for whom the future has a fascination and who delight in the solution of enigmas, from renewing the attempt. In prophecy, instruction is subordinate to moral impression. The occurrence of important events is so predicted as to produce in the minds of the people of God faith that they will certainly come to pass. Enough is made known of their nature, and of the time and mode of their occurrence, to awaken attention, desire, or apprehension, as the case may be; and to secure proper effort on the part of those concerned to be prepared for what is to come to pass. Although such predictions may be variously misinterpreted before their fulfilment; yet when fulfilled, the agreement between the prophecy and the event is seen to be such as to render the divine origin of the prophecy a matter of certainty. Thus with regard to the first advent of Christ, the Old Testament prophecies rendered it certain that a great Redeemer was to appear; that He was to be a Prophet, Priest, and King; that He would deliver his people from their sins, and from the evils under which they groaned; that He was to establish a kingdom which should ultimately absorb all the kingdoms on earth; and that He would render all his people supremely happy and blessed. These predictions had the effect of turning the minds of the whole Jewish nation to the future, in confident expectation that the Deliverer would come; of exciting earnest desire for his advent; and of leading the pious portion of the people to prayerful preparation for that event. Nevertheless, of all the hundreds of thousands to whom these predictions of the Hebrew Scriptures were made known, not a single person, so far as appears, interpreted them aright; yet, when fulfilled, we can almost construct a history of the events from these misunderstood predictions concerning them. Christ was indeed a king, but no such king as the world had ever seen, and such as no man expected; He was a priest, but the only priest that ever lived of whose priesthood he was Himself the victim; He did establish a kingdom, but it was not of this world. It was foretold that Elias should first come and prepare the way of the Lord. He did come; but in a way in which no man did or could have anticipated.

It follows, from what has been said, that prophecy makes a general impression with regard to future events, which is reliable and salutary, while the details remain in obscurity. The Jews were not disappointed in the general impression made on their minds by the predictions relating to the Messiah. It was only in the explanation of details that they failed. The Messiah was a king; He did sit upon the throne of David, but not in the way in which they expected; He is to subdue all nations, not by the sword, as they supposed, but by truth and love; He was to make his people priests and kings, but not worldly princes and satraps. The utter failure of the Old Testament Church in interpreting the prophecies relating to the first advent of Christ, should teach us to be modest and diffident in explaining those which relate to his second coming. We should be satisfied with the great truths which those prophecies unfold, and leave the details to be ex-

plained by the event. This the Church, as a Church, has generally done.

§ 2. *The Common Church Doctrine.*

The common Church doctrine is, first, that there is to be a
second personal, visible, and glorious advent of the Son of God.
Secondly, that the events which are to precede that advent, are

1. The universal diffusion of the Gospel; or, as our Lord expresses it, the ingathering of the elect; this is the vocation of the
Christian Church.

2. The conversion of the Jews, which is to be national. As
their casting away was national, although a remnant was saved;
so their conversion may be national, although some may remain
obdurate.

3. The coming of Antichrist.

Thirdly, that the events which are to attend the second advent
are : —

1. The resurrection of the dead, of the just and of the unjust.

2. The general judgment.

3. The end of the world. And,

4. The consummation of Christ's kingdom.

§ 3. *The Personal Advent of Christ.*

It is admitted that the words " coming of the Lord " are often
used in Scripture for any signal manifestation of his presence
either for judgment or for mercy. When Jesus promised to
manifest Himself to his disciples, " Judas saith unto Him, not
Iscariot, Lord, how is it that thou wilt manifest thyself unto us,
and not unto the world ? Jesus answered and said unto him, If a
man love me he will keep my words : and my Father will love
him, and we will come unto him, and make our abode with him."
(John xiv. 22, 23.) There is a coming of Christ, true and real,
which is not outward and visible. Thus also in the epistle to the
Church in Pergamos it is said : " Repent; or else I will come
unto thee quickly." (Rev. ii. 16.) This form of expression
is used frequently in the Bible. There are, therefore, many
commentators who explain everything said in the New Testament
of the second coming of Christ, of the spiritual manifestation of
his power. Thus Mr. Alger, to cite a single example of this
school, says : " The Hebrews called any signal manifestation of
power — especially any dreadful calamity — a coming of the
Lord. It was a coming of Jehovah when his vengeance strewed

the ground with the corpses of Sennacherib's host; when its
storm swept Jerusalem as with fire, and bore Israel into bondage ;
when its sword came down upon Idumea and was bathed in blood
upon Edom. 'The day of the Lord' is another term of precisely
similar import. It occurs in the Old Testament about fifteen
times. In every instance it means some mighty manifestation of
God's power in calamity. These occasions are pictured forth
with the most astounding figures of speech." [1] On the following
page he says he fully believes that the evangelists and early
Christians understood the language of Christ in reference to his
second coming, as predictions of a personal and visible advent,
connected with a resurrection and a general judgment, but he
more than doubts whether such was the meaning of Christ Himself. (1.) Because he says nothing of a resurrection of the dead.
(2.) The figures which He uses are precisely those which the
Jewish prophets employed in predicting " great and signal events
on the earth." (3.) Because He " fixed the date of the events
He referred to within that generation." Christ he thinks, meant
to teach that his " truths shall prevail and shall be owned as the
criteria of Divine judgment. According to them," he understands
Christ to say, " all the righteous shall be distinguished as my
subjects, and all the iniquitous shall be separated from my kingdom. Some of those standing here shall not taste death till all
these things be fulfilled. Then it will be seen that I am the
Messiah, and that through the eternal principles of truth which I
have proclaimed I shall sit upon a throne of glory, — not literally, in person, as you thought, blessing the Jews and cursing the
Gentiles, but spiritually, in the truth, dispensing joy to good men
and woe to bad men, according to their deserts." It is something
to have it admitted that the Apostles and early Christians believed in the personal advent of Christ. What the Apostles believed we are bound to believe; for St. John said " He that
knoweth God, heareth us." That the New Testament does
teach a second, visible, and glorious appearing of the Son of God,
is plain : —

1. From the analogy between the first and second advents.
The rationalistic Jews would have had precisely the same reasons
for believing in a more spiritual coming of the Messiah as modern
rationalists have for saying that his second coming is to be spiritual. The advent in both cases is predicted in very nearly the
same terms. If, therefore, his first coming was in person and

[1] Alger's *Critical History of the Doctrine of a Future Life.* Philadelphia, 1864, p. 319.

visible, so his second coming must be. The two advents are often spoken of in connection, the one illustrating the other. He came the first time as the Lamb of God bearing the sins of the world; He is to come "the second time, without sin, unto salvation." (Heb. ix. 28.)   God, said the apostle Peter, " shall send Jesus Christ, which before was preached unto you: whom the heaven must receive until the times of restitution of all things, which God hath spoken by the mouth of all his holy prophets since the world began." (Acts iii. 20, 21.) Christ is now invisible to us, having been received up into heaven. He is to remain thus invisible, until God shall send him at the restitution of all things.

2. In many places it is directly asserted that his appearing is to be personal and visible. At the time of his ascension, the angels said to his disciples : " Ye men of Galilee, why stand ye gazing up into heaven ? This same Jesus, which is taken up from you into heaven, shall so come in like manner as ye have seen him go into heaven." (Acts i. 11.) His second coming is to be as visible as his ascension. They saw Him go ; and they shall see Him come. In Matt. xxvi. 64, it is said, " Hereafter shall ye see the Son of Man sitting on the right hand of power, and coming in the clouds of heaven ; " Matt. xxiv. 30, " Then shall all the tribes of the earth mourn, and they shall see the Son of Man coming in the clouds of heaven with power and great glory." Luke xxi. 27, " Then shall they see the Son of Man coming in a cloud."

3. The circumstances attending the second advent prove that it is to be personal and visible. It is to be in the clouds ; with power and great glory ; with the holy angels and all the saints ; and it is to be with a shout and the voice of the archangel.

4. The effects ascribed to his advent prove the same thing. All the tribes of the earth shall mourn ; the dead, both small and great are to arise ; the wicked shall call on the rocks and hills to cover them ; the saints are to be caught up to meet the Lord in the air ; and the earth and the heavens are to flee away at his presence.

5. That the Apostles understood Christ to predict his second coming in person does not admit of doubt. Indeed almost all the rationalistic commentators teach that the Apostles fully believed and even taught that the second advent with all its glorious consequences would occur in their day. Certain it is that they believed that He would come visibly and with great glory, and that

they held his coming as the great object of expectation and desire. Indeed Christians are described as those who " are waiting for the coming of our Lord Jesus Christ" (1 Cor. i. 7) ; as those who are " looking for that blessed hope, and the glorious appearing of the great God and our Saviour Jesus Christ " (Tit. ii. 13) (it is to them who look for Him, He is to " appear the second time, without sin unto salvation," Heb. ix. 28) ; as those who are expecting and earnestly desiring the coming of the day of God. (2 Pet. iii. 12.) It is a marked characteristic of the apostolic writings that they give such prominence to the doctrine of the second advent. " Judge nothing before the time, until the Lord come." (1 Cor. iv. 5.) " Christ the first-fruits ; afterwards they that are Christ's at his coming." (1 Cor. xv. 23.) Ye are our rejoicing " in the day of the Lord Jesus." (2 Cor. i. 14.) " He . . . . will perform it until the day of Jesus Christ." (Phil. i. 6.) " That I may rejoice in the day of Christ." (ii. 16.) " Our conversation is in heaven, from whence also we look for the Saviour, the Lord Jesus Christ." (iii. 20.) " When Christ, who is our life, shall appear, then shall ye also appear with Him in glory." (Col. iii. 4.) ' To wait for his Son from heaven, whom he raised from the dead, even Jesus, which delivered us from the wrath to come." (1 Thess. i. 10.) " What is our hope, ... are not even ye in the presence of our Lord Jesus Christ at his coming ? " (ii. 19.) " Unblamable in holiness . . . . at the coming of our Lord Jesus Christ with all his saints." (iii. 13.) " We which are alive, and remain unto the coming of the Lord . . . . shall be caught up . . . . in the clouds, to meet the Lord in the air : and so shall we ever be with the Lord." (iv. 15–17.) In his second epistle he assures the Thessalonians that they shall have rest, " when the Lord Jesus shall be revealed from heaven." (2 Thess. i. 7.) The coming of Christ, however, he tells them was not at hand ; there must come a great falling away first. Paul said to Timothy, " Keep this commandment without spot, unrebukable, until the appearing of our Lord Jesus Christ." (1 Tim. vi. 14.) " There is laid up for me a crown of righteousness, which the Lord, the righteous judge, shall give me at that day : and not to me only, but unto all them also that love his appearing." (2 Tim. iv. 8.) The epistles of Peter afford the same evidence of the deep hold which the promise of Christ's second coming had taken on the minds of the Apostles and of all the early Christians. He tells his readers that they " are kept by the power of God through faith unto salvation, ready to be revealed in the last time . . . . that the trial of your faith, .

might be found unto praise, and honour, and glory, at the appearing of Jesus Christ." (1 Pet. i. 5–7.)   Men are to " give account
to Him that is ready to judge the quick and the dead." (iv. 5.)
" Rejoice, ... that, when his glory shall be revealed, ye may be
glad also with exceeding joy." (verse 13.) " When the chief Shepherd shall appear, ye shall receive a crown of glory." (v. 4.) " We
have not followed cunningly devised fables, when we made known
unto you the power and coming of our Lord Jesus Christ, but
were eye-witnesses of his majesty." (2 Pet. i. 16).   The transfiguration on the mount was a type and pledge of the glory of the
second advent.   The Apostle warns the disciples that scoffers
would come " saying, Where is the promise of his coming ? for
since the fathers fell asleep, all things continue as they were from
the beginning of the creation."   In answer to this objection, he
reminds them that the threatened deluge was long delayed, but
came at last ; that time is not with God as it is with us ; that
with Him a thousand years are as one day, and one day as a
thousand years.   He repeats the assurance that " the day of
the Lord will come as a thief in the night ; in the which the
heavens shall pass away with a great noise, and the elements
shall melt with fervent heat ; the earth also and the works that
are therein, shall be burned up." (2 Peter iii. 3–10.)

From all these passages, and from the whole drift of the New
Testament, it is plain, (1.) That the Apostles fully believed that
there is to be a second coming of Christ.   (2.) That his coming
is to be in person, visible and glorious.   (3.) That they kept this
great event constantly before their own minds, and urged it on
the attention of the people, as a motive to patience, constancy,
joy, and holy living.   (4.) That the Apostles believed that the
second advent of Christ would be attended by the general resurrection, the final judgment, and the end of the world.

As already intimated, it is objected to this view of the prophecies of the New Testament referring to the Second Advent, —

1. That the first advent of Christ is predicted in the Old Testament in nearly as glowing terms as his second coming is set
forth in the New Testament.   He was to come in the clouds of
heaven ; with great pomp and power ; all nations were to be subject to Him ; all people were to be gathered before Him ; the
stars were to fall from heaven ; the sun was to be darkened, and
the moon to be turned into blood.   These descriptions were not
realized by the event ; and are understood to refer to the great
changes in the state of the world to be effected by his coming.

It is unreasonable, therefore, as it is agreed, to expect anything like a literal fulfilment of these New Testament prophecies.   To this it may be answered, (1.) That in the Old Testament the Messianic period is described as a whole.   The fact that the Messiah was to come and establish an everlasting kingdom which was to triumph over all opposition, and experience a glorious consummation, is clearly foretold.   All these events were, so to speak, included in the same picture ; but the perspective was not preserved.   The prophecies were not intended to give the chronological order of the events foretold.   Hence the consummation of the Messiah's kingdom is depicted as in immediate proximity with his appearance in the flesh.   This led almost all the Jews, and even the disciples of Christ themselves, before the day of Pentecost, to look for the immediate establishment of the Messiah's kingdom in its glory.   Such being the character of the Old Testament prophecies, it cannot be fairly inferred that they have as yet received their full accomplishment ; or that they are now being fulfilled in the silent progress of the Gospel.   They include the past and the present, but much remains to be accomplished in the future more in accordance with their literal meaning.   (2.) The character of the predictions in the New Testament does not admit of their being made to refer to any spiritual coming of Christ or to the constant progress of his Church.   They evidently refer to a single event; to an event in the future, not now in progress ; an event which shall attract the attention of all nations, and be attended by the resurrection of the dead, the complete salvation of the righteous, and the condemnation of the wicked.   (3.) A third answer to the objection under consideration is, that the Apostles, as is conceded, understood the predictions of Christ concerning his second coming, in the way in which they have been understood by the Church, as a whole, from that day to this.

2. A second objection to the common Church view of the eschatology of the New Testament is, that our Lord expressly says that the events which He foretold were to come to pass during that generation.   His words are, " Verily, I say unto you, This generation shall not pass, till all these things be fulfilled." This objection is founded upon the pregnant discourse of Christ recorded in the twenty-fourth and twenty-fifth chapters of Matthew.   It is to be remarked that those chapters contain the answer which Christ gave to three questions addressed to Him by his disciples; first, when the destruction of the temple and of

Jerusalem was to occur ; second, what was to be the sign of his coming ; and third, when the end of the world was to take place. The difficulty in interpreting this discourse is, to determine its relation to these several questions. There are three methods of interpretation which have been applied to this passage. The first assumes that the whole of our Lord's discourse refers but to one question, namely, When was Jerusalem to be destroyed and Christ's kingdom to be inaugurated ; the second adopts the theory of what used to be called the double sense of prophecy ; that is, that the same words or prediction refer to one event in one sense, and to a different event in a higher sense ; the third assumes that one part of our Lord's predictions refers exclusively to one of the questions asked, and that other portions refer exclusively to the other questions.

The rationalistic interpreters adopt the first method and refer everything to the overthrow of the Jewish polity, the destruction of Jerusalem, and the inauguration of the Church which is to do its work of judgment in the earth. Some evangelical interpreters also assume that our Lord answers the three questions put to Him as one, as they constituted in fact but one in the minds of his disciples, since they believed that the three events, the destruction of Jerusalem, the second coming of Christ, and the end of the world, were all to occur together. Thus Luthardt says : "There are three questions according to the words ; but only one in the minds of the disciples, as they did not consider the three events, the destruction of Jerusalem, the second coming of Christ, and the end of the world, as separated chronologically ; but as three great acts in the final drama of the world's history." [1] In this sense our Lord, he adds, answered their inquiries. He does not separate the different subjects, so as to speak first of one and then of another ; but he keeps all ever in view. "It is the method," he says, "of Biblical prophecy, which our Lord observes, always to predict the one great end and all else and what is preparatory, only so far as it stands in connection with that end and appears as one of its elements." [2] Although, therefore, the prophecy of Christ extends to events in the distant future, He could say that that generation should not pass away until all was fulfilled ; for the destruction of Jerusalem was the commencement of that work of judgment which Christ foretold.

[1] *Die Lehre von den letzten Dingen in Abhandlungen und Schriftauslegungen dargestellt* von Chr. Ernst Luthardt, der Theologie Doktor und Professor zu Leipzig. Leipzig, 1861, p. 87.

[2] *Ibid.* pp. 87, 88.

According to this view, the first method of interpretation differs very little from the second of those above mentioned. Both
suppose that the same words or descriptions are intended to refer to
two or more events very different in their nature and in the time
of their occurrence. Isaiah's prediction of the great deliverance
which God was to effect for his people, was so framed as to answer both to the redemption of the Jews from their captivity in
Babylon, and to the greater redemption by the Messiah. It was
in fact and equally a prediction of both events. The former was
the type, and the first step toward the accomplishment of the
other. So also in the fourteenth chapter of Zechariah, the
prophecy of the destruction of Jerusalem, the spiritual redemption, and the final judgment, are blended together. As, therefore, in the Old Testament the Messianic prophecies took in the
whole scope of God's dealings with his people, including their
deliverance from Babylon and their redemption by Christ, so as
to make it doubtful what refers to the former and what to the
latter event; so this discourse of Christ may be considered as
taking in the whole history of his kingdom, including his great
work of judgment in casting out the Jews and calling the Gentiles, as well as the final consummation of his work. Thus everything predicted of the final judgment had its counterpart in what
was fulfilled in that generation.

The third method of interpretation is greatly to be preferred,
if it can be successfully carried out. Christ does in fact answer
the three questions presented by his disciples. He told when the
temple and the city were to be destroyed; it was when they
should see Jerusalem compassed about with armies. He told
them that the sign of the coming of the Son of Man was to be
great defection in the Church, dreadful persecutions, and all but
irresistible temptations, and that with his coming were to be connected the final judgment and the end of the world; but that
the time when those events were to occur, was not given unto
them to know, nor even to the angels of heaven. (Matt. xxiv. 36.)

If this be the method of interpreting these important predictions, then the declaration contained in Matt. xxiv. 34, " This
generation shall not pass, till all these things be fulfilled," must
be restricted to the " all things " spoken of, referring to the destruction of Jerusalem and the inauguration of the Church as
Christ's kingdom on earth. There is, however, high authority
for making ἡ γενεὰ αὕτη, here and in the parallel passages, Mark
xiii. 30 and Luke xxi. 32, refer to Israel as a people or race ; in

this case the meaning would be that the Jews would not cease to be a distinct people until his predictions were fulfilled.[1] There is nothing, therefore, in this discourse of Christ's inconsistent with the common Church doctrine as to the nature and concomitants of his Second Advent.

§ 4. The Calling of the Gentiles.

The first great event which is to precede the second coming of Christ, is the universal proclamation of the Gospel.

1. The first argument in proof of the position that the Gospel must be preached to all nations before the second advent, is founded on the predictions of the Old Testament. It is there distinctly foretold that when the Messiah appeared the Spirit should be poured out on all flesh, and that all men should see the salvation of God. The Messiah was to be a light to lighten the Gentiles, as well as the glory of his people Israel. The feet of those who brought the glad tidings and published peace, were to be beautiful upon the mountains. God said in Hosea ii. 23, " I will say to them which were not my people, Thou art my people ; and they shall say, Thou art my God." And in Isaiah xlv. 22, 23, " Look unto me, and be ye saved, all the ends of the earth : for I am God, and there is none else. I have sworn by myself . . . . that unto me every knee shall bow, every tongue shall swear." That is, the true religion shall prevail over the whole earth. Jehovah shall everywhere be recognized and worshipped as the only true God. It is to be remembered that these and many other passages of like import are quoted and applied by the Apostle to the Gospel dispensation. They are enforced on the attention of those to whom they wrote as showing the Gentiles that the Gospel was designed for them as well as for the Jews ; and to impress upon the Church its obligation to preach the Gospel to every creature under heaven.

2. Christ repeatedly taught that the Gospel was to be preached to all nations before his second coming. Thus in Matt. xxiv. 14, it is said, " This gospel of the kingdom shall be preached in all the world for a witness unto all nations ; and then shall the end come." (Mark xiii. 10) " The gospel must first be published among all nations."

---

[1] Dorner. De Oratione Christi Eschatologica, Tractatus Theologicus. Stuttgart, 1844, pp. 76–86.

C. A. Auberlen, The Prophecies of Daniel and the Revelations of St. John. Translated by Rev. Adolph Saphir, Edinburgh, 1856, p. 354. " The Lord Jesus himself," says Auberlen, " prophesied (Matthew xxiv. 34), that Israel was to be preserved during the entire Church-historical period."

3. Accordingly our Lord after his resurrection, in giving his commission to the Church, said: " Go ye therefore and teach all nations, baptizing them in the name of the Father, and of the Son, and of the Holy Ghost ; teaching them to observe all things whatsoever I have commanded you : and lo, I am with you always, even unto the end of the world." (Matt. xxviii. 19, 20.) In Mark xvi. 15, the commission reads thus: " Go ye into all the world, and preach the gospel to every creature." This commission prescribes the present duty of the Church ; one that is not to be deferred or languidly performed until a new and more effective dispensation be inaugurated. The promise of Christ to be with his Church, as then commissioned, to the end of the world, implies that its obligation to teach the nations is to continue until the final consummation.

4. Having imposed upon his Church the duty to preach the Gospel to every creature under heaven, He endowed it with all the gifts necessary for the proper discharge of this duty, and promised to send his Spirit to render their preaching effectual. " He gave some, Apostles ; and some, prophets ; and some, evangelists ; and some, pastors and teachers." Of these officers some were temporary, their peculiar function being the founding and organizing the Church ; some were permanent. Their common object was the perfecting of the saints. Their mission and duties were and are to continue until " all come in the unity of the faith, and of the knowledge of the Son of God, unto a perfect man, unto the measure of the stature of the fulness of Christ." (Eph. iv. 11–13.) The duties of the ministry, therefore, are to continue until all, that is, all believers, the whole Church, or, as our Lord says, all the elect, are gathered in and brought to the stature of perfection in Christ.

5. The Apostles understood their commission in this sense and entered on their duties with a clear view of the task set before them. Our Lord, in his high-priestly prayer said concerning them, " As thou hast sent me into the world, even so have I also sent them into the world." He would not leave them alone ; He promised to send the Paraclete, the Helper, who should bring all things to their remembrance ; He would give them a mouth and a wisdom which all their adversaries should be unable to gainsay or resist. The Spirit was to abide with them and dwell in them, so that it would not be they who spoke, but the Spirit of the Father who spoke in them ; that Spirit was to convince the world of sin, righteousness, and judgment ; He was to render their

preaching the wisdom and power of God unto salvation. Their
simple duty was to teach ; their commission was, "Go teach all
nations."   One of the great elements of the Papal apostasy was
the idea derived from paganism, that the main design of the
Church is "cultus," worship, and not instruction. The Apostles,
as Peter teaches (Acts i. 22), and as is everywhere else taught
in Scripture, were to be witnesses of Christ ; to bear testimony to
his doctrines, to the facts of his life, to his death, and especially
to his resurrection, on which everything else depended.   As,
however, of themselves they could do nothing, they were required
to attempt nothing, but to abide in Jerusalem, until they were
imbued with power from on high. When thus imbued they
began at once to declare the wonderful works of God to "Par-
thians, and Medes, and Elamites, and the dwellers in Mesopota-
mia, and in Judea, and Cappadocia, in Pontus and Asia, Phry-
gia, and Pamphylia, in Egypt, and in the parts of Libya about
Cyrene, and strangers of Rome, Jews and proselytes, Cretes and
Arabians ; " thus making the first proclamation of the Gospel
after the resurrection of Christ typical of its design and destiny
as the religion of the whole world.

The Apostles accordingly "went everywhere ; " and everywhere taught (1.) That God is not the God of the Jews only,
but also of the Gentiles ; that He is rich in mercy towards all
who call upon him, justifying the circumcision by faith and the
uncircumcision through faith. (2.) That the Gospel, therefore,
was designed and adapted for the whole world ; for all classes of
men ; not only for Jews and Gentiles, but also for the learned
and unlearned, the young and the old, for the wicked and the
righteous. It is the power of God to salvation to every one that
believeth. (3.) Being thus suited to all men, it should be
preached to all men. "How shall they call on Him in whom they
have not believed ? and how shall they believe in Him of
whom they have not heard ? and how shall they hear without a
preacher ? and how shall they preach, except they be sent ? "
(Rom. x. 14, 15.)   Paul glorified his office : he thanked God for
giving him the grace to be the Apostle of the Gentiles. He said
that he was under obligation to preach the Gospel both to the
Greeks and to the Barbarians, to the wise and to the unwise.
He devotes no small portion of his Epistle to the Romans and the
greater portion of the doctrinal part of that to the Ephesians, to
setting forth the purpose of God to bring the Gentiles into his
Church, and to make them equally with the Jews partakers of

the redemption of Christ. He teaches that the middle wall of partition between the two had been broken down, and that the Gentiles were no more " strangers and foreigners, but fellow-citizens with the saints, and of the household of God." (Eph. ii. 19.) The great object of the Epistle to the Hebrews is to show that the Gospel is the substance of which the old dispensation was the shadow; that nothing more glorious, real, and effectual was to be, or could be, so far as the salvation of sinners is concerned. The eternal Son of God, the brightness of the Father's glory, and the express image of his person, had assumed our nature to become the Apostle and High Priest of our profession. There was no hope for those who neglected the great salvation which he announced, and no more sacrifice for sin remained for those who refused to be cleansed by his most precious blood. The final revelation of God's truth, the offering of the infinitely meritorious sacrifice for sin, and the coöperation of the everywhere present and almighty Spirit of God are all made known in the Gospel; and the Bible knows nothing of any other arrangements for the salvation of men. It is evident that the Apostles considered the dispensation of the Spirit under which we are now living, as the only one which was to intervene between the first advent of Christ and the end of the world.

6. In 2 Corinthians iii. the Apostle contrasts the new and old dispensations, showing that the former excels the latter, (1.) Because the one used the ministration of the letter, the other uses that of the spirit. (2.) Because the one was the ministration of death and of condemnation, the other is the ministration of the Spirit and of righteousness; and (3.) Because the one was transient and the other is permanent. " If that which is done away was glorious, much more that which remaineth is glorious." (verse 11.)

7. In Romans xi. 25, Paul teaches that the national conversion of the Jews is not to take place " until the fulness of the Gentiles be come in." The πλήρωμα τῶν ἐθνῶν, is that which makes the number of the Gentiles full; the full complement which the Gentiles are to render to make the number of the elect complete.

This ingathering of the heathen is the special work of the Church. It is a missionary work. It was so understood by the Apostles. Their two great duties were the propagation and defence of the truth. To these they devoted themselves. While they laboured night and day, and travelled hither and thither through all parts of the Roman world, preaching the Gospel;

they laboured no less assiduously in its defence. All the epistles of the New Testament, those of Paul, Peter, John, and James, are directed towards the correction of false doctrine. These two duties of propagating and of defending the truth, the Apostles devolved on their successors. During the apostolic age and for some time after it, the former had the ascendancy; to preach the Gospel to all nations, to bring all men to the knowledge of the truth, was felt to be the special vocation of the Church. Gradually, and especially after the conversion of Constantine and the establishment of Christianity as the religion of the Roman empire, the mind of the Church was directed principally to securing what had been attained; in perfecting its organization and in stating its creed and defending it against the numerous forms of error by which it was assailed.

From this time for long centuries the Church found its hands filled with its internal affairs. Its energies were expended mainly in three directions, in building up a hierarchy with a supreme pontiff, surrounded by ecclesiastical princes, which sought to concentrate in itself all power over the bodies and souls of men; in founding numerous orders of monks; and in the subtleties of metaphysical discussions. The work of missions during this period was almost entirely neglected.

When the Reformation came, the Protestants had as much as they could do to live. They had arrayed against them everywhere the tremendous power of the Romish Church, and in most cases all the power of the State. They had to defend their doctrines against the prejudices and learning of the age; to organize their Churches, and alas! they were distracted among themselves. Under these circumstances it is not to be wondered at that the command, "Go ye into all the world, and preach the gospel to every creature," was almost forgotten. It is only within the last fifty years that the Church has been brought to feel that its great duty is the conversion of the nations. More, probably, has been done in this direction during the last half century than during the preceding five hundred years. It is to be hoped that a new effusion of the Spirit like that of the day of Pentecost may be granted to the Church whose fruits shall as far exceed those of the first effusion as the millions of Christians now alive exceed in number the one hundred and twenty souls then gathered in Jerusalem.

That the conversion of the Gentile world is the work assigned the Church under the present dispensation, and that it is not to fold its hands and await the second coming of Christ to accomplish that work for it, seems evident from what has already been said, (1.) This is the work which Christ commanded his Church to undertake. (2.) He furnished it with all the means necessary for its accomplishment; He revealed the truth which is the power of God unto salvation ; He instituted the ministry to be perpetuated to the end of the world, and promised to endow men from age to age with the gifts and graces necessary for the discharge of its duties, and to grant them his constant presence and assistance. (3.) The Apostles and the Church of that age so understood the work assigned and addressed themselves to it with a devotion and a success, which, had they been continued, the work, humanly speaking, had long since been accomplished. (4.) There is no intimation in the New Testament that the work of converting the world is to be effected by any other means than those now in use. (5.) It is to dishonour the Gospel, and the power of the Holy Spirit, to suppose that they are inadequate to the accomplishment of this work. (6.) The wonderful success of the work of missions in our day goes to prove the fact contended for. Barriers deemed insurmountable have been removed ; facilities of access and intercourse have been increased a hundred fold ; hundreds of missionary stations have been established in every part of the world; many thousands of converts have been gathered into churches and hundreds of thousands of children are under Christian instruction ; the foundations of ancient systems of idolatry have been undermined ; nations lately heathen have become Christian, and are taking part in sending the Gospel to those still sitting in darkness ; and nothing seems wanting to secure the gathering in of the Gentiles, but a revival of the missionary spirit of the apostolic age in the churches of the nineteenth century.

§ 5. *Conversion of the Jews.*

The second great event, which, according to the common faith of the Church, is to precede the second advent of Christ, is the national conversion of the Jews.

First, that there is to be such a national conversion may be argued, —

1. From the original call and destination of that people. God called Abraham and promised that through him, and in his seed, all the nations of the earth should be blessed. He entered into a solemn covenant with him engaging to be his God and the God of his posterity to the latest generations ; and that they

should be his people. These promises have been hitherto fulfilled; God preserved the Hebrews, although comparatively few in numbers amid hostile nations, from destruction or dispersion until the promised seed of Abraham appeared and accomplished his redeeming work. This is an assurance that the other promises relating to this people shall be fully accomplished.

2. The second argument is from the general drift of the Old Testament concerning the chosen people. Those prophecies run through a regular cycle often repeated in different forms. The people are rebuked for their sins and threatened with severe punishment; when that punishment has been inflicted, and the nation brought to repentance, there uniformly follow promises of restoration and favour. Isaiah predicted that for their idolatry the people should be carried into captivity, but that a remnant should be restored to their own land, and their privileges secured to them again. Joel and Zechariah predicted that for their rejection of the Messiah, they should be scattered to the ends of the earth, but that God would bring them back, and that his favour should not be finally withdrawn from them. Thus it is with all the prophets. As these general predictions are familiar to all the readers of the Bible, they need not be specified.

3. There are in the Old Testament express predictions of their national conversion to faith in Him whom they had rejected and crucified. Thus in Zechariah xii. it is said; " I will pour upon the house of David and upon the inhabitants of Jerusalem, the spirit of grace and of supplications; and they shall look on me whom they have pierced, and they shall mourn for him, as one mourneth for his only son, and shall be in bitterness for him, as one that is in bitterness for his first-born." This is to be a national conversion, for it is said " the land shall mourn " every family apart.

4. The most decisive passage, however, bearing on this subject, and one which may be taken " instar omnium," is the eleventh chapter of the Epistle to the Romans. Paul had taught, (1.) That God had cast off the Jews as a nation because they as a nation, represented by the Sanhedrim, the High Priest, the scribes and the Pharisees, by their rulers of every class, and by the popular voice, had rejected Christ. " He came unto his own, and his own received him not." Therefore, as a nation, God rejected them. (2.) This rejection, however, he here teaches, was not entire. There was " a remnant according to the election of grace " who believed in Christ and were received into his kingdom. (3.) This

national rejection of Israel, as it was not entire, so neither was it to be final. It was to continue until the bringing in of the Gentiles. God had made a covenant with Abraham that his posterity should be his people; and " the gifts and calling of God are without repentance." Therefore, although broken off from the olive-tree for the present, they were to be grafted in again. (4.) Thus "all Israel shall be saved." Whether this means the Jews as a nation, or the whole elect people of God including both Jews and Gentiles, may be doubtful. But in either case it is, in view of the context, a promise of the restoration of the Jews as a nation. There is, therefore, to be a national conversion of the Jews.

Second, this conversion is to take place before the second advent of Christ. This the Apostle teaches when he says, that the salvation of the Gentiles was designed to provoke the Jews to jealousy, verse 11; and that the mercy shown to the Gentiles was to be the means of the Jews obtaining mercy, verse 31. The rejection of the Jews was the occasion of the conversion of the Gentiles; and the conversion of the Gentiles is to be the occasion of the restoration of the Jews. On this point Luthardt says: " As our Lord (Matt. xxiii. 39) said: ' Ye shall not see me henceforth, till ye shall say, Blessed is he that cometh in the name of the Lord ' — so it is certain that, when Jesus comes, who will be visible to all the world, as the lightning which cometh out of the east, and shineth even unto the west, whom all eyes, even of those who pierced Him and all kindreds of the earth shall see (Rev. i. 7 ; Zech. xii. 10), — the Jews must have been converted and have become a Christian nation. . . . . And further when Peter (Acts iii. 19–21) exhorts to repentance and conversion until the times of refreshing from the presence of the Lord shall come ; so it appears to be to me beyond all doubt that the conversion of Israel is to precede the Second Advent of Christ." [1]

Are the Jews to be restored to their own Land?

According to one view, the Jews after their conversion are to be restored to the land of their fathers and there constituted a distinct nation. According to another, their restoration to their own land is to precede their conversion. And according to a third view there is to be no such restoration, but they are to be amalgamated with the great body of Christians as they were in the times of the Apostles.

[1] *Lehre von den letzten Dingen*, pp. 71, 72.

In favour of a literal restoration it is urged, —

1. That it is predicted in the Old Testament in the most express terms. Luthardt says a man must " break" the Scriptures who denies such restoration. To him it is certain and undeniable that the Jews are to be brought back to their own land and re-established as a nation.[1]

2. It is argued that the promise of God to Abraham has never yet been fully accomplished. God promised to give to him and to his seed after him all the land from the river of Egypt (understood to be the Nile) to the river Euphrates. They were, however, during all their national history pent up in the narrow strip between the Jordan and the Mediterranean Sea, except for a while when the two and a half tribes dwelt on the eastern side of Jordan. As the promise cannot fail, the time must yet come when the whole region granted to Abraham shall be occupied by his descendants.

3. A presumptive argument is drawn from the strange preservation of the Jews through so many centuries as a distinct people. They have often been compared to a river flowing through the ocean without mingling with its waters. There must be some purpose in this wonderful preservation. That people must have a future corresponding to its marvellous past.

4. Reference is also made to the fact that the land promised to the Jews is now empty, as though waiting for their return. It once teemed with a population counted by millions ; and there is no reason why it may not in the future be as densely inhabited.

The arguments against the assumed restoration of the Jews to the Holy Land are, —

1. The argument from the ancient prophecies is proved to be invalid, because it would prove too much. If those prophecies foretell a literal restoration, they foretell that the temple is to be rebuilt, the priesthood restored, sacrifices again offered, and that the whole Mosaic ritual is to be observed in all its details. (See the prophecies of Ezekiel from the thirty-seventh chapter onward.) We know, however, from the New Testament that the Old Testament service has been finally abolished ; there is to be no new temple made with hands ; no other priest but the high-priest of our profession ; and no other sacrifice but that already offered upon the cross. It is utterly inconsistent with the character of the Gospel that there should be a renewed inauguration of Judaism within the pale of the Christian Church. If it be said

---

[1] *Lehre von den letzten Dingen*, p. 71.

that the Jews are to return to their own land as Jews, and there restore their temple and its service, and then be converted; it may be answered that this is inconsistent with the prophetic representations. They are to be brought to repentance and faith, and to be restored to their land, or, to use the figure employed by the Apostle, grafted again into their own olive-tree, because of their repentance. When Christ comes, " He shall send his angels with a great sound of a trumpet, and they shall gather together his elect from the four winds, from one end of heaven to the other." (Matt. xxiv. 31.) But further than this, in Zechariah xiv., it is predicted that after the restoration, all the nations of the earth " shall go up from year to year to worship the King, the LORD of hosts, and to keep the feast of tabernacles." In Isaiah lxvi. 22, 23, it is said, " As the new heavens and the new earth, which I will make, shall remain before me, saith the LORD, so shall your seed and your name remain. And it shall come to pass, that from one new moon to another, and from one Sabbath to another, shall all flesh come to worship before me, saith the LORD." The literal interpretation of the Old Testament prophecies relating to the restoration of Israel and the future kingdom of Christ, cannot by possibility be carried out; and if abandoned in one point, it cannot be pressed in regard to others.

2. It is undeniable that the ancient prophets in predicting the events of the Messianic period and the future of Christ's kingdom, borrowed their language and imagery from the Old Testament institutions and usages. The Messiah is often called David; his church is called Jerusalem, and Zion; his people are called Israel; Canaan was the land of their inheritance; the loss of God's favour was expressed by saying that they forfeited that inheritance, and restoration to his favour was denoted by a return to the promised land. This usage is so pervading that the conviction produced by it on the minds of Christians is indelible. To them, Zion and Jerusalem are the Church and not the city made with hands. To interpret all that the ancient prophets say of Jerusalem of an earthly city, and all that is said of Israel of the Jewish nation, would be to bring down heaven to earth, and to transmute Christianity into the corrupt Judaism of the apostolic age.

3. Accordingly in the New Testament it is taught, not in poetic imagery, but didactically, in simple, unmistakable prose, that believers are the seed of Abraham; they are his sons; his heirs.; they are the true Israel. (See especially Romans iv. and ix.

and Galatians iii.)   It is not natural descent, that makes a man
a child of Abraham.   " They which are the children of the flesh,
these are not the children of God ; but the children of the promise are counted for the seed." (Rom. ix. 8.)   The Apostle asserts
that the promises are made not to the Israel κατὰ σάρκα, but to the
Israel κατὰ πνεῦμα.   He says in the name of believers, " We are the
circumcision." (Phil. iii. 3.)   " We are Abraham's seed, and heirs
according to the promise." (Gal. iii. 29.)   The promise to Abraham that he should be the father of many nations, did not mean
merely that his natural descendants should be very numerous; but
that all the nations of the earth should have the right to call him
father (Rom. iv. 17) ; for he is " the father of all them that believe, though they be not circumcised." (Rom. iv. 11.)   It would
turn the Gospel upside down ; not only the Apostle's argument
but his whole system would collapse, if what the Bible says of
Israel should be understood of the natural descendants of Abraham to the exclusion of his spiritual children.

4. The idea that the Jews are to be restored to their own land
and there constituted a distinct nation in the Christian Church,
is inconsistent not only with the distinct assertions of the Scriptures, but also with its plainest and most important doctrines.
It is asserted over and over again that the middle wall of partition between Jew and Gentile has been broken down ; that God
has made of the two one ; that Gentile believers are fellow-citizens
of the saints and members of the household of God ; that they
are built up together with the Jews into one temple.   (Eph. ii.
11–22.) " As many of you as have been baptized into Christ
have put on Christ.   There is neither Jew nor Greek, there is
neither bond nor free, there is neither male nor female : for ye
are all one in Christ Jesus.   And if ye be Christ's, then are ye
Abraham's seed, and heirs according to the promise." (Gal. iii.
27–29.) There could not be a more distinct assertion that all difference between the Jew and Gentile has been done away within
the pale of the Christian Church.   This, however, is not a mere
matter of assertion, it is involved in the very nature of the Gospel.   Nothing is plainer from the teachings of Scripture than
that all believers are one body in Christ, that all are the partakers
of the Holy Spirit, and by virtue of their union with Him are
joint and equal partakers of the benefits of his redemption ; that
if there be any difference between them, it is not in virtue of
national or social distinctions, but solely of individual character
and devotion.   That we are all one in Christ Jesus, is a doctrine

which precludes the possibility of the preëminence assigned to the Jews in the theory of which their restoration to their own land, and their national individuality are constituent elements.

5. The Apostles uniformly acted on this principle. They recognize no future for the Jews in which the Gentile Christians are not to participate. As under the old dispensation proselytes from the heathen were incorporated with the Jewish people and all distinction between them and those who were Jews by birth, was lost, so it was under the Gospel. Gentiles and Jews were united in undistinguished and undistinguishable membership in the same Church. And so it has continued to the present day; the two streams, Jewish and Gentile, united in the Apostolic Church, have flowed on as one great river through all ages. As this was by divine ordinance, it is not to be believed that they are to be separated in the future.

6. The restoration of the Jews to their own land and their continued national individuality, is generally associated with the idea that they are to constitute a sort of peerage in the Church of the future, exalted in prerogative and dignity above their fellow believers; and this again is more or less intimately connected with the doctrine that what the Church of the present is to look forward to is the establishment of a kingdom on earth of great worldly splendour and prosperity. For neither of these is there any authority in the didactic portions of the New Testament. There is no intimation that any one class of Christians, or Christians of any one nation or race, are to be exalted over their brethren; neither is there the slightest suggestion that the future kingdom of Christ is to be of earthly splendour. Not only are these expectations without any foundation in the teachings of the Apostles, but they are also inconsistent with the whole spirit of their instructions. They did not exhort believers to look forward to a reign of wealth and power, but to long after complete conformity to the image of Christ, and to pray for the coming of that kingdom which is righteousness, joy, and peace in the Holy Ghost. Any Christian would rejoice to be a servant of Paul, or of John, of a martyr, or of a poor worn-out missionary; but to be servant to a Jew, merely because he is a Jew, is a different affair; unless indeed such should prove to be the will of Christ: then such service would be an honour. It is as much opposed to the spirit of the Gospel that preëminence in Christ's kingdom should be adjudged to any man or set of men on the ground of natural descent, as on the ground of superior stature, physical strength, or wealth.

The Scriptures, then, as they have been generally understood in the Church, teach that before the Second Advent, there is to be the ingathering of the heathen; that the Gospel must be preached to all nations; and also that there is to be a national conversion of the Jews; but it is not to be inferred from this that either all the heathen or all the Jews are to become true Christians. In many cases the conversion may be merely nominal. There will probably enough remain unchanged in heart to be the germ of that persecuting power which shall bring about those days of tribulation which the Bible seems to teach are to immediately precede the coming of the Lord.

§ 6. *Antichrist.*

That Antichrist is to appear before the second coming of Christ, is expressedly asserted by the Apostle in 2 Thessalonians ii. 1–3, " We beseech you . . . . that ye be not soon shaken in mind, or be troubled . . . . as that the day of Christ is at hand. . . . . For that day shall not come, except there come a falling away first, and that man of sin be revealed, the son of perdition." This is clear; but as to who or what Antichrist is, there is no little diversity of opinion.

1. Some understand by that term any antichristian spirit, or power, or person. The Apostle John says, " Little children, it is the last time: and as ye have heard that antichrist shall come, even now are there many antichrists; whereby we know that it is the last time . . . . Who is a liar but he that denieth that Jesus is the Christ? He is antichrist, that denieth the Father and the Son." (1 John ii. 18 and 22.) And again, " Every spirit that confesseth not that Jesus Christ is come in the flesh, is not of God: and this is that spirit of antichrist, whereof ye have heard that it should come; and even now already is it in the world." (iv. 3.) And in 2 John 7, it is said, " Many deceivers are entered into the world, who confess not that Jesus Christ is come in the flesh. This is a deceiver and an antichrist (ὁ πλάνος καὶ ὁ ἀντίχριστος, the deceiver and the antichrist)." Thus our Lord had predicted, " There shall arise false Christs, and false prophets, and shall show great signs and wonders; insomuch that, if it were possible, they shall deceive the very elect." (Matt. xxiv. 24.) And the Apostle Paul in 1 Timothy iv. 1, says: " The Spirit speaketh expessly, that in the latter times some shall depart from the faith, giving heed to seducing spirits, and doctrines of devils." These passages refer to a marked characteristic of

the period between the apostolic age and the second coming of Christ. There were to be many antichrists; many manifestations of malignant opposition to the person and to the work of Christ; many attempts to cast off his authority and to overthrow his kingdom.

2. Besides this general reference to the antichristian spirit which was to manifest itself in different forms and with different degrees of intensity, many believe that there is yet to be a person, in whom the power of the world shall be concentrated, and who will exert all his energies to overthrow Christianity, and to usurp the place of Christ on earth. This is the Antichrist of prophecy; of whom it is assumed that Daniel, Paul, and St. John in the Apocalypse speak. This is the view generally adopted by Romanists and by many eminent evangelical Protestant theologians.

3. The common opinion, however, among Protestants is, that the prophecies concerning Antichrist have special reference to the papacy. This conviction is founded principally on the remarkable prediction contained in Paul's second epistle to the Thessalonians. The Apostle knew that the Thessalonians, in common with other Christians of the early Church, would be exposed to grievous persecutions; to comfort them under their sufferings, to give them patience and to sustain their faith, he referred to the promised second coming of Christ. When the Lord should come all their sorrows would be ended; those who in the meantime had fallen asleep, would not lose their part in the blessing of his second advent. For " we which are alive, and remain unto the coming of the Lord, shall not prevent them which are asleep. For the Lord himself shall descend from heaven with a shout, with the voice of the archangel, and with the trump of God: and the dead in Christ shall rise first: then we which are alive and remain shall be caught up together with them in the clouds, to meet the Lord in the air: and so shall we ever be with the Lord. Wherefore, comfort one another with these words." (1 Thess. iv. 15–17.) These words it seems had been perverted and misinterpreted, by some who were " disorderly, working not at all, but " were " busybodies;" unsettling the minds of the people, turning them off from present duties, as though the day of the Lord were at hand. To correct this abuse, the Apostle writes his second epistle. He does not set the doctrine of the second advent in the background, or say anything to weaken its power as a source of consolation to the suffering believers. On the contrary, he sets forth the glory

of that advent and the richness of the blessings by which it should be attended, in more glowing terms than ever before. " We ourselves," he says, " glory in you in the churches of God, for your patience and faith in all your persecutions and tribulations that ye endure ; which is a manifest token of the righteous judgment of God, that ye may be counted worthy of the kingdom of God, for which ye also suffer ; seeing it is a righteous thing with God to recompense tribulation to them that trouble you ; and to you, who are troubled, rest with us, when the Lord Jesus shall be revealed from heaven with his mighty angels, in flaming fire taking vengeance on them that know not God, and that obey not the Gospel of our Lord Jesus Christ : . . . . when he shall come to be glorified in his saints, and to be admired in all them that believe." (2 Thess. i. 4–10.) All this stands true. Nevertheless the Thessalonians were not to be deceived. The great day of deliverance was not at hand. They had much to do, and much to suffer before that day should come. The time of the second advent was not revealed. In his first epistle he had said, " Of the times and the seasons, brethren, ye have no need that I write unto you. For yourselves know perfectly that the day of the Lord so cometh as a thief in the night." (1 Thess. v. 1, 2.) That being conceded, they should know that great things must occur before that day could come. First, there was to be a great apostasy. As the Church was then in its infancy, and had just begun to make progress among the nations, such language naturally presupposes a much more extended propagation of the Gospel, than had as yet taken place. The second event that was to precede the second advent was the coming of Antichrist, or, in other words, the man of sin was to be revealed.

The first question, to be determined in the interpretation of this prophecy, is, Whether Antichrist is a particular individual, or an institution, a power, or a corporation. Protestants generally adopt the latter view ; because they do not regard any one pope, but the papacy, as the Antichrist of Scripture. In favour of this view it may be urged, (1.) That it is according to the analogy of prophecy to speak of nations, institutions, or kingdoms, as individuals. In Daniel, the ten kings are ten kingdoms or dynasties ; the several beasts which he saw in vision, were not the symbols of particular men, but of nations. When therefore the Apostle speaks of Antichrist as " the man of sin," and " the son of perdition," it is perfectly consistent with Scriptural usage to understand him to refer to an order of men, or to an institution.

(2.) The work assigned to Antichrist in prophecy, extends over far too long a period to be accomplished by one man. (3.) Those who insist that the antichrist here predicted, is an individual man, are forced to admit that what is said in 2 Thessalonians ii. 7 ("He who now letteth, will let, until he be taken out of the way") is to be understood of a power. It is generally understood of the Roman power. Luthardt understands it of the moral power which sustains the right, and therefore is opposed to the reckless disregard of all law, which is one of the characteristics of Antichrist. It is true that he supposes that reference is also made to one of the guardian or protecting angels spoken of by the prophet Daniel. But such an angel is not to be "taken out of the way." And there is nothing in the context or in Paul's writings anywhere to justify the assumption that reference is here had to any angelic personage.

The second question is, Whether the antichrist here described is an ecclesiastical or civil power; whether it is to arise in the Church or in the world. The considerations which are in favour of the former of these assumptions are, —

1. That the designations "man of sin" and "son of perdition" have a religious import, and are more appropriate to an ecclesiastical than to a worldly power or potentate.

2. Antichrist was to have the seat of his power in the "temple of God." It is there he sits. This seems clearly to indicate that it is an ecclesiastical usurping, tyrannical, and persecuting power, that is here depicted. By the temple of God in this passage is generally understood the Church which is so often elsewhere called, and especially by Paul, God's temple. Some, however, suppose that the reference is to the literal temple in Jerusalem; but this supposes, (a.) That the Jews are to be restored to their own land. (b.) That they are to be restored as Jews, or unconverted, and that the temple is to be there rebuilt. (c.) That the Thessalonians knew all this and would understand the Apostle as referring to the temple made with hands; which is to the last degree improbable.

3. His coming is after the working of Satan, with all power and signs and lying wonders. This is not the way in which worldly potentates gain their power; they rely on force. But this is the way, as though traced by the pen of history rather than by the pencil of prophecy, in which the papacy has attained and maintained its fearful ascendancy in the world. Its power has been achieved mainly by fraud, " by the deceivableness of

unrighteousness ; " by forged documents and false pretences ; by claiming that Peter was made primate over the whole Church and the vicar or plenipotentiary of Christ on earth ; that he was the bishop of Rome ; that his successors in that office were his successors in that primacy ; and that as the vicar of Christ he was superior to all earthly potentates, not merely as the spiritual is above the temporal, but as lord of the conscience, authorized to decide what was right and what was wrong for them to do in all their relations as men and as rulers ; which is a claim of absolute dominion. This, however, is a small matter so far as it concerns the things of this world. It was to the mass of the people of little moment whether their absolute sovereign was a bishop or a prince ; whether he resided at Rome or in Paris, whether his authority extended over one nation or over all nations. It is the false claim of the papacy to have supreme authority over the faith of men, to decide for them what they must believe on the pain of eternal perdition, that is the most fearful power ever assumed by sinful men. To this is to be added the false claim to the power to forgive sin. This is, as we have seen, a twofold power, answering to the twofold penalty attached to sin, namely, the eternal penalty as a violation of the divine law, and the penances still due after the remission of the eternal penalty, as satisfactions to divine justice. The former can be obtained only through the intervention or absolution of the priest ; and the latter can be imposed or remitted at the discretion of the Church. This includes power over purgatory, the pains of which are represented as frightful and of indefinite duration. These pains the pope and his subordinates falsely claim the power to alleviate or remit. These claims have no parallel in the history of the world. If such pretensions as these do not constitute the power which makes them Antichrist, then nothing more remains. Any future antichrist that may arise must be a small affair compared to the papacy.

Then again, the Apostle tells us, these portentous claims, these unrighteous deceits, were to be supported by " signs and lying wonders." These have seldom, if ever, been appealed to by worldly powers to support their pretensions. They ever have been and still are among the chief supports of the papacy. There is not a false doctrine which it teaches, or a false assumption which it makes, which is not sustained by " lying wonders." Its whole history is a history of apparitions of the Virgin Mary or of saints and angels ; and of miracles of every possible description from the most stupendous to the most absurd. It has ever acted on the principle " populus vult decipi," and that it is right to deceive them for their own good, or, the good of the Church. The whole system, so far as it is distinctive,[1] is a system of falsehood, or false pretensions, supported by deceit.

4. Antichrist is to be a persecuting power. Is not this true of the papacy? It has been drunk with the blood of the saints. It not only persecutes, but it justifies persecution, and avows to this day its purpose to enforce its dominion by the rack and the stake wherever it has the power. This is involved in its justification of the past, and in its making it a duty to suppress every form of religion but that of Rome. The thirty years' war in Germany; the persistent attempts to exterminate the Piedmontese; the massacres by the Duke of Alva in the Netherlands; the horrors of the inquisition in Spain; the dragonnades and the massacre of St. Bartholomew in France, over which Te Deums were sung in Rome, show that the people of God can hardly have more to suffer under any future antichrist than they have already suffered, and perhaps have yet to suffer, under the papacy.

5. Antichrist, according to the Apostle, was to oppose and exalt himself above all that is called God or is worshipped; " so that he, as God, sitteth in the temple of God, shewing himself that he is God." This is true of no worldly power. It was not true of Antiochus Epiphanes, who is regarded as the type whence the prophetic portrait of Antichrist was drawn. It was not true of any of the Roman emperors. Some of them allowed themselves to be enrolled among the thousand gods of the Pantheon; but this falls very far short of the description here given. It is, however, all true of the papacy, and it is true of no other power which has yet appeared upon earth. Paul does not concern himself with theories, but with facts. It is not that the popes openly profess to be superior to God; or, that in theory they claim to be more than men. It is the practical operation of the system which he describes. The actual facts are first, that the popes claim the honour that is due to God alone; secondly, that they assume the powers which are his exclusive prerogatives; and thirdly, that they supersede the authority of God, putting their own in its place. It is thus they exalt themselves above God.

---

[1] This qualification is necessary. Papists of course hold the truths of natural religion; and many of the distinguishing doctrines of the Gospel. This is to be acknowledged. We are not to deny that truth is truth, because held by Romanists; nor are we to deny, that where truth is, there may be its fruits. While condemning Papacy, Protestants can, and do joyfully admit that there are among Romanists such godly men as St. Bernard, Fénélon, and Pascal, and doubtless thousands more known only unto God.

They assume the honour which belongs to God not merely by claiming to be the vicars of Christ on earth, and by allowing themselves to be addressed as Lord and God, but by exacting the submission of the reason, the conscience, and the life, to their authority. This is the highest tribute which a creature can render the Creator ; and this the popes claim to be their due from all mankind. They claim divine prerogatives as infallible teachers on all questions of faith and practice, and as having the power to forgive sin. And they exalt their authority above that of God by practically setting aside his word, and substituting their decrees and what they put forth as the teachings of the Church. It is a simple and undeniable fact that in all countries under the effective dominion of the pope, the Scriptures are inaccessible to the people, and the faith of the masses reposes not on what the Bible teaches, but on what the Church declares to be true.

Even such a writer as John Henry Newman, in an essay written before his formal adhesion to the Church of Rome, uses such language as the following : The question is, " Has Christ, or has He not, appointed a body representative of Him in earth during his absence ? " This question he answers in the affirmative, and says, " Not even the proof of our Lord's divinity is plainer than that of the Church's commission. Not even the promises to David or to Solomon more evidently belong to Christ, than those to Israel, or Jerusalem, or Sion, belong to the Church. Not even Daniel's prophecies are more exact to the letter, than those which invest the Church with powers which Protestants consider Babylonish. Nay, holy Daniel himself is in no small measure employed on this very subject. He it is who announces a fifth kingdom, like ' a stone cut out without hands,' which ' broke in pieces and consumed ' all former kingdoms, but was itself to ' stand forever.' and to become ' a great mountain,' and ' to fill the whole earth.' He it is also who prophesies that ' the Saints of the most High shall take the kingdom and possess the kingdom forever.' He ' saw in the night visions and behold one like to the Son of Man came with the clouds of heaven, and came to the Ancient of Days, and there was given Him dominion and glory and a kingdom, that all people, nations, and languages should serve Him.' Such too is Isaiah's prophecy, ' Out of Zion shall go forth the law, and the word of the LORD from Jerusalem, and He shall judge among the nations and rebuke many people.' Now Christ Himself was to depart from the earth. He could not then in his own person be intended in these great prophecies ; if He acted

it must be by delegacy."[1] According to the Romanists, therefore, these prophecies, relating to Christ and his kingdom, refer
to the papacy. It is the stone cut out of the mountain without
hands, which is to break in pieces and consume all other kingdoms ; which is to stand forever ; which is to fill the whole earth ;
to which is given dominion, and glory, and a kingdom, that all
people, nations, and languages should serve. If this be not to put
itself in the place of God, it is hard to see how the prophecies
concerning Antichrist can ever be fulfilled.

No more conclusive argument to prove that the papacy is Antichrist, could be constructed, than that furnished by Dr. Newman, himself a Romanist. According to him the prophecies
respecting the glory, the exaltation, the power, and the universal
dominion of Christ, have their fulfilment in the popes. But who
is Antichrist, but the man that puts himself in the place of Christ ;
claiming the honour and the power which belong to God manifest
in the flesh, for himself ? Whoever does this is Antichrist, in the
highest form in which he can appear.

6. Another argument to prove that the Antichrist described by
the Apostle is an ecclesiastical power is that his appearance is the
consequence of a great apostasy. That the apostasy spoken of is a
defection from the truth is plain from the Scriptural usage of the
term (Acts xxi. 21), and from the connection in which it here
occurs. When God brought the heathen upon the people as con-
querors, in punishment of their idolatry, their sufferings were a
judicial consequence of their apostasy, but it cannot be said that
the power of Chaldean or Egyptian oppressors was the fruit of
their defection from the truth. In this case, however, Antichrist
is represented as the ultimate development of the predicted apostasy. If a simple minister should claim to be a priest, and then
one priest assume dominion over many priests, and then one prelate over other prelates, and then one over all, and then that one
claim to be the ruler of the whole world as vicar of Christ,
clothed with his authority, so that the prophecy that all peoples,
nations, and languages should serve the Son of Man, is fulfilled
in him, then indeed we should have a regular development, from
the first step to the last. Bishop Ellicott, though believing Antichrist to be " one single personal being, as truly man as He
whom he impiously opposes," and that he is to be hereafter revealed, still admits that Antichrist is to be "the concluding and

---

[1] *Essays Critical and Historical.* By John Henry Newman, formerly Fellow of Oriel
College, Oxford. London, 1871. *The Protestant Idea of Antichrist*, vol. ii. pp. 173-175.

most appalling phenomenon" of the great apostasy. But if so, he must be an ecclesiastical, and not a worldly power.

7. Again the Apostle says that "the mystery of iniquity doth already work." That is, the principles and spirit had already begun to manifest themselves in the Church, which were to culminate in the revelation of the Man of Sin. How could this be said of a person who was to be a worldly prince, appearing outside of the Church, separated, not only chronologically by ages from the apostolic age, but also logically, from all the causes then in operation. If Antichrist is to be a single person, concentrating in himself all worldly power as a universal monarch, to appear shortly before the end of the world, as is assumed by so many expounders of prophecy, it is hard to see how he was to be the product of the leaven already working in the times of the Apostles.

If however, as Protestants have so generally believed, the papacy is the Antichrist which the Apostle had in his prophetic eye, then this passage is perfectly intelligible. The two elements of which the papacy is the development are the desire of preëminence or lust of power, and the idea of a priesthood, that is, that Christian ministers are mediators whose intervention is necessary to secure access to God, and that they are authorized to make atonement for sin; to which was added the claim to grant absolution. Both these elements were at work in the apostolic age. The papacy is the product of the transfer of Jewish and Pagan ideas to the Christian system. The Jews had a high priest, and all the ministers of the sanctuary were sacrificing priests. The Romans had a " Pontifex Maximus " and the ministers of religion among them were priests. Nothing was more natural and nothing is plainer as a historical fact than that the assumption of a priestly character and functions by the Christian ministry, was one of the earliest corruptions of the Church. And nothing is plainer than that to this assumption the power of the papacy is in a large measure to be attributed. And as to the desire of preëminence, we know that there was, even among the twelve, a contention who should be the greatest. The Apostle John (3 Epistle 9) speaks of Diotrephes, "who loveth to have the preëminence; " and in all the Epistles there is evidence of the struggle for ascendancy on the part of unworthy ministers and teachers. The leaven of iniquity, therefore, was at work in the apostolic age, which concentrated by degrees into the portentous system of the papacy.

8. According to this view, the difficult passage in verses 6 and

7 admits of an easy interpretation. The Apostle there says: " Now ye know what withholdeth, that he might be revealed in his time. For the mystery of iniquity doth already work : only he who now letteth will let, until he be taken out of the way." There was, therefore, at that time an obstacle which prevented the development of the Man of Sin, and would continue to prevent it, as long as it remained as it then was. It is to be noticed that Paul says, " Now ye know what withholdeth." How could the Thessalonians know to what he referred ? only from the Apostle's instructions, or from the nature of the case. The fact however is that they did know, and, therefore, it is probable that knowledge was communicated to others, and was not likely to be soon forgotten. This consideration gives the more weight to the almost unanimous judgment of the early fathers that the obstacle to the development of Antichrist was the Roman empire. While that continued in its vigour it was impossible that an ecclesiastic should become the virtual sovereign of the world. It is a historical fact that the conflict between the Emperors and the Popes for the ascendancy, was continued for ages, and that as the power of the former decreased that of the latter increased.

On the assumption that the Antichrist of which Paul speaks in his Epistle to the Thessalonians, is a powerful worldly monarch hereafter to appear, these verses, the 6th and 7th, present the greatest difficulty. The causes which are to bring such a monarch into the possession of his power were not then in operation ; there was then no obstacle to his manifestation so obvious as to be generally known to Christians, and the removal of which was to be followed at once by his revelation. Even on the assumption that the obstacle of which the Apostle speaks, was not the Roman empire, but rather the regard to law and order deeply fixed in the public mind, which stood in the way of the revelation of the Man of Sin, this difficulty is scarcely lessened. How could the Thessalonians have known that ? How foreign to their minds must have been the thought that a regard for law must be taken out the way before the lawless one could appear. It seems plain that the early fathers were right in their interpretation of the Apostle's language ; and that he meant to say that the appearance of ecclesiastical claimants to universal dominion, was not possible until the Roman empire was effectually broken.

According to Paul's account, Antichrist was to arise in the Church. He was to put forth the most exorbitant claims ; exalt himself above all human authority ; assume to himself the prerogatives of God, demanding a submission due only to God, and virtually setting aside the authority of God, and substituting his own in its place. These assumptions were to be sustained by all manner of unrighteous deceits, by signs, and by lying wonders. This portrait suits the papacy so exactly, that Protestants at least have rarely doubted that it is the Antichrist which the Apostle intended to describe.

Dr. John Henry Newman says, that if Protestants insist on making the Church of Rome Antichrist, they thereby make over all Roman Catholics, past and present, "to utter and hopeless perdition." [1] This does not follow. The Church of Rome is to be viewed under different aspects ; as the papacy, an external organized hierarchy, with the pope, with all his arrogant claims, at its head ; and also as a body of men professing certain religious doctrines. Much may be said of it in the one aspect, which is not true of it in the other. Much may be said of Russia as an empire that cannot be said of all Russians. At one time the first Napoleon was regarded by many as Antichrist; that did not involve the belief that all Frenchmen who acknowledged him as emperor, or all soldiers who followed him as their leader, were the sons of perdition. That many Roman Catholics, past and present, are true Christians, is a palpable fact. It is a fact which no man can deny without committing a great sin. It is a sin against Christ not to acknowledge as true Christians those who bear his image, and whom He recognizes as his brethren. It is a sin also against ourselves. We are not born of God unless we love the children of God. If we hate and denounce those whom Christ loves as members of his own body, what are we? It is best to be found on the side of Christ, let what will happen. It is perfectly consistent, then, for a man to denounce the papacy as the man of sin, and yet rejoice in believing, and in openly acknowledging, that there are, and ever have been, many Romanists who are the true children of God.

Admitting that the Apostle's predictions refer to the Roman pontiffs, it does not follow that the papacy is the only antichrist. St. John says there are many antichrists. Our Lord says many shall come in his name, claiming in one form or another his authority, and endeavouring to take his place by dethroning him. The Apostle John tells us this " is the last time " (1 John ii. 18) in which many antichrists are to appear. This

[1] *The Protestant Idea of Antichrist*, in vol. ii. of his *Essays Critical and Historical*, p. 148.

"last time" extends from the first to the second advent of Christ. This long period lay as one scene before the minds of the prophets. And they tell what was given them to see, not as though they were writing a history, and unfolding events in their historical order, but as describing the figures which they saw, as it were, represented on the same canvass. As Isaiah describes the redemption from Babylon and the redemption by the Messiah as though they were contemporary events, so Joel, in almost the same sentence, connects the effusion of the spirit which attended the first advent of Christ with the great elemental changes which are to attend his second coming. How long the period between the first and second advents of the Son of God is to be protracted is unrevealed. It has already lasted nearly two thousand years, and, for what we know, may last two thousand more. As this long period, crowded with great events, was presented as a whole to the minds of the prophets, it is not surprising that, under the guidance of the Holy Spirit, one should fix on one prominent feature in the scene, and others upon another. Under the divine guidance granted to these holy seers, there could be no error aud no contradiction, but there could hardly fail to be great variety. It would not, therefore, invalidate the account given of Paul's description of Antichrist, if it should be found to differ in some respects from the antichrists of Daniel and of the Apocalypse.

The Antichrist of Daniel.

The reader of the prophecies of Daniel has, at least in many cases, the advantage of a divine interpretation of his predictions. The prophet himself did not understand the import of his visions, and begged to have them explained to him; and his request was, in a measure, granted. Thus in the seventh chapter we read: "I saw in my vision by night, and behold, ... four great beasts came up from the sea, diverse one from another. The first was like a lion ; . . . . a second like to a bear ; another like a leopard ; (and) a fourth beast dreadful and terrible, and strong exceedingly, ... and it had ten horns . . . . And behold there came up among them another little horn, before whom there were three of the first horns plucked up by the roots : and, behold, in this horn were eyes like the eyes of a man, and a mouth speaking great things."

These beasts were, as the explanation states, the symbols of four kingdoms, the Babylonish, the Medo-Persian, the Greek, and the Roman. This last was to be divided into ten kingdoms. That kings in this prophecy mean kingdoms, not individuals, but an organized community under a king, is plain from the nature of the predictions and from the express declaration of the prophet; for he says, in verse 17, that the four beasts are four kings; and in verse 23, that the fourth beast is the fourth kingdom. King and kingdom, therefore, are interchanged as of the same import, After, or in the midst of these ten kingdoms signified by the ten horns, there was to arise another kingdom or power symbolized by the little horn. Of this power it is said: (1.) That it was to be of a different kind from the others. Perhaps, as they were civil or worldly kingdoms, this was to be ecclesiastical. (2.) He was to gain the ascendancy over the other powers; at least three of them were to be plucked up by the roots. (3.) He was to speak great things, or be arrogant in his assumptions. (4.) He was to set himself against God; speaking " great words against the Most High." (5.) He was to persecute the saints; prevail against them and wear them out; and they shall be given into his hands. (6.) This antichristian power was to continue until the judgment, *i. e.*, "until the Ancient of Days came, and judgment was given to the saints of the Most High." (Dan. vii. 22.) In all these particulars the Antichrist of Daniel answers to the description given by St. Paul in 2 Thessalonians. In one point, however, they appear to differ. According to Daniel, the power of Antichrist was to last, or at least his persecution of the saints, only "a time and times and the dividing of a time;" that is, three years and a half. (Compare Rev. xiii. 5, and xi. 2, 3.) This is the interpretation generally adopted. Calvin adopts the principle that in the prophecies definite periods of time are used for periods of indefinite duration. In his Commentary on Daniel he makes the little horn spoken of in the seventh chapter to be Julius Cæsar, and says : " Qui annum putant hic notari per tempus, falluntur meo judicio . . . . Annus sumetur figurate pro tempore aliquo indeterminato." [1] He significantly says : " In numeris non sum Pythagoricus."

There are two answers to this difficulty. The word antichrist may be a generic term, as it seems to have been used by St. John, not referring exclusively to any one individual person, or to any one organization, but to any and every antichristian power, having certain characteristics. So that there may be, as

---

[1] *In Danielem* vii. 20, 25; *Works*, Amsterdam, 1667, vol. v. pp. 109, 113.
[2] *In Danielem* xii. 12; *Ibid.*, p. 205 b.

the Apostle says, many Antichrists.   Hence Daniel may describe one, and Paul another.   Secondly, the same power, retaining all its essential characteristics, may change its form.   If republican France, during the first revolution, was an antichristian nation, it did not necessarily change its character when it became an empire; and what was, or might have been, said of it in prophecy under the one form, might not have answered to what it was under the other form.   During the Middle Ages, bishops were sometimes princes and warriors.   A prophetic description of them, while giving their general characteristics suited to both their ecclesiastical and worldly functions, might say some things of them as warlike princes which did not belong to them as bishops.   However, we do not pretend to be experts in matters of prophecy; our object is simply to state what Paul said of the Antichrist which he had in view, and what Daniel said of the Antichrist which he was inspired to describe.

In the eleventh chapter of Daniel, from the 36th verse to the end, there is a passage which is commonly understood of Antichrist, because what is there said is not true of Antiochus Epiphanes, to whom the former part of the chapter is referred, and is true of Antichrist as described in other places in the Scriptures.   It is not true of Antiochus Epiphanes that he abandoned the gods of his fathers.   On the contrary, his purpose was to force all under his control, the Jews included, to worship those gods.   What is said in verse 36 is in substance what Paul says, in 2 Thessalonians ii. 4, of the Man of Sin.   Daniel says that " the king," whom he describes, " shall do according to his will; and he shall exalt himself, and magnify himself above every god, and shall speak marvellous things against the God of gods, and shall prosper till the indignation be accomplished : for that that is determined shall be done."   This exalting himself " above all that is called god " is the prominent characteristic of Antichrist as he is elsewhere presented in Scripture.

The Antichrist of the Apocalypse.

The Apocalypse seems to be a summing up and expansion of all the eschatological prophecies of the Old Testament, especially of those of Ezekiel, Zechariah and Daniel.   The same symbols, the same forms of expression, the same numbers, the same cycle of events, occur in the New Testament predictions, that are found in those of the Old.   Every one knows that commentators differ not only in their interpretation of the details, but even as to the

whole structure and design of the book of Revelation. Some
regard it as a description in oriental imagery of contemporaneous
events ; others as intended to set forth the different phases of the
spiritual life of the Church ; others as designed to unfold the
leading events in the history of the Church and of the world in
their chronological order ; others again assume that it is a series,
figuratively speaking, of circles ; each vision or series of visions
relating to the same events under different aspects ; the end, and
the preparation for the end, being presented over and over again ;
the great theme being the coming of the Lord, and the triumph
of his Church.[1]

The most commonly accepted view of the general contents of
the book by those who adopt the chronological method is that so
clearly presented in the admirable little work of Dr. James M.
Macdonald (now of Princeton, New Jersey).[2] According to this
view, the introduction is contained in chapters i.–iii. ; part second
relates the Jewish persecutions, and the destruction of that
power, in chapters iv.–xi. 14 ; part third relates the Pagan
persecutions, and the end of the Pagan persecuting power, in
chapters xi. 15–xiii. 10 ; part fourth relates the Papal persecutions and errors, and their end, in chapters xiii. 11–xix. ; and
part fifth relates the latter day of glory, the battle of Gog and
Magog, the final judgment, and the heavenly state, in chapters
xx.–xxii.

Luthardt may be taken as a representative of the advocates of
the theory that the historical sequence of events is not designed to
be set forth in the Apocalypse. The three works of the Apostle

---

[1] *The Prophecies of Daniel and the Revelations of St. John, viewed in their Mutual
Relation, with an Exposition of the Principal Passages.* By Carl August Auberlen, Dr.
Phil., Licentiate and Professor Extraordinarius of Theology in Basil. Edinburgh, 1856.
Auberlen says, on page 359: "The interpretation of the Apocalypse may be reduced to
three grand groups. First, the church-historical view regards the Revelations as a prophetic compendium of Church history." This was the early Church view. Its principal
representative in Germany is Bengel. It is generally adopted by the British and French
interpreters. To this class belong Elliot's *Horæ Apocalypticæ, or a Commentary on the
Apocalypse, Critical and Historical,* second edition, London; 1846; four volumes; and the
work of Gaussen of Geneva, entitled *Daniel le Prophète.* The second class includes the
modern German interpreters, who, denying any real prediction of the future, confine
the views of Daniel and John to their contemporary history. To this class belong Ewald,
De Wette, Lücke, and others. The third group includes those who admit the divine inspiration of the prophecies and acknowledge the prediction of even minute events, but deny
that the Apocalypse was designed to be a detailed history of the future. "Its object is to
represent the great epochs and leading principal powers in the development of the kingdom of God viewed in its relation to the world-kingdoms." (p. 361.) To this class
Auberlen himself belongs, and he has carried out the theory with singular clearness and
ability. His work is excellently translated by the Rev. Adolph Saphir.

[2] *A Key to the Book of Revelation ; with an Appendix.* By James M. Macdonald,
Minister of the Presbyterian Church, Jamaica, L. I. Second edition. New London, 1848

John contained in the New Testament, the Gospel, the Epistles, and the Apocalypse, according to Luthardt, form a beautiful, harmonious whole; as faith, love, and hope mingle into one, so do these writings of St. John, though each has its characteristic; faith is prominent in the Gospel, love in the Epistles, and hope in the Apocalypse. The theme of the Book of Revelation is, — " Behold, He comes." Luthardt admits that commentators differ greatly as to their views of its meaning, and that, at first, it appears very full of enigmas; but he adds, [1] " Whoever is familiar with the ancient prophecies, and gives himself with loving confidence to this book, will soon find the right way, which will lead him safely through all its labyrinths." This is the experience of every commentator so far as he himself is concerned, however he may fail to satisfy his readers that his way is the right one. The main principle of Luthardt's exposition is, " That the Revelation of John does not contemplate the events of history, whether of the Church or of the world. It contemplates the end. We find that the antagonism of the Church and the world, and the issue of the conflict are its contents; the coming of Christ is its theme. The events of history preceding the consummation are taken up only so far as they are connected with the final issue. This consummation is not chronologically unfolded, but is ever taken up anew, in order to lead us by a new way to the end." [2] One thing is certain, namely, that the Apocalypse contains the series of predictions common to all the prophets; the defections of the people of God; persecutions of their enemies; direful judgments on the persecutors; and the final triumph and blessedness of the elect. Under different forms, this is the burden of all the disclosures God has seen fit to make of the fate of his Church here on earth; and this is the burden of the Apocalypse. According to Luthardt, the first vision i. 9–iii. 22, concerns the present state of the Church; the second vision, iv. 1–viii. 1, concerns God and the world; the third vision, viii. 2–xi. 19, concerns the judgment of the world and the consummation of covenant fellowship with God; the fourth vision, xii.–xiv. concerns the Church and the antichristian world power; this contains the vision of the woman, which brought forth the man child; and in xii. 18–xiii. 18, Antichrist and the false prophet; and in xiv. the Church of the end, and the judgment of the antichristian world; and the fifth vision, xv.–xxii. concerns the outpouring of wrath upon the world and the redemption of the Church.

[1] *Die Lehre von den letzten Dingen*, pp. 165-173; see page 173.
[2] *Ibid.*, p. 171.

It is characteristic of the Apocalypse that it takes up and expands the eschatological predictions of the earlier portions of Scripture. What in the Old Testament or in the Epistles of the New Testament, is set forth under one symbol and in the concrete, is in the Apocalypse presented under two or more symbols representing the constituent elements of the whole. Thus the Antichrist is predicted in Daniel under the symbol of " the little horn," and in Paul's Epistle to the Thessalonians under the title of the Man of Sin. Antichrist, as thus portrayed, includes an ecclesiastical and a worldly element; an apostate Church invested with imperial, worldly power. In the Apocalypse these two elements are represented as separate and united; a woman sitting on a beast with ten horns. The woman is the apostate Church ; the beast is the symbol of the world-power by which it is supported. The destruction of the one, therefore, does not involve the destruction of the other. According to the prediction in the eighteenth chapter, the kings of the earth, wearied with the arrogance and assumption of the apostate Church, shall turn against it, waste, and consume it ; that is, despoil it of its external power and glory. The destruction of Babylon, therefore, here predicted, is understood by that diligent student of prophecy, Mr. D. N. Lord, not as implying the overthrow of the Papacy, but its " denationalization" and spoliation.[1]

Throughout the Scriptures the relation between God and his people is illustrated by that of a husband to his wife ; apostasy from God, therefore, is in the ancient prophets called adultery. In the Revelation, the Church, considered as faithful, is called the woman ; as apostate, the adulteress or harlot ; and as glorified, the bride, the Lamb's wife. It is in accordance with the analogy of Scripture that the harlot spoken of in chapters xvii. and xviii. is understood to be the apostate Church. Of this woman it is said : (1.) That she sits on many waters. This is explained in xvii. 15, of her wide spread dominion : " The waters which thou sawest, where the whore sitteth, are peoples, and multitudes, and nations, and tongues." (2.) That she seduced the nations into idolatry ; making the inhabitants of the earth drunk with the wine of her fornication. (3.) That she is sustained in her blasphemous assumption of divine prerogatives and powers by the kings and princes of the earth. She is seen sitting on a scarlet-coloured beast, full of the names of blasphemy, having seven heads and ten horns. In verse 12, these ten horns are said to be ten kings, *i. e.*, in the lan-

[1] *An Exposition of the Apocalypse.* By David N. Lord. New York, 1859, p. 502.

guage of prophecy, ten kingdoms. (4.) That she takes rank among
and above the kings and princes of the earth. She is "arrayed in
purple and scarlet colour, and decked with gold and precious
stones and pearls." (5.) That her riches are above estimate. This
is dwelt upon at length in the eighteenth chapter. (6.) That she
is a persecuting power, "drunken with the blood of the saints,
and with the blood of the martyrs of Jesus." (7.) That the
claims of this persecuting power, as appears from Revelation
xiii. 13, 14, are to be sustained by lying wonders. "He doeth
great wonders, so that he maketh fire come down from heaven on
the earth in the sight of men, and deceiveth them that dwell on
the earth by those miracles which he hath power to do in the
sight of the beast." We find, therefore, in this description all
the traits which in Daniel and the Epistle to the Thessalonians
are ascribed to the Man of Sin, or, ὁ ἀντικείμενος, the Antichrist. It
matters not what this power may be called. "Wheresoever the
carcass is, there will the eagles be gathered together." Any
man; any institution; any organized power which answers to
this prophetic description, comes within the prophetic denunciations here recorded.[1] Neither does it matter what is to happen
after this judgment on the mystical Babylon. Should another
Antichrist arise, essentially worldly in his character, as so many
anticipate, who shall attain universal dominion, and set himself
against God and his Christ with more blasphemous assumptions,
with a more malignant hatred of the Church, and a more de-
moniacal spirit than any of his predecessors, this would not at
all disprove the correctness of the interpretation given above
of St. John's predictions concerning Babylon. On this point,
Maitland says: "The two great powers whose names stand fore-
most in prophecy come into historical contact at a single point.
Where Babylon ends, Antichrist begins: the same ten kings
that destroy the first, give their power to the second. When

---

[1] Auberlen, p. 293, quotes with approbation the following passage from John Michael
Hahn (*Briefe und Lieder über die Offenbarung. Works*, vol. v. § 6, Tübingen, 1820): "The
harlot is not the city of Rome alone, neither is it only the Roman Catholic Church, to the
exclusion of another, but all churches and every church, ours included, namely, all Christendom that is without the Spirit and life of our Lord Jesus, which calls itself Christian,
and has neither Christ's mind nor Spirit." While giving the prophecy this wide scope,
Auberlen, nevertheless, adds, "The Roman Catholic Church is not only accidentally and
'de facto,' but in virtue of its very principle a harlot; she has the lamentable distinction
of being the harlot κατ᾽ ἐξοχήν, the metropolis of whoredom, the mother of harlots (Rev.
xvii. 5); it is she, who, more than others, boasts of herself; I sit a queen, and am no
widow, and shall see no sorrow (xviii. 7), whereas the evangelical (Protestant) Church is,
according to her principle and fundamental creed, a chaste woman; the Reformation was
a protest of the woman against the harlot."

the ten kings shall have burnt Rome, so complete will be the ruin, that no sign of life or habitation will again be found in her. Here, then, is a decisive landmark; Rome is still standing, therefore, Antichrist has not yet come: we are still in the times of Babylon, whether tasting or refusing her golden cup." In this view, that is, in assuming that the Scriptural prophecies respecting Antichrist, have not their full accomplishment in any one antichristian power or personage exclusively, many of the most distinguished eschatologists, as Auberlen and Luthardt, substantially agree. The ancient prediction that Japhet should dwell in the tents of Shem, had its fulfilment every time the descendants of the latter participated in the temporal or spiritual heritage of the children of the former; and had its final and great accomplishment in the sons of Japhet sharing the blessings of redemption, which were to be realized in the line of Shem. In like manner the predictions concerning Antichrist may have had a partial fulfilment in Antiochus Epiphanes, in Nero and Pagan Rome, and in the papacy, and, it may still have a fulfilment in some great antichristian power which is yet to appear. So much, at least, is clear, in the time of Paul there was in the future a great apostasy and an antichristian, arrogant persecuting power, which has been realized, in all its essential characteristics, in the papacy, whatever may happen after Antichrist, in that form, is utterly despoiled and trodden under foot.[1]

[1] *The Apostles' School of Prophetic Interpretation: with its History down to the Present Time.* London, 1849, p. 41. Mr. Maitland, on p. 42, presents the difference between Babylon and Antichrist in the following manner: —

" Babylon is Described.	Antichrist is Described.
As a feminine power.	As a masculine power.
Seductive and abandoned, prevailing through her golden cup.	Ferocious and warlike, enforcing his claims by the sword.
Is succeeded by ten antichristian kings.	A final apostasy provoking Christ's second coming in vengeance.
Is burnt by the ten kings, who afterwards fight against the Lamb.	Destroyed, together with the kings, in the great battle with the Lamb.
Is bewailed by her accomplices in crime.	Leaves none to lament his fall.
Contains some of God's people even to the end.	Fatal to salvation of all his followers.
Established on the seven hills.	Reigns in Jerusalem."

The undue size which this volume has already reached forbids a fuller discussion of this subject. The reader is referred to the American edition of *Smith's Dictionary of the Bible*, under the word "Antichrist," for an elaborate exhibition of the different views which have prevailed in the Church, and for an exhaustive statement of the literature of the subject. *Doctor William Smith's Dictionary of the Bible.* Revised and edited by Professor H. B. Hackett, D.D., with the coöperation of Ezra Abbot, LL. D., Assistant Librarian of Harvard College. New York, 1870.

Roman Catholic Doctrine of Antichrist.

The general opinion in the early Church was that Antichrist was a man of Satanic spirit endowed with Satanic power who should appear before the second coming of Christ. Jerome says, in his Commentary on Daniel : " Let us say what all ecclesiastical writers have handed down, namely, that at the end of the world, when the Roman empire is destroyed, there will be ten kings who will divide the Roman world amongst them ; and there will arise an eleventh little king, who will subdue three of the ten kings, that is, the king of Egypt, of Africa, and of Ethiopia, as we shall hereafter show. And on these being slain the seven others will also submit. 'And behold,' he says, 'in the ram were the eyes of a man.' This is said that we may not suppose him to be a devil or demon, as some have thought, but a man in whom Satan will dwell utterly and bodily. 'And a mouth speaking great things,' for he is ' the man of sin, the son of perdition, who sitteth in the temple of God, making himself as God.' " [1]

Substantially the same view prevailed during the Middle Ages. Some however of the theologians of the Latin Church saw that the development of the Man of Sin was to take place in the Church itself and be connected with a general apostasy from the faith. They were therefore sufficiently bold to teach that the Church of Rome was to fall away, and that the Papacy or some individual pontiff was to become the Antichrist spoken of in Scripture. The abbot Joachim of Floris (died 1202), a Franciscan, put himself in opposition to the worldly spirit of the Church of his time, and his followers, called " Spirituales," came to denounce the Church of Rome as the mystical Babylon of the Apocalypse. This was done with great boldness by John Peter of Oliva (died 1297), whose works were formally condemned as " blasphemous and heretical." Among the passages thus condemned are the following : " The woman here stands for the people and empire of Rome, both as she existed formerly in a

---

[1] "Dicamus quod omnes scriptores ecclesiastici tradiderunt: in consummatione mundi, quando regnum destruendum est Romanorum, decem futuros reges, qui orbem Romanum inter se dividant, et undecimum surrecturum esse regem parvulum, qui tres reges de decem regibus superaturus sit, id est, Ægyptiorum regem, et Africæ et Æthiopiæ, sicut in consequentibus manifestius dicemus. Quibus interfectus, etiam septem alii reges victori colla submittent. ' Et ecce,' ait, ' oculi quasi oculi hominis erant in cornu isto.' Ne eum putemus juxta quorumdam opinionem, vel diabolum esse, vel dæmonem: sed unum de hominibus, in quo totus satanas habitaturus sit corporaliter. ' Et os loquens ingentia (2 Thess. ii.).' Est enim homo peccati, filius perditionis, ita ut in templo Dei sedere audeat, faciens se quasi Deum." In Danielem, vii. 8; Works, edit. Migne, vol. v. p. 531, a, b [667, 668].

state of Paganism, and as she has since existed, holding the faith
of Christ, though by many crimes committing harlotry with this
world. And, therefore, she is called a great harlot ; for, depart-
ing from the faithful worship, the true love and delights of her
Bridegroom, even Christ her God, she cleaves to this world, its
riches and delights ; yea, for their sake she cleaves to the devil,
also to kings, nobles, and prelates, and to all other lovers of this
world." "She saith in her heart, that is, in her pride, I sit a
queen : — I am at rest ; I rule over my kingdom with great
dominion and glory. And I am no widow: — I am not destitute
of glorious bishops and kings." [1]

Not only the poets Dante and Petrarch denounced the corruptions of the Church of Rome, but down to the time of the
Reformation that Church was held up by a succession of theologians or ecclesiastics, as the Babylon of the Apocalypse which
was to be overthrown and rendered desolate.

When the Reformers with one voice pronounced the same
judgment, and, making little distinction between Babylon and
Antichrist, held up the Papacy as the antichristian power predicted by Daniel, by St. Paul, and by St. John, the Romanists laid
out their strength in defending their Church from this denunciation. Bellarmin, the great advocate of the cause of Romanism,
devotes an extended dissertation to the discussion of this subject,
which constitutes the third book of his work, "De Romano Pontifice." The points that he assumes are : First, that the word
"Antichrist" cannot mean, as some Protestants thought, "substitute or vicar" of Christ, but an opponent of Christ. In this
all parties are now agreed. Second, that Antichrist is "unus
homo," and not "genus hominum." The Magdeburg Centuriators[2] said : "Docent [Apostoli] Antichristum non fore unam
aliquam tantum personam, sed integrum regnum, per falsos doc-
tores in templo Dei, hoc est in Ecclesia Dei praesidentes, in urba
magna, quæ habet regnum super reges terræ id est, in Romana
civitate, et imperio Romano, opera diaboli, et fraude, et decep-
tione comparatum." This view Bellarmin undertakes to refute,
controverting the arguments of Calvin and Beza in its support.
In this opinion also the leading Protestant interpreters of the
present day, as above stated, agree. According to the views
already advanced, there may be hereafter a great antichristian

[1] Maitland, *The Apostles' School of Prophetic Interpretation*, p. 340; see also Guericke, *Kirchengeschichte*, 6th edit., Leipzig, 1846, vol. ii. pp. 223–226.
[2] *De Antichristo*, cent. i. lib. ii. cap. iv.; Basle, 1562, vol. i. pp. 434, 435, of second set.

power, concentrated in an individual ruler, who will be utterly
destroyed at the coming of the Lord, and at the same time the
belief may be maintained that the Antichrist described by Daniel
and St. Paul is not a man, but an institution or organized power
such as a kingdom or the papacy.

The third position assumed by Bellarmin is that the Antichrist is still future. In this way he endeavours to make it plain
that the papacy is not Antichrist. But, as just said, even if an
Antichrist, and even the Antichrist κατ᾽ ἐξοχήν, is yet to come, that
would not prove that the papacy is not the power predicted by
the Apostle as the Man of Sin, and the mystical Babylon as predicted in the Apocalypse.

Bellarmin says that the Holy Spirit gives us six signs of Antichrist, from which it is plain that he has not yet appeared. Two
of these signs precede his coming, the universal proclamation of
the Gospel, and the utter destruction of the Roman Empire ; two
are to attend it, namely, the preaching of Enoch and Elias, and
persecutions so severe as to cause the cessation of all public worship of God ; and two are to follow his appearance ; his utter
destruction after three years and a half ; and the end of the world.
The passages on which he relies to prove that Enoch and Elias
are to come and oppose themselves to Antichrist, and to preserve
the elect, are Malachi iv., Ecclesiasticus xliv. and xlviii., Matthew
xvii. 11 (Jesus said, " Elias truly shall first come and restore all
things "), and Revelation xi. 3, where the appearance of the two
witnesses, who were to prophesy two thousand two hundred and
sixty days, is foretold. As modern evangelical interpreters agree
with Bellarmin in so many other points, so they agree with him
in teaching that there is to be a second appearance of Elias, before
the second advent of Christ. Luthardt understands Matthew
xvii. 11 as predicting such reappearance of the Old Testament
prophet. He was to be one, and Moses the other of the two witnesses spoken of in Revelation xi. 3. Of course, says Luthardt,
Elias and Moses are to reappear in the sense in which Elias
appeared in the person of John the Baptist.[1]

Fourthly, according to Bellarmin, Antichrist is to be a Jew,
and probably of the tribe of Dan. He is to claim to be the Messiah, and this claim is to be recognized by the Jews. In virtue
of his Messiahship he sets himself against Christ, and puts himself in his place, and arrogates the reverence, the obedience, the
universal dominion and the absolute authority, which rightfully

---

[1] Luthardt, *Lehre von den letzten Dingen*, p. 46.

belong to the Lord Jesus Christ. The seat of his dominion is to be Jerusalem. In the Temple restored in that city, he is to take his seat as God, and exalt himself above all that is called God. He is called " the little horn," because the Jews are comparatively a small nation. But he is to subdue one kingdom after another until his dominion as a worldly sovereign becomes absolutely universal. The authority urged for this view is principally that of the fathers, many of whom taught that Antichrist was to be a Jew of the tribe of Dan. Appeal was made by those fathers as by their followers to Genesis xlix. 17, where it is said, " Dan shall be a serpent by the way, an adder in the path, that biteth the horse-heels, so that his rider shall fall backward." And also to Revelation vii., because in the enumeration of the tribes from which the hundred and forty and four thousand were sealed, the name of Dan is omitted. Bellarmin argues that Antichrist is to be a Jew from John v. 43 : " I am come in my Father's name and ye (Jews) receive me not : if another shall come in his own name, him ye (Jews) will receive." That is, will receive as the Messiah ; but the Jews, as Bellarmin argues, would never receive as the Messiah any one who was not himself a Jew. The principal Scriptural ground of the opinion that Antichrist is to be a Jew is founded on Revelation xi. 8, where the seat of his dominion is said to be the great city " where also our Lord was crucified." In answer to this argument it may be said, first, that admitting that the literal Jerusalem is to be the seat of the kingdom of Antichrist, it does not follow that either he or his kingdom is to be Jewish. Many interpreters hold that the Jews, instead of being the supporters of Antichrist, are to be the principal objects of his malice, and that it is by persecuting and oppressing them that he is to get possession of their holy city and profane their temple far more atrociously than it was profaned by Antiochus Epiphanes. And secondly, interpreters so different as Hengstenberg and Mr. David N. Lord, agree in understanding the predictions in Revelation xi. to refer not to the literal Jerusalem and its Temple, but to that of which they were the symbols. The New Jerusalem is the symbol of the purified and glorified Church ; the city where our Lord was crucified, the symbol of the worldly and nationalized Church.[1]

---

[1] Mr. Lord says: "The place where Christ was crucified, was an open elevated space without the walls of Jerusalem, and on one of the principal entrances to the city. The street where the dead body of the witnesses is to be placed, represents parts therefore of the ten kingdoms, bearing a relation of conspicuity and importance to the apostate hierarchies, like that which the great entrance to Jerusalem that passed along by the foot of Calvary bore to that city ; — parts of those kingdoms from which those hierarchies largely

Fifthly, as to the doctrine of Antichrist, everything follows, from the assumption that he claims to be Christ. In claiming to be the Messiah predicted by the prophets, he is to claim to be the only object of worship. That he is to admit of no other God, whether true or false, nor of any idols, Bellarmin infers from 2 Thessalonians ii. 2, " He opposeth and exalteth himself above all that is called God or is worshipped." " Certum est," says Bellarmin, " Antichristi persecutionem fore gravissimam et notissimam; ita ut cessent omnes publicæ religionis ceremoniæ et sacrificia . . . . [Daniel xii. docet] Antichristum interdicturum omnem divinum cultum, qui in ecclesiis Christianorum exercetur." [1] Thus also Stapleton says : " Pelli sane poterit in desertam ecclesia, regnante Antichristi, et illo momento temporis in deserta, id est, in locis abitis, in speluncis, in latibulis quo sancti se recipient, non incommode quæretur ecclesia." [2] During the reign of Antichrist, according to the notes to the Romish version of the New Testament on 2 Thessalonians ii., " The external state of the Romish Church, and the public intercourse of the faithful with it, may cease. Yet the due honour and obedience towards the Roman see, and the communion of heart with it, and the secret practice of that communion, and the open confession thereof, if the occasion require, shall not cease." Again on verse 4th it is said, " The great Antichrist who must come towards the world's end, shall abolish all other religions, true and false; and put down the blessed sacrament of the altar, wherein consisteth principally the worship of the true God, and also all idols of the Gentiles." " The oblation of Christ's blood," it is said, " is to be abolished among all the nations and churches in the world."

Finally, concerning the kingdom and wars of Antichrist, the Roman cardinal teaches, (1.) That from small beginnings, he is by fraud and deceit, to attain the kingdom of the Jews. (2.) That he is to subdue and take possession of the three kingdoms of Egypt, Libya, and Ethiopia. (Dan. xi.) (3.) That he is then to reduce to subjection the other seven kingdoms spoken of by the prophet; and (4.) That with an innumerable army, he shall make for a time successful war against all Christians in every part of the world, and finally be overthrown and utterly destroyed, as described in the twentieth chapter of Revelation.

From this review it appears that the doctrine of the Romish the-

derived their sustenance, wealth, and worshippers." *An Exposition of the Apocalypse,* p. 297.

[1] Bellarmin, *De Romano Pontifice,* III. vii.; *Disputationes,* Paris, 1608, vol. i. pp. 721 e, 723 c.

[2] *Princip. Doct.* cap. 2.

ologians concerning Antichrist, agrees with that of a large body
of modern Protestant writers in the following points: (1.) That
he is to be an individual, and not a corporation, or " genus hominum." (2.) That he is to be a worldly potentate. (3.) That he
is to attain universal dominion. (4.) That he is to be, in character, godless and reckless, full of malignity against Christ and his
people. (5.) That by his seductions and persecutions he is to succeed for a time in almost banishing true religion from the world.
(6.) That his reign is to be brief.

The principal difference between the early Protestants and
the modern evangelical interpreters, is, that the former identify
Babylon and Antichrist; that is, they refer to one and the same
power the prophecies of Daniel referring to the little horn; the
description given by the Apostle in 2 Thessalonians ii.; and the
account of the beast in chapter xiii. of the Apocalypse and that
given in chapter xvii. Whereas, the moderns for the most part
distinguish between the two. The papacy they regard as set
forth under the symbol of Babylon; and Antichrist, as a worldly
potentate, under the beast which came up out of the abyss.[1]

The great truth set forth in these prophecies is, that there was
future in the time, not only of Daniel, but also of the Apostles, a
great apostasy in the Church; that this apostasy would be Antichristian (or Antichrist), ally itself with the world and become a
great persecuting power; and that the two elements, the ecclesiastical and the worldly, which enter into this great Antichristian
development, will, sometimes the one and sometimes the other,
become the more prominent; sometimes acting in harmony, and
sometimes opposed one to the other; and, therefore, sometimes
spoken of as one, and sometimes as two distinct powers. Both,
as united or as separate, are to be overtaken with a final destruction when the Lord comes. So much is certain, that any and
every power, be it one or more, which answers to the description
given in Daniel vii. and xi. and in 2 Thessalonians ii. is Antichrist in the Scriptural sense of the term.

According, then, to the common faith of the Church, the three
great events which are to precede the second advent of Christ,
are the universal proclamation of the Gospel or the conversion of
the Gentile world; the national conversion of the Jews; and the
appearance of Antichrist.

[1] Ebrard says, "The Reformers and the early theologians, erred only in this, that they
identified the beast that was to remain three and one half years mentioned in Rev. xiii.
with that mentioned in chap. xvii. That is, they identified the papacy and the Antichristian kingdom." *Christliche Dogmatik*, Königsberg, 1852. vol. ii. p. 736.

CHAPTER IV.

THE CONCOMITANTS OF THE SECOND ADVENT.

THE events which according to the common doctrine of the Church are to attend the second coming of Christ, are first, the general resurrection of the dead; second, the final judgment; third, "the end of the world;" and fourth, the consummation of the kingdom of Christ.

§ 1. *The General Resurrection.*

That there is to be a general resurrection of the just and of the unjust, is not, among Christians, a matter of doubt. Already in the book of Daniel xii. 2, it is said, " Many of them that sleep in the dust of the earth shall awake, some to everlasting life, and some to shame and everlasting contempt. And they that be wise shall shine as the brightness of the firmament; and they that turn many to righteousness, as stars for ever and ever." This prediction our Lord repeats without any limitation. " Marvel not at this : for the hour is coming, in the which all that are in the graves shall hear his voice, and shall come forth ; they that have done good, unto the resurrection of life; and they that have done evil, unto the resurrection of damnation." (John v. 28, 29.) Again: " When the Son of man shall come in his glory, and all the holy angels with him, then shall he sit upon the throne of his glory : and before him shall be gathered all nations." (Matt. xxv. 31, 32.) Paul, in his speech before Felix (Acts xxiv. 15), avowed it as his own faith and that of his fathers that " there shall be a resurrection of the dead, both of the just and unjust." John (Rev. xx. 12, 13) says : " I saw the dead, small and great, stand before God ; and the books were opened : and another book was opened, which is the book of life : and the dead were judged out of those things which were written in the books, according to their works. And the sea gave up the dead which were in it ; and death and hell gave up the dead which were in them."

The Time of this General Resurrection.

The uniform representation of Scripture on this subject is that this general resurrection is to take place " at the last day," or, at the second coming of Christ. The same form of expression is used to designate the time when the people of Christ are to rise, and the time when the general resurrection is to occur. The Bible, if the doubtful passage Revelation xx. 4–6 be excepted, never speaks of any other than one resurrection. The dead, according to the Scriptures, are to rise together, some to everlasting life, and some to shame and everlasting contempt. When Christ comes, all who are in their graves shall come forth, some to the resurrection of life, and others to the resurrection of damnation. When in 1 Thessalonians iv. 16, it is said, " The dead in Christ shall rise first," it does not mean that there are to be two resurrections, one of those who are in Christ, and the other of those who are not in Him. The Apostle is speaking of a different subject. He comforts the Thessalonians with the assurance, that their friends who sleep in Jesus shall not miss their part in the glories of the second advent. Those then alive should not prevent, *i. e.*, precede, those who were asleep ; but, the dead in Christ should rise before those then living should be changed ; and then both should be caught up to meet the Lord in the air. The parallel passage is in 1 Corinthians xv. 51, 52, " We shall not all sleep, but we shall all be changed, in a moment, in the twinkling of an eye, at the last trump : for the trumpet shall sound, and the dead shall be raised incorruptible, and we shall be changed."

In 1 Corinthians xv. 23, 24, the Apostle, when speaking of the resurrection, says : " Every man in his own order : Christ the first fruits ; afterward they that are Christ's at his coming. Then cometh the end." This passage is often understood to teach that the resurrection takes place in the following order : (1.) That of Christ. (2.) That of his people. (3.) Then that of the rest of mankind. And as the resurrection of Christ and that of his people are separated by a long interval ; so the resurrection of the people of God and the general resurrection may also be separated by an interval of greater or less duration. This interpretation supposes that the word " end," as here used, means the end of the resurrection. To this, however, it may be objected, (1.) That it is opposed to the constant " usus loquendi " of the New Testament. The " end," when thus used, always elsewhere means the end of the world. In 1 Peter iv. 7, it is said : " The end of all things is at hand." Matthew xxiv. 6, " The end is not yet;" verse 14, " Then shall the end come." So in Mark xiii. 7, Luke xxi. 9. In all these passages the " end " means the end of the world. (2.) The equivalent expressions serve to explain the meaning of the term. The disciples asked our Lord, " What shall be the sign of Thy coming and of the end of the world?" In answer to that question Christ said that certain things were to happen, but, " the end is not yet;" and afterwards, " then cometh the end." (Matt. xxiv. 3, 6, 14.) The same expression occurs in the same sense, Matthew xiii. 39, xxviii. 20, and elsewhere. (3.) What immediately follows in verse 24, seems decisive in favour of this interpretation. The end spoken of is when Christ shall have delivered up his kingdom; that is, when the whole work of redemption shall have been consummated. (4.) It is further to be remarked that in 1 Corinthians xv. Paul does not make the slightest reference to the resurrection of the wicked, from the beginning to the end of the chapter. The whole concerns the resurrection of believers. That was what the errorists in Corinth denied; and that was what the Apostle undertook to prove to be certain and desirable. Christ certainly rose from the dead; so all his people shall rise; but each in his order; first, Christ, then they who are Christ's; then comes the end; the end of all things. To make this refer to another and general resurrection, would be to introduce a subject entirely foreign to the matter in hand.

Meyer, although he makes τέλος in the 24th verse refer to the resurrection, nevertheless says [1] " That it is the constant doctrine of the New Testament (leaving the Apocalypse out of view), that with the coming of Christ the ' finis hujus sæculi ' is connected, so that the Second Advent is the termination of the ante-messianic, and the commencement of the future world-period."

Luthardt says,[2] " Then, not before the resurrection, . . . comes the end; the end, not of the resurrection, that is the resurrection of others than believers, but the absolute end; the end of history." Whether the end of all things is to follow the resurrection of believers immediately, or long afterwards, is, in his view, a different question. He admits that the common view is that the coming of Christ, the general resurrection of the dead, the general judgment, the end of the world, and the new heavens and new earth, are to occur contemporaneously. His own view is different.

That the New Testament does teach that the general resurrection is to occur at the time of the Second Advent appears: —

[1] *Commentar über das Neue Testament*, 2d edit., Göttingen, 1849, vol. v. p. 323.
[2] *Lehre von den letzten Dingen*, Leipzig, 1861. " 127

1. From such passages as the following ; In the passage in Daniel, quoted above, it is said, that the righteous and the wicked are to rise together; the one to life, the other to shame and everlasting contempt. This passage our Lord reiterates, saying that "the hour is coming, in the which all that are in the graves shall hear his voice, and shall come forth ; they that have done good, unto the resurrection of life; and they that have done evil, unto the resurrection of damnation." (John v. 28, 29.) In Matthew xxv. 31, 32, it is said, that when the Son of Man shall appear in his glory all nations shall stand before him. The same is said in Revelations xx. 12, 13. In 2 Thessalonians i. 7–10, it is taught that when the Lord Jesus shall be revealed from heaven, it will be to take vengeance on those who obey not the Gospel, and to be glorified in all them that believe. In all these passages the resurrection of the righteous is declared to be contemporaneous with that of the wicked.

2. There is another class of passages which teach that the resurrection of the righteous is to take place at "the last day," and, therefore, not a thousand years before that event. Thus Martha, speaking of her brother Lazarus, said, "I know that he shall rise again in the resurrection at the last day." (John xi. 24.) Our Lord, in John vi. 39, says that it is the Father's will "that of all which He hath given me, I should lose nothing, but should raise it up again at the last day." This declaration is repeated in verses 40, 44, 54, comp. xii. 48: "The word that I have spoken, the same shall judge him in the last day." It is true that the expressions "the last time," "the last day," "the end of days," "the end of the world," are often used very indefinitely in Scripture. They often mean nothing more than "hereafter." But this is not true with the phrase ἐν τῇ ἐσχάτῃ ἡμέρᾳ as used in these passages. "In the last day," is a known and definite period. It is to be remembered also that what is predicted to happen on "the last day," is elsewhere said to take place when Christ shall appear in his glory.

3. A third class of passages teach that the resurrection of the saints is to take place at the day of judgment and in connection with that event. According to the common representations of Scripture, when Christ shall come the second time, the dead are to rise, all nations are to be judged, and the present order of things is to cease. The heavens are to retain Christ, "until the times of restitution of all things." (Acts iii. 21.) This ἀποκατάστασις is "die Wiederherstellung aller Dinge in ihren frühern vollkomm-

nern Zustand," [1] the restoration of all things to their original perfect condition. " This consummation may be called a ' restitution,' in allusion to a circle which returns into itself, or more probably because it really involves the healing of all curable disorder and the restoration to communion with the Deity of all that He has chosen to be so restored. Till this great cycle has achieved its revolution, and this great remedial process has accomplished its design, the glorified body of the risen and ascended Christ not only may, but must, as an appointed means of that accomplishment, be resident in heaven, and not on earth." [2]

The general resurrection is represented as connected with the final judgment, in Matthew xxiv. 30, 31, and xxv. 31–46, 2 Thessalonians i. 7–10, and elsewhere. On this point Dr. Julius Müller says: " It is the plain doctrine of Scripture that the general resurrection of the dead contemporaneous with the transfiguration of believers then living on earth is to occur at the end of the world (or of history), at the reappearance of Christ for judgment and for the glorification of his kingdom. . . . . With this consummation of Christ's kingdom, and the therewith connected ἀπολύτρωσις τοῦ σώματος ἡμῶν ἀπὸ τῆς δουλείας τῆς φθορᾶς, the Apostle, in the profound passage, Romans viii. 19–23, sets forth, as also connected with these events, the renovation of the nature of the earth and its exaltation to a participation in the glory of the children of God. As the body of man stands in intimate relation with nature, ... it is scarcely possible to form any idea of the resurrection of the body . . . . without assuming a corresponding exaltation of the external world as the theatre of his new life. This renovation of nature, the new heavens and the new earth, takes for granted, according to the Apostle, the destruction of the world as it now is." [3] With these views, which accord with the common doctrine of the Church, Lange avows his entire agreement. [4]

The only passage which seems to teach that there is to be a first and second resurrection of the body, the former being confined to martyrs and more or fewer of the saints, and the latter including " the rest of the dead," is Revelation xx. 4–6. It must be admitted that that passage, taken by itself, does seem to teach the doctrine founded upon it. But —

[1] De Wette, *Exegetisches Handbuch zum Neuen Testament*, Leipzig, 1845, vol. i. part 4, p. 48.
[2] *The Acts of the Apostles Explained*. By Joseph Addison Alexander. New York, 1857, vol. i. p. 118.
[3] *Studien und Kritiken*, 1835, pp. 783–785.
[4] *Lehre von den letzen Dingen*, Meurs, 1841, pp. 246, 247.

1. It is a sound rule in the interpretation of Scripture that obscure passages should be so explained as to make them agree with those that are plain. It is unreasonable to make the symbolic and figurative language of prophecy and poetry the rule by which to explain the simple didactic prose language of the Bible. It is no less unreasonable that a multitude of passages should be taken out of their natural sense to make them accord with a single passage of doubtful import.

2. It is conceded that the Apocalypse is an obscure book. This almost every reader knows from his own experience; and it is proved to be true, the few who imagine it to be plain to the contrary notwithstanding, by the endless diversity of interpretations to which it has been subjected. This diversity exists not only between commentators of different classes, as rationalistic and orthodox, but between those of the same class, and even of the same school. This remark, which applies to the whole book, applies with special force to the passage under consideration.

3. The Bible speaks of a spiritual, or figurative, as well as of a literal resurrection. This figure is used both in reference to individuals and in reference to communities. The sinner, dead in trespasses and sins, is said to be quickened and raised again in Christ Jesus. (Rom. vi. and Eph. ii.) Whole communities, when elevated from a state of depression and misery, are in prophetic language said to be raised from the dead. (Rom. xi. 15; Is. xxvi. 19.) "Thy dead men shall live, together with my dead body shall they arise. Awake and sing, ye that dwell in dust; for thy dew is as the dew of herbs, and the earth shall cast out the dead." (Ez. xxxvii. 12.) "I will open your graves, and cause you to come up out of your graves, and bring you into the land of Israel." More than this, Elias is said to have lived again in John the Baptist; and, according to a common interpretation, the two witnesses spoken of in the Apocalypse are Moses and Elias, who are to rise not in person, but as represented by men filled with the same spirit, endued with similar gifts, and called to exercise the same offices. It would, therefore, not be inconsistent with the analogy of prophecy if we should understand the Apostle as here predicting that a new race of men were to arise filled with the spirit of the martyrs, and were to live and reign with Christ a thousand years. According to Hengstenberg, the Apostle saw the souls of the martyrs in heaven. There they were enthroned. This was their first resurrection. "There can be no doubt," he

says, " that by the first resurrection we are here primarily to understand that first stage of blessedness." [1]

4. John does not say that the bodies of the martyrs are to be raised from the dead. He says : " I saw the souls of them that were beheaded for the witness of Jesus." The resurrection of tne dead is never thus spoken of in Scripture. There is a sense in which the martyrs are said to live again, but nothing is said of their rising again from their graves. The first resurrection may be spiritual, and the second literal. There may be a time of great prosperity in the Church, in which it will be a great blessing to participate. It is said that there is no force in this argument, as the Apostle does not speak of a resurrection of souls. He simply says he saw the souls of the martyrs ; as in chapter vi. 9, it is said : " I saw under the altar the souls of them that were slain for the word of God." The prophet, according to xx. 4, first saw the martyrs in the state of the dead, and then he saw them alive. The argument, however, is not founded merely on the use of the word " souls," but on the fact that the resurrection of the dead is never spoken of in the Scriptures in the way in which the living again of the martyrs is here described.

5. The common millenarian doctrine is, that there is to be a literal resurrection when Christ shall come to reign in person upon the earth, a thousand years before the end of the world, and that the risen saints are to dwell here and share with Christ in the glories of his reign. But this seems to be inconsistent with what is taught in 1 Corinthians xv. 50. Paul there says : " Now this I say, brethren, that flesh and blood cannot inherit the kingdom of God ; neither doth corruption inherit incorruption." It is here expressly asserted that our bodies as now constituted are not adapted to the state of things which shall exist when the kingdom of God is inaugurated. We must all be changed. From this it follows that the spiritual body is not adapted to our present mode of existence ; that is, it is not suited or designed for an earthly kingdom. Luthardt admits this. He admits that the renovated, or transfigured, body of necessity supposes a renovated earth. He admits also that when the bodies of believers are thus changed they are to be caught up from the earth, and are to dwell with Christ in heaven. When Christ appears, his people are to appear with Him in glory. Bengel, and after him others, endeavour to reconcile these admissions with the theory of

[1] *The Revelation of St. John Expounded*, edit. Edinburgh, 1852, vol. ii. p. 281.

an earthly kingdom of glory, by assuming that risen saints are
to rule this kingdom, not from the literal Jerusalem, but from
heaven. This, however, is to introduce an extra-scriptural and
conjectural idea.

6. It has already been said, when speaking of the restoration
of the Jews to their own land, that this whole theory of a splen-
did earthly kingdom is a relic of Judaism, and out of keeping
with the spirituality of the Gospel.[1]

All this is said with diffidence and submission. The interpretation of unfulfilled prophecy experience teaches is exceedingly precarious. There is every reason to believe that the predictions concerning the second advent of Christ, and the events
which are to attend and follow it, will disappoint the expectations of commentators, as the expectations of the Jews were disappointed in the manner in which the prophecies concerning the
first advent were accomplished.

§ 2. *The Final Judgment.*

The Scriptures abound in passages which set forth God as the
moral ruler of men ; which declare that He will judge the world
in righteousness. The Bible represents Him as the judge of
nations and of individuals ; as the avenger of the poor and the
persecuted. It abounds also in promises and in threatenings,
and in illustrations of the righteous judgments of God. Nothing,
therefore, is plainer than that men in this world are subject to
the moral government of God. Besides this, the Bible also
teaches that there is a future state of reward and punishment, in
which the inequalities and anomalies here permitted shall be
adjusted. According to some, this is all that the Bible teaches
on the subject. What is said of the punishment of the wicked
and of the reward of the righteous is to be understood in this
general way. This is the doctrine of the common school of
Rationalists.[2] Bretschneider[3] admits, however, that reason has
nothing to object to the Church doctrine on this subject properly understood.

---

[1] The interpretation of this whole passage (Rev. xx. 1–6) is thoroughly discussed in the
very able work of the Rev. David Brown, of St. James' Free Church, Glasgow, entitled,
Christ's Second Coming: Will it be Pre-Millenial? chapter x. edit. New York, 1851,
p. 218 ff.

[2] J. A. L. Wegscheider, *Institutiones Theologicæ*, iv. ii. 99; 5th edit. Halle, 1826, p. 614 ff.

[3] *Dogmatik der evangelisch-lutherischen Kirche*, § 172, 3d edit. Leipzig, 1828; vol. ii
p. 445.

A second view of the last judgment assumes it to be a process now in progress. In the Old Testament the Messianic period is spoken of as the "last day," "the last time," "the end of days," "the end of the world," and is represented as a time of conflict and of judgment. The Jews expected that when the Messiah came, the severest judgments would fall upon the heathen, and that the chosen people would be greatly exalted and blessed. This was the day of judgment. Those who give substantially the same interpretation to the Old Testament prophecies, hold that the day of judgment covers the whole period between the first and second advents of Christ.

A third doctrine is that the world in its progress works out all possible manifestations of God, so that according to the stereotyped dictum of Schelling, Die Weltgeschichte ist das Weltgericht; the history of the world is the judgment of the world. Premillenarians use precisely the same words, although not in the same philosophical sense. With them "to judge" is to reign; and when Christ comes to establish his personal reign upon earth, the last judgment will begin, and "the judgment of God is the administration of the government of God." [1]

A fourth theory may be mentioned. There are certain immutable laws, either independent, as some say, of the will of God, or dependent on his voluntary constitution, which secure that the righteous shall be happy and the wicked miserable; and this is all that either reason or Scripture, properly understood, teaches of rewards and punishment.

A fifth doctrine is that the day of judgment is a protracted future dispensation, as just mentioned, to commence with the second advent of Christ, and to continue during the thousand years of his personal reign upon the earth. This theory is connected with the doctrine of the pre-millenial advent of Christ.

The Church Doctrine.

By the Church doctrine is meant that doctrine which is held by the Church universal; by Romanists and Protestants in the West, and by the Greeks in the East. That doctrine includes the following points: —

1. The final judgment is a definite future event (not a protracted process), when the eternal destiny of men and of angels shall be finally determined and publicly manifested. That this is the doctrine of the Bible, is proved by such passages as the

---

[1] *The Last Times*, by Joseph A. Seiss, D. D., Philadelphia, 1866, p. 141.

following : Matthew xi. 24, " It shall be more tolerable for the land of Sodom in the day of judgment, than for thee ; " Matthew xiii. 30, " Let both grow together until the harvest : and in the time of harvest I will say to the reapers, Gather ye together first the tares, and bind them in bundles to burn them : but gather the wheat into my barn ; " verse 39, " The harvest is the end of the world, and the reapers are the angels ; " verse 49, " So shall it be at the end of the world : the angels shall come forth, and sever the wicked from among the just ; " John xii. 48, " The word that I have spoken, the same shall judge him in the last day ; " Acts xviii. 31, God " hath appointed a day in the which He will judge the world in righteousness ; " Romans ii. 5, " The day of wrath and revelation of the righteous judgment of God ; " and 1 Corinthians iv. 5, " Judge nothing before the time, until the Lord come." It is true that the word " day " in Scripture is often used for an indefinite period ; as " the day of the Lord," is the time of the Lord. And, therefore, it does not follow from the use of this word, that the judgment is to be commenced and ended in the space of twenty-four hours. Nevertheless, the way in which the word is used in this connection, and the circumstances with which the judgment is connected, show that a definite and limited period, and not a protracted dispensation, is intended by the term. The appearance of Christ, the resurrection of the dead, and the gathering of the nations, are not events which are to be protracted through years or centuries.

2. Christ is to be the judge. John v. 22, 23, " The Father judgeth no man, but hath committed all judgment unto the Son ; that all men should honour the Son, even as they honour the Father ; " verse 27, " And hath given Him authority to execute judgment also, because He is the Son of Man." Peter, in Acts x. 34–43, says that God " anointed Jesus of Nazareth with the Holy Ghost and with power ; " had " raised " Him from the dead " and shewed Him openly," and " commanded us to preach unto the people, and to testify that it is He which was ordained of God to be the Judge of quick and dead." Paul, in his speech on Mars' Hill, tells the Athenians that God " hath appointed a day, in the which He will judge the world in righteousness, by that man whom He hath ordained ; whereof He hath given assurance unto all men, in that He hath raised Him from the dead." (Acts xvii. 31.) And in 2 Corinthians v. 10, he says, " We must all appear before the judgment-seat of Christ." Our Lord says that He will say to the wicked, " Depart from me, ye that work iniquity."

(Matt. v. 23 ; Luke xiii. 27.) In all the graphic descriptions given in the New Testament of the process of the final judgment, Christ is represented as acting as the judge. On this point it is to be observed : (1.) That He is set forth as acting on his own authority ; and not merely as the " Bevollmächter," or plenipotentiary of God. Everywhere in the New Testament, our responsibility is said to be to Him. We are to stand before his judgment-seat. He will say, " Depart from me, ye cursed." It is He, who is to bring every secret thing into judgment. (2.) He is qualified thus to sit in judgment on men and angels ; because He is omniscient, and infinite in justice and mercy. (3.) It is especially appropriate that the man Christ Jesus, God manifest in the flesh, should be the judge of all men. He has this authority committed to Him because He is the Son of man ; because, although in the form of God, and thinking it no robbery to be equal with God, He humbled Himself to be found in fashion as a man. This is part of his exaltation, due to Him because He consented to become obedient unto death. It is meet that He who stood condemned at the bar of Pilate, should sit enthroned on the seat of universal judgment. It is a joy and ground of special confidence to all believers, that He who loved them and gave Himself for them, shall be their judge on the last day.

3. This judgment is to take place at the second coming of Christ and at the general resurrection. Therefore it is not a process now in progress ; it does not take place at death ; it is not a protracted period prior to the general resurrection. A few of the passages bearing on this point are the following : In the parable of the wheat and the tares (Matt. xiii. 37–43), already referred to, we are taught that the final separation between the righteous and the wicked is to take place at the end of the world, when the Son of Man shall send forth his angels to gather out of his kingdom all things that offend. This implies that the general resurrection, the second advent, and the last judgment, are contemporaneous events. The Bible knows nothing of three personal advents of Christ: one at the time of the incarnation ; a second before the millennium ; and a third to judge the world. He who came in the flesh, is to come a second time without sin unto salvation. Matthew xvi. 27, " The Son of Man shall come in the glory of his Father, with his angels ; and then He shall reward every man according to his works." Matthew xxiv. 29–35, teaches that when the sign of the Son of Man appears in the heavens, all the tribes of the earth shall mourn, and the elect shall be gathered in.

Matthew xxv. 31–46 sets forth the whole process of the judgment. When the Son of Man shall come in his glory, all nations shall be gathered before Him, and He shall separate them as a shepherd divideth the sheep from the goats; and then shall He say to those on his right hand, Come, ye blessed of my Father; and to those on the left, Depart from me, ye cursed. 1 Corinthians iv. 5, " Judge nothing before the time, until the Lord come, who both will bring to light the hidden things of darkness, and will make manifest the counsels of the hearts: and then shall every man have praise of God." When Christ comes, the general judgment is to occur. In 2 Thessalonians i. 7–10, it is taught that when the Lord Jesus Christ shall be revealed from heaven, it will be for the double purpose of taking vengeance on them that know not God, and of being glorified in all them that believe. In 2 Timothy iv. 1, it is said: The Lord Jesus Christ " shall judge the quick and the dead at his appearing, and his kingdom." In the fifteenth chapter of First Corinthians, the Apostle expressly teaches that corruption cannot inherit incorruption, that our present vile bodies must be changed before they can enter the kingdom of God; and this change from the natural to the spiritual, from mortal to immortal, is to take place at the last trump; and in Philippians iii. 20, 21, he says it is to occur when Christ comes from heaven, who shall fashion our bodies like unto his own glorious body. In all these different ways it is taught that the general judgment is to take place at the second coming of Christ.

4. The persons to be judged are men and angels. In several passages already quoted it is said that Christ is to come to judge " the quick and the dead;" in others it is said, " all nations are to stand before Him;" in others, that " we must all appear before the judgment-seat of Christ;" in others again it is said that " He will render to every man according to his works." This judgment, therefore, is absolutely universal; it includes both small and great; and all the generations of men. With regard to the evil angels, it is said that God " delivered them into chains of darkness, to be reserved unto judgment." (2 Pet. ii. 4.) Satan is said to be the God of this world. The conflict in which believers are engaged in this life, is with principalities and powers and spiritual wickedness in heaven, ἐν τοῖς ἐπουρανίοις. This conflict is to continue until the Second Advent, when Satan and his angels are to be cast into the pit.

The older theologians speculated on the manner in which the

judgment is to be arranged, so as to admit of the countless millions of human beings who shall have lived from the beginning of the world to the final consummation being so congregated as to be all gathered before the throne of the Son of Man. The common answer to that difficulty was that the throne is to be so exalted and so glorious as to be visible, as are the sun and moon, from a large part of the earth's surface at the same time. These, however, are questions about which we need give ourselves no concern; these descriptions of the judgment are designed to teach us moral truths, and not the physical phenomena by which the solemn adjudication on the destiny of men is to be attended.

5. The ground or matter of judgment is said to be the " deeds done in the body," men are to be judged " according to their works ; " " the secrets of the heart " are to be brought to light. God's judgment will not be founded on the professions, or the relations of men, or on the appearance or reputation which they sustain among their fellows ; but on their real character and on their acts, however secret and covered from the sight of men those acts may have been. God will not be mocked and cannot be deceived ; the character of every man will be clearly revealed. (1.) In the sight of God. (2.) In the sight of the man himself. All self deception will be banished. Every man will see himself as he appears in the sight of God. His memory will probably prove an indelible register of all his sinful acts and thoughts and feelings. His conscience will be so enlightened as to recognize the justice of the sentence which the righteous judge shall pronounce upon him. All whom Christ condemns will be self-condemned. (3.) There will be such a revelation of the character of every man to all around him, or to all who know him, as shall render the justice of the sentence of condemnation or acquittal apparent. Beyond this the representations of Scripture do not require us to go.

Besides these general representations of Scripture that the character and conduct of men is the ground on which the final sentence is to be pronounced, there is clear intimation in the Word of God, that, so far as those who hear the Gospel are concerned their future destiny depends on the attitude which they assume to Christ. He came to his own, and his own received Him not ; but to as many as received Him, to them gave He power to become the sons of God. He is God manifest in the flesh ; He came into the world to save sinners ; all who receive Him as their God and Saviour, are saved ; all who refuse to recognize and trust

Him, perish. They are condemned already, because they have not believed in the name of the only begotten Son of God. He that believeth on the Son hath everlasting life; he that believeth not the Son shall not see life; but the wrath of God abideth on him. Whosoever shall confess me before men, him will I also confess before my Father who is in heaven. But whosoever shall deny me before men, him will I also deny before my Father which is in heaven. When the Jews asked our Lord, What shall we do that we might work the works of God? his answer was, "This is the work of God, that ye believe on him whom He hath sent." In the solemn account given of the last judgment in Matthew xxv. 31–46, the inquest concerns the conduct of men towards Christ. And the Apostle says, If any man love not the Lord Jesus Christ let him be Anathema Maranatha. The special ground of condemnation, therefore, under the Gospel is unbelief; the refusal to receive Christ in the character in which He is presented for our acceptance.

6. Men are to be judged according to the light which they have severally enjoyed. The servant that knew his Lord's will, and did it not, shall be beaten with many stripes; but he that knew it not, shall be beaten with few stripes. " For unto whomsoever much is given, of him shall be much required." Our Lord says that it shall be more tolerable, in the day of judgment, for Tyre and Sidon, than for the men of his generation. Paul says that the heathen are inexcusable, because that when they knew God, they glorified Him not as God; and he lays down the principle that they who sin without law, shall be judged without law; and that they who have sinned in the law shall be judged by the law.

7. At the judgment of the last day the destiny of the righteous and of the wicked shall be unalterably determined. Each class shall be assigned to its final abode. This is taught in the solemn words : " These shall go away into everlasting punishment : but the righteous into life eternal."

How far the descriptions of the process of the last judgment, given in the Bible, are to be understood literally, it is useless to inquire. Two things are remarkable about the prophecies of Scripture, which have already been accomplished. The one is that the fulfilment has, in many cases, been very different from that which a literal interpretation led men to anticipate. The other is, that in some cases they have been fulfilled even to the most minute details. These facts should render us modest in our interpretation of those predictions which remain to be accomplished; satisfied that what we know not now we shall know hereafter.

§ 3. *The End of the World.*

The principal passages of Scriptures relating to the final consummation or the end of the world, are the following: Psalm cii. 25, 26, " Of old hast thou laid the foundation of the earth; and the heavens are the work of thy hands. They shall perish, but thou shalt endure; yea, all of them shall wax old as a garment; as a vesture shalt thou change them, and they shall be changed." Isaiah li. 6, " Lift up your eyes to the heavens, and look upon the earth beneath; for the heavens shall vanish away like smoke, and the earth shall wax old like a garment." Isaiah lxv. 17, " Behold, I create new heavens, and a new earth: and the former shall not be remembered nor come into mind." Luke xxi. 33, " Heaven and earth shall pass away: but my words shall not pass away." Romans viii. 19–21, " The earnest expectation of the creature (κτίσις, creation) waiteth for the manifestation of the sons of God. For the creature was made subject to vanity, not willingly, but by reason of him who hath subjected the same in hope, because the creature itself also shall be delivered from the bondage of corruption into the glorious liberty of the children of God." 2 Peter iii. 6–13, " The world that then was, being overflowed with water, perished: but the heavens and earth which are now, by the same word are kept in store, reserved unto fire against the day of judgment and perdition of ungodly men. . . . . The day of the Lord will come as a thief in the night; in the which the heavens shall pass away with a great noise, and the elements shall melt with fervent heat; the earth also, and the works that are therein shall be burned up. . . . . Nevertheless we, according to his promise, look for new heavens and a new earth, wherein dwelleth righteousness." Revelation xx. 11, " I saw a great white throne, and Him that sat on it, from whose face the earth and the heaven fled away; and there was found no place for them." Revelation xxi. 1, " I saw a new heaven and a new earth: for the first heaven and the first earth were passed away; and there was no more sea."

Remarks.

1. These passages are not to be understood as predicting great political and moral revolutions. It is possible that some of them might bear that interpretation; but others are evidently intended to be understood in a more literal sense. This is especially the

case with 2 Peter iii. 6–13, in which the Apostle contrasts the destruction of the world by the waters of the deluge with the destruction by fire which is still future. If the fact be established that the Scriptures anywhere clearly predict the destruction of the world at the last day, that fact becomes a rule for the interpretation of the more doubtful passages. There is nothing in this predicted destruction of our earth out of analogy with the course of nature. Stars once clearly visible in the firmament, after a brief period of unusual splendour, have disappeared; to all appearance they have been burnt up. Scientific men tell us that there is abundant evidence that the earth was once in a state of fusion; and there are causes in operation which are adequate to reduce it to that state again, whenever God sees fit to put them into operation.

2. The destruction here foretold is not annihilation. (*a.*) The world is to be burnt up; but combustion is not a destruction of substance. It is merely a change of state or condition. (*b.*) The destruction of the world by water and its destruction by fire are analogous events; the former was not annihilation, therefore the second is not. (*c.*) The destruction spoken of is elsewhere called a παλιγγενεσία, regeneration (Matt. xix. 28); an ἀποκατάστασις, a restoration (Acts iii. 21); a deliverance from the bondage of corruption (Rom. viii. 21). The Apostle teaches that our vile bodies are to be fashioned like unto the glorious body of Christ, and that a similar change is to take place in the world we inhabit. There are to be new heavens and a new earth, just as we are to have new bodies. Our bodies are not to be annihilated, but changed. (*d.*) There is no evidence, either from Scripture or experience, that any substance has ever been annihilated. If force be motion, it may cease; but cessation of motion is not annihilation, and the common idea in our day, among men of science, is that no force is ever lost; it is, as they say, only transformed. However this may be, it is a purely gratuitous assumption that any substance has ever passed out of existence. In all the endless and complicated changes which have been going on, from the beginning, in our earth and throughout the universe, nothing, so far as known, has ever ceased to be. Of course He who creates can destroy; the question, however, concerns the purpose, and not the power of God; and He has never, either in his word or in his works, revealed his purpose to destroy anything He has once created.

Many of the old theologians, especially among the Lutherans,

understood the Bible to teach the absolute annihilation of our
world. Schmid [1] states as the Lutheran doctrine that the world
is to be reduced to nothing (in Nichts sich auflösen). He quotes
Baier, Hollaz, and Quenstedt in support of this view. Quenstedt [2]
says : " Forma consummationis hujus non in nuda qualitatum
immutatione, alteratione seu innovatione, sed in ipsius substantiæ mundi totali abolitione et in nihilum reductione consistit."
Gerhard [3] takes the same view : " Formam consummationis dicimus fore non nudam qualitatum alterationem, sed ipsius substantiæ abolitionem, adeoque totalem annihilationem, ut sic terminus
a quo consummationis sive destructionis sit ' esse,' terminus vero
ad quem ' non esse ' sive nihil." He admits, however, that many
of the fathers and Luther himself were on the other side. He
quotes Irenæus, Cyril of Jerusalem, Jerome, Augustine, and
Chrysostom, as in favour of mutation and against annihilation.
Luther was wont to say : " The heavens have their work-day
clothes on ; hereafter they will have on their Sunday garments."
Most of the Reformed theologians generally oppose the idea of
annihilation. Turrettin certainly does.[4] One of his questions is :
" Qualis futuris sit mundi interitus ? An per ultimam conflagra-
tionem sit annihilandus, an instaurandus et renovandus ? " He
argues throughout in favour of the latter.

3. The subject of the change which is to take place at the last
day is not the whole material universe, but our earth and what
pertains to it. (a.) It is true the Bible says : " Heaven and
earth are to pass away," and by heaven and earth the Scriptures
often mean the universe ; and it would therefore be consistent
with the language of Scripture to hold that the whole universe is
to be changed at the last day. It was natural that this interpretation should be put upon the language of the Bible so long as
our earth was regarded as the central body of the universe and
sun, moon, and stars as subordinate luminaries, intended simply
for the benefit of the inhabitants of our world. " Wenn der
Tanz," says Strauss,[5] " zu Ende ist, bläst der Wirth die Lichter
aus." The case however assumes a different aspect when we
know that our earth and even our solar system is a mere speck in
the immensity of God's works. It is one of the unmistakable

---

[1] *Die Dogmatik der evangelisch-lutherischen Kirche*, von Heinrich Schmid, Professor der
Theologie in Erlangen; Frankfort and Erlangen, 1853; p. 506.
[2] *Theologia Didactico-Polemica*, edit. Leipzig, 1715.
[3] *Loci Theologici*, xxx. v. 37; Tübingen, 1779, vol. xx. pp. 51, 52.
[4] *Institutio*, xx. v.; edit. Edinburgh, 1847, vol. iii. p. 506.
[5] *Dogmatik*, § 104; Tübingen, 1841, vol. ii. p. 665.

evidences of the divine origin of the Scriptures, that they are
written on such a high level that all the mutations of human
science take place beneath them without ever coming into collision with their teachings. They could be read by those who
believed that the sun moves round the earth, without their convictions being shocked by their statements ; and they can be read
by us who know that the earth moves round the sun, with the
same satisfaction and confidence. Whether the heaven and earth
which are to pass away are the whole material universe, or only
our earth and its atmospheric heavens, the language of the Scripture leaves undecided. Either view is perfectly consistent with
the meaning of the words employed. The choice between the
two views is to be determined by other considerations. (b.) The
à priori probability is overwhelming in favour of the more limited interpretation. Anything so stupendous as the passing away
of the whole universe as the last act of the drama of human history would be altogether out of keeping. (c.) The Bible concerns man. The earth was cursed for his transgression. That
curse is to be removed when man's redemption is completed.
The κτίσις that was made subject to vanity for man's sin, is our
earth ; and our earth is the κτίσις which is to be delivered from
the bondage of corruption. The change to be effected is in the
dwelling-place of man. (d.) According to the Apostle Peter, it
is the world which once was destroyed by water, that is to be
consumed by fire. But although the predictions of Scripture
concern only our earth, it does not follow that the material universe is to last forever. As it is not from eternity, it probably
will not last forever. It may be only one of the grand exhibitions of the wonderful working of God in the field of infinite
space, and in the course of unending ages.

4. The result of this change is said to be the introduction of
a new heavens and a new earth. This is set forth not only in the
use of these terms, but in calling the predicted change " a regeneration," " a restoration," a deliverance from the bondage of corruption and an introduction into the glorious liberty of the Son
of God. This earth, according to the common opinion, that is,
this renovated earth, is to be the final seat of Christ's kingdom.
This is the new heavens ; this is the New Jerusalem, the Mount
Zion in which are to be gathered the general assembly and church
of the first-born, which are written in heaven ; the spirits of just
men made perfect ; this is the heavenly Jerusalem ; the city of
the living God ; the kingdom prepared for his people before the
foundation of the world.

5. It is of course, in itself, no matter of interest what portion of space these new heavens and new earth are to occupy, or of what materials they are to be formed. As the resurrection bodies of believers are to be human bodies they must have a local habitation, although it be one not made with hands eternal in the heavens. All we know about it is that it will be glorious, and adapted to the spiritual bodies which those in Christ are to receive when He comes the second time unto salvation.

§ 4. *The Kingdom of Heaven.*

In the account given of the final judgment in Matthew xxv. 31–46, we are told that the King shall " say to those on his right hand, Come, ye blessed of my Father, inherit the kingdom prepared for you from the foundation of the world."

1. In the Old Testament it was predicted that God would set up a kingdom, which was to be universal and everlasting.

2. Of this kingdom the Messiah was to be the head. He is everywhere in the Old Testament set forth as a king. (See Gen. xlix. 10; Num. xxiv. 17; 2 Sam. vii 16; Is. ix. 6, 7; xi.; lii.; liii.; Mich. iv.; and Psalms ii.; xlv.; lxxii.; and cx.)

3. It is called, for obvious reasons, in the Scriptures, indifferently, the kingdom of God, the kingdom of Christ, the kingdom of the Son of Man (Matt. xiii. 41) and the kingdom of heaven.

4. It is described in the prophets in the most glowing terms, in figures borrowed partly from the paradisiacal state of man, and partly from the state of the theocracy during the reign of Solomon.

5. This kingdom belongs to Christ, not as the Logos, but as the Son of Man, the Theanthropos; God manifest in the flesh.

6. Its twofold foundation, as presented in the Bible, is the possession on the part of Christ of all divine attributes, and his work of redemption. (Heb. i. 3; Phil. ii. 6–11.) It is because He being equal with God, " humbled Himself, and became obedient unto death, even the death of the cross," that " God also hath highly exalted Him, and given Him a name which is above every name : that at the name of Jesus every knee should bow, of things in heaven, and things in earth, and things under the earth , and that every tongue should confess that Jesus Christ is Lord, to the glory of God the Father." All power in heaven and earth has been given into his hands; and all things, τὰ πάντα, the universe, put under his feet. Even the angels are his ministering spirits, sent by Him to minister to those who shall be heirs of salvation.

7. This messianic or mediatorial kingdom of Christ, being thus comprehensive, is presented in different aspects in the Word of God. Viewed as extending over all creatures, it is a kingdom of power, which, according to 1 Corinthians xv. 24, He shall deliver up to God even the Father, when his mediatorial work is accomplished. Viewed in relation to his own people on earth it is the kingdom of grace. They all recognize Him as their absolute proprietor and sovereign. They all confide in his protection, and devote themselves to his service. He rules in them and reigns over them, and subdues all their and his enemies. Viewed in relation to the whole body of the redeemed, when the work of redemption is consummated, it is the kingdom of glory, the kingdom of heaven, in the highest sense of the words. In this view his kingdom is everlasting. His headship over his people is to continue forever, and his dominion over those whom He has purchased with his blood shall never end.

8. As this kingdom is thus manifold, so also it is, in some of its aspects, progressive. It is represented in Scripture as passing through different stages. In prophecy it is spoken of as a stone cut out without hands, which became a great mountain and filled the whole earth. In Daniel vii. 14, it is said of the Messiah that to Him " there was given dominion, and glory, and a kingdom, that all people, nations, and languages, should serve Him." So, too, in Psalm ii. 8, it is written of Him, " Ask of me, and I shall give thee the heathen for thine inheritance, and the uttermost parts of the earth for thy possession ; " in Psalm lxxii. 11, " All nations shall serve Him ; " verse 17, " All nations shall call Him blessed ; " in Psalm lxxxvi. 9, " All nations whom thou hast made shall come and worship before thee, O Lord ; and shall glorify thy name ; " in Isaiah xlix. 6, " I will also give thee for a light to the Gentiles, that thou mayest be my salvation unto the end of the earth ; " in Habakkuk ii. 14, " The earth shall be filled with the knowledge of the glory of the LORD, as the waters cover the sea ; " and in Malachi i. 11, " From the rising of the sun even unto the going down of the same, my name shall be great among the Gentiles." The Scriptures abound with passages of similar import. It is not only asserted that the kingdom of Christ is to attain this universal extension by slow degrees, but its gradual progress is illustrated in various ways. Our Lord compares his kingdom to a grain of mustard-seed, which is indeed the least of all seeds ; but when it is grown it is the greatest among herbs ; and to leaven which a woman took, and hid in three measures of meal, till the whole was leavened.

9. Although God has always had a kingdom upon earth, yet the kingdom of which the prophets speak began in its messianic form when the Son of God came in the flesh. John the Baptist, the forerunner of Christ, came preaching that the kingdom of God was at hand. Our Lord Himself, it is said, went from village to village, preaching the kingdom of God. (Luke iv. 43; viii. 1.) When asked by Pilate whether He was a king, he "answered, Thou sayest that I am a king. To this end was I born, and for this cause came I into the world." (John xviii. 37). The Apostles wherever they went "testified the kingdom of God." (Acts xxviii. 23.) Their business was to call upon men to receive the Lord Jesus as the Christ, the anointed and predicted Messiah or king of his people, and to worship, love, trust and obey Him as such. They were, therefore, accused of acting contrary to "the decrees of Cæsar, saying that there is another king, one Jesus." (Acts xvii. 7.) Men are exhorted to seek first the kingdom of God, as a present good. It is compared to a pearl or treasure, for which it were wise for a man to sacrifice everything. Every believer receives Christ as his king. Those who receive Him in sincerity constitute his kingdom, in the sense in which the loyal subjects of an earthly sovereign constitute his kingdom. Those who profess allegiance to Christ as king constitute his visible kingdom upon earth. Nothing, therefore, can be more opposed to the plain teaching of the New Testament, than that the kingdom of Christ is yet future and is not to be inaugurated until his second coming. This is to confound its consummation with its commencement.

10. As to the nature of this kingdom, our Lord Himself teaches us that it is not of this world. It is not analogous to the kingdoms which exist among men. It is not a kingdom of earthly splendour, wealth, or power. It does not concern the civil or political affairs of men, except in their moral relations. Its rewards and enjoyments are not the good things of this world. It is said to consist in "righteousness, and peace, and joy in the Holy Ghost." (Rom. xiv. 17.) Christ told his hearers, "The kingdom of God is within you." The condition of admission into that kingdom is regeneration (John iii. 5), conversion (Matt. xviii. 3), holiness of heart and life, for the unrighteous shall not inherit the kingdom of God; nor thieves, nor drunkards, nor revilers, nor extortioners (1 Cor. vi. 9, 10; Gal. v. 21; Eph. v. 5).

11. This kingdom, in the interval between the first and second

advents of Christ, is said to be like a field in which the wheat
and tares are to grow together until the harvest, which is the
end of the world. Then "the Son of Man shall send forth his
angels, and they shall gather out of his kingdom all things that
offend, and them which do iniquity ; and shall cast them into a
furnace of fire : there shall be wailing and gnashing of teeth.
Then shall the righteous shine forth as the sun in the kingdom of
their Father." (Matt. xiii. 41–43.) Experience concurs with
Scripture in teaching that the kingdom of Christ passes through
many vicissitudes ; that it has its times of depression and its seasons of exaltation and prosperity. About this in the past, there
can be no doubt. Prophecy sheds a sufficiently clear light on
the future to teach us, not only that this alternation is to continue to the end, but, more definitely, that before the second
coming of Christ there is to be a time of great and long continued
prosperity, to be followed by a season of decay and of suffering,
so that when the Son of Man comes he shall hardly find faith on
the earth. It appears from passages already quoted that all
nations are to be converted ; that the Jews are to be brought in
and reingrafted into their own olive-tree ; and that their restoration is to be the occasion and the cause of a change from death
unto life ; that is, analogous to the change of a body mouldering
in the grave to one instinct with joyous activity and power. Of
this period the ancient prophets speak in terms adapted to raise
the hopes of the Church to the highest pitch. It is true it is difficult to separate, in their descriptions, what refers to "this latter
day of glory" from what relates to the kingdom of Christ as
consummated in heaven. So also it was difficult for the ancient
people of God to separate what, in the declarations of their
prophets, referred to the redemption of the people from Babylon
from what referred to the greater redemption to be effected by
the Messiah. In both cases enough is plain to satisfy the Church.
There was a redemption from Babylon, and there was a redemption by Christ ; and in like manner, it is hoped, there is to be a
period of millenial glory on earth, and a still more glorious consummation of the Church in heaven. This period is called a
millennium because in Revelation it is said to last a thousand
years, an expression which is perhaps generally understood literally. Some however think it means a protracted season of
indefinite duration, as when it is said that one day is with the
Lord as a thousand years. Others, assuming that in the prophetic language a day stands for a year, assume that the so-called

millennium is to last three hundred and sixty-five thousand years. During this period, be it longer or shorter, the Church is to enjoy a season of peace, purity, and blessedness such as it has never yet experienced.

The principal reason for assuming that the prophets predict a glorious state of the Church prior to the second advent, is, that they represent the Church as being thus prosperous and glorious on earth. But we know that when Christ comes again the heavens and earth are to pass away, and that no more place will be found for them. The seat of the Church, after the second coming, is not to be the earth, but a new heavens and a new earth. As therefore the Scriptures teach that the kingdom of Christ is to extend over all the earth ; that all nations are to serve Him ; and that all people shall call Him blessed ; it is to be inferred that these predictions refer to a state of things which is to exist before the second coming of Christ. This state is described as one of spiritual prosperity ; God will pour out his Spirit upon all flesh ; knowledge shall everywhere abound ; wars shall cease to the ends of the earth, and there shall be nothing to hurt or destroy in all my holy mountain, saith the Lord. This does not imply that there is to be neither sin nor sorrow in the world during this long period, or that all men are to be true Christians. The tares are to grow together with the wheat until the harvest. The means of grace will still be needed ; conversion and sanctification will be then what they ever have been. It is only a higher measure of the good which the Church has experienced in the past that we are taught to anticipate in the future. This however is not the end. After this and after the great apostasy which is to follow, comes the consummation.

The Consummation.

12. When Christ comes again it will be to be admired in all them that believe. Those who are then alive will be changed, in the twinkling of an eye ; their corruptible shall put on incorruption, and their mortal shall put on immortality. Those who are in the graves shall hear the voice of the Son of Man and come forth to the resurrection of life, their bodies fashioned like unto the glorious body of the Son of God. Thus changed, both classes shall be ever with the Lord.

The place of the final abode of the righteous is sometimes called a house ; as when the Saviour said : " In my Father's house are many mansions " (John xiv. 2) ; sometimes " a city,

which hath foundations, whose builder and maker is God." (Heb.
xi. 10.) Under this figure it is called the new or heavenly Jerusalem, so gorgeously described in the twenty-first chapter of the
Apocalypse. Sometimes it is spoken of as "a better country, that
is an heavenly" (Heb. xi. 16) ; a country through which flows
the river of the water of life, and " on either side of the river
was there the tree of life, which bare twelve manner of fruits,
and yielded her fruit every month : and the leaves of the tree
were for the healing of the nations. And there shall be no more
curse : but the throne of God and of the Lamb shall be in it ;
and his servants shall serve Him : and they shall see his face ,
and his name shall be in their foreheads. And there shall be no
night there : and they need no candle, neither light of the sun ;
for the Lord God giveth them light : and they shall reign for
ever and ever." (Rev. xxii. 2–5.) Sometimes the final abode
of the redeemed is called a "new heavens and a new earth."
(2 Pet. iii. 13.)

As to the blessedness of this heavenly state we know that it is
inconceivable : " Eye hath not seen, nor ear heard, neither have
entered into the heart of man, the things which God hath prepared for them that love Him." (1 Cor. ii. 9.)

> " We know not, O we know not,
>   What joys await us there;
>   What radiancy of glory,
>   What bliss beyond compare."

We know however : (1.) That this incomprehensible blessedness of heaven shall arise from the vision of God. This vision
is beatific. It beatifies. It transforms the soul into the divine
image ; transfusing into it the divine life, so that it is filled with
the fulness of God. This vision of God is in the face of Jesus
Christ, in whom dwells the plenitude of the divine glory bodily.
God is seen in fashion as a man ; and it is this manifestation of
God in the person of Christ that is inconceivably and intolerably
ravishing. Peter, James, and John became as dead men when
they saw his glory, for a moment, in the holy mount. (2.) The
blessedness of the redeemed will flow not only from the manifestation of the glory, but also of the love of God ; of that love,
mysterious, unchangeable, and infinite, of which the work of
redemption is the fruit. (3.) Another element of the future
happiness of the saints is the indefinite enlargement of all their
faculties. (4.) Another is their entire exemption from all sin
and sorrow. (5.) Another is their intercourse and fellowship

with the high intelligences of heaven ; with patriarchs, prophets, apostles, martyrs, and all the redeemed. (6.) Another is constant increase in knowledge and in the useful exercise of all their powers. (7.) Another is the secure and everlasting possession of all possible good. And, (8.) Doubtless the outward circumstances of their being will be such as to minister to their increasing blessedness.

§ 5. *The Theory of the Pre-millennial Advent.*

The common doctrine of the Church stated above, is that the conversion of the world, the restoration of the Jews, and the destruction of Antichrist are to precede the second coming of Christ, which event will be attended by the general resurrection of the dead, the final judgment, the end of the world, and the consummation of the Church. In opposition to this view the doctrine of a pre-millennial advent of Christ has been extensively held from the days of the Apostles to the present time.[1] According to this view, (1.) The nations are not to be converted, nor are the Jews to be restored to their standing in the Church, until the second coming of Christ. (2.) His advent is to be personal and glorious. (3.) He will establish Himself in Jerusalem as the head of a visible, external kingdom. (4.) When He comes, the martyrs, as some say, or, as others believe, all who sleep in Jesus, shall be raised from the dead and associated with Him in this earthly kingdom. (5.) The Jews are to be converted, restored to their

---

[1] There recently appeared in the *Presbyterian*, a series of articles signed "Twisse," understood to be from the pen of the Rev. Dr. Duffield of Princeton, New Jersey, designed to sustain the doctrine of the pre-millennial advent of Christ, and especially to disprove "the doctrine of a millennial era of universal righteousness and peace on earth before" the second coming of Christ. The arguments summarily stated by the writer are the following: "(1.) Were the doctrine true, it would undoubtedly be prominent in the New Testament, and especially in the Apostolical Epistles. The fact is, it is not only not prominent, but, so far as we are informed, the advocates of the doctrine do not pretend to find in the Epistles the slightest allusion to it. (2.) The uniform and abundant teaching of the New Testament as to the condition of the Church and of the world during the present dispensation — that is, until the advent — forbid the expectation of such a millennium. (3.) The advent itself, not the millennium, is prominently presented in the New Testament as 'the blessed hope' of the Church, and is uniformly referred to as an event near at hand, ever imminent, to be 'looked for' with longing expectation. (4.) The Saviour's repeated command to 'watch' for his coming, because we 'know not the hour,' is inconsistent with the idea of a millennium intervening. (5.) The New Testament teaches repeatedly and unequivocally that the advent and the manifestation of the Messianic kingdom are to be synchronous events. (6.) The Apostolic Church, under the instruction of those holy men who spoke and wrote as they were moved by the Holy Ghost, was millennarian. (7.) The Church, for two centuries immediately succeeding the Apostles, was millennarian. (8.) The doctrine of a millennium before the advent is not to be found in the standards of any of the Churches of the Reformation; by several it is expressly repudiated. It is a modern novelty, suggested but one hundred and fifty years ago by Whitby, and avowedly as 'a new hypothesis.'"

own land, invested with special honours and prerogatives, and made the instruments of the conversion of the world. (6.) This kingdom is to be one of great splendour, prosperity, and blessedness, and is to continue a thousand years; which, however, as stated above, is understood in different senses. (7.) After the expiration of the millennium, the general resurrection of the dead, the end of the world, and the final consummation of the Church are to occur. Such are the general features of the scheme which, with many modifications as to details, is known as the pre-millennial advent theory.

The leading objections to this doctrine have been already presented in the discussions of the several topics included under the general head of eschatology. They may be summarily stated as follows: —

1. It is a Jewish doctrine. The principles adopted by its advocates in the interpretation of prophecy, are the same as those adopted by the Jews at the time of Christ; and they have led substantially to the same conclusions. The Jews expected that when the Messiah came He would establish a glorious earthly kingdom at Jerusalem; that those who had died in the faith should be raised from the dead to share in the blessings of the Messiah's reign; that all nations and peoples on the face of the whole earth should be subject to them; and that any nation that did not serve them should be destroyed. All the riches and honours of the world were to be at their disposal. The event disappointed these expectations; and the principles of prophetic interpretation on which those expectations were founded were proved to be incorrect.

2. This theory is inconsistent with the Scriptures, inasmuch as it teaches that believers only are to rise from the dead when Christ comes; whereas the Bible declares that when He appears all who are in the graves shall hear his voice, and shall come forth; they that have done good unto the resurrection of life; and they that have done evil unto the resurrection of damnation.

3. The Bible teaches that when Christ comes all nations shall appear at his bar for judgment. This theory teaches that the final judgment will not occur until after the millennium. It may be said that the judgment is to commence at the second advent and continue during the reign of a thousand years. But the general judgment cannot occur before the general resurrection, and as the general resurrection, according to this theory, is not to take place until after the millennium, so neither can the general judgment.

4. The Scriptures teach that when Christ comes the second time without sin unto salvation, then the Church shall enter on its everlasting state of exaltation and glory. Those in Christ who have departed this life shall be raised from the dead and be clothed with their spiritual bodies, and those who are alive shall be changed in a moment, and thus they shall be ever with the Lord. According to this theory, instead of heaven awaiting the risen saints, they are to be introduced into a mere worldly kingdom.[1]

5. It is inconsistent with all the representations given of the glory and blessedness of departed saints, to assume that at the resurrection they are to be brought down to a lower state of existence, degraded from heaven to earth. The millennium may be a great advance on the present state of the Church ; but, exalt it as you may, it is far below heaven. This argument bears, at least, against the patristic doctrine of the millennium.

6. The view presented by pre-millennarians of the kingdom of Christ on earth is, in many respects, inconsistent with the Scriptural account of its nature. (*a.*) It is to be a worldly kingdom. (*b.*) Its blessedness is to consist largely in worldly prosperity. Although the modern advocates of the doctrine have eliminated the grosser elements included in the theory of many of the fathers on this subject, nevertheless the essential earthly character of the kingdom remains. Men are not to be like the angels. Births and deaths are to go on, not only during the millennium, but without end. Not that the glorified believers who have been raised from the dead are to marry and be given in marriage, but the race of men is to continue indefinitely to increase in the future as it has increased in the past.[2] (*c.*) The Bible teaches

---

[1] It is true that pre-millennialists differ very much on this point. The common opinion in the early Church was that the risen saints are to live and reign a thousand years with Christ on earth ; but some say that the glorified believers are to be in heaven ; others, that they are to appear from time to time on earth, as Christ did, during the forty days which intervened between his resurrection and ascension ; and others appear to teach that glorified saints are to rule over unglorified humanity without being revealed to those over whom they reign.

[2] See passages cited from distinguished millennarians on this point in Rev. David Brown's *Christ's Second Coming*, pp. 167–173. Mr. David N. Lord devotes to this subject two chapters of his book on *The Coming and Reign of Christ*. New York, 1858. He says (p. 151), that the Scriptures teach that the earth is " to continue forever, and that mankind are forever to occupy it, and multiply in an endless succession of generations; and that it is to be the scene of Christ's everlasting kingdom and reign." He argues this from the covenant made with Noah; from the promise made to Abraham that his seed should forever possess the land of Canaan; and from the promise made to David that his seed should sit on his throne and reign forever. This perpetuity of the human race on the earth and in the flesh, he considers one of the most clearly revealed purposes of God concerning the family of man. Instead of the number of the redeemed being nearly made up, he holds that they are to go on multiplying through all eternity.

that the distinction between the Jews and Gentiles is abolished in the kingdom of Christ. This theory teaches that after the second advent that distinction is to continue and to be made greater than ever before. The temple at Jerusalem is to be rebuilt; the sacrifices restored; and all the details of the Mosaic ritual, as described in Ezekiel, again introduced. (*d.*) The Bible teaches that after the end of the world, as described in 2 Peter iii. 10 and in the Apocalypse, there are to be a new heavens and a new earth. This theory teaches the " earth's eternal perpetuity." [1] " The dissolving fires of which Peter speaks," we are told, " are for ' the perdition of ungodly men ; ' and not for the utter depopulation and destruction of the whole world. . . . . Men and nations will survive them and still continue to live in the flesh." [2]

7. This theory disparages the Gospel. " The more common opinion," says Dr. McNeile, " is, that this is the final dispensation, and that by a more copious outpouring of the Holy Spirit it will magnify itself, and swell into the universal blessedness predicted by the prophets, carrying with it Jews and Gentiles, even the whole world, in one glorious flock under one shepherd, Jesus Christ the Lord. This is reiterated from pulpit, press, and platform. It is the usual climax of missionary exhortation, or rather missionary prophecy." [3] " The universal prevalence of religion hereafter to be enjoyed," says Mr. Brooks, " is not to be effected by any increased impetus given by the present means of evangelizing the nations, but by a stupendous display of Divine wrath upon all the apostate and ungodly." [4] Wrath, however, never converted a single soul, and never will. " The Scriptures," according to Mr. Tyso, " do state the design of the Gospel, and what it is to effect; but they never say it is to convert the world. Its powers have been tried for eighteen hundred years, and it has never yet truly converted one nation, one city, one town, nor even a single village." [5] In the work of Rev. David Brown on the Second Advent,[6] abundant evidence is advanced from the writings of Mr. Brooks, Dr. McNeile, and the Rev. Mr. Bickersteth, to show that those gentlemen teach that the Scriptures " are to be superseded " in the millennium. Other means, probably, as they

---

[1] *The Last Times and the Great Consummation.* By Joseph A. Seiss, D.D. Philadelphia and London, 1866. p. 73. On p. 75, the author says, " The earth shall not pass away."
[2] Seiss, *ut supra*, p. 211.
[3] *Lectures on the Prophecies Relative to the Jewish Nation*, 1st. edit., 1830, p. 72.
[4] *Elements of Prophetic Interpretation*, pp. 227, 228.
[5] *Defence of the Personal Reign of Christ.* 1841. pp. 41, 42.   [6] pp. 311–315.

say, other revelations are to be made for the salvation of men. Any theory which thus disparages the gospel of the grace of God must be false. Christ's commission to his Church was to preach the Gospel to every creature under heaven; Paul says, the Gospel is the power of God unto salvation; that, though a stumbling-block to the Jew and foolishness to the Greek, it is the wisdom of God and the power of God; that it has pleased God by the foolishness of preaching to save them that believe; and he plainly teaches (Rom. x. 11–15) that there is no other means of salvation. Wrath, judgments, displays of visible glory, and miracles are not designed for the conversion of souls, nor are they adapted to that end.

8. Another objection to the pre-millennial theory is the want of consistency in its advocates and the conflicting conclusions to which they come. They profess to adopt the principle of literal interpretation. They interpret literally the prophecies relating to the return of the Jews to their own land; which promise to them as a nation dominion over all the other nations of the earth, the rebuilding of the Temple and the restoration of the Temple-service, the greatest worldly prosperity, and even the everlasting perpetuity of their nation in the highest state of blessedness here on earth and "in the flesh." Yet they are forced to abandon their literalism when they come to the interpretation of the prophecies which predict that all the nations of the earth are to go up to Jerusalem every month, and even on every Sabbath. And more than this, they go to the extreme of figurative or spiritual interpretation in explaining the prophecies which refer to the end of the world. The Apostle Peter says in express terms: "The heavens shall pass away with a great noise, and the elements shall melt with fervent heat, the earth also and the works that are therein shall be burned up." This they deny. They say that it is only certain nations who are to be destroyed; that the earth is not to be depopulated; that the final conflagration will produce less change or injury than the deluge did.[1]

The utmost confusion also prevails in the views of pre-millennarians as to the nature of the kingdom of Christ. According to one view Christ and his risen and glorified saints are to dwell visibly on the earth and reign for a thousand years; according to another, the risen saints are to be in heaven, and not on earth any more than the angels now are; nevertheless the subjects of the first resurrection, although dwelling in heaven, are to govern

[1] *The Last Times*, J. A. Seiss, D. D., p. 74.

the earth ; according to another it is the converted Jewish nation restored to their own land, who are to be the governors of the world ; according to another, the Bible divides men into three classes : the Gentiles, the Jews, and the Church of God. The prophecies relating to the millennium are understood to refer to the relative condition of the Jews and Gentiles in this world, and not to the risen and glorified believers. Another view seems to be, that this earth, changed no more by the fires of the last day than it was by the waters of the deluge, is to be the only heaven of the redeemed. Dr. Cumming and Dr. Seiss say they wish no better heaven than this earth free from the curse and from sin. The latter says : [1] " My faith is, that these very hills and valleys shall yet be made glad with the songs of a finished redemption, and this earth yet become the bright, blessed, and everlasting homestead of men made glorious and immortal in body and in soul." Still another view is that there are two heavens, one here and one above ; two Jerusalems, both to continue forever, the one on earth and the other in heaven ; the one made with hands, the other without hands ; both glorious and blessed, but the earthly far inferior to the heavenly ; they are like concentric circles, one within the other ; both endless. Men will continue forever, on earth, living and dying ; happy but not perfect, needing regeneration and sanctification ; and, when they die, will be translated to the kingdom which is above.

It seems therefore that the torch of the literalist is an " ignis fatuus," leading those who follow it, they know not whither. Is it not better to abide by the plain doctrinal teaching of the Bible, rather than to trust to the uncertain expositions of unfulfilled prophecies ? What almost all Christians believe is : (1.) That all nations shall be converted unto God. Jesus shall reign from the rising to the setting of the sun. (2.) That the Jews shall be reingrafted into their own olive-tree and acknowledge our Lord to be their God and Saviour. (3.) That all Antichristian powers shall be destroyed. (4.) That Christ shall come again in person and with great glory ; the dead shall be raised, those who have done good unto the resurrection of life, those who have done evil unto the resurrection of damnation ; and, (5.) That the righteous clothed in their glorified bodies shall then inherit the kingdom prepared for them from the foundation of the world ; and the wicked be consigned to their final doom.

[1] *The Last Times*, p. 72.

Did the Apostles expect the Second Advent in their Day ?

The simple facts on this subject are : (1.) That the coming of the Messiah and the establishment of his kingdom was the great object of expectation and desire for the people of God from the beginning of the world. It was the great subject of prophecy and promise under the old dispensation. The ancient saints are described (as Christians now are) as those who were constantly hoping for the coming of the Lord. (Eph. ii. 12 ; Acts xxvi. 6, 7.) The dying thief said : " Lord, remember me, when thou comest into thy kingdom." The last question put to our Lord by his disciples was : " Lord wilt thou at this time restore again the kingdom to Israel." (2.) As the Messiah came at first as a man of sorrows, to make Himself a sacrifice for sin, He promised to come a second time without sin unto salvation, to raise the dead and to gather all his people into his everlasting home. His second coming therefore was to Christians what his first coming was to the Old Testament saints ; the constant object of expectation and desire. (3.) As the time of the second advent was unrevealed either to men or angels, the early Christians hoped it might occur in their day. The Apostles themselves no doubt at first cherished that expectation. (4.) To the Apostle Paul, however, it was revealed that the day of the Lord was not to come until a great apostasy had occurred. (5.) Nevertheless as the Apostolic Christians did not know how long that apostasy was to continue, their constant prayer was, O Lord come quickly. The Apostles continued to hold up the second advent as an impending event, the moral impression of which ought to be to raise the affections of the people from the world and fix them on the things unseen and eternal. Those who urge the fact that the New Testament writers speak of the day of the Lord as at hand, and exhort believers to watch and pray for his advent, as a proof that the Apostles believed that it might occur at once, that no events then future must come to pass before Christ came, forget that what inspired men said God said. If God, who knew that Christ was not to come for at least eighteen centuries after his ascension, could say to his people : " The day of the Lord is at hand." " Watch therefore, for ye know neither the day nor the hour wherein the Son of Man cometh," then that language was appropriate even on the assumption that those who used it knew that the second advent was not to occur for thousands of years ; for a thousand years are with God as one day, and one day as a thousand years. The Church waited four thousand years for the first advent; we may be content to wait God's time for the second.[1]

§ 6. *Future Punishment.*

Our Lord in his account of the final judgment says, that the wicked shall go away into everlasting punishment; but the righteous into life eternal.

The sufferings of the finally impenitent, according to the Scriptures, arise: (1.) From the loss of all earthly good. (2.) From exclusion from the presence and favour of God. (3.) From utter reprobation, or the final withdrawal from them of the Holy Spirit. (4.) From the consequent unrestrained dominion of sin and sinful passions. (5.) From the operations of conscience. (6.) From despair. (7.) From their evil associates. (8.) From their external circumstances; that is, future suffering is not exclusively the natural consequences of sin, but also includes positive inflictions. (9.) From their perpetuity.

There seems to be no more reason for supposing that the fire spoken of in Scripture is to be literal fire, than that the worm that never dies is literally a worm. The devil and his angels who are to suffer the vengeance of eternal fire, and whose doom the finally impenitent are to share, have no material bodies to be acted upon by elemental fire. As there are to be degrees in the glory and blessedness of heaven, as our Lord teaches us in the parable of the ten talents, so there will be differences as to degree in the sufferings of the lost: some will be beaten with few stripes, some with many.

The Duration of Future Punishment.

On this subject the following opinions have been held: —

1. It is assumed that the design of punishment is reformation, and that it is effective to that end. The time will, therefore, come when all sinful creatures, whether men or angels, shall be purged from all corruption, and restored to the image and favour of God. This was the doctrine of Origen in the early Church.

---

[1] Millennarians are not consistent in urging the objection considered in the text, as some at least of their own number teach that important events yet future must occur before the establishment of Christ's kingdom. For example, Rev. John Cox, Minister of the Gospel, Woolwich, in his *Thoughts on the Coming and Kingdom of our Lord Jesus Christ*, devotes the third chapter of that work to prove tnat the entire destruction of the Papacy, of Mohammedanism, and of the tyrannical kingdoms of the world, and the restoration of the Jews to their own land, must precede the kingdom of Christ. See *The Literalist*, vol. v, p. 26 ff. *The Literalist* is a collection, in five octavo volumes, of the publications of the leading English pre-millennarians. Published by Orrin Rogers, Philadelphia, 1840 and 1841.

Other restorationists rest their hope of the ultimate salvation of all men, not on the purifying effect of suffering, but on the efficacy of the death of Christ. If He died for all, they infer, all will be saved.

2. Others hold that future punishment is only hypothetically everlasting. That is, the wicked will suffer forever if they continue to sin forever. But, if the Spirit continues to strive with men in the world to come, or, as others believe, if plenary ability belongs to the very nature of a rational creature, then we may assume that some, perhaps many, perhaps all, in the course of ages, will repent and turn unto God and live.

3. Others again teach that the sufferings of the impenitent are only relatively endless ; that is, it will forever be true that their condition will be inferior to what it would have been had they been better men.

4. Others hold that the life promised to the righteous is immortality, and that the death threatened against the wicked is the extinction of life, or, the cessation of conscious existence. The soul will die in the future world, just as the body dies here. It ceases to act ; it ceases to feel ; it ceases to be. This death of the soul is called eternal, because life is never to be restored. The punishment of the wicked is, therefore, in a sense, everlasting. It is a final and everlasting forfeiture of all good. Thus Cicero [1] calls death " sempiternum malum," and Lucretius [2] speaks of a " mors immortalis." This second death may be very painful and protracted. The finally impenitent, may, and doubtless will, suffer for a longer or shorter period, and to a less or greater degree, before the final extinction of their being. And thus there shall be a future retribution, answering all the ends of justice. [3]

5. The common doctrine is, that the conscious existence of the soul after the death of the body is unending ; that there is no repentance or reformation in the future world ; that those who depart this life unreconciled to God, remain forever in this state of alienation, and therefore are forever sinful and miserable. This is the doctrine of the whole Christian Church, of the Greeks, of the Latins, and of all the great historical Protestant bodies.

---

[1] *Tusculanarum Disputationum*, I. xlii. 100; *Works*, edit. Leipzig, 1850, p. 1057, b.

[2] See Lucretius, *De Rerum Natura*, iii. 517–519, edit. London, 1712, p. 144.

[3] This theory is advocated with confidence, as well as with ability and learning, by Henry Constable, A. M., Prebendary of Cork, in his tract on *The Duration and Nature of Future Punishment*, Reprinted from the Second London Edition," New Haven, Conn., 1872. And much more elaborately in *Debt and Grace as related to the Doctrine of a Future Life*. By C. F. Hudson. Fifth Edition. Boston: 1859.

It is obvious that this is a question which can be decided only by divine revelation. No one can reasonably presume to decide how long the wicked are to suffer for their sins upon any general principles of right and wrong. The conditions of the problem are not within our grasp. What the infinitely wise and good God may see fit to do with his creatures ; or what the exigencies of a government embracing the whole universe and continuing throughout eternal ages, may demand, it is not for such worms of the dust as we are, to determine. If we believe the Bible to be the Word of God, all we have to do is to ascertain what it teaches on this subject, and humbly submit.

1. It is an almost invincible presumption that the Bible does teach the unending punishment of the finally impenitent, that all Christian churches have so understood it. There is no other way in which this unanimity of judgment can be accounted for. To refer it to some philosophical speculation which had gained ascendancy in the Church, such as the dualism of good and evil as two coeternal and necessary principles, or the Platonic doctrine of the inherent immortality and indestructible nature of the human soul, would be to assign a cause altogether inadequate to the effect. Much less can this general consent be accounted for on the ground that the doctrine in question is congenial to the human mind, and is believed for its own sake, without any adequate support from Scripture. The reverse is the case. It is a doctrine which the natural heart revolts from and struggles against, and to which it submits only under stress of authority. The Church believes the doctrine because it must believe it, or renounce faith in the Bible and give up all the hopes founded upon its promises. There is no doctrine in support of which this general consent can be pleaded, which can be shown not to be taught in the Bible. The doctrines of the Trinity, the divinity of Christ, the personality of the Holy Spirit, the sinfulness of men, and others of a like kind, are admitted to be Scriptural even by those who do not believe them. The argument now urged, does not suppose the Church to be infallible ; nor that the authority of the Church is the ground of faith ; it only assumes that what the great body of the competent readers of a plain book take to be its meaning, must be its meaning.

It is unreasonable to account for the general reception of the doctrine in question on the ground of church authority. It was universally received before the external Church arrogated to itself the right to dictate to the people of God what they must believe ;

and it continued to be received when, at the Reformation, the authority of the Church was repudiated, and the Scriptures were declared to be the only infallible rule of faith and practice. Any man, therefore, assumes a fearful responsibility who sets himself in opposition to the faith of the Church universal.

2. It is admitted that the doctrine of the perpetuity of the future punishment of the wicked was held by the Jews under the old dispensation, and at the time of Christ. Neither our Lord nor his Apostles ever contradicted that doctrine. They reproved the false teachers of their day for doctrinal errors on many points, but they never corrected their faith in this doctrine. They never teach anything inconsistent with it. Their recorded instructions give no ground for a belief either of the final restoration of all rational creatures to the favour of God, or of the annihilation of the wicked. The passages which are appealed to by Universalists in support of their doctrine admit of a natural and simple interpretation in harmony with the general teaching of the Bible on this subject. For example, in Ephesians i. 10, it is said to be the purpose of God to bring into one harmonious whole (or, as it is expressed in Colossians i. 20, to reconcile unto Himself) all things, *i. e.*, all, who are in heaven and who are on earth. The question is, who, or what are the all, who are to be reconciled unto God? This question must be answered by a reference to the nature of the thing spoken of, and to the analogy of Scripture. It cannot mean absolutely " all things," the whole universe, including sun, moon, and stars, for they are not susceptible of reconciliation to God. For the same reason it cannot mean all sensitive creatures, including irrational animals. Nor can it mean all rational creatures, including the holy angels; for they do not need reconciliation. Nor can it mean all fallen rational creatures, for it is expressly taught, Hebrews ii. 16, that Christ did not come to redeem fallen angels. Nor can it mean all men, for the Bible teaches elsewhere that all men are not reconciled to God; and Scripture cannot contradict Scripture; for that would be for God to contradict Himself. The " all " intended is the " all " spoken of in the context; the whole body of the people of God; all the objects of redemption.

Restorationists appeal also to Romans v. 18: " As by the offence of one judgment came upon all men to condemnation; even so by the righteousness of one the free gift came upon all men unto justification of life." This is made to mean, that as all men are condemned for Adam's offence, so all men are justified

for the righteousness of Christ. The same interpretation is put
upon the parallel passage in 1 Corinthians xv. 22: "As in Adam
all die, even so in Christ shall all be made alive." In both these
passages, however, the "all" is necessarily limited by the context.
It is the all who are in Adam, that die ; and the all who are in
Christ, that are made alive. Restorationists limit the word to all
men, or to all fallen creatures, in obedience to what they suppose to be the analogy of Scripture ; and this is all that is done
by the orthodox. The only question is, What do the Scriptures
elsewhere teach ? If they clearly teach that all men and fallen
angels are to be saved, then these passages must be interpreted
accordingly ; but if they teach that all men are not saved, then
these passages cannot be understood to assert the contrary. Of
themselves they decide nothing. They may be understood in
two ways ; which is their real meaning depends on what is taught
elsewhere.

The same remark may be made in reference to other passages
which Universalists rely upon. Thus in 1 Corinthians xv. 25, it
is said that Christ "must reign, until He hath put all enemies
under his feet." This may mean that He must reign until all sin
and misery are banished from the universe ; but this is not its
necessary meaning, for Satan may be subdued without being
either converted or annihilated. In like manner, in 1 Timothy
ii. 4, it is said God "will have all men to be saved ; " if the word
will, θέλει, here means *to purpose*, then the passage teaches that all
men shall ultimately be certainly saved. But if the word means
here what it does in Matthew xxvii. 43, to have complacency in,
(εἰ θέλει αὐτόν,) then it teaches only what the Bible everywhere
else teaches, namely, that God is love ; that He delights not in
the death of sinners. It is to pervert, and to misinterpret the
Word of God, to make one passage contradict another simply
because the language used admits of an explanation which brings
them into conflict. The question is not, What certain words may
mean ? but, What were they intended to mean as used in certain
connections ?

If Christ and his Apostles did not teach that all men are to be
saved, neither did they teach that the wicked are to be annihilated.
Mr. Constable, in his work above referred to, lays down the principle that the language of the Scriptures, especially of the New
Testament, is to be interpreted according to the "usus loquendi"
of the Greek writers. We are to go to our classical dictionaries
to learn the meaning of the words they use. From this principle

he infers that as the word ζωή, *life*, in ordinary Greek, means continued existence, and θανατός, *death*, the cessation of existence, such is their meaning in the Scriptures. Therefore, when in the Bible eternal life is promised to the righteous, immortality is promised to them ; and when eternal death is threatened against the wicked, annihilation is declared to be their doom. A Greek-speaking people, he says, could attach no other meaning to such language. In like manner as the words which we translate to destroy, or cause to perish, mean to blot out of existence, the inference is that when the wicked are said to be destroyed, or to perish, it can only mean that they are annihilated.

On this it may be remarked, —

1. That the rule of interpretation here laid down is obviously incorrect, and its application would reduce the doctrines of the Bible to the level of heathenism. If Greek words as used in Scripture express no higher ideas than on the lips of Pagans, then we can have only the thoughts of Pagans in the Bible. On this principle, how could the Gospel be preached to heathen ? to the Hindoos, for example, if they were forbidden to attach to the words God, sin, repentance, and a holy life, no other ideas than those suggested by the corresponding terms of their own language ? The Bible, so far as written in Greek, must be understood as Greek. But the " usus loquendi " of every language varies more or less in different ages, and as spoken by different tribes and nations. Every one admits that Hellenistic Greek has a usage distinguishing it from the language of the classics. The language of the Bible must explain the language of the Bible. It has a " usus loquendi " of its own. It is, however, not true that the words life and death (ζωή and θάνατος) are in any language used only in the limited sense which Mr. Constable's argument would assign to them. When the poet said, " dum vivimus vivamus," he surely did not mean to say, ' while we continue to exist, let us continue to exist.' The Scriptures written in the language of men use words as men are accustomed to use them, literally or figuratively, and in senses suited to the nature of the subjects to which they are applied. The word life means one thing when used of plants, another when used of animals, and another when spoken of in reference to the soul of man. The death of a plant is one thing, the death of an immortal soul is something entirely different. That the words life and death are not confined to the limited sense in which annihilationists would take them, hardly needs to be proved. The Scriptures every-

where recognize the distinction, in reference to men, between animal, intellectual, and spiritual life. A man may have the two former and be destitute of the latter. God quickens those dead in trespasses and sins ; that is, he imparts spiritual life to those who are in the full vigour of their animal and intellectual being. Therefore we are told that the favour of God is life ; that to know God is eternal life ; that to be spiritually minded is life ; and that to be carnally minded is death. The Apostle tells the Colossians : " Ye are dead, and your life is hid with Christ in God." He says to the Galatians : " I live ; yet not I, but Christ liveth in me." Those who " live in pleasure " are said to be " dead while they live." No one believes that the word life in such Scriptural phrases as " the bread of life," " the water of life," " the tree of life," " the crown of life," means only continued existence. The word, when used of the soul of man, means not only conscious being, but a normal state of being in the likeness, fellowship, and enjoyment of God. And in like manner the word death, when spoken of the soul, means alienation or separation from God ; and when that separation is final it is eternal death. This is so plain that it never has been doubted, except for the purpose of supporting the doctrine of the annihilation of the wicked.

2. The same remark applies to the use of the words destroy and perish. To destroy is to ruin. The nature of that ruin depends on the nature of the subject of which it is predicated. A thing is ruined when it is rendered unfit for use ; when it is in such a state that it can no longer answer the end for which it was designed. A ship at sea, dismasted, rudderless, with its sides battered in, is ruined, but not annihilated. It is a ship still. A man destroys himself when he ruins his health, squanders his property, debases his character, and renders himself unfit to act his part in life. A soul is utterly and forever destroyed when it is reprobated, alienated from God, rendered a fit companion only for the devil and his angels. This is a destruction a thousandfold more fearful than annihilation. The earnestness with which the doctrine of the unending punishment of the wicked is denounced by those who reject it, should convince them that its truth is the only rational solution of the fact that Christ and his Apostles did not condemn it.

3. But Christ and the Apostles not only failed to correct the teachings of the Jews of their day concerning the everlasting punishment of the wicked, but they themselves also taught that

doctrine in the most explicit and solemn manner. It is asserted affirmatively that future punishment is everlasting; in the negative form that it can never end; that there is in the future world an impassable gulf between the righteous and the wicked; and that there are sins which can never be forgiven either in this life or in the life to come. Thus if words can teach this doctrine it is taught in the Bible from the beginning to the end. In the Old Testament, the prophet says (Is. xxxiii. 14): "The sinners in Zion are afraid; fearfulness hath surprised the hypocrites; who among us shall dwell with the devouring fire? who among us shall dwell with everlasting burnings." In Isaiah lxvi. 24 it is said of those who should be excluded from the new heavens and the new earth which the prophet had predicted, "that their worm shall not die, neither shall their fire be quenched." "Hell," however, "is of both worlds, so that in the same essential sense, although in different degrees, it may be said both of him who is still living but accursed, and of him who perished centuries ago, that his worm dieth not and his fire is not quenched." [1] The prophet Daniel (xii. 2) says of the wicked, that they "shall awake . . . . to shame and everlasting contempt." In Luke iii. 17 it is said that Christ shall "gather the wheat into his garner; but the chaff He will burn with fire unquenchable." In Mark ix. 42–48 our Lord says that it is better "to enter into life maimed, than, having two hands, to go into hell, into the fire that never shall be quenched: where their worm dieth not, and the fire is not quenched." These awful words fell three times, in one discourse, from the lips of mercy, to give them the greater effect. Christ wept over Jerusalem. Why did He not avert its doom? Simply because it would not have been right. So He may weep over the doom of the impenitent wicked; and yet leave them to their fate. It is no more possible that the cup should pass from their lips than that it should have been taken from the trembling hand of the Son of God himself. The latter spectacle was far more appalling in the eyes of angels than the lake of fire prepared for the devil and his angels.

The Judge on the last day, we are told, will say to those on the left hand: "Depart from me, ye cursed, into everlasting fire." "And these shall go away into everlasting punishment: but the righteous into life eternal." The same word is used in both clauses; the wicked are to go εἰς κόλασιν αἰώνιον; and the

---

[1] *The Prophecies of Isaiah Translated and Explained.* By Joseph Addison Alexander. New York, 1865, vol. ii. p. 482.

righteous εἰς ζωὴν αἰώνιον; it must have the same sense in both. (Matt. xxv. 41, 46.) In John iii. 36 it is said: "He that believeth on the Son hath everlasting life: and he that believeth not the Son, shall not see life; but the wrath of God abideth on him." Paul teaches us in 2 Thessalonians i. 9 that when Christ comes the wicked "shall be punished with everlasting destruction from the presence of the Lord, and from the glory of his power." Jude (verse 6) says that the angels which kept not their first estate are "reserved in everlasting chains under darkness, unto the judgment of the great day. Even as Sodom and Gomorrah . . . . are set forth for an example, suffering the vengeance of eternal fire." Of apostates, he says (verses 12, 13) there is reserved for them "the blackness of darkness forever." In Revelation xiv. 9–11, those who worship the beast and his image or receive his mark, shall "be tormented with fire and brimstone in the presence of the holy angels, and in the presence of the Lamb: and the smoke of their torment ascendeth up forever and ever: and they have no rest day nor night." Nearly the same words are repeated in chapters xix. 1–3, 20; xx. 10.

It is objected to the argument founded on these passages that the word "everlasting" is sometimes used in Scripture of periods of limited duration. In reference to this objection it may be remarked, (1.) That the Hebrew and Greek words rendered in our version eternal, or everlasting, mean duration whose termination is unknown. When used in reference to perishable things, as when the Bible speaks of "the everlasting hills," they simply indicate indefinite existence, that is, existence to which there is no known or assignable limit. But when used in reference to that which is either in its own nature imperishable, or of which the unending existence is revealed, as the human soul, or in reference to that which we have no authority from other sources to assign a limit to, as the future blessedness of the saints, then the words are to be taken in their literal sense. If, because we sometimes say we give a man a thing forever, without intending that he is to possess it to all eternity, it were argued that the word forever expresses limited duration, every one would see that the inference was unfounded. If the Bible says that the sufferings of the lost are to be everlasting, they are to endure forever, unless it can be shown either that the soul is not immortal or that the Scriptures elsewhere teach that those sufferings are to come to an end. No one argues that the blessedness of the righteous will cease after a term of years, because the word everlasting is sometimes used of things which do not continue forever. Our Lord teaches that the punishment of the wicked is everlasting, in the same sense that the blessedness of the saints is everlasting. (2.) It is to be remembered, that admitting the word " everlasting" to be ever so ambiguous, the Bible says that the worm never dies, and the fire is never quenched. We have therefore the direct assertion of the word of God that the sufferings of the lost are unending. All the modes of expression used to set forth the perpetuity of the salvation of believers and the everlasting duration of the kingdom of Christ, are employed to teach the perpetuity of the future punishment of the wicked. If that doctrine, therefore, be not taught in the Scriptures, it is difficult to see how it could be taught in human language.

4. A fourth argument on this subject is drawn from passages in which the doctrine is implied, although not directly asserted. This includes those passages which teach that there is no repentance, no forgiveness, no change of state in the future world. This is done, for example, in our Lord's parable of the rich man and Lazarus, in which He teaches that there is no possibility of passing from hell to heaven. So, also, we are taught that those who die in sin remain sinful forever. And our Lord says, it would be better for a man had he never been born, than that he should incur the guilt of offending any of the little ones who believe on Him. This, at least, is conclusive against the doctrine of universal salvation; for if, after any period of suffering, an eternity of happiness awaits a man, his being born is an unspeakable blessing.

Rationalists say that it is very impolitic for Christians to represent the everlasting punishment of the wicked as a doctrine of the Bible. This is undoubtedly true. And so Paul felt that it was very impolitic to preach the doctrine of the Cross. He knew that doctrine to be a stumbling-block to the Jew and foolishness to the Greek. He knew that had he preached the common sense doctrine of salvation by works, the offence of the cross would have ceased. Nevertheless, he knew that the doctrine of Christ crucified was the wisdom of God and the power of God unto salvation. He knew that it was not his business to make a Gospel, but to declare that Gospel which had been taught Him, by the revelation of Jesus Christ. It would be well if all who call themselves Christians, should learn that it is not their business to believe and teach what they may think true or right, but what God in his Holy Word has seen fit to reveal.

Objections.

It is urged that it cannot be consistent with the justice of God to inflict a really infinite penalty on such a creature as man. It is very obvious to remark on this subject : —

1. That we are incompetent judges of the penalty which sin deserves. We have no adequate apprehension of its inherent guilt, of the dignity of the person against whom it is committed, or of the extent of the evil which it is suited to produce. The proper end of punishment is retribution and prevention. What is necessary for that end, God only knows ; and, therefore, the penalty which He imposes on sin is the only just measure of its ill desert.

2. If it be inconsistent with the justice of God that men should perish for their sins, then redemption is not a matter of grace, or undeserved mercy. Deliverance from an unjust penalty, is a matter of justice. Nothing, however, is plainer from the teaching of Scripture, and nothing is more universally and joyfully acknowledged by all Christians, than that the whole plan of redemption, the mission, the incarnation, and the sufferings and death of the Son of God for the salvation of sinners, is a wonderful exhibition of the love of God which passes knowledge. But if justice demand that all men should be saved, then salvation is a matter of justice ; and then all the songs of gratitude and praise from the redeemed, whether in heaven or on earth, must at once cease.

3. It is often said that sin is an infinite evil because committed against a person of infinite dignity, and therefore deserves an infinite penalty. To this it is answered, that as sin is an act or state of a finite subject, it must of necessity be itself finite. Men are apt to involve themselves in contradictions when they attempt to reason about the infinite. The word is so vague and so comprehensive, and our ideas of what it is intended to express are so inadequate, that we are soon lost when we seek to make it a guide in forming our judgments. If the evil of a single sin, and that the smallest, lasts forever, it is in one sense an infinite evil, although in comparison with other sins, or with the whole mass of sin ever committed, it may appear a mere trifle. The guilt of sin is infinite in the sense that we can set no limits to its turpitude or to the evil which it is adapted to produce.

4. Relief on this subject is sought from the consideration that as the lost continue to sin forever they may justly be punished forever. To this, however, it is answered that the retributions of

eternity are threatened for the sins done in the body. This is true; nevertheless, it is also true, first, that sin in its nature is alienation and separation from God; and as God is the source of all holiness and happiness, separation from Him is of necessity the forfeiture of all good; secondly, that this separation is from its nature final and consequently involves endless sinfulness and misery. It is thus final, unless on the assumption of the unde- served and supernatural intervention of God as in the case of the redemption of man; and thirdly, it is also true that from the nature of the case "the carnal mind is death." Degradation and misery are inseparably connected with sin. As long as rational creatures are sinful, they must be degraded and miserable. There is no law of nature more immutable than this. If men do not expect God to reverse the laws of nature to secure their exemp- tion from wanton transgression of those laws, why should they expect Him to reverse the still more immutable laws of our moral constitution and of his moral government? The doom of the fallen angels teaches us that one act of rebellion against God is fatal, whether we say that all they have suffered since, and all they are to suffer forever, is the penalty of that one act, or the inevitable consequence of the condition into which that one act brought them, makes no difference.

The Goodness of God.

A still more formidable objection is drawn from the goodness of God. It is said to be inconsistent with his benevolence that He should allow any of his creatures to be forever miserable. The answer to this is: —

1. That it is just as impossible that God should do a little wrong as a great one. If He has permitted such a vast amount of sin and misery to exist in the world, from the fall of Adam to the present time, how can we say that it is inconsistent with his goodness, to allow them to continue to exist? How do we know that the reasons, so to speak, which constrained God to allow his children to be sinful and miserable for thousands of years, may not constrain Him to permit some of them to remain miserable forever? If the highest glory of God and the good of the uni- verse have been promoted by the past sinfulness and misery of men, why may not those objects be promoted by what is declared to be future?

2. We have reason to believe, as urged in the first volume of this work, and as often urged elsewhere, that the number of the

finally lost in comparison with the whole number of the saved will be very inconsiderable.   Our blessed Lord, when surrounded by the innumerable company of the redeemed, will be hailed as the " Salvator Hominum," the Saviour of Men, as the Lamb that bore the sins of the world.

3. It should constrain us to humility, and to silence on this subject, that the most solemn and explicit declarations of the everlasting misery of the wicked recorded in the Scriptures, fell from the lips of Him, who, though equal with God, was found in fashion as a man, and humbled Himself unto death, even the death of the cross, for us men and for our salvation.